Hymnbook 1982

the hymns together with accompaniments from
The Hymnal 1982

The Church Hymnal Corporation
800 Second Avenue, New York, New York 10017

Copyright Acknowledgments will be found on page 1021 ff.

Hymnbook 1982

Contents

Indexes

Preface

In the past several decades, the renewal of the spiritual life of the Church has created a pressing need for new hymnody and liturgical music. This has served as a catalyst for a world-wide outburst of creative liturgical and musical activity of a magnitude perhaps unparalleled since the Reformation. *The Hymnal 1982*, the culmination of more than a decade of work by the Standing Commission on Church Music, incorporates many of the riches of this contemporary renaissance. This hymnal is a response to the challenge of the Church's mission to spread the Good News of Jesus Christ to a changed and changing world.

The Hymnal 1982 is a revision of *The Hymnal 1940*, and as such stands on the foundation laid by The Joint Commission on Revision of the Hymnal. The precepts guiding that commission led to a comprehensive book of unusual appeal and excellence which served as a model for a number of hymnals produced since the middle of the twentieth century.

As an initial step in its revision process, the Standing Commission on Church Music developed a philosophical statement expressing the Commission's commitment to maintain and enhance the rich repertoire which constitutes the singing tradition of the people of God. This commitment led to the development of the following objectives:

- to prepare a body of texts which presents the Christian faith with clarity and integrity;
- to restore music which has lost some of its melodic, rhythmic, or harmonic vitality through prior revision;
- to reflect the nature of today's Church by including the works of contemporary artists and works representing many cultures;
- to strengthen ecumenical relationships through the inclusion of texts and tunes used by other Christian traditions;
- to create a hymnal embodying both practicality and esthetic excellence.

The Hymnal 1982 retains the best of the past and sets forth many riches of our own time. The Commission looked for theological orthodoxy, poetic beauty, and integrity of meaning. At the same time the Commission was especially concerned that the hymnody affirm "the participation of all in the Body of Christ the Church, while recognizing our diverse natures as children of God." This work has resulted in the sensitive alteration of texts which "could be interpreted as either pejorative or discriminatory," while preserving the artistic quality and intent of the originals. Language deemed "obscure or so changed in the contemporary usage as to have a different meaning"* has been clarified. Texts and music which reflect the pluralistic nature of the Church have been included, affording the use of Native American, Afro-American, Hispanic, and Asian material. Study and research into historic hymnody have led to the inclusion of chant tunes in rhythmic forms, of early settings of chorales and Psalter tunes, and of tunes whose roots lie deep in the treasury of American folk hymnody.

Often, consistency of style and practice seemed a less important goal than a representation of the wonderful variety of materials that are available. The recent renaissance of hymn-writing imparts rich benefits to *The Hymnal 1982*. The Commission drew many new hymns from the wealth of available material and commissioned authors and composers to write hymns on themes for which nothing suitable could be found. Here we must record gratitude for the work of the late F. Bland Tucker, a poet and priest whose wisdom and skills enhanced the work of the commissions which produced both this book and *The Hymnal 1940*.

In designing *The Hymnal 1982*, the Commission sought to create a book which is comprehensive and musically practical. Most tunes which are used more than once appear in different keys or harmonizations. Further variety in the performance of hymns is facilitated by descants and alternative accompaniments. The use of instruments in addition to the organ is encouraged through the inclusion, where appropriate, of guitar chords and bell and percussion parts. Details on notation and performance appear in the general performance notes in the Accompaniment Edition and with some individual hymns.

The Commission gave serious thought to the evaluation of texts for theological and literary merit by consultants representing congregations across the country before reaching final decisions on the contents of the book. In addition, the testing of new tunes in liturgical settings over an extended period of time determined their appropriateness for congregational singing.

The Commission gratefully acknowledges the contributions of Carl P. Daw, Jr., Georgia M. Joyner, Marilyn J. Keiser, Anne K. Le Croy, J. Waring McCrady, James McGregor, Bruce Neswick, Charles P. Price, McNeil Robinson II, F. Bland Tucker†, and John E. Williams, Jr.

The Hymnal 1982 is truly a book of and for the people, reflecting their involvement in its creation and responding to their desire for new songs with which to praise God. May God prosper this handiwork!

Geoffrey Butcher
Charles J. Child, Jr.
Robert H. Cochrane
Elizabeth Morris Downie
Carol Morey Foster
Raymond F. Glover
Jerry D. Godwin
Eric S. Greenwood
William M. Hale
Marion J. Hatchett
David J. Hurd, Jr.
Roy F. Kehl
James H. Litton
Richard T. Proulx
Arthur Rhea
Walter C. Righter
Russell Schulz-Widmar
Frederic P. Williams
Alec Wyton

†Deceased

*Report of the Standing Commission on Church Music to the 1982 General Convention of the Episcopal Church.

Hymns

1

1 Fa - ther, we praise thee, now the night is o - ver, ac - tive and watch-ful, stand we all be - fore thee; sing - ing we of - fer prayer and med - i - ta - tion: thus we a - dore thee.
2 Mon - arch of all things, fit us for thy man - sions; ban - ish our weak - ness, health and whole - ness send - ing; bring us to hea - ven, where thy saints u - nit - ed joy with - out end - ing.
3 All ho - ly Fa - ther, Son, and e - qual Spi - rit, Trin - i - ty bless - ed, send us thy sal - va - tion; thine is the glo - ry, gleam - ing and re - sound - ing through all cre - a - tion.

Alternative tune: *Nocte surgentes*, 2.

Words: Latin, 10th cent.; tr. Percy Dearmer (1867-1936)

Music: *Christe sanctorum*, melody from *Antiphoner*, 1681; harm. Ralph Vaughan Williams (1872-1958)

𝅗𝅥 = 63

11 11. 11 5

1 Fa - ther, we praise thee, now the night is o - ver, ac - tive and
2 Mon - arch of all things, fit us for thy man - sions; ban - ish our
3 All ho - ly Fa - ther, Son, and e - qual Spi - rit, Trin - i - ty
(Accompaniment optional)
watch - ful, stand we all be - fore thee; sing - ing we of - fer
weak - ness, health and whole-ness send - ing; bring us to hea - ven,
bless - ed, send us thy sal - va - tion; thine is the glo - ry,
prayer and med - i - ta - tion: thus we a - dore thee.
where thy saints u - nit - ed joy with - out end - ing.
gleam-ing and re - sound - ing through all cre - a - tion.

Alternative tune: *Christe sanctorum,* 1.

Words: Latin, 10th cent.; tr. Percy Dearmer (1867-1936)
Music: *Nocte surgentes,* plainsong, Mode 3, Nevers MS., 13th cent.; ver. Schola Antiqua, 1983; acc. Roy Kehl (b. 1935)

𝅗𝅥 = 80
11 11. 11 5

1 Now that the day - light fills the sky, we
2 Our hearts and lips may he re - strain; keep
3 From e - vil may he guard our eyes, our
4 that we, when this new day is gone, and
5 To God the Fa - ther, heaven - ly Light, to

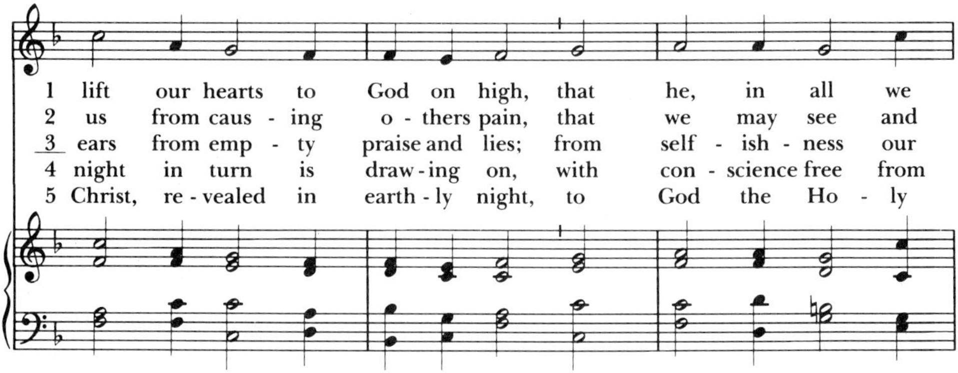
1 lift our hearts to God on high, that he, in all we
2 us from caus - ing o - thers pain, that we may see and
3 ears from emp - ty praise and lies; from self - ish - ness our
4 night in turn is draw - ing on, with con - science free from
5 Christ, re - vealed in earth - ly night, to God the Ho - ly

1 do or say, would keep us free from harm this day:
2 serve his Son, and grow in love for ev - ery - one.
3 hearts re - lease, that we may serve, and know his peace;
4 sin and blame, may praise and bless his ho - ly Name.
5 Ghost we raise our e - qual and un - ceas - ing praise.

Alternative tunes: *Verbum supernum prodiens,* 4; *Herr Jesu Christ* (isometric), 310.

Words: Latin, 6th cent.; st. 1, tr. John Mason Neale (1818-1866); sts. 2-4, tr. Peter Scagnelli (b. 1949). St. 5, Charles Coffin (1676-1749); tr. John Chandler (1806-1876)

Music: *Herr Jesu Christ,* melody from *Cantionale Germanicum,* 1628; harm. *Gothaischen Cantional,* 1651, alt.

♩= 152
LM

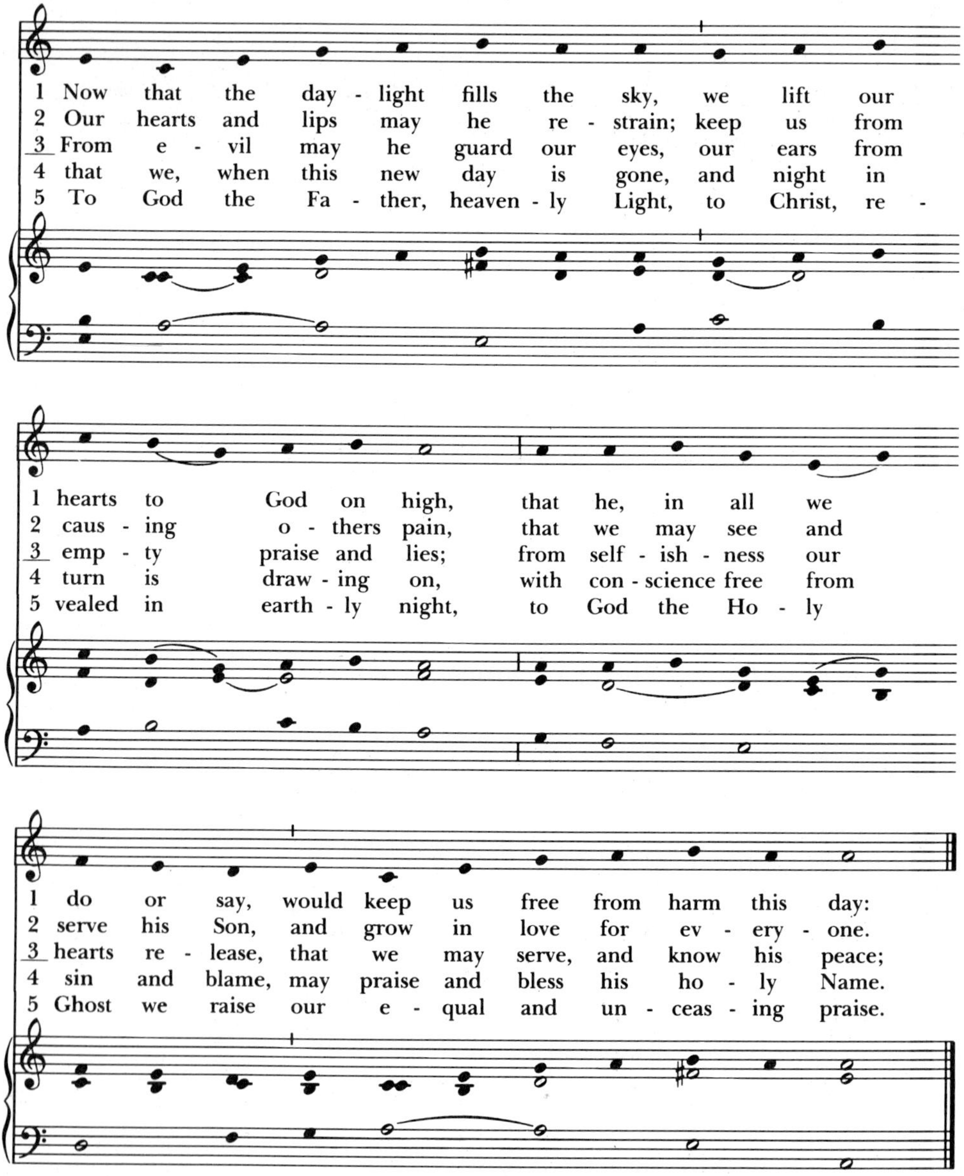
1 Now that the day - light fills the sky, we lift our
2 Our hearts and lips may he re - strain; keep us from
3 From e - vil may he guard our eyes, our ears from
4 that we, when this new day is gone, and night in
5 To God the Fa - ther, heaven - ly Light, to Christ, re -
1 hearts to God on high, that he, in all we
2 caus - ing o - thers pain, that we may see and
3 emp - ty praise and lies; from self - ish - ness our
4 turn is draw - ing on, with con - science free from
5 vealed in earth - ly night, to God the Ho - ly
1 do or say, would keep us free from harm this day:
2 serve his Son, and grow in love for ev - ery - one.
3 hearts re - lease, that we may serve, and know his peace;
4 sin and blame, may praise and bless his ho - ly Name.
5 Ghost we raise our e - qual and un - ceas - ing praise.

Another accompaniment, 311. Alternative tune: *Herr Jesu Christ,* 3.

Words: Latin, 6th cent.; st. 1, tr. John Mason Neale (1818-1866); sts. 2-4, tr. Peter Scagnelli (b. 1949). St. 5, Charles Coffin (1676-1749); tr. John Chandler (1806-1876)

Music: *Verbum supernum prodiens,* plainsong, Mode 2, Nevers MS., 13th cent.; acc. Howard Don Small (b. 1932)

LM

1 O splen - dor of God's glo - ry bright, O thou that
2 O thou true Sun of heaven - ly love, pour down thy
3 With prayer the Fa - ther we im - plore: O Fa - ther,
4 to guide what - e'er we no - bly do, with love all
*5 All laud to God the Fa - ther be; all praise, e -
1 bring - est light from light, O Light of Light, light's
2 ra - diance from a - bove: the Spi - rit's sanc - ti -
3 glo - rious ev - er - more, we plead with thee for
4 en - vy to sub - due, to give us grace our
5 ter - nal Son, to thee; all glo - ry to the
1 liv - ing spring, O Day, all days il - lu - mi - ning,
2 fy - ing beam up - on our earth - ly sen - ses stream.
3 grace and power to con - quer in temp - ta - tion's hour,
4 wrongs to bear, to make ill for - tune turn to fair.
5 Spi - rit raise in e - qual and un - end - ing praise.

Alternative tune: *Puer nobis,* 124 and 193.

Words: Ambrose of Milan (340-397); tr. Robert Seymour Bridges (1844-1930), alt.
Music: *Splendor paternae gloriae,* plainsong, Mode 1, Worcester MS., 13th cent.; acc. Richard Proulx (b. 1937) LM

1 Christ, whose glo - ry fills the skies,
2 Dark and cheer - less is the morn
3 Vis - it then this soul of mine!
Christ, the true, the on - ly Light,
un - ac - com - pan - ied by thee;
Pierce the gloom of sin and grief!
Sun of Right-eous-ness, a - rise! Tri-umph o'er the
joy - less is the day's re - turn, till thy mer - cy's
Fill me, ra - dian - cy di - vine; scat - ter all my

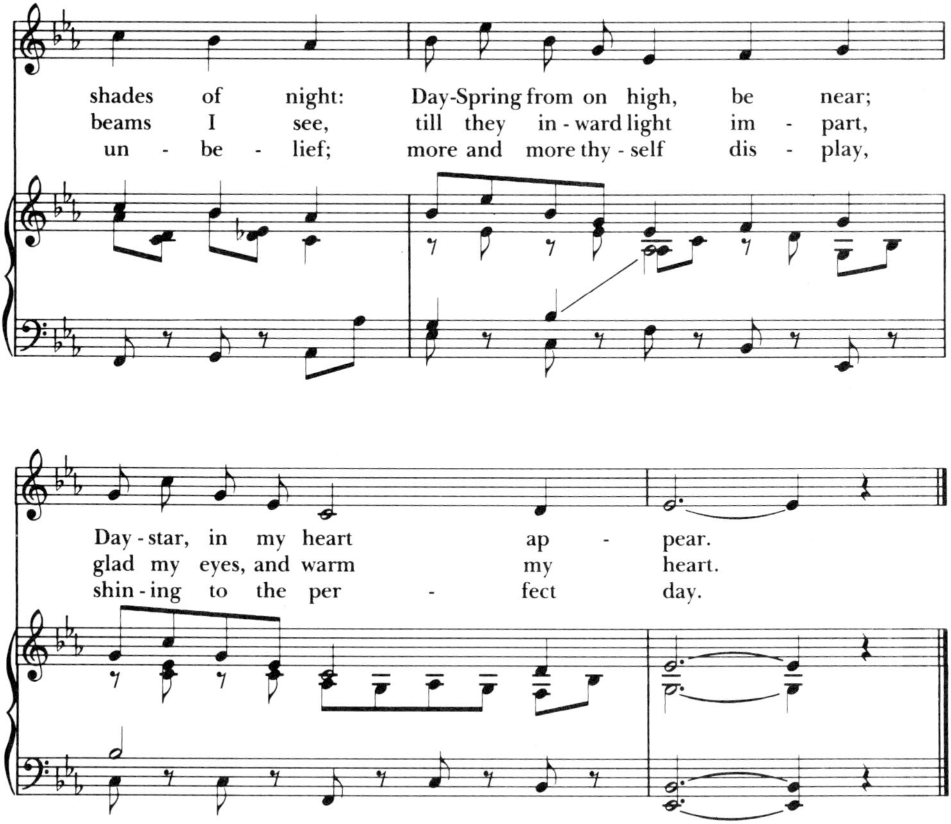
shades of night: Day-Spring from on high, be near;
beams I see, till they in-ward light im - part,
un - be - lief; more and more thy - self dis - play,
Day - star, in my heart ap - pear.
glad my eyes, and warm my heart.
shin - ing to the per - fect day.

Alternative tune: *Ratisbon*, 7.

Words: Charles Wesley (1707-1788)
Music: *Christ Whose Glory*, Malcolm Williamson (b. 1931)

♩= 72
77. 77. 77

1 Christ, whose glo - ry fills the skies, Christ, the true, the
2 Dark and cheer - less is the morn un - ac - com - pan -
3 Vis - it then this soul of mine! Pierce the gloom of
on - ly Light, Sun of Right - eous - ness, a - rise!
ied by thee; joy - less is the day's re - turn,
sin and grief! Fill me, ra - dian - cy di - vine;
Tri - umph o'er the shades of night: Day - spring from on
till thy mer - cy's beams I see, till they in - ward
scat - ter all my un - be - lief; more and more thy -
high, be near; Day - star, in my heart ap - pear.
light im - part, glad my eyes, and warm my heart.
self dis - play, shin - ing to the per - fect day.

Alternative tune: *Christ Whose Glory,* 6.

Words: Charles Wesley (1707-1788)
Music: *Ratisbon,* melody from *Geystliche gesangk Buchleyn,* 1524; adapt. att. William Henry Havergal (1793-1870); harm. William Henry Havergal (1793-1870), alt.

𝅗𝅥=60
77. 77. 77

Unison or harmony
C Am Dm Em Fmaj7 C
1 Morn-ing has bro - ken like the first morn - ing,
2 Sweet the rain's new fall sun - lit from hea - ven,
3 Mine is the sun - light! Mine is the morn - ing
Am Em Fmaj7 C Gsus4 G
black-bird has spo - ken like the first bird.
like the first dew - fall on the first grass.
born of the one light E - den saw play!
Em Am Dm C Am Gsus4 G
Praise for the sing - ing! Praise for the morn - ing!
Praise for the sweet - ness of the wet gar - den,
Praise with e - la - tion, praise ev - ery morn - ing,
Em C Am Dm G Csus4 C
Praise for them, spring - ing! fresh from the Word!
sprung in com - plete - ness where his feet pass.
God's re - cre - a - tion of the new day!

Words: Eleanor Farjeon (1881-1965), alt.
Music: *Bunessan,* Gaelic melody; harm. Alec Wyton (b. 1921)

𝅗𝅥. = 50
55. 54. D

Fm(Em) D♭(C) E♭(D) A♭(G) Fm(Em) D♭(C)
*1 Not here for high and ho - ly things we ren - der thanks to
*2 the roy - al robes of au - tumn moors, the gold - en gates of
*3 of faith and hope and love un-dimmed, un - dy - ing still through
4 A - wake, a - wake to love and work! The lark is in the
5 Come, let thy voice be one with theirs, shout with their shout of
6 to give and give, and give a - gain, what God hath giv - en
A♭(G) A♭(G) B♭m(Am) E♭(D) A♭(G)
1 thee, but for the com - mon things of earth, the
2 spring, the vel - vet of soft sum - mer nights, the
3 death, the re - sur - rec - tion of the world, what
4 sky, the fields are wet with dia - mond dew, the
5 praise; see how the gi - ant sun soars up, great
6 thee; to spend thy - self nor count the cost; to

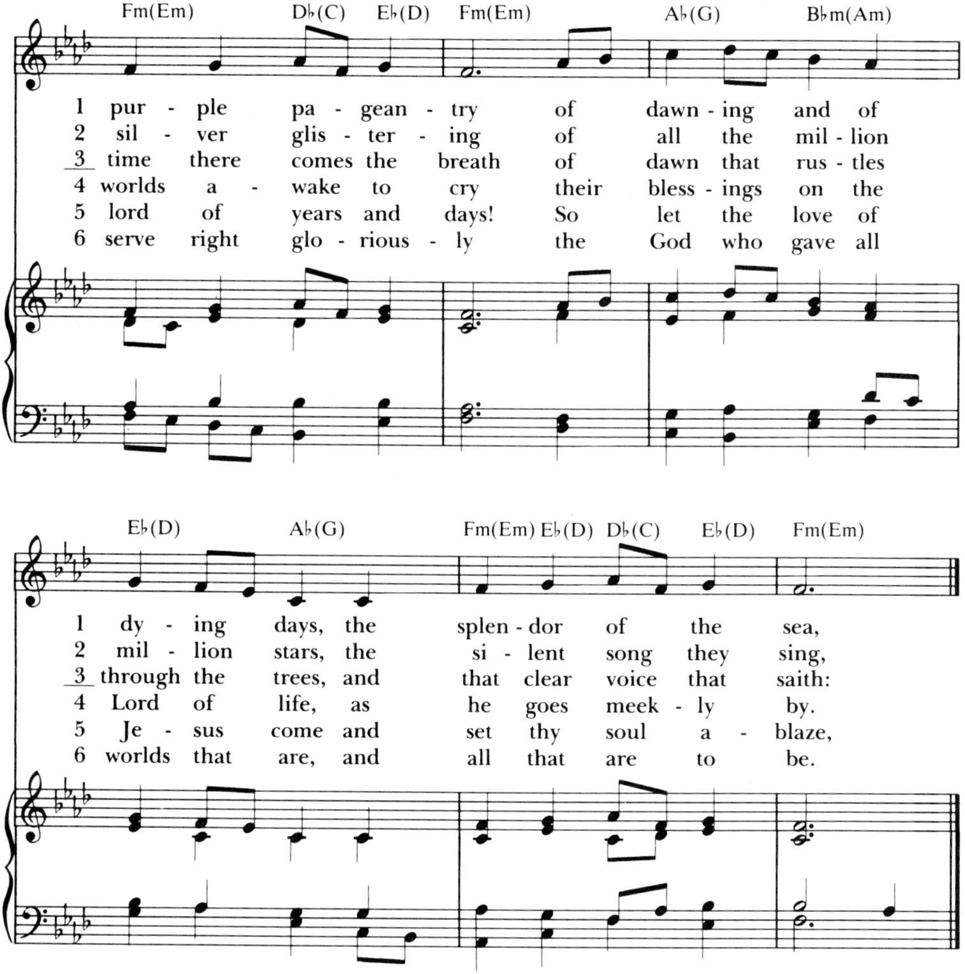
Fm(Em) D♭(C) E♭(D) Fm(Em) A♭(G) B♭m(Am)
1 pur - ple pa - gean - try of dawn - ing and of
2 sil - ver glis - ter - ing of all the mil - lion
3 time there comes the breath of dawn that rus - tles
4 worlds a - wake to cry their bless - ings on the
5 lord of years and days! So let the love of
6 serve right glo - rious - ly the God who gave all
E♭(D) A♭(G) Fm(Em) E♭(D) D♭(C) E♭(D) Fm(Em)
1 dy - ing days, the splen - dor of the sea,
2 mil - lion stars, the si - lent song they sing,
3 through the trees, and that clear voice that saith:
4 Lord of life, as he goes meek - ly by.
5 Je - sus come and set thy soul a - blaze,
6 worlds that are, and all that are to be.

Fm (capo 1, Em). Keyboard and guitar should not sound together. The melody may be sung as a two-part canon at distances of either two or four beats. Another harmonization, 583.

Words: Geoffrey Anketel Studdert-Kennedy (1883-1929)
Music: *Morning Song,* melody att. Elkanah Kelsay Dare (1782-1826); harm. Charles Winfred Douglas (1867-1944)

♩= 92
86. 86. 86

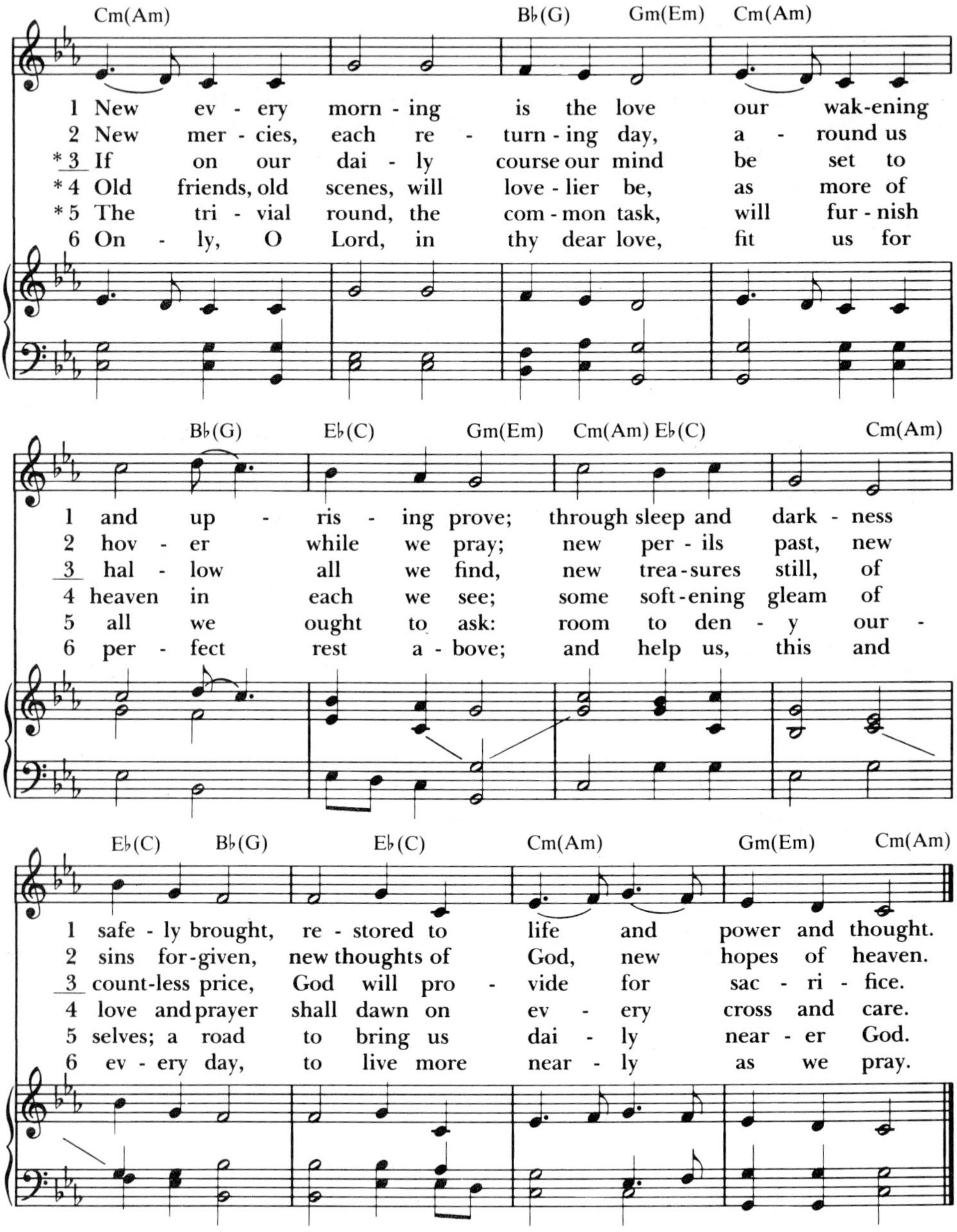
Cm(Am) Bb(G) Gm(Em) Cm(Am)
1 New ev - ery morn - ing is the love our wak-ening
2 New mer - cies, each re - turn - ing day, a - round us
*3 If on our dai - ly course our mind be set to
*4 Old friends, old scenes, will love - lier be, as more of
*5 The tri - vial round, the com - mon task, will fur - nish
6 On - ly, O Lord, in thy dear love, fit us for
Bb(G) Eb(C) Gm(Em) Cm(Am) Eb(C) Cm(Am)
1 and up - ris - ing prove; through sleep and dark - ness
2 hov - er while we pray; new per - ils past, new
3 hal - low all we find, new trea - sures still, of
4 heaven in each we see; some soft - ening gleam of
5 all we ought to ask: room to den - y our -
6 per - fect rest a - bove; and help us, this and
Eb(C) Bb(G) Eb(C) Cm(Am) Gm(Em) Cm(Am)
1 safe - ly brought, re - stored to life and power and thought.
2 sins for - given, new thoughts of God, new hopes of heaven.
3 count - less price, God will pro - vide for sac - ri - fice.
4 love and prayer shall dawn on ev - ery cross and care.
5 selves; a road to bring us dai - ly near - er God.
6 ev - ery day, to live more near - ly as we pray.

Cm (capo 3, Am). Another harmonization, 163. Alternative tune: *Melcombe,* 531.

Words: John Keble (1792-1866)
Music: *Kedron,* melody att. Elkanah Kelsay Dare (1782-1826); harm. *The Southern Harmony,* 1835; adapt. *Hymnal 1982*

𝅗𝅥 = 58
LM

1 A - wake, my soul, and with the sun thy
2 Lord, I my vows to thee re - new; dis -
3 Di - rect, con - trol, sug - gest, this day, all
*4 Praise God, from whom all bless - ings flow; praise
dai - ly stage of du - ty run; shake off dull sloth, and
perse my sins as morn - ing dew; guard my first springs of
I de - sign, or do, or say; that all my powers, with
him, all crea - tures here be - low; praise him a - bove, ye
joy - ful rise to pay thy morn - ing sac - ri - fice:
thought and will, and with thy - self my spi - rit fill.
all their might, in thy sole glo - ry may u - nite.
heaven - ly host: praise Fa - ther, Son, and Ho - ly Ghost.

Words: Thomas Ken (1637-1711), alt.
Music: *Morning Hymn*, melody François Hippolyte Barthélémon (1741-1808); harm. *The Church Hymnal for the Church Year*, 1917

𝅗𝅥 = 52
LM

Noonday

1 The gold - en sun lights up the sky, im - part - ing
2 At the third hour you took your cross, you stum-bled,
3 At the third hour your faith - ful band was clothed with
4 O God, cre - a tion's rul - ing force, O Je - sus,
vi - gor to the day. A - mid our cus - tom - ar - y
Lord, be - neath its weight. Now help us bear our dai - ly
power on Pen - te - cost. Be - stow your Spi - rit on us
cru - ci - fied for us, O Spi - rit, love's life - giv - ing
round, we of - fer you our prayer and praise.
load and strive to fol - low where you lead.
now, and give us strength to do your will.
ray, we praise and bless you ev - ery hour.

Alternative tune: *Verbum supernum prodiens,* 13.

Words: Charles P. Price (b. 1920)
Music: *Danby,* English melody; adapt. and harm. Ralph Vaughan Williams (1872-1958)

𝅗𝅥=52
LM

Noonday

13

1 The golden sun lights up the sky, imparting vigor to the day. Amid our customary round, we offer you our prayer and praise.
2 At the third hour you took your cross, you stumbled, Lord, beneath its weight. Now help us bear our daily load and strive to follow where you lead.
3 At the third hour your faithful band was clothed with power on Pentecost. Bestow your Spirit on us now, and give us strength to do your will.
4 O God, creation's ruling force, O Jesus, crucified for us, O Spirit, love's life-giving ray, we praise and bless you every hour.

Alternative tunes: *Danby*, 12; *Verbum supernum prodiens* (Nevers), 4.

Words: Charles P. Price (b. 1920)
Music: *Verbum supernum prodiens*, plainsong, Mode 8, Einsiedeln MS., 13th cent.; acc. Richard P. Solly (b.1952)

LM

1 O God, cre - a - tion's se - cret force, your - self un -
2 Grant us, when this short life is past, the glo - rious
*3 Al - might - y Fa - ther, hear our cry through Je - sus
moved, all mo - tion's source, you, from the morn till eve - ning's
eve - ning that shall last; that, by a ho - ly death at -
Christ, our Lord Most High, whom with the Spi - rit we a -
ray, through all its chan - ges guide the day:
tained, e - ter - nal glo - ry may be gained.
dore for ev - er and for ev - er - more.

Alternative tune: *Te lucis ante terminum,* 15.

Words: Ambrose of Milan (340-397); tr. John Mason Neale (1818-1866), alt.
St. 3, James Waring McCrady (b. 1938)

Music: *O Heiland, reiss,* melody from *Rheinfelsisches Deutsches Catholisches Gesangbuch,* 1666; harm. *Orgelbuch Zum Gesangbuch Der Evangelisch-Reformierten Kirchen Der Deutschsprachigen Schweiz,* 1926

♩= 112
LM

1 O God, cre - a - tion's se - cret force, your - self un -
2 Grant us, when this short life is past, the glo - rious
*3 Al - might - y Fa - ther, hear our cry through Je - sus
moved, all mo - tion's source, you, from the morn till
eve - ning that shall last; that, by a ho - ly
Christ, our Lord Most High, whom with the Spi - rit
eve - ning's ray, through all its chan - ges guide the day:
death at - tained, e - ter - nal glo - ry may be gained.
we a - dore for ev - er and for ev - er - more.

Alternative tune: *O Heiland, reiss,* 14.

Words: Ambrose of Milan (340-397); tr. John Mason Neale (1818-1866), alt.
St. 3, James Waring McCrady (b. 1938)

Music: *Te lucis ante terminum,* plainsong, Mode 8, *Antiphonale Sarisburiense,* Vol. II;
acc. Gerard Farrell (b. 1919)

LM

16

1 Now let us sing our praise to God with fer - vent
2 For at this hour to all the world the grace of
3 So daz - zling is its ho - ly light, it puts the
4 All glo - ry be to you, Lord Christ, who, con - quering
heart and rea - dy mind: each day the sun at
true sal - va - tion came: the Lamb of God re -
noon - day sun in shade. Then let us all with
death, reign glo - rious - ly with God, Cre - a - tor
ze - nith calls the faith - ful to their noon - day prayers.
stored our peace by vir - tue of his sav - ing cross.
joy em - brace the flam - ing splen - dor of such grace.
of all things and with the Spi - rit, Com - fort - er.

Alternative tune: *Solemnis haec festivitas,* 17.

Words: Latin; ver. *Hymnal 1982.* St. 4, Anne K. LeCroy (b. 1930)
Music: *Dicamus laudes Domino,* plainsong, Mode 5, Nevers MS., 13th cent.; acc. David Hurd (b. 1950) LM

1 Now let us sing our praise to God with fer - vent
2 For at this hour to all the world the grace of
3 So daz - zling is its ho - ly light, it puts the
4 All glo - ry be to you, Lord Christ, who, con - quering

heart and rea - dy mind: each day the sun at
true sal - va - tion came: the Lamb of God re -
noon - day sun in shade. Then let us all with
death, reign glo - rious - ly with God, Cre - a - tor

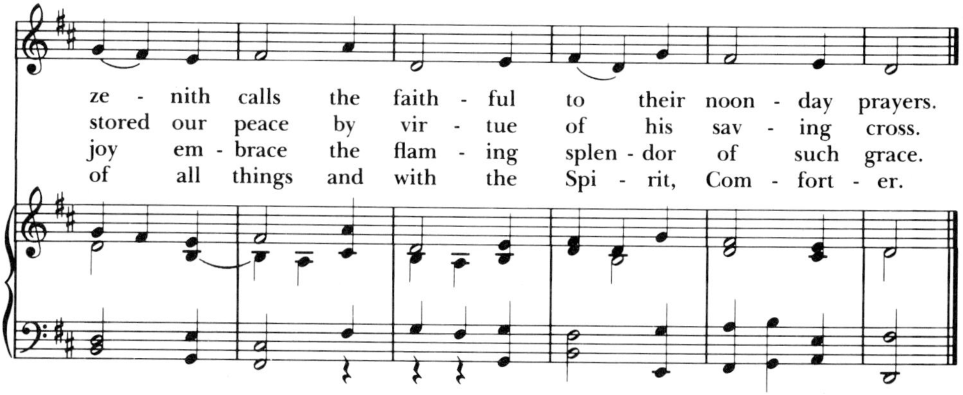
ze - nith calls the faith - ful to their noon - day prayers.
stored our peace by vir - tue of his sav - ing cross.
joy em - brace the flam - ing splen - dor of such grace.
of all things and with the Spi - rit, Com - fort - er.

Alternative tune: *Dicamus laudes Domino,* 16.

Words: Latin; ver. *Hymnal 1982.* St. 4, Anne K. LeCroy (b. 1930)
Music: *Solemnis haec festivitas,* melody from *Graduale,* 1685; harm. Arthur Hutchings (b. 1906)

𝅗𝅥. = 44
LM

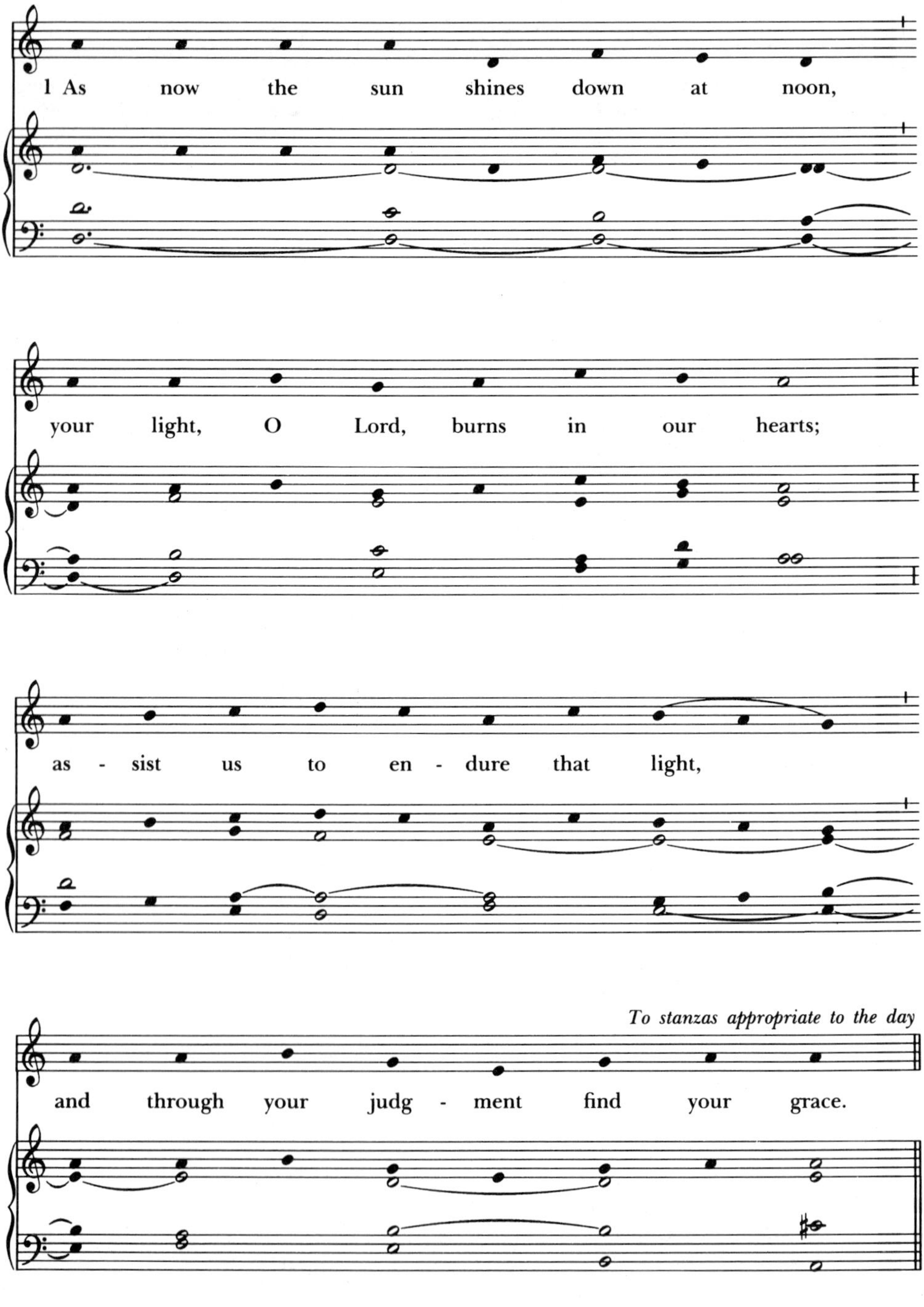
1 As now the sun shines down at noon,
your light, O Lord, burns in our hearts;
as - sist us to en - dure that light,
To stanzas appropriate to the day
and through your judg - ment find your grace.

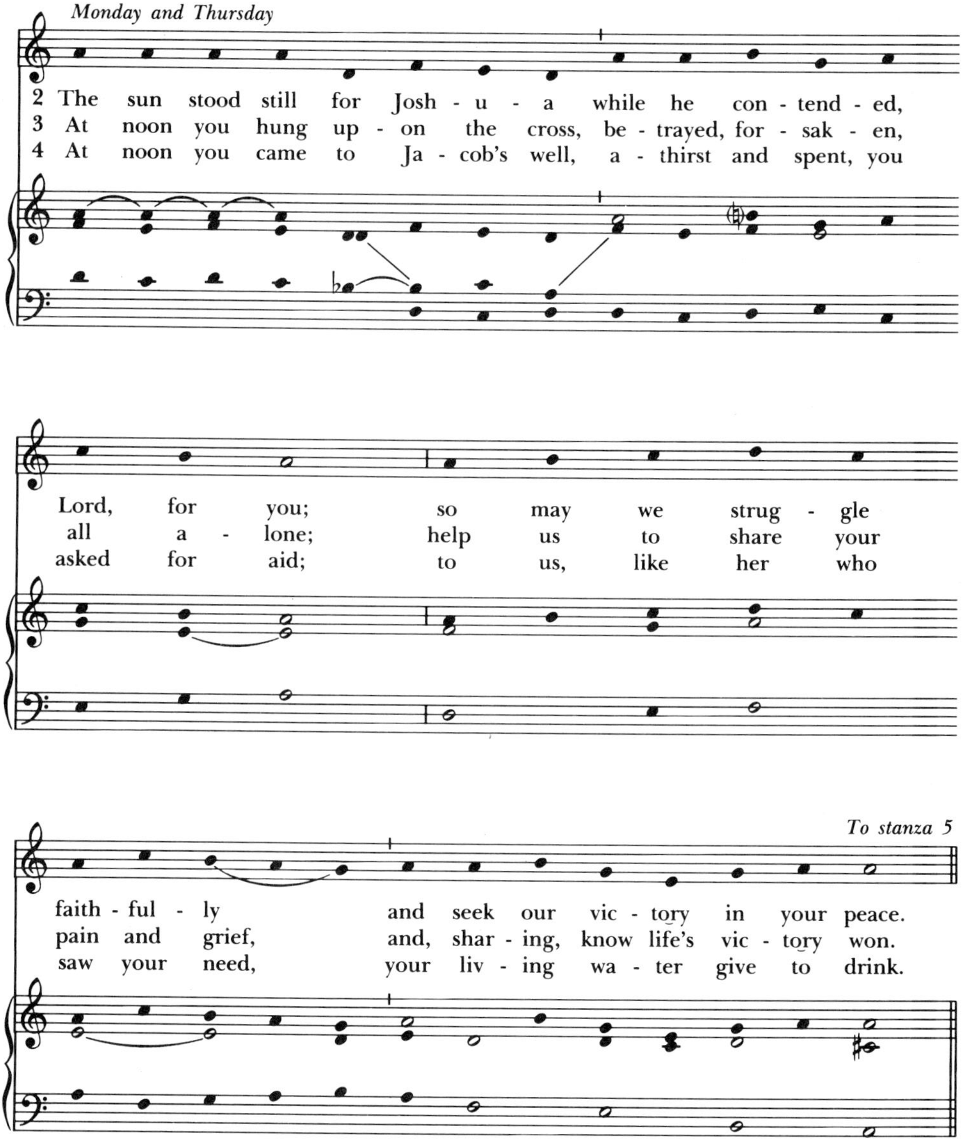
Monday and Thursday
2 The sun stood still for Josh - u - a while he con - tend - ed,
3 At noon you hung up - on the cross, be - trayed, for - sak - en,
4 At noon you came to Ja - cob's well, a - thirst and spent, you
Lord, for you; so may we strug - gle
all a - lone; help us to share your
asked for aid; to us, like her who
To stanza 5
faith - ful - ly and seek our vic - tory in your peace.
pain and grief, and, shar - ing, know life's vic - tory won.
saw your need, your liv - ing wa - ter give to drink.

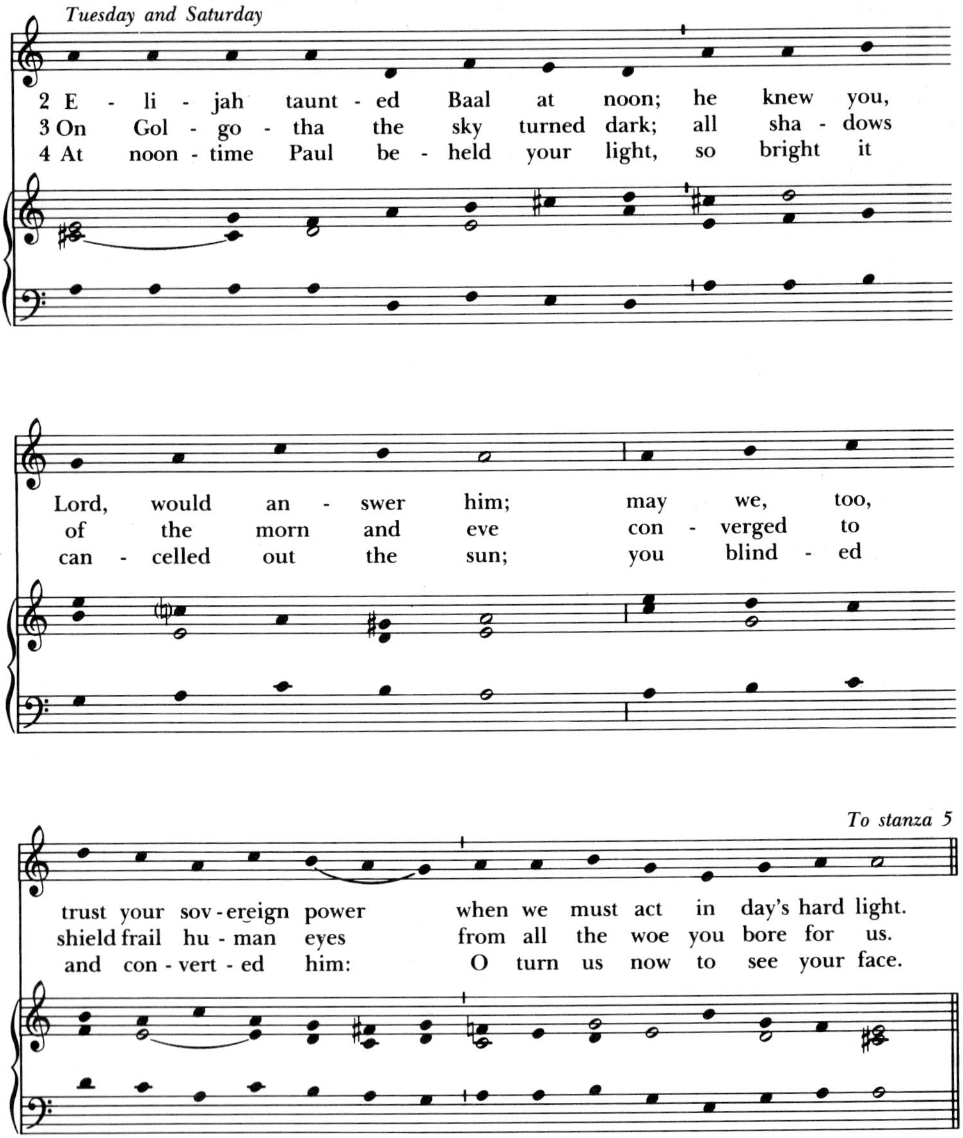
Tuesday and Saturday
2 E - li - jah taunt - ed Baal at noon; he knew you,
3 On Gol - go - tha the sky turned dark; all sha - dows
4 At noon - time Paul be - held your light, so bright it
Lord, would an - swer him; may we, too,
of the morn and eve con - verged to
can - celled out the sun; you blind - ed
To stanza 5
trust your sov - ereign power when we must act in day's hard light.
shield frail hu - man eyes from all the woe you bore for us.
and con - vert - ed him: O turn us now to see your face.

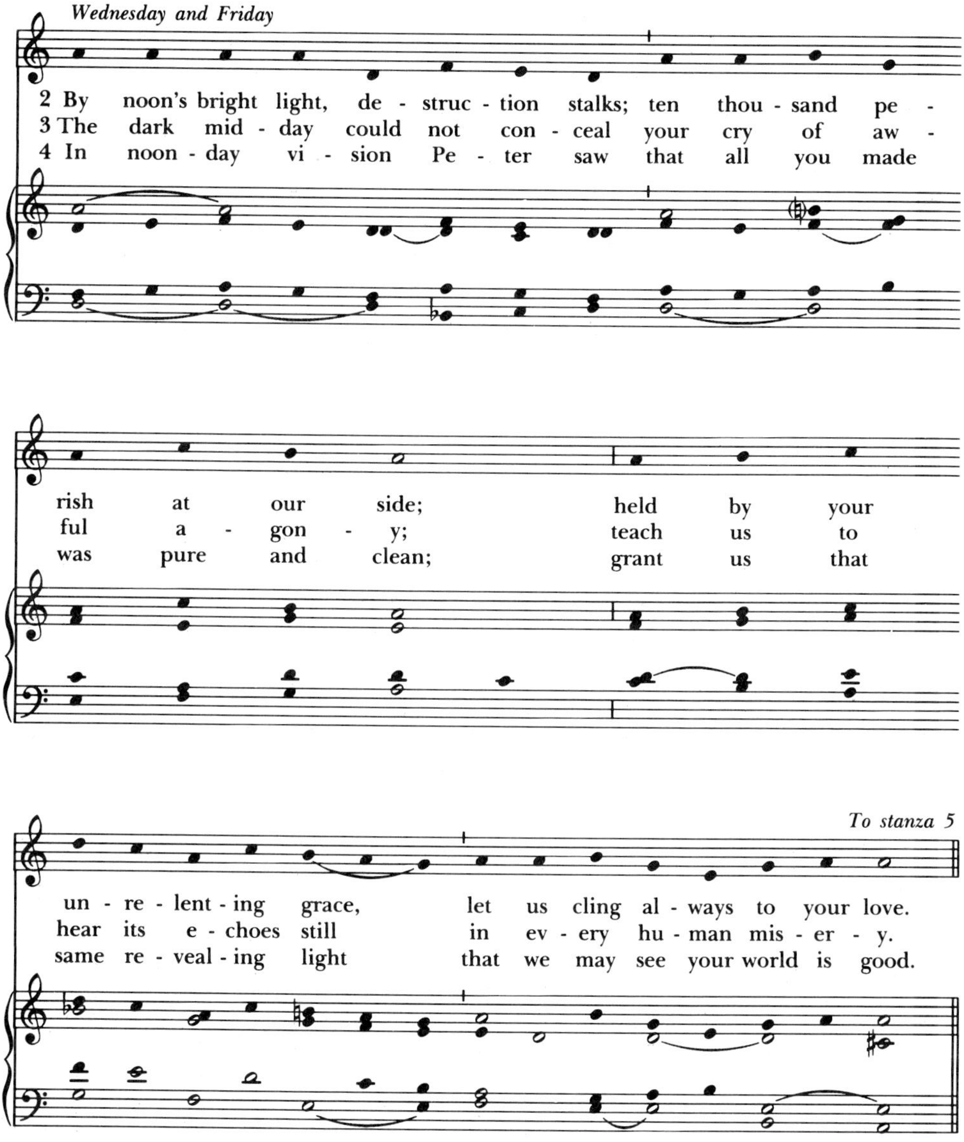
Wednesday and Friday
2 By noon's bright light, de - struc - tion stalks; ten thou - sand pe - rish at our side; held by your un - re - lent - ing grace, let us cling al - ways to your love.
3 The dark mid - day could not con - ceal your cry of aw - ful a - gon - y; teach us to hear its e - choes still in ev - ery hu - man mis - er - y.
4 In noon - day vi - sion Pe - ter saw that all you made was pure and clean; grant us that same re - veal - ing light that we may see your world is good.
To stanza 5

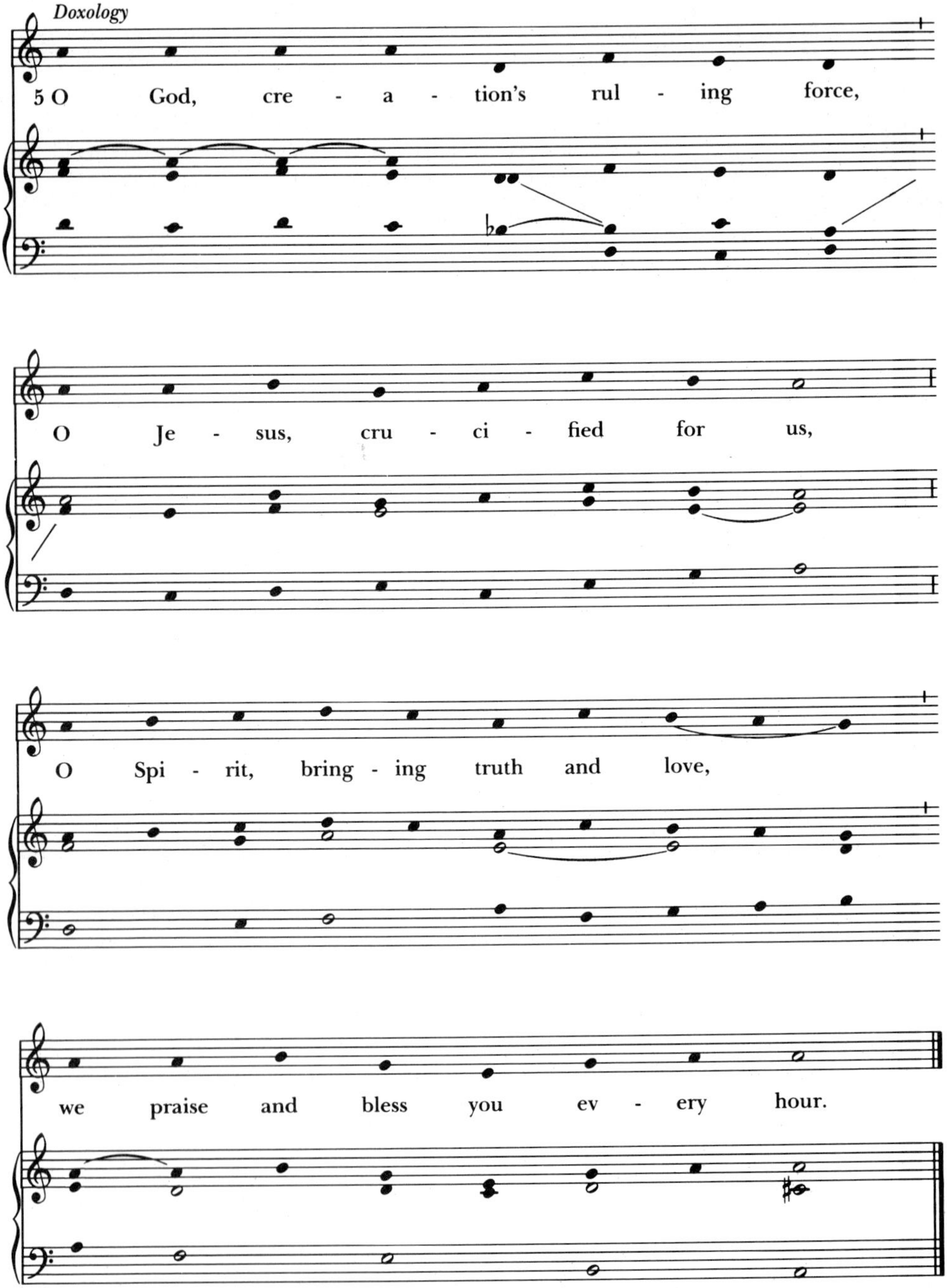
Doxology
5 O God, cre - a - tion's rul - ing force,
O Je - sus, cru - ci - fied for us,
O Spi - rit, bring - ing truth and love,
we praise and bless you ev - ery hour.

Other accompaniments, 134 and 650.

Words: Charles P. Price (b. 1920) and Carl P. Daw, Jr. (b. 1944)
Music: *Jesu dulcis memoria,* plainsong, Mode 2; acc. McNeil Robinson II (b. 1943)

LM

1 Now Ho - ly Spi - rit, ev - er One with God the
2 Let mouth and tongue, mind, sense, and strength God's might - y
*3 Al - might - y Fa - ther, hear our cry through Je - sus
Fa - ther and the Son, pour forth in - to our
ac - tions tell at length; let love in flames of
Christ, our Lord Most High, whom with the Spi - rit
hearts, we pray, the full - ness of your grace to - day.
liv - ing fire the hearts of all the world in - spire.
we a - dore for ev - er and for ev - er - more.

Alternative tune: *Wareham,* 20.

Words: Ambrose of Milan (340-397); ver. *Hymnal 1982.* St. 3, James Waring McCrady (b. 1938)
Music: *Nunc Sancte nobis Spiritus,* plainsong, Mode 5, Verona MS., 12th cent.; acc. Gerard Farrell (b. 1919) LM

1 Now Ho - ly Spi - rit, ev - er One
2 Let mouth and tongue, mind, sense, and strength
*3 Al - might - y Fa - ther, hear our cry
with God the Fa - ther and the Son,
God's might - y ac - tions tell at length;
through Je - sus Christ, our Lord Most High,
pour forth in - to our hearts, we pray,
let love in flames of liv - ing fire
whom with the Spi - rit we a - dore
the full - ness of your grace to - day.
the hearts of all the world in - spire.
for ev - er and for ev - er - more.

This music with descant, 137. Alternative tune: *Nunc Sancte nobis Spiritus,* 19.

Words: Ambrose of Milan (340-397); ver. *Hymnal 1982.* St. 3, James Waring McCrady (b. 1938)
Music: *Wareham,* melody William Knapp (1698-1768), alt.; harm. *Hymns Ancient and Modern,* 1875, after James Turle (1802-1882)

♩=96
LM

1 O God of truth, O Lord of might,
2 Quench now on earth the flames of strife;
* 3 Al - might - y Fa - ther, hear our cry
you or - der time and change a - right,
from pas - sion's heat pre - serve our life;
through Je - sus Christ, our Lord Most High,
you send the ear - ly morn - ing ray,
and while you keep our bo - dy whole,
whom with the Spi - rit we a - dore
and light the glow of per - fect day:
pour heal - ing peace up - on our soul.
for ev - er and for ev - er - - more.

Alternative tune: *Rector potens, verax Deus,* 22.

Words: Ambrose of Milan (340-397); tr. John Mason Neale (1818-1866), alt.
St. 3, James Waring McCrady (b. 1938)
Music: *Song 34,* melody and bass Orlando Gibbons (1583-1625); harm. *The English Hymnal,* 1906, alt.

♩=88
LM

1 O God of truth, O Lord of might, you or - der
2 Quench now on earth the flames of strife; from pas - sion's
*3 Al - might - y Fa - ther, hear our cry through Je - sus
time and change a - right, you send the ear - ly
heat pre - serve our life; and while you keep our
Christ, our Lord Most High, whom with the Spi - rit
morn - ing ray, and light the glow of per - fect day:
bo - dy whole, pour heal - ing peace up - on our soul.
we a - dore for ev - er and for ev - er - more.

Alternative tune: *Song 34*, 21.

Words: Ambrose of Milan (340-397); tr. John Mason Neale (1818-1866), alt.
St. 3, James Waring McCrady (b. 1938)

Music: *Rector potens, verax Deus*, plainsong, Mode 1, *Klosterneuburger Hymnar*, 1336; acc. Roy F. Kehl (b. 1935)

LM

Alternative accompaniment

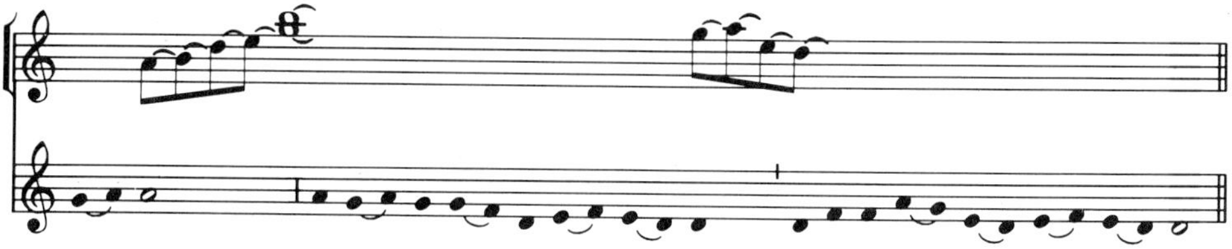

Simultaneous ostinati patterns

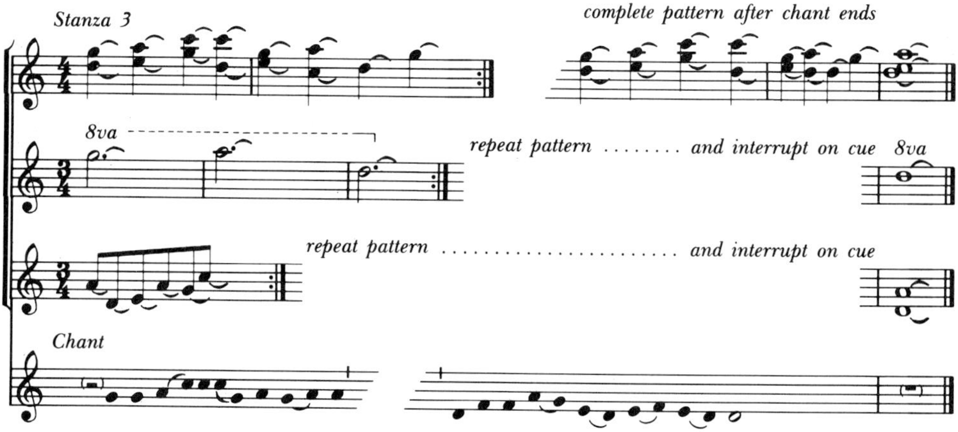

The ostinati should be played in a tempo independent of the chant; in the ostinati, ♪=♩. After the chant ends, complete the first ostinato before giving the cue for the final chord; that cue interrupts the other ostinati for the chord. The ostinato for stanza 2 may be used alone for selected stanzas.

Music: *Rector potens, verax Deus,* plainsong, Mode 1, *Klosterneuburger Hymnar,* 1336; acc. David Shuler (b. 1954)

Noonday

1 The fleet - ing day is near - ly gone;
2 At prayer time, near the Tem - ple gate,
3 With "It is fi - nished" on your lips,
4 O God, cre - a - tion's rul - ing force,
we har - vest what the morn - ing sowed.
A - pos - tles made a lame man walk.
at that ninth hour you died for us.
O Je - sus, cru - ci - fied for us,
Now grant us un - di - mi - nished strength
They gave him heal - ing in your Name;
In - spire us by your dy - ing breath
O Spi - rit, bring - ing power and health,
to stand and do what still re - mains.
now give us grace to walk your way.
to live for you and do your will.
we praise and bless you ev - ery hour.

Words: Charles P. Price (b. 1920)
Music: *Du meiner Seelen*, from *Cantica Spiritualia*, 1847

♩. = 52
LM

1 The day thou gav - est, Lord, is end - ed,
2 We thank thee that thy Church, un - sleep - ing
3 As o'er each con - ti - nent and is - land
4 So be it, Lord; thy throne shall nev - er,
the dark - ness falls at thy be - hest;
while earth rolls on - ward in - to light,
the dawn leads on an - oth - er day,
like earth's proud em - pires, pass a - way;
to thee our morn - ing hymns a - scend - ed,
through all the world her watch is keep - ing
the voice of prayer is nev - er si - lent,
thy king - dom stands, and grows for ev - er,
thy praise shall sanc - ti - fy our rest.
and rests not now by day or night.
nor dies the strain of praise a - way.
till all thy crea - tures own thy sway.

This hymn may be used in the morning by omitting stanza 1.

Words: John Ellerton (1826-1893)
Music: *St. Clement,* Clement Cottevill Scholefield (1839-1904)

♩= 100
98. 98

1 2
1 O gra - cious Light, Lord Je - sus Christ, in you the Fa - ther's
2 Now sun - set comes, but light shines forth, the lamps are lit to
3 Wor - thy are you of end - less praise, O Son of God, Life -
glo - ry shone. Im - mor - tal, ho - ly, blest is he, and
pierce the night. Praise Fa - ther, Son, and Spi - rit: God who
giv - ing Lord; where - fore you are through all the earth and
For canon only
blest are you, his ho - ly Son. (his Ho - ly Son.)
dwells in the e - ter - nal light. (e - ter - nal light.)
in the high - est heaven a - dored. (est heaven a - dored.)

This hymn may be sung unaccompanied as a four-part canon at a distance of one measure.
Alternative tune: *Conditor alme,* 26.

Words: Greek, 3rd cent.; tr. F. Bland Tucker (1895-1984); para. of *O Gracious Light*
Music: *The Eighth Tune,* Thomas Tallis (1505?-1585); adapt. *Hymnal 1982*

♩=76
LM

26

1 O gra - cious Light, Lord Je - sus Christ, in you the
2 Now sun - set comes, but light shines forth, the lamps are
3 Wor - thy are you of end - less praise, O Son of
Fa - ther's glo - ry shone. Im - mor - tal, ho - ly,
lit to pierce the night. Praise Fa - ther, Son, and
God, Life - giv - ing Lord; where - fore you are through
blest is he, and blest are you, his ho - ly Son.
Spi - rit: God who dwells in the e - ter - nal light.
all the earth and in the high - est heaven a - dored.

This melody may be sung in rhythmic form: ♪ ♩ ♪ ♩. Alternative tune: *The Eighth Tune,* 25.

Words: Greek, 3rd cent.; tr. F. Bland Tucker (1895-1984); para. of *O Gracious Light*
Music: *Conditor alme siderum,* plainsong, Mode 4; acc. Bruce Neswick (b. 1956)

LM

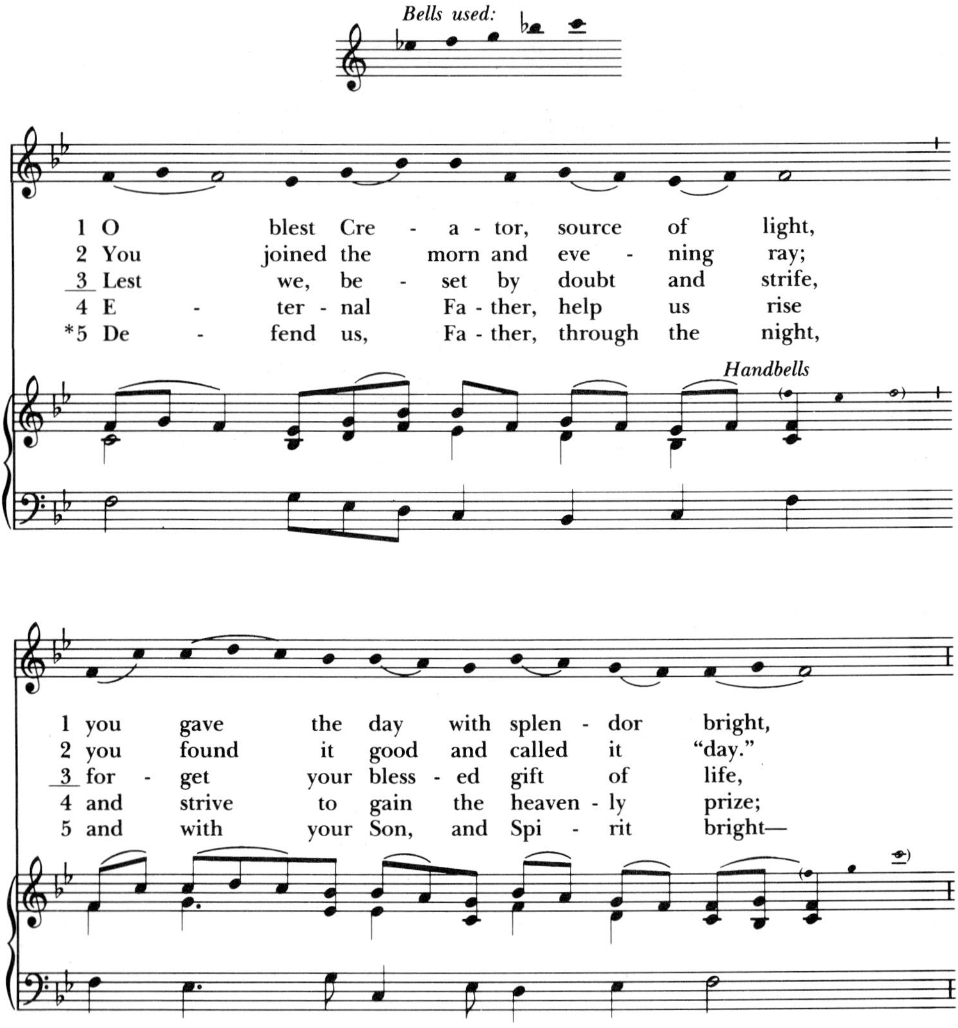
Bells used:
1 O blest Cre - a - tor, source of light,
2 You joined the morn and eve - ning ray;
3 Lest we, be - set by doubt and strife,
4 E - ter - nal Fa - ther, help us rise
*5 De - fend us, Fa - ther, through the night,
Handbells
1 you gave the day with splen - dor bright,
2 you found it good and called it "day."
3 for - get your bless - ed gift of life,
4 and strive to gain the heaven - ly prize;
5 and with your Son, and Spi - rit bright—

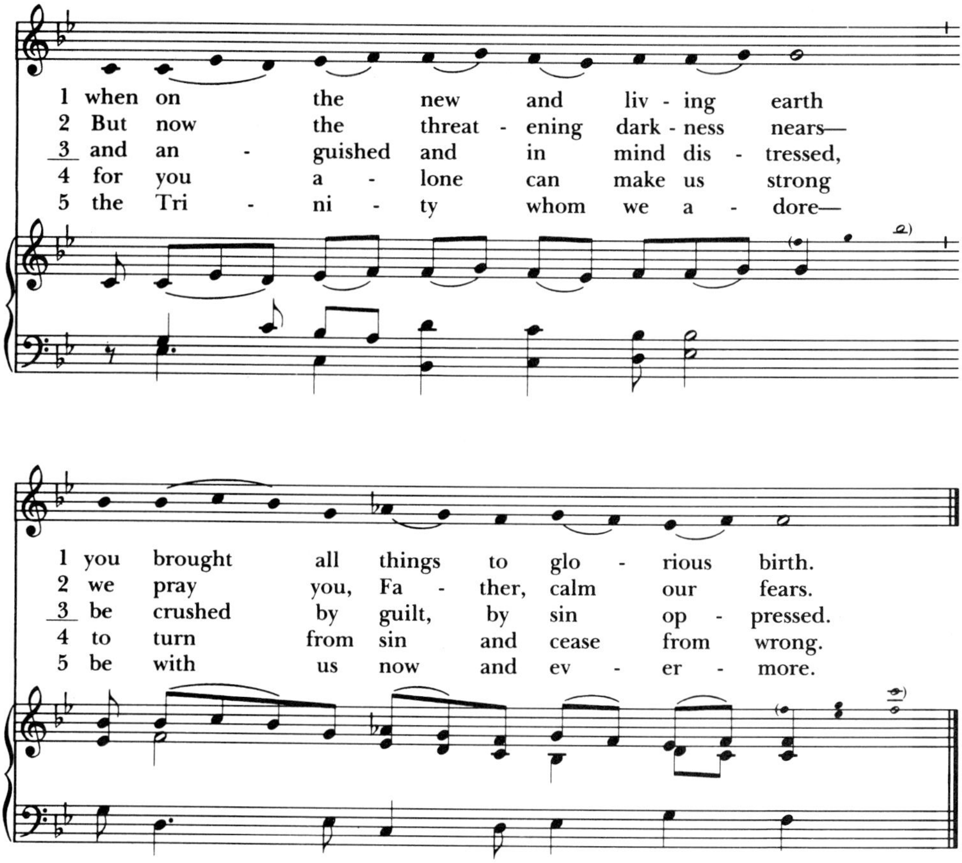
1 when on the new and liv - ing earth
2 But now the threat - ening dark - ness nears—
3 and an - guished and in mind dis - tressed,
4 for you a - lone can make us strong
5 the Tri - ni - ty whom we a - dore—
1 you brought all things to glo - rious birth.
2 we pray you, Fa - ther, calm our fears.
3 be crushed by guilt, by sin op - pressed.
4 to turn from sin and cease from wrong.
5 be with us now and ev - er - more.

The handbell notes are optional. Alternative tune: *Bromley*, 28.

Words: Latin, 6th cent.; tr. Anne K. LeCroy (b. 1930), alt.
Music: *Lucis Creator optime,* plainsong, Mode 8, Verona MS., 11th cent.; acc. David Dahl (b. 1937) LM

1 O blest Cre - a - tor, source of light, you gave the
2 You joined the morn and eve - ning ray; you found it
3 Lest we, be - set by doubt and strife, for - get your
4 E - ter - nal Fa - ther, help us rise and strive to
*5 De - fend us, Fa - ther, through the night, and with your
1 day with splen - dor bright, when on the new and
2 good and called it "day." But now the threat - ening
3 bless - ed gift of life, and an - guished and in
4 gain the heaven - ly prize; for you a - lone can
5 Son, and Spi - rit bright— the Tri - ni - ty whom
1 liv - ing earth you brought all things to glo - rious birth.
2 dark - ness nears— we pray you, Fa - ther, calm our fears.
3 mind dis - tressed, be crushed by guilt, by sin op - pressed.
4 make us strong to turn from sin and cease from wrong.
5 we a - dore— be with us now and ev - er - more.

Alternative tune: *Lucis Creator optime,* 27.

Words: Latin, 6th cent.; tr. Anne K. LeCroy (b. 1930), alt.
Music: *Bromley,* Franz Joseph Haydn (1732-1809)

♩= 108
LM

1 O Trin - i - ty of bless - ed light, O U - ni -
2 To thee our morn - ing song of praise, to thee our
3 To God the Fa - ther, heaven-ly Light, to Christ re -
ty of prince - ly might, the fier - y sun now
eve - ning prayer we raise; O grant us with thy
vealed in earth - ly night, to God the Ho - ly
goes his way; shed thou with - in our hearts thy ray.
saints on high to praise thee through e - ter - ni - ty.
Ghost we raise our e - qual and un - ceas - ing praise.

Alternative tune: *O Lux beata Trinitas,* 30.

Words: Latin, 6th cent.; tr. John Mason Neale (1818-1866). St. 3, Charles Coffin (1676-1749); tr. John Chandler (1806-1876)

Music: *Bromley,* Franz Joseph Haydn (1732-1809)

♩= 108
LM

1 O Trin - i - ty of bless - ed light,
2 To thee our morn-ing song of praise,
3 To God the Fa - ther, heaven - ly Light,
O U - ni - ty of prince - ly might,
to thee our eve - ning prayer we raise;
to Christ re - vealed in earth - ly night,
the fier - y sun now goes his way;
O grant us with thy saints on high
to God the Ho - ly Ghost we raise

shed thou with - in our hearts thy ray.
to praise thee through e - ter - ni - ty.
our e - qual and un - ceas - ing praise.

Alternative tune: *Bromley*, 29.

Words: Latin, 6th cent.; tr. John Mason Neale (1818-1866). St. 3, Charles Coffin (1676-1749); tr. John Chandler (1806-1876)

Music: *O lux beata Trinitas*, plainsong, Mode 8; acc. Alec Wyton (b. 1921) LM

1 Most Ho - ly God, the Lord of heaven, who in the
2 for you the daz - - zling star shines forth which in its
3 The day de - parts, the eve - ning stars se - rene - ly
4 You, Ho - ly One, Cre - a - tor, Lord, you in the
5 Like sun and day, shine in our hearts; like moon and
1 high arched sky has placed the sun that flames up from the
2 gleam - ing path de - clares the won - ders of your glo - rious
3 light the dark - ening sky; the moon with cool re - flect - ed
4 pri - mal world once set the bound-aries of the day and
5 night, give lov - ing peace. Free us from bonds of blind-ing
1 east and brings the splen - dors of the dawn:
2 power, and beck - ons us to wor - ship you.
3 glow will bring the si - lenc - es of night.
4 night and or - dered sea - sons in their round.
5 sin and guide us on our path to you.

Alternative tune: *Immense caeli Conditor*, 32.

Words: Latin; tr. Ann K. LeCroy (b. 1930)
Music: *Dunedin*, Vernon Griffiths (b. 1894)

𝅗𝅥=60
LM

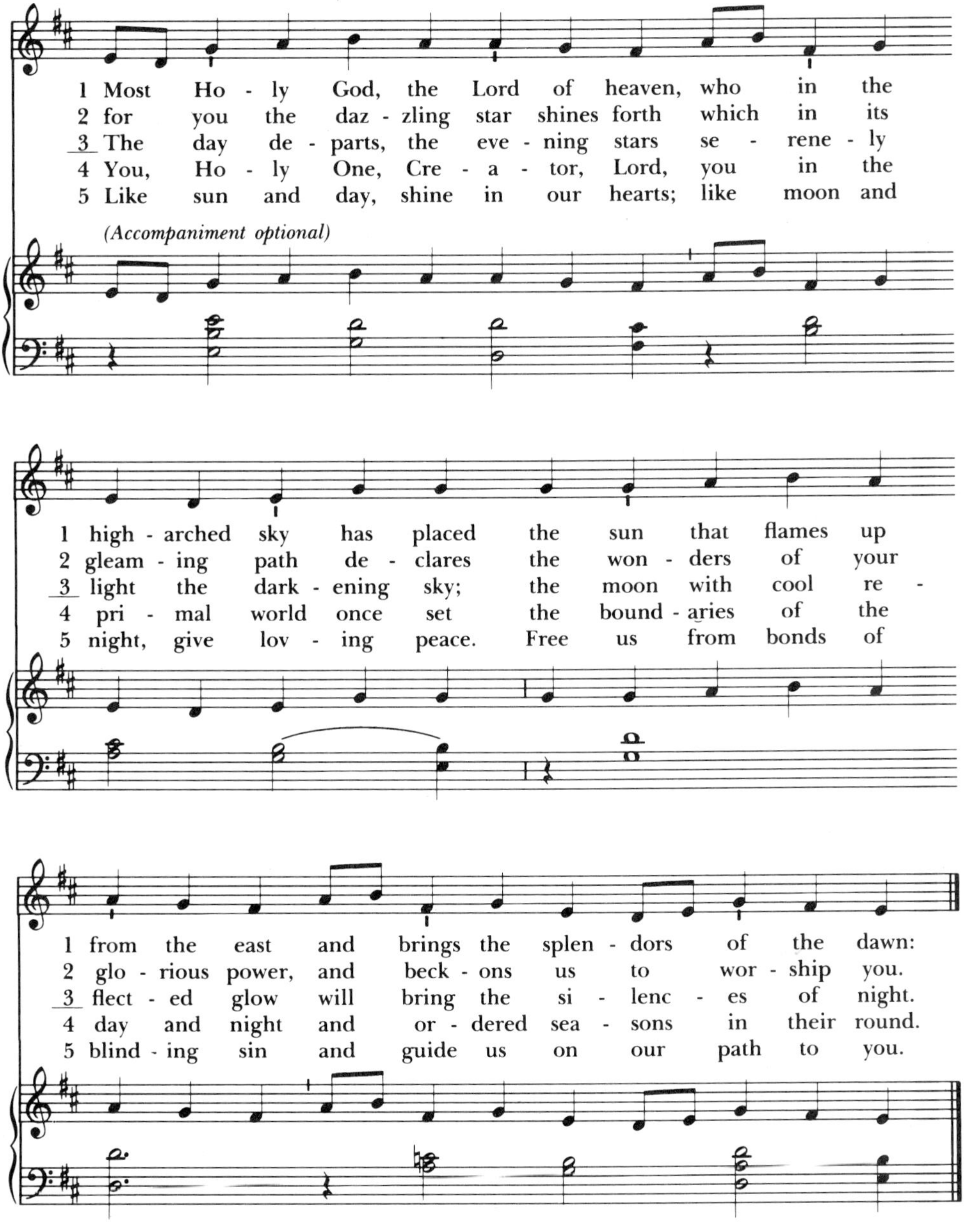
1 Most Ho - ly God, the Lord of heaven, who in the
2 for you the daz - zling star shines forth which in its
3 The day de - parts, the eve - ning stars se - rene - ly
4 You, Ho - ly One, Cre - a - tor, Lord, you in the
5 Like sun and day, shine in our hearts; like moon and
(Accompaniment optional)
1 high - arched sky has placed the sun that flames up
2 gleam - ing path de - clares the won - ders of your
3 light the dark - ening sky; the moon with cool re -
4 pri - mal world once set the bound - aries of the
5 night, give lov - ing peace. Free us from bonds of
1 from the east and brings the splen - dors of the dawn:
2 glo - rious power, and beck - ons us to wor - ship you.
3 flect - ed glow will bring the si - lenc - es of night.
4 day and night and or - dered sea - sons in their round.
5 blind - ing sin and guide us on our path to you.

Alternative tune: *Dunedin*, 31.

Words: Latin; tr. Anne K. LeCroy (b. 1930)
Music: *Immense caeli Conditor*, plainsong, Mode 1; ver. Schola Antiqua, 1983; acc. Roy Kehl (b. 1935)

𝅗𝅥 = 60
LM

1 Christ, might - y Sa - vior, Light of all cre - a - tion, you make the
2 Now comes the day's end as the sun is set - ting: mir - ror of
3 There - fore we come now eve - ning rites to of - fer, joy - ful - ly
4 Give heed, we pray you, to our sup - pli - ca - tion: that you may
5 Though bo - dies slum - ber, hearts shall keep their vi - gil, for ev - er
1 day - time ra - diant with the sun - light and to the night give
2 day - break, pledge of re - sur - rec - tion; while in the hea - vens
3 chant - ing ho - ly hymns to praise you, with all cre - a - tion
4 grant us par - don for of - fens - es, strength for our weak hearts,
5 rest - ing in the peace of Je - sus, in light or dark - ness
1 glit - ter - ing a - dorn - ment, stars in the hea - vens.
2 choirs of stars ap - pear - ing hal - low the night - fall.
3 join - ing hearts and voic - es sing - ing your glo - ry.
4 rest for ach - ing bo - dies, sooth - ing the wear - y.
5 wor - ship - ing our Sa - vior now and for ev - er.

Alternative tunes: *Innisfree Farm,* 34; *Mighty Savior,* 35.

Words: Mozarabic, 10th cent.; tr. Alan G. McDougall (1895-1964); rev. Anne K. LeCroy (b. 1930)
Music: *Christe, Lux mundi,* plainsong, Mode 7, Freiburg MS., 14th cent.; acc. Richard Proulx (b. 1937) 11. 11. 11. 5

34

1 Christ, might - y Sa - vior, Light of all cre - a - tion, you make the
2 Now comes the day's end as the sun is set - ting: mir - ror of
3 There - fore we come now eve - ning rites to of - fer, joy - ful - ly
4 Give heed, we pray you, to our sup - pli - ca - tion: that you may
5 Though bo - dies slum - ber, hearts shall keep their vi - gil, for ev - er
1 day - time ra - diant with the sun - light and to the night give
2 day - break, pledge of re - sur-rec - tion; while in the hea - vens
3 chant - ing ho - ly hymns to praise you, with all cre - a - tion
4 grant us par - don for of-fens - es, strength for our weak hearts,
5 rest - ing in the peace of Je - sus, in light or dark - ness
1 glit - ter - ing a - dorn - ment, stars in the hea - vens.
2 choirs of stars ap - pear - ing hal - low the night - fall.
3 join - ing hearts and voic - es sing - ing your glo - ry.
4 rest for ach - ing bo - dies, sooth - ing the wear - y.
5 wor-ship-ing our Sa - vior now and for ev - er.

Alternative tunes: *Christe, Lux mundi,* 33; *Mighty Savior,* 35.

Words: Mozarabic, 10th cent.; tr. Alan G. McDougall (1895-1964); rev. Anne K. LeCroy (b. 1930) ♩=56

Music: *Innisfree Farm,* Richard Wayne Dirksen (b. 1921) 11. 11. 11. 5

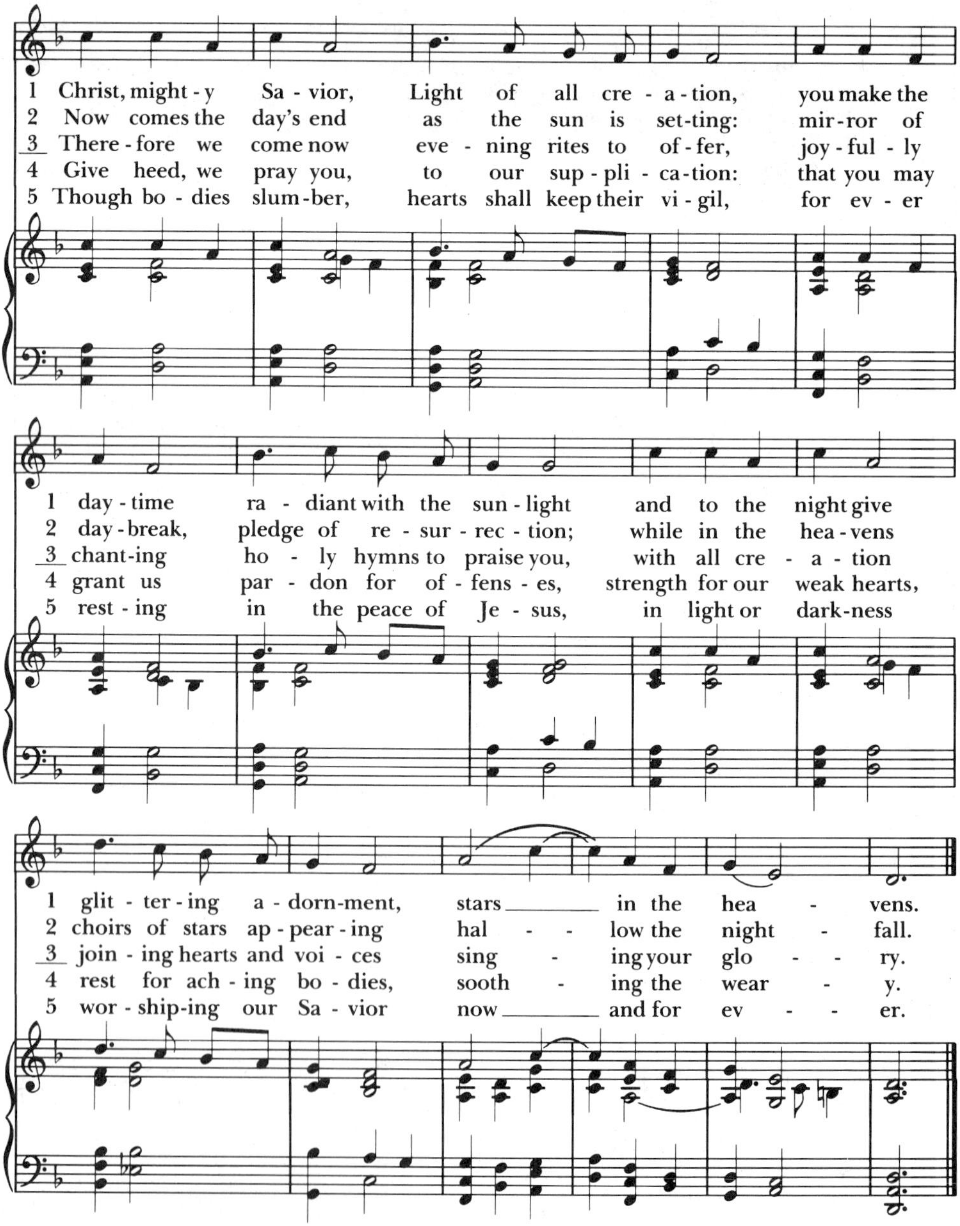
1 Christ, might - y Sa - vior, Light of all cre - a - tion, you make the
2 Now comes the day's end as the sun is set-ting: mir-ror of
3 There - fore we come now eve - ning rites to of - fer, joy - ful - ly
4 Give heed, we pray you, to our sup - pli - ca - tion: that you may
5 Though bo - dies slum - ber, hearts shall keep their vi - gil, for ev - er
1 day - time ra - diant with the sun - light and to the night give
2 day - break, pledge of re - sur - rec - tion; while in the hea - vens
3 chant - ing ho - ly hymns to praise you, with all cre - a - tion
4 grant us par - don for of - fens - es, strength for our weak hearts,
5 rest - ing in the peace of Je - sus, in light or dark - ness
1 glit - ter - ing a - dorn - ment, stars ___ in the hea - vens.
2 choirs of stars ap - pear - ing hal - low the night - fall.
3 join - ing hearts and voi - ces sing - ing your glo - ry.
4 rest for ach - ing bo - dies, sooth - ing the wear - y.
5 wor - ship - ing our Sa - vior now ___ and for ev - er.

Alternative tunes: *Christe, Lux mundi,* 33; *Innisfree Farm,* 34.

Words: Mozarabic, 10th cent.; tr. Alan G. McDougall; (1895-1964) rev. Anne K. LeCroy (b. 1930)
Music: *Mighty Savior,* David Hurd (b. 1950)

♩= 100
11. 11. 11. 5

36

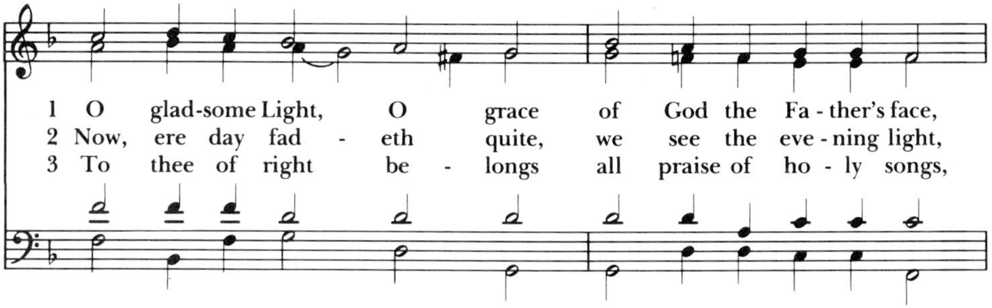
1 O glad-some Light, O grace of God the Fa - ther's face,
2 Now, ere day fad - eth quite, we see the eve - ning light,
3 To thee of right be - longs all praise of ho - ly songs,

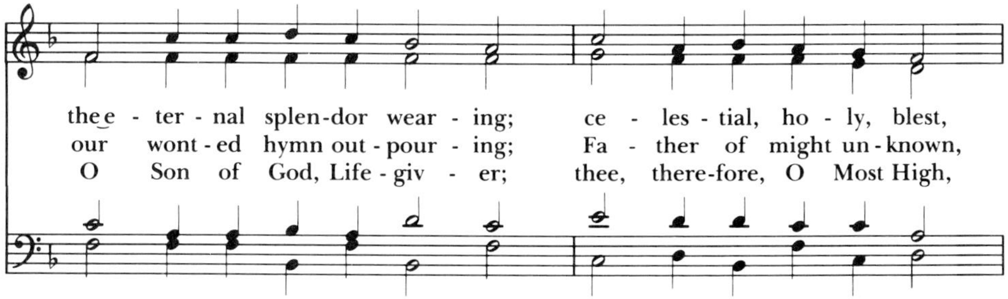
the e - ter - nal splen-dor wear - ing; ce - les - tial, ho - ly, blest,
our wont - ed hymn out - pour - ing; Fa - ther of might un - known,
O Son of God, Life - giv - er; thee, there-fore, O Most High,

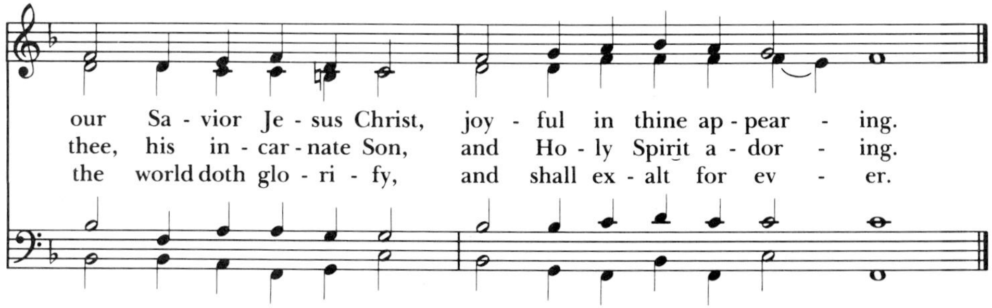
our Sa - vior Je - sus Christ, joy - ful in thine ap - pear - ing.
thee, his in - car - nate Son, and Ho - ly Spirit a - dor - ing.
the world doth glo - ri - fy, and shall ex - alt for ev - er.

Words: Greek, 3rd cent.; tr. Robert Seymour Bridges (1844-1930); para. of *O Gracious Light*
Music: *Le Cantique de Siméon*, melody Louis Bourgeois (1510?-1561?); harm. Claude Goudimel (1514-1572)

𝅗𝅥 = 50
667. 667

Evening

1 O bright-ness of the im - mor - tal Fa - ther's face,
2 the sun is sink - ing now, and one by one
3 Worth-y art thou at all times to re - ceive
most ho - ly, heaven-ly, blest, Lord Je - sus Christ, in whom his
the lamps of eve - ning shine; we hymn the e - ter - nal Fa - ther,
our hal-lowed prais - es, Lord. O Son of God, be thou, in
truth and grace are vi - si - bly ex - pressed:
and the Son, and Ho - ly Ghost di - vine.
whom we live, through all the world a - dored.

Words: Greek, 3rd cent.; tr. Edward W. Eddis (1825-1905); para. of *O Gracious Light*
Music: *Evening Hymn*, Gerald Near (b. 1942)

♩=100
10 6. 10 6

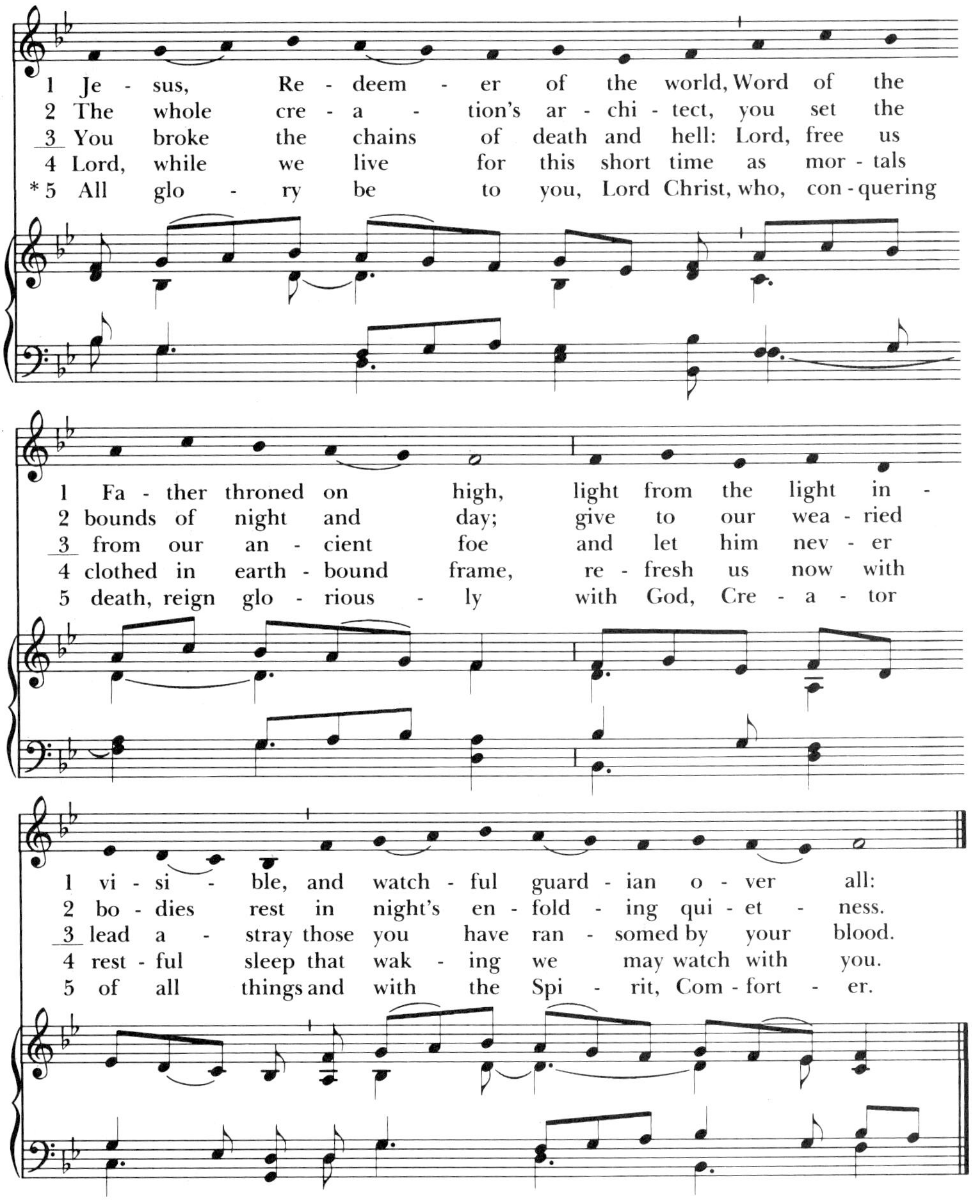
1 Je - sus, Re - deem - er of the world, Word of the
2 The whole cre - a - tion's ar - chi - tect, you set the
3 You broke the chains of death and hell: Lord, free us
4 Lord, while we live for this short time as mor - tals
*5 All glo - ry be to you, Lord Christ, who, con - quering
1 Fa - ther throned on high, light from the light in -
2 bounds of night and day; give to our wea - ried
3 from our an - cient foe and let him nev - er
4 clothed in earth - bound frame, re - fresh us now with
5 death, reign glo - rious - ly with God, Cre - a - tor
1 vi - si - ble, and watch - ful guard - ian o - ver all:
2 bo - dies rest in night's en - fold - ing qui - et - ness.
3 lead a - stray those you have ran - somed by your blood.
4 rest - ful sleep that wak - ing we may watch with you.
5 of all things and with the Spi - rit, Com - fort - er.

Other accompaniments, 236. Alternative tunes: *Wilderness*, 39; *Jesu, nostra redemptio* (syllabic rhythm), 233.

Words: Latin, 10th cent.; ver. *Hymnal 1982*. St. 5, Anne LeCroy (b. 1930)
Music: *Jesu, nostra redemptio*, plainsong, Mode 8, Worcester MS., 13th cent.; acc. Richard P. Solly (b. 1952)

LM

1 Je - sus, Re - deem - er of the world, Word of the
2 The whole cre - a - tion's ar - chi - tect, you set the
3 You broke the chains of death and hell: Lord, free us
4 Lord, while we live for this short time as mor - tals
*5 All glo - ry be to you, Lord Christ, who, con-quering
1 Fa - ther throned on high, light from the light in - vi - si -
2 bounds of night and day; give to our wea-ried bo - dies
3 from our an - cient foe and let him nev - er lead a -
4 clothed in earth - bound frame, re - fresh us now with rest - ful
5 death, reign glo - rious - ly with God, Cre - a - tor of all
1 ble, and watch - ful guard - ian o - ver all;
2 rest in night's en - fold - ing qui - et - ness.
3 stray those you have ran - somed by your blood.
4 sleep that wak - ing we may watch with you.
5 things and with the Spi - rit, Com - fort - er.

Alternative tune: *Jesu, nostra redemptio,* 38.

Words: Latin, 10th cent.; ver. *Hymnal 1982.* St. 5, Anne K. LeCroy (b. 1930)
Music: *Wilderness,* Reginald Sparshatt Thatcher (1888-1957)

𝅗𝅥=63
LM

Compline

40

1 O Christ, you are both light and day, you drive a -
2 We pray you, O most ho - ly Lord, to be our
3 Al - though our eyes in sleep be closed, let hearts in
4 De - fend - er of us all, look down; re - pel our
*5 O Christ, Re - deem - er of the world, O God, our
1 way the sha - dowed night; as Day - star you pre -
2 guard - ian while we sleep; be - stow on us who
3 con - stant vi - gil watch; with your right hand you
4 dread, ma - li - cious foe; di - rect your faith - ful
5 Ma - ker and our end, O Spi - rit, bond of
1 cede the dawn, the Her - ald of the light to come.
2 rest in you the bless - ing of a qui - et night.
3 will pro - tect those who be - lieve and trust in you.
4 house - hold Lord, whom you have pur - chased with your blood.
5 peace and love, to you be thanks and end - less praise.

Alternative tune: *Compline*, 41.

Words: Latin, 6th cent.; ver. *Hymnal 1982.* St. 5, Charles P. Price (b. 1920)
Music: *Christe, qui Lux es et dies*, plainsong, Mode 2, *Mailander Hymnen*, 15th cent; acc. James McGregor (b. 1930)

LM

1 O Christ, you are both light and day,
2 We pray you, O most ho - ly Lord,
3 Al - though our eyes in sleep be closed,
4 De - fend - er of us all, look down;
*5 O Christ, Re - deem - er of the world,
1 you drive a - way the sha - dowed night;
2 to be our guard - ian while we sleep;
3 let hearts in con - stant vi - gil watch;
4 re - pel our dread, ma - li - cious foe;
5 O God, our Ma - ker and our end,
1 as Day - star you pre - cede the dawn,
2 be - stow on us who rest in you
3 with your right hand you will pro - tect
4 di - rect your faith - ful house - hold, Lord,
5 O Spi - rit, bond of peace and love,

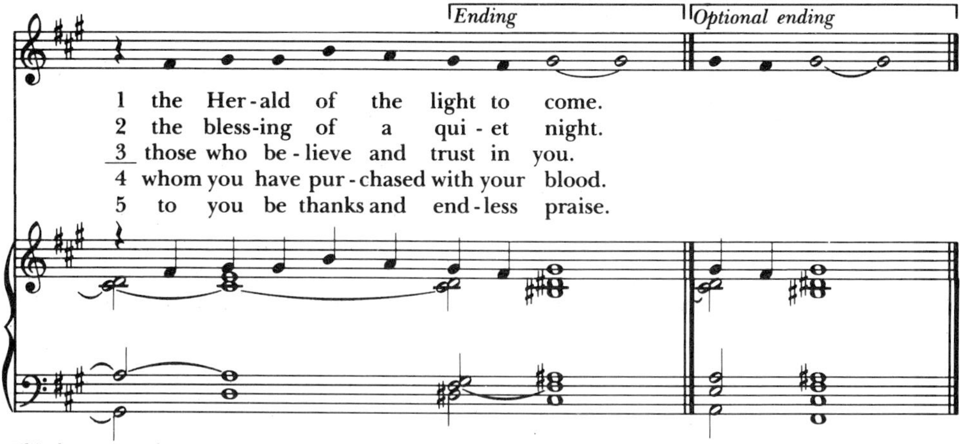
Ending
Optional ending
1 the Her-ald of the light to come.
2 the bless-ing of a qui-et night.
3 those who be-lieve and trust in you.
4 whom you have pur-chased with your blood.
5 to you be thanks and end-less praise.

This hymn may be sung unaccompanied. The accompaniment may be performed without pedal. When 16′ pedal sound is desired, the optional ending should be used. Alternative tune: *Christe, qui Lux es et dies,* 40.

Words: Latin, 6th cent.; ver. *Hymnal 1982.* St. 5, Charles P. Price (b. 1920) 𝅗𝅥=𝅝=56
Music: *Compline,* David Hurd (b. 1950) LM

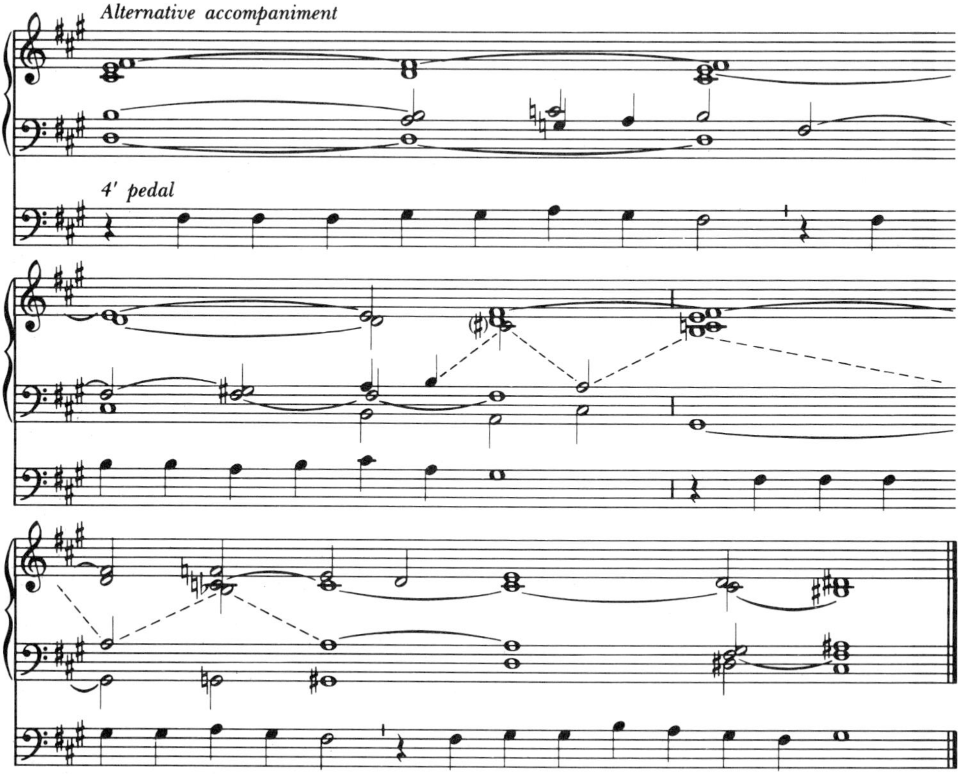
Alternative accompaniment
4′ pedal
(♯)

Music: *Compline,* David Hurd (b. 1950) 𝅗𝅥=𝅝=56

1 Now the day is o - ver, night is draw - ing nigh,
2 Je - sus, give the wear - y calm and sweet re - pose;
3 Grant to lit - tle child - ren vis - ions bright of thee;
4 Com - fort eve - ry suf - ferer watch-ing late in pain;
5 Through the long night watch - es may thine an - gels spread

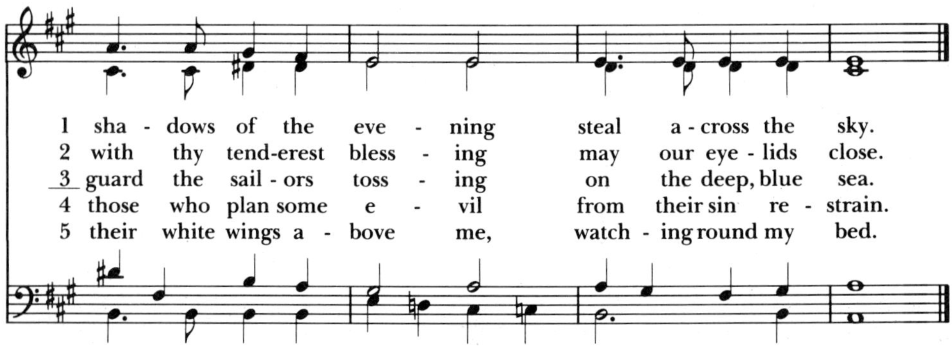
1 sha - dows of the eve - ning steal a - cross the sky.
2 with thy tend-erest bless - ing may our eye - lids close.
3 guard the sail - ors toss - ing on the deep, blue sea.
4 those who plan some e - vil from their sin re - strain.
5 their white wings a - bove me, watch - ing round my bed.

1 eve - ning steal a - cross the sky.
2 bless-ing may our eye - - lids close.
3 toss - ing on the deep, blue sea.
4 e - vil from their sin re - strain.
5 bove me, watch-ing round my bed.

6 When the morning wakens,
then may I arise
pure, and fresh, and sinless
in thy holy eyes.

Words: Sabine Baring-Gould (1834-1924), alt.
Music: *Merrial,* Joseph Barnby (1838-1896)

𝅗𝅥=48
65.65

43

1 2
1 All praise to thee, my God, this night, for all the bless - ings
2 For - give me, Lord, for thy dear Son, the ill that I this
3 O may my soul on thee re - pose, and with sweet sleep mine
4 Praise God, from whom all bless - ings flow; praise him, all crea - tures
of the light: keep me, O keep me, King of kings, be -
day have done; that with the world, my - self, and thee, I,
eye - lids close; sleep that shall me more vi - gorous make to
here be - low; praise him a - bove, ye heaven - ly host: praise
For canon only
neath thine own al - might - y wings. (al - might - y wings.)
ere I sleep, at peace may be. (at peace may be.)
serve my God when I a - wake. (when I a - wake.)
Fa - ther, Son, and Ho - ly Ghost. (and Ho - ly Ghost.)

This hymn may be sung unaccompanied as a four-part canon at a distance of one measure.

Words: Thomas Ken (1637-1711)
Music: *The Eighth Tune,* Thomas Tallis (1505?-1585); adapt. *Hymnal 1982*

♩= 76
LM

1 To you be - fore the close of day, Cre - a - tor
2 Save us from trou - bled, rest - less sleep, from all ill
3 A health - y life we ask of you, the fire of
4 Al - might - y Fa - ther, hear our cry through Je - sus
of all things, we pray that in your con - - stant
dreams your child-ren keep; so calm our minds that
love in us re - new, and when the dawn new
Christ, our Lord Most High, whom with the Spi - - rit
clem - en - cy our guard and keep - er you would be.
fears may cease and rest - ed bo - dies wake in peace.
light will bring your praise and glo - ry we shall sing.
we a - dore for ev - er and for ev - er - more.

Alternative tune: *Te lucis ante terminum* (Sarum ferial), 45.

Words: Latin, 6th cent.; ver. *Hymnal 1982.* St. 4, James Waring McCrady (b. 1938)
Music: *Te lucis ante terminum,* plainsong, Mode 8, *Antiphonale Sarisburiense,* Vol. II; acc. Gerard Farrell (b. 1919)

LM

1 To you be - fore the close of day, Cre - a - tor
2 Save us from trou - bled, rest - less sleep, from all ill
3 A health - y life we ask of you, the fire of
4 Al - might - y Fa - ther, hear our cry through Je - sus
of all things, we pray that in your con - stant
dreams your child - ren keep; so calm our minds that
love in us re - new, and when the dawn new
Christ, our Lord Most High, whom with the Spi - rit
clem - en - cy our guard and keep - er you would be.
fears may cease and rest - ed bo - dies wake in peace.
light will bring your praise and glo - ry we shall sing.
we a - dore for ev - er and for ev - er - more.

Alternative tune: *Te lucis ante terminum* (Sarum), 44.

Words: Latin, 6th cent.; ver. *Hymnal 1982*. St. 4, James Waring McCrady (b. 1938)
Music: *Te lucis ante terminum*, plainsong, Mode 8; acc. James McGregor (b. 1930)

LM

1 The du - teous day now clos - eth, each flower and tree re -
2 Now all the heaven-ly splen - dor breaks forth in star - light
3 Though long our mor - tal blind - ness has missed God's lov - ing -
pos - eth, shade creeps o'er wild and wood: let
ten - der from myr - iad worlds un - known; and
kind - ness and plunged us in - to strife; yet
us, as night is fall - ing, on God our Ma - ker
we, this mar - vel see - ing, for - get our sel - fish
when life's day is o - ver, shall death's fair night dis -
call - - ing, give thanks to him, the Giv - er good.
be - - ing for joy of beau - ty not our own.
cov - - er the fields of ev - er - last - ing life.

Words: Paul Gerhardt (1607-1676); tr. Robert Seymour Bridges (1844-1930) and others
Music: *O Welt, ich muss dich lassen,* melody att. Heinrich Isaac (1450?-1517); harm. Johann Sebastian Bach (1685-1750)

𝅗𝅥=66
776. 778

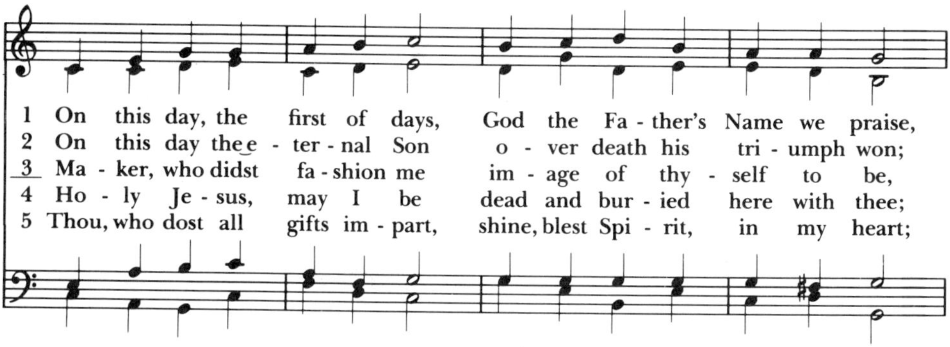
1 On this day, the first of days, God the Fa - ther's Name we praise,
2 On this day the e - ter - nal Son o - ver death his tri - umph won;
3 Ma - ker, who didst fa - shion me im - age of thy - self to be,
4 Ho - ly Je - sus, may I be dead and bur - ied here with thee;
5 Thou, who dost all gifts im - part, shine, blest Spi - rit, in my heart;

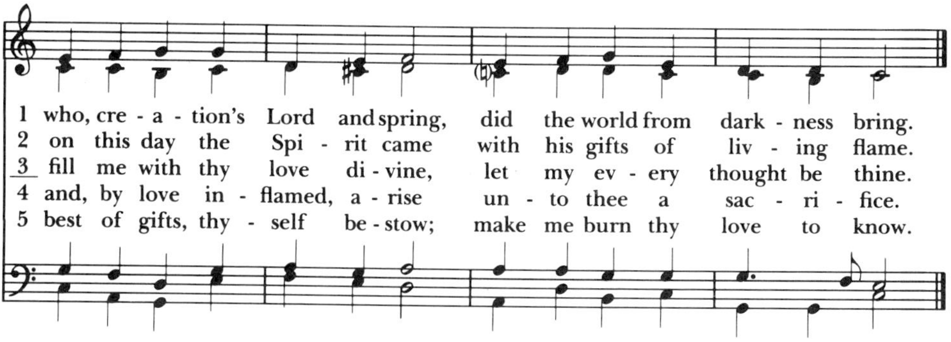
1 who, cre - a - tion's Lord and spring, did the world from dark - ness bring.
2 on this day the Spi - rit came with his gifts of liv - ing flame.
3 fill me with thy love di - vine, let my ev - ery thought be thine.
4 and, by love in - flamed, a - rise un - to thee a sac - ri - fice.
5 best of gifts, thy - self be - stow; make me burn thy love to know.

6 God, the blessed Three in One
dwell within my heart alone;
thou dost give thyself to me:
help me give myself to thee.

Stanzas 1 and 2 may be sung as a sequence hymn.

Words: Latin; tr. Henry Williams Baker (1821-1877), alt.
Music: *Gott sei Dank,* melody from *Geistreiches Gesangbuch,* 1704;
adapt. and harm. William Henry Havergal (1793-1870), alt.

𝅗𝅥 = 52
77. 77

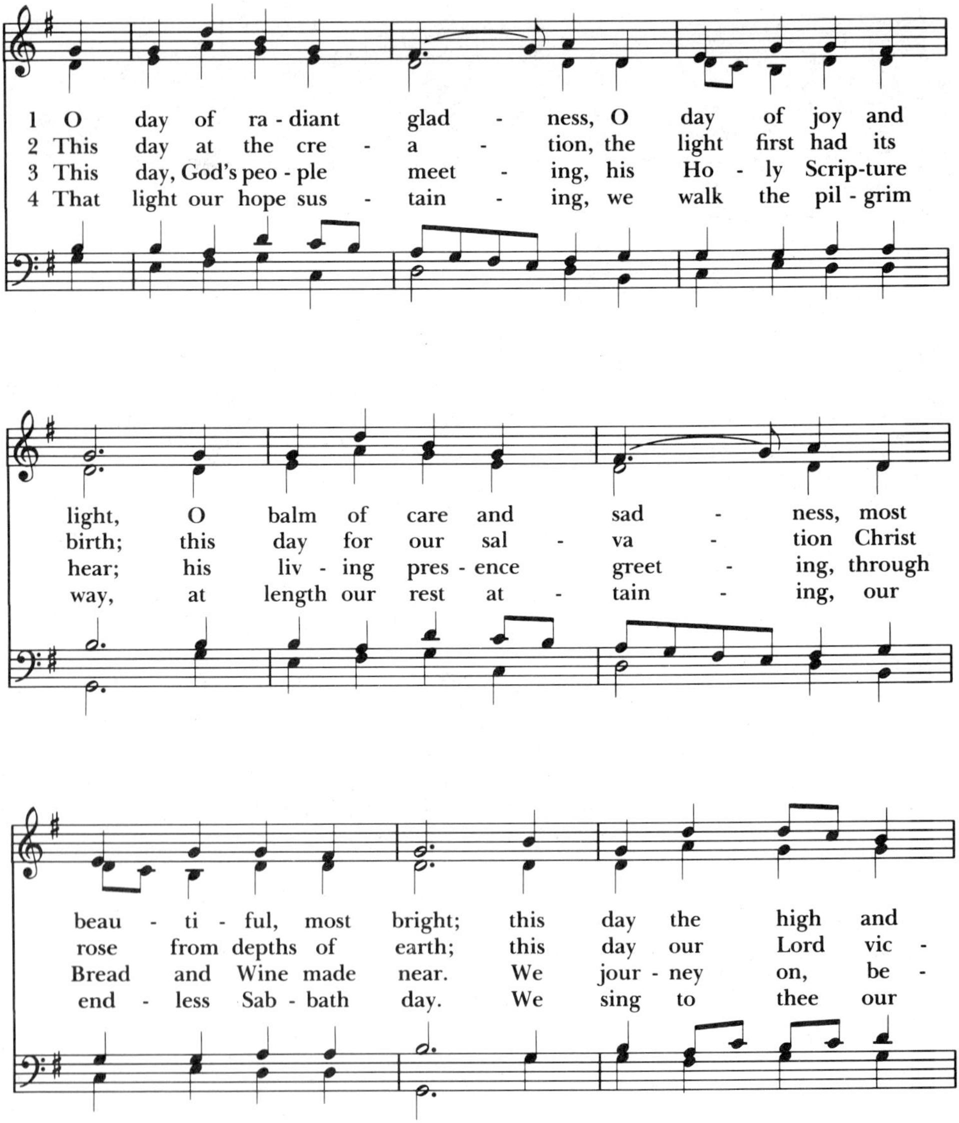
1 O day of ra - diant glad - ness, O day of joy and
2 This day at the cre - a - tion, the light first had its
3 This day, God's peo - ple meet - ing, his Ho - ly Scrip-ture
4 That light our hope sus - tain - ing, we walk the pil - grim
light, O balm of care and sad - ness, most
birth; this day for our sal - va - tion Christ
hear; his liv - ing pres - ence greet - ing, through
way, at length our rest at - tain - ing, our
beau - ti - ful, most bright; this day the high and
rose from depths of earth; this day our Lord vic -
Bread and Wine made near. We jour - ney on, be -
end - less Sab - bath day. We sing to thee our

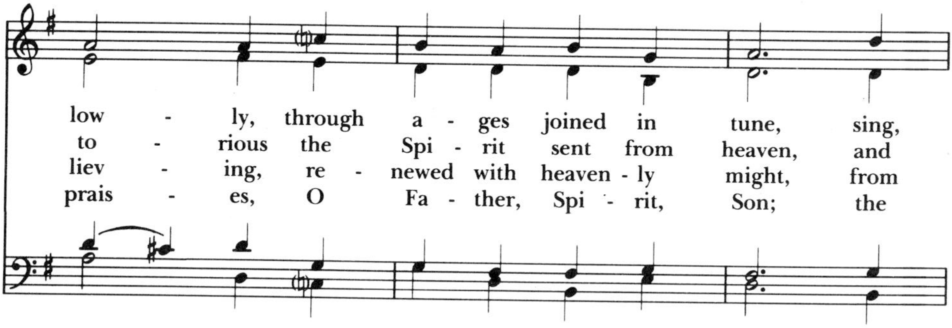
low - ly, through a - ges joined in tune, sing,
to - rious the Spi - rit sent from heaven, and
liev - ing, re - newed with heaven - ly might, from
prais - es, O Fa - ther, Spi - rit, Son; the

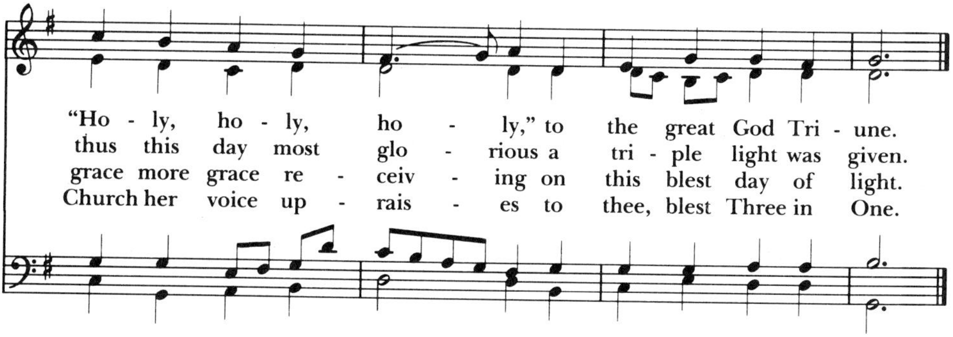
"Ho - ly, ho - ly, ho - ly," to the great God Tri - une.
thus this day most glo - rious a tri - ple light was given.
grace more grace re - ceiv - ing on this blest day of light.
Church her voice up - rais - es to thee, blest Three in One.

Another harmonization, 616.

Words: Sts. 1-2, Christopher Wordsworth (1807-1885), alt.; st. 3, Charles P. Price (b. 1920); st. 4, *Hymnal 1982*

Music: *Es flog ein kleins Waldvögelein,* German folk song; harm. George Ratcliffe Woodward (1848-1934)

𝅗𝅥 = 54

76. 76. D

1 Come, let us with our Lord a - rise, our Lord who made both
2 This is the day the Lord hath made that all may see his
3 Then let us ren - der him his own, with sol - emn prayer ap -
earth and skies, who died to save the world he made
love dis-played, may feel his re - sur - rec - tion's power
proach the throne, with meek-ness hear the gos - pel word,
and rose tri - um - phant from the dead; he rose, the
and rise a - gain to fall no more, in per - fect
with thanks his dy - ing love re - cord; our joy - ful

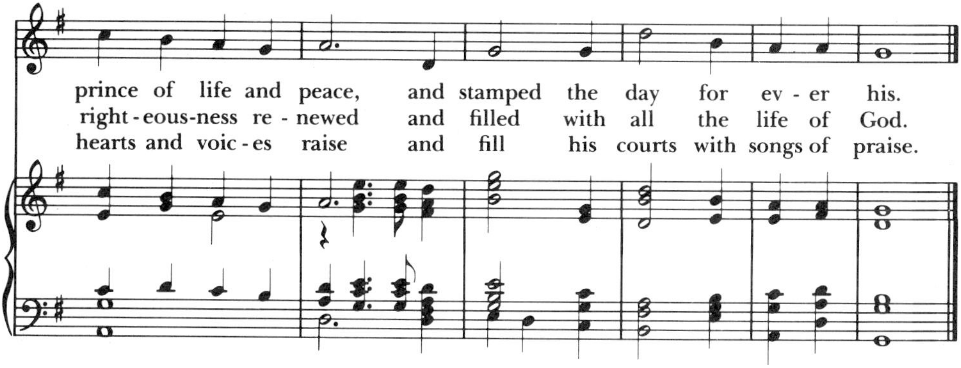
prince of life and peace, and stamped the day for ev - er his.
right - eous-ness re - newed and filled with all the life of God.
hearts and voic - es raise and fill his courts with songs of praise.

Words: Charles Wesley (1707-1788)
Music: *Meadville,* Walter Pelz (b. 1926); adapt. W. Thomas Jones (b. 1956)

♩= 112
88. 88. 88

Sunday

50

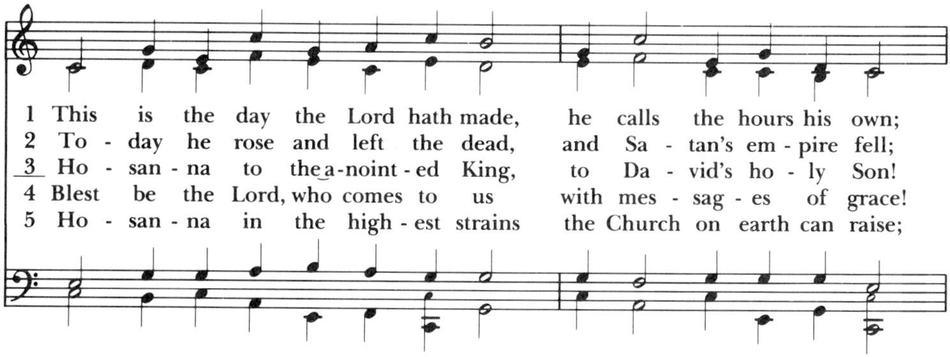
1 This is the day the Lord hath made, he calls the hours his own;
2 To - day he rose and left the dead, and Sa - tan's em - pire fell;
3 Ho - san - na to the a-noint - ed King, to Da - vid's ho - ly Son!
4 Blest be the Lord, who comes to us with mes - sag - es of grace!
5 Ho - san - na in the high - est strains the Church on earth can raise;

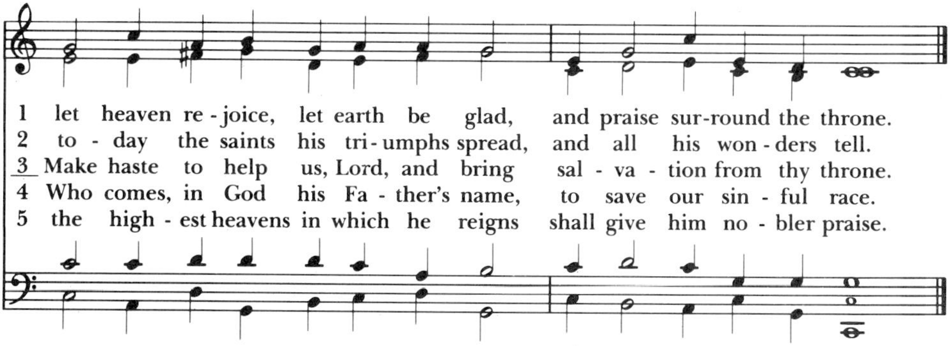
1 let heaven re - joice, let earth be glad, and praise sur-round the throne.
2 to - day the saints his tri - umphs spread, and all his won - ders tell.
3 Make haste to help us, Lord, and bring sal - va - tion from thy throne.
4 Who comes, in God his Fa - ther's name, to save our sin - ful race.
5 the high - est heavens in which he reigns shall give him no - bler praise.

Stanzas 1 and 2 may be sung as a sequence hymn. This music in D, 677.

Words: Isaac Watts (1674-1748), alt.
Music: *London New,* melody from *The Psalmes of David in Prose and Meter,* 1635, alt.; harm. John Playford (1623-1686)

♩= 88
CM

1 We the Lord's peo - ple, heart and voice u - nit - ing, praise him who
2 This is the Lord's house, home of all his peo - ple, school for the
3 This is the Lord's day, day of God's own mak - ing, day of cre -
4 In the Lord's ser - vice bread and wine are of - fered, that Christ may
called us out of sin and dark - ness in - to his own light,
faith - ful, ref - uge for the sin - ner, rest for the pil - grim,
a - tion, day of re - sur - rec - tion, day of the Spi - rit,
take them, bless them, break, and give them to all his peo - ple,
that he might a - noint us a roy - al priest-hood.
ha - ven for the wea - ry; all find a wel - come.
sign of hea - ven's ban - quet, day for re - joic - ing.
his own life im - part - ing, food ev - er - last - ing.

Words: John E. Bowers (b. 1923), alt.
Music: *Decatur Place*, Richard Wayne Dirksen (b. 1921)

♩=84
11. 11. 11. 5

1 This day at thy cre - at - ing word first o'er the earth the light was poured; O Lord, this day up - on us shine and fill our souls with light di - vine.
2 This day the Lord for sin - ners slain in might vic - to - rious rose a - gain; O Je - sus, may we lift - ed be from death of sin to life in thee!
3 This day the Ho - ly Spi - rit came with fier - y tongues of clo - ven flame; O Spi - rit, fill our hearts this day with grace to hear and grace to pray.
4 All praise to God the Fa - ther be, all praise, e - ter - nal Son, to thee, whom, with the Spi - rit, we a - dore for ev - er and for ev - er - more.

Words: William Walsham How (1823-1897), alt.
Music: *Rushford,* Henry G. Ley (1887-1962)

𝅗𝅥=54
LM

1 Once he came in bless - ing, all our ills re - dress - ing;
2 Still he comes with - in us, still his voice would win us
3 Thus, if thou canst name him, not a - shamed to claim him,
4 One who thus en - dur - eth bright re - ward se - cur - eth.
came in like - ness low - ly, Son of God most ho - ly;
from the sins that hurt us, would to Truth con - vert us:
but wilt trust him bold - ly nor dost love him cold - ly,
Come, then, O Lord Je - sus, from our sins re - lease us;
bore the cross to save us, hope and free - dom gave us.
not in tor - ment hold us, but in love en - fold us.
he will then re - ceive thee, heal thee, and for - give thee.
let us here con - fess thee till in heaven we bless thee.

Words: Jan Roh (1485?-1547); tr. Catherine Winkworth (1827-1878), alt.
Music: *Gottes Sohn ist kommen,* melody Michael Weisse (d. 1534); harm. Jack W. Burnam (b. 1946)

𝅗𝅥=60
66. 66. 66

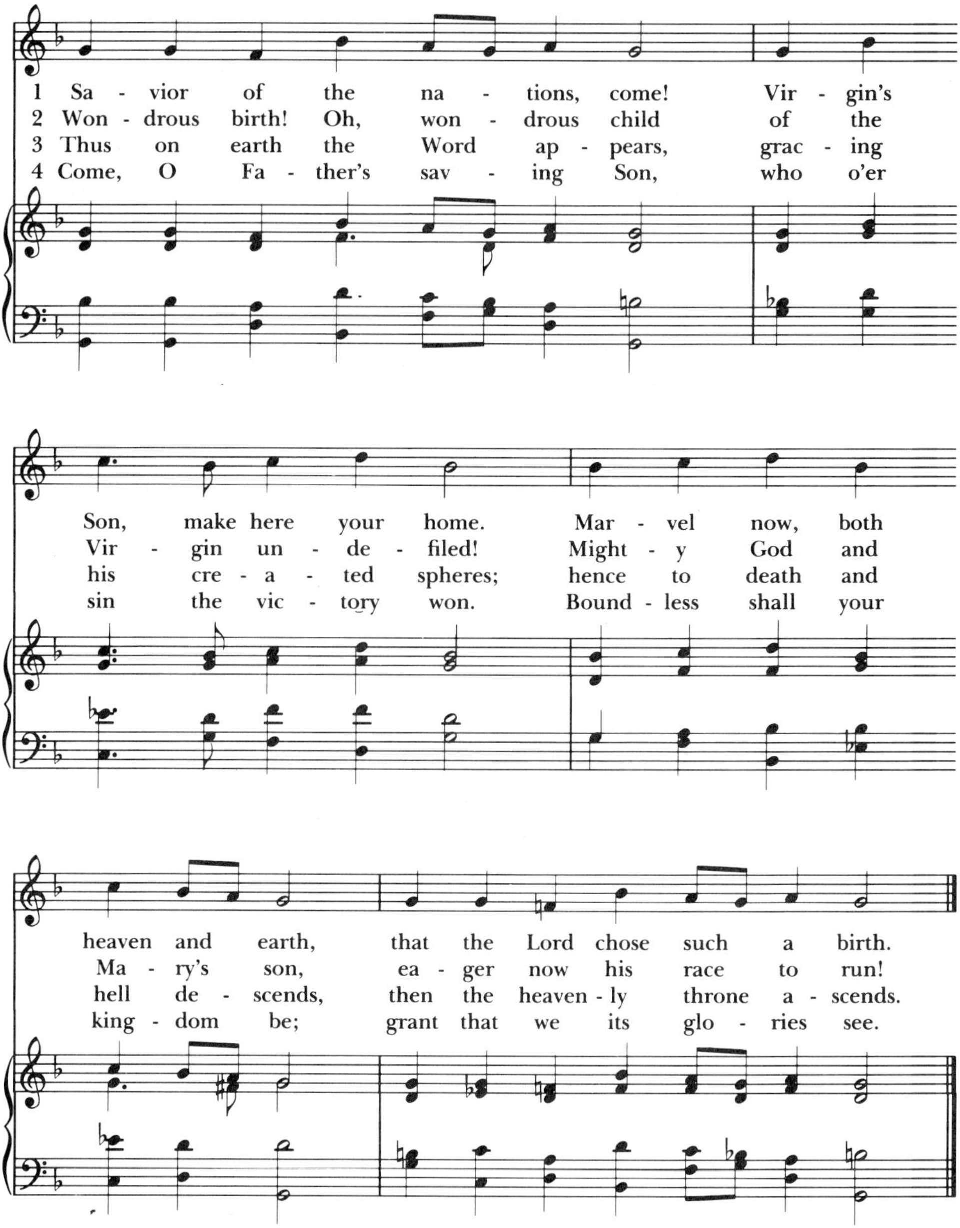
1 Sa - vior of the na - tions, come! Vir - gin's
2 Won - drous birth! Oh, won - drous child of the
3 Thus on earth the Word ap - pears, grac - ing
4 Come, O Fa - ther's sav - ing Son, who o'er
Son, make here your home. Mar - vel now, both
Vir - gin un - de - filed! Might - y God and
his cre - a - ted spheres; hence to death and
sin the vic - tory won. Bound - less shall your
heaven and earth, that the Lord chose such a birth.
Ma - ry's son, ea - ger now his race to run!
hell de - scends, then the heaven - ly throne a - scends.
king - dom be; grant that we its glo - ries see.

Words: Martin Luther (1483-1546) after Ambrose of Milan (340-397);
tr. William M. Reynolds (1812-1876) and James Waring McCrady (b. 1938)

Music: *Nun komm, der Heiden Heiland,* melody from *Erfurt Enchiridia,* 1524;
harm. Melchior Vulpius (1560?-1616)

𝅗𝅥 = 44
77. 77

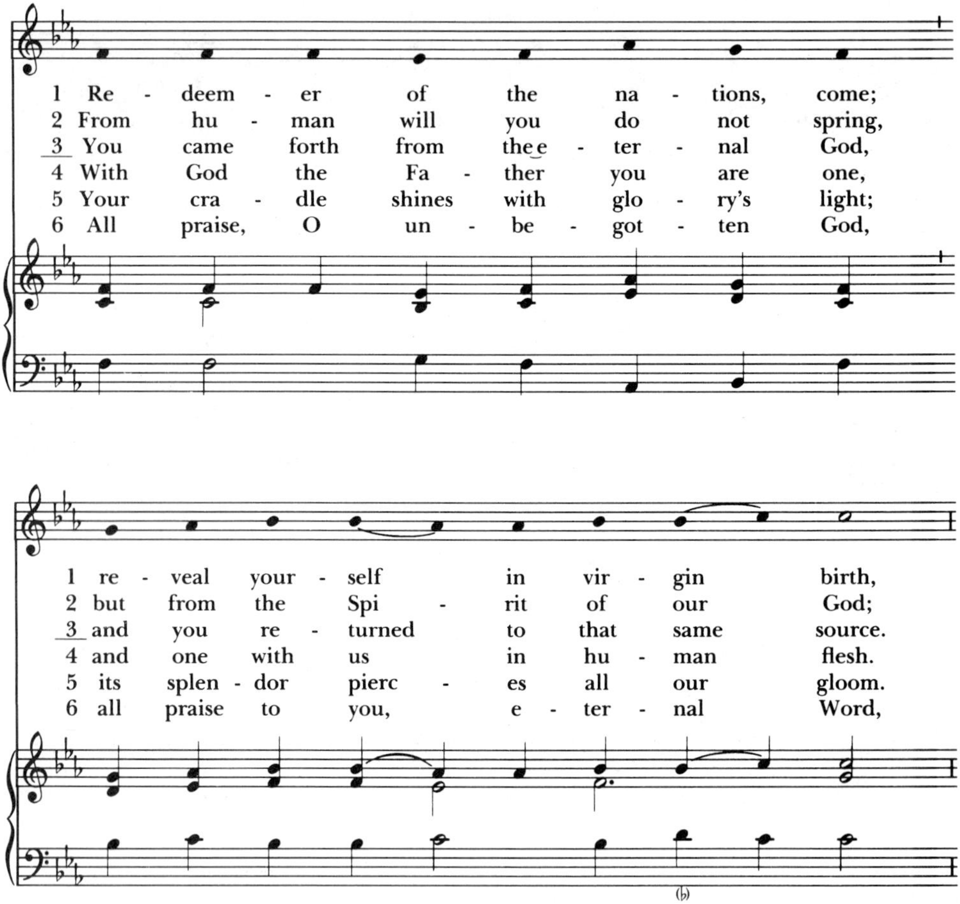
1 Re - deem - er of the na - tions, come;
2 From hu - man will you do not spring,
3 You came forth from the e - ter - nal God,
4 With God the Fa - ther you are one,
5 Your cra - dle shines with glo - ry's light;
6 All praise, O un - be - got - ten God,
1 re - veal your - self in vir - gin birth,
2 but from the Spi - rit of our God;
3 and you re - turned to that same source.
4 and one with us in hu - man flesh.
5 its splen - dor pierc - es all our gloom.
6 all praise to you, e - ter - nal Word,

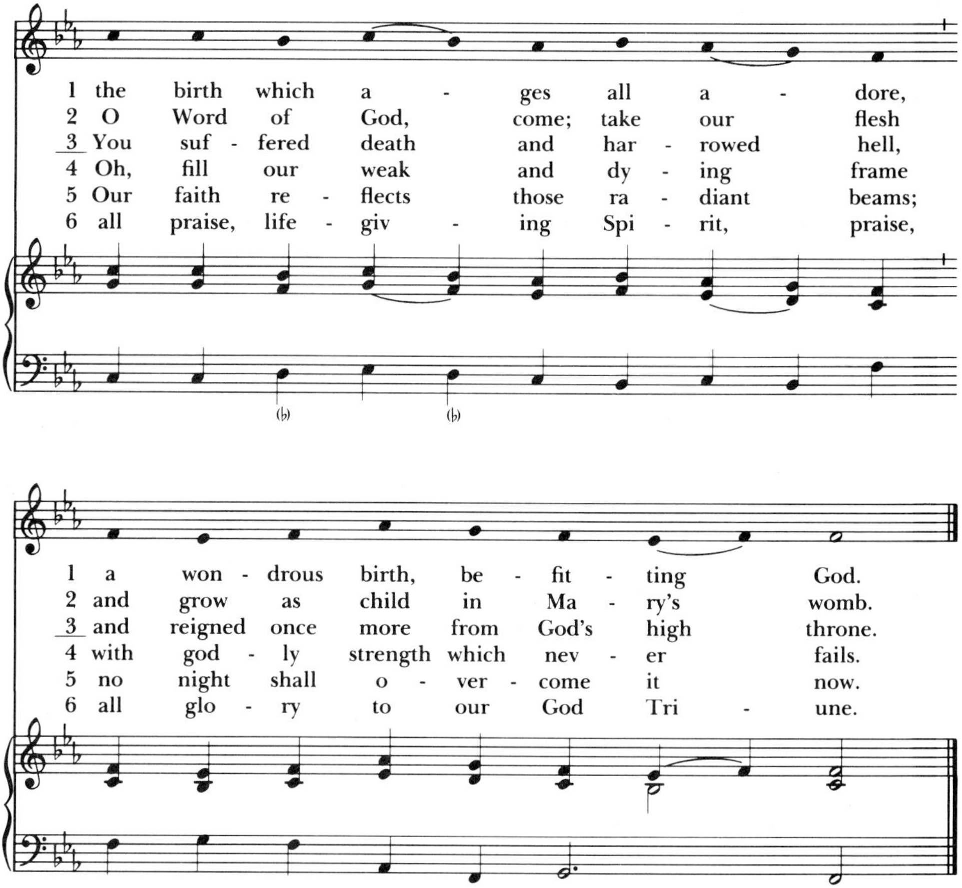
1 the birth which a - ges all a - dore,
2 O Word of God, come; take our flesh
3 You suf - fered death and har - rowed hell,
4 Oh, fill our weak and dy - ing frame
5 Our faith re - flects those ra - diant beams;
6 all praise, life - giv - ing Spi - rit, praise,
(♭)
(♭)
1 a won - drous birth, be - fit - ting God.
2 and grow as child in Ma - ry's womb.
3 and reigned once more from God's high throne.
4 with god - ly strength which nev - er fails.
5 no night shall o - ver - come it now.
6 all glo - ry to our God Tri - une.

Alternative tune: *Puer nobis,* 124.

Words: Att. Ambrose of Milan (340-397); tr. Charles P. Price (b. 1920)
Music: *Veni Redemptor gentium,* plainsong, Mode 1, Einsiedeln MS., 12th cent.; acc. David Hurd (b. 1950) LM

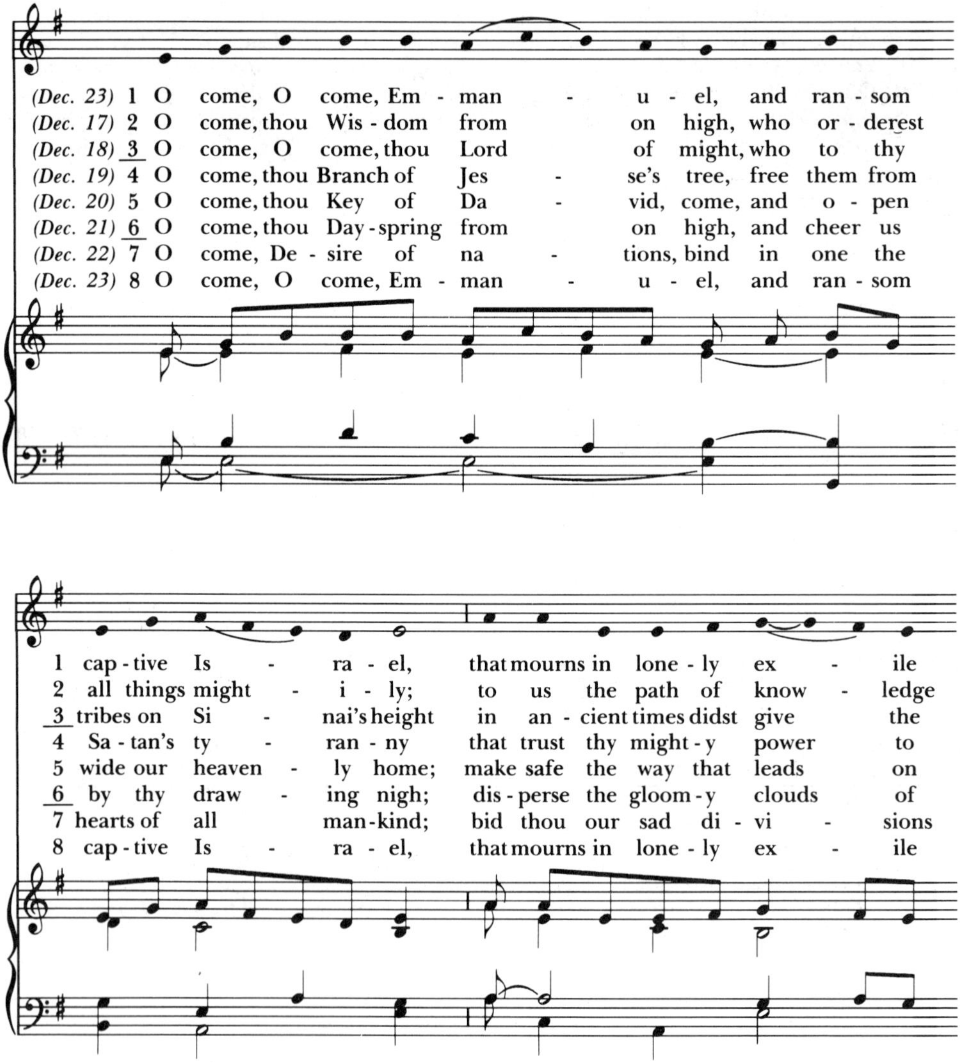
(Dec. 23) 1 O come, O come, Em - man - u - el, and ran - som
(Dec. 17) 2 O come, thou Wis - dom from on high, who or - derest
(Dec. 18) 3 O come, O come, thou Lord of might, who to thy
(Dec. 19) 4 O come, thou Branch of Jes - se's tree, free them from
(Dec. 20) 5 O come, thou Key of Da - vid, come, and o - pen
(Dec. 21) 6 O come, thou Day-spring from on high, and cheer us
(Dec. 22) 7 O come, De - sire of na - tions, bind in one the
(Dec. 23) 8 O come, O come, Em - man - u - el, and ran - som
1 cap - tive Is - ra - el, that mourns in lone - ly ex - ile
2 all things might - i - ly; to us the path of know - ledge
3 tribes on Si - nai's height in an - cient times didst give the
4 Sa - tan's ty - ran - ny that trust thy might - y power to
5 wide our heaven - ly home; make safe the way that leads on
6 by thy draw - ing nigh; dis - perse the gloom - y clouds of
7 hearts of all man-kind; bid thou our sad di - vi - sions
8 cap - tive Is - ra - el, that mourns in lone - ly ex - ile

1 here un - til the Son of God ap - pear.
2 show, and teach us in her ways to go.
3 law, in cloud, and ma - jes - ty, and awe.
4 save, and give them vic - tory o'er the grave.
5 high, and close the path to mis - er - y.
6 night, and death's dark shad - ow put to flight.
7 cease, and be thy - self our King of Peace.
8 here un - til the Son of God ap - pear.
Re - joice! Re - joice!

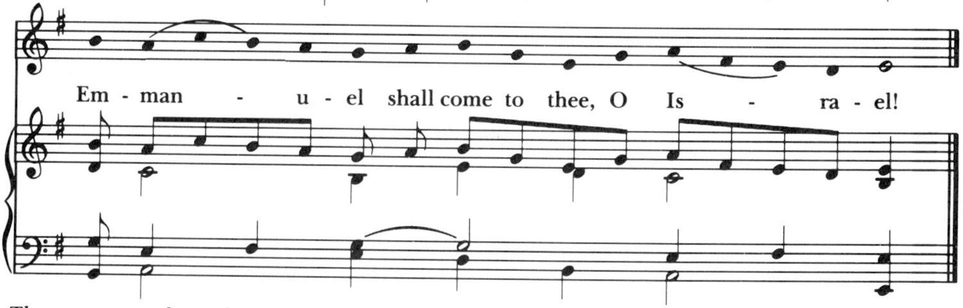
Em - man - u - el shall come to thee, O Is - ra - el!

The stanzas may be used as antiphons with "The Song of Mary" on the dates given.

Words: Latin, ca. 9th cent.; ver. *Hymnal 1940,* alt.
Music: *Veni, veni, Emmanuel,* plainsong, Mode 1, *Processionale,* 15th cent.; adapt. Thomas Helmore (1811-1890); acc. Richard Proulx (b. 1937)

LM with Refrain

Alternative accompaniment

This accompaniment may be used for selected stanzas and may be played an octave lower.

Music: *Veni, veni, Emmanuel,* plainsong, Mode 1, *Processionale,* 15th cent.; adapt. Thomas Helmore (1811-1890); acc. Richard Proulx (b. 1937)

1 Lo! he comes, with clouds de - scend - ing, once for
2 Ev - ery eye shall now be - hold him, robed in
3 Those dear to - kens of his pas - sion still his
4 Yea, a - men! let all a - dore thee, high on
our sal - va - tion slain; thou - sand thou - sand
dread-ful ma - jes - ty; those who set at
daz - zling bo - dy bears, cause of end - less
thine e - ter - nal throne; Sa - vior, take the
saints at - tend - ing swell the tri - umph of his
nought and sold him, pierced, and nailed him to the
ex - ul - ta - tion to his ran - somed wor - ship -
power and glo - ry; claim the king - dom for thine

train: Al - le - lu - ia! Al - le - lu - ia!
tree, deep - ly wail - ing, deep - ly wail - ing,
ers; with what rap - ture, with what rap - ture,
own: Al - le - lu - ia! Al - le - lu - ia!

Al - le - lu - ia! Christ the Lord re - turns to reign.
deep - ly wail - ing, shall the true Mes - si - ah see.
with what rap - ture gaze we on those glo - rious scars!
Al - le - lu - ia! Thou shalt reign, and thou a - lone.

Alternative tune: *St. Thomas*, 58.

Words: Charles Wesley (1707-1788)
Music: *Helmsley*, melody Augustine Arne (1710-1778);
harm. Ralph Vaughan Williams (1872-1958), alt.

𝅗𝅥=60
87. 87. 12 7

1 Lo! he comes, with clouds de - scend - ing, once for our sal -
2 Ev - ery eye shall now be - hold him, robed in dread - ful
3 Those dear to - kens of his pas - sion still his daz - zling
4 Yea, a - men! let all a - dore thee, high on thine e -
va - tion slain; thou - sand thou - sand saints at - tend - ing
ma - jes - ty; those who set at nought and sold him,
bo - dy bears, cause of end - less ex - ul - ta - tion
ter - nal throne; Sa - vior, take the power and glo - ry;
swell the tri - umph of his train: Al - le - lu - ia!
pierced, and nailed him to the tree, deep - ly wail - ing,
to his ran - somed wor - ship - ers; with what rap - ture,
claim the king - dom for thine own: Al - le - lu - ia!
Al - le - lu - ia! Christ the Lord re - turns to reign.
deep - ly wail - ing, shall the true Mes - si - ah see.
with what rap - ture gaze we on those glo - rious scars!
Al - le - lu - ia! Thou shalt reign, and thou a - lone.

Alternative tune: *Helmsley*, 57.

Words: Charles Wesley (1707-1788)
Music: *St. Thomas*, melody att. John Francis Wade (1711-1786); harm. att. Vincent Francis Novello (1781-1861)

𝅗𝅥 = 48
87. 87

Descant
2 Wak - ened by the sol - emn warn - ing, from earth's bond - age let us rise;
5 Hon - or, glo - ry, might, and bless - ing to the Fa - ther and the Son,
1 Hark! a thrill - ing voice is sound - ing: "Christ is nigh," it seems to say;
2 Wak - ened by the sol - emn warn - ing, from earth's bond - age let us rise;
3 Lo! the Lamb, so long ex - pect - ed, comes with par - don down from heaven;
4 so when next he comes with glo - ry, and the world is wrapped in fear,
5 Hon - or, glo - ry, might, and bless - ing to the Fa - ther and the Son,
2 Christ, our sun, all sloth dis - pel - ling, shines up - on the morn - ing skies.
5 with the ev - er - last - ing Spi - rit while un - end - ing a - ges run.
1 "Cast a - way the works of dark - ness, O ye chil - dren of the day."
2 Christ, our sun, all sloth dis - pel - ling, shines up - on the morn - ing skies.
3 let us haste, with tears of sor - row, one and all to be for - given;
4 may he with his mer - cy shield us, and with words of love draw near.
5 with the ev - er - last - ing Spi - rit while un - end - ing a - ges run.

Words: Latin, ca. 6th cent.; tr. *Hymns Ancient and Modern,* 1861, alt.
Music: *Merton,* William Henry Monk (1823-1889); desc. Alan Gray (1855-1935)

𝅗𝅥=46
87. 87

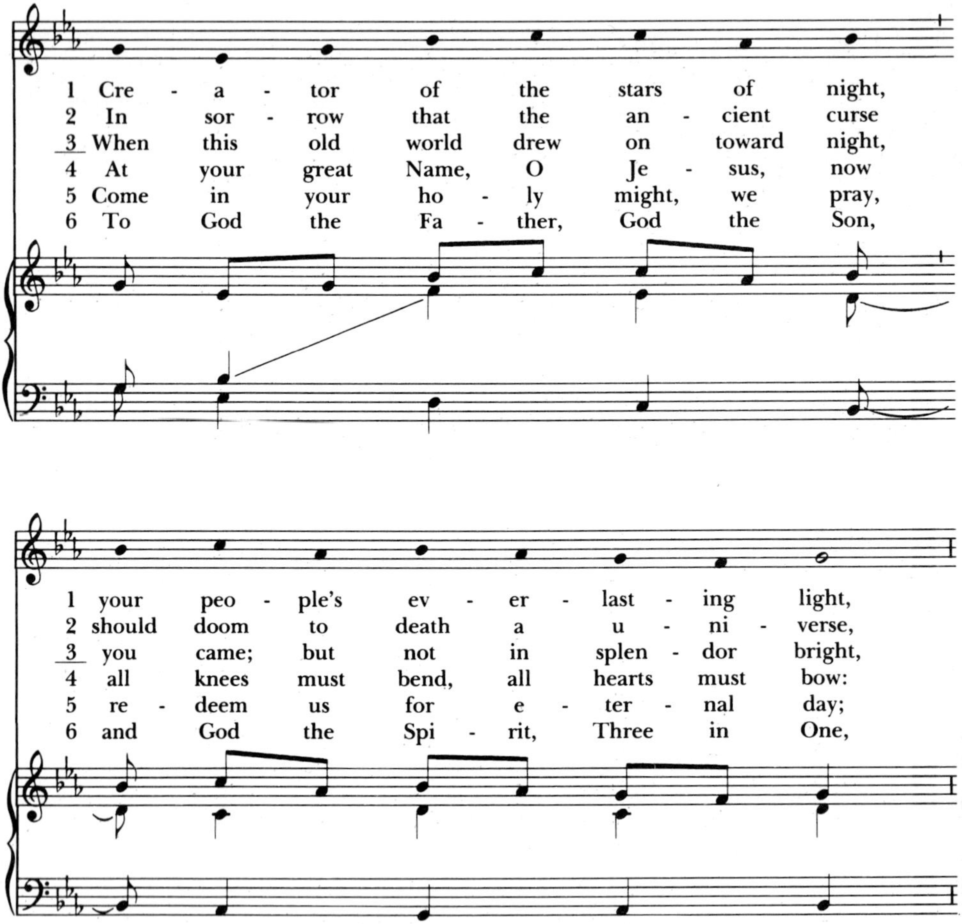
1 Cre - a - tor of the stars of night, your peo - ple's ev - er - last - ing light,
2 In sor - row that the an - cient curse should doom to death a u - ni - verse,
3 When this old world drew on toward night, you came; but not in splen - dor bright,
4 At your great Name, O Je - sus, now all knees must bend, all hearts must bow:
5 Come in your ho - ly might, we pray, re - deem us for e - ter - nal day;
6 To God the Fa - ther, God the Son, and God the Spi - rit, Three in One,

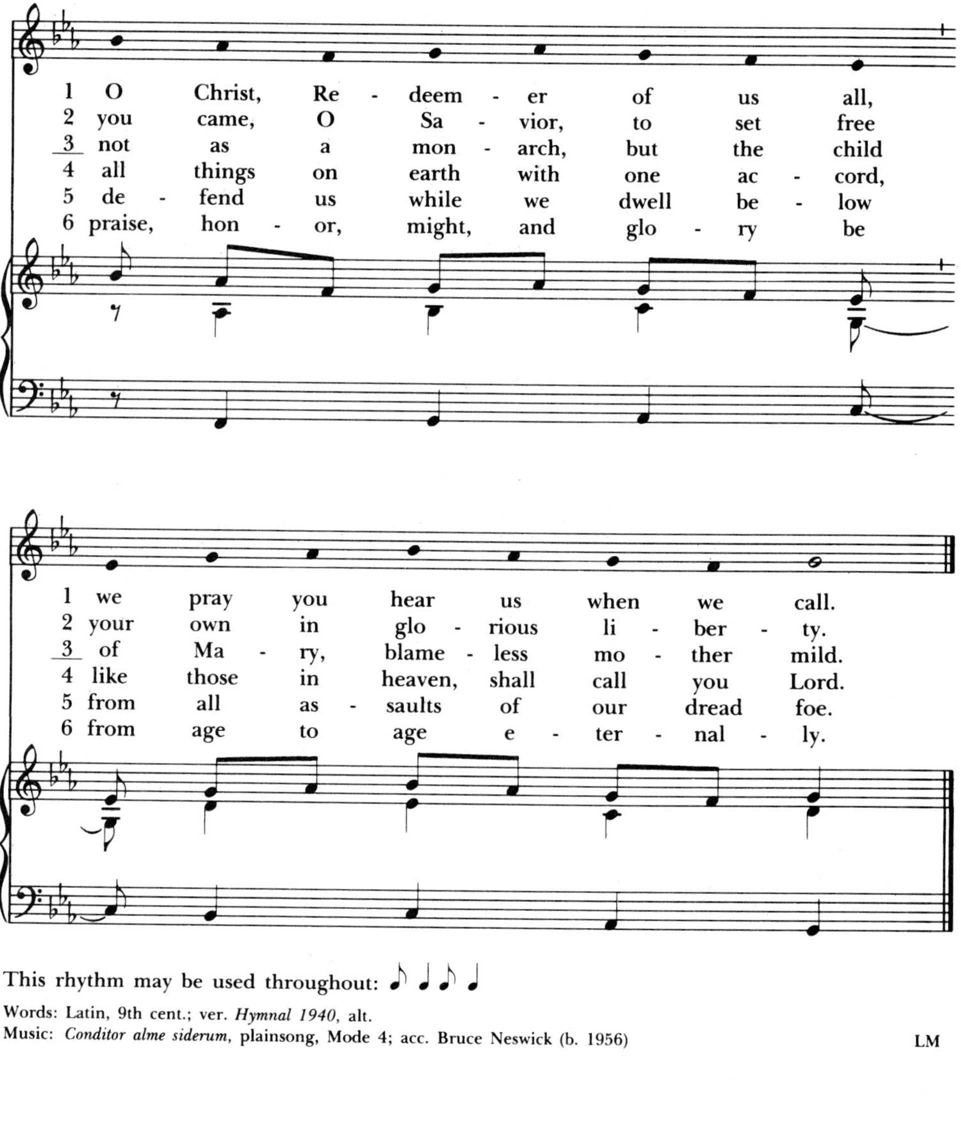
1 O Christ, Re - deem - er of us all,
2 you came, O Sa - vior, to set free
3 not as a mon - arch, but the child
4 all things on earth with one ac - cord,
5 de - fend us while we dwell be - low
6 praise, hon - or, might, and glo - ry be
1 we pray you hear us when we call.
2 your own in glo - rious li - ber - ty.
3 of Ma - ry, blame - less mo - ther mild.
4 like those in heaven, shall call you Lord.
5 from all as - saults of our dread foe.
6 from age to age e - ter - nal - ly.

This rhythm may be used throughout:

Words: Latin, 9th cent.; ver. *Hymnal 1940*, alt.
Music: *Conditor alme siderum*, plainsong, Mode 4; acc. Bruce Neswick (b. 1956) LM

1 "Sleep-ers, wake!" A voice a - stounds us, the
2 Zi - on hears the watch - men sing - ing; her
3 Lamb of God, the heavens a - dore you; let
shout of ram - part - guards sur - rounds us: "A -
heart with joy - ful hope is spring - ing, she
saints and an - gels sing be - fore you, as
wake, Je - ru - sa - lem, a - rise!" Mid - night's peace their
wakes and hur - ries through the night. Forth he comes, her
harps and cym - bals swell the sound. Twelve great pearls, the
cry has bro - ken, their ur - gent sum - mons clear - ly spo -
Bride - groom glo - rious in strength of grace, in truth vic - to -
ci - ty's por - tals: through them we stream to join the im - mor -

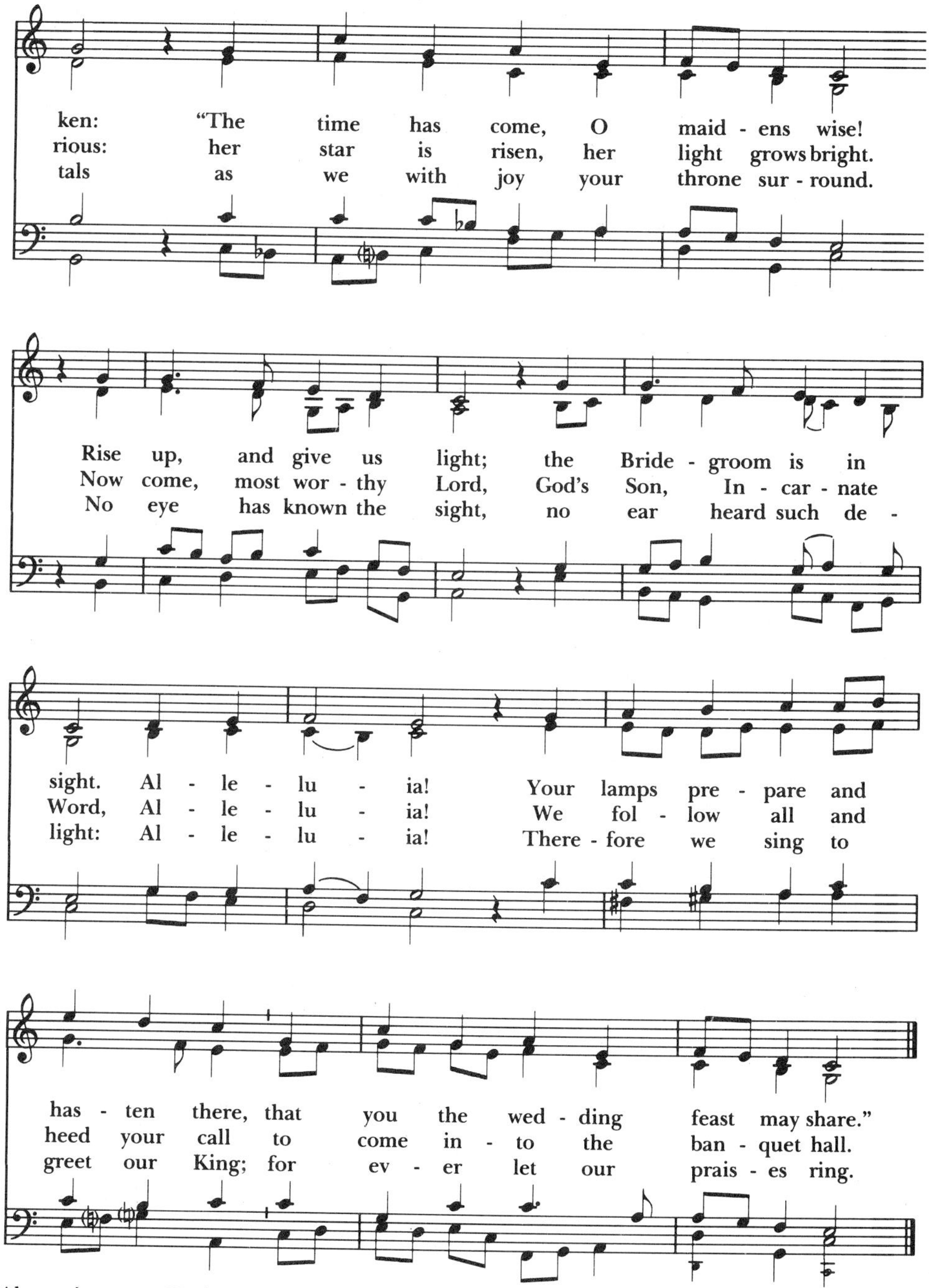
ken: "The time has come, O maid - ens wise!
rious: her star is risen, her light grows bright.
tals as we with joy your throne sur - round.
Rise up, and give us light; the Bride - groom is in
Now come, most wor - thy Lord, God's Son, In - car - nate
No eye has known the sight, no ear heard such de -
sight. Al - le - lu - ia! Your lamps pre - pare and
Word, Al - le - lu - ia! We fol - low all and
light: Al - le - lu - ia! There - fore we sing to
has - ten there, that you the wed - ding feast may share."
heed your call to come in - to the ban - quet hall.
greet our King; for ev - er let our prais - es ring.

Alternative tune: *Wachet auf* (rhythmic), 62.

Words: Philipp Nicolai (1556-1608); tr. Carl P. Daw, Jr. (b. 1944)
Music: *Wachet auf,* melody Hans Sachs (1494-1576); adapt. Philipp Nicolai (1556-1608); arr. and harm. Johann Sebastian Bach (1685-1750)

♩=69
Irr.

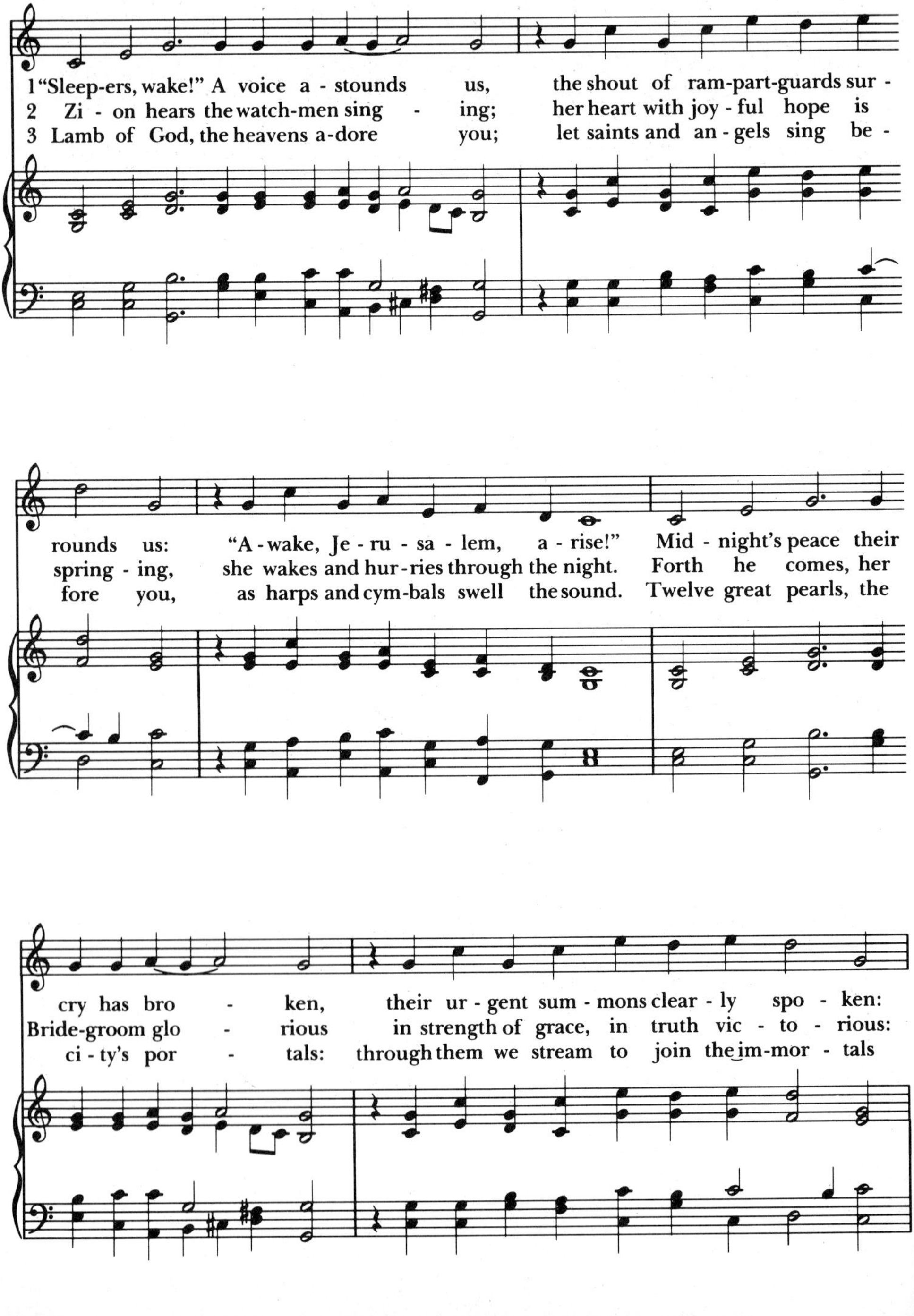
1 "Sleep-ers, wake!" A voice a - stounds us, the shout of ram-part-guards sur -
2 Zi - on hears the watch-men sing - ing; her heart with joy - ful hope is
3 Lamb of God, the heavens a-dore you; let saints and an - gels sing be -
rounds us: "A - wake, Je - ru - sa - lem, a - rise!" Mid - night's peace their
spring - ing, she wakes and hur - ries through the night. Forth he comes, her
fore you, as harps and cym-bals swell the sound. Twelve great pearls, the
cry has bro - ken, their ur - gent sum - mons clear - ly spo - ken:
Bride-groom glo - rious in strength of grace, in truth vic - to - rious:
ci - ty's por - tals: through them we stream to join the im-mor - tals

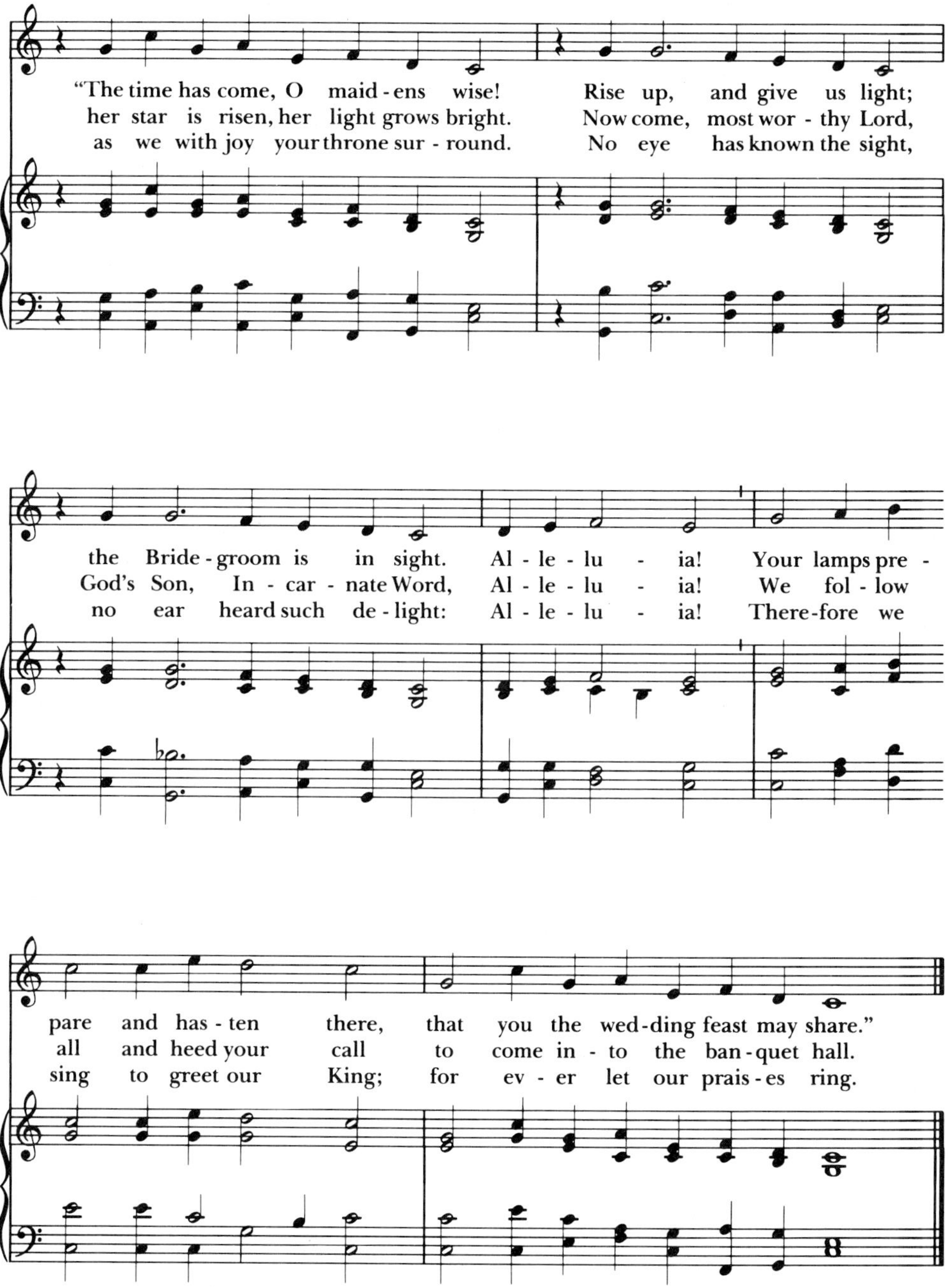
"The time has come, O maid-ens wise! Rise up, and give us light;
her star is risen, her light grows bright. Now come, most wor-thy Lord,
as we with joy your throne sur-round. No eye has known the sight,
the Bride-groom is in sight. Al-le-lu-ia! Your lamps pre-
God's Son, In-car-nate Word, Al-le-lu-ia! We fol-low
no ear heard such de-light: Al-le-lu-ia! There-fore we
pare and has-ten there, that you the wed-ding feast may share."
all and heed your call to come in-to the ban-quet hall.
sing to greet our King; for ev-er let our prais-es ring.

Alternative tune: *Wachet auf* (isometric), 61.

Words: Philipp Nicolai (1556-1608); tr. Carl P. Daw, Jr. (b. 1944)
Music: *Wachet auf,* melody Hans Sachs (1494-1576); adapt. Philipp Nicolai (1556-1608); harm. Jakob Praetorius (1586-1651)

𝅗𝅥=69
Irr.

63

1 O heaven - ly Word, e - ter - nal Light, be - got - ten
2 pour light up - on us from a - bove, and fire our
3 and when, as judge, thou draw - est nigh the se - crets
4 O let us not, for e - vil past, be driv - en
*5 To God the Fa - ther, God the Son, and God the
1 of the Fa - ther's might, who in these lat - ter
2 hearts with ar - dent love, that, as we hear thy
3 of our hearts to try, to rec - om - pense each
4 from thy face at last, but with thy saints for
5 Spi - rit, ev - er One, praise, hon - or, might, and
1 days wast born for bless - ing to a world for - lorn;
2 truth to - day, all wrong de - sires may burn a - way;
3 hid - den sin and bid the saints their reign be - gin;
4 ev - er - more be - hold thee, love thee, and a - dore.
5 glo - ry be from age to age e - ter - nal - ly.

Another accompaniment, 311. Alternative tune: *O Heiland, reiss,* 64.

Words: Latin, ca. 7th cent.; tr. *Hymnal 1982*
Music: *Verbum supernum prodiens,* plainsong, Mode 2, Nevers MS., 13th cent.; acc. Howard Don Small (b. 1932)

LM

1 O heaven - ly Word, e - ter - nal Light, be - got - ten
2 pour light up - on us from a - bove, and fire our
3 and when, as judge, thou draw - est nigh the se - crets
4 O let us not, for e - vil past, be driv - en
*5 To God the Fa - ther, God the Son, and God the
1 of the Fa - ther's might, who in these lat - ter days wast
2 hearts with ar - dent love, that, as we hear thy truth to -
3 of our hearts to try, to rec - om - pense each hid - den
4 from thy face at last, but with thy saints for ev - er -
5 Spi - rit, ev - er One, praise, hon - or, might, and glo - ry
1 born for bless - ing to a world for - lorn;
2 day, all wrong de - sires may burn a - way;
3 sin and bid the saints their reign be - gin;
4 more be - hold thee, love thee, and a - dore.
5 be from age to age e - ter - nal - ly.

Alternative tune: *Verbum supernum prodiens* (Nevers), 63.

Words: Latin, ca. 7th cent.; tr. *Hymnal 1982*
Music: *O Heiland, reiss,* melody from *Rheinfelsisches Deutsches Catholisches Gesangbuch,* 1666; harm. *Orgelbuch Zum Gesangbuch Der Evangelisch-Reformierten Kirchen Der Deutschsprachigen Schweiz,* 1926

♩= 112
LM

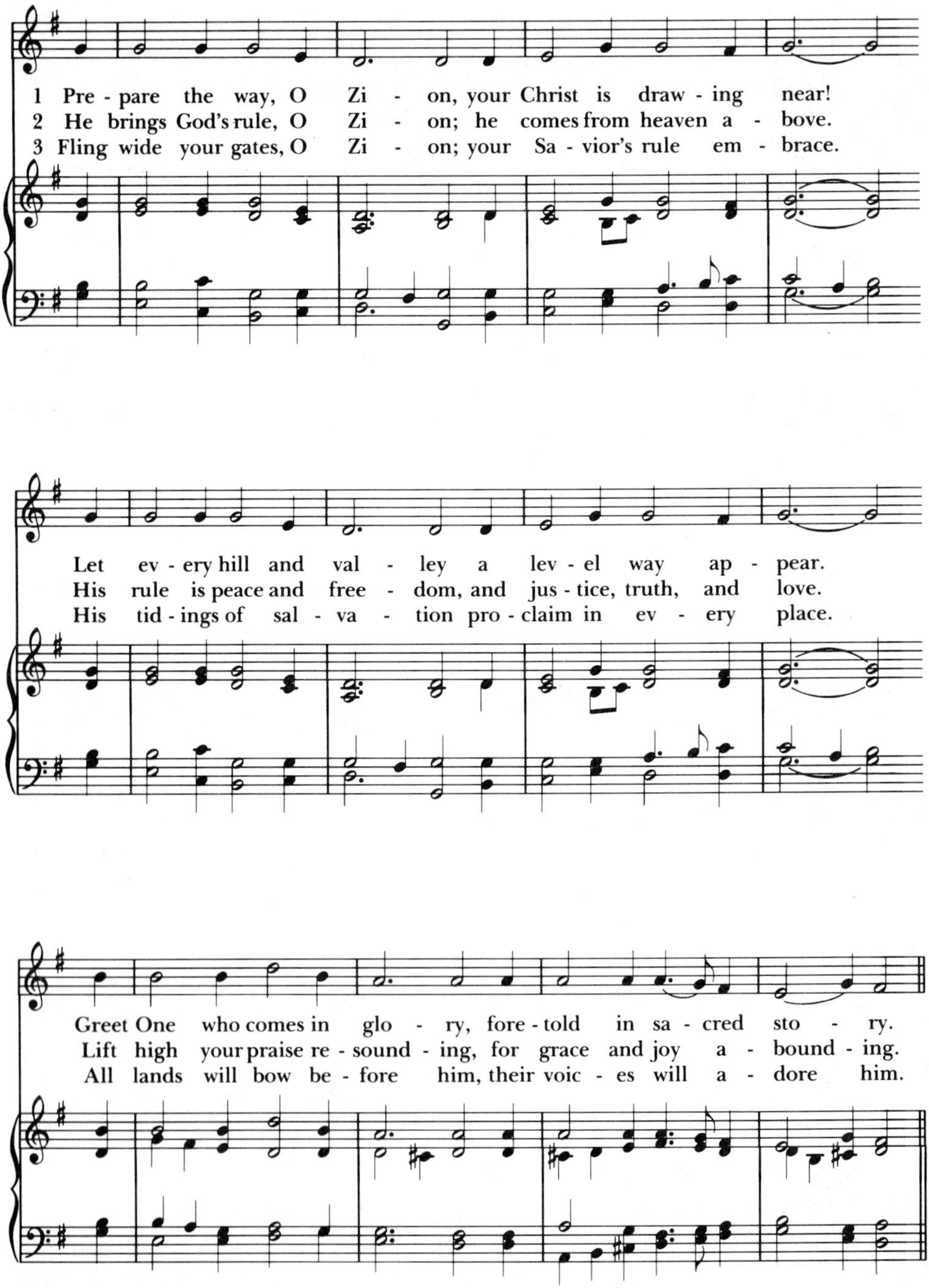
1 Pre - pare the way, O Zi - on, your Christ is draw - ing near!
2 He brings God's rule, O Zi - on; he comes from heaven a - bove.
3 Fling wide your gates, O Zi - on; your Sa - vior's rule em - brace.
Let ev - ery hill and val - ley a lev - el way ap - pear.
His rule is peace and free - dom, and jus - tice, truth, and love.
His tid - ings of sal - va - tion pro - claim in ev - ery place.
Greet One who comes in glo - ry, fore - told in sa - cred sto - ry.
Lift high your praise re - sound - ing, for grace and joy a - bound - ing.
All lands will bow be - fore him, their voic - es will a - dore him.

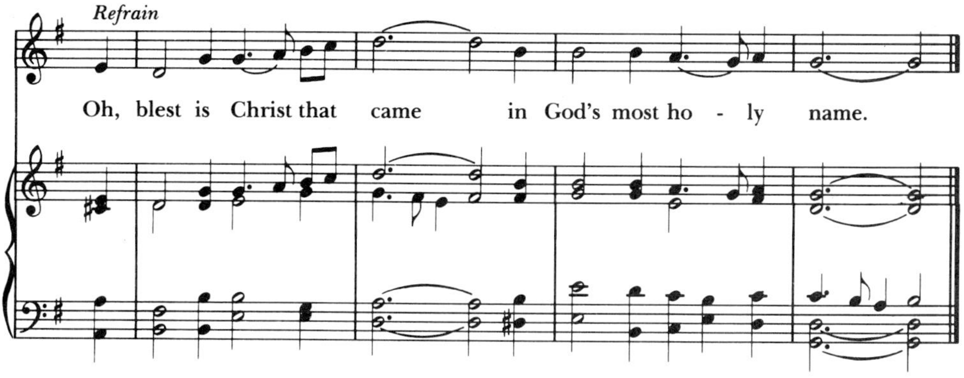
Refrain
Oh, blest is Christ that came in God's most ho - ly name.

Words: Frans Mikael Franzen (1772-1847); tr. composite; adapt. Charles P. Price (b. 1920)
Music: *Bereden väg för Herran,* melody from *Then Swenska Psalmboken,* 1697; harm. *Koralbok för Svenska Kyrkan,* 1939, alt.

𝅗𝅥. = 52
76. 76. 77 with Refrain

Advent 66

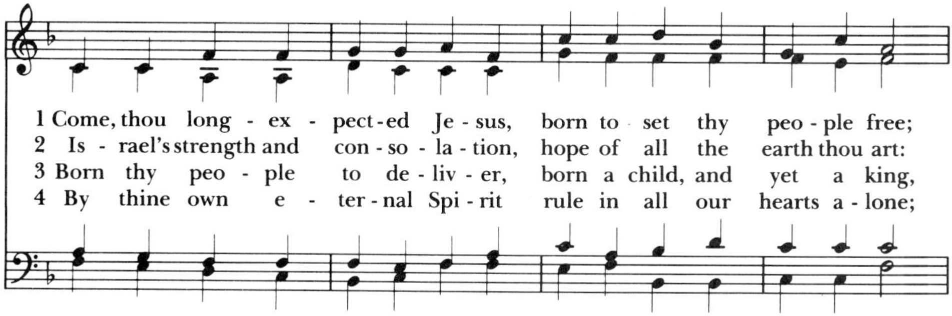
1 Come, thou long - ex - pect-ed Je - sus, born to set thy peo - ple free;
2 Is - rael's strength and con - so - la - tion, hope of all the earth thou art:
3 Born thy peo - ple to de - liv - er, born a child, and yet a king,
4 By thine own e - ter - nal Spi - rit rule in all our hearts a - lone;

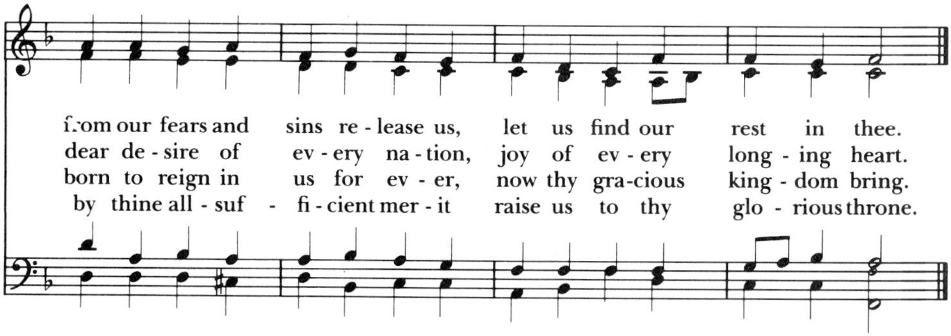
from our fears and sins re - lease us, let us find our rest in thee.
dear de - sire of ev - ery na - tion, joy of ev - ery long - ing heart.
born to reign in us for ev - er, now thy gra-cious king - dom bring.
by thine all - suf - fi - cient mer - it raise us to thy glo - rious throne.

Another harmonization, 127.

Words: Charles Wesley (1707-1788)
Music: *Stuttgart,* melody from *Psalmodia Sacra, oder Andächtige und Schöne Gesange,* 1715; adapt. and harm. William Henry Havergal (1793-1870), alt.

♩= 80
87. 87

1 Com - fort, com - fort ye my peo - ple, speak ye peace, thus
2 Hark, the voice of one that cri - eth in the des - ert
3 Make ye straight what long was crook - ed, make the rough - er
saith our God; com - fort those who sit in dark - ness mourn - ing
far and near, call - ing us to new re - pent - ance since the
pla - ces plain; let your hearts be true and hum - ble, as be -
'neath their sor - rows' load. Speak ye to Je - ru - sa - lem
king - dom now is here. Oh, that warn - ing cry o - bey!
fits his ho - ly reign. For the glo - ry of the Lord

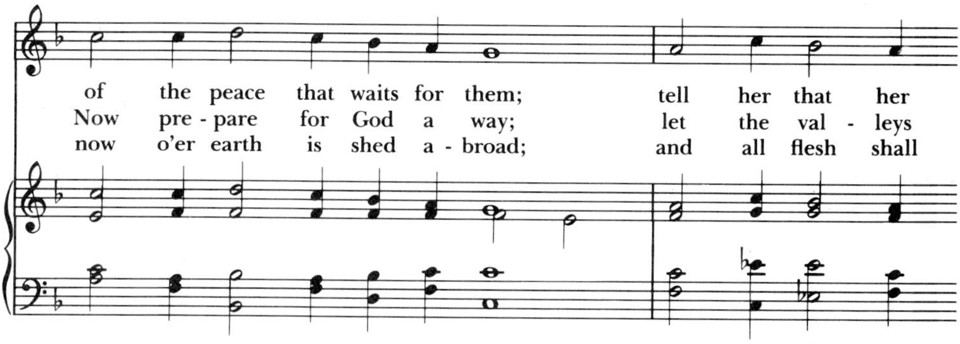
of the peace that waits for them; tell her that her
Now pre - pare for God a way; let the val - leys
now o'er earth is shed a - broad; and all flesh shall

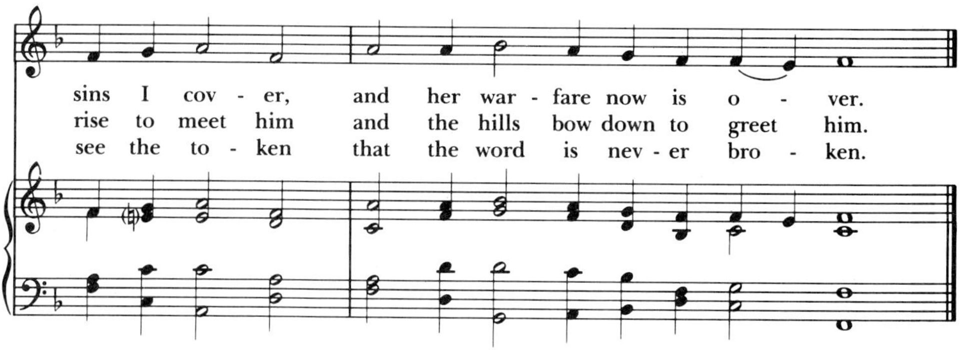
sins I cov - er, and her war - fare now is o - ver.
rise to meet him and the hills bow down to greet him.
see the to - ken that the word is nev - er bro - ken.

Words: Johann G. Olearius (1611-1684); tr. Catherine Winkworth (1827-1878), alt.
Music: *Psalm 42*, melody and bass Claude Goudimel (1514-1572); harm. *Hymnal 1982*

𝅗𝅥=68
87. 87. 77. 88

1 Re - joice! re - joice, be - liev - ers, and let your lights ap - pear!
2 See that your lamps are burn - ing, re - ple - nish them with oil;
3 Our hope and ex - pec - ta - tion, O Je - sus, now ap - pear;
The eve-ning is ad - vanc - ing, and dark-er night is near.
look now for your sal - va - tion, the end of sin and toil.
a - rise, thou Sun so longed for, a - bove this dark-ened sphere!
The Bride-groom is a - ris - ing, and soon he will draw nigh;
The mar - riage-feast is wait - ing, the gates wide o - pen stand;
With hearts and hands up - lift - ed, we plead, O Lord, to see
up, watch in ex - pec - ta - tion! at mid - night comes the cry.
rise up, ye heirs of glo - ry, the Bride-groom is at hand!
the day of earth's re - demp - tion, and ev - er be with thee!

Another harmonization, 607.

Words: Laurentius Laurenti (1660-1722); tr. Sarah B. Findlater (1823-1907), alt. ♩=60

Music: *Llangloffan*, melody from *Hymnau a Thonau er Gwasanaeth yr Eglwys yng Nghymru*, 1865 76. 76. D

1 What is the cry - ing at Jor - dan? Who
2 Who then shall stir in this dark - ness, pre -
3 Lord, give us grace to a - wake us, to
4 Now comes the day of sal - va - tion, in
hears, O God, the ___ pro - phe - cy? Dark is the
pare for joy in the win - ter night? Mor - tal in
see the branch that be - gins to bloom; in great hu -
joy and ter - ror the Word is born! God gives him -
sea - son, dark our hearts and shut ___ to mys - ter - y.
dark - ness we lie down, blind - heart - ed see - ing no light.
mil - i - ty is hid all heaven in a lit - tle room.
self in - to our lives; O let ___ sal - va - tion dawn!

Words: Carol Christopher Drake (b. 1933), alt.
Music: *St. Mark's, Berkeley,* Irish melody from *Danta De: Hymns to God, Ancient and Modern;* harm. Norman Mealy (b. 1923)

𝅗𝅥 = 54
88. 86

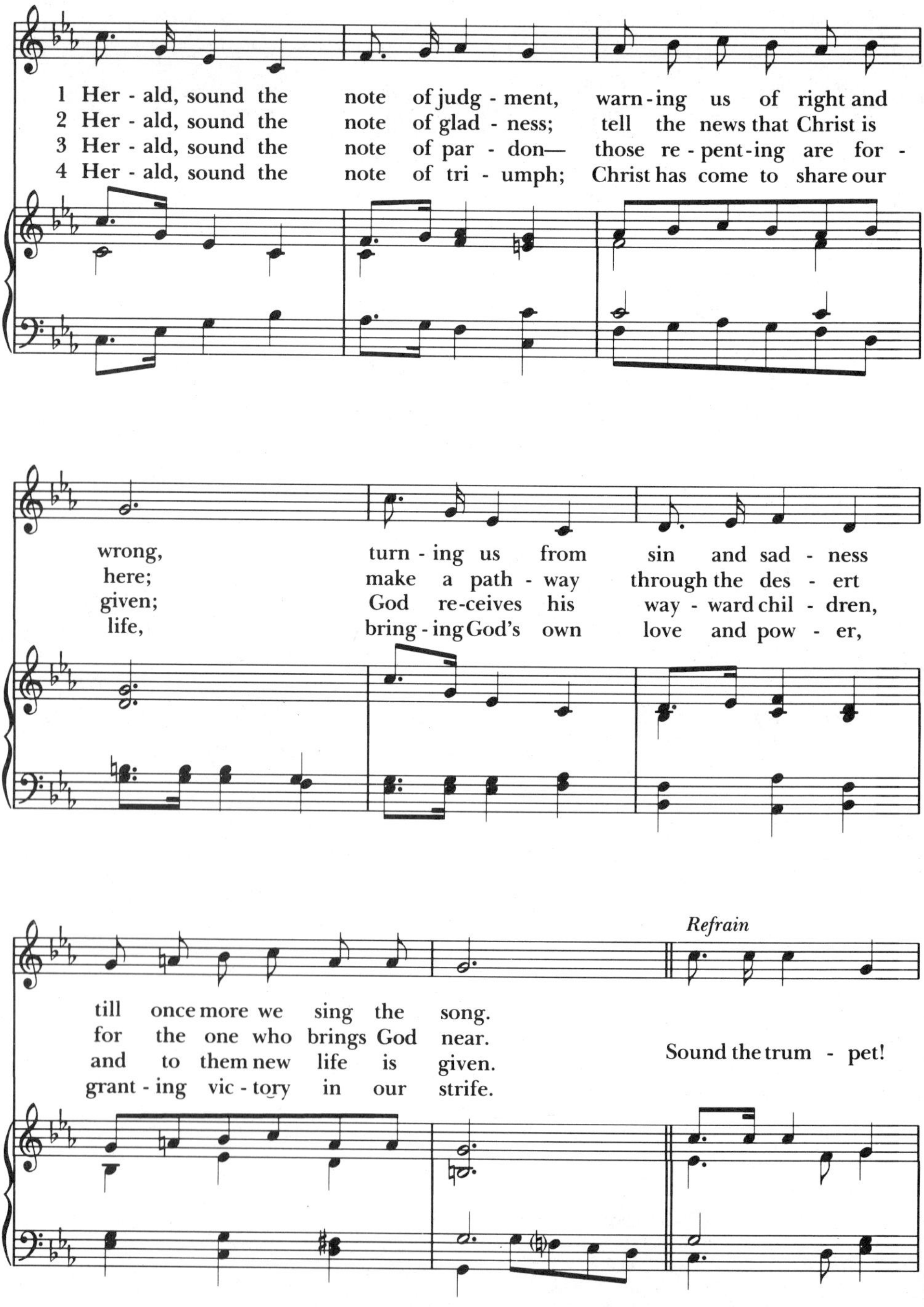
1 Her - ald, sound the note of judg - ment, warn - ing us of right and wrong, turn - ing us from sin and sad - ness till once more we sing the song.
2 Her - ald, sound the note of glad - ness; tell the news that Christ is here; make a path - way through the des - ert for the one who brings God near.
3 Her - ald, sound the note of par - don— those re - pent - ing are for - given; God re-ceives his way - ward chil - dren, and to them new life is given.
4 Her - ald, sound the note of tri - umph; Christ has come to share our life, bring - ing God's own love and pow - er, grant - ing vic - tory in our strife.
Refrain
Sound the trum - pet!

Tell the mes - sage! Christ, the Sa - vior King, has come!

Words: Moir A. J. Waters (1906-1980), alt.
Music: *Herald, Sound,* Robert Powell (b. 1932)

♩=80
87. 87 with Refrain

Advent

71

1 Hark! the glad sound! the Sa - vior comes, the Sa - vior
2 He comes, the pris - oners to re - lease in Sa - tan's
3 He comes, the bro - ken heart to bind, the bleed-ing
4 Our glad ho - san - nas, Prince of Peace, thy wel - come
prom - ised long: let ev - ery heart pre -
bond - age held; the gates of brass be -
soul to cure; and with the trea - sures
shall pro - claim; and heaven's e - ter - nal
pare a throne, and ev - ery voice a song.
fore him burst, the i - ron fet - ters yield.
of his grace to en - rich the hum - ble poor.
arch - es ring with thy be - lov - ed Name.

Alternative tune: *Richmond,* 72.

Words: Philip Doddridge (1702-1751)
Music: *Bristol,* from *The Whole Booke of Psalmes,* 1621

♩=88
CM

Descant
4 Our glad ho - san - nas, Prince of Peace, thy wel - come shall pro - claim; and heaven's e - ter - nal arch - es ring with thy be - lov - ed Name.
1 Hark! the glad sound! the Sa - vior comes, the Sa - vior prom - ised long; let ev - ery heart pre - pare a throne, and ev - ery voice a song.
2 He comes, the pris - oners to re - lease in Sa - tan's bond - age held; the gates of brass be - fore him burst, the i - ron fet - ters yield.
3 He comes, the bro - ken heart to bind, the bleed - ing soul to cure; and with the trea - sures of his grace to en - rich the hum - ble poor.
4 Our glad ho - san - nas, Prince of Peace, thy wel - come shall pro - claim; and heaven's e - ter - nal arch - es ring with thy be - lov - ed Name.

Alternative tune: *Bristol,* 71.

Words: Philip Doddridge (1702-1751)
Music: *Richmond,* melody Thomas Haweis (1734-1820); adapt. Samuel Webbe (1740-1816); harm. *Hymns Ancient and Modern, Revised,* 1950; desc. Craig Sellar Lang (1891-1971)

♩=76
CM

73

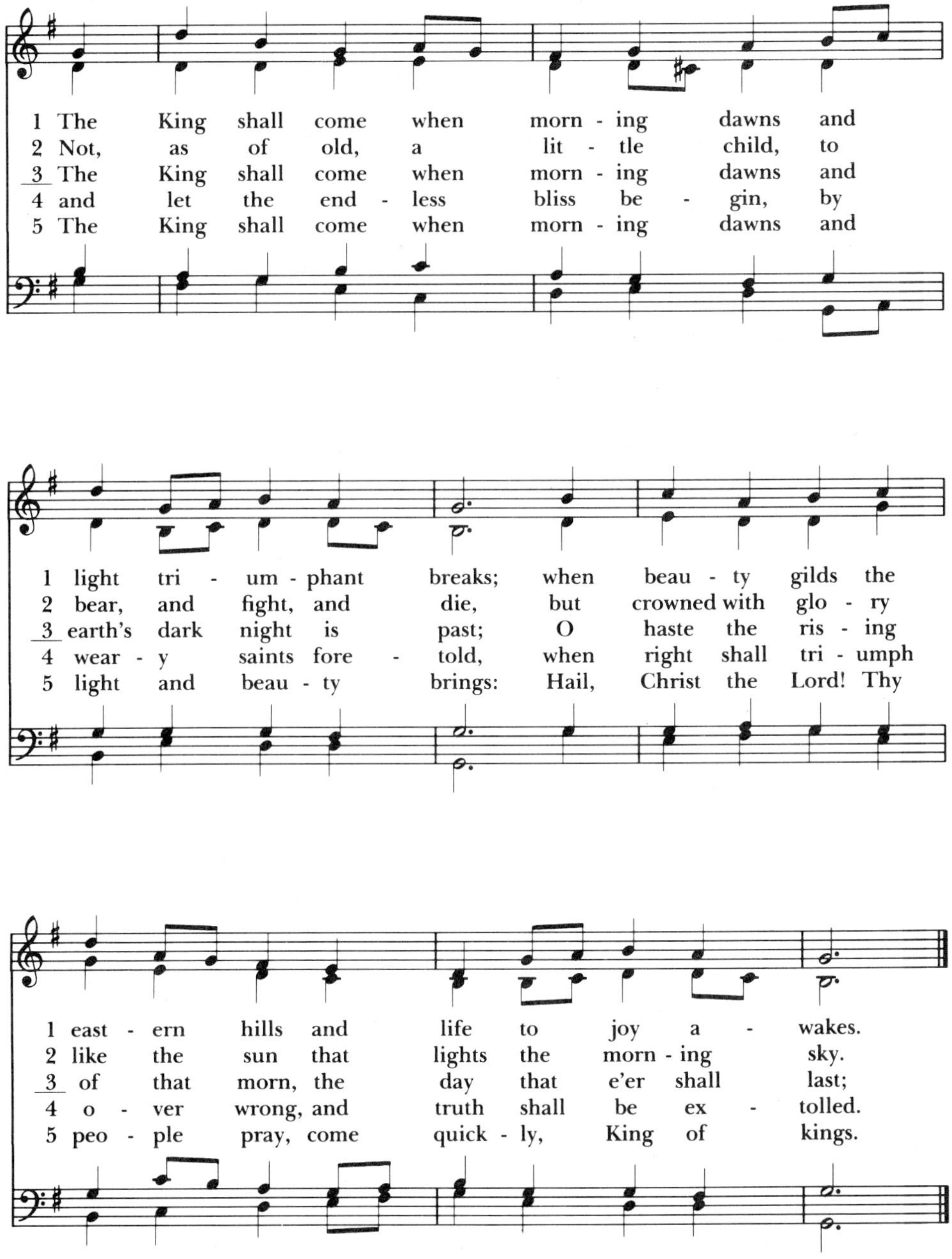
1 The King shall come when morn - ing dawns and
2 Not, as of old, a lit - tle child, to
3 The King shall come when morn - ing dawns and
4 and let the end - less bliss be - gin, by
5 The King shall come when morn - ing dawns and
1 light tri - um - phant breaks; when beau - ty gilds the
2 bear, and fight, and die, but crowned with glo - ry
3 earth's dark night is past; O haste the ris - ing
4 wear - y saints fore - told, when right shall tri - umph
5 light and beau - ty brings: Hail, Christ the Lord! Thy
1 east - ern hills and life to joy a - wakes.
2 like the sun that lights the morn - ing sky.
3 of that morn, the day that e'er shall last;
4 o - ver wrong, and truth shall be ex - tolled.
5 peo - ple pray, come quick - ly, King of kings.

Words: Greek; tr. John Brownlie (1859-1925), alt.
Music: *St. Stephen,* William Jones (1726-1800), alt.

♩= 84
CM

Descant
3 Blest be the King whose com - ing is in the name of God! He on - ly to the hum - ble re - veals the face of God. All power is his, all glo - ry! All
1 Blest be the King whose com - ing is in the name of God! For him let doors be o - pened, no hearts a - gainst him barred! Not robed in roy - al splen - dor, in
2 Blest be the King whose com - ing is in the name of God! By those who tru - ly lis - ten his voice is tru - ly heard; pi - ty the proud and haugh - ty, who
3 Blest be the King whose com - ing is in the name of God! He on - ly to the hum - ble re - veals the face of God. All power is his, all glo - ry! All
4 Blest be the King whose com - ing is in the name of God! He of - fers to the bur - dened the rest and grace they need. Gen - tle is he and hum - ble! And

things are in his hand, all a - ges and all
power and pomp, comes he; but clad as are the
have not learned to heed the Christ who is the
things are in his hand, all a - ges and all
light his yoke shall be, for he would have us
peo - ples, till time it - self shall end!
poor - est, such his hu - mil - i - ty!
Prom - ise, who has a - tone - ment made.
peo - ples, till time it - self shall end!
bear it so he can make us free!

Another harmonization, 154.

Words: Frederico J. Pagura (b. 1923); tr. F. Pratt Green (b. 1903), alt.
Music: *Valet will ich dir geben,* melody Melchior Teschner (1584-1635) alt.; harm. and desc. Ronald Arnatt (b. 1930)

𝅗𝅥 = 54
76. 76 D

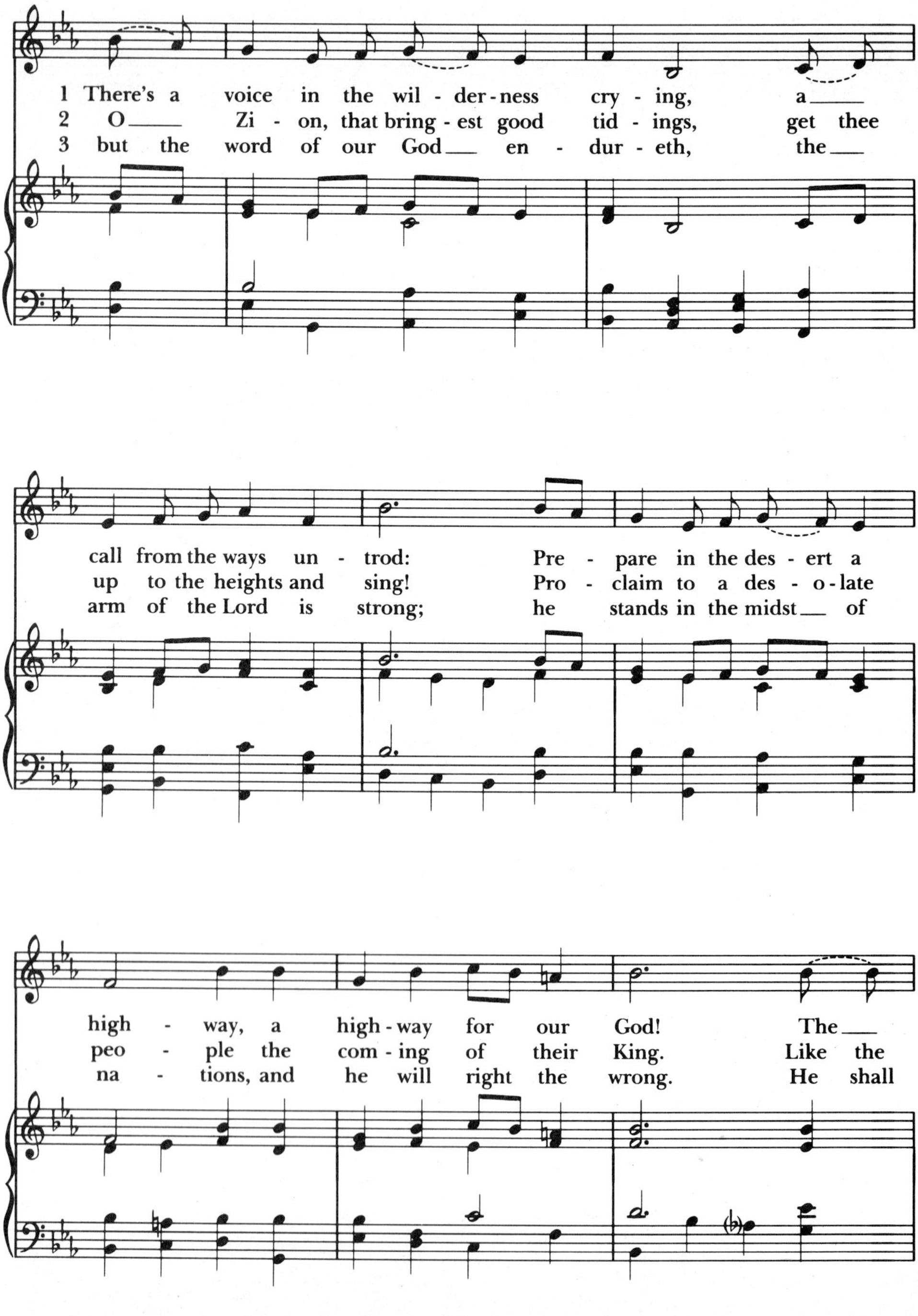
1 There's a voice in the wil - der - ness cry - ing, a___
2 O___ Zi - on, that bring - est good tid - ings, get thee
3 but the word of our God___ en - dur - eth, the___
call from the ways un - trod: Pre - pare in the des - ert a
up to the heights and sing! Pro - claim to a des - o - late
arm of the Lord is strong; he stands in the midst___ of
high - way, a high - way for our God! The___
peo - ple the com - ing of their King. Like the
na - tions, and he will right the wrong. He shall

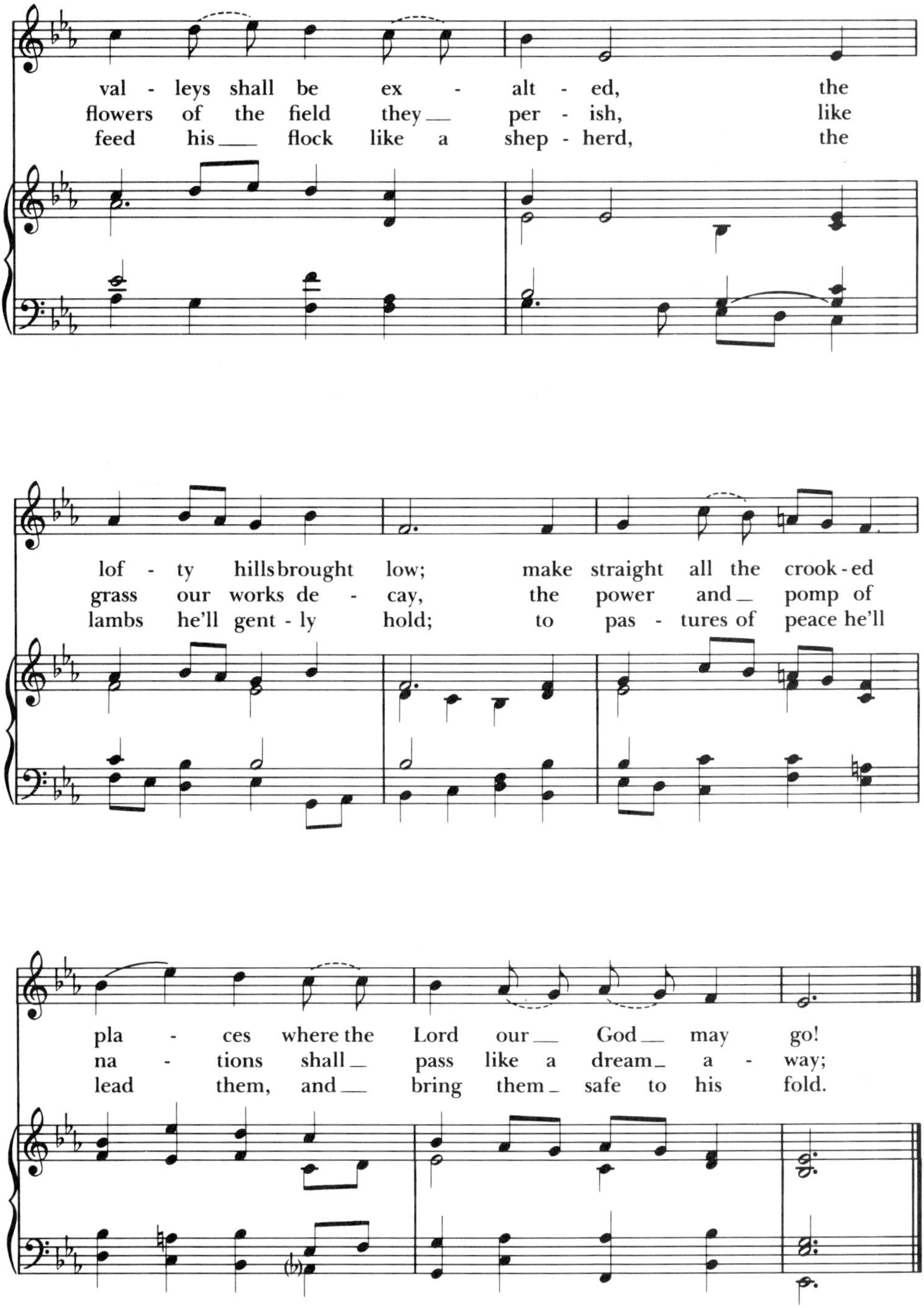
valleys shall be exalted, the
flowers of the field they perish, like
feed his flock like a shepherd, the
lofty hills brought low; make straight all the crooked
grass our works decay, the power and pomp of
lambs he'll gently hold; to pastures of peace he'll
places where the Lord our God may go!
nations shall pass like a dream away;
lead them, and bring them safe to his fold.

Words: James Lewis Milligan (1876-1961), alt.
Music: *Ascension,* Henry Hugh Bancroft (b. 1904)

𝅗𝅥 = 56
Irr.

1 On Jor - dan's bank the Bap - tist's cry an -
2 Then cleansed be ev - ery breast from sin; make
3 For thou art our sal - va - tion, Lord, our
4 To heal the sick stretch out thine hand, and
5 All praise, e - ter - nal Son, to thee, whose
1 noun - ces that the Lord is nigh; a - wake and heark - en,
2 straight the way for God with - in, and let each heart pre -
3 ref - uge, and our great re - ward; with - out thy grace we
4 bid the fall - en sin - ner stand; shine forth, and let thy
5 ad - vent doth thy peo - ple free; whom with the Fa - ther
1 for he brings glad tid - ings of the King of kings.
2 pare a home where such a might - y guest may come.
3 waste a - way like flowers that with - er and de - cay.
4 light re - store earth's own true love - li - ness once more.
5 we a - dore and Ho - ly Spi - rit ev - er - more.

Words: Charles Coffin (1676-1749); tr. Charles Winfred Douglas (1867-1944), after John Chandler (1806-1876); alt.
Music: *Winchester New,* melody from *Musicalishes Hand-Buch,* 1690; harm. William Henry Monk (1823-1889), alt.

♩=84
LM

77

1 From east to west, from shore to shore, let
2 Be - hold, the world's cre - a - tor wears the
3 For this how won - drous - ly he wrought! A
4 And while the an - gels in the sky sang
5 All glo - ry for this bless - ed morn to
1 ev - ery heart a - wake and sing the ho - ly child whom
2 form and fa - shion of a slave; our ve - ry flesh our
3 maid in low - ly hu - man place be - came, in ways be -
4 praise a - bove the si - lent field, to shep - herds poor the
5 God the Fa - ther ev - er be; all praise to thee, O
1 Ma - ry bore, the Christ, the ev - er - last - ing King.
2 Ma - ker shares, his fal - len crea - tures all to save.
3 yond all thought, the cho - sen ves - sel of his grace.
4 Lord Most High, the one great Shep - herd, was re - vealed.
5 Vir - gin - born, all praise, O Ho - ly Ghost, to thee.

Words: Caelius Sedulius (5th cent.); tr. John Ellerton (1826-1893), alt.
Music: *Vom Himmel kam der Engel Schar*, melody source unknown; acc. Carol Doran (b. 1936)

𝅗𝅥. = 48
LM

Unison or harmony
1 O lit - tle town of Beth - le - hem, how still we see thee
2 For Christ is born of Ma - ry; and gath - ered all a -
3 How si - lent - ly, how si - lent - ly, the won - drous gift is
*4 Where child - ren pure and hap - py pray to the bless - ed
5 O ho - ly Child of Beth - le - hem, de - scend to us, we
1 lie! A - bove thy deep and dream - less sleep the
2 bove, while mor - tals sleep, the an - gels keep their
3 given! So God im - parts to hu - man hearts the
4 Child, where mis - er - y cries out to thee, Son
5 pray; cast out our sin and en - ter in, be
1 si - lent stars go by; yet in thy dark streets
2 watch of won - dering love. O morn - ing stars, to -
3 bless - ings of his heaven. No ear may hear his
4 of the mo - ther mild; where char - i - ty stands
5 born in us to - day. We hear the Christ - mas

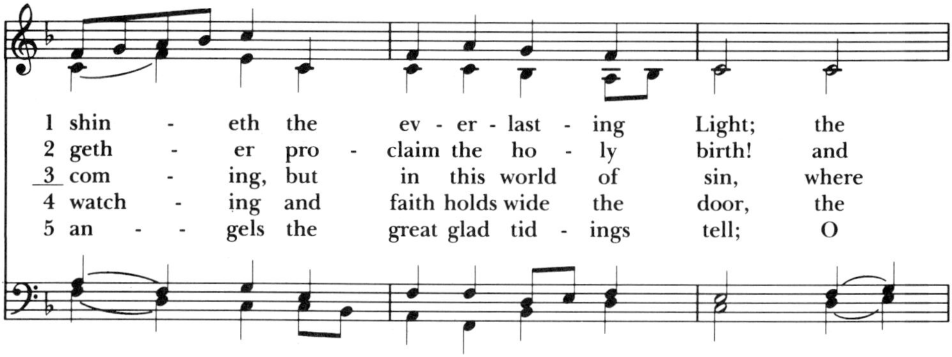
1 shin - eth the ev - er - last - ing Light; the
2 geth - er pro - claim the ho - ly birth! and
3 com - ing, but in this world of sin, where
4 watch - ing and faith holds wide the door, the
5 an - - gels the great glad tid - ings tell; O

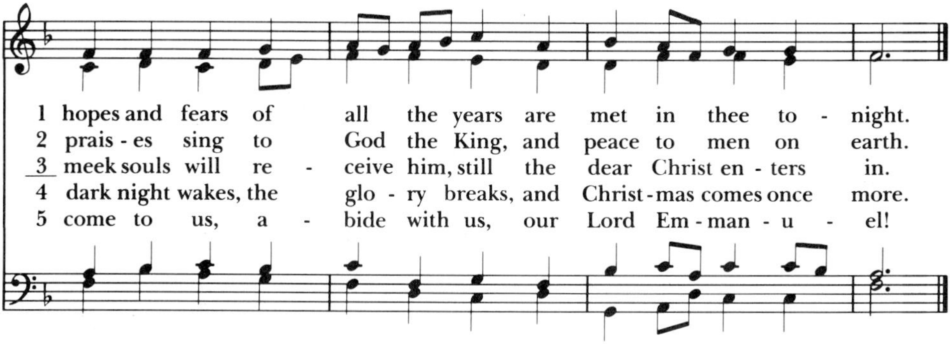
1 hopes and fears of all the years are met in thee to - night.
2 prais - es sing to God the King, and peace to men on earth.
3 meek souls will re - ceive him, still the dear Christ en - ters in.
4 dark night wakes, the glo - ry breaks, and Christ - mas comes once more.
5 come to us, a - bide with us, our Lord Em - man - u - el!

Alternative tune: *St. Louis*, 79.

Words: Phillips Brooks (1835-1893) — 𝅗𝅥 = 48

Music: *Forest Green*, English melody; adapt. and harm. Ralph Vaughan Williams (1872-1958) — CMD

1 O lit - tle town of Beth - le - hem, how still we see thee
2 For Christ is born of Ma - ry; and gath - ered all a -
3 How si - lent - ly, how si - lent - ly, the won - drous gift is
*4 Where child - ren pure and hap - py pray to the bless - ed
5 O ho - ly Child of Beth - le - hem, de - scend to us, we
1 lie! A - bove thy deep and dream - less sleep the
2 bove, while mor - tals sleep, the an - gels keep their
3 given! So God im - parts to hu - man hearts the
4 Child, where mis - er - y cries out to thee, Son
5 pray; cast out our sin and en - ter in, be
1 si - lent stars go by; yet in thy dark streets
2 watch of won - dering love. O morn - ing stars, to -
3 bless - ings of his heaven. No ear may hear his
4 of the mo - ther mild; where char - i - ty stands
5 born in us to - day. We hear the Christ - mas

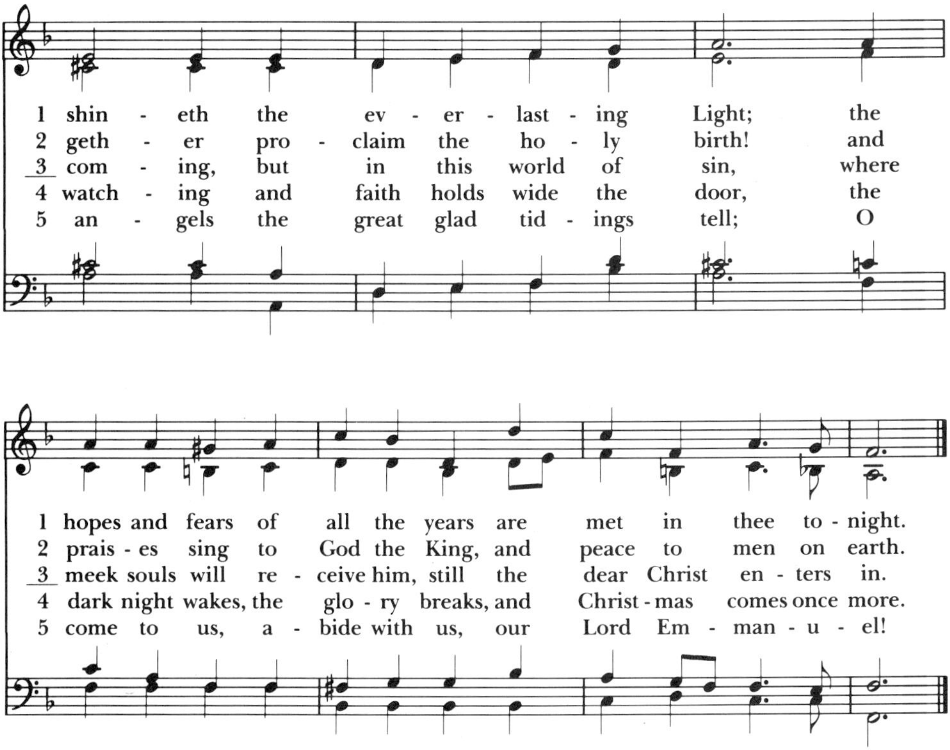
1 shin - eth the ev - er - last - ing Light; the
2 geth - er pro - claim the ho - ly birth! and
3 com - ing, but in this world of sin, where
4 watch - ing and faith holds wide the door, the
5 an - gels the great glad tid - ings tell; O
1 hopes and fears of all the years are met in thee to - night.
2 prais - es sing to God the King, and peace to men on earth.
3 meek souls will re - ceive him, still the dear Christ en - ters in.
4 dark night wakes, the glo - ry breaks, and Christ - mas comes once more.
5 come to us, a - bide with us, our Lord Em - man - u - el!

Alternative tune: *Forest Green,* 78.

Words: Phillips Brooks (1835-1893)
Music: *St. Louis,* Lewis H. Redner (1831-1908)

𝅗𝅥 = 48
CMD

1 From heaven a - bove to earth I come to bring good
2 to you this night is born a child of Ma - ry,
3 This is the Christ, God's Son most high, who hears your
4 The bless - ing which the Fa - ther planned the Son holds
news to ev - ery - one! Glad tid - ings of great
cho - sen vir - gin mild; this new - born child of
sad and bit - ter cry; he will him - self your
in his in - fant hand, that in his king - dom,
joy I bring to all the world, and glad - ly sing:
low - ly birth shall be the joy of all the earth.
Sa - vior be and from all sin will set you free.
bright and fair, you may with us his glo - ry share.

Words: Martin Luther (1483-1546); tr. *Lutheran Book of Worship*, 1978
Music: *Vom Himmel hoch*, melody from *Geistliche lieder auffs new gebessert und gemehrt*, 1539; harm. Hans Leo Hassler (1564-1612)

𝅗𝅥=50
LM

1 Lo, how a Rose e'er bloom-ing from ten-der stem hath sprung!
2 I-sa-iah 'twas fore-told it, the Rose I have in mind,
*3 O Flower, whose fra-grance ten-der with sweet-ness fills the air,
Of Jes-se's lin-eage com-ing as seers of old have sung.
with Ma-ry we be-hold it, the Vir-gin Mo-ther kind.
dis-pel in glo-rious splen-dor the dark-ness ev-ery-where;
It came, a blos-som bright, a-mid the
To show God's love a-right, she bore to
true man, yet ve-ry God, from sin and
cold of win-ter, when half spent was the night.
us a Sa-vior, when half spent was the night.
death now save us, and share our ev-ery load.

Words: St. 1-2, German, 15th cent.; tr. Theodore Baker (1851-1934). st. 3, Friedrich Layritz (1808-1859); tr. Harriet Reynolds Krauth Spaeth (1845-1925); ver. *Hymnal 1940*

Music: *Es ist ein Ros*, melody from *Alte Catholische Geistliche Kirchengesäng*, 1599; harm. Michael Praetorius (1571-1621)

𝅗𝅥 = 50

76. 76. 676

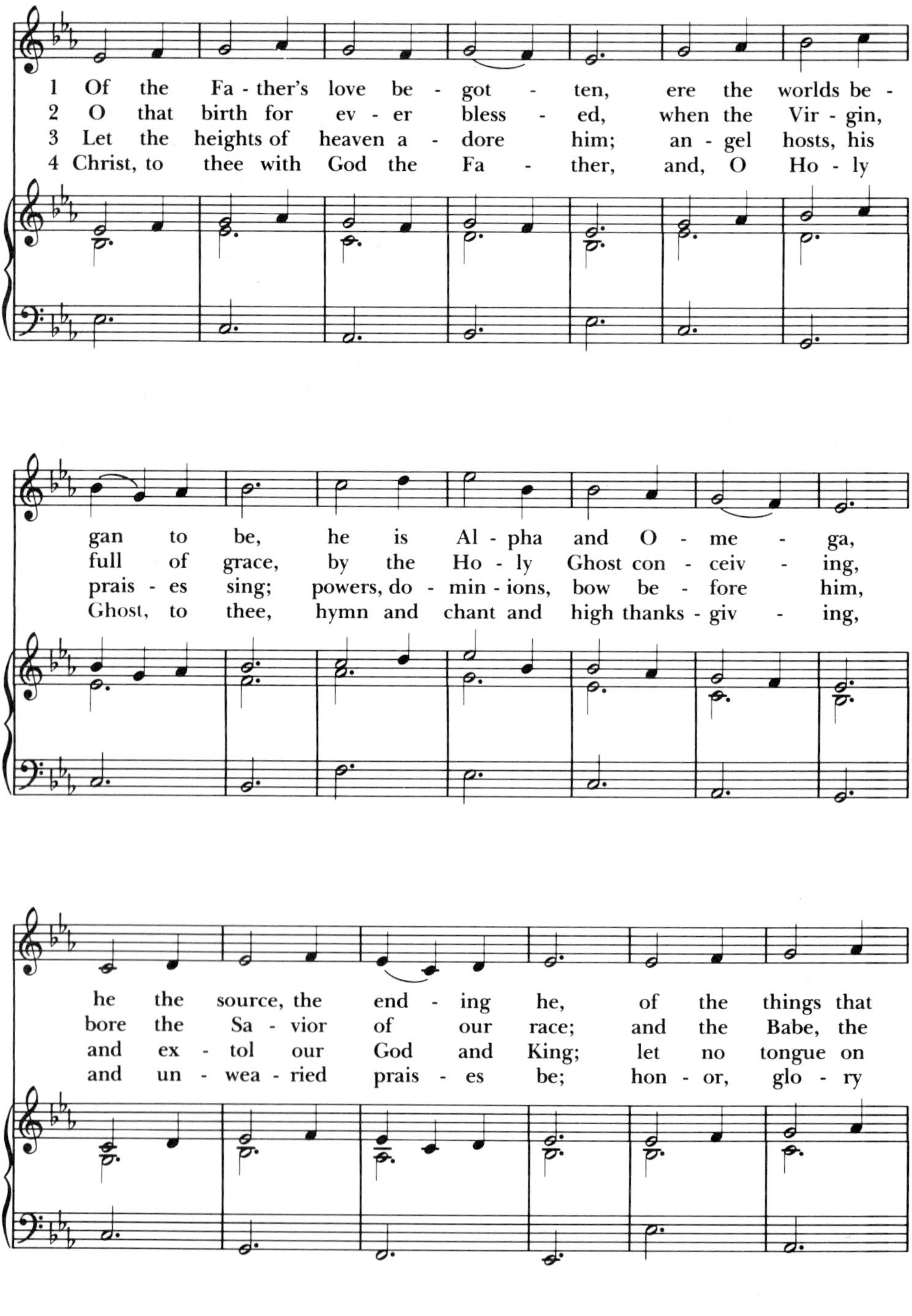
1 Of the Fa - ther's love be - got - ten, ere the worlds be -
2 O that birth for ev - er bless - ed, when the Vir - gin,
3 Let the heights of heaven a - dore him; an - gel hosts, his
4 Christ, to thee with God the Fa - ther, and, O Ho - ly
gan to be, he is Al - pha and O - me - ga,
full of grace, by the Ho - ly Ghost con - ceiv - ing,
prais - es sing; powers, do - min - ions, bow be - fore him,
Ghost, to thee, hymn and chant and high thanks - giv - ing,
he the source, the end - ing he, of the things that
bore the Sa - vior of our race; and the Babe, the
and ex - tol our God and King; let no tongue on
and un - wea - ried prais - es be; hon - or, glo - ry

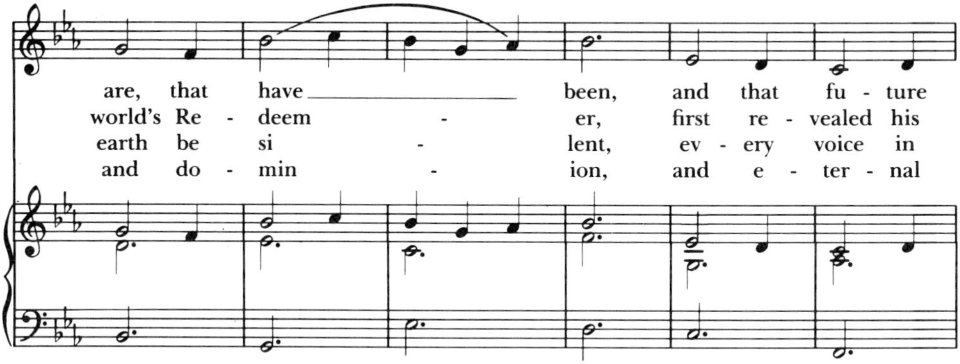
are, that have been, and that fu - ture
world's Re - deem - er, first re - vealed his
earth be si - lent, ev - ery voice in
and do - min - ion, and e - ter - nal

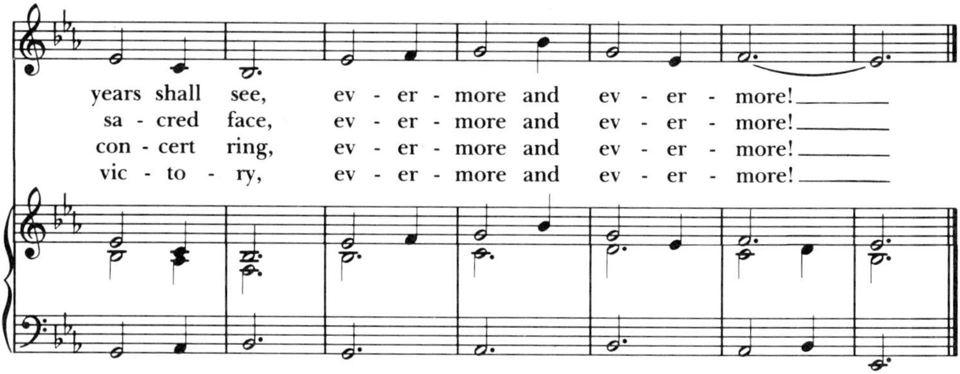
years shall see, ev - er - more and ev - er - more!
sa - cred face, ev - er - more and ev - er - more!
con - cert ring, ev - er - more and ev - er - more!
vic - to - ry, ev - er - more and ev - er - more!

This hymn may be performed in equal note values: ♩ ♩ ♩ ♩

Words: Marcus Aurelius Clemens Prudentius (348-410?); tr. John Mason Neale (1818-1866)
and Henry Williams Baker (1821-1877), alt.

Music: *Divinum mysterium,* Sanctus trope, 11th cent; adapt. *Piae Cantiones*, 1582; acc. Bruce Neswick (b. 1956)

𝅗𝅥. = 60
87. 87. 87 with Refrain

1 O come, all ye faith - ful, joy - ful and tri - um - phant, O
2 God from God, Light from Light e - ter - nal,
3 Sing, choirs of an - gels, sing in ex - ul - ta - tion,
*4 See how the shep - herds, sum-moned to his cra - dle,
*5 Child, for us sin - ners poor and in the man - ger,
1 come ye, O come ye to Beth - le - hem;
2 lo! he ab - hors not the Vir - gin's womb;
3 sing, all ye ci - ti - zens of heaven a - bove;
4 leav - ing their flocks, draw nigh to gaze;
5 we would em - brace thee, with love and awe;
1 come, and be - hold him, born the King of an - gels;
2 on - ly - be - got - ten Son of the Fa - ther;
3 glo - ry to God, glo - ry in the high - est;
4 we too will thith - er bend our joy - ful foot - steps;
5 who would not love thee, lov - ing us so dear - ly?
Refrain
O come, let us a - dore him, O come, let us a -

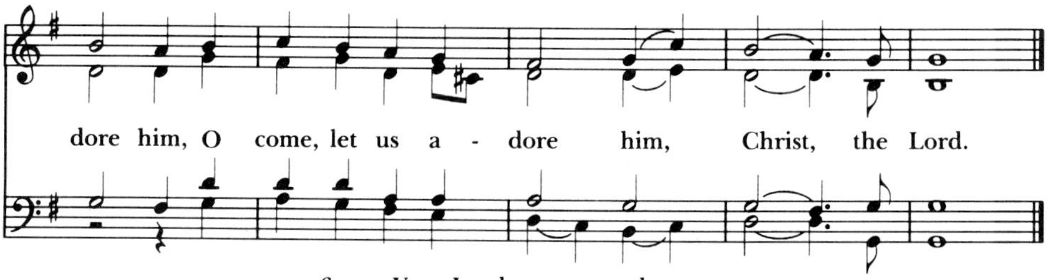
dore him, O come, let us a - dore him, Christ, the Lord.

6 Yea, Lord, we greet thee,
born this happy morning;
Jesus, to thee be glory given;
Word of the Father,
now in flesh appearing;

Refrain

Words: John Francis Wade (1711-1786); tr. Frederick Oakeley (1802-1880) and others
Music: *Adeste fideles,* present form of melody att. John Francis Wade (1711-1786); harm. *The English Hymnal,* 1906

𝅗𝅥=54
Irr.

Christmas 84

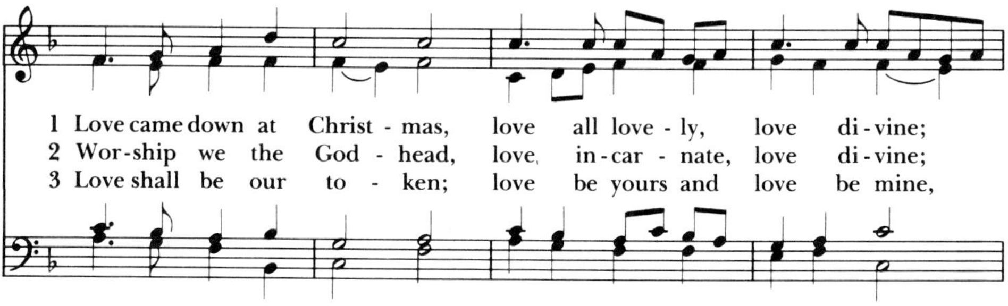
1 Love came down at Christ - mas, love all love - ly, love di - vine;
2 Wor-ship we the God - head, love, in - car - nate, love di - vine;
3 Love shall be our to - ken; love be yours and love be mine,

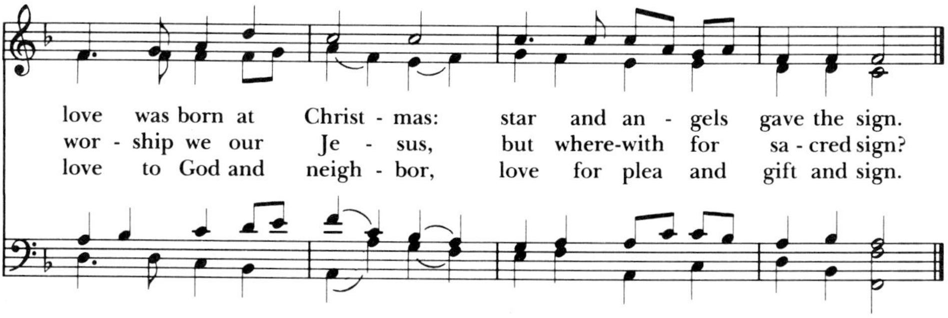
love was born at Christ - mas: star and an - gels gave the sign.
wor - ship we our Je - sus, but where-with for sa - cred sign?
love to God and neigh - bor, love for plea and gift and sign.

Words: Christina Rossetti (1830-1894), alt.
Music: *Gartan,* melody from *Petrie Collection of Irish Melodies, Part II,* 1902; harm. David Evans (1874-1948)

𝅗𝅥=46
67. 67

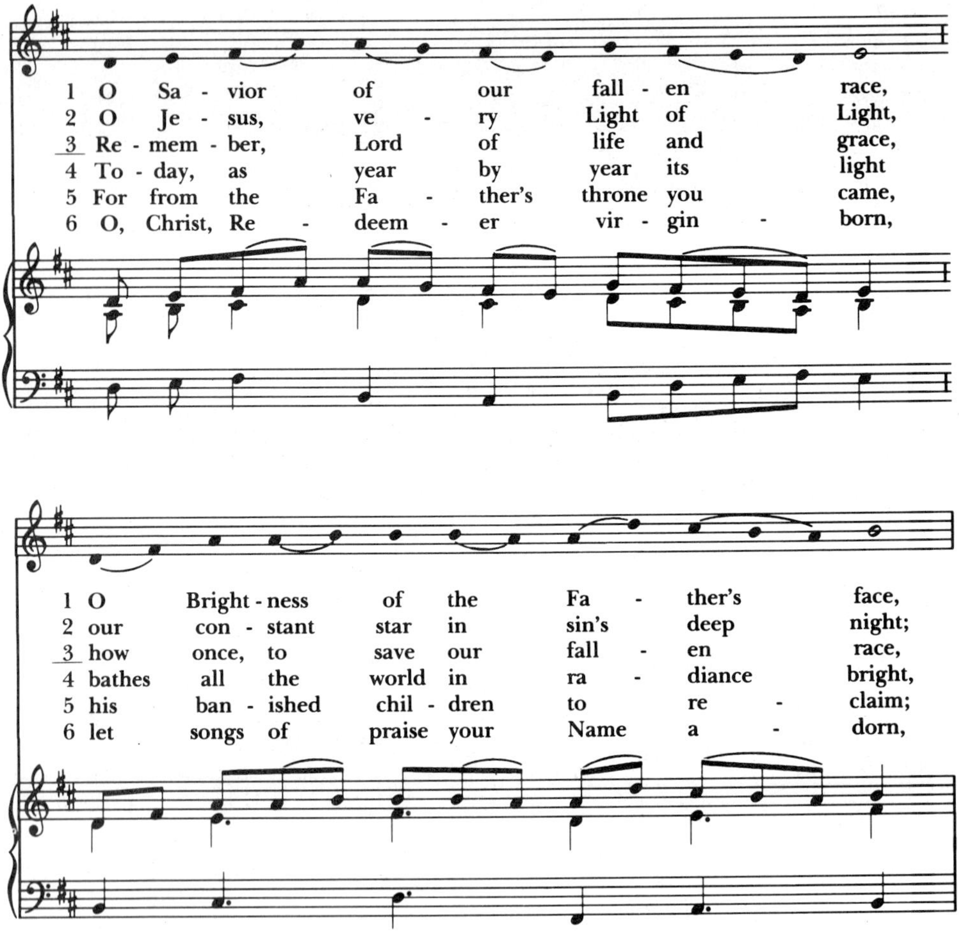
1 O Sa - vior of our fall - en race,
2 O Je - sus, ve - ry Light of Light,
3 Re - mem - ber, Lord of life and grace,
4 To - day, as year by year its light
5 For from the Fa - ther's throne you came,
6 O, Christ, Re - deem - er vir - gin - born,
1 O Bright - ness of the Fa - ther's face,
2 our con - stant star in sin's deep night;
3 how once, to save our fall - en race,
4 bathes all the world in ra - diance bright,
5 his ban - ished chil - dren to re - claim;
6 let songs of praise your Name a - dorn,

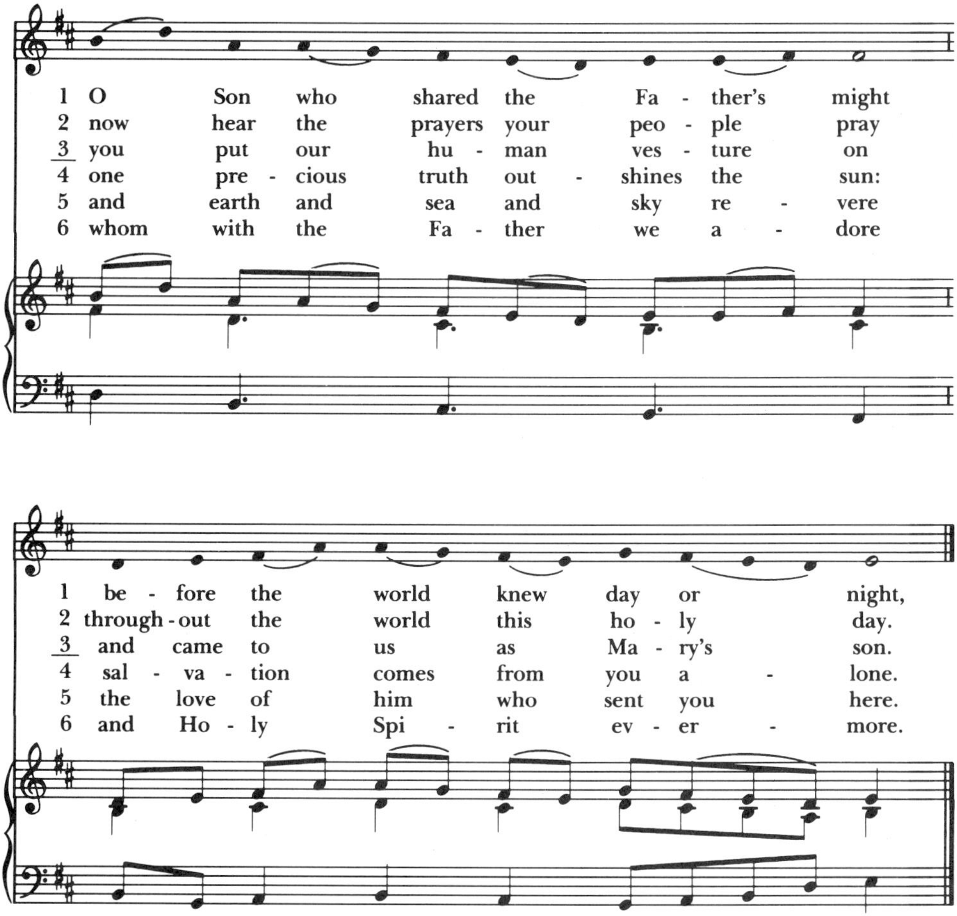
1 O Son who shared the Fa - ther's might
2 now hear the prayers your peo - ple pray
3 you put our hu - man ves - ture on
4 one pre - cious truth out - shines the sun:
5 and earth and sea and sky re - vere
6 whom with the Fa - ther we a - dore
1 be - fore the world knew day or night,
2 through - out the world this ho - ly day.
3 and came to us as Ma - ry's son.
4 sal - va - tion comes from you a - lone.
5 the love of him who sent you here.
6 and Ho - ly Spi - rit ev - er - more.

Alternative tune: *Gonfalon Royal,* 86.

Words: Latin, ca. 6th cent.; tr. Gilbert E. Doan (b. 1930)
Music: *Christe, Redemptor omnium,* plainsong, Mode 1; acc. Bruce Neswick (b. 1956) LM

1 O Sa - vior of our fall - en race,
2 O Je - sus, ve - ry Light of Light,
3 Re - mem - ber, Lord of life and grace,
4 To - day, as year by year its light
5 For from the Fa - ther's throne you came,
6 O Christ, Re - deem - er vir - gin - born,

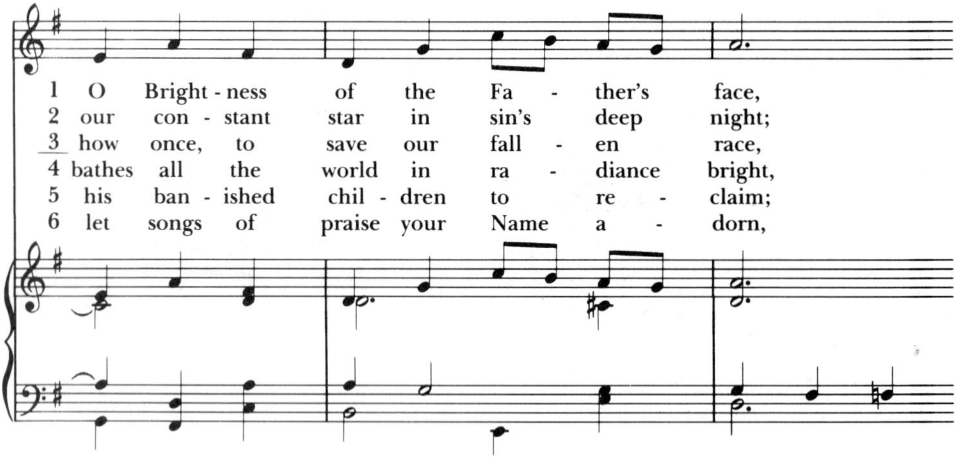
1 O Bright - ness of the Fa - ther's face,
2 our con - stant star in sin's deep night;
3 how once, to save our fall - en race,
4 bathes all the world in ra - diance bright,
5 his ban - ished chil - dren to re - claim;
6 let songs of praise your Name a - dorn,

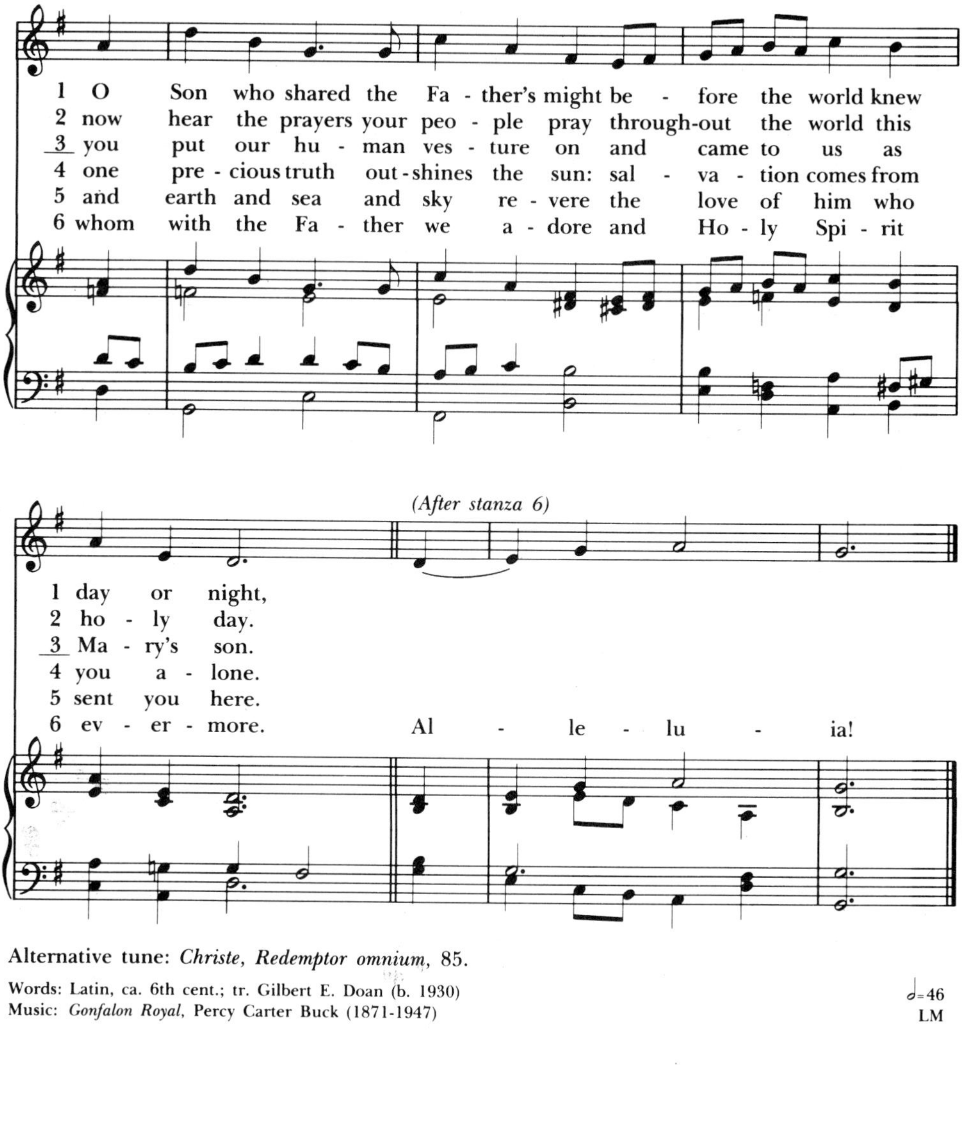
1 O Son who shared the Fa - ther's might be - fore the world knew
2 now hear the prayers your peo - ple pray through-out the world this
3 you put our hu - man ves - ture on and came to us as
4 one pre - cious truth out - shines the sun: sal - va - tion comes from
5 and earth and sea and sky re - vere the love of him who
6 whom with the Fa - ther we a - dore and Ho - ly Spi - rit
(After stanza 6)
1 day or night,
2 ho - ly day.
3 Ma - ry's son.
4 you a - lone.
5 sent you here.
6 ev - er - more. Al - le - lu - ia!

Alternative tune: *Christe, Redemptor omnium,* 85.

Words: Latin, ca. 6th cent.; tr. Gilbert E. Doan (b. 1930)
Music: *Gonfalon Royal,* Percy Carter Buck (1871-1947)

𝅗𝅥 = 46
LM

1 Hark! the her - ald an - gels sing glo - ry to the new-born King!
2 Christ, by high - est heaven a - dored; Christ, the ev - er - last - ing Lord;
3 Mild he lays his glo - ry by, born that we no more may die,
Peace on earth and mer - cy mild, God and sin - ners rec - on - ciled!
late in time be - hold him come, off - spring of the Vir-gin's womb.
born to raise us from the earth, born to give us sec - ond birth.
Joy - ful, all ye na - tions, rise, join the tri-umph of the skies;
Veiled in flesh the God-head see; hail the in-car - nate De - i - ty.
Risen with heal-ing in his wings, light and life to all he brings,
with the an - gel - ic host pro - claim Christ is born in Beth - le - hem!
Pleased as man with us to dwell; Je - sus, our Em - man - u - el!
hail, the Sun of Right-eous - ness! hail, the heaven-born Prince of Peace!

Refrain
Hark! the her - ald an - gels sing glo - ry to the new-born King!

Words: Charles Wesley (1707-1788), alt.
Music: *Mendelssohn,* Felix Mendelssohn (1809-1847); adapt. William H. Cummings (1831-1915)

𝅗𝅥=54
77. 77. D with Refrain

Christmas

88

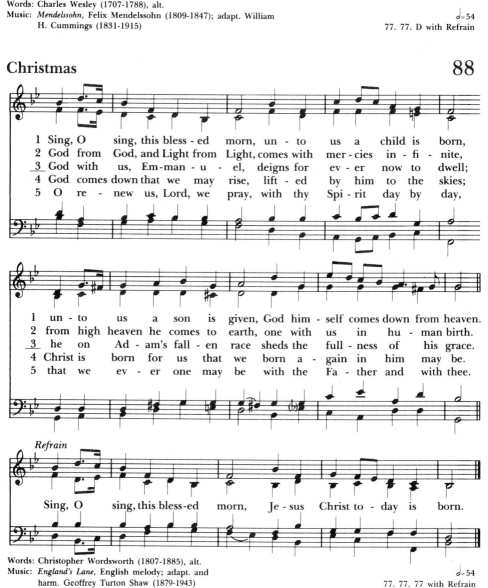

1 Sing, O sing, this bless - ed morn, un - to us a child is born,
2 God from God, and Light from Light, comes with mer - cies in - fi - nite,
3 God with us, Em - man - u - el, deigns for ev - er now to dwell;
4 God comes down that we may rise, lift - ed by him to the skies;
5 O re - new us, Lord, we pray, with thy Spi - rit day by day,
1 un - to us a son is given, God him - self comes down from heaven.
2 from high heaven he comes to earth, one with us in hu - man birth.
3 he on Ad - am's fall - en race sheds the full - ness of his grace.
4 Christ is born for us that we born a - gain in him may be.
5 that we ev - er one may be with the Fa - ther and with thee.
Refrain
Sing, O sing, this bless - ed morn, Je - sus Christ to - day is born.

Words: Christopher Wordsworth (1807-1885), alt.
Music: *England's Lane,* English melody; adapt. and harm. Geoffrey Turton Shaw (1879-1943)

𝅗𝅥=54
77. 77. 77 with Refrain

1 It came up - on the mid - night clear, that
2 Still through the clov - en skies they come with
3 Yet with the woes of sin and strife the
4 For lo! the days are haste - ning on, by
glo - rious song of old, from an - gels bend - ing
peace - ful wings un - furled, and still their heaven - ly
world has suf - fered long; be - neath the heaven - ly
pro - phets seen of old, when with the ev - er -
near the earth to touch their harps of gold:
mu - sic floats o'er all the wea - ry world;
hymn have rolled two thou - sand years of wrong;
cir - cling years shall come the time fore - told,
"Peace on the earth, good will to men, from
a - bove its sad and low - ly plains they
and war - ring hu - man - kind hears not the
when peace shall o - ver all the earth its

heaven's all - gra - cious King." The world in sol - emn
bend on hov - ering wing, and ev - er o'er its
tid - ings which they bring; O hush the noise and
an - cient splen - dors fling, and all the world give
still - ness lay to hear the an - gels sing.
Ba - bel - sounds the bless - ed an - gels sing.
cease your strife and hear the an - gels sing!
back the song which now the an - gels sing.

Alternative tune: *Noel,* 90.

Words: Edmund H. Sears (1810-1876), alt.
Music: *Carol,* Richard Storrs Willis (1819-1900)

♩. = 52
CMD

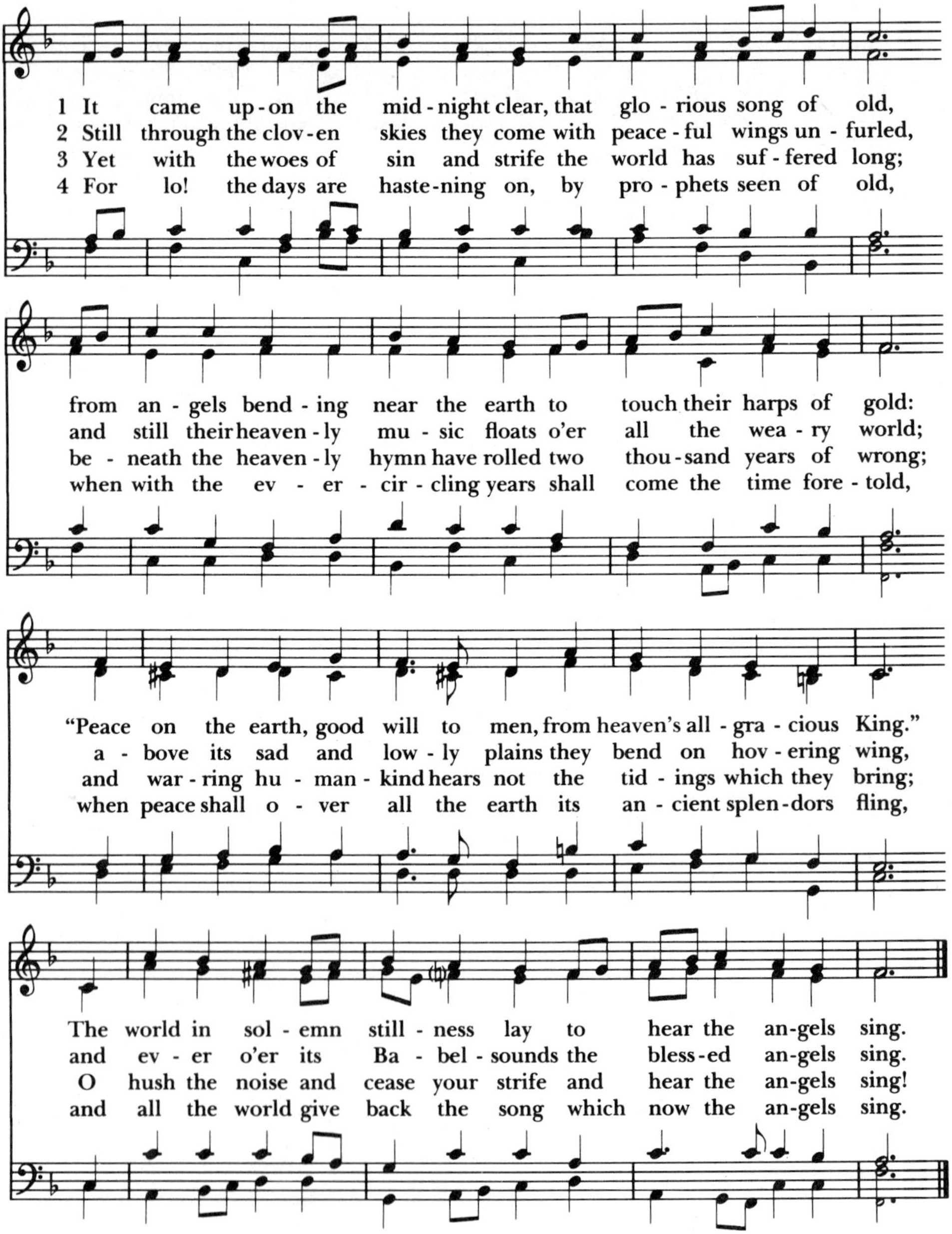
1 It came up-on the mid-night clear, that glo-rious song of old,
2 Still through the clov-en skies they come with peace-ful wings un-furled,
3 Yet with the woes of sin and strife the world has suf-fered long;
4 For lo! the days are haste-ning on, by pro-phets seen of old,
from an-gels bend-ing near the earth to touch their harps of gold:
and still their heaven-ly mu-sic floats o'er all the wea-ry world;
be-neath the heaven-ly hymn have rolled two thou-sand years of wrong;
when with the ev-er-cir-cling years shall come the time fore-told,
"Peace on the earth, good will to men, from heaven's all-gra-cious King."
a-bove its sad and low-ly plains they bend on hov-ering wing,
and war-ring hu-man-kind hears not the tid-ings which they bring;
when peace shall o-ver all the earth its an-cient splen-dors fling,
The world in sol-emn still-ness lay to hear the an-gels sing.
and ev-er o'er its Ba-bel-sounds the bless-ed an-gels sing.
O hush the noise and cease your strife and hear the an-gels sing!
and all the world give back the song which now the an-gels sing.

Alternative tune: *Carol,* 89.

Words: Edmund H. Sears (1810-1876), alt.
Music: *Noel,* English melody; adapt. Arthur Seymour Sullivan (1842-1900)

𝅗𝅥=60
CMD

Break forth, O beau-teous heaven-ly light, and ush-er in the
morn-ing; O shep-herds, greet that glo-rious sight, our
Lord a crib a-dorn-ing. This child, this lit-tle
help-less boy, shall be our con-fi-dence and joy, the
power of Sa-tan break-ing, our peace e-ter-nal mak-ing.

Words: Johann Rist (1607-1667); ver. *Hymnal 1982*
Music: *Ermuntre dich,* melody Johann Schop (d. 1665?), alt.;
harm. Johann Sebastian Bach (1685-1750)

♩=64
87. 87. 88. 77

1 On this day earth shall ring with the song chil - dren sing to the Lord, Christ our King, born on earth to
2 His the doom, ours the mirth; when he came down to earth Beth - le - hem saw his birth; ox and ass be -
3 God's bright star, o'er his head, Wise Men three to him led; kneel they low by his bed, lay their gifts be -
4 On this day an - gels sing; with their song earth shall ring, prais - ing Christ, hea - ven's King, born on earth to

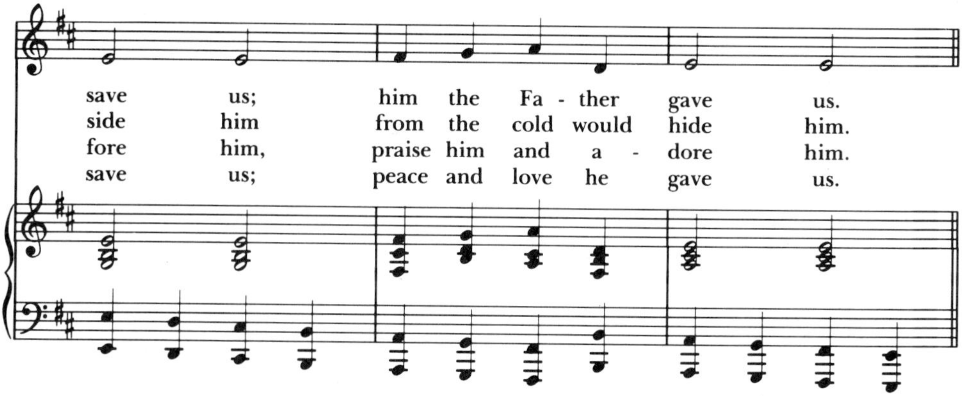
save us; him the Fa - ther gave us.
side him from the cold would hide him.
fore him, praise him and a - dore him.
save us; peace and love he gave us.

Refrain
Id - e - o - o - o, Id - e - o - o - o,

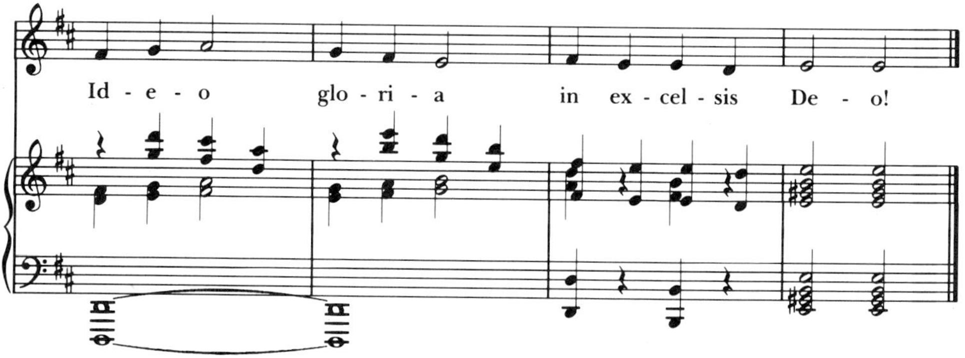
Id - e - o glo - ri - a in ex - cel - sis De - o!

"Ideo gloria in excelsis Deo!" is Latin for "Therefore, glory to God in the highest!"

Words: *Piae Cantiones,* 1582; tr. Jane M. Joseph (1894-1929)
Music: *Personent hodie,* melody from *Piae Cantiones,* 1582;
harm. Gustav Theodore Holst (1874-1934)

𝅗𝅥 = 60
666. 66 with Refrain

1 An - gels, from the realms of glo - ry, wing your flight o'er all the earth; ye, who sang cre - a - tion's sto - ry, now pro - claim Mes - si - ah's birth:
2 Shep - herds in the field a - bid - ing, watch - ing o'er your flocks by night, God with you is now re - sid - ing; yon - der shines the in - fant Light:
3 Sa - ges, leave your con - tem - pla - tions; bright - er vi - sions beam a - far: seek the great De - sire of na - tions; ye have seen his na - tal star:
4 Saints be - fore the al - tar bend - ing, watch - ing long in hope and fear, sud - den - ly the Lord, de - scend - ing, in his tem - ple shall ap - pear:
Refrain
come and wor - ship, come and wor - ship, wor - ship Christ, the new - born King.

This music in A with descant, 368.

Words: James Montgomery (1771-1854), alt.
Music: *Regent Square,* Henry Thomas Smart (1813-1879)

𝅗𝅥=56
87. 87. 87

94

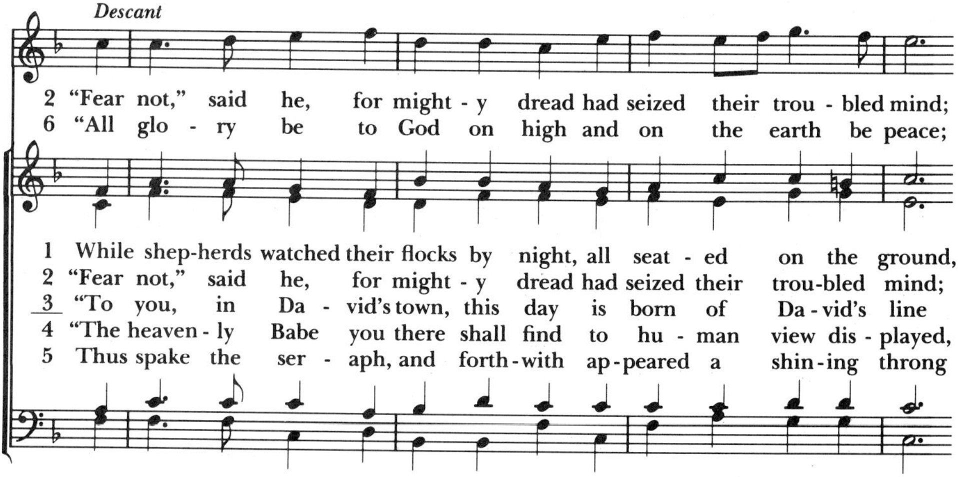
Descant
2 "Fear not," said he, for might - y dread had seized their trou - bled mind;
6 "All glo - ry be to God on high and on the earth be peace;
1 While shep-herds watched their flocks by night, all seat - ed on the ground,
2 "Fear not," said he, for might - y dread had seized their trou-bled mind;
3 "To you, in Da - vid's town, this day is born of Da - vid's line
4 "The heaven - ly Babe you there shall find to hu - man view dis - played,
5 Thus spake the ser - aph, and forth-with ap-peared a shin-ing throng

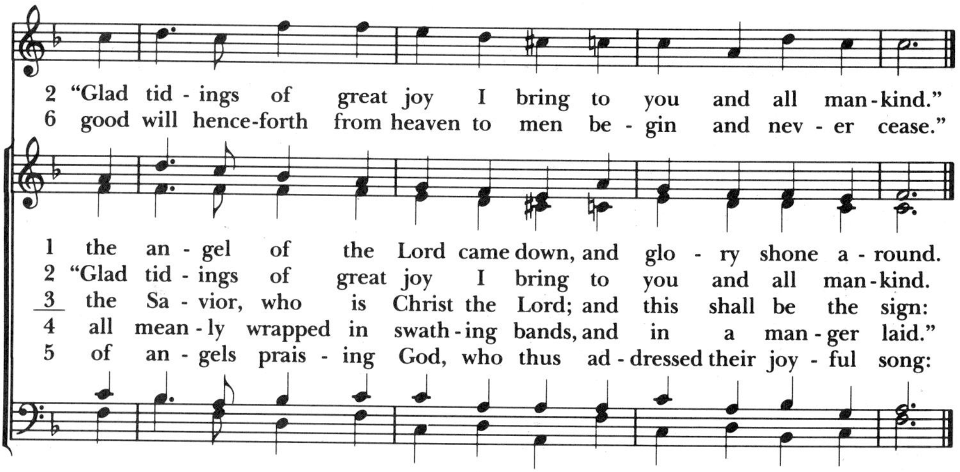
2 "Glad tid - ings of great joy I bring to you and all man-kind."
6 good will hence-forth from heaven to men be - gin and nev - er cease."
1 the an - gel of the Lord came down, and glo - ry shone a - round.
2 "Glad tid - ings of great joy I bring to you and all man-kind.
3 the Sa - vior, who is Christ the Lord; and this shall be the sign:
4 all mean - ly wrapped in swath - ing bands, and in a man - ger laid."
5 of an - gels prais - ing God, who thus ad - dressed their joy - ful song:

6 "All glory be to God on high
and on the earth be peace;
good will henceforth from heaven to men
begin and never cease."

Alternative tune: *Hampton*, 95.

Words: Nahum Tate (1625-1715)
Music: *Winchester Old*, melody from *The Whole Booke of Psalmes*, 1592; harm. *Hymns Ancient and Modern*, 1922; desc. Craig Sellar Lang (1891-1971)

♩=80
CM

1 While shep - herds watched their flocks by night, all
3 "To you, in Da - vid's town, this day is
5 Thus spake the ser - aph, and forth - with ap -
seat - ed on the ground, the an - gel of the
born of Da - vid's line the Sa - vior, who is
peared a shin - ing throng of an - gels prais - ing
Lord came down, and glo - ry shone a - round.
Christ the Lord; and this shall be the sign:
God, who thus ad - dressed their joy - ful song:

2 "Fear not," said he, for might - y dread had
4 "The heaven - ly Babe you there shall find to
6 "All glo - ry be to God on high and
seized their trou - bled mind; "Glad tid - ings of great
hu - man view dis - played, all mean - ly wrapped in
on the earth be peace; good will hence - forth from
joy I bring to you and all man - kind.
swath - ing bands, and in a man - ger laid."
heaven to men be - gin and nev - er cease."

Alternative tune: *Winchester Old,* 94

Words: Nahum Tate (1625-1715)
Music: *Hampton,* McNeil Robinson II (b. 1943)

♩=88
CM

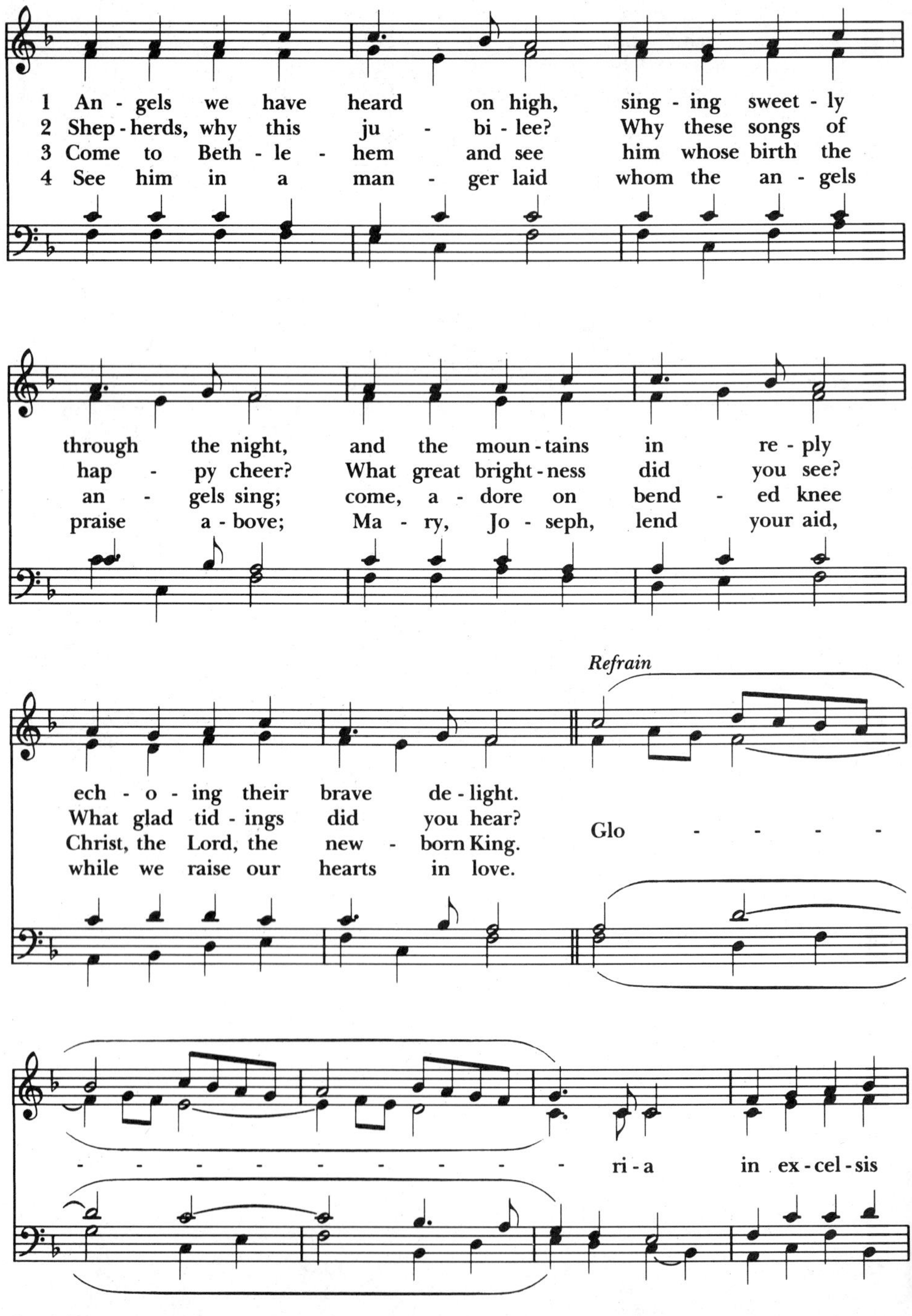
1 An - gels we have heard on high, sing - ing sweet - ly
2 Shep - herds, why this ju - bi - lee? Why these songs of
3 Come to Beth - le - hem and see him whose birth the
4 See him in a man - ger laid whom the an - gels
through the night, and the moun - tains in re - ply
hap - py cheer? What great bright - ness did you see?
an - gels sing; come, a - dore on bend - ed knee
praise a - bove; Ma - ry, Jo - seph, lend your aid,
ech - o - ing their brave de - light.
What glad tid - ings did you hear?
Christ, the Lord, the new - born King.
while we raise our hearts in love.
Refrain
Glo - - - - - - - - - - - - - - - - - ri - a in ex - cel - sis

De - o. Glo - - - - - - -
- ri - a in ex - cel - sis De - o.

Words: French carol; tr. James Chadwick (1813-1882), alt.
Music: *Gloria,* French carol; arr. Edward Shippen Barnes (1887-1958)

𝅗𝅥=58
77. 77 with Refrain

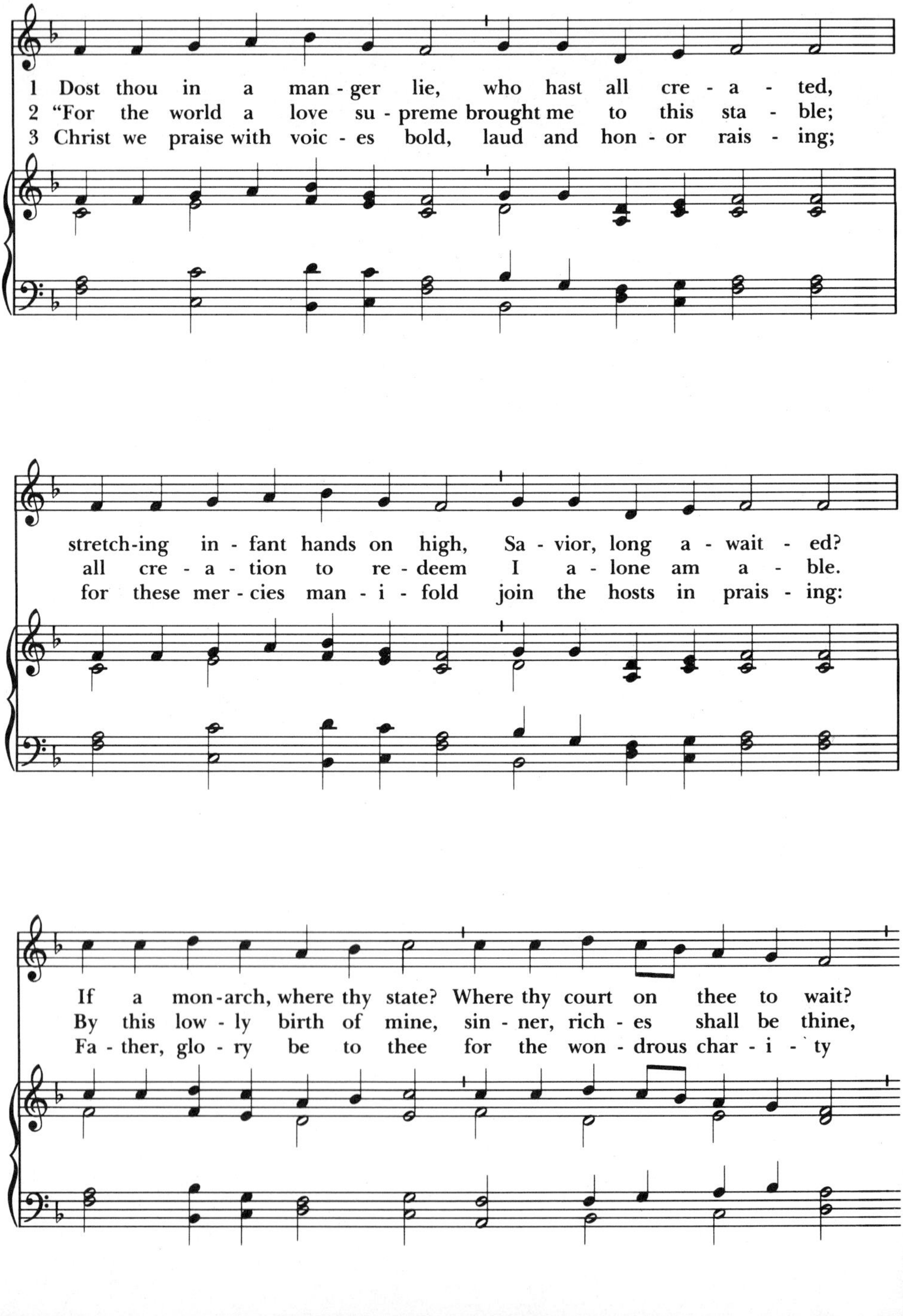
1 Dost thou in a man - ger lie, who hast all cre - a - ted,
2 "For the world a love su - preme brought me to this sta - ble;
3 Christ we praise with voic - es bold, laud and hon - or rais - ing;
stretch-ing in - fant hands on high, Sa - vior, long a - wait - ed?
all cre - a - tion to re - deem I a - lone am a - ble.
for these mer - cies man - i - fold join the hosts in prais - ing:
If a mon-arch, where thy state? Where thy court on thee to wait?
By this low - ly birth of mine, sin - ner, rich - es shall be thine,
Fa - ther, glo - ry be to thee for the won - drous char - i - ty

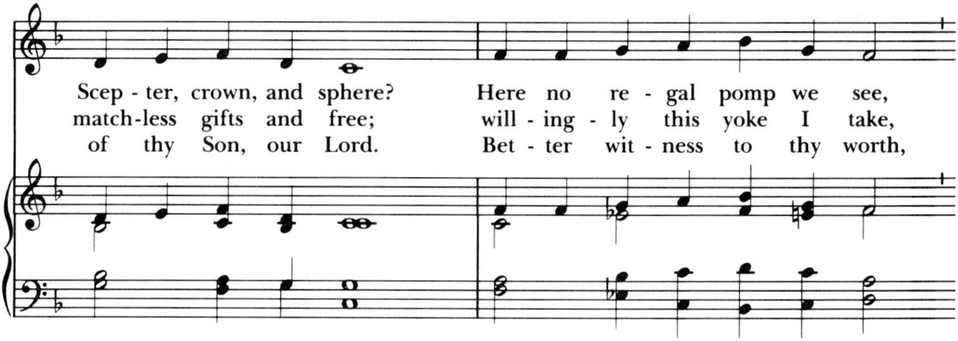
Scep - ter, crown, and sphere? Here no re - gal pomp we see,
match-less gifts and free; will - ing - ly this yoke I take,
of thy Son, our Lord. Bet - ter wit - ness to thy worth,

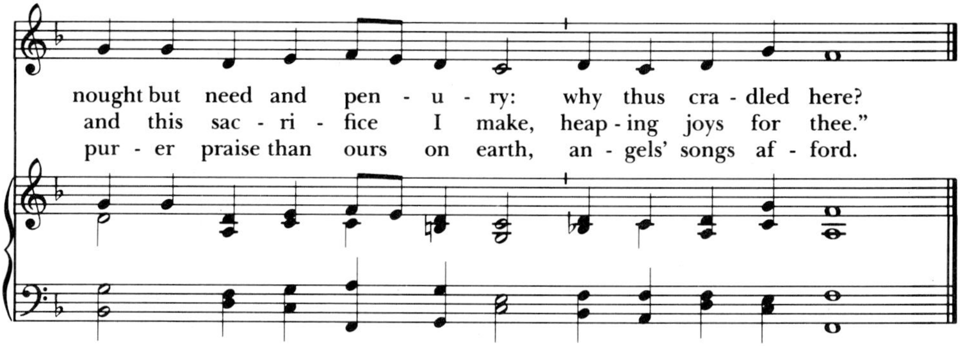
nought but need and pen - u - ry: why thus cra - dled here?
and this sac - ri - fice I make, heap - ing joys for thee."
pur - er praise than ours on earth, an - gels' songs af - ford.

Words: Jean Mauburn (1460-1503); tr. Elizabeth Rundle Charles (1828-1896) and others
Music: *Dies est laetitiae,* melody from *Piae Cantiones*, 1582; harm. Jack W. Burnam (b. 1946)

= 60
76. 76. 775. 775

1. Un - to us a boy is born! The King of all cre -
a - tion, came he to a world for - lorn, the
Lord of ev - ery na - - - tion.
2. Cra - dled in a stall was he with sleep - y cows and

ass - es; but the ve - ry beasts could see that
he all men sur - pass - - - es.
3. He - rod then with fear was filled; "A prince," he said, "in
Jew - ry!" All the lit - tle boys he killed at

Beth-lehem in his fu - - - ry.
4. Now may Ma - ry's son, who came so long a - go to
love us, lead us all with hearts a - flame un -
to the joys a - bove us.

5. Un - to us a boy is born! The King of all cre -
Great: Trumpet
Swell
Ped.
a - tion, came he to a world for - lorn, the
Swell
Lord of ev - ery na - - - tion.
Great: Trumpet

The accompaniment for stanza 1 may be used for all stanzas.

Words: Latin carol, 15th cent.; tr. Percy Dearmer (1867-1936), alt.

Music: *Puer nobis nascitur,* melody from *Piae Cantiones,* 1582; harm. Geoffrey Turton Shaw (1879-1943)

𝅗𝅥=60

77. 77

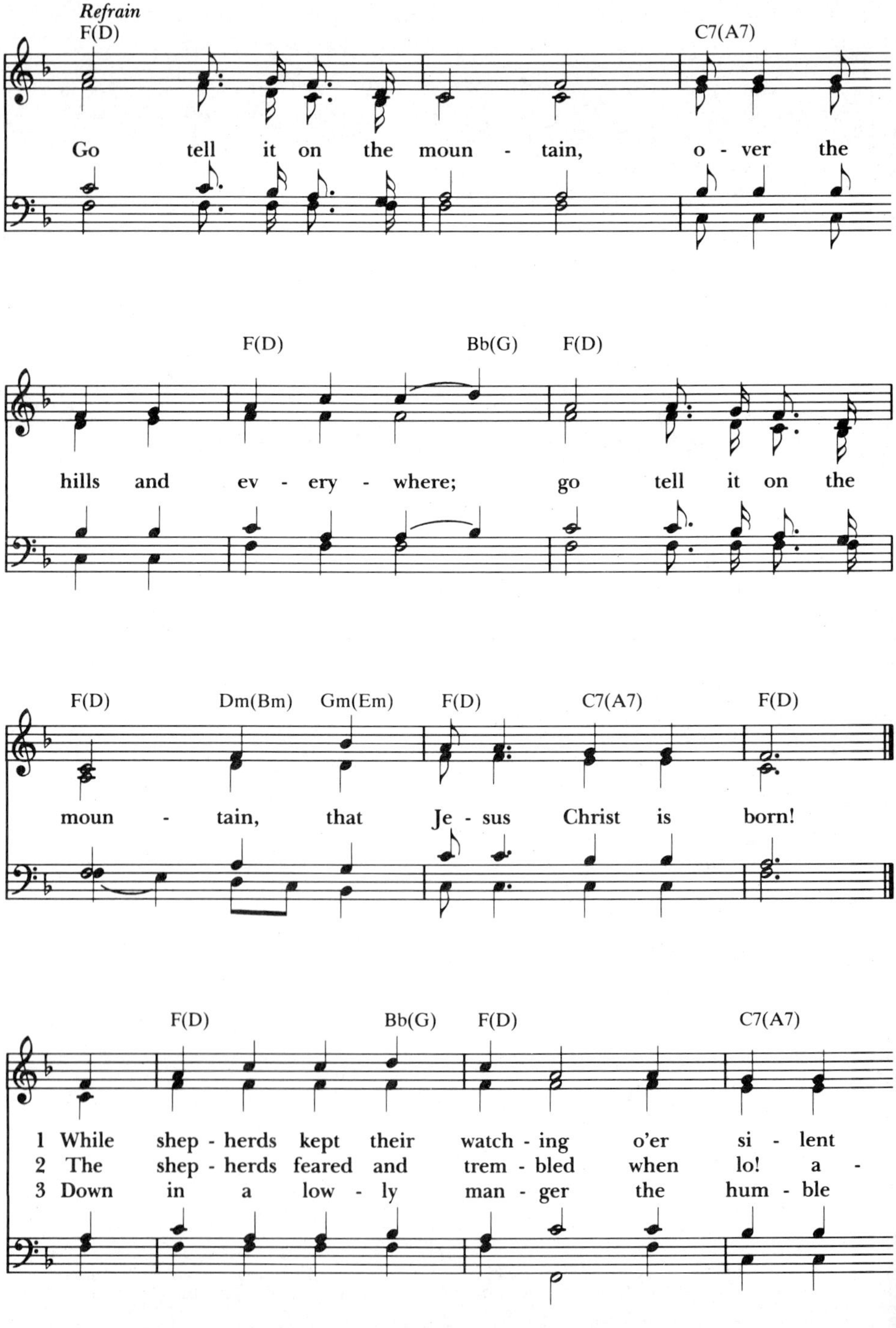
Refrain
F(D) C7(A7)
Go tell it on the moun - tain, o - ver the
F(D) Bb(G) F(D)
hills and ev - ery - where; go tell it on the
F(D) Dm(Bm) Gm(Em) F(D) C7(A7) F(D)
moun - tain, that Je - sus Christ is born!
F(D) Bb(G) F(D) C7(A7)
1 While shep - herds kept their watch - ing o'er si - lent
2 The shep - herds feared and trem - bled when lo! a -
3 Down in a low - ly man - ger the hum - ble

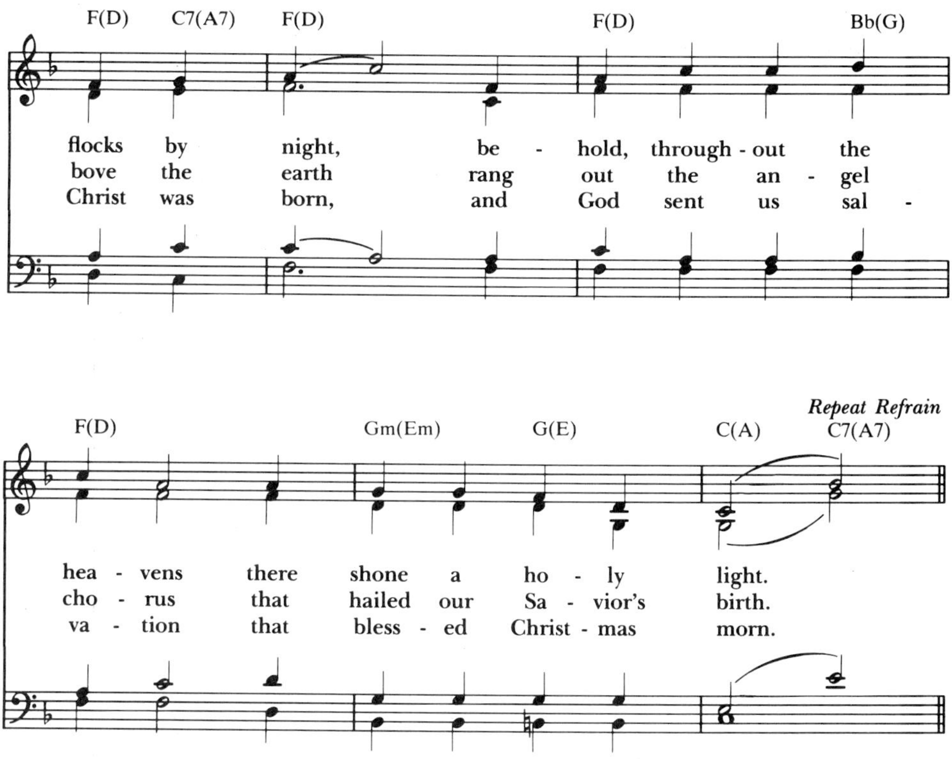
F(D) C7(A7) F(D) F(D) Bb(G)
flocks by night, be - hold, through - out the
bove the earth rang out the an - gel
Christ was born, and God sent us sal -
Repeat Refrain
F(D) Gm(Em) G(E) C(A) C7(A7)
hea - vens there shone a ho - ly light.
cho - rus that hailed our Sa - vior's birth.
va - tion that bless - ed Christ - mas morn.

F(capo 3, D)

Words: Afro-American spiritual, 19th cent., adapt. John W. Work (b. 1901)
Music: *Go Tell It on the Mountain,* Afro-American spiritual, 19th cent.; arr. Horace Clarence Boyer (b. 1935)

𝅗𝅥=60
76. 76 with Refrain

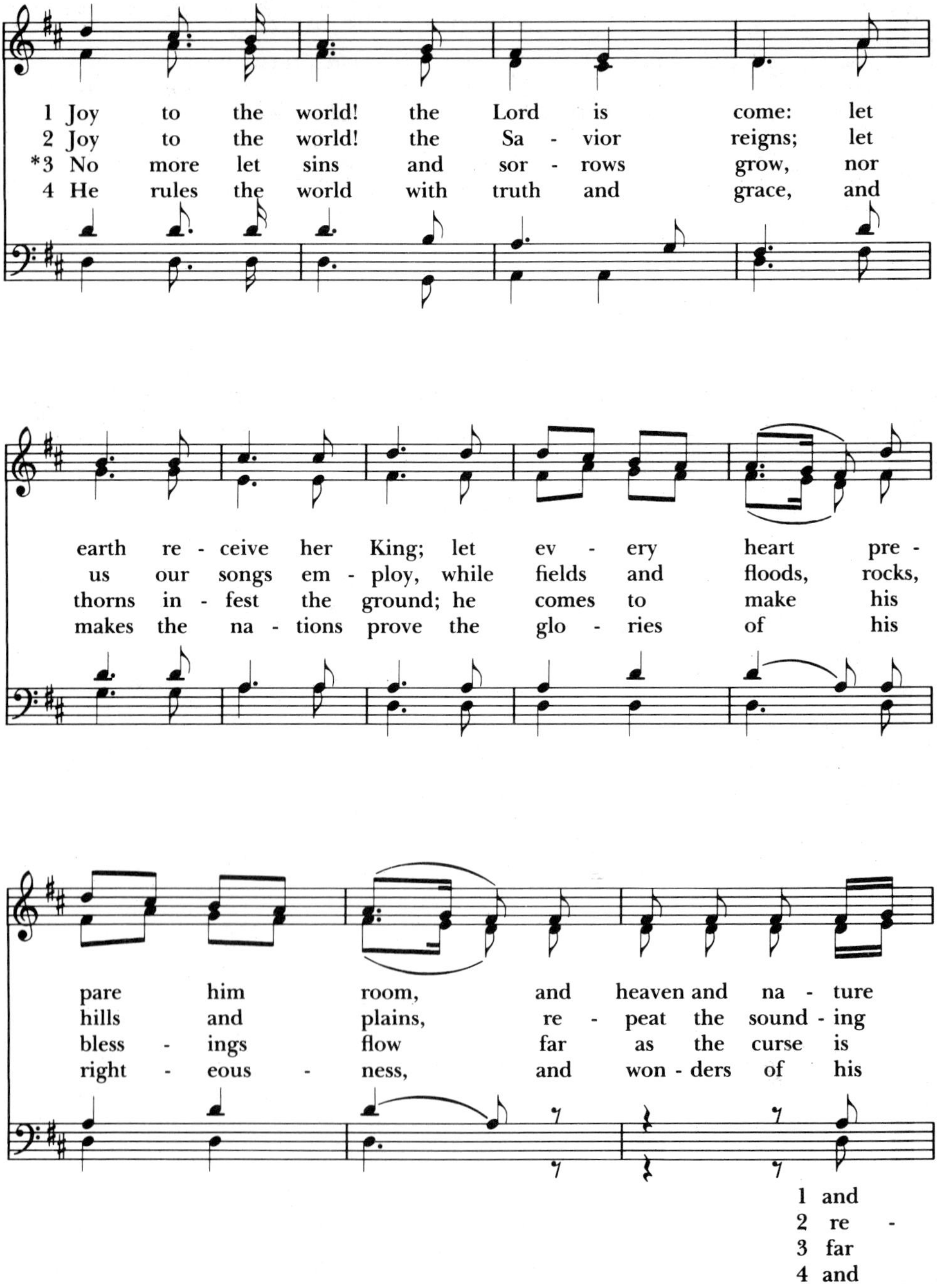
1 Joy to the world! the Lord is come: let
2 Joy to the world! the Sa - vior reigns; let
*3 No more let sins and sor - rows grow, nor
4 He rules the world with truth and grace, and
earth re - ceive her King; let ev - ery heart pre -
us our songs em - ploy, while fields and floods, rocks,
thorns in - fest the ground; he comes to make his
makes the na - tions prove the glo - ries of his
pare him room, and heaven and na - ture
hills and plains, re - peat the sound - ing
bless - ings flow far as the curse is
right - eous - ness, and won - ders of his
1 and
2 re -
3 far
4 and

sing, and heaven and na - ture sing, and heaven and na - ture sing, and heaven and na - ture
joy, re - peat the sound - ing joy, re - peat the sound - ing joy, re - peat the sound - ing
found, far as the curse is found, far as the curse is found, far as the curse is
love, and won - ders of his love, and won - ders of his love, and won - ders of his
heaven, and heaven and na - ture sing.
peat, re - peat the sound - ing joy.
as, far as the curse is found.
won - ders, won - ders of his love.
sing,
joy,
found,
love,

Words: Isaac Watts (1674-1748), alt.
Music: *Antioch,* George Frideric Handel (1685-1759); adapt. and arr. Lowell Mason (1792-1872)

♩=96
CM with Repeat

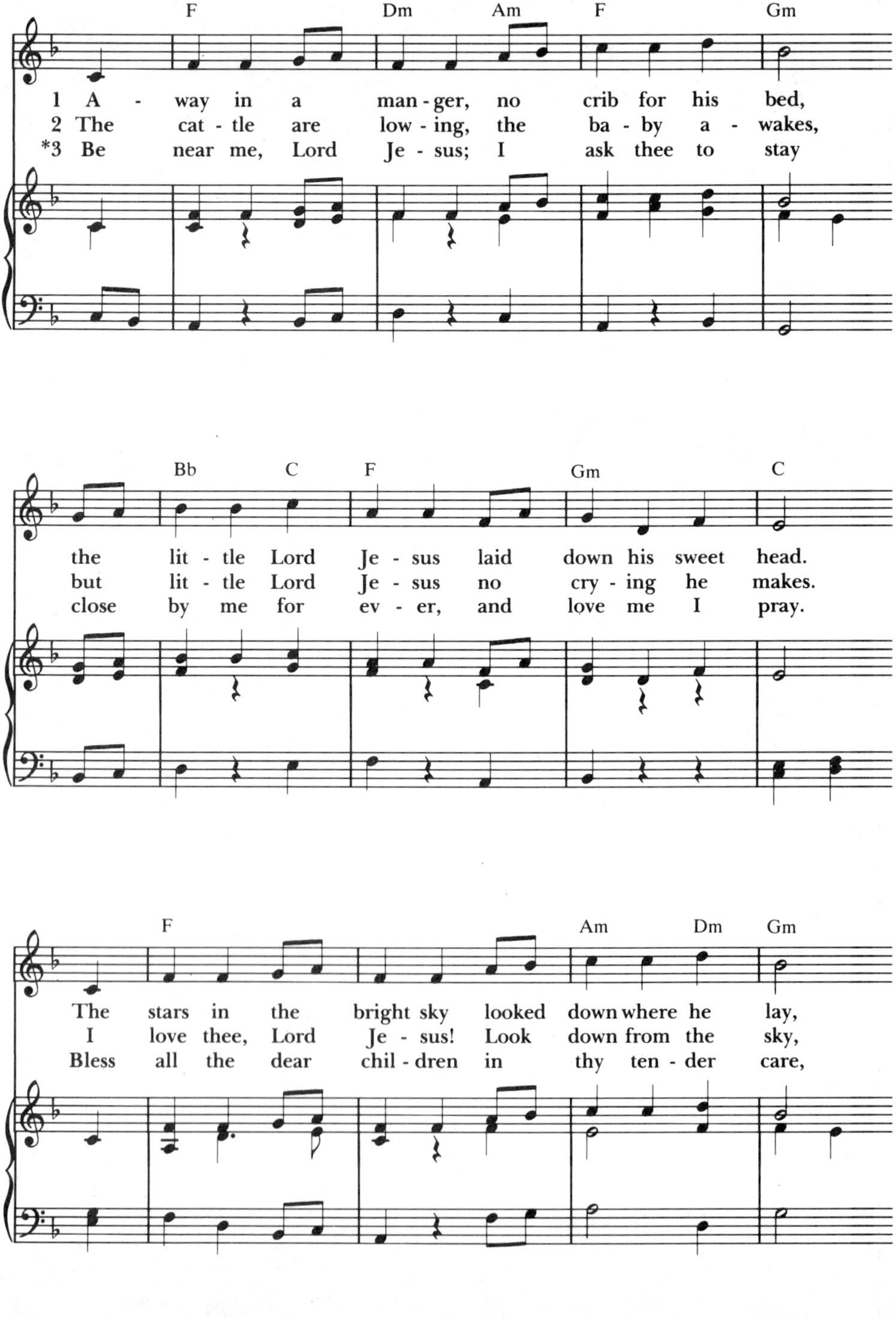
F Dm Am F Gm
1 A - way in a man - ger, no crib for his bed,
2 The cat - tle are low - ing, the ba - by a - wakes,
*3 Be near me, Lord Je - sus; I ask thee to stay
Bb C F Gm C
the lit - tle Lord Je - sus laid down his sweet head.
but lit - tle Lord Je - sus no cry - ing he makes.
close by me for ev - er, and love me I pray.
F Am Dm Gm
The stars in the bright sky looked down where he lay,
I love thee, Lord Je - sus! Look down from the sky,
Bless all the dear chil - dren in thy ten - der care,

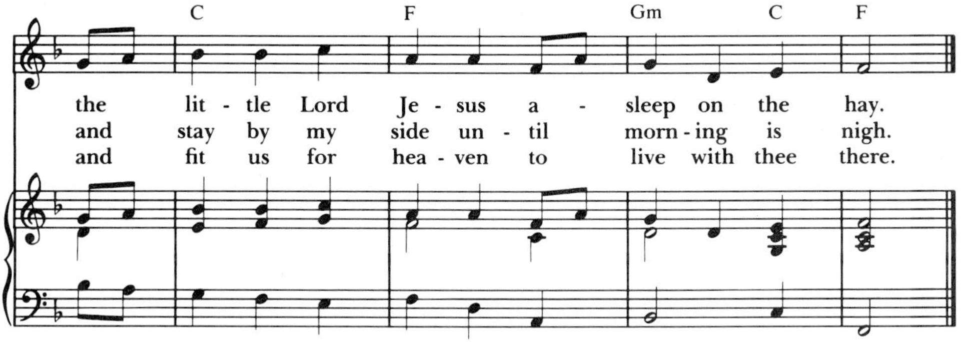
C F Gm C F
the lit - tle Lord Je - sus a - sleep on the hay.
and stay by my side un - til morn - ing is nigh.
and fit us for hea - ven to live with thee there.

Words: Traditional carol
Music: *Cradle Song*, melody William James Kirkpatrick (1838-1921); harm. Ralph Vaughan Williams (1872-1958)

♩=84
11 11. 11 11

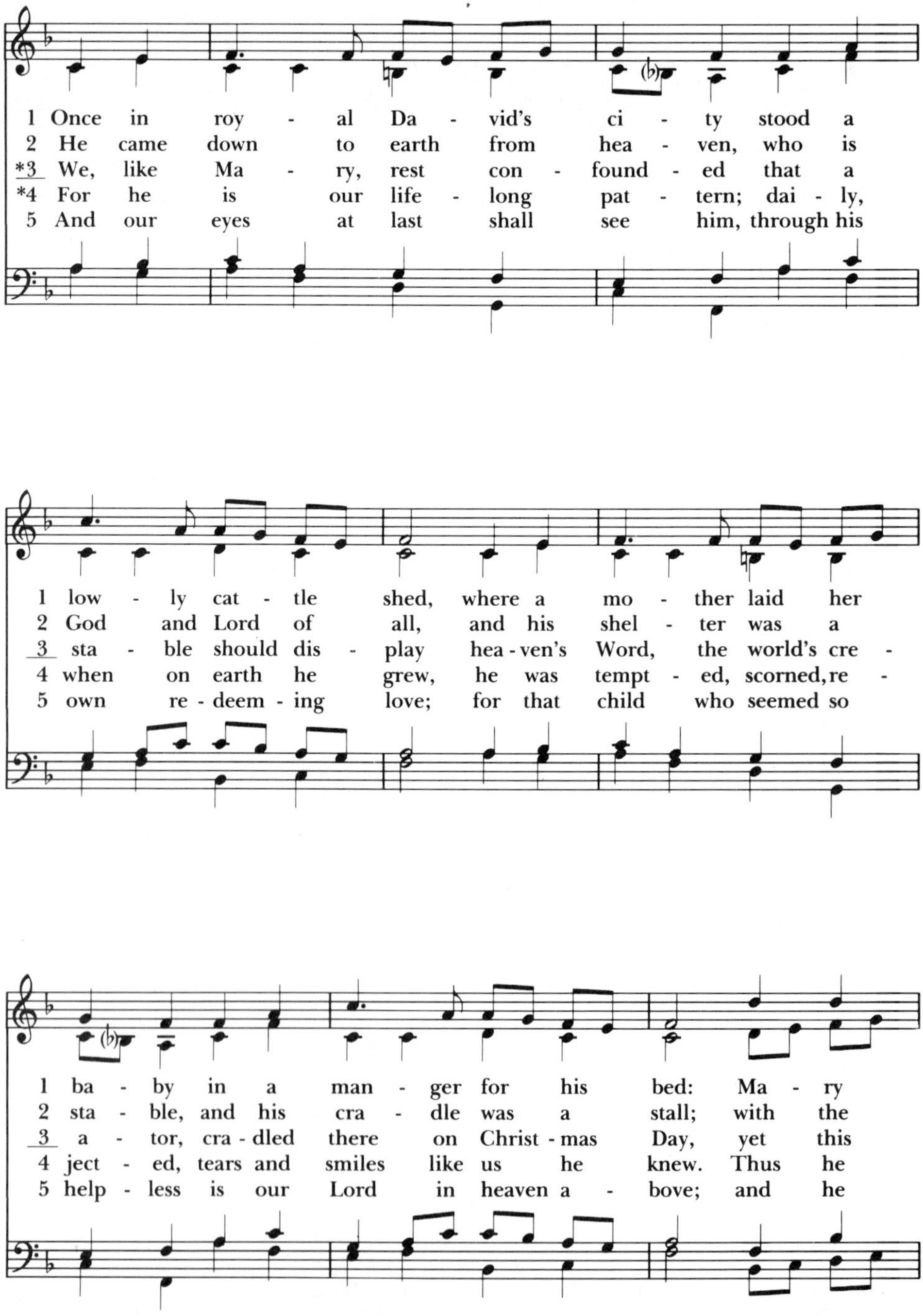
1 Once in roy - al Da - vid's ci - ty stood a
2 He came down to earth from hea - ven, who is
*3 We, like Ma - ry, rest con - found - ed that a
*4 For he is our life - long pat - tern; dai - ly,
5 And our eyes at last shall see him, through his
1 low - ly cat - tle shed, where a mo - ther laid her
2 God and Lord of all, and his shel - ter was a
3 sta - ble should dis - play hea - ven's Word, the world's cre -
4 when on earth he grew, he was tempt - ed, scorned, re -
5 own re - deem - ing love; for that child who seemed so
1 ba - by in a man - ger for his bed: Ma - ry
2 sta - ble, and his cra - dle was a stall; with the
3 a - tor, cra - dled there on Christ - mas Day, yet this
4 ject - ed, tears and smiles like us he knew. Thus he
5 help - less is our Lord in heaven a - bove; and he

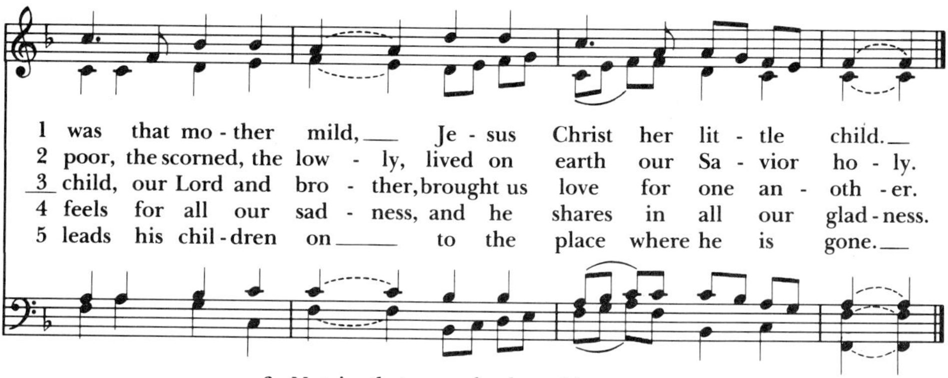
1 was that mo - ther mild, Je - sus Christ her lit - tle child.
2 poor, the scorned, the low - ly, lived on earth our Sa - vior ho - ly.
3 child, our Lord and bro - ther, brought us love for one an - oth - er.
4 feels for all our sad - ness, and he shares in all our glad - ness.
5 leads his chil - dren on to the place where he is gone.

6 Not in that poor lowly stable,
with the oxen standing round,
we shall see him; but in heaven,
where his saints his throne surround:
Christ, revealed to faithful eye,
set at God's right hand on high.

Words: Sts. 1-2 and 4-6, Cecil Frances Alexander (1818-1895), alt.;
st. 3, James Waring McCrady (b. 1938)
Music: *Irby*, melody Henry John Gauntlett (1805-1876); harm. Arthur Henry Mann (1850-1929)

♩= 69
87. 87. 77

Bells used:
Bells
1 A child is born in Beth - le - hem, Al - le - lu - ia! there -
2 The babe with - in a man - ger poor, Al - le - lu - ia! will
3 Up - on this joy - ful ho - ly night, Al - le - lu - ia! we
4 We praise you, Ho - ly Trin - i - ty, Al - le - lu - ia! a -
fore re - joice Je - ru - sa - lem, Al - le - lu -
rule the world for ev - er - more, Al - le - lu -
bless your Name, O Lord of Light, Al - le - lu -
dor - ing you e - ter - nal - ly. Al - le - lu -

Refrain
ia, al - le - lu - ia!
ia, al - le - lu - ia!
ia, al - le - lu - ia!
ia, al - le - lu - ia!
Come, join the an - gel throng in songs of
joy, in one ac - cord a - dor - ing Christ the Lord.

The low voice of the handbell part may be omitted.

Words: Latin, 14th cent.; tr. Ruth Fox Hume (1922-1980), alt.
Music: *Puer natus in Bethlehem,* plainsong, Mode 1, *Benedictine Processional,* 14th cent.; acc. David Hurd (b. 1950)

𝅗𝅥. = 72
88 with Alleluias and Refrain

1 A sta - ble lamp is light - ed Whose
2 (This) child through Da-vid's ci - ty Shall
3 (Yet) he shall be for - sak - en, And
4 (But) now, as at the end - ing, The
glow shall wake the sky; The stars shall bend their voic - es, And
ride in tri - umph by; The palm shall strew its branch - es, And
yield - ed up to die; The sky shall groan and dark - en, And
low is lift - ed high; The stars shall bend their voic - es, And
ev - ery stone shall cry. And ev - ery stone shall
ev - ery stone shall cry. And ev - ery stone shall
ev - ery stone shall cry. And ev - ery stone shall
ev - ery stone shall cry. And ev - ery stone shall

cry, And straw like gold shall shine; A barn shall har - bor
cry. Though hea - vy, dull, and dumb, And lie with-in the
cry, For ston - y hearts of men: God's blood up - on the
cry, In prais - es of the Child By whose de-scent a -
hea - ven, A stall be-come a shrine.
road - way To pave his king - dom come.
spear - head, God's love re-fused a - gain.
mong us The worlds are rec - on - ciled.
1-3
2 This
3 Yet
4 But
1-3

Words: © Richard Wilbur (b. 1921)
Music: *Andújar,* David Hurd (b. 1950)

♩. = 66
76. 76. 66. 76

105

Christmas

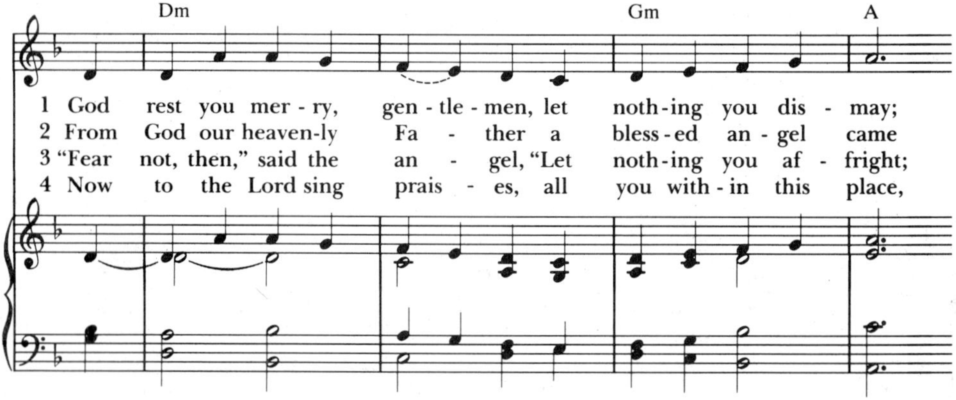
Dm Gm A
1 God rest you mer-ry, gen-tle-men, let noth-ing you dis-may;
2 From God our heaven-ly Fa-ther a bless-ed an-gel came
3 "Fear not, then," said the an-gel, "Let noth-ing you af-fright;
4 Now to the Lord sing prais-es, all you with-in this place,

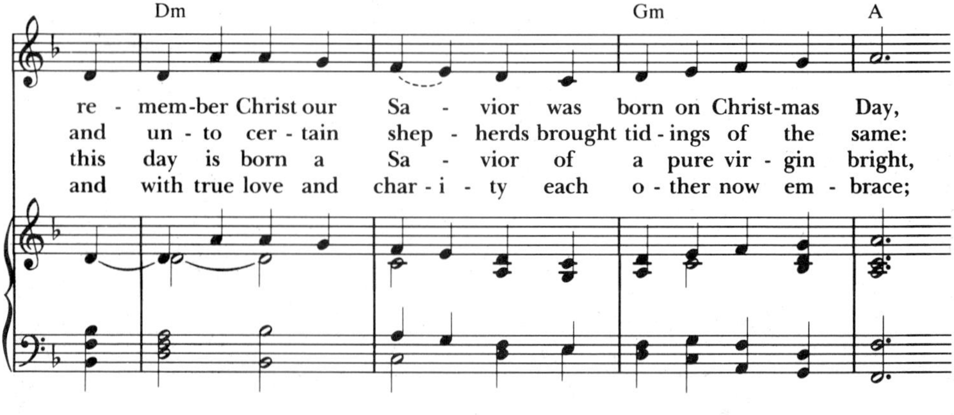
Dm Gm A
re-mem-ber Christ our Sa-vior was born on Christ-mas Day,
and un-to cer-tain shep-herds brought tid-ings of the same:
this day is born a Sa-vior of a pure vir-gin bright,
and with true love and char-i-ty each o-ther now em-brace;

Gm Dm Am Dm C
to save us all from Sa-tan's power when we were gone a-stray.
how that in Beth-le-hem was born the Son of God by name.
to free all those who trust in him from Sa-tan's power and might."
this ho-ly tide of Christ-mas doth bring re-deem-ing grace.
Refrain
F C Dm
O tid-ings of com-fort and joy, com-fort and
C F Gm A Dm
joy; O tid-ings of com-fort and joy!

Keyboard and guitar should not sound together.

Words: London carol, 18th cent.
Music: *God Rest You Merry,* melody from *Little Book of Christmas Carols,* ca. 1850; harm. Charles Winfred Douglas (1867-1944)

𝅗𝅥=69
76. 76. 86 with Refrain

1 Chris - tians, a - wake, sa - lute the hap - py morn
2 Then to the watch - ful shep - herds it was told,
*3 He spoke, and straight - way the ce - les - tial choir
*4 In Beth - le - hem the hap - py shep - herds sought
5 Let us, like these good shep - herds, then em - ploy
1 where - on the Sa - vior of the world was born;
2 who heard the an - gel - ic her - ald's voice: "Be - hold,
3 in hymns of joy, un - known be - fore, con - spire;
4 to see the won - der God for us had wrought,
5 our grate - ful voic - es to pro - claim the joy;
1 rise to a - dore the mys - ter - y of love,
2 I bring good tid - ings of a Sa - vior's birth
3 the prais - es of re - deem - ing love they sang,
4 and found, with Jo - seph and the bless - ed maid,
5 trace we the Babe, who hath re - trieved our loss,

1 which hosts of an - gels chant - ed from a - bove;
2 to you and all the na - tions on the earth:
3 and heaven's whole orb with al - le - lu - ias rang;
4 her Son, the Sa - vior, in a man - ger laid;
5 from his poor man - ger to his bit - ter cross;
1 with them the joy - ful tid - ings first be - gun of
2 this day hath God ful - filled his prom - ised word, this
3 God's high - est glo - ry was their an - them still, peace
4 a - mazed, the won - drous sto - ry they pro - claim, the
5 tread - ing his steps, as - sist - ed by his grace, till
1 God In - car - nate and the Vir - gin's Son.
2 day is born a Sa - vior, Christ the Lord."
3 on the earth, and un - to men good will.
4 ear - liest her - alds of the Sa - vior's name.
5 our first heaven - ly state a - gain takes place.

6 Then may we hope, the angelic thrones among,
to sing, redeemed, a glad triumphal song;
he that was born upon this joyful day
around us all his glory shall display;
saved by his love, incessant we shall sing
eternal praise to heaven's almighty King.

Words: John Byrom (1692-1763), alt.
Music: *Yorkshire*, John Wainwright (1723-1768)

𝅗𝅥 = 88
10 10. 10 10. 10 10

1 Good Chris-tian friends, re - joice with heart and soul and voice;
2 Good Chris-tian friends, re - joice with heart and soul and voice;
3 Good Chris-tian friends, re - joice with heart and soul and voice;
give ye heed to what we say: Je - sus Christ is born to - day;
now ye hear of end - less bliss; Je - sus Christ was born for this!
now ye need not fear the grave: Je - sus Christ was born to save!
ox and ass be - fore him bow, and he is in the man - ger now.
He hath o - pened hea - ven's door, and we are blest for ev - er-more.
Calls you one and calls you all to gain his ev - er - last - ing hall.
Christ is born to - day! Christ is born to - day!
Christ was born for this! Christ was born for this!
Christ was born to save! Christ was born to save!

Words: John Mason Neale (1818-1866), alt.
Music: *In dulci jubilo,* German carol, 14th cent.; harm. Charles Winfred Douglas (1867-1944)

𝅗𝅥. = 60
66. 77. 78. 55

108

1 Now yield we thanks and praise to Christ en - throned in glo - ry,
2 What tri - bute shall we pay to him who came in weak - ness,
and on this day of days tell out re - demp-tion's sto - ry,
and in a man - ger lay to teach his peo - ple meek - ness?
who tru - ly have be - lieved that on this bless - ed morn,
Let ev - ery house be bright; let prais - es nev - er cease;
in ho - li - ness con - ceived, the Son of God was born.
with mer-cies in - fi - nite our Christ hath brought us peace.

Words: Howard Chandler Robbins (1876-1952)
Music: *Was frag' ich nach der Welt,* melody Ahasuerus Fritsch (1629-1701); harm. Johann Sebastian Bach (1685-1750)

♩=76
67. 67. 66. 66

1 The first No - well the an-gel did say was to cer - tain poor
2 They look - ed up and saw a star shin-ing in the
3 And by the light of that same star three wise men
4 This star drew nigh to the north - west, o'er Beth - le -
5 Then en - tered in those wise men three full rev - erent-
1 shep-herds in fields as they lay; in fields as they lay,
2 east be - yond them far, and to the earth it
3 came from coun - try far; to seek for a king was
4 hem it took its rest, and there it did both
5 ly up - on their knee, and of - fered there in
1 keep-ing their sheep, on a cold win-ter's night that was so deep.
2 gave great light, and so it con - tin - ued both day and night.
3 their in - tent, and to fol - low the star wher - ev - er it went.
4 stop and stay right o - ver the place where Je - sus lay.
5 his pres - ence their gold, and myrrh, and frank - in - cense.
Refrain
No - well, No - well, No - well, No - well,

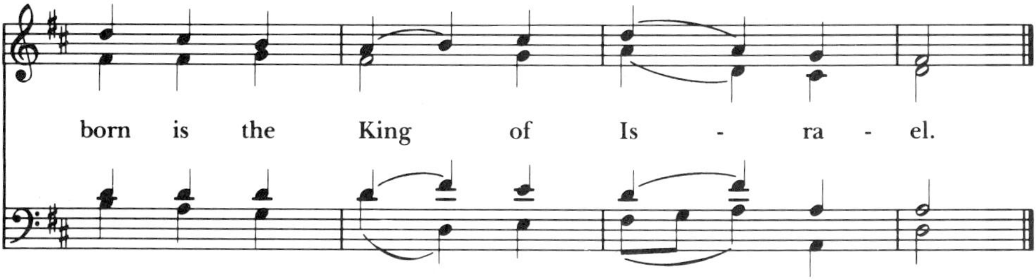
born is the King of Is - ra - el.

6 Then let us all with one accord
sing praises to our heavenly Lord;
that hath made heaven and earth of nought,
and with his blood our life hath bought.

Refrain

Words: English carol, 18th cent.
Music: *The First Nowell,* English carol, 17th cent.; harm. John Stainer (1840-1901)

♩= 108
Irr. with Refrain

Alternative Refrain
Descant (others unison)

No - well, No - well, No - well, No - well,

born is the King of Is - ra - el.

Music: *The First Nowell,* English carol, 17th cent.; harm. and desc. Healey Willan (1880-1968)

♩= 108

G C G D
1 The snow lay on the ground, the stars shone bright,
2 'Twas Ma - ry, daugh - ter pure of ho - ly Anne,
3 Saint Jo - seph, too, was by to tend the child;
4 And thus that man - ger poor be - came a throne;
C G G D G
when Christ our Lord was born on Christ - mas night. Ve -
that brought in - to this world the God made man. She
to guard him, and pro - tect his mo - ther mild; the
for he whom Ma - ry bore was God the Son. O
G C G D
ni - te a - do - re - mus Do - mi - num. Ve -
laid him in a stall at Beth - le - hem; the
an - gels hov - ered round, and sang this song, Ve -
come, then, let us join the heaven - ly host; to

C Am G D7 G Dsus2 D G
Refrain
ni - te a - do - re - mus Do - mi - num.
ass and ox - en shared the roof with them.
ni - te a - do - re - mus Do - mi - num.
praise the Fa - ther, Son, and Ho - ly Ghost.
Ve -
G Am E Am
ni - te a - do - re - mus Do - mi - num. Ve -
D7 C G D7 G
ni - te a - do - re - mus Do - mi - num.

Words: Source unknown, 19th cent.
Music: *Venite adoremus*, melody adapt. Charles Winfred Douglas (1867-1944); harm. Leo Sowerby (1895-1968)

♩. = 92
Irr. with Refrain

Christmas

1 Silent night, holy night, all is calm,
2 Silent night, holy night, shepherds quake
3 Silent night, holy night, Son of God,

all is bright round yon virgin mother and child.
at the sight, glories stream from heaven afar,
love's pure light radiant beams from thy holy face,

Holy infant, so tender and mild, sleep in heavenly
heavenly hosts sing alleluia; Christ, the Savior, is
with the dawn of redeeming grace, Jesus, Lord, at thy

peace. Sleep in heavenly peace.
born! Christ, the Savior, is born!
birth. Jesus, Lord, at thy birth.

Bb (capo 3,G)

Words: Joseph Mohr (1792-1848); tr. John Freeman Young (1820-1885)
Music: *Stille Nacht*, melody Franz Xaver Gruber (1787-1863); harm. Carl H. Reinecke (1824-1910)

♩=96

Irr.

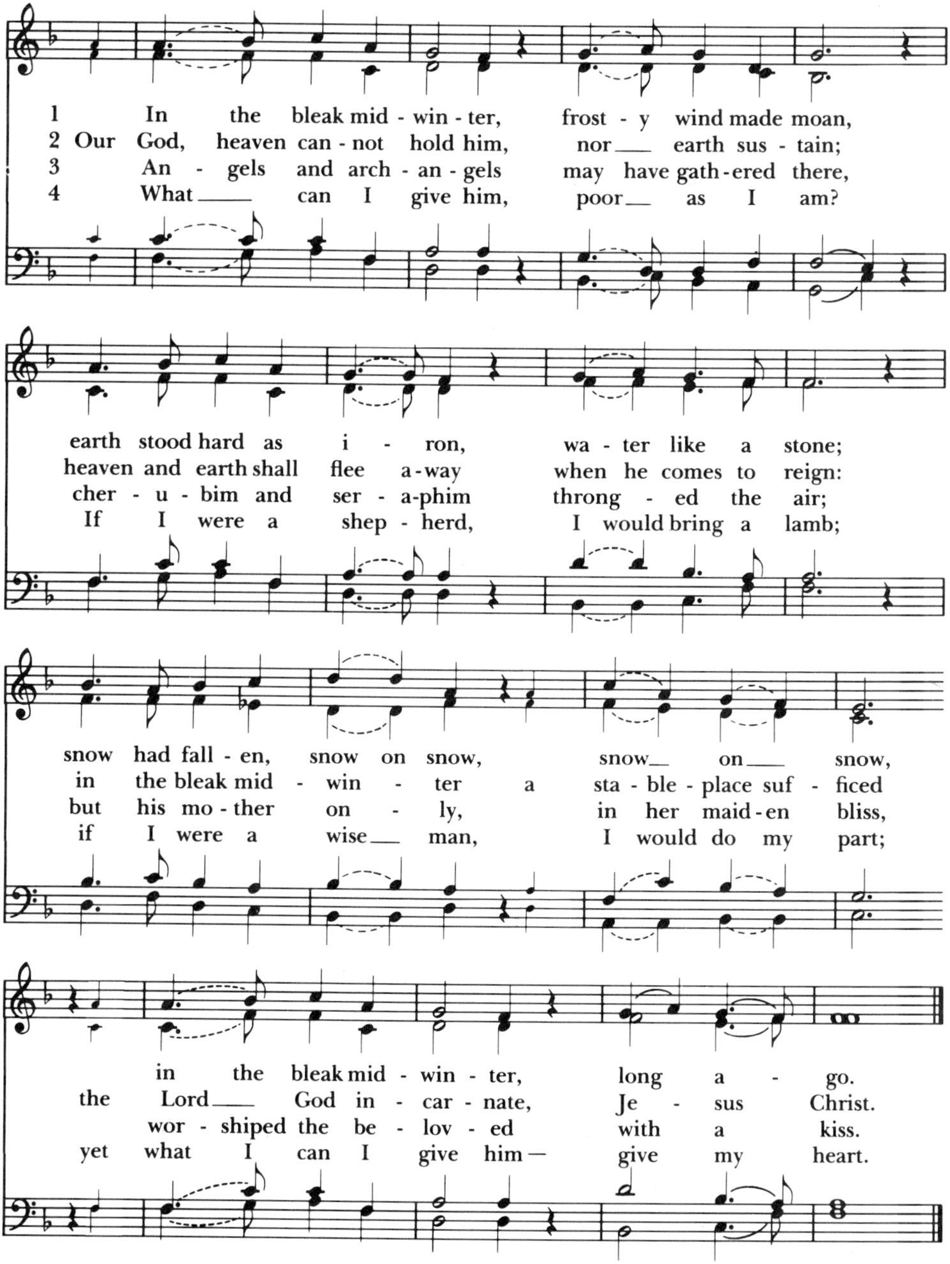
1 In the bleak mid - win - ter, frost - y wind made moan,
2 Our God, heaven can - not hold him, nor earth sus - tain;
3 An - gels and arch - an - gels may have gath - ered there,
4 What can I give him, poor as I am?
earth stood hard as i - ron, wa - ter like a stone;
heaven and earth shall flee a - way when he comes to reign:
cher - u - bim and ser - a-phim throng - ed the air;
If I were a shep - herd, I would bring a lamb;
snow had fall - en, snow on snow, snow on snow,
in the bleak mid - win - ter a sta - ble - place suf - ficed
but his mo - ther on - ly, in her maid - en bliss,
if I were a wise man, I would do my part;
in the bleak mid - win - ter, long a - go.
the Lord God in - car - nate, Je - sus Christ.
wor - shiped the be - lov - ed with a kiss.
yet what I can I give him— give my heart.

Words: Christina Rossetti (1830-1894)
Music: *Cranham,* Gustav Theodore Holst (1874-1934)

𝅗𝅥=50
Irr.

D A G E7 D A7
1 Duér-
2 No
1 Oh,
2 You
Introduction/Interlude
D A7 D G D
1 me - te, Ni - ño lin - do, en los bra - zos del a -
2 te - mas al rey He - ro - des que na - da te ha de ha -
1 sleep now, ho - ly ba - by, with your head a - gainst my
2 need not fear King He - rod, he will bring no harm to
Bm D Bm
1 mor mien - tras que duer - me y des - can - sa la
2 cer; en los bra - zos de tu ma - dre y ahí
1 breast; mean - while the pangs of my sor - row are
2 you; so rest in the arms of your mo - ther who

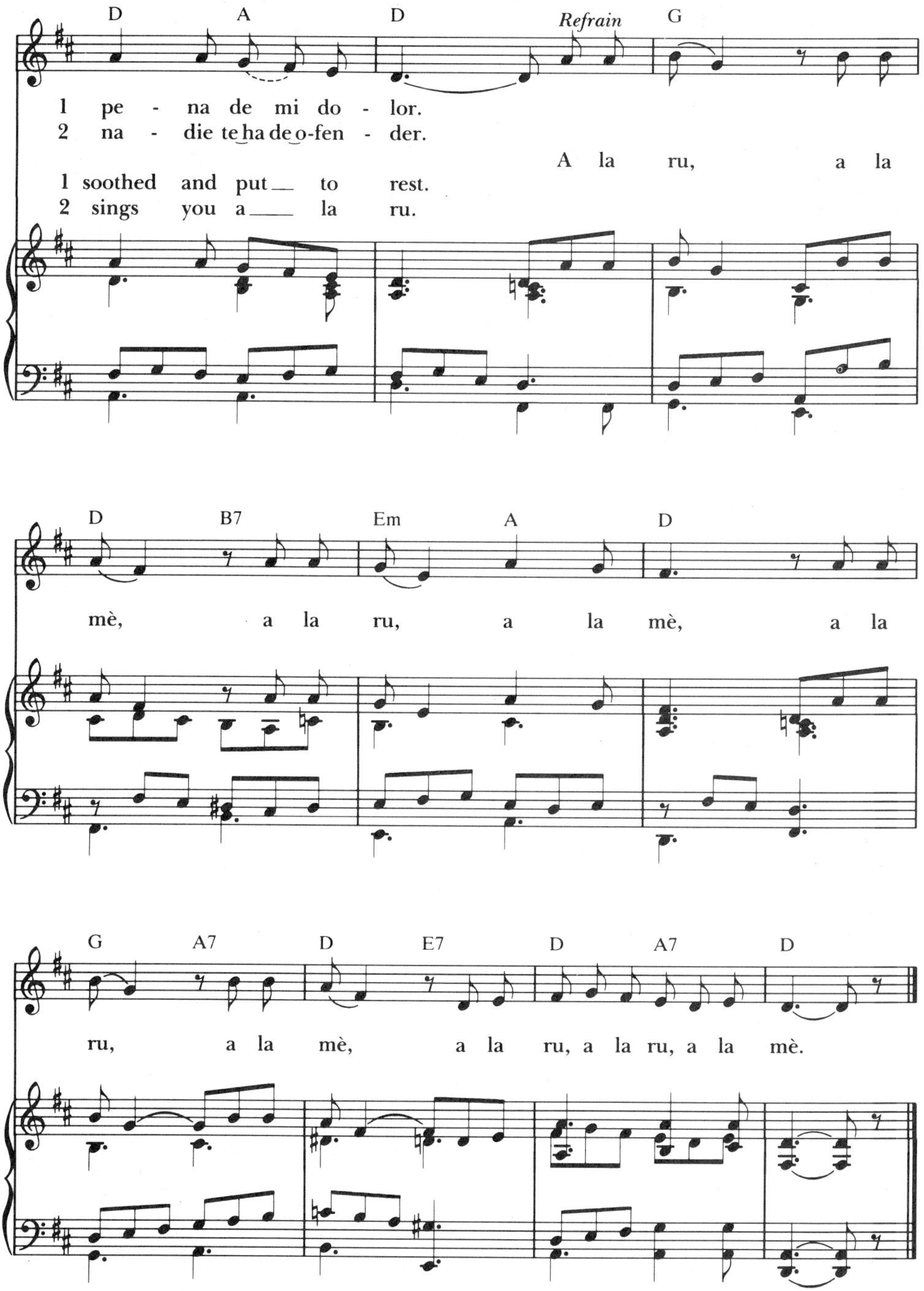
D A D Refrain G
1 pe - na de mi do - lor.
2 na - die te ha de o-fen - der.
1 soothed and put to rest.
2 sings you a la ru.
A la ru, a la
D B7 Em A D
mè, a la ru, a la mè, a la
G A7 D E7 D A7 D
ru, a la mè, a la ru, a la ru, a la mè.

Keyboard and guitar should not sound together.

Words: Hispanic folk song; tr. John Donald Robb (b. 1892), alt.
Music: *A la ru*, Hispanic folk melody; arr. John Donald Robb (b. 1892)

♩. = 48
Irr. with Refrain

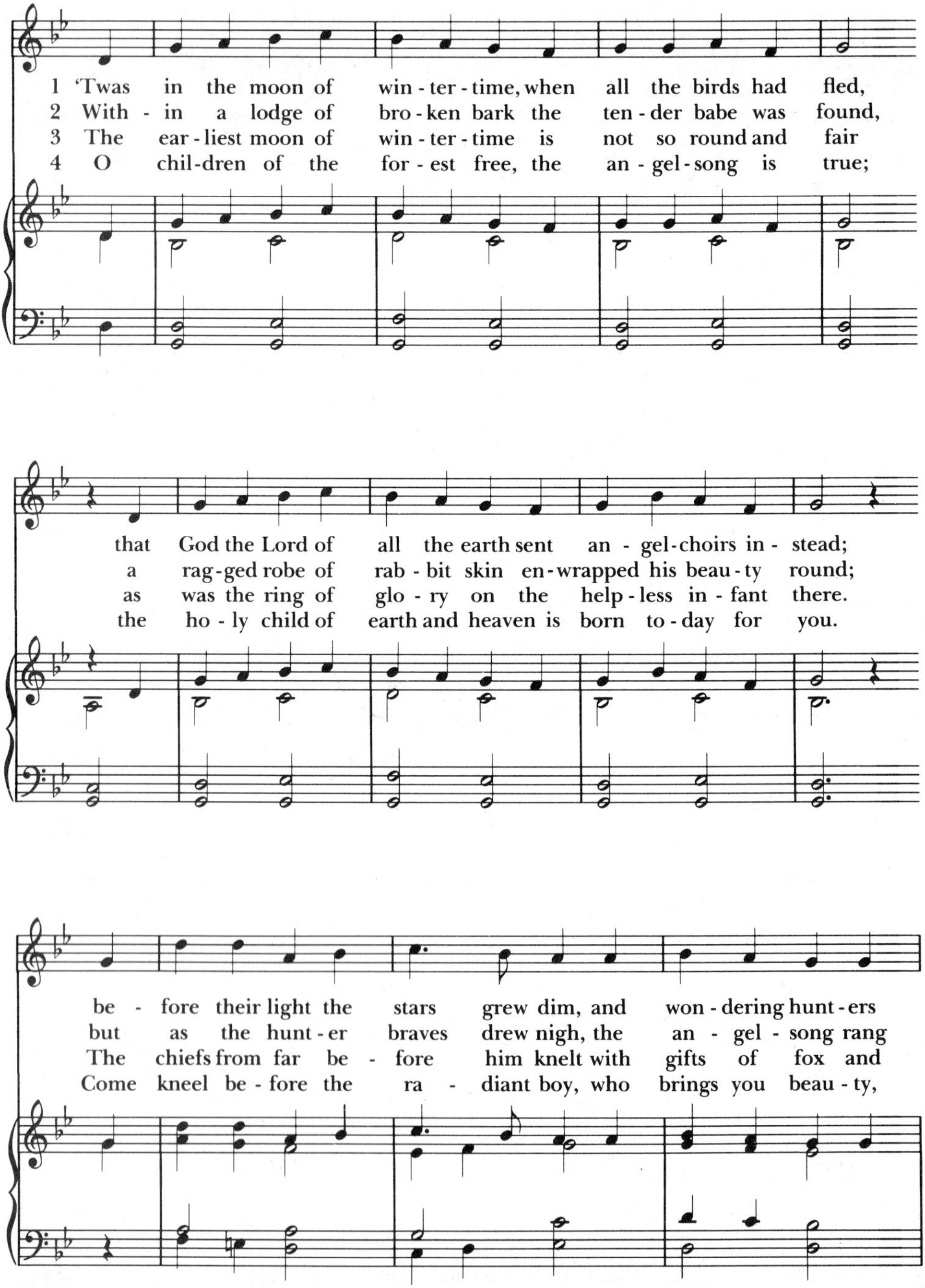
1 'Twas in the moon of win - ter - time, when all the birds had fled,
2 With - in a lodge of bro - ken bark the ten - der babe was found,
3 The ear - liest moon of win - ter - time is not so round and fair
4 O chil-dren of the for - est free, the an - gel - song is true;
that God the Lord of all the earth sent an - gel-choirs in - stead;
a rag-ged robe of rab - bit skin en-wrapped his beau - ty round;
as was the ring of glo - ry on the help - less in - fant there.
the ho - ly child of earth and heaven is born to - day for you.
be - fore their light the stars grew dim, and won - dering hunt - ers
but as the hunt - er braves drew nigh, the an - gel - song rang
The chiefs from far be - fore him knelt with gifts of fox and
Come kneel be - fore the ra - diant boy, who brings you beau - ty,

Refrain
heard the hymn:
loud and high:
bea - ver - pelt.
peace, and joy.
Je - sus your King is born, Je - sus is
born, in ex - cel - sis glo - ri - a.

This hymn may be sung unaccompanied or with light percussion.

Words: Jesse Edgar Middleton (1872-1960), alt.
Music: *Une jeune pucelle,* French folk melody, 16th cent.;
harm. Frederick Jackisch (b. 1922)

𝅗𝅥 = 60
86. 86. 88 with Refrain

Alternative accompaniment
Introduction

1. 'Twas in the moon of

win-ter-time, when all the birds had fled, that God the Lord of
all the earth sent an-gel-choirs in-stead; be-fore their light the
stars grew dim, and won-dering hunt-ers heard the hymn:
Refrain
Je-sus your
King is born, Je-sus is born, in ex-cel-sis glo-ri-

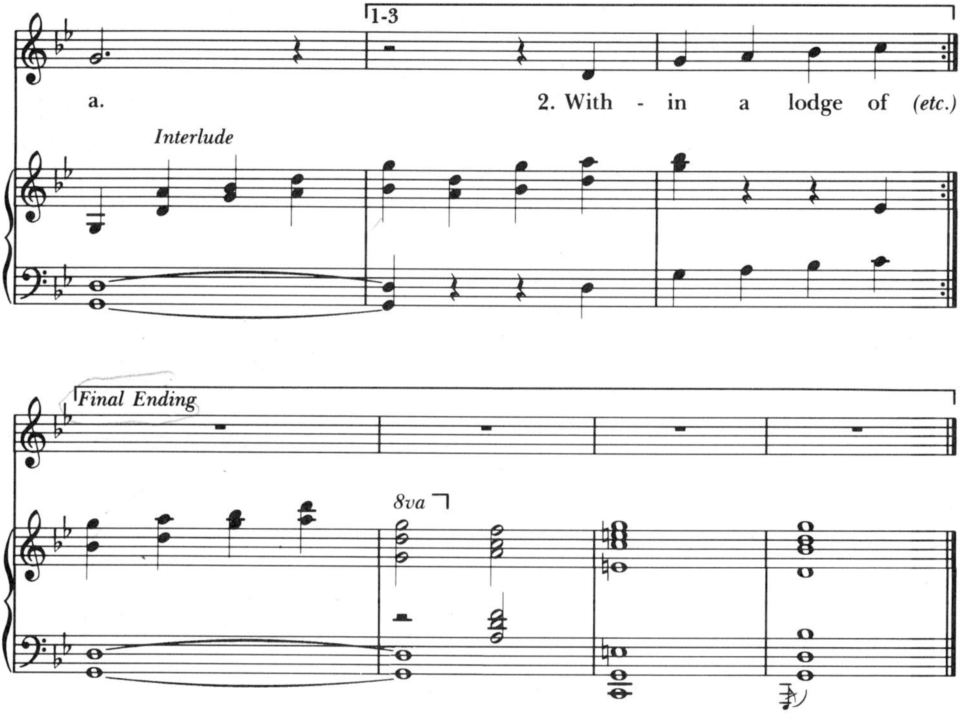
1-3
a.
2. With - in a lodge of (etc.)
Interlude
Final Ending
8va

2 Within a lodge of broken bark
the tender babe was found,
a ragged robe of rabbit skin
enwrapped his beauty round;
but as the hunter braves drew nigh,
the angel-song rang loud and high:

Refrain

3 The earliest moon of winter-time
is not so round and fair
as was the ring of glory on
the helpless infant there.
The chiefs from far before him knelt
with gifts of fox and beaver-pelt.

Refrain

4 O children of the forest free,
the angel song is true;
the holy child of earth and heaven
is born today for you.
Come kneel before the radiant boy,
who brings you beauty, peace, and joy.

Refrain

Words: Jess Edgar Middleton (1872-1960), alt.
Music: *Une jeune pucelle,* French folk melody, 16th cent.; harm. Healey Willan (1880-1968)

𝅗𝅥 = 60
86. 86. 88 with Refrain

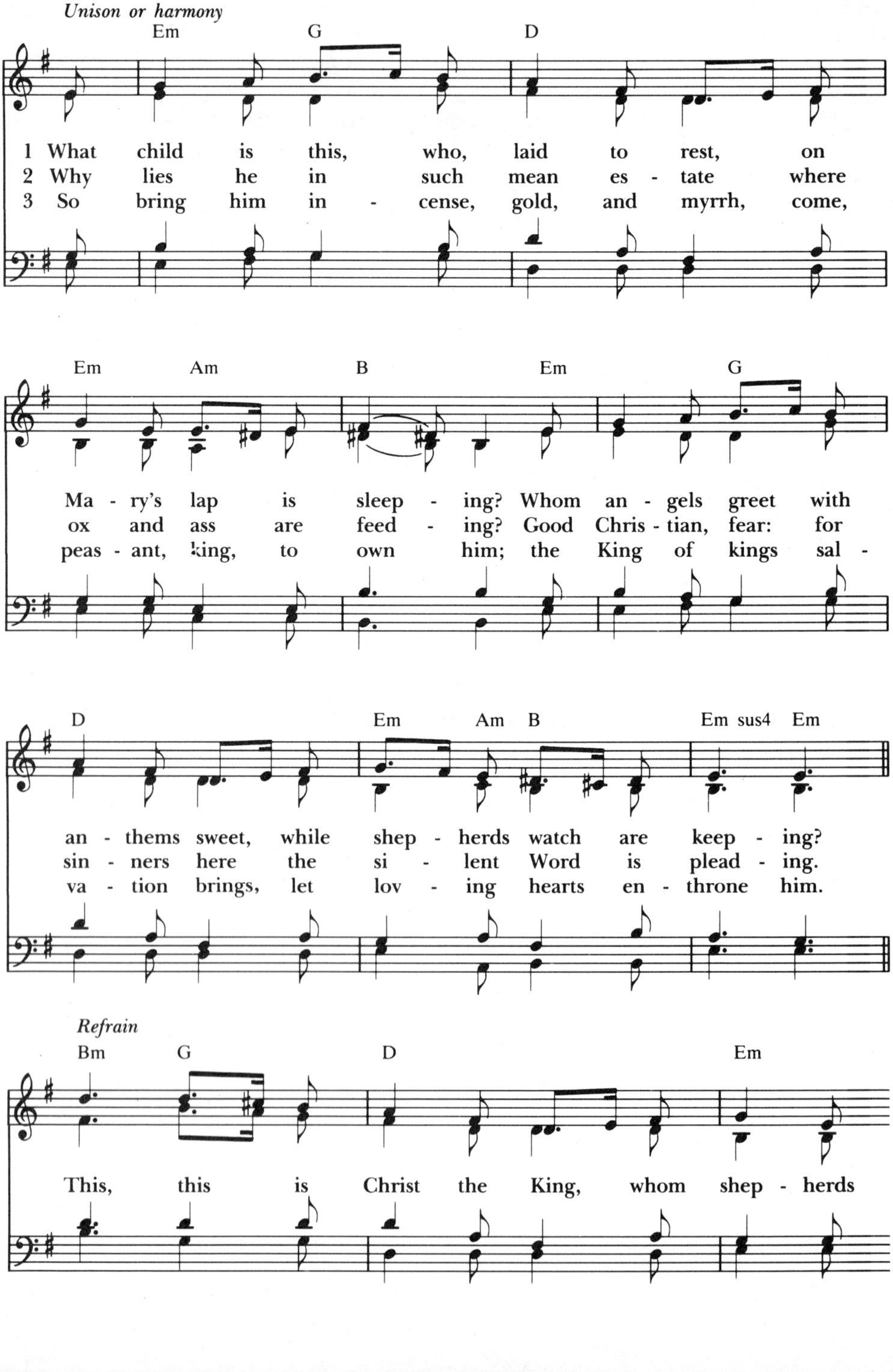
Unison or harmony
Em G D
1 What child is this, who, laid to rest, on
2 Why lies he in such mean es - tate where
3 So bring him in - cense, gold, and myrrh, come,
Em Am B Em G
Ma - ry's lap is sleep - ing? Whom an - gels greet with
ox and ass are feed - ing? Good Chris - tian, fear: for
peas - ant, king, to own him; the King of kings sal -
D Em Am B Em sus4 Em
an - thems sweet, while shep - herds watch are keep - ing?
sin - ners here the si - lent Word is plead - ing.
va - tion brings, let lov - ing hearts en - throne him.
Refrain
Bm G D Em
This, this is Christ the King, whom shep - herds

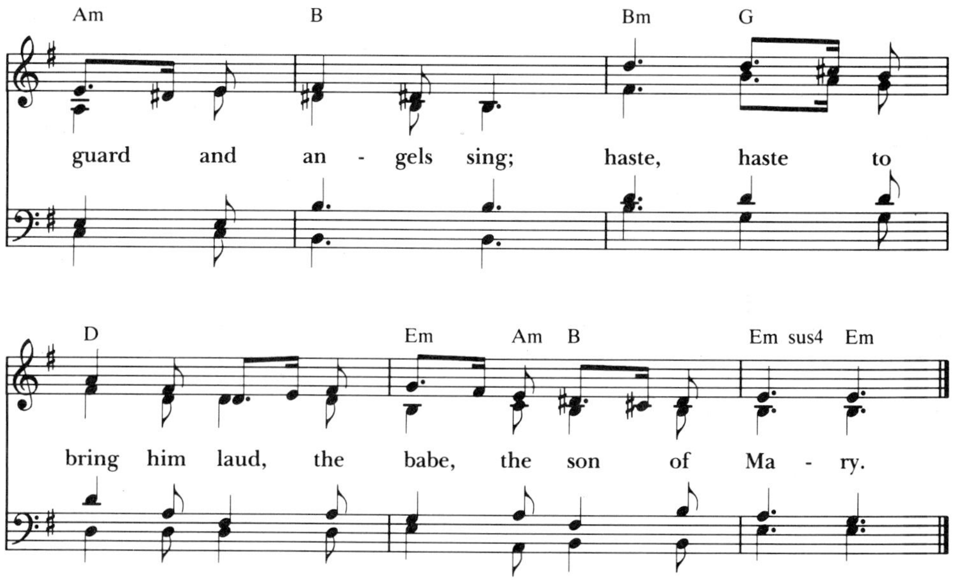
Am B Bm G
guard and an - gels sing; haste, haste to
D Em Am B Em sus4 Em
bring him laud, the babe, the son of Ma - ry.

Words: William Chatterton Dix (1837-1898)
Music: *Greensleeves*, English melody; harm. *Christmas Carols New and Old*, 1871

♩. = 48
87. 87 with Refrain

116

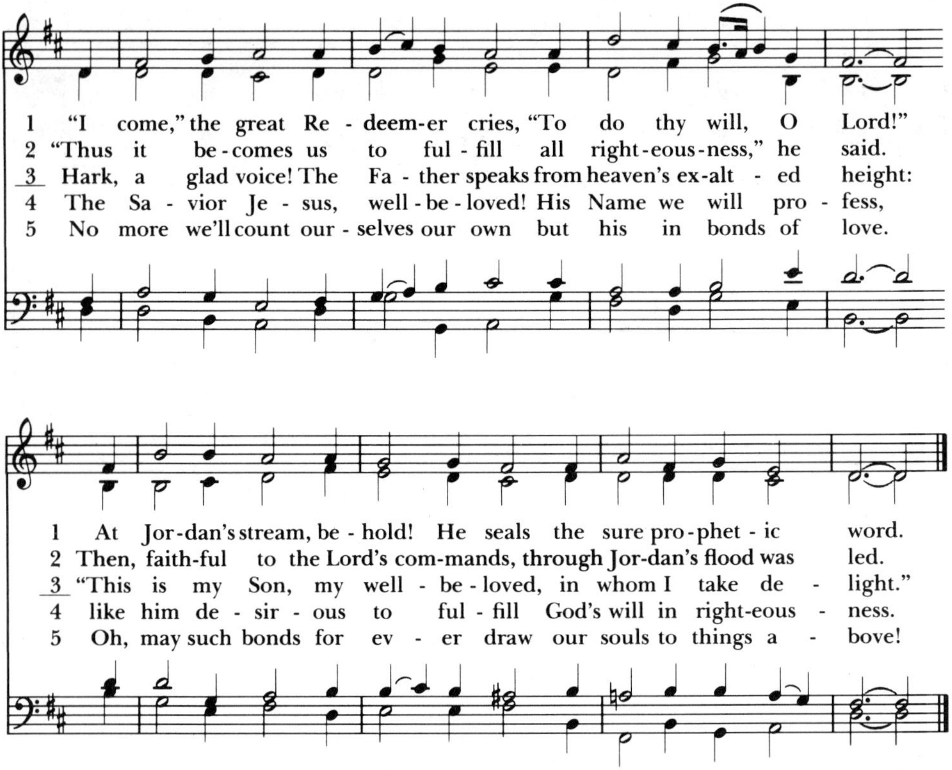
1 "I come," the great Re - deem-er cries, "To do thy will, O Lord!"
2 "Thus it be-comes us to ful - fill all right-eous-ness," he said.
3 Hark, a glad voice! The Fa - ther speaks from heaven's ex-alt - ed height:
4 The Sa - vior Je - sus, well - be - loved! His Name we will pro - fess,
5 No more we'll count our - selves our own but his in bonds of love.
1 At Jor-dan's stream, be - hold! He seals the sure pro-phet - ic word.
2 Then, faith-ful to the Lord's com-mands, through Jor-dan's flood was led.
3 "This is my Son, my well - be - loved, in whom I take de - light."
4 like him de - sir - ous to ful - fill God's will in right-eous - ness.
5 Oh, may such bonds for ev - er draw our souls to things a - bove!

Words: *Christian Hymnbook,* 1865, alt.
Music: *This Endris Nyght,* English melody; harm. Ralph Vaughan Williams (1872-1958)

𝅗𝅥. = 48
CM

117

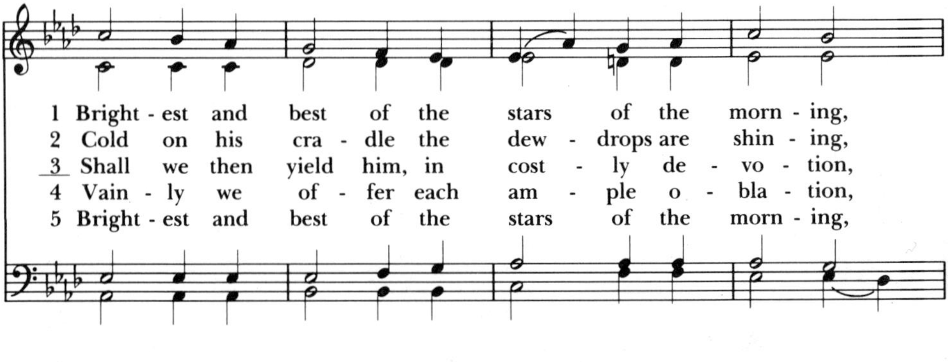
1 Bright - est and best of the stars of the morn - ing,
2 Cold on his cra - dle the dew - drops are shin - ing,
3 Shall we then yield him, in cost - ly de - vo - tion,
4 Vain - ly we of - fer each am - ple o - bla - tion,
5 Bright - est and best of the stars of the morn - ing,

1 dawn on our dark - ness, and lend us thine aid;
2 low lies his head with the beasts of the stall;
3 o - dors of E - dom, and of - ferings di - vine,
4 vain - ly with gifts would his fa - vor se - cure,
5 dawn on our dark - ness, and lend us thine aid;
1 star of the east, the hor - i - zon a - dorn - ing,
2 an - gels a - dore him in slum - ber re - clin - ing,
3 gems of the moun - tain, and pearls of the o - cean,
4 rich - er by far is the heart's a - dor - a - tion,
5 star of the east, the hor - i - zon a - dorn - ing,
1 guide where our in - fant Re - deem - er is laid.
2 Ma - ker and Mon - arch and Sa - vior of all.
3 myrrh from the for - est, and gold from the mine?
4 dear - er to God are the prayers of the poor.
5 guide where our in - fant Re - deem - er is laid.

Alternative tune: *Star in the East,* 118.

Words: Reginald Heber (1783-1826), alt.
Music: *Morning Star,* James Proctor Harding (1850-1911)

𝅗𝅥 = 60
11 10. 11 10

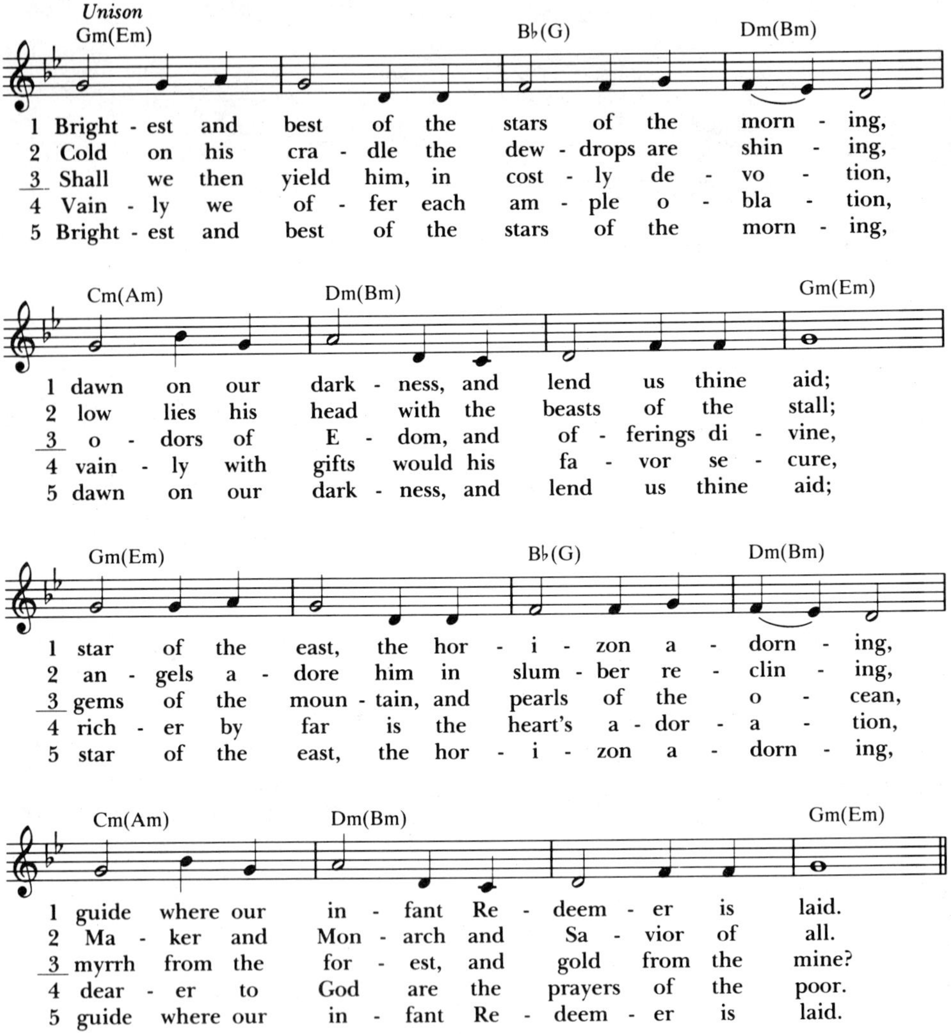
Unison
Gm(Em) Bb(G) Dm(Bm)
1 Bright - est and best of the stars of the morn - ing,
2 Cold on his cra - dle the dew - drops are shin - ing,
3 Shall we then yield him, in cost - ly de - vo - tion,
4 Vain - ly we of - fer each am - ple o - bla - tion,
5 Bright - est and best of the stars of the morn - ing,
Cm(Am) Dm(Bm) Gm(Em)
1 dawn on our dark - ness, and lend us thine aid;
2 low lies his head with the beasts of the stall;
3 o - dors of E - dom, and of - ferings di - vine,
4 vain - ly with gifts would his fa - vor se - cure,
5 dawn on our dark - ness, and lend us thine aid;
Gm(Em) Bb(G) Dm(Bm)
1 star of the east, the hor - i - zon a - dorn - ing,
2 an - gels a - dore him in slum - ber re - clin - ing,
3 gems of the moun - tain, and pearls of the o - cean,
4 rich - er by far is the heart's a - dor - a - tion,
5 star of the east, the hor - i - zon a - dorn - ing,
Cm(Am) Dm(Bm) Gm(Em)
1 guide where our in - fant Re - deem - er is laid.
2 Ma - ker and Mon - arch and Sa - vior of all.
3 myrrh from the for - est, and gold from the mine?
4 dear - er to God are the prayers of the poor.
5 guide where our in - fant Re - deem - er is laid.

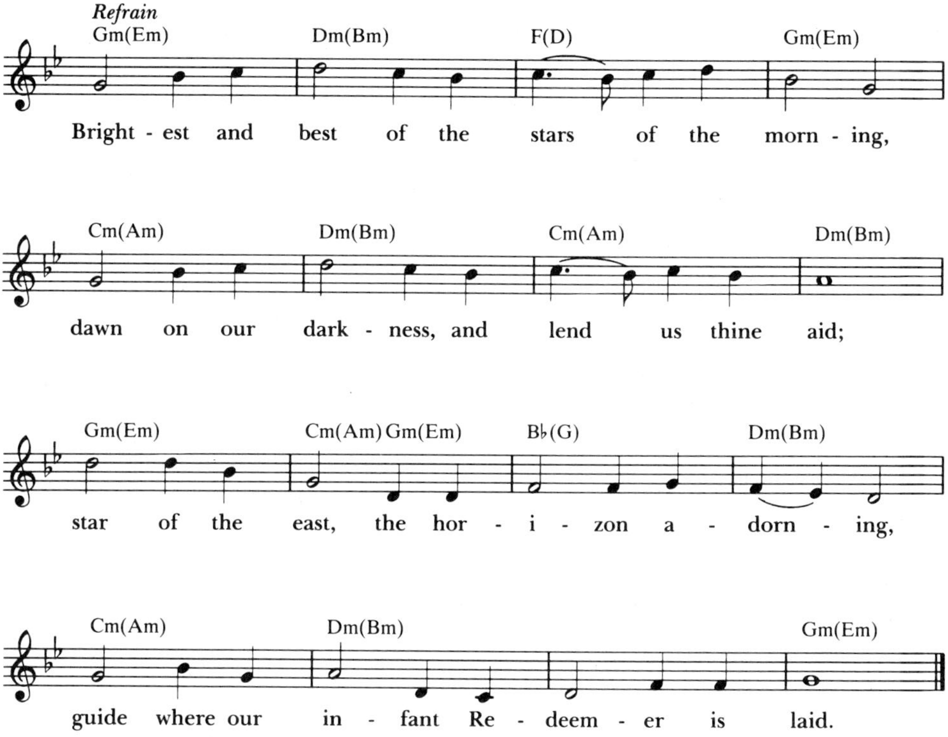
Refrain
Gm(Em) Dm(Bm) F(D) Gm(Em)
Bright - est and best of the stars of the morn - ing,
Cm(Am) Dm(Bm) Cm(Am) Dm(Bm)
dawn on our dark - ness, and lend us thine aid;
Gm(Em) Cm(Am) Gm(Em) B♭(G) Dm(Bm)
star of the east, the hor - i - zon a - dorn - ing,
Cm(Am) Dm(Bm) Gm(Em)
guide where our in - fant Re - deem - er is laid.

Gm(capo 3, Em). Either of the following harmonizations may accompany unison singing.
Alternative tune: *Morning Star,* 117.

Words: Reginald Heber (1783-1826), alt.
Music: *Star in the East,* from *The Southern Harmony,* 1835

♩= 76
11 10. 11 10 with Refrain

Harmony (the melody is in the tenor)

1 Bright - est and best of the stars of the morn - ing,
2 Cold on his cra - dle the dew - drops are shin - ing,
3 Shall we then yield him, in cost - ly de - vo - tion,
4 Vain - ly we of - fer each am - ple o - bla - tion,
5 Bright - est and best of the stars of the morn - ing,
1 dawn on our dark - ness, and lend us thine aid;
2 low lies his head with the beasts of the stall;
3 o - dors of E - dom, and of - ferings di - vine,
4 vain - ly with gifts would his fa - vor se - cure,
5 dawn on our dark - ness, and lend us thine aid;
1 star of the east, the hor - i - zon a - dorn - ing,
2 an - gels a - dore him in slum - ber re - clin - ing,
3 gems of the moun - tain, and pearls of the o - cean,
4 rich - er by far is the heart's a - dor - a - tion,
5 star of the east, the hor - i - zon a - dorn - ing,
1 guide where our in - fant Re - deem - er is laid.
2 Ma - ker and Mon - arch and Sa - vior of all.
3 myrrh from the for - est, and gold from the mine?
4 dear - er to God are the prayers of the poor.
5 guide where our in - fant Re - deem - er is laid.

Refrain
Bright - est and best of the stars of the morn - ing,
dawn on our dark - ness, and lend us thine aid;
star of the east, the hor - i - zon a - dorn - ing,
guide where our in - fant Re - deem - er is laid.

Words: Reginald Heber (1783-1826), alt.
Music: *Star in the East,* from *The Southern Harmony,* 1835

♩= 76
11 10. 11 10 with Refrain

Music: *Star in the East,* melody from *The Southern Harmony,* 1835; harm. Thomas Foster (b. 1938) 𝅗𝅥 = 76

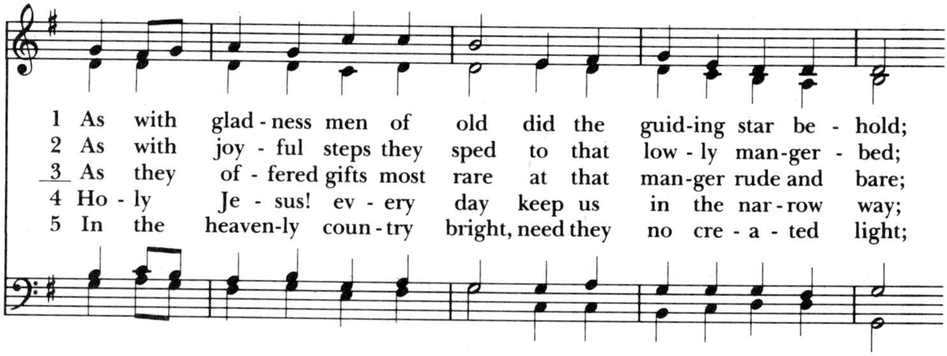
1 As with glad-ness men of old did the guid-ing star be-hold;
2 As with joy-ful steps they sped to that low-ly man-ger-bed;
3 As they of-fered gifts most rare at that man-ger rude and bare;
4 Ho-ly Je-sus! ev-ery day keep us in the nar-row way;
5 In the heaven-ly coun-try bright, need they no cre-a-ted light;

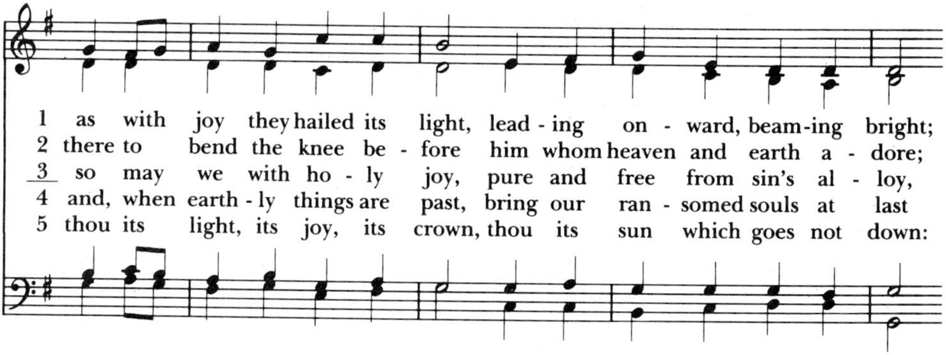
1 as with joy they hailed its light, lead-ing on-ward, beam-ing bright;
2 there to bend the knee be-fore him whom heaven and earth a-dore;
3 so may we with ho-ly joy, pure and free from sin's al-loy,
4 and, when earth-ly things are past, bring our ran-somed souls at last
5 thou its light, its joy, its crown, thou its sun which goes not down:

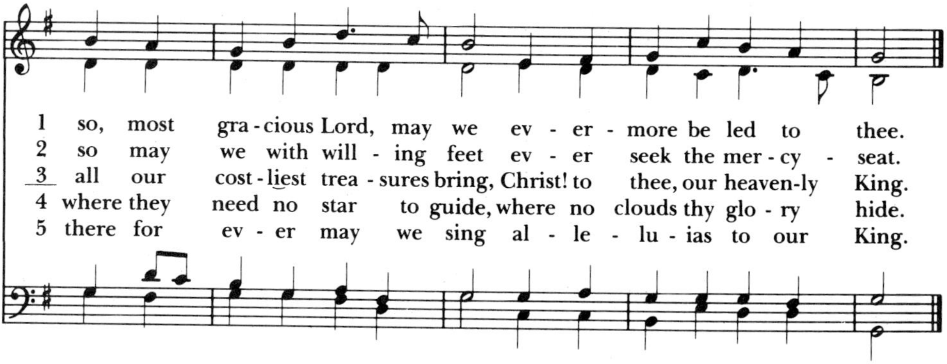
1 so, most gra-cious Lord, may we ev-er-more be led to thee.
2 so may we with will-ing feet ev-er seek the mer-cy-seat.
3 all our cost-liest trea-sures bring, Christ! to thee, our heaven-ly King.
4 where they need no star to guide, where no clouds thy glo-ry hide.
5 there for ev-er may we sing al-le-lu-ias to our King.

Words: William Chatterton Dix (1837-1898)
Music: *Dix*, melody Conrad Kocher (1786-1872); arr. William Henry Monk (1823-1889); harm. *The English Hymnal*, 1906

𝅗𝅥 = 50
77. 77. 77

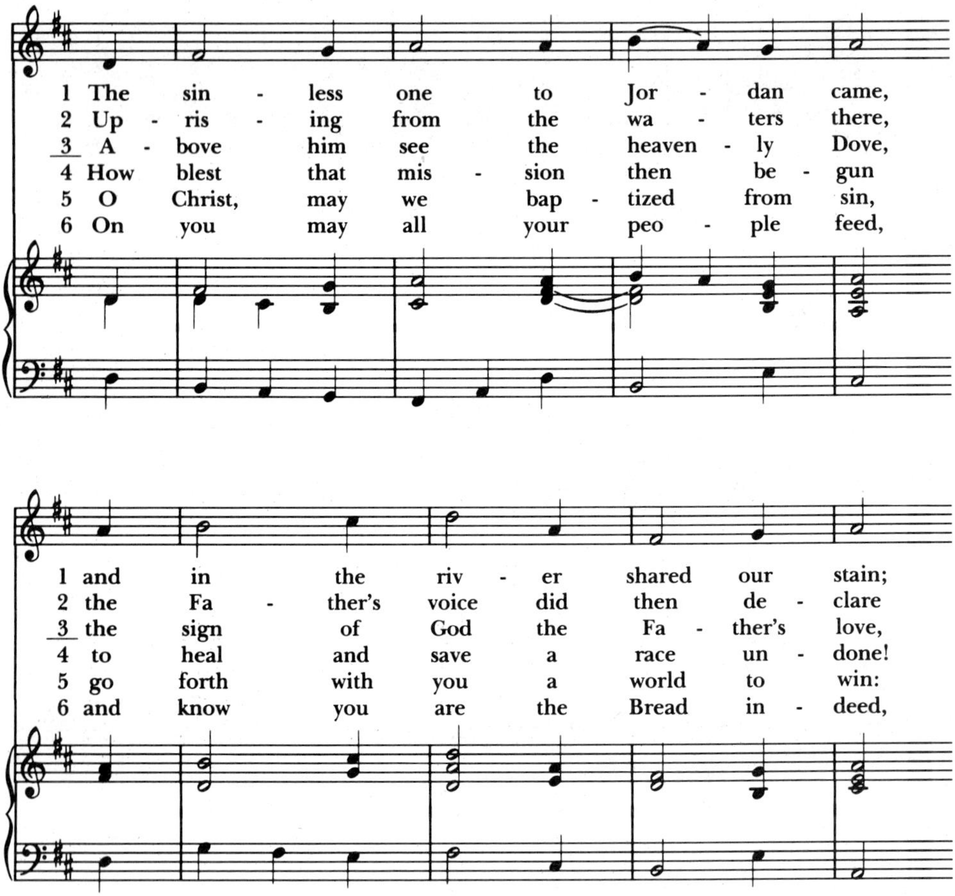
1 The sin - less one to Jor - dan came,
2 Up - ris - ing from the wa - ters there,
3 A - bove him see the heaven - ly Dove,
4 How blest that mis - sion then be - gun
5 O Christ, may we bap - tized from sin,
6 On you may all your peo - ple feed,
1 and in the riv - er shared our stain;
2 the Fa - ther's voice did then de - clare
3 the sign of God the Fa - ther's love,
4 to heal and save a race un - done!
5 go forth with you a world to win:
6 and know you are the Bread in - deed,

1 God's right - eous - ness he thus ful - filled,
2 that Christ, the Son of God, had come
3 now by the Ho - ly Spi - rit shed
4 Straight to the wil - der - ness he goes
5 grant us the Ho - ly Spi - rit's power
6 who gives e - ter - nal life to those
1 and chose the path his Fa - ther willed.
2 to lead his scat - tered peo - ple home.
3 up - on the Son's a - noint - ed head.
4 to wres - tle with his peo - ple's foes.
5 to shield us in tem - ta - tion's hour.
6 that with you died, and with you rose.

Words: George B. Timms (b. 1910), alt.
Music: *Solemnis haec festivitas,* melody from *Graduale,* 1685; harm. Arthur Hutchings (b. 1906)

𝅗𝅥. = 44
LM

121

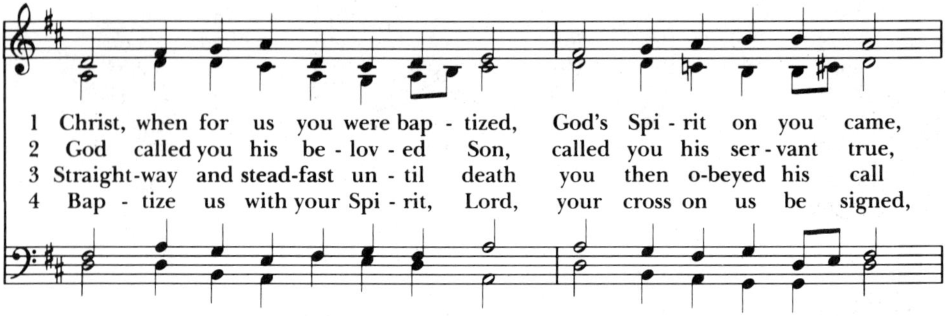
1 Christ, when for us you were bap - tized, God's Spi - rit on you came,
2 God called you his be - lov - ed Son, called you his ser - vant true,
3 Straight-way and stead-fast un - til death you then o-beyed his call
4 Bap - tize us with your Spi - rit, Lord, your cross on us be signed,

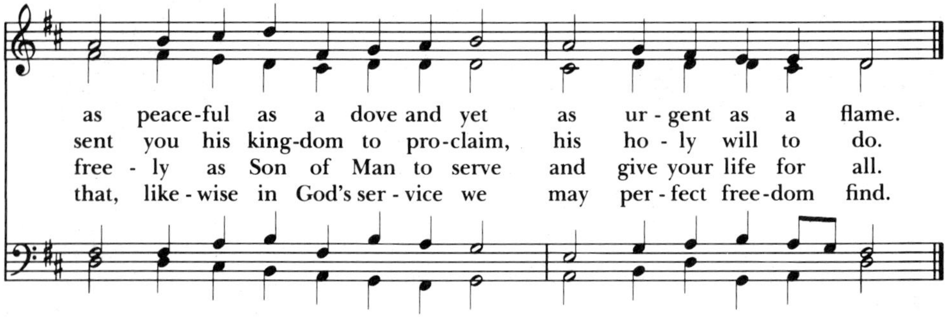
as peace-ful as a dove and yet as ur - gent as a flame.
sent you his king-dom to pro-claim, his ho - ly will to do.
free - ly as Son of Man to serve and give your life for all.
that, like - wise in God's ser - vice we may per - fect free-dom find.

Words: F. Bland Tucker (1895-1984), rev.
Music: *Caithness,* melody from *The Psalmes of David in Prose and Meeter,* 1635; harm. *The English Hymnal,* 1906

♩= 88
CM

122

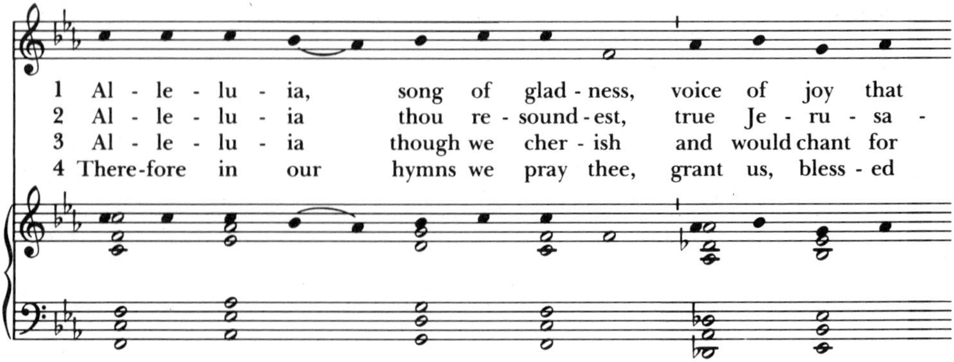
1 Al - le - lu - ia, song of glad - ness, voice of joy that
2 Al - le - lu - ia thou re - sound - est, true Je - ru - sa -
3 Al - le - lu - ia though we cher - ish and would chant for
4 There-fore in our hymns we pray thee, grant us, bless - ed

can - not die; al - le - lu - ia is the an - them
lem and free; al - le - lu - ia, joy - ful mo - ther,
ev - er - more al - le - lu - ia in our sing - ing,
Trin - i - ty, at the last to keep thine Eas - ter
ev - er raised by choirs on high; in the house of
all thy chil - dren sing with thee; but by Bab - y -
let us for a while give o'er, as our Sa - vior
with thy faith - ful saints on high; there to thee for
God a - bid - ing thus they sing e - ter - nal - ly.
lon's sad wa - ters mourn-ing ex - iles now are we.
in his fast - ing plea - sures of the world for - bore.
ev - er sing - ing al - le - lu - ia joy - ful - ly.

The doubling of the melody may be omitted. Another accompaniment, 519. Alternative tunes: *Tibi, Christe, splendor Patris,* 123; *Dulce Carmen,* 559; *Urbs beata Jerusalem* (proportional rhythm), 622.

Words: Latin, 11th cent.; tr. John Mason Neale (1818-1866), alt.
Music: *Urbs beata Jerusalem,* plainsong, Mode 2, Nevers MS., 13th cent.; acc. Jackson Hill (b. 1941) 87. 87. 87

Bells used:
Handbells
1 Al - le - lu - ia, song of glad - ness, voice of joy that
2 Al - le - lu - ia thou re - sound - est, true Je - ru - sa -
3 Al - le - lu - ia though we cher - ish and would chant for
4 There - fore in our hymns we pray thee, grant us, bless - ed
Tambourine
Drum
Finger cymbals, triangle, etc.
can - not die; al - le - lu - ia is the an - them
lem and free; al - le - lu - ia, joy - ful mo - ther,
ev - er - more al - le - lu - ia in our sing - ing,
Trin - i - ty, at the last to keep thine Eas - ter
tr

ev - er raised by choirs on high; in the house of
all thy chil - dren sing with thee; but by Bab - y -
let us for a while give o'er, as our Sa - vior
with thy faith - ful saints on high; there to thee for
God a - bid - ing thus they sing e - ter - nal - ly.
lon's sad wa - ters mourn - ing ex - iles now are we.
in his fast - ing plea - sures of the world for - bore.
ev - er sing - ing al - le - lu - ia joy - ful - ly.

This hymn may also be accompanied by playing the handbell part (an octave higher) and the melody on a keyboard instrument. Alternative tunes: *Urbs beata Jerusalem* (equalist rhythm), 122; *Dulce Carmen*, 559.

Words: Latin, 11th cent.; tr. John Mason Neale (1818-1866), alt.
Music: *Tibi, Christe, splendor Patris,* plainsong, Mode 2, Moissac MS., 12th cent.; ver. Schola Antiqua, 1983; acc. Richard Proulx (b. 1937)

♩=96
87. 87. 87

Alternative accompaniment

Music: *Tibi, Christe, splendor Patris,* plainsong, Mode 2, Moissac MS., 12th cent.; ver. Schola Antiqua, 1983; acc. Jackson Hill (b. 1941)

♩=96
87. 87. 87

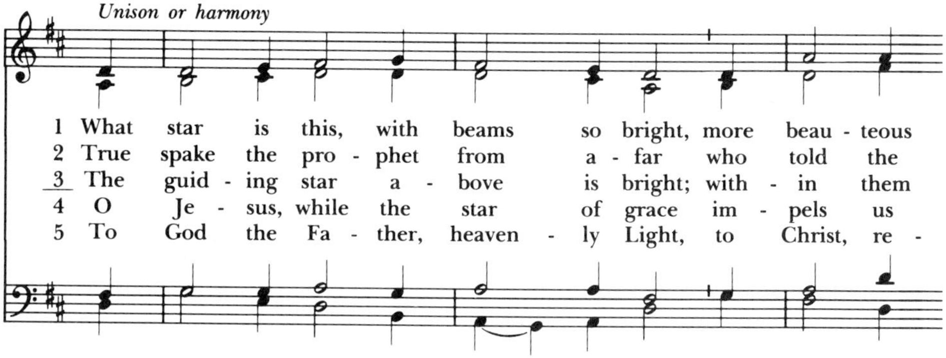
Unison or harmony
1 What star is this, with beams so bright, more beau - teous
2 True spake the pro - phet from a - far who told the
3 The guid - ing star a - bove is bright; with - in them
4 O Je - sus, while the star of grace im - pels us
5 To God the Fa - ther, heaven - ly Light, to Christ, re -

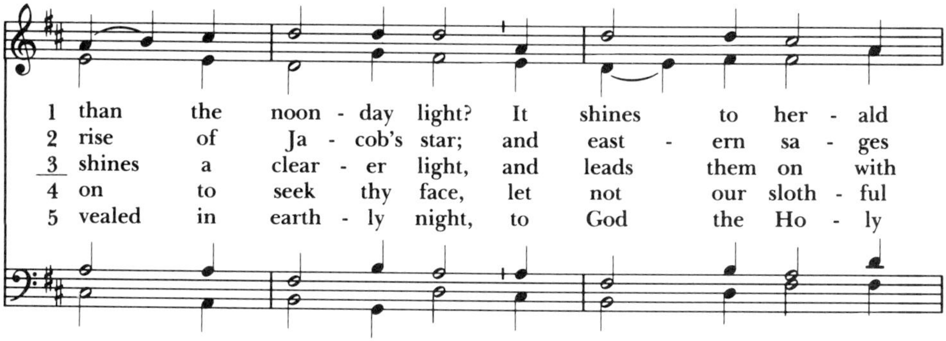
1 than the noon - day light? It shines to her - ald
2 rise of Ja - cob's star; and east - ern sa - ges
3 shines a clear - er light, and leads them on with
4 on to seek thy face, let not our sloth - ful
5 vealed in earth - ly night, to God the Ho - ly

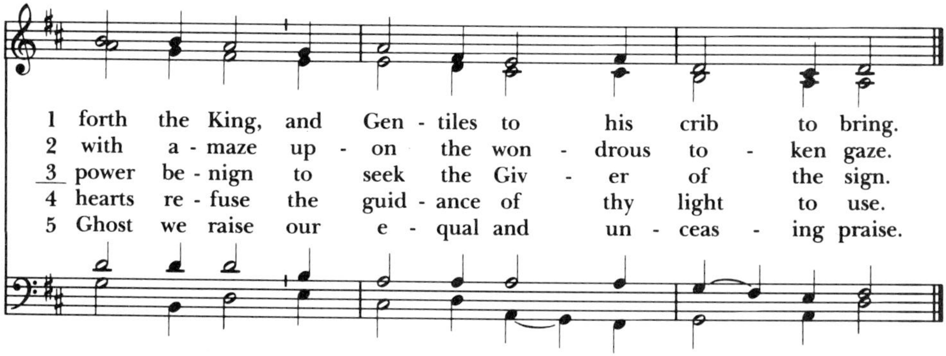
1 forth the King, and Gen - tiles to his crib to bring.
2 with a - maze up - on the won - drous to - ken gaze.
3 power be - nign to seek the Giv - er of the sign.
4 hearts re - fuse the guid - ance of thy light to use.
5 Ghost we raise our e - qual and un - ceas - ing praise.

Another harmonization, 193.

Words: Charles Coffin (1676-1749); tr. *Hymns Ancient and Modern,* 1861, after John Chandler (1807-1876), alt.
Music: *Puer nobis,* melody from Trier MS., 15th cent.; adapt. Michael Praetorius (1571-1621); harm. *Cowley Carol Book,* 1902

𝅗𝅥. = 50
LM

125 Epiphany

1 The peo - ple who in dark - ness walked have seen a glo - rious light;
2 To hail thy ris - ing, Sun of life, the ga - thering na - tions come,
3 To us the prom-ised Child is born, to us the Son is given;
4 His name shall be the Prince of Peace for ev - er - more a - dored,
5 His power in - creas - ing still shall spread, his reign no end shall know;

1 on them broke forth the heaven-ly dawn who dwelt in death and night.
2 joy - ous as when the reap - ers bear their har - vest trea - sures home.
3 him shall the tribes of earth o - bey, and all the hosts of heaven.
4 the Won - der - ful, the Coun - sel - lor, the might-y God and Lord.
5 jus - tice shall guard his throne a - bove, and peace a - bound be - low.

Alternative tune: *Dundee,* 126.

Words: John Morison (1749-1798), alt.; para. of Isaiah 9:2-7 — 𝅗𝅥=60
Music: *Perry,* Leo Sowerby (1895-1968), alt. — CM

126 Epiphany

1 The peo - ple who in dark - ness walked have seen a glo - rious light;
2 To hail thy ris - ing, Sun of life, the ga - thering na - tions come,
3 To us the prom-ised Child is born, to us the Son is given;
4 His name shall be the Prince of Peace for ev - er - more a - dored,
5 His power in - creas - ing still shall spread, his reign no end shall know;

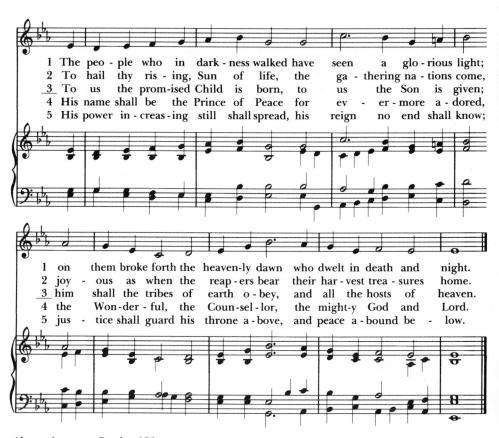

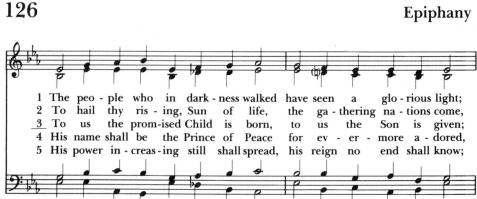

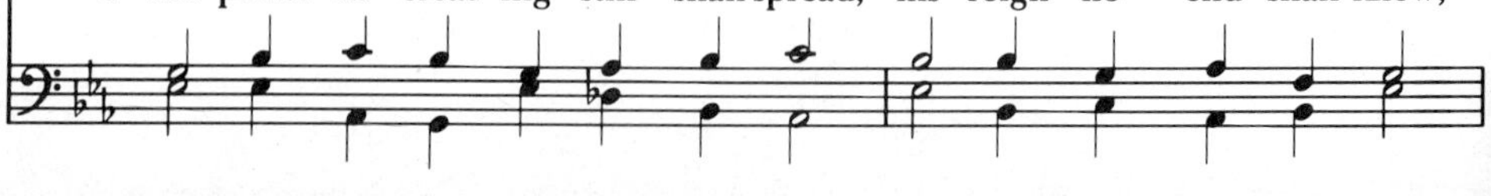

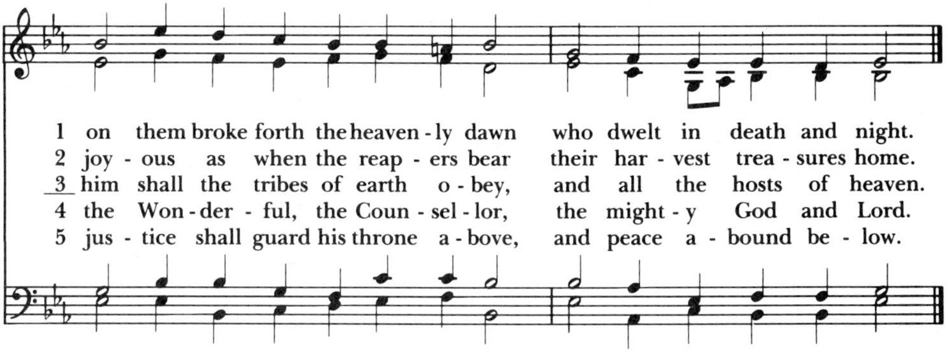
1 on them broke forth the heaven-ly dawn who dwelt in death and night.
2 joy-ous as when the reap-ers bear their har-vest trea-sures home.
3 him shall the tribes of earth o-bey, and all the hosts of heaven.
4 the Won-der-ful, the Coun-sel-lor, the might-y God and Lord.
5 jus-tice shall guard his throne a-bove, and peace a-bound be-low.

A fauxbourdon setting, 709. Alternative tune: *Perry*, 125.

Words: John Morison (1749-1798), alt.; para. of Isaiah 9:2-7
Music: *Dundee*, melody *The CL Psalmes of David*, 1615; harm. Thomas Ravenscroft (1592?-1635?), alt.

♩=88
CM

Epiphany

127

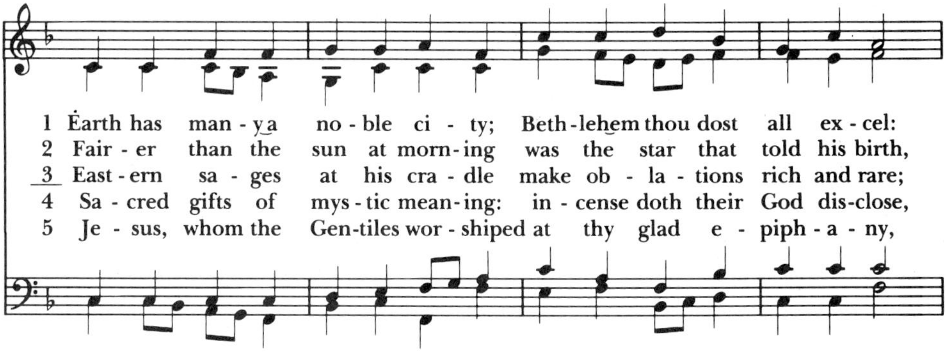
1 Earth has man-y a no-ble ci-ty; Beth-lehem thou dost all ex-cel:
2 Fair-er than the sun at morn-ing was the star that told his birth,
3 East-ern sa-ges at his cra-dle make ob-la-tions rich and rare;
4 Sa-cred gifts of mys-tic mean-ing: in-cense doth their God dis-close,
5 Je-sus, whom the Gen-tiles wor-shiped at thy glad e-piph-a-ny,

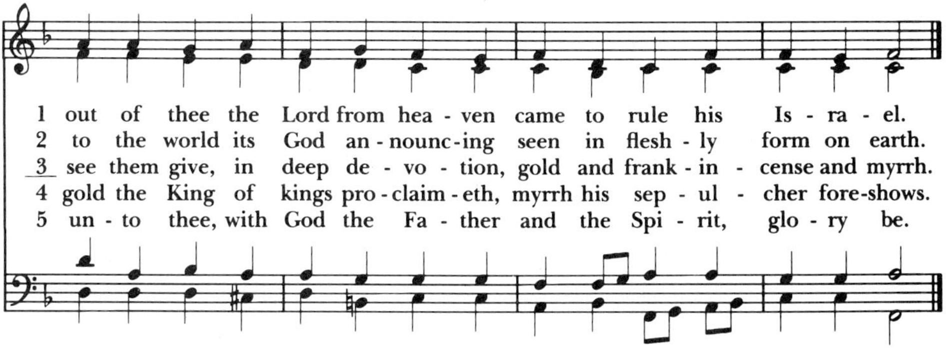
1 out of thee the Lord from hea-ven came to rule his Is-ra-el.
2 to the world its God an-nounc-ing seen in flesh-ly form on earth.
3 see them give, in deep de-vo-tion, gold and frank-in-cense and myrrh.
4 gold the King of kings pro-claim-eth, myrrh his sep-ul-cher fore-shows.
5 un-to thee, with God the Fa-ther and the Spi-rit, glo-ry be.

Other harmonizations, 66 and 414.

Words: Marcus Aurelius Clemens Prudentius (348-410?); tr. *Hymns Ancient and Modern*, 1861, alt.
Music: *Stuttgart*, melody from *Psalmodia Sacra, oder Andächtige und Schöne Gesänge*, 1715; adapt. William Henry Havergal (1793-1870); harm. K. D. Smith (b. 1928)

♩=80
87. 87

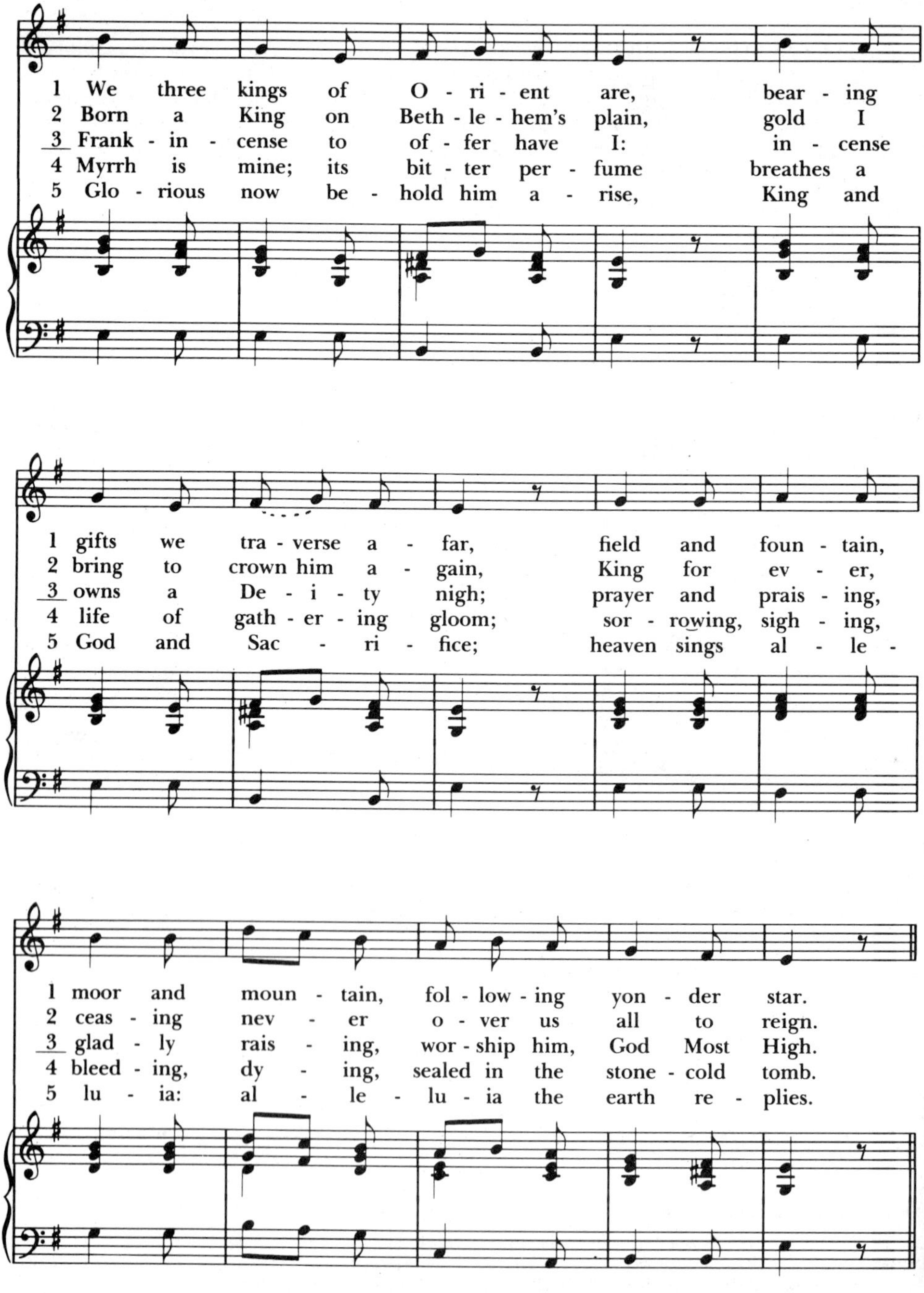
1 We three kings of O - ri - ent are, bear - ing
2 Born a King on Beth - le - hem's plain, gold I
3 Frank - in - cense to of - fer have I: in - cense
4 Myrrh is mine; its bit - ter per - fume breathes a
5 Glo - rious now be - hold him a - rise, King and
1 gifts we tra - verse a - far, field and foun - tain,
2 bring to crown him a - gain, King for ev - er,
3 owns a De - i - ty nigh; prayer and prais - ing,
4 life of gath - er - ing gloom; sor - rowing, sigh - ing,
5 God and Sac - ri - fice; heaven sings al - le -
1 moor and moun - tain, fol - low - ing yon - der star.
2 ceas - ing nev - er o - ver us all to reign.
3 glad - ly rais - ing, wor - ship him, God Most High.
4 bleed - ing, dy - ing, sealed in the stone - cold tomb.
5 lu - ia: al - le - lu - ia the earth re - plies.

Refrain
O star of wonder, star of night,
star with royal beauty bright;
westward leading, still proceeding,
guide us to thy perfect light!
Interlude

The stanzas may be sung by three soloists: 1 and 5 by the ensemble; 2-4 by individuals; and the refrain by all.

Words: John Henry Hopkins, Jr. (1820-1891), alt.
Music: *Three Kings of Orient,* John Henry Hopkins, Jr. (1820-1891)

♩. = 54
88. 446 with Refrain

129

1 Christ up - on the moun - tain peak stands a - lone in glo - ry blaz - ing; let us, if we dare to speak, with the saints and an - gels praise him. Al - le - lu - ia!
2 Trem-bling at his feet we saw Mo - ses and E - li - jah speak - ing. All the pro - phets and the Law shout through them their joy - ful greet - ing. Al - le - lu - ia!
3 Swift the cloud of glo - ry came. God pro - claim - ing in its thun - der Je - sus as his Son by name! Na - tions cry a - loud in won - der! Al - le - lu - ia!
4 This is God's be - lov - ed Son! Law and pro - phets fade be - fore him; first and last and on - ly One, let cre - a - tion now a - dore him! Al - le - lu - ia!

Alternative tune: *Shillingford,* 130.

Words: Brian A. Wren (b. 1936)
Music: *Mowsley,* Cyril Vincent Taylor (b. 1907)

𝅗𝅥 = 66
78. 78 with Alleluia

1 Christ up - on the moun-tain peak stands a - lone in glo - ry
2 Trem-bling at his feet we saw Mo - ses and E - li - jah
3 Swift the cloud of glo - ry came. God pro-claim-ing in its
4 This is God's be - lov - ed Son! Law and pro-phets fade be -
blaz - ing; let us, if we dare to speak,
speak - ing. All the pro - phets and the Law
thun - der Je - sus as his Son by name!
fore him; first and last and on - ly One,
with the saints and an-gels praise him. Al - le - lu - ia!
shout through them their joy-ful greet - ing. Al - le - lu - ia!
Na - tions cry a - loud in won - der! Al - le - lu - ia!
let cre - a - tion now a - dore him! Al - le - lu - ia!

Alternative tune: *Mowsley,* 129.

Words: Brian A. Wren (b. 1936)
Music: *Shillingford,* Peter Cutts (b. 1937)

♩=96
78. 78 with Alleluia

1 When Christ's ap - pear - ing was made known, King
2 The east - ern sa - ges saw from far and
3 With - in the Jor - dan's sa - cred flood the
4 Oh, what a mir - a - cle di - vine, when
5 All glo - ry, Je - sus, be to thee for
1 He - rod trem - bled for his throne; but he who of - fers
2 fol - lowed on his guid - ing star; by light their way to
3 heaven - ly Lamb in meek - ness stood, that he, to whom no
4 wa - ter red - dened in - to wine! He spoke the word, and
5 this thy glad e - piph - a - ny: whom with the Fa - ther
1 heaven - ly birth sought not the king - doms of this earth.
2 Light they trod, and by their gifts con - fessed their God.
3 sin was known, might cleanse his peo - ple from their own.
4 forth it flowed in streams that na - ture ne'er be - stowed.
5 we a - dore and Ho - ly Ghost for ev - er - more.

Alternative tune: *Erhalt uns, Herr* (rhythmic), 132.

Words: Caelius Sedulius (5th cent.); st. 1, tr. *The Hymn Book of the Anglican Church of Canada and the United Church of Canada,* 1971; sts. 2-5, tr. John Mason Neale (1818-1866), alt.

Music: *Vom Himmel kam der Engel Schar,* melody source unknown; harm. Carol Doran (b. 1936)

𝅗𝅥=48
LM

1 When Christ's ap - pear - ing was made known, King He - rod
2 The east - ern sa - ges saw from far and fol - lowed
3 With - in the Jor - dan's sa - cred flood the heaven - ly
4 Oh, what a mir - a - cle di - vine, when wa - ter
5 All glo - ry, Je - sus, be to thee for this thy
1 trem - bled for his throne; but he who of - fers
2 on his guid - ing star; by light their way to
3 Lamb in meek - ness stood, that he, to whom no
4 red - dened in - to wine! He spoke the word, and
5 glad e - piph - a - ny: whom with the Fa - ther
1 heaven - ly birth sought not the king - doms of this earth.
2 Light they trod, and by their gifts con - fessed their God.
3 sin was known, might cleanse his peo - ple from their own.
4 forth it flowed in streams that na - ture ne'er be - stowed.
5 we a - dore and Ho - ly Ghost for ev - er - more.

Alternative tunes: *Vom Himmel kam der Engel Schar,* 77; *Erhalt uns, Herr* (isometric), 143.

Words: Caelius Sedulius (5th cent.); st. 1, tr. *The Hymn Book of the Anglican Church of Canada and the United Church of Canada,* 1971; sts. 2-5, tr. John Mason Neale (1818-1866), alt.

Music: *Erhalt uns, Herr,* melody from *Geistliche Lieder,* 1543; harm. Hans Leo Hassler (1564-1612)

♩=80
LM

1 O Light of Light, Love giv - en birth; Je - sus, Re -
2 Two pro - phets, who had faith to see, with your e -
deem - er of the earth: More
lect found com - pa - ny; the
bright than day your face did show, your
heavens a - bove your glo - ry named, your

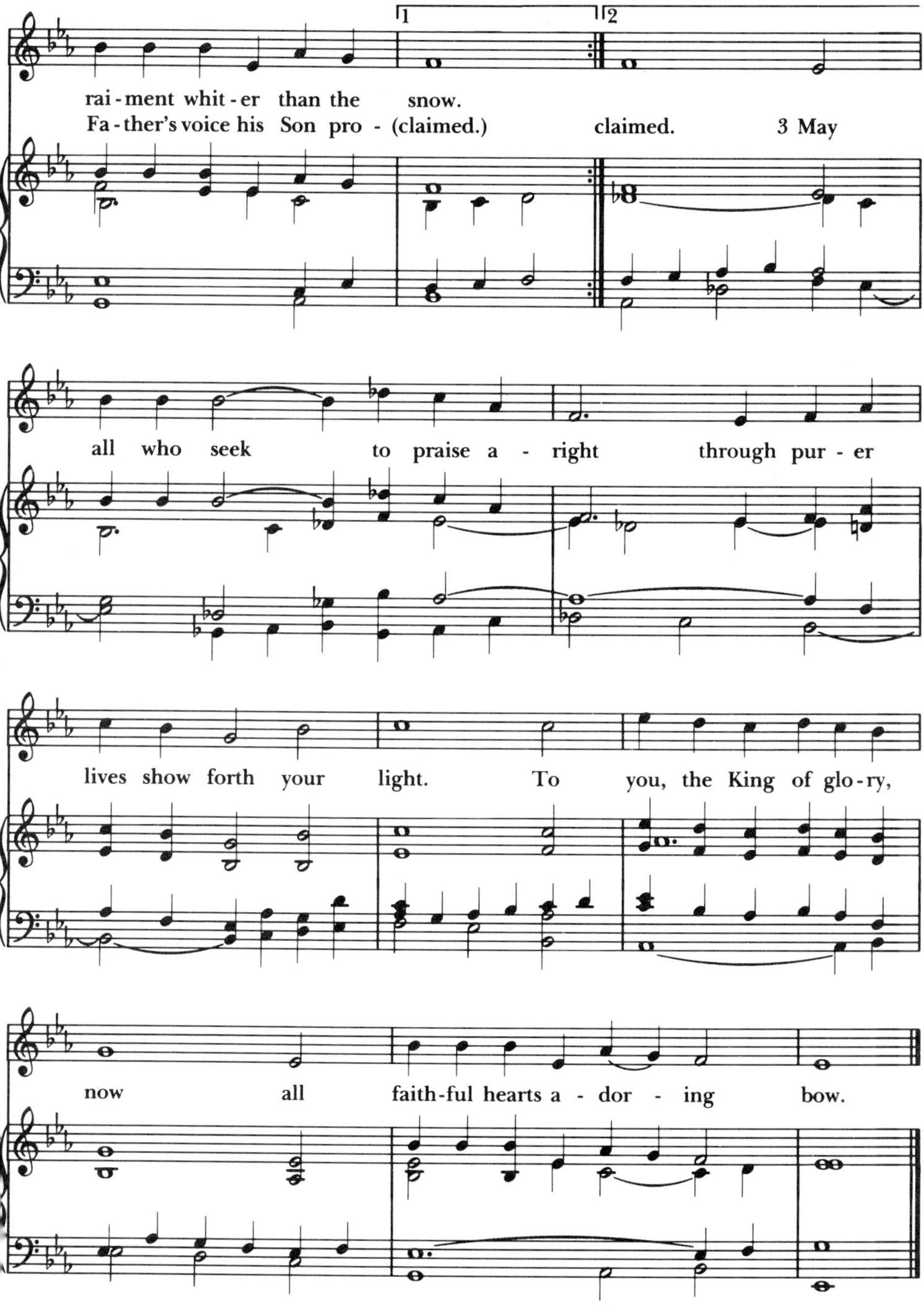
1
2
rai - ment whit - er than the snow.
Fa - ther's voice his Son pro - (claimed.) claimed. 3 May
all who seek to praise a - right through pur - er
lives show forth your light. To you, the King of glo - ry,
now all faith - ful hearts a - dor - ing bow.

Alternative tune: *Jesu dulcis memoria,* 134.

Words: Latin, 10th cent.; tr. Laurence Housman (1865-1959), alt.
Music: *Elmhurst,* Cary Ratcliff (b. 1953)

𝅗𝅥=72
LM

1 O light of Light, Love giv - en birth; Je - sus, Re - deem - er
2 Two pro - phets, who had faith to see, with your e - lect found
3 May all who seek to praise a - right through pur - er lives show
of the earth: more bright than day your face did
com - pa - ny; the heavens a - bove your glo - ry
forth your light. To you, the King of glo - ry,
show, your rai - ment whit - er than the snow.
named, your Fa - ther's voice his Son pro - claimed.
now all faith - ful hearts a - dor - ing bow.

Other accompaniments, 18 and 650. Alternative tune: *Elmhurst,* 133.

Words: Latin, 10th cent.; tr. Laurence Housman (1865-1959), alt.
Music: *Jesu dulcis memoria,* plainsong, Mode 2; acc. James McGregor (b. 1930) LM

1 Songs of thank-ful - ness and praise, Je - sus, Lord, to thee we raise,
2 Man - i - fest at Jor - dan's stream, Pro-phet, Priest, and King su - preme;
3 Man - i - fest in mak - ing whole pal - sied limbs and faint - ing soul;
4 Man - i - fest on moun - tain height, shin - ing in re - splen-dent light,
Man - i - fest - ed by the star to the sa - ges from a - far;
and at Ca - na, wed - ding-guest, in thy God - head man - i - fest;
man - i - fest in val - iant fight, quell - ing all the dev - il's might;
where dis - ci - ples filled with awe thy trans - fi - gured glo - ry saw.
branch of roy - al Da - vid's stem in thy birth at Beth - le - hem;
man - i - fest in power di - vine, chang - ing wa - ter in - to wine;
man - i - fest in gra - cious will, ev - er bring - ing good from ill;
When from there thou led - dest them stead - fast to Je - ru - sa - lem,
an - thems be to thee ad - dressed, God in man made man - i - fest.
an - thems be to thee ad - dressed, God in man made man - i - fest.
an - thems be to thee ad - dressed, God in man made man - i - fest.
cross and Eas - ter Day at - test God in man made man - i - fest.

Words: Sts. 1-3, Christopher Wordsworth (1807-1885); st. 4, F. Bland Tucker (1895-1984) 𝅗𝅥=48
Music: *Salzburg*, melody Jakob Hintze (1622-1702); harm. Johann Sebastian Bach (1685-1750) 77. 77. D

1 O won - drous type! O vi - sion fair
2 With Mo - ses and E - li - jah nigh
3 With shin - ing face and bright ar - ray,
4 And faith - ful hearts are raised on high
5 O Fa - ther, with the e - ter - nal Son,
1 of glo - ry that the Church may share,
2 the in - car - nate Lord holds con - verse high;
3 Christ deigns to man - i - fest to - day
4 by this great vi - sion's mys - ter - y;
5 and Ho - ly Spi - rit, ev - er One,
1 which Christ up - on the moun - tain shows,
2 and from the cloud, the Ho - ly One
3 what glo - ry shall be theirs a - bove
4 for which in joy - ful strains we raise
5 vouch - safe to bring us by thy grace

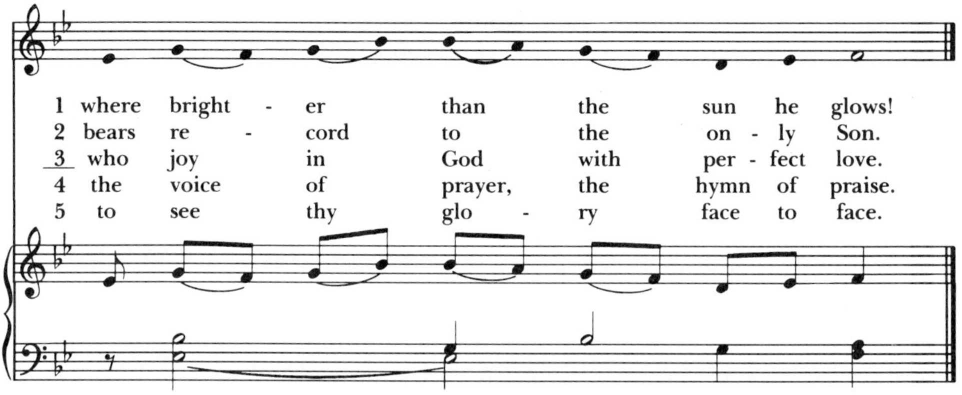
1 where bright - er than the sun he glows!
2 bears re - cord to the on - ly Son.
3 who joy in God with per - fect love.
4 the voice of prayer, the hymn of praise.
5 to see thy glo - ry face to face.

Another accompaniment, 220. Alternative tune: *Wareham,* 137.

Words: Latin, 15th cent.; tr. *Hymns Ancient and Modern,* 1861, after John Mason Neale (1818-1866), alt.
Music: *Aeterne Rex altissime,* plainsong, Mode 1, *Zisterzienser Hymnar,* 14th cent.; acc. Roy F. Kehl (b. 1935) LM

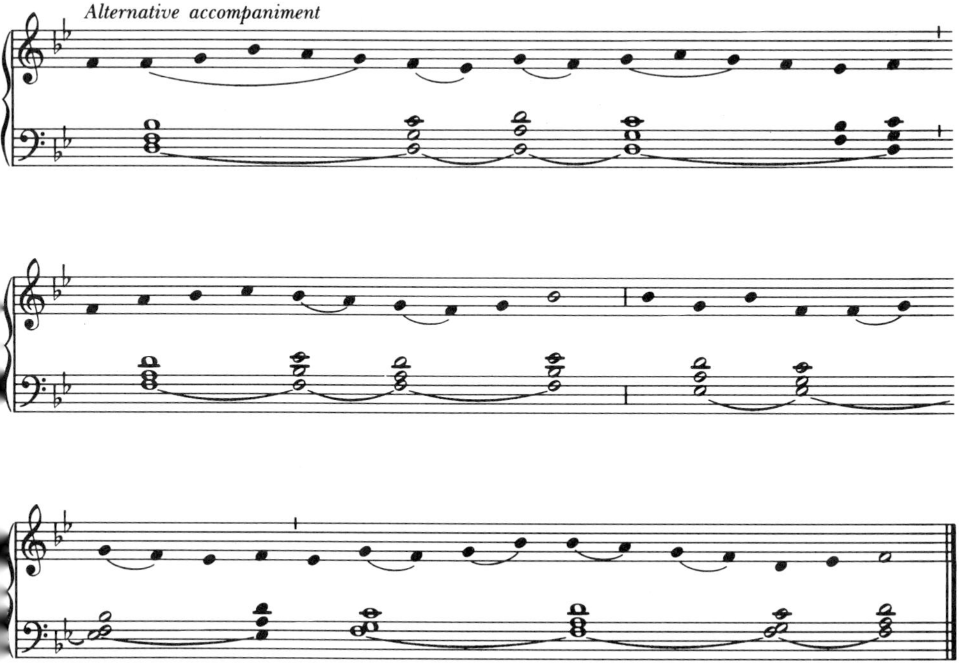
Alternative accompaniment

Music: *Aeterne Rex altissime,* plainsong, Mode 1, *Zisterzienser Hymnar,* 14th cent.; acc. Thomas Foster (b. 1938)

Descant
4 And faith - ful hearts are raised on high by this great
1 O won - drous type! O vi - sion fair of glo - ry
2 With Mo - ses and E - li - jah nigh the in - car - nate
3 With shin - ing face and bright ar - ray, Christ deigns to
4 And faith - ful hearts are raised on high by this great
5 O Fa - ther, with the e - ter - nal Son, and Ho - ly
vi - sion's mys - ter - y; for which in joy - ful
1 that the Church may share, which Christ up - on the
2 Lord holds con - verse high; and from the cloud, the
3 man - i - fest to - day what glo - ry shall be
4 vi - sion's mys - ter - y; for which in joy - ful
5 Spi - rit, ev - er One, vouch - safe to bring us

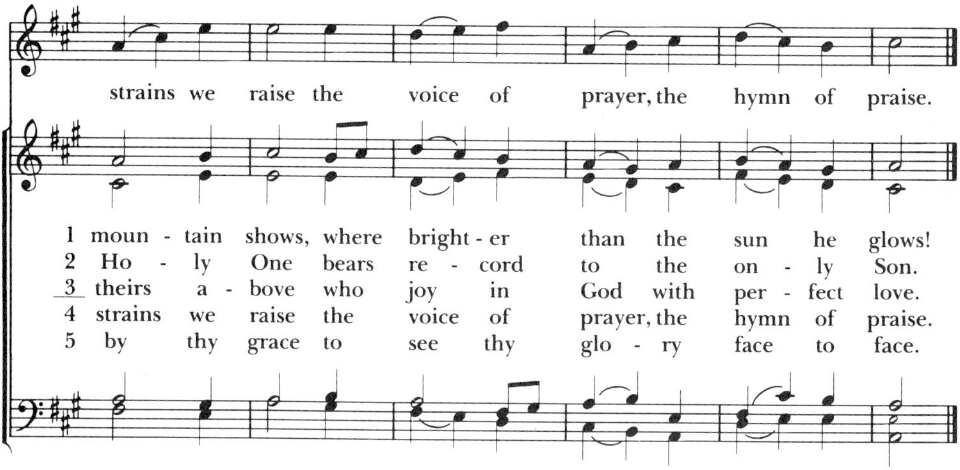
strains we raise the voice of prayer, the hymn of praise.
1 moun - tain shows, where bright - er than the sun he glows!
2 Ho - ly One bears re - cord to the on - ly Son.
3 theirs a - bove who joy in God with per - fect love.
4 strains we raise the voice of prayer, the hymn of praise.
5 by thy grace to see thy glo - ry face to face.

Alternative tune: *Aeterne Rex altissime,* 136.

Words: Latin, 15th cent.; tr. *Hymns Ancient and Modern,* 1861, after John Mason Neale (1818-1866), alt.
Music: *Wareham,* melody William Knapp (1698-1768), alt.; harm. *Hymns Ancient and Modern,* 1875, after James Turle (1802-1882); desc. Sydney Hugo Nicholson (1875-1947)

♩=96
LM

Epiphany

138

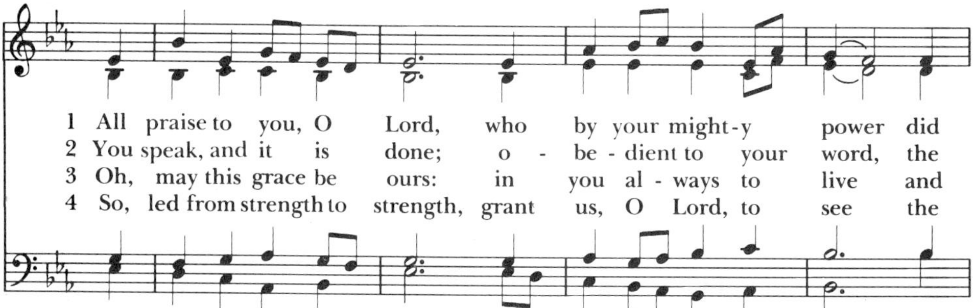
1 All praise to you, O Lord, who by your might-y power did
2 You speak, and it is done; o - be - dient to your word, the
3 Oh, may this grace be ours: in you al - ways to live and
4 So, led from strength to strength, grant us, O Lord, to see the

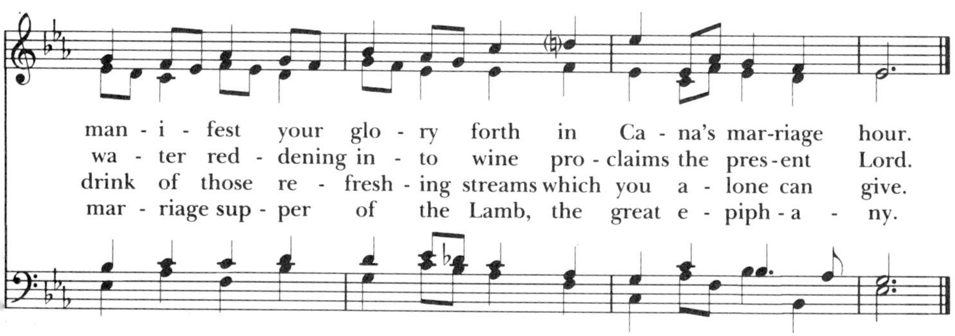
man - i - fest your glo - ry forth in Ca - na's mar-riage hour.
wa - ter red - dening in - to wine pro - claims the pres-ent Lord.
drink of those re - fresh - ing streams which you a - lone can give.
mar - riage sup - per of the Lamb, the great e - piph - a - ny.

Words: Hyde W. Beadon (1812-1891), alt.
Music: *Carlisle,* Charles Lockhart (1745-1815)

𝅗𝅥=88
SM

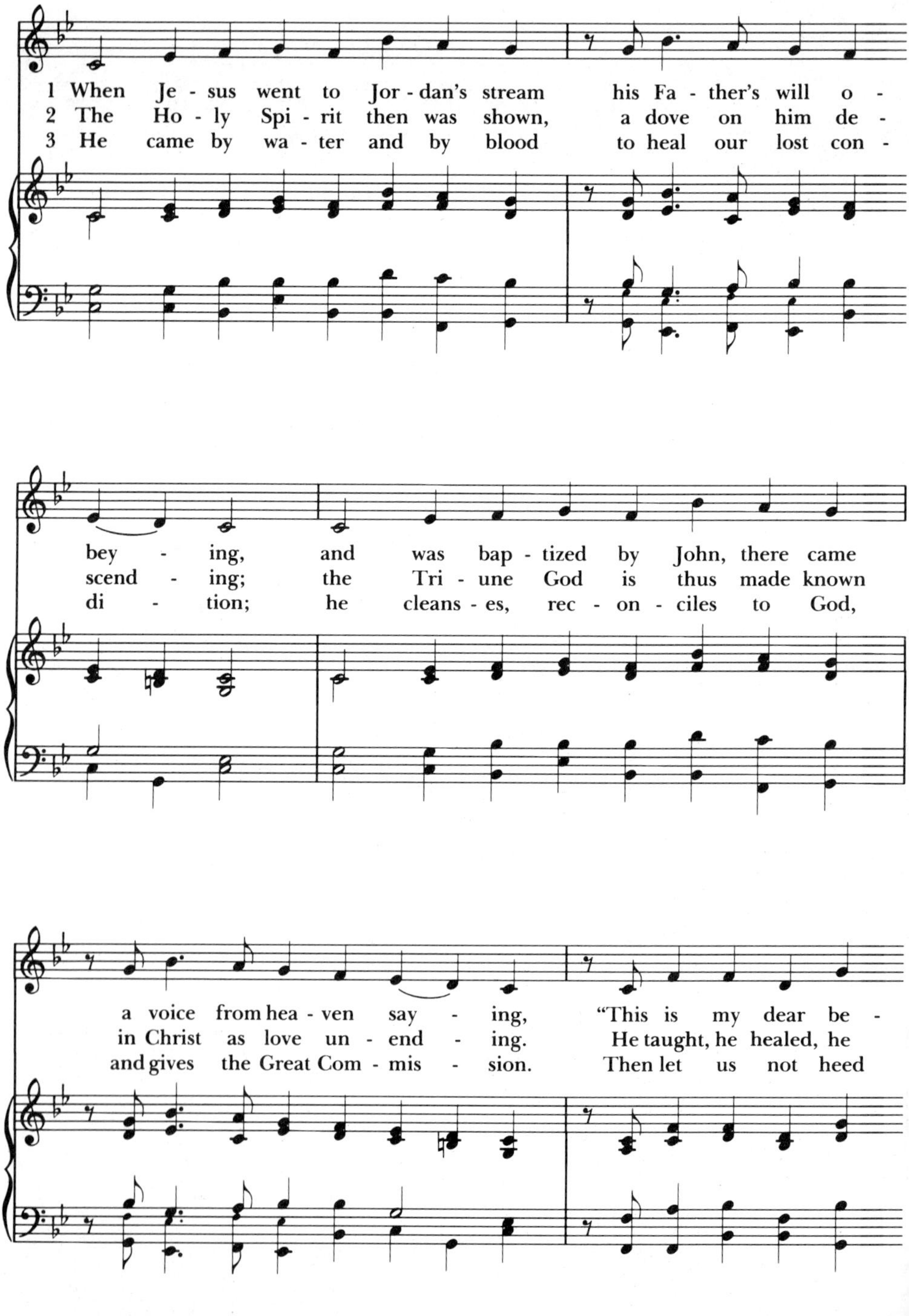
1 When Je - sus went to Jor - dan's stream his Fa - ther's will o -
2 The Ho - ly Spi - rit then was shown, a dove on him de -
3 He came by wa - ter and by blood to heal our lost con -
bey - ing, and was bap - tized by John, there came
scend - ing; the Tri - une God is thus made known
di - tion; he cleans - es, rec - on - ciles to God,
a voice from hea - ven say - ing, "This is my dear be -
in Christ as love un - end - ing. He taught, he healed, he
and gives the Great Com - mis - sion. Then let us not heed

lov - ed Son up - on whom rests my fa - vor."
raised the dead, yet, in his great en - deav - or
world - ly lies nor rest up - on our mer - it,
And till God's will is ful - ly done he will not bend or
to save us, his own blood was shed; but death could hold him
but trust in Christ who will bap - tize with wa - ter and the
wa - ver, for he is Christ the Sa - vior.
nev - er. He rose, and lives for ev - er.
Spi - rit that we may life in - her - it.

Words: Martin Luther (1483-1546); para. F. Bland Tucker (1895-1984), rev.
Music: *Christ unser Herr zum Jordan kam,* melody from *Geystliche gesangk Buchleyn,* 1524; harm. Lucas Osiander (1534-1604)

𝅗𝅥=48
87. 87. 87. 877

1 Wilt thou for-give that sin, where I be - gun,
2 Wilt thou for-give that sin, by which I won
3 I have a sin of fear that when I've spun
which is my sin, though it were done be - fore?
o - thers to sin, and made my sin their door?
my last thread, I shall per - ish on the shore;
Wilt thou for-give those sins through which I run,
Wilt thou for-give that sin which I did shun
swear by thy-self, that at my death thy Son

and do run still, though still I do de - plore?
a year or two, but wal - lowed in a score?
shall shine as he shines now, and here - to - fore.
When thou hast done, thou hast not done,
When thou hast done, thou hast not done,
And hav - ing done that, thou hast done,
for I have more.
for I have more.
I fear no (more.) more.
1-2
Final Ending

Alternative tune: *So giebst du nun,* 141.

Words: John Donne (1573-1631)
Music: *Donne,* melody and bass John Hilton (1599-1657), alt.; harm. Roy F. Kehl (b. 1935), after Elizabeth Poston (b. 1905)

𝅗𝅥=48
10 10. 10 10. 84

1 Wilt thou for-give that sin, where I be - gun,
2 Wilt thou for-give that sin, by which I won
3 I have a sin of fear that when I've spun
which is my sin, though it were done be - fore?
o - thers to sin, and made my sin their door?
my last thread, I shall per - ish on the shore;
Wilt thou for-give those sins through which I run,
Wilt thou for-give that sin which I did shun
swear by thy-self, that at my death thy Son
and do run still, though still I do de-plore?
a year or two, but wal - lowed in a score?
shall shine as he shines now, and here - to-fore.
3

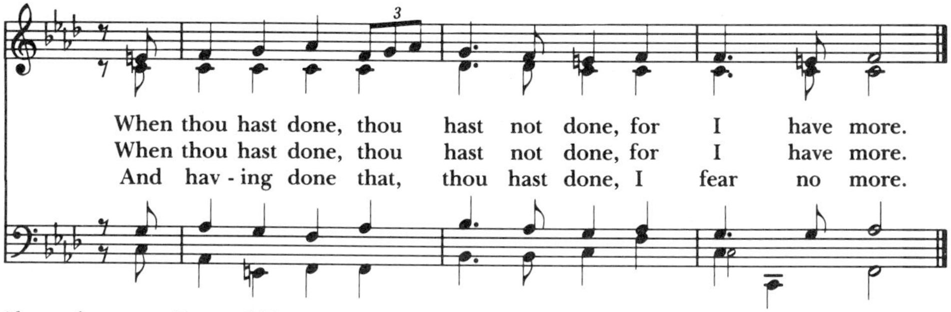
When thou hast done, thou hast not done, for I have more.
When thou hast done, thou hast not done, for I have more.
And hav-ing done that, thou hast done, I fear no more.

Alternative tune: *Donne,* 140.

Words: John Donne (1573-1631)
Music: *So giebst du nun,* melody from *Geist und Lehr-reiches Kirchen und Haus Buch,* 1694; harm. Johann Sebastian Bach (1685-1750)

𝅗𝅥=80
10 10. 10 10. 84

142

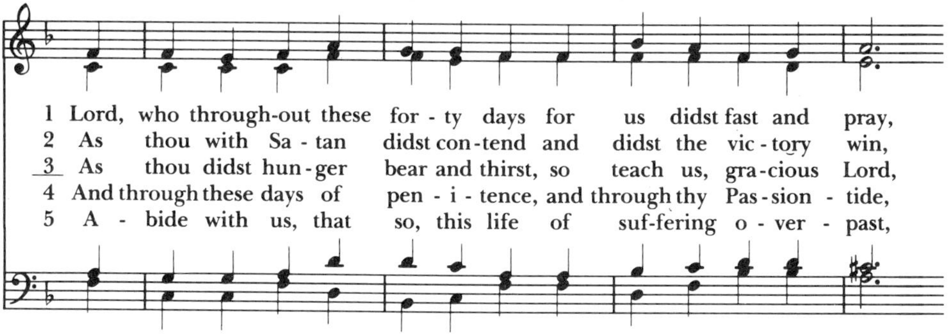
1 Lord, who through-out these for-ty days for us didst fast and pray,
2 As thou with Sa-tan didst con-tend and didst the vic-tory win,
3 As thou didst hun-ger bear and thirst, so teach us, gra-cious Lord,
4 And through these days of pen-i-tence, and through thy Pas-sion-tide,
5 A-bide with us, that so, this life of suf-fering o-ver-past,

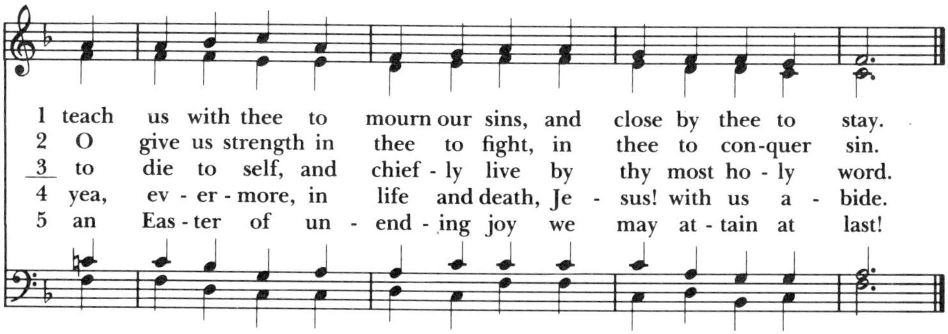
1 teach us with thee to mourn our sins, and close by thee to stay.
2 O give us strength in thee to fight, in thee to con-quer sin.
3 to die to self, and chief-ly live by thy most ho-ly word.
4 yea, ev-er-more, in life and death, Je-sus! with us a-bide.
5 an Eas-ter of un-end-ing joy we may at-tain at last!

Alternative tune: *St. Flavian* (original rhythm), 332.

Words: Claudia Frances Hernaman (1838-1898)
Music: *St. Flavian,* melody from *Day's Psalter,* 1562; adapt. and harm. Richard Redhead (1820-1901)

♩=80
CM

1 The glo - ry of these for - ty days we
2 A - lone and fast - ing Mo - ses saw the
3 So Dan - iel trained his mys - tic sight, de -
4 Then grant us, Lord, like them to be full
*5 O Fa - ther, Son, and Spi - rit blest, to
1 cel - e - brate with songs of praise; for Christ, through whom all
2 lov - ing God who gave the law; and to E - li - jah,
3 liv - ered from the li - ons' might; and John, the Bride-groom's
4 oft in fast and prayer with thee; our spi - rits strength-en
5 thee be ev - ery prayer ad - dressed, who art in three-fold
1 things were made, him - self has fast - ed and has prayed.
2 fast - ing, came the steeds and char - i - ots of flame.
3 friend, be - came the her - ald of Mes - si - ah's name.
4 with thy grace, and give us joy to see thy face.
5 Name a - dored, from age to age, the on - ly Lord.

Alternative tune: *Erhalt uns, Herr* (rhythmic), 132.

Words: Latin, 6th cent.; tr. Maurice F. Bell (1862-1947), alt.
Music: *Erhalt uns, Herr,* melody from *Geistliche Lieder,* 1543; harm. Johann Sebastian Bach (1685-1750)

♩.= 80
LM

1 Lord Je - sus, Sun of Right - eous - ness, shine
2 Give guid - ance to our wan - dering ways, for -
3 Lord, grant that we in pen - i - tence may
4 Now near - er draws the day of days when
5 The u - ni - verse your glo - ry shows, blest

1 in our hearts, we pray; dis - pel the gloom that
2 give us, Lord, our sin; re - store us by your
3 of - fer you our praise, and through your sav - ing
4 par - a - dise shall bloom, when we shall be at
5 Fa - ther, Spi - rit, Son; we shall ac - claim your

1 shades our minds and be to us as day.
2 lov - ing care to peace and joy with - in.
3 sac - ri - fice re - ceive your gift of grace.
4 one with you, Lord, ris - en from the tomb.
5 ma - jes - ty, e - ter - nal Three in One.

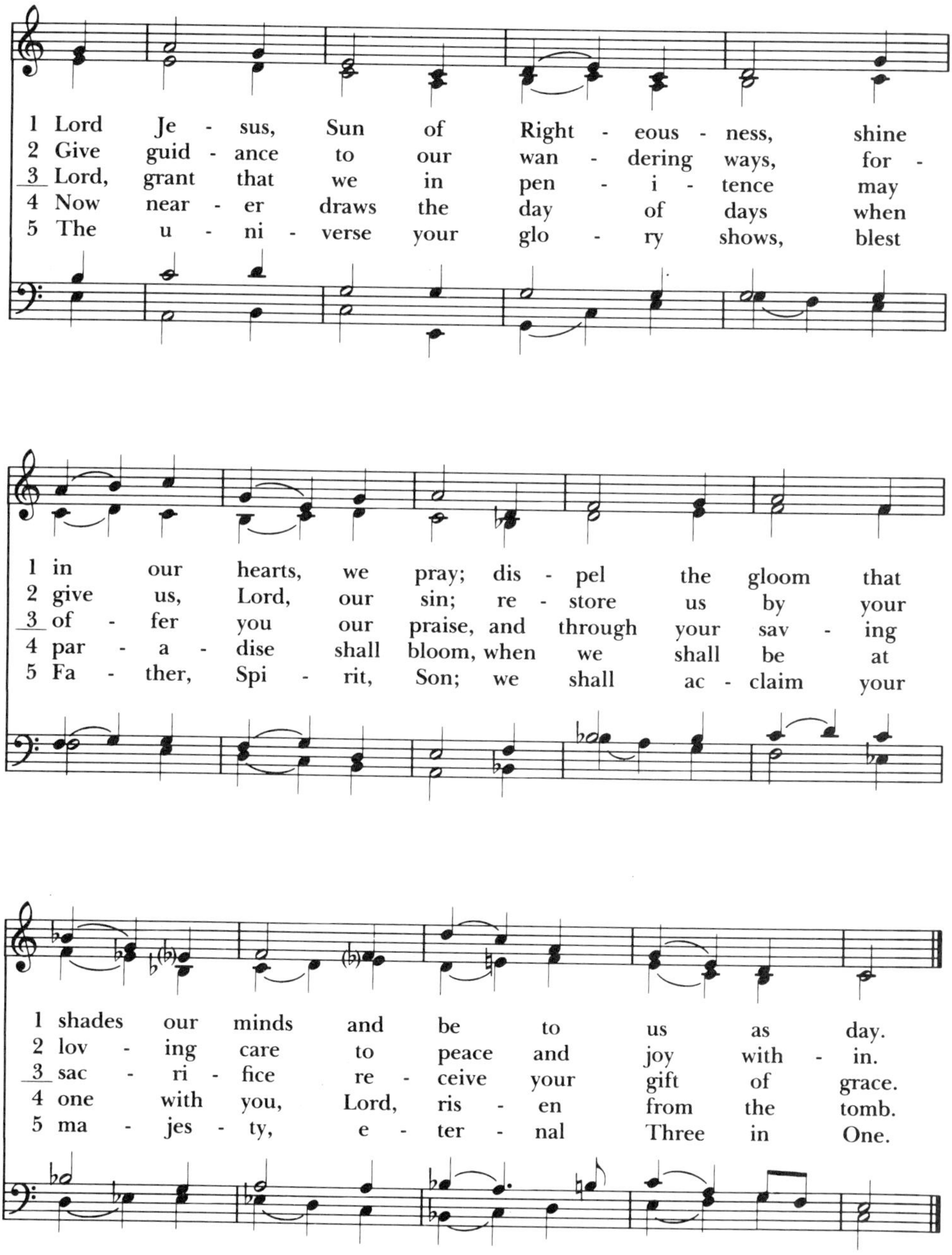

Words: Latin; tr. Anne K. LeCroy (b. 1930)
Music: *Cornhill*, Harold Darke (1888-1976), alt.

♩. =40
CM

1 Now quit your care and anx-ious fear and wor - ry; for
2 To bow the head in sack-cloth and in ash - es, or
3 For is not this the fast that I have cho - sen? (The
4 For right-eous - ness and peace will show their fa - ces to
5 Then shall your light break forth as doth the morn - ing; your
1 schemes are vain and fret-ting brings no gain. Lent calls to
2 rend the soul, such grief is not Lent's goal; but to be
3 pro - phet spoke) To shat-ter ev - ery yoke, of wick - ed -
4 those who feed the hun-gry in their need, and wrongs re -
5 health shall spring, the friends you make shall bring God's glo - ry
1 prayer, to trust and ded - i - ca - tion; God brings new beau - ty
2 led to where God's glo - ry flash - es, his beau - ty to come
3 ness the griev-ous bands to loos - en, op - pres-sion put to
4 dress, who build the old waste pla - ces, and in the dark-ness
5 bright, your way through life a - dorn - ing; and love shall be the

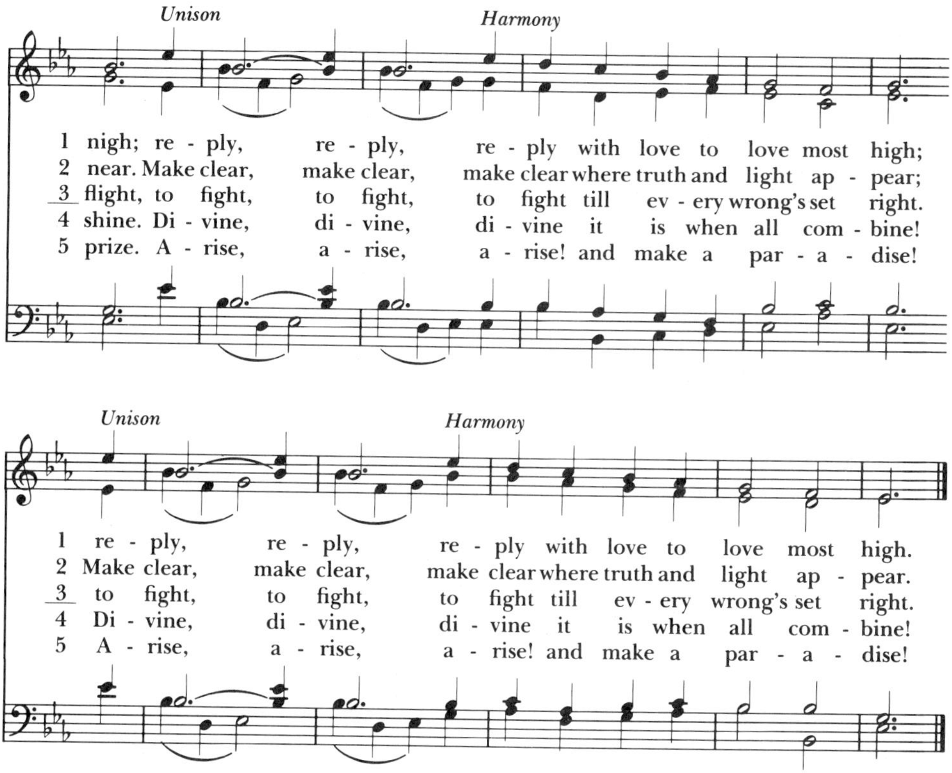
Unison
Harmony
1 nigh; re - ply, re - ply, re - ply with love to love most high;
2 near. Make clear, make clear, make clear where truth and light ap - pear;
3 flight, to fight, to fight, to fight till ev - ery wrong's set right.
4 shine. Di - vine, di - vine, di - vine it is when all com - bine!
5 prize. A - rise, a - rise, a - rise! and make a par - a - dise!
Unison
Harmony
1 re - ply, re - ply, re - ply with love to love most high.
2 Make clear, make clear, make clear where truth and light ap - pear.
3 to fight, to fight, to fight till ev - ery wrong's set right.
4 Di - vine, di - vine, di - vine it is when all com - bine!
5 A - rise, a - rise, a - rise! and make a par - a - dise!

Words: Percy Dearmer (1867-1936), alt.
Music: *Quittez, Pasteurs,* French carol; harm. Martin Fallas Shaw (1875-1958)

𝅗𝅥 = 72
Irr.

1 Now let us all with one ac - cord,
2 The cov - e - nant, so long re - vealed
3 Your love, O Lord, our sin - ful race
4 Re - mem - ber, Lord, though frail we be,
5 There - fore, we pray you, Lord, for - give;
1 in com - pa - ny with a - ges past,
2 to those of faith in for - mer time,
3 has not re - turned, but fal - si - fied;
4 in your own im - age were we made;
5 so when our wan - derings here shall cease,
1 keep vi - gil with our heaven - ly Lord
2 Christ by his own ex - am - ple sealed,
3 au - thor of mer - cy, turn your face
4 help us, lest in anx - i - e - ty,
5 we may with you for ev - er live,

1 in his temp - ta - tion and his fast.
2 the Lord of love, in love sub - lime.
3 and grant re - pent - ance for our pride.
4 we cause your Name to be be - trayed.
5 in love and u - ni - ty and peace.

Alternative tune: *Bourbon,* 147.

Words: Att. Gregory the Great (540-604); tr. *Praise the Lord,* 1972, alt.
Music: *Ex more docti mystico,* plainsong, Mode 2, Verona MS., 12th cent.; acc. Roy F. Kehl (b. 1935) LM

Alternative accompaniment

The chords on the upper staff may be played by handbells.

Bells used:

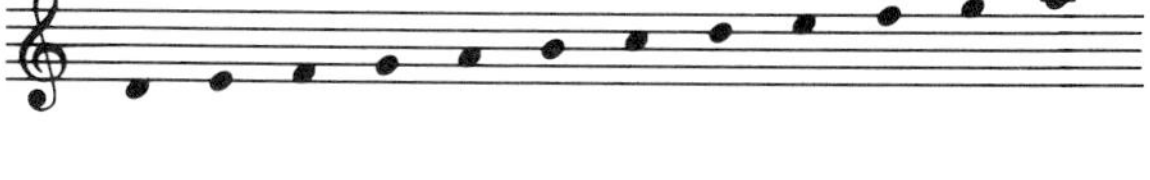

Music: *Ex more docti mystico,* plainsong, Mode 2, Verona MS., 12th cent.; acc. Morgan F. Simmons (b. 1929)

1 Now let us all with one ac - cord, in
2 The cov - e - nant, so long re - vealed to
3 Your love, O Lord, our sin - ful race has
4 Re - mem - ber, Lord, though frail we be, in
5 There - fore, we pray you, Lord, for - give; so
1 com - pa - ny with a - ges past, keep vi - gil with our
2 those of faith in for - mer time, Christ by his own ex -
3 not re - turned, but fal - si - fied; au - thor of mer - cy,
4 your own im - age were we made; help us, lest in anx -
5 when our wan - derings here shall cease, we may with you for
1 heaven-ly Lord in his temp - ta - tion and his fast.
2 am - ple sealed, the Lord of love, in love sub - lime.
3 turn your face and grant re - pent - ance for our pride.
4 i - e - ty, we cause your Name to be be - trayed.
5 ev - er live, in love and u - ni - ty and peace.

Another harmonization, 675. Alternative tune: *Ex more docti mystico,* 146.

Words: Att. Gregory the Great (540-604); tr. *Praise the Lord,* 1972, alt.
Music: *Bourbon,* melody att. Freeman Lewis (1780-1859); harm. Thomas Foster (b. 1938)

♩=69
LM

1 Cre - a - tor of the earth and skies, to whom the
2 We have not known you: to the skies our mon - u -
3 We have not loved you: far and wide the wreck-age
4 For this, our fool - ish con - fi - dence, our pride of
5 Teach us to know and love you, Lord, and hum - bly
1 words of life be - long, grant us your truth to make us
2 ments of fol - ly soar, and all our self - wrought mis - er -
3 of our ha-tred spreads, and e - vils wrought by hu - man
4 know - ledge and our sin, we come to you in pen - i -
5 fol - low in your way. Speak to our souls the quick - ening
1 wise; grant us your power to make us strong.
2 ies have made us trust our - selves the more.
3 pride re - coil on un - re - pent - ant heads.
4 tence; in us the work of grace be - gin.
5 word, and turn our dark - ness in - to day.

Words: David W. Hughes (1911-1967), alt.
Music: *Uffingham*, melody and bass Jeremiah Clarke (1670-1707), alt.; harm. *Songs for Liturgy and More Hymns and Spiritual Songs*, 1971

♩ = 108
LM

Unison or harmony
1 E - ter - nal Lord of love, be - hold your Church
2 So dai - ly dy - ing to the way of self;
3 If dead in you, so in you we a - rise,
walk - ing once more the pil - grim way of Lent,
so dai - ly liv - ing to your way of love,
you the first - born of all the faith - ful dead;
led by your cloud by day, by night your fire,
we walk the road, Lord Je - sus, that you trod,
and as through ston - y ground the green shoots break,
moved by your love and toward your pres - ence bent:
know - ing our - selves bap - tized in - to your death:
glo - rious in spring - time dress of leaf and flower,

far off yet here— the goal of all de - sire.
so we are dead and live with you in God.
so in the Fa - ther's glo - ry shall we wake.

Words: Thomas H. Cain (b. 1931)
Music: *Old 124th*, melody *Pseaumes octante trois de David*, 1551; harm. Charles Winfred Douglas (1867-1944)

♩=96
10 10. 10 10 10

150

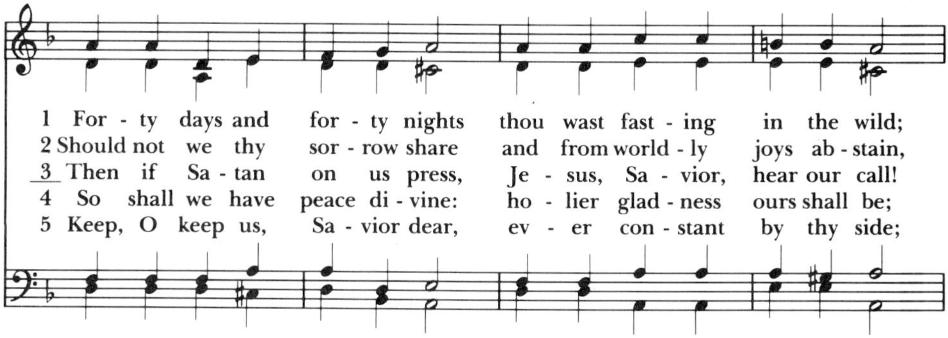
1 For - ty days and for - ty nights thou wast fast - ing in the wild;
2 Should not we thy sor - row share and from world - ly joys ab - stain,
3 Then if Sa - tan on us press, Je - sus, Sa - vior, hear our call!
4 So shall we have peace di - vine: ho - lier glad - ness ours shall be;
5 Keep, O keep us, Sa - vior dear, ev - er con - stant by thy side;

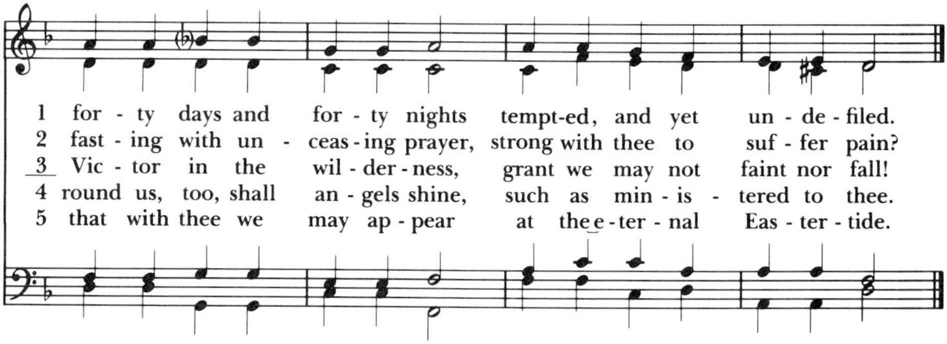
1 for - ty days and for - ty nights tempt-ed, and yet un - de - filed.
2 fast - ing with un - ceas - ing prayer, strong with thee to suf - fer pain?
3 Vic - tor in the wil - der - ness, grant we may not faint nor fall!
4 round us, too, shall an - gels shine, such as min - is - tered to thee.
5 that with thee we may ap - pear at the e - ter - nal Eas - ter - tide.

Words: George Hunt Smyttan (1822-1870), alt.
Music: *Aus der Tiefe rufe ich*, melody att. Martin Herbst (1654-1681), alt.; harm. William Henry Monk (1823-1889)

𝅗𝅥=52
77. 77

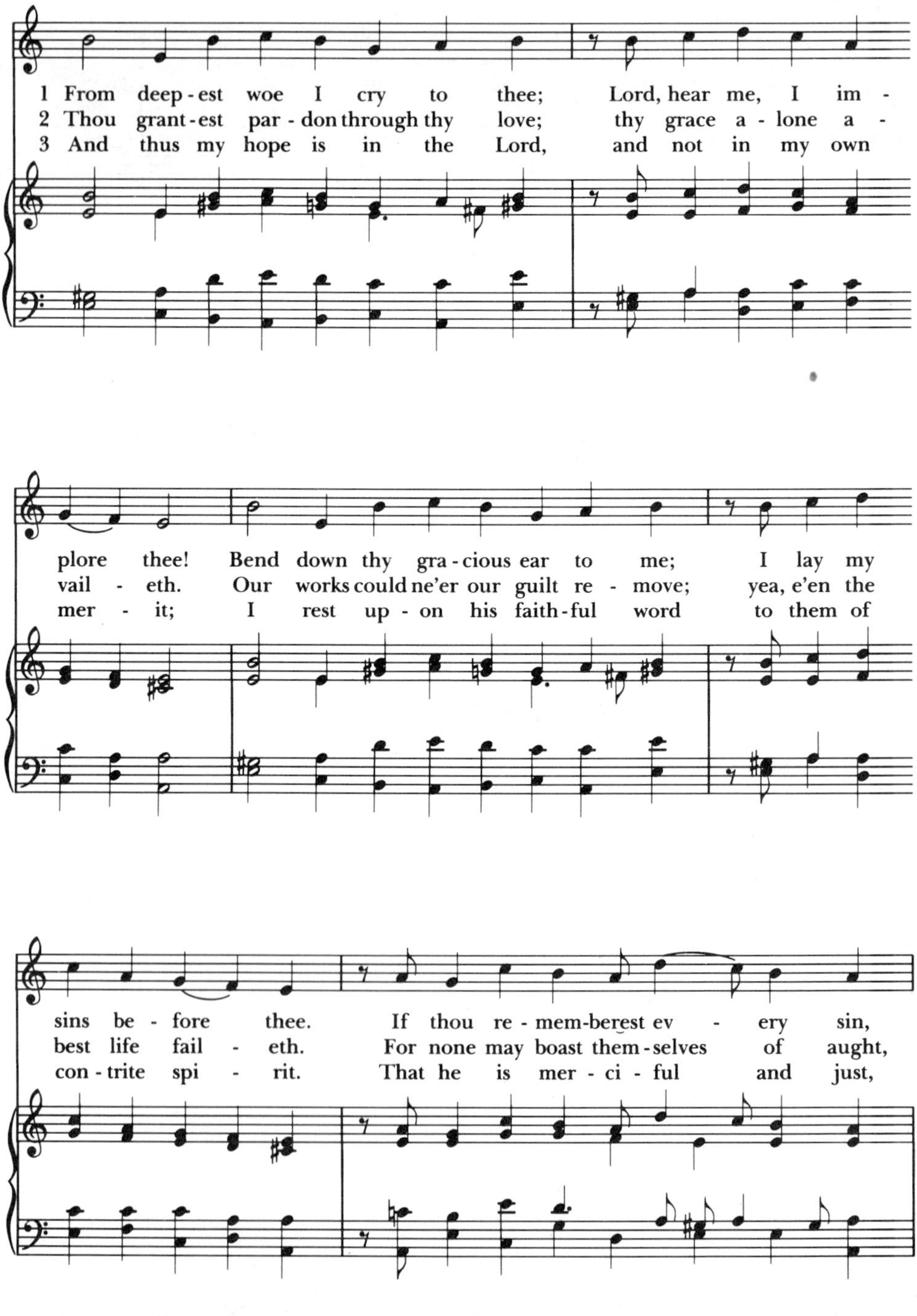
1 From deep-est woe I cry to thee; Lord, hear me, I im-
2 Thou grant-est par-don through thy love; thy grace a-lone a-
3 And thus my hope is in the Lord, and not in my own
plore thee! Bend down thy gra-cious ear to me; I lay my
vail-eth. Our works could ne'er our guilt re-move; yea, e'en the
mer-it; I rest up-on his faith-ful word to them of
sins be-fore thee. If thou re-mem-berest ev-ery sin,
best life fail-eth. For none may boast them-selves of aught,
con-trite spi-rit. That he is mer-ci-ful and just,

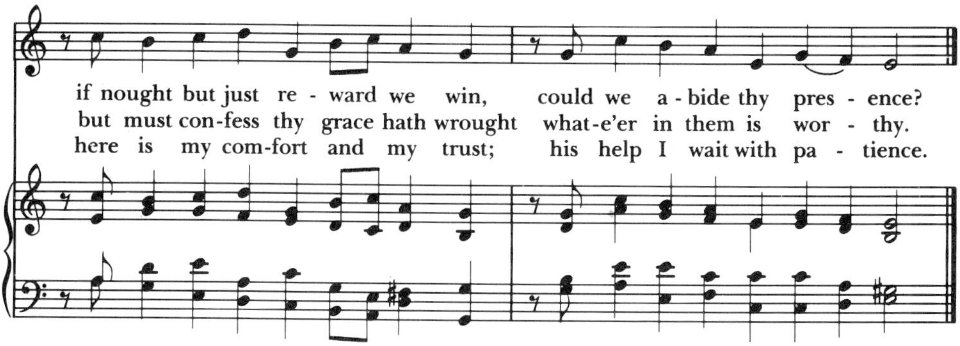
if nought but just re - ward we win, could we a - bide thy pres - ence?
but must con-fess thy grace hath wrought what-e'er in them is wor - thy.
here is my com-fort and my trust; his help I wait with pa - tience.

Words: Martin Luther (1483-1546); tr. Catherine Winkworth (1827-1878), alt.; based on Psalm 130
Music: *Aus tiefer Not,* melody att. Martin Luther (1483-1546); harm. Johann Herman Schein (1586-1630), alt.

♩=88
87. 87. 887

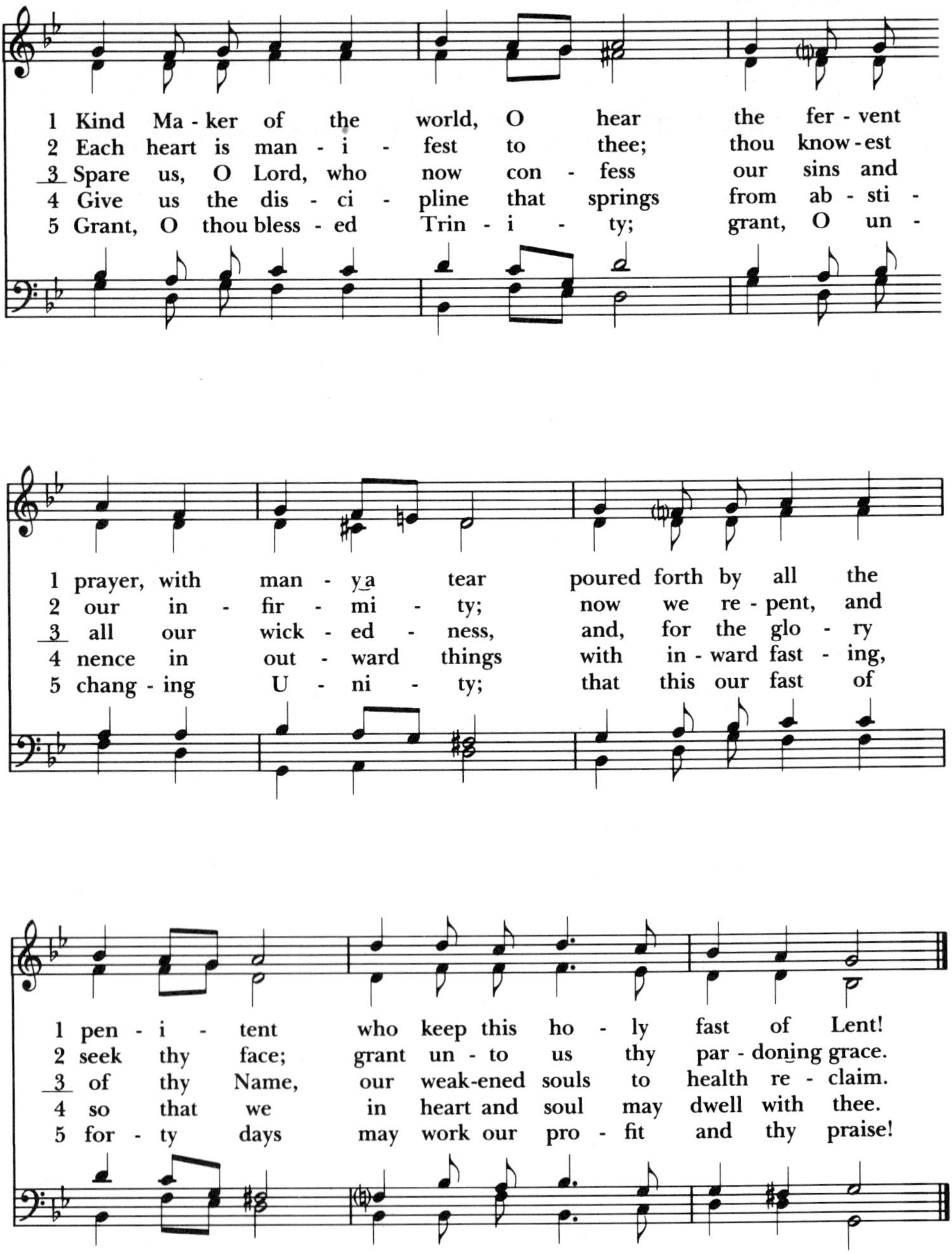
1 Kind Ma - ker of the world, O hear the fer - vent
2 Each heart is man - i - fest to thee; thou know - est
3 Spare us, O Lord, who now con - fess our sins and
4 Give us the dis - ci - pline that springs from ab - sti -
5 Grant, O thou bless - ed Trin - i - ty; grant, O un -
1 prayer, with man - y a tear poured forth by all the
2 our in - fir - mi - ty; now we re - pent, and
3 all our wick - ed - ness, and, for the glo - ry
4 nence in out - ward things with in - ward fast - ing,
5 chang - ing U - ni - ty; that this our fast of
1 pen - i - tent who keep this ho - ly fast of Lent!
2 seek thy face; grant un - to us thy par - doning grace.
3 of thy Name, our weak-ened souls to health re - claim.
4 so that we in heart and soul may dwell with thee.
5 for - ty days may work our pro - fit and thy praise!

Words: Att. Gregory the Great (540-604); ver. *Hymnal 1940,* alt.
Music: *A la venue de Noël,* melody from *Fleurs des noëls,* 1535

𝅗𝅥=76
LM

Opening Anthem

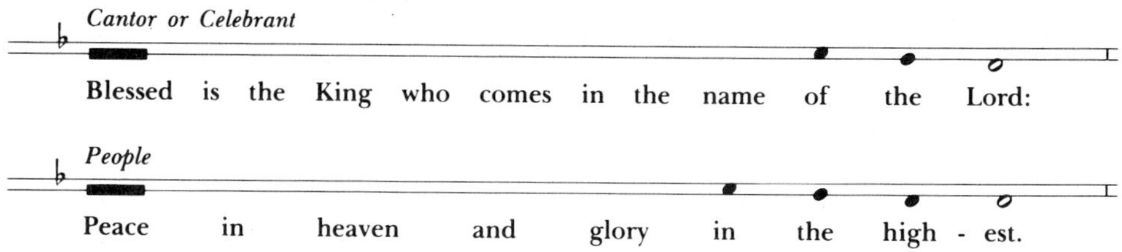
Cantor or Celebrant
Blessed is the King who comes in the name of the Lord:
People
Peace in heaven and glory in the high - est.

Blessing over the Branches

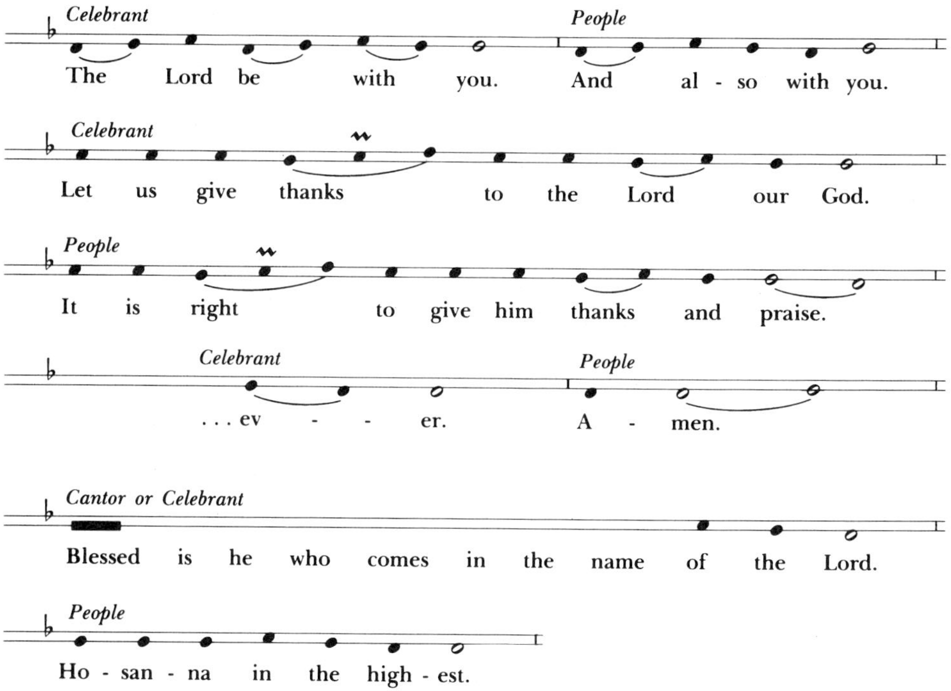
Celebrant
The Lord be with you.
People
And al - so with you.
Celebrant
Let us give thanks to the Lord our God.
People
It is right to give him thanks and praise.
Celebrant
. . . ev - - er.
People
A - men.
Cantor or Celebrant
Blessed is he who comes in the name of the Lord.
People
Ho - san - na in the high - est.

At the Procession

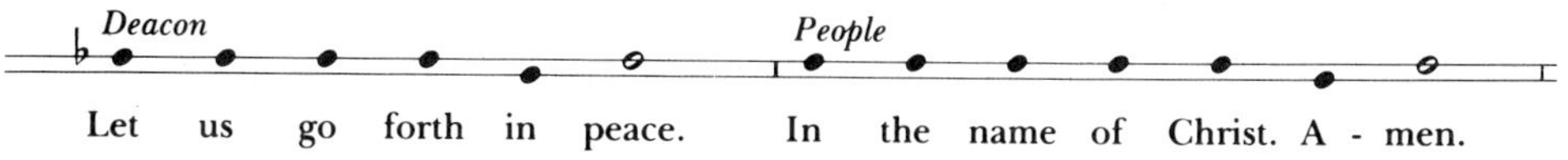
Deacon
Let us go forth in peace.
People
In the name of Christ. A - men.

154 The Liturgy of the Palms: Processional

Refrain
All glo - ry, laud, and hon - or to thee, Re-deem-er, King!
to whom the lips of chil - dren made sweet ho - san - nas ring.
1 Thou art the King of Is - ra - el, thou Da - vid's roy - al Son,
2 The com - pa - ny of an - gels is prais - ing thee on high;
3 The peo - ple of the He - brews with palms be - fore thee went;
4 To thee be - fore thy pas - sion they sang their hymns of praise;
5 Thou didst ac - cept their prais - es; ac - cept the prayers we bring,
Repeat Refrain
1 who in the Lord's Name com - est, the King and Bless - ed One.
2 and we with all cre - a - tion in cho - rus make re - ply.
3 our praise and prayers and an - thems be - fore thee we pre - sent.
4 to thee, now high ex - alt - ed, our mel - o - dy we raise.
5 who in all good de - light - est, thou good and gra - cious King.

The stanzas may be sung by choir alone or alternately by contrasted groups; all sing the refrain.
Another harmonization, 74. Alternative tune: *Gloria, laus, et honor,* 155.

Words: Theodulph of Orleans (d. 821); tr. John Mason Neale (1818-1866), alt.
Music: *Valet will ich dir geben,* melody Melchior Teschner (1584-1635), alt.; harm. William Henry Monk (1823-1889)

𝅗𝅥=54
76. 76. D

Bells used:
optional
Refrain (sung by all)
Bells
All glo - ry, laud, and hon - or to thee, Re - deem - er,
Tambourine
Drum; Finger Cymbals
King! to whom the lips of chil - dren made sweet ho - san - nas ring.
tr
Cantor or choir
1 Thou art the King of Is - ra - el, thou Da - vid's roy - al Son,
2 The com - pa - ny of an - gels is prais - ing thee on high;
3 The peo - ple of the He - brews with palms be - fore thee went;
4 To thee be - fore thy pas - sion they sang their hymns of praise;
5 Thou didst ac - cept their prais - es; ac - cept the prayers we bring,
Repeat Refrain
1 who in the Lord's Name com - est, the King and Bless - ed One.
2 and we with all cre - a - tion in cho - rus make re - ply.
3 our praise and prayers and an - thems be - fore thee we pre - sent.
4 to thee, now high ex - alt - ed, our mel - o - dy we raise.
5 who in all good de - light - est, thou good and gra - cious King.

Alternative tune: *Valet will ich dir geben,* 154.

Words: Theodulph of Orleans (d. 821); tr. John Mason Neale (1818-1866), alt.
Music: *Gloria, laus, et honor,* plainsong, Mode 1, Einsiedeln MS. and St. Gall MS., 10th cent.; ver. Schola Antiqua, 1983; acc. Richard Proulx (b. 1937)

𝅗𝅥 = 96
76. 76 with Refrain

1 Ride on! ride on in ma - jes - ty! Hark! all the
2 Ride on! ride on in ma - jes - ty! In low - ly
3 Ride on! ride on in ma - jes - ty! The an - gel
4 Ride on! ride on in ma - jes - ty! Thy last and
5 Ride on! ride on in ma - jes - ty! In low - ly
1 tribes ho - san - na cry; thy hum - ble beast pur - sues his
2 pomp ride on to die; O Christ, thy tri - umphs now be -
3 ar - mies of the sky look down with sad and won-dering
4 fierc - est strife is nigh; the Fa - ther on his sap - phire
5 pomp ride on to die; bow thy meek head to mor - tal
1 road with palms and scat - tered gar - ments strowed.
2 gin o'er cap - tive death and con - quered sin.
3 eyes to see the ap - proach - ing sac - ri - fice.
4 throne ex - pects his own a - noint - ed Son.
5 pain, then take, O God, thy power, and reign.

Alternative tune: *Winchester New*, 391.

Words: Henry Hart Milman (1791-1868), alt.
Music: *The King's Majesty*, Graham George (b. 1912)

𝅗𝅥=52
LM

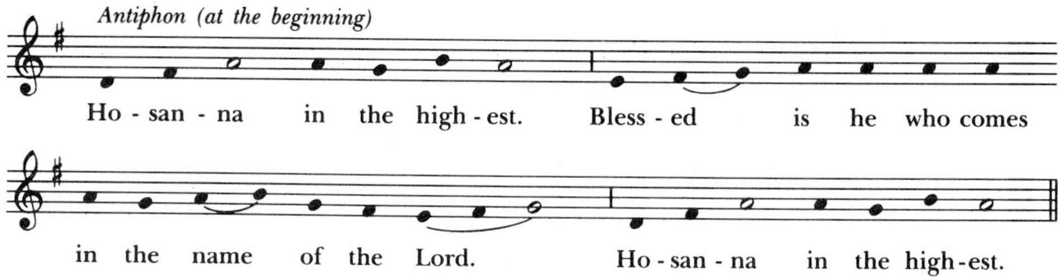
Antiphon (at the beginning)
Ho - san - na in the high - est. Bless - ed is he who comes
in the name of the Lord. Ho - san - na in the high - est.

(The concluding phrase of the antiphon, "Hosanna in the highest," may be repeated as a Refrain after each verse.)

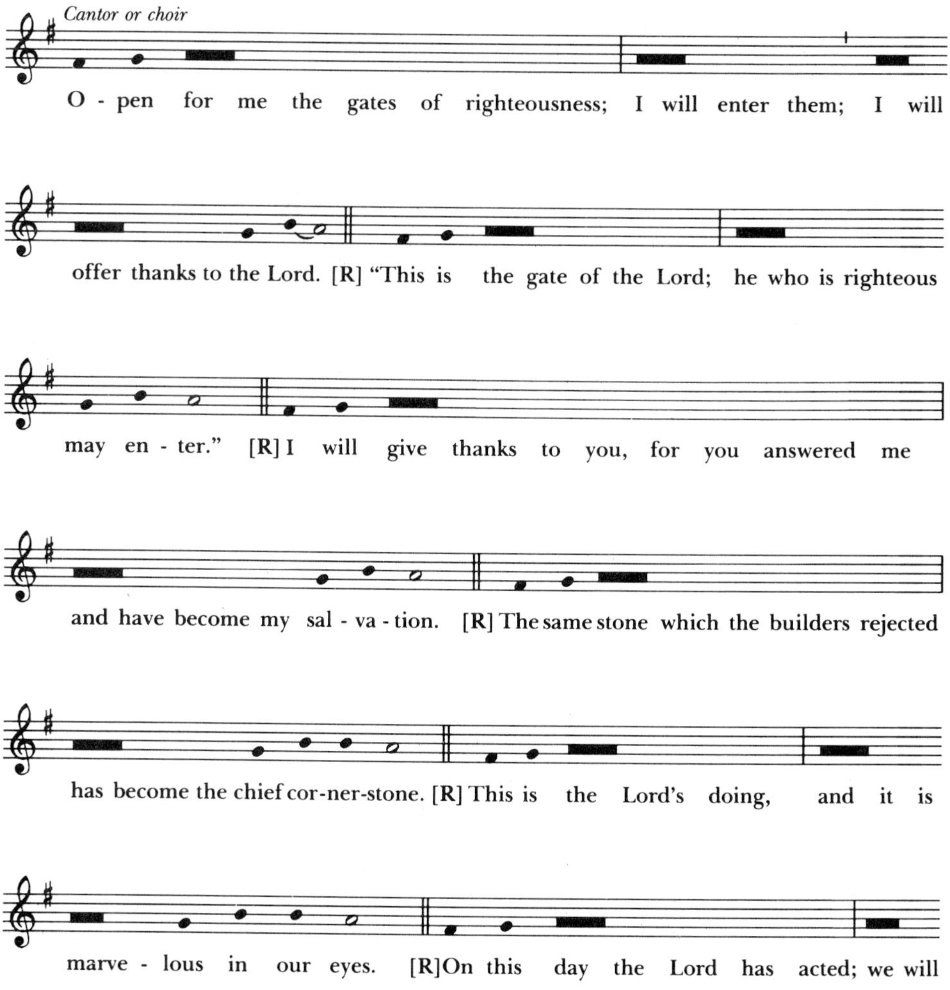
Cantor or choir
O - pen for me the gates of righteousness; I will enter them; I will
offer thanks to the Lord. [R] "This is the gate of the Lord; he who is righteous
may en - ter." [R] I will give thanks to you, for you answered me
and have become my sal - va - tion. [R] The same stone which the builders rejected
has become the chief cor-ner-stone. [R] This is the Lord's doing, and it is
marve - lous in our eyes. [R] On this day the Lord has acted; we will

rejoice and be glad in it. [R] Ho-san - na, Lord, hosanna! Lord, send us
now suc-cess. [R] Bless-ed is he who comes in the name of the Lord; we bless you
from the house of the Lord. [R] God is the Lord; he has shined upon us;
form a procession with branches up to the horns of the al - tar. [R]
"You are my God, and I will thank you; You are my God, and I will ex-alt you." [R]
Give thanks to the Lord, for he is good; his mercy endures for ev - er. [R]
Antiphon (at the end)
Ho - san - na in the high - est. Bless - ed is he who comes
in the name of the Lord. Ho - san - na in the high-est.

Words: Psalm 118:19-29
Music: Ancient Gallican chant; adapt. Howard E. Galley (b. 1929)

1 Ah, ho - ly Je - sus, how hast thou of - fend - ed, that man to
2 Who was the guilt - y? Who brought this up - on thee? A - las, my
3 Lo, the Good Shep - herd for the sheep is of - fered; the slave hath
4 For me, kind Je - sus, was thy in - car - na - tion, thy mor - tal
5 There-fore, kind Je - sus, since I can - not pay thee, I do a -
1 judge thee hath in hate pre - tend - ed? By foes de - rid - ed,
2 trea - son, Je - sus, hath un - done thee. 'Twas I, Lord Je - sus,
3 sin - ned, and the Son hath suf - fered; for our a - tone - ment,
4 sor - row, and thy life's ob - la - tion; thy death of an - guish
5 dore thee, and will ev - er pray thee, think on thy pi - ty
1 by thine own re - ject - ed, O most af - flict - ed.
2 I it was de - nied thee: I cru - ci - fied thee.
3 while we noth - ing heed - ed, God in - ter - ced - ed.
4 and thy bit - ter pas - sion, for my sal - va - tion.
5 and thy love un - swerv - ing, not my de - serv - ing.

Words: Johann Heermann (1585-1647); tr. Robert Seymour Bridges (1844-1930) 𝅗𝅥=52

Music: *Herzliebster Jesu,* Johann Cruger (1598-1662), alt. 11 11. 11 5

1 At the cross her vig - il keep - ing, stood the mourn - ful
2 With what pain and des - o - la - tion, with what grief and
3 Him she saw for our sal - va - tion mocked with cru - el
4 Who, on Christ's dear mo - ther gaz - ing, pierced by an - guish
5 Je - sus, may her deep de - vo - tion stir in me the
1 mo - ther weep - ing, where he hung, the dy - ing Lord:
2 res - ig - na - tion, Mar - y watched her dy - ing son.
3 ac - cla - ma - tion, scourged, and crowned with thorns en - twined;
4 so a - maz - ing, born of wo - man, would not weep?
5 same e - mo - tion, Fount of love, Re - deem - er kind;
1 there she wait - ed in her an - guish, see - ing Christ in
2 Deep the woe of her af - flic - tion, when she saw the
3 saw him then from judg - ment tak - en, and in death by
4 Who, on Christ's dear mo - ther think - ing, such a cup of
5 that my heart fresh ar - dor gain - ing, and a pur - er

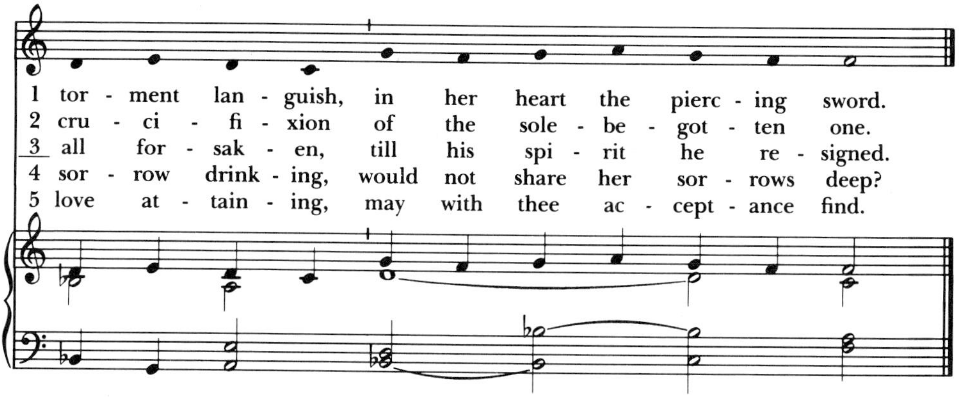
1 tor - ment lan - guish, in her heart the pierc - ing sword.
2 cru - ci - fi - xion of the sole - be - got - ten one.
3 all for - sak - en, till his spi - rit he re - signed.
4 sor - row drink - ing, would not share her sor - rows deep?
5 love at - tain - ing, may with thee ac - cept - ance find.

Words: Latin, 13th cent.; ver. *Hymnal 1982*
Music: *Stabat Mater dolorosa,* melody from *Maintzisch Gesangbuch,* 1661;
harm. Charles Winfred Douglas (1867-1944)

1 Cross of Je - sus, cross of sor - row, where the
2 Here the King of all the a - ges, throned in
3 O mys - ter - ious con - de - scend - ing! O a -
4 Cross of Je - sus, cross of sor - row, where the
blood of Christ was shed, per - fect Man on
light ere worlds could be, robed in mor - tal
ban - don - ment sub - lime! Ve - ry God him -
blood of Christ was shed, per - fect Man on
thee did suf - fer, per - fect God on thee has bled!
flesh is dy - ing, cru - ci - fied by sin for me.
self is bear - ing all the suf - fer - ings of time!
thee did suf - fer, per - fect God on thee has bled!

Words: William J. Sparrow-Simpson (1860-1952)
Music: *Cross of Jesus,* John Stainer (1840-1901)

𝅗𝅥=48
87. 87

1 The flam - ing ban - ners of our King ad - vance through
2 A Ro - man sol - dier drew a spear to mix his
3 The crowd would have been sat - is - fied to see a
4 With what strange light the rough trunk shone, its pur - ple
5 The best are shamed be - fore that wood; the worst gain
(Accompaniment optional)
1 his self - of - fer - ing. He lived to rob death
2 blood with wa - ter clear. That blood re - tains its
3 pro - phet cru - ci - fied. They stum - bled on a
4 limbs a roy - al throne, its load a roy - al
5 pow - er to be good. O grant, most bless - ed
1 of its sting; he died e - ter - nal life to bring.
2 liv - ing power; the wa - ter cleans - es to this hour.
3 mys - ter - y: Mes - si - ah reign - ing from a tree.
4 trea - sur - y: the ran - som of a world set free.
5 Trin - i - ty, that all may share the vic - to - ry.

Alternative tune: *Vexilla Regis prodeunt* (equalist rhythm), 162.

Words: Venantius Honorius Fortunatus (540?-600?); para. John Webster Grant (b. 1919)
Music: *Vexilla Regis prodeunt*, plainsong, Mode 1, Rome MS., 12th cent.; ver. Schola Antiqua, 1983; acc. David Hurd (b. 1950)

♩= 100
LM

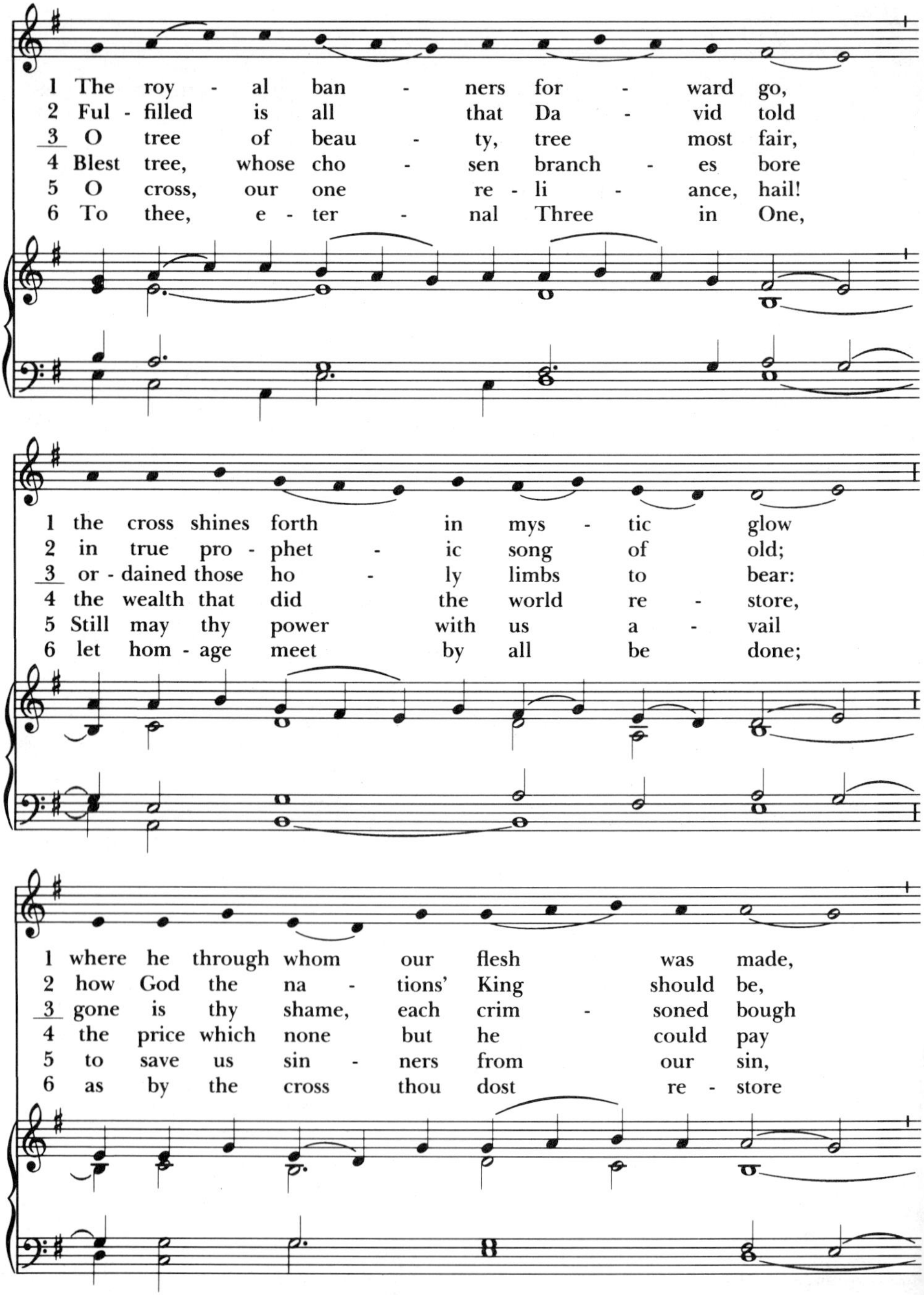
1 The roy - al ban - ners for - ward go,
2 Ful - filled is all that Da - vid told
3 O tree of beau - ty, tree most fair,
4 Blest tree, whose cho - sen branch - es bore
5 O cross, our one re - li - ance, hail!
6 To thee, e - ter - nal Three in One,
1 the cross shines forth in mys - tic glow
2 in true pro - phet - ic song of old;
3 or - dained those ho - ly limbs to bear:
4 the wealth that did the world re - store,
5 Still may thy power with us a - vail
6 let hom - age meet by all be done;
1 where he through whom our flesh was made,
2 how God the na - tions' King should be,
3 gone is thy shame, each crim - soned bough
4 the price which none but he could pay
5 to save us sin - ners from our sin,
6 as by the cross thou dost re - store

1 in that same flesh our ran - som paid.
2 for God is reign - ing from the tree.
3 pro - claims the King of glo - ry now.
4 to spoil the spoil - er of his prey.
5 God's right - eous - ness for all to win.
6 so rule and guide us ev - er - more.

Alternative tune: *Vexilla Regis prodeunt* (proportional), 161.

Words: Venantius Honorius Fortunatus (540?-600?); ver. *Hymnal 1982*
Music: *Vexilla Regis prodeunt,* plainsong, Mode 1, Rome MS., 12th cent.; acc. David Hurd (b. 1950) LM

Alternative accompaniment

Music: *Vexilla Regis prodeunt,* plainsong, Mode 1, Rome MS., 12th cent.; acc. Richard Proulx (b. 1937)

1 Sun - set to sun - rise chang - es now, for
2 E'en though the sun with - holds its light, lo!
3 Here in o'er - whelm - ing fi - nal strife the
God doth make his world a - new; on the Re - deem - er's
a more heaven - ly lamp shines here, and from the cross on
Lord of life hath vic - to - ry, and sin is slain, and
thorn-crowned brow the won - ders of that dawn we view.
Cal - vary's height gleams of e - ter - ni - ty ap - pear.
death brings life, and earth in - her - its hea - ven's key.

Another harmonization, 10.

Words: Clement of Alexandria (170?-220?); para. Howard Chandler Robbins (1876-1952), alt.
Music: *Kedron*, melody att. Elkanah Kelsay Dare (1782-1826); harm. Alec Wyton (b. 1921)

𝅗𝅥=58
LM

1 A - lone thou go - est forth, O Lord, in
2 Our sins, not thine, thou bear - est, Lord; make
3 This is earth's dark - est hour, but thou dost
4 Grant us with thee to suf - fer pain that,
sac - ri - fice to die; is this thy sor - row
us thy sor - row feel, till through our pit - y
light and life re - store; then let all praise be
as we share this hour, thy cross may bring us
nought to us who pass un - heed - ing by?
and our shame love an - swers love's ap - peal.
giv - en thee who liv - est ev - er - more.
to thy joy and re - sur - rec - tion power.

Words: Peter Abelard (1079-1142); tr. F. Bland Tucker (1895-1984)
Music: *Bangor,* from *A Compleat Melody or Harmony of Zion,* 1734

♩= 72
CM

1 Sing, my tongue, the glo - rious bat - tle;
2 Thir - ty years a - mong us dwell - ing,
3 He en - dures the nails, the spit - ting,
4 Faith - ful cross! a - bove all o - ther,
5 Bend thy boughs, O tree of glo - ry!
*6 Praise and hon - or to the Fa - ther,

1 of the might - y con - flict sing;
2 his ap - point - ed time ful - filled,
3 vin - e - gar, - and spear, and reed;
4 one and on - ly no - ble tree!
5 Thy re - lax - ing sin - ews bend;
6 praise and hon - or to the Son,

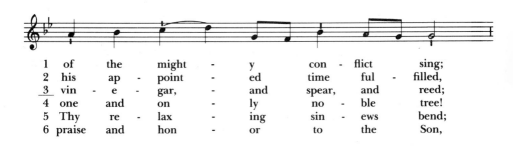

1 tell the tri - umph of the vic - tim,
2 born for this, he meets his pas - sion,
3 from that ho - ly bo - dy bro - ken
4 None in fo - liage, none in blos - som,
5 for a - while the an - cient ri - gor
6 praise and hon - or to the Spi - rit,

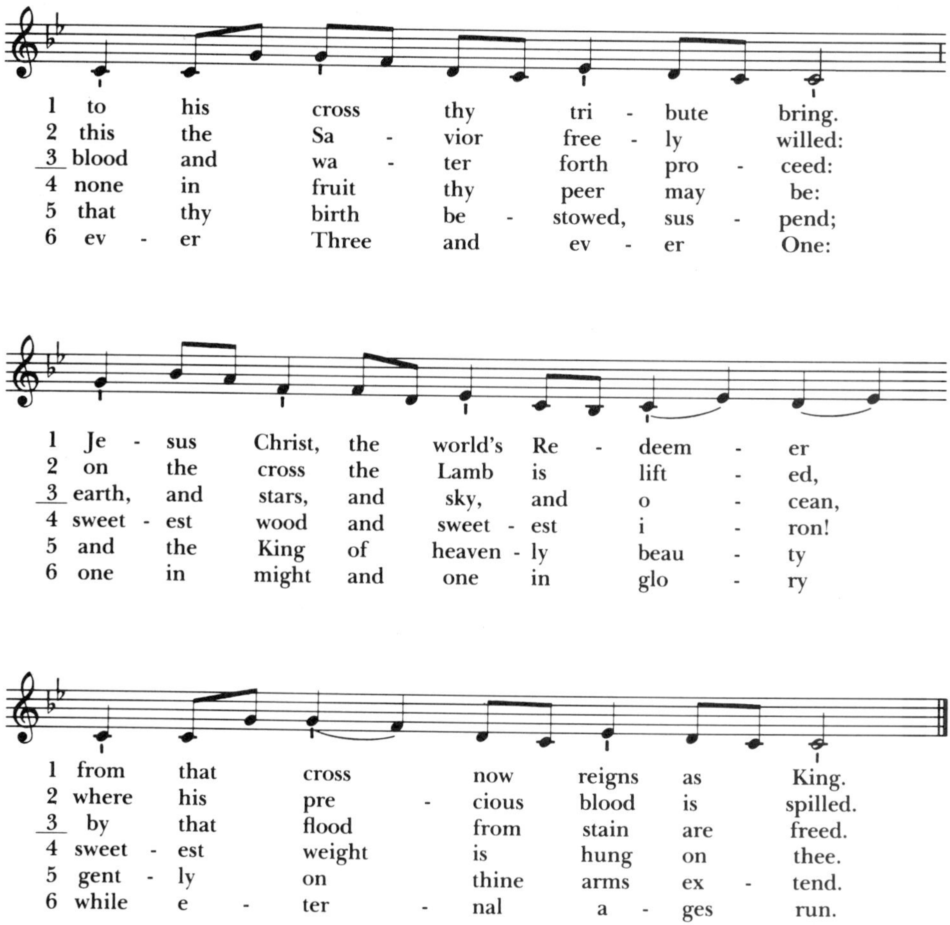
1 to his cross thy tri - bute bring.
2 this the Sa - vior free - ly willed:
3 blood and wa - ter forth pro - ceed:
4 none in fruit thy peer may be:
5 that thy birth be - stowed, sus - pend;
6 ev - er Three and ev - er One:
1 Je - sus Christ, the world's Re - deem - er
2 on the cross the Lamb is lift - ed,
3 earth, and stars, and sky, and o - cean,
4 sweet - est wood and sweet - est i - ron!
5 and the King of heaven - ly beau - ty
6 one in might and one in glo - ry
1 from that cross now reigns as King.
2 where his pre - cious blood is spilled.
3 by that flood from stain are freed.
4 sweet - est weight is hung on thee.
5 gent - ly on thine arms ex - tend.
6 while e - ter - nal a - ges run.

Alternative tune: *Pange lingua,* Mode 3 (equalist rhythm), 166.

Words: Venantius Honorius Fortunatus (540?-600?); ver. *Hymnal 1982,* after John Mason Neale (1818-1866)

Music: *Pange lingua,* plainsong, Mode 1, St. Gall MS., 10th cent.; ver. Schola Antiqua, 1983 — 87. 87. 87

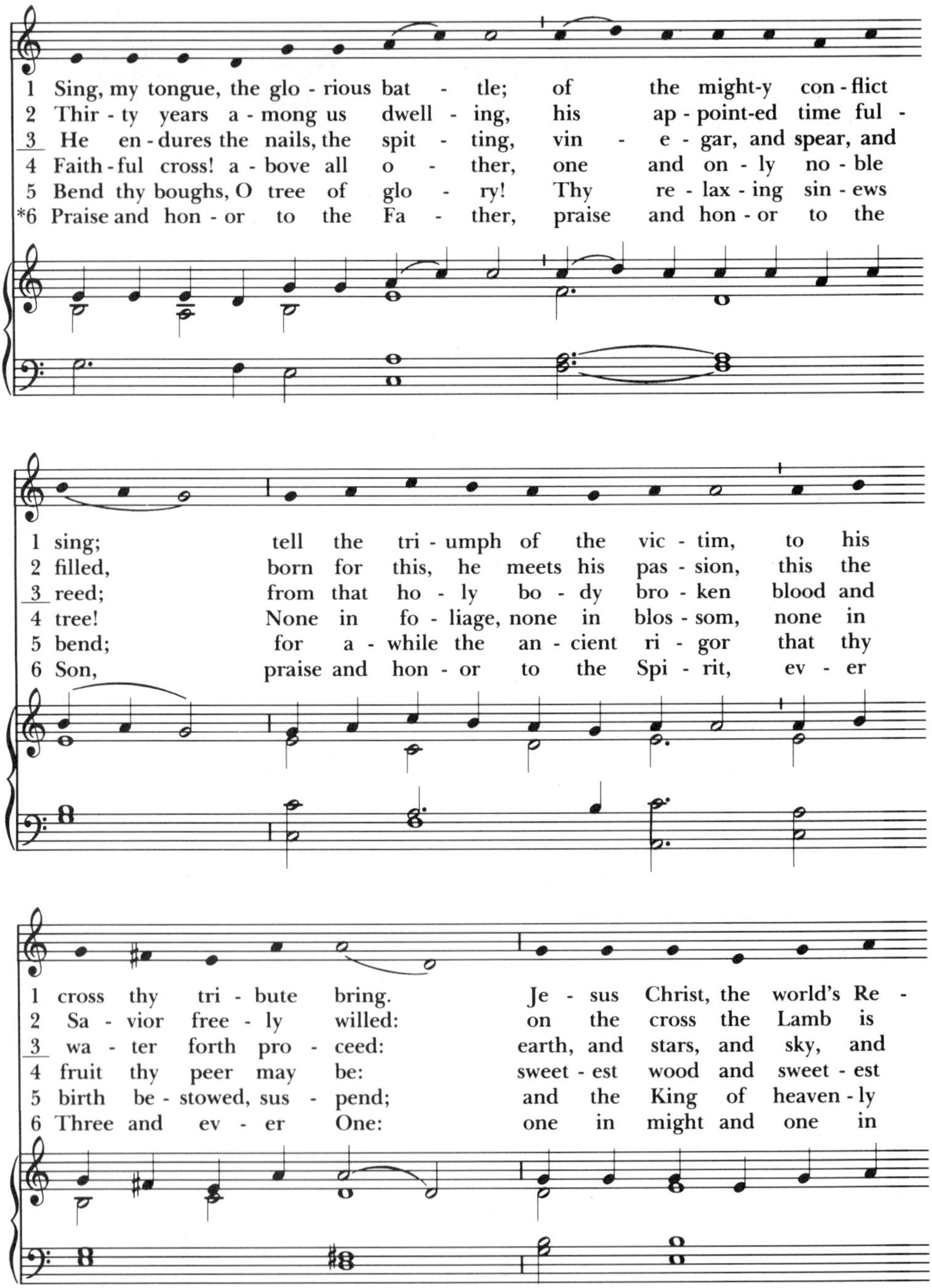
1 Sing, my tongue, the glo - rious bat - tle; of the might-y con - flict
2 Thir - ty years a - mong us dwell - ing, his ap - point-ed time ful -
3 He en - dures the nails, the spit - ting, vin - e - gar, and spear, and
4 Faith - ful cross! a - bove all o - ther, one and on - ly no - ble
5 Bend thy boughs, O tree of glo - ry! Thy re - lax - ing sin - ews
*6 Praise and hon - or to the Fa - ther, praise and hon - or to the
1 sing; tell the tri - umph of the vic - tim, to his
2 filled, born for this, he meets his pas - sion, this the
3 reed; from that ho - ly bo - dy bro - ken blood and
4 tree! None in fo - liage, none in blos - som, none in
5 bend; for a - while the an - cient ri - gor that thy
6 Son, praise and hon - or to the Spi - rit, ev - er
1 cross thy tri - bute bring. Je - sus Christ, the world's Re -
2 Sa - vior free - ly willed: on the cross the Lamb is
3 wa - ter forth pro - ceed: earth, and stars, and sky, and
4 fruit thy peer may be: sweet - est wood and sweet - est
5 birth be - stowed, sus - pend; and the King of heaven - ly
6 Three and ev - er One: one in might and one in

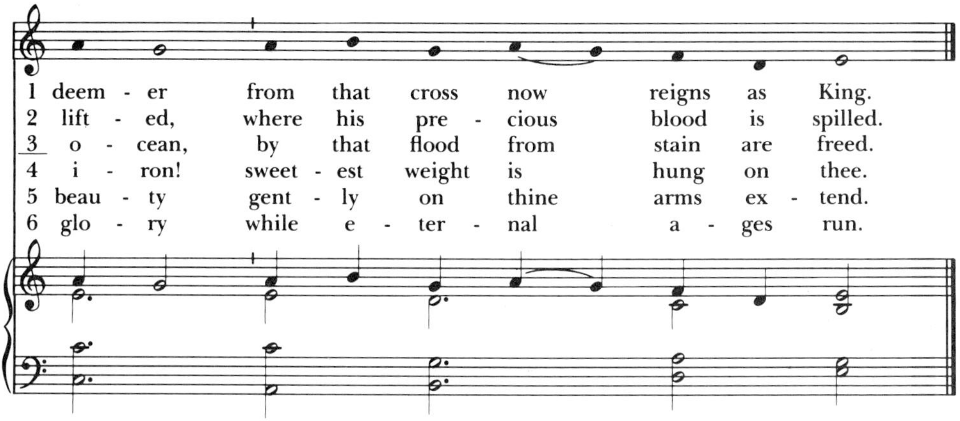
1 deem - er from that cross now reigns as King.
2 lift - ed, where his pre - cious blood is spilled.
3 o - cean, by that flood from stain are freed.
4 i - ron! sweet - est weight is hung on thee.
5 beau - ty gent - ly on thine arms ex - tend.
6 glo - ry while e - ter - nal a - ges run.

Another accompaniment, 329. Alternative tune: *Pange lingua,* Mode 1 (modal rhythm), 165.

Words: Venantius Honorius Fortunatus (540?-600?); ver. *Hymnal 1982,*
after John Mason Neale (1818-1866)

Music: *Pange lingua,* plainsong, Mode 3, *Zisterzienser Hymnar,* 14th cent.; acc. David Hurd (b. 1950) 87. 87. 78

Alternative accompaniment

Music: *Pange lingua,* plainsong, Mode 3, *Zisterzienser Hymnar,* 14th cent.; acc. *Hymnal 1940*

167

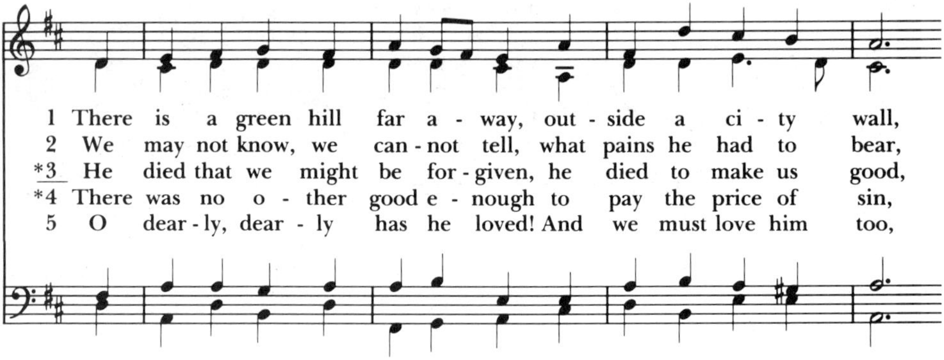
1 There is a green hill far a - way, out - side a ci - ty wall,
2 We may not know, we can - not tell, what pains he had to bear,
*3 He died that we might be for - given, he died to make us good,
*4 There was no o - ther good e - nough to pay the price of sin,
5 O dear - ly, dear - ly has he loved! And we must love him too,

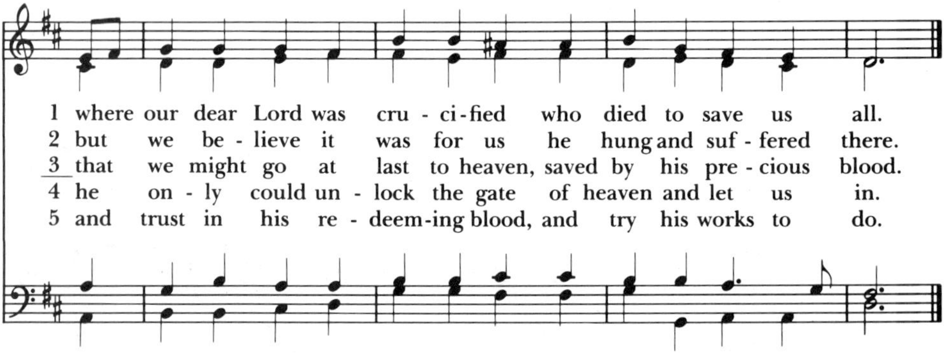
1 where our dear Lord was cru - ci - fied who died to save us all.
2 but we be - lieve it was for us he hung and suf - fered there.
3 that we might go at last to heaven, saved by his pre - cious blood.
4 he on - ly could un - lock the gate of heaven and let us in.
5 and trust in his re - deem - ing blood, and try his works to do.

Words: Cecil Frances Alexander (1818-1895), alt.
Music: *Horsley,* William Horsley (1774-1858)

𝅗𝅥=48
CM

168

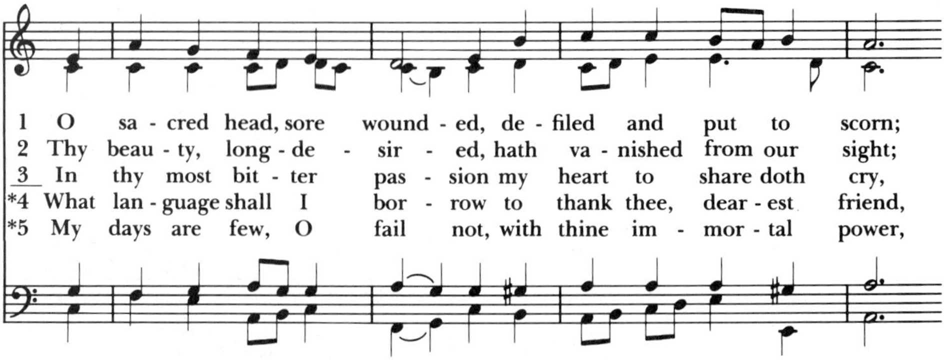
1 O sa - cred head, sore wound - ed, de - filed and put to scorn;
2 Thy beau - ty, long - de - sir - ed, hath va - nished from our sight;
3 In thy most bit - ter pas - sion my heart to share doth cry,
*4 What lan - guage shall I bor - row to thank thee, dear - est friend,
*5 My days are few, O fail not, with thine im - mor - tal power,

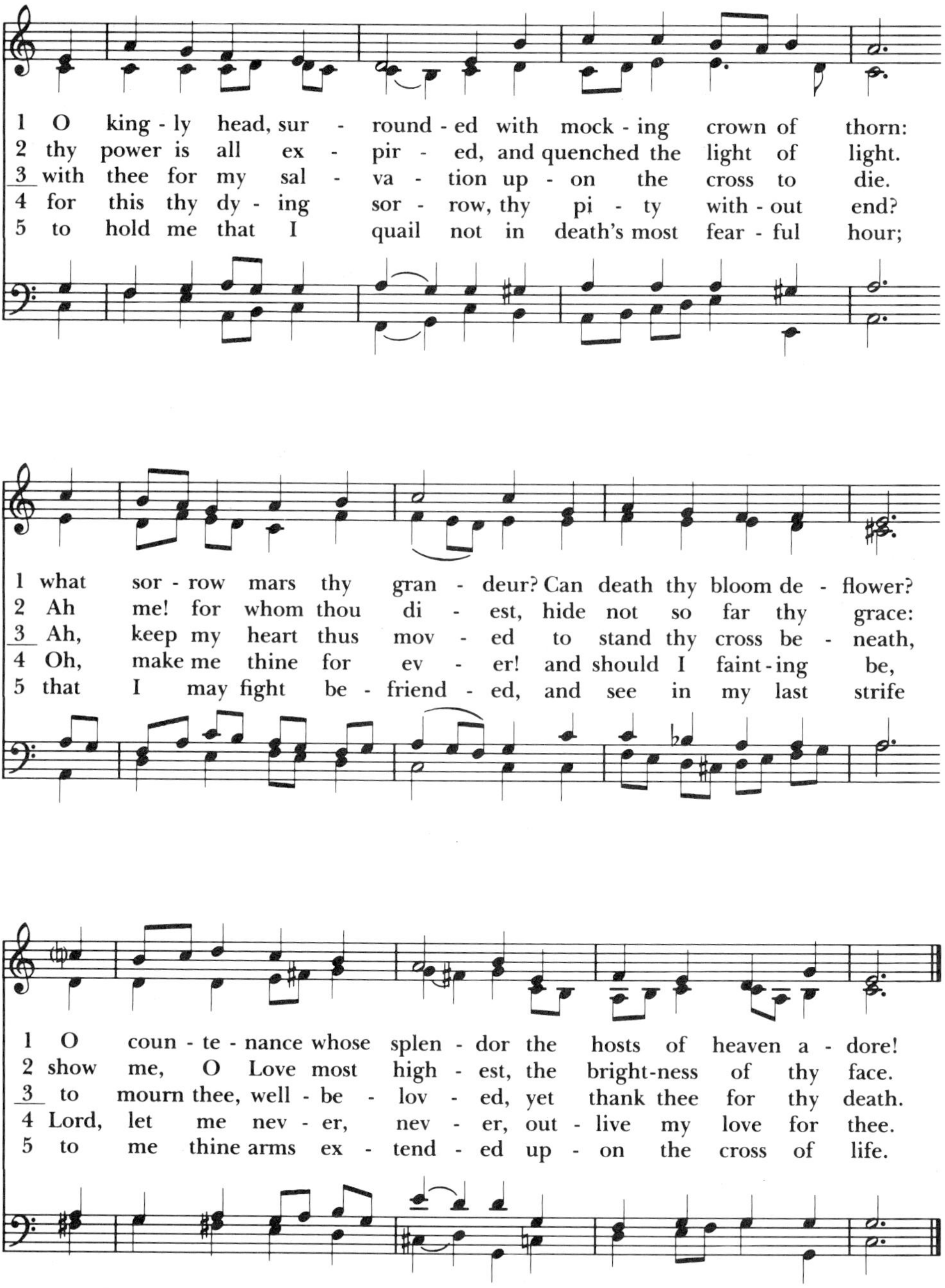
1 O king - ly head, sur - round - ed with mock - ing crown of thorn:
2 thy power is all ex - pir - ed, and quenched the light of light.
3 with thee for my sal - va - tion up - on the cross to die.
4 for this thy dy - ing sor - row, thy pi - ty with - out end?
5 to hold me that I quail not in death's most fear - ful hour;
1 what sor - row mars thy gran - deur? Can death thy bloom de - flower?
2 Ah me! for whom thou di - est, hide not so far thy grace:
3 Ah, keep my heart thus mov - ed to stand thy cross be - neath,
4 Oh, make me thine for ev - er! and should I faint - ing be,
5 that I may fight be - friend - ed, and see in my last strife
1 O coun - te - nance whose splen - dor the hosts of heaven a - dore!
2 show me, O Love most high - est, the bright-ness of thy face.
3 to mourn thee, well - be - lov - ed, yet thank thee for thy death.
4 Lord, let me nev - er, nev - er, out - live my love for thee.
5 to me thine arms ex - tend - ed up - on the cross of life.

Alternative tune: *Herzlich tut mich verlangen* (rhythmic), 169.

Words: Paul Gerhardt (1607-1676); sts. 1-3 and 5, tr. Robert Seymour Bridges (1844-1930); st. 4, tr. James Waddell Alexander (1804-1859), alt.

Music: *Herzlich tut mich verlangen [Passion Chorale]*, Hans Leo Hassler (1564-1612); adapt. and harm. Johann Sebastian Bach (1685-1750)

𝅗𝅥 = 72
76. 76. D

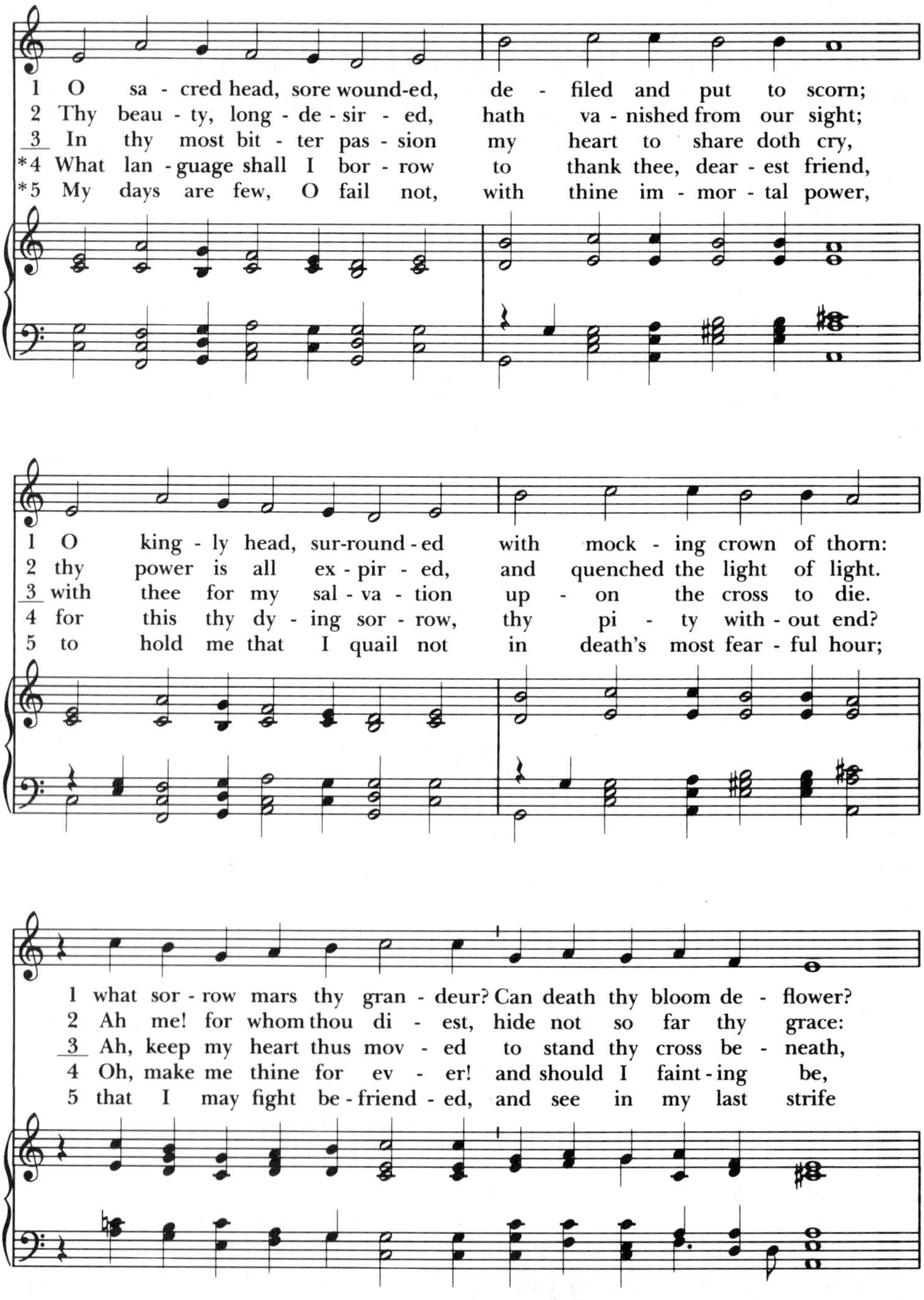
1 O sa - cred head, sore wound-ed, de - filed and put to scorn;
2 Thy beau - ty, long - de - sir - ed, hath va - nished from our sight;
3 In thy most bit - ter pas - sion my heart to share doth cry,
*4 What lan - guage shall I bor - row to thank thee, dear - est friend,
*5 My days are few, O fail not, with thine im - mor - tal power,
1 O king - ly head, sur-round - ed with mock - ing crown of thorn:
2 thy power is all ex - pir - ed, and quenched the light of light.
3 with thee for my sal - va - tion up - on the cross to die.
4 for this thy dy - ing sor - row, thy pi - ty with - out end?
5 to hold me that I quail not in death's most fear - ful hour;
1 what sor - row mars thy gran - deur? Can death thy bloom de - flower?
2 Ah me! for whom thou di - est, hide not so far thy grace:
3 Ah, keep my heart thus mov - ed to stand thy cross be - neath,
4 Oh, make me thine for ev - er! and should I faint - ing be,
5 that I may fight be - friend - ed, and see in my last strife

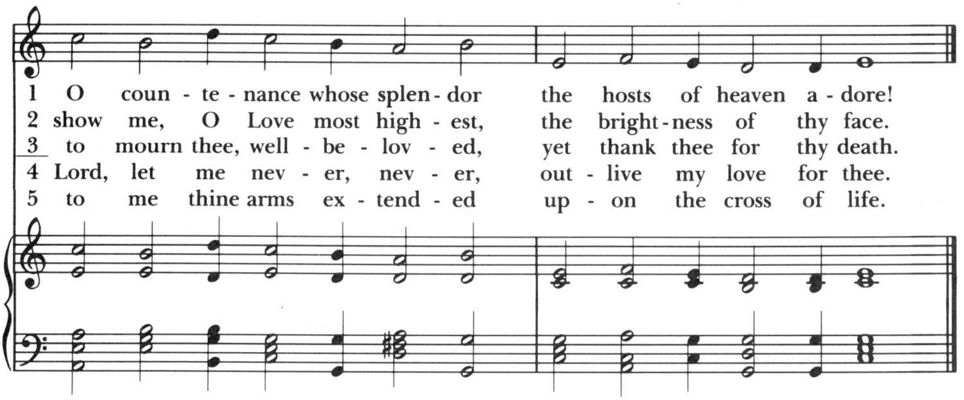
1 O coun - te - nance whose splen - dor the hosts of heaven a - dore!
2 show me, O Love most high - est, the bright - ness of thy face.
3 to mourn thee, well - be - lov - ed, yet thank thee for thy death.
4 Lord, let me nev - er, nev - er, out - live my love for thee.
5 to me thine arms ex - tend - ed up - on the cross of life.

Alternative tune: *Herzlich tut mich verlangen [Passion Chorale]* (isometric), 168.

Words: Paul Gerhardt (1607-1676); sts. 1-3 and 5, tr. Robert Seymour Bridges (1844-1930); st. 4, tr. James Waddell Alexander (1804-1859), alt.

𝅗𝅥 = 56

Music: *Herzlich tut mich verlangen,* Hans Leo Hassler (1564-1612)

76. 76. D

1 To mock your reign, O dear - est Lord, they made a crown of thorns;
2 In mock ac - claim, O gra - cious Lord, they snatched a pur - ple cloak,
3 A scep - tered reed, O pa - tient Lord, they thrust in - to your hand,
set you with taunts a - long that road from which no one re - turns.
your pas - sion turned, for all they cared, in - to a sol - dier's joke.
and act - ed out their grim cha - rade to its ap - point - ed end.
*
They did not know, as we do now, that glo - rious is your crown;
They did not know, as we do now, that though we mer - it blame
They did not know, as we do now, though em - pires rise and fall,
that thorns would flower up - on your brow, your sor - rows heal our own.
you will your robe of mer - cy throw a - round our na - ked shame.
your King - dom shall not cease to grow till love em - bra - ces all.

**The bracketed notes are to be treated as triplet groups.* This music in E, 692.

Words: F. Pratt Green (b. 1903), alt.
Music: *The Third Tune,* Thomas Tallis (1505?-1585); ed. John Wilson (b. 1905)

♩=82
CMD

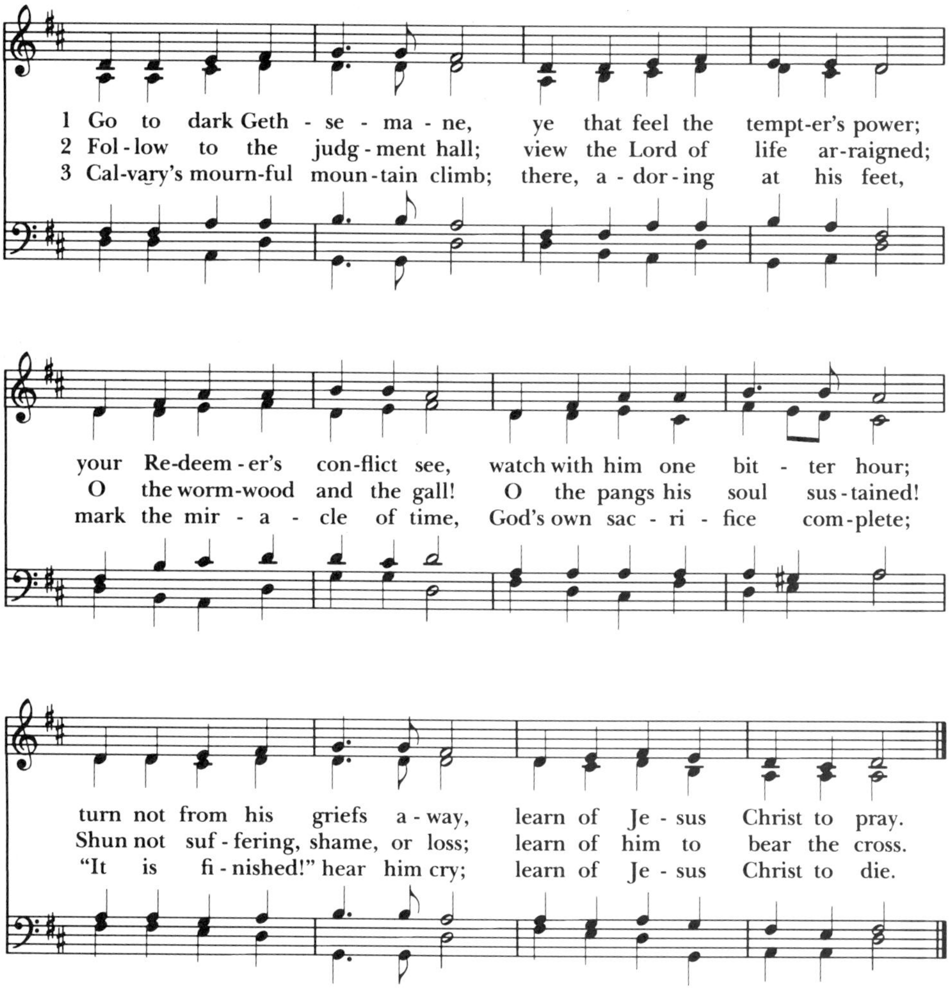
1 Go to dark Geth - se - ma - ne, ye that feel the tempt-er's power;
2 Fol - low to the judg - ment hall; view the Lord of life ar-raigned;
3 Cal-vary's mourn-ful moun-tain climb; there, a - dor - ing at his feet,
your Re-deem - er's con-flict see, watch with him one bit - ter hour;
O the worm-wood and the gall! O the pangs his soul sus - tained!
mark the mir - a - cle of time, God's own sac - ri - fice com-plete;
turn not from his griefs a - way, learn of Je - sus Christ to pray.
Shun not suf - fering, shame, or loss; learn of him to bear the cross.
"It is fi - nished!" hear him cry; learn of Je - sus Christ to die.

Words: James Montgomery (1771-1854)
Music: *Petra,* Richard Redhead (1820-1901)

𝅗𝅥=48
77. 77. 77

1 Were you there when they cru - ci - fied my Lord? Were you
2 Were you there when they nailed him to the tree? Were you
*3 Were you there when they pierced him in the side? Were you
4 Were you there when they laid him in the tomb? Were you
there when they cru - ci - fied my Lord? Oh!
there when they nailed him to the tree? Oh!
there when they pierced him in the side? Oh!
there when they laid him in the tomb? Oh!
Some - times it caus - es me to trem - ble, trem - ble,
Some - times it caus - es me to trem - ble, trem - ble,
Some - times it caus - es me to trem - ble, trem - ble,
Some - times it caus - es me to trem - ble, trem - ble,
trem - ble. Were you there when they cru - ci - fied my Lord?
trem - ble. Were you there when they nailed him to the tree?
trem - ble. Were you there when they pierced him in the side?
trem - ble. Were you there when they laid him in the tomb?

Words: Afro-American spiritual
Music: *Were You There*, Afro-American spiritual; harm. Charles Winfred Douglas (1867-1944)

𝅗𝅥=40
Irr.

1 O sor - row deep! Who would not weep
2 The Pas - chal Lamb, like I - saac's ram,
3 Blest shall they be e - ter - nal - ly
4 O Je - sus blest, my help and rest,
with heart - felt pain and sigh - ing!
in blood was of - fered for us,
who pon - der in their weep - ing
with tears I pray thee, hear me:
slightly slower
God the Fa - ther's on - ly Son
pour - ing out his life that he
that the glo - rious Prince of Life
now, and e - ven un - to death,
in the tomb is ly - ing.
might to life re - store us.
should in death be sleep - ing.
dear - est Lord, be near me.

Words: St. 1, Friedrich von Spee (1591-1635); tr. Charles Winfred Douglas (1867-1944). Sts. 2-3, James Waring McCrady (b. 1938). St. 4, Johann Rist (1607-1667); tr. Charles Winfred Douglas (1867-1944)

Music: *O Traurigkeit,* melody and bass *Himlischer Lieder,* 1641, alt.; harm. *Hymnal 1982*

𝅗𝅥=60

447. 76

1 At the Lamb's high feast we sing praise to our vic - to - rious King,
2 Where the Pas - chal blood is poured, death's dark an - gel sheathes his sword;
3 Might - y vic - tim from on high, hell's fierce powers be - neath thee lie;
4 Eas - ter tri - umph, Eas - ter joy, these a - lone do sin de - stroy.
who hath washed us in the tide flow - ing from his pierc - ed side;
Is - rael's hosts tri - um - phant go through the wave that drowns the foe.
thou hast con - quered in the fight, thou hast brought us life and light:
From sin's power do thou set free souls new - born, O Lord, in thee.
praise we him, whose love di - vine gives his sa - cred Blood for wine,
Praise we Christ, whose blood was shed, Pas - chal vic - tim, Pas - chal bread;
now no more can death ap - pall, now no more the grave en - thrall;
Hymns of glo - ry, songs of praise, Fa - ther, un - to thee we raise:
gives his Bo - dy for the feast, Christ the vic - tim, Christ the priest.
with sin - cer - i - ty and love eat we man - na from a - bove.
thou hast o - pened par - a - dise, and in thee thy saints shall rise.
ris - en Lord, all praise to thee with the Spi - rit ev - er be.

Words: Latin, 1632; tr. Robert Campbell (1814-1868), alt.
Music: *Salzburg,* melody Jakob Hintze (1622-1702); harm. Johann Sebastian Bach (1685-1750)

𝅗𝅥=48
77. 77. D

Refrain
Hail thee, fes - ti - val day! blest day that art hal-lowed for -
ev - er, day where-on Christ a - rose, break - ing the
king - dom of death.
First time only
death.
2

1 Lo, the fair beau - ty of earth, from the death of the win - ter a - ris - ing! Ev - ery good gift of the year now with its Mas - ter re - turns:
3 Dai - ly the love - li - ness grows, a - dorned with the glo - ry of blos - som; hea - ven her gates un - bars, fling - ing her in - crease of light:
5 God the Cre - a - tor, the Lord, who rul - est the earth and the hea - vens, guard us from harm with - out, cleanse us from e - vil with - in:
7 Spi - rit of life and of power, now flow in us, fount of our be - ing, light that dost light - en all, life that in all dost a - bide:
Repeat Refrain

2 He who was nailed to the cross is___ Lord and the
4 Rise from the grave now, O Lord, who art au - thor of
6 Je - sus the health of the world, en - light - en our
8 Praise to the Giv - er of good! Thou___ Love who art
ru - ler of na - ture; all things cre - a - ted on
life and cre - a - tion. Tread - ing the path - way of
minds, thou Re - deem - er, Son of the Fa - ther su -
au - thor of con - cord, pour out thy balm on our
Repeat Refrain
earth sing to the glo - ry of God:
death, life thou be - stow - est on all:
preme, on - ly - be - got - ten of God:
souls, or - der our ways in thy peace:

The refrain may be sung once by choir alone and repeated by all. The stanzas may be sung by choir alone, alternately by contrasted groups, or by all.

Words: Venantius Honorius Fortunatus (540?-600?); tr. *The English Hymnal,* 1906, alt. 𝅗𝅥=56

Music: *Salve festa dies,* Ralph Vaughan Williams (1872-1958) 79. 77 with Refrain

1 O-ver the cha - os of the emp-ty wa - ters hov-ered the
2 By the same Spi - rit we, re-gen-er - at - ed in-to the
3 By the same Spi - rit we are called to wor - ship God our Cre -
Spi - rit, bring-ing forth cre - a - tion; so from the emp - ty
bo - dy of our ris - en Sa - vior, seek through the pow - er
a - tor, Sa - vior, Sanc-ti - fi - er, of whom the glo - ry,
tomb the Sec-ond Ad - am is-sued tri - um - phant.
of the new cre - a - tion life ev - er - last - ing.
in both earth and hea - ven, is man - i - fest - ed.

Alternative tune: *Bickford,* 177.

Words: Sts. 1-2, *A Monastic Breviary,* 1976; st. 3, *Hymnal 1982*
Music: *West Park,* Robert Roth (b. 1928)

♩= 126
11 11. 11 5

1 O - ver the cha - os of the emp - ty wa - ters hov - ered the Spi - rit, bring-ing forth cre - a - tion; so from the emp - ty tomb the Sec - ond Ad - am is - sued tri-um - phant.
2 By the same Spi - rit we, re - gen - er - at - ed in - to the bo - dy of our ris - en Sa - vior, seek through the pow - er of the new cre - a - tion life ev - er-last - ing.
3 By the same Spi - rit we are called to wor - ship God our Cre - a - tor, Sa - vior, Sanc - ti - fi - er, of whom the glo - ry, in both earth and hea - ven, is man - i - fest - ed.

Alternative tune: *West Park,* 176.

Words: Sts. 1-2, *A Monastic Breviary,* 1976; st. 3, *Hymnal 1982*
Music: *Bickford,* Hank Beebe (b. 1926)

♩=84
11 11. 11 5

Descant

Al - le - lu - ia, al - le -

Refrain E(D) C#m(Bm) F#m(Em)

Al - le - lu - ia, al - le - lu - ia! Give thanks to the

lu - ia, al - le - lu - ia!

Bm(Am) E(D) C#m(Bm)

ris - en Lord. Al - le - lu - ia, al - le - lu - ia! Give

1-4 Final Ending

Praise to his Name. Name.

F#m(Em) B(A) E(D) E(D)

praise to his Name. Name.

E(D)
C♯m(Bm)
F♯m(Em)
B(A)
1 Je - sus is Lord of all the earth.
2 Spread the good news o'er all the earth:
3 We have been cru - ci - fied with Christ.
4 Come, let us praise the liv - ing God,
E(D)
C♯m(Bm)
F♯m(Em)
B(A)
Repeat Refrain
He is the King of cre - a - tion.
Je - sus has died and has ris - en.
Now we shall live for ev - er.
joy - ful - ly sing to our Sa - vior.
Al-le -

E(capo 2, D). The descant may be sung after stanzas 3 and 4.

Words: Donald Fishel (b. 1950)
Music: *Alleluia No. 1,* Donald Fishel (b. 1950); arr. Betty Pulkingham (b. 1928), Charles Mallory (b. 1950) and George Mims (b. 1938)

♩=72
88 with Refrain

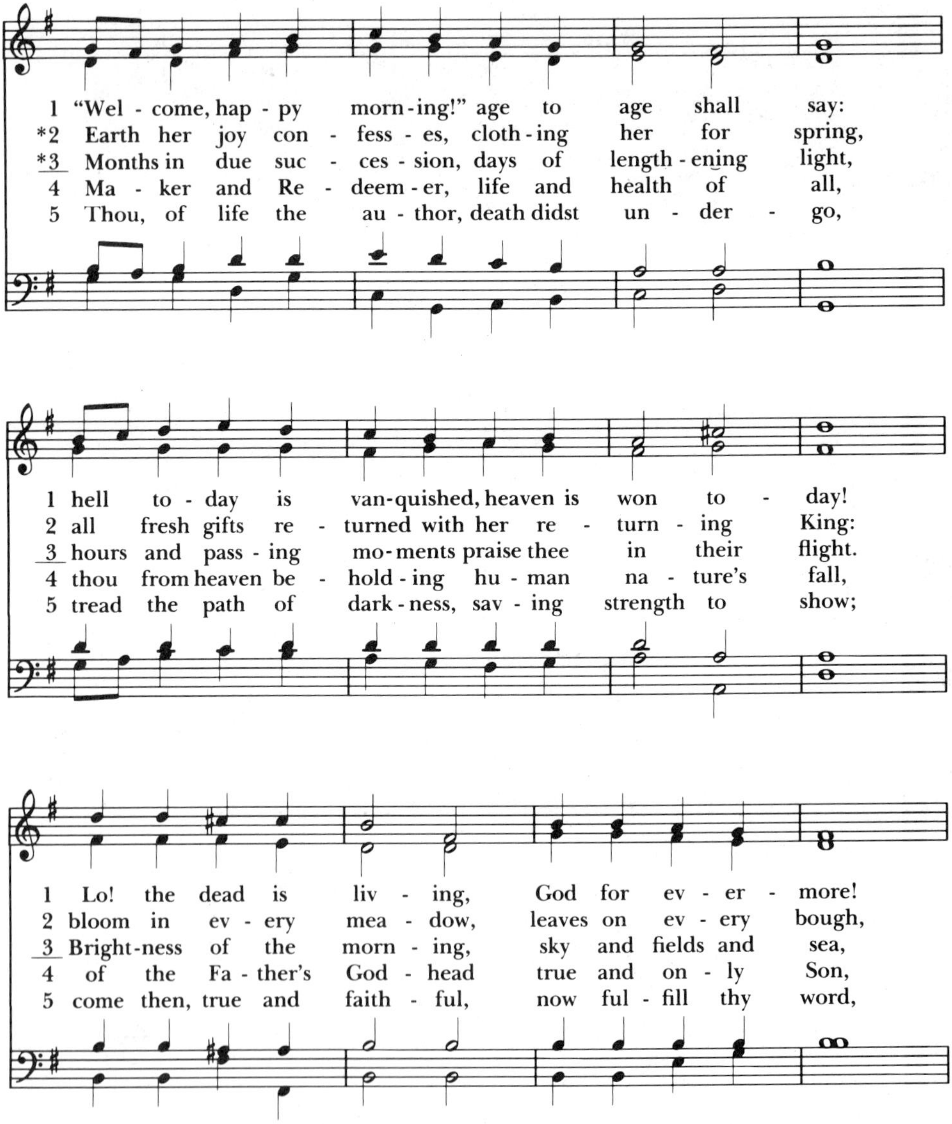
1 "Wel - come, hap - py morn - ing!" age to age shall say:
*2 Earth her joy con - fess - es, cloth - ing her for spring,
*3 Months in due suc - ces - sion, days of length - ening light,
4 Ma - ker and Re - deem - er, life and health of all,
5 Thou, of life the au - thor, death didst un - der - go,
1 hell to - day is van-quished, heaven is won to - day!
2 all fresh gifts re - turned with her re - turn - ing King:
3 hours and pass - ing mo-ments praise thee in their flight.
4 thou from heaven be - hold - ing hu - man na - ture's fall,
5 tread the path of dark - ness, sav - ing strength to show;
1 Lo! the dead is liv - ing, God for ev - er - more!
2 bloom in ev - ery mea - dow, leaves on ev - ery bough,
3 Bright-ness of the morn - ing, sky and fields and sea,
4 of the Fa - ther's God - head true and on - ly Son,
5 come then, true and faith - ful, now ful - fill thy word,

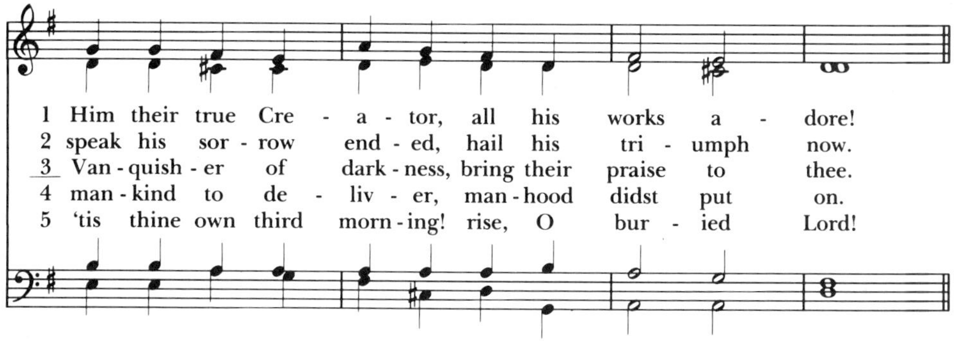
1 Him their true Cre - a - tor, all his works a - dore!
2 speak his sor - row end - ed, hail his tri - umph now.
3 Van - quish - er of dark - ness, bring their praise to thee.
4 man - kind to de - liv - er, man - hood didst put on.
5 'tis thine own third morn - ing! rise, O bur - ied Lord!

Refrain

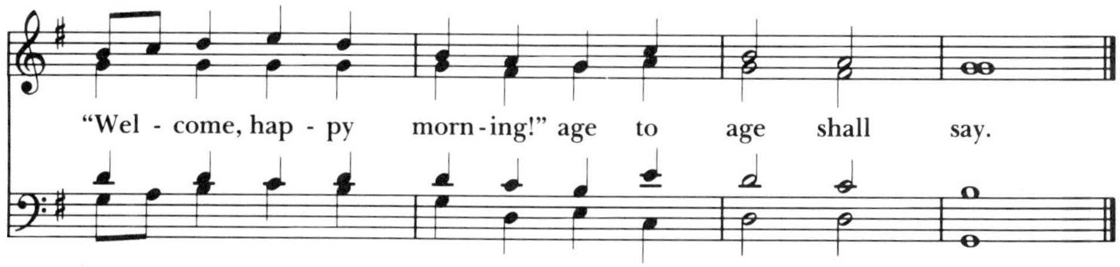
"Wel - come, hap - py morn - ing!" age to age shall say.

6 Loose the souls long prisoned, bound with Satan's chain;
all that now is fallen raise to life again;
show thy face in brightness, bid the nations see;
bring again our daylight: day returns with thee!

Refrain

Words: Venantius Honorius Fortunatus (540?-600?); tr. John Ellerton (1826-1893), alt. 𝅗𝅥=54
Music: *Fortunatus*, Arthur Seymour Sullivan (1842-1900) 11 11. 11 11. 11

1 He is ris - en, he is ris - en! Tell it out with
2 Come, ye sad and fear - ful - heart - ed, with glad smile and
*3 Come, with high and ho - ly hymn - ing, hail our Lord's tri -
4 He is ris - en, he is ris - en! He hath o - pened
joy - ful voice: he has burst his three days' pris - on;
ra - diant brow! Death's long sha - dows have de - part - ed;
um - phant day; not one dark - some cloud is dim - ming
hea - ven's gate: we are free from sin's dark pris - on,
let the whole wide earth re - joice: death is con - quered,
Je - sus' woes are o - ver now, and the pas - sion
yon - der glo - rious morn - ing ray, break - ing o'er the
ris - en to a ho - lier state; and a bright - er
we are free, Christ has won the vic - to - ry.
that he bore— sin and pain can vex no more.
pur - ple east, sym - bol of our Eas - ter feast.
Eas - ter beam on our long - ing eyes shall stream.

Words: Cecil Frances Alexander (1818-1895), alt.
Music: *Unser Herrscher*, Joachim Neander (1650-1680)

𝅗𝅥=52
87. 87. 77

Descant
4 Soon shall each rap - tured tongue his
1 A - wake and sing the song of
2 Sing of his dy - ing love, his
3 You pil - grims on the road to
4 Soon shall each rap - tured tongue his
end - less praise pro - claim, and sing in sweet - er
Mo - ses and the Lamb; wake ev - ery heart and
re - sur - rec - tion power; sing how he in - ter -
Zi - on's ci - ty, sing, re - joic - ing in the
end - less praise pro - claim, and sing in sweet - er
notes the song of Mo - ses and the Lamb.
ev - ery tongue to praise the Sa - vior's name.
cedes a - bove for those whose sins he bore.
Lamb of God, to Christ the e - ter - nal King.
notes the song of Mo - ses and the Lamb.

Words: William Hammond (1719-1783), alt.
Music: *St. Ethelwald,* William Henry Monk (1823-1889)

𝅗𝅥=56
SM

1 Christ is a - live! Let Chris - tians sing. His cross stands
2 Christ is a - live! No long - er bound to dis - tant
3 Not throned a - bove, re - mote - ly high, un - touched, un -
4 In ev - ery in - sult, rift, and war where co - lor,
5 Christ is a - live! His Spi - rit burns through this and
1 emp - ty to the sky. Let streets and homes with
2 years in Pal - es - tine, he comes to claim the
3 moved by hu - man pains, but dai - ly, in the
4 scorn or wealth di - vide, he suf - fers still, yet
5 ev - ery fu - ture age, till all cre - a - tion
1 prais - es ring. His love in death shall nev - er die.
2 here and now and con - quer ev - ery place and time.
3 midst of life, our Sa - vior with the Fa - ther reigns.
4 loves the more, and lives, though ev - er cru - ci - fied.
5 lives and learns his joy, his jus - tice, love, and praise.

Words: Brian A. Wren (b. 1936), rev.
Music: *Truro,* melody from *Psalmodia Evangelica, Part II,* 1789; harm. Lowell Mason (1792-1872), alt.

𝅗𝅥=96
LM

All
1. Chris-tians, to the Pas-chal vic-tim of-fer your thank-ful prais-es!
Men
2. A lamb the sheep re-deem-eth: Christ, who on-ly is sin-less,
rec-on-cil-eth sin-ners to the Fa-ther.
Trebles
3. Death and life have con-tend-ed in that com-bat stu-pen-dous:

the Prince of life, who died, reigns im - mor - tal.
Men
4. Speak, Ma - ry, de - clar - ing what thou saw - est, way - far - ing:
Trebles
5. "The tomb of Christ, who is liv - ing, the glo - ry of
Je - sus' re - sur - rec - tion;
6. bright an - gels at - test - ing,

the shroud and nap - kin rest - ing. 7. Yea, Christ my hope is a -
ris - en; to Gal - i - lee he will go be - fore you."
All
8. Christ in - deed from death is ris - en, our new life ob - tain - ing;
have mer - cy, vic - tor King, ev - er reign - ing!

A - men. Al - le - lu - ia!

The melody may be played on a solo stop (reed or cornet).

Words: Wigbert [Wipo of Burgundy] (d. 1050?); tr. *The Antiphoner and Grail,* 1880, alt.
Music: *Victimae Paschali laudes,* plainsong, Mode 1; melody att. Wigbert [Wipo of Burgundy] (d. 1050?); acc. Richard Proulx (b. 1937) Irr.

184

Easter

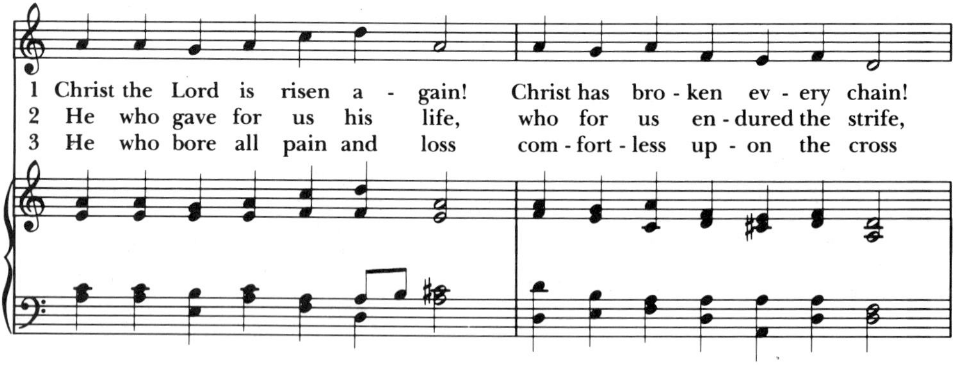
1 Christ the Lord is risen a - gain! Christ has bro - ken ev - ery chain!
2 He who gave for us his life, who for us en - dured the strife,
3 He who bore all pain and loss com - fort - less up - on the cross

Now through all the world it rings that the Lamb is King of kings.
takes our sin and guilt a - way that with an - gels we may say:
is ex - alt - ed now to save, wrest - ing vic - tory from the grave.

Refrain
Al - le - lu - ia!
Al - le - lu - ia! Al - le - lu - ia, al - le - lu - ia,
Al - le - lu - ia!
al - le - lu - ia! Christ, our Pas - chal Lamb in - deed,
Christ, to - day your peo - ple feed. Al - le - lu - ia!

This melody is based on Victimae Paschali laudes, 183. *The two hymns may be sung in alternation between two groups (or solists). One group (or soloist) sings the* Victimae *(transposed a whole step lower), pausing after stanzas 3, 7 and 8. At these points another group (or soloist) sings successive thirds of* Christ is erstanden.

Words: Michael Weisse (1480-1534); tr. Catherine Winkworth (1827-1878), alt.
Music: *Christ ist erstanden,* melody from *Geistliche Lieder,* 1533;
harm. after Hans Leo Hassler (1564-1612)

𝅗𝅥=66
77. 77. 4 with Refrain

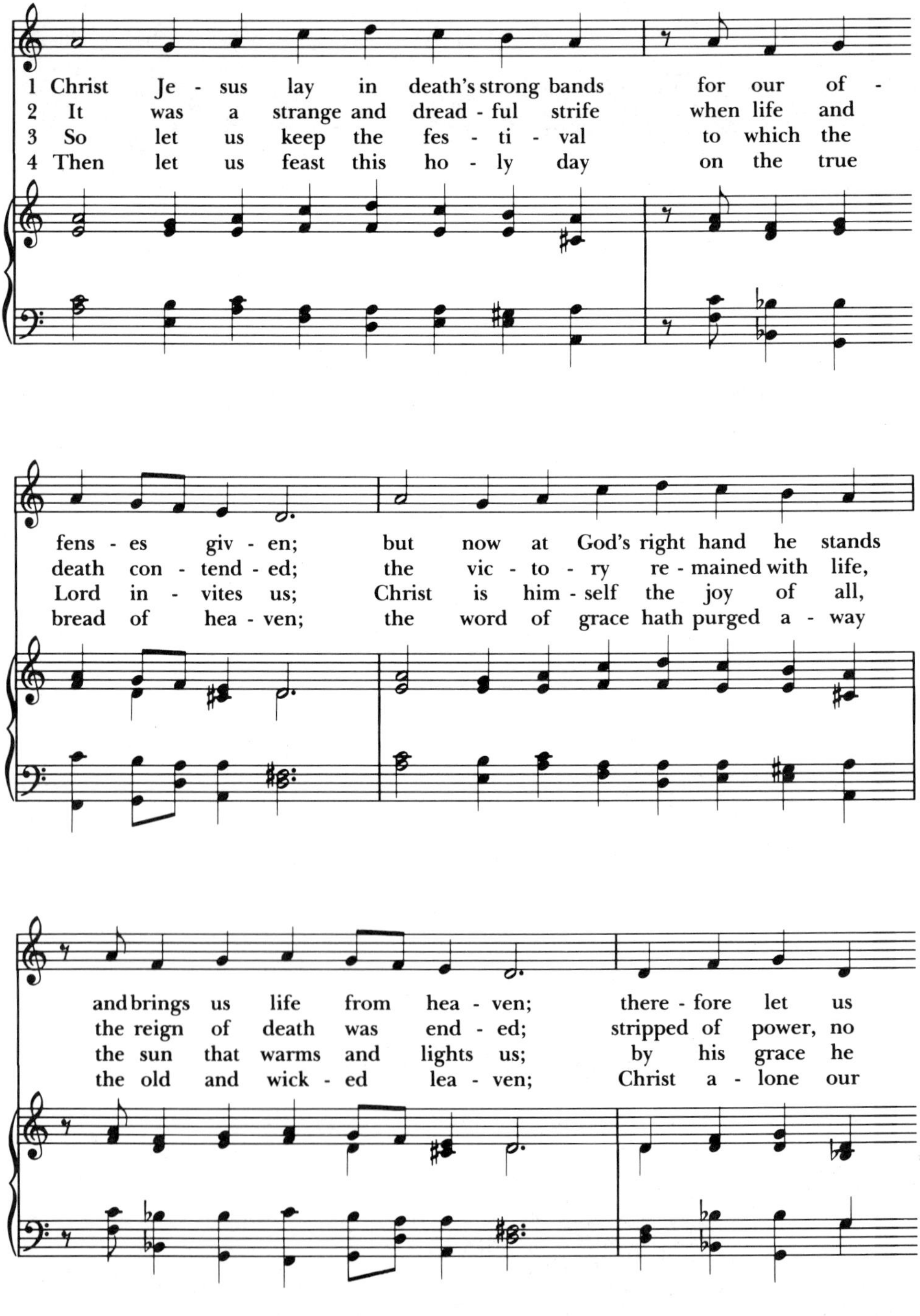

1 Christ Je - sus lay in death's strong bands for our of -
2 It was a strange and dread - ful strife when life and
3 So let us keep the fes - ti - val to which the
4 Then let us feast this ho - ly day on the true

fens - es giv - en; but now at God's right hand he stands
death con - tend - ed; the vic - to - ry re - mained with life,
Lord in - vites us; Christ is him - self the joy of all,
bread of hea - ven; the word of grace hath purged a - way

and brings us life from hea - ven; there - fore let us
the reign of death was end - ed; stripped of power, no
the sun that warms and lights us; by his grace he
the old and wick - ed lea - ven; Christ a - lone our

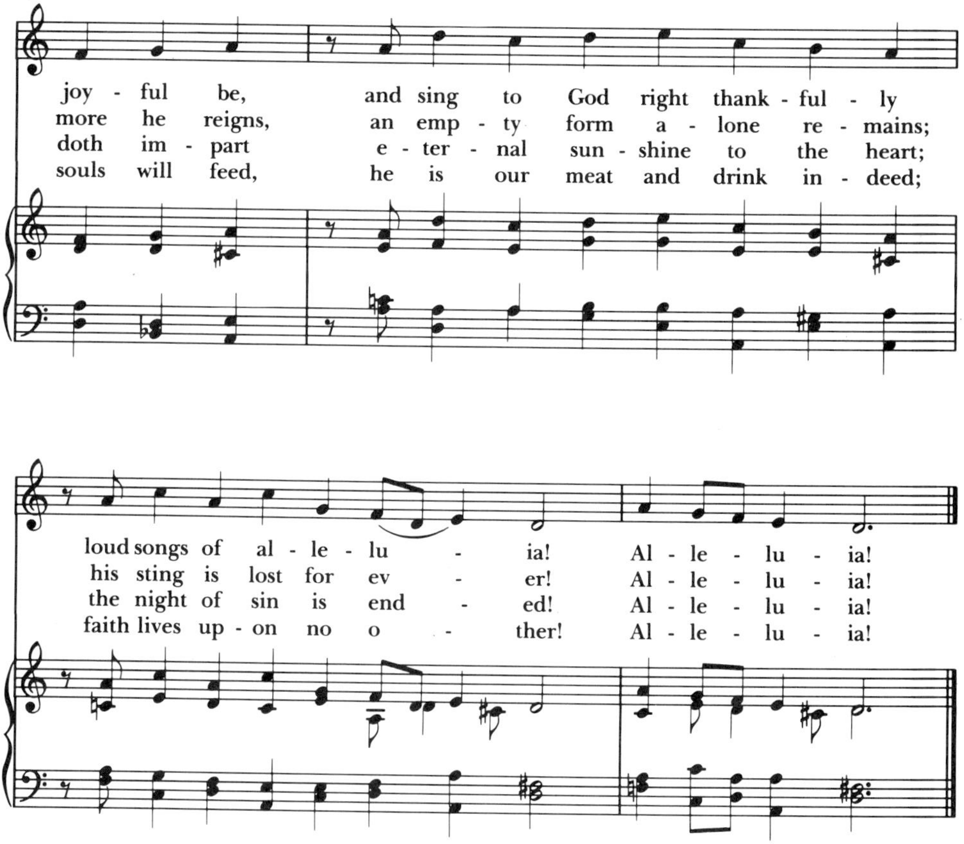
joy - ful be, and sing to God right thank - ful - ly
more he reigns, an emp - ty form a - lone re - mains;
doth im - part e - ter - nal sun - shine to the heart;
souls will feed, he is our meat and drink in - deed;
loud songs of al - le - lu - ia! Al - le - lu - ia!
his sting is lost for ev - er! Al - le - lu - ia!
the night of sin is end - ed! Al - le - lu - ia!
faith lives up - on no o - ther! Al - le - lu - ia!

Alternative tune: *Christ lag in Todesbanden* (isometric), 186.

Words: Martin Luther (1483-1546); tr. Richard Massie (1800-1887), alt.
Music: *Christ lag in Todesbanden,* melody from *Geystliche gesangk Buchleyn,* 1524; harm. *Hymnal 1982,* after Hans Leo Hassler (1564-1612)

𝅗𝅥 = 48
87. 87. 78. 74

1 Christ Je - sus lay in death's strong bands for
2 It was a strange and dread - ful strife when
3 So let us keep the fes - ti - val to
4 Then let us feast this ho - ly day on
our of - fens - es giv - en; but now at God's right
life and death con - tend - ed; the vic - to - ry re -
which the Lord in - vites us; Christ is him - self the
the true bread of hea - ven; the word of grace hath
hand he stands and brings us life from hea - ven;
mained with life, the reign of death was end - ed;
joy of all, the sun that warms and lights us;
purged a - way the old and wick - ed lea - ven;
there - fore let us joy - ful be, and sing to
stripped of power, no more he reigns, an emp - ty
by his grace he doth im - part e - ter - nal
Christ a - lone our souls will feed, he is our

God right thank - ful - ly loud songs of al - le -
form a - lone re - mains; his sting is lost for
sun - shine to the heart; the night of sin is
meat and drink in - deed; faith lives up - on no
lu - ia! Al - le - lu - ia!
ev - er! Al - le - lu - ia!
end - ed! Al - le - lu - ia!
o - ther! Al - le - lu - ia!

Alternative tune: *Christ lag in Todesbanden* (rhythmic), 185.

Words: Martin Luther (1483-1546); tr. Richard Massie (1800-1887), alt.
Music: *Christ lag in Todesbanden,* melody from *Geystliche gesangk Buchleyn,* 1524; adapt. and harm. Johann Sebastian Bach (1685-1750)

♩=66
87. 87. 78. 74

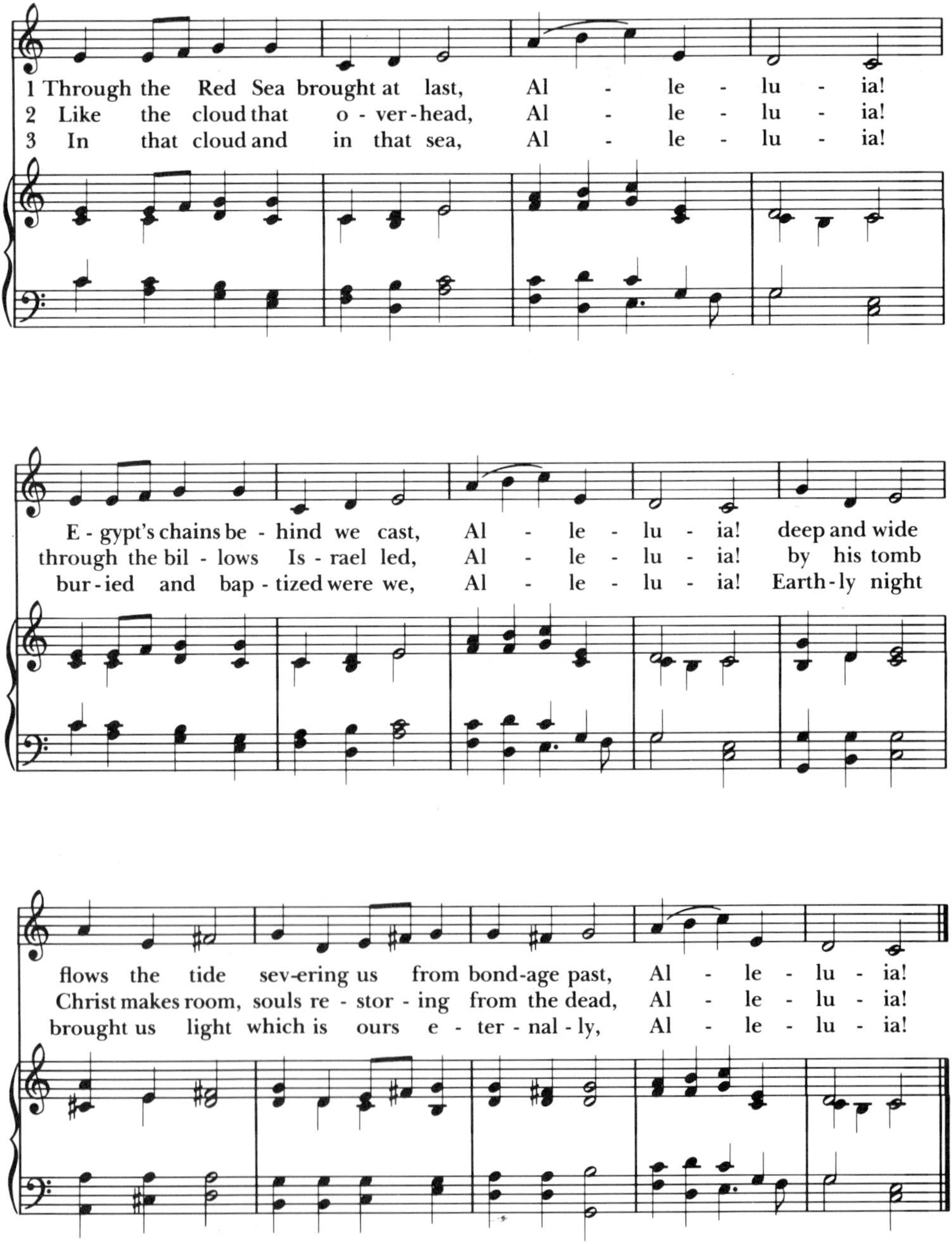
1 Through the Red Sea brought at last, Al - le - lu - ia!
2 Like the cloud that o - ver - head, Al - le - lu - ia!
3 In that cloud and in that sea, Al - le - lu - ia!
E - gypt's chains be - hind we cast, Al - le - lu - ia! deep and wide
through the bil - lows Is - rael led, Al - le - lu - ia! by his tomb
bur - ied and bap - tized were we, Al - le - lu - ia! Earth - ly night
flows the tide sev-ering us from bond - age past, Al - le - lu - ia!
Christ makes room, souls re - stor - ing from the dead, Al - le - lu - ia!
brought us light which is ours e - ter - nal - ly, Al - le - lu - ia!

Words: Ronald A. Knox (1888-1957)
Music: *Straf mich nicht,* melody from *Hundert Arien,* 1694; harm. Alastair Cassels-Brown (b. 1927)

𝅗𝅥=60
76. 76. 676

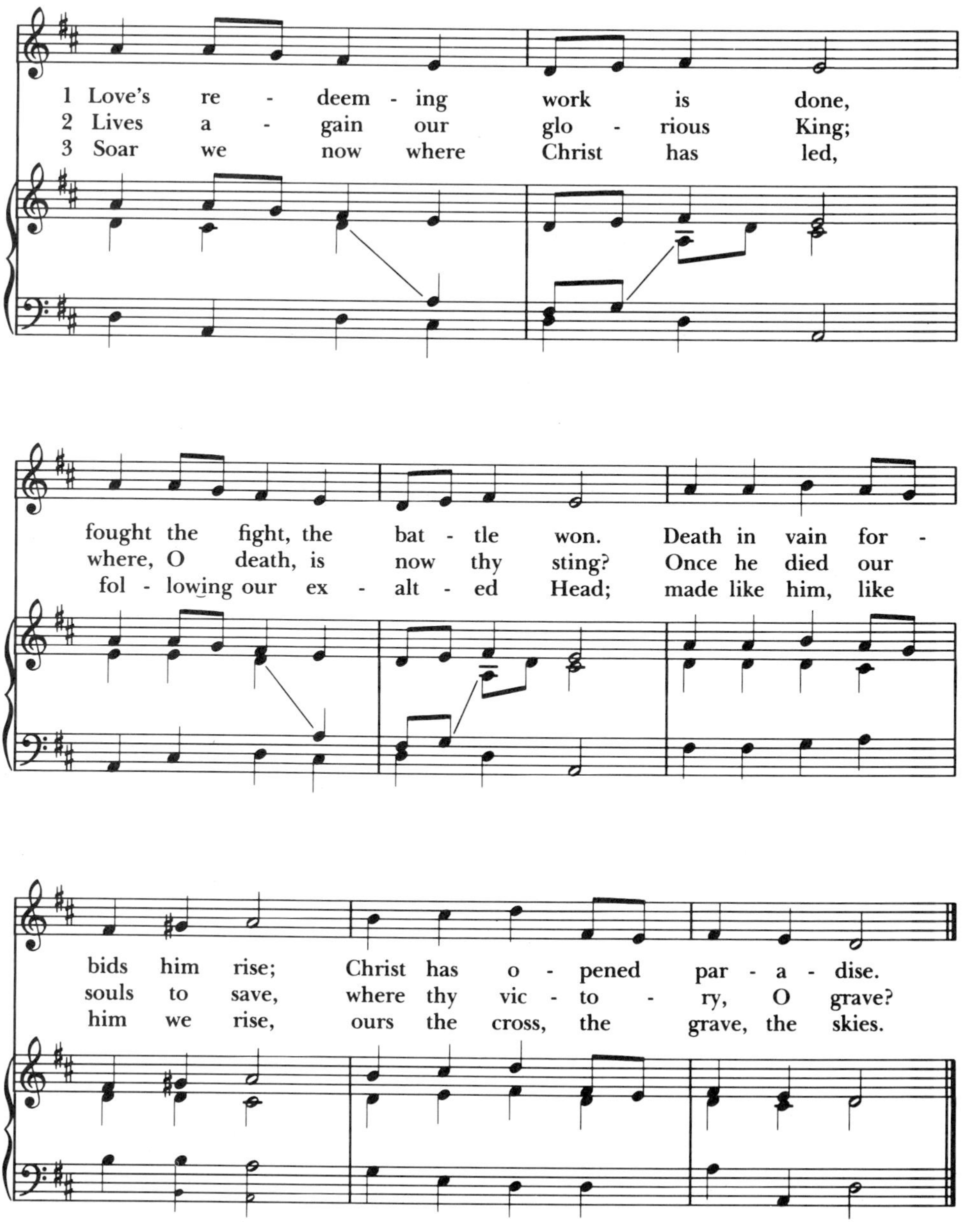
1 Love's re - deem - ing work is done,
2 Lives a - gain our glo - rious King;
3 Soar we now where Christ has led,
fought the fight, the bat - tle won. Death in vain for -
where, O death, is now thy sting? Once he died our
fol - lowing our ex - alt - ed Head; made like him, like
bids him rise; Christ has o - pened par - a - dise.
souls to save, where thy vic - to - ry, O grave?
him we rise, ours the cross, the grave, the skies.

Alternative tune: *Resurrexit,* 189.

Words: Charles Wesley (1707-1788), alt.
Music: *Savannah,* from *Harmonia Sacra,* ca. 1760

♩=96
77. 77

1 Love's re - deem-ing work is done, fought the fight, the
2 Lives a - gain our glo-rious King; where, O death, is
3 Soar we now where Christ has led, fol - lowing our ex -
bat - tle won. Death in vain for - bids him rise;
now thy sting? Once he died our souls to save,
alt - ed Head; made like him, like him we rise,
Christ has o - pened par - a - dise. Al - le-lu - ia, al - le - lu -
where thy vic - to - ry, O grave? Al - le-lu - ia, al - le - lu -
ours the cross, the grave, the skies. Al - le-lu - ia, al - le - lu -

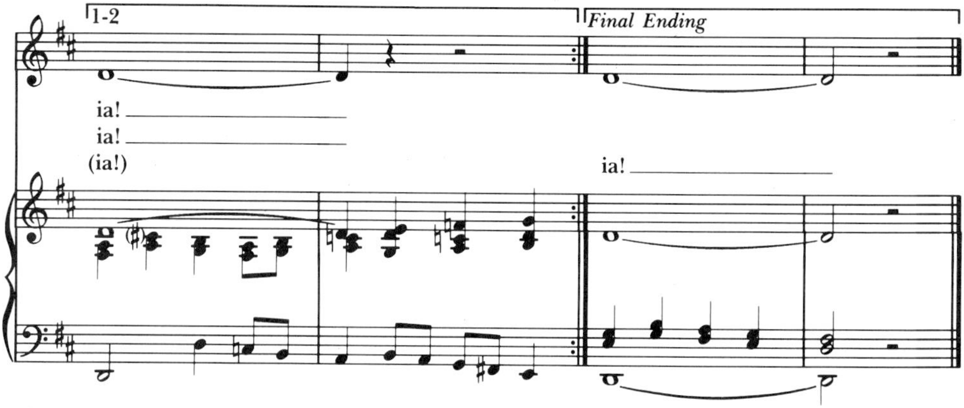

Alternative tune: *Savannah*, 188.

Words: Charles Wesley (1707-1788), alt.
Music: *Resurrexit*, Robert Sherlaw Johnson (b. 1932)

𝅗𝅥 = 52
77. 77 with Alleluias

Alternative accompaniment

Music: *Resurrexit*, Robert Sherlaw Johnson (b. 1932)

𝅗𝅥 = 52

1 Lift your voice re - joic - ing, Ma - ry, Christ has
2 Raise your wea - - ry eye - lids, Ma - ry, see him
3 Life is yours for ev - er, Ma - ry, for your
ris - en from the tomb; on the cross a suf - fering
liv - ing ev - er - more; see his coun - te - nance how
light is come once more and the strength of death is
vic - tim, now as vic - tor he is come. Whom your
gra - cious, see the wounds for you he bore. All the
bro - ken; now your songs of joy out - pour. End - ed

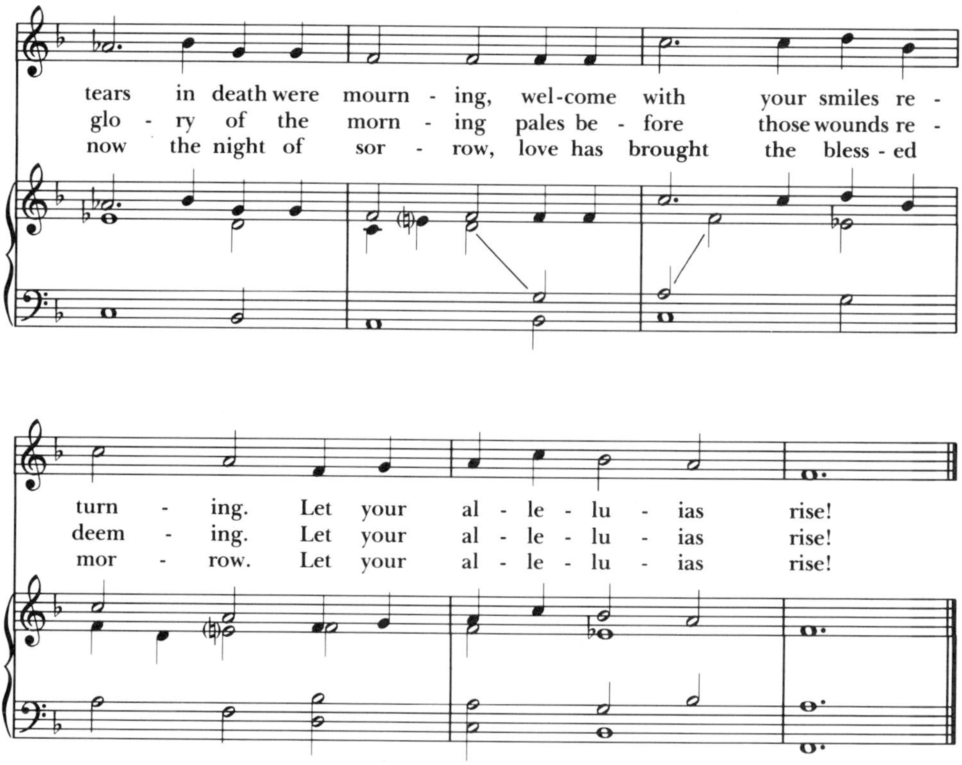
tears in death were mourn - ing, wel-come with your smiles re -
glo - ry of the morn - ing pales be - fore those wounds re -
now the night of sor - row, love has brought the bless - ed
turn - ing. Let your al - le - lu - ias rise!
deem - ing. Let your al - le - lu - ias rise!
mor - row. Let your al - le - lu - ias rise!

Words: Latin; tr. Elizabeth Rundle Charles (1828-1896), alt.
Music: *Fisk of Gloucester*, Thomas Foster (b. 1938)

𝅗𝅥 = 76
87. 87. 887

1 Al - le - lu - ia, al - le - lu - ia! Hearts and voic - es heaven-ward raise:
2 Now the i - ron bars are bro - ken, Christ from death to life is born,
3 Christ is ris - en, Christ, the first-fruits of the ho - ly har - vest - field,
4 Christ is ris - en, we are ris - en! Shed up - on us heaven-ly grace,
5 Al - le - lu - ia, al - le - lu - ia! Glo - ry be to God on high;
1 sing to God a hymn of glad - ness, sing to God a hymn of praise.
2 glo - rious life, and life im - mor - tal, on his re - sur - rec - tion morn.
3 which will all its full a - bun - dance at his sec - ond com - ing yield:
4 rain and dew and gleams of glo - ry from the bright - ness of thy face;
5 Al - le - lu - ia! to the Sa - vior who has won the vic - to - ry;
1 He, who on the cross a vic - tim, for the world's sal - va - tion bled,
2 Christ has tri - umphed, and we con - quer by his might - y en - ter - prise:
3 then the gold - en ears of har - vest will their heads be - fore him wave,
4 that, with hearts in hea - ven dwell - ing, we on earth may fruit - ful be,
5 Al - le - lu - ia! to the Spi - rit, fount of love and sanc - ti - ty:

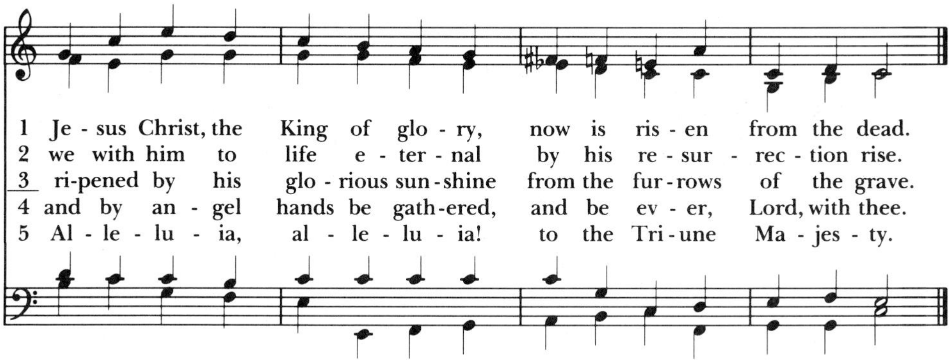
1 Je - sus Christ, the King of glo - ry, now is ris - en from the dead.
2 we with him to life e - ter - nal by his re - sur - rec - tion rise.
3 ri-pened by his glo - rious sun - shine from the fur - rows of the grave.
4 and by an - gel hands be gath-ered, and be ev - er, Lord, with thee.
5 Al - le - lu - ia, al - le - lu - ia! to the Tri - une Ma - jes - ty.

Alternative tune: *Hyfrydol,* 460.

Words: Christopher Wordsworth (1807-1885), alt.
Music: *Lux eoi,* Arthur Seymour Sullivan (1842-1900)

𝅗𝅥 = 56
87. 87. D

Unison or harmony
1 This joy - ful Eas - ter - tide, a - way with sin and sor - row! My Love, the Cru - ci - fied, hath sprung to life this mor - row.
2 Death's flood hath lost its chill, since Je - sus crossed the riv - er: Lord of all life, from ill my pass - ing life de - liv - er.
3 My flesh in hope shall rest, and for a sea - son slum - ber, till trump from east to west shall wake the dead in num - ber.
Refrain
Had Christ, that once was slain, ne'er burst his three-day pris - on, our faith had been in

vain; but now is Christ a - ris - en, a - ris - en, a -

ris - en, a - ris - - - en.

Words: George R. Woodward (1848-1934), alt.
Music: *Vruechten,* melody from *Psalmen,* 1685; harm. Charles Wood (1866-1926)

𝅗𝅥=60
67. 67 with Refrain

1 That Eas - ter day with joy was bright, the
2 His ris - en flesh with ra - diance glowed; his
3 O Je - sus, King of gen - tle - ness, do
4 O Lord of all, with us a - bide in
5 All praise, O ris - en Lord, we give to
1 sun shone out with fair- er light, when, to their long - ing
2 wound - ed hands and feet he showed; those scars their sol - emn
3 thou thy - self our hearts pos-sess that we may give thee
4 this our joy - ful Eas- ter-tide; from ev - ery wea - pon
5 thee, who, dead, a - gain dost live; to God the Fa - ther
1 eyes re-stored, the a - pos - tles saw their ris - en Lord.
2 wit - ness gave that Christ was ris - en from the grave.
3 all our days the will - ing tri - bute of our praise.
4 death can wield thine own re-deemed for ev - er shield.
5 e - qual praise, and God the Ho - ly Ghost, we raise.

Another accompaniment, 124.

Words: Latin, 5th cent.; ver. *Hymnal 1940*
Music: *Puer nobis*, melody from Trier MS., 15th cent.; adapt. Michael Praetorius (1571-1621); harm. *Hymns Ancient and Modern, Revised,* 1950

𝅗𝅥. = 50
LM

Alternative accompaniment for keyboard, bells, Orff instruments, etc.

Finger cymbals may sound on the first beat of each measure.

Music: *Puer nobis,* melody from Trier MS., 15th cent.; adapt. Michael Praetorius (1571-1621); acc. John F. Erickson (b. 1938)

𝅗𝅥=50

1 Je - sus lives! thy ter - rors now can no long - er, death, ap -
2 Je - sus lives! for us he died; then, a - lone to Je - sus
3 Je - sus lives! our hearts know well nought from us his love shall
4 Je - sus lives! to him the throne o - ver all the world is
pall us; Je - sus lives! by this we know thou, O
liv - ing, pure in heart may we a - bide, glo - ry
sev - er; life, nor death, nor powers of hell tear us
giv - en: may we go where he has gone, rest and
grave, canst not en - thrall us. Al - le - lu - ia!
to our Sa - vior giv - ing. Al - le - lu - ia!
from his keep - ing ev - er. Al - le - lu - ia!
reign with him in hea - ven. Al - le - lu - ia!

Alternative tune: *Mowsley*, 195.

Words: Christian Furchtegott Gellert (1715-1769); tr. Frances Elizabeth Cox (1812-1897), alt.
Music: *St. Albinus*, Henry John Gauntlett (1805-1876)

𝅗𝅥=50
78. 78 with Alleluia

195

1 Je - sus lives! thy ter - rors now can no long - er,
2 Je - sus lives! for us he died; then, a - lone to
3 Je - sus lives! our hearts know well nought from us his
4 Je - sus lives! to him the throne o - ver all the
death, ap - pall us; Je - sus lives! by this we know
Je - sus liv - ing, pure in heart may we a - bide,
love shall sev - er; life, nor death, nor powers of hell
world is giv - en: may we go where he has gone,
thou, O grave, canst not en - thrall us. Al - le - lu - ia!
glo - ry to our Sa - vior giv - ing. Al - le - lu - ia!
tear us from his keep - ing ev - er. Al - le - lu - ia!
rest and reign with him in hea - ven. Al - le - lu - ia!

Alternative tune: *St. Albinus*, 194.

Words: Christian Furchtegott Gellert (1715-1769); tr. Frances Elizabeth Cox (1812-1897), alt. 𝅗𝅥=66

Music: *Mowsley*, Cyril Vincent Taylor (b. 1907) 78. 78 with Alleluia

Introduction/Interlude
f
f
1 Look there! the Christ, our Bro-ther, comes re - splen-dent from the gal-lows tree __ and what he brings in
2 Good Je - sus Christ in - side his pain looked down Gol - go - tha's ston-y slope _ and let the blood flow
3 Good Je - sus Christ, our Bro-ther, died in dark - est hurt up - on the tree __ to of - fer us the
4 Look there! the Christ, our Bro-ther, comes re - splen-dent from the gal-lows tree __ and what he brings in

his hurt hands is life on life for you and me.
from his flesh to fill the springs of liv - ing hope.
worlds of light that live in-side the Trin - i - ty.
his hurt hands is life on life for you and me.
Refrain
Joy! (joy) joy! (joy) joy to the heart and all in this good day's dawn-
ad. lib
- ing! Joy! (joy) joy! (joy) joy to the heart and
all in this good day's dawn -ing!
f
sfz

The stanzas may be sung by choir or cantor alone. The right hand may play the vocal line instead of the ostinato. Alternative tune: *Grand Prairie,* 197.

Words: John Bennett (b. 1920), alt.
Music: *Petrus,* William Albright (b. 1944)

♩= 152
LM with Refrain

1 Look there! the Christ, our Bro - ther,
2 Good Je - sus Christ in - side his
3 Good Je - sus Christ, our Bro - ther,
4 Look there! the Christ, our Bro - ther,
comes re - splen-dent from the gal-lows tree and what he
pain looked down Gol - go-tha's ston-y slope and let the
died in dark-est hurt up-on the tree to of-fer
comes re - splen-dent from the gal-lows tree and what he
brings in his hurt hands is life on life for you and
blood flow from his flesh to fill the springs of liv - ing
us the worlds of light that live in - side the Trin - i -
brings in his hurt hands is life on life for you and

Refrain
me.
hope.
ty.
me.
Joy! joy! joy to the
heart and all in this good day's dawn - ing!

Alternative tune: *Petrus,* 196.

Words: John Bennett (b. 1920), alt.
Music: *Grand Prairie,* Peter Cutts (b. 1937)

𝅗𝅥=80
LM with Refrain

1 Thou hallowed chosen morn of praise, that best and greatest shinest: fair Easter, queen of all the days, of seasons, best, divinest! Christ rose from death; and we adore for ever and for evermore.
2 Come, let us taste the vine's new fruit, for heavenly joy preparing; today the branches with the root in resurrection sharing: whom as true God our hymns adore for ever and for evermore.

Words: John of Damascus (8th cent.); tr. John Mason Neale (1818-1866), alt.
Music: *Mach's mit mir, Gott,* melody from *Das ander Theil des andern newen Operis Geistlicher Deutscher Lieder,* 1605; adapt., att., and harm. Johann Hermann Schein (1586-1630)

𝅗𝅥. = 42
87. 87. 88

199

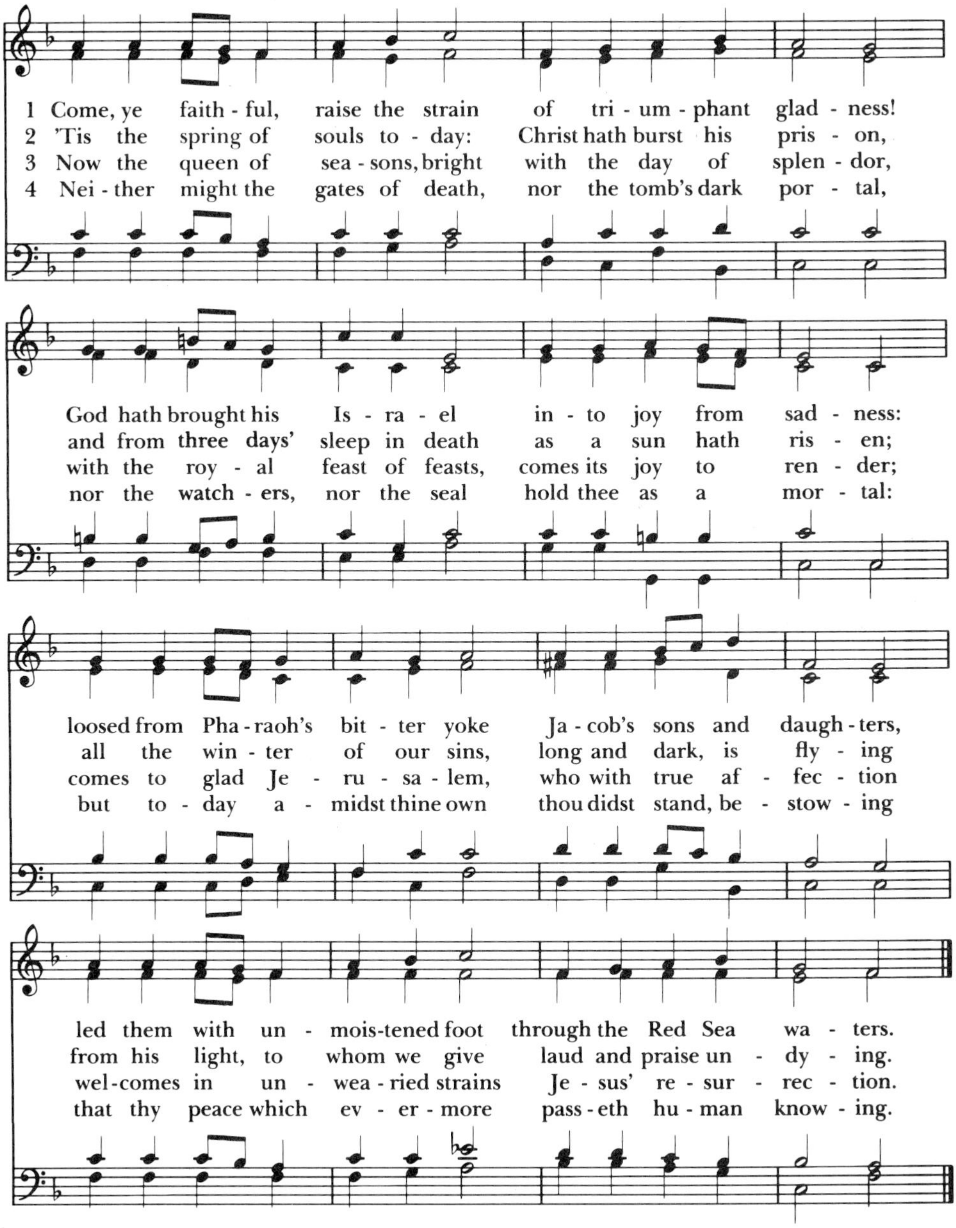
1 Come, ye faith - ful, raise the strain of tri - um - phant glad - ness!
2 'Tis the spring of souls to - day: Christ hath burst his pris - on,
3 Now the queen of sea - sons, bright with the day of splen - dor,
4 Nei - ther might the gates of death, nor the tomb's dark por - tal,
God hath brought his Is - ra - el in - to joy from sad - ness:
and from three days' sleep in death as a sun hath ris - en;
with the roy - al feast of feasts, comes its joy to ren - der;
nor the watch - ers, nor the seal hold thee as a mor - tal:
loosed from Pha - raoh's bit - ter yoke Ja - cob's sons and daugh - ters,
all the win - ter of our sins, long and dark, is fly - ing
comes to glad Je - ru - sa - lem, who with true af - fec - tion
but to - day a - midst thine own thou didst stand, be - stow - ing
led them with un - mois-tened foot through the Red Sea wa - ters.
from his light, to whom we give laud and praise un - dy - ing.
wel-comes in un - wea - ried strains Je - sus' re - sur - rec - tion.
that thy peace which ev - er - more pass - eth hu - man know - ing.

Alternative tune: *Gaudeamus pariter*, 200.

Words: John of Damascus (8th cent.); tr. John Mason Neale (1818-1866), alt.
Music: *St. Kevin*, Arthur Seymour Sullivan (1842-1900)

𝅗𝅥=63
76. 76. D

1 Come, ye faith - ful, raise the strain of tri - um - phant glad - ness!
2 'Tis the spring of souls to - day: Christ hath burst his pris - on,
3 Now the queen of sea - sons, bright with the day of splen - dor,
4 Nei - ther might the gates of death, nor the tomb's dark por - tal,
God hath brought his Is - ra - el in - to joy from sad - ness:
and from three days' sleep in death as a sun hath ris - en;
with the roy - al feast of feasts, comes its joy to ren - der;
nor the watch - ers, nor the seal hold thee as a mor - tal:
loosed from Pha - roah's bit - ter yoke Ja - cob's sons and daugh - ters,
all the win - ter of our sins, long and dark, is fly - ing
comes to glad Je - ru - sa - lem, who with true af - fec - tion
but to - day a - midst thine own thou didst stand, be - stow - ing

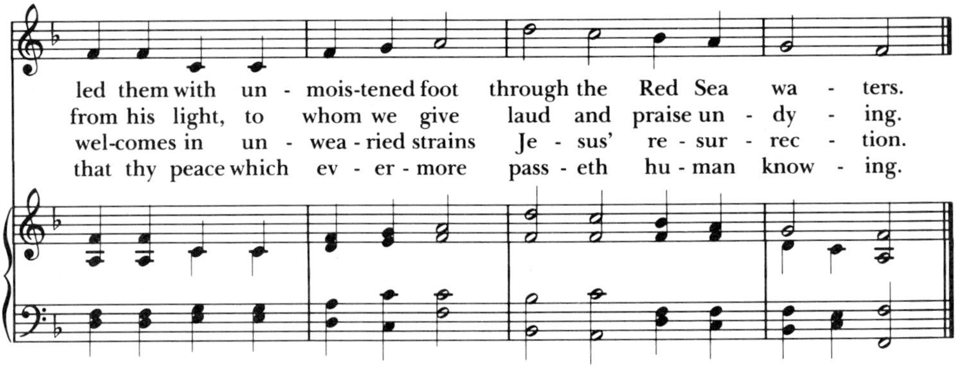
led them with un - mois-tened foot through the Red Sea wa - ters.
from his light, to whom we give laud and praise un - dy - ing.
wel-comes in un - wea - ried strains Je - sus' re - sur - rec - tion.
that thy peace which ev - er - more pass - eth hu - man know - ing.

Alternative tune: *St. Kevin,* 199.

Words: John of Damascus (8th cent.); tr. John Mason Neale (1818-1866), alt.
Music: *Gaudeamus pariter,* melody from *Medieval [German or] Bohemian Carol Melody,* 1544; harm. *Songs of Syon,* 1904

♩= 80
76. 76. D

1 On earth has dawned this day of days, where - on the
2 At ear - ly morn, with spi - ces rare, the wo - men
3 "Whom seek ye here?" the an - gel said; "The Lord is
4 So let our songs to hea - ven wing, the vault with
faith - ful give God praise! For Christ is ris - en from the tomb,
three as - sem - bled there, all to a - noint fair Ma - ry's Son,
ris - en from the dead; see where he lay; let joy be - gin,
al - le - lu - ias ring, in praise of Christ, our ris - en Lord;
and light and joy have con - quered doom. Al - le - lu - ia!
who o - ver death had vic - tory won. Al - le - lu - ia!
the tomb is emp - ty: en - ter in!" Al - le - lu - ia!
new life to all he doth af - ford. Al - le - lu - ia!

Words: Nikolaus Hermann (1480?-1561); tr. Charles Sanford Terry (1864-1936), alt.
Music: *Erschienen ist der herrlich Tag*, melody Nikolaus Hermann (1480?-1561); harm. *Hymnal 1982*

𝅗𝅥. = 48
LM with Alleluia

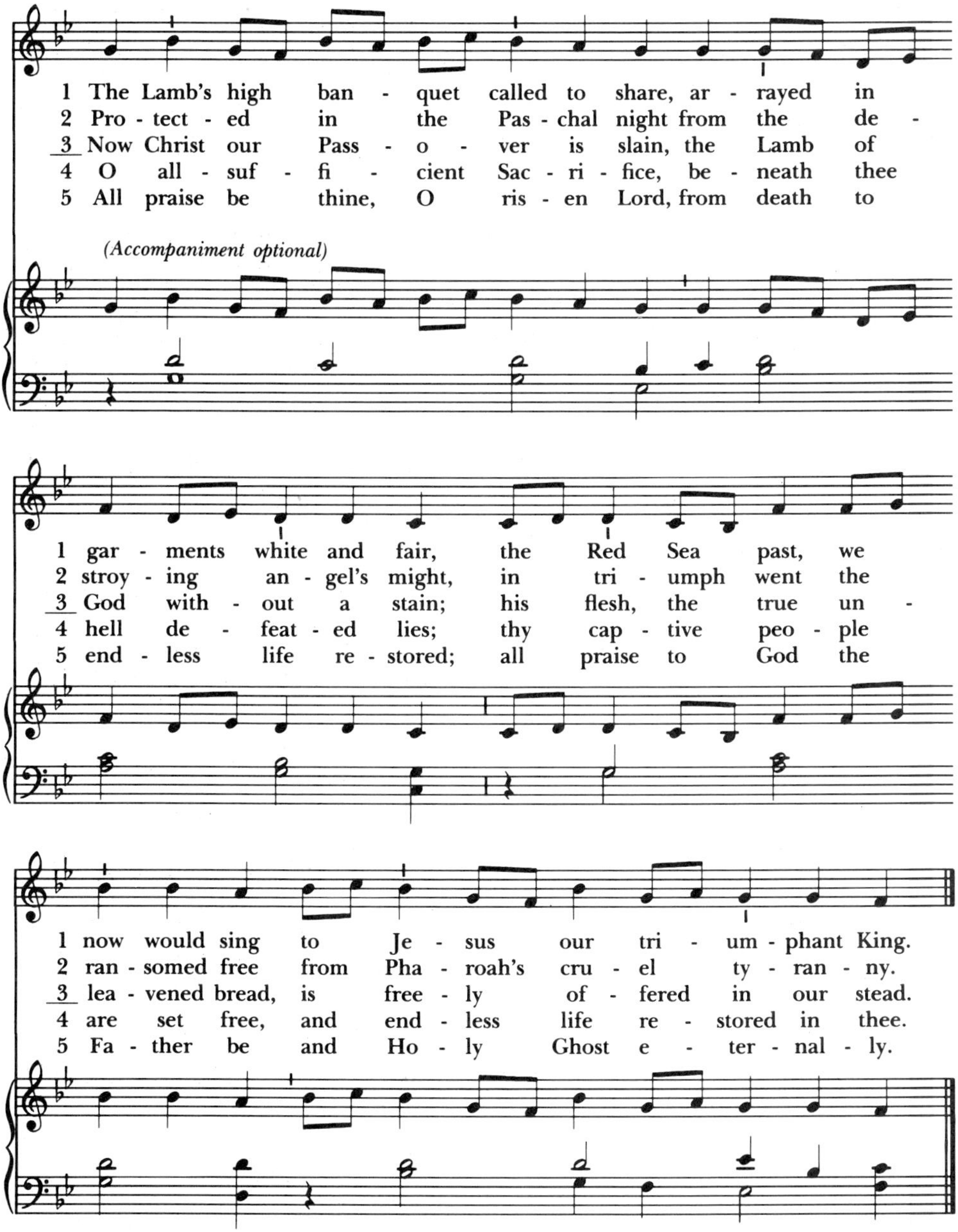
1 The Lamb's high ban - quet called to share, ar - rayed in
2 Pro - tect - ed in the Pas - chal night from the de -
3 Now Christ our Pass - o - ver is slain, the Lamb of
4 O all - suf - fi - cient Sac - ri - fice, be - neath thee
5 All praise be thine, O ris - en Lord, from death to
(Accompaniment optional)
1 gar - ments white and fair, the Red Sea past, we
2 stroy - ing an - gel's might, in tri - umph went the
3 God with - out a stain; his flesh, the true un -
4 hell de - feat - ed lies; thy cap - tive peo - ple
5 end - less life re - stored; all praise to God the
1 now would sing to Je - sus our tri - um - phant King.
2 ran - somed free from Pha - roah's cru - el ty - ran - ny.
3 lea - vened bread, is free - ly of - fered in our stead.
4 are set free, and end - less life re - stored in thee.
5 Fa - ther be and Ho - ly Ghost e - ter - nal - ly.

Words: Latin, 7th-8th cent.; tr. John Mason Neale (1818-1866) and others
Music: *Ad cenam Agni providi,* plainsong, Mode 8, Paris MS., 12th cent.; ver. A. Gregory Murray (b. 1905) acc. Roy F. Kehl (b. 1935)

♩=100
LM

Antiphon (at the beginning)
Al - le - lu - ia, al - le - lu - ia!
Al - le - lu - ia, al - le - lu - ia!
1 O sons and daugh-ters, let us sing! The King of heaven, the
2 That Eas - ter morn, at break of day, the faith - ful wo - men
3 An an - gel clad in white they see, who sat and spake un -
4 That night the a - pos - tles met in fear; a - midst them came their
5 On this most ho - ly day of days, to God your hearts and
1 glo - rious King, o'er death and hell rose tri - umph - ing.
2 went their way to seek the tomb where Je - sus lay.
3 to the three, "Your Lord doth go to Gal - i - lee."
4 Lord most dear, and said, "My peace be on all here."
5 voic - es raise, in laud and ju - bi - lee and praise.

1 Al - le - lu - ia, al - le - lu - ia!
2 Al - le - lu - ia, al - le - lu - ia!
3 Al - le - lu - ia, al - le - lu - ia!
4 Al - le - lu - ia, al - le - lu - ia!
5 Al - le - lu - ia, al - le - lu - ia! [Ant.]
Antiphon (at the end)
Al - le - lu - ia, al - le - lu - ia!
Al - le - lu - ia, al - le - lu - ia!

Alternative tune: *O filii et filiae* (chant), 206.

Words: Att. Jean Tisserand (15th cent.); tr. John Mason Neale (1818-1866)
Music: *O filii et filiae,* melody from *Airs sur les hymnes sacrez, odes et noëls,* 1623; harm. *Hymnal 1982*

𝅗𝅥. = 48
888 with Alleluias

1 Now the green blade ris - eth from the bur - ied grain,
2 In the grave they laid him, Love whom hate had slain,
3 Forth he came at Eas - ter, like the ris - en grain,
4 When our hearts are win - try, griev - ing, or in pain,
wheat that in dark earth man-y days has lain; love lives a -
think - ing that nev - er he would wake a - gain, laid in the
he that for three days in the grave had lain, quick from the
thy touch can call us back to life a - gain, fields of our
gain, that with the dead has been:
earth like grain that sleeps un - seen:
dead my ris - en Lord is seen:
hearts that (dead and bare have been:)
1-3
Refrain
Love is come a - gain like

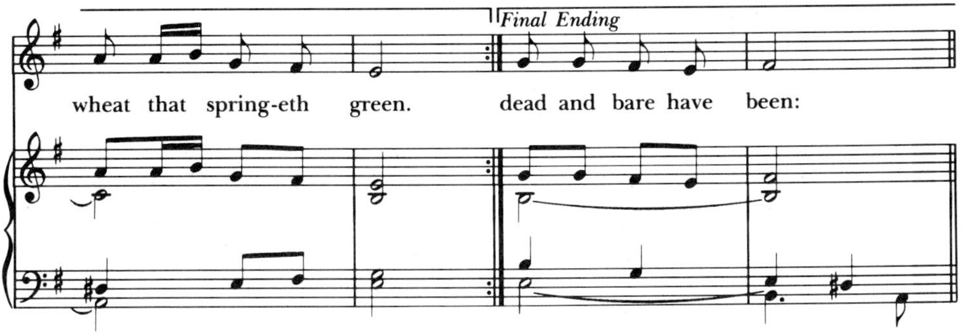
Final Ending
wheat that spring-eth green.
dead and bare have been:

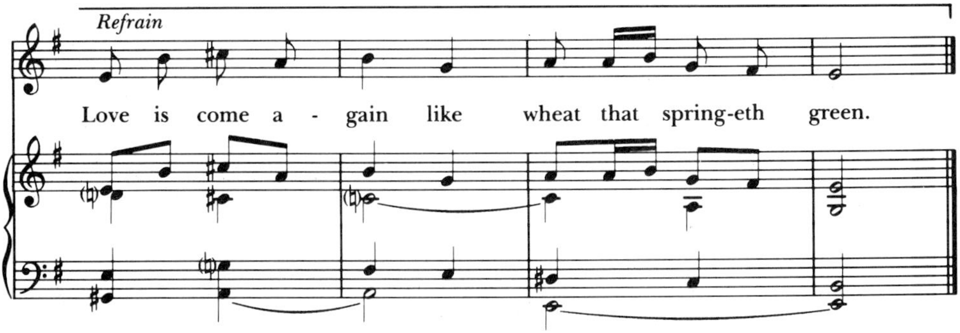
Refrain
Love is come a - gain like wheat that spring-eth green.

Words: John Macleod Campbell Crum (1872-1958), alt.
Music: *Noël nouvelet,* medieval French carol; harm. Marcel Dupré (1886-1971); adapt. Roy F. Kehl (b. 1935)

𝅗𝅥 = 76
11 10. 10 11

Alternative accompaniment

Music: *Noël nouvelet*, medieval French carol; harm. George Mims (b. 1938)

𝅗𝅥=76

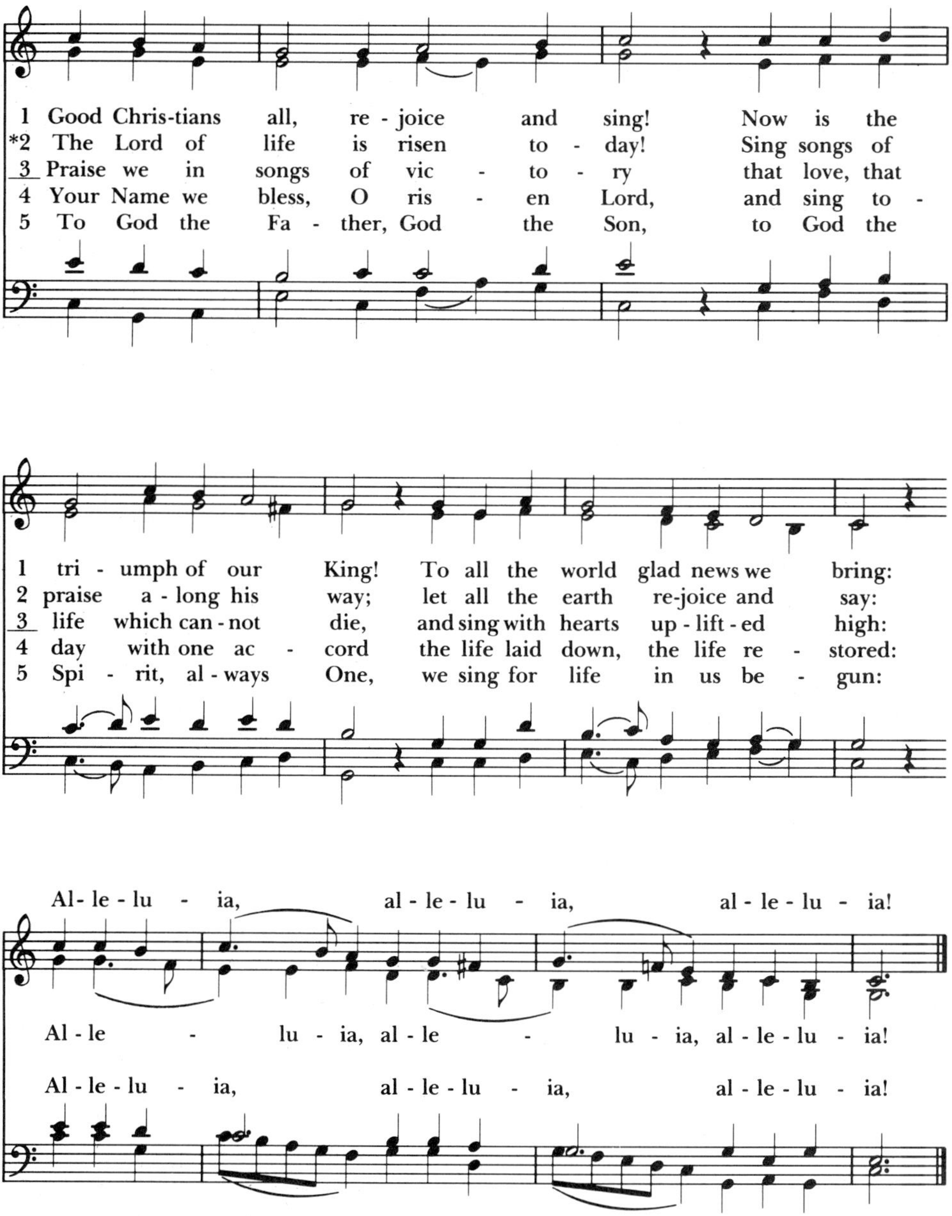
1 Good Chris-tians all, re - joice and sing! Now is the
*2 The Lord of life is risen to - day! Sing songs of
3 Praise we in songs of vic - to - ry that love, that
4 Your Name we bless, O ris - en Lord, and sing to -
5 To God the Fa - ther, God the Son, to God the
1 tri - umph of our King! To all the world glad news we bring:
2 praise a - long his way; let all the earth re-joice and say:
3 life which can - not die, and sing with hearts up - lift - ed high:
4 day with one ac - cord the life laid down, the life re - stored:
5 Spi - rit, al - ways One, we sing for life in us be - gun:
Al - le - lu - ia, al - le - lu - ia, al - le - lu - ia!
Al - le - lu - ia, al - le - lu - ia, al - le - lu - ia!
Al - le - lu - ia, al - le - lu - ia, al - le - lu - ia!

The stanzas may be sung in unison and the Alleluias in harmony.

Words: Cyril A. Alington (1872-1955), alt. St. 5, Norman Mealy (b. 1923)
Music: *Gelobt sei Gott,* Melchior Vulpius (1560?-1616)

𝅗𝅥. = 44
888 with Alleluias

Antiphon (at the beginning)
Gm(Em) Dm sus4 (Bm sus4) Gm(Em) Dm(Bm) F(D) Gm(Em)
Al - le - lu - ia, al - le - lu - ia, al - le - lu - ia!
Gm(Em) Gm7(Em7) Cm(Am) Gm(Em)
1 O sons and daugh - ters, let us sing!
2 That night the a - pos - tles met in fear;
3 When Thom - as first the tid - ings heard,
4 "My pierc - ed side, O Thom - as, see;
5 No long - er Thom - as then de - nied,
6 How blest are they who have not seen,
Gm(Em) Bb(G) F(D) Gm(Em)
1 The King of heaven, the glo - rious King,
2 a - midst them came their Lord most dear,
3 how they had seen the ris - en Lord,
4 my hands, my feet, I show to thee;
5 he saw the feet, the hands, the side;
6 and yet whose faith has con - stant been,

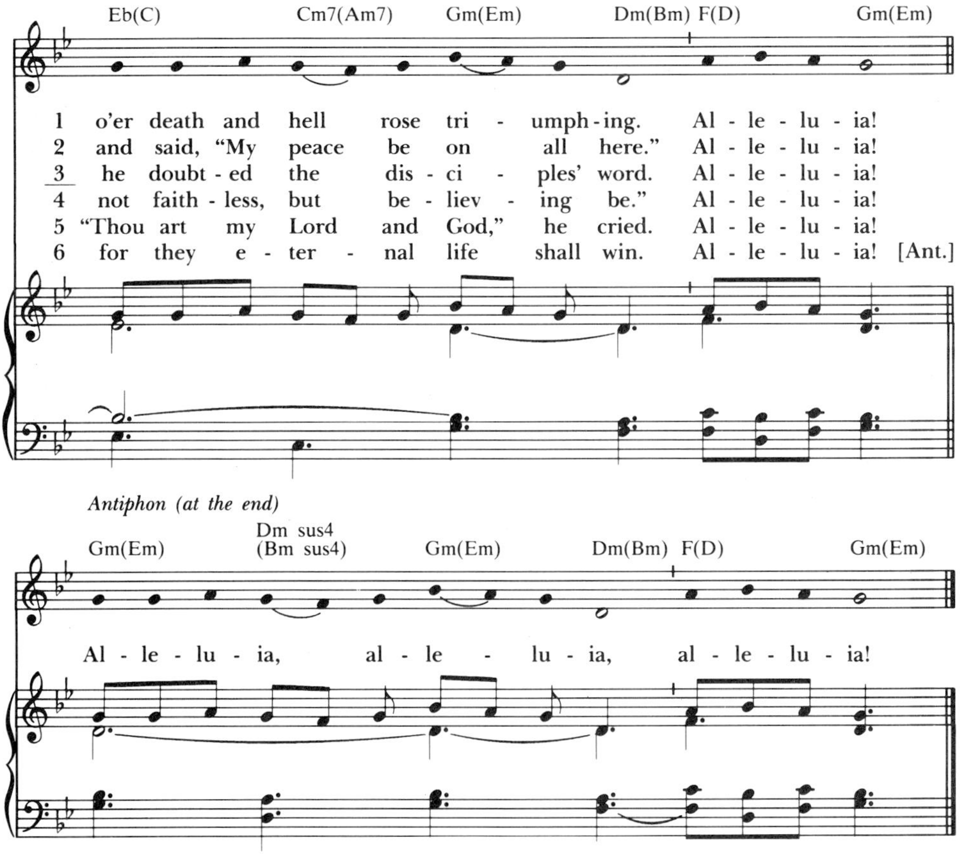
Eb(C) Cm7(Am7) Gm(Em) Dm(Bm) F(D) Gm(Em)
1 o'er death and hell rose tri - umph - ing. Al - le - lu - ia!
2 and said, "My peace be on all here." Al - le - lu - ia!
3 he doubt - ed the dis - ci - ples' word. Al - le - lu - ia!
4 not faith - less, but be - liev - ing be." Al - le - lu - ia!
5 "Thou art my Lord and God," he cried. Al - le - lu - ia!
6 for they e - ter - nal life shall win. Al - le - lu - ia! [Ant.]
Antiphon (at the end)
Gm(Em) Dm sus4 (Bm sus4) Gm(Em) Dm(Bm) F(D) Gm(Em)
Al - le - lu - ia, al - le - lu - ia, al - le - lu - ia!

Gm(capo 3, Em). Alternative tune: *O filii et filiae* (carol), 203. *This hymn is for the Second Sunday of Easter and St. Thomas' Day. The alternative accompaniment may be used for some stanzas.*

Words: Att. Jean Tisserand (15th cent.); tr. John Mason Neale (1818-1866)
Music: *O filii et filiae,* melody from *Airs sur les hymnes sacrez, odes et noëls,* 1623; acc. Richard Proulx (b. 1937)

888 with Alleluias

Alternative accompaniment
Antiphon (at the beginning)

Antiphon (at the end)

Music: *O filii et filiae,* melody from *Airs sur les hymnes sacrez, odes et noëls,* 1623; acc. Richard Proulx (b. 1937)

207 Easter

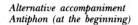

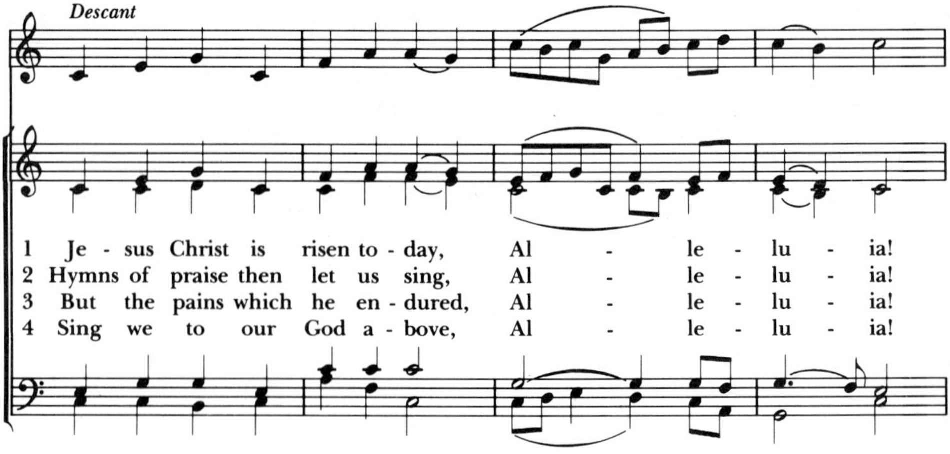
Descant
1 Je - sus Christ is risen to - day, Al - le - lu - ia!
2 Hymns of praise then let us sing, Al - le - lu - ia!
3 But the pains which he en - dured, Al - le - lu - ia!
4 Sing we to our God a - bove, Al - le - lu - ia!

our tri - um - phant ho - ly day, Al - le - lu - ia!
un - to Christ, our heaven - ly King, Al - le - lu - ia!
our sal - va - tion have pro - cured, Al - le - lu - ia!
praise e - ter - nal as his love, Al - le - lu - ia!
who did once up - on the cross, Al - le - lu - ia!
who en - dured the cross and grave, Al - le - lu - ia!
now a - bove the sky he's King, Al - le - lu - ia!
praise him, all ye heaven - ly host, Al - le - lu - ia!
suf - fer to re - deem our loss. Al - le - lu - ia!
sin - ners to re - deem and save. Al - le - lu - ia!
where the an - gels ev - er sing. Al - le - lu - ia!
Fa - ther, Son, and Ho - ly Ghost. Al - le - lu - ia!

Words: Latin, 14th cent.; tr. *Lyra Davidica,* 1708, alt. St. 4, Charles Wesley (1707-1788)
Music: *Easter Hymn,* from *Lyra Davidica,* 1708; adapt. *The Compleat Psalmodist,* 1749, alt., desc. *Hymns Ancient and Modern, Revised,* 1950

𝅗𝅥 = 60
77. 77 with Alleluias

Antiphon (at the beginning)
Al - le - lu - ia, al - le - lu - ia, al - le - lu - ia!
Ped.
1 The strife is o'er, the bat - tle done, the vic - to - ry of life is won; the song of tri - umph has be - gun. Al - le - lu - ia!
2 The powers of death have done their worst, but Christ their le - gions hath dis - persed: let shout of ho - ly joy out - burst. Al - le - lu - ia!
*3 The three sad days are quick - ly sped, he ris - es glo - rious from the dead: all glo - ry to our ris - en Head! Al - le - lu - ia!
4 He closed the yawn - ing gates of hell, the bars from heaven's high por - tals fell; let hymns of praise his tri - umphs tell! Al - le - lu - ia!
5 Lord! by the stripes which wound - ed thee, from death's dread sting thy serv - ants free, that we may live and sing to thee. Al - le - lu - ia! [Ant.]

Antiphon (at the end)
Al - le - lu - ia, al - le - lu - ia, al - le - lu - ia!
Ped.

Words: Latin, 1695; tr. Francis Pott (1832-1909), alt.
Music: *Victory,* Giovanni Pierluigi da Palestrina (1525-1594); adapt. and arr. William Henry Monk (1823-1889)

♩= 112
888 with Alleluias

209

1 We walk by faith, and not by sight; no gra - cious words we hear from him who spoke as none e'er spoke; but we be - lieve him near.
2 We may not touch his hands and side, nor fol - low where he trod; but in his prom - ise we re - joice; and cry, "My Lord and God!"
3 Help then, O Lord, our un - be - lief; and may our faith a - bound, to call on you when you are near, and seek where you are found:
4 that, when our life of faith is done, in realms of clear - er light we may be - hold you as you are, with full and end - less sight.

Words: Henry Alford (1810-1871), alt.
Music: *St. Botolph,* Gordon Slater (1896-1979)

𝅗𝅥. = 40
CM

Descant
3 Now let the heavens be joy - ful, let earth her song be - gin,
the round world keep high tri - umph, and all that is there - in;
let all things seen and un - seen their notes to - geth - er blend,
1 The day of re - sur - rec - tion! Earth, tell it out a - broad;
the Pass - o - ver of glad - ness, the Pass - o - ver of God.
From death to life e - ter - nal, from earth un - to the sky,
2 Our hearts be pure from e - vil, that we may see a - right
the Lord in rays e - ter - nal of re - sur - rec - tion light;
and, lis - tening to his ac - cents, may hear so calm and plain
3 Now let the heavens be joy - ful, let earth her song be - gin,
the round world keep high tri - umph, and all that is there - in;
let all things seen and un - seen their notes to - geth - er blend,

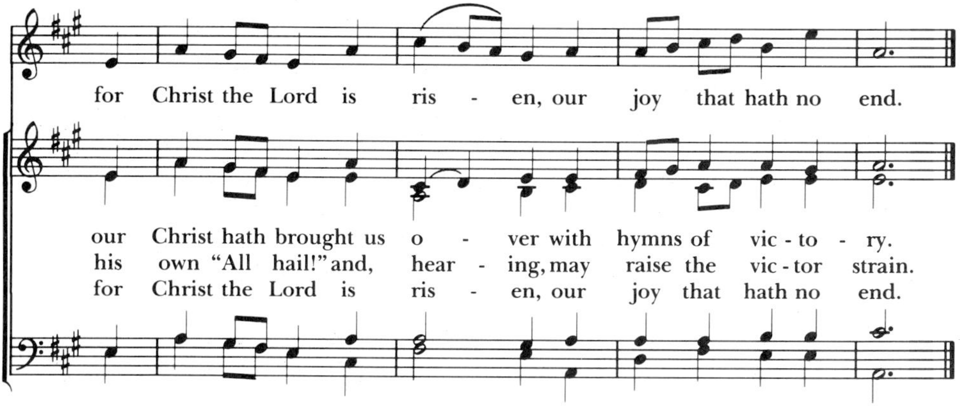
for Christ the Lord is ris - en, our joy that hath no end.
our Christ hath brought us o - ver with hymns of vic - to - ry.
his own "All hail!" and, hear - ing, may raise the vic - tor strain.
for Christ the Lord is ris - en, our joy that hath no end.

Words: John of Damascus (8th cent.); tr. John Mason Neale (1818-1866), alt.
Music: *Ellacombe*, melody from *Gesangbuch . . . der Herzogl. Wirtembergischen katolischen Hofkapelle*, 1784, alt.; adapt. *Katholisches Gesangbuch*, 1863; harm. William Henry Monk (1823-1889); desc. Cyril Winn (1884-1973)

𝅗𝅥 = 54

76. 76. D

1 The whole bright world re - joic - es now, Hi - lar - i - ter,
2 Then shout be - neath the rac - ing skies, Hi - lar - i - ter,
3 And all you liv - ing things make praise, Hi - lar - i - ter,
4 To Fa - ther, Son, and Ho - ly Ghost— Hi - lar - i - ter,
hi - lar - i - ter! The birds do sing on ev - ery bough,
hi - lar - i - ter! To him who rose that we might rise,
hi - lar - i - ter! He guid - eth you on all your ways,
hi - lar - i - ter! Our God most high, our joy and boast.
Al - le - lu - ia, al - le - lu - ia!
Al - le - lu - ia, al - le - lu - ia!
Al - le - lu - ia, al - le - lu - ia!
Al - le - lu - ia, al - le - lu - ia!

"Hilariter" is Latin for "joyfully" and is pronounced "hi-lair-i-tair" in this hymn.

Words: Friedrich von Spee (1591-1635); tr. Percy Dearmer (1867-1936)
Music: *Hilariter,* Richard Wayne Dirksen (b. 1921)

♩= 132
888 with Alleluias

1 A - wake, a - rise, lift up your voice, let
2 Oh, with what glad - ness and sur - prise the
3 those hands of lib - eral love in - deed in
4 His en - e - mies had sealed the stone as
5 O Dead a - rise! O Friend - less stand by
1 Eas - ter mu - sic swell; re - joice in Christ, a -
2 saints their Sa - vior greet; nor will they trust their
3 in - fi - nite de - gree, those feet still free to
4 Pi - late gave them leave, lest dead and friend - less
5 ser - a - phim a - dored! O Sol - i - tude a -
1 gain re - joice and on his prais - es dwell.
2 ears and eyes but by his hands and feet,
3 move and bleed for mil - lions and for me.
4 and a - lone he should their skill de - ceive.
5 gain com - mand your host from heaven re - stored!

This music in F, 72.

Words: Christopher Smart (1722-1771), alt.
Music: *Richmond,* melody Thomas Haweis (1734-1820); adapt. Samuel Webbe (1740-1816)

♩=76
CM

213

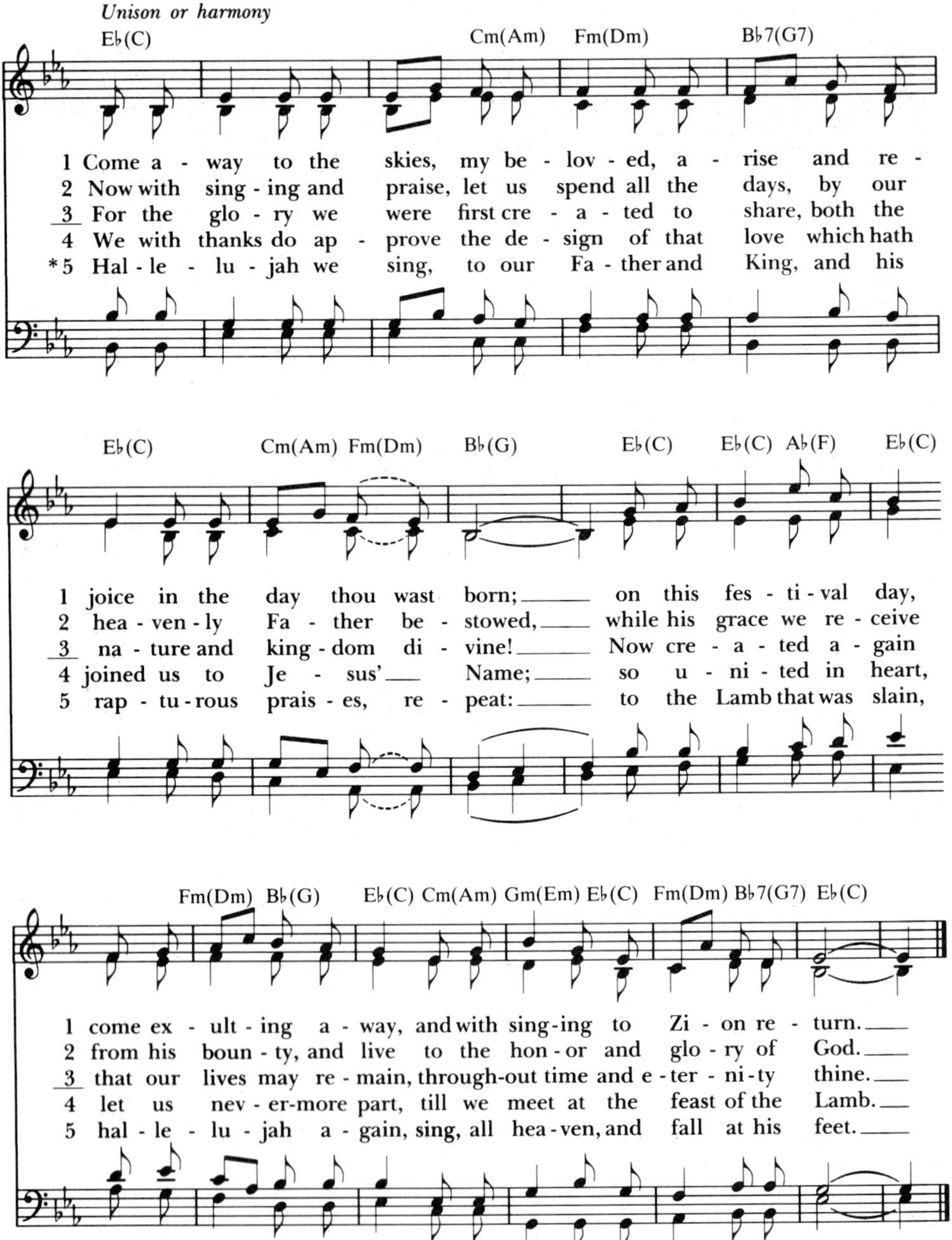
Unison or harmony
Eb(C) Cm(Am) Fm(Dm) Bb7(G7)
1 Come a - way to the skies, my be - lov - ed, a - rise and re -
2 Now with sing - ing and praise, let us spend all the days, by our
3 For the glo - ry we were first cre - a - ted to share, both the
4 We with thanks do ap - prove the de - sign of that love which hath
*5 Hal - le - lu - jah we sing, to our Fa - ther and King, and his
Eb(C) Cm(Am) Fm(Dm) Bb(G) Eb(C) Eb(C) Ab(F) Eb(C)
1 joice in the day thou wast born; on this fes - ti - val day,
2 hea - ven - ly Fa - ther be - stowed, while his grace we re - ceive
3 na - ture and king - dom di - vine! Now cre - a - ted a - gain
4 joined us to Je - sus' Name; so u - ni - ted in heart,
5 rap - tu - rous prais - es, re - peat: to the Lamb that was slain,
Fm(Dm) Bb(G) Eb(C) Cm(Am) Gm(Em) Eb(C) Fm(Dm) Bb7(G7) Eb(C)
1 come ex - ult - ing a - way, and with sing - ing to Zi - on re - turn.
2 from his boun - ty, and live to the hon - or and glo - ry of God.
3 that our lives may re - main, through-out time and e - ter - ni - ty thine.
4 let us nev - er-more part, till we meet at the feast of the Lamb.
5 hal - le - lu - jah a - gain, sing, all hea - ven, and fall at his feet.

Eb (capo 3, C).

Words: Anon., *The Southern Harmony*, 1835, alt.
Music: *Middlebury*, melody from *The Southern Harmony*, 1835; harm. Jack W. Burnam (b. 1946)

♩=96
669. 669

Alternative accompaniment in E for handbells

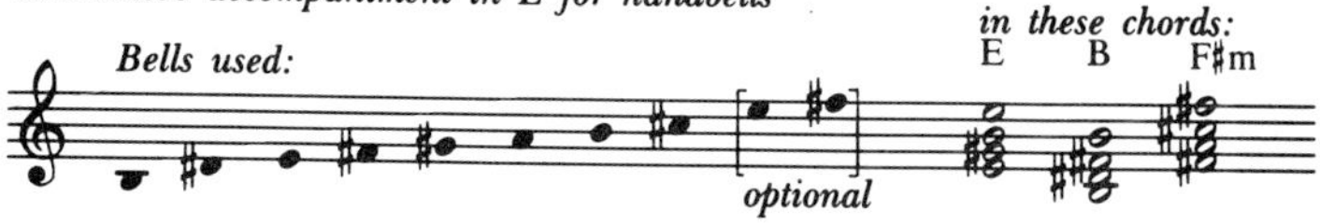

Ring chords with the melody as indicated, 1.v.:

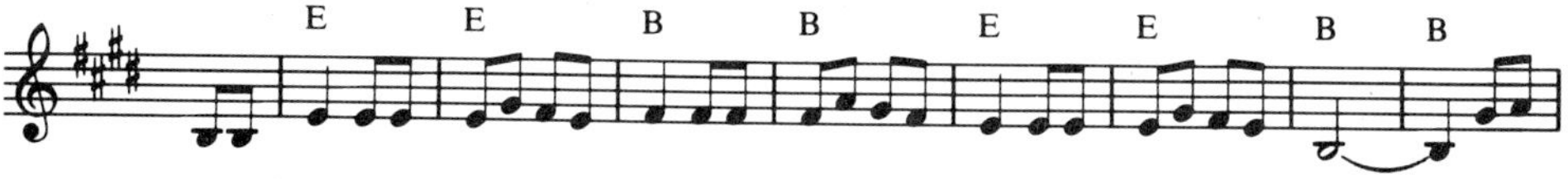

This key is especially suitable for children.

Music: *Middlebury,* melody from *The Southern Harmony,* 1835; acc. Marilyn J. Keiser (b. 1941)

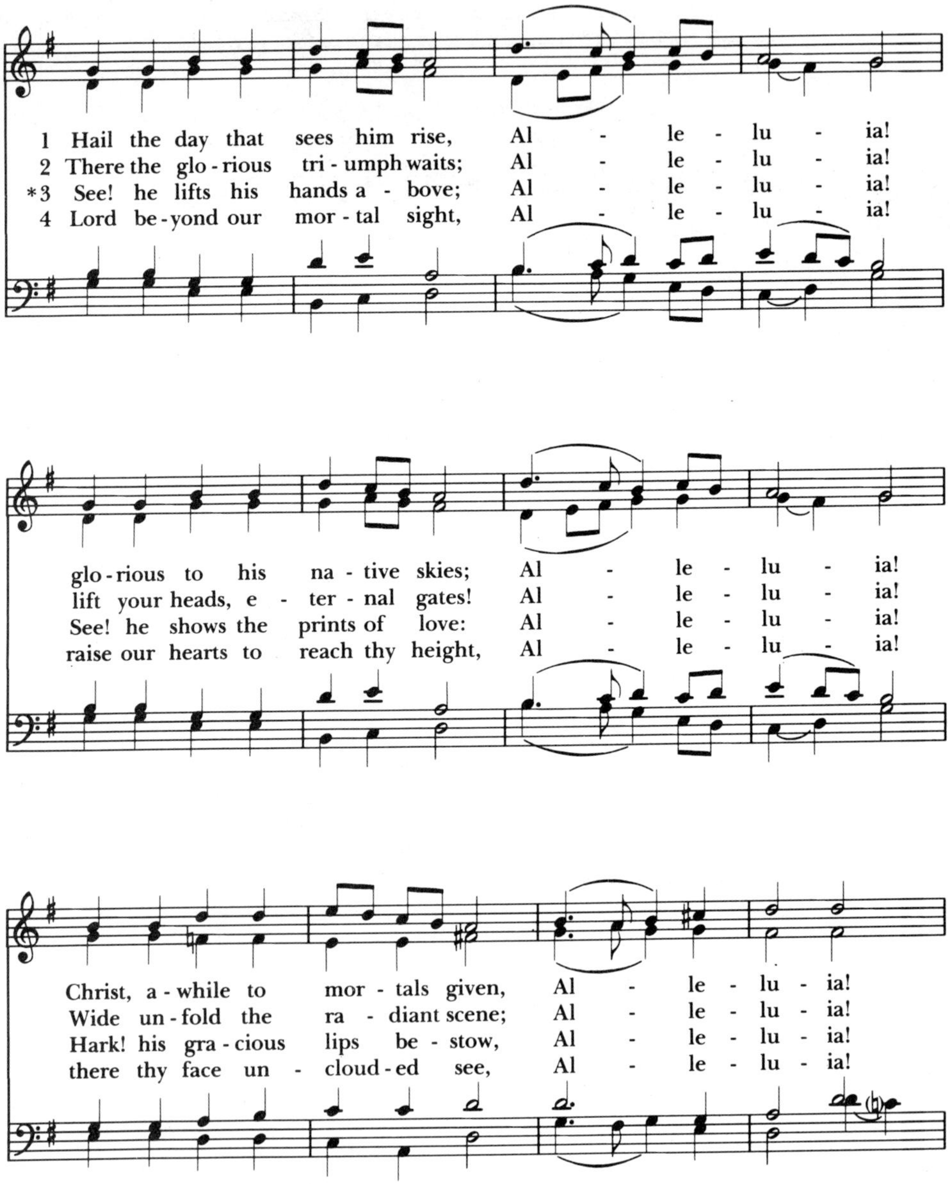
1 Hail the day that sees him rise, Al - le - lu - ia!
2 There the glo - rious tri - umph waits; Al - le - lu - ia!
*3 See! he lifts his hands a - bove; Al - le - lu - ia!
4 Lord be - yond our mor - tal sight, Al - le - lu - ia!
glo - rious to his na - tive skies; Al - le - lu - ia!
lift your heads, e - ter - nal gates! Al - le - lu - ia!
See! he shows the prints of love: Al - le - lu - ia!
raise our hearts to reach thy height, Al - le - lu - ia!
Christ, a - while to mor - tals given, Al - le - lu - ia!
Wide un - fold the ra - diant scene; Al - le - lu - ia!
Hark! his gra - cious lips be - stow, Al - le - lu - ia!
there thy face un - cloud - ed see, Al - le - lu - ia!

en - ters now the high - est heaven! Al - le - lu - ia!
take the King of glo - ry in! Al - le - lu - ia!
bless-ings on his Church be - low. Al - le - lu - ia!
find our heaven of heavens in thee. Al - le - lu - ia!

Words: Charles Wesley (1707-1788), alt.
Music: *Llanfair,* Robert Williams (1781-1821)

𝅗𝅥=72
77. 77 with Alleluias

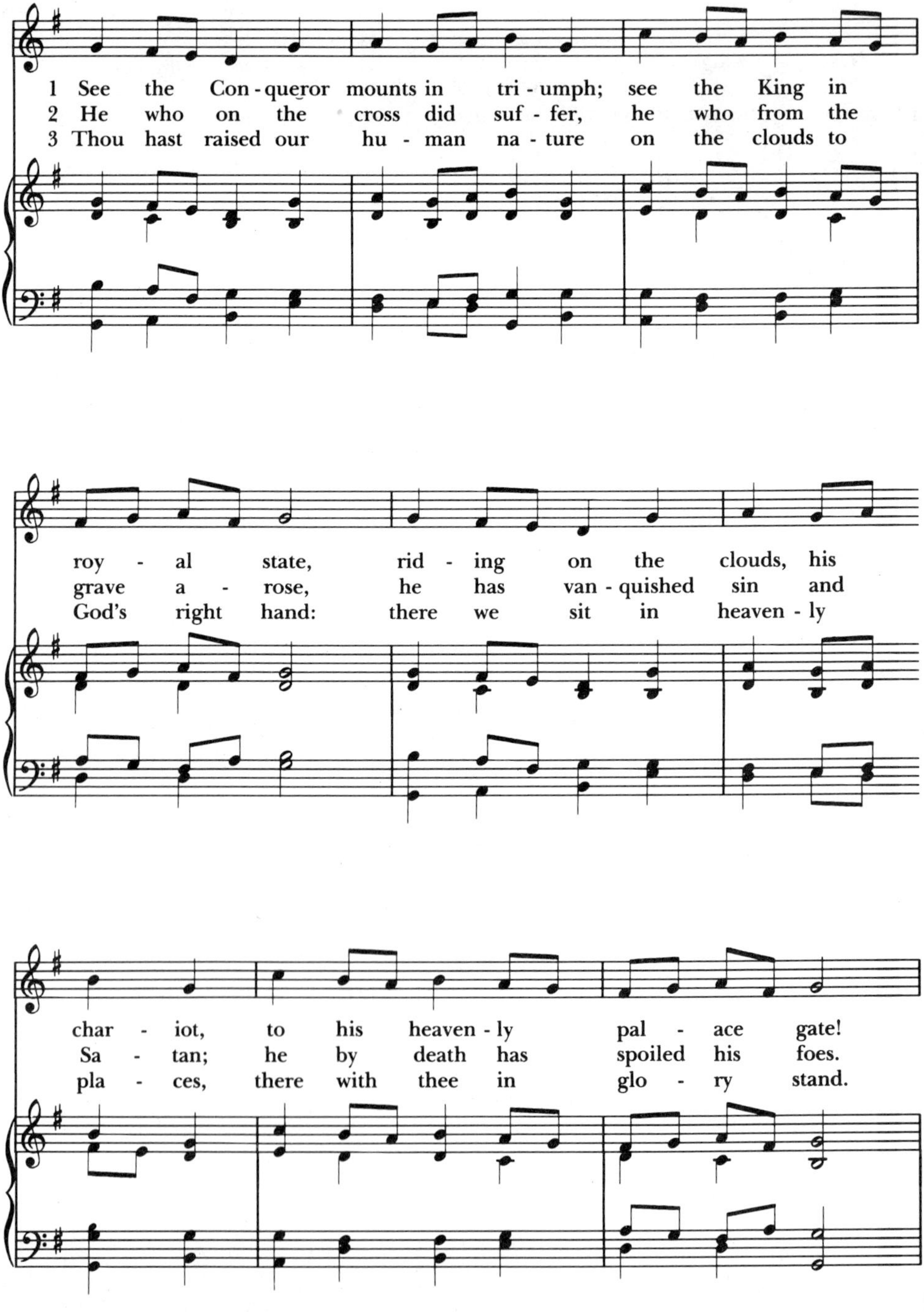
1 See the Con-quer-or mounts in tri-umph; see the King in
2 He who on the cross did suf-fer, he who from the
3 Thou hast raised our hu-man na-ture on the clouds to
roy-al state, rid-ing on the clouds, his
grave a-rose, he has van-quished sin and
God's right hand: there we sit in heaven-ly
char-iot, to his heaven-ly pal-ace gate!
Sa-tan; he by death has spoiled his foes.
pla-ces, there with thee in glo-ry stand.

Hark! the choirs of an - gel voic - es joy - ful al - le - lu - ias sing, and the por - tals high are lift - ed to re - ceive their heaven - ly King.
While he lifts his hands in bless - ing, he is part - ed from his friends; while their ea - ger eyes be - hold him, he up - on the clouds a - scends.
Je - sus reigns, a - dored by an - gels; Man with God is on the throne; might - y Lord, in thine as - cen - sion, we by faith be - hold our own.

Another harmonization, 495.

Words: Christopher Wordsworth (1807-1885), alt.
Music: *In Babilone,* melody from *Oude en Nieuwe Hollantse Boerenlities en Contradanseu,* 1710; harm. Charles Winfred Douglas (1867-1944)

𝅗𝅥=84
87. 87. D

Refrain
Hail thee, fes - ti - val day! blest day that art hal-lowed for
ev - er, day when the Christ a - scends, high in the
First time only
2
hea - vens to reign. reign.

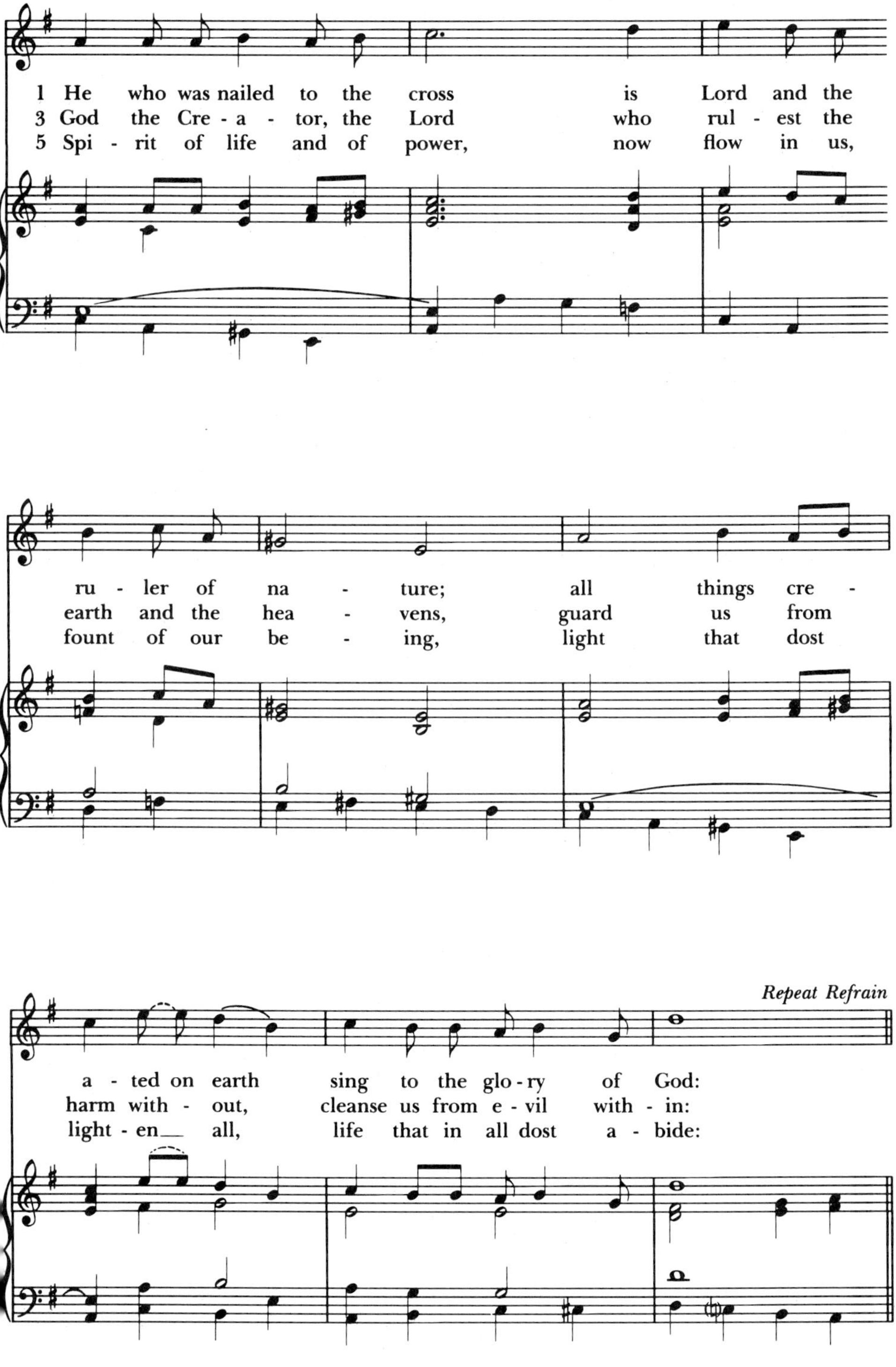
1 He who was nailed to the cross is Lord and the
3 God the Cre - a - tor, the Lord who rul - est the
5 Spi - rit of life and of power, now flow in us,
ru - ler of na - ture; all things cre -
earth and the hea - vens, guard us from
fount of our be - ing, light that dost
Repeat Refrain
a - ted on earth sing to the glo - ry of God:
harm with - out, cleanse us from e - vil with - in:
light - en all, life that in all dost a - bide:

2 Dai - ly the love - li - ness grows, a - dorned with the
4 Je - sus the health of the world, en - light - en our
6 Praise to the Giv - er of good! Thou Love who art
glo - ry of blos - som; hea - ven her gates un -
minds, thou Re - deem - er, Son of the Fa - ther su -
au - thor of con - cord, pour out thy balm on our
bars, fling - ing her in - crease of light:
preme, on - ly - be - got - ten of God:
souls, or - der our ways in thy peace:
Repeat Refrain

The refrain may be sung once by choir alone and repeated by all. The stanzas may be sung by choir alone, alternately by contrasted groups, or by all. This music in F, 175.

Words: Venantius Honorius Fortunatus (540?-600?); tr. *The English Hymnal*, 1906, alt.
Music: *Salve festa dies*, Ralph Vaughan Williams (1872-1958)

𝅗𝅥 = 56
79. 79 with Refrain

1 A hymn of glo - ry let us sing, new hymns through -
2 You are a pre - sent joy, O Lord; you will be
3 O ris - en Christ, a - scend - ed Lord, all praise to
out the world shall ring; by a new way none
ev - er our re - ward; and great the light in
you let earth ac - cord, who are, while end - less
ev - er trod Christ takes his place— the throne of God!
you we see to guide us to e - ter - ni - ty.
a - ges run, with Fa - ther and with Spi - rit, One.

Alternative tune: *Deo gracias,* 218.

Words: The Venerable Bede (673-735); sts. 1-2, tr. Elizabeth Rundle Charles (1828-1896), alt.; st. 3, tr. Benjamin Webb (1819-1885), alt.

Music: *Jam lucis orto sidere,* plainsong, Mode 1, *Mailander Hymnen,* 15th cent.; acc. Bruce Neswick (b. 1956)

LM

Fanfare
1 A hymn of glo - ry let us sing, new
2 You are a pre - sent joy, O Lord; you
3 O ris - en Christ, a - scend-ed Lord, all
hymns through-out the world shall ring; by a new way none
will be ev - er our re - ward; and great the light in
praise to you let earth ac - cord, who are, while end - less

ev - er trod Christ takes his place— the throne of God!
you we see to guide us to e - ter - ni - ty. Al -
a - ges run, with Fa - ther and with Spi - rit, One.
- le - lu - ia, al - le - lu - ia, al - le -
lu - ia, al - le - lu - ia, al - le - lu - ia!

The fanfare may be used as introduction, interlude, and conclusion. Another Harmonization, 449.
Alternative tune: *Jam lucis orto sidere,* 217.

Words: The Venerable Bede (673-735); sts. 1-2, tr. Elizabeth Rundle Charles (1828-1896), alt.;
st. 3, tr. Benjamin Webb (1819-1885), alt.

Music: *Deo gracias,* English ballad melody, Trinity College MS., 15th cent.;
harm. Richard Proulx (b. 1937), based on E. Power Biggs (1906-1977)

♩= 104
LM with Alleluias

Unison or harmony
1 The Lord a - scend - eth up on high, the Lord hath tri - umphed
2 The heavens with joy re - ceive their Lord, by saints, by an - gel
3 Our great High Priest hath gone be - fore, up - on his Church his
glo - rious - ly, in power and might ex - cel - ling;
hosts a - dored; O day of ex - ul - ta - tion!
grace to pour; and still his love he giv - eth.
the grave and hell are cap - tive led. Lo! he re -
O earth, a - dore thy glo - rious King! His ris - ing,
O may our hearts to him a - scend; may all with -
turns, our glo - rious Head, to his e - ter - nal dwell - ing.
his as - cen - sion sing with grate - ful a - dor - a - tion!
in us up - ward tend to him who ev - er liv - eth!

Words: Arthur T. Russell (1806-1874), alt.
Music: *Ach Herr, du allerhöchster Gott,* Michael Praetorius (1571-1621)

𝅗𝅥. = 44
887. 887

1 O Lord Most High, e - ter - nal King, by thee re - deemed thy praise we sing. The bonds of death are burst by thee, and grace has won the vic - to - ry.
2 A - scend - ing to the Fa - ther's throne thou claim'st the king - dom as thine own; and an - gels won - der when they see how changed is our hu - man - i - ty.
3 Be thou our joy, O Might - y Lord, as thou wilt be our great re - ward; let all our glo - ry be in thee both now and through e - ter - ni - ty.
4 O ris - en Christ, a - scend - ed Lord, all praise to thee let earth ac - cord, who art, while end - less a - ges run, with Fa - ther and with Spi - rit, One.

Another accompaniment, 136. Alternative tune: *Gonfalon Royal,* 221.

Words: Medieval Latin; sts. 1-3, tr. F. Bland Tucker (1895-1984); st. 4, tr. Benjamin Webb (1819-1885)
Music: *Aeterne Rex altissime,* plainsong, Mode 1, *Zisterzienser Hymnar,* 14th cent.; acc. Richard Solly (b. 1952) LM

1 O Lord Most High, e - ter - nal King, by thee re -
2 A - scend - ing to the Fa - ther's throne thou claim'st the
3 Be thou our joy, O might - y Lord, as thou wilt
4 O ris - en Christ, a - scend - ed Lord, all praise to
deemed thy praise we sing. The bonds of death are
king - dom as thine own; and an - gels won - der
be our great re - ward; let all our glo - ry
thee let earth ac - cord, who art, while end - less
burst by thee, and grace has won the vic - to - ry.
when they see how changed is our hu - man - i - ty.
be in thee both now and through e - ter - ni - ty.
a - ges run, with Fa - ther and with Spi - rit, One.

After stanza 4
Al - le - lu - ia!

Alternative tune: *Aeterne Rex altissime,* 220.

Words: Medieval Latin; sts. 1-3, tr. F. Bland Tucker (1895-1984); st. 4, tr. Benjamin Webb (1819-1885)
Music: *Gonfalon Royal,* Percy Carter Buck (1871-1947)

𝅗𝅥=46
LM

Ascension

222

1 Re - joice, the Lord of life a - scends in tri - umph from earth's bat - tle - field: his strife with hu - man ha - tred ends, as sin and death their con - quests yield.
2 No more his mor - tal form we see; he reigns in - vis - i - ble but near: for in the midst of two or three he makes his glo - rious pres - ence clear.
3 He reigns, but with a love that shares the trou - bles of our earth - ly life; he takes up - on his heart the cares, the pain, and shame of hu - man strife.
4 He reigns in heaven un - til the hour when he, who once was cru - ci - fied, shall come in all love's glo - rious power to rule the world for which he died.

Words: Albert F. Bayly (1901-1984)
Music: *Parker,* Horatio Parker (1864-1919)

𝅗𝅥=50
LM

1 Hail this joy - ful day's re - turn, hail the
2 Like to clo - ven tongues of flame on the
3 Lord, to you your peo - ple bend; un - to
4 You who did our fore - bears guide, with their
Pen - te - cos - tal morn, morn when our a -
twelve the Spi - rit came— tongues, that earth may
us your Spi - rit send; bless - ings of this
chil - dren still a - bide; grant us par - don,
scend - ed Lord on his Church his Spi - rit poured!
hear their call, fire, that love may burn in all.
sa - cred day grant us, dear - est Lord, we pray.
grant us peace, till our earth - ly wan - derings cease.

Alternative tune: *Sonne der Gerechtigkeit,* 224.

Words: Att. Hilary of Poitiers (4th cent.); tr. Robert Campbell (1814-1868), alt.
Music: *Beata nobis gaudia,* plainsong, Mode 1, *Zisterzienser Hymnar,* 14th cent.; acc. Gerard Farrell (b. 1919)

77. 77

224

1 Hail this joy - ful day's re - turn, hail the Pen - te - cos - tal morn,
2 Like to clo - ven tongues of flame on the twelve the Spi - rit came—
3 Lord, to you your peo - ple bend; un - to us your Spi - rit send;
4 You who did our fore - bears guide, with their chil - dren still a - bide;
morn when our a - scend - ed Lord on his Church his Spi - rit poured! Al - le - lu - ia!
tongues, that earth may hear their call, fire, that love may burn in all. Al - le - lu - ia!
bless - ings of this sa - cred day grant us, dear - est Lord, we pray. Al - le - lu - ia!
grant us par - don, grant us peace, till our earth - ly wan - derings cease. Al - le - lu - ia!

Alternative tune: *Beata nobis gaudia,* 223.

Words: Att. Hilary of Poitiers (4th cent.); tr. Robert Campbell (1814-1868), alt.
Music: *Sonne der Gerechtigkeit,* melody from *Bohemian Brethren, Kirchengeseng,* 1566; harm. Jan O. Bender (b. 1909)

𝅗𝅥 = 96
77. 77 with Alleluia

Refrain
Hail thee, fes - ti - val day! blest day that art hal-lowed for
ev - er, day when the Ho - ly Ghost shone in the
First time only
2
world with God's grace. grace.

1 Lo, in the like - ness of fire, on those who a - wait his ap - pear - ing, he whom the Lord fore - told sud - den - ly, swift - ly de - scends:
3 Hark! for in myr - i - ad tongues Christ's own, his cho - sen a - pos - tles, preach to the ends of the earth Christ and his won - der - ful works:
Repeat Refrain

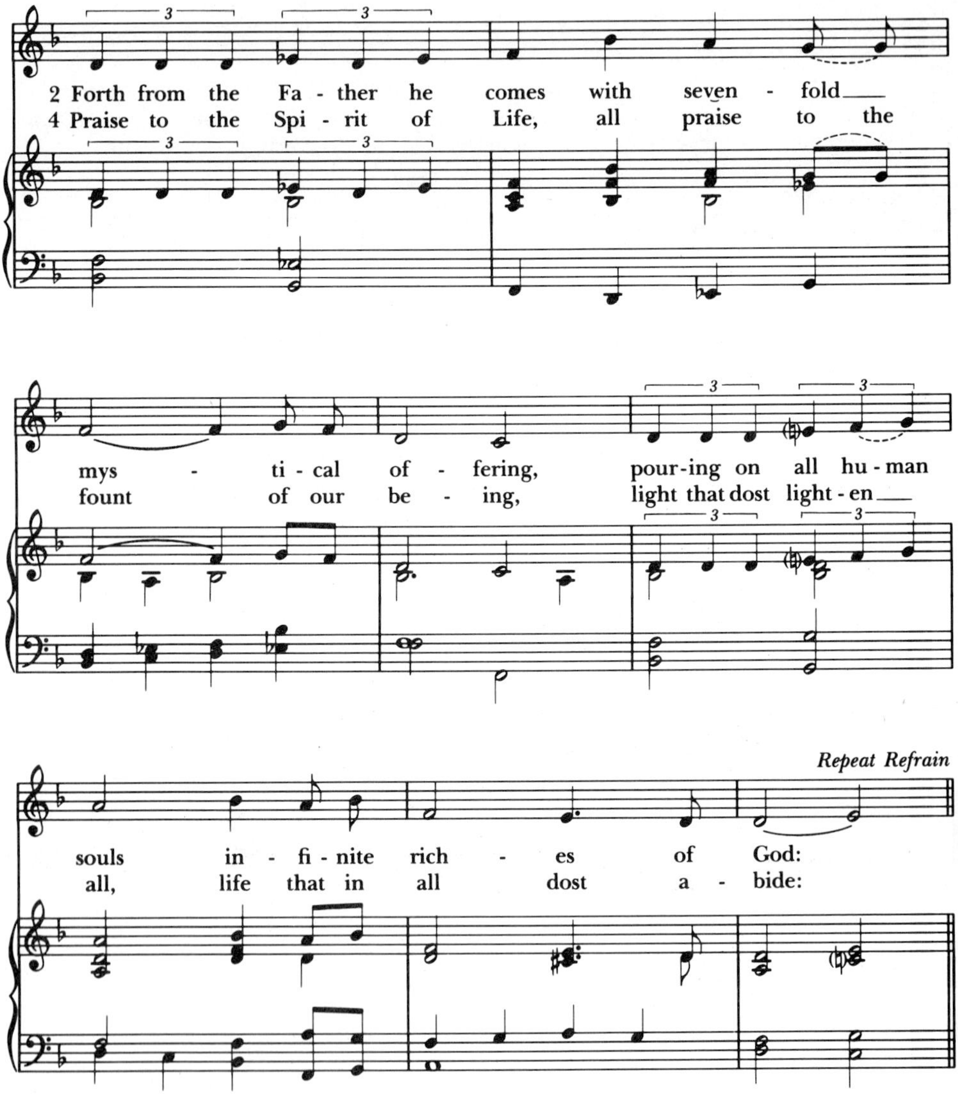
2 Forth from the Fa - ther he comes with seven - fold
4 Praise to the Spi - rit of Life, all praise to the
mys - ti - cal of - fering,
fount of our be - ing,
pour-ing on all hu - man
light that dost light - en
souls in - fi - nite rich - es of God:
all, life that in all dost a - bide:
Repeat Refrain

The refrain may be sung once by choir alone and repeated by all. The stanzas may be sung by choir alone, alternately by contrasted groups, or by all. This music in G, 216.

Words: Venantius Honorius Fortunatus (540?-600?); tr. *English Hymnal*, 1906, alt.
Music: *Salve festa dies*, Ralph Vaughan Williams (1872-1958)

𝅗𝅥=56
Irr.

1. Come, thou Ho - ly Spi - rit bright; come with thy ce - les - tial
light; pour on us thy love di - vine. Come, pro -
tec - tor of the poor; come, thou source of bless - ings
sure; come with - in our hearts to shine. 2. Thou, of

com - fort - ers the best, thou, the soul's most wel - come
guest, of our peace thou art the sign. In our
la - bor, be our aid; in our sum - mer, cool - ing
shade. Ev - ery bit - ter tear re - fine.

3. Bright - er than the noon - day sun, fill our lives which Christ has
won; fill our hearts and make them thine. Where thou
art not, we have nought: all our word and deed and
thought twist - ed from thy true de - sign. 4. Bend the

stub - born heart and will; melt the fro - zen, warm the
chill; rule us by thy judg-ment's line. Cleanse us
with thy heal - ing power; what is bar - ren bring to
flower; to thy love our sins con - sign.

5. To thy peo - ple who a - dore and con - fess thee ev - er -
more, thy blest seven - fold gift as -
sign. Grant us thy sal - va - tion, Lord, bound - less
mer - cy our re - ward, joys which earth and heaven en - twine.

Alternative tune: ***Arbor Street*, 227.**

Words: Latin, 12th cent.; tr. Charles P. Price (b. 1920); tr. of *Veni Sancte Spiritus*

Music: *Veni Sancte Spiritus*, plainsong, Mode 1, *Dublin Troper*, ca. 1360; acc. Adriaan Engels (b. 1906)

𝅗𝅥. = 50

777. 777

1 Come, thou Holy Spirit bright; come with thy celestial light; pour on us thy love divine. Come, protector
2 (Thou,) of comforters the best, thou, the soul's most welcome guest, of our peace thou art the sign. In our labor,
3 (Bright)-er than the noonday sun, fill our lives which Christ has won; fill our hearts and make them thine. Where thou art not,
4 (Bend) the stubborn heart and will; melt the frozen, warm the chill; rule us by thy judgment's line. Cleanse us with thy
5 (To) thy people who adore and confess thee evermore, thy blest sevenfold gift assign. Grant us thy sal-

1 of the poor; come, thou source of bless-ings sure;
2 be our aid; in our sum-mer, cool-ing shade.
3 we have nought: all our word and deed and thought
4 heal - ing power; what is bar-ren bring to flower;
5 va - tion, Lord, bound - less mer-cy our re - ward,
1 come with-in our hearts to shine. 2 Thou,
2 Ev-ery bit - ter tear re - fine. 3 Bright
3 twist-ed from thy true de - sign. 4 Bend
4 to thy love our sins con - sign. 5 To
5 joys which earth and heaven en - (twine.)
1-4
Final Ending
5 twine.

Alternative tune: *Veni Sancte Spiritus*, 226.

Words: Latin, 12th cent.; tr. Charles P. Price (b. 1920); tr. of *Veni Sancte Spiritus*
Music: *Arbor Street*, William Albright (b. 1944)

♩= 116
777. 777

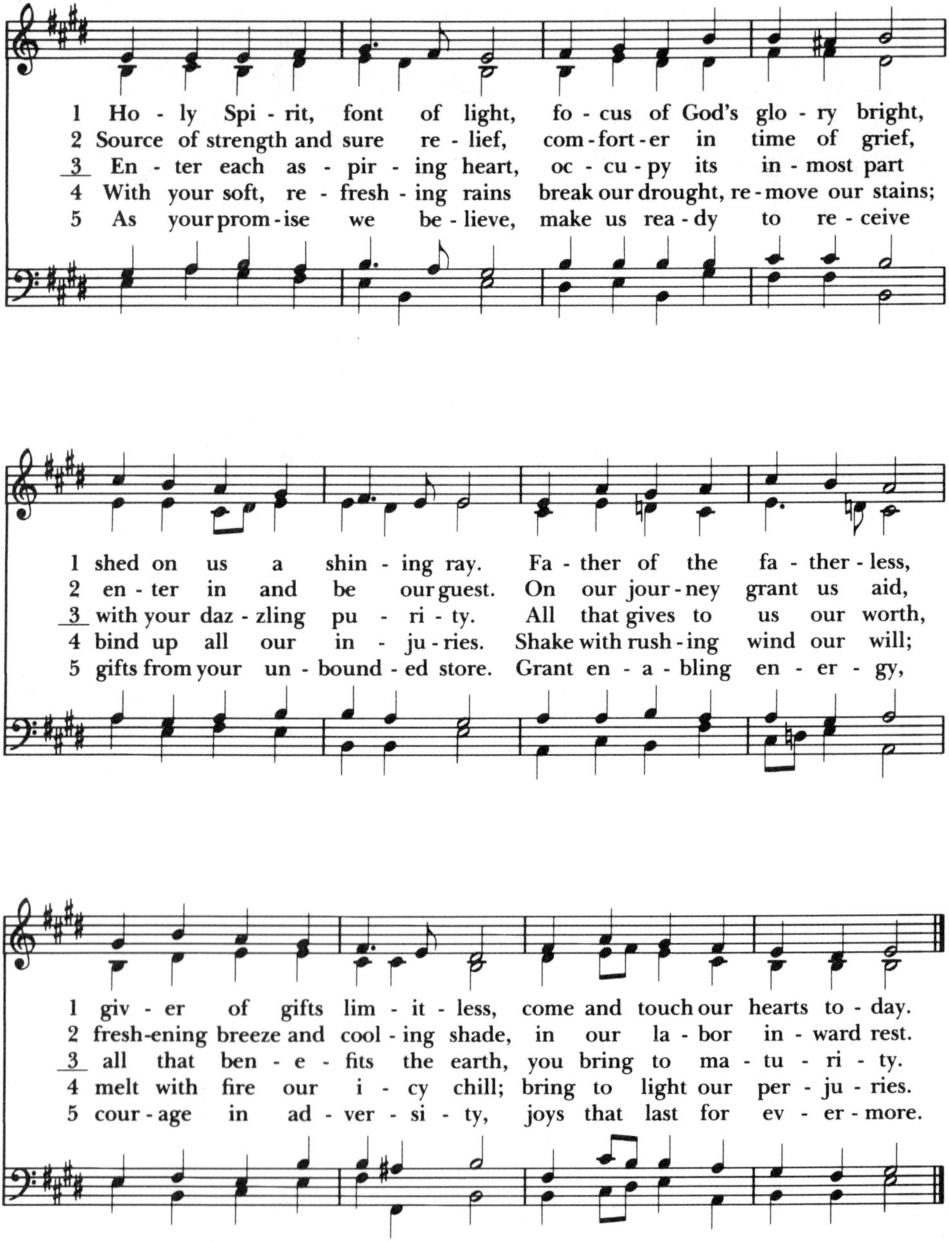
1 Ho - ly Spi - rit, font of light, fo - cus of God's glo - ry bright,
2 Source of strength and sure re - lief, com - fort - er in time of grief,
3 En - ter each as - pir - ing heart, oc - cu - py its in - most part
4 With your soft, re - fresh - ing rains break our drought, re - move our stains;
5 As your prom - ise we be - lieve, make us rea - dy to re - ceive
1 shed on us a shin - ing ray. Fa - ther of the fa - ther - less,
2 en - ter in and be our guest. On our jour - ney grant us aid,
3 with your daz - zling pu - ri - ty. All that gives to us our worth,
4 bind up all our in - ju - ries. Shake with rush - ing wind our will;
5 gifts from your un - bound - ed store. Grant en - a - bling en - er - gy,
1 giv - er of gifts lim - it - less, come and touch our hearts to - day.
2 fresh-ening breeze and cool - ing shade, in our la - bor in - ward rest.
3 all that ben - e - fits the earth, you bring to ma - tu - ri - ty.
4 melt with fire our i - cy chill; bring to light our per - ju - ries.
5 cour - age in ad - ver - si - ty, joys that last for ev - er - more.

Words: Latin, 12th cent.; tr. John Webster Grant (b. 1919), alt.; tr. of *Veni Sancte Spiritus*
Music: *Webbe,* melody from *An Essay on the Church Plain Chant,* 1782; adapt. att. Samuel Webbe (1740-1816), alt.; harm. *Hymns Ancient and Modern,* 1916

𝅗𝅥=52
777. 777

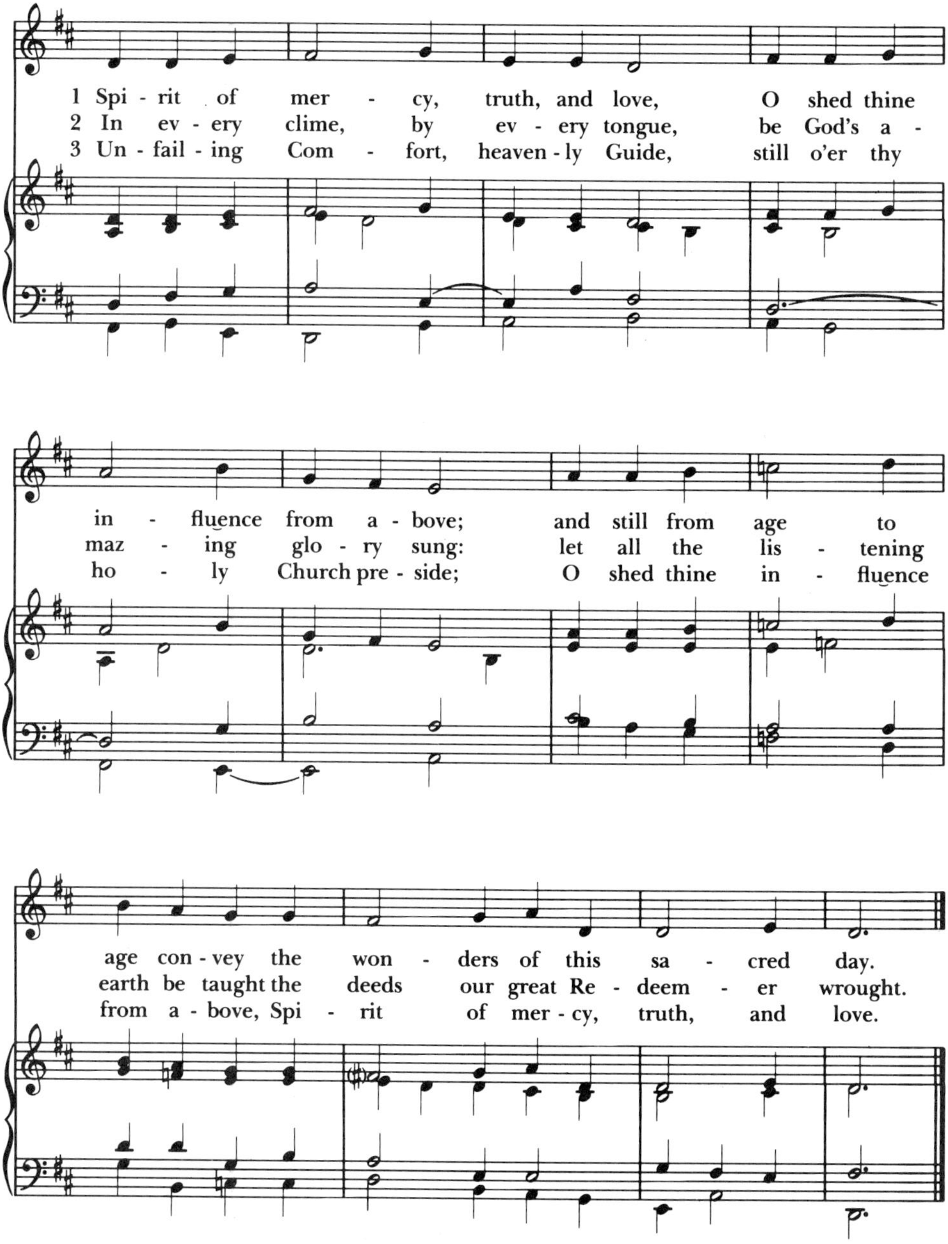
1 Spi - rit of mer - cy, truth, and love, O shed thine
2 In ev - ery clime, by ev - ery tongue, be God's a -
3 Un - fail - ing Com - fort, heaven - ly Guide, still o'er thy
in - fluence from a - bove; and still from age to
maz - ing glo - ry sung: let all the lis - tening
ho - ly Church pre - side; O shed thine in - fluence
age con - vey the won - ders of this sa - cred day.
earth be taught the deeds our great Re - deem - er wrought.
from a - bove, Spi - rit of mer - cy, truth, and love.

Alternative tune: *Melcombe,* 531.

Words: Anon., *Psalms, Hymns and Anthems,* 1774, alt.
Music: *Cornish,* M. Lee Suitor (b. 1942)

♩= 112
LM

1 A might - y sound from hea - ven at Pen - te - cost there came,
2 In Sa - lem's street was gath - ered a crowd from man-y a land,
3 Then come, all Chris - tian peo - ple, keep fes - ti - val to - day,
and filled the place of meet - ing with rush-ing wind and flame:
and all in their own tongues did the Gos - pel un - der - stand:
for God the Ho - ly Spi - rit dwells with the Church al - way:
what Christ had prom - ised now oc - curred as each A - pos - tle
for by the tri - umph of the Son the curse of Bab - el
and grieve him not, O Chris-tian soul, his grace with - in shall
spoke the word be - neath the Spi - rit's thun - der, and to the
was un - done when God did send the Spi - rit; so to the
make you whole in bo - dy, mind, and spi - rit, un - til you

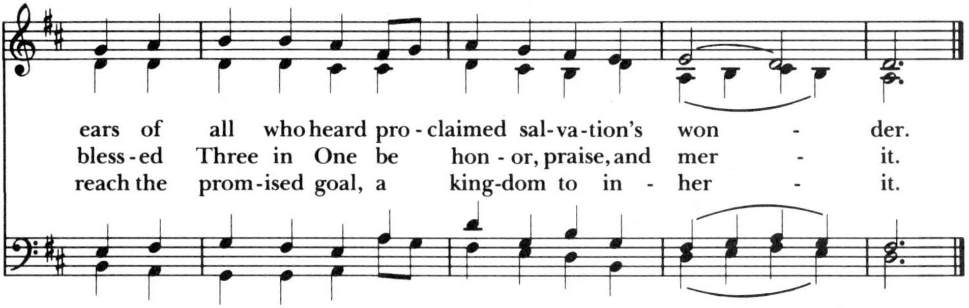
ears of all who heard pro-claimed sal-va-tion's won - der.
bless-ed Three in One be hon-or, praise, and mer - it.
reach the prom-ised goal, a king-dom to in - her - it.

Words: George B. Timms (b. 1910), alt. ♩= 126
Music: *Song of the Holy Spirit,* Dutch melody; harm. Alec Wyton (b. 1921) 76. 76. 887. 87

1 By all your saints still striv - ing, for all your saints at rest,
2 (Insert the stanza appropriate to the day)
3 Then let us praise the Fa - ther and wor - ship God the Son
your ho - ly Name, O Je - sus, for ev - er - more be blessed.
and sing to God the Spi - rit, e - ter - nal Three in One,
You rose, our King vic - to - rious, that they might wear the crown
till all the ran - somed num - ber who stand be - fore the throne

and ev - er shine in splen - dor re - flect - ed from your throne.
a - scribe all power and glo - ry and praise to God a - lone.

Saints' Days. Alternative tunes: *Nyland,* 232; *Ach Gott von Himmelreiche,* 235; *Munich,* 255.

Words: Horatio Bolton Nelson (1823-1913); ver. *Hymnal 1982* 𝅗𝅥=60

Music: *King's Lynn,* English melody; adapt. and harm. Ralph Vaughan Williams (1872-1958) 76. 76. D

Saint Andrew *November 30*

All praise, O Lord, for Andrew,
the first to follow you;
he witnessed to his brother,
"This is Messiah true."
You called him from his fishing
upon Lake Galilee;
he rose to meet your challenge,
"Leave all and follow me."

Saint Thomas *December 21*

All praise, O Lord, for Thomas
whose short-lived doubtings prove
your perfect two-fold nature,
the depth of your true love.
To all who live with questions
a steadfast faith afford;
and grant us grace to know you,
made flesh, yet God and Lord.

Saint Stephen *December 26*

All praise, O Lord, for Stephen
who, martyred, saw you stand
to help in time of torment,
to plead at God's right hand.
Like you, our suffering Savior,
his enemies he blessed,
with "Lord, receive my spirit,"
his faith, in death, confessed.

Saint John *December 27*

For John, your loved disciple,
exiled to Patmos' shore,
and for his faithful record,
we praise you evermore;
praise for the mystic vision
his words to us unfold.
Instill in us his longing,
your glory to behold.

The Holy Innocents *December 28*

Praise for your infant martyrs,
whom your mysterious love
called early from life's conflicts
to share your peace above.
O Rachel, cease your weeping;
they're free from pain and cares.
Lord, grant us crowns as brilliant
and lives as pure as theirs.

Confession of Saint Peter *January 18*

We praise you, Lord, for Peter,
so eager and so bold:
thrice falling, yet repentent,
thrice charged to feed your fold.
Lord, make your pastors faithful
to guard your flock from harm
and hold them when they waver
with your almighty arm.

Conversion of Saint Paul *January 25*

Praise for the light from heaven
and for the voice of awe,
praise for the glorious vision
the persecutor saw.
O Lord, for Paul's conversion,
we bless your Name today.
Come shine within our darkness
and guide us in the Way.

Saint Matthias *February 24*

For one in place of Judas,
the apostles sought God's choice:
the lot fell to Matthias
for whom we now rejoice.
May we like true apostles
your holy Church defend,
and not betray our calling
but serve you to the end.

Saint Joseph *March 19*

All praise, O God, for Joseph,
the guardian of your Son,
who saved him from King Herod
when safety there was none.
He taught the trade of builder,
when they to Nazareth came,
and Joseph's love made "Father"
to be, for Christ, God's Name.

Saint Mark *April 25*

For Mark, O Lord, we praise you,
the weak by grace made strong:
his witness in his Gospel
becomes victorious song.
May we, in all our weakness,
receive your power divine,
and all, as faithful branches
grow strong in you, the Vine.

Saint Philip and Saint James *May 1*

We praise you, Lord, for Philip,
blest guide to Greek and Jew,
and for young James the faithful,
who heard and followed you.
O grant us grace to know you,
the victor in the strife,
that we with all your servants
may wear the crown of life.

Saint Barnabas *June 11*

For Barnabas we praise you,
who kept your law of love
and, leaving earthly treasures,
sought riches from above.
O Christ, our Lord and Savior,
let gifts of grace descend,
that your true consolation
may through the world extend.

The Nativity of Saint John the Baptist *June 24*

All praise for John the Baptist,
forerunner of the Word,
our true Elijah, making
a highway for the Lord.
The last and greatest prophet,
he saw the dawning ray
of light that grows in splendor
until the perfect day.

Saint Peter and Saint Paul *June 29*

We praise you for Saint Peter;
we praise you for Saint Paul.
They taught both Jew and Gentile
that Christ is all in all.
To cross and sword they yielded
and saw the kingdom come:
O God, your two apostles,
won life through martyrdom.

Saint Mary Magdalene *July 22*

All praise for Mary Magdalene,
whose wholeness was restored
by you, her faithful Master,
her Savior and her Lord.
On Easter morning early,
a word from you sufficed:
her faith was first to see you,
her Lord, the risen Christ.

Saint James *July 25*

O Lord, for James, we praise you,
who fell to Herod's sword.
He drank the cup of suffering
and thus fulfilled your word.
Lord, curb our vain impatience
for glory and for fame,
equip us for such sufferings
as glorify your Name.

Saint Mary the Virgin *August 15*

We sing with joy of Mary
whose heart with awe was stirred
when, youthful and unready,
she heard the angel's word;
yet she her voice upraises,
God's glory to proclaim,
as once for our salvation
your mother she became.

Saint Bartholomew *August 24*

Praise for your blest apostle
surnamed Bartholomew;
we know not his achievements
but know that he was true,
for he at the ascension
was an apostle still.
May we discern your presence
and seek, like him, your will.

Saint Matthew *September 21*

We praise you, Lord, for Matthew,
whose gospel words declare
that, worldly gain forsaking,
your path of life we share.
From all unrighteous mammon,
O raise our eyes anew,
that we, whate'er our station
may rise and follow you.

Saint Luke *October 18*

For Luke, beloved physician,
all praise, whose Gospel shows
the healer of the nations,
the one who shares our woes.
Your wine and oil, O Savior,
upon our spirits pour,
and with true balm of Gilead
anoint us evermore.

1 By all your saints still striv - ing, for all your saints at rest,
2 (Insert the stanza appropriate to the day)
3 Then let us praise the Fa - ther and wor-ship God the Son
your ho - ly Name, O Je - sus for ev - er - more be blessed.
and sing to God the Spi - rit, e - ter - nal Three in One,
You rose, our King vic - to - rious, that they might wear the crown
till all the ran - somed num - ber who stand be - fore the throne

and ev - er shine in splen - dor re - flect - ed from your throne.
a - scribe all power and glo - ry and praise to God a - lone.

Saints' Days. Alternative tunes: *King's Lynn,* 231; *Ach Gott von Himmelreich,* 235; *Munich,* 255.

Words: Horatio Bolton Nelson (1823-1913); ver. *Hymnal 1982*
Music: *Nyland,* Finnish folk melody; adapt. and harm. David Evans (1874-1948)

𝅗𝅥 = 48
76. 76. D

Saint James of Jerusalem *October 23*

Praise for the Lord's own brother,
 James of Jerusalem;
he saw the risen Savior
 and placed his faith in him.
Presiding at the council
 that set the Gentiles free,
he welcomed them as kindred
 on equal terms to be.

Saint Simon and Saint Jude *October 28*

Praise, Lord, for your apostles,
 Saint Simon and Saint Jude.
One love, one hope, impelled them
 to tread the way, renewed.
May we with zeal as earnest
 the faith of Christ maintain,
be bound in love together,
 and life eternal gain.

All Saints' Day *November 1*

Apostles, prophets, martyrs,
 and all the noble throng
who wear the spotless raiment
 and raise the ceaseless song:
for them and those whose witness
 is only known to you—
by walking in their footsteps
 we give you praise anew.

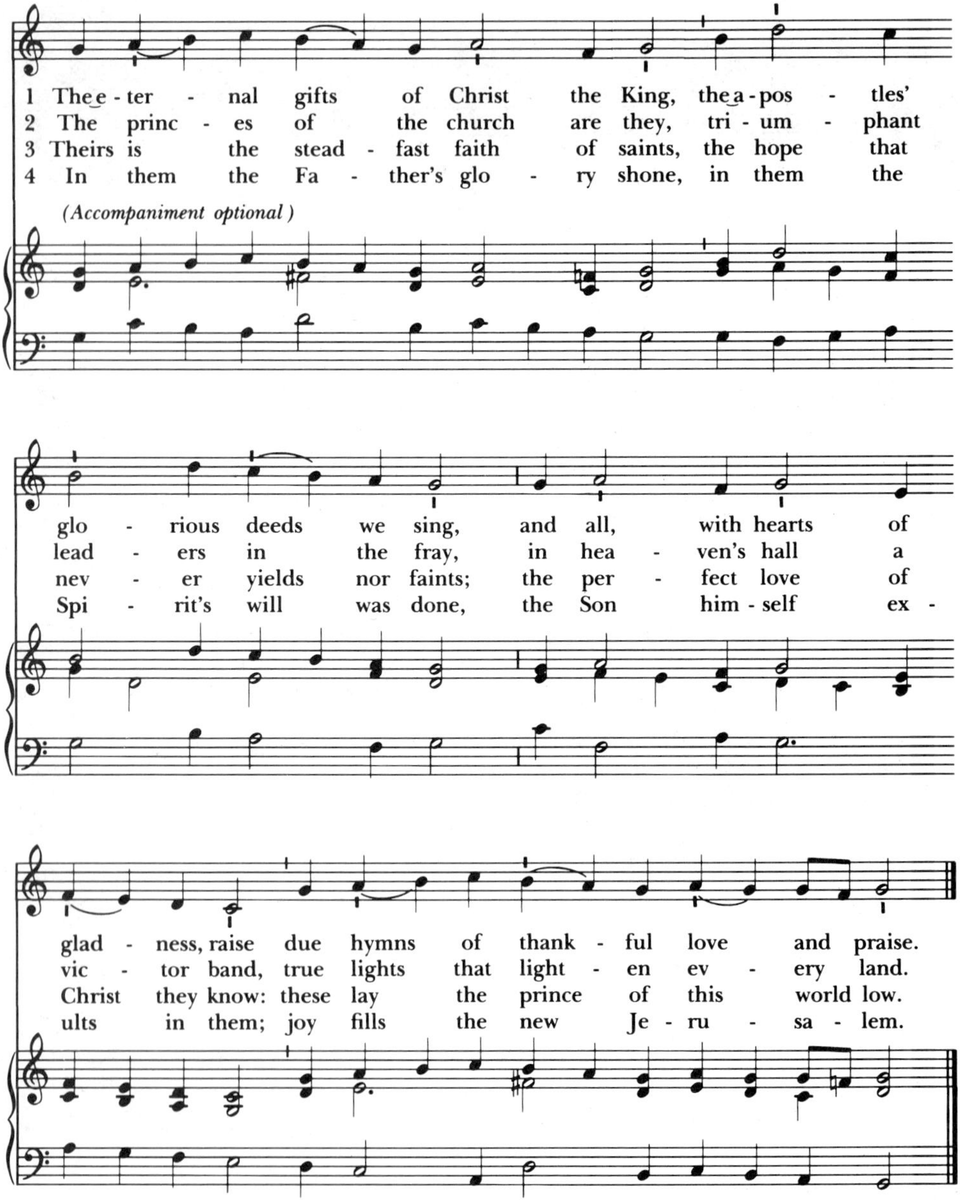
1 The e - ter - nal gifts of Christ the King, the a - pos - tles'
2 The princ - es of the church are they, tri - um - phant
3 Theirs is the stead - fast faith of saints, the hope that
4 In them the Fa - ther's glo - ry shone, in them the
(Accompaniment optional)
glo - rious deeds we sing, and all, with hearts of
lead - ers in the fray, in hea - ven's hall a
nev - er yields nor faints; the per - fect love of
Spi - rit's will was done, the Son him - self ex -
glad - ness, raise due hymns of thank - ful love and praise.
vic - tor band, true lights that light - en ev - ery land.
Christ they know: these lay the prince of this world low.
ults in them; joy fills the new Je - ru - sa - lem.

Alternative tunes: *Gonfalon Royal*, 234; *Jesu, nostra redemptio* (equalist rhythm), 236.

Words: Ambrose of Milan (340-397); ver. *Hymnal 1940*, alt.
Music: *Jesu, nostra redemptio*, plainsong, Mode 8, Worcester MS., 13th cent.; ver. A. Gregory Murray (b. 1905); acc. David Hurd (b. 1950)

♩=116
LM

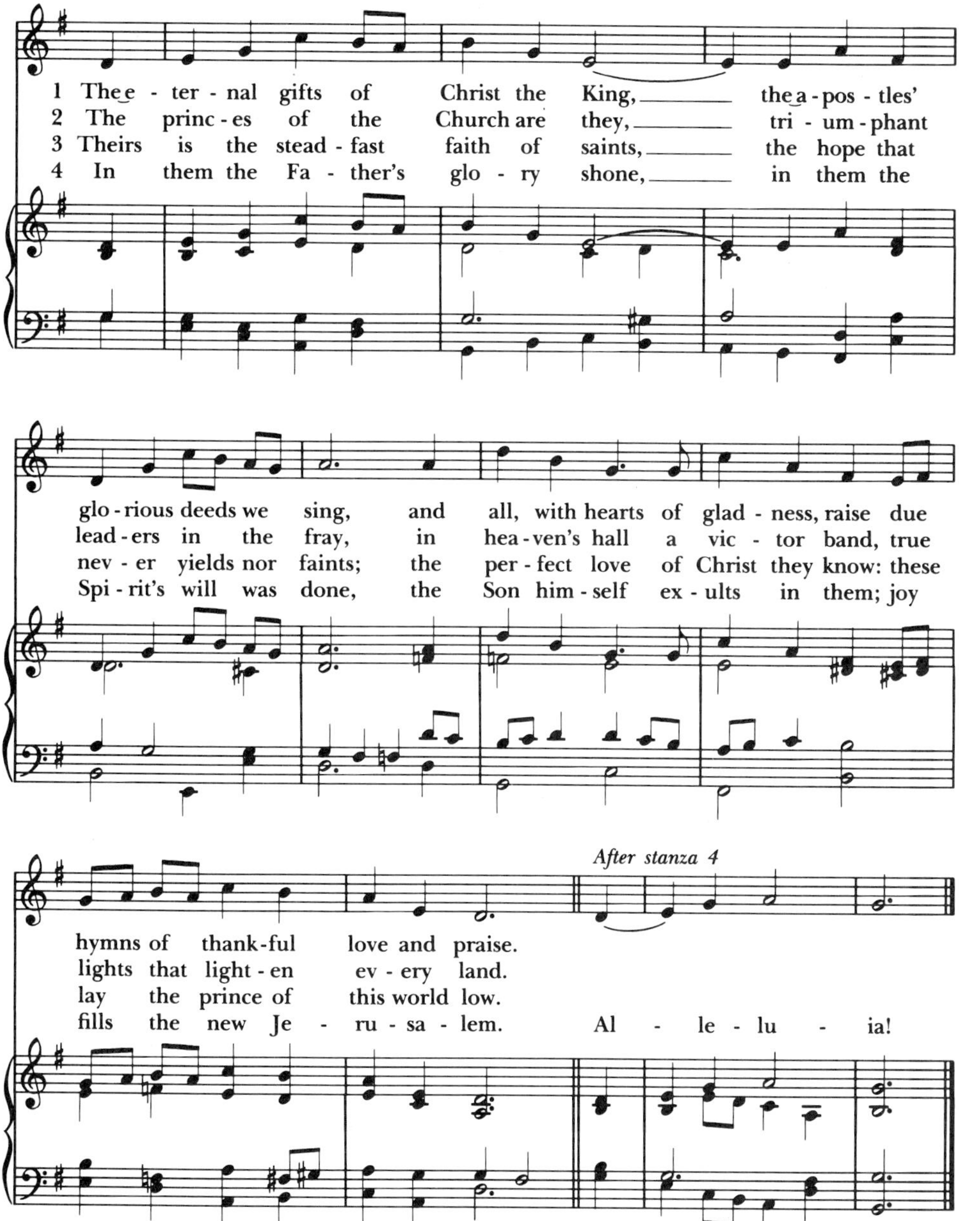
1 The e - ter - nal gifts of Christ the King, the a - pos - tles' glo - rious deeds we sing, and all, with hearts of glad - ness, raise due hymns of thank - ful love and praise.
2 The princ - es of the Church are they, tri - um - phant lead - ers in the fray, in hea - ven's hall a vic - tor band, true lights that light - en ev - ery land.
3 Theirs is the stead - fast faith of saints, the hope that nev - er yields nor faints; the per - fect love of Christ they know: these lay the prince of this world low.
4 In them the Fa - ther's glo - ry shone, in them the Spi - rit's will was done, the Son him - self ex - ults in them; joy fills the new Je - ru - sa - lem.
After stanza 4
Al - le - lu - ia!

Apostles. Alternative tune: *Jesu, nostra redemptio* (syllabic rhythm), 233.

Words: Ambrose of Milan (340-397); ver. *Hymnal 1940*, alt.
Music: *Gonfalon Royal*, Percy Carter Buck (1871-1947)

𝅗𝅥=46
LM

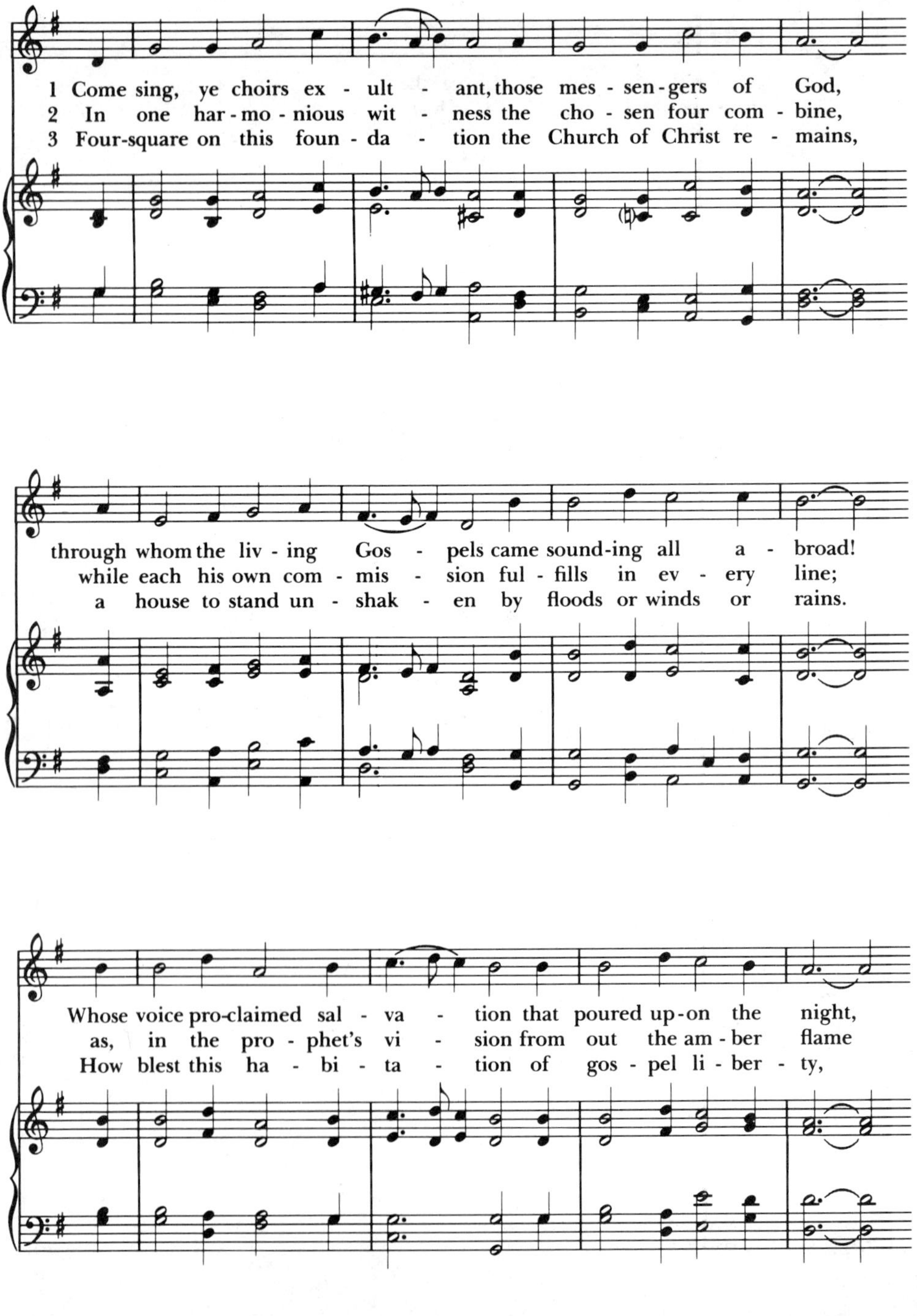
1 Come sing, ye choirs ex - ult - ant, those mes - sen - gers of God,
2 In one har - mo - nious wit - ness the cho - sen four com - bine,
3 Four-square on this foun - da - tion the Church of Christ re - mains,
through whom the liv - ing Gos - pels came sound - ing all a - broad!
while each his own com - mis - sion ful - fills in ev - ery line;
a house to stand un - shak - en by floods or winds or rains.
Whose voice pro-claimed sal - va - tion that poured up - on the night,
as, in the pro - phet's vi - sion from out the am - ber flame
How blest this ha - bi - ta - tion of gos - pel li - ber - ty,

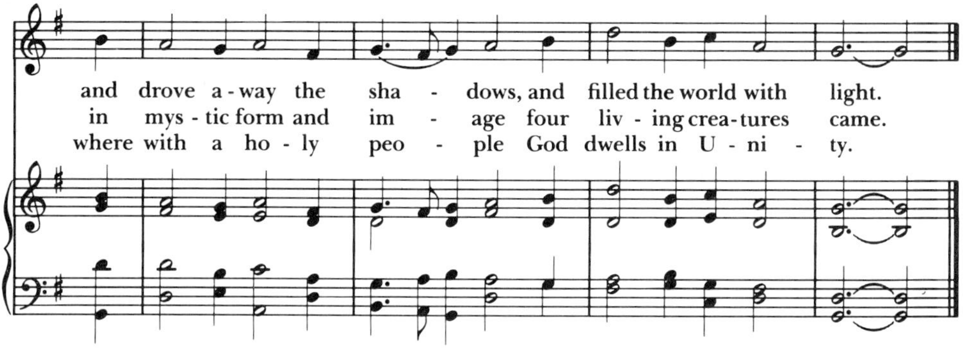
and drove a-way the sha - dows, and filled the world with light.
in mys-tic form and im - age four liv-ing crea-tures came.
where with a ho-ly peo - ple God dwells in U-ni - ty.

Evangelists.

Words: Latin, 12th cent.; tr. Jackson Mason (1833-1889), alt.
Music: *Ach Gott, vom Himmelreiche,* melody Michael Praetorius (1571-1621); harm. George Ratcliffe Woodward (1848-1934), after Michael Praetorius (1571-1621); adapt. *Hymnnal 1982*

𝅗𝅥 = 58
76. 76. D

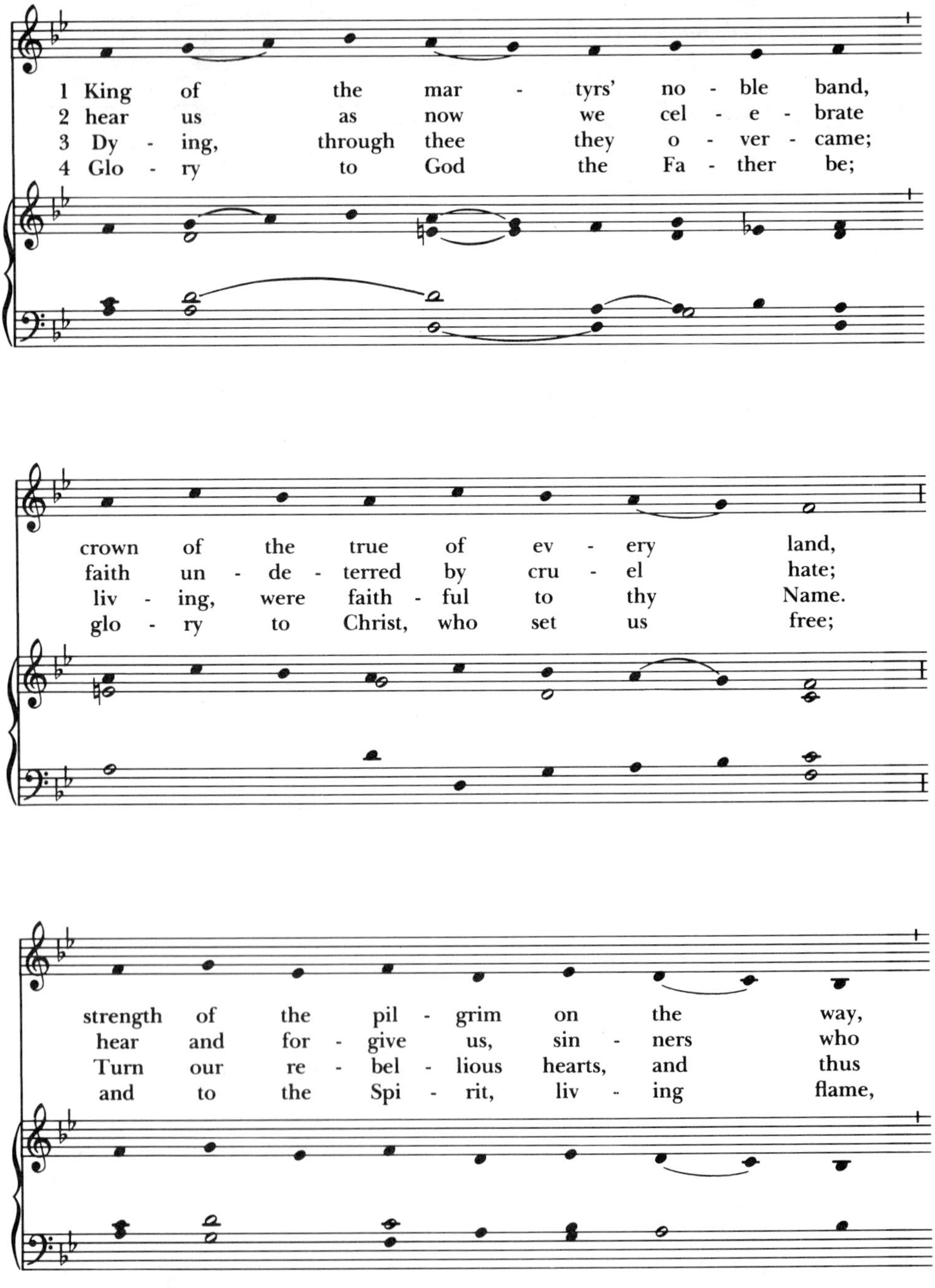
1 King of the mar - tyrs' no - ble band,
2 hear us as now we cel - e - brate
3 Dy - ing, through thee they o - ver - came;
4 Glo - ry to God the Fa - ther be;
crown of the true of ev - ery land,
faith un - de - terred by cru - el hate;
liv - ing, were faith - ful to thy Name.
glo - ry to Christ, who set us free;
strength of the pil - grim on the way,
hear and for - give us, sin - ners who
Turn our re - bel - lious hearts, and thus
and to the Spi - rit, liv - ing flame,

bea - con by night and cloud by day:
are bur - dened by the wrong we do.
win a like vic - to - ry in us.
glo - ry un - ceas - ing we pro - claim.

Martyrs. Another accompaniment, 38. Alternative tune: *Jesu nostra redemptio* (syllabic rhythm), 233

Words: Latin; tr. John Webster Grant (b. 1919), alt.
Music: *Jesu, nostra redemptio,* plainsong, Mode 8, Worcester MS., 13th cent.; acc. Howard Don Small (b. 1932) LM

Alternative accompaniment in higher key
Descant

Chant

Handbells or solo instrument may play either the plainsong melody or the descant; or the melody may be played on the pedal at 4′.

Music: *Jesu, nostra redemptio,* plainsong Mode 8, Worcester MS., 13th cent.; acc. Morgan F. Simmons (b. 1929)

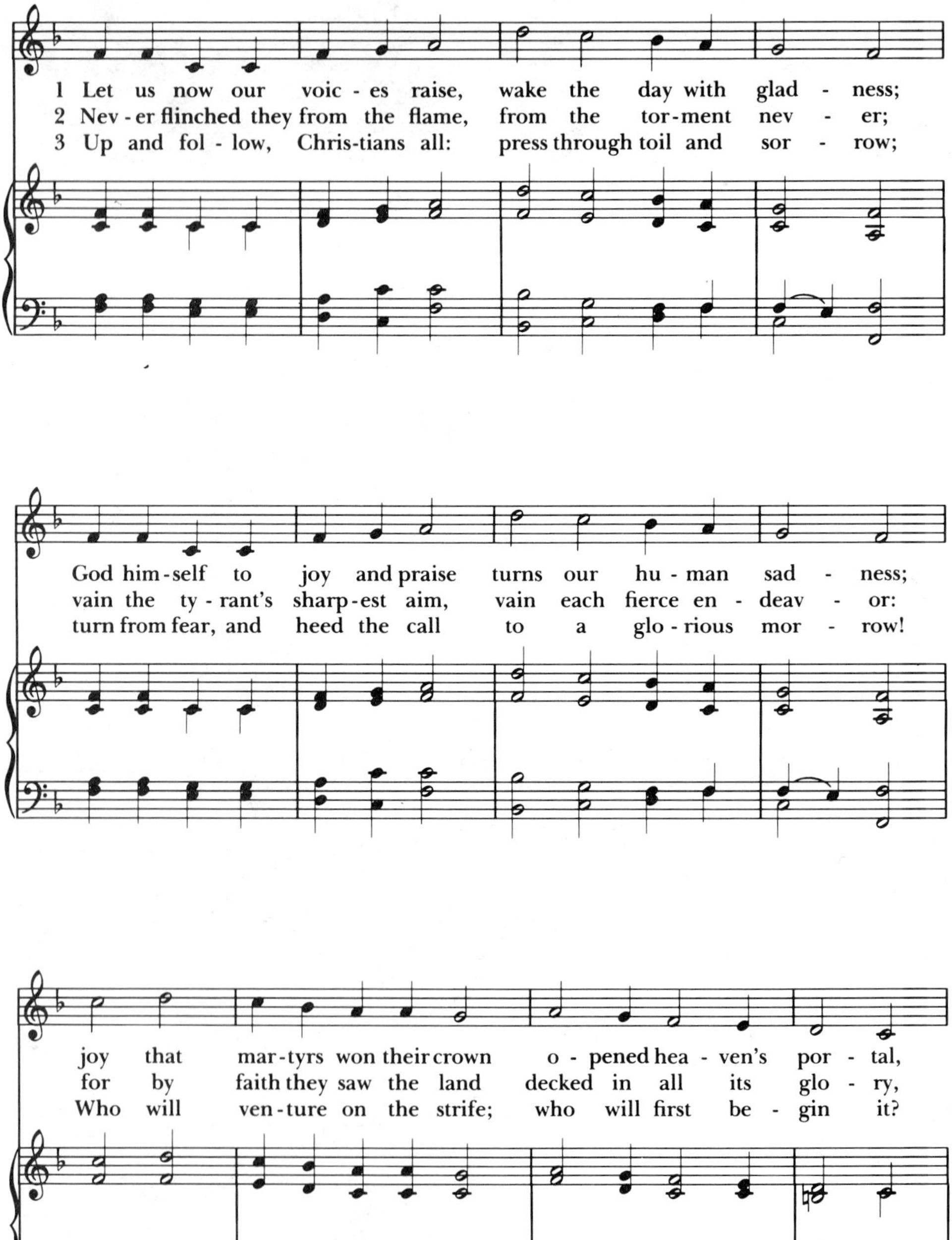
1 Let us now our voic - es raise, wake the day with glad - ness;
2 Nev - er flinched they from the flame, from the tor - ment nev - er;
3 Up and fol - low, Chris - tians all: press through toil and sor - row;
God him - self to joy and praise turns our hu - man sad - ness;
vain the ty - rant's sharp - est aim, vain each fierce en - deav - or:
turn from fear, and heed the call to a glo - rious mor - row!
joy that mar - tyrs won their crown o - pened hea - ven's por - tal,
for by faith they saw the land decked in all its glo - ry,
Who will ven - ture on the strife; who will first be - gin it?

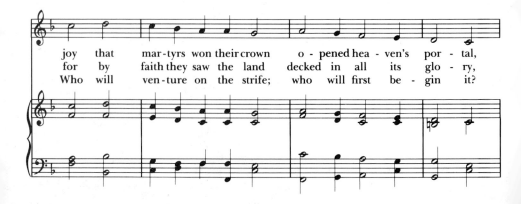

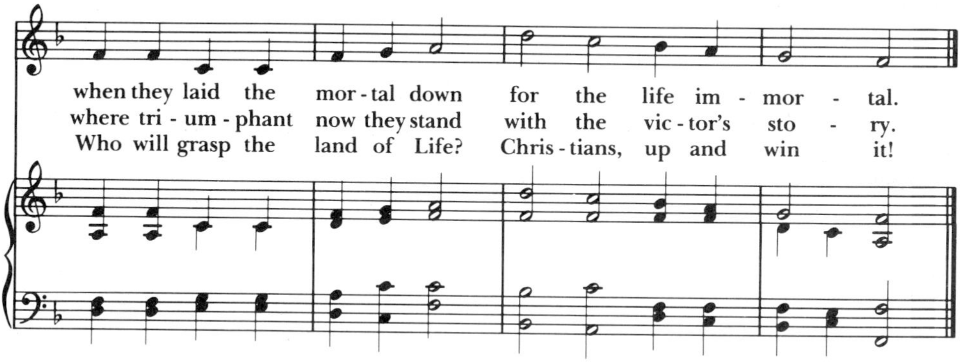
when they laid the mor - tal down for the life im - mor - tal.
where tri - um - phant now they stand with the vic - tor's sto - ry.
Who will grasp the land of Life? Chris - tians, up and win it!

Martyrs.

Words: Joseph the Hymnographer (9th cent.); tr. John Mason Neale (1818-1866), alt.
Music: *Gaudeamus pariter,* melody from *Medieval [German or] Bohemian Carol Melody,* 1544; harm. *Songs of Syon,* 1904

♩= 80
76. 76. D

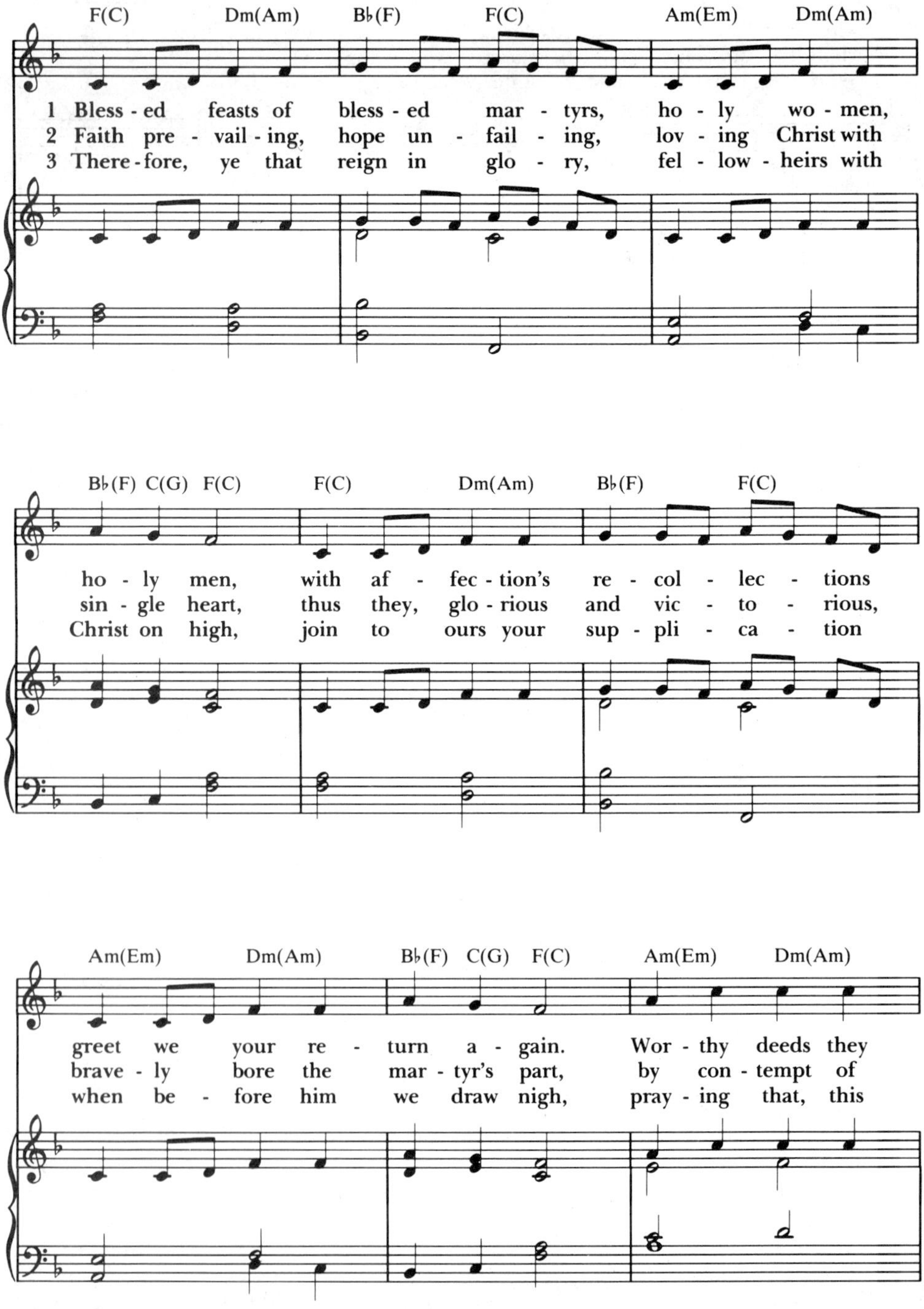
F(C) Dm(Am) B♭(F) F(C) Am(Em) Dm(Am)
1 Bless - ed feasts of bless - ed mar - tyrs, ho - ly wo - men,
2 Faith pre - vail - ing, hope un - fail - ing, lov - ing Christ with
3 There - fore, ye that reign in glo - ry, fel - low - heirs with
B♭(F) C(G) F(C) F(C) Dm(Am) B♭(F) F(C)
ho - ly men, with af - fec - tion's re - col - lec - tions
sin - gle heart, thus they, glo - rious and vic - to - rious,
Christ on high, join to ours your sup - pli - ca - tion
Am(Em) Dm(Am) B♭(F) C(G) F(C) Am(Em) Dm(Am)
greet we your re - turn a - gain. Wor - thy deeds they
brave - ly bore the mar - tyr's part, by con - tempt of
when be - fore him we draw nigh, pray - ing that, this

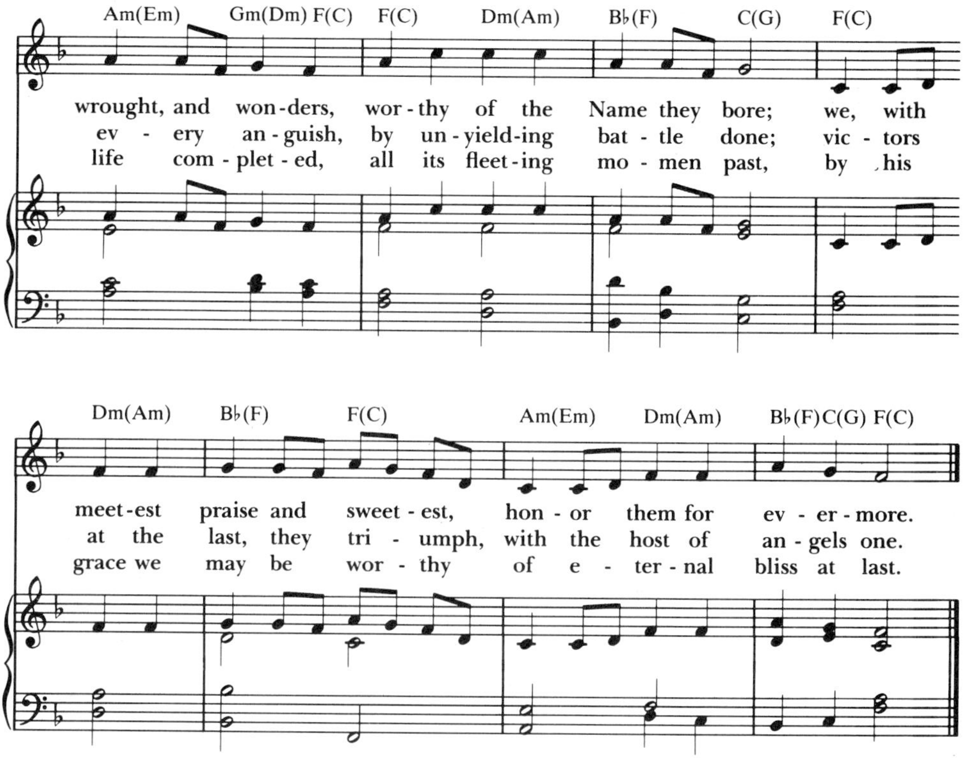
Am(Em) Gm(Dm) F(C) F(C) Dm(Am) B♭(F) C(G) F(C)
wrought, and won-ders, wor-thy of the Name they bore; we, with
ev - ery an-guish, by un-yield-ing bat-tle done; vic-tors
life com-plet-ed, all its fleet-ing mo-men past, by his
Dm(Am) B♭(F) F(C) Am(Em) Dm(Am) B♭(F) C(G) F(C)
meet-est praise and sweet-est, hon-or them for ev-er-more.
at the last, they tri-umph, with the host of an-gels one.
grace we may be wor-thy of e-ter-nal bliss at last.

Martyrs. F (capo 5, C) Another harmonization, 580. Alternative tune: *Alta Trinità beata,* 239.

Words: Latin, 12th cent.; tr. John Mason Neale (1818-1866), alt. 𝅗𝅥=52

Music: *Holy Manna,* melody from *The Southern Harmony,* 1835; acc. Margaret W. Mealy (b. 1922) 87. 87. D

Unison or harmony
1 Bless - ed feasts of bless - ed mar - tyrs, ho - ly wo - men,
2 Faith pre - vail - ing, hope un - fail - ing, lov - ing Christ with
3 There - fore, ye that reign in glo - ry, fel - low - heirs with
ho - ly men, with af - fec - tion's re - col - lec - tions greet we
sin - gle heart, thus they, glo - rious and vic - to - rious, brave - ly
Christ on high, join to ours your sup - pli - ca - tion when be -
your re - turn a - gain. Wor - thy deeds they wrought and won - ders,
bore the mar - tyr's part, by con - tempt of ev - ery an - guish,
fore him we draw nigh, pray - ing that, this life com - plet - ed,
wor - thy of the Name they bore; we, with meet - est
by un - yield - ing bat - tle done; vic - tors at the
all its fleet - ing mo - ments past, by his grace we

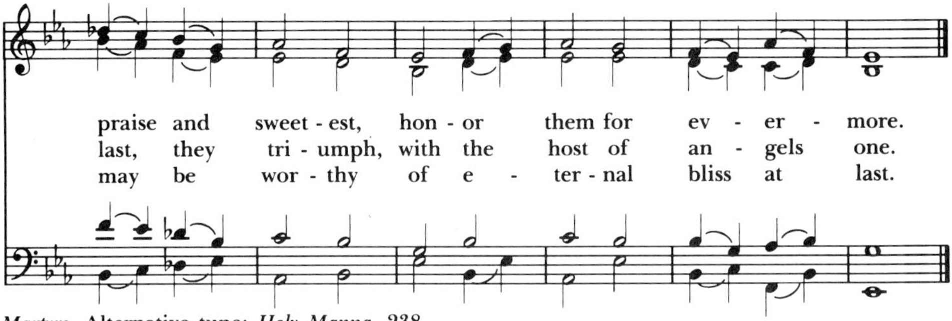
praise and sweet - est, hon - or them for ev - er - more.
last, they tri - umph, with the host of an - gels one.
may be wor - thy of e - ter - nal bliss at last.

Martyrs. Alternative tune: *Holy Manna,* 238.

Words: Latin, 12th cent.; tr. John Mason Neale (1818-1866), alt.
Music: *Alta Trinità beata,* melody from *Laudi Spirituali,* 14th cent.; adapt. and harm. Charles Burney (1726-1814)

𝅗𝅥=58
87. 87. D

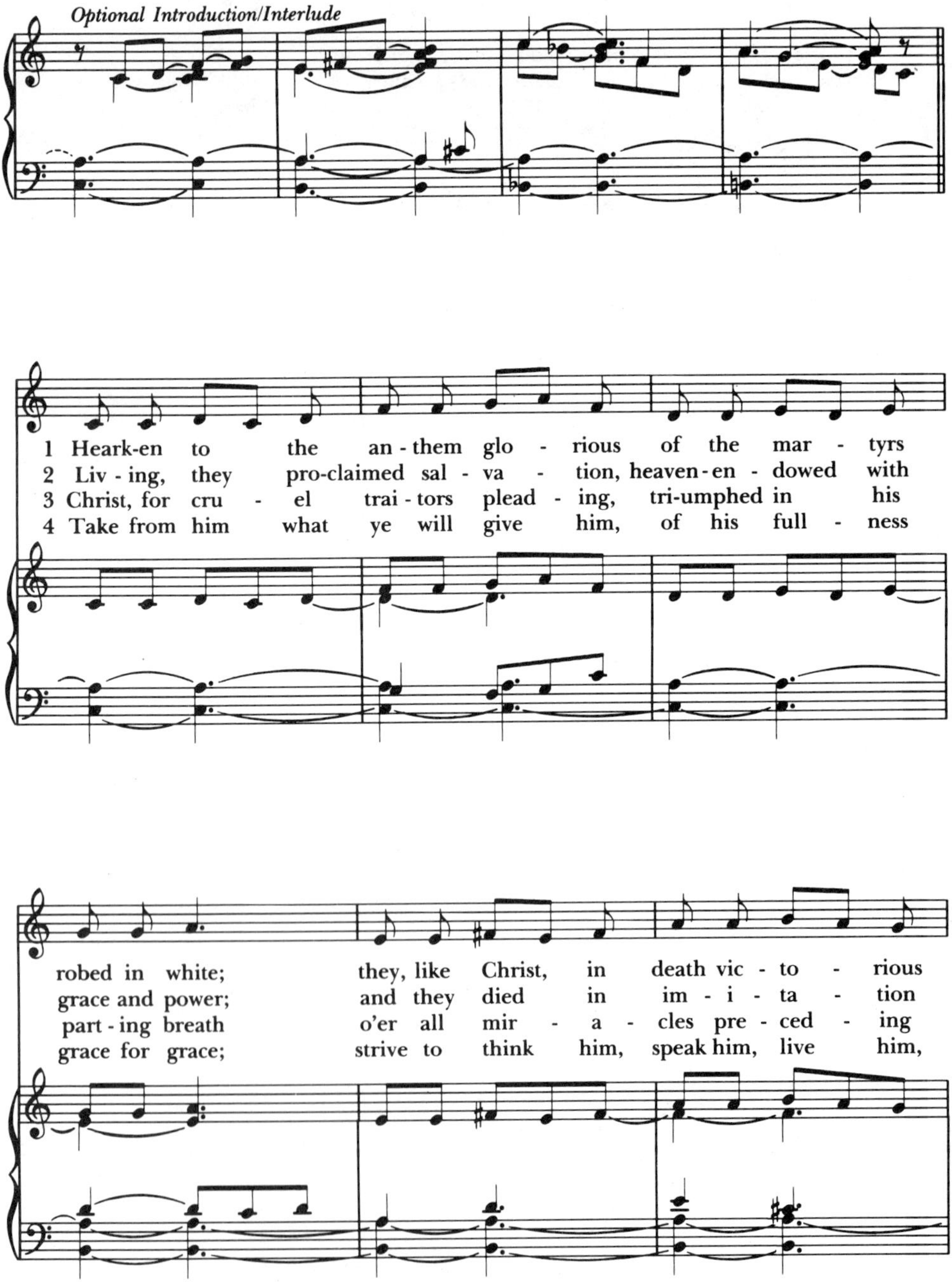
Optional Introduction/Interlude
1 Heark-en to the an-them glo - rious of the mar - tyrs
2 Liv - ing, they pro-claimed sal - va - tion, heaven-en - dowed with
3 Christ, for cru - el trai-tors plead - ing, tri-umphed in his
4 Take from him what ye will give him, of his full - ness
robed in white; they, like Christ, in death vic - to - rious
grace and power; and they died in im - i - ta - tion
part-ing breath o'er all mir - a - cles pre - ced - ing
grace for grace; strive to think him, speak him, live him,

dwell for ev - er in the light.
of their Sa - vior's fi - nal hour.
his in - es - ti - ma - ble death.
till you find him face to face.

Martyrs. The C♯ applies to the final stanza only. Alternative tunes: *Laus Deo,* 241; *Merton,* 59.

Words: Christopher Smart (1722-1771), alt.
Music: *Faciem ejus videtis,* David Thompson Childs (b. 1938)

♪ = 138
87. 87

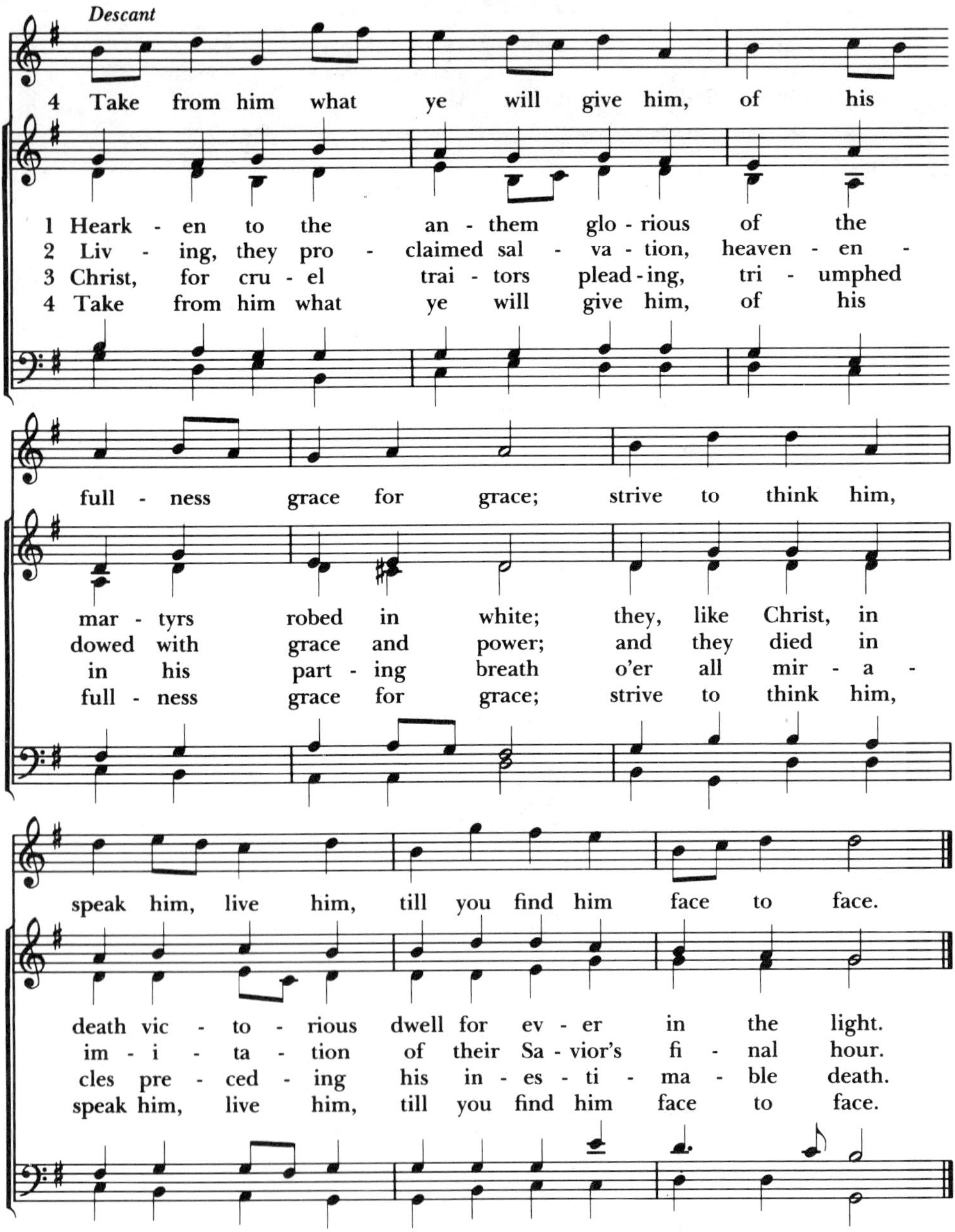
Descant
4 Take from him what ye will give him, of his
1 Heark - en to the an - them glo - rious of the
2 Liv - ing, they pro - claimed sal - va - tion, heaven - en -
3 Christ, for cru - el trai - tors plead - ing, tri - umphed
4 Take from him what ye will give him, of his
full - ness grace for grace; strive to think him,
mar - tyrs robed in white; they, like Christ, in
dowed with grace and power; and they died in
in his part - ing breath o'er all mir - a -
full - ness grace for grace; strive to think him,
speak him, live him, till you find him face to face.
death vic - to - rious dwell for ev - er in the light.
im - i - ta - tion of their Sa - vior's fi - nal hour.
cles pre - ced - ing his in - es - ti - ma - ble death.
speak him, live him, till you find him face to face.

Martyrs. Alternative tunes: *Faciem ejus videtis,* 240; *Merton,* 59.

Words: Christopher Smart (1722-1771), alt.
Music: *Laus Deo,* Richard Redhead (1820-1901); desc. Percy William Whitlock (1903-1946)

𝅗𝅥=46
87. 87

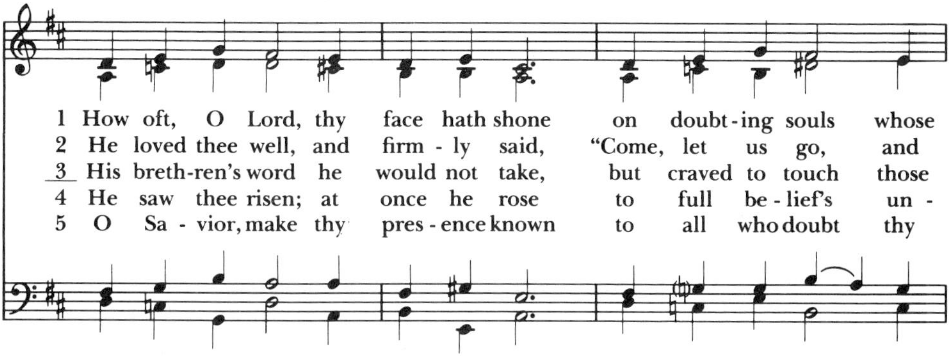
1 How oft, O Lord, thy face hath shone on doubt-ing souls whose
2 He loved thee well, and firm - ly said, "Come, let us go, and
3 His breth-ren's word he would not take, but craved to touch those
4 He saw thee risen; at once he rose to full be - lief's un -
5 O Sa - vior, make thy pres - ence known to all who doubt thy

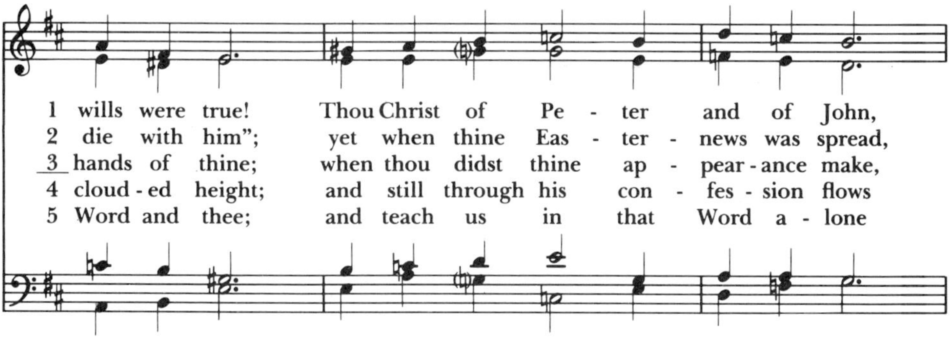
1 wills were true! Thou Christ of Pe - ter and of John,
2 die with him"; yet when thine Eas - ter - news was spread,
3 hands of thine; when thou didst thine ap - pear - ance make,
4 cloud - ed height; and still through his con - fes - sion flows
5 Word and thee; and teach us in that Word a - lone

1 thou art the Christ of Thom - as too.
2 mid all its light his faith was dim.
3 he saw, and hailed his Lord Di - vine.
4 to Chris - tian souls thy life and light.
5 to find the truth that sets us free.

Saint Thomas (December 21). This music in E♭, 466.

Words: William Bright (1824-1901), alt.
Music: *Jacob,* Jane Manton Marshall (b. 1924)

♩=76
LM

1 When Ste-phen, full of power and grace, went forth through-out the
2 When Ste-phen preached a - gainst the laws and by those laws was
3 When Ste-phen, young and doomed to die, fell crushed be - neath the
4 Let me, O Lord, thy cause de - fend, a knight with - out a
land, he bore no shield be - fore his face, no
tried, he had no friend to plead his cause, no
stones, he had no curse nor venge - ful cry for
sword; no shield I ask, no faith - ful friend, no
wea - pon in his hand; but on - ly in his
spokes - man at his side; but on - ly in his
those who broke his bones; but on - ly in his
ven - geance, no re - ward; but on - ly in my

heart a flame and on his lips a sword where -
heart a flame and on his eyes a light where -
heart a flame and on his lips a prayer that
heart a flame and in my soul a dream, so
with he smote and o - ver - came the foe - men of the Lord.
with God's day - break to pro - claim and rend the veils of night.
God, in sweet for - give - ness' name, should un - der - stand and spare.
that the stones of earth - ly shame a jew - eled crown may seem.

Saint Stephen (December 26).

Words: Jan Struther (1901-1953), alt.
Music: *Salvation,* melody from *Kentucky Harmony,* 1816; harm. *Songs for Liturgy and More Hymns and Spiritual Songs,* 1971

𝅗𝅥=54
CMD

Alternative harmonization

This hymn may be sung in unison or two parts, with or without accompaniment.

Music: *Salvation*, melody from *Kentucky Harmony*, 1816; harm. Eugene W. Hancock (b. 1929) 𝅗𝅥=54

1 Come, pure hearts, in joy - ful mea - sure sing of those who
2 See the riv - ers four that glad - den, with their streams, the
3 O that we, thy truth con - fess - ing, and thy ho - ly
spread the trea - sure in the ho - ly Gos - pels shrined;
bet - ter E - den plant - ed by our Lord most dear;
word pos - sess - ing, Je - sus may thy love a - dore;
bless - ed tid - ings of sal - va - tion, peace on earth their
Christ the foun - tain, these the wa - ters; drink, O Zi - ion's
un - to thee our voic - es rais - ing, thee with all thy
proc - la - ma - tion, love from God to lost man - kind.
son and daugh - ters, drink, and find sal - va - tion here.
ran - somed prais - ing, ev - er and for ev - er - more.

Evangelists.

Words: Latin, 12th cent.; tr. *Hymns Ancient and Modern,* 1861, after Robert Campbell (1814-1868), alt.
Music: *Alles ist an Gottes Segen,* melody att. Johann Balthasar König (1691-1758), alt.; harm. Johann Löhner (1645-1705), after chorale version by Johann Sebastian Bach (1685-1750)

𝅗𝅥=52
887. 887

1 Praise God for John, e - van - ge - list, who bore the Spi - rit's
2 Your great I AM's Saint John re - cords, signs of your grace di -
3 O Word made flesh, your deeds and words re - fresh our hearts like
sword, whose words re - flect, like ea - gles' wings, the
vine: "I am the way, the truth, the life; the
dew. Our thanks we raise that all John wrote bears
glo - ry of our Lord. Your bright - ness, O e -
light; the liv - ing vine; your soul's true bread; thirst -
wit - ness, Lord, to you. We praise you that John's
ter - nal Word, A - pos - tle John un - furled, the
quench - ing stream. All these I am, and more: the
voice still lives your glo - ry to pro - claim where -

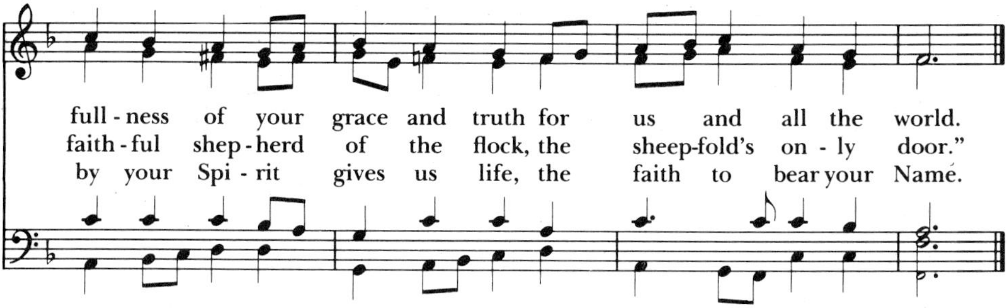
full - ness of your grace and truth for us and all the world.
faith - ful shep - herd of the flock, the sheep-fold's on - ly door."
by your Spi - rit gives us life, the faith to bear your Name.

Saint John (December 27). Alternative tune: *Halifax,* 459.

Words: F. Samuel Janzow (b. 1913)
Music: *Noel,* English melody; adapt. Arthur Seymour Sullivan (1842-1900)

𝅗𝅥 = 60
CMD

246

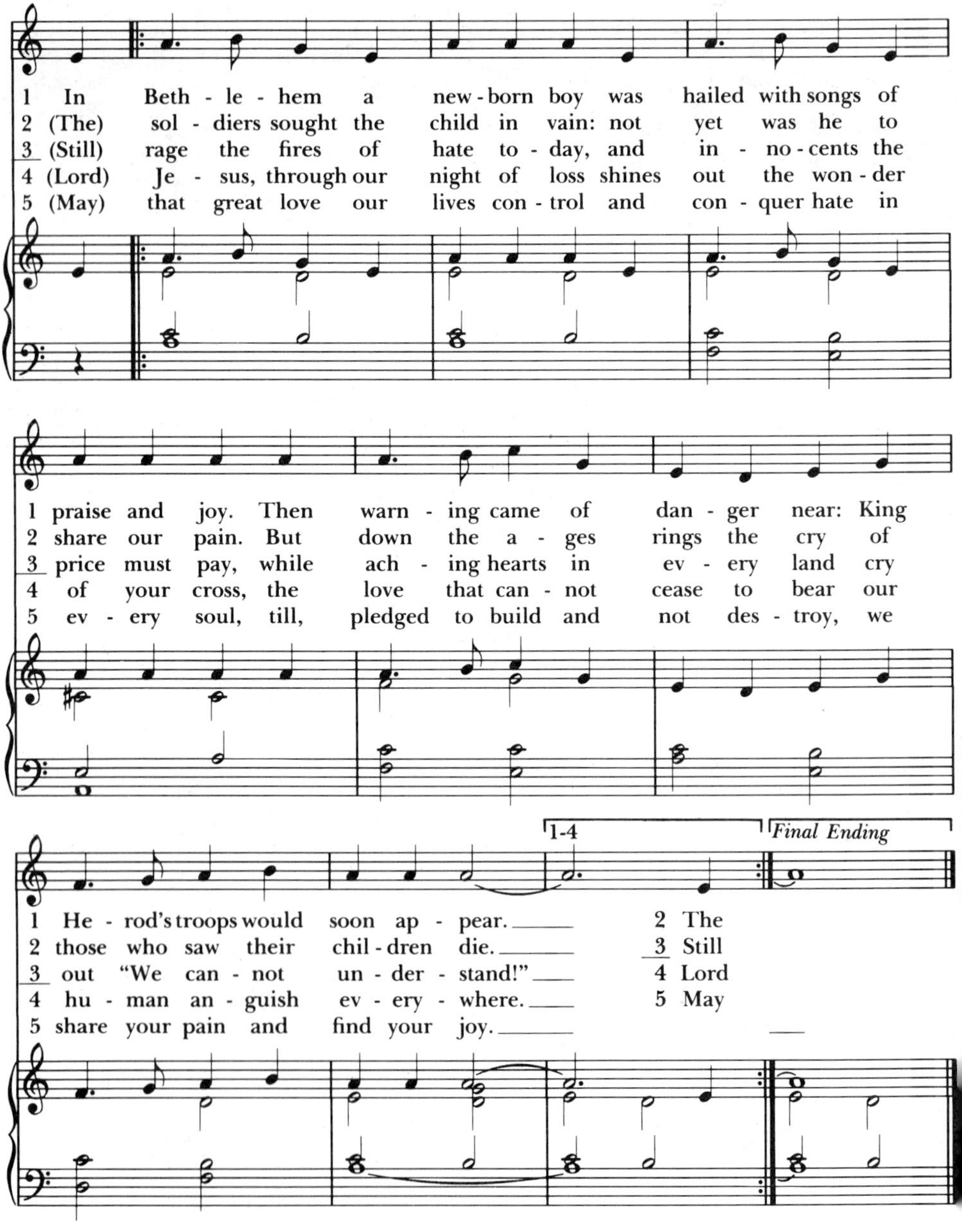
1 In Beth-le-hem a new-born boy was hailed with songs of
2 (The) sol-diers sought the child in vain: not yet was he to
3 (Still) rage the fires of hate to-day, and in-no-cents the
4 (Lord) Je-sus, through our night of loss shines out the won-der
5 (May) that great love our lives con-trol and con-quer hate in
1 praise and joy. Then warn-ing came of dan-ger near: King
2 share our pain. But down the a-ges rings the cry of
3 price must pay, while ach-ing hearts in ev-ery land cry
4 of your cross, the love that can-not cease to bear our
5 ev-ery soul, till, pledged to build and not des-troy, we
1-4
Final Ending
1 He-rod's troops would soon ap-pear.
2 those who saw their chil-dren die.
3 out "We can-not un-der-stand!"
4 hu-man an-guish ev-ery-where.
5 share your pain and find your joy.
2 The
3 Still
4 Lord
5 May

Holy Innocents (December 28).

Words: Rosamond E. Herklots (b. 1905)
Music: *In Bethlehem*, Wilbur Held (b. 1914)

𝅗𝅥 = 50
LM

Burden
Lul - ly, lul - lay, thou lit-tle tin - y child, bye - bye, lul -
ly lul - lay.
1 O sis - ters, too, how may we do
2 He - rod the King, in his ra - ging
3 That woe is me, poor child for thee!
for to pre - serve this day this poor young - ling for
charg - ed he hath this day his men of might, in
And ev - ery morn and day, for thy part - ing nor
Repeat Burden after verse 3
whom we sing bye - bye, lul - ly lul - - lay?
his own sight, all young chil - dren to slay.
say nor sing bye - bye, lul - ly lul - - lay.

Holy Innocents (December 28).

Words: Coventry carol, 15th cent.
Music: *Coventry Carol,* melody from *Pageant of the Shearmen and Tailors,* 15th cent.; harm. Martin Fallas Shaw (1875-1958)

♩= 84
44. 6 D with Refrain

1 To the Name of our sal - va - tion laud and hon - or
2 Je - sus is the Name we trea - sure; Name be - yond what
3 'Tis the Name that who - so preach - eth speaks like mu - sic
4 There-fore we, in love a - dor - ing, this most bless - ed
let us pay, which for man - y a gen - er - a - tion
words can tell; Name of glad - ness, Name of plea - sure,
to the ear; who in prayer this Name be - seech - eth
Name re - vere, ho - ly Je - sus, thee im - plor - ing
hid in God's fore - know-ledge lay; but with ho - ly
ear and heart de - light - ing well; Name of sweet - ness,
sweet - est com - fort find - eth near; who its per - fect
so to write it in us here that here - af - ter,
ex - ul - ta - tion we may sing a - loud to - day.
pass - ing mea - sure, sav - ing us from sin and hell.
wis - dom reach - eth, heaven - ly joy pos - ess - eth here.
heaven-ward soar - ing, we may sing with an - gels there.

Holy Name; New Year (January 1). Alternative tune: *Grafton,* 249.

Words: Latin, 15th cent.; tr. *Hymns Ancient and Modern,* 1861
Music: *Oriel,* Caspar Ett (1788-1847)

𝅗𝅥=46
87. 87. 87

1 To the Name of our sal - va - tion laud and hon - or
2 Je - sus is the Name we trea - sure; Name be - yond what
3 'Tis the Name that who - so preach-eth speaks like mu - sic
4 There-fore we, in love a - dor - ing, this most bless - ed
let us pay, which for man - y a gen - er - a - tion
words can tell; Name of glad - ness, Name of plea - sure,
to the ear; who in prayer this Name be - seech-eth
Name re - vere, ho - ly Je - sus, thee im - plor - ing
hid in God's fore - know - ledge lay; but with ho - ly
ear and heart de - light - ing well; Name of sweet - ness,
sweet-est com-fort find - eth near; who its per - fect
so to write it in us here that here - af - ter,
ex - ul - ta - tion we may sing a - loud to - day.
pass - ing mea - sure, sav - ing us from sin and hell.
wis - dom reach-eth, heaven-ly joy pos - sess - eth here.
heaven-ward soar - ing, we may sing with an - gels there.

Holy Name; New Year (January 1). Alternative tune: *Oriel,* 248.

Words: Latin, 15th cent.; tr. *Hymns Ancient and Modern,* 1861
Music: *Grafton,* melody from *Chants ordinaires de l'Office Divin,* 1881; harm. *Songs of Praise,* 1925

♩=69
87. 87. 87

A D G Em A
1 Now greet the swift - ly chang - ing year with
2 For Je - sus came to wage sin's war; this
3 His love a - bun - dant far ex - ceeds the
4 With such a Lord to lead our way in
5 "All glo - ry be to God on high and
D G Em A C D
1 joy and pen - i - tence sin - cere; re - joice, re - joice, with
2 Name of names for us he bore; re - joice, re - joice, with
3 vol - ume of a whole year's needs; re - joice, re - joice, with
4 haz - ard and pros - per - i - ty, what need we fear in
5 peace on earth," the an - gels cry; re - joice, re - joice, with
G A D G A7 D
1 thanks em - brace an - oth - er year of grace.
2 thanks em - brace an - oth - er year of grace.
3 thanks em - brace an - oth - er year of grace.
4 earth or space in this new year of grace?
5 thanks em - brace an - oth - er year of grace.

Holy Name; New Year (January 1). The melody may be sung in canon at a distance of one measure.

Words: Slovak, 17th cent.; tr. Jaroslav J. Vajda (b. 1919), alt.
Music: *Sixth Night*, Alfred V. Fedak (b. 1953)

♩. = 80
88. 86

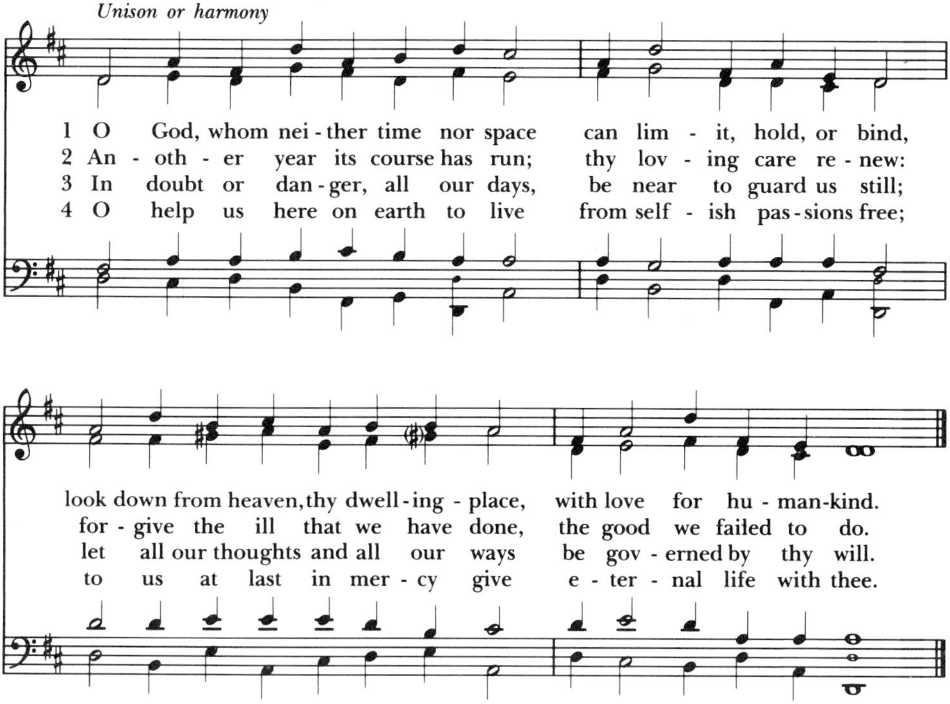
Unison or harmony
1 O God, whom nei - ther time nor space can lim - it, hold, or bind,
2 An - oth - er year its course has run; thy lov - ing care re - new:
3 In doubt or dan - ger, all our days, be near to guard us still;
4 O help us here on earth to live from self - ish pas - sions free;
look down from heaven, thy dwell - ing - place, with love for hu - man-kind.
for - give the ill that we have done, the good we failed to do.
let all our thoughts and all our ways be gov - erned by thy will.
to us at last in mer - cy give e - ter - nal life with thee.

Holy Name; New Year (January 1). This hymn may be used at other times by omitting stanza 2.
This music in C, 50.

Words: Horace Smith (1836-1922) and others
Music: *London New,* melody from *The Psalmes of David in Prose and Meeter,* 1635, alt.; harm. John Playford (1623-1686)

♩= 88
CM

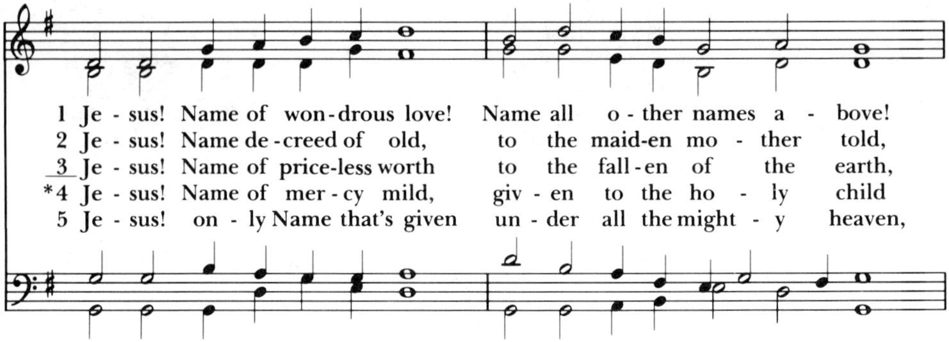
1 Je - sus! Name of won-drous love! Name all o - ther names a - bove!
2 Je - sus! Name de - creed of old, to the maid-en mo - ther told,
3 Je - sus! Name of price-less worth to the fall - en of the earth,
*4 Je - sus! Name of mer - cy mild, giv - en to the ho - ly child
5 Je - sus! on - ly Name that's given un - der all the might - y heaven,

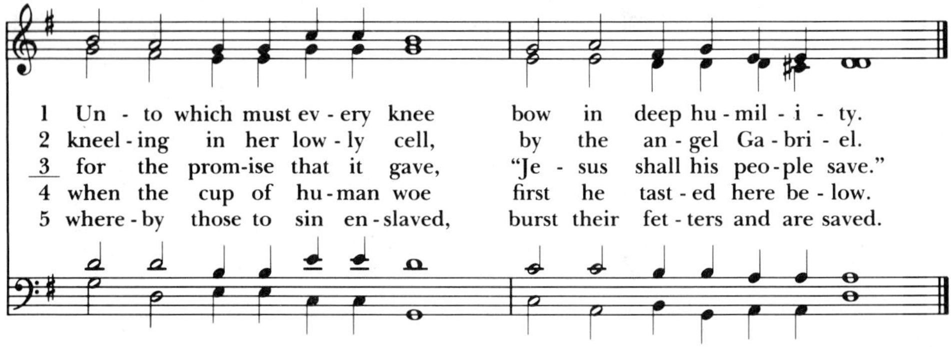
1 Un - to which must ev - ery knee bow in deep hu - mil - i - ty.
2 kneel - ing in her low - ly cell, by the an - gel Ga - bri - el.
3 for the prom-ise that it gave, "Je - sus shall his peo - ple save."
4 when the cup of hu - man woe first he tast - ed here be - low.
5 where - by those to sin en - slaved, burst their fet - ters and are saved.

6 Jesus! Name of wondrous love!
Human Name of God above;
pleading only this we flee,
helpless, O our God, to thee.

Holy Name; New Year (January 1).

Words: William Walsham How (1823-1897), alt. 𝅗𝅥=58

Music: *Louez Dieu*, from *Les cent cinquante Pseaumes de David*, 1564, alt. 77. 77

1 Give us the wings of faith to rise with - in the
2 We ask them whence their vic - tory came; they, with u -
3 They marked the foot - steps that he trod, his zeal in -
4 Our glo - rious Lead - er claims our praise for his own
veil, and see the saints a - bove, how great their joys, how
ni - ted breath, as - cribe their con - quest to the Lamb, their
spired their quest, and fol - lowing their in - car - nate God, they
pat - tern given; while the long cloud of wit - ness - es show
bright their glo - ries be.
tri - umph to his death.
reached the prom - ised rest.
the same path to (heaven.)
Optional interlude between stanzas
Ending
(be.)
(death.)
(rest.)
heaven.

Saints' Days; All Saints' Day (November 1). This music in C, 604.

Words: Isaac Watts (1674-1748), alt.
Music: *San Rocco,* Derek Williams (b. 1945)

𝅗𝅥=48
CM

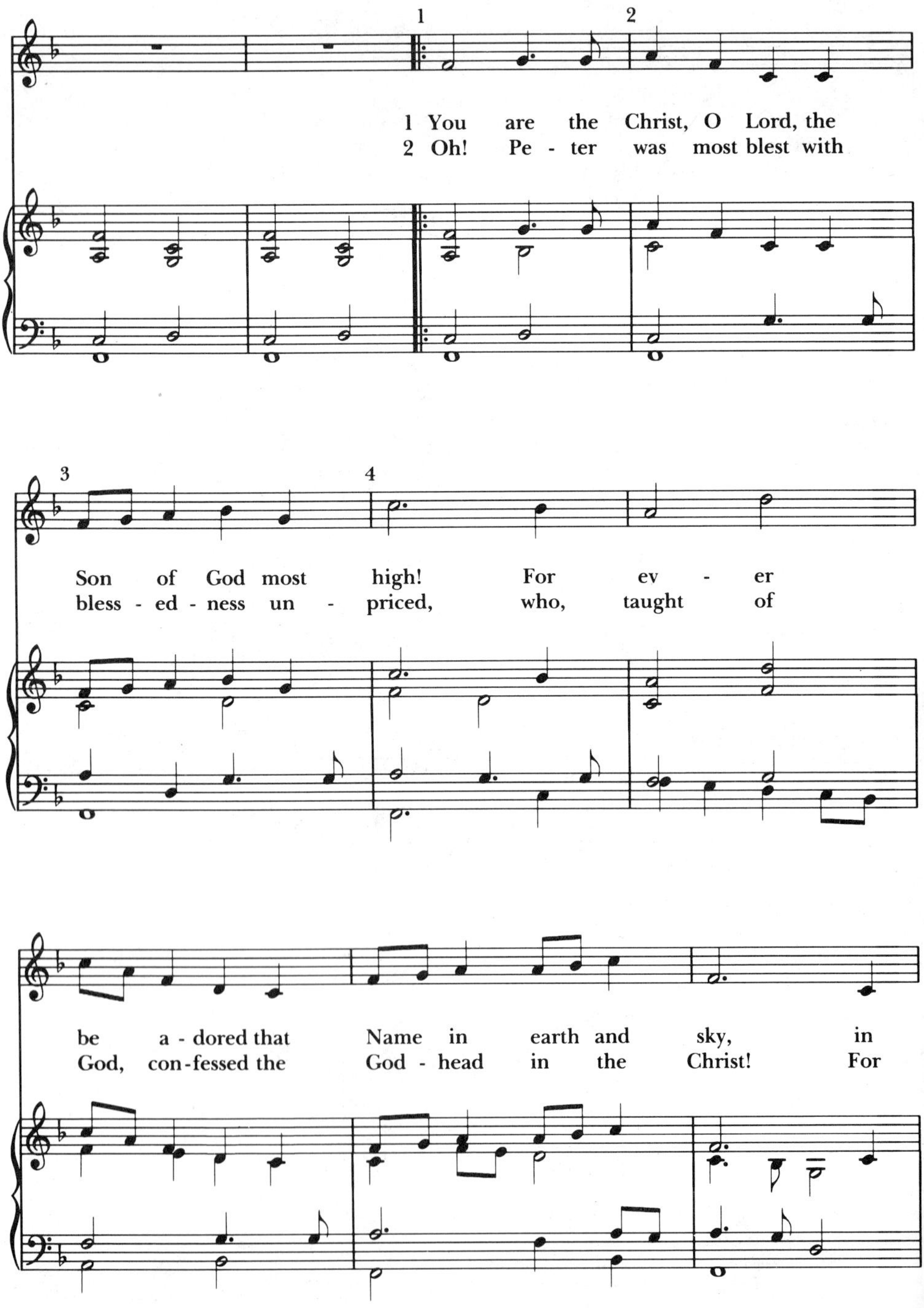
1
2
1 You are the Christ, O Lord, the
2 Oh! Pe - ter was most blest with
3
4
Son of God most high! For ev - er
bless - ed - ness un - priced, who, taught of
be a - dored that Name in earth and sky, in
God, con-fessed the God - head in the Christ! For

which, though mor - tal strength may fail, the saints of God at
of your Church, Lord, you made known this saint a true foun -

for canon only
last pre - vail!
da - tion-stone.

Confession of Saint Peter (January 18). This hymn may be sung as a two- or four-part canon with entrances alternating between treble and male voices.

Words: William Walsham How (1823-1897)
Music: *Wyngate Canon*, Richard Wayne Dirksen (b. 1921)

𝅗𝅥 = 72
66. 66. 88

1 We sing the glo - rious con - quest be - fore Da - mas - cus' gate,
2 O Voice that spoke with - in him; O strong, re - prov - ing Word;
3 Your grace, by ways mys - te - rious, our sin - ful wrath can bind,
when Saul, the church - 's spoil - er came spread - ing fear and hate.
O Love that sought and held him a pris - oner of his Lord;
and in those least ex - pect - ed true ser - vants you can find.
God's light shone down from hea - ven and broke a - cross the path.
help us to know your king - ship that we, in ev - ery hour,
In us you seek dis - ci - ples to share your cross and crown
His pres - ence pierced and blind - ed the zeal - ot in his wrath.
in all that may con - front us, will trust your hid - den power.
and give you fi - nal ser - vice in glo - ry at your throne.

Conversion of Saint Paul (January 25). This music in E♭, 632.

Words: John Ellerton (1826-1893), alt.
Music: *Munich,* melody from *Neu-vermehrtes und zu Ubung Christl. Gottseligkeit eingerichtetes Meiningisches Gesangbuch,* 1693; adapt. and harm. Felix Mendelssohn (1809-1847)

𝅗𝅥 = 50
76. 76. D

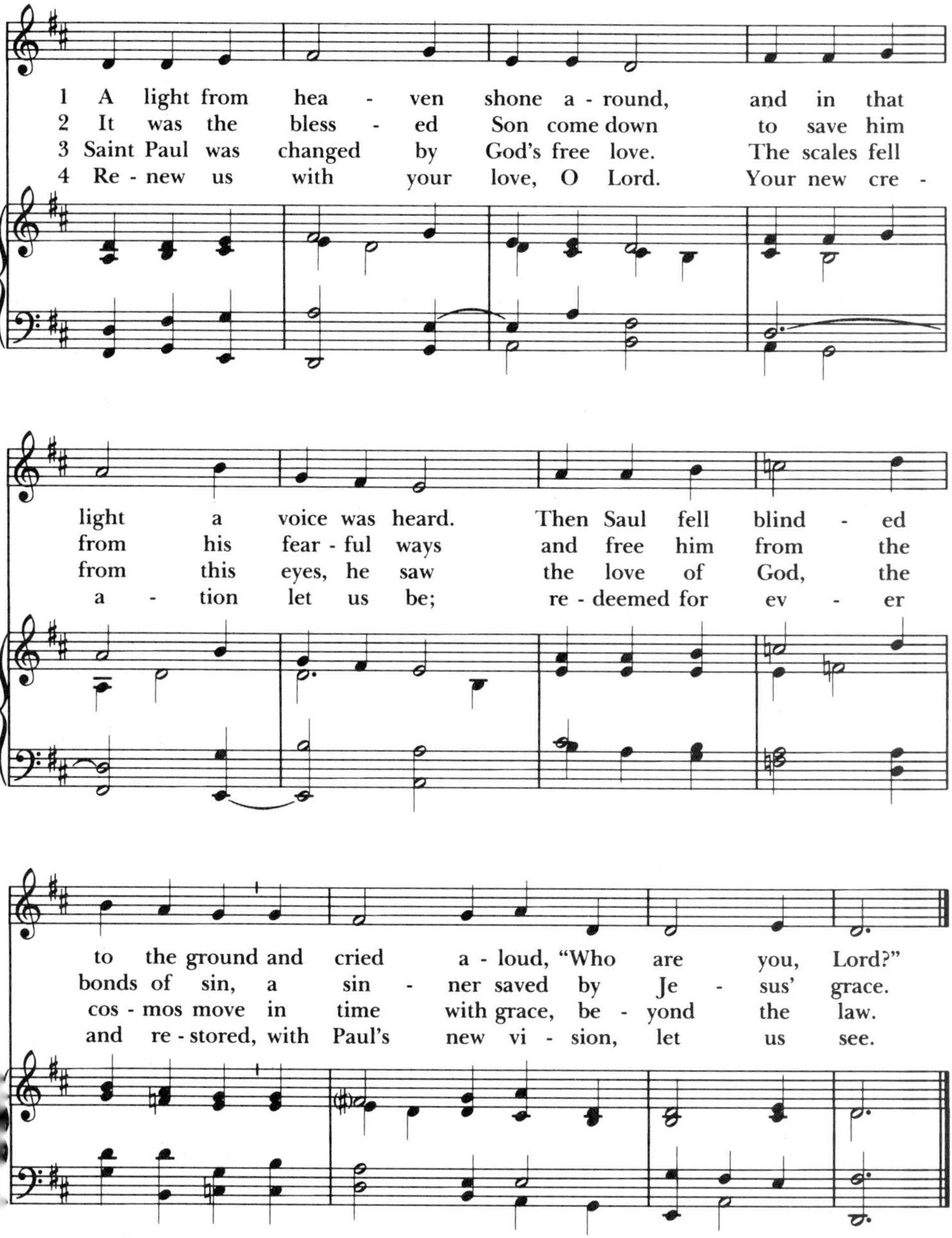
1 A light from hea - ven shone a - round, and in that
2 It was the bless - ed Son come down to save him
3 Saint Paul was changed by God's free love. The scales fell
4 Re - new us with your love, O Lord. Your new cre -
light a voice was heard. Then Saul fell blind - ed
from his fear - ful ways and free him from the
from this eyes, he saw the love of God, the
a - tion let us be; re - deemed for ev - er
to the ground and cried a - loud, "Who are you, Lord?"
bonds of sin, a sin - ner saved by Je - sus' grace.
cos - mos move in time with grace, be - yond the law.
and re - stored, with Paul's new vi - sion, let us see.

Conversion of Saint Paul (January 25).

Words: Gracia Grindal (b. 1943), alt.
Music: *Cornish,* M. Lee Suitor (b. 1942)

♩=112
LM

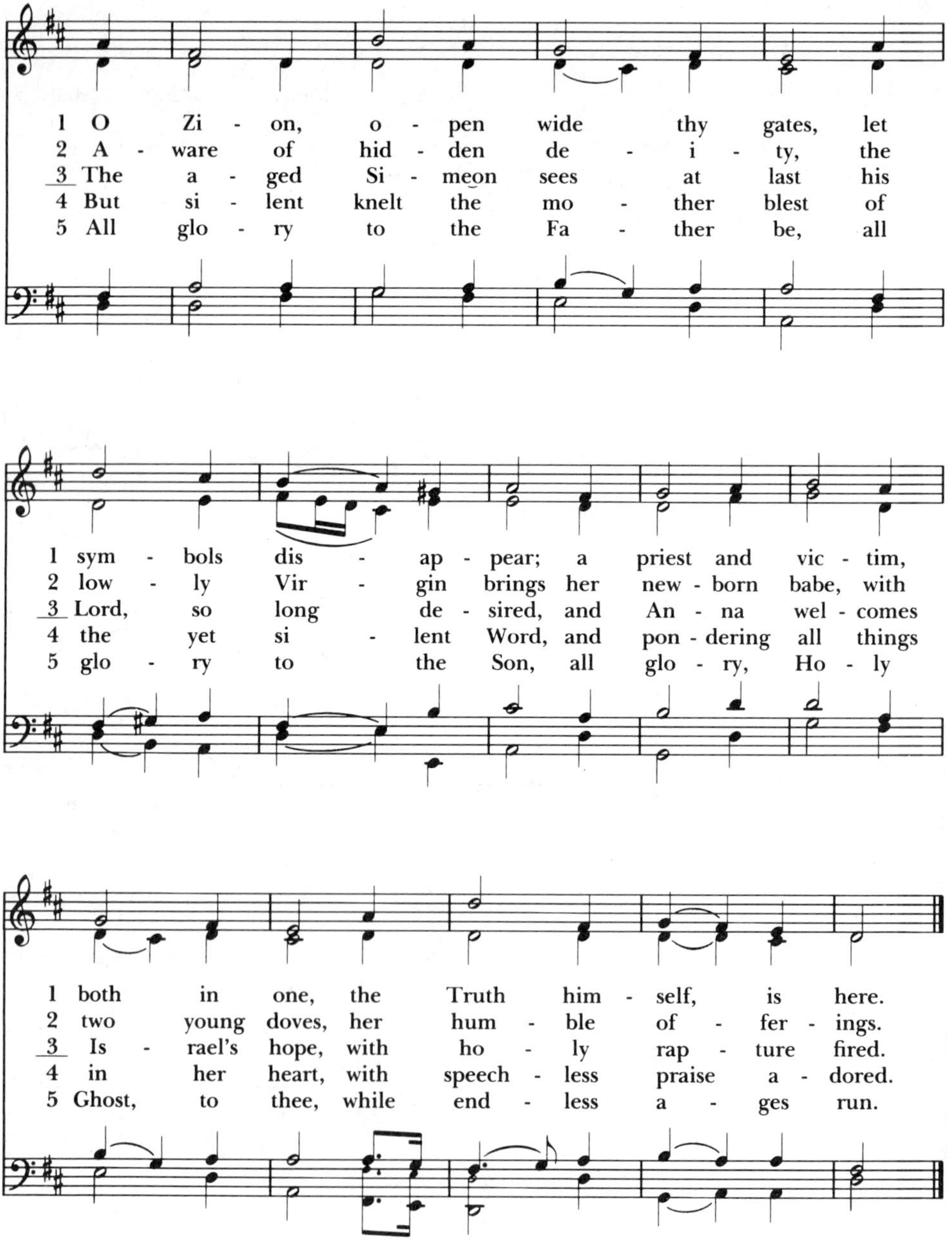
1 O Zi - on, o - pen wide thy gates, let
2 A - ware of hid - den de - i - ty, the
3 The a - ged Si - meon sees at last his
4 But si - lent knelt the mo - ther blest of
5 All glo - ry to the Fa - ther be, all
1 sym - bols dis - ap - pear; a priest and vic - tim,
2 low - ly Vir - gin brings her new - born babe, with
3 Lord, so long de - sired, and An - na wel - comes
4 the yet si - lent Word, and pon - dering all things
5 glo - ry to the Son, all glo - ry, Ho - ly
1 both in one, the Truth him - self, is here.
2 two young doves, her hum - ble of - fer - ings.
3 Is - rael's hope, with ho - ly rap - ture fired.
4 in her heart, with speech - less praise a - dored.
5 Ghost, to thee, while end - less a - ges run.

The Presentation (February 2).

Words: Jean Baptiste de Santeüil (1630-1697); tr. Edward Caswall (1814-1878), alt.
Music: *Edmonton*, from *Harmonia Sacra*, ca. 1760; harm. *Hymnal 1982*

♩= 96
CM

Alternative harmonization

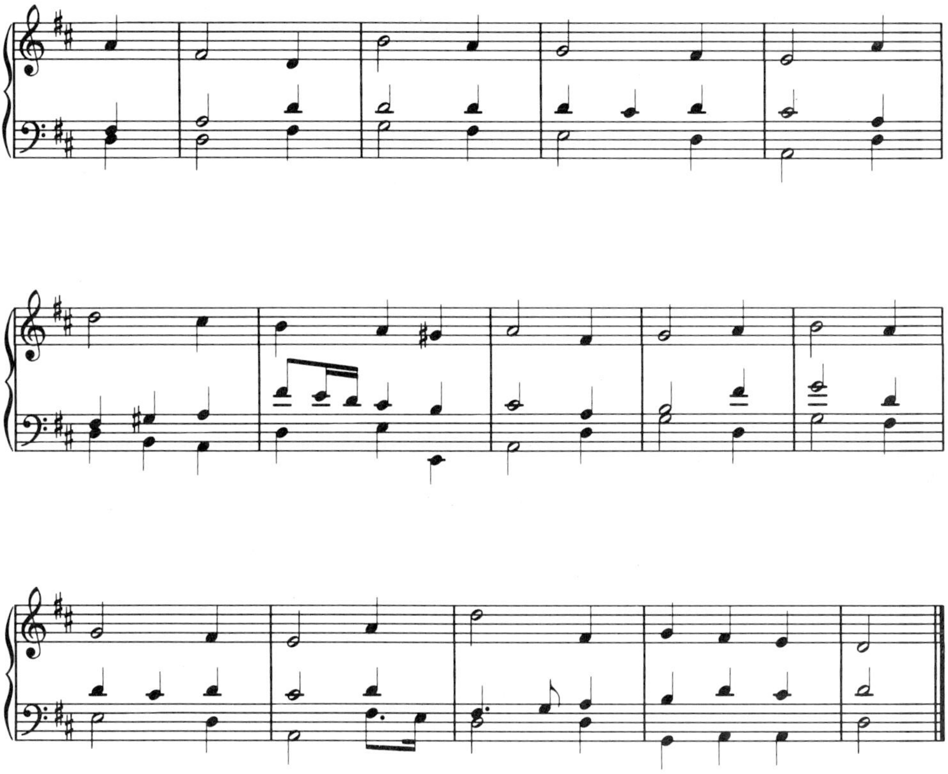

Music: *Edmonton*, melody and bass from *Harmonia Sacra*, ca. 1760 ♩= 96

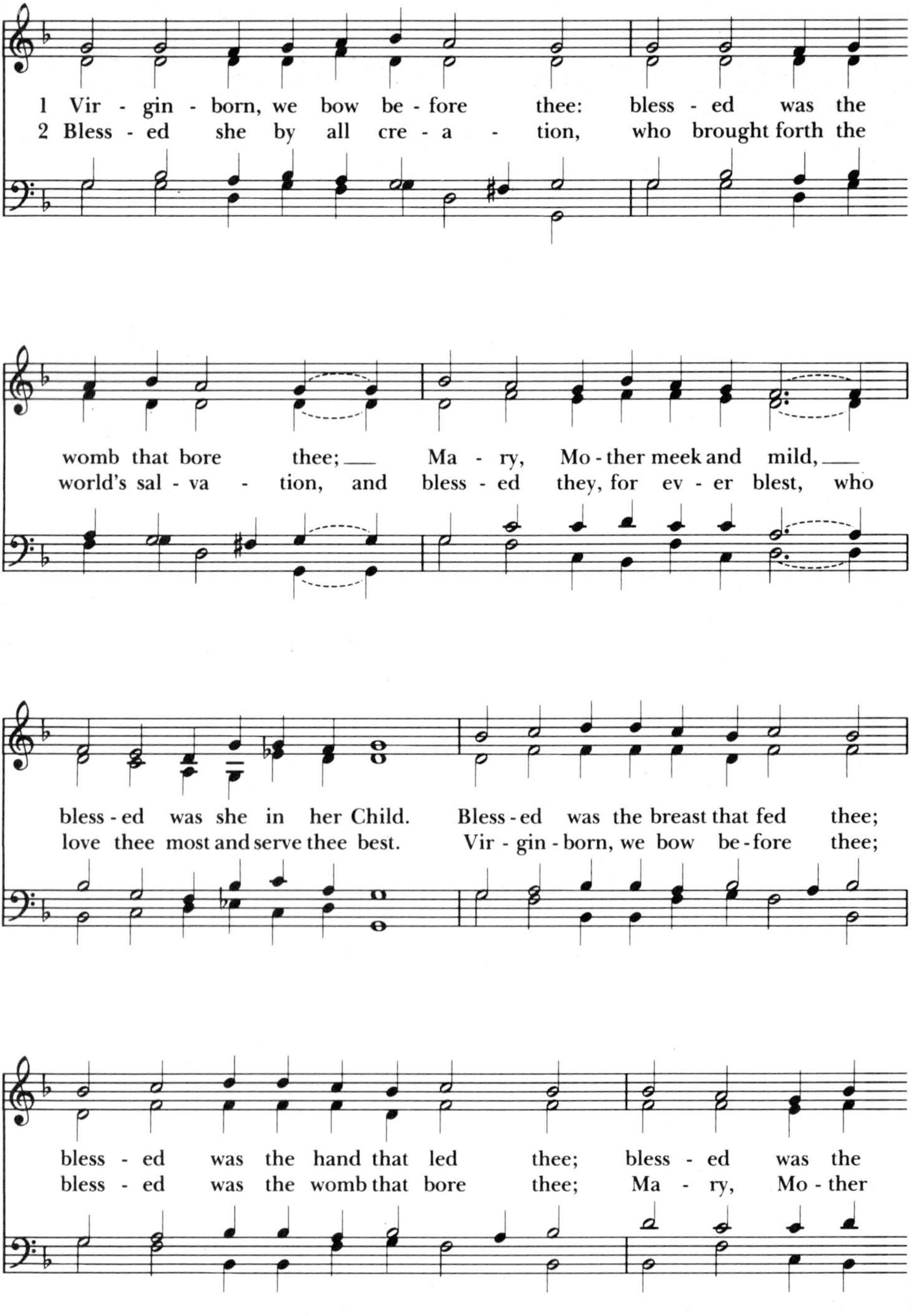
1 Vir - gin - born, we bow be - fore thee: bless - ed was the
2 Bless - ed she by all cre - a - tion, who brought forth the
womb that bore thee; Ma - ry, Mo - ther meek and mild,
world's sal - va - tion, and bless - ed they, for ev - er blest, who
bless - ed was she in her Child.
love thee most and serve thee best.
Bless - ed was the breast that fed thee;
Vir - gin - born, we bow be - fore thee;
bless - ed was the hand that led thee; bless - ed was the
bless - ed was the womb that bore thee; Ma - ry, Mo - ther

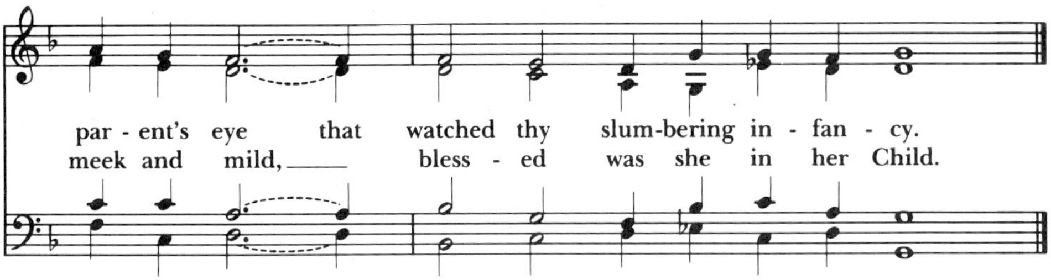
par - ent's eye that watched thy slum-bering in - fan - cy.
meek and mild, bless - ed was she in her Child.

The Presentation (February 2); The Annunciation (March 25).

Words: Reginald Heber (1783-1826)
Music: *Psalm 86,* Claude Goudimel (1514-1572), alt.

𝅗𝅥=58
88. 77. D

259

1 Hail to the Lord who comes, comes to his tem - ple gate;
2 but, borne up - on the throne of Ma - ry's gen - tle breast,
3 There Jo - seph at her side in rev - erent won - der stands;
4 O Light of all the earth, thy chil - dren wait for thee!
not with his an - gel host, not in his king - ly state;
watched by her du - teous love, in her fond arms at rest,
and, filled with ho - ly joy, old Si - meon in his hands
Come to thy tem - ples here, that we, from sin set free,
no shouts pro-claim him nigh, no crowds his com - ing wait;
thus to his Fa - ther's house he comes, the heaven - ly guest.
takes up the prom - ised child, the glo - ry of all lands.
be - fore thy Fa - ther's face may all pre - sent - ed be!

The Presentation (February 2).

Words: John Ellerton (1826-1893), alt.
Music: *Old 120th,* melody from *The Whole Booke of Psalmes,* 1570; harm. Thomas Ravenscroft (1592?-1635?), after Richard Allison (16th cent.); adapt. Ralph Vaughan Williams (1872-1958)

♩=88
66. 66. 66

260

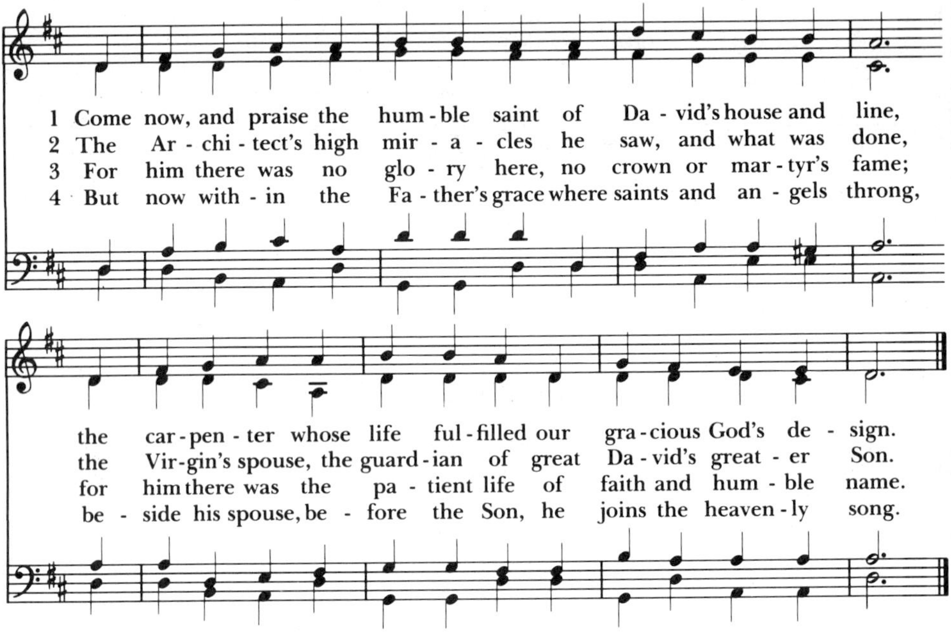
1 Come now, and praise the hum-ble saint of Da-vid's house and line,
2 The Ar-chi-tect's high mir-a-cles he saw, and what was done,
3 For him there was no glo-ry here, no crown or mar-tyr's fame;
4 But now with-in the Fa-ther's grace where saints and an-gels throng,
the car-pen-ter whose life ful-filled our gra-cious God's de-sign.
the Vir-gin's spouse, the guard-ian of great Da-vid's great-er Son.
for him there was the pa-tient life of faith and hum-ble name.
be-side his spouse, be-fore the Son, he joins the heaven-ly song.

Saint Joseph (March 19).

Words: George W. Williams (b. 1922)
Music: *Tallis' Ordinal,* Thomas Tallis (1505?-1585)

♩=80
CM

261

Holy Days and Various Occasions

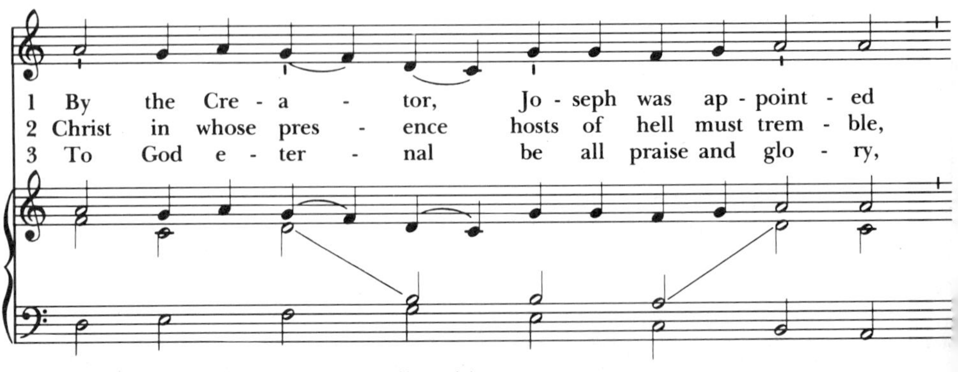
1 By the Cre-a-tor, Jo-seph was ap-point-ed
2 Christ in whose pres-ence hosts of hell must trem-ble,
3 To God e-ter-nal be all praise and glo-ry,

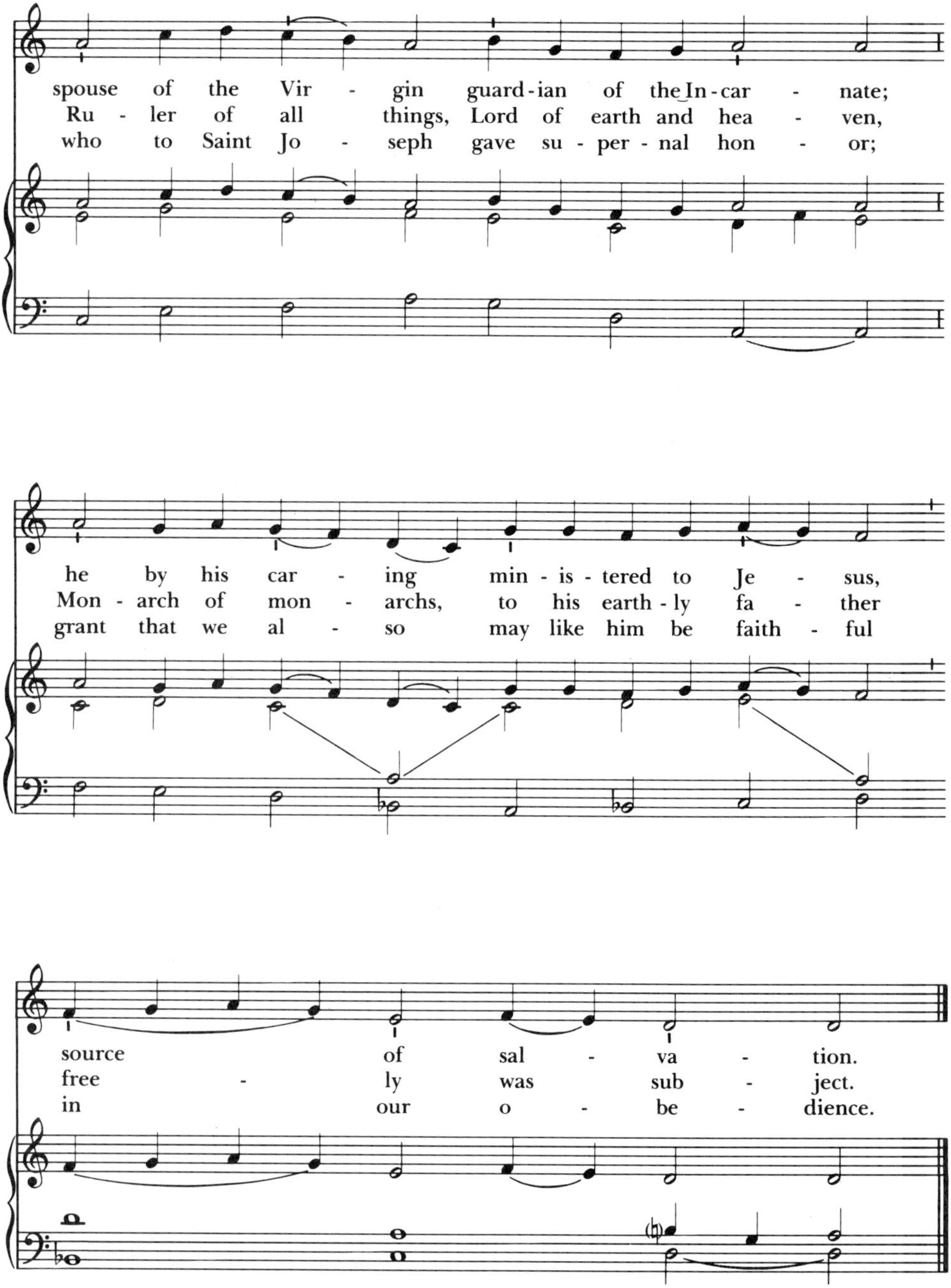
spouse of the Vir - gin guard-ian of the In-car - nate;
Ru - ler of all things, Lord of earth and hea - ven,
who to Saint Jo - seph gave su-per-nal hon - or;
he by his car - ing min-is-tered to Je - sus,
Mon-arch of mon - archs, to his earth-ly fa - ther
grant that we al - so may like him be faith - ful
source of sal - va - tion.
free - ly was sub - ject.
in our o - be - dience.
(♮)

Saint Joseph (March 19). Another accompaniment, 283. Alternative tune: *Bickford,* 262.

Words: Hieronimo Casanate (d. 1700); tr. *Hymnal 1982*
Music: *Caelitum Joseph,* plainsong, Mode 1, Worcester MS., 13th cent; ver. Schola Antiqua, 1983; acc. Thomas Foster (b. 1938)

𝅗𝅥=84
11 11. 11 5

1 By the Cre - a - tor, Jo - seph was ap - point - ed spouse of the
2 Christ in whose pres - ence hosts of hell must trem - ble, Ru - ler of
3 To God e - ter - nal be all praise and glo - ry, who to Saint
Vir - gin, guard-ian of the In - car - nate; he by his car - ing
all things, Lord of earth and hea - ven, Mon - arch of mon - archs,
Jo - seph gave su - per - nal hon - or; grant that we al - so
min - is - tered to Je - sus, source of sal - va - tion.
to his earth - ly fa - ther free - ly was sub - ject.
may like him be faith - ful in our o - be - dience.

Saint Joseph (March 19). Alternative tune: *Caelitum Joseph,* 261.

Words: Hieronimo Casanate (d. 1700); tr. *Hymnal 1982*
Music: *Bickford,* Hank Beebe (b. 1926)

♩=84
11 11. 11 5

1 The Word whom earth and sea and sky a - dore and
2 To Ma - ry the Arch - an - gel came and God's new
3 Blest in the mes - sage Ga - briel brought, blest in the
4 Lord Je - sus, Vir - gin - born, to thee e - ter - nal
laud and mag - ni - fy, whose might they show, whose
mes - sage did pro - claim, "Hail, Ma - ry, you shall
work the Spi - rit wrought, most blest to bring to
praise and glo - ry be, whom with the Fa - ther
praise they tell, in Ma - ry's bo - dy deigned to dwell.
bear a son who shall be called the Ho - ly One."
hu - man birth the long - de - sired of all the earth.
we a - dore and Ho - ly Spi - rit ev - er-more.

The Annunciation (March 25). Alternative tune: *Song 34,* 264.

Words: Latin, 7th-8th cent.; sts. 1 and 3-4, tr. *Hymns Ancient and Modern,* 1861, after John Mason Neale (1818-1866); st. 2, tr. Anne K. LeCroy (b. 1930)
Music: *Quem terra, pontus, aethera,* plainsong, Mode 2, *Mailander Hymnen,* 15th cent.; acc. Bruce Neswick (b. 1956)

LM

1 The Word whom earth and sea and sky a - dore and laud and
2 To Ma - ry the Arch - an - gel came and God's new mes - sage
3 Blest in the mes - sage Ga - briel brought, blest in the work the
4 Lord Je - sus, Vir - gin - born, to thee e - ter - nal praise and
mag - ni - fy, whose might they show, whose praise they
did pro - claim, "Hail, Ma - ry, you shall bear a
Spi - rit wrought, most blest to bring to hu - man
glo - ry be, whom with the Fa - ther we a -
tell, in Ma - ry's bo - dy deigned to dwell.
son who shall be called the Ho - ly One."
birth the long - de - sired of all the earth.
dore and Ho - ly Spi - rit ev - er - more.

The Annunciation (March 25). Alternative tune: *Quem terra, pontus, aethera,* 263.

Words: Latin, 7th-8th cent.; sts. 1 and 3-4, tr. *Hymns Ancient and Modern,* 1861, after John Mason Neale (1818-1866); st. 2, tr. Anne K. LeCroy (b. 1930)

Music: *Song 34,* melody and bass Orlando Gibbons (1583-1625); harm. *The English Hymnal,* 1906, alt.

♩= 88
LM

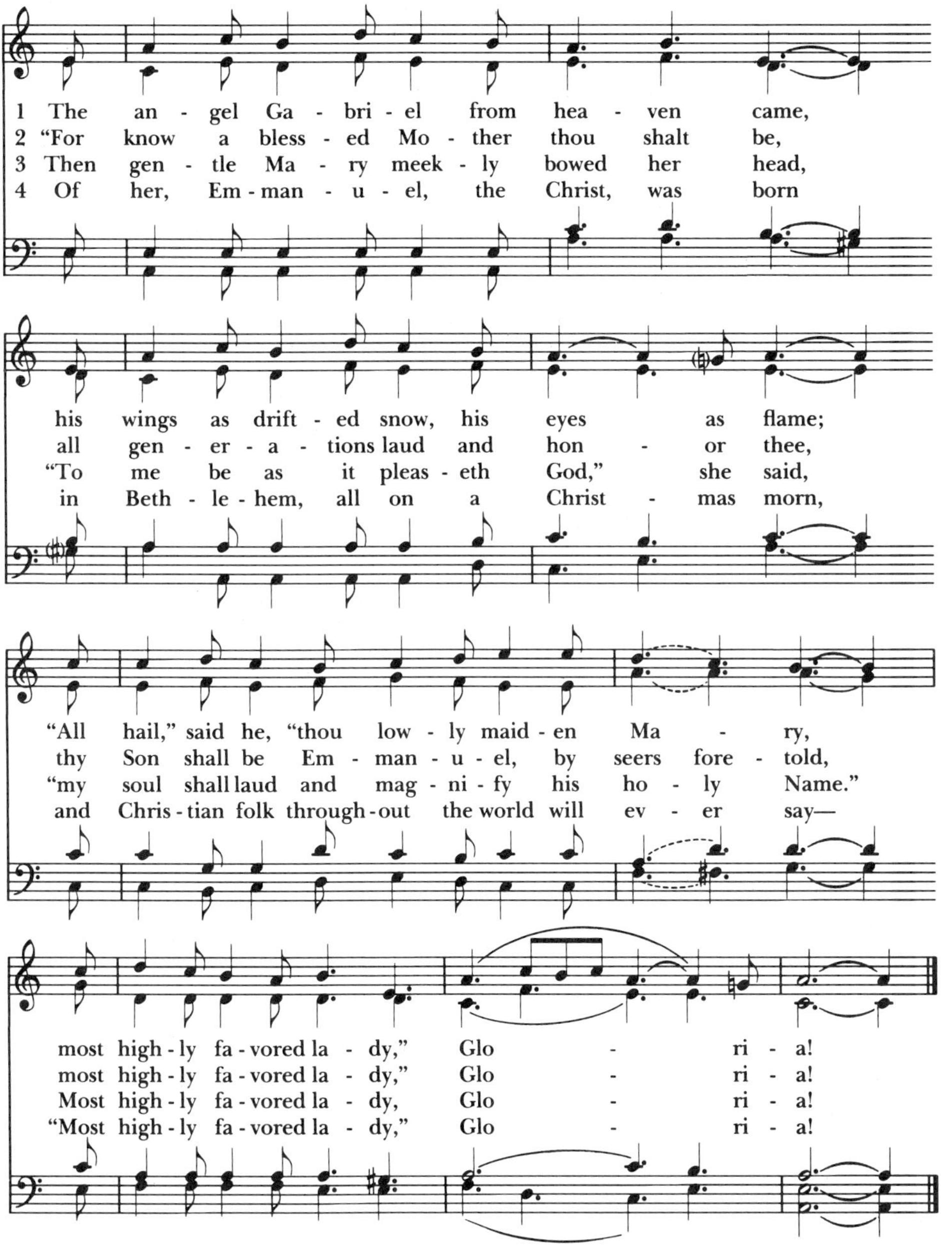
1 The an - gel Ga - bri - el from hea - ven came,
2 "For know a bless - ed Mo - ther thou shalt be,
3 Then gen - tle Ma - ry meek - ly bowed her head,
4 Of her, Em - man - u - el, the Christ, was born
his wings as drift - ed snow, his eyes as flame;
all gen - er - a - tions laud and hon - or thee,
"To me be as it pleas - eth God," she said,
in Beth - le - hem, all on a Christ - mas morn,
"All hail," said he, "thou low - ly maid - en Ma - ry,
thy Son shall be Em - man - u - el, by seers fore - told,
"my soul shall laud and mag - ni - fy his ho - ly Name."
and Chris - tian folk through - out the world will ev - er say—
most high - ly fa - vored la - dy," Glo - ri - a!
most high - ly fa - vored la - dy," Glo - ri - a!
Most high - ly fa - vored la - dy, Glo - ri - a!
"Most high - ly fa - vored la - dy," Glo - ri - a!

The Annunciation (March 25).

Words: Basque carol; para. Sabine Baring-Gould (1834-1924)
Music: *Gabriel's Message,* Basque carol; harm. Edgar Pettman (1865-1943)

♩. = 66
10 10. 12. 10

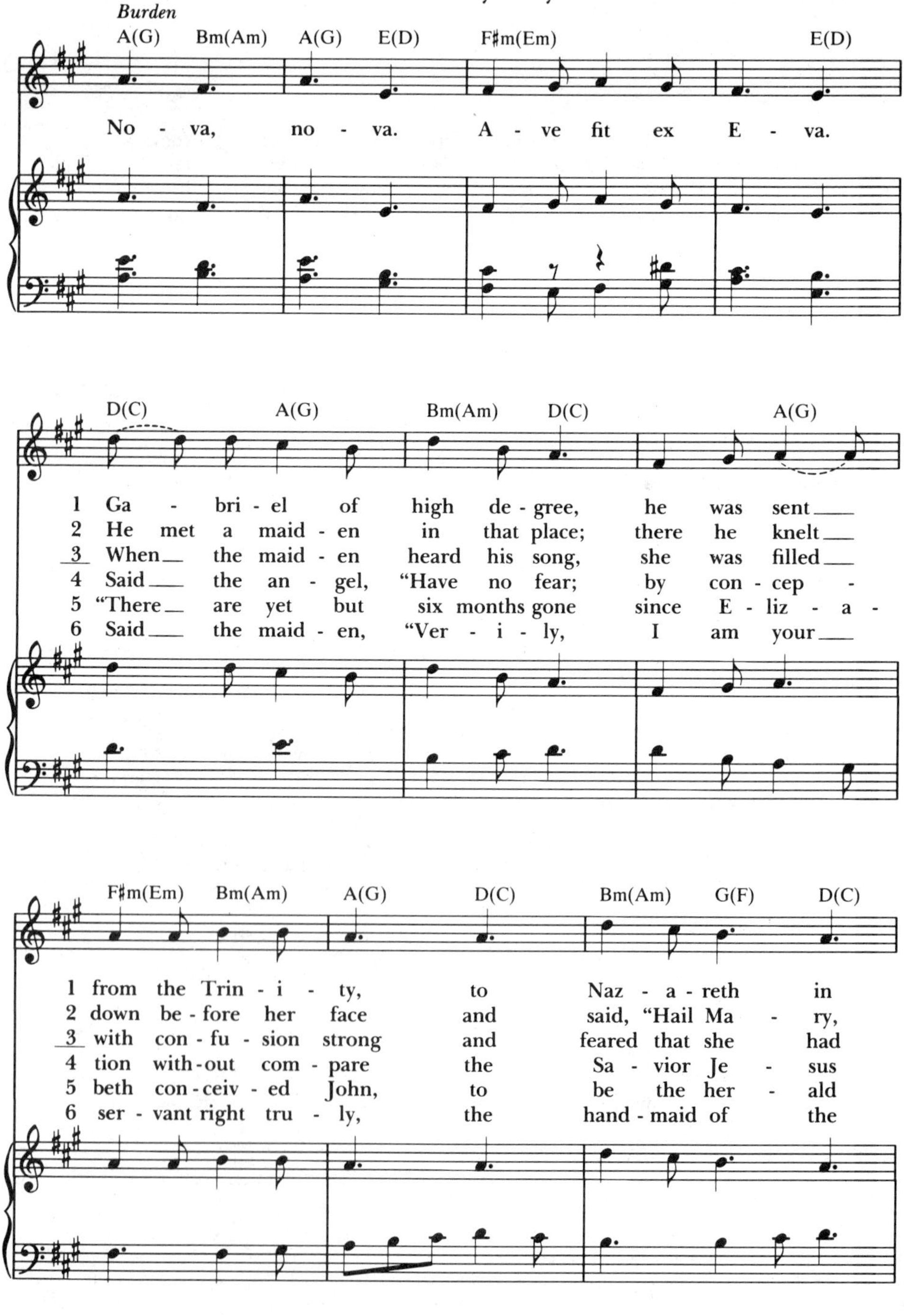
Burden
A(G) Bm(Am) A(G) E(D) F♯m(Em) E(D)
No - va, no - va. A - ve fit ex E - va.
D(C) A(G) Bm(Am) D(C) A(G)
1 Ga - bri - el of high de - gree, he was sent
2 He met a maid - en in that place; there he knelt
3 When the maid - en heard his song, she was filled
4 Said the an - gel, "Have no fear; by con - cep -
5 "There are yet but six months gone since E - liz - a -
6 Said the maid - en, "Ver - i - ly, I am your
F♯m(Em) Bm(Am) A(G) D(C) Bm(Am) G(F) D(C)
1 from the Trin - i - ty, to Naz - a - reth in
2 down be - fore her face and said, "Hail Ma - ry,
3 with con - fu - sion strong and feared that she had
4 tion with - out com - pare the Sa - vior Je - sus
5 beth con - ceiv - ed John, to be the her - ald
6 ser - vant right tru - ly, the hand - maid of the

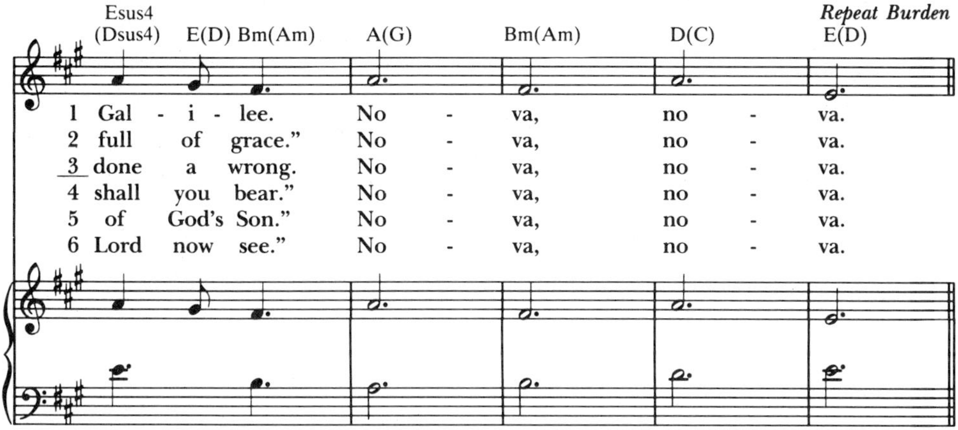
Esus4
(Dsus4) E(D) Bm(Am) A(G) Bm(Am) D(C)
Repeat Burden
E(D)
1 Gal - i - lee. No - va, no - va.
2 full of grace." No - va, no - va.
3 done a wrong. No - va, no - va.
4 shall you bear." No - va, no - va.
5 of God's Son." No - va, no - va.
6 Lord now see." No - va, no - va.

The Annunciation (March 25). The following burden and final line may be used with each stanza: "Tidings! Tidings! Promise of salvation!" and "Tidings! Tidings!". Accompaniment by guitar or keyboard is optional.

Words: Hunterian MS. 83, 15th cent.; adapt. Carl P. Daw, Jr. (b. 1944) ♩. = 100
Music: *Nova, nova,* melody Hunterian MS.83, 15th cent.; harm. Jack W. Burnam (b. 1946) Irr. with Refrain

267

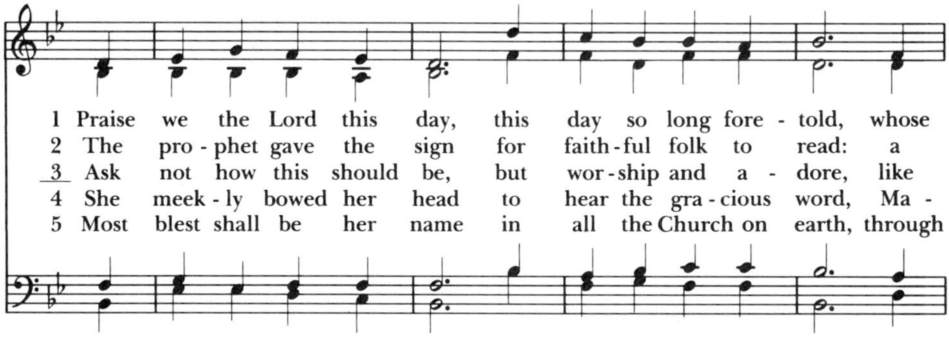
1 Praise we the Lord this day, this day so long fore - told, whose
2 The pro - phet gave the sign for faith - ful folk to read: a
3 Ask not how this should be, but wor - ship and a - dore, like
4 She meek - ly bowed her head to hear the gra - cious word, Ma -
5 Most blest shall be her name in all the Church on earth, through

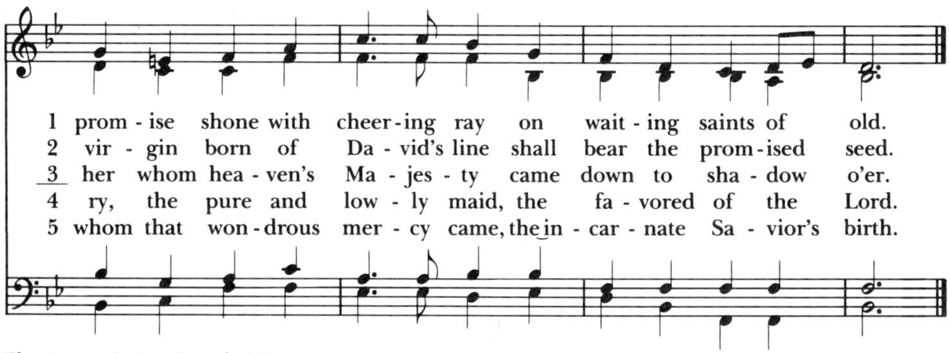
1 prom - ise shone with cheer - ing ray on wait - ing saints of old.
2 vir - gin born of Da - vid's line shall bear the prom - ised seed.
3 her whom hea - ven's Ma - jes - ty came down to sha - dow o'er.
4 ry, the pure and low - ly maid, the fa - vored of the Lord.
5 whom that won - drous mer - cy came, the in - car - nate Sa - vior's birth.

The Annunciation (March 25).

Words: Anon., *Hymns for the Festivals and Saints' Days of the Church of England,* 1846, alt. 𝅗𝅥 = 46
Music: *St. George,* Henry John Gauntlett (1805-1876) SM

Introduction/Interlude
Descant
4 "Mag - ni - fi - cat
an - i - ma me - a
1 Ye who claim the faith of Je - sus, sing the won - ders that were done when the love of God the
2 Bless - ed were the cho - sen peo - ple out of whom the Lord did come; bless - ed was the land of
3 There-fore let all faith - ful peo - ple sing the hon - or of her name; let the Church, in her fore -
4 "Mag - ni - fy, my soul, God's great - ness; in my Sa - vior I re - joice; all the a - ges call me

Do - mi - num. Mag - ni - fi - cat, mag - ni - fi - cat."
Fa - ther o - ver sin the vic - tory won, when he made the Vir - gin Ma - ry mo - ther of his on - ly Son.
prom - ise fa - shioned for his earth - ly home; but more bless - ed far the mo - ther, she who bore him in her womb.
shad - owed, part in her thanks - giv - ing claim; what Christ's mo - ther sang in glad - ness let Christ's peo - ple sing the same:
bless - ed, in his praise I lift my voice; he has cast down all the might - y and the low - ly are his choice."
Conclusion

The Annunciation (March 25); The Visitation (May 31). Alternative tune: *Den des Vaters Sinn geboren*, 269.

Words: Sts. 1-3, Vincent Stuckey Stratton Coles (1845-1929), alt; st. 4, F. Bland Tucker (1895-1984), metrical *Magnificat*
Music: *Julion,* David Hurd (b. 1950)

♩= 72
87. 87. 87

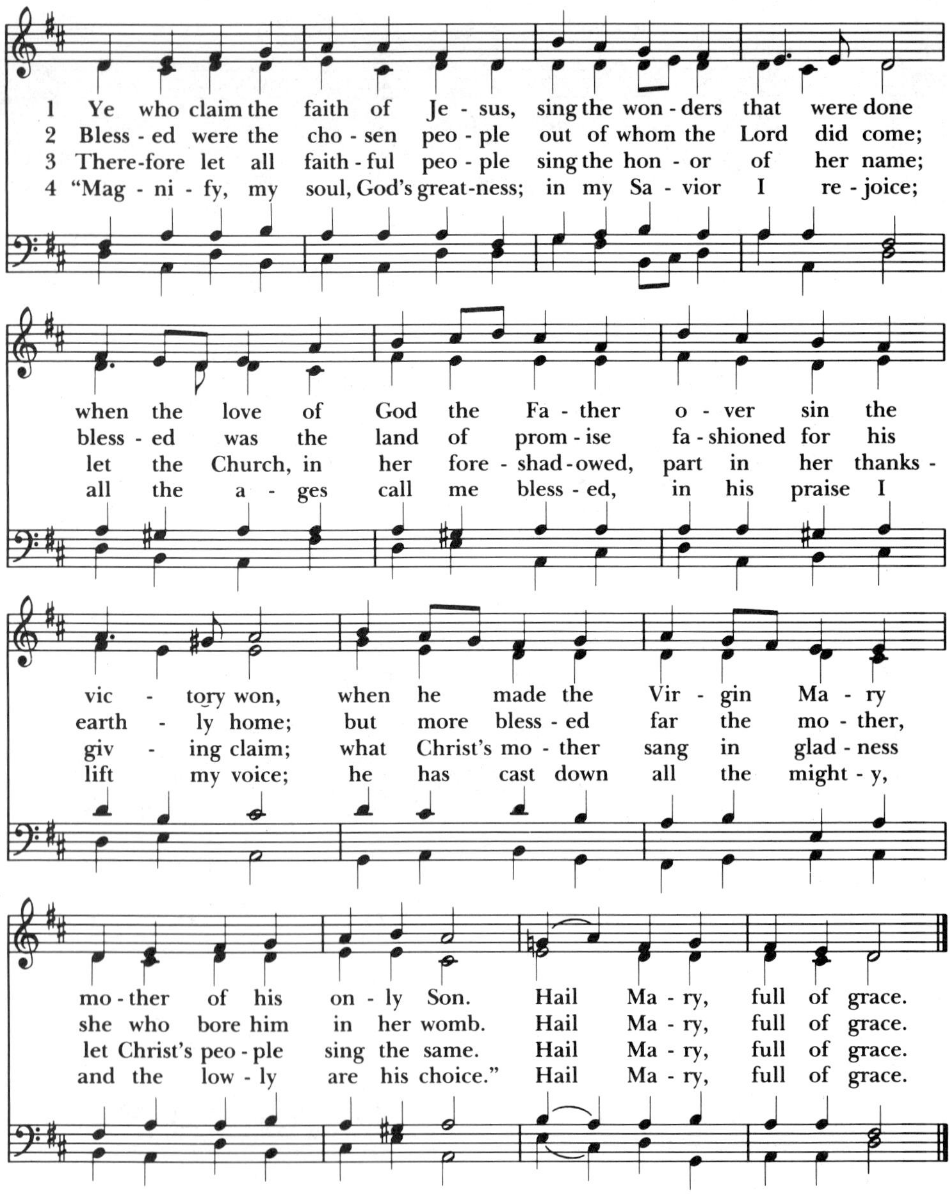
1 Ye who claim the faith of Je - sus, sing the won - ders that were done
2 Bless - ed were the cho - sen peo - ple out of whom the Lord did come;
3 There-fore let all faith - ful peo - ple sing the hon - or of her name;
4 "Mag - ni - fy, my soul, God's great-ness; in my Sa - vior I re - joice;
when the love of God the Fa - ther o - ver sin the
bless - ed was the land of prom - ise fa - shioned for his
let the Church, in her fore - shad - owed, part in her thanks -
all the a - ges call me bless - ed, in his praise I
vic - tory won, when he made the Vir - gin Ma - ry
earth - ly home; but more bless - ed far the mo - ther,
giv - ing claim; what Christ's mo - ther sang in glad - ness
lift my voice; he has cast down all the might - y,
mo - ther of his on - ly Son. Hail Ma - ry, full of grace.
she who bore him in her womb. Hail Ma - ry, full of grace.
let Christ's peo - ple sing the same. Hail Ma - ry, full of grace.
and the low - ly are his choice." Hail Ma - ry, full of grace.

The Annunciation (March 25); The Visitation (May 31). Alternative tune: *Julion,* 268.

Words: Sts. 1-3, Vincent Stuckey Stratton Coles (1845-1929), alt; st. 4, F. Bland Tucker (1895-1984), metrical *Magnificat*

Music: *Den des Vaters Sinn geboren,* melody from *Hundert Arien,* 1694; harm. Conrad Kocher (1786-1872)

𝅗𝅥=46

87. 87. 87 with Refrain

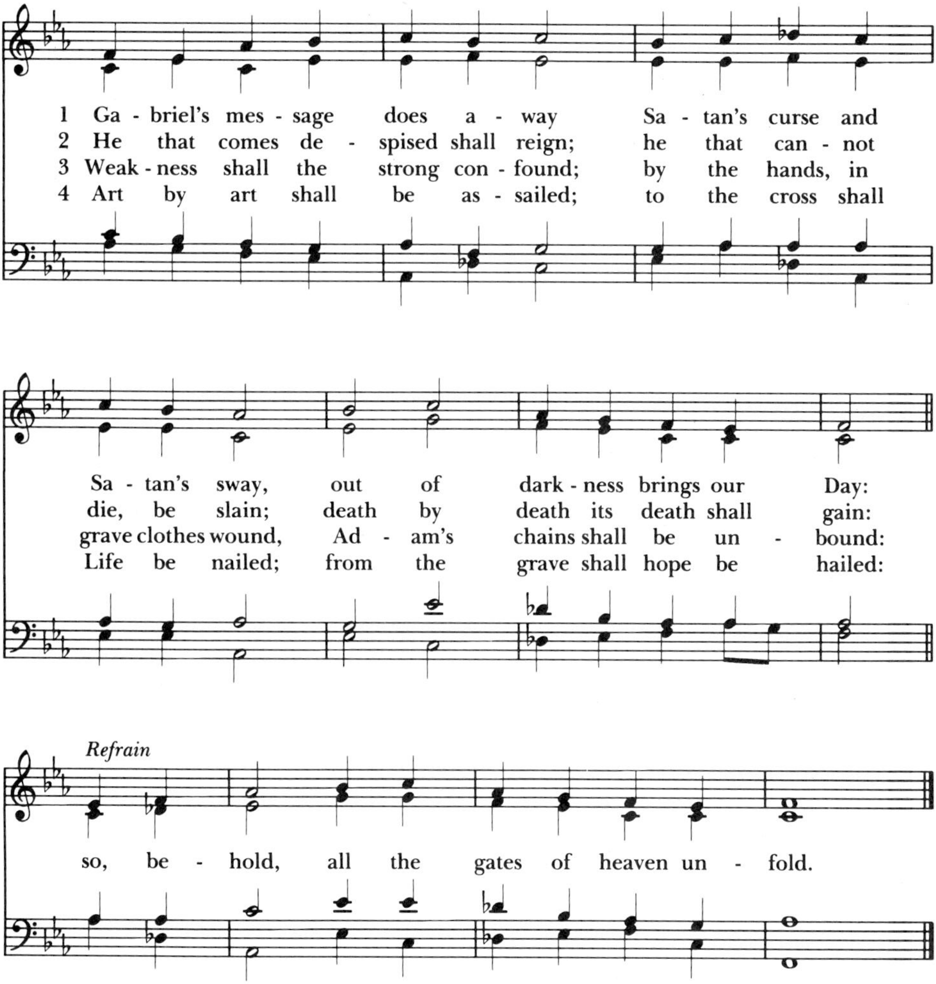
1 Ga - briel's mes - sage does a - way Sa - tan's curse and Sa - tan's sway, out of dark - ness brings our Day:
2 He that comes de - spised shall reign; he that can - not die, be slain; death by death its death shall gain:
3 Weak - ness shall the strong con - found; by the hands, in grave clothes wound, Ad - am's chains shall be un - bound:
4 Art by art shall be as - sailed; to the cross shall Life be nailed; from the grave shall hope be hailed:
Refrain
so, be - hold, all the gates of heaven un - fold.

The Annunciation (March 25).

Words: *Piae cantiones*, 1582; tr. John Mason Neale (1818-1866)
Music: *Angelus emittitur*, melody from *Piae Cantiones*, 1582; harm. Richard Runciman Terry (1865-1938)

𝅗𝅥=69
777 with Refrain

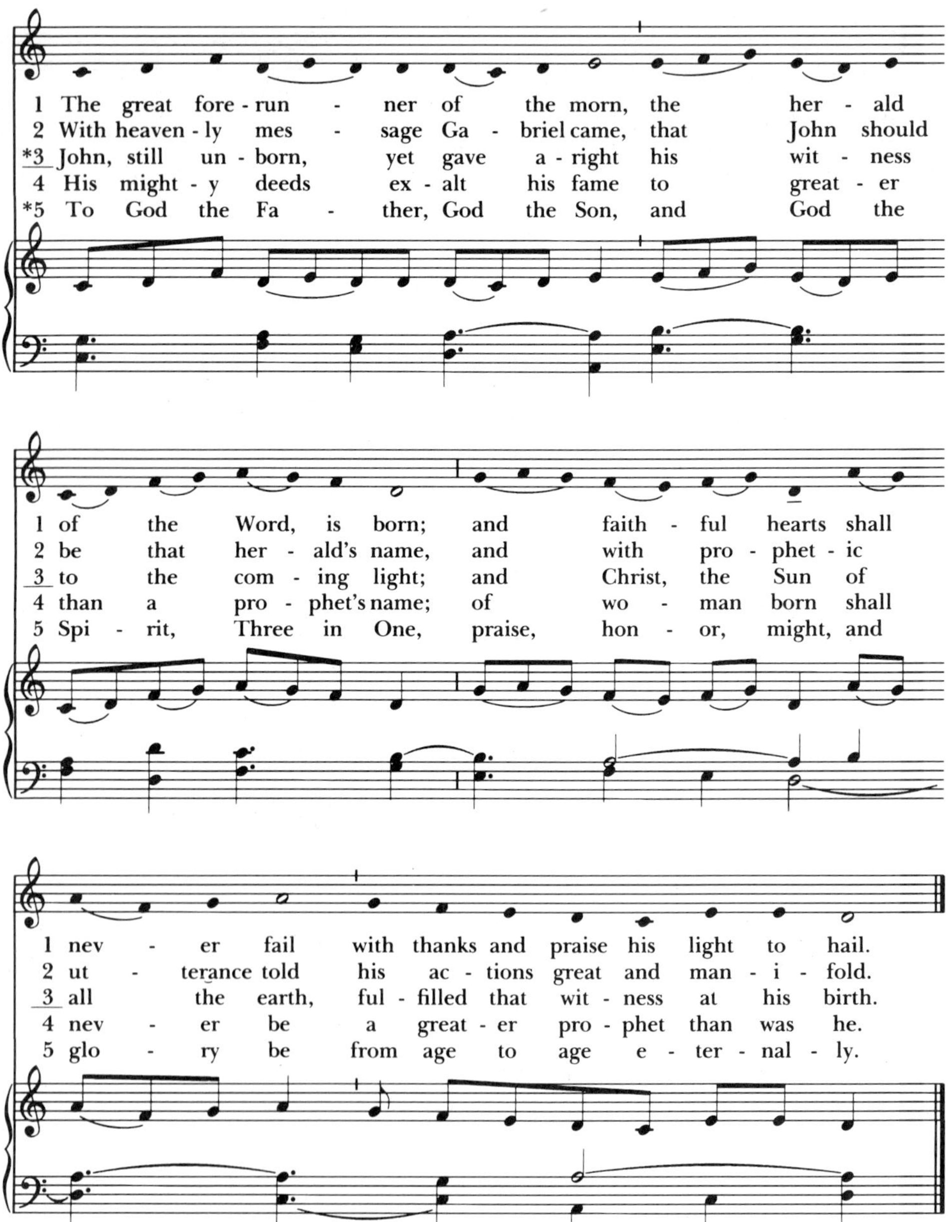
1 The great fore - run - ner of the morn, the her - ald
2 With heaven - ly mes - sage Ga - briel came, that John should
*3 John, still un - born, yet gave a - right his wit - ness
4 His might - y deeds ex - alt his fame to great - er
*5 To God the Fa - ther, God the Son, and God the
1 of the Word, is born; and faith - ful hearts shall
2 be that her - ald's name, and with pro - phet - ic
3 to the com - ing light; and Christ, the Sun of
4 than a pro - phet's name; of wo - man born shall
5 Spi - rit, Three in One, praise, hon - or, might, and
1 nev - er fail with thanks and praise his light to hail.
2 ut - terance told his ac - tions great and man - i - fold.
3 all the earth, ful - filled that wit - ness at his birth.
4 nev - er be a great - er pro - phet than was he.
5 glo - ry be from age to age e - ter - nal - ly.

The Nativity of Saint John the Baptist (June 24). Alternative tune: *The Truth from Above,* 272.

Words: The Venerable Bede (673-735); tr. John Mason Neale (1818-1866), alt.
Music: *Ut queant laxis,* plainsong, Mode 2, Theoretikerquellen MS., 12th cent.; acc. Richard Proulx (b. 1937) LM

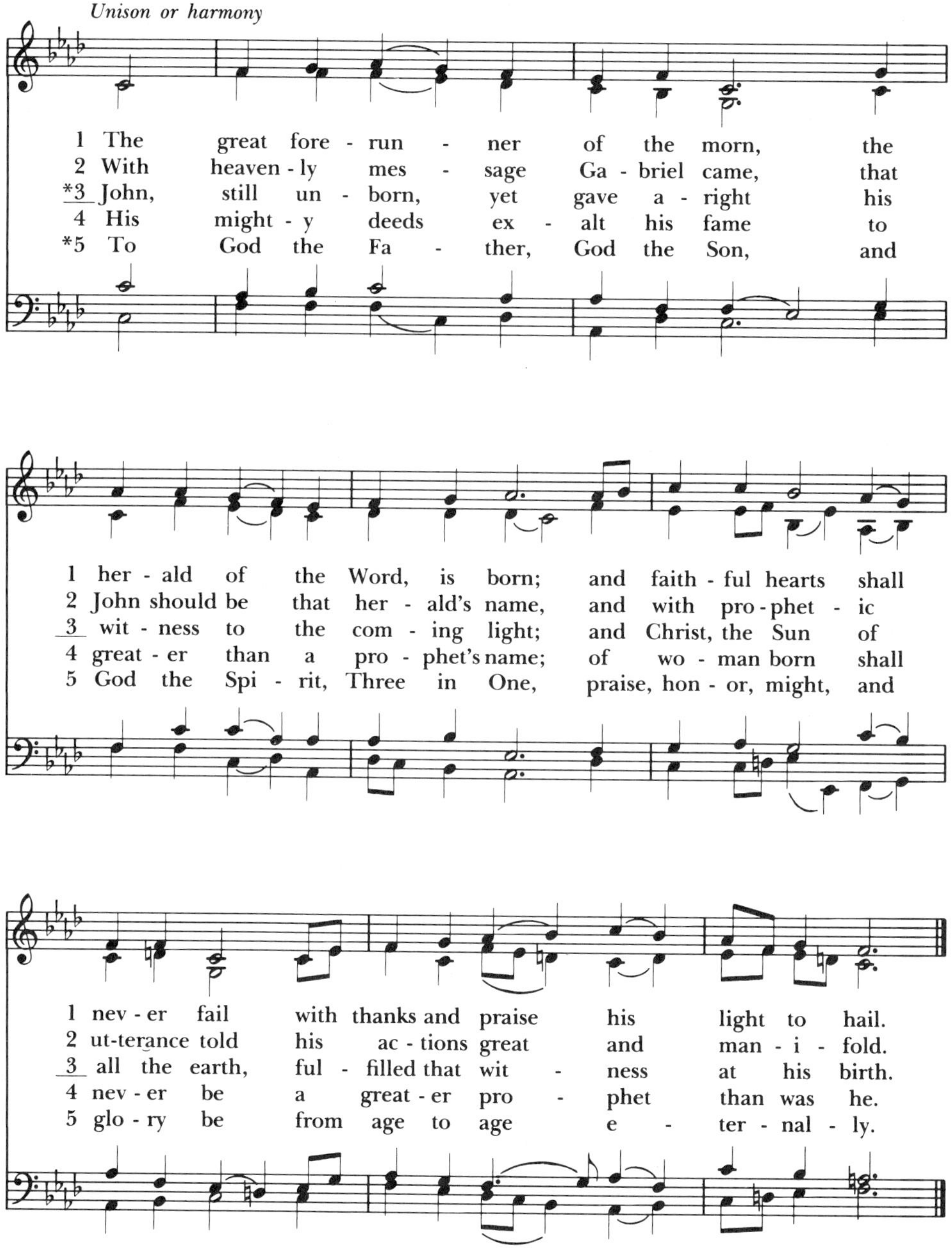
Unison or harmony
1 The great fore - run - ner of the morn, the
2 With heaven - ly mes - sage Ga - briel came, that
*3 John, still un - born, yet gave a - right his
4 His might - y deeds ex - alt his fame to
*5 To God the Fa - ther, God the Son, and
1 her - ald of the Word, is born; and faith - ful hearts shall
2 John should be that her - ald's name, and with pro - phet - ic
3 wit - ness to the com - ing light; and Christ, the Sun of
4 great - er than a pro - phet's name; of wo - man born shall
5 God the Spi - rit, Three in One, praise, hon - or, might, and
1 nev - er fail with thanks and praise his light to hail.
2 ut-terance told his ac - tions great and man - i - fold.
3 all the earth, ful - filled that wit - ness at his birth.
4 nev - er be a great - er pro - phet than was he.
5 glo - ry be from age to age e - ter - nal - ly.

The Nativity of Saint John the Baptist (June 24). Alternative tune: *Ut queant laxis,* 271.

Words: The Venerable Bede (673-735); tr. John Mason Neale (1818-1866), alt.
Music: *The Truth From Above,* English melody; harm. Ralph Vaughan Williams (1872-1958)

♩=100
LM

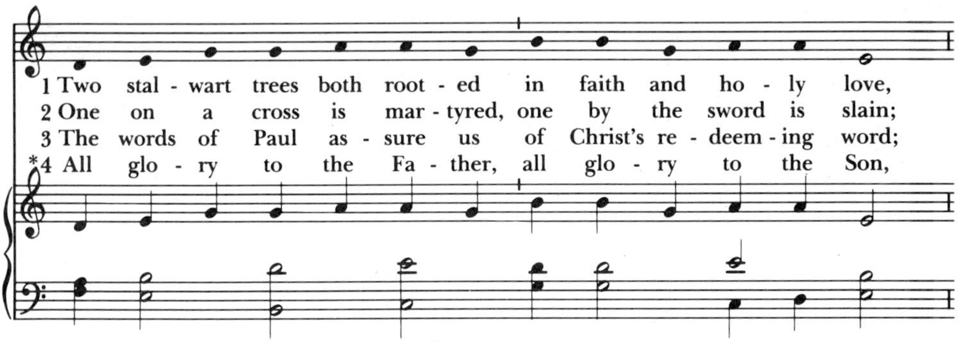
1 Two stal - wart trees both root - ed in faith and ho - ly love,
2 One on a cross is mar - tyred, one by the sword is slain;
3 The words of Paul as - sure us of Christ's re - deem - ing word;
*4 All glo - ry to the Fa - ther, all glo - ry to the Son,

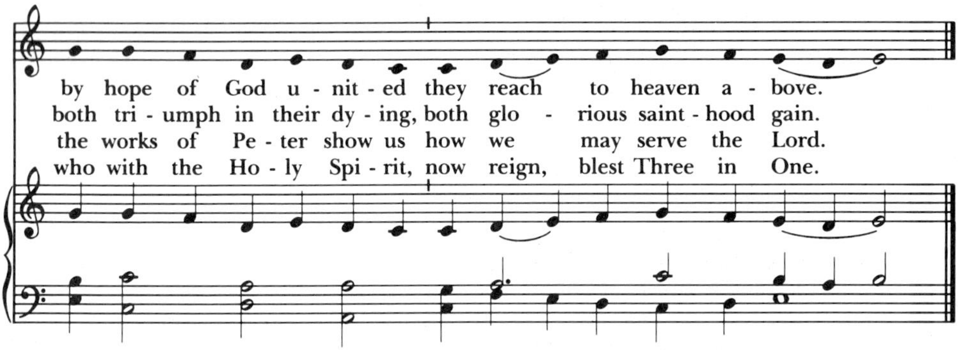
by hope of God u - nit - ed they reach to heaven a - bove.
both tri - umph in their dy - ing, both glo - rious saint - hood gain.
the works of Pe - ter show us how we may serve the Lord.
who with the Ho - ly Spi - rit, now reign, blest Three in One.

Saint Peter and Saint Paul (June 29). Alternative tune: *De eersten zijn de laatsten,* 274.

Words: Latin; tr. Anne K. LeCroy (b. 1930)
Music: *Ave caeli janua,* plainsong, Mode 4, Moissac MS., 12th cent.; acc. David Hurd (b. 1950) 76. 76

1 Two stal - wart trees both root - ed in
2 One on a cross is mar - tyred, one
3 The words of Paul as - sure us of
*4 All glo - ry to the Fa - ther, all
faith and ho - ly love, by hope of God u -
by the sword is slain; both tri - umph in their
Christ's re-deem - ing word; the works of Pe - ter
glo - ry to the Son, who with the Ho - ly
nit - ed they reach to heaven a - bove.
dy - ing, both glo - rious saint - hood gain.
show us how we may serve the Lord.
Spi - rit, now reign, blest Three in One.

Saint Peter and Saint Paul (June 29). Alternative tune: *Ave caeli janua,* 273.

Words: Latin; tr. Anne K. LeCroy (b. 1930)
Music: *De eersten zijn de laatsten,* Frederik August Mehrtens (b. 1922)

𝅗𝅥. = 48
76. 76

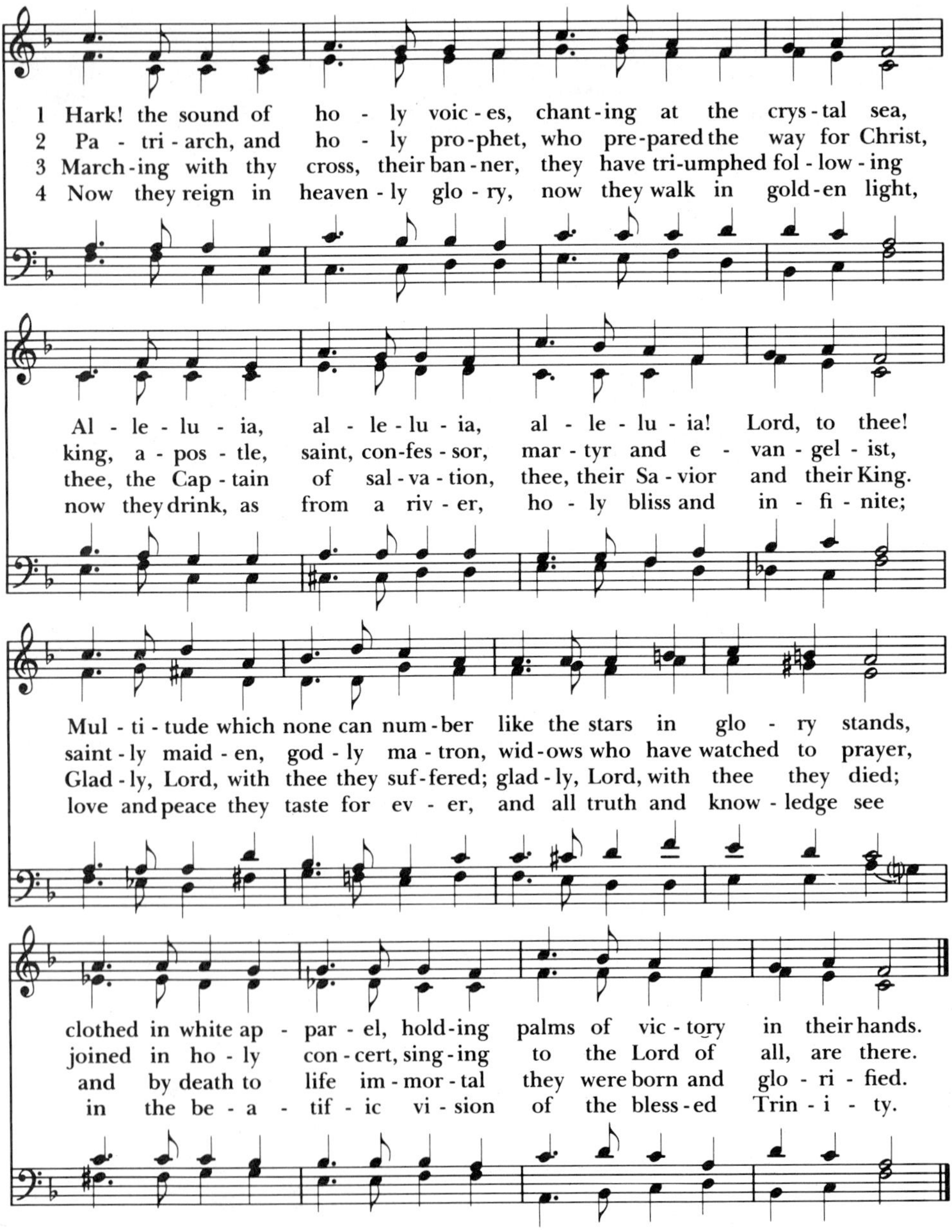
1 Hark! the sound of ho - ly voic - es, chant - ing at the crys - tal sea,
2 Pa - tri - arch, and ho - ly pro - phet, who pre - pared the way for Christ,
3 March - ing with thy cross, their ban - ner, they have tri - umphed fol - low - ing
4 Now they reign in heaven - ly glo - ry, now they walk in gold - en light,
Al - le - lu - ia, al - le - lu - ia, al - le - lu - ia! Lord, to thee!
king, a - pos - tle, saint, con - fes - sor, mar - tyr and e - van - gel - ist,
thee, the Cap - tain of sal - va - tion, thee, their Sa - vior and their King.
now they drink, as from a riv - er, ho - ly bliss and in - fi - nite;
Mul - ti - tude which none can num - ber like the stars in glo - ry stands,
saint - ly maid - en, god - ly ma - tron, wid - ows who have watched to prayer,
Glad - ly, Lord, with thee they suf - fered; glad - ly, Lord, with thee they died;
love and peace they taste for ev - er, and all truth and know - ledge see
clothed in white ap - par - el, hold - ing palms of vic - to - ry in their hands.
joined in ho - ly con - cert, sing - ing to the Lord of all, are there.
and by death to life im - mor - tal they were born and glo - ri - fied.
in the be - a - tif - ic vi - sion of the bless - ed Trin - i - ty.

Saints' Days; All Saints' Day (November 1). Alternative tune: *In Babilone*, 495.

Words: Christopher Wordsworth (1807-1885)
Music: *Moultrie*, Gerard Francis Cobb (1838-1904)

𝅗𝅥=54
87. 87. D

D A G Bm A D
1 For thy blest saints, a no - ble throng, who fell by
2 For James who left his fa - ther's side, not lin - gering
3 he stood with thee be - side the dead; he climbed the
4 he knelt be - neath the ol - ive shade; he drank thy
5 Lord, may we learn to drink thy cup, and meek and
G D A A D
1 fire and sword, or ear - ly died or
2 by the sea: he heard what could not
3 mount with thee, and saw the glo - ry
4 cup of pain; and slain by He - rod's
5 firm be found, when thou shalt come to
Bm D A G A D
1 flour - ished long, we praise thy Name, O Lord.
2 be de - nied, thy sum - mons, "Fol - low me";
3 round thy head, one of thy cho - sen three;
4 flash - ing blade, he saw thy face a - gain.
5 take us up where thine e - lect are crowned.

Saint James (July 25). Keyboard and guitar should not sound together. Alternative tune: *St. James,* 457.

Words: Cecil Frances Alexander (1818-1895), alt.

Music: *Dunlap's Creek,* melody Freeman Lewis (1780-1859); harm. Margaret W. Mealy (b. 1922)

𝅗𝅥 = 69

CM

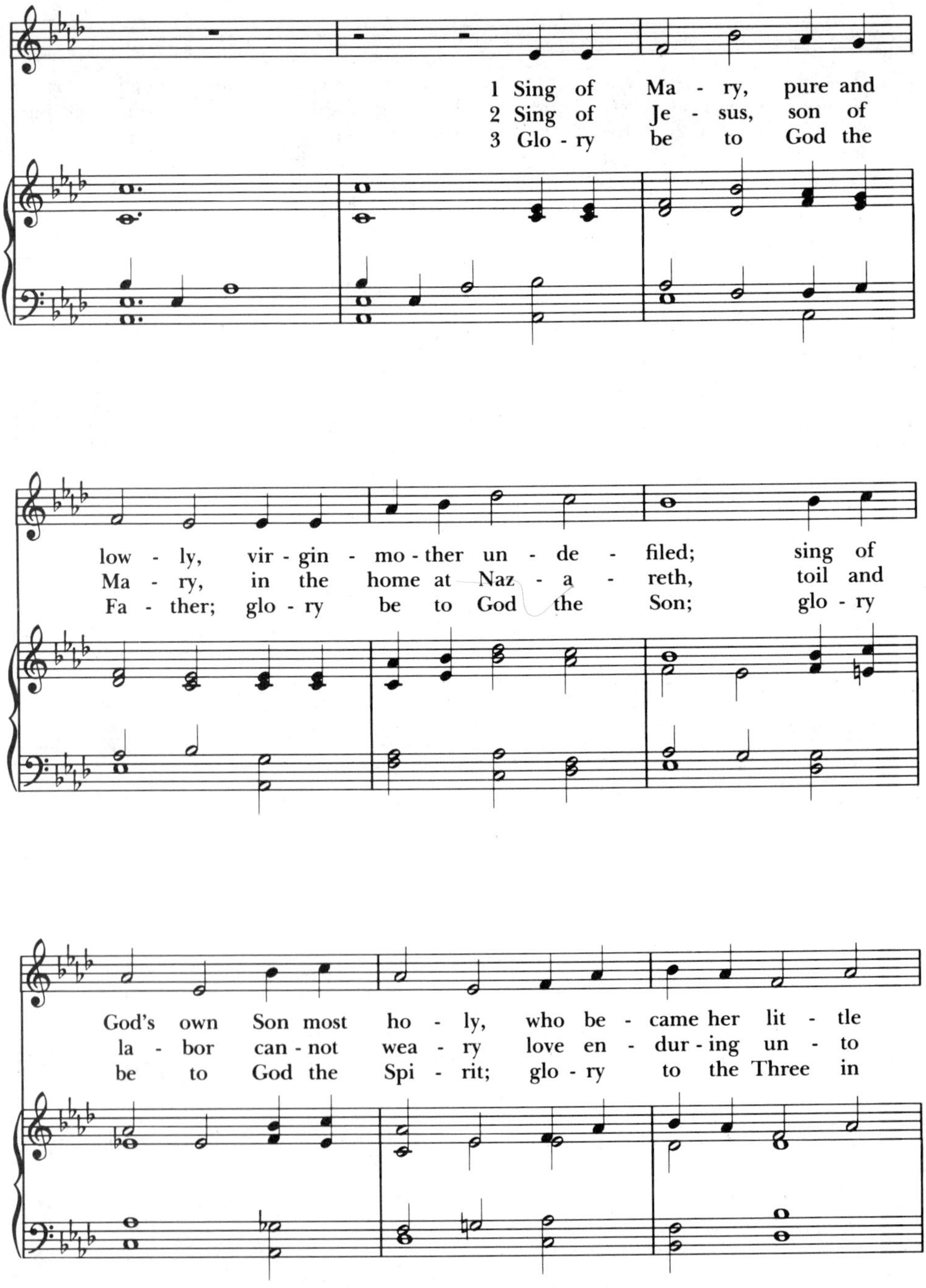
1 Sing of Ma - ry, pure and low - ly, vir - gin - mo - ther un - de - filed; sing of God's own Son most ho - ly, who be - came her lit - tle
2 Sing of Je - sus, son of Ma - ry, in the home at Naz - a - reth, toil and la - bor can - not wea - ry love en - dur - ing un - to
3 Glo - ry be to God the Fa - ther; glo - ry be to God the Son; glo - ry be to God the Spi - rit; glo - ry to the Three in

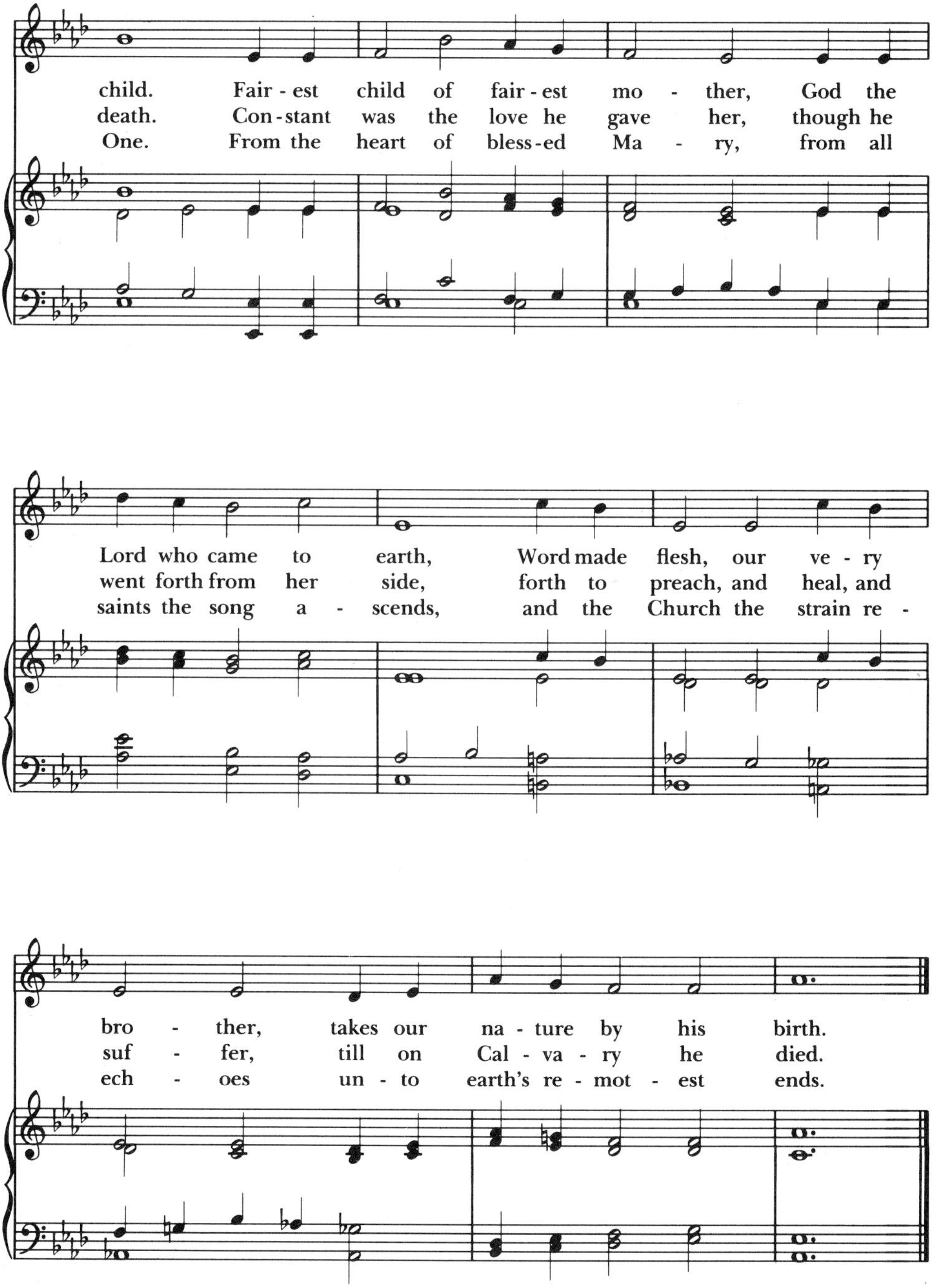
child. Fair-est child of fair-est mo-ther, God the Lord who came to earth, Word made flesh, our ve-ry bro-ther, takes our na-ture by his birth.
death. Con-stant was the love he gave her, though he went forth from her side, forth to preach, and heal, and suf-fer, till on Cal-va-ry he died.
One. From the heart of bless-ed Ma-ry, from all saints the song a-scends, and the Church the strain re-ech-oes un-to earth's re-mot-est ends.

Saint Mary the Virgin (August 15). Alternative tune: *Pleading Savior,* 586.

Words: Roland Ford Palmer (b. 1891)
Music: *Raquel,* Skinner Chávez-Melo (b. 1944)

𝅗𝅥 = 84
87. 87. D

1 Sing we of the bless - ed Mo-ther who re - ceived the an - gel's
2 Sing we, too, of Ma - ry's sor-rows, of the sword that pierced her
3 Sing a - gain the joys of Ma - ry when she saw the ris - en
4 Sing the chief-est joy of Ma - ry when on earth her work was
word, and o - be - dient to the sum - mons bore in
through, when be - neath the cross of Je - sus she his
Lord, and in prayer with Christ's a - pos - tles, wait - ed
done, and the Lord of all cre - a - tion brought her
love the in - fant Lord; sing we of the joys of
weight of suf - fering knew, looked up - on her Son and
on his prom - ised word; from on high the blaz - ing
to his heaven - ly home; where, raised high with saints and
Ma - ry at whose breast the child was fed who is
Sa - vior reign - ing from the aw - ful tree, saw the
glo - ry of the Spi - rit's pres - ence came, heaven - ly
an - gels, in Je - ru - sa - lem a - bove, she be -

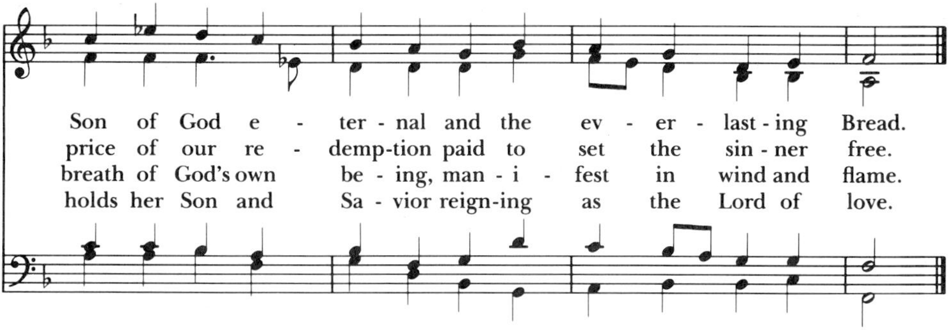
Son of God e - ter - nal and the ev - er - last - ing Bread.
price of our re - demp-tion paid to set the sin - ner free.
breath of God's own be - ing, man - i - fest in wind and flame.
holds her Son and Sa - vior reign-ing as the Lord of love.

Saint Mary the Virgin (August 15). Alternative tune: *Abbot's Leigh,* 379.

Words: George B. Timms (b. 1910), alt. — 𝅗𝅥=52
Music: *Rustington,* Charles Hubert Hastings Parry (1848-1918) — 87. 87. D

Holy Days and Various Occasions

279

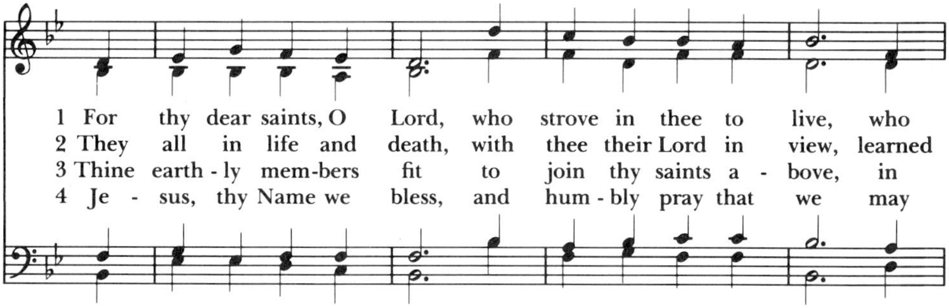
1 For thy dear saints, O Lord, who strove in thee to live, who
2 They all in life and death, with thee their Lord in view, learned
3 Thine earth - ly mem-bers fit to join thy saints a - bove, in
4 Je - sus, thy Name we bless, and hum - bly pray that we may

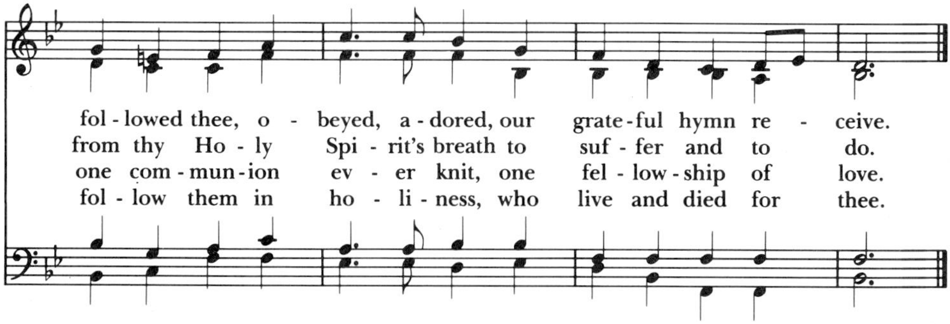
fol - lowed thee, o - beyed, a - dored, our grate-ful hymn re - ceive.
from thy Ho - ly Spi - rit's breath to suf - fer and to do.
one com - mun - ion ev - er knit, one fel - low - ship of love.
fol - low them in ho - li - ness, who live and died for thee.

Saints' Days; All Saints' Day (November 1).

Words: Richard Mant (1776-1848), alt. — 𝅗𝅥=46
Music: *St. George,* Henry John Gauntlett (1805-1876) — SM

1 God of saints, to whom the num - ber of the star - ry
2 In the roll of your a - pos - tles stands the name Bar -
3 All his faith and prayer and pa - tience, all his toil - ing
4 There are named the bless - ed faith - ful of the new Je -
host is known: man - y saints by earth for -
thol - o - mew, for this faith - ful saint we
and his strife, all are veiled from us, but
ru - sa - lem. When Christ comes a - gain in
got - ten live for ev - er round your throne.
of - fer, year by year, our thanks to you.
writ - ten in the Lamb's great book of life.
glo - ry, num - ber us, we pray, with them.

Saint Bartholomew (August 24).

Words: John Ellerton (1826-1893), alt.
Music: *Halton Holgate,* William Boyce (1711-1779)

𝅗𝅥 = 50
87. 87

1 He sat to watch o'er cus - toms paid, a
2 But grace with - in his heart had stirred, there
3 E - nough, when thou wast pass - ing by, to
4 O wise ex - change! with these to part, and
man of scorned and hard-ening trade, a - like the sym - bol
need - ed but the time - ly word; it came, true Lord of
hear thy voice, to meet thine eye; he rose, re - spon - sive
lay up trea - sures in the heart; let them of Mat - thew's
and the tool of for - eign mas - ter's hat - ed rule.
souls, from thee, that roy - al sum - mons, "Fol - low me."
to the call, and left his task, his gains, his all.
wealth par - take, who yield up all for Je - sus' sake.

Saint Matthew (September 21).

Words: William Bright (1824-1901), alt.
Music: *Breslau,* melody from *Lochamer Gesangbuch,* 1450?, alt.; harm. after Felix Mendelssohn (1804-1847)

𝅗𝅥=46
LM

1 Christ, the fair glo - ry of the ho - ly
2 Send thine arch - an - gel Mi - chael to our
3 Send thine arch - an - gel Ga - bri - el, the
4 Send from the hea - vens Ra - phael thine arch -
5 May the blest mo - ther of our God and
6 Fa - ther Al - might - y, Son, and Ho - ly
1 an - gels, ma - ker of all things,
2 suc - cor; peace - ma - ker bless - ed,
3 might - y; her - ald of hea - ven,
4 an - gel, health - bring - er bless - ed,
5 Sa - vior, may the ce - les - tial
6 Spi - rit, God ev - er bless - ed,
1 ru - ler of all na - tions, grant of thy
2 may he ban - ish from us striv - ing and
3 may he, from us mor - tals, drive ev - ery
4 aid - ing ev - ery suf - ferer, that, in thy
5 com - pa - ny of an - gels, may the as -
6 hear our thank - ful prais - es; thine is the

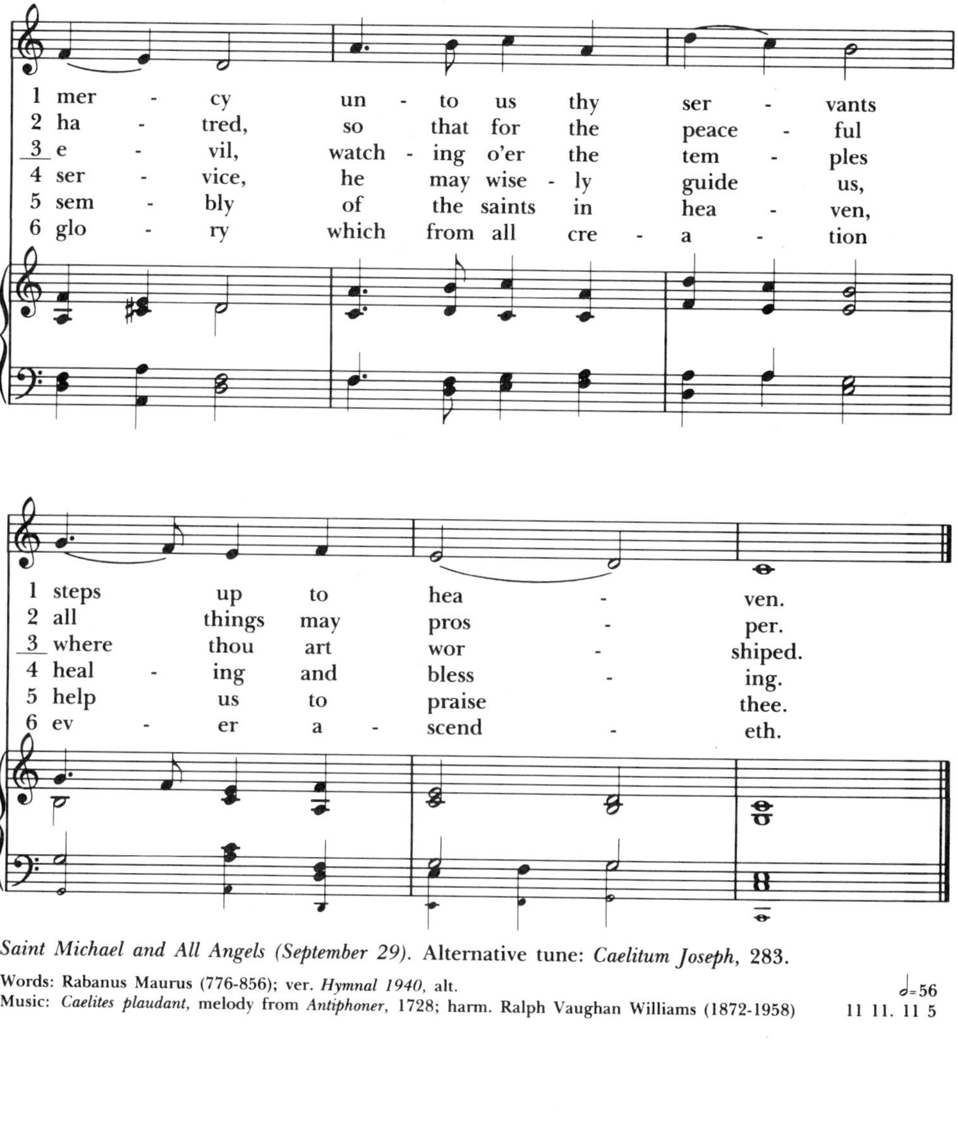
1 mer - cy un - to us thy ser - vants
2 ha - tred, so that for the peace - ful
3 e - vil, watch - ing o'er the tem - ples
4 ser - vice, he may wise - ly guide us,
5 sem - bly of the saints in hea - ven,
6 glo - ry which from all cre - a - tion
1 steps up to hea - ven.
2 all things may pros - per.
3 where thou art wor - shiped.
4 heal - ing and bless - ing.
5 help us to praise thee.
6 ev - er a - scend - eth.

Saint Michael and All Angels (September 29). Alternative tune: *Caelitum Joseph,* 283.

Words: Rabanus Maurus (776-856); ver. *Hymnal 1940,* alt.

Music: *Caelites plaudant,* melody from *Antiphoner,* 1728; harm. Ralph Vaughan Williams (1872-1958)

𝅗𝅥=56

11 11. 11 5

1 Christ, the fair glo - ry of the ho - ly
2 Send thine arch - an - gel Mi - chael to our
3 Send thine arch - an - gel Ga - bri - el, the
4 Send from the hea - vens Ra - phael thine arch -
5 May the blest mo - ther of our God and
6 Fa - ther Al - might - y, Son, and Ho - ly
1 an - gels, ma - ker of all things,
2 suc - cor; peace - ma - ker bless - ed,
3 might - y; her - ald of hea - ven,
4 an - gel, health - bring - er bless - ed,
5 Sa - vior, may the ce - les - tial
6 Spi - rit, God ev - er bless - ed,
1 ru - ler of all na - tions, grant of thy
2 may he ban - ish from us striv - ing and
3 may he, from us mor - tals, drive ev - ery
4 aid - ing ev - ery suf - ferer, that, in thy
5 com - pa - ny of an - gels, may the as -
6 hear our thank - ful prais - es; thine is the

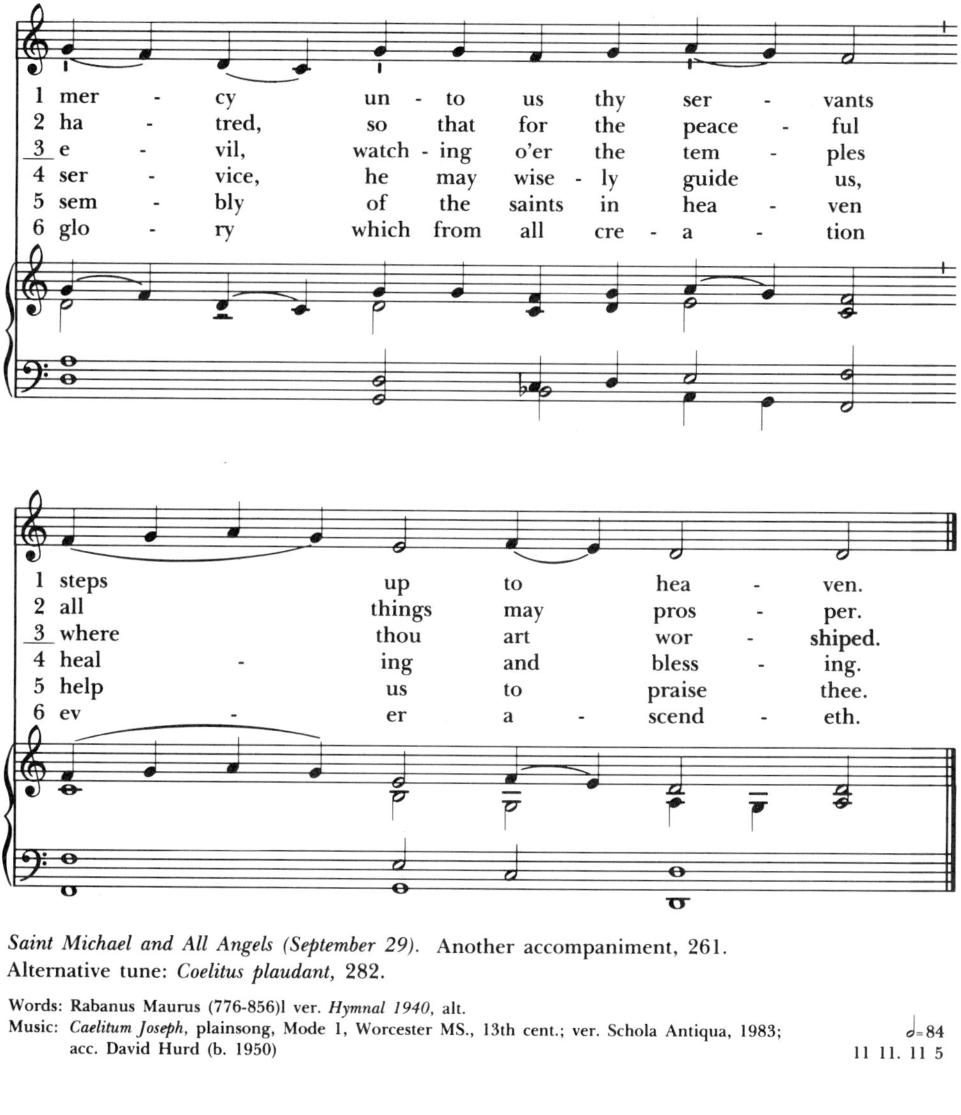
1 mer - cy un - to us thy ser - vants
2 ha - tred, so that for the peace - ful
3 e - vil, watch - ing o'er the tem - ples
4 ser - vice, he may wise - ly guide us,
5 sem - bly of the saints in hea - ven
6 glo - ry which from all cre - a - tion
1 steps up to hea - ven.
2 all things may pros - per.
3 where thou art wor - shiped.
4 heal - ing and bless - ing.
5 help us to praise thee.
6 ev - er a - scend - eth.

Saint Michael and All Angels (September 29). Another accompaniment, 261.
Alternative tune: *Coelitus plaudant,* 282.

Words: Rabanus Maurus (776-856)l ver. *Hymnal 1940,* alt.
Music: *Caelitum Joseph,* plainsong, Mode 1, Worcester MS., 13th cent.; ver. Schola Antiqua, 1983; acc. David Hurd (b. 1950)

𝅗𝅥 = 84
11 11. 11 5

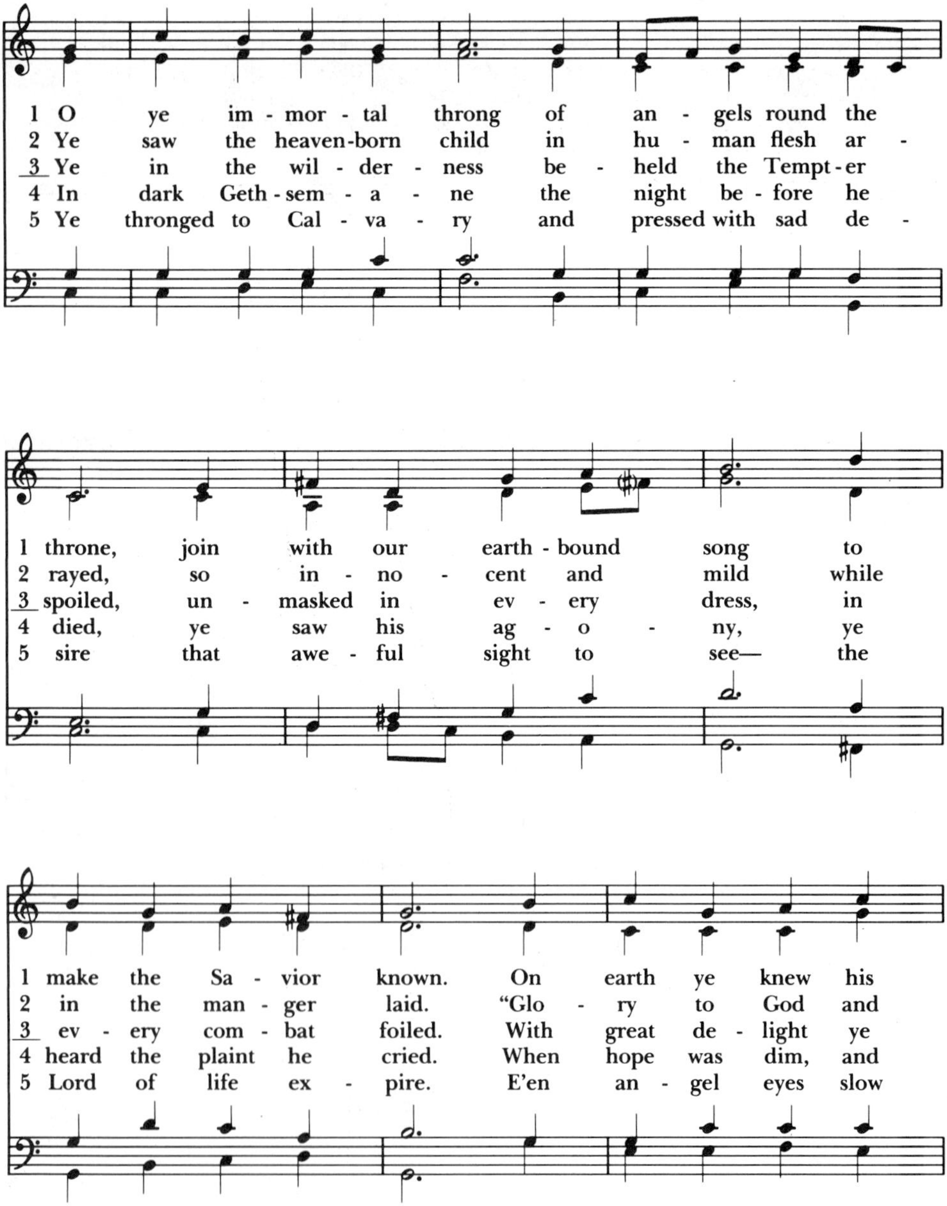
1 O ye im - mor - tal throng of an - gels round the
2 Ye saw the heaven-born child in hu - man flesh ar -
3 Ye in the wil - der - ness be - held the Tempt - er
4 In dark Geth - sem - a - ne the night be - fore he
5 Ye thronged to Cal - va - ry and pressed with sad de -
1 throne, join with our earth - bound song to
2 rayed, so in - no - cent and mild while
3 spoiled, un - masked in ev - ery dress, in
4 died, ye saw his ag - o - ny, ye
5 sire that awe - ful sight to see— the
1 make the Sa - vior known. On earth ye knew his
2 in the man - ger laid. "Glo - ry to God and
3 ev - ery com - bat foiled. With great de - light ye
4 heard the plaint he cried. When hope was dim, and
5 Lord of life ex - pire. E'en an - gel eyes slow

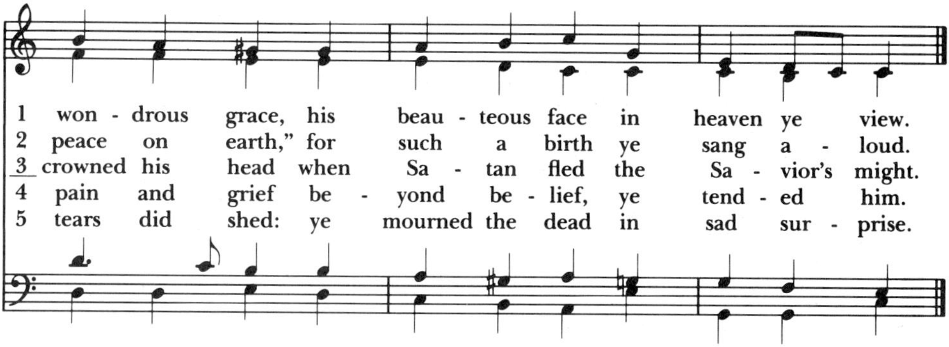
1 won - drous grace, his beau - teous face in heaven ye view.
2 peace on earth," for such a birth ye sang a - loud.
3 crowned his head when Sa - tan fled the Sa - vior's might.
4 pain and grief be - yond be - lief, ye tend - ed him.
5 tears did shed: ye mourned the dead in sad sur - prise.

6 Around his sacred tomb
a willing watch ye kept;
till out from death's vast room,
up from the grave, he leapt.
Ye rolled the stone,
and all adored
your rising Lord
with joy unknown.

7 When all arrayed in light
the shining conqueror rode,
ye hailed his wondrous flight
up to the throne of God.
And waved around
your golden wings,
and struck your strings
of sweetest sound.

8 The joyous notes pursue
and louder anthems raise;
while mortals sing with you
their own Redeemer's praise.
With equal flame
and equal art,
do thou my heart
extol his Name.

Saint Michael and All Angels (September 29).

Words: Sts. 1-3 and 5-8, Philip Doddridge (1702-1751), alt; st. 4, Charles P. Price (b. 1920)
Music: *Croft's 136th,* melody and bass William Croft (1678-1727);
harm. *Hymns Ancient and Modern, Revised,* 1950

♩= 88
66. 66. 44. 44

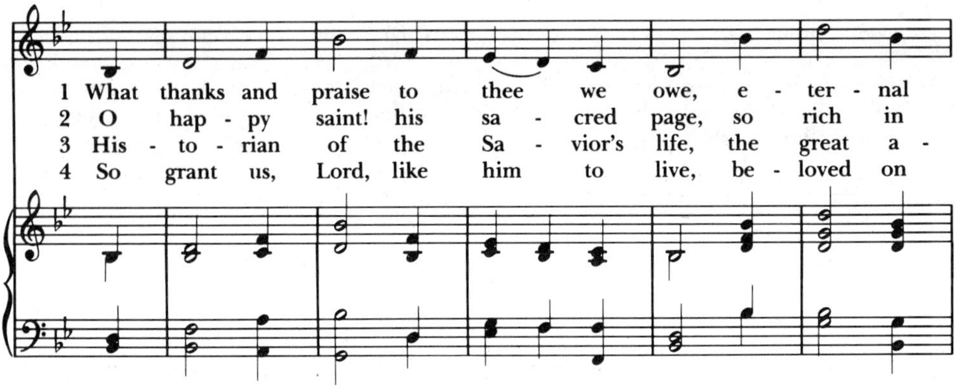
1 What thanks and praise to thee we owe, e - ter - nal
2 O hap - py saint! his sa - cred page, so rich in
3 His - to - rian of the Sa - vior's life, the great a -
4 So grant us, Lord, like him to live, be - loved on

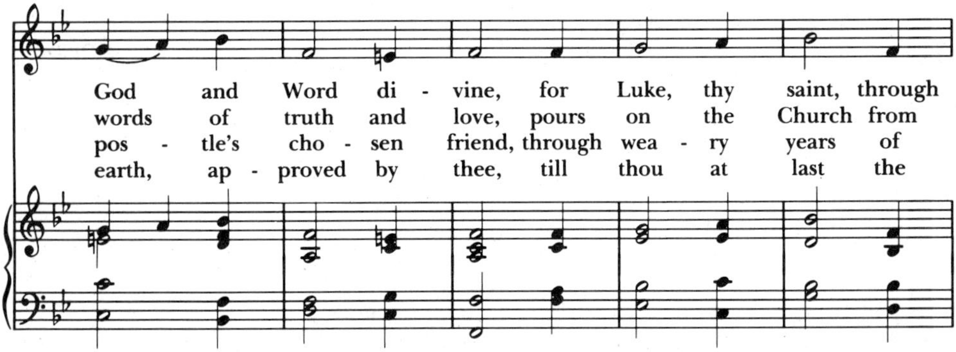
God and Word di - vine, for Luke, thy saint, through
words of truth and love, pours on the Church from
pos - tle's cho - sen friend, through wea - ry years of
earth, ap - proved by thee, till thou at last the

whom we know so man - y gra - cious words of thine.
age to age the heal - ing unc - tion from a - bove.
toil and strife was still found faith - ful to the end.
sum - mons give, and we, with him, thy face shall see.

Saint Luke (October 18).

Words: William Dalrymple Maclagan (1826-1910), alt.
Music: *Deus tuorum militum,* melody from *Antiphoner,* 1753; adapt. *The English Hymnal,* 1906, alt.; harm. after Basil Harwood (1859-1949)

𝅗𝅥. =40
LM

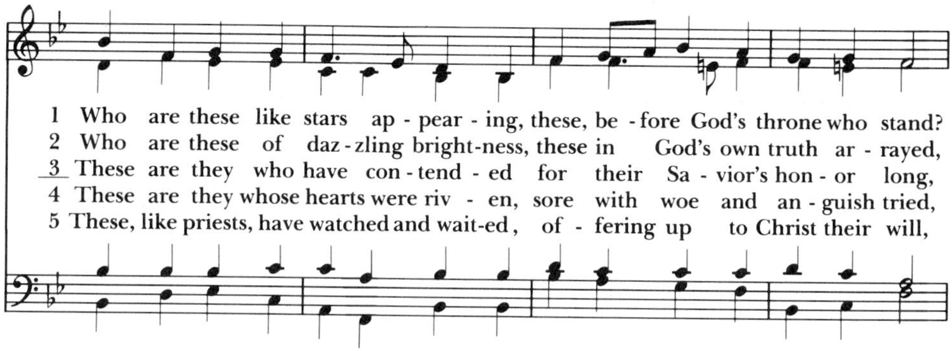
1 Who are these like stars ap - pear - ing, these, be - fore God's throne who stand?
2 Who are these of daz - zling bright-ness, these in God's own truth ar - rayed,
3 These are they who have con - tend - ed for their Sa - vior's hon - or long,
4 These are they whose hearts were riv - en, sore with woe and an - guish tried,
5 These, like priests, have watched and wait-ed, of - fering up to Christ their will,

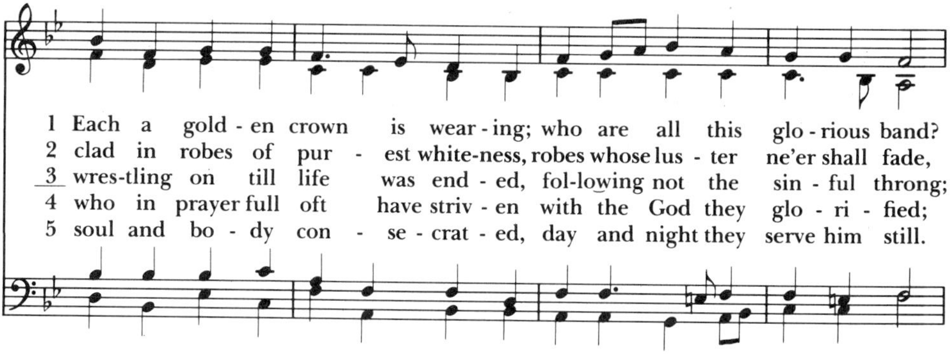
1 Each a gold - en crown is wear - ing; who are all this glo - rious band?
2 clad in robes of pur - est white-ness, robes whose lus - ter ne'er shall fade,
3 wres-tling on till life was end - ed, fol-lowing not the sin - ful throng;
4 who in prayer full oft have striv - en with the God they glo - ri - fied;
5 soul and bo - dy con - se - crat - ed, day and night they serve him still.

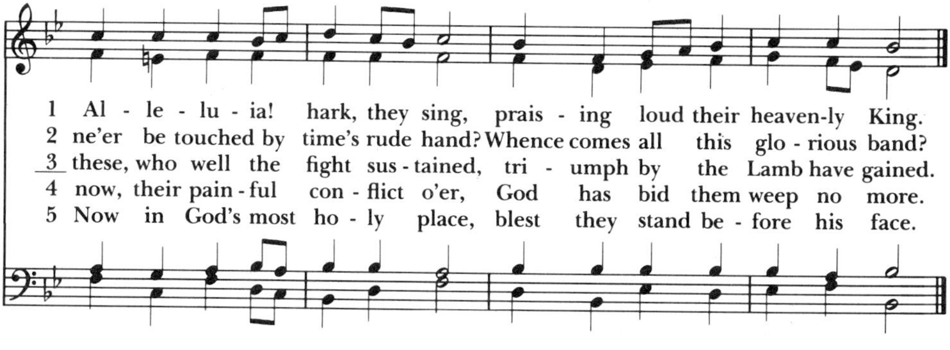
1 Al - le - lu - ia! hark, they sing, prais - ing loud their heaven-ly King.
2 ne'er be touched by time's rude hand? Whence comes all this glo - rious band?
3 these, who well the fight sus - tained, tri - umph by the Lamb have gained.
4 now, their pain - ful con - flict o'er, God has bid them weep no more.
5 Now in God's most ho - ly place, blest they stand be - fore his face.

All Saints' Day (November 1).

Words: Theobald Heinrich Schenck (1656-1727); tr. Frances Elizabeth Cox (1812-1897), alt.
Music: *Zeuch mich, zeuch mich,* melody from *Geistreiches Gesang-buch,* 1698; harm. William Henry Monk (1823-1889), alt.

𝅗𝅥=50
87. 87. 77

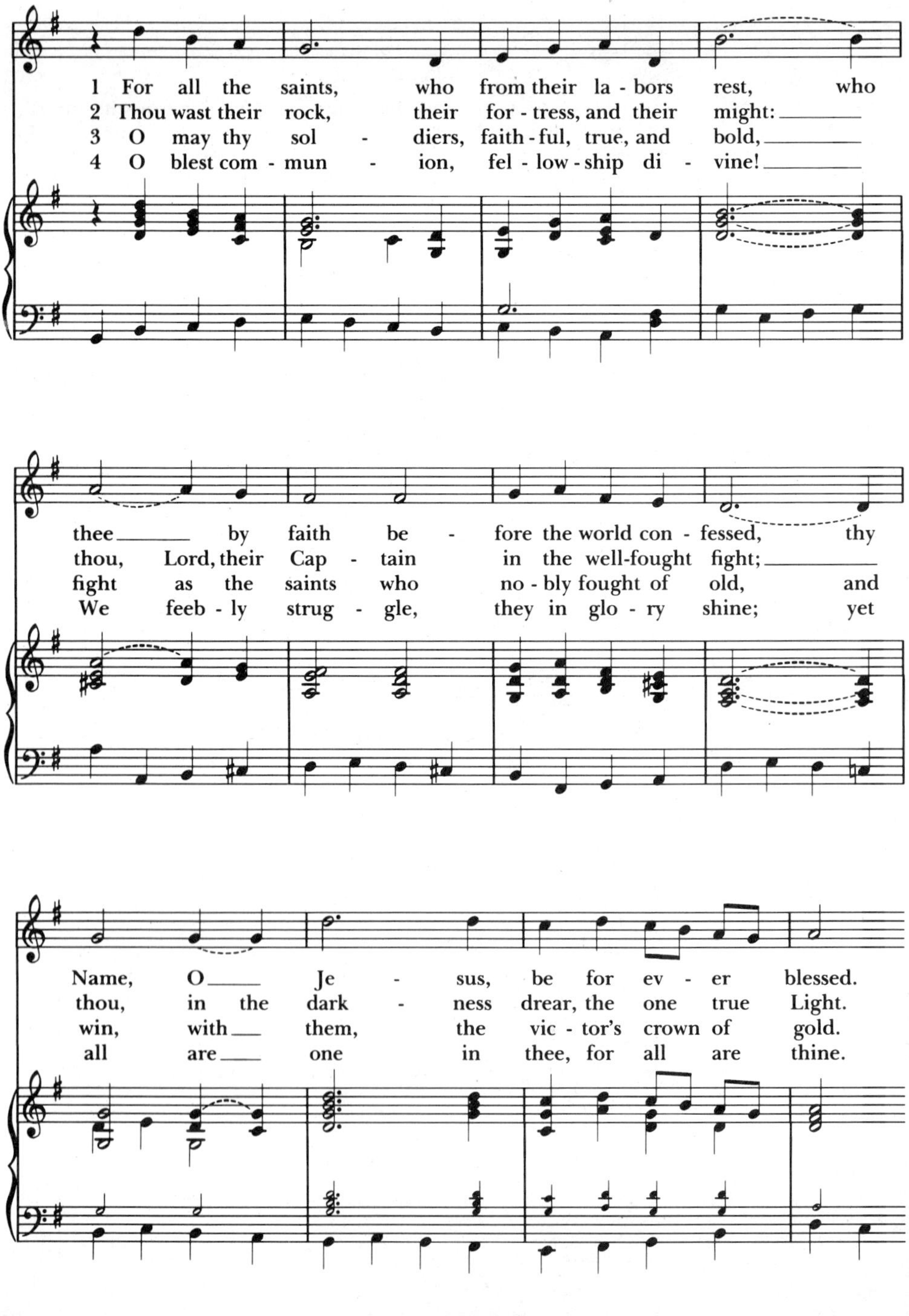
1 For all the saints, who from their la - bors rest, who
2 Thou wast their rock, their for - tress, and their might:
3 O may thy sol - diers, faith - ful, true, and bold,
4 O blest com - mun - ion, fel - low - ship di - vine!
thee by faith be - fore the world con - fessed, thy
thou, Lord, their Cap - tain in the well-fought fight;
fight as the saints who no - bly fought of old, and
We feeb - ly strug - gle, they in glo - ry shine; yet
Name, O Je - sus, be for ev - er blessed.
thou, in the dark - ness drear, the one true Light.
win, with them, the vic - tor's crown of gold.
all are one in thee, for all are thine.

Al - le - lu - ia, al - le - lu - ia!

*5 And when the strife is fierce, the war-fare long, steals on the ear the
*6 The gold-en eve-ning bright-ens in the west; soon, soon to faith-ful

dis-tant tri-umph song, and hearts are ___ brave a-gain, and arms are
war-riors com-eth rest; ___ sweet is the calm of par-a-dise the

strong.
blest. Al - le - lu - ia. al - le - lu - ia!

*7 But lo! there breaks a yet more glo-rious day; the
*8 From earth's wide bounds, from o-cean's far-thest coast, through
saints tri - umph - ant rise in bright ar - ray; the
gates of pearl streams in the count-less host,
King of glo - ry pass-es on his way.
sing - ing to Fa - ther, Son, and Ho - ly Ghost,
Al - le - lu - ia, al - le - lu - ia!

All Saints' Day (November 1).

Words: William Walsham How (1823-1897)
Music: *Sine Nomine*, Ralph Vaughan Williams (1872-1958)

𝅗𝅥 = 60
10 10 10 with Alleluias

1 Praise to God, im - mor - tal praise, for the love that crowns our days;
2 All the plen - ty sum - mer pours; au - tumn's rich o'er - flow - ing stores;
3 As thy pros-pering hand hath blessed, may we give thee of our best;
boun - teous source of ev - ery joy, let thy praise our tongues em - ploy:
flocks that whit - en all the plain; yel - low sheaves of ri - pened grain:
and by deeds of kind - ly love for thy mer - cies grate - ful prove;
all to thee, our God, we owe, source whence all our bless-ings flow.
Lord, for these our souls shall raise grate - ful vows and sol - emn praise.
sing - ing thus through all our days praise to God, im - mor - tal praise.

Thanksgiving Day.

Words: Anna Laetitia Barbauld (1743-1825)
Music: *Dix,* melody Conrad Kocher (1786-1872); arr. William Henry Monk (1823-1889); harm. *The English Hymnal,* 1906

𝅗𝅥=50
77. 77. 77

1 Our Fa - ther, by whose ser - vants our house was built of
2 The change - ful years un - rest - ing their si - lent course have
3 They reap not where they la - bored; we reap what they have
old, whose hand hath crowned her chil - dren with
sped, new com - rades ev - er bring - ing in
sown: our har - vest may be gar - nered by
bless - ings man - i - fold, for thine un - fail - ing
com - rades' steps to tread: and some are long for -
a - ges yet un - known. The days of old have
mer - cies far - strewn a - long our way, with
got - ten, long spent their hopes and fears; safe
dowered us with gifts be - yond all praise: our

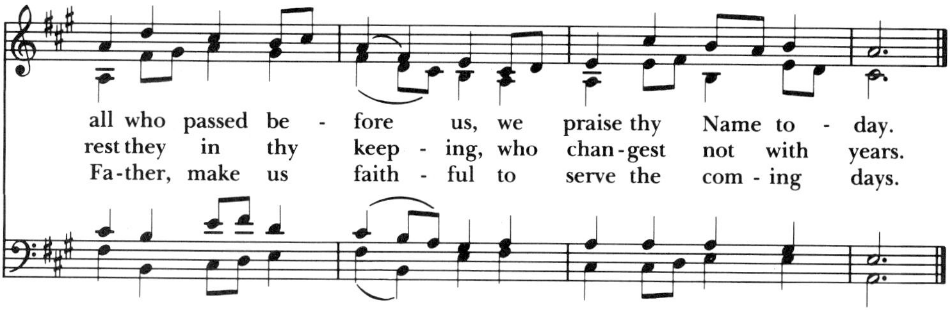
all who passed be - fore us, we praise thy Name to - day.
rest they in thy keep - ing, who chan - gest not with years.
Fa-ther, make us faith - ful to serve the com - ing days.

On the Anniversary of the Dedication of a Church. Alternative tune: *Llangloffan,* 607.

Words: George Wallace Briggs (1875-1959)
Music: *Wolvercote,* William Harold Ferguson (1874-1950)

𝅗𝅥 = 52
76. 76. D

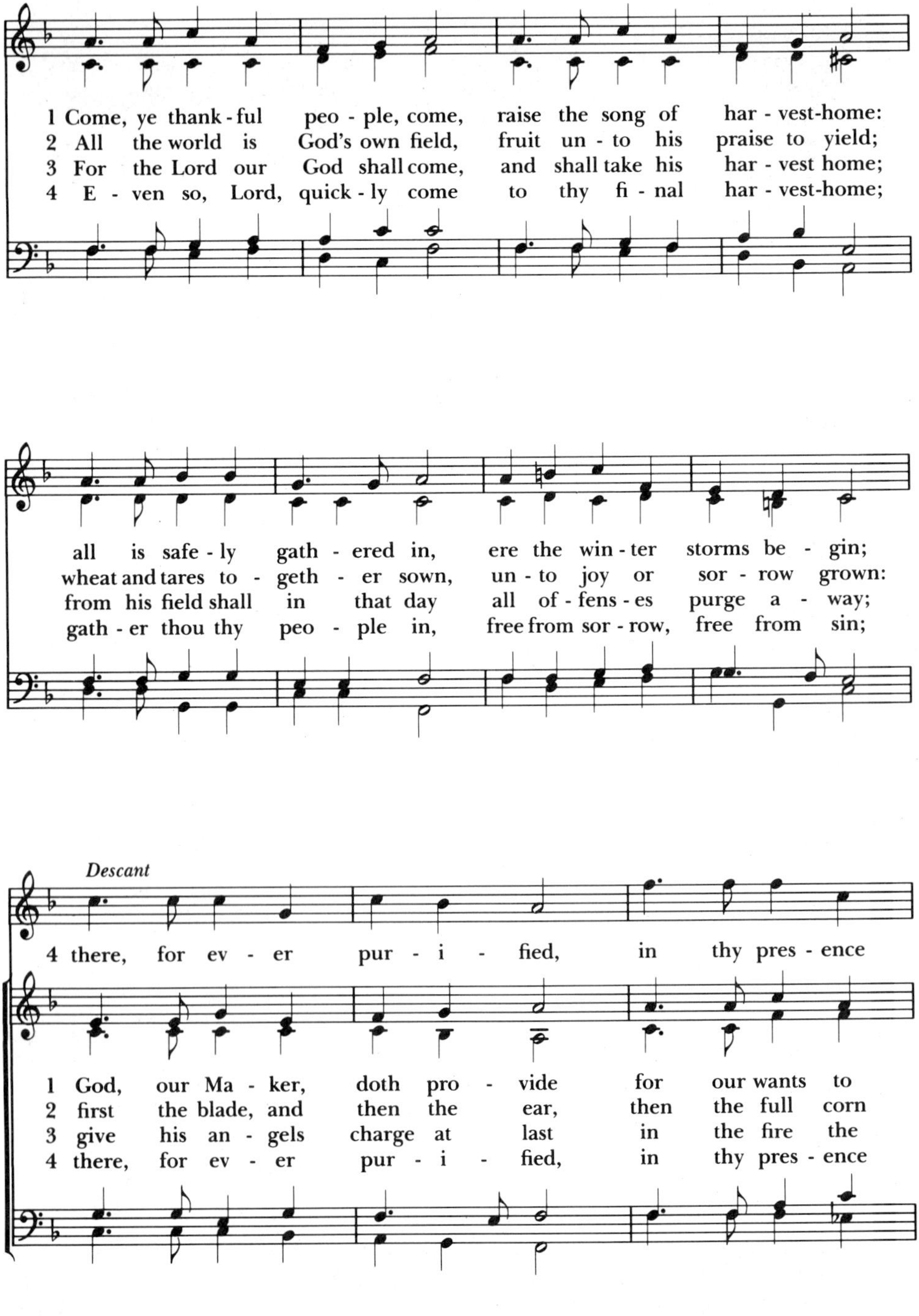
1 Come, ye thank - ful peo - ple, come, raise the song of har - vest-home:
2 All the world is God's own field, fruit un - to his praise to yield;
3 For the Lord our God shall come, and shall take his har - vest home;
4 E - ven so, Lord, quick - ly come to thy fi - nal har - vest-home;
all is safe - ly gath - ered in, ere the win - ter storms be - gin;
wheat and tares to - geth - er sown, un - to joy or sor - row grown:
from his field shall in that day all of - fens - es purge a - way;
gath - er thou thy peo - ple in, free from sor - row, free from sin;
Descant
4 there, for ev - er pur - i - fied, in thy pres - ence
1 God, our Ma - ker, doth pro - vide for our wants to
2 first the blade, and then the ear, then the full corn
3 give his an - gels charge at last in the fire the
4 there, for ev - er pur - i - fied, in thy pres - ence

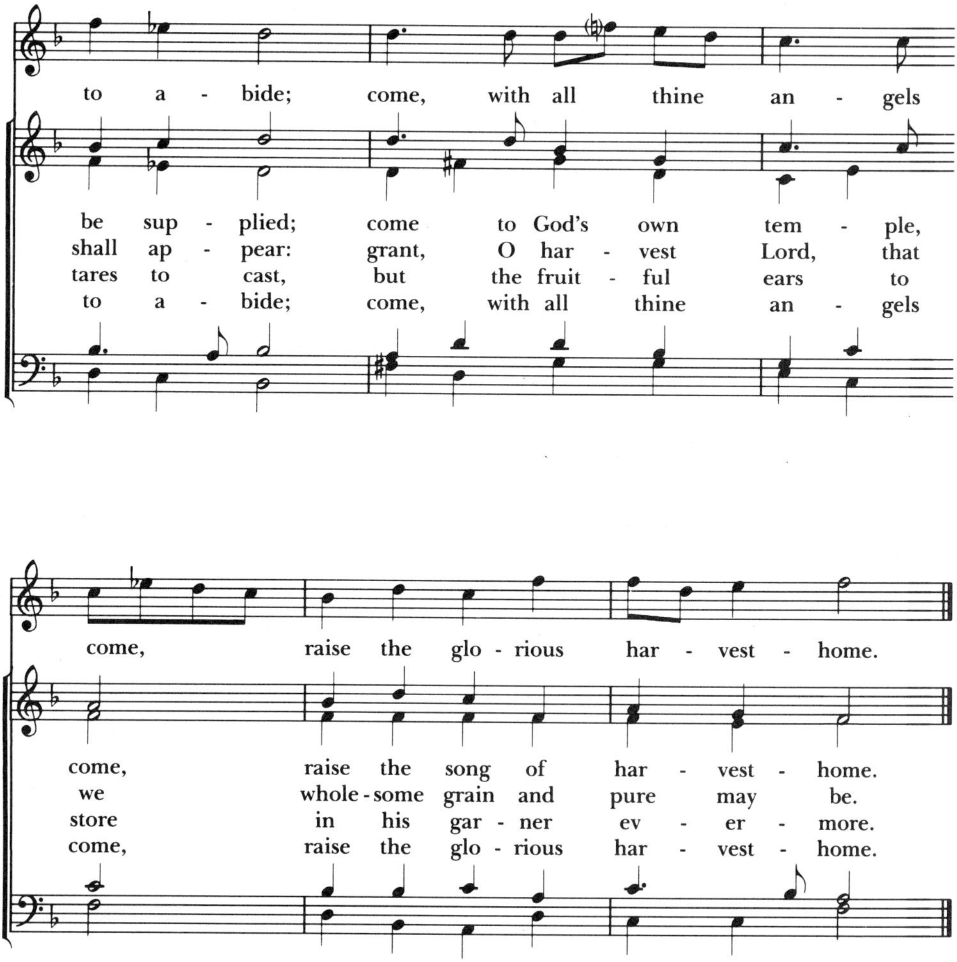
to a - bide; come, with all thine an - gels
be sup - plied; come to God's own tem - ple,
shall ap - pear: grant, O har - vest Lord, that
tares to cast, but the fruit - ful ears to
to a - bide; come, with all thine an - gels
come, raise the glo - rious har - vest - home.
come, raise the song of har - vest - home.
we whole-some grain and pure may be.
store in his gar - ner ev - er - more.
come, raise the glo - rious har - vest - home.

Thanksgiving Day.

Words: Henry Alford (1810-1871), alt.

Music: *St. George's, Windsor,* George Job Elvey (1816-1893); desc. Craig Sellar Lang (1891-1971)

𝅗𝅥 = 54

77. 77. D

1 We plow the fields, and scat - ter the good seed on the land,
2 He on - ly is the Ma - ker of all things near and far;
3 We thank thee, then, O Fa - ther, for all things bright and good,
but it is fed and wa - tered by God's al - might - y hand;
he paints the way - side flow - er, he lights the eve - ning star;
the seed - time and the har - vest, our life, our health, our food:
he sends the snow in win - ter, the warmth to swell the grain,
the winds and waves o - bey him, by him the birds are fed;
the gifts we have to of - fer are what thy love im - parts,
the breez - es and the sun - shine, and soft re - fresh - ing rain.
much more to us, his chil - dren, he gives our dai - ly bread.
but chief - ly thou de - sir - est our hum - ble thank - ful hearts.

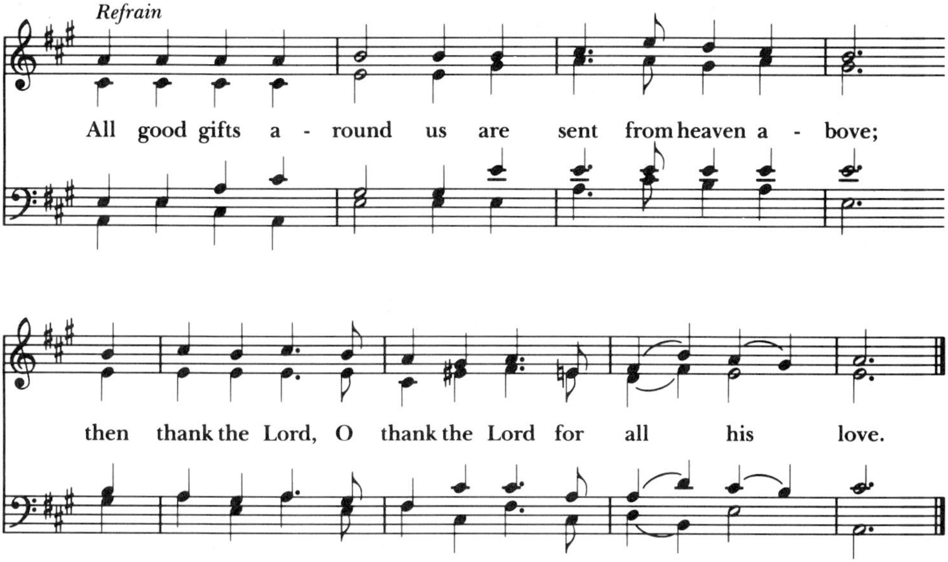
Refrain
All good gifts a - round us are sent from heaven a - bove;
then thank the Lord, O thank the Lord for all his love.

Thanksgiving Day.

Words: Matthias Claudius (1740-1815); tr. Jane Montgomery Campbell (1817-1878), alt.
Music: *Wir pflugen,* Johann Abraham Peter Schulz (1747-1800)

𝅗𝅥=54
76. 76. D with Refrain

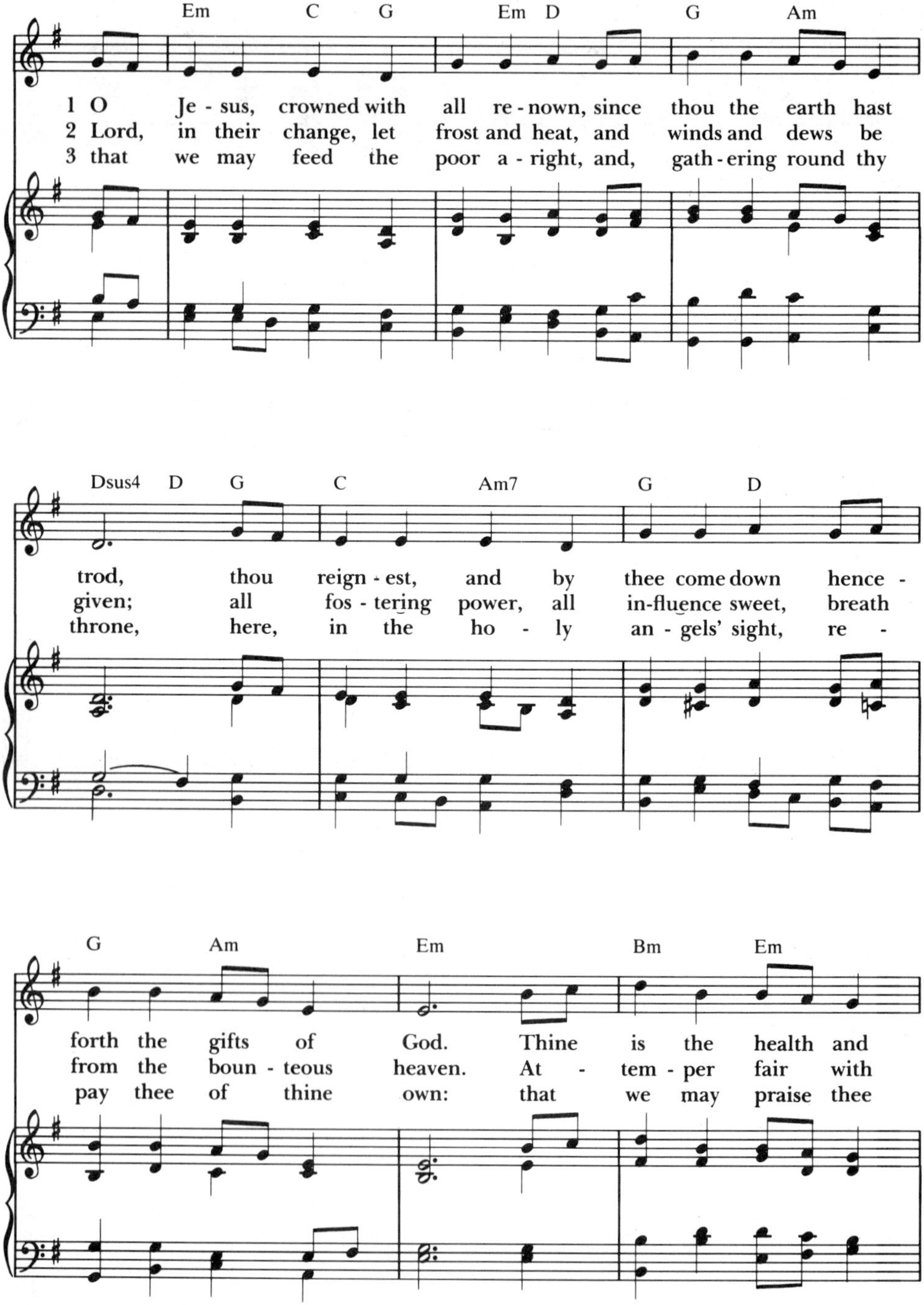
Em C G Em D G Am
1 O Je - sus, crowned with all re - nown, since thou the earth hast
2 Lord, in their change, let frost and heat, and winds and dews be
3 that we may feed the poor a - right, and, gath - ering round thy
Dsus4 D G C Am7 G D
trod, thou reign - est, and by thee come down hence -
given; all fos - tering power, all in-fluence sweet, breath
throne, here, in the ho - ly an - gels' sight, re -
G Am Em Bm Em
forth the gifts of God. Thine is the health and
from the boun - teous heaven. At - tem - per fair with
pay thee of thine own: that we may praise thee

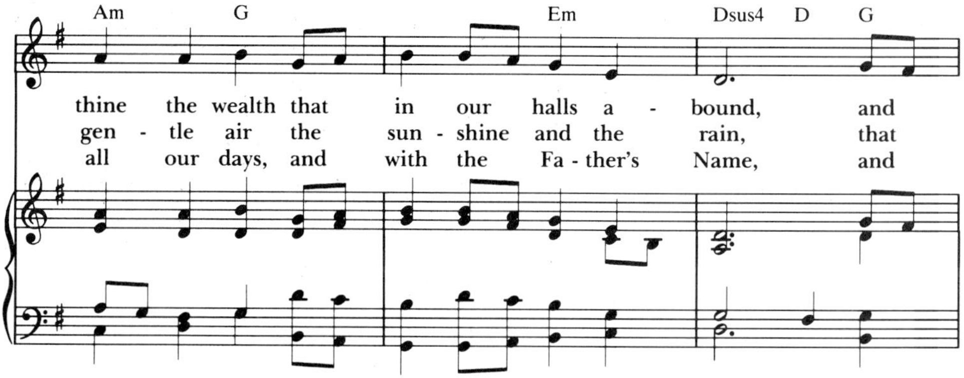
Am G Em Dsus4 D G
thine the wealth that in our halls a - bound, and
gen - tle air the sun - shine and the rain, that
all our days, and with the Fa - ther's Name, and

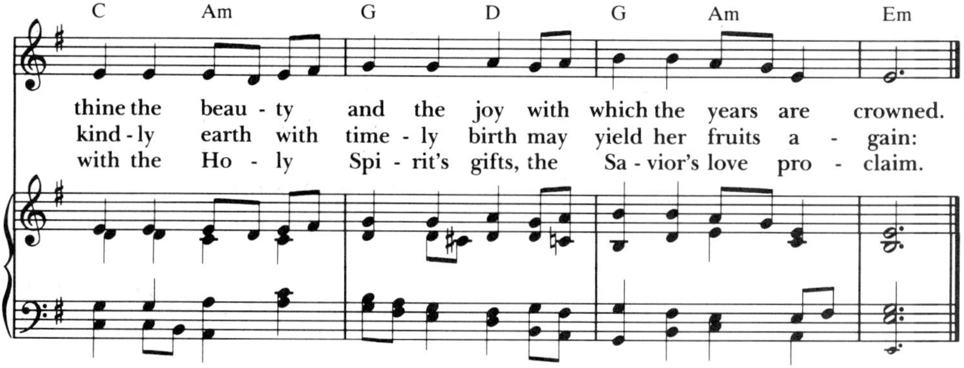
C Am G D G Am Em
thine the beau - ty and the joy with which the years are crowned.
kind - ly earth with time - ly birth may yield her fruits a - gain:
with the Ho - ly Spi - rit's gifts, the Sa - vior's love pro - claim.

Rogation Days. Keyboard and guitar should not sound together.

Words: Edward White Benson (1829-1896), alt.
Music: *Kingsfold,* English melody; adapt. and harm. Ralph Vaughan Williams (1872-1958)

𝅗𝅥 = 50
CMD

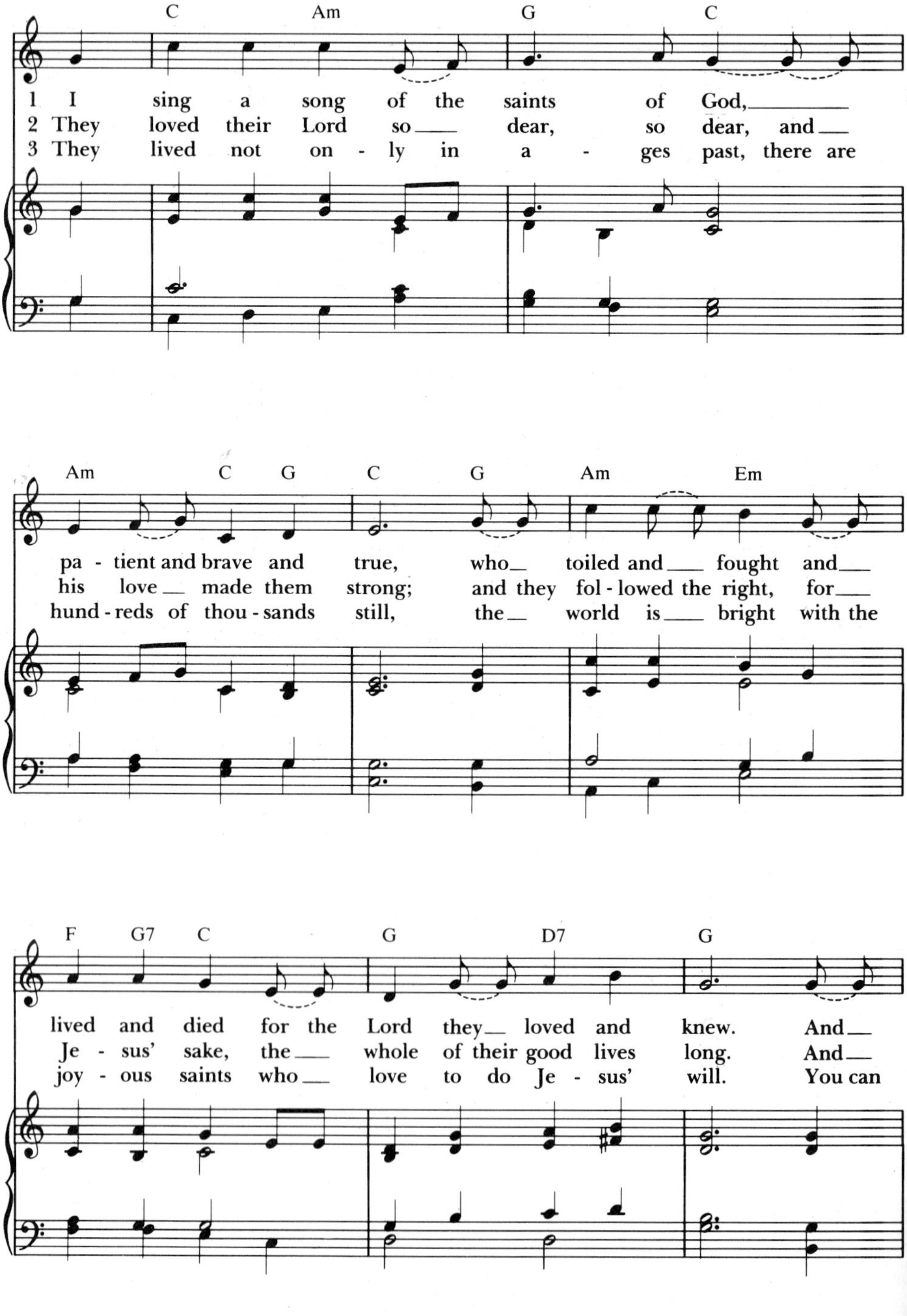
C Am G C
1 I sing a song of the saints of God,
2 They loved their Lord so dear, so dear, and
3 They lived not on - ly in a - ges past, there are
Am C G C G Am Em
pa - tient and brave and true, who toiled and fought and
his love made them strong; and they fol - lowed the right, for
hund - reds of thou - sands still, the world is bright with the
F G7 C G D7 G
lived and died for the Lord they loved and knew. And
Je - sus' sake, the whole of their good lives long. And
joy - ous saints who love to do Je - sus' will. You can

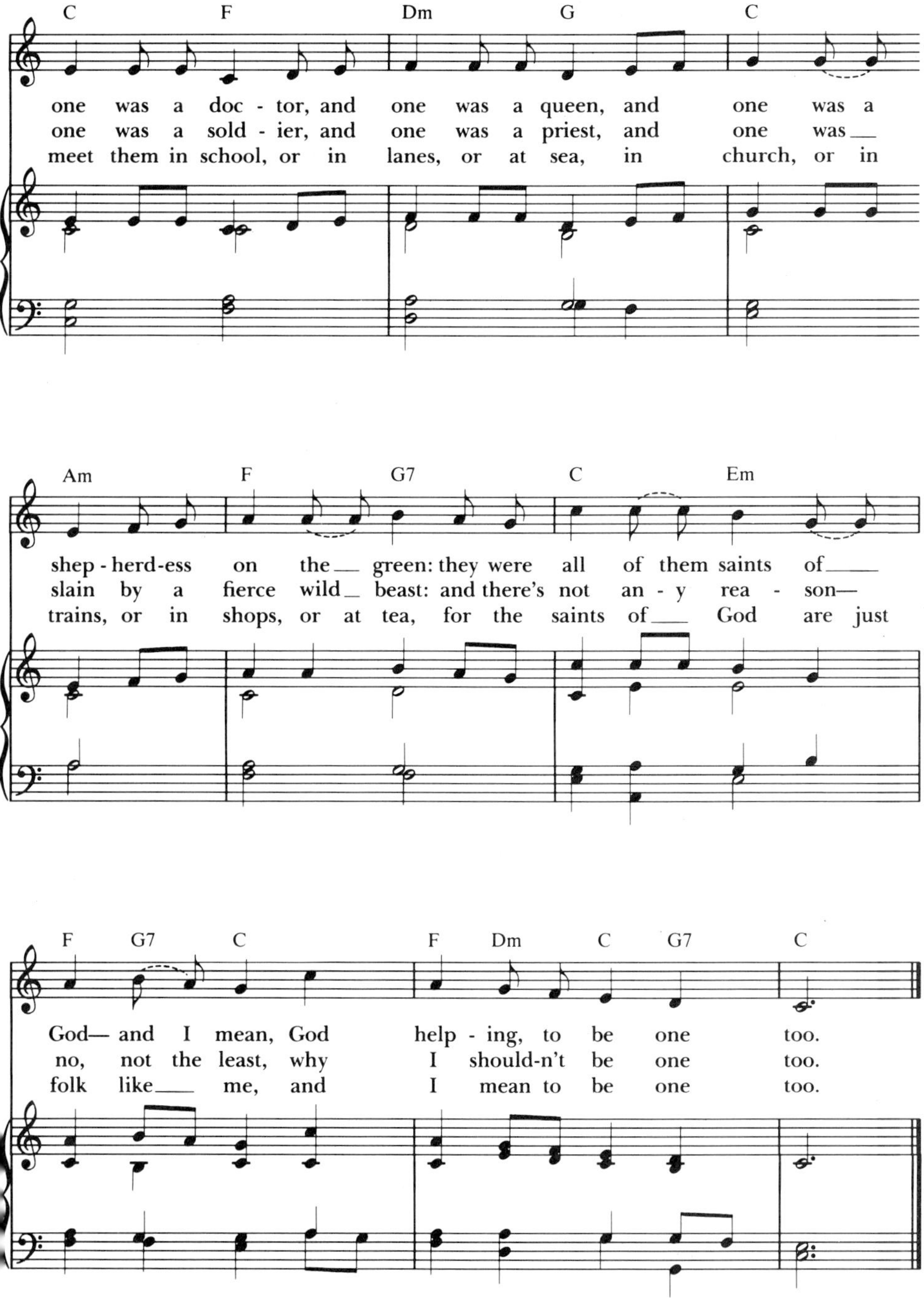
C F Dm G C
one was a doc - tor, and one was a queen, and one was a
one was a sold - ier, and one was a priest, and one was
meet them in school, or in lanes, or at sea, in church, or in
Am F G7 C Em
shep - herd - ess on the green: they were all of them saints of
slain by a fierce wild beast: and there's not an - y rea - son—
trains, or in shops, or at tea, for the saints of God are just
F G7 C F Dm C G7 C
God— and I mean, God help - ing, to be one too.
no, not the least, why I should-n't be one too.
folk like me, and I mean to be one too.

Saints' Days; All Saints' Day (November 1).

Words: Lesbia Scott (b. 1898), alt.
Music: *Grand Isle,* John Henry Hopkins (1861-1945)

𝅗𝅥 = 60
Irr.

1 Bap - tized in wa - ter, sealed by the Spi - rit,
2 Bap - tized in wa - ter, sealed by the Spi - rit,
3 Bap - tized in wa - ter, sealed by the Spi - rit,
cleansed by the blood of Christ our King: heirs of sal - va - tion,
dead in the tomb with Christ our King: one with his ris - ing,
marked with the sign of Christ our King: born of one Fa - ther,
trust - ing his prom - ise, faith - ful - ly now God's praise we sing.
freed and for - giv - en, thank - ful - ly now God's praise we sing.
we are his chil - dren, joy - ful - ly now God's praise we sing.

Words: Michael Saward (b. 1932), alt.
Music: *Point Loma,* David Charles Walker (b. 1938)

♪ = 138
558. 558

295

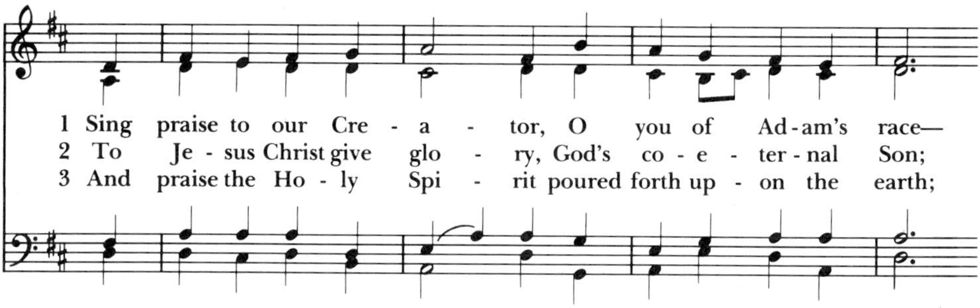
1 Sing praise to our Cre - a - tor, O you of Ad-am's race—
2 To Je - sus Christ give glo - ry, God's co - e - ter-nal Son;
3 And praise the Ho - ly Spi - rit poured forth up - on the earth;

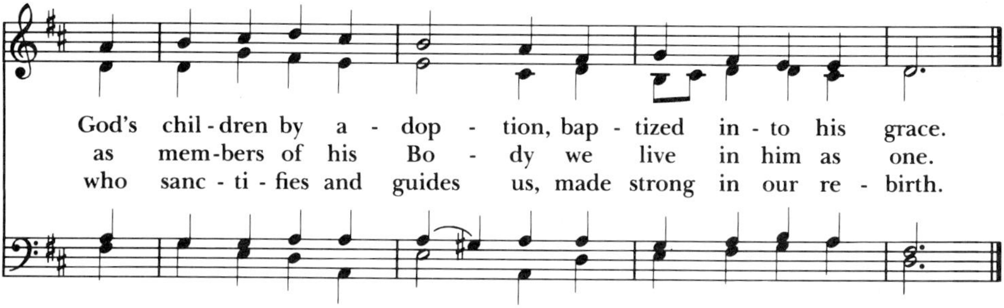
God's chil-dren by a - dop - tion, bap - tized in - to his grace.
as mem-bers of his Bo - dy we live in him as one.
who sanc - ti - fies and guides us, made strong in our re - birth.

Words: Mark Evans (b. 1916), alt.
Music: *Christus, der ist mein Leben,* melody Melchior Vulpius (1560?-1616); harm. after Melchior Vulpius (1560?-1616)

♩= 84
76. 76

1 We know that Christ is raised and dies no more. Em-braced by
2 We share by wa - ter in his sav-ing death. Re-born we
3 The Fa-ther's splen-dor clothes the Son with life. The Spi-rit's
4 A new cre - a - tion comes to life and grows as Christ's new
death he broke its fear-ful hold; and our de-spair he turned to
share with him an Eas-ter life as liv-ing mem-bers of a
pow-er shakes the Church of God. Bap-tized we live with God the
bo-dy takes on flesh and blood. The u-ni-verse re-stored and
blaz-ing joy.
liv-ing Christ.
Three in One.
whole will sing:
1-3
Al-le-lu-ia!

Final Ending
Al - le - lu - ia! A - men.

This music in G, 420; this music with descant, 477.

Words: John Brownlow Geyer (b. 1932), alt.
Music: *Engelberg*, Charles Villiers Stanford (1852-1924)

𝅗𝅥 = 48
10 10 10 with Alleluia

1 De - scend, O Spi - rit, purg - ing flame,
2 For - bid us not this sec - ond birth;
brand us this day with Je - sus' Name!
grant un - to us the great - er worth!
Con - firm our faith, con - sume our doubt;
En - list us in your ser - vice Lord;
sign us as Christ's, with - in, with - out.
bap - tize all na - tions with your Word.

Alternative tune: *Erhalt uns, Herr* (rhythmic), 132.

Words: Scott Francis Brenner (b. 1903), alt.
Music: *Erhalt uns Herr*, melody from *Geistliche Lieder*, 1543; harm. Johann Sebastian Bach (1685-1750)

♩=80
LM

1 All who be - lieve and are bap - tized shall see the Lord's sal -
2 With one ac - cord, O God, we pray: grant us thy Ho - ly
va - tion; bap-tized in - to the death of Christ, each is a
Spi - rit; help us in our in - fir - mi - ty through Je - sus'
new cre - a - tion. Through Christ's re-demp-tion we shall stand a-mong the
blood and mer - it. Grant us to grow in grace each day that as is
glo - rious heaven - ly band of ev - ery tribe and na - tion.
prom - ised here we may e - ter - nal life in - her - it.

Alternative tune: *Mit Freuden zart,* 408.

Words: Thomas Hansen Kingo (1634-1703); tr. George Alfred Taylor Rygh (1860-1942), alt. 𝅗𝅥=56
Music: *Es ist das Heil,* Hans Leo Hassler (1564-1612), alt. 87. 87. 887

1 Spi - rit of God, un - leashed on earth
2 You came in power; the Church was born;
3 With burn - ing words of vic - tory won
with rush of wind and roar of flame!
O Ho - ly Spi - rit, come a - gain!
in - spire our hearts grown cold with fear,
With tongues of fire saints spread good news;
From liv - ing wa - ters raise new saints;
re - vive in us bap - tis - mal grace,
earth, kin - dling, blazed her loud ac - claim.
let new tongues hail the ris - en Lord.
and fan our smol - dering lives to flame.

Words: John W. Arthur (1922-1980), alt.
Music: *Lledrod,* melody from *Llyfr Tonau Cynnulleidfaol,* 1859; harm. *Hymnal 1940*

𝅗𝅥=60
LM

1 Glo - ry, love, and praise, and hon - or for our food
2 Thank-ful for our ev - ery bless - ing, let us sing
3 He dis - pels our sin and sad - ness, life im - parts,
now be - stowed ren - der we the Do - nor.
Christ the Spring, nev - er, nev - er ceas - ing.
cheers our hearts, fills with food and glad - ness.
Boun - teous God, we now con - fess thee: God, who thus
Source of all our gifts and gra - ces, Christ we own;
Who him - self for all hath giv - en, us he feeds,
bless - est us, right it is to bless thee.
Christ a - lone calls for all our prais - es.
us he leads to a feast in hea - ven.

Words: Charles Wesley (1707-1788), alt.
Music: *Benifold,* Francis B. Westbrook (1903-1975)

𝅗𝅥=52
8. 33. 6. D

Bread of the world, in mer - cy bro - ken, Wine of the
soul, in mer - cy shed, by whom the words of life were
spo - ken, and in whose death our sins are dead:
look on the heart by sor - row bro - ken, look on the

tears by sin - ners shed; and be thy feast to us the
to - ken that by thy grace our souls are fed.

Other harmonizations, 302 and 413.

Words: Reginald Heber (1783-1826)
Music: *Rendez à Dieu*, melody att. Louis Bourgeois (1510?-1561?); harm. Claude Goudimel (1514-1572), alt.

♩= 96
98. 98. D

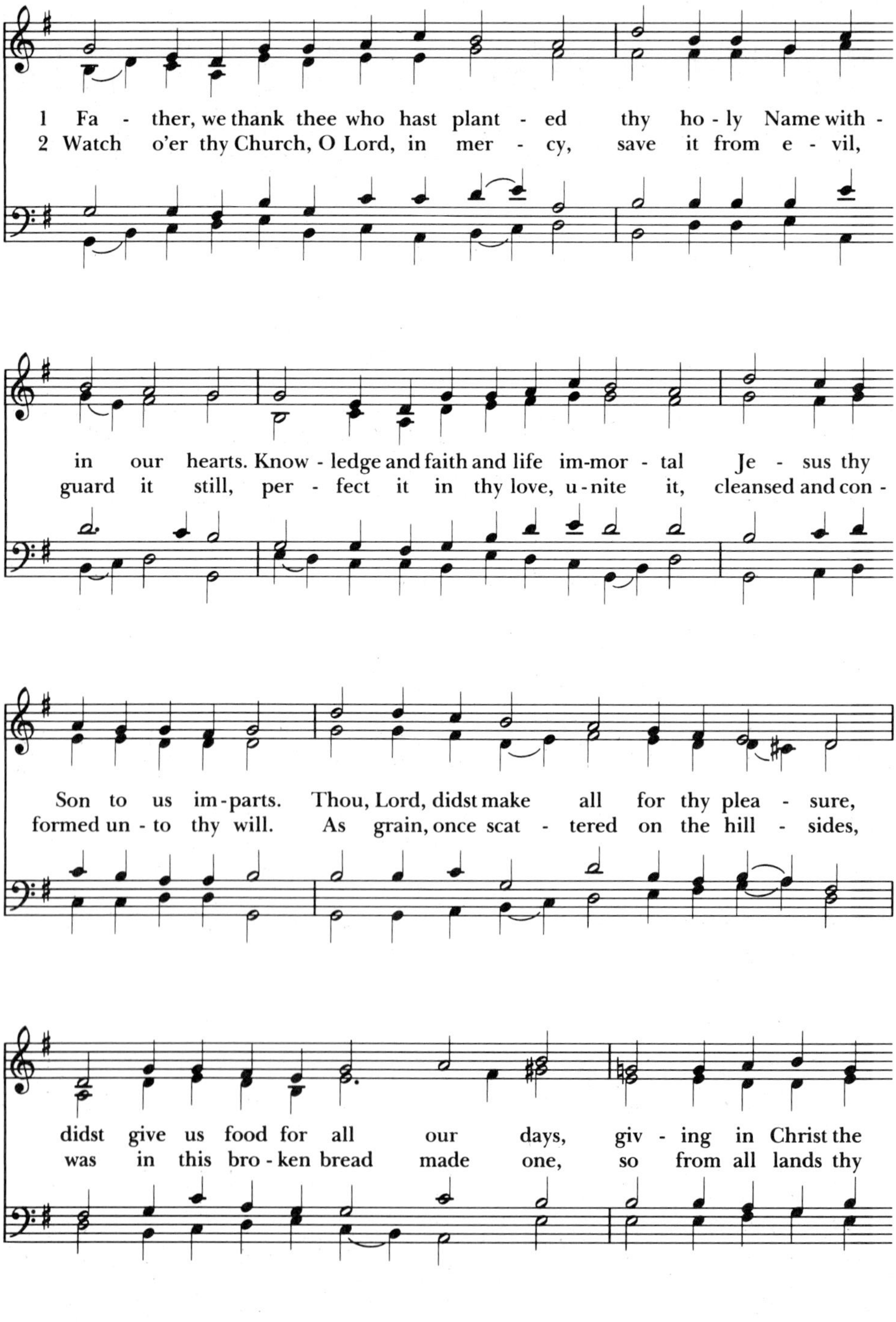
1 Fa - ther, we thank thee who hast plant - ed thy ho - ly Name with -
2 Watch o'er thy Church, O Lord, in mer - cy, save it from e - vil,
in our hearts. Know - ledge and faith and life im-mor - tal Je - sus thy
guard it still, per - fect it in thy love, u - nite it, cleansed and con -
Son to us im - parts. Thou, Lord, didst make all for thy plea - sure,
formed un - to thy will. As grain, once scat - tered on the hill - sides,
didst give us food for all our days, giv - ing in Christ the
was in this bro - ken bread made one, so from all lands thy

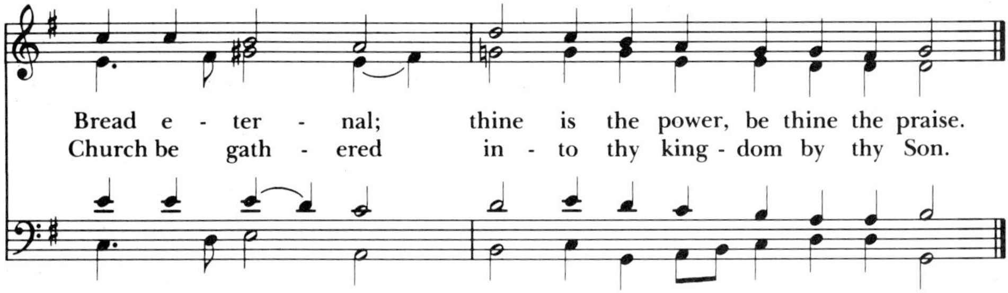
Bread e - ter - nal; thine is the power, be thine the praise.
Church be gath - ered in - to thy king - dom by thy Son.

Other harmonizations, 301 and 413. Alternative tune: *Albright,* 303.

Words: Greek, ca. 110; tr. F. Bland Tucker (1895-1984), rev. ♩= 96

Music: *Rendez à Dieu,* melody and harm. att. Louis Bourgeois (1510?-1561?) 98. 98. D

1 Fa - ther, we thank thee
2 Thou, Lord, didst make all
3 Watch o'er thy Church, O
4 As grain, once scat - tered
pp
8va
who hast plant - ed thy ho - ly
for thy plea - sure, didst give us
Lord, in mer - cy, save it from
on the hill - sides, was in this
8va

Name with - in our hearts. Know-ledge and
food for all our days, giv - ing in
e - vil, guard it still, per - fect it
bro - ken bread made one, so from all
8va
8va
8va
8va
faith and life im - mor - tal Je - sus thy
Christ the bread e - ter - nal; thine is the
in thy love, u - nite it, cleansed and con -
lands thy Church be gath - ered in - to thy
8va

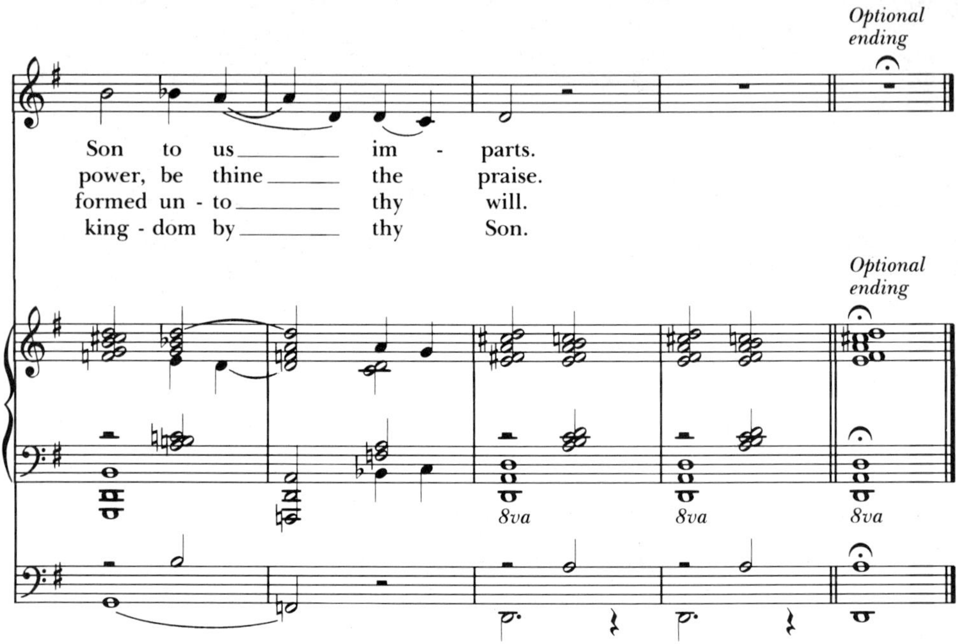
Optional ending
Son to us im - parts.
power, be thine the praise.
formed un - to thy will.
king - dom by thy Son.
Optional ending
8va
8va
8va

Optional Instrumental Ostinato

(Played by at least three of the following instruments. Duplications are possible.)

Harp
Glockenspiel
Celesta
Vibraphone
Piano (poss. 4-hand)
Chimes (Tub. Bells)
Organ Chimes
Glass Harmonica
Handbells
Carillon
Acoustic Guitar (harmonics)
Antique Cymbals (tuned)
Tuned Goblets (arco)
Toy Piano (chromatic)
Prepared Tape (Bell or Bell-like sounds)
Electric Piano

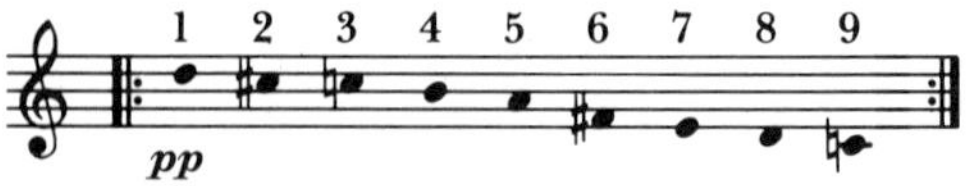

Performance of ostinato: Play the 9 pitches in the given order, and in any register (except lower): do not damp. Play steadily in any tempo (MM 52-120): each player should choose a different tempo. Starting with the first note only, add one note, in series, to each repetition, i.e., note 1, note 1 + 2, 1 + 2 + 3 . . . 1 to 9. When the complete series is attained, reverse the process, subtracting one pitch at a time from the end of the series, i.e., 1 to 9, 1 to 8 . . . note 1. When the cycle is complete, begin again without interruption. The instruments begin shortly before the organ and at the end they continue briefly after the organ stops; instruments should blend as much as possible in order to create an overall "celestial" effect.

Alternative tune: *Rendez à Dieu*, 302.

Words: Greek, ca. 110; tr. F. Bland Tucker (1895-1984), rev.
Music: *Albright*, William Albright (b. 1944)

Flowing (𝅗𝅥=60)
98. 98

Unison or harmony

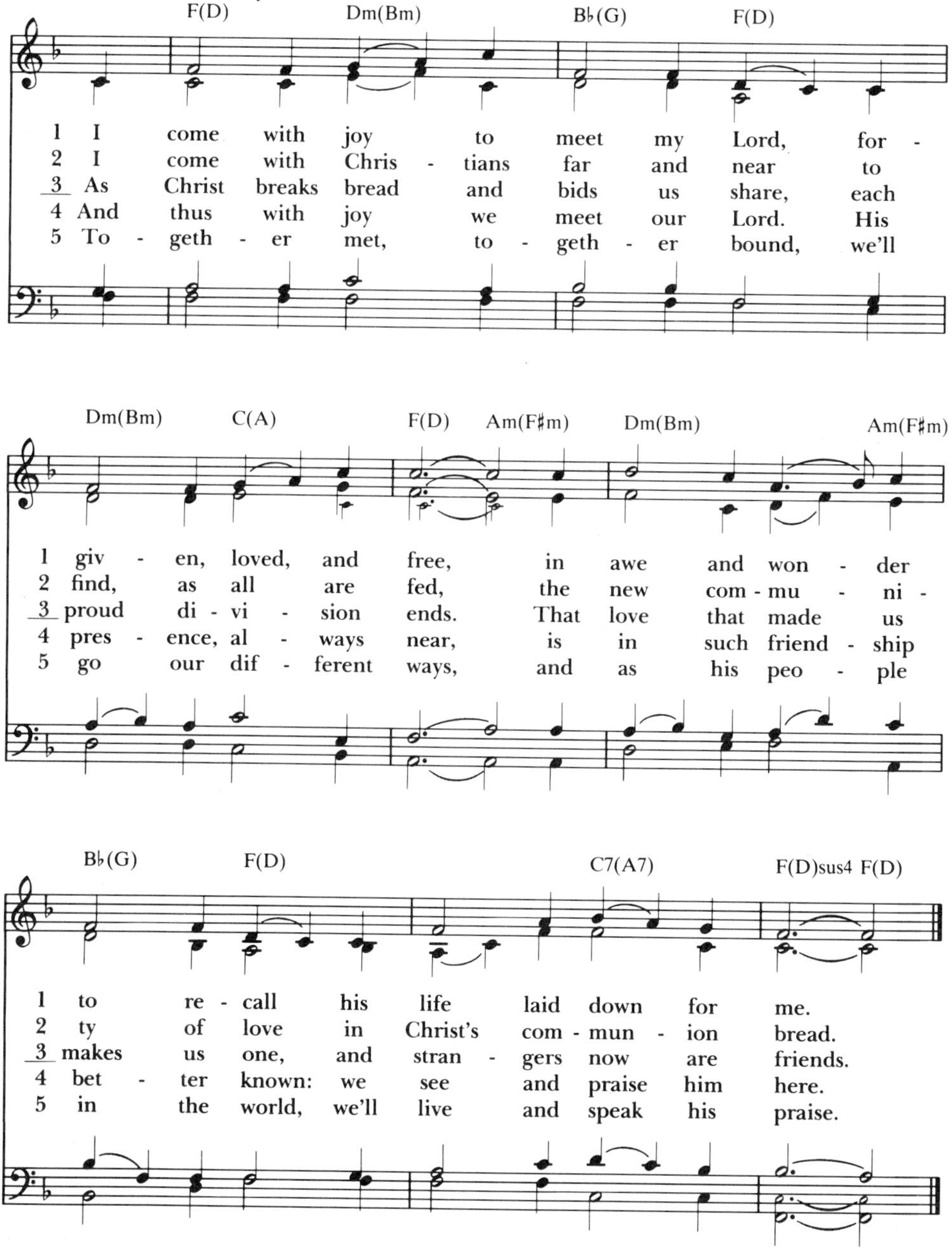
F(D) Dm(Bm) B♭(G) F(D)
1 I come with joy to meet my Lord, for -
2 I come with Chris - tians far and near to
3 As Christ breaks bread and bids us share, each
4 And thus with joy we meet our Lord. His
5 To - geth - er met, to - geth - er bound, we'll
Dm(Bm) C(A) F(D) Am(F♯m) Dm(Bm) Am(F♯m)
1 giv - en, loved, and free, in awe and won - der
2 find, as all are fed, the new com - mu - ni -
3 proud di - vi - sion ends. That love that made us
4 pres - ence, al - ways near, is in such friend - ship
5 go our dif - ferent ways, and as his peo - ple
B♭(G) F(D) C7(A7) F(D)sus4 F(D)
1 to re - call his life laid down for me.
2 ty of love in Christ's com - mun - ion bread.
3 makes us one, and stran - gers now are friends.
4 bet - ter known: we see and praise him here.
5 in the world, we'll live and speak his praise.

F (capo 3, D). Keyboard and guitar should not sound together.

Words: Brian A. Wren (b. 1936), alt.
Music: *Land of Rest,* American folk melody; adapt. and harm. Annabel Morris Buchanan (1889-1983)

𝅗𝅥. = 50
CM

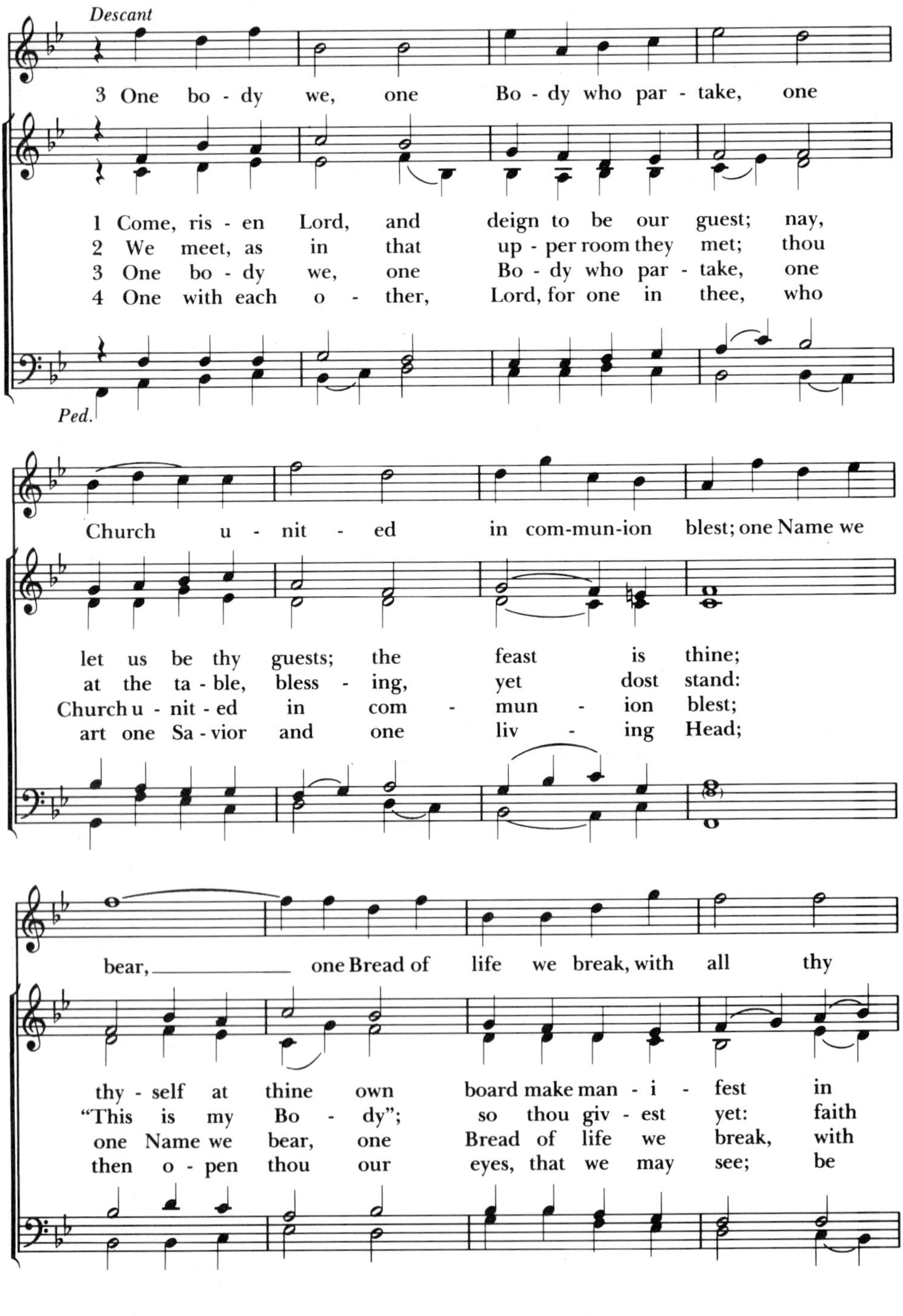
Descant
3 One bo - dy we, one Bo - dy who par - take, one
1 Come, ris - en Lord, and deign to be our guest; nay,
2 We meet, as in that up - per room they met; thou
3 One bo - dy we, one Bo - dy who par - take, one
4 One with each o - ther, Lord, for one in thee, who
Ped.
Church u - nit - ed in com-mun-ion blest; one Name we
let us be thy guests; the feast is thine;
at the ta - ble, bless - ing, yet dost stand:
Church u - nit - ed in com - mun - ion blest;
art one Sa - vior and one liv - ing Head;
bear, one Bread of life we break, with all thy
thy - self at thine own board make man - i - fest in
"This is my Bo - dy"; so thou giv - est yet: faith
one Name we bear, one Bread of life we break, with
then o - pen thou our eyes, that we may see; be

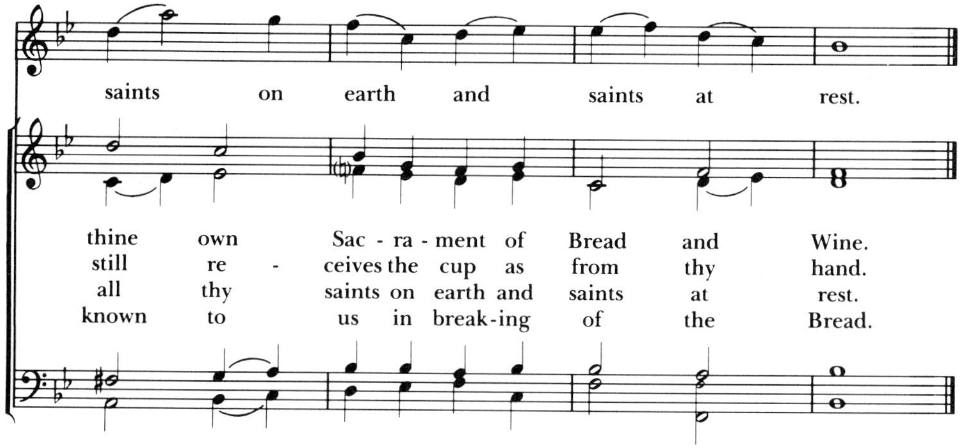
saints on earth and saints at rest.
thine own Sac - ra - ment of Bread and Wine.
still re - ceives the cup as from thy hand.
all thy saints on earth and saints at rest.
known to us in break-ing of the Bread.

Alternative tune: *Sursum Corda*, 306.

Words: George Wallace Briggs (1875-1959), alt.
Music: *Rosedale*, Leo Sowerby (1895-1968)

𝅗𝅥=50
10 10. 10 10

1 Come, ris - en Lord, and deign to be our guest;
2 We meet, as in that up - per room they met;
3 One bo - dy we, one Bo - dy who par - take,
4 One with each o - ther, Lord, for one in thee,
nay, let us be thy guests; the feast is thine;
thou at the ta - ble, bless - ing, yet dost stand:
one Church u - nit - ed in com - mun - ion blest;
who art one Sa - vior and one liv - ing Head;
thy - self at thine own board make man - i - fest
"This is my Bo - dy"; so thou giv - est yet:
one Name we bear, one Bread of life we break,
then o - pen thou our eyes, that we may see;

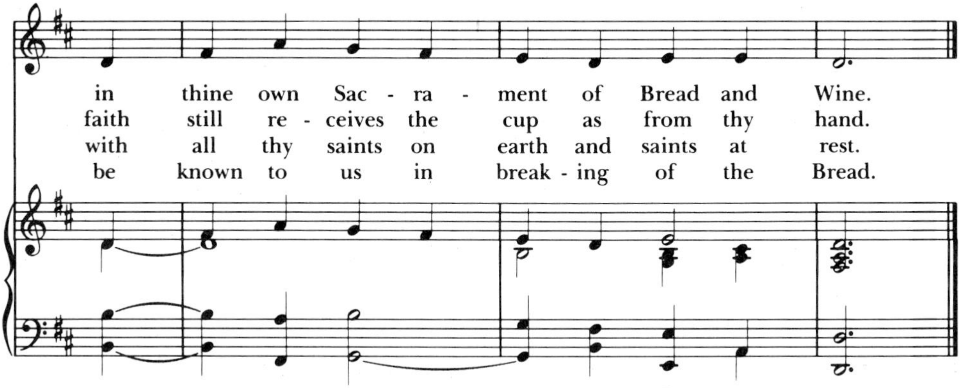
in thine own Sac - ra - ment of Bread and Wine.
faith still re - ceives the cup as from thy hand.
with all thy saints on earth and saints at rest.
be known to us in break - ing of the Bread.

Alternative tune: *Rosedale,* 305.

Words: George Wallace Briggs (1875-1959), alt. ♩= 52
Music: *Sursum Corda,* Alfred Morton Smith (1879-1971) 10 10. 10 10

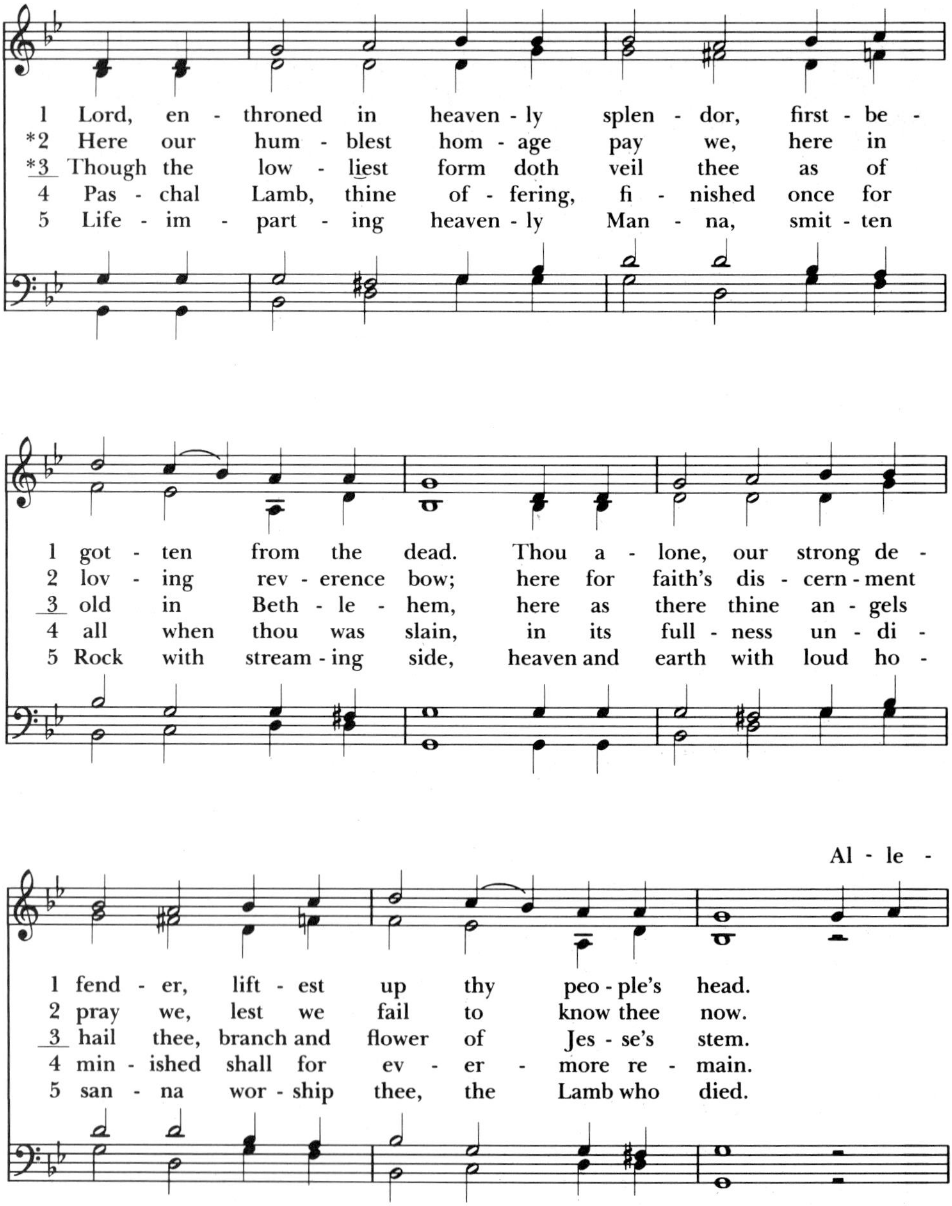
1 Lord, en - throned in heaven - ly splen - dor, first - be -
*2 Here our hum - blest hom - age pay we, here in
*3 Though the low - liest form doth veil thee as of
4 Pas - chal Lamb, thine of - fering, fi - nished once for
5 Life - im - part - ing heaven - ly Man - na, smit - ten
1 got - ten from the dead. Thou a - lone, our strong de -
2 lov - ing rev - erence bow; here for faith's dis - cern - ment
3 old in Beth - le - hem, here as there thine an - gels
4 all when thou was slain, in its full - ness un - di -
5 Rock with stream - ing side, heaven and earth with loud ho -
Al - le -
1 fend - er, lift - est up thy peo - ple's head.
2 pray we, lest we fail to know thee now.
3 hail thee, branch and flower of Jes - se's stem.
4 min - ished shall for ev - er - more re - main.
5 san - na wor - ship thee, the Lamb who died.

lu - ia! Al - le - lu - ia! Al - le -
Al - le - lu - ia! Al - le - lu - ia!
lu - ia!
Al - le - lu - ia!
1 Je - sus, true and liv - ing
2 Thou art here, we ask not
3 We in wor - ship join with
4 Cleans - ing us from ev - ery
5 Risen, a - scend - ed, glo - ri -
1 bread! Je - sus, true and liv - ing bread!
2 how. Thou are here, we ask not how.
3 them. We in wor - ship join with them.
4 stain. Cleans - ing us from ev - ery stain.
5 fied! Risen, a - scend - ed, glo - ri - fied!

Words: George Hugh Bourne (1840-1925), alt.
Music: *Bryn Calfaria,* melody William Owen (1813-1893); harm. *Christian Hymns,* 1977

𝅗𝅥=72
87. 87. 12 77

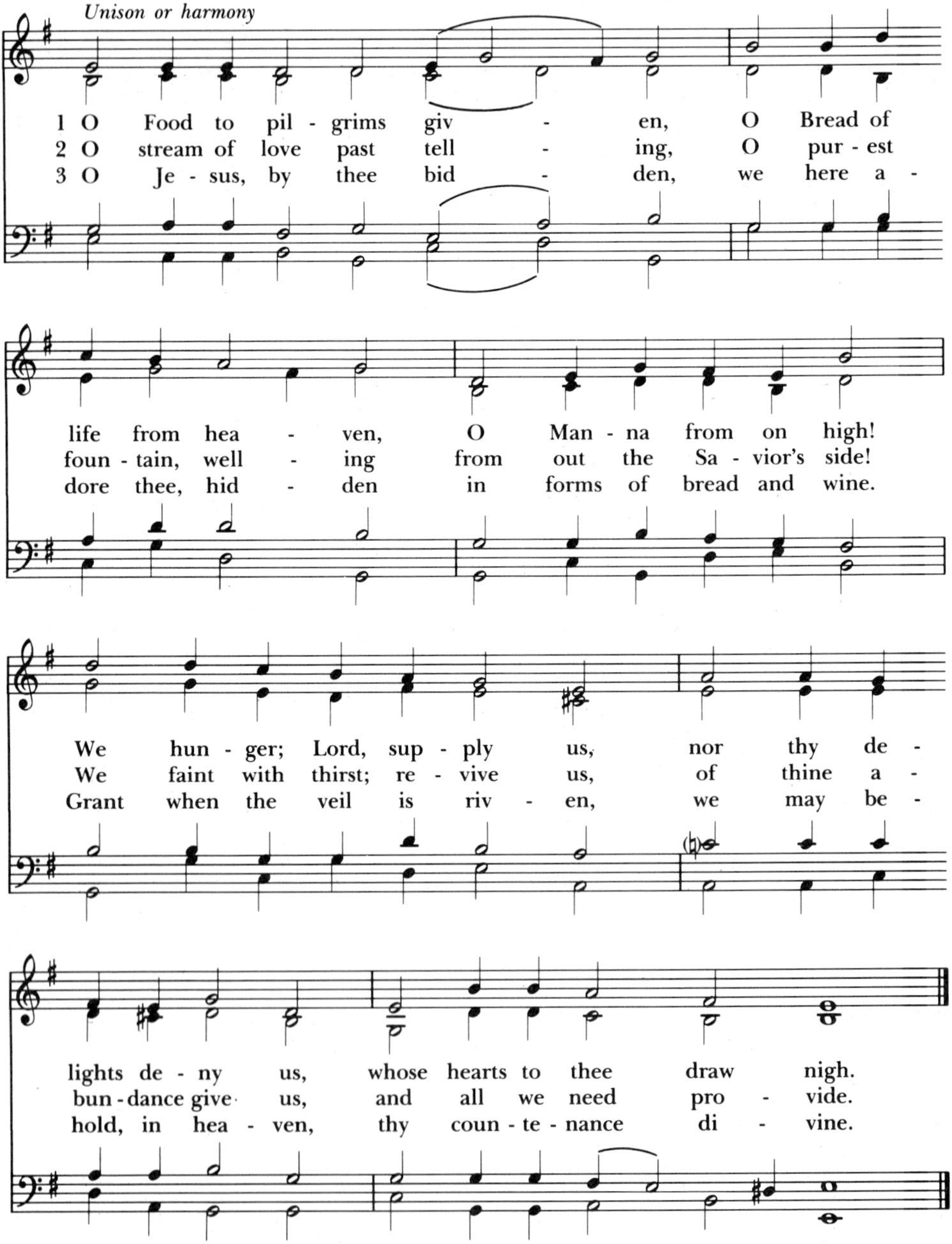
Unison or harmony
1 O Food to pil - grims giv - en, O Bread of
2 O stream of love past tell - ing, O pur - est
3 O Je - sus, by thee bid - den, we here a -
life from hea - ven, O Man - na from on high!
foun - tain, well - ing from out the Sa - vior's side!
dore thee, hid - den in forms of bread and wine.
We hun - ger; Lord, sup - ply us, nor thy de -
We faint with thirst; re - vive us, of thine a -
Grant when the veil is riv - en, we may be -
lights de - ny us, whose hearts to thee draw nigh.
bun - dance give us, and all we need pro - vide.
hold, in hea - ven, thy coun - te - nance di - vine.

Alternative tune: *O Welt, ich muss dich lassen,* 309.

Words: Latin, 1661; tr. John Athelstan Laurie Riley (1858-1945), alt.
Music: *Psalm 6,* from *Les cent cinquante Pseaumes de David,* 1564, alt.

♩=92
776. D

1 O Food to pil - grims giv - en, O Bread of life from
2 O stream of love past tell - ing, O pur - est foun - tain,
3 O Je - sus, by thee bid - den, we here a - dore thee,
hea - ven, O Man - na from on high! We
well - ing from out the Sa - vior's side! We
hid - den in forms of bread and wine. Grant
hun - ger; Lord, sup - ply us, nor thy de - lights de -
faint with thirst; re - vive us, of thine a - bun - dance
when the veil is riv - en, we may be - hold, in
ny us, whose hearts to thee draw nigh.
give us, and all we need pro - vide.
hea - ven, thy coun - te - nance di - vine.

Alternative tune: *Psalm 6,* 308.

Words: Latin, 1661; tr. John Athelstan Laurie Riley (1858-1945), alt.
Music: *O Welt, ich muss dich lassen,* present form of melody att. Heinrich Isaac (1450?-1517), alt.; harm. Johann Sebastian Bach (1685-1750)

𝅗𝅥=72
776. D

1 O sav - ing Vic - tim, o - pening wide the
2 All praise and thanks to thee a - scend for

gate of heaven to us be - low, our foes press on from
ev - er - more, blest One in Three; O grant us life that

ev - ery side, thine aid sup - ply, thy strength be - stow.
shall not end in our true na - tive land with thee.

Alternative tunes: *Verbum supernum prodiens (Nevers)*, 311; *Herr Jesu Christ* (rhythmic), 3.

Words: Att. Thomas Aquinas (1225?-1274); tr. Edward Caswall (1814-1878), alt.
Music: *Herr Jesu Christ*, melody from *Cantionale Germanicum*, 1628; adapt. and harm.
 Johann Sebastian Bach (1685-1750)

♩=152
LM

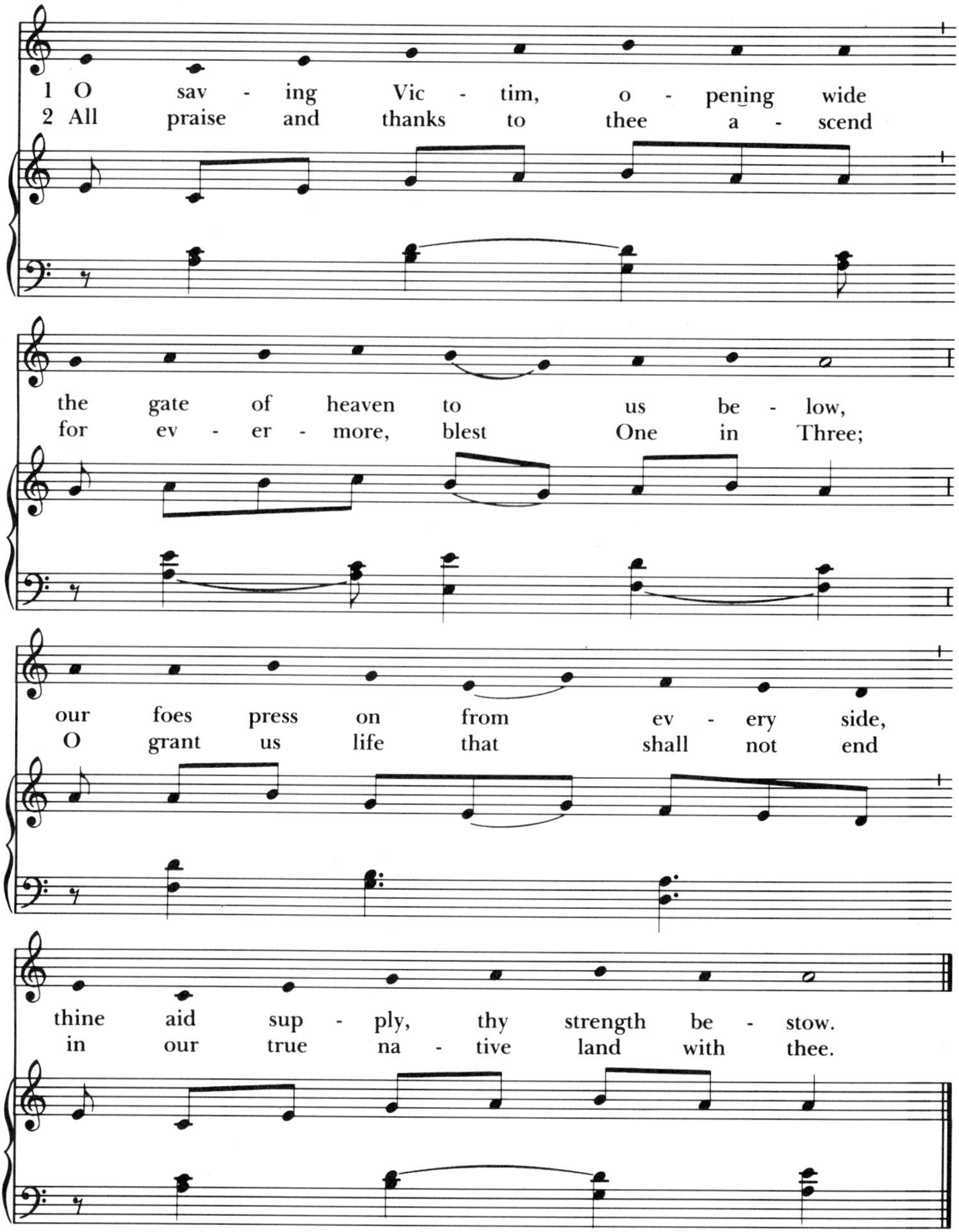
1 O sav - ing Vic - tim, o - pening wide
2 All praise and thanks to thee a - scend
the gate of heaven to us be - low,
for ev - er - more, blest One in Three;
our foes press on from ev - ery side,
O grant us life that shall not end
thine aid sup - ply, thy strength be - stow.
in our true na - tive land with thee.

Another accompaniment, 4. Alternative tune: *Herr Jesu Christ* (isometric), 310.

Words: Att. Thomas Aquinas (1225?-1274); tr. Edward Caswall (1814-1878), alt.
Music: *Verbum supernum prodiens,* plainsong, Mode 2, Nevers MS., 13th cent.; acc. Roy Kehl (b. 1935) LM

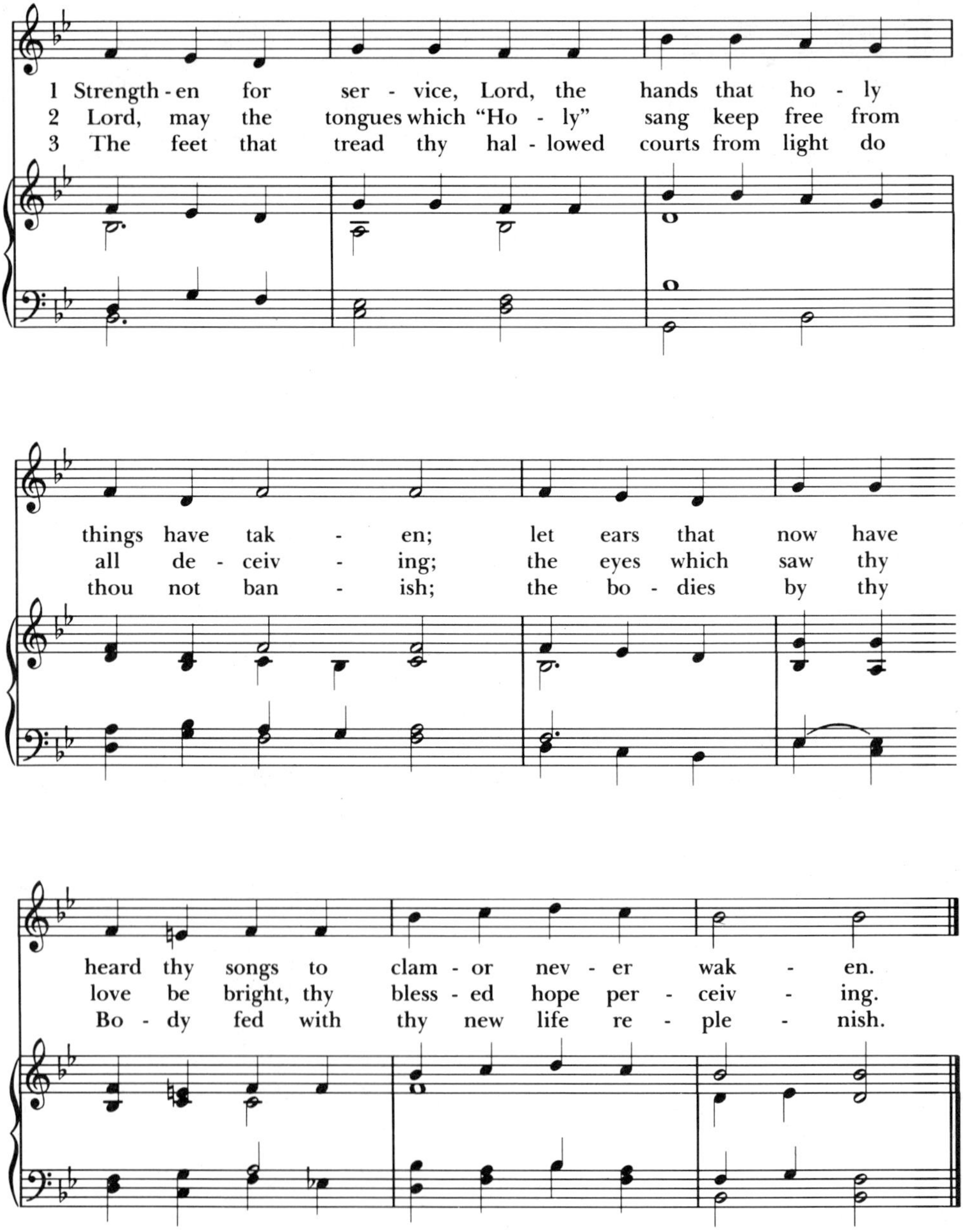
1 Strength - en for ser - vice, Lord, the hands that ho - ly
2 Lord, may the tongues which "Ho - ly" sang keep free from
3 The feet that tread thy hal - lowed courts from light do
things have tak - en; let ears that now have
all de - ceiv - ing; the eyes which saw thy
thou not ban - ish; the bo - dies by thy
heard thy songs to clam - or nev - er wak - en.
love be bright, thy bless - ed hope per - ceiv - ing.
Bo - dy fed with thy new life re - ple - nish.

Words: Syriac Liturgy of Malabar; tr. Charles William Humphreys (1840-1921); alt. Percy Dearmer (1867-1936)
Music: *Malabar,* David McKinley Williams (1887-1978)

𝅗𝅥=50
87. 87

1 Let thy Blood in mer - cy poured, let thy gra - cious
2 Thou didst die that I might live; bless - ed Lord, thou
3 By the thorns that crowned thy brow, by the spear-wound
4 Wilt thou own the gift I bring? All my pen - i -
Bo - dy bro - ken, be to me, O gra - cious Lord,
cam'st to save me; all that love of God could give
and the nail - ing, by the pain and death, I now
tence I give thee; thou art my ex - alt - ed King,
of thy bound-less love the to - ken.
Je - sus by his sor - rows gave me.
claim, O Christ, thy love un - fail - ing.
of thy match-less love for - give me.
Refrain
Thou didst give thy - self for me, now I give my - self to thee.

Words: John Brownlie (1859-1925)
Music: *Jesus, meine Zuversicht,* melody Johann Cruger (1598-1662); harm. after *The Chorale Book for England,* 1863

♩=76
78. 78. 77

1 Hum - bly I a - dore thee, Ver - i - ty un - seen,
2 Taste and touch and vi - sion to dis - cern thee fail;
3 O me - mo - rial won - drous of the Lord's own death;
4 Je - sus, whom now hid - den, I by faith be - hold,
who thy glo - ry hid - est 'neath these sha - dows mean;
faith, that comes by hear - ing, pierc - es through the veil.
liv - ing Bread that giv - est all thy crea - tures breath,
what my soul doth long for, that thy word fore - told:
lo, to thee sur - ren - dered, my whole heart is bowed,
I be - lieve what - e'er the Son of God hath told;
grant my spi - rit ev - er by thy life may live,
face to face thy splen - dor, I at last shall see,

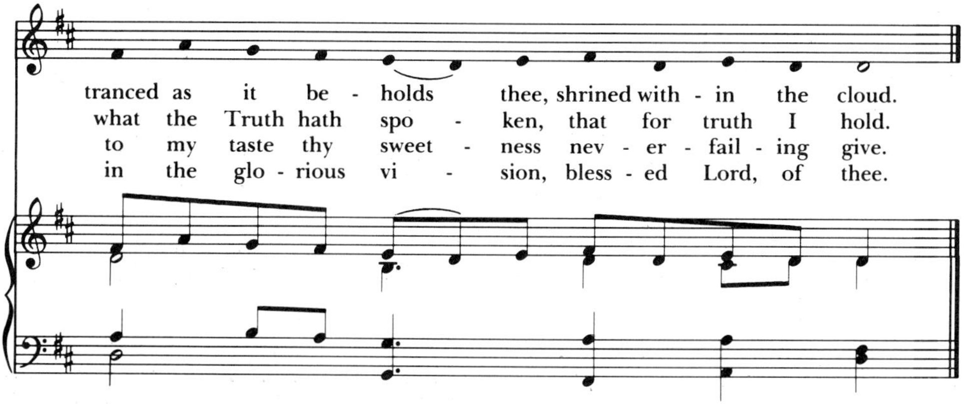
tranced as it be - holds thee, shrined with - in the cloud.
what the Truth hath spo - ken, that for truth I hold.
to my taste thy sweet - ness nev - er - fail - ing give.
in the glo - rious vi - sion, bless - ed Lord, of thee.

Another accompaniment, 357.

Words: Att. Thomas Aquinas (1225?-1274); sts. 1-3, tr. *Hymnal 1940;* st. 4, tr. *Hymnal 1982*
Music: *Adoro devote,* French church melody, Mode 5, *Processionale,* 1697;
acc. Charles Winfred Douglas (1867-1944), alt.

11 11. 11 11

Unison or harmony
1 Thou, who at thy first Eu - cha - rist didst pray
2 For all thy Church, O Lord, we in - ter - cede;
3 So, Lord, at length when sac - ra - ments shall cease,
that all thy Church might be for ev - er one,
make thou our sad di - vi - sions soon to cease;
may we be one with all thy Church a - bove,
grant us at ev - ery Eu - cha - rist to say
draw us the near - er each to each, we plead,
one with thy saints in one un - bro - ken peace,
with long - ing heart and soul, "Thy will be done."
by draw - ing all to thee, O Prince of Peace;
one with thy saints in one un - bound - ed love;

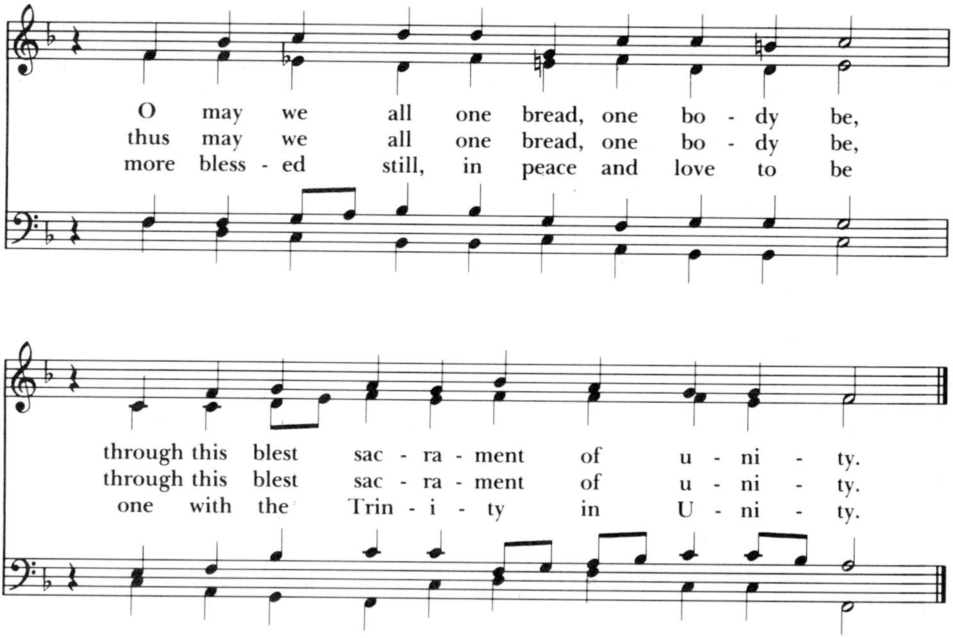
O may we all one bread, one bo - dy be,
thus may we all one bread, one bo - dy be,
more bless - ed still, in peace and love to be
through this blest sac - ra - ment of u - ni - ty.
through this blest sac - ra - ment of u - ni - ty.
one with the Trin - i - ty in U - ni - ty.

Words: William Harry Turton (1856-1938)
Music: *Song 1*, melody and bass Orlando Gibbons (1583-1625); harm. Ralph Vaughan Williams (1872-1958), alt.

♩= 90
10 10. 10 10. 10 10

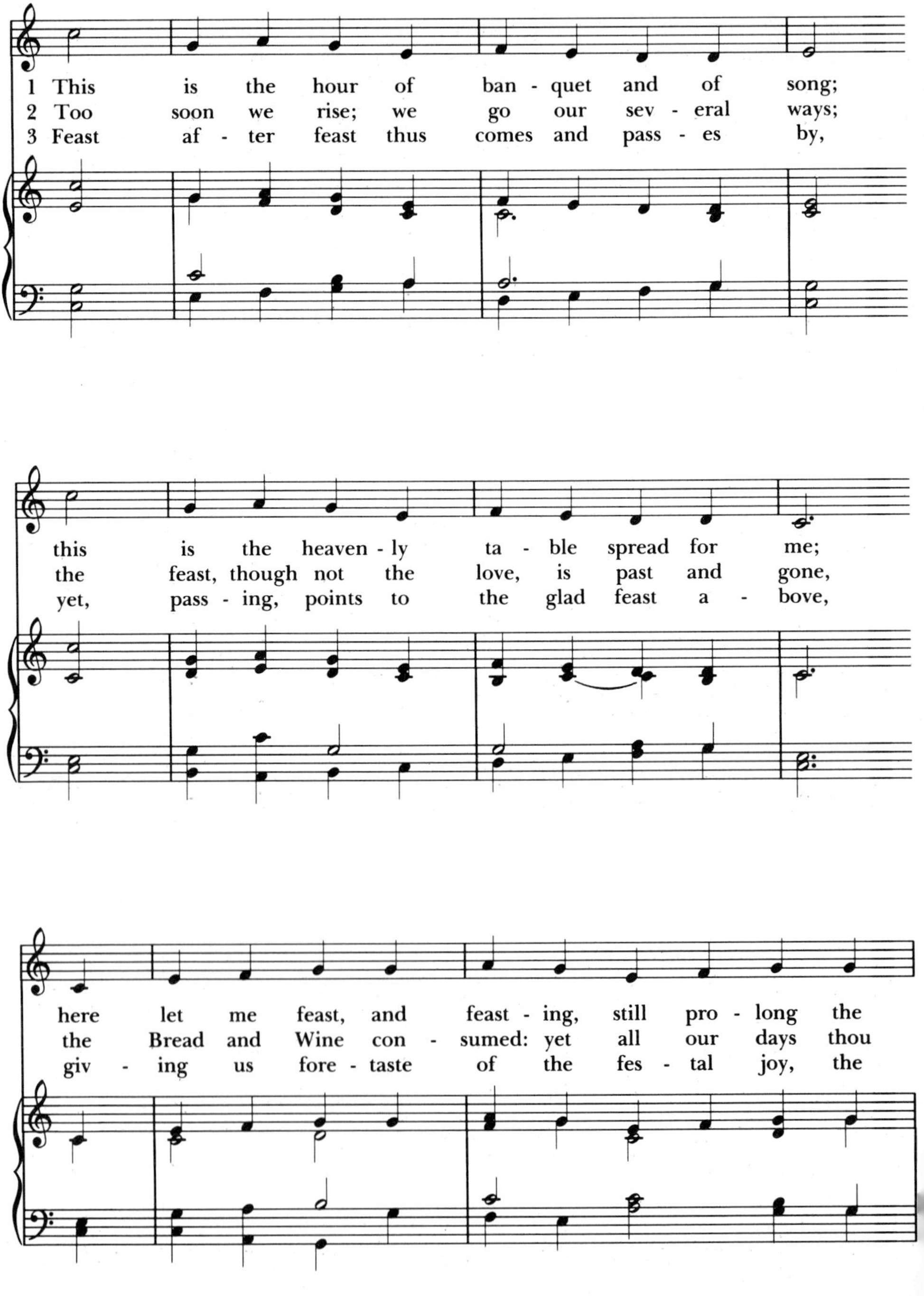
1 This is the hour of ban - quet and of song;
2 Too soon we rise; we go our sev - eral ways;
3 Feast af - ter feast thus comes and pass - es by,
this is the heaven - ly ta - ble spread for me;
the feast, though not the love, is past and gone,
yet, pass - ing, points to the glad feast a - bove,
here let me feast, and feast - ing, still pro - long the
the Bread and Wine con - sumed: yet all our days thou
giv - ing us fore - taste of the fes - tal joy, the

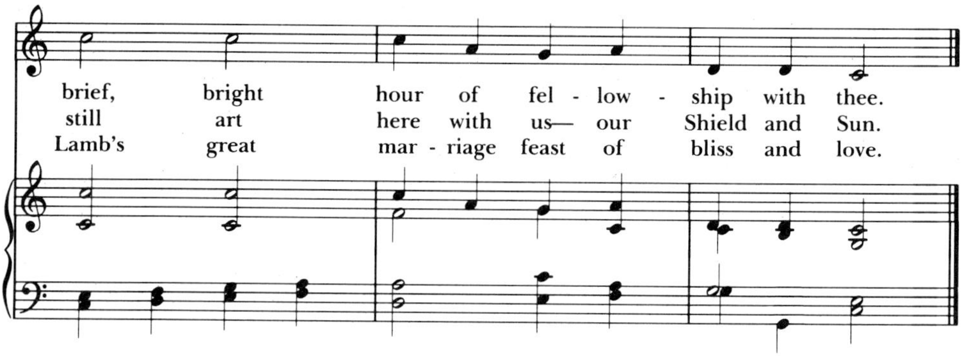
brief, bright hour of fel - low - ship with thee.
still art here with us— our Shield and Sun.
Lamb's great mar - riage feast of bliss and love.

Alternative tune: *Morestead*, 317.

Words: Horatius Bonar (1808-1889), alt.
Music: *Canticum refectionis*, David McKinley Williams (1887-1978)

𝅗𝅥 = 54
10 10. 10 10

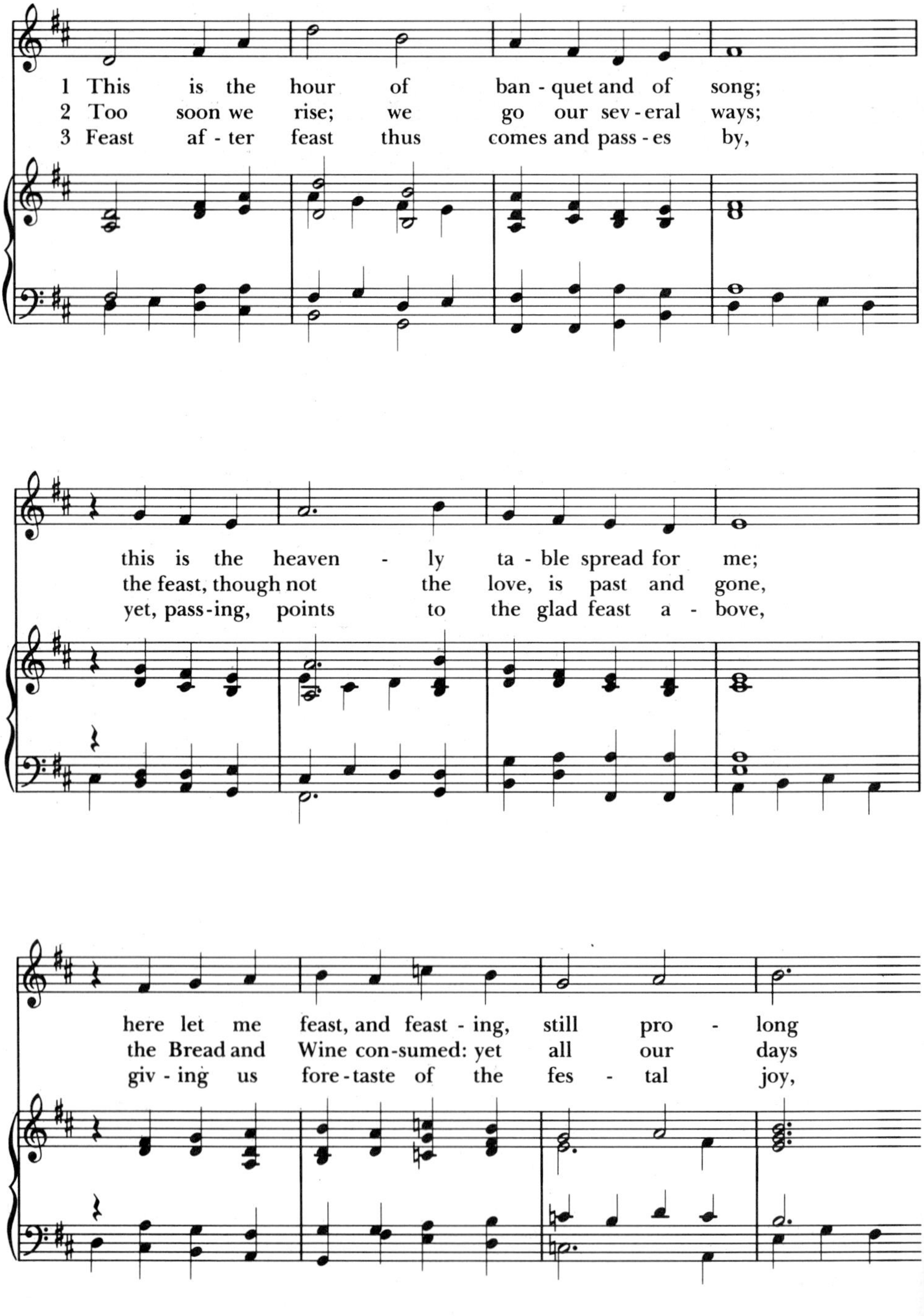
1 This is the hour of ban - quet and of song;
2 Too soon we rise; we go our sev - eral ways;
3 Feast af - ter feast thus comes and pass - es by,
this is the heaven - ly ta - ble spread for me;
the feast, though not the love, is past and gone,
yet, pass-ing, points to the glad feast a - bove,
here let me feast, and feast - ing, still pro - long
the Bread and Wine con-sumed: yet all our days
giv - ing us fore-taste of the fes - tal joy,

the brief, bright hour of fel - low - ship with thee.
thou still art here with us—our Shield and Sun.
the Lamb's great mar-riage feast of bliss and love.

Alternative tune: *Canticum refectionis*, 316.

Words: Horatius Bonar (1808-1889), alt.
Music: *Morestead*, Sidney Watson (b. 1903)

𝅗𝅥 = 60
10 10. 10 10

1 Here, O my Lord, I see thee face to face;
2 Here would I feed up - on the Bread of God;
3 I have no help but thine; nor do I need
4 Mine is the sin, but thine the right-eous - ness;
here would I touch and han - dle things un - seen;
here drink with thee the roy - al Wine of heaven;
an - oth - er arm save thine to lean up - on;
mine is the guilt, but thine the cleans-ing Blood.
here grasp with firm - er hand e - ter - nal grace,
here would I lay a - side each earth - ly load,
it is e - nough, my Lord, e - nough in - deed;
Here is my robe, my ref - uge, and my peace;

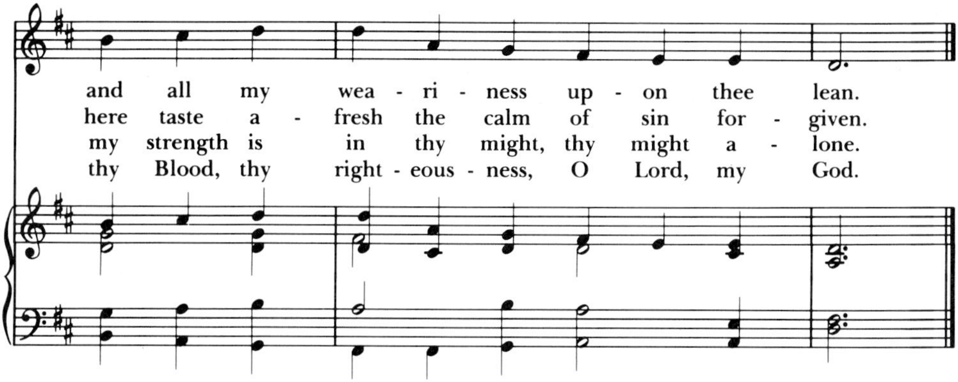
and all my wea - ri - ness up - on thee lean.
here taste a - fresh the calm of sin for - given.
my strength is in thy might, thy might a - lone.
thy Blood, thy right - eous - ness, O Lord, my God.

Words: Horatius Bonar (1808-1889)
Music: *Nyack*, Warren Swenson (b. 1937)

♩= 88
10 10. 10 10

1 You, Lord, we praise in songs of cel - e - bra - tion for this
2 You, Lord, in our stead to the grave de - scend - ed when by
tambourine
drum
feast of our sal - va - - tion. Here at your
sin our life was end - - ed. No great - er
tr

ta - ble ev - ery life you nour - ish; by your grace we
love than this to you could bind us; dai - ly still your
all may flour - ish. Ky - ri - e e - le - i - son.
mer-cies find us. Ky - ri - e e - le - i - son.
tr tr tr tr

In the light of your In-car - na - tion, all cre -
Bind our hearts as one we im - plore you, who a -
a - tion knows the love of God, and in
dore you and con - fess your Name. Thus may
tr
tr

you finds re - lease that we all might
we ev - er be yours in peace and
tr
tr
tr

live in peace. Ky - ri - e e - le - i - son.
u - ni - ty. Ky - ri - e e - le - i - son.
tr
tr

The keyboard accompaniment is optional.

Words: Russell Schulz-Widmar (b. 1944), based on German folk hymn and Martin Luther (1483-1546)
Music: *Gott sei gelobet,* melody from *Miltenberger Processionale,* 15th cent. adapt. *Geistliche Gesangbüchlein,* 1524, alt.; harm. *Hymnal 1982,* after Hans Leo Hassler (1496-1570); perc. David Hurd (b. 1950)

𝅗𝅥=58
Irr.

1 Zi - on, praise thy Sa - vior, sing - ing hymns with ex - ul - ta - tion ring - ing, praise thy King and Shep - herd true.
Hon - or Christ, thy voice up - rais - ing, who sur - pass - eth all thy prais - ing; nev - er canst thou reach his due.
2 Let the Bread, life - giv - ing, liv - ing, be our theme of glad thanks - giv - ing, now in truth be - fore thee set;
as of old the Lord pro - vid - ed when the twelve, di - vine - ly guid - ed, at the ho - ly ta - ble met.

3 What he did, at sup - per seat - ed, Christ or - dained to be re - peat - ed, his me - mo - rial ne'er to cease;
4 Full and clear sing out thy prais - ing, gra - cious hymns of joy up - rais - ing in thy heart and soul to - day;
his com - mand for guid - ance tak - ing, bread and wine we hal - low, mak - ing thus our sac - ri - fice of peace.
for to - day the new ob - la - tion of the new King's rev - e - la - tion bids us feast in glad ar - ray.

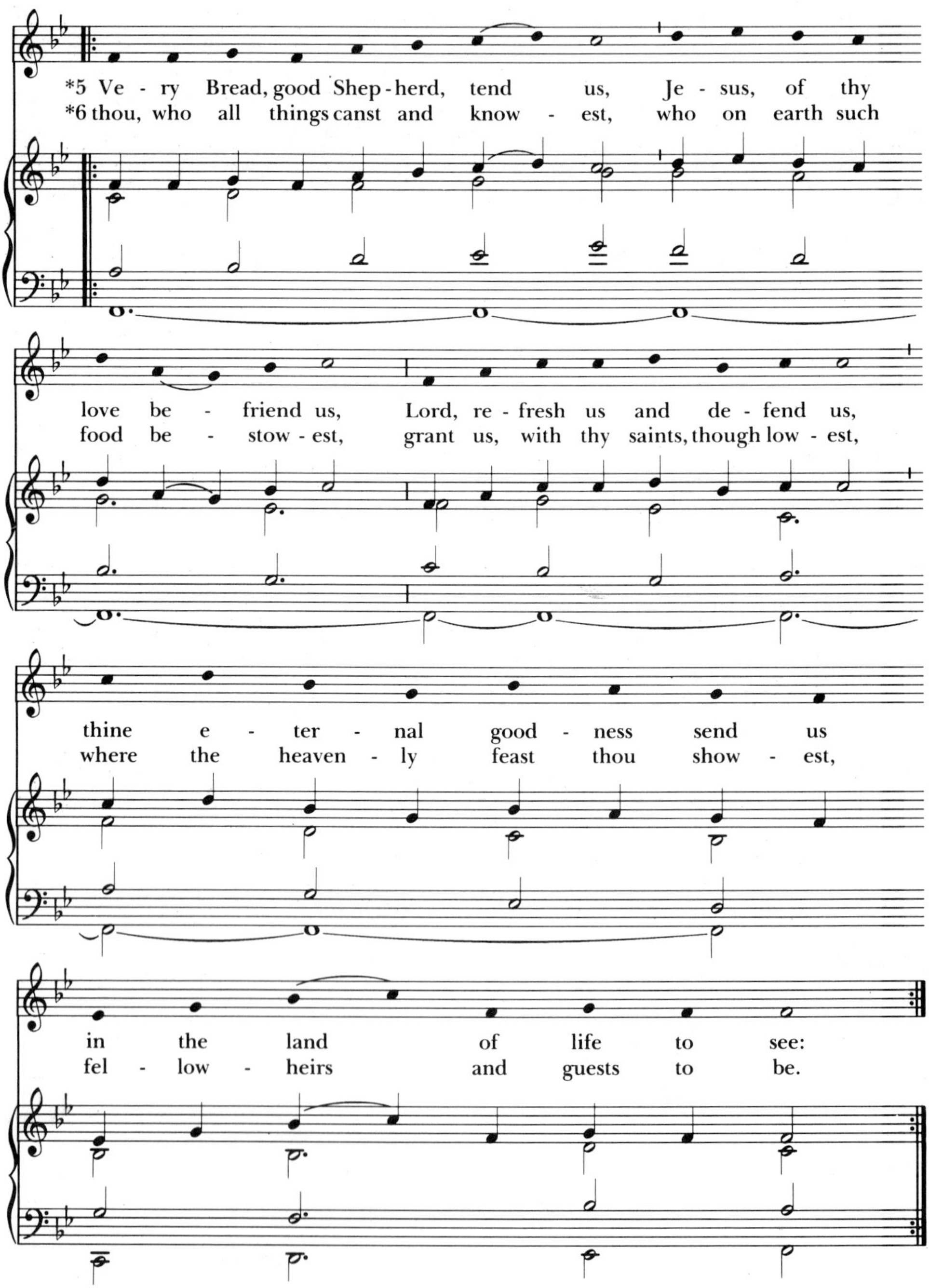
*5 Ve - ry Bread, good Shep - herd, tend us, Je - sus, of thy
*6 thou, who all things canst and know - est, who on earth such
love be - friend us, Lord, re - fresh us and de - fend us,
food be - stow - est, grant us, with thy saints, though low - est,
thine e - ter - nal good - ness send us
where the heaven - ly feast thou show - est,
in the land of life to see:
fel - low - heirs and guests to be.

When stanzas 5 and 6 are omitted, stanzas 1 through 4 may be sung to the tune of stanza 1, or the tunes of stanzas 1 and 2 may be repeated for stanzas 3 and 4.

Words: Att. Thomas Aquinas (1225?-1274); tr. *Hymnal 1940;* rev. *Hymnal 1982*
Music: *Lauda Sion Salvatorem,* plainsong, Mode 7, 12th cent.; acc. David Hurd (b. 1950) 887. 887

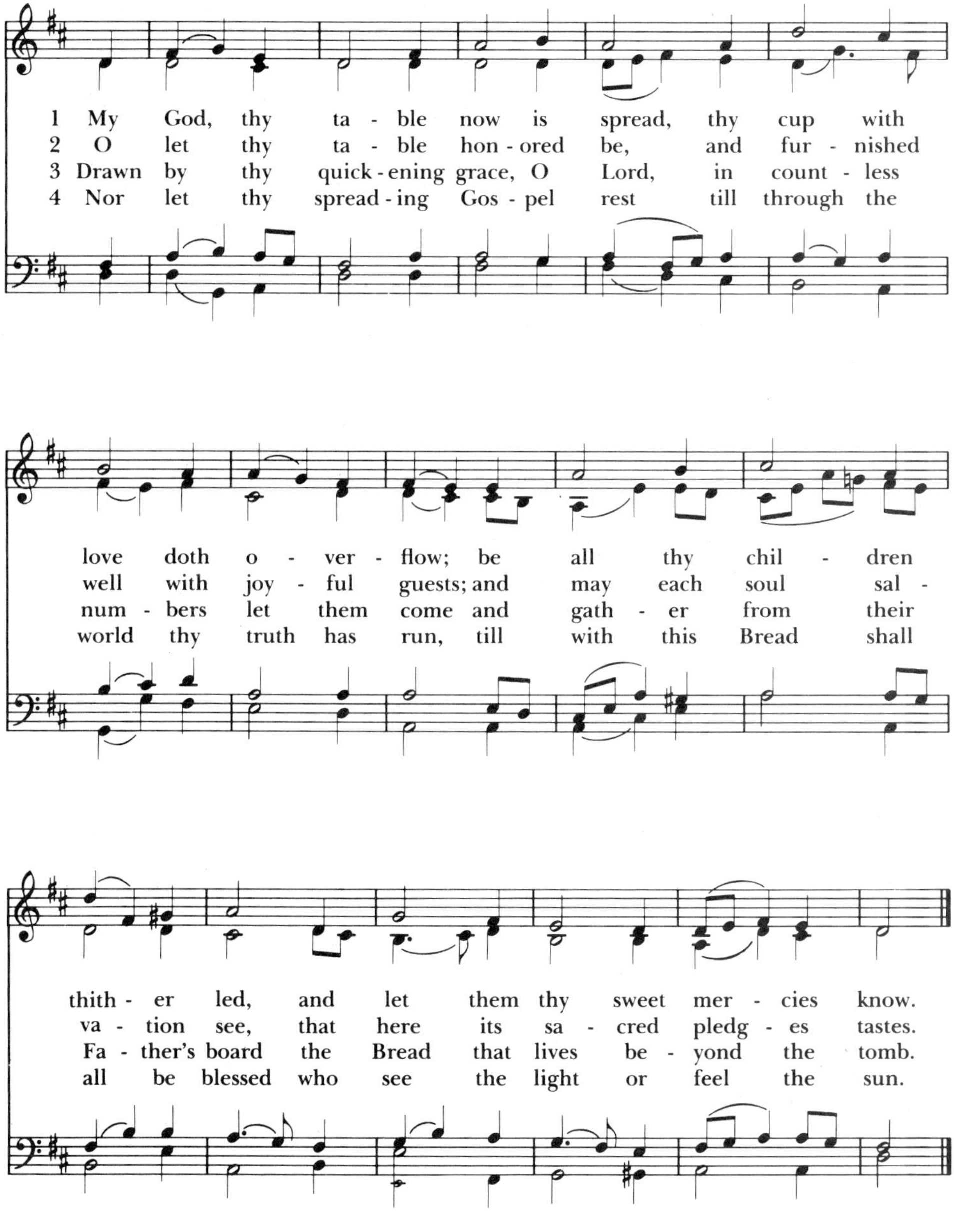
1 My God, thy ta - ble now is spread, thy cup with
2 O let thy ta - ble hon - ored be, and fur - nished
3 Drawn by thy quick - ening grace, O Lord, in count - less
4 Nor let thy spread - ing Gos - pel rest till through the
love doth o - ver - flow; be all thy chil - dren
well with joy - ful guests; and may each soul sal -
num - bers let them come and gath - er from their
world thy truth has run, till with this Bread shall
thith - er led, and let them thy sweet mer - cies know.
va - tion see, that here its sa - cred pledg - es tastes.
Fa - ther's board the Bread that lives be - yond the tomb.
all be blessed who see the light or feel the sun.

Another harmonization, 474.

Words: Sts. 1-3, Philip Doddridge (1702-1751), alt.; st. 4, Isaac Watts (1674-1748), alt.
Music: *Rockingham,* melody from *Second Supplement to Psalmody in Miniature,* ca. 1780; adapt. Edward Miller (1731-1807); harm. Samuel Webbe (1740-1816)

𝅗𝅥 = 100
LM

1 When Je - sus died to save us, a word, an act he gave us; and still that word is spo - ken, and still the bread is bro - ken. 2 He
was the Word that spake it, he took the bread and brake it, and what that Word did make it, I do be - lieve and take it.
1
Final Ending

Words: St. 1, F. Bland Tucker (1895-1984); st. 2, att. John Donne (1573-1631)
Music: *Tucker,* David Hurd (b. 1950)

♩= 100
77. 77

1 Bread of heaven, on thee we feed, for thy Flesh is
2 Vine of heaven, thy Blood sup-plies this blest cup of
meat in-deed; ev - er may our souls be fed
sac - ri - fice; Lord, thy wounds our heal - ing give,
with this true and liv - ing Bread; day by day with
to thy cross we look and live: Je - sus, may we
strength sup-plied, through the life of him who died.
ev - er be graft - ed, root - ed, built in thee.

Words: Josiah Conder (1789-1855), alt.
Music: *Jesu, Jesu, du mein Hirt,* melody Paul Heinlein (1626-1686); harm. *The English Hymnal,* 1906

𝅗𝅥=48
77. 77. 77

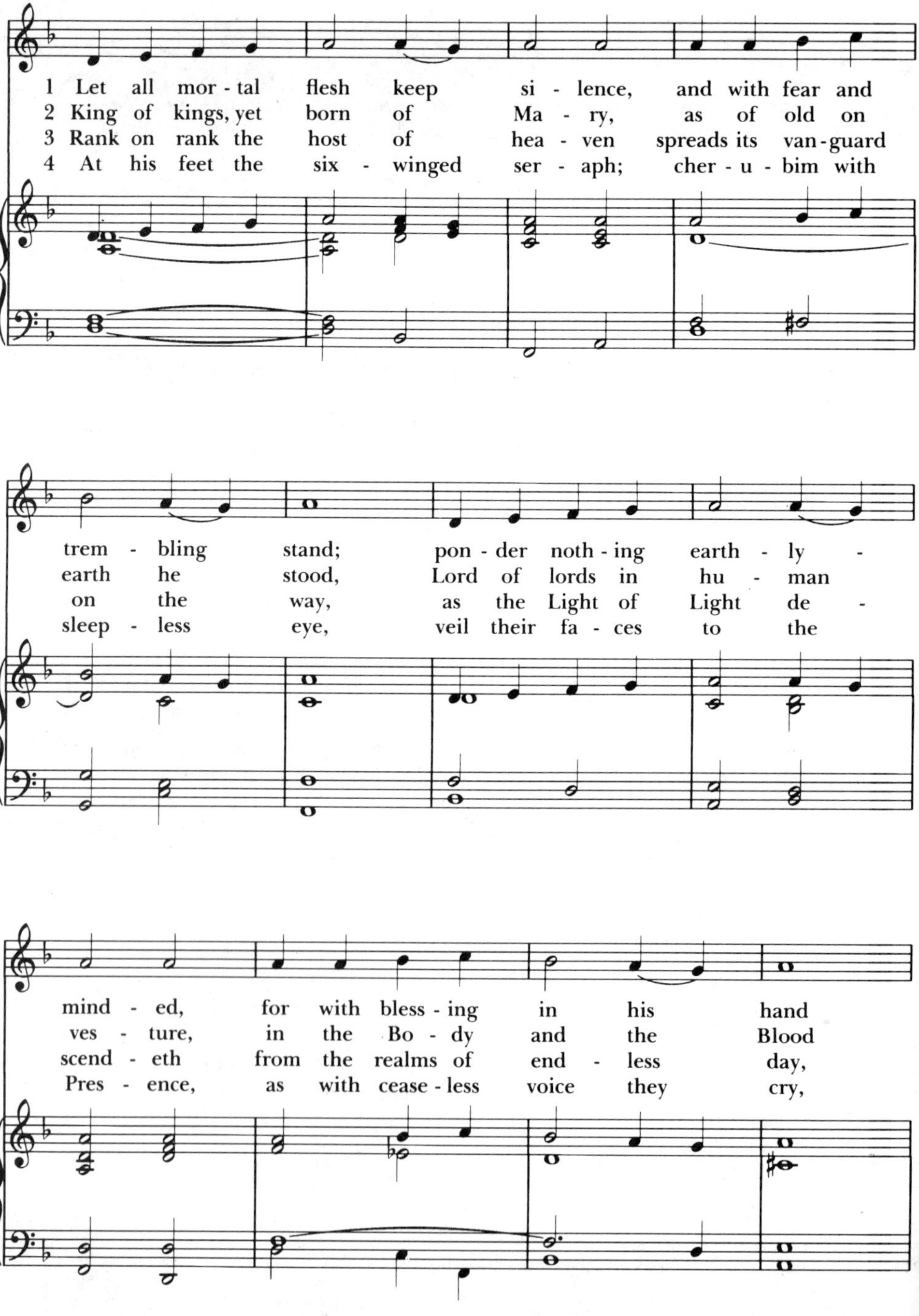
1 Let all mor - tal flesh keep si - lence, and with fear and
2 King of kings, yet born of Ma - ry, as of old on
3 Rank on rank the host of hea - ven spreads its van - guard
4 At his feet the six - winged ser - aph; cher - u - bim with
trem - bling stand; pon - der noth - ing earth - ly -
earth he stood, Lord of lords in hu - man
on the way, as the Light of Light de -
sleep - less eye, veil their fa - ces to the
mind - ed, for with bless - ing in his hand
ves - ture, in the Bo - dy and the Blood
scend - eth from the realms of end - less day,
Pres - ence, as with cease - less voice they cry,

Christ our God to earth de - scend - eth, our full hom - age to de - mand.
he will give to all the faith - ful his own self for heaven - ly food.
that the powers of hell may va - nish as the dark - ness clears a - way.
"Al - le - lu - ia, al - le - lu - ia! Al - le - lu - ia, Lord Most High!"

Words: Liturgy of St. James; para. Gerard Moultrie (1829-1885)
Music: *Picardy*, French carol, 17th cent.; melody from *Chansons populaires des Provinces de France*, 1860; harm. after *The English Hymnal*, 1906

𝅗𝅥 = 56
87. 87. 87

1 Let us break bread to - geth-er on our knees;
2 Let us drink wine to - geth-er on our knees;
let us break bread to - geth-er on our knees;
let us drink wine to - geth-er on our knees;
Refrain
when I fall on my knees, with my face to the ris-ing sun, O
Lord, have mer-cy on me.
1
2

3 Let us praise God to-geth-er on our knees;
let us praise God to-geth-er on our knees;
Refrain
when I fall on my knees, with my face to the ris-ing sun, O
Lord, have mer-cy on me.

Words: Afro-American spiritual
Music: *Let Us Break Bread,* Afro-American spiritual; harm. David Hurd (b. 1950)

♩= 96
10 10 with Refrain

1 From glo - ry to glo - ry ad - vanc - ing, we
2 Thanks - giv - ing, and glo - ry and wor - ship, and
praise thee, O Lord; thy Name with the Fa - ther and
bless - ing and love, one heart and one song have the
Spi - rit be ev - er a - dored. From strength un - to
saints up - on earth and a - bove. O Lord, ev - er -

strength we go for - ward on Zi - on's high -
more to thy ser - vants thy pres - ence be
way, to ap - pear be - fore God in the
nigh; ev - er fit us by ser - vice on
ci - ty of in - fi - nite day.
earth for thy ser - vice on high.

The small notes in the vocal part and the G♯ in the final chord are recommended for stanza 2.

Words: Liturgy of St. James; tr. Charles William Humphreys (1840-1921)
Music: *St. Keverne,* Craig Sellar Lang (1891-1971), alt.

♩=54
14 14. 14 15

327

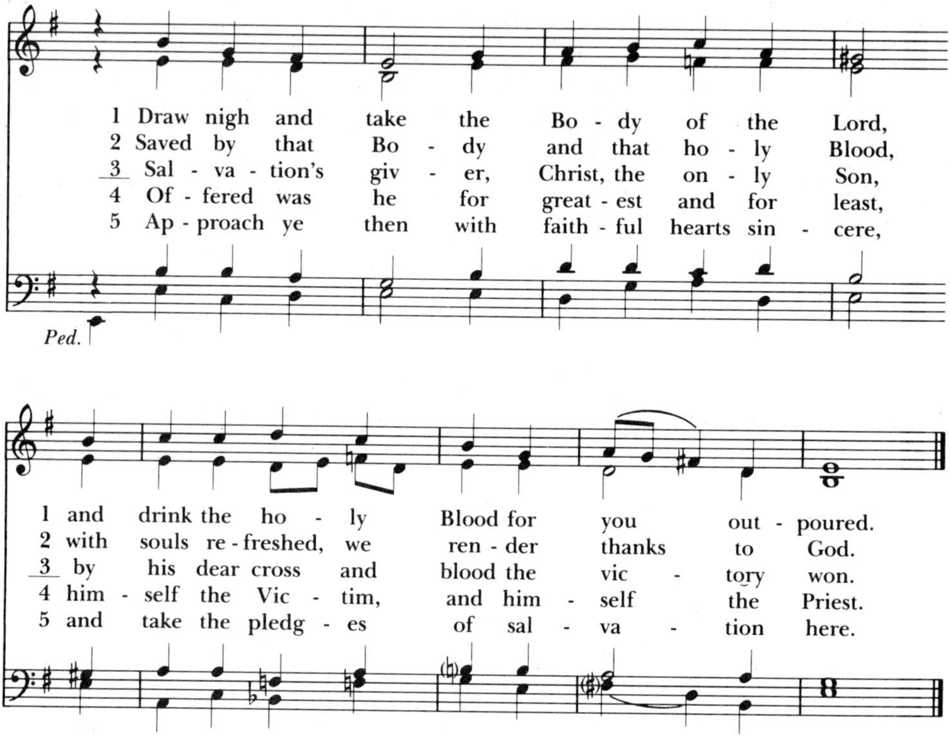
1 Draw nigh and take the Bo - dy of the Lord,
and drink the ho - ly Blood for you out - poured.
2 Saved by that Bo - dy and that ho - ly Blood,
with souls re - freshed, we ren - der thanks to God.
3 Sal - va - tion's giv - er, Christ, the on - ly Son,
by his dear cross and blood the vic - tory won.
4 Of - fered was he for great - est and for least,
him - self the Vic - tim, and him - self the Priest.
5 Ap - proach ye then with faith - ful hearts sin - cere,
and take the pledg - es of sal - va - tion here.
Ped.

6 He that his saints in this world rules and shields
to all believers life eternal yields;

7 with heavenly bread he makes the hungry whole,
gives living waters to the thirsting soul.

8 Alpha-Omega, unto whom shall bow
all nations at the doom, is with us now.

Alternative tune: *Song 46,* 328.

Words: *Bangor Antiphoner,* ca. 690; tr. John Mason Neale (1818-1866), alt.
Music: *Palmer Church,* David Ashley White (b. 1944)

♩=84-92
10. 10

328

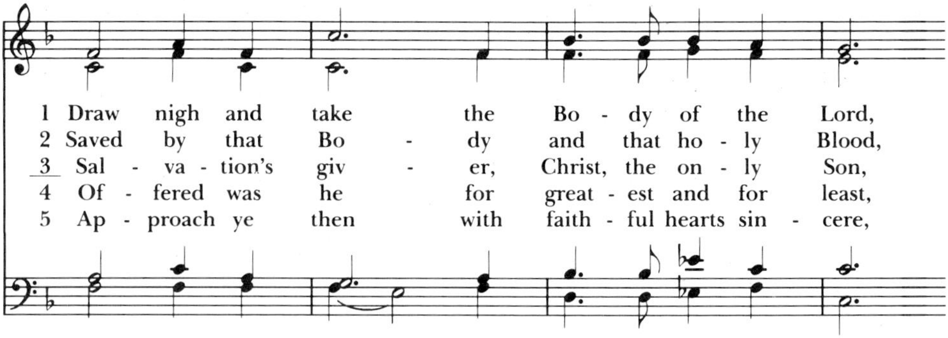
1 Draw nigh and take the Bo - dy of the Lord,
2 Saved by that Bo - dy and that ho - ly Blood,
3 Sal - va - tion's giv - er, Christ, the on - ly Son,
4 Of - fered was he for great - est and for least,
5 Ap - proach ye then with faith - ful hearts sin - cere,

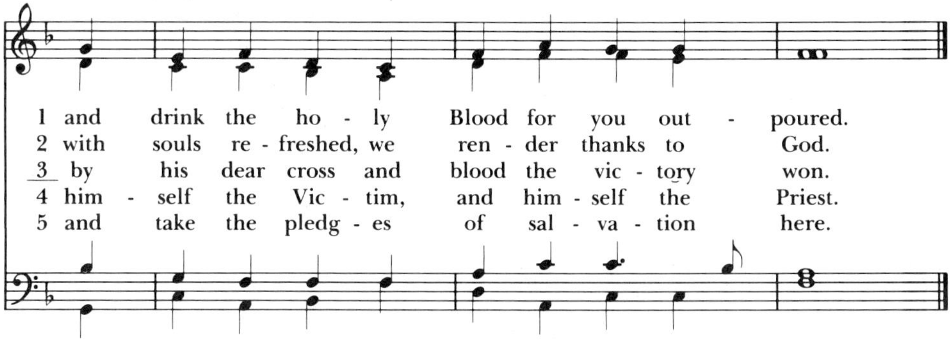
1 and drink the ho - ly Blood for you out - poured.
2 with souls re - freshed, we ren - der thanks to God.
3 by his dear cross and blood the vic - tory won.
4 him - self the Vic - tim, and him - self the Priest.
5 and take the pledg - es of sal - va - tion here.

6 He that his saints in this world rules and shields
to all believers life eternal yields;

7 with heavenly bread he makes the hungry whole,
gives living waters to the thirsting soul.

8 Alpha-Omega, unto whom shall bow
all nations at the doom, is with us now.

Alternative tune: *Palmer Church,* 327.

Words: *Bangor Antiphoner,* ca. 690; tr. John Mason Neale (1818-1866), alt. — 𝅗𝅥=46
Music: *Song 46,* melody and bass Orlando Gibbons (1583-1625); harm. *The English Hymnal,* 1906 — 10. 10

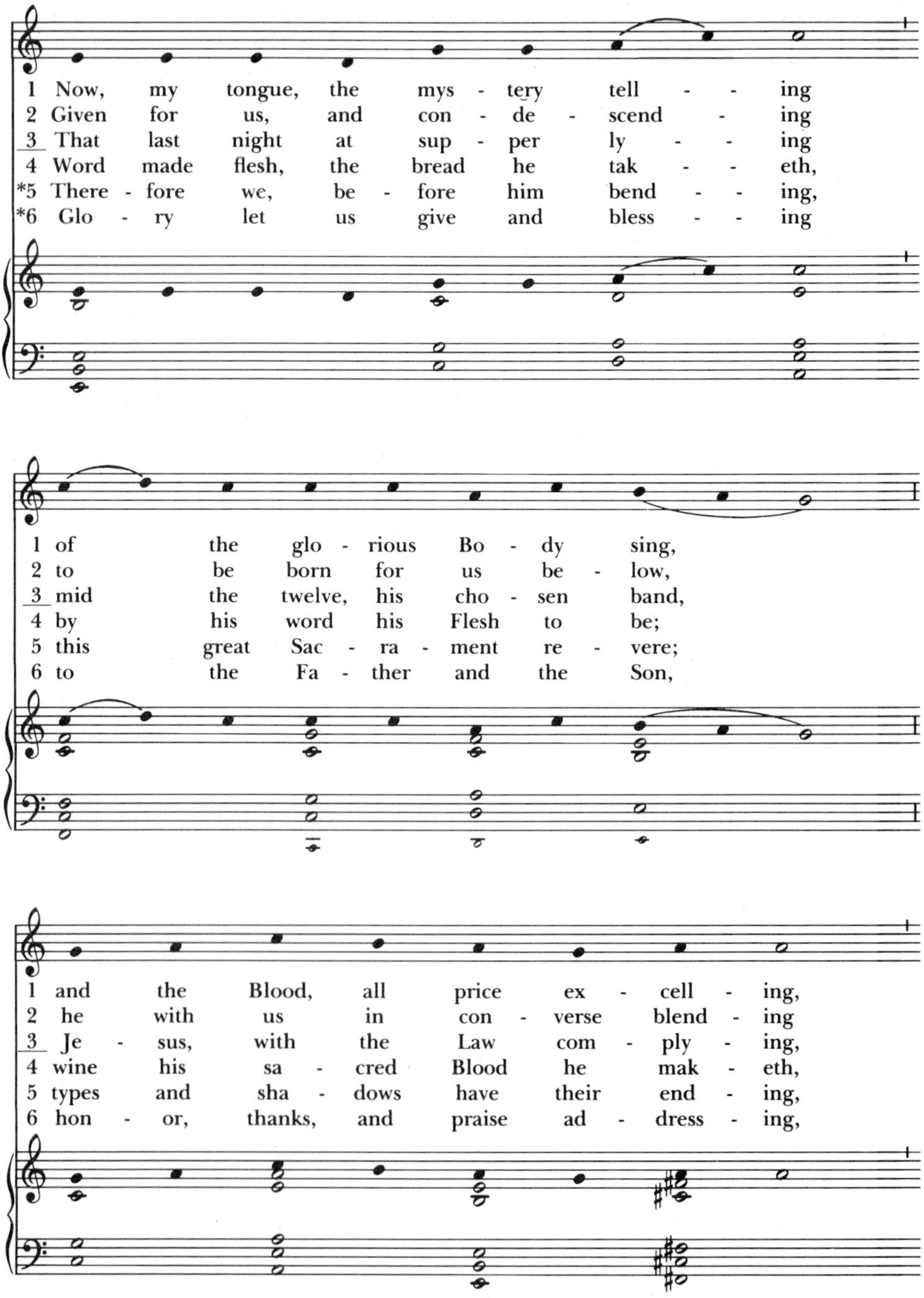
1 Now, my tongue, the mys - tery tell - - ing
2 Given for us, and con - de - scend - ing
3 That last night at sup - per ly - - ing
4 Word made flesh, the bread he tak - - eth,
*5 There - fore we, be - fore him bend - - ing,
*6 Glo - ry let us give and bless - - ing
1 of the glo - rious Bo - dy sing,
2 to be born for us be - low,
3 mid the twelve, his cho - sen band,
4 by his word his Flesh to be;
5 this great Sac - ra - ment re - vere;
6 to the Fa - ther and the Son,
1 and the Blood, all price ex - cell - ing,
2 he with us in con - verse blend - ing
3 Je - sus, with the Law com - ply - ing,
4 wine his sa - cred Blood he mak - eth,
5 types and sha - dows have their end - ing,
6 hon - or, thanks, and praise ad - dress - ing,

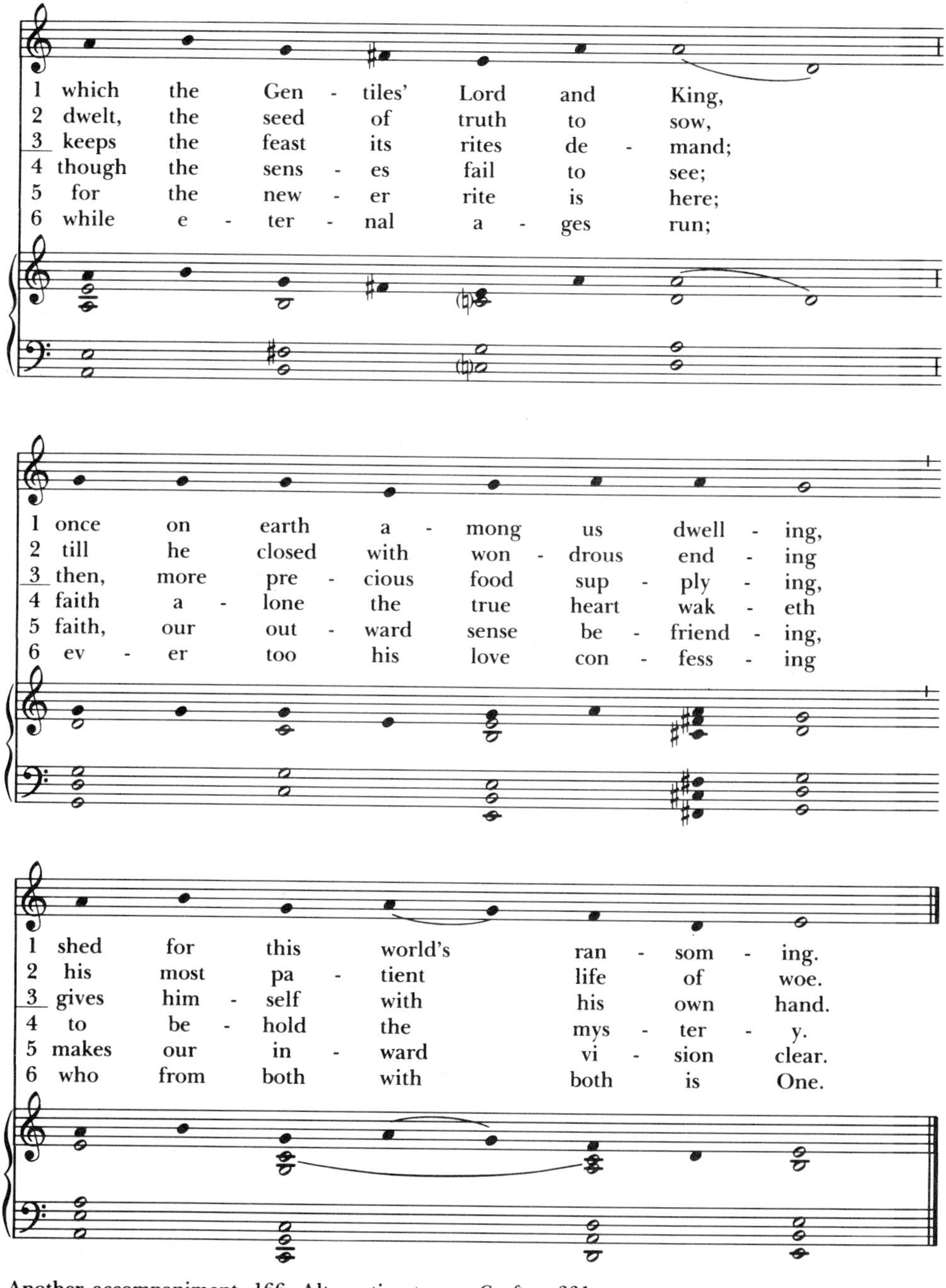
1 which the Gen - tiles' Lord and King,
2 dwelt, the seed of truth to sow,
3 keeps the feast its rites de - mand;
4 though the sens - es fail to see;
5 for the new - er rite is here;
6 while e - ter - nal a - ges run;
1 once on earth a - mong us dwell - ing,
2 till he closed with won - drous end - ing
3 then, more pre - cious food sup - ply - ing,
4 faith a - lone the true heart wak - eth
5 faith, our out - ward sense be - friend - ing,
6 ev - er too his love con - fess - ing
1 shed for this world's ran - som - ing.
2 his most pa - tient life of woe.
3 gives him - self with his own hand.
4 to be - hold the mys - ter - y.
5 makes our in - ward vi - sion clear.
6 who from both with both is One.

Another accompaniment, 166. Alternative tunes: *Grafton,* 331; *Tantum ergo sacramentum,* 330; *St. Thomas,* 58.

Words: Att. Thomas Aquinas (1225?-1274); ver. *Hymnal 1940,* rev.
Music: *Pange lingua,* plainsong, Mode 3, *Zisterzienser Hymnar,* 14th cent.; acc. Jackson Hill (b. 1941)

87. 87. 87

5 There-fore we, be - fore him bend - ing,
6 Glo - ry let us give and bless - ing
this great Sac - ra - ment re - vere;
to the Fa - ther and the Son,
types and sha - dows have their end - - ing,
hon - or, thanks, and praise ad - dress - ing,
for the new - er rite is here;
while e - ter - nal a - ges run;

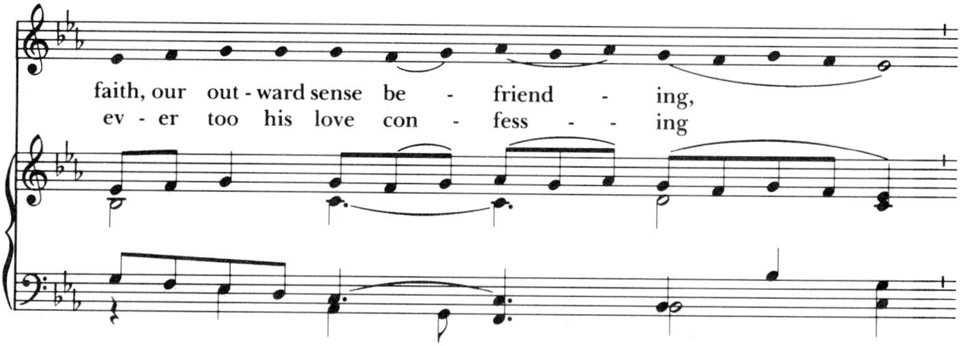
faith, our out - ward sense be - friend - ing,
ev - er too his love con - fess - - ing

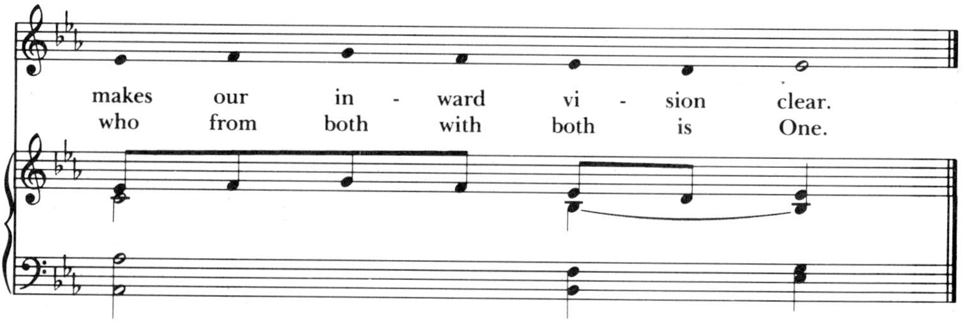
makes our in - ward vi - sion clear.
who from both with both is One.

These are stanzas from the hymns found at 329 *and* 331.

Alternative tunes: *Grafton,* 331; *Pange lingua,* 329; *St. Thomas,* 58.

Words: Att. Thomas Aquinas (1225?-1274); ver. *Hymnal 1940*

Music: *Tantum ergo Sacramentum,* plainsong, Mode 5, *Zisterzienser Hymnar,* 14th cent.; acc. *Hymnal 1940* 87. 87. 87

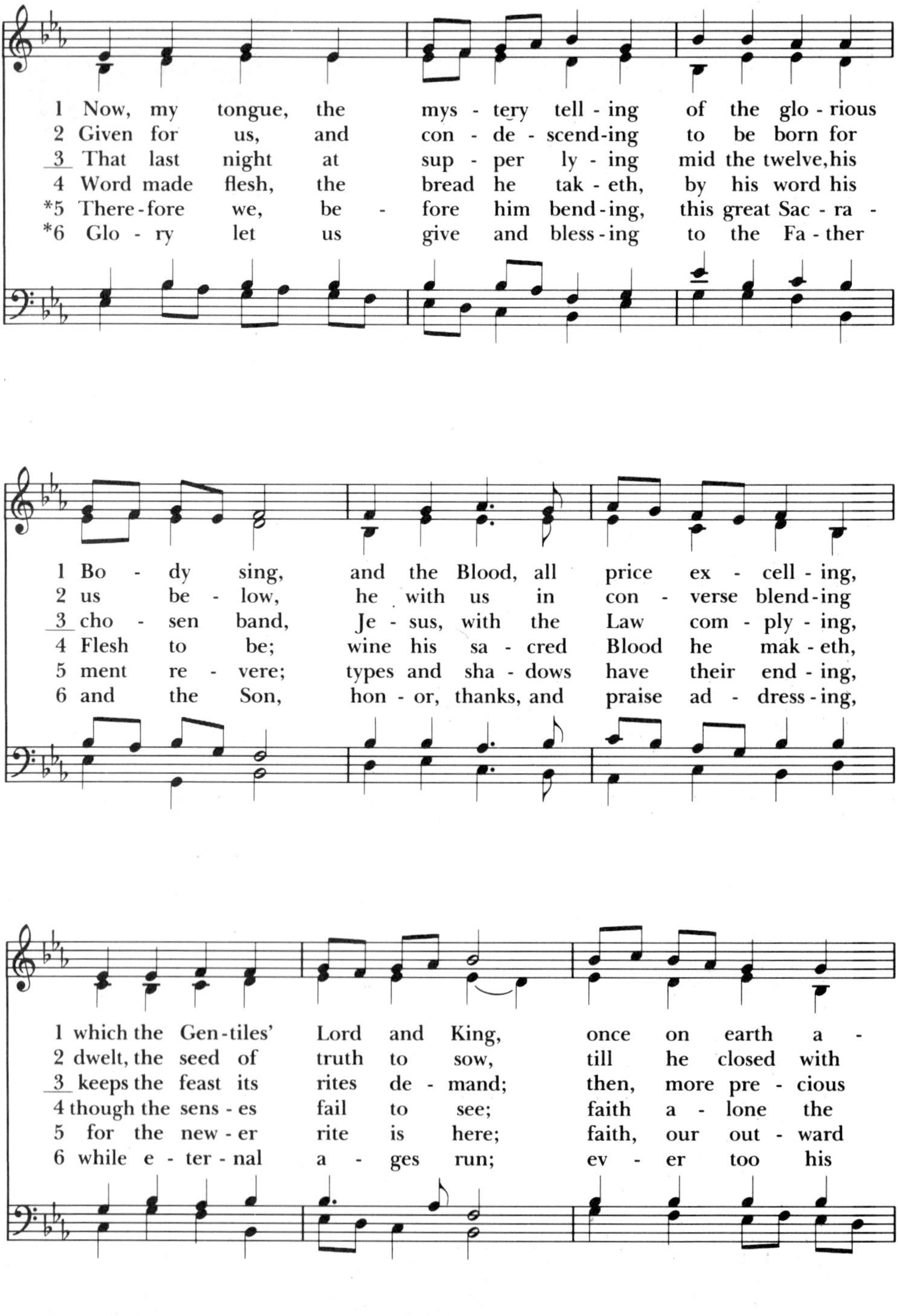
1 Now, my tongue, the mys - tery tell - ing of the glo - rious
2 Given for us, and con - de - scend-ing to be born for
3 That last night at sup - per ly - ing mid the twelve, his
4 Word made flesh, the bread he tak - eth, by his word his
*5 There-fore we, be - fore him bend-ing, this great Sac - ra -
*6 Glo - ry let us give and bless-ing to the Fa - ther
1 Bo - dy sing, and the Blood, all price ex - cell - ing,
2 us be - low, he with us in con - verse blend-ing
3 cho - sen band, Je - sus, with the Law com - ply - ing,
4 Flesh to be; wine his sa - cred Blood he mak - eth,
5 ment re - vere; types and sha - dows have their end - ing,
6 and the Son, hon - or, thanks, and praise ad - dress-ing,
1 which the Gen-tiles' Lord and King, once on earth a -
2 dwelt, the seed of truth to sow, till he closed with
3 keeps the feast its rites de - mand; then, more pre - cious
4 though the sens - es fail to see; faith a - lone the
5 for the new - er rite is here; faith, our out - ward
6 while e - ter - nal a - ges run; ev - er too his

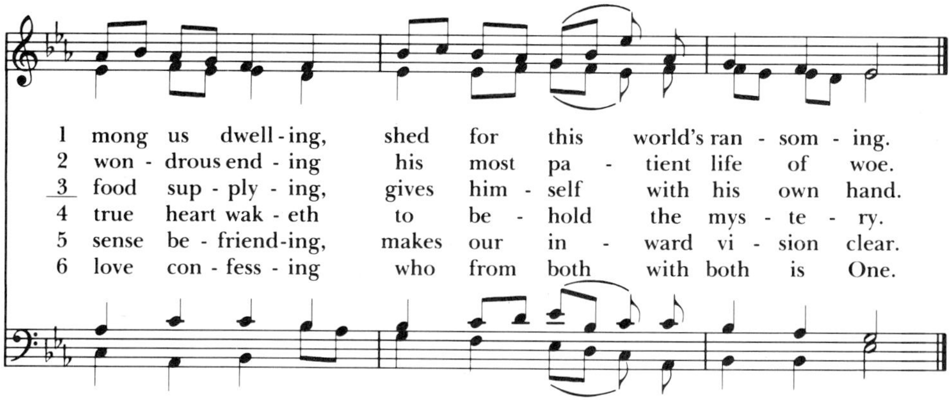
1 mong us dwell - ing, shed for this world's ran - som - ing.
2 won - drous end - ing his most pa - tient life of woe.
3 food sup - ply - ing, gives him - self with his own hand.
4 true heart wak - eth to be - hold the mys - te - ry.
5 sense be - friend-ing, makes our in - ward vi - sion clear.
6 love con - fess - ing who from both with both is One.

Alternative tunes: *Pange lingua,* 329; *Tantum ergo sacramentum,* 330; *St. Thomas,* 58.

Words: Att. Thomas Aquinas (1225?-1274); ver. *Hymnal 1940,* rev.
Music: *Grafton,* melody from *Chants ordinaires de l'Office Divin,* 1881; harm. *Songs of Praise,* 1925

♩=69
87. 87. 87

Holy Eucharist

332

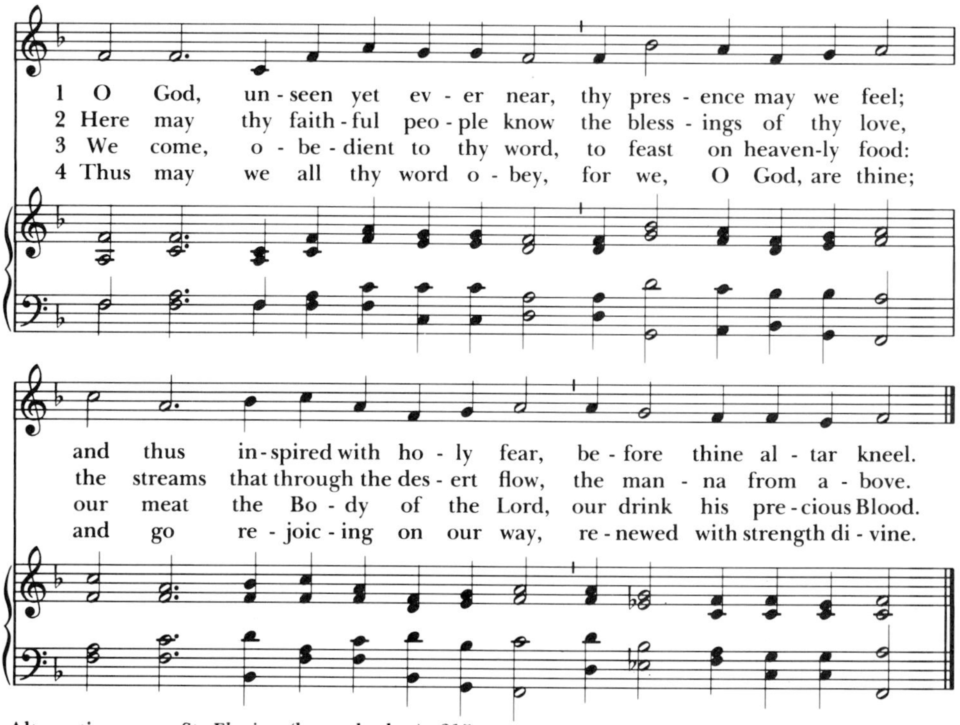
1 O God, un - seen yet ev - er near, thy pres - ence may we feel;
2 Here may thy faith - ful peo - ple know the bless - ings of thy love,
3 We come, o - be - dient to thy word, to feast on heaven-ly food:
4 Thus may we all thy word o - bey, for we, O God, are thine;
and thus in - spired with ho - ly fear, be - fore thine al - tar kneel.
the streams that through the des - ert flow, the man - na from a - bove.
our meat the Bo - dy of the Lord, our drink his pre - cious Blood.
and go re - joic - ing on our way, re - newed with strength di - vine.

Alternative tune: *St. Flavian* (later rhythm), 615.

Words: Edward Osler (1798-1863)
Music: *St. Flavian,* from *Day's Psalter,* 1562

♩=80
CM

Now the si - lence Now the peace Now the emp - ty hands up -
lift - ed Now the kneel - ing Now the plea Now the Fa - ther's
arms in wel - come Now the hear - ing Now the power Now the
ves - sel brimmed for pour - ing Now the Bo - dy Now the Blood

Now the joy - ful cel - e - bra - tion Now the wed - ding
Now the songs Now the heart for - giv - en leap - ing Now the
Spi - rit's vis - i - ta - tion Now the Son's e - piph - an - y
Now the Fa - ther's bless - ing Now Now Now

Words: Jaroslav J. Vajda (b. 1919)
Music: *Now,* Carl Flentge Schalk (b. 1929)

♩. = 60
Irr.

1 Praise the Lord, rise up re - joic - ing, wor - ship, thanks, de -
2 Scat - tered flock, one shep - herd shar - ing, lost and lone - ly,
3 Sins for - giv - en, wrong for - giv - ing, we go forth a -
vo - tion voic - ing; glo - ry be to God on high!
one voice hear - ing, ears at - ten - tive to your word;
lert and liv - ing in your Spi - rit, strong and free.
Christ, your cross and pas - sion shar - ing, by this Eu - cha -
by your Blood new life re - ceiv - ing, in your Bo - dy,
Part - ners in your new cre - a - tion, seek - ing peace in
rist de - clar - ing yours the fi - nal vic - to - ry.
firm be - liev - ing, we are yours, and you the Lord.
ev - ery na - tion, may we faith - ful fol - lowers be.

Words: Howard Charles Adie Gaunt (b. 1902), alt.
Music: *Alles ist an Gottes Segen,* melody att. Johann Balthasar König (1691-1758), alt.; harm. Johann Löhner (1645-1705), after chorale ver. Johann Sebastian Bach (1685-1750)

𝅗𝅥=52
887. 887

A(G)
C♯m(Bm)
1 I am the bread of life; they who
2 Bread that I will give is my
3 less you eat of the
4 I am the re - sur - rec - tion,
5 Lord we be - lieve that
D(C)
E(D)
1 come to me shall not hun - ger; they who be -
2 Flesh for the life of the world, and they who
3 Flesh of the Son of Man and
4 I am the life. They who be -
5 you are the Christ, the
A(G)
C♯m(Bm)
D(C)
A(G)
1 lieve in me shall not thirst. No one can come to
2 eat of this bread, they shall live for
3 drink of his Blood, you shall not have life with -
4 lieve in me, e - ven if they
5 Son of God who has

D(C)
Bm(Am)
E(D)
1 me__ un - less the__ Fa - ther draw them.
2 ev - er,__ they shall__ live for ev - er.
3 in you, you shall not have life with - in you.
4 die,__ they shall__ live for ev - er.
5 come__ in - to__ the__ world.__
Descant
And I will raise them up, and I will raise them
Refrain
A(G)
E(D)
A(G)
D(C)
And I will raise them up, and I will raise them

up, and I will raise them up on the
E(D)
A(G)
D(C)
up, and I will raise them up on the
last day. 5 Yes, day.
1-4
Final Ending
A(G) E(D) A(G) A(G)
last day.
2 The
3 Un-
4
5 Yes,
day.

A (capo 2, G). The descant may be sung after stanzas 4 and 5.

Words: Suzanne Toolan (b. 1927); adapt. of John 6
Music: *I Am the Bread of Life,* Suzanne Toolan (b. 1927); arr. Betty Pulkingham (b. 1928)

𝅗𝅥 = 69
Irr. with Refrain

1 Come with us, O bless - ed Je - sus, with us ev - er -
*2 Come with us, O might - y Sa - vior, God from God, and
*3 Come with us, O King of glo - ry, by an - gel - ic
more to be; and though leav - ing now thine
Light from Light; thou art God, thy glo - ry
voic - es praised; in our hearts as in thy
al - tar, let us nev - er - more leave thee.
veil - ing, so that we may bear the sight.
hea - ven, be en - rap - tured an - thems raised.
Be thou one with us for ev - er, in our life thy
Now we go to seek and serve thee, through our work as
Let the might - y cho - rus ev - er sing its glad ex -

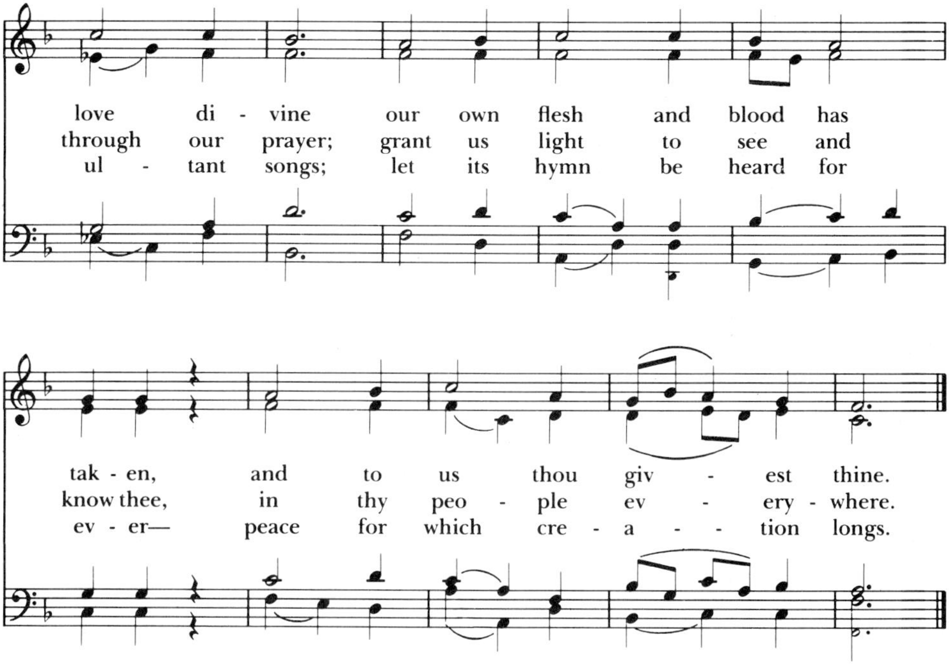
love di - vine our own flesh and blood has
through our prayer; grant us light to see and
ul - tant songs; let its hymn be heard for
tak - en, and to us thou giv - est thine.
know thee, in thy peo - ple ev - ery - where.
ev - er— peace for which cre - a - - tion longs.

Words: John Henry Hopkins, Jr. (1820-1891) and Charles P. Price (b. 1920)
Music: *Werde munter*, Johann Schop (d. 1665?); arr. and harm. Johann Sebastian Bach (1685-1750)

♩= 88
87. 87. D

1 And now, O Fa - ther, mind - ful of the love that
2 Look Fa - ther, look on his a - noint - ed face, and
*3 And then for those, our dear - est and our best, by
*4 And so we come; O draw us to thy feet, most
bought us, once for all, on Cal - vary's tree, and hav - ing with us
on - ly look on us as found in him; look not on our mis -
this pre - vail - ing pres-ence we ap - peal; O fold them clos - er
pa - tient Sa - vior, who canst love us still! And by this food, so
him that pleads a - bove, we here pre - sent, we here spread
us - ings of thy grace, our prayer so lan - guid, and our
to thy mer - cy's breast! O do thine ut - most for their
awe - some and so sweet, de - liv - er us from ev - ery
forth to thee, that on - ly of - fering per - fect in thine
faith so dim: for lo! be - tween our sins and their re -
soul's true weal! From taint - ing mis - chief keep them pure and
touch of ill: in thine own ser - vice make us glad and

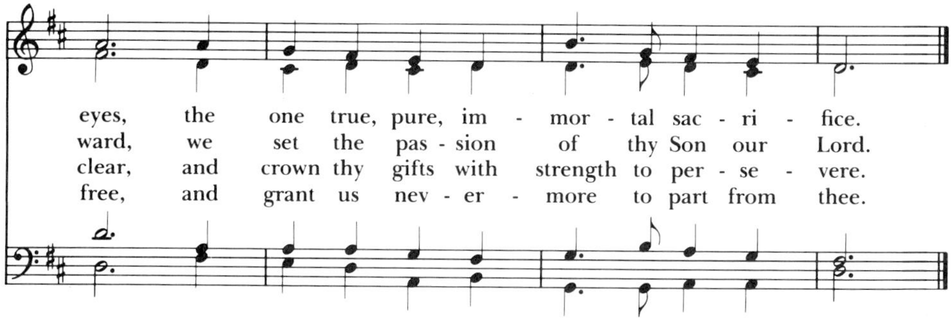
eyes, the one true, pure, im - mor - tal sac - ri - fice.
ward, we set the pas - sion of thy Son our Lord.
clear, and crown thy gifts with strength to per - se - vere.
free, and grant us nev - er - more to part from thee.

Words: William Bright (1824-1901), alt.
Music: *Unde et memores*, William Henry Monk (1823-1889)

𝅗𝅥=52
10 10. 10 10. 10 10

Holy Eucharist

338

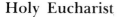

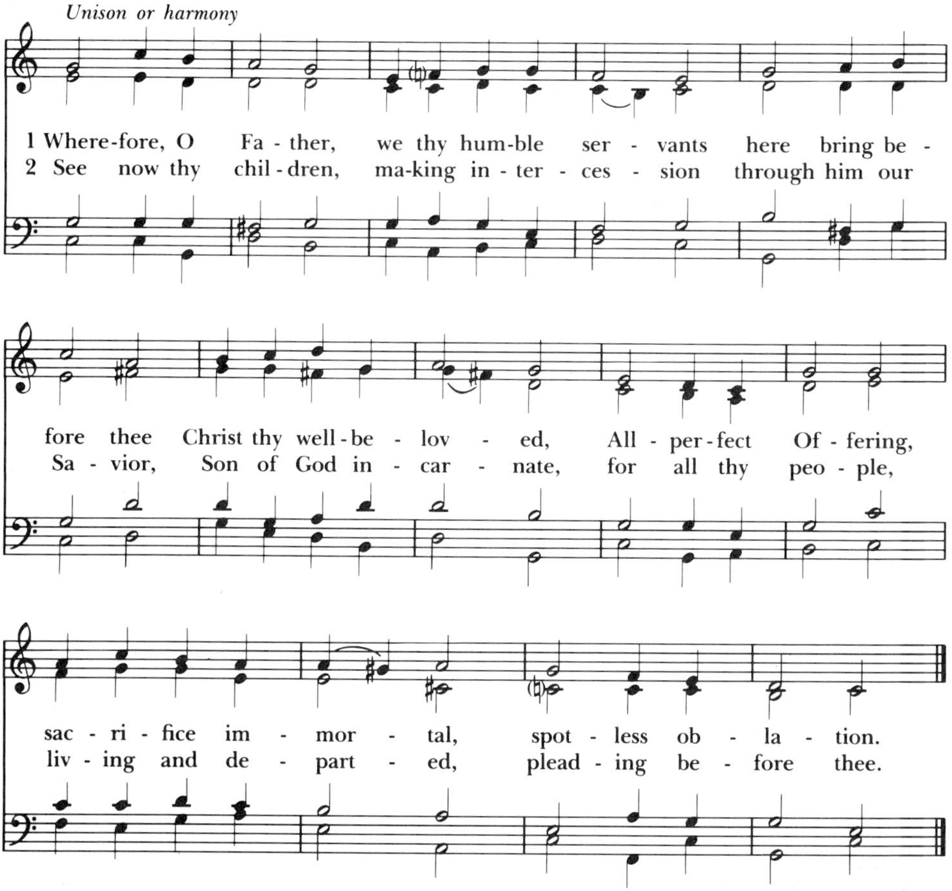
Unison or harmony
1 Where-fore, O Fa - ther, we thy hum-ble ser - vants here bring be - fore thee Christ thy well-be - lov - ed, All - per-fect Of - fering, sac - ri - fice im - mor - tal, spot - less ob - la - tion.
2 See now thy chil - dren, ma-king in - ter - ces - sion through him our Sa - vior, Son of God in - car - nate, for all thy peo - ple, liv - ing and de - part - ed, plead - ing be - fore thee.

Words: William Henry Hammond Jervois (1852-1905)
Music: *Lobet den Herren*, melody Johann Cruger (1598-1662); harm. Friedrich Layriz (1808-1859)

𝅗𝅥=58
11 11. 11 5

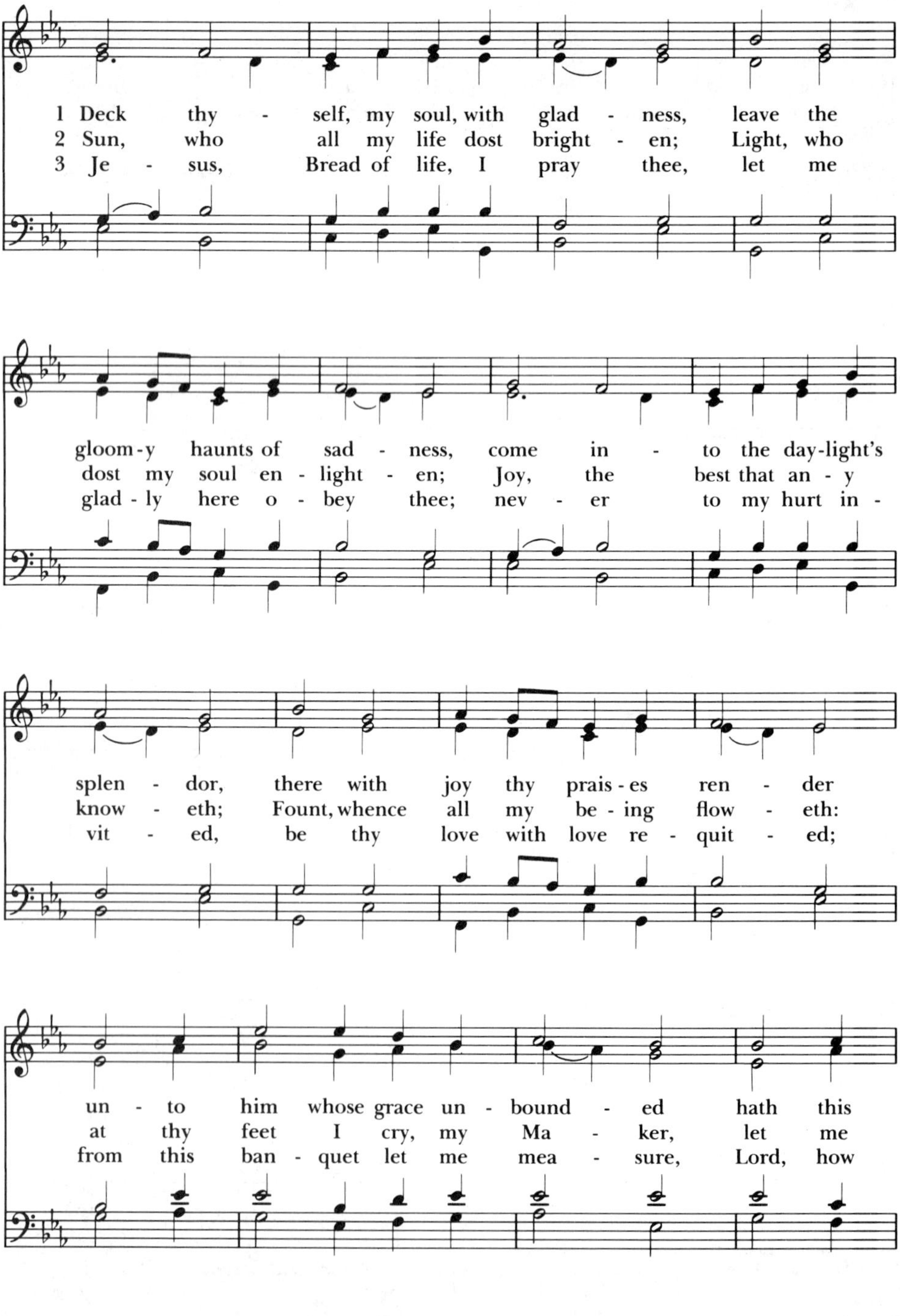
1 Deck thy - self, my soul, with glad - ness, leave the
2 Sun, who all my life dost bright - en; Light, who
3 Je - sus, Bread of life, I pray thee, let me
gloom-y haunts of sad - ness, come in - to the day-light's
dost my soul en - light - en; Joy, the best that an - y
glad - ly here o - bey thee; nev - er to my hurt in -
splen - dor, there with joy thy prais - es ren - der
know - eth; Fount, whence all my be - ing flow - eth:
vit - ed, be thy love with love re - quit - ed;
un - to him whose grace un - bound - ed hath this
at thy feet I cry, my Ma - ker, let me
from this ban - quet let me mea - sure, Lord, how

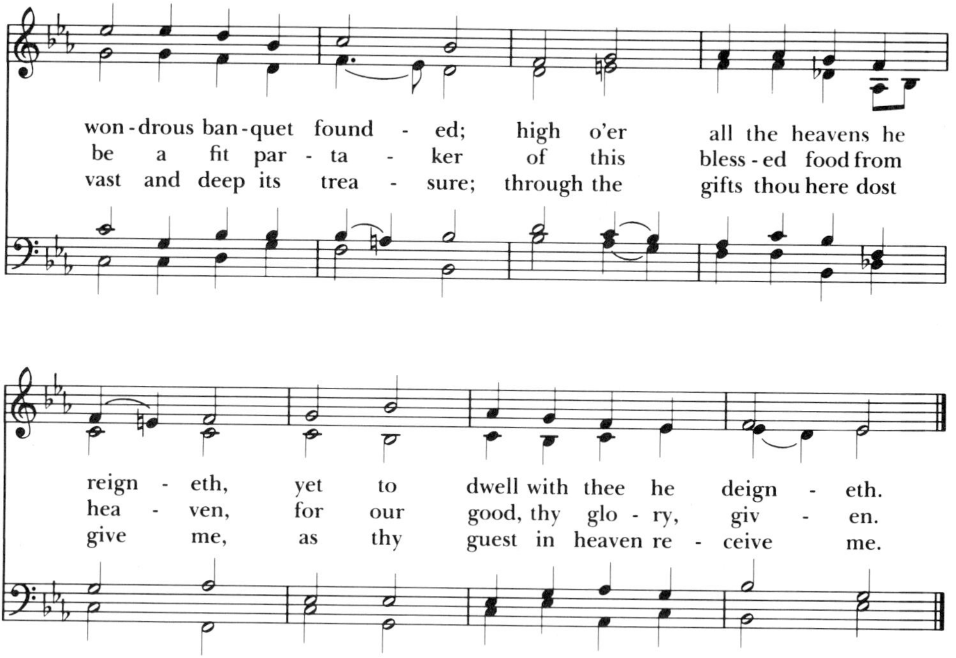
won-drous ban-quet found - ed; high o'er all the heavens he
be a fit par - ta - ker of this bless-ed food from
vast and deep its trea - sure; through the gifts thou here dost
reign - eth, yet to dwell with thee he deign - eth.
hea - ven, for our good, thy glo - ry, giv - en.
give me, as thy guest in heaven re - ceive me.

Words: Johann Franck (1618-1677); tr. Catherine Winkworth (1827-1878), alt.
Music: *Schmücke dich,* melody Johann Cruger (1598-1662); harm. *The English Hymnal,* 1906

𝅗𝅥=48
LMD

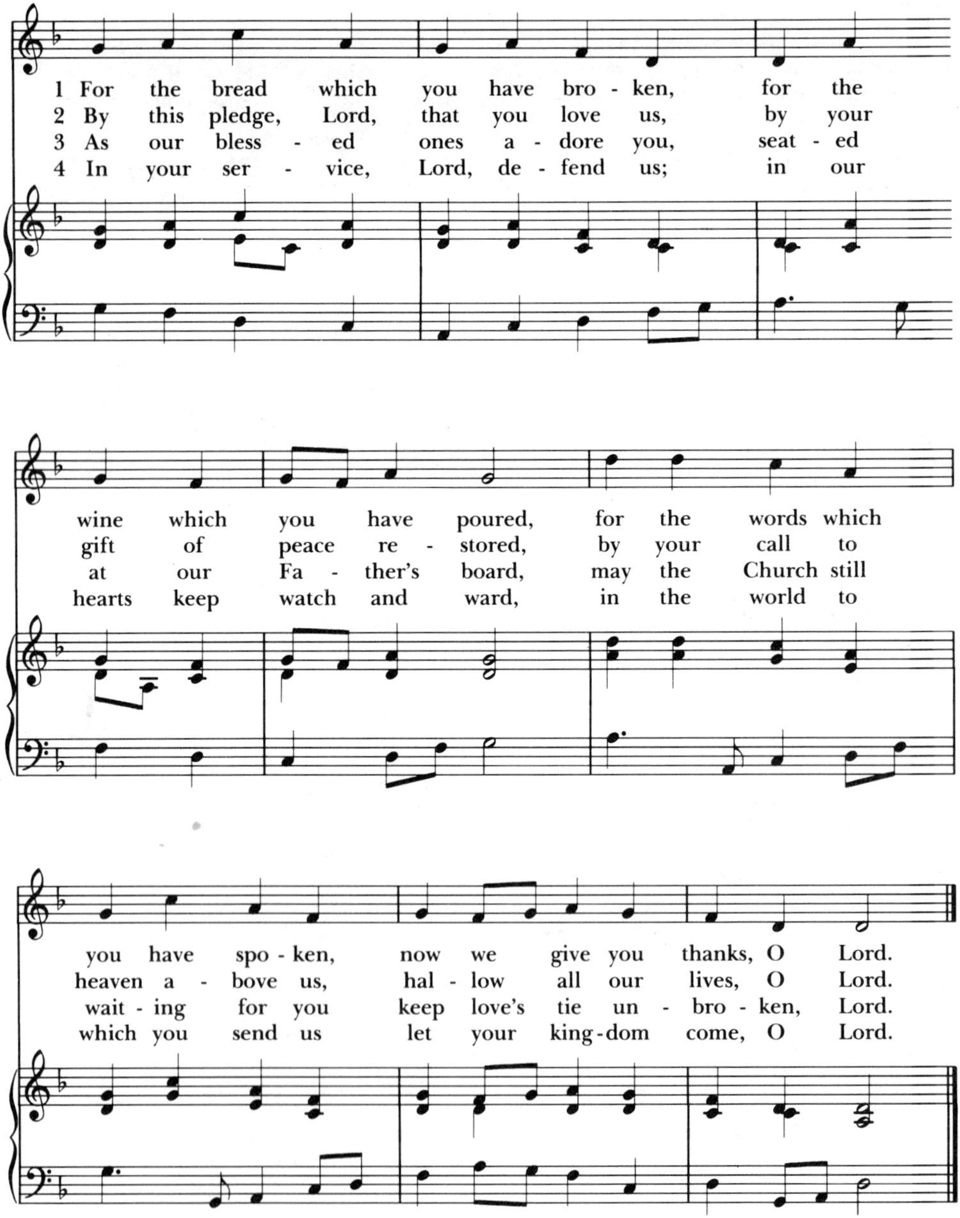
1 For the bread which you have bro - ken, for the
2 By this pledge, Lord, that you love us, by your
3 As our bless - ed ones a - dore you, seat - ed
4 In your ser - vice, Lord, de - fend us; in our
wine which you have poured, for the words which
gift of peace re - stored, by your call to
at our Fa - ther's board, may the Church still
hearts keep watch and ward, in the world to
you have spo - ken, now we give you thanks, O Lord.
heaven a - bove us, hal - low all our lives, O Lord.
wait - ing for you keep love's tie un - bro - ken, Lord.
which you send us let your king - dom come, O Lord.

Alternative tune: *Omni die,* 341.

Words: Louis F. Benson (1855-1930), alt.
Music: *Beng-Li,* I-to Loh (b. 1936)

♩=c. 80
87. 87

1 For the bread which you have bro - ken, for the
2 By this pledge, Lord, that you love us, by your
3 As our bless - ed ones a - dore you, seat - ed
4 In your ser - vice, Lord, de - fend us; in our
wine which you have poured, for the words which you have
gift of peace re - stored, by your call to heaven a -
at our Fa - ther's board, may the Church still wait - ing
hearts keep watch and ward, in the world to which you
spo - ken, now we give you thanks, O Lord.
bove us, hal - low all our lives, O Lord.
for you keep love's tie un - bro - ken, Lord.
send us let your king - dom come, O Lord.

Alternative tune: *Beng-Li,* 340.

Words: Louis F. Benson (1855-1930), alt.
Music: *Omni die,* melody from *Gross Catolisch Gesangbuch,* 1631; harm. William Smith Rockstro (1823-1895)

𝅗𝅥=63
87. 87

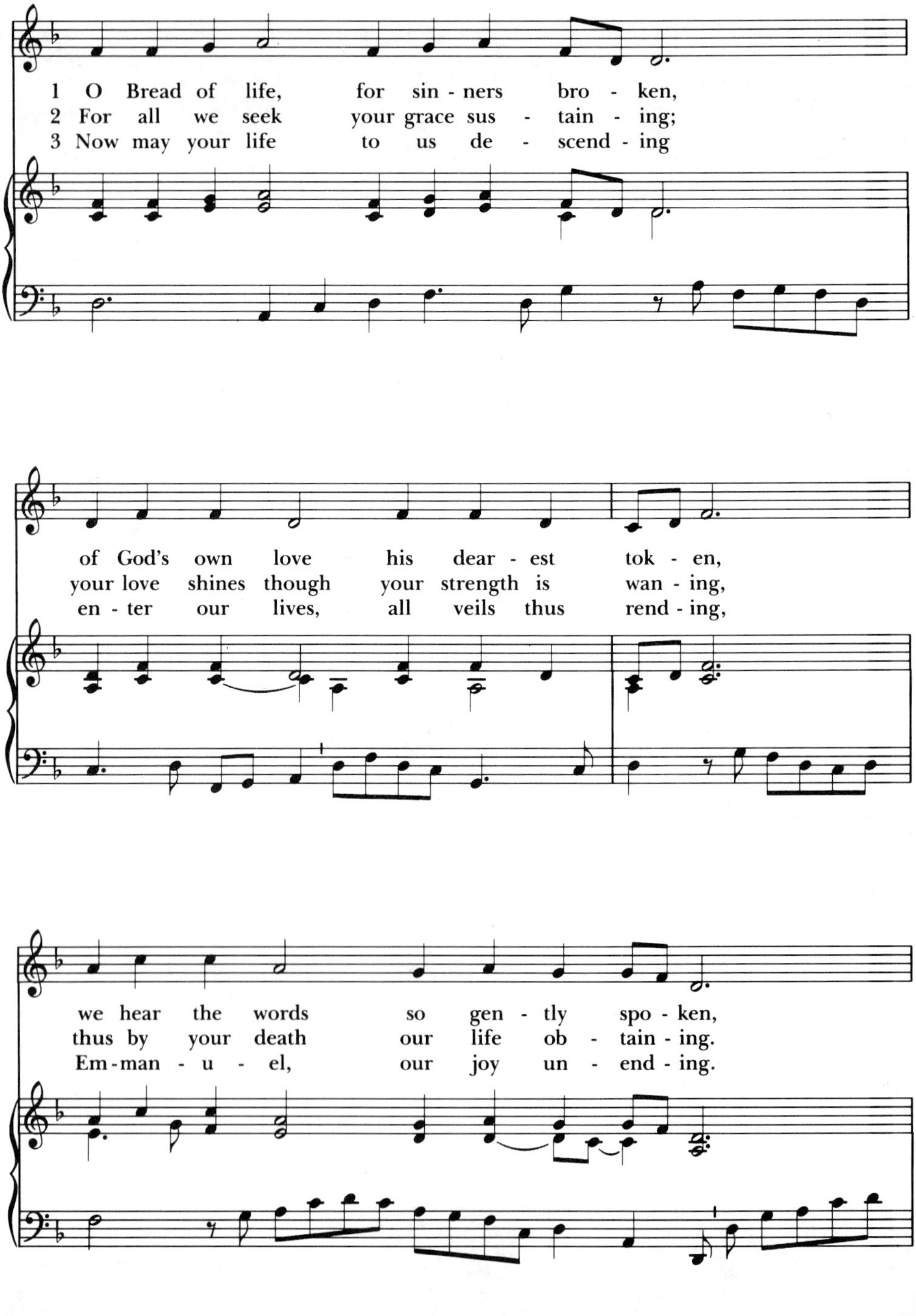
1 O Bread of life, for sin - ners bro - ken,
2 For all we seek your grace sus - tain - ing;
3 Now may your life to us de - scend - ing
of God's own love his dear - est tok - en,
your love shines though your strength is wan - ing,
en - ter our lives, all veils thus rend - ing,
we hear the words so gen - tly spo - ken,
thus by your death our life ob - tain - ing.
Em - man - u - el, our joy un - end - ing.

"Do this for me in my re - mem-brance."
"Come un - to me, you hea - vy la - den."
"I am with you, this day and ev - er."

Words: Timothy T'ing Fang Lew (1892-1947); tr. Frank W. Price (1895-1974), alt.
Music: *Sheng En*, melody Su Yin-Lan (20th cent.); harm. I-to Loh (b. 1936)

♩= c. 84
99. 99

1 Shep-herd of souls, re - fresh and bless thy cho-sen
2 We would not live by bread a - lone, but by thy
3 Be known to us in break - ing bread, and do not
4 Lord, sup with us in love di - vine, thy Bo - dy
pil - grim flock with man - na in the
word of grace, in strength of which we
then de - part; Sa - vior, a - bide with
and thy Blood, that liv - ing bread, that
wil - der - ness, with wa - ter from the rock.
trav - el on to our a - bid - ing - place.
us, and spread thy ta - ble in our heart.
heaven - ly wine, be our im - mor - tal food.

Another harmonization, 510. Alternative tune: *Dundee,* 526.

Words: James Montgomery (1771-1854), alt.
Music: *St. Agnes,* melody John Bacchus Dykes (1823-1876); harm. Richard Proulx (b. 1937), after John Bacchus Dykes (1823-1876)

♩= 108
CM

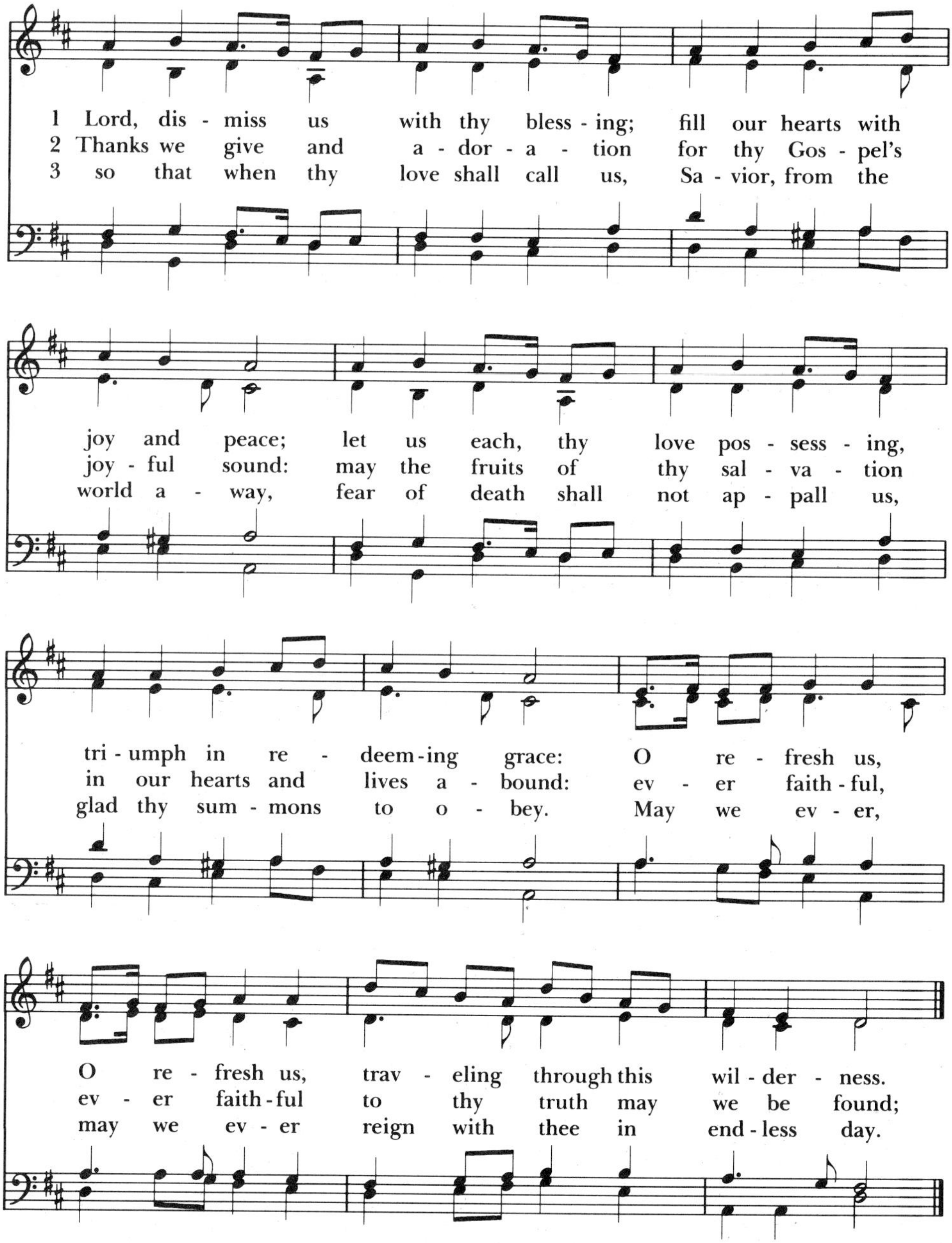
1 Lord, dis - miss us with thy bless - ing; fill our hearts with
2 Thanks we give and a - dor - a - tion for thy Gos - pel's
3 so that when thy love shall call us, Sa - vior, from the
joy and peace; let us each, thy love pos - sess - ing,
joy - ful sound: may the fruits of thy sal - va - tion
world a - way, fear of death shall not ap - pall us,
tri - umph in re - deem - ing grace: O re - fresh us,
in our hearts and lives a - bound: ev - er faith - ful,
glad thy sum - mons to o - bey. May we ev - er,
O re - fresh us, trav - eling through this wil - der - ness.
ev - er faith - ful to thy truth may we be found;
may we ev - er reign with thee in end - less day.

Words: Att. John Fawcett (1739/40-1817)
Music: *Sicilian Mariners*, Sicilian melody; first published *The European Magazine and London Review*, 1792, alt.

♩=69
87. 87. 87

1 Sa - vior, a - gain to thy dear Name we raise
*2 Grant us thy peace up - on our home-ward way;
3 Grant us thy peace through - out our earth - ly life;
4 thy peace in life, the balm of ev - ery pain;
with one ac - cord our part - ing hymn of praise;
with thee be - gan, with thee shall end the day:
peace to thy Church from er - ror and from strife;
thy peace in death, the hope to rise a - gain;
guard thou the lips from sin, the hearts from shame,
from harm and dan - ger keep thy chil - dren free,
peace to our land, the fruit of truth and love;
then, when thy voice shall bid our con - flict cease,
that in this house have called up - on thy Name.
for dark and light are both a - like to thee.
peace in each heart, thy Spi - rit from a - bove:
call us, O Lord, to thine e - ter - nal peace.

Words: John Ellerton (1826-1893), alt.
Music: *Ellers*, Edward John Hopkins (1818-1901)

𝅗𝅥=48
10 10. 10 10

Unison or harmony
1 Com - plet - ed, Lord, the Ho - ly Mys - ter - ies,
2 Here we have tast - ed in - fi - nite de - lights,
3 Through God's good grace these Mys - ter - ies are ours,
as far as lies with - in our mor - tal power!
be - held a - far that life which soon shall be;
or - dained by thee, the ev - er - last - ing Son;
Thy death re - mem - bered, feed - ing thus on thee,
oh, count us wor - thy, Christ, thy joys to share
blest by the Spi - rit, breath and flame of life,
we here have known the re - sur - rec - tion hour.
for ev - er in e - ter - ni - ty with thee.
to whom be praise while end - less a - ges run.

Words: Liturgy of St. Basil; tr. Cyril E. Pocknee (1906-1980)
Music: *Song 4*, Orlando Gibbons (1583-1625), alt.

♩= 84
10 10. 10 10

1 Go forth for God; go ___ to the world in peace;
2 Go forth for God; go ___ to the world in love;
3 Go forth for God; go ___ to the world in strength;
4 Go forth for God; go ___ to the world in joy;
be of good cour - age, armed with heaven - ly grace,
strength-en the faint, give cour - age to the weak;
hold fast the good, be ur - gent for the right;
to serve God's peo - ple ev - ery day and hour,

in God's good Spi - rit dai - ly to in - crease, till in his king - dom we be - hold his face.
help the af - flict - ed; rich - ly from a - bove his love sup - plies the grace and power we seek.
ren - der to no one e - vil; Christ at length shall o - ver - come all dark - ness with his light.
and serv - ing Christ, our ev - ery gift em - ploy, re - joic - ing in the Ho - ly Spi - rit's power.

Alternative tune: *Woodlands,* 438.

Words: John Raphael Peacey (1896-1971) and *English Praise,* 1975, alt.
Music: *Litton,* Erik Routley (1917-1982)

𝅗𝅥 = 52
10 10. 10 10

1 Lord, we have come at your own in - vi - ta - tion,
2 Here, at your ta - ble, con - firm our in - ten - tion
3 When, at your ta - ble, each time of re - turn - ing,
4 So, in the world where each du - ty as - signed us
cho - sen by you, to be coun - ted as friends:
ev - er to cher - ish the gifts you pro - vide;
vows are re - newed, and our cour - age re - stored:
gives us the chance to cre - ate or des - troy,
yours is the strength that sus - tains our vo - ca - tion,
teach us to serve with-out pride or pre - ten - sion,
may we in - creas - ing - ly glo - ry in learn - ing
help us to make those de - ci - sions that bind us,

ours a com - mit - ment we know nev - er ends.
led by your Spi - rit, de - fend - er and guide.
all that it means to ac - cept you as Lord.
Lord, to your - self, in o - be - dience and joy.

Another harmonization, 623.

Words: F. Pratt Green (b. 1903), rev.
Music: *O quanta qualia,* melody from *Antiphoner,* 1681; harm. *Hymns Ancient and Modern, Historical Edition,* 1909

𝅗𝅥 = 54
10 10. 10 10

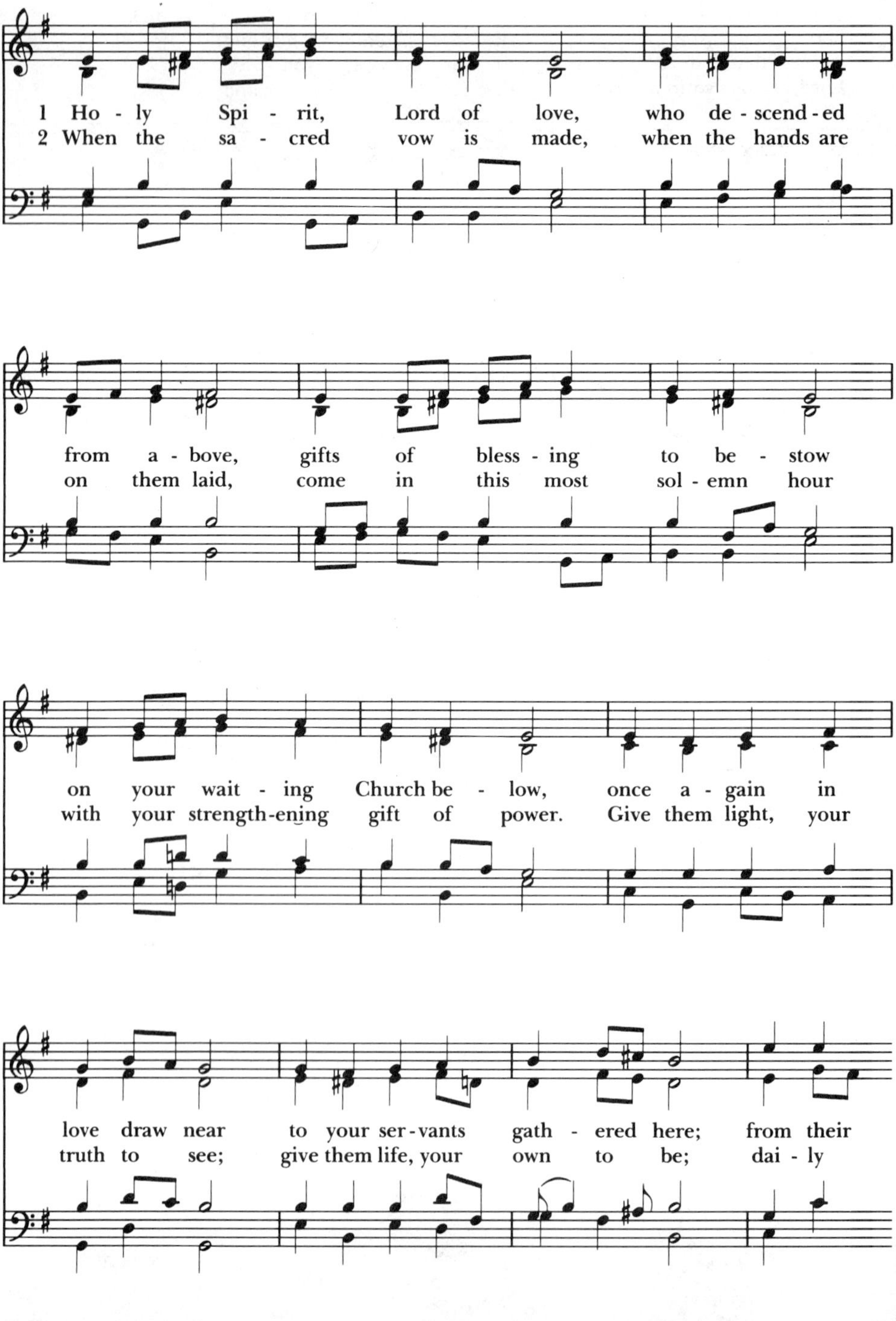
1 Ho - ly Spi - rit, Lord of love, who de - scend - ed
2 When the sa - cred vow is made, when the hands are
from a - bove, gifts of bless - ing to be - stow
on them laid, come in this most sol - emn hour
on your wait - ing Church be - low, once a - gain in
with your strength-ening gift of power. Give them light, your
love draw near to your ser - vants gath - ered here; from their
truth to see; give them life, your own to be; dai - ly

bright bap - tis - mal day you have led them on their way.
power to con-quer sin; pa - tient faith, the crown to win.

This music in d, 640.

Words: William Dalrymple Maclagen (1826-1910), alt.
Music: *Aberystwyth,* Joseph Parry (1841-1903)

𝅗𝅥 = 44
77. 77. D

1 O God of love, to thee we bow, and pray for these be - fore thee now, that, close-ly knit in ho - ly vow, they may in thee be one.
2 What-ev - er comes to be their share of quick-ening joy or bur-dening care, in power to do and grace to bear, may they in thee be one.
3 E - ter - nal love, with them a - bide; through change and chance be thou their guide, let noth-ing in this life di - vide those whom thou mak - est one.

Words: William Vaughan Jenkins (1868-1920), alt.
Music: *St. Mary Magdalene,* Gerre Hancock (b. 1934)

𝅗𝅥=c. 60
888. 6

1 May the grace of Christ our Sa - vior, and the Fa - ther's bound - less love, with the Ho - ly Spi - rit's fa - vor, rest up - on them from a - bove.
2 Thus may they a - bide in un - ion with each o - ther and the Lord, and pos - sess, in sweet com - mun - ion, joys which earth can - not af - ford.

Words: John Newton (1725-1807), alt.
Music: *Halton Holgate,* William Boyce (1711-1779)

𝅗𝅥=50
87. 87

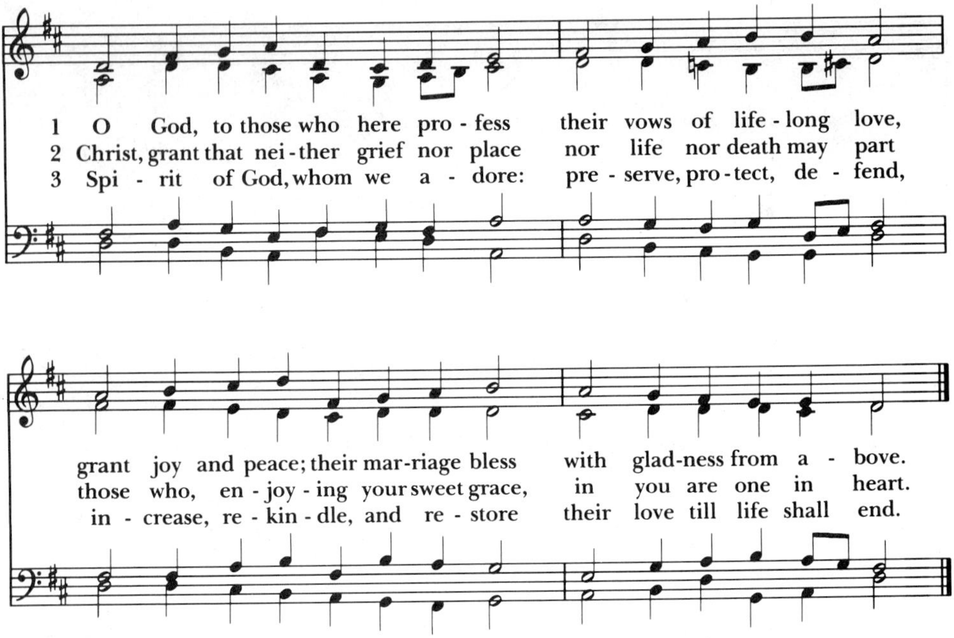
1 O God, to those who here pro - fess their vows of life - long love,
2 Christ, grant that nei - ther grief nor place nor life nor death may part
3 Spi - rit of God, whom we a - dore: pre - serve, pro - tect, de - fend,
grant joy and peace; their mar-riage bless with glad-ness from a - bove.
those who, en - joy - ing your sweet grace, in you are one in heart.
in - crease, re - kin - dle, and re - store their love till life shall end.

Words: Sts. 1 and 3, Charles P. Price (b. 1920); st. 2, Charles Wesley (1707-1788), alt.
Music: *Caithness,* melody from *The Psalmes of David in Prose and Meeter,* 1635; harm. *The English Hymnal,* 1906

♩=88
CM

1 Your love, O God, has called us here,
2 O gra - cious God, you con - se - crate
3 O God of love, in - spire our life,
for all love finds its source in you,
all that is love - ly, good, and true.
re - veal your will in all we do;
the per - fect love that casts out fear,
Bless those who in your pres - ence wait
join ev - ery hus - band, ev - ery wife
the love that Christ makes ev - er new.
and ev - ery day their love re - new.
in mu - tual love and love for you.

This music with descant, 137.

Words: Russell Schulz-Widmar (b. 1944)
Music: *Wareham,* melody William Knapp (1698-1768); harm. *Hymns Ancient and Modern,* 1875, after James Turle (1802-1882)

♩=96
LM

1. In - to par - a - dise may the an - gels lead you.
At your com - ing may the mar-tyrs re - ceive you,
and bring you in - to the ho - ly ci - ty Je - ru - sa - lem.
2. May the choirs of an - gels wel - come you,

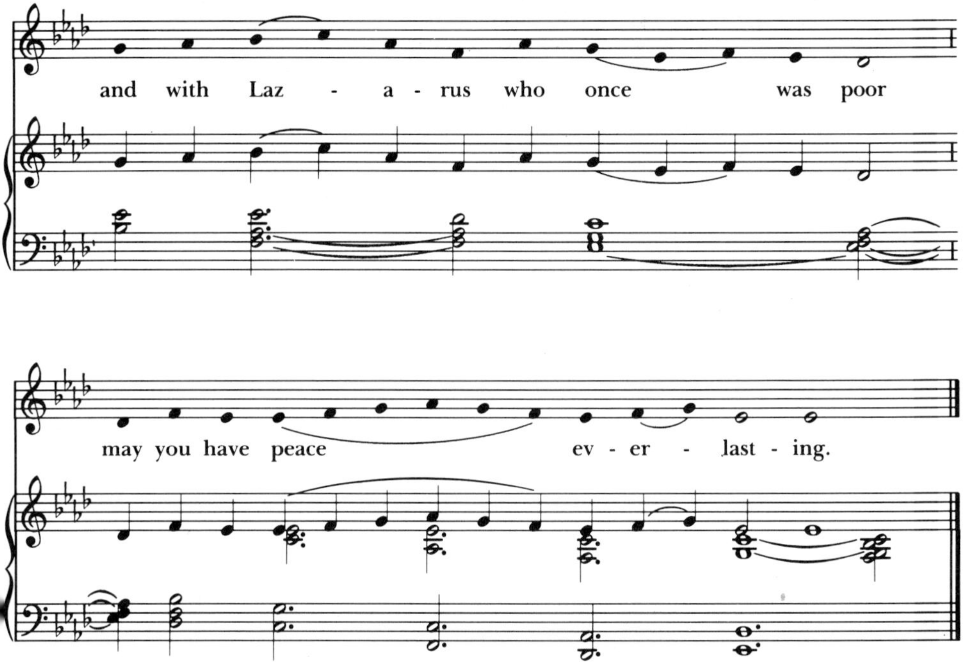
and with Laz - a - rus who once was poor
may you have peace ev - er - last - ing.

Words: Latin; tr. *The Book of Common Prayer*, 1979, and Theodore Marier (b. 1912)
Music: *In paradisum*, plainsong, Mode 7 and Mode 8; *Graduale Romanum*, 1974;
acc. David Hurd (b. 1950)

Irr.

Alternative accompaniment

Music: ***In paradisum,*** plainsong, Mode 7 and Mode 8; *Graduale Romanum,* 1974; acc. Richard Proulx (b. 1937)

Give rest, O Christ, to your ser - vant(s) with your
saints, where sor - row and pain are no more, nei - ther
sigh - ing, but life ev - er - last - ing.
Fine
You on - ly are im - mor - tal, the cre - a - tor
and ma - ker of man - kind; and we are mor - tal,

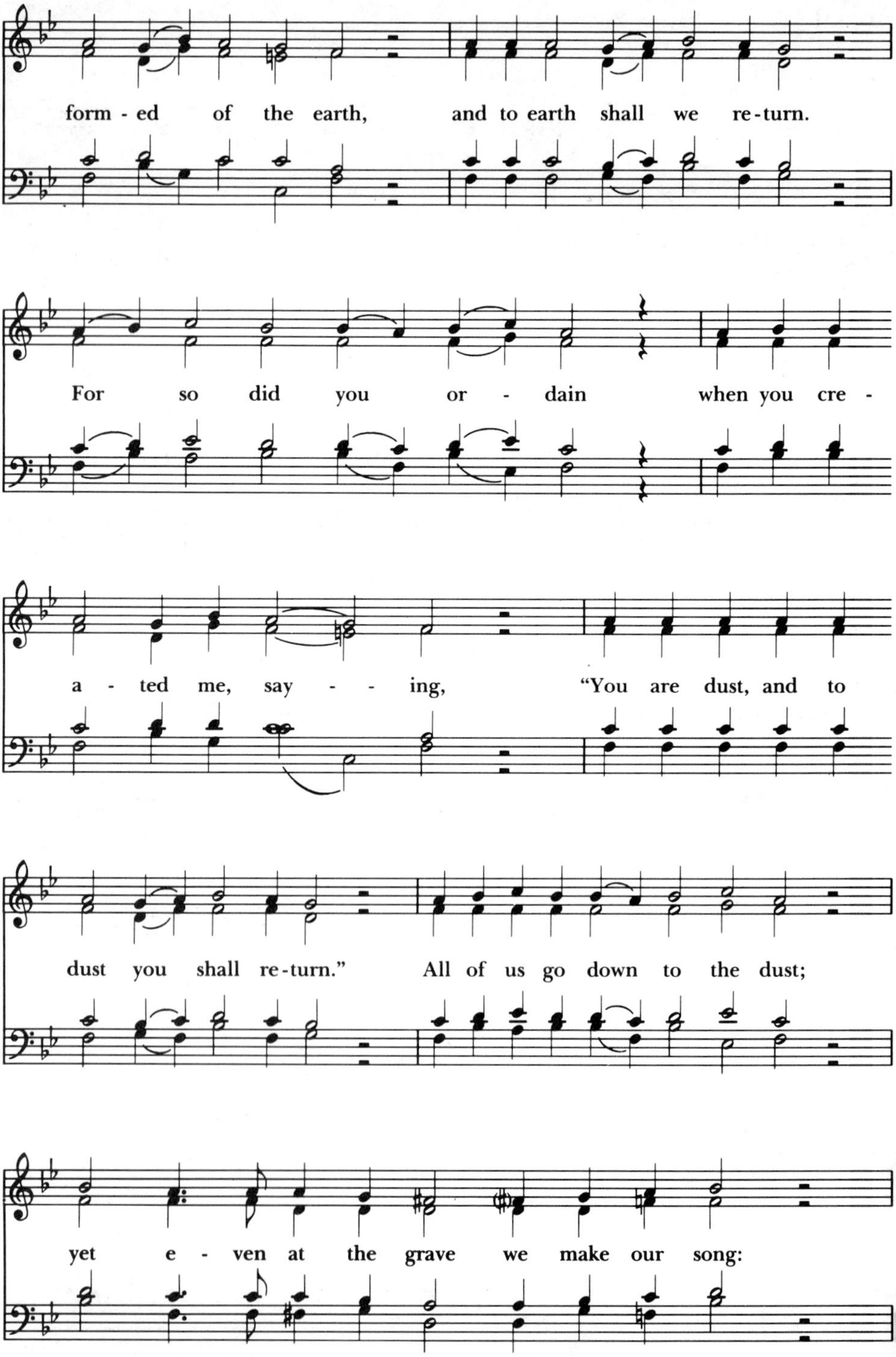
form - ed of the earth, and to earth shall we re - turn.
For so did you or - dain when you cre -
a - ted me, say - - - ing, "You are dust, and to
dust you shall re - turn." All of us go down to the dust;
yet e - ven at the grave we make our song:

D.C. al Fine
Al - le - lu - ia, al - le - lu - ia, al - le - lu - ia.

Words: Eastern Orthodox Memorial Service; tr. *The Book of Common Prayer,* 1979
Music: *Kontakion [Kievan chant],* from Eastern Orthodox Memorial Service; ed. Walter Parratt (1841-1924), alt. Irr.

Burial

356

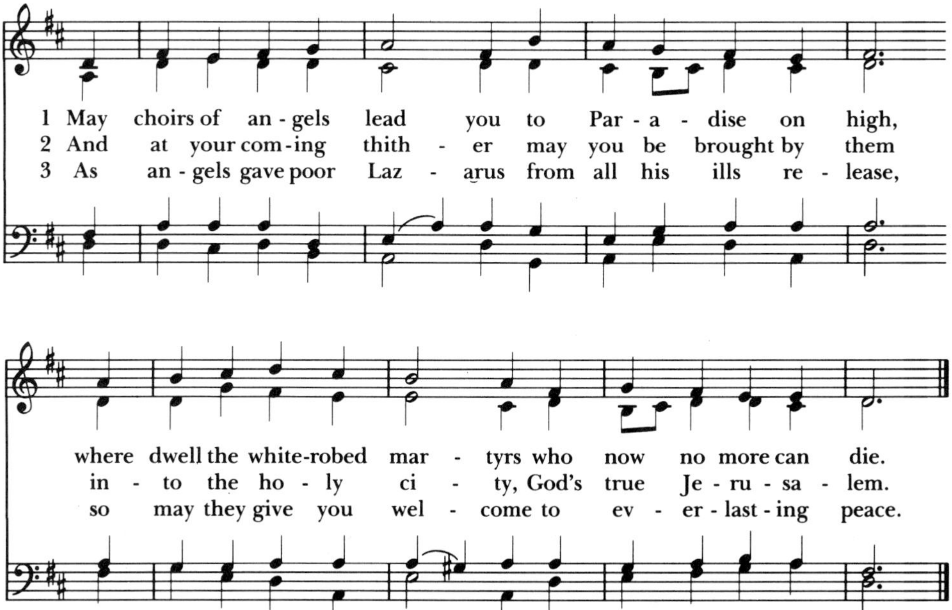
1 May choirs of an - gels lead you to Par - a - dise on high,
2 And at your com - ing thith - er may you be brought by them
3 As an - gels gave poor Laz - a-rus from all his ills re - lease,
where dwell the white-robed mar - tyrs who now no more can die.
in - to the ho - ly ci - ty, God's true Je - ru - sa - lem.
so may they give you wel - come to ev - er - last - ing peace.

Words: Latin; tr. F. Bland Tucker (1895-1984)
Music: *Christus, der ist mein Leben,* melody Melchior Vulpius (1560?-1616); harm. after Melchior Vulpius (1560?-1616)

♩=84
76. 76

1 Je - sus, Son of Ma - ry, fount of life a - lone,
3 Of - ten were they wound - ed in the dead - ly strife;
now we hail thee pres - ent on thine al - tar throne.
heal them, Good Phy - si - cian, with the balm of life.
Hum - bly we a - dore thee, Lord of end - less might,
Ev - ery taint of e - vil, frail - ty and de - cay,
in the mys - tic sym - bols veiled from earth - ly sight.
good and gra - cious Sa - vior, cleanse and purge a - way.

2 Think, O Lord, in mer - cy on the souls of those
4 Rest e - ter - nal grant them, af - ter wea - ry fight;
who, in faith gone from us, now in death re - pose.
shed on them the ra - diance of thy heaven - ly light.
Here mid stress and con - flict toils can nev - er cease;
Lead them on - ward, up - ward, to the ho - ly place,
there, the war - fare end - ed, bid them rest in peace.
where thy saints made per - fect gaze up - on thy face.

Another accompaniment, 314.

Words: Edmund Stuart Palmer (1856-1931)
Music: *Adoro devote,* French church melody, Mode 5, *Processionale,* 1697;
acc. Richard Proulx (b. 1937)

11 11. 11 11

1 Christ the Vic - to - ri - ous, give to your ser - vants
2 On - ly Im - mor - tal One, Might - y Cre - a - tor!
3 God - spo - ken pro - phe - cy, word at cre - a - tion:
4 Christ the Vic - to - ri - ous, give to your ser - vants
rest with your saints in the re - gions of light.
We are your crea - tures and chil - dren of earth.
"You came from dust and to dust shall re - turn."
rest with your saints in the re - gions of light.
Grief and pain end - ed, and sigh - ing no long - er,
From earth you formed us, both glo - rious and mor - tal,
Yet at the grave shall we raise up our glad song,
Grief and pain end - ed, and sigh - ing no long - er,
there may they find ev - er - last - ing life.
and to the earth shall we all re - turn.
"Al - le - lu - ia, al - le - lu - ia!"
there may they find ev - er - last - ing life.

This music in D. 569.

Words: Carl P. Daw, Jr. (b. 1944)
Music: *Russia*, Alexis Lvov (1799-1870)

𝅗𝅥=58
11 10. 11 9

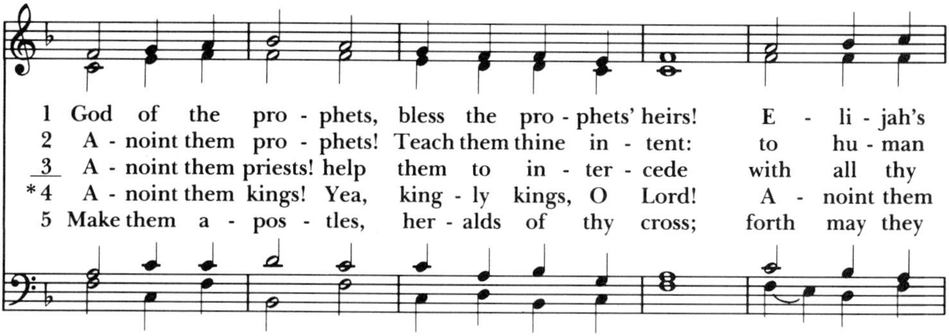
1 God of the pro - phets, bless the pro - phets' heirs! E - li - jah's
2 A - noint them pro - phets! Teach them thine in - tent: to hu - man
3 A - noint them priests! help them to in - ter - cede with all thy
*4 A - noint them kings! Yea, king - ly kings, O Lord! A - noint them
5 Make them a - pos - tles, her - alds of thy cross; forth may they

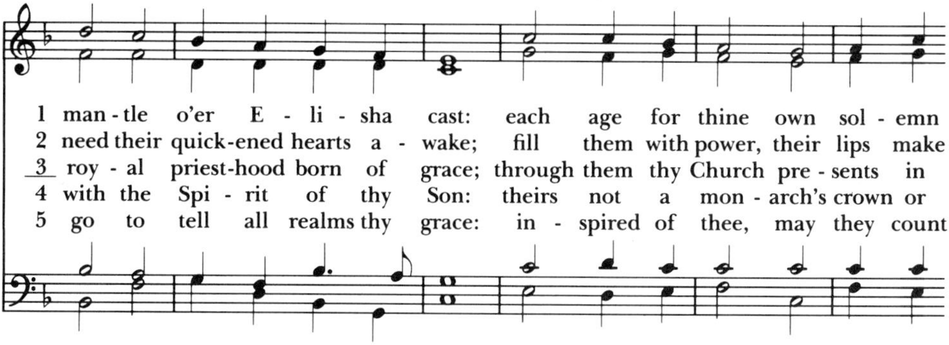
1 man - tle o'er E - li - sha cast: each age for thine own sol - emn
2 need their quick-ened hearts a - wake; fill them with power, their lips make
3 roy - al priest-hood born of grace; through them thy Church pre - sents in
4 with the Spi - rit of thy Son: theirs not a mon - arch's crown or
5 go to tell all realms thy grace: in - spired of thee, may they count

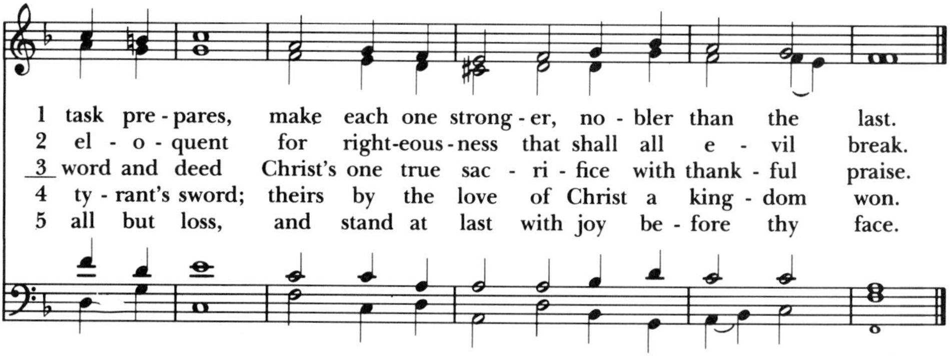
1 task pre - pares, make each one strong - er, no - bler than the last.
2 el - o - quent for right-eous - ness that shall all e - vil break.
3 word and deed Christ's one true sac - ri - fice with thank - ful praise.
4 ty - rant's sword; theirs by the love of Christ a king - dom won.
5 all but loss, and stand at last with joy be - fore thy face.

Words: St. 1-2 and 4-5, Denis Wortman (1835-1922), alt.; st. 3, Carl P. Daw, Jr. (b. 1944)
Music: *Toulon,* melody from *Pseaumes octante trois de David,* 1551, abridged; harm. Charles Winfred Douglas (1867-1944)

♩=96
10 10. 10 10

Consecration of a Church

1 On - ly - be - got - ten, Word of God e -
2 This is thy tem - ple; here thy pres - ence -
3 Here in our sick - ness heal - ing grace a -
*4 Hal - lowed this dwell - ing where the Lord a -
5 Lord, we be - seech thee, as we throng thy
6 God in three Per - sons, Fa - ther ev - er -
1 ter - nal, Lord of cre - a - tion, mer - ci - ful and
2 cham - ber; here may thy ser - vants, at the mys - tic
3 bound - eth, light in our blind - ness, in our toil re -
4 bid - eth, this is none o - ther than the gate of
5 tem - ple, by thy past bless - ings, by thy pres - ent
6 last - ing, Son co - e - ter - nal, ev - er - bless - ed
1 might - y, hear now thy ser - vants when their joy - ful
2 ban - quet, hum - bly a - dor - ing, take thy Bo - dy
3 fresh - ment: sin is for - giv - en, hope o'er fear pre -
4 hea - ven; strang - ers and pil - grims, seek - ing homes e -
5 boun - ty, fa - vor thy chil - dren, and with ten - der
6 Spi - rit, thine be the glo - ry, praise, and a - dor -

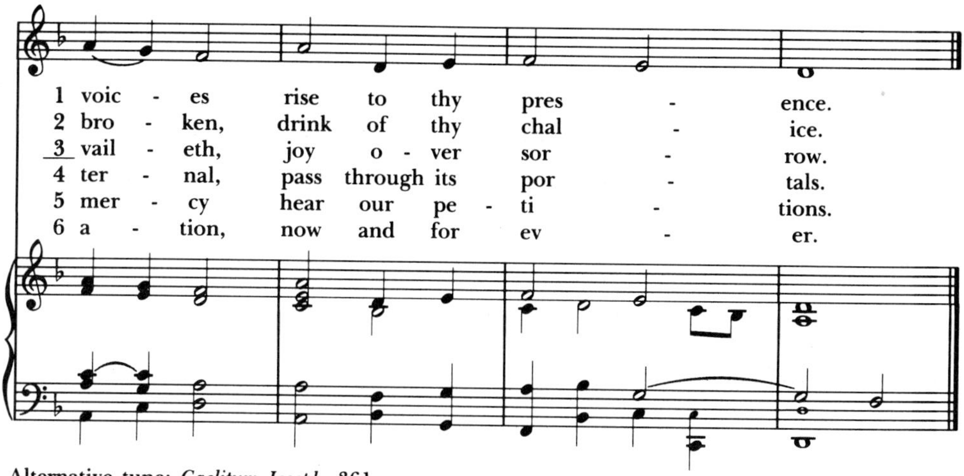
1 voic - es rise to thy pres - ence.
2 bro - ken, drink of thy chal - ice.
3 vail - eth, joy o - ver sor - row.
4 ter - nal, pass through its por - tals.
5 mer - cy hear our pe - ti - tions.
6 a - tion, now and for ev - er.

Alternative tune: *Caelitum Joseph,* 361.

Words: Latin, ca. 9th cent.; tr. Maxwell Julius Blacker (1822-1888)
Music: *Rouen,* melody from *Vesperale,* 1746; harm. Healey Willan (1880-1968)

𝅗𝅥 = 54
11 11. 11 5

1 On - ly - be - got - ten, Word of God e - ter - nal,
2 This is thy tem - ple; here thy pres - ence-cham - ber;
3 Here in our sick - ness heal - ing grace a - bound - eth,
*4 Hal - lowed this dwell - ing where the Lord a - bid - eth,
5 Lord, we be - seech thee, as we throng thy tem - ple,
6 God in three Per - sons, Fa - ther ev - er - last - ing,
1 Lord of cre - a - tion, mer - ci - ful and might - y,
2 here may thy ser - vants, at the mys - tic ban - quet,
3 light in our blind - ness, in our toil re - fresh - ment:
4 this is none o - ther than the gate of hea - ven;
5 by thy past bless - ings, by thy pres - ent boun - ty,
6 Son co - e - ter - nal, ev - er - bless - ed Spi - rit,
1 hear now thy ser - vants when their joy - ful voic - es
2 hum - bly a - dor - ing, take thy Bo - dy bro - ken,
3 sin is for - giv - en, hope o'er fear pre - vail - eth,
4 strang - ers and pil - grims seek - ing homes e - ter - nal,
5 fa - vor thy chil - dren, and with ten - der mer - cy
6 thine be the glo - ry, praise, and a - dor - a - tion,

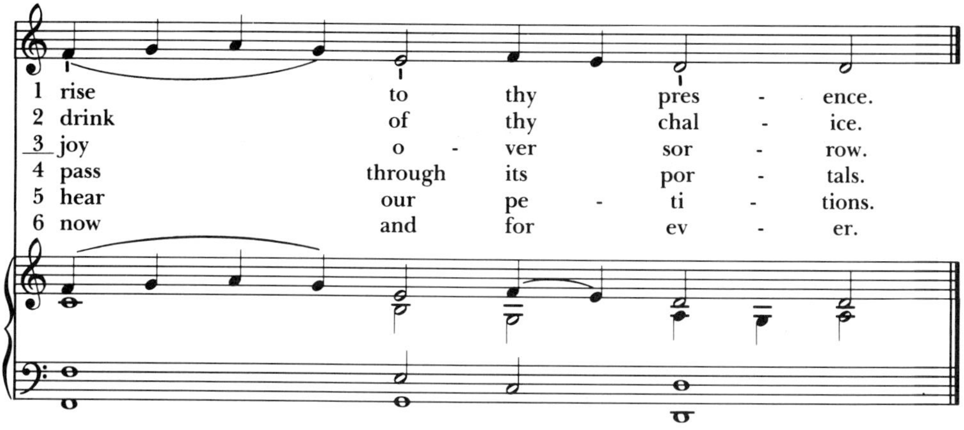
1 rise to thy pres - ence.
2 drink of thy chal - ice.
3 joy o - ver sor - row.
4 pass through its por - tals.
5 hear our pe - ti - tions.
6 now and for ev - er.

Another accompaniment, 261. Alternative tune: *Rouen*, 360.

Words: Latin, ca. 9th cent.; tr. Maxwell Julius Blacker (1822-1888)
Music: *Caelitum Joseph*, plainsong, Mode 1, Worcester MS., 13th cent.; ver. Schola Antiqua, 1983; acc. David Hurd (b. 1950)

𝅗𝅥 = 84
11 11. 11 5

Alternative accompaniment

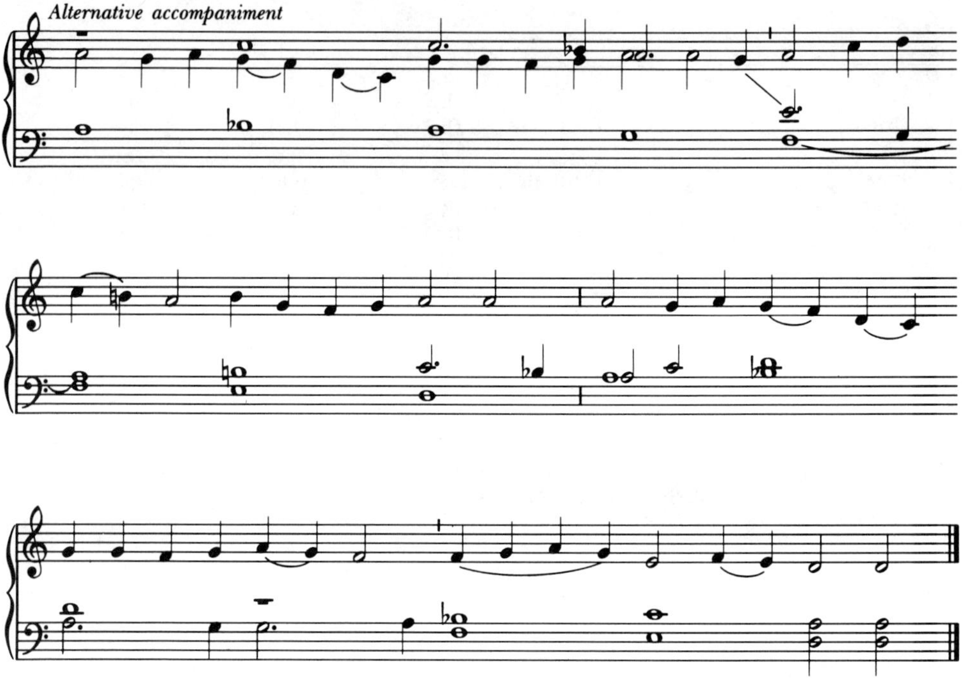

Music: *Caelitim Joseph,* plainsong, Mode 1, Worcester MS., 13th cent.; ver. Schola Antiqua, 1983; acc. John Blackley (b. 1936)

𝅗𝅥=84

1 Ho - ly, ho - ly ho - ly! Lord___ God Al - might - y!
*2 Ho - ly, ho - ly, ho - ly! All the saints a - dore thee,
3 Ho - ly, ho - ly, ho - ly! Though the dark-ness hide thee,
4 Ho - ly, ho - ly, ho - ly! Lord___ God Al - might - y!
Ear - ly in the morn - ing our song shall rise to thee:
cast - ing down their gold - en crowns a - round the glass - y sea;
though the sin - ful hu - man eye thy glo - ry may not see,
All thy works shall praise thy Name, in earth, and sky, and sea;
Ho - ly, ho - ly, ho - ly! Mer - ci - ful and might - y,
cher - u - bim and ser - a - phim fall - ing down be - fore thee,
on - ly thou art ho - ly; there is none be - side thee,
Ho - ly, ho - ly, ho - ly! Mer - ci - ful and might - y,
God in three Per - sons, bless - ed Trin - i - ty.
which wert, and art, and ev - er - more shalt be.
per - fect in power, in love, and pu - ri - ty.
God in three Per - sons, bless - ed Trin - i - ty.

Words: Reginald Heber (1783-1826), alt.
Music: *Nicaea,* John Bacchus Dykes (1823-1876)

𝅗𝅥 = 52
11 12. 12 10

1 An-cient of Days, who sit - test throned in glo - ry,
2 O ho - ly Fa - ther, who hast led thy chil - dren
5 O Tri-une God, with heart and voice a - dor - ing,
to thee all knees are bent, all voic - es pray;
in all the a - ges with the fire and cloud,
praise we the good - ness that doth crown our days;
thy love has blessed the wide world's won - drous sto - ry
through seas dry - shod, through wea - ry wastes be - wil - dering
pray we that thou wilt hear us, still im - plor - ing

1-2
Final Ending
with light and life since E - den's dawn-ing day.
to thee in rev - erent love our hearts are bowed.
thy love and fa - vor, kept to us al - (ways.) ways.
3 O ho-ly Je - sus, Lord of our sal - va - tion, call-ing the least,
4 O Ho-ly Ghost, the Lord and the Life - giv - er, thine is the quick -
the last, the lost to thee, sum-mon-ing all to share thy new cre-
ening power that gives in - crease: from thee have flowed, as from a might - y
a - tion, thou, Lord, by death hast won life's vic - to - ry.
riv - er, our faith and hope, our fel - low-ship and peace.

Words: William Croswell Doane (1832-1913), alt.
Music: *Coburn*, Alec Wyton (b. 1921)

𝅗𝅥=60
11 10. 11 10

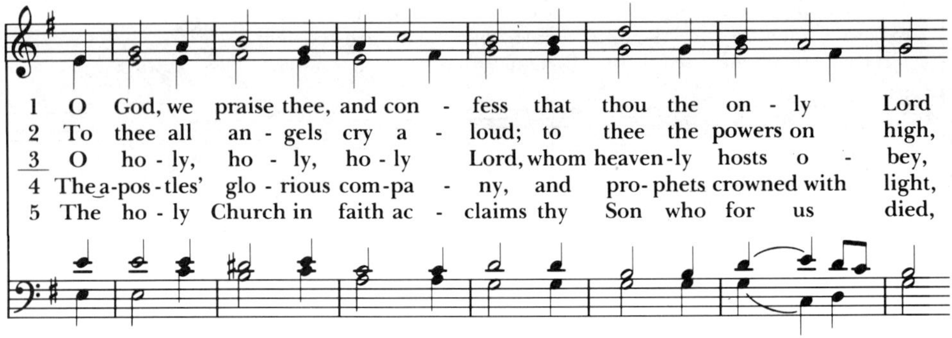
1 O God, we praise thee, and con - fess that thou the on - ly Lord
2 To thee all an - gels cry a - loud; to thee the powers on high,
3 O ho - ly, ho - ly, ho - ly Lord, whom heaven-ly hosts o - bey,
4 The a-pos-tles' glo - rious com-pa - ny, and pro-phets crowned with light,
5 The ho - ly Church in faith ac - claims thy Son who for us died,

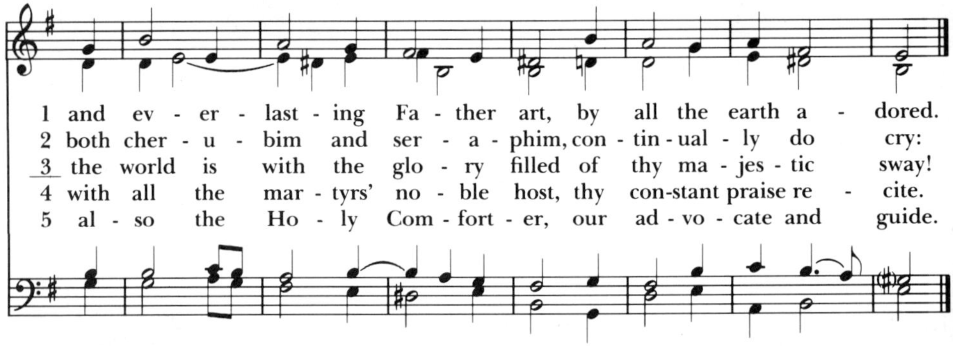
1 and ev - er - last - ing Fa - ther art, by all the earth a - dored.
2 both cher - u - bim and ser - a - phim, con - tin - ual - ly do cry:
3 the world is with the glo - ry filled of thy ma - jes - tic sway!
4 with all the mar - tyrs' no - ble host, thy con-stant praise re - cite.
5 al - so the Ho - ly Com - fort - er, our ad - vo - cate and guide.

*6 Thou art the King of glory, Christ,
the everlasting Son;
humbly thou cam'st to set us free,
nor Virgin womb didst shun.

*7 When thou hadst overcome death's sting
and opened heaven's door,
thou didst ascend to God's right hand
in glory evermore.

*8 When thou shalt come to be our judge,
bring us whom thou hast bought
to dwell on high with all thy saints
in joy surpassing thought.

The G♯ may be reserved for the final stanza.

Words: Para. of *Te Deum;* sts. 1-5, *A Supplement to the New Version of the Psalms of David,* 1698, alt.; sts. 6-8, ver. *Hymnal 1982*

Music: *Manchester,* melody and bass Thomas Ravenscroft (1592?-1635?); harm. *Hymnal 1982*

𝅗𝅥. = 42
CM

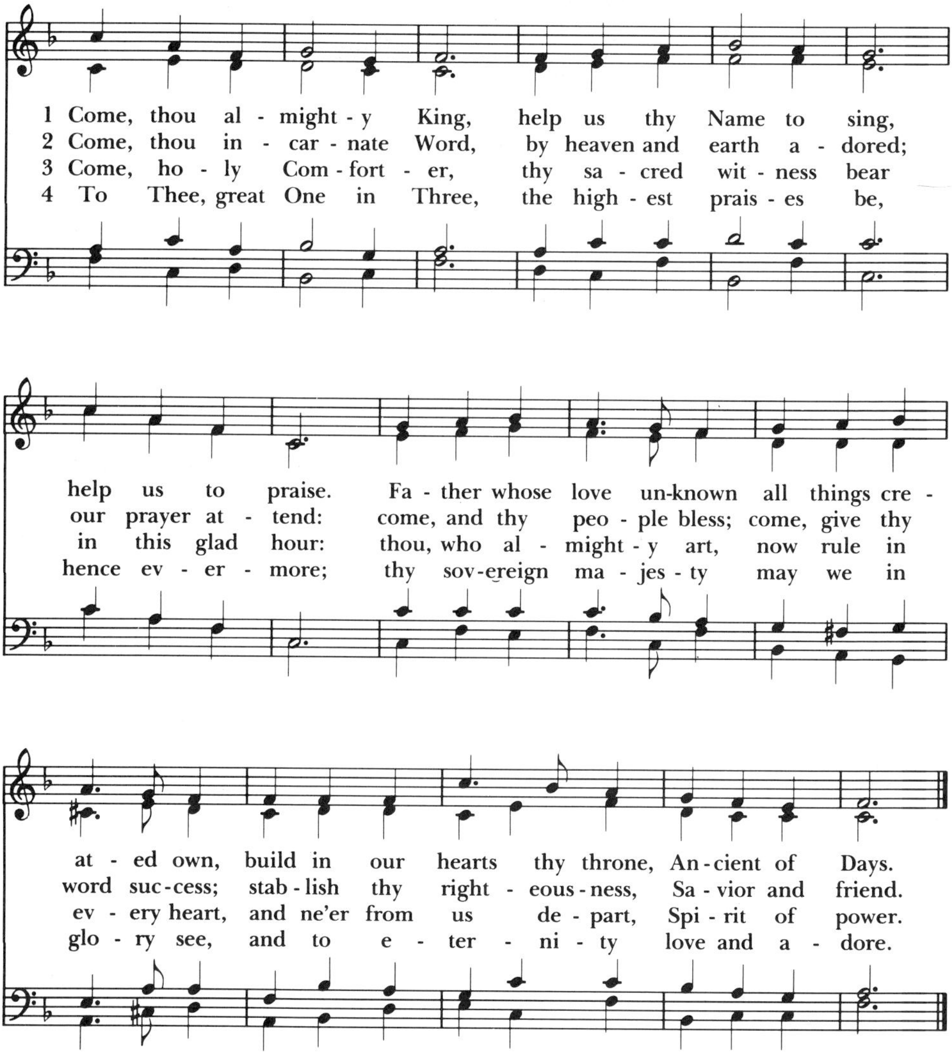
1 Come, thou al - might - y King, help us thy Name to sing,
2 Come, thou in - car - nate Word, by heaven and earth a - dored;
3 Come, ho - ly Com - fort - er, thy sa - cred wit - ness bear
4 To Thee, great One in Three, the high - est prais - es be,
help us to praise. Fa - ther whose love un-known all things cre -
our prayer at - tend: come, and thy peo - ple bless; come, give thy
in this glad hour: thou, who al - might - y art, now rule in
hence ev - er - more; thy sov-ereign ma - jes - ty may we in
at - ed own, build in our hearts thy throne, An - cient of Days.
word suc - cess; stab - lish thy right - eous - ness, Sa - vior and friend.
ev - ery heart, and ne'er from us de - part, Spi - rit of power.
glo - ry see, and to e - ter - ni - ty love and a - dore.

This music in G, 537.

Words: Anon. ca. 1757, alt.
Music: *Moscow,* Felice de Giardini (1716-1796); harm. *The New Hymnal,* 1916, based on *Hymns Ancient and Modern,* 1875, and Lowell Mason (1792-1872)

𝅗𝅥. = 40
664. 6664

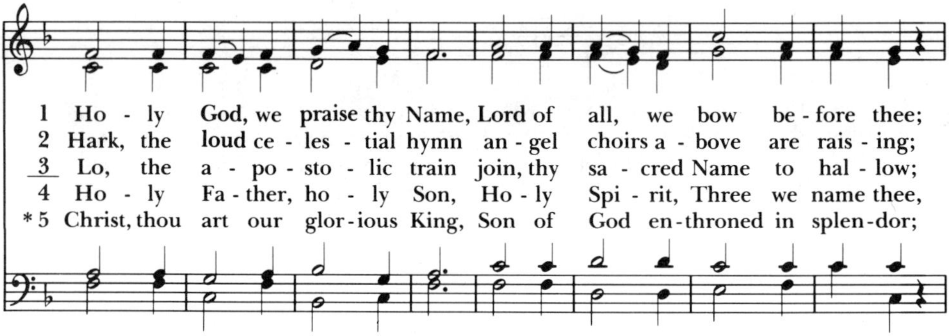
1 Ho - ly God, we praise thy Name, Lord of all, we bow be - fore thee;
2 Hark, the loud ce - les - tial hymn an - gel choirs a - bove are rais - ing;
3 Lo, the a - po - sto - lic train join, thy sa - cred Name to hal - low;
4 Ho - ly Fa - ther, ho - ly Son, Ho - ly Spi - rit, Three we name thee,
*5 Christ, thou art our glor - ious King, Son of God en - throned in splen - dor;

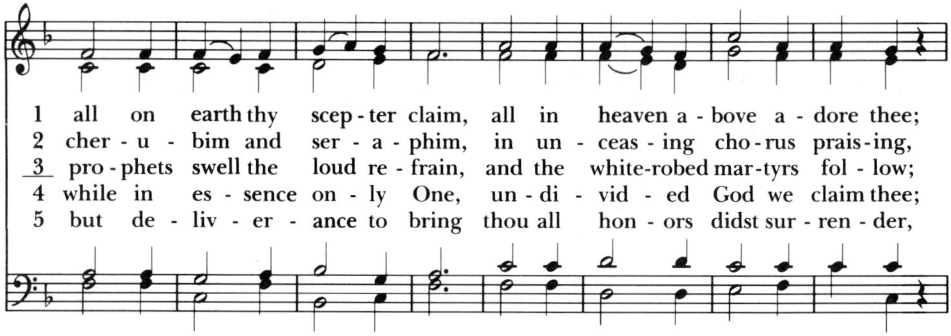
1 all on earth thy scep - ter claim, all in heaven a - bove a - dore thee;
2 cher - u - bim and ser - a - phim, in un - ceas - ing cho - rus prais - ing,
3 pro - phets swell the loud re - frain, and the white-robed mar - tyrs fol - low;
4 while in es - sence on - ly One, un - di - vid - ed God we claim thee;
5 but de - liv - er - ance to bring thou all hon - ors didst sur - ren - der,

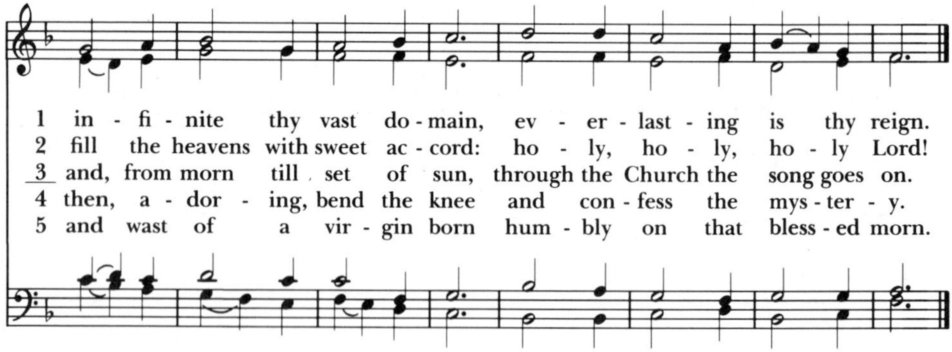
1 in - fi - nite thy vast do - main, ev - er - last - ing is thy reign.
2 fill the heavens with sweet ac - cord: ho - ly, ho - ly, ho - ly Lord!
3 and, from morn till set of sun, through the Church the song goes on.
4 then, a - dor - ing, bend the knee and con - fess the mys - ter - y.
5 and wast of a vir - gin born hum - bly on that bless - ed morn.

*6 Thou didst take the sting from death,
Son of God, as Savior given;
on the cross thy dying breath
opened wide the realm of heaven.
In the glory of that land
thou art set at God's right hand.

*7 As our judge thou wilt appear.
Savior, who hast died to win us.
help thy servants, drawing near.
Lord, renew our hearts within us.
Grant that with thy saints we may
dwell in everlasting day.

Words: Para. of *Te Deum;* sts. 1-4, Ignaz Franz (1719-1790); tr. Clarence Walworth (1820-1900).
Sts. 5-7, F. Bland Tucker (1895-1984)

Music: *Grosser Gott,* melody from *Katholisches Gesangbuch,* 1686; alt. *Cantate,* 1851;
harm. Charles Winfred Douglas (1867-1944), after Conrad Kocher (1786-1872)

𝅗𝅥. = 44
78. 78. 77

1 Round the Lord in glo - ry seat - ed cher - u - bim and ser - a - phim
2 Heaven is still with glo - ry ring-ing, earth takes up the an - gels' cry,
3 "Lord, thy glo - ry fills the hea - ven, earth is with thy full - ness stored;
filled his tem-ple, and re - peat - ed each to each the al - ter - nate hymn:
"Ho - ly, ho - ly, ho - ly," sing-ing, "Lord of hosts, the Lord Most High."
un - to thee be glo - ry giv - en, ho - ly, ho - ly, ho - ly, Lord."
"Lord, thy glo - ry fills the hea-ven, earth is with thy full - ness stored;
With his ser - aph train be - fore him, with his ho - ly Church be - low,
Thus thy glo - rious Name con - fess-ing, with thine an - gel hosts we cry
un - to thee be glo - ry giv - en, ho - ly, ho - ly, ho - ly Lord."
thus u - nite we to a - dore him, bid we thus our an - them flow:
"Ho - ly, ho - ly, ho - ly," bless-ing thee, the Lord of hosts Most High.

Words: Richard Mant (1776-1848)
Music: *Rustington*, Charles Hubert Hastings Parry (1848-1918)

𝅗𝅥=52
87. 87. D

Descant
4 God the Lord, through ev - ery na-tion let thy won-drous mer-cies shine. In the song of thy sal - va - tion ev - ery tongue and race com-bine. Great Je-ho-vah,
1 Ho - ly Fa - ther, great Cre - a - tor, source of mer - cy, love, and peace, look up - on the Me - di - a - tor, clothe us with his right-eous-ness; heaven - ly Fa - ther,
2 Ho - ly Je - sus, Lord of glo - ry, whom an - gel - ic hosts pro-claim, while we hear thy won - drous sto - ry, meet and wor - ship in thy Name, dear Re-deem - er,
3 Ho - ly Spi - rit, Sanc - ti - fi - er, come with unc - tion from a - bove, touch our hearts with sa - cred fire, fill them with the Sa - vior's love. Source of com - fort,
4 God the Lord, through ev - ery na - tion let thy won-drous mer - cies shine. In the song of thy sal - va - tion ev - ery tongue and race com - bine. Great Je - ho - vah,

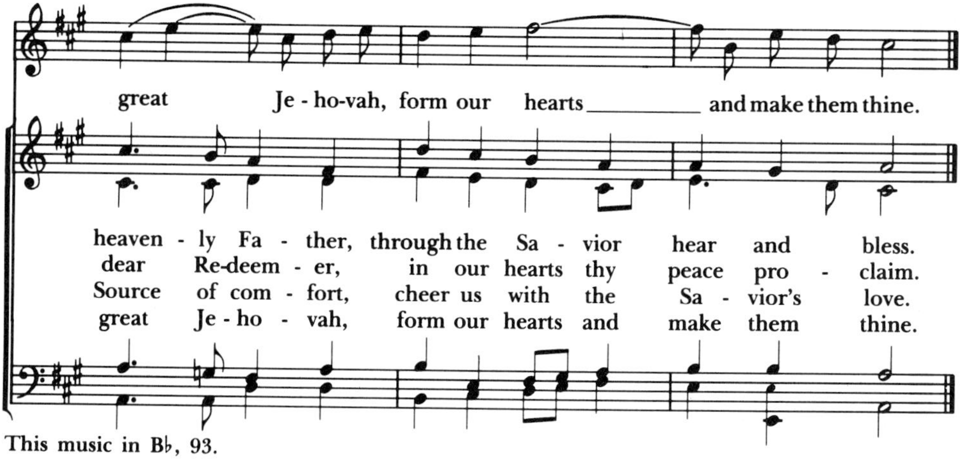
great Je - ho-vah, form our hearts and make them thine.
heaven - ly Fa - ther, through the Sa - vior hear and bless.
dear Re-deem - er, in our hearts thy peace pro - claim.
Source of com - fort, cheer us with the Sa - vior's love.
great Je - ho - vah, form our hearts and make them thine.

This music in B♭, 93.

Words: Alexander Viets Griswold (1766-1843), alt.
Music: *Regent Square,* Henry Thomas Smart (1813-1879); desc. Craig Sellar Lang (1891-1971)

𝅗𝅥 = 56
87. 87. 87

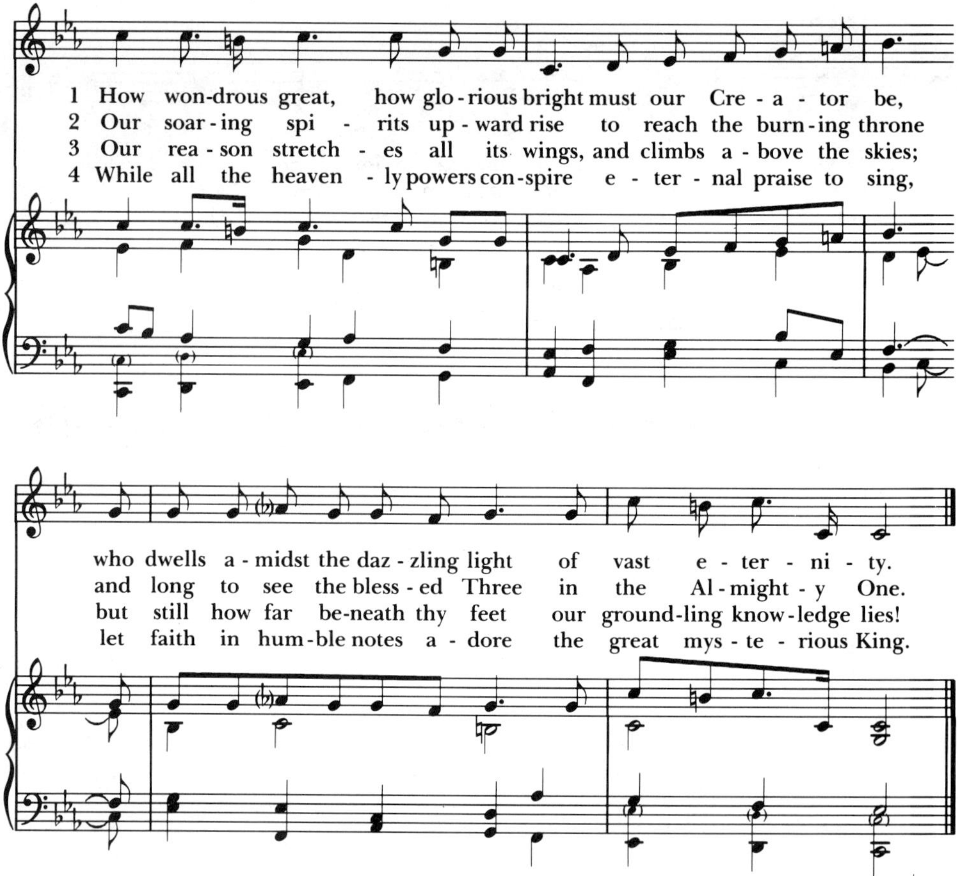
1 How won-drous great, how glo-rious bright must our Cre-a-tor be,
2 Our soar-ing spi-rits up-ward rise to reach the burn-ing throne
3 Our rea-son stretch-es all its wings, and climbs a-bove the skies;
4 While all the heaven-ly powers con-spire e-ter-nal praise to sing,
who dwells a-midst the daz-zling light of vast e-ter-ni-ty.
and long to see the bless-ed Three in the Al-might-y One.
but still how far be-neath thy feet our ground-ling know-ledge lies!
let faith in hum-ble notes a-dore the great mys-te-rious King.

Words: Isaac Watts (1674-1748), alt.; st. 3, alt. Caryl Micklem (b. 1925)
Music: *Shorney,* Alec Wyton (b. 1921)

♩=63
CM

Alternative accompaniment

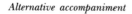

Music: *Shorney,* Alec Wyton (b. 1921) ♩=63

The Holy Trinity 370

1. I bind un - to my - self to - day the strong Name
of the Trin - i - ty, by in - vo - ca - tion
of the same, the Three in One, and One in Three.

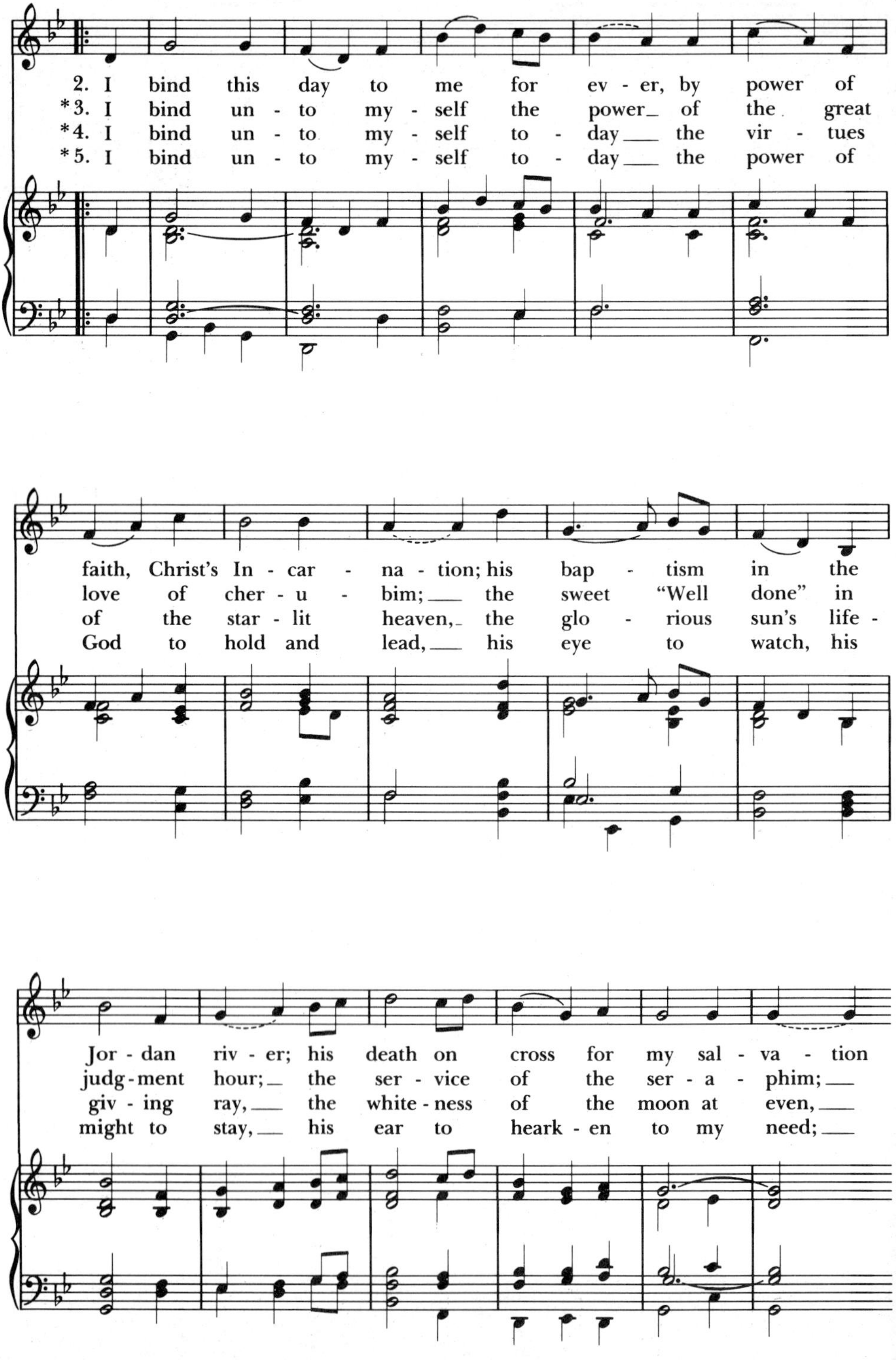
2. I bind this day to me for ev - er, by power of
*3. I bind un - to my - self the power of the great
*4. I bind un - to my - self to - day the vir - tues
*5. I bind un - to my - self to - day the power of
faith, Christ's In - car - na - tion; his bap - tism in the
love of cher - u - bim; the sweet "Well done" in
of the star - lit heaven, the glo - rious sun's life -
God to hold and lead, his eye to watch, his
Jor - dan riv - er; his death on cross for my sal - va - tion
judg - ment hour; the ser - vice of the ser - a - phim;
giv - ing ray, the white - ness of the moon at even,
might to stay, his ear to heark - en to my need;

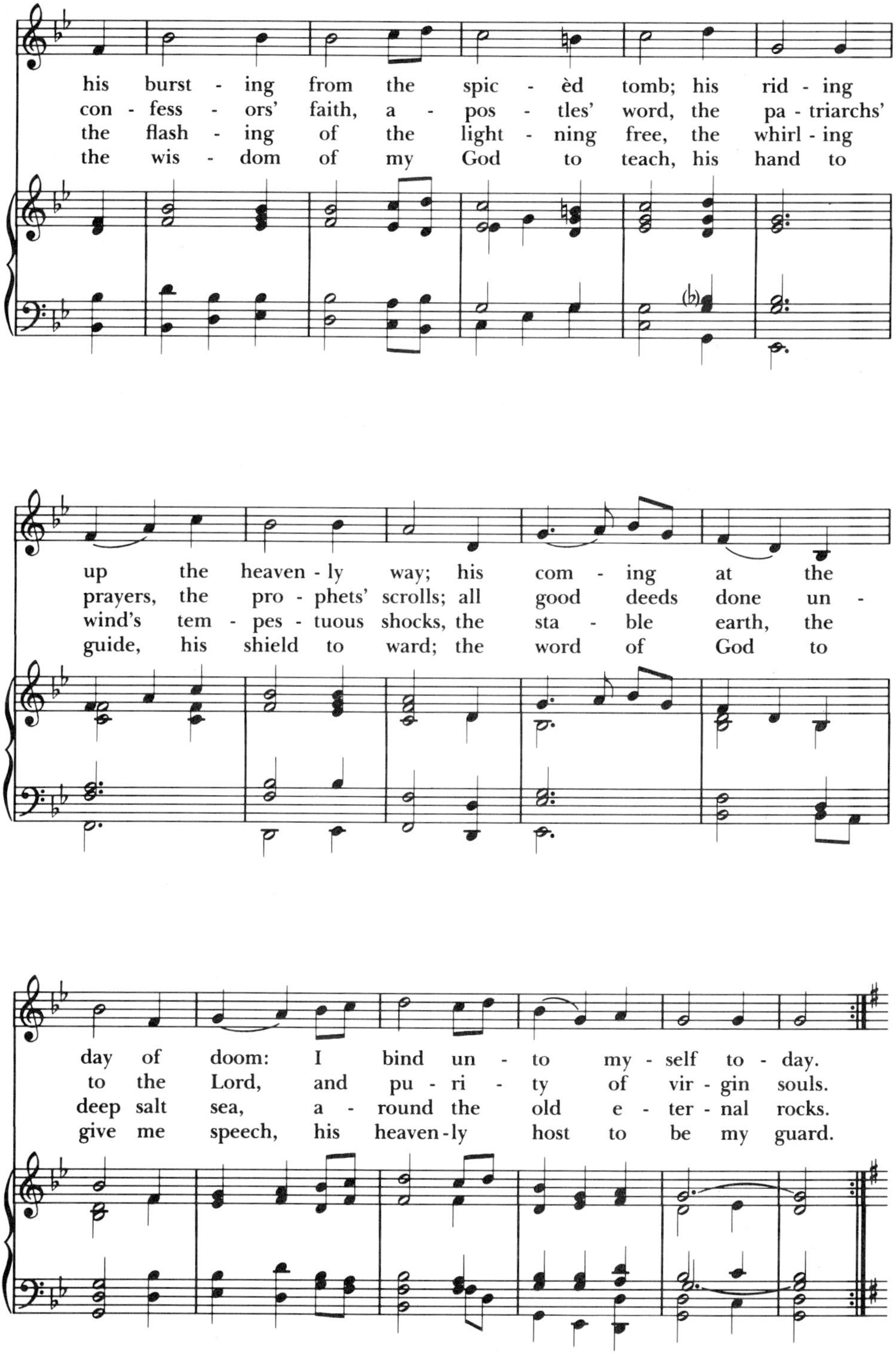
his burst - ing from the spic - èd tomb; his rid - ing
con - fess - ors' faith, a - pos - tles' word, the pa - triarchs'
the flash - ing of the light - ning free, the whirl - ing
the wis - dom of my God to teach, his hand to
up the heaven - ly way; his com - ing at the
prayers, the pro - phets' scrolls; all good deeds done un -
wind's tem - pes - tuous shocks, the sta - ble earth, the
guide, his shield to ward; the word of God to
day of doom: I bind un - to my - self to - day.
to the Lord, and pu - ri - ty of vir - gin souls.
deep salt sea, a - round the old e - ter - nal rocks.
give me speech, his heaven - ly host to be my guard.

*6. Christ be with me, Christ with-in me, Christ be-hind me, Christ be-fore me,
Christ be-neath me, Christ a-bove me, Christ in qui-et, Christ in dan-ger,
Christ be-side me, Christ to win me, Christ to com-fort and re-store me,
Christ in hearts of all that love me, Christ in mouth of friend and stran-ger.
7. I bind un-to my-self the Name, the strong Name
of the Trin-i-ty, by in-vo-ca-tion

of the same, the Three in One, and One in Three.
Of whom all na - ture hath cre - a - tion, e - ter - nal
Fa - ther, Spi - rit, Word: praise to the Lord of
my sal - va - tion, sal - va - tion is of Christ the Lord.

Words: Att. Patrick (372-466); tr. Cecil Frances Alexander (1818-1895)
Music: *St. Patrick's Breastplate,* Irish melody; adapt. Charles Villiers Stanford (1852-1924); St. 6, *Deirdre,* Irish melody; harm. Ralph Vaughan Williams (1872-1958)

o. = 44
♩ = 72
LMD

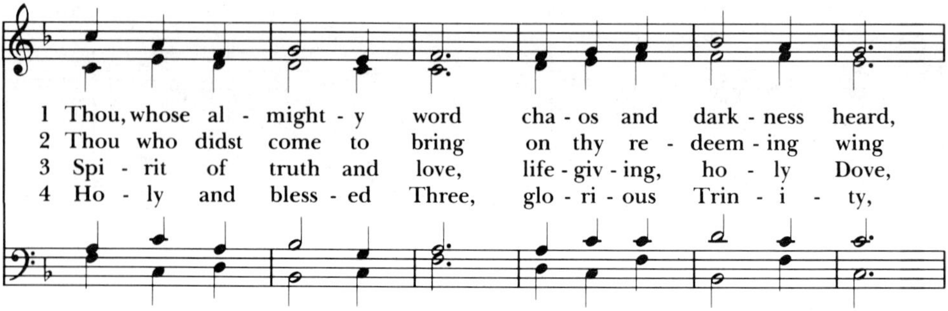
1 Thou, whose al - might - y word cha - os and dark - ness heard,
2 Thou who didst come to bring on thy re - deem - ing wing
3 Spi - rit of truth and love, life - giv - ing, ho - ly Dove,
4 Ho - ly and bless - ed Three, glo - ri - ous Trin - i - ty,

and took their flight; hear us, we hum - bly pray, and, where the
heal - ing and sight, health to the sick in mind, sight to the
speed forth thy flight! Move on the wa - ters' face bear - ing the
wis - dom, love, might; bound - less as o - cean tide, roll - ing in

Gos - pel day sheds not its glo - rious ray, let there be light!
in - ly blind, now to all hu - man-kind, let there be light!
gifts of grace, and, in earth's dark - est place, let there be light!
full - est pride, through the world, far and wide, let there be light!

This music in G, 537.

Words: John Marriott (1780-1825), alt.
Music: *Moscow*, Felice de Giardini (1716-1796); harm. *The New Hymnal*, 1916, based on *Hymns Ancient and Modern*, 1875, and Lowell Mason (1792-1872)

𝅗𝅥. = 40
664. 6664

372

1 Praise to the liv - ing God! All prais - ed be his Name
2 Form - less, all love - ly forms de - clare his love - li - ness;
3 His Spi - rit flow - eth free, high surg - ing where it will:
4 E - ter - nal life hath he im - plant - ed in the soul;
who was, and is, and is to be, for ay the same.
ho - ly, no ho - li - ness of earth can his ex - press.
in pro-phet's word he spoke of old; he speak - eth still.
his love shall be our strength and stay while a - ges roll.
The one e - ter - nal God ere aught that now ap - pears:
Lo, he is Lord of all. Cre - a - tion speaks his praise,
Es - tab-lished is his law, and change - less it shall stand,
Praise to the liv - ing God! All prais - ed be his Name
the first, the last, be - yond all thought his time - less years!
and ev - ery-where a - bove, be - low, his will o - beys.
deep writ up - on the hu - man heart, on sea, on land.
who was, and is, and is to be, for ay the same.

Words: Medieval Jewish liturgy; tr. Max Landsberg (1845-1928) and Newton M. Mann (1836-1926) — 𝅗𝅥=48

Music: *Leoni,* Hebrew melody; harm. *Hymns Ancient and Modern,* 1875, alt. — 66. 84. D

1 Praise the Lord! ye heavens a - dore him; praise him an - gels in the
2 Praise the Lord! for he is glo - rious; nev - er shall his prom - ise
height; sun and moon, re - joice be - fore him; praise him, all ye
fail; God hath made his saints vic - to - rious; sin and death shall
stars of light. Praise the Lord! for he hath spo - ken;
not pre - vail. Praise the God of our sal - va - tion!
worlds his might - y voice o - beyed; laws which nev - er shall be
Hosts on high, his power pro - claim; heaven and earth, and all cre -

bro - ken for their guid-ance he hath made.
a - tion, laud and mag - ni - fy his Name.

Alternative tune: *Austria*, 522.

Words: Anon., *Foundling Hospital Psalms and Hymns*, 1797; para. of Psalm 148
Music: *Daniel's Tune*, David N. Johnson (b. 1922)

𝅗𝅥 = 72
87. 87. D

Praise to God

374

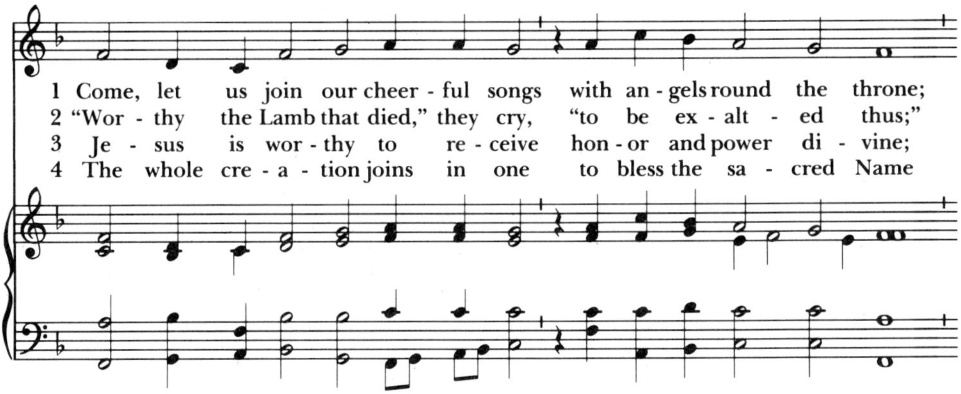
1 Come, let us join our cheer - ful songs with an - gels round the throne;
2 "Wor - thy the Lamb that died," they cry, "to be ex - alt - ed thus;"
3 Je - sus is wor - thy to re - ceive hon - or and power di - vine;
4 The whole cre - a - tion joins in one to bless the sa - cred Name

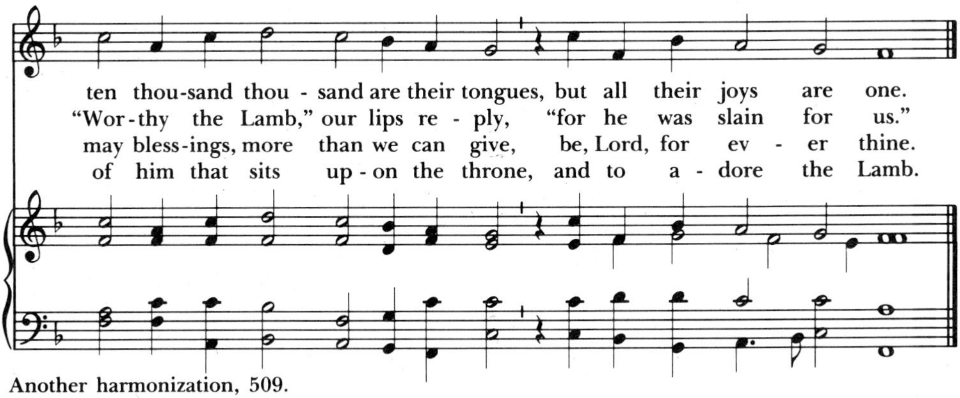
ten thou-sand thou - sand are their tongues, but all their joys are one.
"Wor-thy the Lamb," our lips re - ply, "for he was slain for us."
may bless-ings, more than we can give, be, Lord, for ev - er thine.
of him that sits up - on the throne, and to a - dore the Lamb.

Another harmonization, 509.

Words: Isaac Watts (1674–1748); para. of *A Song to the Lamb*
Music: *Nun danket all und bringet Ehr,* att. Johann Cruger (1598–1662), alt.

𝅗𝅥 = 58
CM

Praise to God

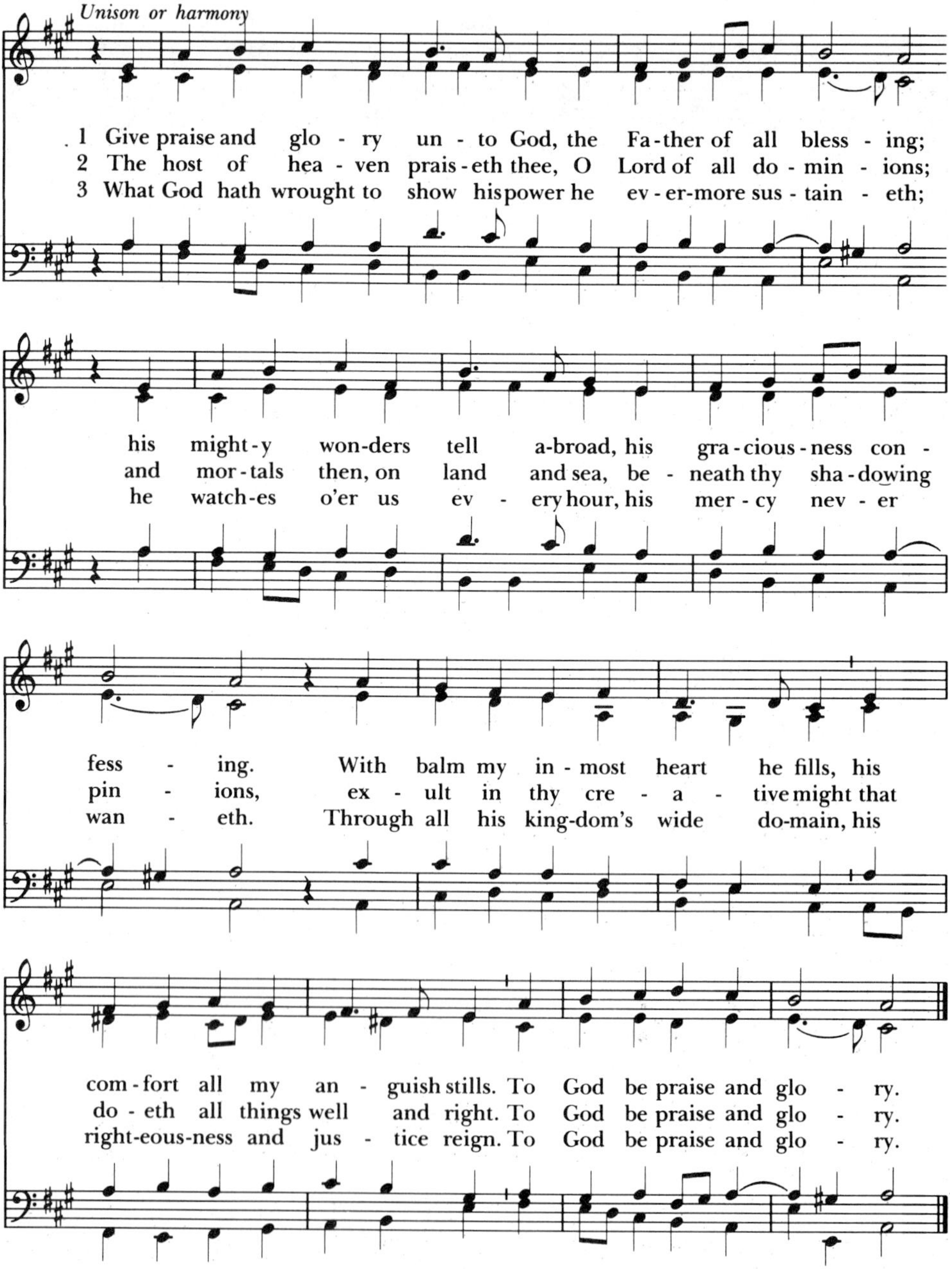
Unison or harmony
1 Give praise and glo - ry un - to God, the Fa-ther of all bless - ing;
2 The host of hea - ven prais-eth thee, O Lord of all do - min - ions;
3 What God hath wrought to show his power he ev-er-more sus - tain - eth;
his might-y won-ders tell a-broad, his gra-cious-ness con -
and mor-tals then, on land and sea, be - neath thy sha-dowing
he watch-es o'er us ev - ery hour, his mer - cy nev - er
fess - ing. With balm my in - most heart he fills, his
pin - ions, ex - ult in thy cre - a - tive might that
wan - eth. Through all his king-dom's wide do-main, his
com-fort all my an - guish stills. To God be praise and glo - ry.
do - eth all things well and right. To God be praise and glo - ry.
right-eous-ness and jus - tice reign. To God be praise and glo - ry.

Words: Johann Jacob Schütz (1640-1690); tr. Arthur William Farlander (1898-1952) and Charles Winfred Douglas (1867-1944), alt.

Music: *Du Lebensbrot Herr Jesu Christ,* Peter Sohren (1630?-1692?); adapt. Johann Anastasius Freylinghausen (1670-1739), alt.

𝅗𝅥=50
87. 87. 887

1 Joy - ful, joy - ful, we a - dore thee, God of glo - ry, Lord of love;
2 All thy works with joy sur-round thee, earth and heaven re - flect thy rays,
3 Thou art giv - ing and for - giv - ing, ev - er bless - ing, ev - er blest,
hearts un - fold like flowers be-fore thee, prais - ing thee, their sun a - bove.
stars and an - gels sing a-round thee, cen - ter of un - bro - ken praise.
well - spring of the joy of liv - ing, o - cean-depth of hap - py rest!
Melt the clouds of sin and sad - ness; drive the dark of doubt a - way;
field and for - est, vale and moun-tain, bloom - ing mea-dow, flash - ing sea,
Thou our Fa - ther, Christ our Bro - ther: all who live in love are thine;
giv - er of im - mor - tal glad-ness, fill us with the light of day.
chant - ing bird and flow - ing foun-tain, call us to re - joice in thee.
teach us how to love each o - ther, lift us to the joy di-vine.

Words: Henry Van Dyke (1852-1933)
Music: *Hymn to Joy*, Ludwig van Beethoven (1770-1827); adapt. Edward Hodges (1796-1867), alt.

𝅗𝅥=60
87. 87. D

Praise to God

Unison or harmony

1 All peo - ple that on earth do dwell, sing to the Lord with
2 Know that the Lord is God in - deed; with - out our aid he
3 O en - ter then his gates with praise, ap - proach with joy his
4 For why? the Lord our God is good, his mer - cy is for
*5 To Fa - ther, Son, and Ho - ly Ghost, the God whom heaven and

1 cheer - ful voice: him serve with mirth, his praise forth
2 did us make: we are his folk, he doth us
3 courts un - to; praise, laud, and bless his Name al -
4 ev - er sure; his truth at all times firm - ly
5 earth a - dore, from men and from the an - gel

1 tell, come ye be - fore him and re - joice.
2 feed, and for his sheep he doth us take.
3 ways, for it is seem - ly so to do.
4 stood, and shall from age to age en - dure.
5 host be praise and glo - ry ev - er - more.

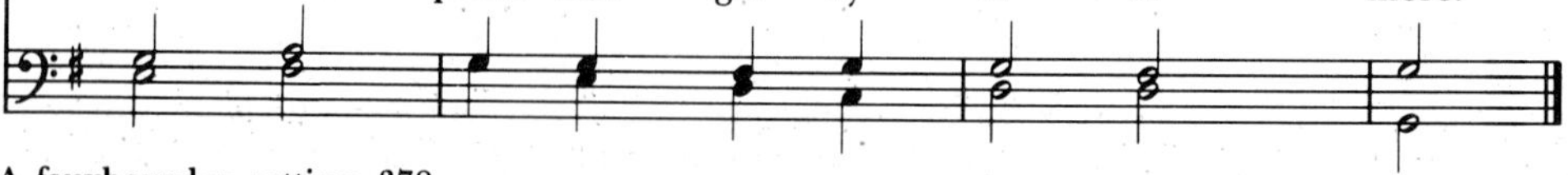

A fauxbourdon setting, 378.

Words: William Kethe (d. 1608?); para. of Psalm 100
Music: *Old 100th,* melody from *Pseaumes octante trois de David,* 1551, alt.; harm. after Louis Bourgeois (1510?-1561?)

𝅗𝅥 = 50
LM

Praise to God

378

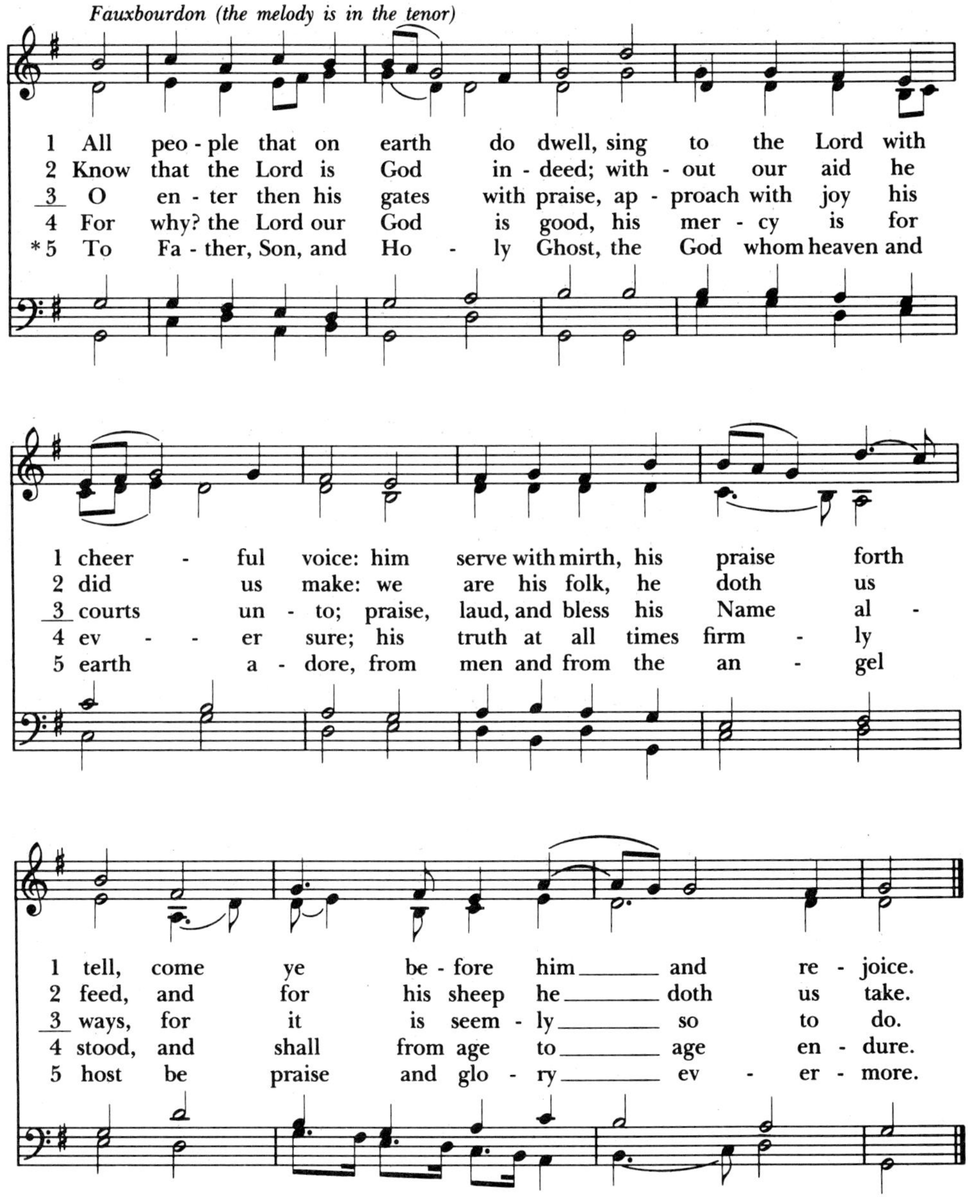
Fauxbourdon (the melody is in the tenor)
1 All peo - ple that on earth do dwell, sing to the Lord with
2 Know that the Lord is God in - deed; with - out our aid he
3 O en - ter then his gates with praise, ap - proach with joy his
4 For why? the Lord our God is good, his mer - cy is for
*5 To Fa - ther, Son, and Ho - ly Ghost, the God whom heaven and
1 cheer - ful voice: him serve with mirth, his praise forth
2 did us make: we are his folk, he doth us
3 courts un - to; praise, laud, and bless his Name al -
4 ev - - er sure; his truth at all times firm - ly
5 earth a - dore, from men and from the an - gel
1 tell, come ye be - fore him and re - joice.
2 feed, and for his sheep he doth us take.
3 ways, for it is seem - ly so to do.
4 stood, and shall from age to age en - dure.
5 host be praise and glo - ry ev - er - more.

Another harmonization, 377.

Words: William Kethe (d. 1608?); para. of Psalm 100
Music: *Old 100th*, melody from *Pseaumes octante trois de David*, 1551, alt.; fauxbourdon and harm. John Dowland (1563-1626), alt.

𝅗𝅥=50
LM

1 God is Love, let heaven a - dore him; God is Love, let
2 God is Love; and love en - folds us, all the world in
3 God is Love; and though with blind-ness sin af - flicts all
earth re - joice; let cre - a - tion sing be - fore him
one em - brace: with un - fail - ing grasp God holds us,
hu - man life, God's e - ter - nal lov - ing - kind-ness
and ex - alt him with one voice. God who laid the earth's foun -
ev - ery child of ev - ery race. And when hu - man hearts are
guides us through our earth - ly strife. Sin and death and hell shall
da - tion, God who spread the heavens a - bove, God who breathes through
break-ing un - der sor - row's i - ron rod, then we find that
nev - er o'er us fi - nal tri - umph gain; God is Love, so

all cre - a - tion: God is Love, e - ter - nal Love.
self - same ach - ing deep with - in the heart of God.
Love for ev - er o'er the u - ni - verse must reign.

This music in D, 511.

Words: Timothy Rees (1874-1939), alt.
Music: *Abbot's Leigh*, Cyril Vincent Taylor (b. 1907)

♩=92
87. 87. D

Praise to God

380

1 From all that dwell be - low the skies let
2 E - ter - nal are thy mer - cies, Lord, and
*3 Praise God, from whom all bless - ings flow; praise
the Cre - a - tor's praise a - rise! Let the Re - deem - er's
truth e - ter - nal is thy word: thy praise shall sound from
him, all crea - tures here be - low; praise him a - bove, ye
Name be sung through ev - ery land, by ev - ery tongue!
shore to shore till suns shall rise and set no more.
heaven - ly host: praise Fa - ther, Son, and Ho - ly Ghost.

A fauxbourdon setting, 378.

Words: Isaac Watts (1674-1748), para. of Psalm 117. St. 3, Thomas Ken (1637-1711)
Music: *Old 100th*, melody from *Pseaumes octante trois de David*, 1551, alt.; harm. after Louis Bourgeois (1510?-1561?)

𝅗𝅥=50
LM

1 Thy strong word did cleave the dark - ness; at thy
2 Lo, on those who dwelt in dark - ness, dark as
3 Thy strong word be - speaks us right - eous; bright with
4 God the Fa - ther, Light - Cre - a - tor, to thee
speak - ing it was done; for cre - a - ted
night and deep as death, broke the light of
thine own ho - li - ness, glo - rious now, we
laud and hon - or be; to thee, Light of
light we thank thee, while thine or - dered sea - sons run:
thy sal - va - tion, breathed thine own life - giv - ing breath:
press toward glo - ry, and our lives our hopes con - fess:
Light be - got - ten, praise be sung e - ter - nal - ly;

3
Al - le - lu - ia, al - le - lu - ia! Praise to
Al - le - lu - ia, al - le - lu - ia! Praise to
Al - le - lu - ia, al - le - lu - ia! Praise to
Ho - ly Spi - rit, Light - Re - veal - er, glo - ry,
thee who light dost send! Al - le - lu - ia,
thee who light dost send! Al - le - lu - ia,
thee who light dost send! Al - le - lu - ia,
glo - ry be to thee; mor - tals, an - gels,
al - le - lu - ia! Al - le - lu - ia with - out end!
al - le - lu - ia! Al - le - lu - ia with - out end!
al - le - lu - ia! Al - le - lu - ia with - out end!
now and ev - er praise the Ho - ly Tri - ni - ty.

The Alleluias in stanzas 1-3 may be sung antiphonally.

Words: Martin H. Franzmann (1907-1976)
Music: *Ton-y-Botel,* Thomas John Williams (1869-1944)

𝅗𝅥 = 92
87. 87. D

1 King of glo - ry, King of peace, I will love thee;
2 Where-fore with my ut - most art, I will sing thee;
3 Seven whole days, not one in seven, I will praise thee;
Tenor or soprano ad libitum
3 Seven whole days, not one in seven, I will praise thee;
and that love may nev - er cease, I will move thee.
and the cream of all my heart, I will bring thee.
in my heart, though not in heaven, I can raise thee.
in my heart, though not in heaven, I can raise thee.

Thou hast grant-ed my re-quest, thou hast heard me;
Though my sins a-gainst me cried, thou didst clear me;
Small it is in this poor sort to en-roll thee;
Small it is in this poor sort to en-roll thee;
thou didst note my work-ing breast, thou hast spared me.
and a-lone, when they re-plied, thou didst hear me.
e'en e-ter-ni-ty's too short to ex-tol thee.
e'en e-ter-ni-ty's too short to ex-tol thee.

Words: George Herbert (1593-1633)
Music: *General Seminary*, David Charles Walker (b. 1938)

𝅗𝅥 = 56
74. 74. D

383 Praise to God

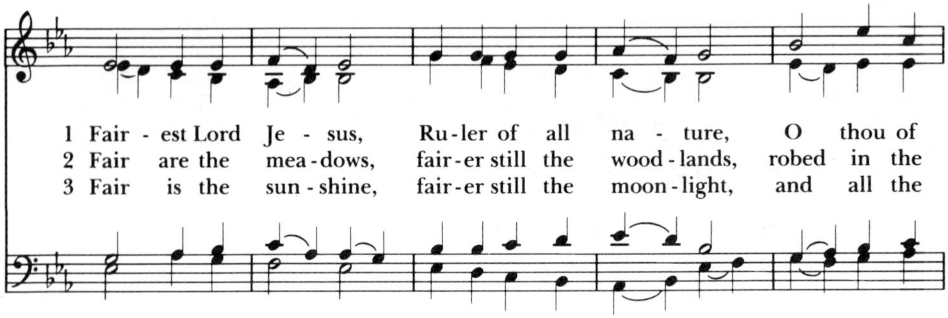
1 Fair - est Lord Je - sus, Ru-ler of all na - ture, O thou of
2 Fair are the mea-dows, fair-er still the wood-lands, robed in the
3 Fair is the sun-shine, fair-er still the moon-light, and all the

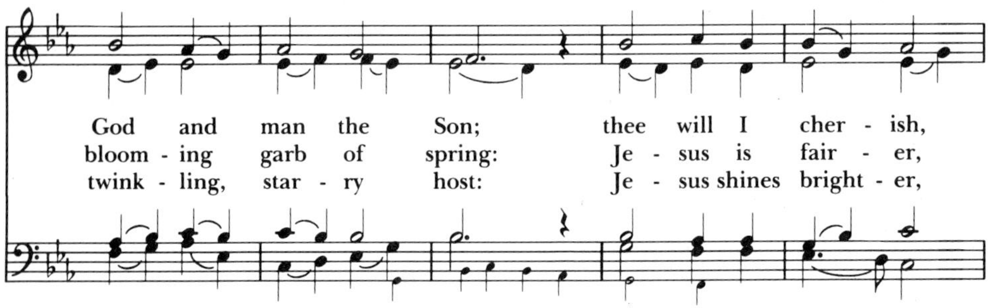
God and man the Son; thee will I cher - ish,
bloom - ing garb of spring: Je - sus is fair - er,
twink - ling, star - ry host: Je - sus shines bright - er,

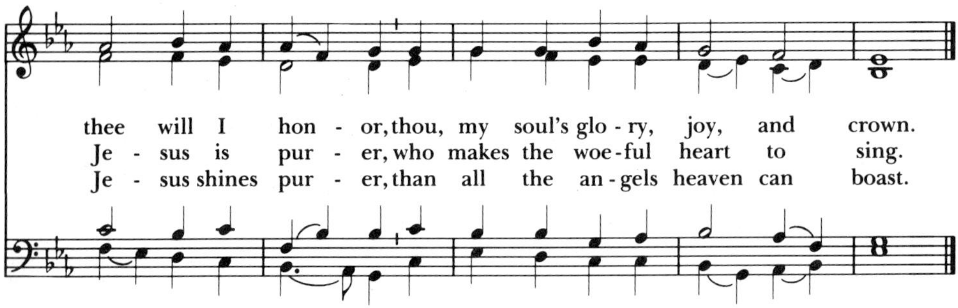
thee will I hon - or, thou, my soul's glo - ry, joy, and crown.
Je - sus is pur - er, who makes the woe-ful heart to sing.
Je - sus shines pur - er, than all the an-gels heaven can boast.

Alternative tune: *Schönster Herr Jesu,* 384.

Words: German composite; tr. pub. New York, 1850, alt. 𝅗𝅥.=48
Music: *St. Elizabeth,* melody from *Schlesische Volkslieder,* 1842; harm. Thomas Tertius Noble (1867-1953) 568. 558

384 Praise to God

1 Fair - est Lord Je - sus, Ru - ler of all na - ture,
2 Fair are the mea - dows, fair - er still the wood - lands,
3 Fair is the sun - shine, fair - er still the moon - light, and

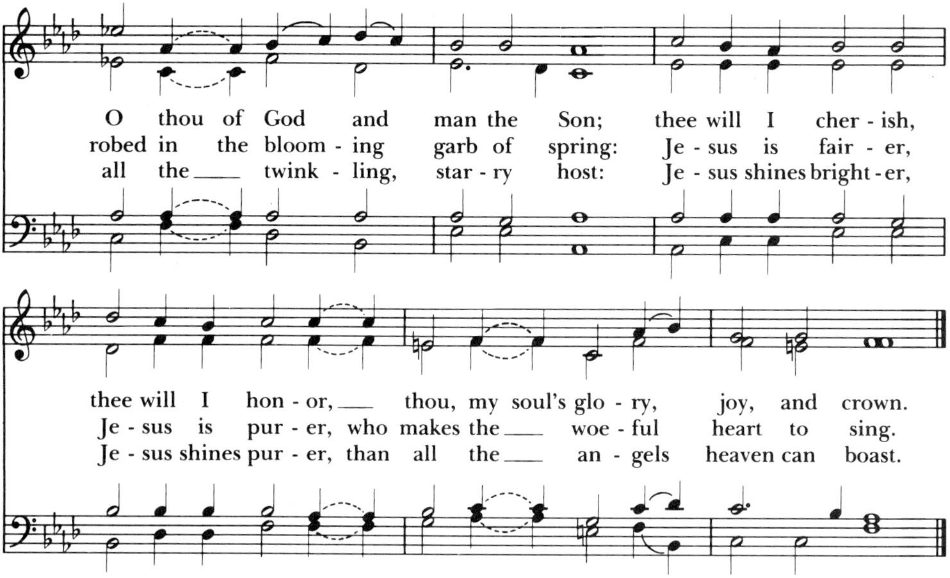
O thou of God and man the Son; thee will I cher - ish,
robed in the bloom - ing garb of spring: Je - sus is fair - er,
all the ___ twink - ling, star - ry host: Je - sus shines bright - er,
thee will I hon - or, ___ thou, my soul's glo - ry, joy, and crown.
Je - sus is pur - er, who makes the ___ woe - ful heart to sing.
Je - sus shines pur - er, than all the ___ an - gels heaven can boast.

Alternative tune: *St. Elizabeth,* 383.

Words: German composite; tr. pub. New York, 1850, alt. 𝅗𝅥 = 52
Music: *Schönster Herr Jesu,* melody from *Münster Gesangbuch,* 1677; harm. *The English Hymnal,* 1906 568. 558

Praise to God 385

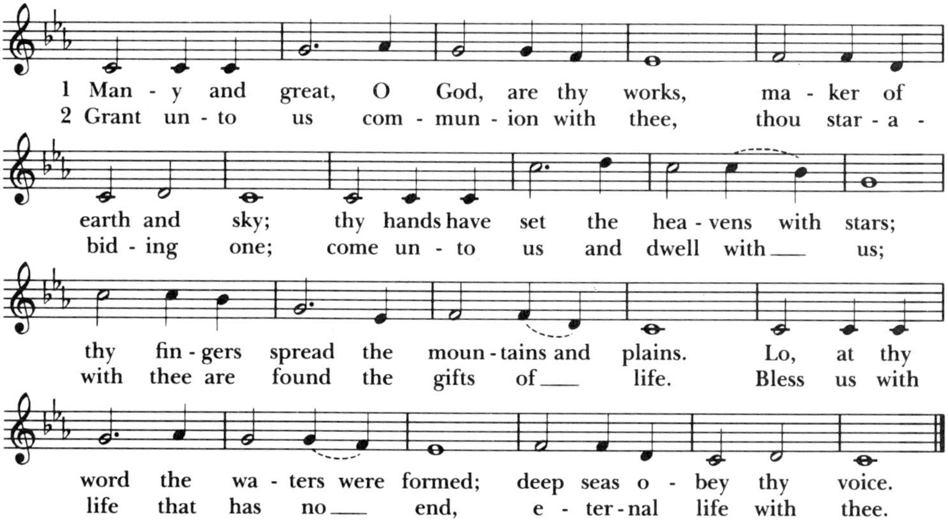
1 Man - y and great, O God, are thy works, ma - ker of
2 Grant un - to us com - mun - ion with thee, thou star - a -
earth and sky; thy hands have set the hea - vens with stars;
bid - ing one; come un - to us and dwell with ___ us;
thy fin - gers spread the moun - tains and plains. Lo, at thy
with thee are found the gifts of ___ life. Bless us with
word the wa - ters were formed; deep seas o - bey thy voice.
life that has no ___ end, e - ter - nal life with thee.

Suggested percussion part for hand drum or tom-tom: ♩ ♩ ♩ ♩

Words: American folk hymn; rev. Philip Frazier (1892-1964), alt. 𝅗𝅥 = 66
Music: *Dakota Indian Chant [Lacquiparle],* Native American melody 96. 99. 96

1 We sing of God, the might - y source of all things; the stu -
*2 Tell them I AM, the Lord God said, to Mo - ses while on
3 Glo - rious the sun in mid ca - reer; glo - rious the as - sem - bled
4 Glo - rious, most glo - rious, is the crown of him that brought sal -
pen - dous force on which all strength de - pends; from
earth in dread and smit - ten to the heart, at
fires ap - pear; glo - rious the com - et's train: glo -
va - tion down by meek - ness, Ma - ry's son; seers
whose right arm, be - neath whose eyes, all pe - riod, power, and
once, a - bove, be - neath, a - round, all na - ture with - out
rious the trum - pet and a - larm; glo - rious the al - might - y
that stu - pen - dous truth be - lieved, and now the match - less
en - ter - prise com - men - ces, reigns, and ends.
voice or sound re - plied, O Lord, thou art.
stretched - out arm; glo - rious the en - rap - tured main:
deed's a - chieved, de - ter - mined, dared, and done.

Alternative tune: *Magdalen College*, 387.

Words: Christopher Smart (1722-1771), alt.
Music: *Cornwall*, Samuel Sebastian Wesley (1810-1876)

𝅗𝅥 = 50
886. 886

1 We sing of God, the might - y source of all things;
*2 Tell them I AM, the Lord God said, to Mo - ses
3 Glo - rious the sun in mid ca - reer; glo - rious the as -
4 Glo - rious, most glo - rious, is the crown of him that
the stu - pen - dous force on which all strength de - pends;
while on earth in dread and smit - ten to the heart,
sem - bled fires ap - pear; glo - rious the com - et's train:
brought sal - va - tion down by meek - ness, Ma - ry's son;
from whose right arm, be - neath whose eyes, all pe - riod,
at once, a - bove, be - neath, a - round, all na - ture
glo - rious the trum - pet and a - larm; glo - rious the al -
seers that stu - pen - dous truth be - lieved, and now the
power, and en - ter - prise com - men - ces, reigns, and ends.
with - out voice or sound re - plied, O Lord, thou art.
might - y stretched-out arm; glo - rious the en - rap - tured main:
match - less deed's a - chieved, de - ter - mined, dared, and done.

Alternative tune: *Cornwall,* 386.

Words: Christopher Smart (1722-1771), alt.
Music: *Magdalen College,* William Hayes (1706-1777)

𝅗𝅥 = 56
886. 886

1 O wor - ship the King, all glo - rious a - bove!
2 O tell of his might! O sing of his grace!
3 The earth, with its store of won - ders un - told,
4 Thy boun - ti - ful care, what tongue can re - cite?
5 Frail chil - dren of dust, and fee - ble as frail,
1 O grate - ful - ly sing his power and his love!
2 Whose robe is the light, whose can - o - py space.
3 Al - might - y, thy power hath found - ed of old,
4 It breathes in the air; it shines in the light;
5 in thee do we trust, nor find thee to fail;
1 Our shield and de - fend - er, the An - cient of Days,
2 His char - iots of wrath the deep thun - der - clouds form,
3 hath stab - lished it fast by a change - less de - cree,
4 it streams from the hills, it de - scends to the plain,
5 thy mer - cies, how ten - der! how firm to the end!

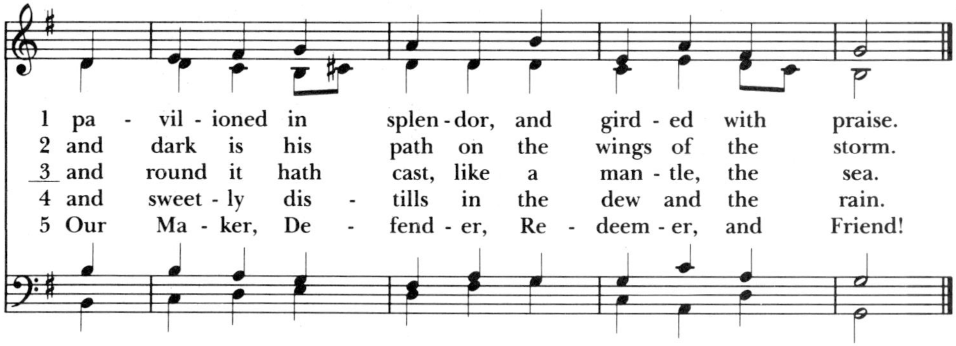
1 pa - vil - ioned in splen - dor, and gird - ed with praise.
2 and dark is his path on the wings of the storm.
3 and round it hath cast, like a man - tle, the sea.
4 and sweet - ly dis - tills in the dew and the rain.
5 Our Ma - ker, De - fend - er, Re - deem - er, and Friend!

Words: Robert Grant (1779-1838)
Music: *Hanover,* att. William Croft (1678-1727)

♩= 108
10 10. 11 11

Praise to God

389

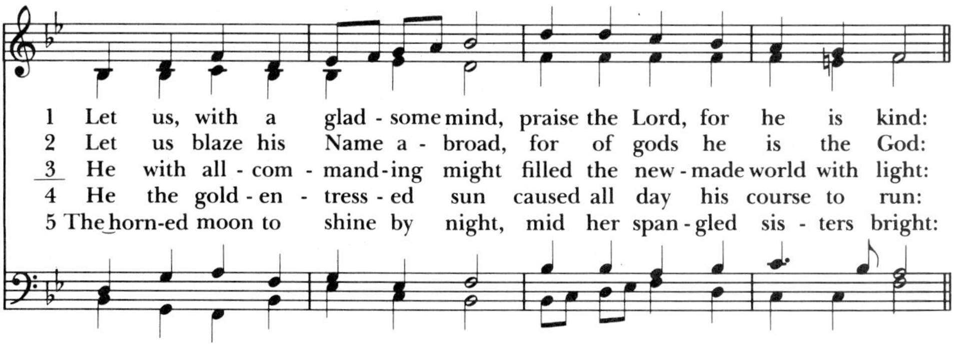
1 Let us, with a glad - some mind, praise the Lord, for he is kind:
2 Let us blaze his Name a - broad, for of gods he is the God:
3 He with all - com - mand - ing might filled the new - made world with light:
4 He the gold - en - tress - ed sun caused all day his course to run:
5 The horn-ed moon to shine by night, mid her span - gled sis - ters bright:

Refrain
for his mer-cies ay en - dure, ev - er faith-ful, ev - er sure.

6 All things living he doth feed,
his full hand supplies their need:

Refrain

7 Let us, with a gladsome mind,
praise the Lord, for he is kind:

Refrain

Words: John Milton (1608-1674); para. Psalm 136
Music: *Monkland,* melody from *Freylinghausen,* 1704; adapt. John Antes (1740-1811); arr. John Bernard Wilkes (1785-1869)

𝅗𝅥= 66
77. 77

Descant
4 Praise to the Lord! O let all that is in me a - dore him! All that hath life and breath come now with prais-es be - fore him! Let the a - men sound_ from his
1 Praise to the Lord, the Al - might - y, the King of cre - a - tion; O my soul, praise him, for he is thy health and sal - va - tion: join the great throng, psal - ter - y,
2 Praise to the Lord; o - ver all things he glo - rious - ly reign - eth: borne as on ea - gle-wings, safe - ly his saints he sus - tain - eth. Hast thou not seen how all thou
3 Praise to the Lord, who doth pros - per thy way and de - fend thee; sure - ly his good - ness and mer - cy shall ev - er at - tend thee; pon - der a - new what the Al -
4 Praise to the Lord! O let all that is in me a - dore him! All that hath life and breath come now with prais-es be - fore him! Let the a - men sound from his

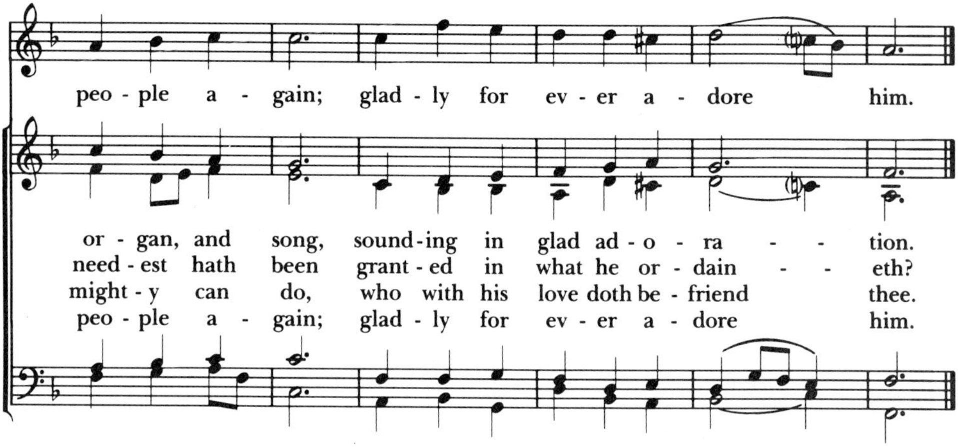
peo - ple a - gain; glad - ly for ev - er a - dore him.
or - gan, and song, sound-ing in glad ad - o - ra - - tion.
need - est hath been grant - ed in what he or - dain - - eth?
might - y can do, who with his love doth be - friend thee.
peo - ple a - gain; glad - ly for ev - er a - dore him.

Words: Joachim Neander (1650-1680); tr. *Hymnal 1940,* alt.
Music: *Lobe den Herren,* melody from *Erneuerten Gesangbuch,* 1665; harm. *The Chorale Book for England,* 1863; desc. Craig Sellar Lang (1891-1971)

𝅗𝅥. = 40
14 14. 478

1 Be - fore the Lord's e - ter - nal throne, ye
2 His sov - ereign power with - out our aid formed
3 We are his peo - ple, we his care, our
4 We'll crowd thy gates with thank - ful songs, high
5 Wide as the world is thy com - mand, vast
1 na - tions, bow with sa - cred joy; know that the Lord is
2 us of clay and gave us breath; and when like wan-dering
3 souls, and all our mor - tal frame: what last - ing hon - ors
4 as the heaven our voic - es raise; and earth, with her ten
5 as e - ter - ni - ty thy love; firm as a rock thy
1 God a - lone; he can cre - ate, and he des - troy.
2 sheep we strayed, he saved us from the power of death.
3 shall we rear, al - might - y Ma - ker, to thy Name?
4 thou - sand tongues, shall fill thy courts with sound - ing praise.
5 truth must stand, when roll - ing years shall cease to move.

Words: Isaac Watts (1674-1748), alt.; para. of Psalm 100
Music: *Winchester New*, melody from *Musicalishes Hand-Buch*, 1690; harm. William Henry Monk (1823-1889)

♩=84
LM

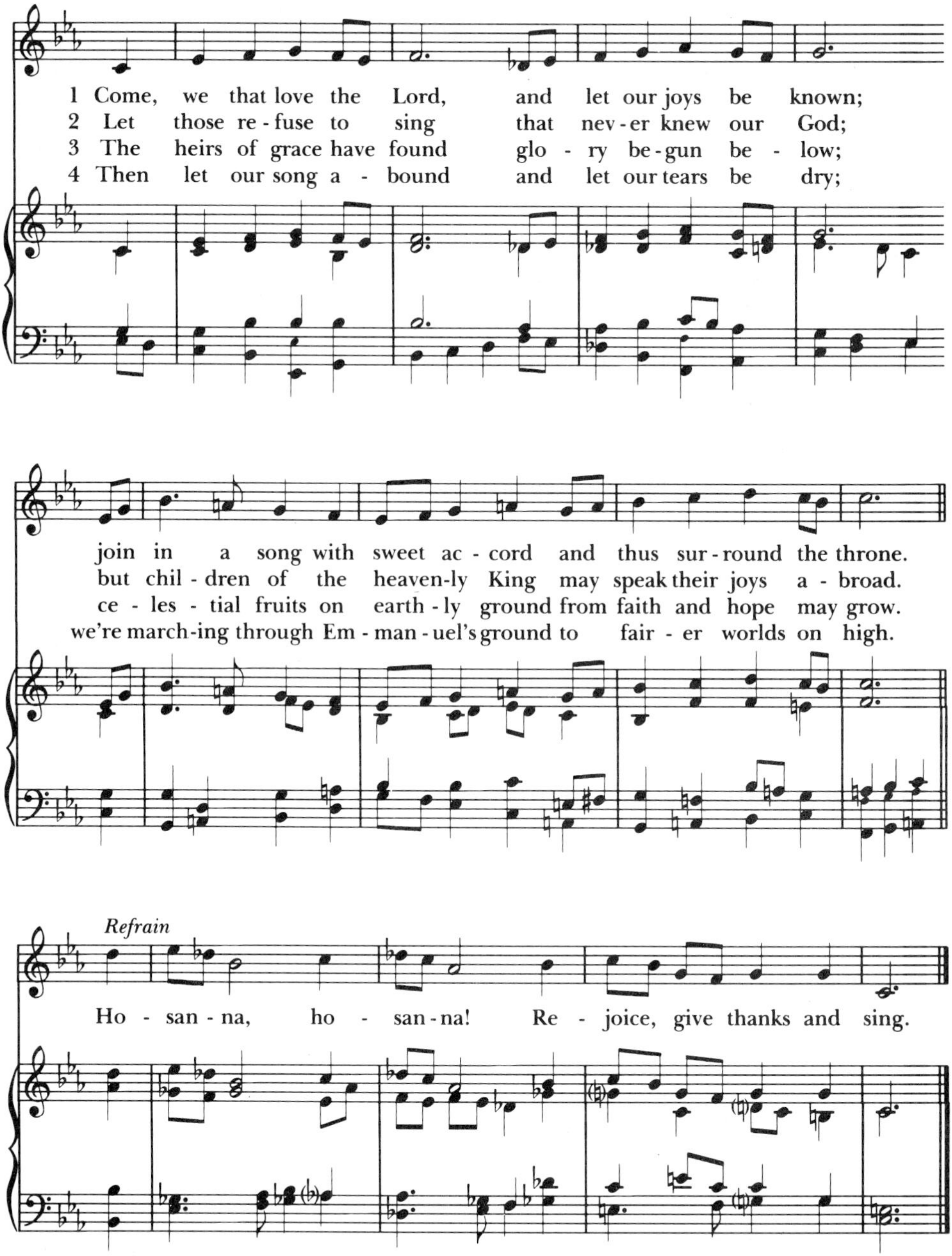
1 Come, we that love the Lord, and let our joys be known;
2 Let those re-fuse to sing that nev-er knew our God;
3 The heirs of grace have found glo-ry be-gun be-low;
4 Then let our song a-bound and let our tears be dry;
join in a song with sweet ac-cord and thus sur-round the throne.
but chil-dren of the heaven-ly King may speak their joys a-broad.
ce-les-tial fruits on earth-ly ground from faith and hope may grow.
we're march-ing through Em-man-uel's ground to fair-er worlds on high.
Refrain
Ho-san-na, ho-san-na! Re-joice, give thanks and sing.

Words: Isaac Watts (1674-1748), alt.
Music: *Vineyard Haven*, Richard Wayne Dirksen (b. 1921)

𝅗𝅥 = 54
SM with Refrain

393 Praise to God

1 Praise our great and gra-cious Lord, call up-on his ho-ly Name;
raising hymns in glad ac-cord, all his might-y acts pro-claim:
how he leads his cho-sen un-to Ca-naan's prom-ised land,
how the word we have heard firm and change-less still shall stand.
2 God has given the cloud by day, given the mov-ing fire by night;
guides his Is-rael on their way from the dark-ness in-to light.
God it is who grants us sure re-treat and ref-uge nigh;
light of dawn leads us on: 'tis the Day-spring from on high.
𝅗𝅥=48

Words: Harriet Auber (1773-1862), alt.
Music: *Maoz Zur*, Hebrew melody; adapt. and arr. Eric Werner (b. 1901)

77. 77. 67. 67

Praise to God 394

1 Cre - at - ing God, your fin - gers trace the bold de -
2 Sus - tain - ing God, your hands up - hold earth's mys-teries
3 Re - deem - ing God, your arms em - brace all now de -
4 In - dwell - ing God, your gos - pel claims one fam - ily
signs of farth - est space; let sun and moon and stars and
known or yet un - told; let wa - ter's fra - gile blend with
spised for creed or race; let peace, de - scend - ing like a
with a bil - lion names; let ev - ery life be touched by
light and what lies hid - den praise your might.
air, en - a - bling life, pro - claim your care.
dove, make known on earth your heal - ing love.
grace un - til we praise you face to face.

Alternative tune: *King*, 395.

Words: Jeffery Rowthorn (b. 1934), alt.
Music: *Wilderness*, Reginald Sparshatt Thatcher (1888-1957)

𝅗𝅥 = 63
LM

Praise to God

Introduction/Interlude
1 Cre - at - ing God, your fin - gers trace the
2 Sus - tain - ing God, your hands up - hold earth's
3 Re - deem - ing God, your arms em - brace all
4 In - dwell - ing God, your gos - pel claims one
bold de - signs of farth - est space; let sun and
mys - teries known or yet un - told; let wa - ter's
now de - spised for creed or race; let peace, de -
fam - ily with a bil - lion names; let ev - ery

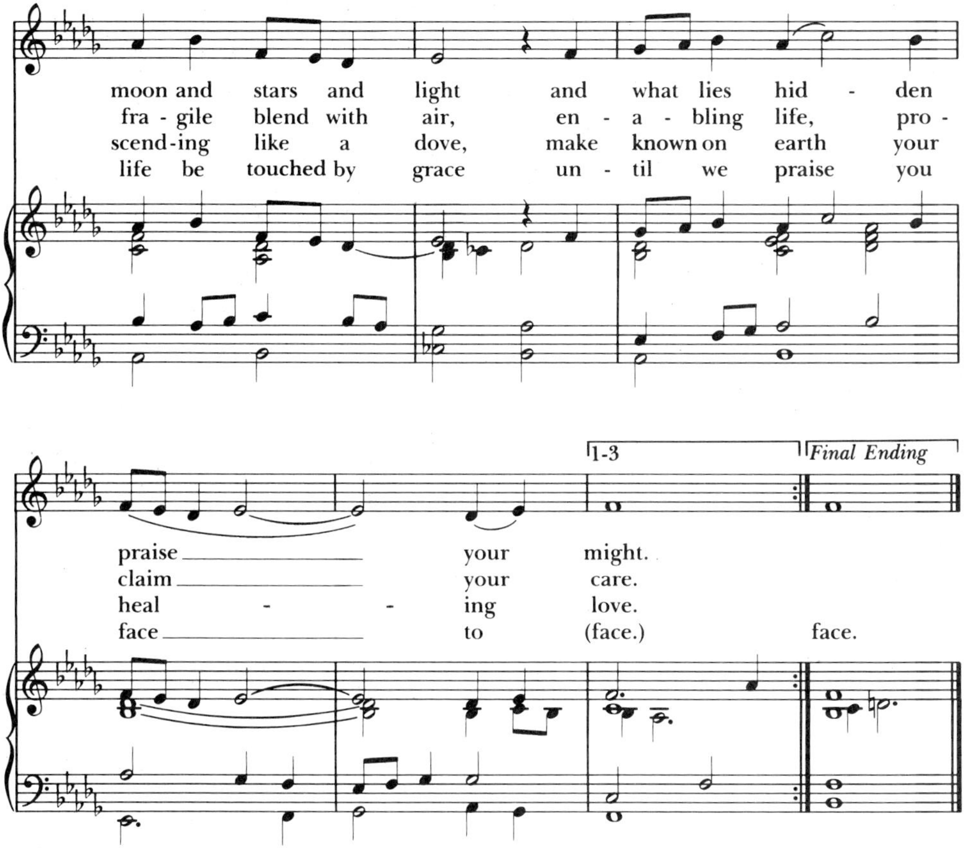
moon and stars and light and what lies hid - den praise your might.
fra - gile blend with air, en - a - bling life, pro - claim your care.
scend-ing like a dove, make known on earth your heal - ing love.
life be touched by grace un - til we praise you face to (face.) face.
1-3
Final Ending

Alternative tune: *Wilderness*, 394.

Words: Jeffery Rowthorn (b. 1934), alt.
Music: *King*, David Hurd (b. 1950)

𝅗𝅥 = 60
LM

1 Now thank we all our God, with heart, and hands, and voic - es,
2 O may this boun - teous God through all our life be near us!
3 All praise and thanks to God the Fa - ther now be giv - en,
who won-drous things hath done, in whom his world re - joic - es;
with ev - er - joy - ful hearts and bless - ed peace to cheer us;
the Son, and him who reigns with them in high - est hea - ven,
who from our mo - ther's arms hath blessed us on our way
and keep us in his grace, and guide us when per - plexed,
e - ter - nal, Tri - une God, whom earth and heaven a - dore;

with count-less gifts of love, and still is ours to - day.
and free us from all ills in this world and the next.
for thus it was, is now, and shall be, ev - er - more.

Alternative tune: *Nun danket alle Gott* (isometric), 397.

Words: Martin Rinckart (1586-1649); tr. Catherine Winkworth (1827-1878), alt. 𝅗𝅥 = 60

Music: *Nun danket alle Gott,* melody Martin Rinckart (1586-1649); harm. Johann Cruger (1598-1662) 67. 67. 66. 66

1 Now thank we all our God, with heart, and hands, and voic - es,
2 O may this boun - teous God through all our life be near us!
3 All praise and thanks to God the Fa - ther now be giv - en,
who won-drous things hath done, in whom his world re - joic - es;
with ev - er - joy - ful hearts and bless - ed peace to cheer us;
the Son, and him who reigns with them in high - est hea - ven,
who from our mo - ther's arms hath blessed us on our way
and keep us in his grace, and guide us when per - plexed,
e - ter - nal, Tri - une God, whom earth and heaven a - dore;
with count-less gifts of love, and still is ours to - day.
and free us from all ills in this world and the next.
for thus it was, is now, and shall be, ev - er - more.

Alternative tune: *Nun danket alle Gott* (rhythmic), 396.

Words: Martin Rinckart (1586-1649); tr. Catherine Winkworth (1827-1878), alt.
Music: *Nun danket alle Gott*, melody Johann Cruger (1598-1662); harm. William Henry Monk (1823-1889), after Felix Mendelssohn (1809-1847)

𝅗𝅥 = 66
67. 67. 66. 66

1 I sing the al-might - y power of God, that made the moun-tains rise,
2 I sing the good - ness of the Lord, that filled the earth with food;
3 There's not a plant or flower be - low, but makes thy glo - ries known;
that spread the flow - ing seas a - broad and built the lof - ty skies.
he formed the crea-tures with his Word, and then pro-nounced them good.
and clouds a - rise, and tem - pests blow, by or - der from thy throne;
I sing the wis - dom that or - dained the sun to rule the day;
Lord, how thy won - ders are dis - played, wher - e'er I turn my eye,
while all that bor - rows life from thee is ev - er in thy care,
the moon shines full at his com-mand, and all the stars o - bey.
if I sur - vey the ground I tread, or gaze up - on the sky!
and ev - ery - where that I could be, thou, God, art pres-ent there.

Words: Isaac Watts (1674-1748), alt.
Music: *Forest Green*, English melody; adapt. and harm. Ralph Vaughan Williams (1872-1958)

𝅗𝅥=48
CMD

Descant
3 Your heaven - ly Fa - ther praise, ac - claim his
1 To God with glad - ness sing, your Rock and Sa - vior
2 He cra - dles in his hand the heights and depths of
3 Your heaven - ly Fa - ther praise, ac - claim his on - ly
on - ly Son, your voic - es raise to him who
bless; in - to his tem - ple bring your songs of
earth; he made the sea and land, he brought the
Son, your voice in hom - age raise to him who

makes all one, O Dove on
thank - - ful - ness! O God of might, to
world to birth! O God Most High, we
makes all one! O Dove of peace, on
us de - scend joy in - crease!
you we sing, en - throned as King on hea - ven's height!
are your sheep; on us you keep your shep - herd's eye!
us de - scend that strife may end and joy in - crease!

Alternative tune: *Darwall's 148th,* 625.

Words: James Quinn (b. 1919), alt.; para. of Psalm 95 (Venite)
Music: *Camano,* Richard Proulx (b. 1937)

♩=c. 96
66. 66. 44. 44

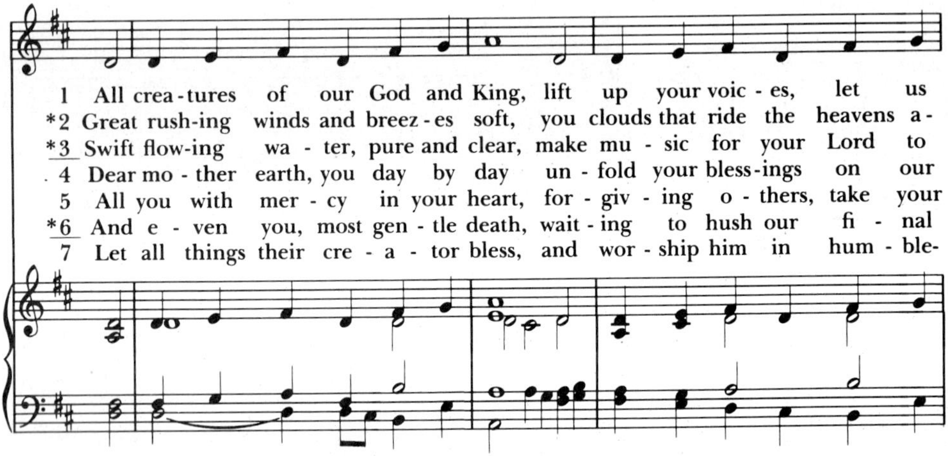
1 All crea-tures of our God and King, lift up your voic-es, let us
*2 Great rush-ing winds and breez-es soft, you clouds that ride the heavens a-
*3 Swift flow-ing wa-ter, pure and clear, make mu-sic for your Lord to
4 Dear mo-ther earth, you day by day un-fold your bless-ings on our
5 All you with mer-cy in your heart, for-giv-ing o-thers, take your
*6 And e-ven you, most gen-tle death, wait-ing to hush our fi-nal
7 Let all things their cre-a-tor bless, and wor-ship him in hum-ble-

1 sing: Al-le-lu-ia, al-le-lu-ia! Bright burn-ing
2 loft, O___ praise him, Al-le-lu-ia! Fair ris-ing
3 hear, Al-le-lu-ia, al-le-lu-ia! Fire, so in-
4 way, O___ praise him, Al-le-lu-ia! All flowers and
5 part, O___ sing now: Al-le-lu-ia! All you that
6 breath, O___ praise him, Al-le-lu-ia! You lead back
7 ness, O___ praise him, Al-le-lu-ia! Praise God the

1 sun with gold - en beams, pale sil - ver moon that gen - tly gleams,
2 morn, with praise re - joice, stars night - ly shin - ing, find a voice,
3 tense and fierce - ly bright, you give to us both warmth and light,
4 fruits that in you grow, let them his glo - ry al - so show:
5 pain and sor - row bear, praise God, and cast on him your care:
6 home the child of God, for Christ our Lord that way has trod:
7 Fa - ther, praise the Son, and praise the Spi - rit, Three in One:
Refrain
O praise him, O praise him, Al - le - lu - ia,
al - le - lu - ia, al - le - lu - - ia!

The refrain may be sung antiphonally, by phrase; all join in the final Alleluia. This music in E♭, 618.

Words: Francis of Assisi (1182-1226); tr. William H. Draper (1855-1933), alt.
Music: *Lasst uns erfreuen*, melody from *Auserlesene Catholische Geistliche Kirchengeseng*, 1623; adapt. and harm. Ralph Vaughan Williams (1872-1958)

𝅗𝅥 = 72
88. 44. 88 with Refrain

1 The God of A-braham praise, who reigns en - throned a - bove;
2 He by him - self hath sworn: we on his oath de - pend;
3 There dwells the Lord, our King, the Lord, our Right - eous - ness,
4 The God who reigns on high the great arch - an - gels sing,
5 The whole tri - um - phant host give thanks to God on high;
1 An - cient of ev - er - last - ing days, and God of love;
2 we shall, on ea - gle - wings up - borne, to heaven a - scend:
3 tri - um-phant o'er the world and sin, the Prince of Peace;
4 and "Ho - ly, ho - ly, ho - ly," cry, "Al - might - y King!
5 "Hail, Fa - ther, Son, and Ho - ly Ghost!" they ev - er cry;
1 the Lord, the great I AM, by earth and heaven con - fessed:
2 we shall be - hold his face, we shall his power a - dore,
3 on Zi - on's sa - cred height his king - dom he main - tains,
4 Who was, and is, the same, and ev - er - more shall be:
5 hail, A-braham's Lord di - vine! With heaven our songs we raise;

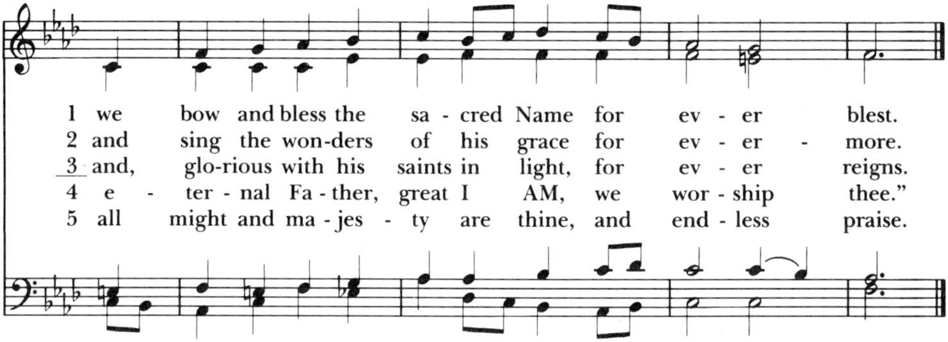
1 we bow and bless the sa - cred Name for ev - er blest.
2 and sing the won-ders of his grace for ev - er - more.
3 and, glo-rious with his saints in light, for ev - er reigns.
4 e - ter - nal Fa - ther, great I AM, we wor - ship thee."
5 all might and ma - jes - ty are thine, and end - less praise.

Words: Thomas Olivers (1725-1799), alt.
Music: *Leoni,* Hebrew melody; harm. *Hymns Ancient and Modern,* 1875, alt.

𝅗𝅥 = 48
66. 84. D

Antiphon
Unison
Let all the world in ev - ery cor - ner
Harmony
sing, my God and King! 1. The heavens are not too
high, his praise may thith - er fly; the earth is not too
Antiphon
Unison
low, his prais - es there may grow. Let all the
ped.
world in ev - ery cor - ner sing, my God and

Harmony
King! 2. The Church with psalms must shout, no door can keep them
out; but, a - bove all, the heart must bear the
Antiphon
Unison
long - est part. Let all the world in
ped.
ev - ery cor - ner sing, my God and King!

Alternative tune: *MacDougall,* 403.

Words: George Herbert (1593-1633)
Music: *Augustine,* Erik Routley (1917-1982)

♩=116
66. 66 with Refrain

Introduction
I
Let all the world in ev - ery cor - ner
sing, my God and King!
II
Let all the world in ev - ery cor - ner

All
sing, my God and King!
1 The heavens are not too high, his praise may thith - er fly; the earth is not too low, his prais - es there may grow.
2 The Church with psalms must shout, no door can keep them out; but, a - bove all, the heart must bear the long - est part.
Let

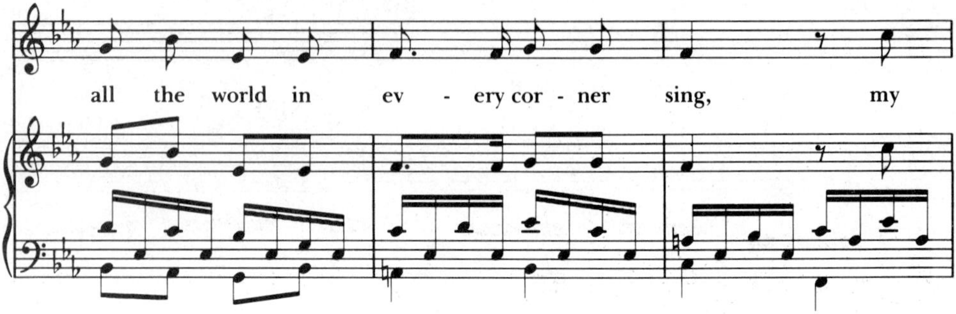
all the world in ev - ery cor - ner sing, my

1
God and King!
Interlude

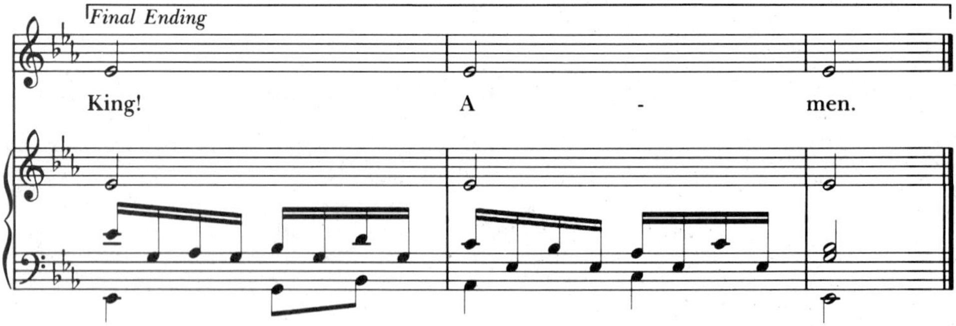
Final Ending
King! A - men.

Alternative tune: *Augustine,* 402.

Words: George Herbert (1593-1633)
Music: *MacDougall,* Calvin Hampton (1938-1984)

♩=76
66. 66 with Refrain

1 We will ex - tol you, ev - er - bless - ed Lord; your ho - ly
2 Age shall to age pass on the end - less song, tell - ing the
3 You, Lord, are gra - cious, mer - ci - ful to all, close to your
Name for ev - er be a - dored; each day we live our
won - ders which to you be - long, your might - y acts with
chil - dren when on you they call; and slow to an - ger,
psalm to you we raise; you, God and King, are wor - thy of all
joy and fear re - late; praise we your glo - ry while on you we
mer - ci - ful and kind, in your com - pas - sion we your bless-ings
praise, great and un - search - a - ble in all your ways.
wait, glad in the know - ledge of your love so great.
find. We love you with our heart and strength and mind.

The first stanza may be repeated at the end.

Words: J. Nichol Grieve, alt.; para. of Psalm 145
Music: *Old 124th,* melody from *Pseaumes octante trois de David,* 1551; harm. Charles Winfred Douglas (1867-1944)

♩=96
10 10. 10 10 10

Descant
All things bright and beau - ti - ful, crea-tures great and small,
Refrain
G C Am D C D G
All things bright and beau - ti - ful, all crea-tures great and small,
all things wise and won - der - ful, God made them all.
G E D Am D C D G
all things wise and won - der - ful, the Lord God made them all.

G G7 C Am D A7 D
1 Each lit - tle flower that o - pens, each lit - tle bird that sings,
2 The pur - ple - head - ed moun - tain, the riv - er run - ning by,
3 The cold wind in the win - ter, the pleas-ant sum - mer sun,
4 He gave us eyes to see them, and lips that we might tell
Repeat Refrain
G Em Am D G D G
he made their glow - ing col - ors, he made their ti - ny wings.
the sun - set, and the morn - ing that bright - ens up the sky.
the ripe fruits in the gar - den, he made them ev - ery one.
how great is God Al - might - y, who has made all things well.

Words: Cecil Frances Alexander (1818-1895)
Music: *Royal Oak*, melody from *The Dancing Master*, 1686;
adapt. and harm. Martin Fallas Shaw (1875-1958); desc. Richard Proulx (b. 1937)

𝅗𝅥 = 66
76. 76 with Refrain

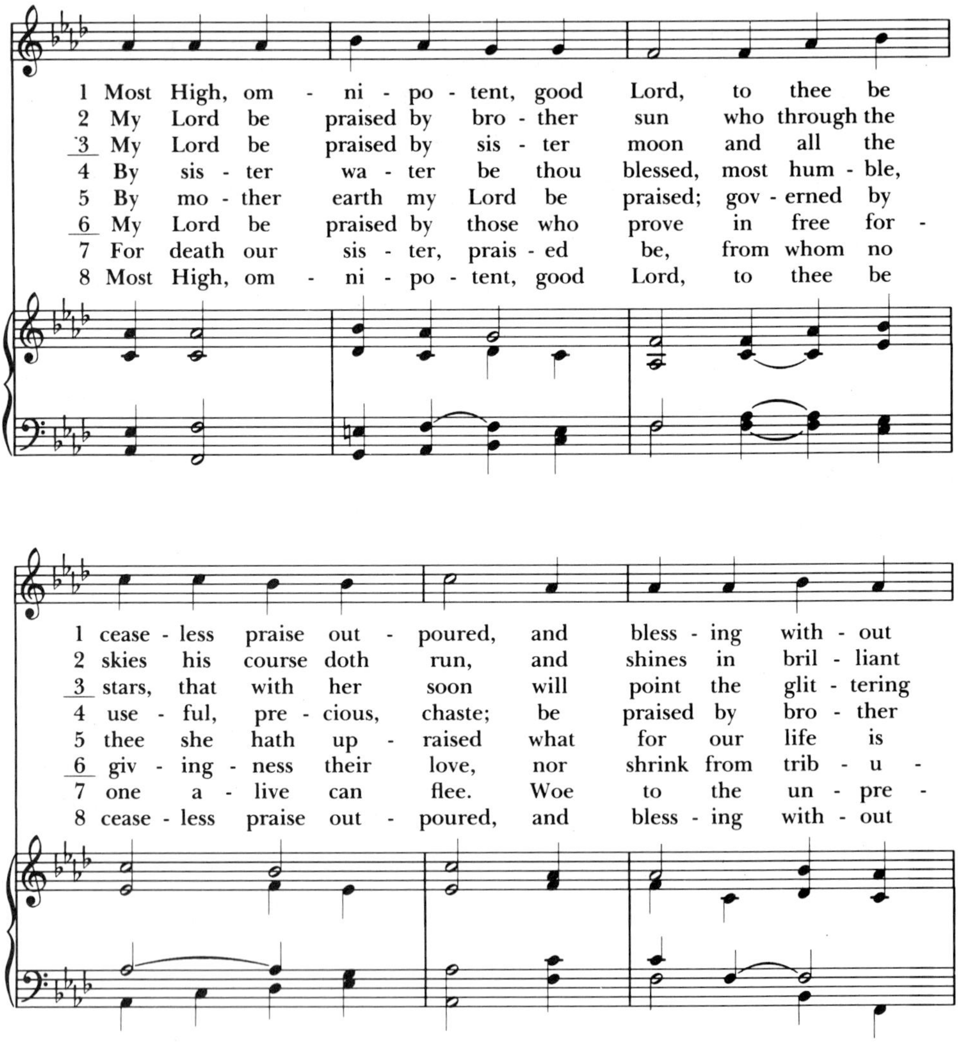
1 Most High, om - ni - po - tent, good Lord, to thee be
2 My Lord be praised by bro - ther sun who through the
3 My Lord be praised by sis - ter moon and all the
4 By sis - ter wa - ter be thou blessed, most hum - ble,
5 By mo - ther earth my Lord be praised; gov - erned by
6 My Lord be praised by those who prove in free for -
7 For death our sis - ter, prais - ed be, from whom no
8 Most High, om - ni - po - tent, good Lord, to thee be
1 cease - less praise out - poured, and bless - ing with - out
2 skies his course doth run, and shines in bril - liant
3 stars, that with her soon will point the glit - tering
4 use - ful, pre - cious, chaste; be praised by bro - ther
5 thee she hath up - raised what for our life is
6 giv - ing - ness their love, nor shrink from trib - u -
7 one a - live can flee. Woe to the un - pre -
8 cease - less praise out - poured, and bless - ing with - out

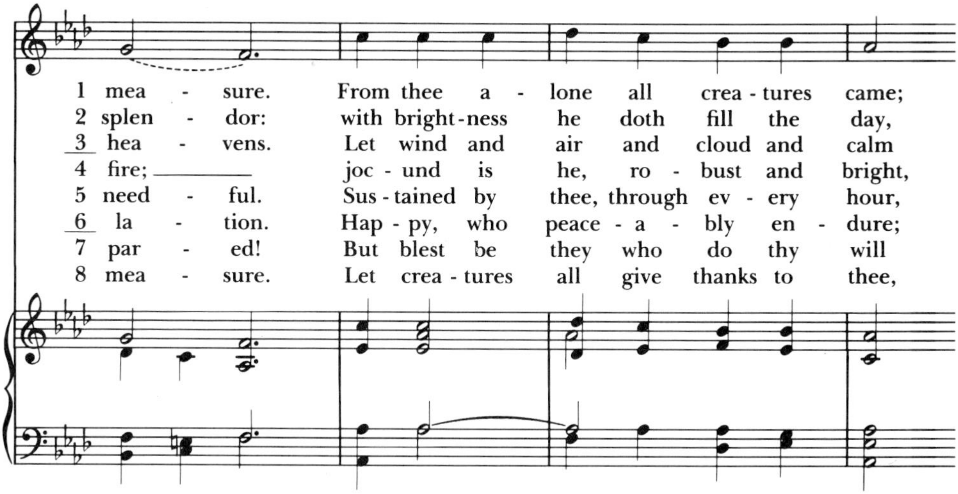
1 mea - sure. From thee a - lone all crea - tures came;
2 splen - dor: with bright-ness he doth fill the day,
3 hea - vens. Let wind and air and cloud and calm
4 fire; joc - und is he, ro - bust and bright,
5 need - ful. Sus-tained by thee, through ev - ery hour,
6 la - tion. Hap - py, who peace - a - bly en - dure;
7 par - ed! But blest be they who do thy will
8 mea - sure. Let crea - tures all give thanks to thee,

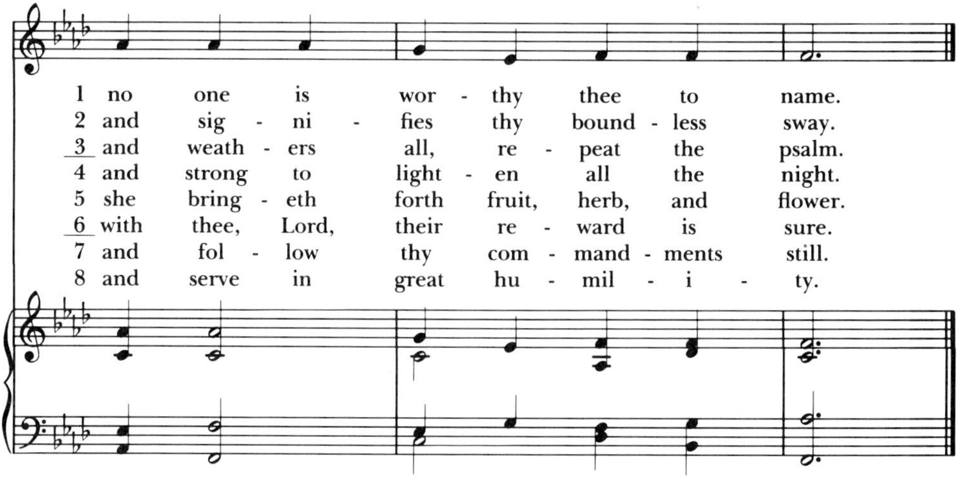
1 no one is wor - thy thee to name.
2 and sig - ni - fies thy bound - less sway.
3 and weath - ers all, re - peat the psalm.
4 and strong to light - en all the night.
5 she bring - eth forth fruit, herb, and flower.
6 with thee, Lord, their re - ward is sure.
7 and fol - low thy com - mand - ments still.
8 and serve in great hu - mil - i - ty.

This hymn may be sung by alternating groups, with all singing the first and final stanzas.
Alternative tune: *Lukkason,* 407.

Words: Francis of Assisi (1182-1226); tr. Howard Chandler Robbins (1876-1952), alt. — 𝅗𝅥=58
Music: *Assisi,* Alfred Morton Smith (1879-1971) — 887. 88

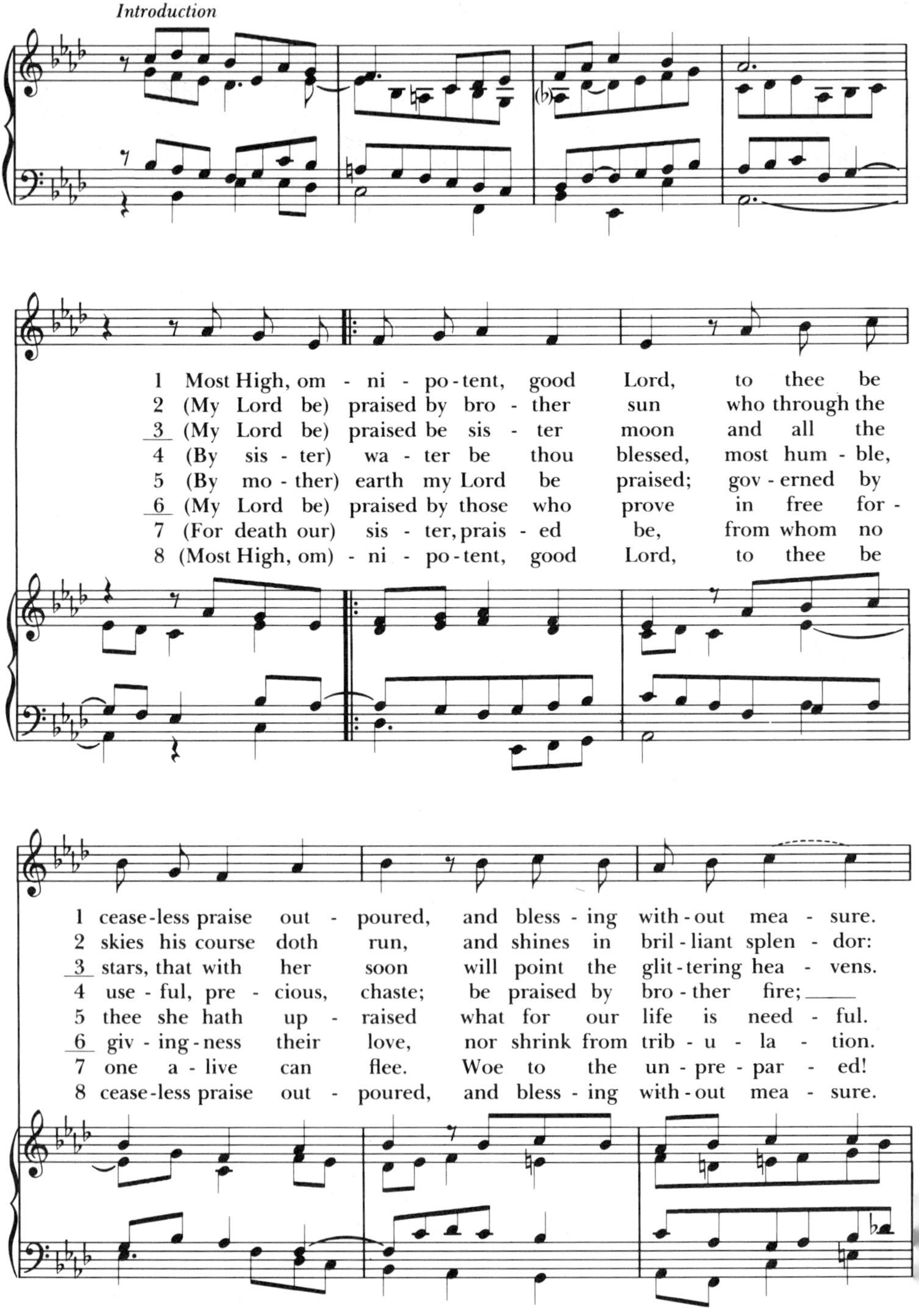
Introduction
1 Most High, om - ni - po-tent, good Lord, to thee be
2 (My Lord be) praised by bro - ther sun who through the
3 (My Lord be) praised be sis - ter moon and all the
4 (By sis - ter) wa - ter be thou blessed, most hum - ble,
5 (By mo - ther) earth my Lord be praised; gov - erned by
6 (My Lord be) praised by those who prove in free for -
7 (For death our) sis - ter, prais - ed be, from whom no
8 (Most High, om) - ni - po-tent, good Lord, to thee be
1 cease-less praise out - poured, and bless - ing with-out mea - sure.
2 skies his course doth run, and shines in bril - liant splen - dor:
3 stars, that with her soon will point the glit-tering hea - vens.
4 use - ful, pre - cious, chaste; be praised by bro - ther fire;
5 thee she hath up - raised what for our life is need - ful.
6 giv - ing-ness their love, nor shrink from trib - u - la - tion.
7 one a - live can flee. Woe to the un - pre - par - ed!
8 cease-less praise out - poured, and bless - ing with-out mea - sure.

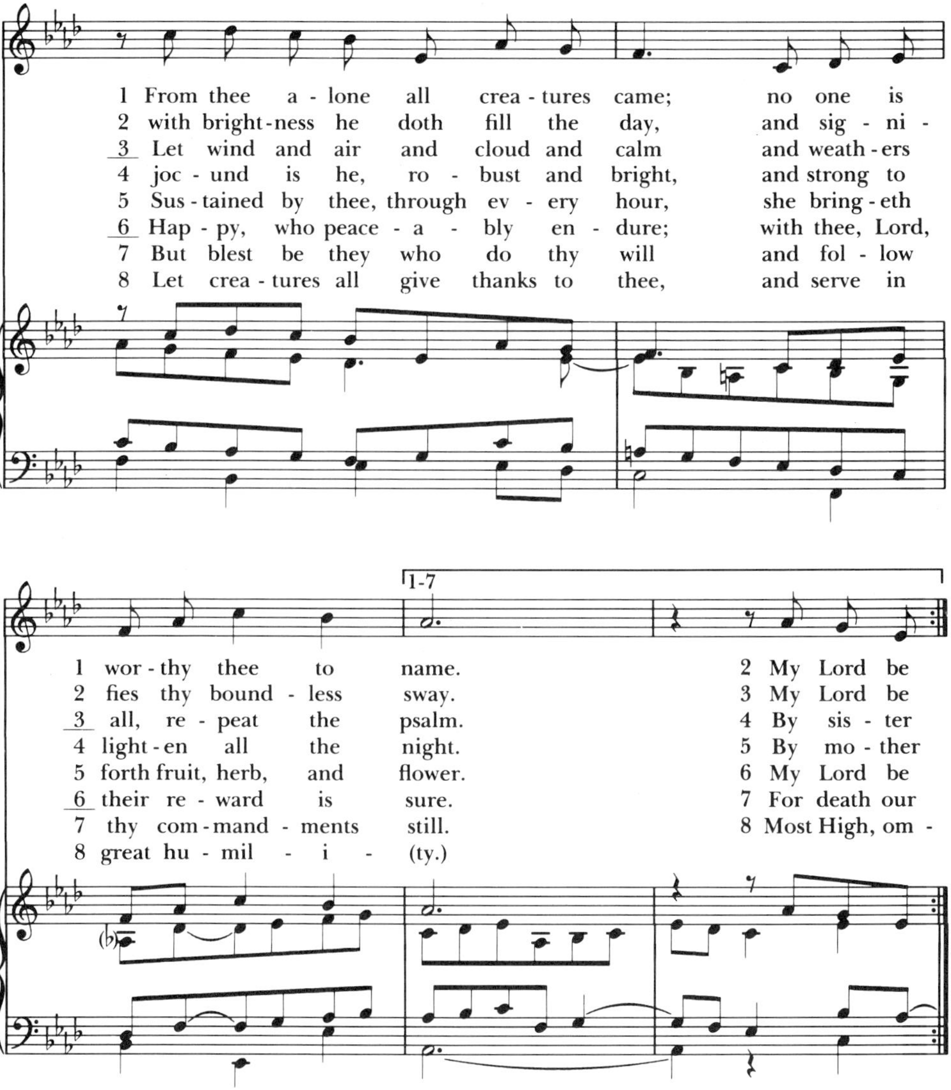
1 From thee a - lone all crea - tures came; no one is
2 with bright - ness he doth fill the day, and sig - ni -
3 Let wind and air and cloud and calm and weath - ers
4 joc - und is he, ro - bust and bright, and strong to
5 Sus - tained by thee, through ev - ery hour, she bring - eth
6 Hap - py, who peace - a - bly en - dure; with thee, Lord,
7 But blest be they who do thy will and fol - low
8 Let crea - tures all give thanks to thee, and serve in
1-7
1 wor - thy thee to name. 2 My Lord be
2 fies thy bound - less sway. 3 My Lord be
3 all, re - peat the psalm. 4 By sis - ter
4 light - en all the night. 5 By mo - ther
5 forth fruit, herb, and flower. 6 My Lord be
6 their re - ward is sure. 7 For death our
7 thy com - mand - ments still. 8 Most High, om -
8 great hu - mil - i - (ty.)

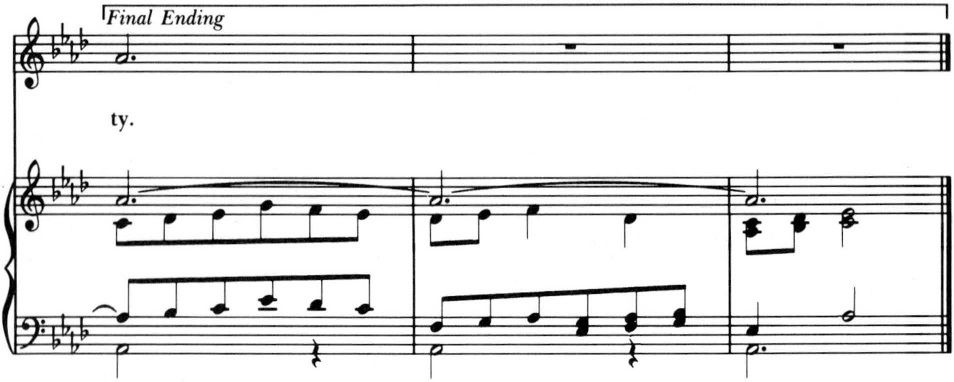
Final Ending
ty.

This hymn may be sung by alternating groups, with all singing the first and final stanzas.
Alternative tune: *Assisi,* 406.

Words: Francis of Assisi (1182-1226); tr. Howard Chandler Robbins (1876-1952), alt. ♩=66
Music: *Lukkason,* Calvin Hampton (1938-1984) 887. 88

408 Praise to God

1 Sing praise to God who reigns a - bove, the God of all cre -
2 What God's al - might - y power hath made, his gra - cious mer - cy
3 Let all who name Christ's ho - ly Name give God all praise and

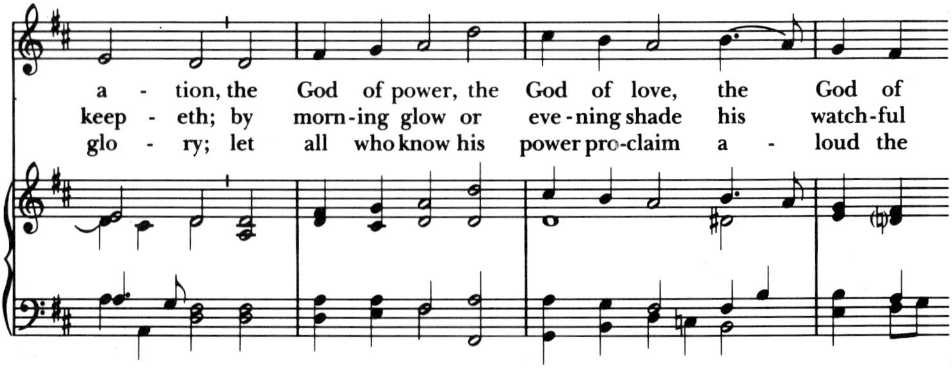
a - tion, the God of power, the God of love, the God of
keep - eth; by morn - ing glow or eve - ning shade his watch - ful
glo - ry; let all who know his power pro - claim a - loud the

1 our sal - va - tion; with heal-ing balm my soul he fills, and
2 eye ne'er sleep - eth. With - in the king-dom of his might, lo!
3 won - drous sto - ry! Cast each false i - dol from its throne, the

ev-ery faith - less mur-mur stills: to God all praise and glo - ry.
all is just and all is right: to God all praise and glo - ry.
Lord is God, and he a - lone: to God all praise and glo - ry.

This music in D♭, 598.

Words: Johann Jacob Schütz (1640-1690); tr. Frances Elizabeth Cox (1812-1897), alt.
Music: *Mit Freuden zart,* melody from "Une pastourelle gentille," 1529; adapt. *Pseaumes cinquante de David,* 1547, and *Kirchengeseng darinnen die Heubtartickel des Christlichen Glaubens gefasset,* 1566; harm. Ralph Vaughan Williams (1872-1958), after Heinrich Reimann (19th cent.)

𝅗𝅥 = 66
87. 87. 887

Unison or harmony
1 The spa - cious fir - ma - ment on high,
2 Soon as the eve - ning shades pre - vail,
3 What though in sol - emn si - lence all
with all the blue e - ther - eal sky,
the moon takes up the won - drous tale,
move round the dark ter - res - trial ball?
and span - gled heavens, a shin - ing frame,
and night - ly to the lis - tening earth
What though no re - - al voice nor sound
their great O - rig - i - nal pro - claim.
re - peats the sto - ry of her birth:
a - mid their ra - diant orbs be found?

The un - wea - ried sun from day to day
whilst all the stars that round her burn,
In rea - son's ear they all re - joice,
does his Cre - a - tor's power dis - play;
and all the plan - ets in their turn,
and ut - ter forth a glo - rious voice;
and pub - lish - es to ev - ery land
con - firm the ti - dings, as they roll
for ev - er sing - ing as they shine,
the work of an al - might - y hand.
and spread the truth from pole to pole.
"The hand that made us is di - vine."

Words: Joseph Addison (1672-1719); para. of Psalm 19:1-6
Music: *Creation*, Franz Joseph Haydn (1732-1809);
adapt. *Dulcimer, or New York Collection of Sacred Music*, 1850, alt.

𝅗𝅥=63
LMD

1. Praise, my soul, the King of hea - ven; to his feet thy trib-ute bring;
ran-somed, healed, re - stored, for - giv-en, ev - er - more his prais-es sing:
Al - le - lu - ia, al - le - lu - ia! Praise the ev - er - last-ing King.
2. Praise him for his grace and fa - vor to his peo-ple in dis - tress;

praise him still, the same as ev - er, slow to chide, and swift to bless:
Al - le - lu - ia, al - le - lu - ia! Glo-rious in his faith-ful - ness.
3. Fa-ther - like he tends and spares us; well our fee-ble frame he knows;
in his hand he gen-tly bears us, res-cues us from all our foes.

Al - le - lu - ia, al - le - lu - ia! Wide-ly yet his mer-cy flows.
Descant
4. An-gels, help us to a - dore him; ye be - hold him face to face;
4. An-gels, help us to a - dore him; ye be - hold him face to face;
sun and moon, bow down be - fore him, dwell - ers all in time and space.
sun and moon, bow down be - fore him, dwell - ers all in time and space.

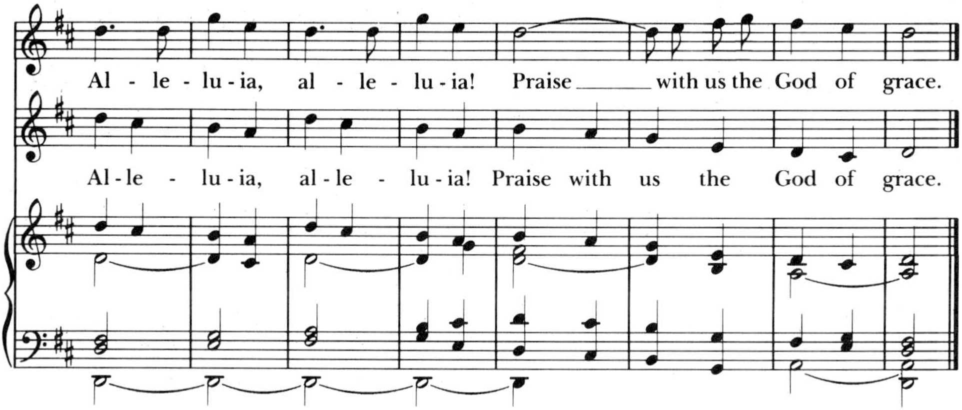
Al - le - lu - ia, al - le - lu - ia! Praise ___ with us the God of grace.
Al - le - lu - ia, al - le - lu - ia! Praise with us the God of grace.

The accompaniment for stanza 2 may be used for all stanzas.

Words: Henry Francis Lyte (1793-1847), alt.
Music: *Lauda anima,* John Goss (1800-1880); desc. Craig Sellar Lang (1891-1971)

𝅗𝅥 = 50
87. 87. 87

Praise to God

411

1 O bless the Lord, my soul! His grace to thee pro - claim!
2 O bless the Lord, my soul! His mer - cies bear in mind!
3 He will not al - ways chide; he will with pa - tience wait;
4 He par - dons all thy sins, pro - longs thy fee - ble breath;
5 He clothes thee with his love, up - holds thee with his truth;

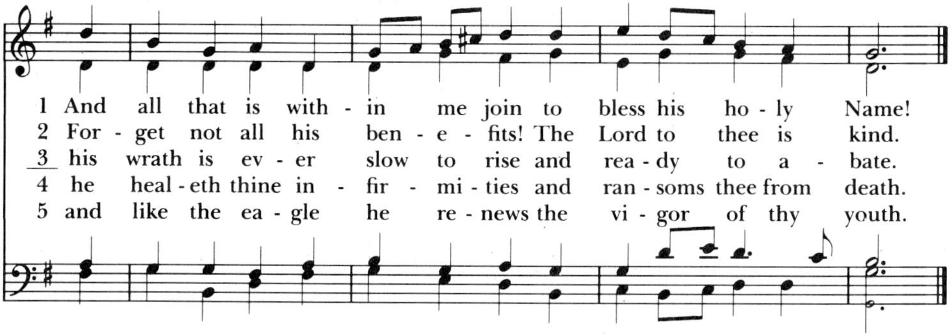
1 And all that is with - in me join to bless his ho - ly Name!
2 For - get not all his ben - e - fits! The Lord to thee is kind.
3 his wrath is ev - er slow to rise and rea - dy to a - bate.
4 he heal - eth thine in - fir - mi - ties and ran - soms thee from death.
5 and like the ea - gle he re - news the vi - gor of thy youth.

6 Then bless his holy Name,
whose grace hath made thee whole,
whose loving-kindness crowns thy days:
O bless the Lord, my soul!

This music in F, 524.

Words: James Montgomery (1771-1854); para. of Psalm 103:1-5
Music: *St. Thomas (Williams),* melody Aaron Williams (1731-1776); harm. Lowell Mason (1792-1872)

♩ = 84
SM

1 Earth and all stars, loud rush - ing plan - ets, sing to the
2 Hail, wind, and rain, loud blow - ing snow - storms, sing to the
3 Trum - pet and pipes, loud clash - ing cym - bals, sing to the
4 En - gines and steel, loud pound-ing ham - mers, sing to the
5 Class-rooms and labs, loud boil - ing test - tubes, sing to the
6 Know-ledge and truth, loud sound-ing wis - dom, sing to the
1 Lord a new song! O vic - to - ry,
2 Lord a new song! Flow - ers and trees,
3 Lord a new song! Harp, lute, and lyre,
4 Lord a new song! Lime - stone and beams,
5 Lord a new song! Ath - lete and band,
6 Lord a new song! Daugh - ter and son,

1 loud shout - ing ar - my, sing to the Lord a new song!
2 loud rus - tling dry leaves, sing to the Lord a new song!
3 loud hum - ming cel - los, sing to the Lord a new song!
4 loud build - ing work - ers, sing to the Lord a new song!
5 loud cheer - ing peo - ple, sing to the Lord a new song!
6 loud pray - ing mem - bers, sing to the Lord a new song!
Refrain
He has done mar - - vel - ous things.
I, too, will praise him with a new song!

Words: Herbert F. Brokering (b. 1926)
Music: *Earth and All Stars,* David N. Johnson (b. 1922)

♩=c. 132
45. 7. D with Refrain

Praise to God

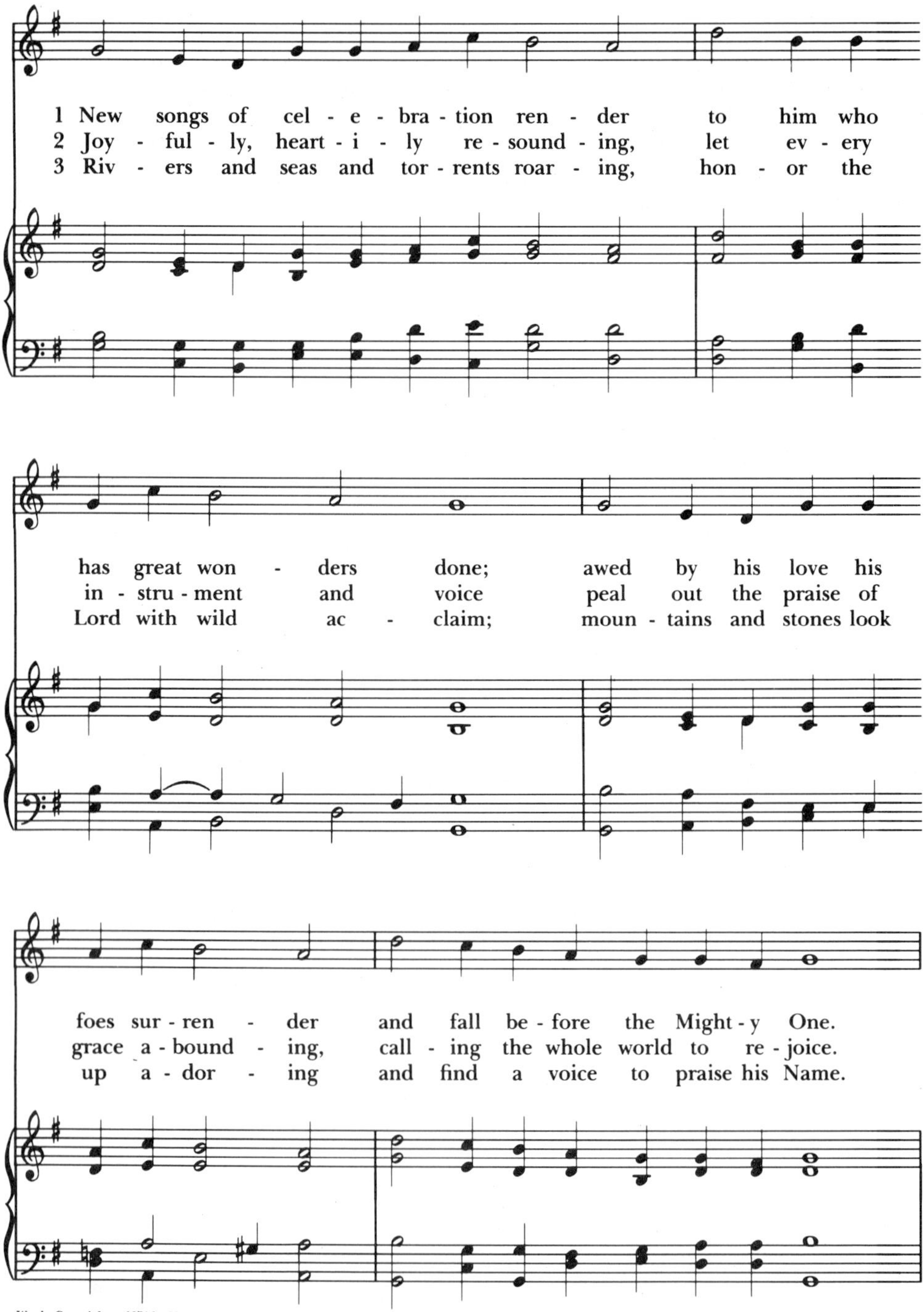
1 New songs of cel - e - bra - tion ren - der to him who
2 Joy - ful - ly, heart - i - ly re - sound - ing, let ev - ery
3 Riv - ers and seas and tor - rents roar - ing, hon - or the
has great won - ders done; awed by his love his
in - stru - ment and voice peal out the praise of
Lord with wild ac - claim; moun - tains and stones look
foes sur - ren - der and fall be - fore the Might - y One.
grace a - bound - ing, call - ing the whole world to re - joice.
up a - dor - ing and find a voice to praise his Name.

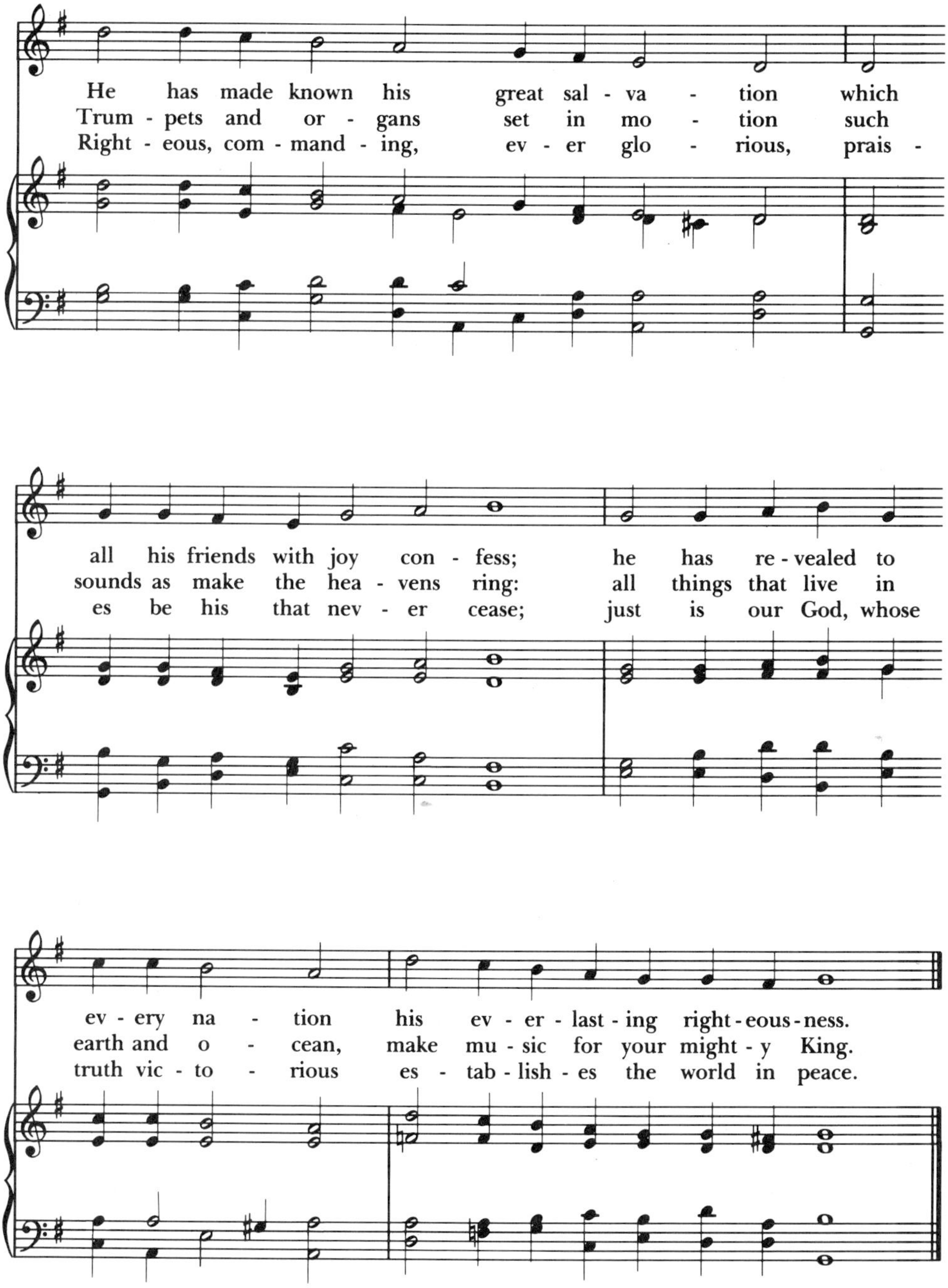
He has made known his great sal - va - tion which
Trum - pets and or - gans set in mo - tion such
Right - eous, com - mand - ing, ev - er glo - rious, prais -
all his friends with joy con - fess; he has re - vealed to
sounds as make the hea - vens ring: all things that live in
es be his that nev - er cease; just is our God, whose
ev - ery na - tion his ev - er - last - ing right - eous - ness.
earth and o - cean, make mu - sic for your might - y King.
truth vic - to - rious es - tab - lish - es the world in peace.

Other harmonizations, 301 and 302.

Words: Erik Routley (1917-1982); para. of Psalm 98
Music: *Rendez à Dieu,* melody att. Louis Bourgeois (1510?-1561?)
harm. Erik Routley (1917-1982)

♩=96
98. 98. D

Descant
6 All thy works, O Lord, shall bless thee; thee shall all thy
1 God, my King, thy might con - fess - ing, ev - er will I
2 Hon - or great our God be - fit - teth; who his ma - jes -
3 They shall talk of all thy glo - ry, on thy might and
4 Nor shall fail from mem-ory's trea - sure works by love and
5 Full of kind - ness and com - pas - sion, slow to an - ger,
saints a - dore: King su - preme shall they con - fess thee,
1 bless thy Name; day by day thy throne ad - dress - ing,
2 ty can reach? Age to age his works trans - mit - teth,
3 great - ness dwell, speak of thy dread acts the sto - ry,
4 mer - cy wrought, works of love sur - pass - ing mea - sure,
5 vast in love, God is good to all cre - a - tion;

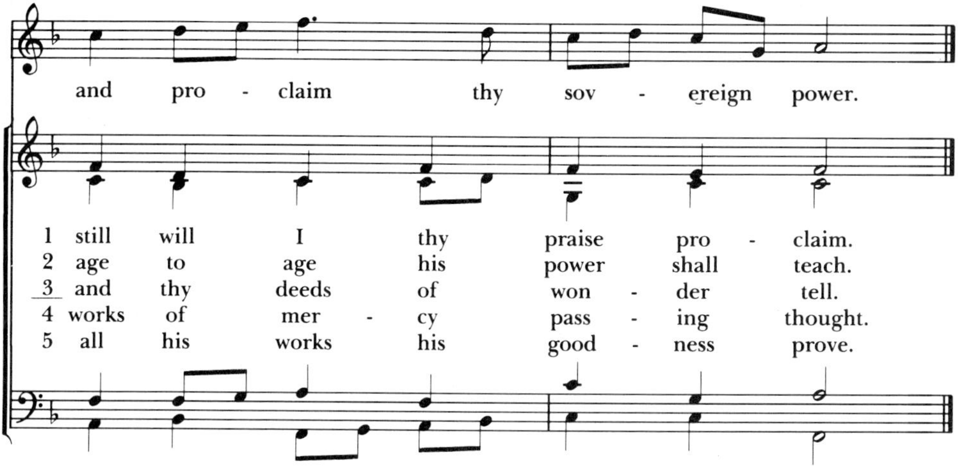
and pro - claim thy sov - ereign power.
1 still will I thy praise pro - claim.
2 age to age his power shall teach.
3 and thy deeds of won - der tell.
4 works of mer - cy pass - ing thought.
5 all his works his good - ness prove.

6 All thy works, O Lord, shall bless thee;
thee shall all thy saints adore:
King supreme shall they confess thee,
and proclaim thy sovereign power.

Another harmonization, 127.

Words: Richard Mant (1776-1848); para. of Psalm 145;1-12
Music: *Stuttgart,* melody from *Psalmodia Sacra, oder Andächtige und Schöne Gesänge,* 1715; adapt. and harm. William Henry Havergal (1793-1870), alt.; desc. John Wilson (b. 1905)

♩= 80
87. 87

1 When all thy mer - cies, O my God, my ris - ing soul sur - veys,
2 O how shall words with e - qual warmth the grat - i - tude de - clare,
3 Ten thou-sand thou - sand pre - cious gifts my dai - ly thanks em - ploy;
4 When na - ture fails, and day and night di - vide thy works no more,
5 Through all e - ter - ni - ty, to thee a joy - ful song I'll raise;

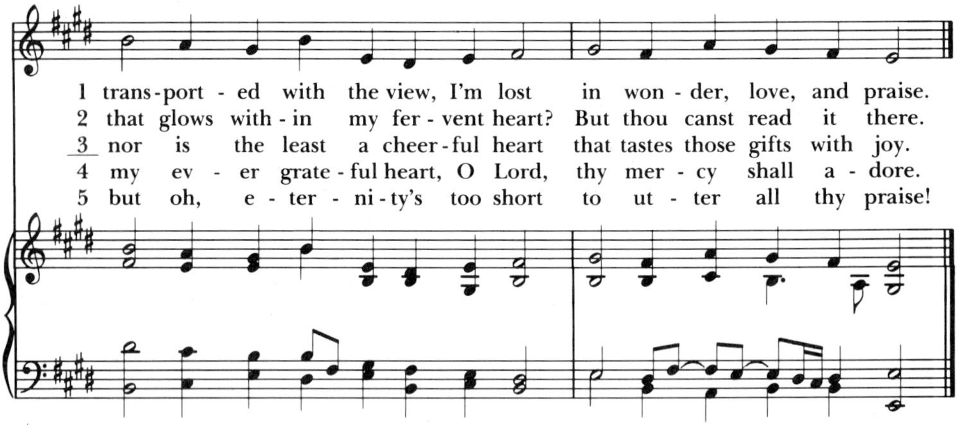
1 trans-port - ed with the view, I'm lost in won - der, love, and praise.
2 that glows with - in my fer - vent heart? But thou canst read it there.
3 nor is the least a cheer - ful heart that tastes those gifts with joy.
4 my ev - er grate - ful heart, O Lord, thy mer - cy shall a - dore.
5 but oh, e - ter - ni - ty's too short to ut - ter all thy praise!

Words: Joseph Addison (1672-1719), alt.
Music: *Durham,* melody and bass Thomas Ravenscroft (1592?-1635?); harm. *Hymnal 1982*

♩=80
CM

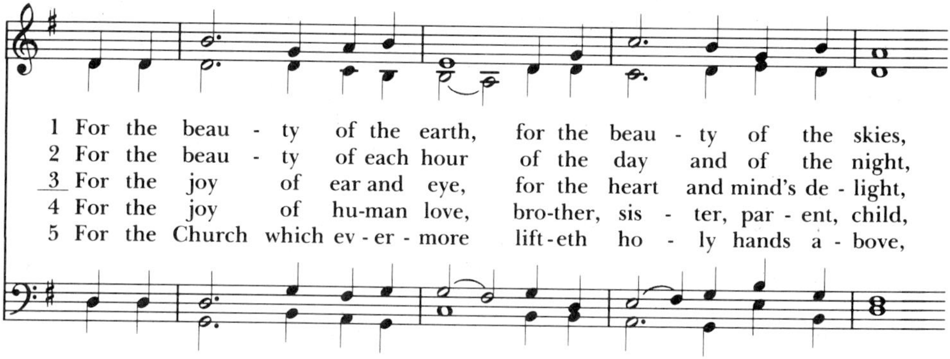
1 For the beau - ty of the earth, for the beau - ty of the skies,
2 For the beau - ty of each hour of the day and of the night,
3 For the joy of ear and eye, for the heart and mind's de - light,
4 For the joy of hu-man love, bro-ther, sis - ter, par - ent, child,
5 For the Church which ev - er - more lift-eth ho - ly hands a - bove,

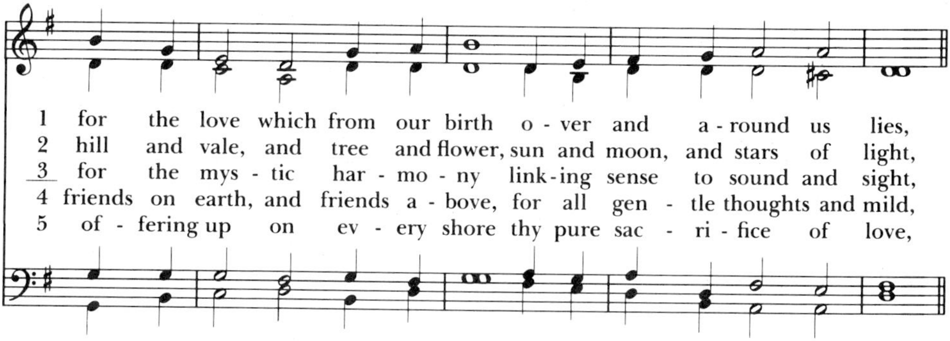
1 for the love which from our birth o - ver and a - round us lies,
2 hill and vale, and tree and flower, sun and moon, and stars of light,
3 for the mys - tic har - mo - ny link-ing sense to sound and sight,
4 friends on earth, and friends a - bove, for all gen - tle thoughts and mild,
5 of - fering up on ev - ery shore thy pure sac - ri - fice of love,

Refrain
Christ our God, to thee we raise this our hymn of grate-ful praise.

6 For each perfect gift of thine
to the world so freely given,
faith and hope and love divine,
peace on earth and joy in heaven,

Refrain

This music in A♭, 538. Alternative tune: *Dix,* 288.

Words: Folliot Sandford Pierpoint (1835-1917), alt.
Music: *Lucerna Laudoniae,* David Evans (1874-1948)

𝅗𝅥 = 84
77. 77 with Refrain

Antiphon
This is the feast of vic-to-ry for our God.
Al-le-lu-ia, al-le-lu-ia, al-le-lu-ia!
1 Wor-thy is Christ, the Lamb who was slain, whose
2 Pow-er, rich-es, wis-dom, and strength, and
3 Sing with all the peo-ple of God, and
4 Bless-ing, hon-or, glo-ry, and might be to
5 For the Lamb who was slain has be-

1 blood set us free to be peo - ple of God. [Ant.]
2 hon - or, bless - ing, and glo - ry are his. [Ant.]
3 join in the hymn of all cre - a - tion. [Ant.]
4 God and the Lamb for ev - er. A - men. [Ant.]
5 gun his reign. Al - le - lu - ia! [Ant.]
Final Antiphon
This is the feast of vic - to - ry for our God.
Al - le - lu - ia, al - le - lu - ia, al - le - lu - ia!

Alternative tune: *Raymond,* 418.

Words: Revelation 5:12-13; adapt. John W. Arthur (1922-1980)
Music: *Festival Canticle,* Richard Hillert (b. 1923)

𝅗𝅥=56
Irr. with Refrain

Antiphon

This is the feast of vic-to-ry for our God. Al-le-
lu - ia, al - le - lu - ia!
1. Wor-thy is Christ, the Lamb who was slain, whose
blood set us free to be peo - ple of God.

Antiphon
This is the feast of vic-to-ry for our God. Al-le-lu-ia, al-le-lu-ia!
2. Pow-er, rich-es, wis-dom and strength, and hon-or, bless-ing, and glo-ry are his.

Antiphon
This is the feast of vic-to-ry for our God. Al-le-lu-ia, al-le-lu-ia!
3. Sing with all the peo-ple of God, and join in the hymn of all cre-a-tion.
Antiphon
This is the feast of vic-to-ry for our

God. Al - le - lu - ia, al - le - lu - ia!
4. Bless - ing, hon - or, glo - ry, and might be to
God and the Lamb for ev - er. A - men.
Antiphon
This is the feast of vic - to - ry for our God. Al - le -

lu - ia, al - le - lu - ia!
5. For the Lamb who was slain has be-gun his reign.
Final Antiphon
Al - le - lu - ia!
This is the feast of vic-to-ry for our God.
Al - le - lu - ia, al - le - lu - ia!
3

Alternative tune: *Festival Canticle*, 417.

Words: Revelation 5:12-13; adapt. John W. Arthur (1922-1980)
Music: *Raymond*, Peter R. Hallock (b. 1923)

♩=c. 72
Irr. with Refrain

1 Lord of all be - ing, throned a - far, thy glo - ry
2 Sun of our life, thy quick - ening ray sheds on our
3 Lord of all life, be - low, a - bove, whose light is
4 Grant us thy truth to make us free, and kin - dling
flames from sun and star; cen - ter and soul of
path the glow of day; star of our hope, thy
truth, whose warmth is love, be - fore thy ev - er -
hearts that burn for thee, till all thy liv - ing
ev - ery sphere, yet to each lov - ing heart how near!
soft - ened light cheers the long watch - es of the night.
blaz - ing throne we ask no lus - ter of our own.
al - tars claim one ho - ly light, one heaven - ly flame.

Words: Oliver Wendell Holmes (1809-1894)
Music: *Mendon,* from *Methodist Harmonist,* 1821; adapt. and harm. Lowell Mason (1792-1872)

♩= 96
LM

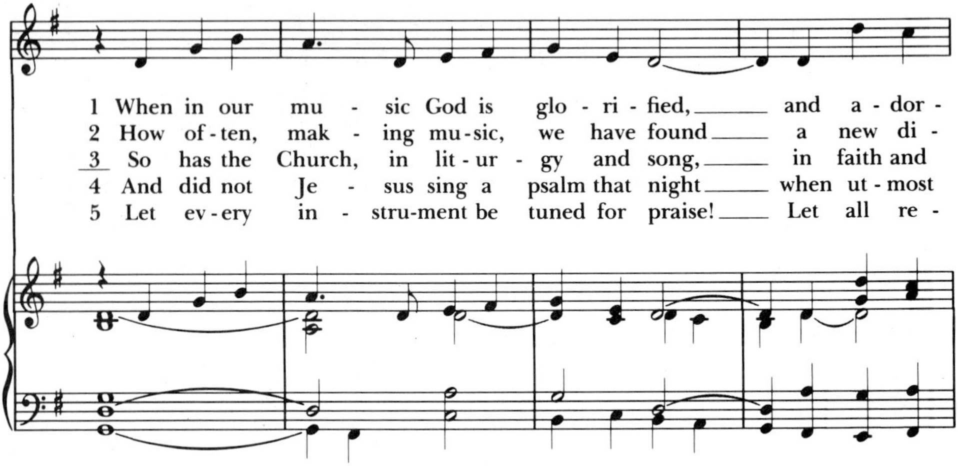
1 When in our mu - sic God is glo - ri - fied, and a - dor -
2 How of - ten, mak - ing mu - sic, we have found a new di -
3 So has the Church, in lit - ur - gy and song, in faith and
4 And did not Je - sus sing a psalm that night when ut - most
5 Let ev - ery in - stru-ment be tuned for praise! Let all re -

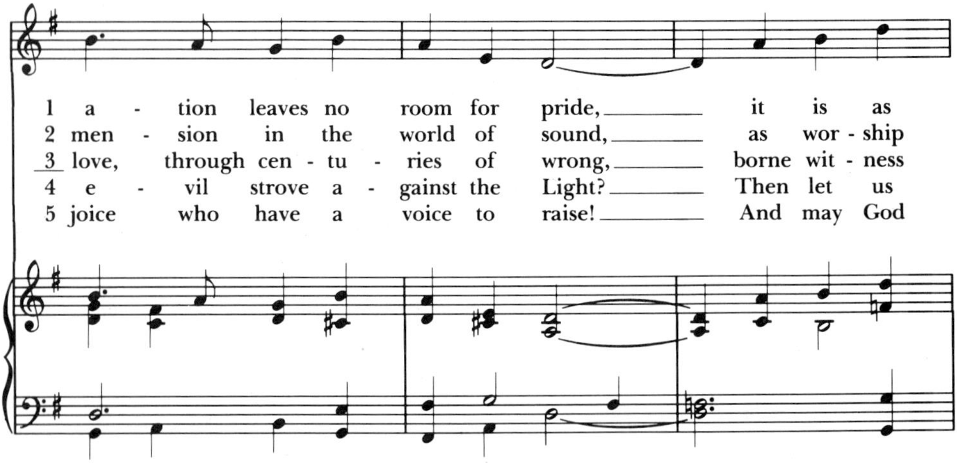
1 a - tion leaves no room for pride, it is as
2 men - sion in the world of sound, as wor - ship
3 love, through cen - tu - ries of wrong, borne wit - ness
4 e - vil strove a - gainst the Light? Then let us
5 joice who have a voice to raise! And may God

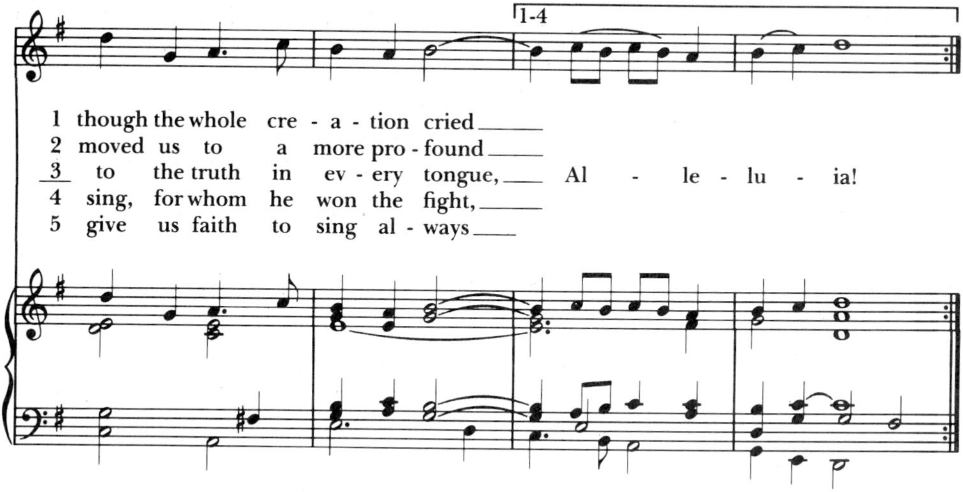
1-4
1 though the whole cre - a - tion cried
2 moved us to a more pro - found
3 to the truth in ev - ery tongue,
4 sing, for whom he won the fight,
5 give us faith to sing al - ways
Al - le - lu - ia!

Final Ending
Al - le - lu - ia! A - men.

This music in F, 296; this music in F with descant, 477.

Words: F. Pratt Green (b. 1903)
Music: *Engelberg,* Charles Villiers Stanford (1852-1924)

𝅗𝅥=48
10 10 10 with Alleluia

1 All glo - ry be to God on high, and peace on earth from
2 O Lamb of God, Lord Je - sus Christ, whom God the Fa - ther
3 You on - ly are the Ho - ly One, who came for our sal -
hea - ven, and God's good will un - fail - ing - ly be
gave us, who for the world was sac - ri - ficed up -
va - tion, and on - ly you are God's true Son, who
to all peo - ple giv - en. We bless, we wor - ship
on the cross to save us; and, as you sit at
was be - fore cre - a - tion. You, on - ly, Christ, as

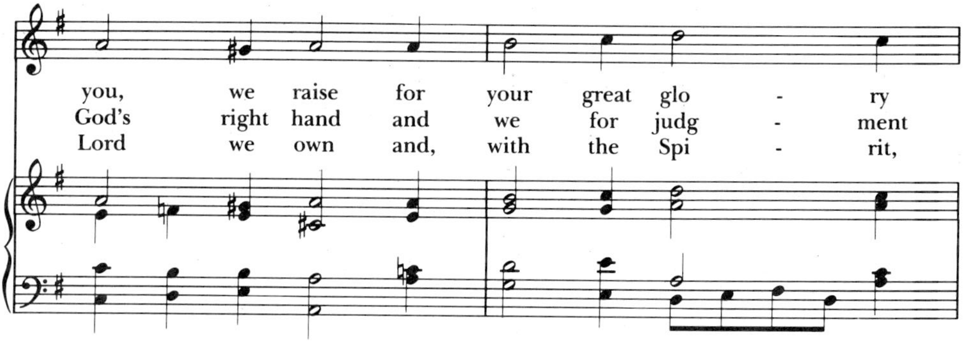
you, we raise for your great glo - ry
God's right hand and we for judg - ment
Lord we own and, with the Spi - rit,

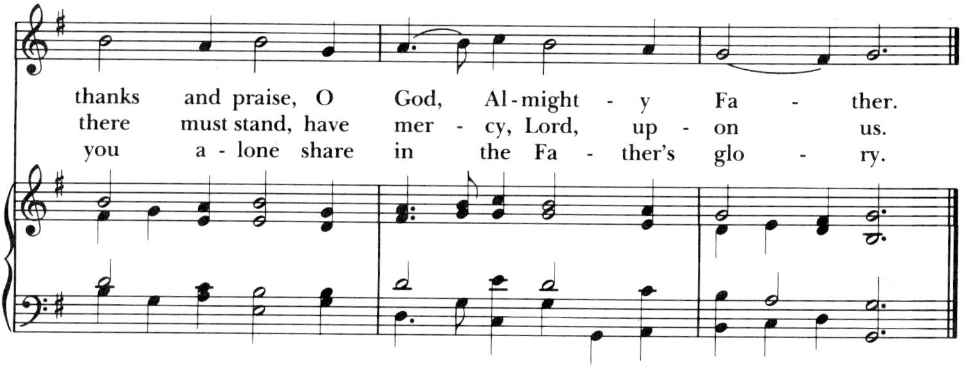
thanks and praise, O God, Al-might - y Fa - ther.
there must stand, have mer - cy, Lord, up - on us.
you a - lone share in the Fa - ther's glo - ry.

Words: Nikolaus Decius (1490?-1541); tr. F. Bland Tucker (1895-1984), rev.;
para. of *Gloria in excelsis*

Music: *Allein Gott in der Höh,* melody att. Nikolaus Decius (1490?-1541);
harm. Hieronymous Praetorius (1560?-1629)

𝅗𝅥. = 48
87. 87. 887

1 Not far be - yond the sea, nor high a - bove the heavens, but
2 Root - ed and ground - ed in thy love, with saints on earth and
3 Help us to press on toward that mark, and, though our vi - sion
ve - ry high thy voice, O God, is heard. For
saints a - bove we join in full ac - cord: to
now is dark, to live by what we see. So,
each new step of faith we take thou hast more truth and
know the breadth, length, depth, and height, the cru - ci - fied and
when we see thee face to face, thy truth and light our
light to break forth from thy Ho - ly Word.
ris - en might of Christ, the in - car - nate Word.
dwell - ing - place for ev - er - more shall be.

Words: George B. Caird (1917-1984), alt.
Music: *Cornwall,* Samuel Sebastian Wesley (1810-1876)

𝅗𝅥=50
886. 886

1 Im - mor - tal, in - vis - i - ble, God on - ly wise,
2 Un - rest - ing, un - hast - ing, and si - lent as light,
3 To all life thou giv - est, to both great and small;
4 Thou reign - est in glo - ry, thou rul - est in light,
in light in - ac - ces - si - ble hid from our eyes,
nor want - ing, nor wast - ing, thou rul - est in might;
in all life thou liv - est, the true life of all;
thine an - gels a - dore thee, all veil - ing their sight;
most bless - ed, most glo - rious, the An - cient of Days,
thy jus - tice like moun - tains high soar - ing a - bove
we blos - som and flour - ish, like leaves on the tree,
all laud we would ren - der: O help us to see
al - might - y, vic - tor - ious, thy great Name we praise.
thy clouds, which are foun - tains of good - ness and love.
then with - er and per - ish; but nought chan - geth thee.
'tis on - ly the splen - dor of light hid - eth thee.

Words: Walter Chalmers Smith (1824-1908), alt.
Music: *St. Denio,* Welsh hymn, from *Caniadau y Cyssegr,* 1839; adapt. John Roberts (1822-1877); harm. *The English Hymnal,* 1906, alt.

𝅗𝅥. = 40
11 11. 11 11

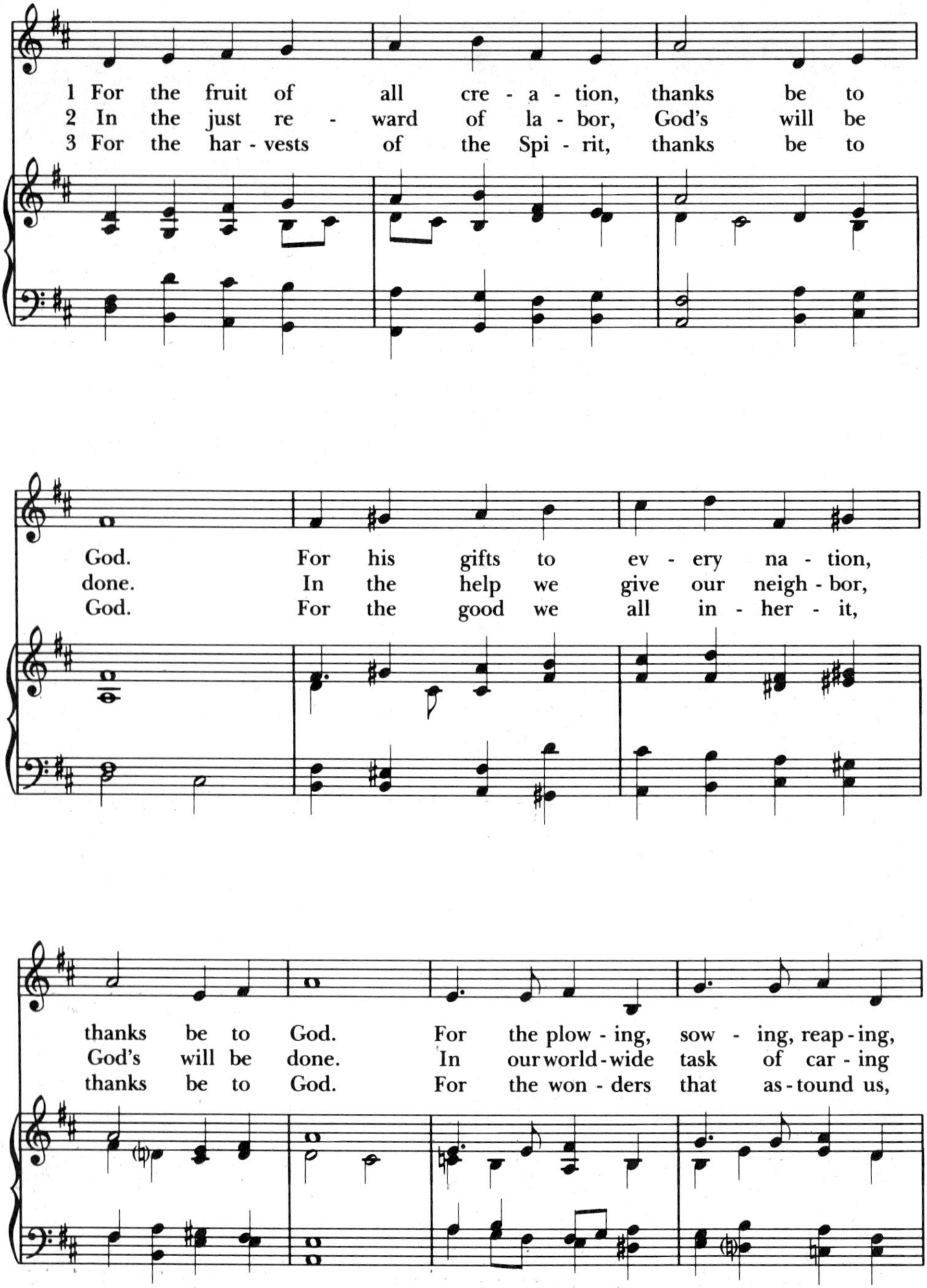
1 For the fruit of all cre - a - tion, thanks be to God.
2 In the just re - ward of la - bor, God's will be done.
3 For the har - vests of the Spi - rit, thanks be to God.
For his gifts to ev - ery na - tion,
In the help we give our neigh - bor,
For the good we all in - her - it,
thanks be to God.
God's will be done.
thanks be to God.
For the plow - ing, sow - ing, reap - ing,
In our world - wide task of car - ing
For the won - ders that as - tound us,

si - lent growth while we are sleep - ing, fu - ture needs in
for the hun - gry and de - spair - ing, in the har - vests
for the truths that still con-found us, most of all that
earth's safe-keep - ing, thanks be to God.
we are shar - ing, God's will be done.
love has found us, thanks be to God.

Words: F. Pratt Green (b. 1903), alt.
Music: *East Acklam,* Francis Jackson (b. 1917)

𝅗𝅥 = 54
84. 84. 888. 4

425 Praise to God

1 Sing now with joy un - to the Lord, for he has tri - umphed glo - rious - ly! The horse, the rid - er, and the sword he cast in - to the rag - ing sea.
2 God is our strength, he is our song, he saved us from our en - e - my. All praise and thanks to him be - long who came to set his peo - ple free.
3 He on - ly is the might - y Lord. He on - ly can des - troy the foe. He on - ly is to be a - dored for he a - lone can strength be - stow.

Words: Anon., ca. 1976, alt.; based on Exodus 15:1-2
Music: *Adon Olam*, Eliezer Gerovitch (1844-1914)

𝅗𝅥=52
LM

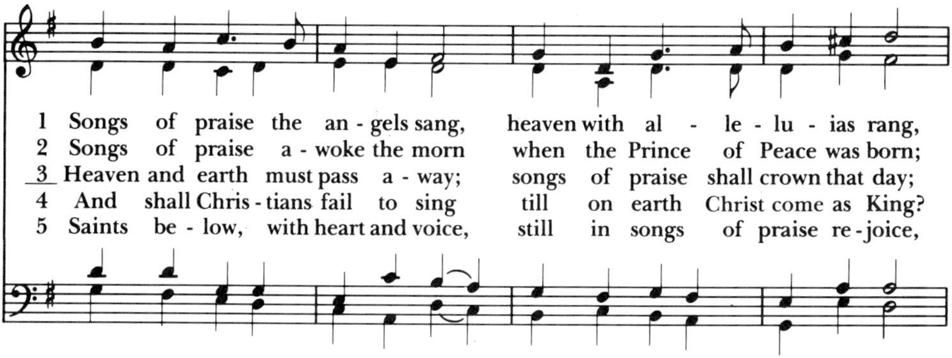
1 Songs of praise the an - gels sang, heaven with al - le - lu - ias rang,
2 Songs of praise a - woke the morn when the Prince of Peace was born;
3 Heaven and earth must pass a - way; songs of praise shall crown that day;
4 And shall Chris - tians fail to sing till on earth Christ come as King?
5 Saints be - low, with heart and voice, still in songs of praise re - joice,

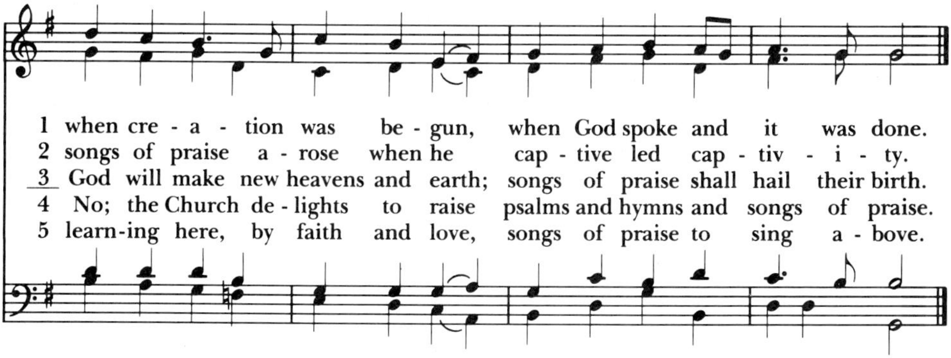
1 when cre - a - tion was be - gun, when God spoke and it was done.
2 songs of praise a - rose when he cap - tive led cap - tiv - i - ty.
3 God will make new heavens and earth; songs of praise shall hail their birth.
4 No; the Church de - lights to raise psalms and hymns and songs of praise.
5 learn-ing here, by faith and love, songs of praise to sing a - bove.

6 Borne upon their latest breath,
songs of praise shall conquer death;
then, amidst eternal joy,
songs of praise their powers employ.

Words: James Montgomery (1771-1854), alt.
Music: *Northampton,* Charles John King (1859-1934)

o=48
77. 77

1 When morn-ing gilds the skies, my heart, a-wak-ing, cries,
2 When mirth for mu-sic longs, this is my song of songs:
3 No love-lier an-ti-phon in all high heaven is known
4 Ye na-tions of man-kind, in this your con-cord find:
5 Sing, suns and stars of space, sing, ye that see his face,
1 may Je-sus Christ be praised! When eve-ning sha-dows fall,
2 may Je-sus Christ be praised! God's ho-ly house of prayer
3 than, Je-sus Christ be praised! There to the e-ter-nal Word
4 may Je-sus Christ be praised! Let all the earth a-round
5 sing, Je-sus Christ be praised! God's whole cre-a-tion o'er,
1 this rings my cur-few call, may Je-sus Christ be praised!
2 hath none that can com-pare with: Je-sus Christ be praised!
3 the e-ter-nal psalm is heard: may Je-sus Christ be praised!
4 ring joy-ous with the sound: may Je-sus Christ be praised!
5 both now and ev-er-more shall Je-sus Christ be praised!

Words: German, ca. 1800; tr. Robert Seymour Bridges (1844-1930), alt.
Music: *Laudes Domini*, Joseph Barnby (1838-1896)

𝅗𝅥 = 58
666. 666

1 O all ye works of God, now come to thank him
2 O sun and moon and stars of heaven, your end - less
3 O heat and cold, O night and day, O storms and
4 O earth and sea, O all that live in wa - ter
5 O let his peo - ple bless the Lord like right - eous
1 and a - dore; O an - gels, sing and
2 praise out - pour; O chang - ing sea - sons,
3 thun - der's roar, O fields and for - ests,
4 or on shore, O men and wo - men,
5 souls of yore; let those of ho - ly,
1 bless the Lord and praise him ev - er - more.
2 bless the Lord and praise him ev - er - more.
3 bless the Lord and praise him ev - er - more.
4 bless the Lord and praise him ev - er - more.
5 hum - ble heart come praise him ev - er - more.

6 So let us glorify and bless
the God we bow before,
the Father, Holy Spirit, Son,
and praise him evermore.

Words: F. Bland Tucker (1895-1984), rev.; para. of *A Song of Creation*
Music: *Irish*, melody from *Hymns and Sacred Poems*, 1749; harm. *The English Hymnal*, 1906

𝅗𝅥. = 40
CM

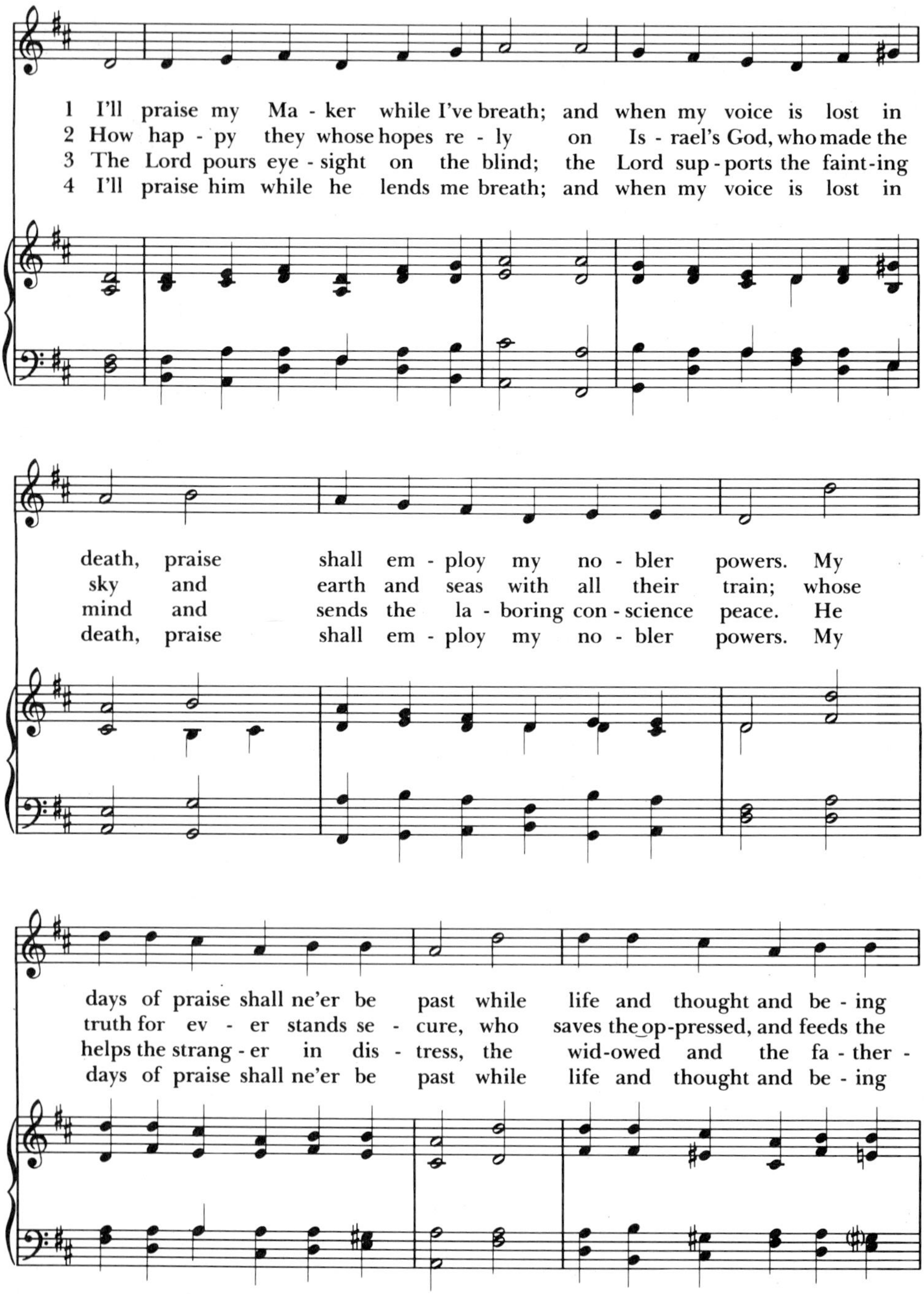
1 I'll praise my Ma - ker while I've breath; and when my voice is lost in
2 How hap - py they whose hopes re - ly on Is - rael's God, who made the
3 The Lord pours eye - sight on the blind; the Lord sup - ports the faint-ing
4 I'll praise him while he lends me breath; and when my voice is lost in
death, praise shall em - ploy my no - bler powers. My
sky and earth and seas with all their train; whose
mind and sends the la - boring con - science peace. He
death, praise shall em - ploy my no - bler powers. My
days of praise shall ne'er be past while life and thought and be - ing
truth for ev - er stands se - cure, who saves the op-pressed, and feeds the
helps the strang - er in dis - tress, the wid-owed and the fa - ther -
days of praise shall ne'er be past while life and thought and be - ing

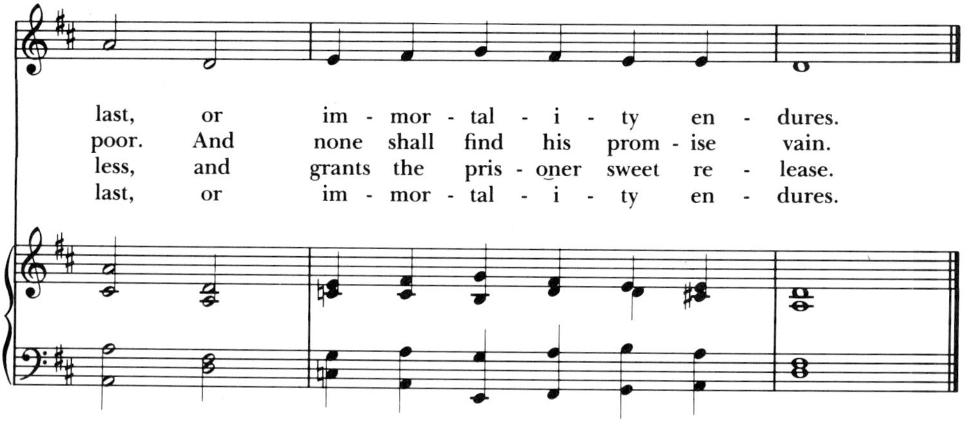
last, or im - mor - tal - i - ty en - dures.
poor. And none shall find his prom - ise vain.
less, and grants the pris - oner sweet re - lease.
last, or im - mor - tal - i - ty en - dures.

Words: Isaac Watts (1674-1748); alt. John Wesley (1703-1791), alt.; para. of Psalm 146 ♩ = 88
Music: *Old 113th,* melody from *Strassburger Kirchenamt,* 1525; harm. Vicar Earle Copes (b. 1921) 88. 88. 88

1 Come, O come, our voic - es raise, sound-ing God Al -
2 Sound the trum - pet, touch the lute, let no tongue nor
3 Come ye all be - fore his face, in this cho - rus
4 Let, in praise of God, the sound run a nev - er -
5 So this huge wide orb we see shall one choir, one
6 Thus our song shall o - ver-climb all the bounds of
might - y's praise; hith - er bring in one con - sent
string be mute, nor a voice-less crea - ture found,
take your place; and a - mid the mor - tal throng,
end - ing round, that our songs of praise may be
tem - ple be; where in such a praise-ful tone
space and time; come, then, come, our voic - es raise,

heart, and voice, and in - stru - ment. Al - le - lu - ia!
that hath nei - ther note nor sound. Al - le - lu - ia!
be you mas - ters of the song. Al - le - lu - ia!
ev - er - last - ing, as is he. Al - le - lu - ia!
we will sing what he hath done. Al - le - lu - ia!
sound - ing God Al - might - y's praise. Al - le - lu - ia!

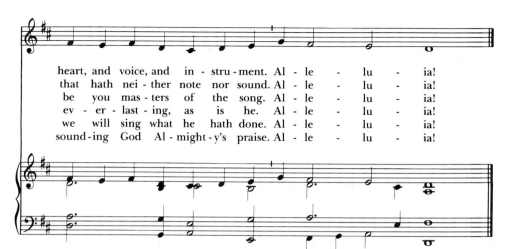

Words: George Wither (1588-1667), alt.
Music: *Sonne der Gerechtigkeit,* melody from *Bohemian Brethren, Kirchengeseng,* 1566; harm. Jan O. Bender (b. 1909)

𝅗𝅥 = 96
77. 77. with Alleluia

1 The stars de-clare his glo - ry; the vault of hea-ven springs
2 The dawn re-turns in splen - dor, the hea - vens burn and blaze,
3 So shine the Lord's com - mand - ment to make the sim - ple wise;
4 So or - der too this life of mine, di - rect it all my days;
mute wit - ness of the Mas-ter's hand in all cre - at - ed
the ris - ing sun re - news the race that mea - sures all our
more sweet than hon - ey to the taste, more rich than an - y
the med - i - ta - tions of my heart be in - no - cence and
things, and through the si - lenc - es of space
days, and writes in fire a - cross the skies
prize, a law of love with - in our hearts,
praise, my rock, and my re - deem - ing Lord,

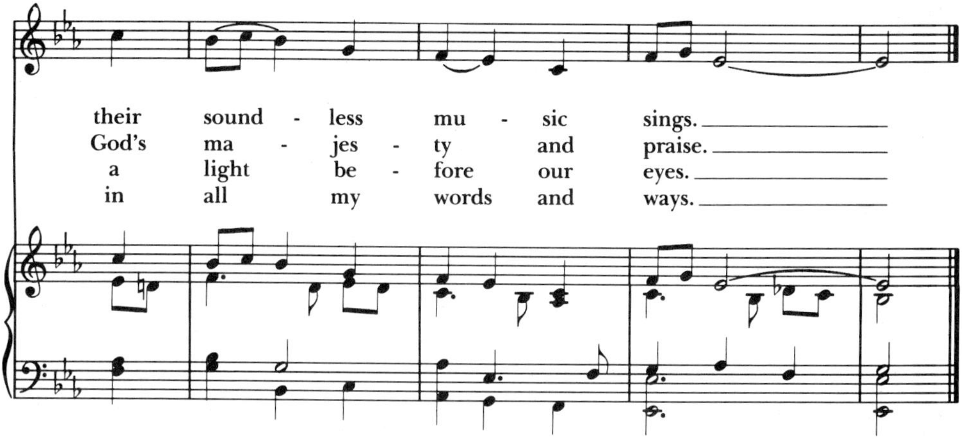
their sound - less mu - sic sings.
God's ma - jes - ty and praise.
a light be - fore our eyes.
in all my words and ways.

Words: Timothy Dudley-Smith (b. 1926); para. of Psalm 19
Music: *Aldine,* Richard Proulx (b. 1937)

♩=c. 72
76. 86. 86

1 O praise ye the Lord! Praise him in the height;
2 O praise ye the Lord! Praise him up - on earth,
*3 O praise ye the Lord! All things that give sound;
4 O praise ye the Lord! Thanks - giv - ing and song
re - joice in his word, ye an - gels of light;
in tune - ful ac - cord, all ye of new birth;
each ju - bi - lant chord re - ech - o a - round;
to him be out - poured all a - ges a - long!
ye hea - vens, a - dore him by whom ye were made,
praise him who hath brought you his grace from a - bove,
loud or - gans, his glo - ry forth tell in deep tone,
For love in cre - a - tion, for hea - ven re - stored,
and wor - ship be - fore him, in bright - ness ar - rayed.
praise him who hath taught you to sing of his love.
and sweet harp, the sto - ry of what he hath done.
for grace of sal - va - tion, O praise ye the Lord!
(♭)

Words: Henry Williams Baker (1821-1877), alt.; based on Psalms 148 and 150
Music: *Laudate Dominum*, Charles Hubert Hastings Parry (1848-1918)

♩= 108
10 10. 11 11

Alternative accompaniment for stanza 4 in unison

Music: *Laudate Dominum,* Charles Hubert Hastings Parry (1848-1918)

♩= 88

1 We gath - er to - geth - er to ask the Lord's bless - ing;
2 Be - side us to guide us, our God with us join - ing,
3 We all do ex - tol thee, thou lead - er tri - um - phant,
he chas - tens and has - tens his will to make known;
or - dain - ing main - tain - ing his king - dom di - vine;
and pray that thou still our de - fend - er wilt be.
the wick - ed op - press - ing now cease from dis - tress - ing:
so from the be - gin - ning the fight we were win - ning:
Let thy con - gre - ga - tion es - cape trib - u - la - tion:
sing prais - es to his Name; he for - gets not his own.
thou, Lord, wast at our side: all ___ glo - ry be thine!
thy Name be ev - er praised! O ___ Lord, make us free!

Words: Anon. 1625; tr. Theodore Baker (1851-1934)
Music: *Kremser*, from *Nederlandtsch Gedenckclank*, 1626; arr. Eduard Kremser (1838-1914)

𝅗𝅥 = 46
12 11. 12 11

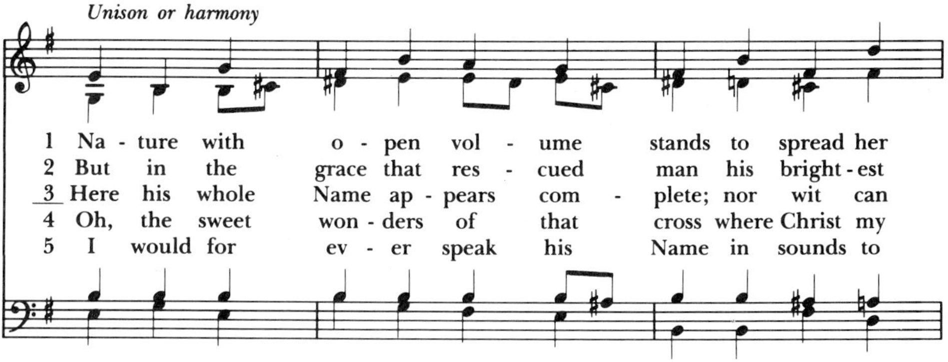
Unison or harmony
1 Na - ture with o - pen vol - ume stands to spread her
2 But in the grace that res - cued man his bright - est
3 Here his whole Name ap - pears com - plete; nor wit can
4 Oh, the sweet won - ders of that cross where Christ my
5 I would for ev - er speak his Name in sounds to

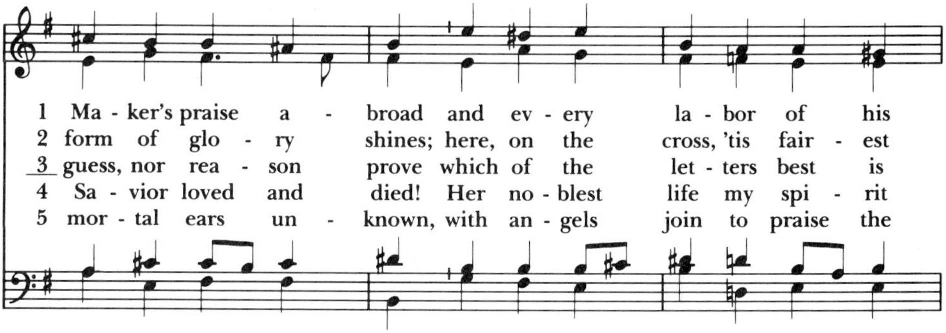
1 Ma - ker's praise a - broad and ev - ery la - bor of his
2 form of glo - ry shines; here, on the cross, 'tis fair - est
3 guess, nor rea - son prove which of the let - ters best is
4 Sa - vior loved and died! Her no - blest life my spi - rit
5 mor - tal ears un - known, with an - gels join to praise the

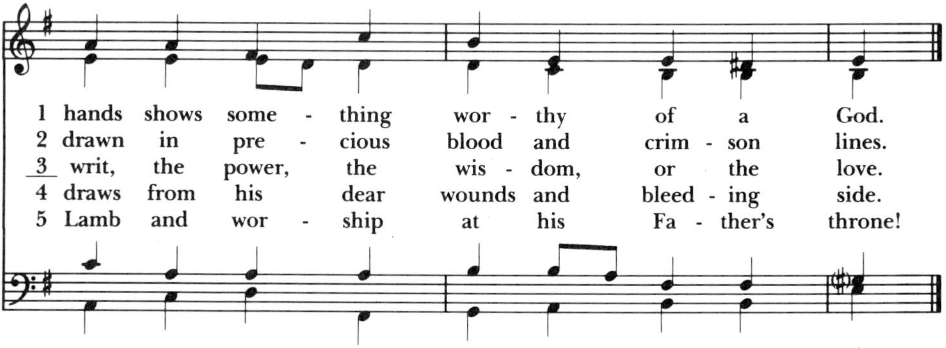
1 hands shows some - thing wor - thy of a God.
2 drawn in pre - cious blood and crim - son lines.
3 writ, the power, the wis - dom, or the love.
4 draws from his dear wounds and bleed - ing side.
5 Lamb and wor - ship at his Fa - ther's throne!

This music in e♭, 578. *The G♯ in the final chord should be reserved for stanza 5.*

Words: Isaac Watts (1674-1748) ♩=88

Music: *Eltham,* melody Nathaniel Gawthorn (18th cent.); harm. Samuel Sebastian Wesley (1810-1876) LM

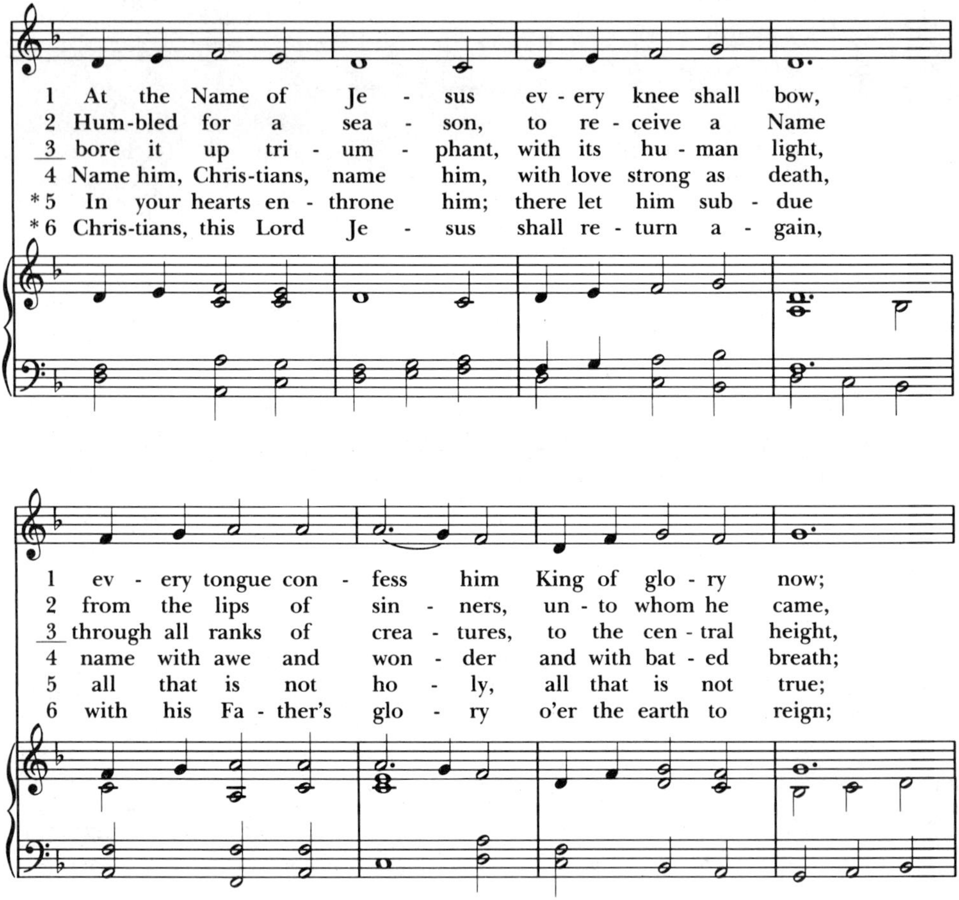
1 At the Name of Je - sus ev - ery knee shall bow,
2 Hum-bled for a sea - son, to re - ceive a Name
3 bore it up tri - um - phant, with its hu - man light,
4 Name him, Chris-tians, name him, with love strong as death,
*5 In your hearts en - throne him; there let him sub - due
*6 Chris-tians, this Lord Je - sus shall re - turn a - gain,
1 ev - ery tongue con - fess him King of glo - ry now;
2 from the lips of sin - ners, un - to whom he came,
3 through all ranks of crea - tures, to the cen - tral height,
4 name with awe and won - der and with bat - ed breath;
5 all that is not ho - ly, all that is not true;
6 with his Fa - ther's glo - ry o'er the earth to reign;

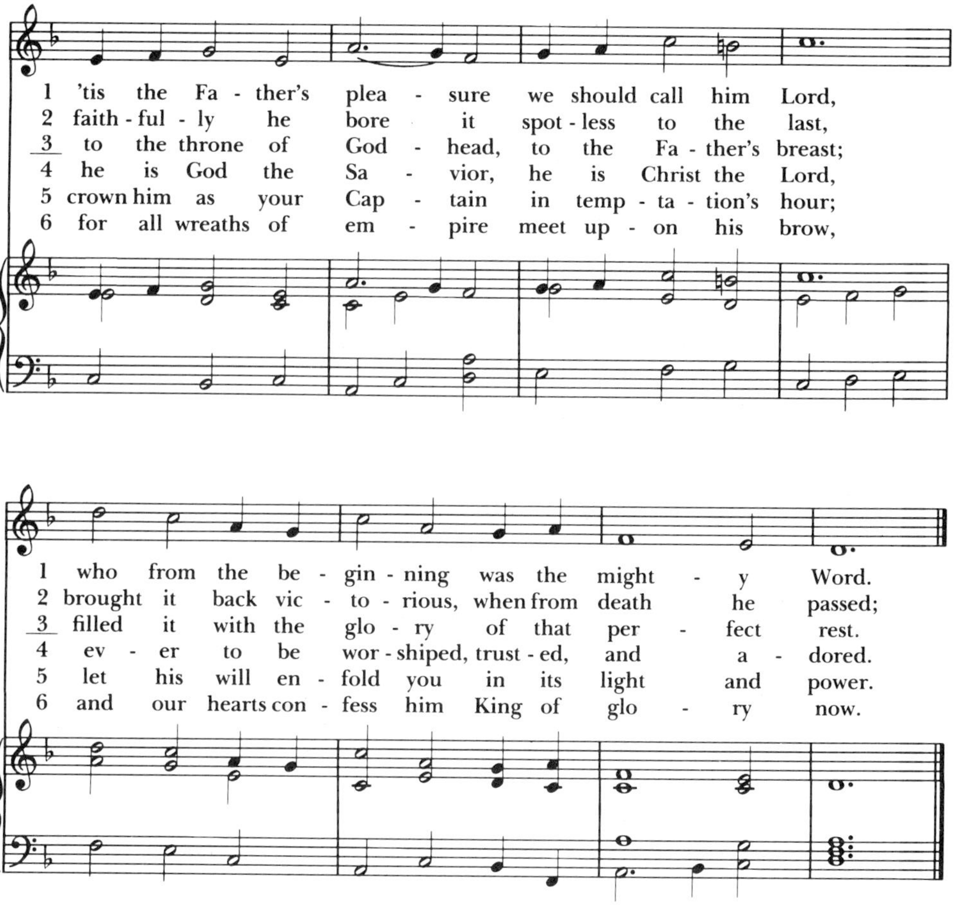
1 'tis the Fa - ther's plea - sure we should call him Lord,
2 faith - ful - ly he bore it spot - less to the last,
3 to the throne of God - head, to the Fa - ther's breast;
4 he is God the Sa - vior, he is Christ the Lord,
5 crown him as your Cap - tain in temp - ta - tion's hour;
6 for all wreaths of em - pire meet up - on his brow,
1 who from the be - gin - ning was the might - y Word.
2 brought it back vic - to - rious, when from death he passed;
3 filled it with the glo - ry of that per - fect rest.
4 ev - er to be wor - shiped, trust - ed, and a - dored.
5 let his will en - fold you in its light and power.
6 and our hearts con - fess him King of glo - ry now.

Words: Caroline Maria Noel (1817-1877), alt.
Music: *King's Weston*, Ralph Vaughan Williams (1872-1958)

♩= 104
65. 65. D

1 Lift up your heads, ye might - y gates; be - hold the
2 O blest the land, the ci - ty blest, where Christ the
3 Fling wide the por - tals of your heart; make it a
*4 Re - deem - er come! I o - pen wide my heart to
5 So come, my Sov - ereign; en - ter in! Let new and
1 King of glo - ry waits! The King of kings is
2 ru - ler is con - fessed! O hap - py hearts and
3 tem - ple, set a - part from earth - ly use for
4 thee: here, Lord, a - bide! Let me thy in - ner
5 no - bler life be - gin; thy Ho - ly Spi - rit
1 draw - ing near; the Sa - vior of the world is here.
2 hap - py homes to whom this King of tri - umph comes!
3 heaven's em - ploy, a - dorned with prayer and love and joy.
4 pres - ence feel: thy grace and love in me re - veal.
5 guide us on, un - til the glo - rious crown be won.

Words: Georg Weissel (1590-1635); tr. Catherine Winkworth (1827-1878)
Music: *Truro,* melody from *Psalmodia Evangelica, Part II,* 1789; harm. Lowell Mason (1792-1872), alt.

𝅗𝅥=96
LM

1 Tell out, my soul, the great-ness of the Lord!
2 Tell out, my soul, the great-ness of his Name!
3 Tell out, my soul, the great-ness of his might!
4 Tell out, my soul, the glo - ries of his word!
Un - num - bered bless - ings give my spi - rit voice;
Make known his might, the deeds his arm has done;
Powers and do - min - ions lay their glo - ry by.
Firm is his prom - ise, and his mer - cy sure.
ten - der to me the prom - ise of his word;
his mer - cy sure, from age to age the same;
Proud hearts and stub - born wills are put to flight,
Tell out, my soul, the great - ness of the Lord
in God my Sa - vior shall my heart re - joice.
his ho - ly Name— the Lord, the Might - y One.
the hun - gry fed, the hum - ble lift - ed high.
to chil-dren's chil - dren and for ev - er - more!

Alternative tune: *Woodlands,* 438.

Words: Timothy Dudley-Smith (b. 1926); based on *The Song of Mary*
Music: *Birmingham,* from *Repository of Sacred Music, Part II,* 1813; harm. *Songs of Praise,* 1925

𝅗𝅥 = 50
10 10. 10 10

1 Tell out, my soul, the great-ness of the Lord! Un-
2 Tell out, my soul, the great-ness of his Name! Make
3 Tell out, my soul, the great-ness of his might! Powers
4 Tell out, my soul, the glo-ries of his word! Firm
num-bered bless-ings give my spi-rit voice; ten-der to
known his might, the deeds his arm has done; his mer-cy
and do-min-ions lay their glo-ry by. Proud hearts and
is his prom-ise, and his mer-cy sure. Tell out, my
me the prom-ise of his word; in
sure, from age to age the same; his
stub-born wills are put to flight, the
soul, the great-ness of the Lord to

God my Sa - vior shall my heart re - joice.
ho - ly Name— the Lord, the Might - y One.
hun - gry fed, the hum - ble lift - ed high.
chil - dren's chil - dren and for ev - er - more!

Alternative tune: *Birmingham,* 437.

Words: Timothy Dudley-Smith (b. 1926); based on *The Song of Mary* 𝅗𝅥=52
Music: *Woodlands,* Walter Greatorex (1877-1949), alt. 10 10. 10 10

Alternative accompaniment

Music: *Woodlands,* Walter Greatorex (1877-1949) 𝅗𝅥=52

Unison
Dm Am Dm C Dm Am Dm
1 What won-drous love is this, O my soul, O my soul! What
2 To God and to the Lamb, I will sing, I will sing, to
3 And when from death I'm free, I'll sing on, I'll sing on, and
F Dm C Dm C Dm F Dm
won-drous love is this, O my soul! What won-drous love is this that
God and to the Lamb, I will sing. To God and to the Lamb who
when from death I'm free, I'll sing on. And when from death I'm free I'll
F Am Dm Dm Am Dm C
caused the Lord of bliss to lay a - side his crown for my
is the great I AM, while mil - lions join the theme, I will
sing and joy - ful be, and through e - ter - ni - ty I'll sing
Dm Am Dm F Am Dm C Dm
soul, for my soul, to lay a - side his crown for my soul.
sing, I will sing, while mil - lions join the theme I will sing.
on, I'll sing on, and through e - ter - ni - ty I'll sing on.

Keyboard and guitar should not sound together. Either of the following harmonizations may accompany unison singing.

Words: American folk hymn, ca. 1835
Music: *Wondrous Love*, from *The Southern Harmony*, 1835

𝅗𝅥=60
12 9. 12. 12 9

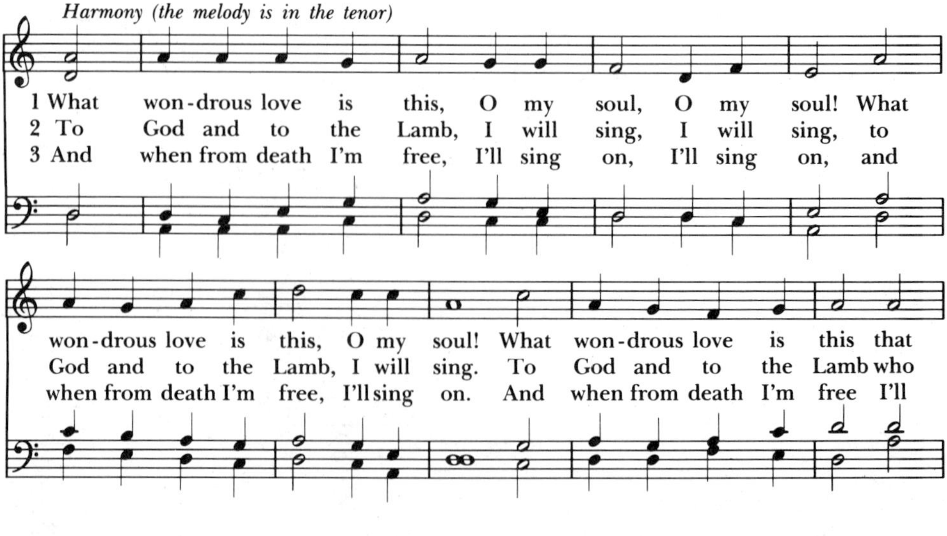
Harmony (the melody is in the tenor)
1 What won-drous love is this, O my soul, O my soul! What
2 To God and to the Lamb, I will sing, I will sing, to
3 And when from death I'm free, I'll sing on, I'll sing on, and
won-drous love is this, O my soul! What won-drous love is this that
God and to the Lamb, I will sing. To God and to the Lamb who
when from death I'm free, I'll sing on. And when from death I'm free I'll

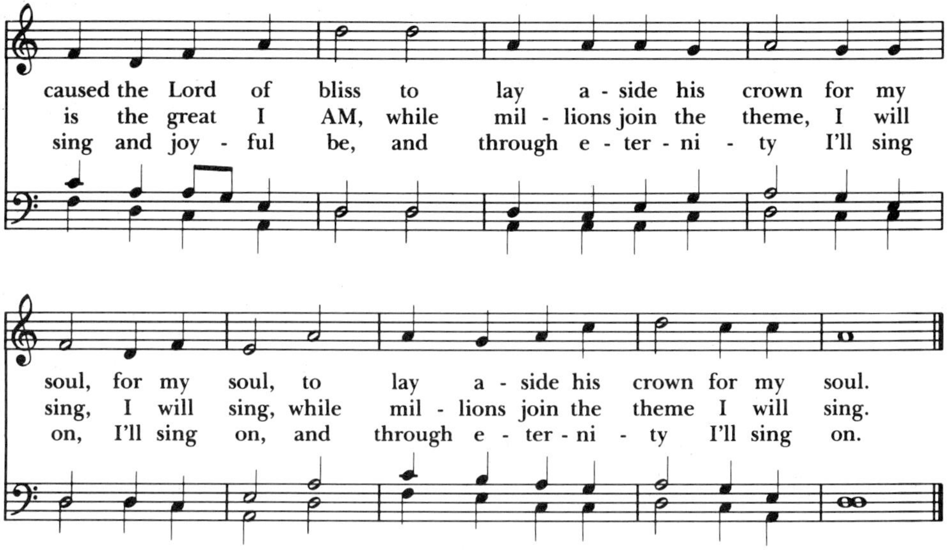
caused the Lord of bliss to lay a - side his crown for my
is the great I AM, while mil - lions join the theme, I will
sing and joy - ful be, and through e - ter - ni - ty I'll sing
soul, for my soul, to lay a - side his crown for my soul.
sing, I will sing, while mil - lions join the theme I will sing.
on, I'll sing on, and through e - ter - ni - ty I'll sing on.

Words: American folk hymn, ca. 1835 — 𝅗𝅥=60

Music: *Wondrous Love,* from *The Southern Harmony,* 1835 — 12 9. 12. 12 9

Alternative accompaniment

Music: *Wondrous Love,* melody from *The Southern Harmony,* 1835; harm. Carlton R. Young (b. 1926) — 𝅗𝅥=60

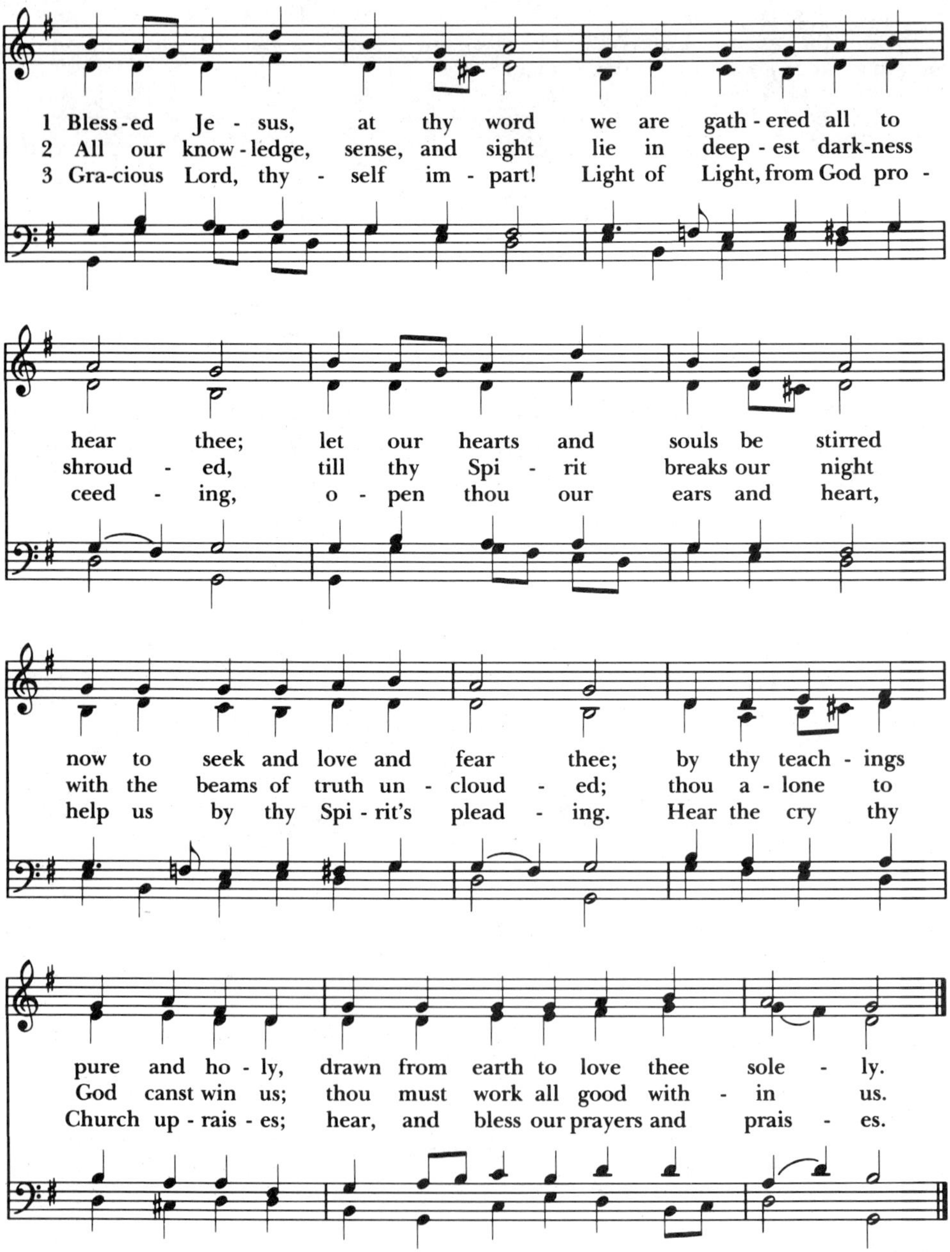
1 Bless-ed Je - sus, at thy word we are gath - ered all to
2 All our know - ledge, sense, and sight lie in deep - est dark-ness
3 Gra-cious Lord, thy - self im - part! Light of Light, from God pro -
hear thee; let our hearts and souls be stirred
shroud - ed, till thy Spi - rit breaks our night
ceed - ing, o - pen thou our ears and heart,
now to seek and love and fear thee; by thy teach - ings
with the beams of truth un - cloud - ed; thou a - lone to
help us by thy Spi - rit's plead - ing. Hear the cry thy
pure and ho - ly, drawn from earth to love thee sole - ly.
God canst win us; thou must work all good with - in us.
Church up - rais - es; hear, and bless our prayers and prais - es.

Words: Tobias Clausnitzer (1619-1684); tr. Catherine Winkworth (1827-1878), alt.
Music: *Liebster Jesu,* melody Johann Rudolph Ahle (1625-1673); alt. *Das grosse Cantional: oder Kirchen-Gesangbuch,* 1687; harm. George Herbert Palmer (1846-1926)

𝅗𝅥=46
78. 78. 88

1 In the cross of Christ I glo - ry, tower - ing
2 When the woes of life o'er - take me, hopes de -
3 When the sun of bliss is beam - ing light and
4 Bane and bless - ing, pain and plea - sure, by the
*5 In the cross of Christ I glo - ry, tower - ing
1 o'er the wrecks of time; all the light of
2 ceive, and fears an - noy, nev - er shall the
3 love up - on my way, from the cross the
4 cross are sanc - ti - fied; peace is there that
5 o'er the wrecks of time; all the light of
1 sa - cred sto - ry gath - ers round its head sub - lime.
2 cross for - sake me: lo, it glows with peace and joy.
3 ra - diance stream - ing adds new lus - ter to the day.
4 knows no mea - sure, joys that through all time a - bide.
5 sa - cred sto - ry gath - ers round its head sub - lime.

Alternate tunes: *Tomter*, 442; *Charlestown*, 571.

Words: John Bowring (1792-1872)
Music: *Rathbun*, Ithamar Conkey (1815-1867)

𝅗𝅥. = 42
87. 87

1 In the cross of Christ I glo - ry, tower - ing o'er the
2 When the woes of life o'er - take me, hopes de - ceive, and
3 When the sun of bliss is beam - ing light and love up -
4 Bane and bless - ing, pain and plea - sure, by the cross are
*5 In the cross of Christ I glo - ry, tower - ing o'er the
1 wrecks of time; all the light of sa - cred
2 fears an - noy, nev - er shall the cross for -
3 on my way, from the cross the ra - diance
4 sanc - ti - fied; peace is there that knows no
5 wrecks of time; all the light of sa - cred
1 sto - ry gath - ers round its head sub - lime.
2 sake me: lo, it glows with peace and joy.
3 stream - ing adds new lus - ter to the day.
4 mea - sure, joys that through all time a - bide.
5 sto - ry gath - ers round its head sub - lime.

Alternate tunes: *Rathbun* 441; *Charlestown,* 571.

Words: John Bowring (1792-1872)
Music: *Tomter,* Bruce Neswick (b. 1956)

♩=96
87. 87

1 From God Christ's de - i - ty came forth, his man - hood from hu -
2 He joined with guests at wed - ding feast, yet in the wil - der -
3 The dis - so - lute he did not scorn, nor turn from those who
4 He did not dis - re - gard the sick; to sim - ple ones his
5 Who then, my Lord, com-pares to you? The Watch - er slept, the
1 man - i - ty; his priest-hood from Mel - chi - ze - dek, his
2 ness did fast; he taught with - in the tem - ple's gates; his
3 were in sin; he for the right - eous did re - joice but
4 word was given; and he de - scend - ed to the earth and
5 Great was small, the Pure bap - tized, the Life who died, the
1 roy - al - ty from Da - vid's tree: praised be his One - ness.
2 peo - ple saw him die at last: praised be his teach - ing.
3 bade the fall - en to come in: praised be his mer - cy.
4 his work done, went up to heaven: praised be his com - ing.
5 King a - based to hon - or all: praised be your glo - ry.

Words: Ephrem of Edessa (4th cent.); tr. John Howard Rhys (b. 1917); adapt. and alt. F. Bland Tucker (1895-1984)
Music: *Salem Harbor,* Ronald Arnatt (b. 1930)

𝅗𝅥 = 52-60
88. 88. 5

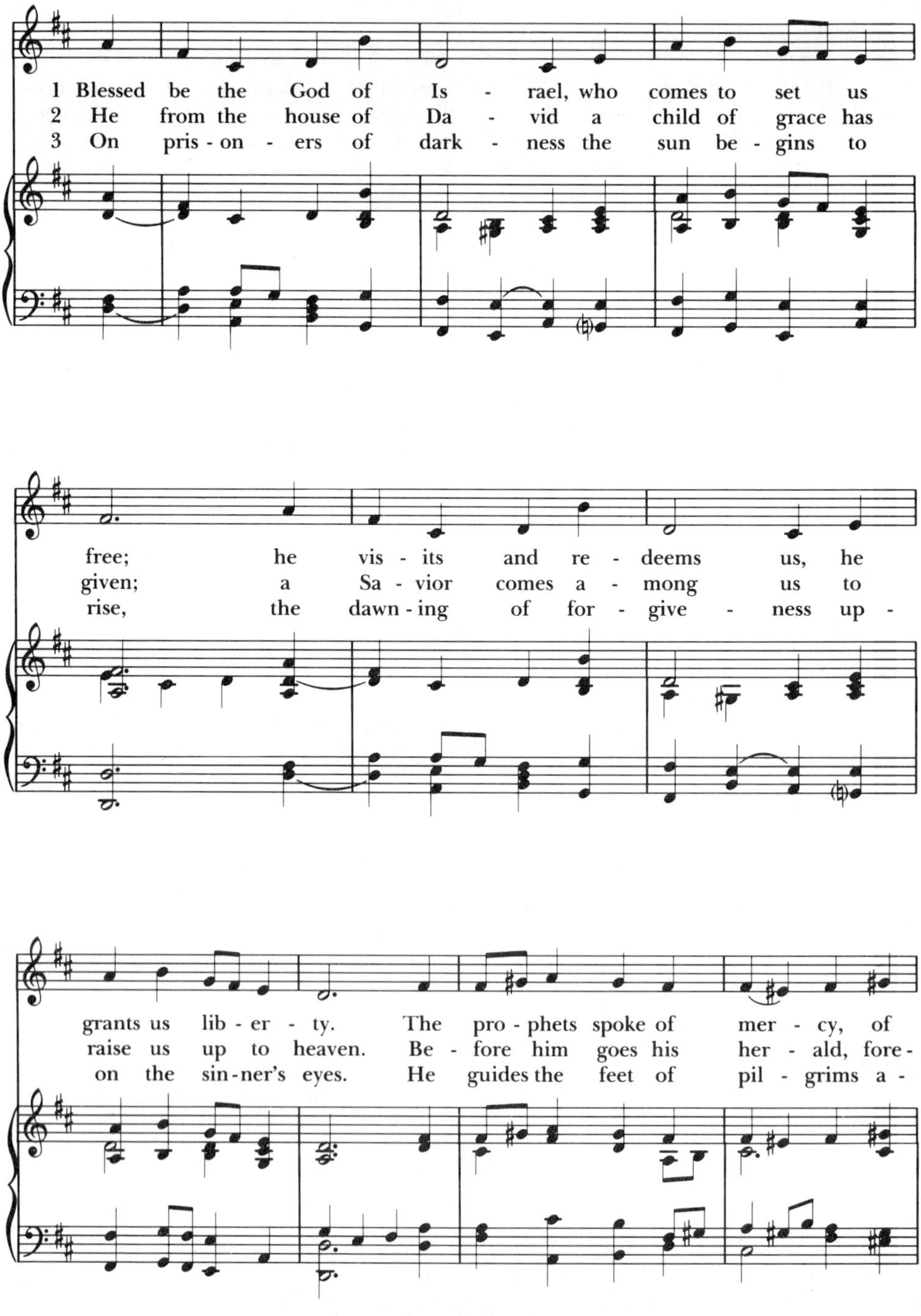
1 Blessed be the God of Is - rael, who comes to set us
2 He from the house of Da - vid a child of grace has
3 On pris - on - ers of dark - ness the sun be - gins to
free; he vis - its and re - deems us, he
given; a Sa - vior comes a - mong us to
rise, the dawn - ing of for - give - ness up -
grants us lib - er - ty. The pro - phets spoke of mer - cy, of
raise us up to heaven. Be - fore him goes his her - ald, fore -
on the sin - ner's eyes. He guides the feet of pil - grims a -

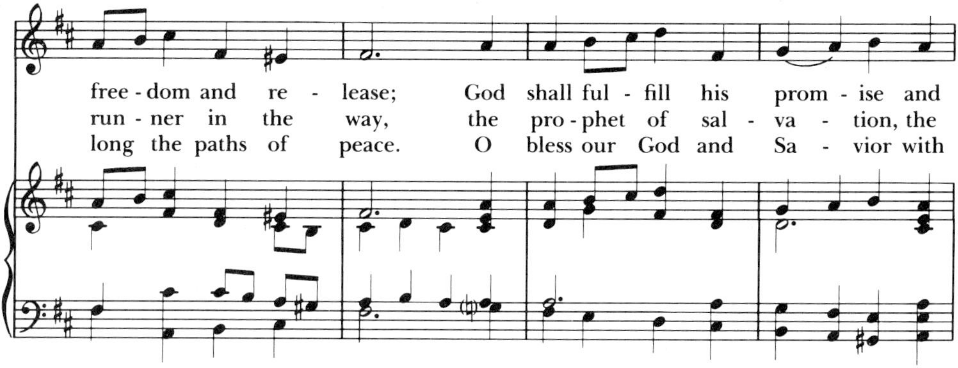
free - dom and re - lease; God shall ful - fill his prom - ise and
run - ner in the way, the pro - phet of sal - va - tion, the
long the paths of peace. O bless our God and Sa - vior with

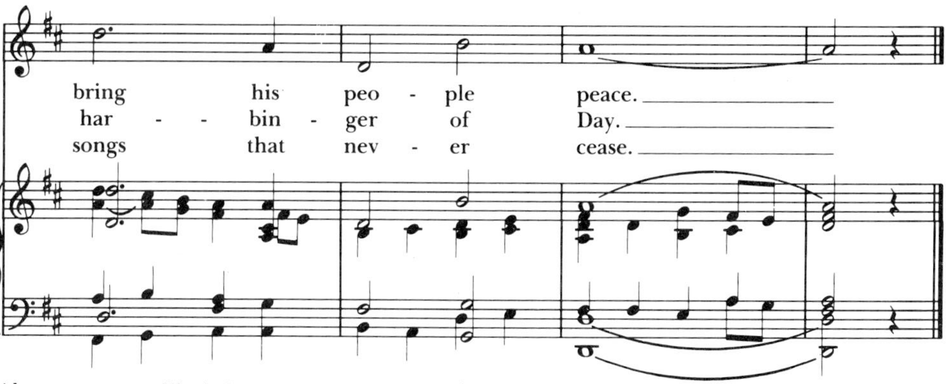
bring his peo - ple peace.
har - - bin - ger of Day.
songs that nev - er cease.

Alternate tunes: *King's Lynn,* 591; *Forest Green,* 705.

Words: Michael A. Perry (b. 1942), alt.; para. of *The Song of Zechariah*
Music: *Thornbury,* Basil Harwood (1859-1949)

𝅗𝅥 = 52
76. 76. D

1 Praise to the Ho - liest in the height, and in the
2 O lov - ing wis - dom of our God! When all was
3 O wis - est love! that flesh and blood, which did in
4 and that the high - est gift of grace should flesh and
5 Praise to the Ho - liest in the height, and in the
1 depth be praise; in all his words most
2 sin and shame, a sec - ond Ad - am
3 Ad - am fail, should strive a - fresh a -
4 blood re - fine: God's pres - ence and his
5 depth be praise; in all his words most
1 won - der - ful, most sure in all his ways!
2 to the fight and to the res - cue came.
3 gainst the foe, should strive, and should pre - vail;
4 ve - ry self, and es - sence all - di - vine.
5 won - der - ful, most sure in all his ways!

Alternative tunes: *Newman,* 446; *Richmond,* 212.

Words: John Henry Newman (1801-1890), alt.
Music: *Gerontius,* John Bacchus Dykes (1823-1876)

♩= 108
CM

1 Praise to the Ho - liest in the height, and in the
2 O lov - ing wis - dom of our God! When all was
3 O wis - est love! that flesh and blood, which did in
4 and that the high - est gift of grace should flesh and
5 Praise to the Ho - liest in the height, and in the
1 depth be praise; in all his words most
2 sin and shame, a sec - ond Ad - am
3 Ad - am fail, should strive a - fresh a -
4 blood re - fine: God's pres - ence and his
5 depth be praise; in all his words most
1 won - der - ful, most sure in all his ways!
2 to the fight and to the res - cue came.
3 gainst the foe, should strive, and should pre - vail;
4 ve - ry self, and es - sence all - di - vine.
5 won - der - ful most sure in all his ways!

Alternative tunes: *Gerontius,* 445; *Richmond,* 212.

Words: John Henry Newman (1801-1890), alt.
Music: *Newman,* Richard Runciman Terry (1865-1938)

♩= 108
CM

Jesus Christ our Lord

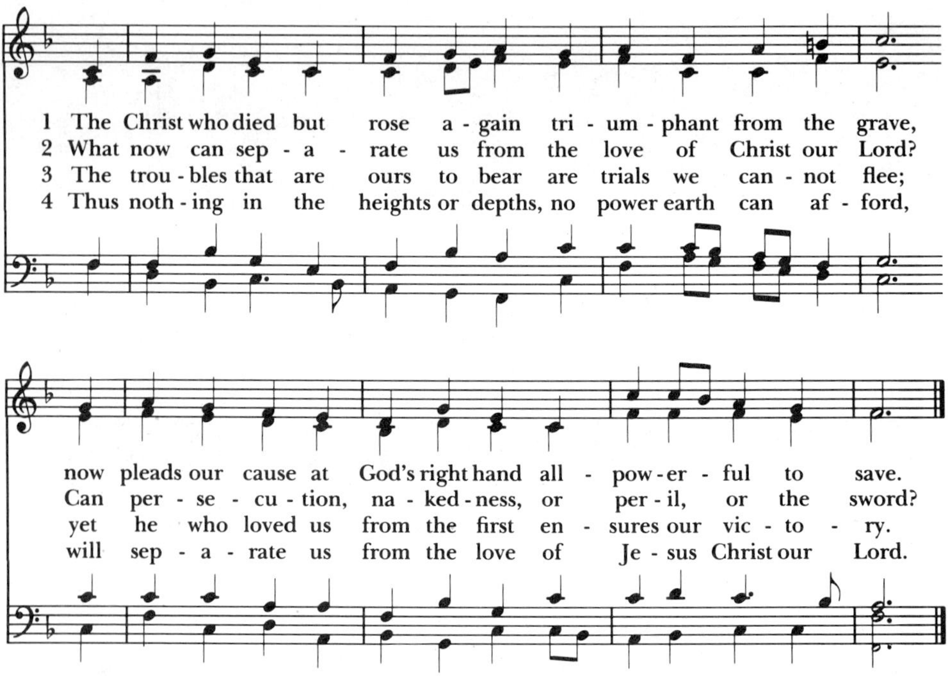

1 The Christ who died but rose a - gain tri - um - phant from the grave,
2 What now can sep - a - rate us from the love of Christ our Lord?
3 The trou - bles that are ours to bear are trials we can - not flee;
4 Thus noth - ing in the heights or depths, no power earth can af - ford,
now pleads our cause at God's right hand all - pow - er - ful to save.
Can per - se - cu - tion, na - ked - ness, or per - il, or the sword?
yet he who loved us from the first en - sures our vic - to - ry.
will sep - a - rate us from the love of Je - sus Christ our Lord.

This music in G, 483.

Words: Granton Douglas Hay (b. 1943), alt.; based on *Paraphrases*, 1781; para. of Romans 8:34-39
Music: *St. Magnus,* melody from *Divine Companion,* 1707; harm. William Henry Monk (1823-1889), after John Pyke Hullah (19th cent.) ♩=84 CM

Jesus Christ our Lord

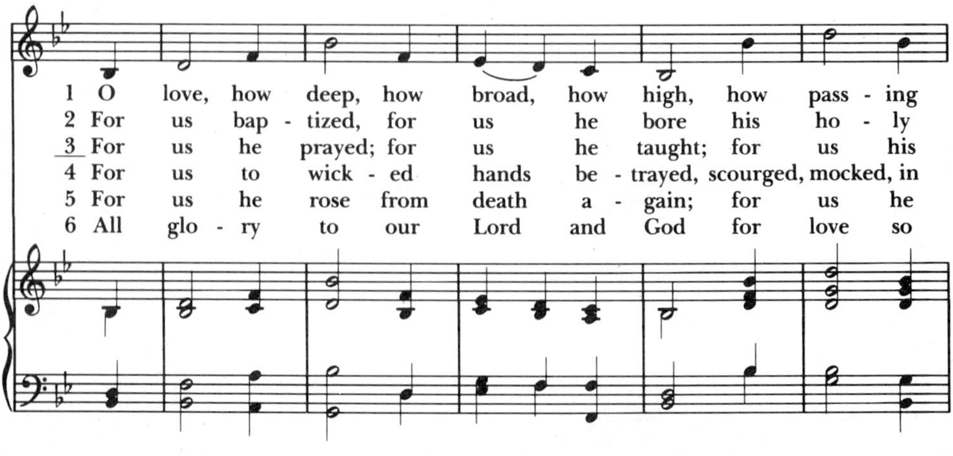

1 O love, how deep, how broad, how high, how pass - ing
2 For us bap - tized, for us he bore his ho - ly
3 For us he prayed; for us he taught; for us his
4 For us to wick - ed hands be - trayed, scourged, mocked, in
5 For us he rose from death a - gain; for us he
6 All glo - ry to our Lord and God for love so

1 thought and fan - ta - sy, that God, the Son of
2 fast and hun - gered sore; for us temp - ta - tions
3 dai - ly works he wrought: by words and signs and
4 pur - ple robe ar - rayed, he bore the shame - ful
5 went on high to reign; for us he sent his
6 deep, so high, so broad; the Trin - i - ty whom
1 God, should take our mor - tal form for mor - tals' sake.
2 sharp he knew; for us the tempt - er o - ver - threw.
3 ac - tions, thus still seek - ing not him - self, but us.
4 cross and death; for us gave up his dy - ing breath.
5 Spi - rit here to guide, to strength-en, and to cheer.
6 we a - dore for ev - er and for ev - er - more.

Alternative tune: *Deo gracias*, 218 and 449.

Words: Latin, 15th cent.; tr. Benjamin Webb (1819-1885), alt.

Music: *Deus tuorum militum*, from *Antiphoner*, 1753; adapt. *The English Hymnal*, 1906, alt.; harm. after Basil Harwood (1859-1949)

𝅗𝅥. = 40

LM

1 O love, how deep, how broad, how high, how pass - ing
2 For us bap - tized, for us he bore his ho - ly
3 For us he prayed; for us he taught; for us his
4 For us to wick - ed hands be - trayed, scourged, mocked, in
5 For us he rose from death a - gain; for us he
6 All glo - ry to our Lord and God for love so
1 thought and fan - ta - sy, that God, the Son of
2 fast and hun - gered sore; for us temp - ta - tions
3 dai - ly works he wrought: by words and signs and
4 pur - ple robe ar - rayed, he bore the shame - ful
5 went on high to reign; for us he sent his
6 deep, so high, so broad; the Trin - i - ty whom

1 God, should take our mor - tal form for mor- tals' sake.
2 sharp he knew; for us the tempt - er o - ver - threw.
3 ac - tions, thus still seek - ing not him - self, but us.
4 cross and death; for us gave up his dy - ing breath.
5 Spi - rit here to guide, to strength - en, and to cheer.
6 we a - dore for ev - er and for ev - er - more.

Another harmonization, 218. Alternative tune: *Deus tuorum militum*, 448.

Words: Latin, 15th cent.; tr. Benjamin Webb (1819-1885), alt.
Music: *Deo gracias*, English ballad melody, Trinity College MS., 15th cent.; harm. *Hymns Ancient and Modern, Revised*, 1950

♩= 104
LM

Alternative accompaniment (the melody is in the bass clef)

Music: *Deo gracias*, English ballad melody, Trinity College MS., 15th cent.

♩= 104

Descant
6 Let ev - ery kin - dred, ev - ery tribe, on this ter - res - trial
1 All hail the power of Je - sus' Name! Let an - gels pros-trate
2 Crown him ye mar - tyrs of our God, who from his al - tar
3 Hail him, the Heir of Da - vid's line, whom Da - vid Lord did
*4 Ye heirs of Is - rael's cho - sen race, ye ran - somed of the
*5 Sin - ners, whose love can ne'er for - get the worm-wood and the
ball, to him a - scribe, and
1 fall; bring forth the roy - al di - a - dem, and
2 call: praise him whose way of pain ye trod, and
3 call, the God in - car - nate, Man di - vine, and
4 fall, hail him who saves you by his grace, and
5 gall, go, spread your tro - phies at his feet, and

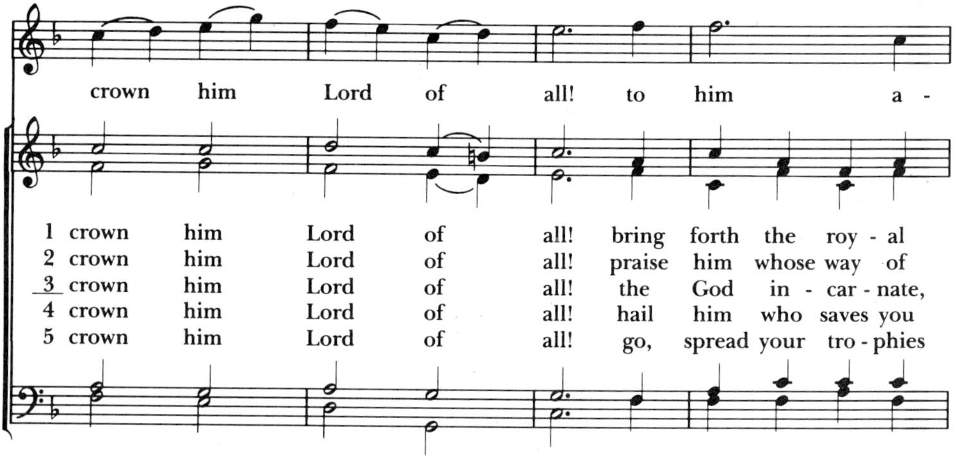
crown him Lord of all! to him a -
1 crown him Lord of all! bring forth the roy - al
2 crown him Lord of all! praise him whose way of
3 crown him Lord of all! the God in - car - nate,
4 crown him Lord of all! hail him who saves you
5 crown him Lord of all! go, spread your tro - phies

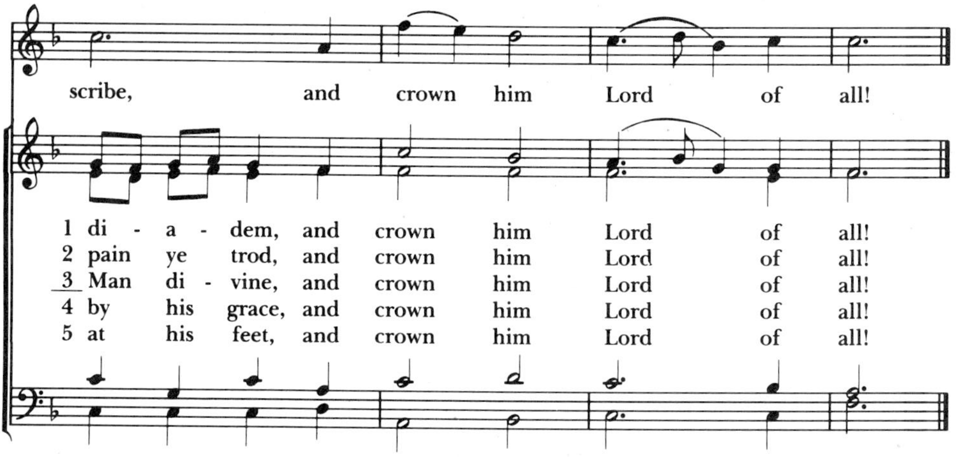
scribe, and crown him Lord of all!
1 di - a - dem, and crown him Lord of all!
2 pain ye trod, and crown him Lord of all!
3 Man di - vine, and crown him Lord of all!
4 by his grace, and crown him Lord of all!
5 at his feet, and crown him Lord of all!

6 Let every kindred, every tribe,
on this terrestrial ball,
to him all majesty ascribe,
and crown him Lord of all!

Alternative tune: *Miles Lane,* 451.

Words: Edward Perronet (1726-1792), alt.
Music: *Coronation,* Oliver Holden (1765-1844), alt.; desc. Michael E. Young (b. 1939)

𝅗𝅥=54
86. 86. 86

1 All hail the power of Je - sus' Name! Let an - gels
2 Crown him, ye mar - tyrs of our God, who from his
3 Hail him, the Heir of Da - vid's line, whom Da - vid
*4 Ye heirs of Is - rael's cho - sen race, ye ran - somed
*5 Sin - ners, whose love can ne'er for - get the worm - wood
1 pros - trate fall; bring forth the roy - al di - a - dem,
2 al - tar call: praise him whose way of pain ye trod,
3 Lord did call, the God in - car - nate, Man di - vine,
4 of the fall, hail him who saves you by his grace,
5 and the gall, go, spread your tro - phies at his feet,
Refrain
and crown him, crown him, crown him, crown him Lord of all!

6 Let every kindred, every tribe,
on this terrestrial ball,
to him all majesty ascribe,

Refrain

Alternative tune: *Coronation,* 450.

Words: Edward Perronet (1726-1792), alt.
Music: *Miles Lane,* William Shrubsole (1760-1806)

𝅗𝅥=50
868 with Refrain

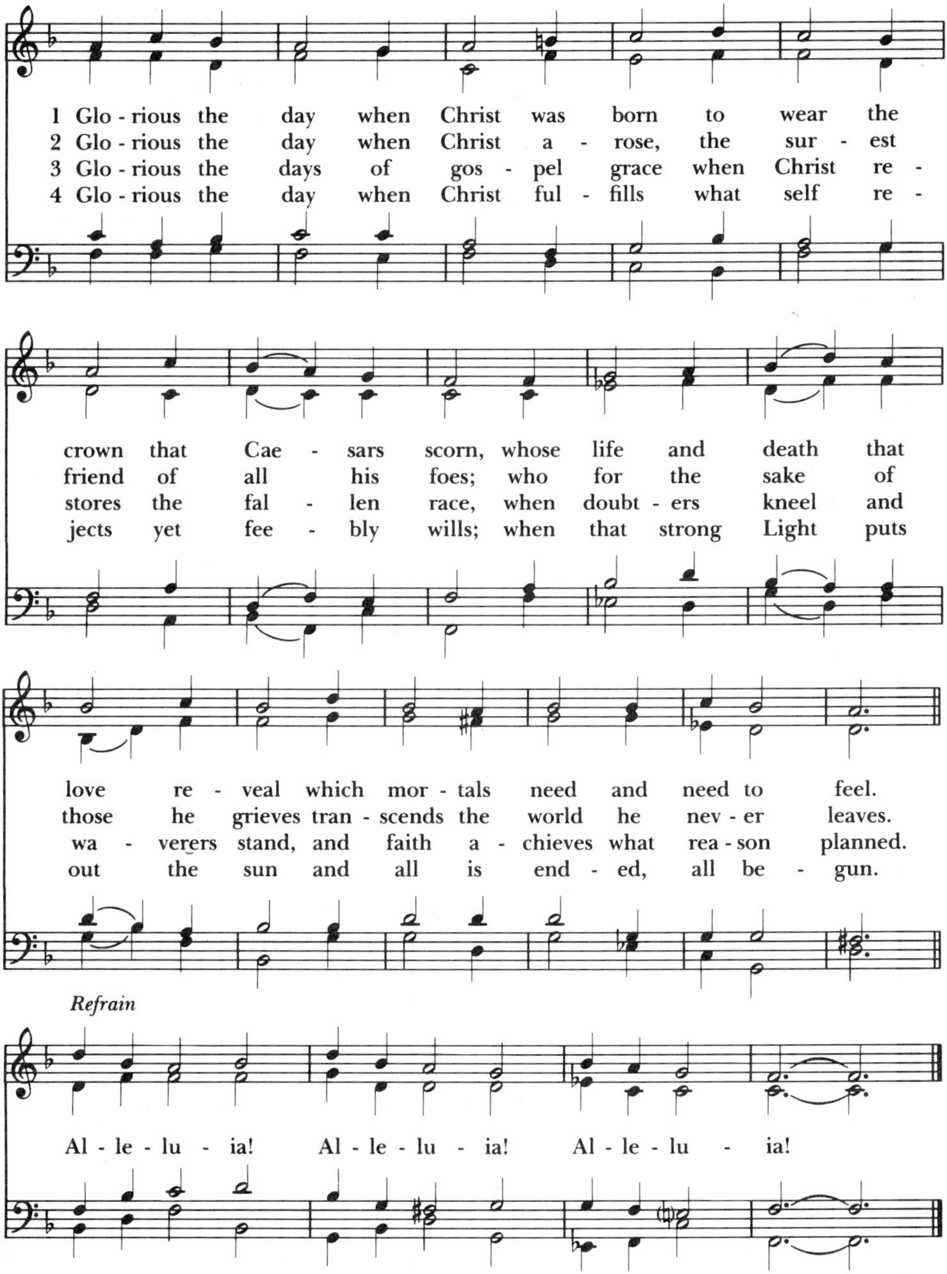
1 Glo - rious the day when Christ was born to wear the
2 Glo - rious the day when Christ a - rose, the sur - est
3 Glo - rious the days of gos - pel grace when Christ re -
4 Glo - rious the day when Christ ful - fills what self re -
crown that Cae - sars scorn, whose life and death that
friend of all his foes; who for the sake of
stores the fal - len race, when doubt - ers kneel and
jects yet fee - bly wills; when that strong Light puts
love re - veal which mor - tals need and need to feel.
those he grieves tran - scends the world he nev - er leaves.
wa - verers stand, and faith a - chieves what rea - son planned.
out the sun and all is end - ed, all be - gun.
Refrain
Al - le - lu - ia! Al - le - lu - ia! Al - le - lu - ia!

Words: F. Pratt Green (b. 1903), rev.
Music: *Frohlockt mit Freud*, Heinrich Schütz (1585-1672), alt.

𝅗𝅥=46
LM with Alleluias

C7(A7) F(D) Gm7(Em7) F(D) Gm7(Em7) C7(A7)
1 As Ja - cob with trav - el was wea - ry one day, at
2 The lad - der is long, it is strong and well - made, has stood
3 Come, let us a - scend! All may climb it who will, for the
4 And when we ar - rive at the ha - ven of rest, we shall
F(D) Gm7(Em7) F(D) G7(E7) C(A) Dm7(Bm7) C(A) F(D)
night on a stone for a pil - low he lay; he
hun - dreds of years and is not yet de - cayed; man - y
an - gels of Ja - cob are guard - ing it still; and re -
hear the glad words, "Come to me all the blest, here are
F(D) NC Gm7(Em7) C7(A7)
saw in a vi - sion a lad - der so high, that its
mil - lions have climbed it and reached Zi - on's hill, man - y
mem - ber, each step that by faith we pass o'er, man - y
re - gions of light, here are man - sions of bliss." Who would

F(D) F(D) Gm7(Em7) F(D) B♭(G) F(D)
foot was on earth and its top in the sky:
mil - lions by faith now are climb - ing it still:
pro - phets and mar - tyrs have trod it be - fore:
not want to climb such a lad - der as this:
Refrain
C7(A7) F(D) Gm7(Em7) F(D) G7(E7) C(A) Dm7(Bm7) C7(A7)
Al - le - lu - ia to Je - sus, who died on the tree and has
F(D) Gm7(Em7) F(D) G7(E7) C(A) C(A) F(D)
raised up a lad - der of mer - cy for me, and has
C7(A7) F(D) Gm7(Em7) F(D)
raised up a lad - der of mer - cy for me.

F(capo 3, D)

Words: English carol, ca. 18th cent.
Music: *Jacob's Ladder*, English folk melody; harm. Jack Noble White (b. 1938)

𝅗𝅥 = 60
Irr. with Refrain

Unison or harmony
1 Je - sus came, a - dored by an - gels, came with peace from
2 Je - sus comes a - gain in mer - cy, when our hearts are
3 Je - sus comes to hearts re - joic - ing, bring - ing news of
4 Je - sus comes on clouds tri - um - phant, when the heavens shall
realms on high; Je - sus came for our re - demp - tion,
bowed with care; Je - sus comes a - gain in an - swer
sins for - given; Je - sus comes in sounds of glad - ness,
pass a - way; Je - sus comes a - gain in glo - ry;
low - ly came on earth to die: Al - le - lu - ia,
to our ear - nest heart - felt prayer: Al - le - lu - ia,
lead - ing souls re - deemed to heaven; Al - le - lu - ia,
let us then our hom - age pay: Al - le - lu - ia,
al - le - lu - ia! came in deep hu - mil - i - ty.
al - le - lu - ia! comes to save us from de - spair.
al - le - lu - ia! now the gate of death is riven.
al - le - lu - ia! till the dawn of end - less day.

Words: Godfrey Thring (1823-1903), alt.
Music: *Lowry,* Gerald Near (b. 1942)

𝅗𝅥 = 54
87. 87 with Alleluia

1 O Love of God, how strong and true, e - ter - nal
2 O wide-em - brac - ing, won - drous Love, we read thee
3 We read thee best in him who came to bear for
4 We read thy power to bless and save e'en in the
and yet ev - er new; un-com-pre - hend - ed and un -
in the sky a - bove; we read thee in the earth be -
us the cross of shame, sent by the Fa - ther from on
dark - ness of the grave; still more in re - sur-rec-tion
bought, be - yond all know-ledge and all thought.
low, in seas that swell and streams that flow.
high, our life to live, our death to die.
light we read the full - ness of thy might.

Alternative tune: *de Tar*, 456.

Words: Horatius Bonar (1808-1889)
Music: *Dunedin*, Vernon Griffiths (b. 1894)

𝅗𝅥=60
LM

1 O Love of God, how strong and true,
2 (O wide-em - brac - ing, won - drous) Love,
3 (We read thee best in him who) came
4 (We read thy power to bless and) save
e - ter - nal and yet ev - er new;
we read thee in the sky a - bove;
to bear for us the cross of shame,
e'en in the dark - ness of the grave;
un - com - pre - hend - ed and un - bought,
we read thee in the earth be - low,
sent by the Fa - ther from on high,
still more in re - sur - rec - tion light

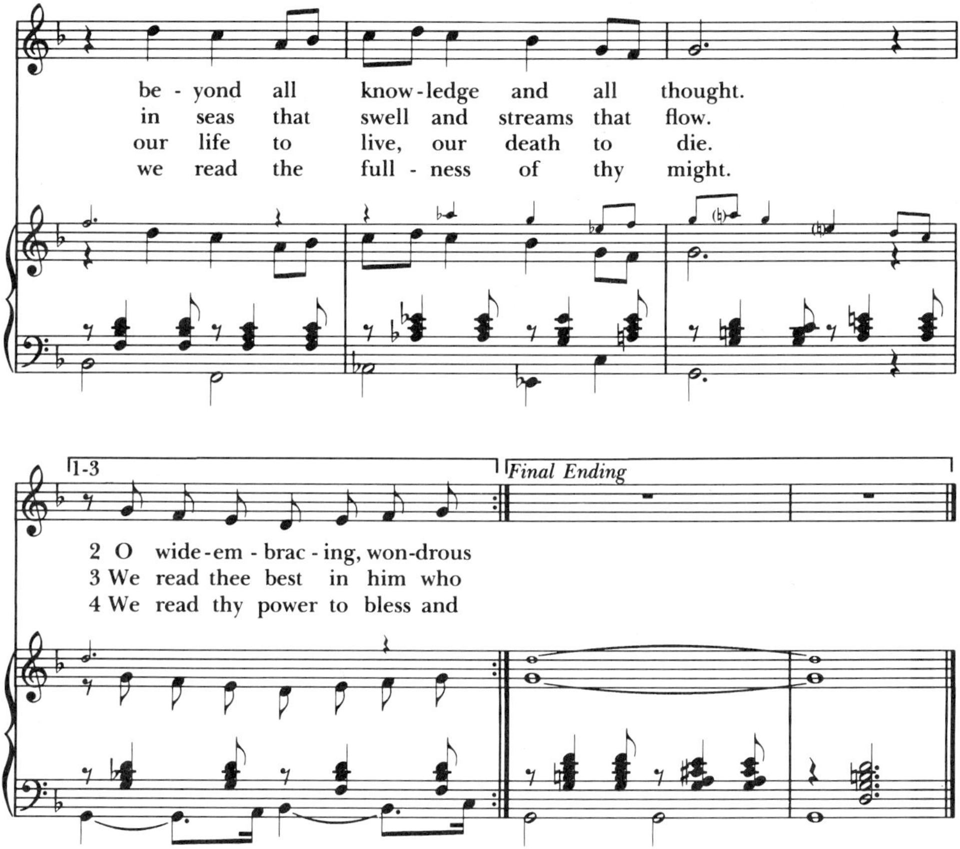
be - yond all know - ledge and all thought.
in seas that swell and streams that flow.
our life to live, our death to die.
we read the full - ness of thy might.
1-3
Final Ending
2 O wide - em - brac - ing, won - drous
3 We read thee best in him who
4 We read thy power to bless and

The obbligato in the right hand of the accompaniment may be played by an assistant, sung by sopranos, or played on a solo instrument. Alternative tune: *Dunedin,* 455.

Words: Horatius Bonar (1808-1889)
Music: *de Tar,* Calvin Hampton (1938-1984)

♩= 72
LM

1 Thou art the Way, to thee a - lone from
2 Thou art the Truth, thy word a - lone true
3 Thou art the Life, the rend - ing tomb pro -
4 Thou art the Way, the Truth, the Life: grant
sin and death we flee; and all who would the
wis - dom can im - part; thou on - ly canst in -
claims thy con - quering arm; and those who put their
us that way to know, that truth to keep, that
Fa - ther seek, must seek him, Lord, by thee.
form the mind and pu - ri - fy the heart.
trust in thee nor death nor hell shall harm.
life to win, whose joys e - ter - nal flow.

Words: George Washington Doane (1799-1859), alt.
Music: *St. James,* Raphael Courteville (d. 1735)

♩=84
CM

Unison or harmony

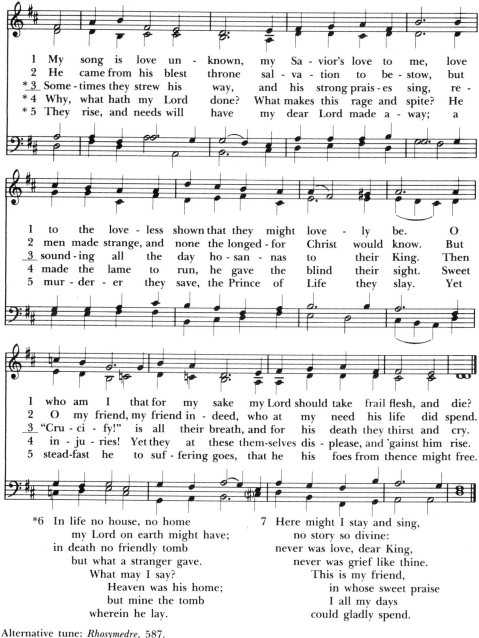

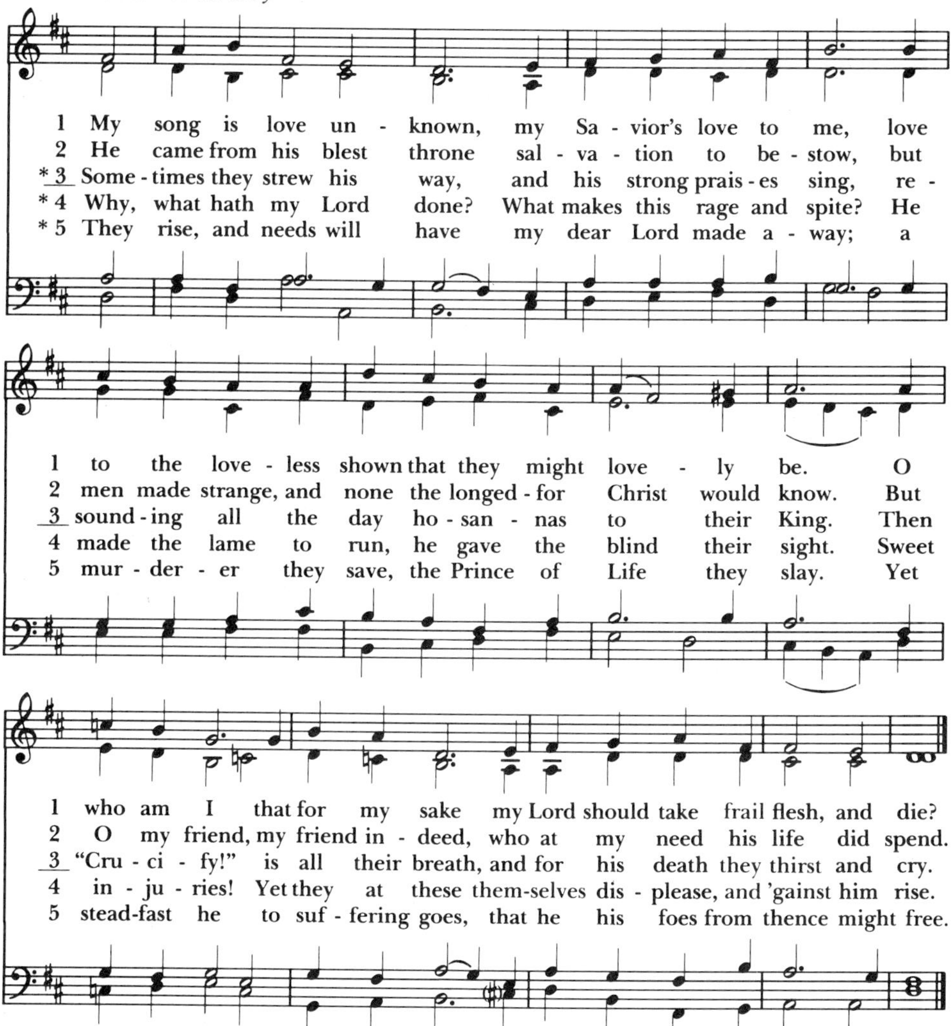
1 My song is love un - known, my Sa - vior's love to me, love
2 He came from his blest throne sal - va - tion to be - stow, but
* 3 Some - times they strew his way, and his strong prais - es sing, re -
* 4 Why, what hath my Lord done? What makes this rage and spite? He
* 5 They rise, and needs will have my dear Lord made a - way; a
1 to the love - less shown that they might love - ly be. O
2 men made strange, and none the longed - for Christ would know. But
3 sound - ing all the day ho - san - nas to their King. Then
4 made the lame to run, he gave the blind their sight. Sweet
5 mur - der - er they save, the Prince of Life they slay. Yet
1 who am I that for my sake my Lord should take frail flesh, and die?
2 O my friend, my friend in - deed, who at my need his life did spend.
3 "Cru - ci - fy!" is all their breath, and for his death they thirst and cry.
4 in - ju - ries! Yet they at these them-selves dis - please, and 'gainst him rise.
5 stead-fast he to suf - fering goes, that he his foes from thence might free.

*6 In life no house, no home
my Lord on earth might have;
in death no friendly tomb
but what a stranger gave.
What may I say?
Heaven was his home;
but mine the tomb
wherein he lay.

7 Here might I stay and sing,
no story so divine:
never was love, dear King,
never was grief like thine.
This is my friend,
in whose sweet praise
I all my days
could gladly spend.

Alternative tune: *Rhosymedre*, 587.

Words: Samuel Crossman (1624-1683), alt.
Music: *Love Unknown*, John Ireland (1879-1962)

𝅗𝅥=54
66. 66. 44. 44

Introduction
1 And have the bright im - men - si - ties re - ceived our ris - en Lord, where light-years frame the Plei - a - des and point O - ri - on's
2 The heaven that hides him from our sight knows nei - ther near nor far: an al - tar can - dle sheds its light as sure - ly as a

sword? Do flam - ing suns his foot - steps trace through
star; and where his lov - ing peo - ple meet to
cor - ri - dors sub - lime, the Lord of in - ter -
share the gift di - vine, there stands he with un -
Interlude/Conclusion
stel - lar space and Con - quer - or of time?
hur - rying feet; there heaven - ly splen - dors shine.

The Introduction, Interlude, and Conclusion may be omitted.

Words: Howard Chandler Robbins (1876-1952)
Music: *Halifax*, George Frideric Handel (1685-1759); adapt. and arr. David Hurd (b. 1950)

♩= 138
CMD

1 Al - le - lu - ia! sing to Je - sus! his the
*2 Al - le - lu - ia! not as or - phans are we
3 Al - le - lu - ia! Bread of Hea - ven, thou on
4 Al - le - lu - ia! King e - ter - nal, thee the
*5 Al - le - lu - ia! sing to Je - sus! his the
1 scep - ter, his the throne; Al - le - lu - ia! his the
2 left in sor - row now; Al - le - lu - ia! he is
3 earth our food, our stay! Al - le - lu - ia! here the
4 Lord of lords we own: Al - le - lu - ia! born of
5 scep - ter his the throne; Al - le - lu - ia! his the
1 tri - umph, his the vic - to - ry a - lone; Hark! the
2 near us, faith be - lieves, nor ques - tions how: though the
3 sin - ful flee to thee from day to day: In - ter -
4 Ma - ry, earth thy foot - stool, heaven thy throne: thou with -
5 tri - umph, his the vic - to - ry a - lone; Hark! the

1 songs of peace - ful Zi - on thun - der like a
2 cloud from sight re - ceived him, when the for - ty
3 ces - sor, friend of sin - ners, earth's Re - deem - er,
4 in the veil hast en - tered, robed in flesh, our
5 songs of ho - ly Zi - on thun - der like a
1 might - y flood; Je - sus out of ev - ery
2 days were o'er, shall our hearts for - get his
3 plead for me, where the songs of all the
4 great High Priest: thou on earth both Priest and
5 might - y flood; Je - sus out of ev - ery
1 na - tion hath re - deemed us by his blood.
2 prom - ise, "I am with you ev - er - more"?
3 sin - less sweep a - cross the crys - tal sea.
4 Vic - tim in the eu - cha - ris - tic feast.
5 na - tion hath re - deemed us by his blood.

Alternative tune: *Alleluia,* 461.

Words: William Chatterton Dix (1837-1898)
Music: *Hyfrydol,* Rowland Hugh Prichard (1811-1887)

♩=112
87. 87. D

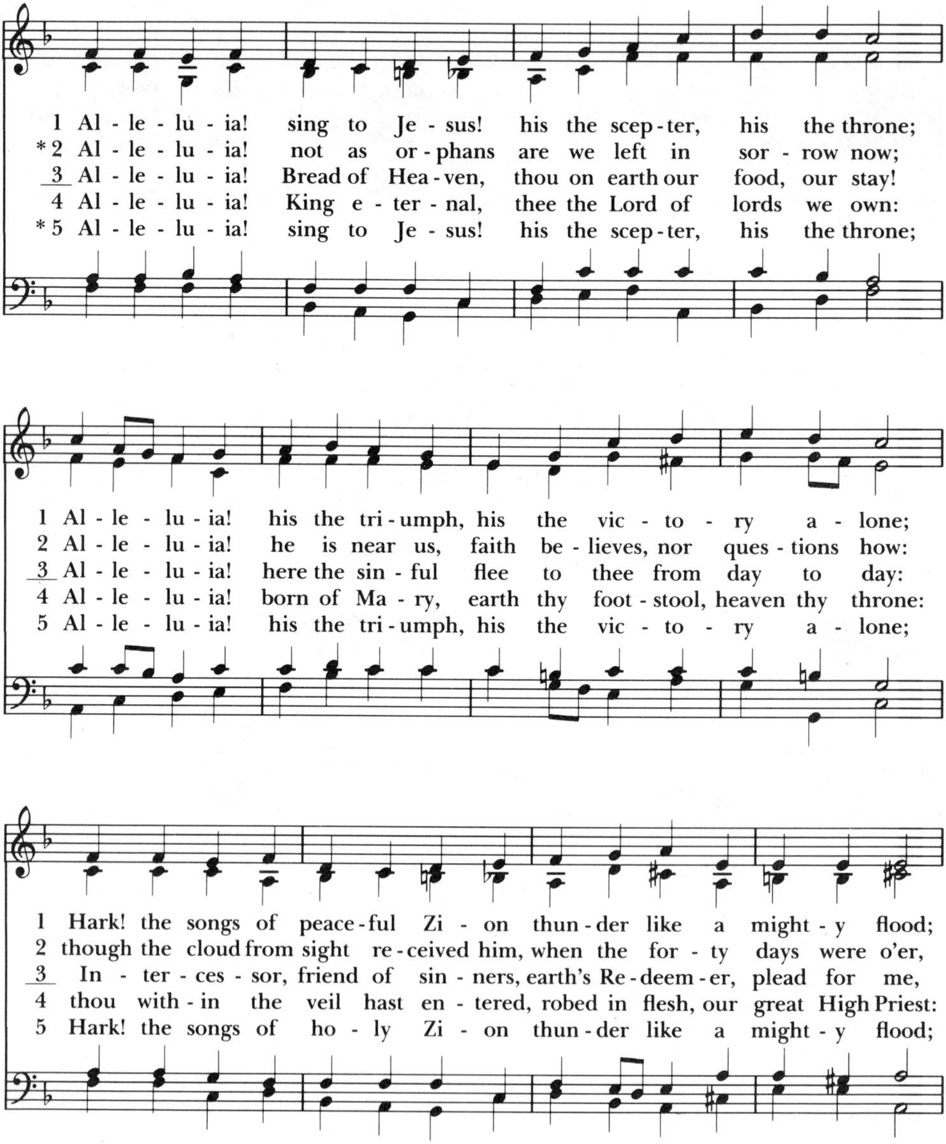
1 Al - le - lu - ia! sing to Je - sus! his the scep - ter, his the throne;
*2 Al - le - lu - ia! not as or - phans are we left in sor - row now;
3 Al - le - lu - ia! Bread of Hea - ven, thou on earth our food, our stay!
4 Al - le - lu - ia! King e - ter - nal, thee the Lord of lords we own:
*5 Al - le - lu - ia! sing to Je - sus! his the scep - ter, his the throne;
1 Al - le - lu - ia! his the tri - umph, his the vic - to - ry a - lone;
2 Al - le - lu - ia! he is near us, faith be - lieves, nor ques - tions how:
3 Al - le - lu - ia! here the sin - ful flee to thee from day to day:
4 Al - le - lu - ia! born of Ma - ry, earth thy foot - stool, heaven thy throne:
5 Al - le - lu - ia! his the tri - umph, his the vic - to - ry a - lone;
1 Hark! the songs of peace - ful Zi - on thun - der like a might - y flood;
2 though the cloud from sight re - ceived him, when the for - ty days were o'er,
3 In - ter - ces - sor, friend of sin - ners, earth's Re - deem - er, plead for me,
4 thou with - in the veil hast en - tered, robed in flesh, our great High Priest:
5 Hark! the songs of ho - ly Zi - on thun - der like a might - y flood;

1 Je - sus out of ev - ery na - tion hath re-deemed us by his blood.
2 shall our hearts for - get his prom - ise, "I am with you ev - er - more"?
3 where the songs of all the sin - less sweep a - cross the crys - tal sea.
4 thou on earth both Priest and Vic - tim in the eu - cha - ris - tic feast.
5 Je - sus out of ev - ery na - tion hath re-deemed us by his blood.

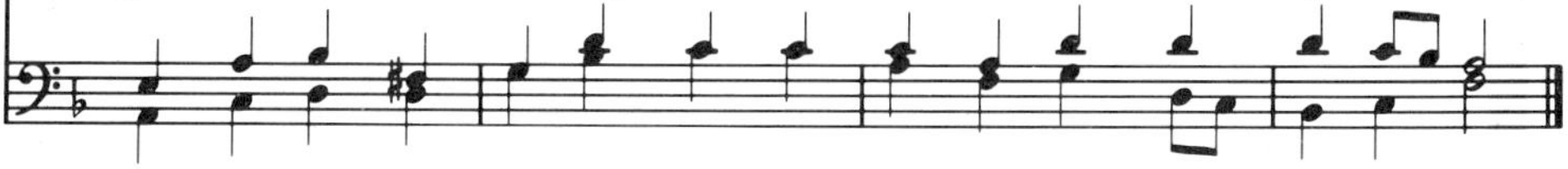

Alternative tune: *Hyfrydol,* 460.

Words: William Chatterton Dix (1837-1898)
Music: *Alleluia,* Samuel Sebastian Wesley (1810-1876)

𝅗𝅥.=54
87. 87. D

Jesus Christ our Lord

462

1 The Lord will come and not be slow, his foot - steps can - not err;
2 Truth from the earth, like to a flower, shall bud and blos - som show;
3 Rise, God, judge thou the earth in might, this wick - ed earth re - dress;
4 The na - tions all whom thou hast made shall come, and all shall frame
5 For great thou art, and won - ders great by thy strong hand are done:

1 be - fore him right-eous - ness shall go, his roy - al har - bin - ger.
2 and jus - tice, from her heaven - ly bower, look down on us be - low.
3 for thou art he who shalt by right the na - tions all pos - sess.
4 to bow them low be - fore thee, Lord, and glo - ri - fy thy Name.
5 thou in thy ev - er - last - ing seat re - main - est God a - lone.

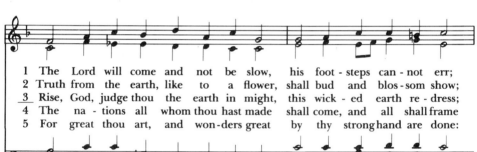

Words: John Milton (1608-1674), alt.
Music: *York,* melody from *The CL Psalmes of David,* 1615; adapt. *The Whole Booke of Psalmes,* 1621; harm. John Milton, Sr. (1563?-1647)

𝅘𝅥=84
CM

1 He is the Way. Fol-low him through the Land of Un - like -
2 (He is the) Truth. Seek_ him in the King - dom of An -
3 (He is the) Life. Love_ him in the World ___ of the
ness; ___ you will see rare_ beasts ___ and have_ u -
xi - e - ty: you will come to a great ci - ty that has___ ex -
Flesh: ___ and ___ at your_ mar - riage all its oc -
1-2
Final Ending
nique ___ ad - ven - tures. 2 He is the
pec - ted your re - turn for years. 3 He is the
ca - sions shall dance for (joy.) joy.

Alternative tune: *New Dance,* 464.

Words: W. H. Auden (1907-1973)
Tune: *Hall,* David Hurd (b. 1950)

𝅗𝅥. = 66
Irr.

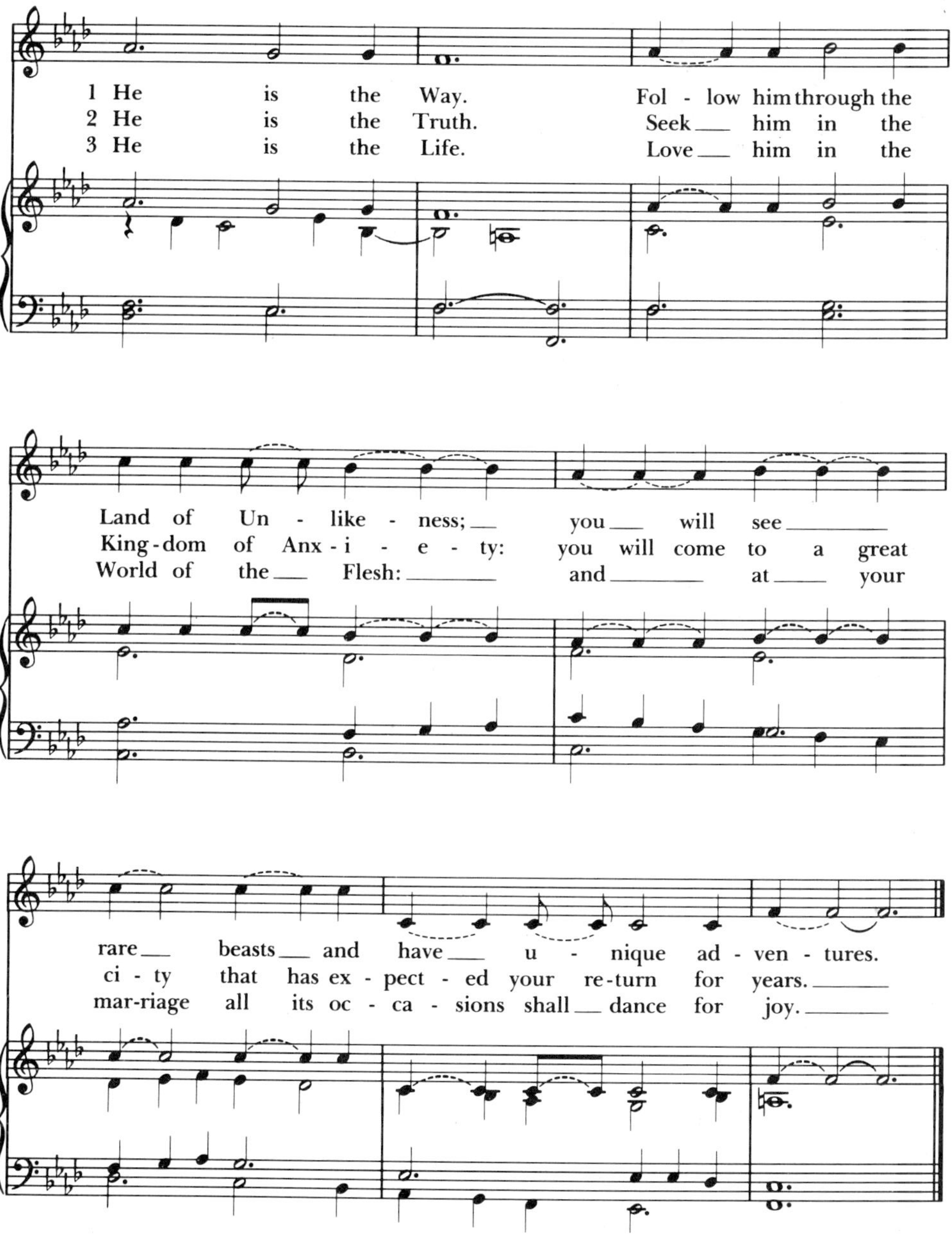
1 He is the Way. Fol - low him through the
2 He is the Truth. Seek ___ him in the
3 He is the Life. Love ___ him in the
Land of Un - like - ness; ___ you ___ will see ___
King - dom of Anx - i - e - ty: you will come to a great
World of the ___ Flesh: ___ and ___ at ___ your
rare ___ beasts ___ and have ___ u - nique ad - ven - tures.
ci - ty that has ex - pect - ed your re - turn for years. ___
mar - riage all its oc - ca - sions shall ___ dance for joy. ___

Alternative tune: *Hall,* 463.

Words: W. H. Auden (1907-1973)
Music: *New Dance,* Richard Wetzel (b. 1935)

𝅗𝅥. = 44
Irr.

465 Jesus Christ our Lord

Unison or harmony

1 E - ter - nal light, shine in my heart; e - ter - nal hope, lift up my eyes; e - ter - nal power, be my sup - port; e - ter - nal wis - dom, make me wise.
2 E - ter - nal life, raise me from death; e - ter - nal bright - ness, help me see; e - ter - nal Spi - rit, give me breath; e - ter - nal Sa - vior, come to me:
3 un - til by your most cost - ly grace, in - vit - ed by your ho - ly word, at last I come be - fore your face to know you, my e - ter - nal God.

Alternative tune: *Jacob,* 466.

Words: Christopher Idle (b. 1938); from a prayer of Alcuin (735?-804) — 𝅗𝅥=54
Music: *Ach bleib bei uns,* melody Samuel Scheidt (1587-1654); harm. Seth Calvisius (1556-1615) — LM

466 Jesus Christ our Lord

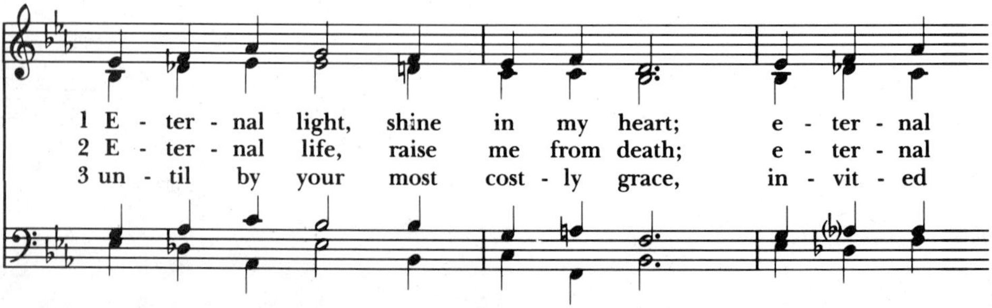
1 E - ter - nal light, shine in my heart; e - ter - nal
2 E - ter - nal life, raise me from death; e - ter - nal
3 un - til by your most cost - ly grace, in - vit - ed

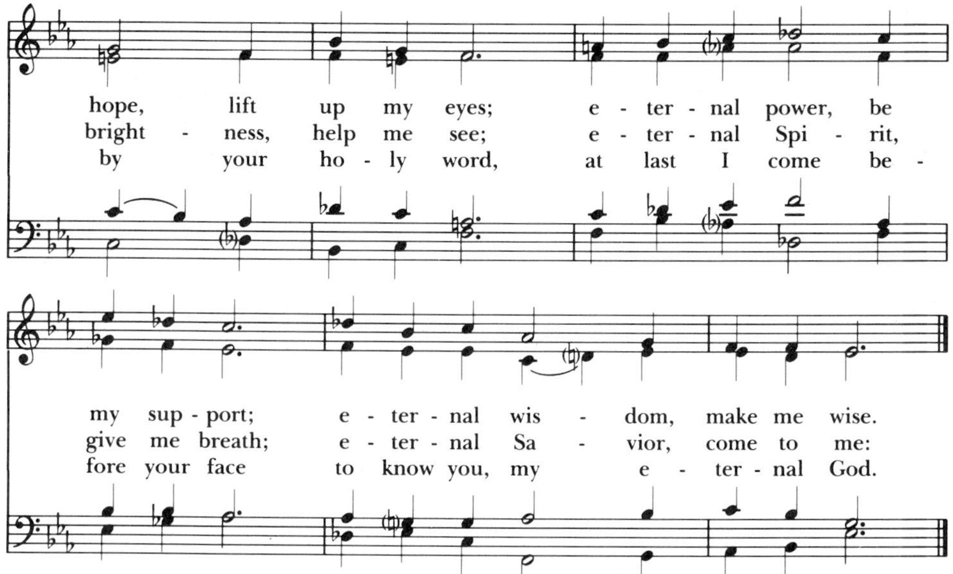
hope, lift up my eyes; e - ter - nal power, be
bright - ness, help me see; e - ter - nal Spi - rit,
by your ho - ly word, at last I come be -
my sup - port; e - ter - nal wis - dom, make me wise.
give me breath; e - ter - nal Sa - vior, come to me:
fore your face to know you, my e - ter - nal God.

This music in D, 242. Alternative tune: *Ach bleib bei uns*, 465.

Words: Christopher Idle (b. 1938); from a prayer by Alcuin (735?-804)
Music: *Jacob*, Jane Manton Marshall (b. 1924)

𝅗𝅥 = 76
LM

Jesus Christ our Lord

467

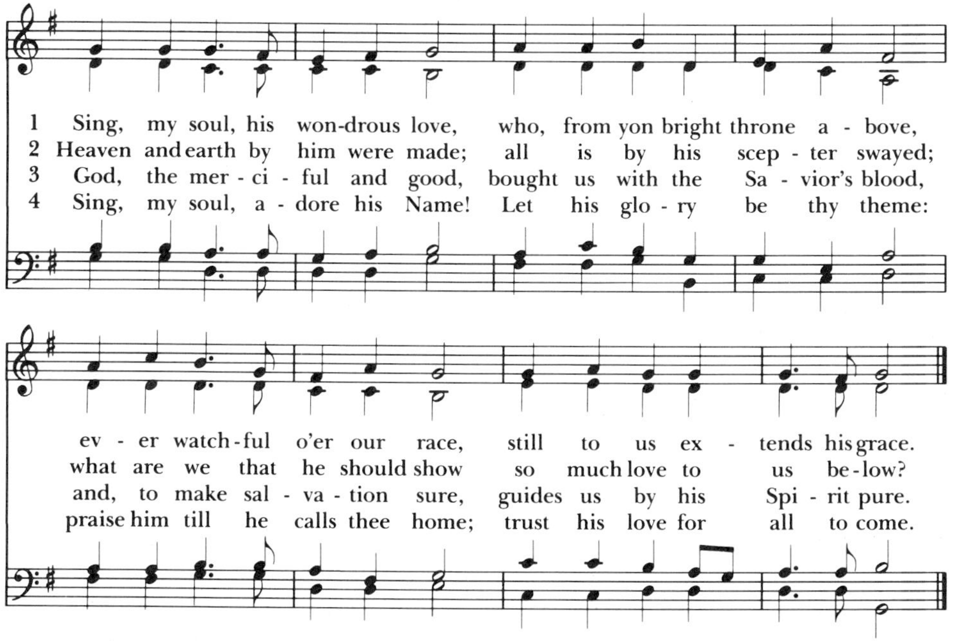
1 Sing, my soul, his won-drous love, who, from yon bright throne a - bove,
2 Heaven and earth by him were made; all is by his scep - ter swayed;
3 God, the mer - ci - ful and good, bought us with the Sa - vior's blood,
4 Sing, my soul, a - dore his Name! Let his glo - ry be thy theme:
ev - er watch-ful o'er our race, still to us ex - tends his grace.
what are we that he should show so much love to us be-low?
and, to make sal - va - tion sure, guides us by his Spi - rit pure.
praise him till he calls thee home; trust his love for all to come.

Words: Anon., 1800, alt.
Music: *St. Bees*, John Bacchus Dykes (1823-1876)

𝅗𝅥 = 50
77. 77

Solo
All
1 It was poor lit - tle Je - sus, yes, yes;
2 It was poor lit - tle Je - sus, yes, yes;
3 It was poor lit - tle Je - sus, yes, yes;
4 It was poor lit - tle Je - sus, yes, yes;
Solo
All
he was born on Christ - mas, yes, yes;
child of Ma - ry, yes, yes;
they nailed him to the cross, Lord, yes, yes;
he's ris - en from dark - ness, yes, yes;
Solo
All
and laid in a man - ger, yes, yes;
did - n't have a cra - dle, yes, yes;
they hung him with a rob - ber, yes yes;
he's 'scend - ed in - to glo - ry, yes, yes;

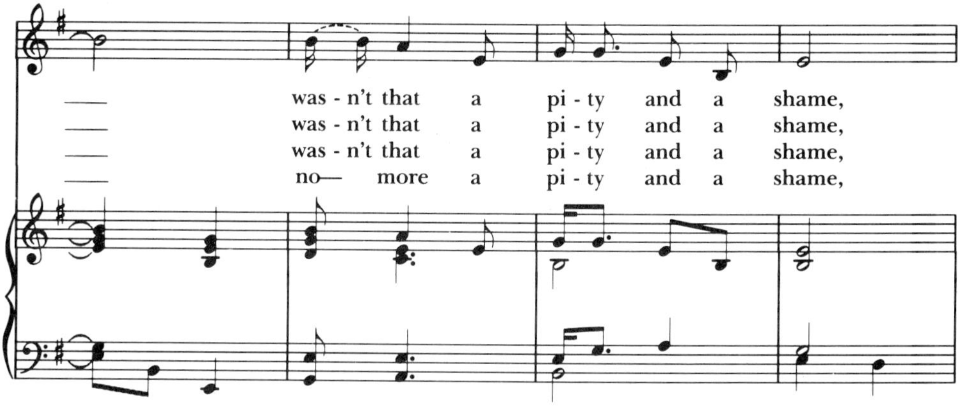
was - n't that a pi - ty and a shame,
was - n't that a pi - ty and a shame,
was - n't that a pi - ty and a shame,
no— more a pi - ty and a shame,

Lord, Lord, was - n't that a pi - ty and a shame?
Lord, Lord, was - n't that a pi - ty and a shame?
Lord, Lord, was - n't that a pi - ty and a shame?
Lord, Lord, no— more a pi - ty and a shame.

Words: Afro-American spiritual
Music: *Poor Little Jesus,* Afro-American spiritual; melody from *Songs and Games of American Children, 1884-1911;* acc. Jack W. Burnam (b. 1946)

♩=63
Irr. with Refrain

Jesus Christ our Lord 469

Introduction

Descant for flute or violin (last time only)
1 There's a wide-ness in God's mer - cy like the wide - ness
2 There is no place where earth's sor - rows are more felt than
3 For the love of God is broad - er than the mea - sure
of the sea; there's a kind - ness in his jus -
up in heaven; there is no place where earth's fail -
of the mind; and the heart of the E - ter -
tice, which is more than lib - er - ty. There is wel - come
ings have such kind - ly judg-ment given. There is plen - ti -
nal is most won - der - ful - ly kind. If our love were

for the sin - ner, and more gra - ces for the good; there is mer - cy
ful re-demp-tion in the blood that has been shed; there is joy for
but more faith-ful, we should take him at his word; and our life would
with the Sa - vior; there is heal - ing in his blood.
all the mem-bers in the sor - rows of the Head.
be thanks-giv - ing for the good-ness of the Lord.
Interlude/Conclusion
*

**Descant instrument may play this interlude each time.* Alternative tune: *Beecher*, 470.

Words: Frederick William Faber (1814-1863), alt.
Music: *St. Helena*, Calvin Hampton (1938-1984)

♩=93
87. 87. D

1 There's a wide-ness in God's mer - cy like the wide-ness of the sea;
2 There is no place where earth's sor - rows are more felt than up in heaven;
3 For the love of God is broad - er than the mea-sure of the mind;
there's a kind-ness in his jus-tice, which is more than lib - er - ty.
there is no place where earth's fail-ings have such kind - ly judg-ment given.
and the heart of the E - ter-nal is most won-der-ful - ly kind.
There is wel-come for the sin - ner, and more gra - ces for the good;
There is plen - ti - ful re - demp-tion in the blood that has been shed;
If our love were but more faith-ful, we should take him at his word;
there is mer - cy with the Sa -vior; there is heal - ing in his blood.
there is joy for all the mem-bers in the sor - rows of the Head.
and our life would be thanks-giv-ing for the good-ness of the Lord.

Alternative tune: *St. Helena,* 469.

Words: Frederick William Faber (1814-1863), alt.
Music: *Beecher,* John Zundel (1815-1882), alt.

𝅗𝅥=52
87. 87. D

1 We sing the praise of him who died, of
2 In - scribed up - on the cross we see in
3 The cross: it takes our guilt a - way, and
4 It makes the cow - ard spi - rit brave, and
5 The balm of life, the cure of woe, the
1 him who died up - on the cross; the sin - ner's hope let
2 shin - ing let - ters, God is love: he bears our sins up -
3 holds the faint - ing spi - rit up; it cheers with hope the
4 nerves the fee - ble arm for fight; it takes its ter - ror
5 mea - sure and the pledge of love, the sin - ner's ref - uge
1 sin de - ride; for this we count the world but loss.
2 on the tree: he brings us mer - cy from a - bove.
3 gloom - y day, and sweet - ens ev - ery bit - ter cup.
4 from the grave, and gilds the bed of death with light.
5 here be - low, the an - gel's theme in heaven a - bove.

Words: Thomas Kelly (1769-1855), alt.
Music: *Breslau,* melody from *Lochamer Gesangbuch,* ca. 1450; harm. Felix Mendelssohn (1809-1847)

𝅗𝅥=46
LM

1 Hope of the world, thou Christ of great com - pas - sion,
2 Hope of the world, God's gift from high - est hea - ven,
3 Hope of the world, a - foot on dust - y high - ways,
4 Hope of the world, who by thy cross didst save us
5 Hope of the world, O Christ, o'er death vic - to - rious,
1 speak to our fear - ful hearts by con - flict rent.
2 bring - ing to hun - gry souls the bread of life,
3 show - ing to wan - dering souls the path of light,
4 from death and dark de - spair, from sin and guilt,
5 who by this sign didst con - quer grief and pain,
1 Save us, thy peo - ple, from con - sum - ing pas - sion,
2 still let thy Spi - rit un - to us be giv - en
3 walk thou be - side us lest the tempt - ing by - ways
4 we rend - er back the love thy mer - cy gave us;
5 we would be faith - ful to thy gos - pel glo - rious;

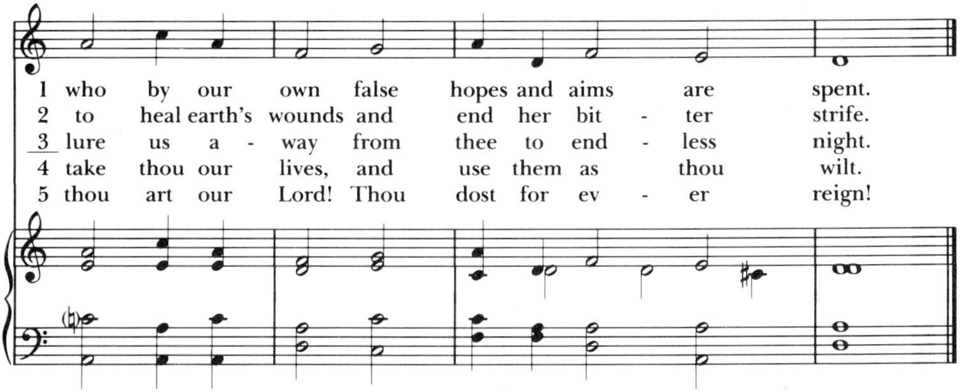
1 who by our own false hopes and aims are spent.
2 to heal earth's wounds and end her bit - ter strife.
3 lure us a - way from thee to end - less night.
4 take thou our lives, and use them as thou wilt.
5 thou art our Lord! Thou dost for ev - er reign!

Words: Georgia Harkness (1891-1974)
Music: *Donne secours,* melody from *Trente quatre pseaumes de David*, 1551;
harm. Claude Goudimel (1514-1572), alt.

𝅗𝅥 = 56
11 10. 11 10

Descant
Lift high the cross, the love of Christ pro - claim
Refrain
Lift high the cross, the love of Christ pro - claim
till all the world a - dore his sa - cred Name.
till all the world a - dore his sa - cred Name.
1 Led on their way by this tri - um - phant sign,
2 Each new - born ser - vant of the Cru - ci - fied
3 O Lord, once lift - ed on the glo - rious tree,
4 So shall our song of tri - umph ev - er be:

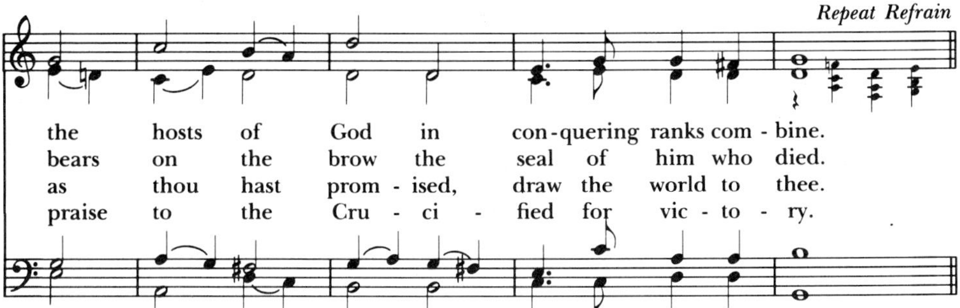
Repeat Refrain
the hosts of God in con-quering ranks com - bine.
bears on the brow the seal of him who died.
as thou hast prom - ised, draw the world to thee.
praise to the Cru - ci - fied for vic - to - ry.

Words: George William Kitchin (1827-1912); alt. Michael Robert Newbolt (1874-1956)
Music: *Crucifer*, Sydney Hugo Nicholson (1875-1947); desc. Richard Proulx (b. 1937)

𝅗𝅥 = 69
10 10 with Refrain

Jesus Christ our Lord

474

1 When I sur - vey the won - drous cross where the young
2 For - bid it, Lord, that I should boast, save in the
3 See, from his head, his hands, his feet, sor - row and
4 Were the whole realm of na - ture mine, that were an
Prince of Glo - ry died, my rich - est gain I
cross of Christ my God: all the vain things that
love flow min - gled down! Did e'er such love and
of - fering far too small; love so a - maz - ing,
count but loss, and pour con - tempt on all my pride.
charm me most, I sac - ri - fice them to his blood.
sor - row meet, or thorns com - pose so rich a crown?
so di - vine, de - mands my soul, my life, my all.

Another harmonization, 321.

Words: Isaac Watts (1674-1748)
Music: *Rockingham*, from *Second Supplement to Psalmody in Miniature*, ca. 1780; harm. Edward Miller (1731-1807)

♩ = 100
LM

1. God him-self is with us; let us all a - dore him,
2 Glad - ly, Lord, we of - fer thine to be for ev - er,
3 Thou per-vad - est all things; let thy rad-iant beau - ty
4 Come, a - bide with - in me; let my soul, like Ma - ry,
and with awe ap - pear be - fore him. God is here with -
soul and life and each en - deav - or. Help us to sur -
light mine eyes to see my du - ty. As the ten - der
be thine earth - ly sanc - tu - ar - y. Come, in - dwell - ing
in us; souls in si - lence fear him, hum - bly, fer - vent -
rend - er earth's de - ceit - ful trea - sures, pride of life, and
flow - ers ea - ger - ly un - fold them, to the sun - light
Spi - rit, with trans - fi - guring splen - dor; love and hon - or
ly draw near him. Now his own who have known
sin - ful plea - sures: thou a - lone shalt be known
calm - ly hold them, so let me qui - et - ly
will I ren - der. Where I go here be - low,

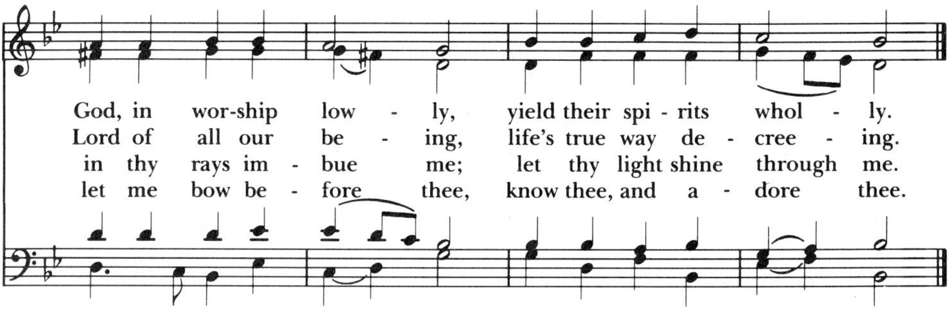
God, in wor-ship low - ly, yield their spi - rits whol - ly.
Lord of all our be - ing, life's true way de - cree - ing.
in thy rays im - bue me; let thy light shine through me.
let me bow be - fore thee, know thee, and a - dore thee.

Words: Gerhardt Tersteegen (1697-1769); tr. *Hymnal 1940*, alt.;
st. 3, tr. Henry Sloane Coffin (1877-1954)
Music: *Tysk*, from *Psalm und Choralbuch*, 1719

𝅗𝅥=50
668. 668. 666

Jesus Christ our Lord

476

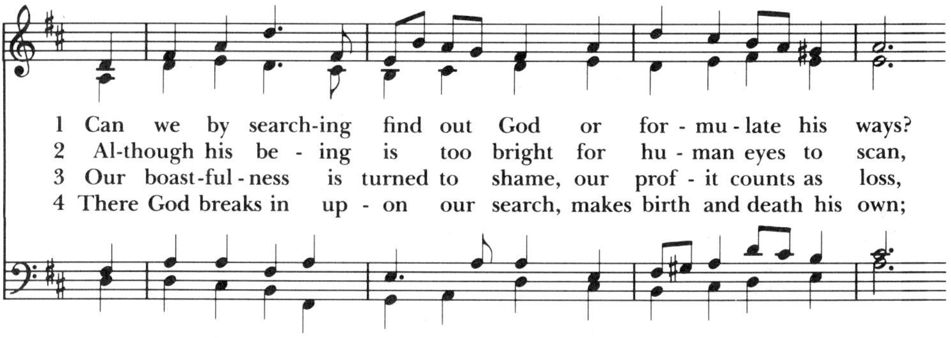
1 Can we by search-ing find out God or for - mu - late his ways?
2 Al-though his be - ing is too bright for hu - man eyes to scan,
3 Our boast-ful - ness is turned to shame, our prof - it counts as loss,
4 There God breaks in up - on our search, makes birth and death his own;

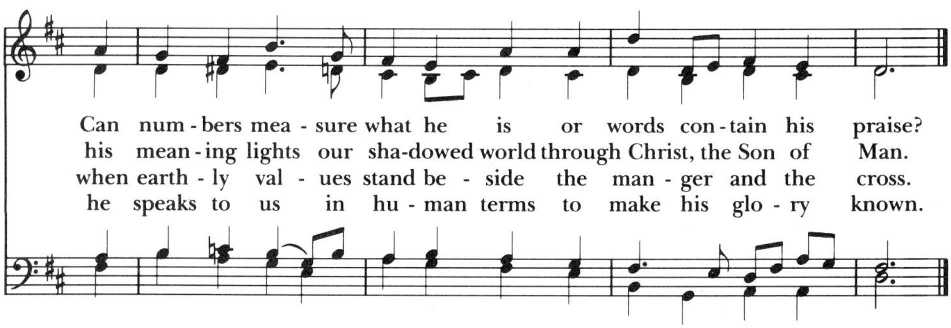
Can num - bers mea - sure what he is or words con - tain his praise?
his mean - ing lights our sha-dowed world through Christ, the Son of Man.
when earth - ly val - ues stand be - side the man - ger and the cross.
he speaks to us in hu - man terms to make his glo - ry known.

Words: Elizabeth Cosnett (b. 1936), alt.
Music: *Epworth*, melody att. Charles Wesley (1757-1834), alt.;
harm. Martin Fallas Shaw (1875-1958), alt.

𝅗𝅥=48
CM

Descant
5 Let every tongue confess with one accord — Jesus Christ is Lord;
1 All praise to thee, for thou, O King divine, didst yield the glory that of right was thine,
2 Thou cam'st to us in lowliness of thought; by thee the outcast and the poor were sought;
3 Let this mind be in us which was in thee, who wast a servant that we might be free,
4 Wherefore, by God's eternal purpose, thou art high exalted o'er all creatures now,
5 Let every tongue confess with one accord in heaven and earth that Jesus Christ is Lord;

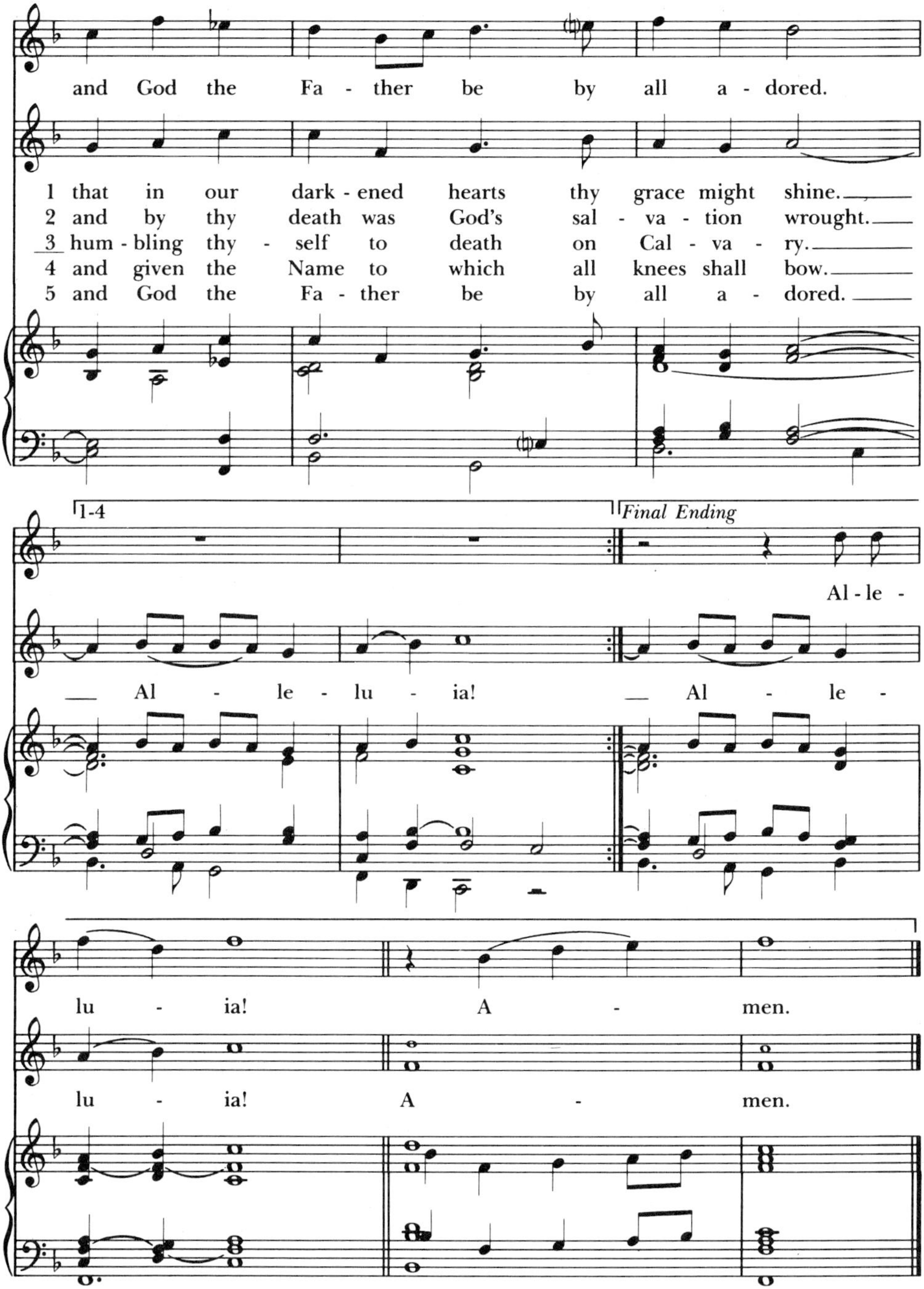

and God the Fa - ther be by all a - dored.
1 that in our dark - ened hearts thy grace might shine.
2 and by thy death was God's sal - va - tion wrought.
3 hum - bling thy - self to death on Cal - va - ry.
4 and given the Name to which all knees shall bow.
5 and God the Fa - ther be by all a - dored.
1-4
Final Ending
Al - le -
Al - le - lu - ia!
Al - le -
lu - ia! A - men.
lu - ia! A - men.

This music in G, 420. Alternative tune: *Sine nomine,* 233.

Words: F. Bland Tucker (1895-1984)
Music: *Engelberg,* Charles Villiers Stanford (1852-1924); desc. Richard Proulx (b. 1937)

𝅗𝅥=48
10 10 10 with Alleluia

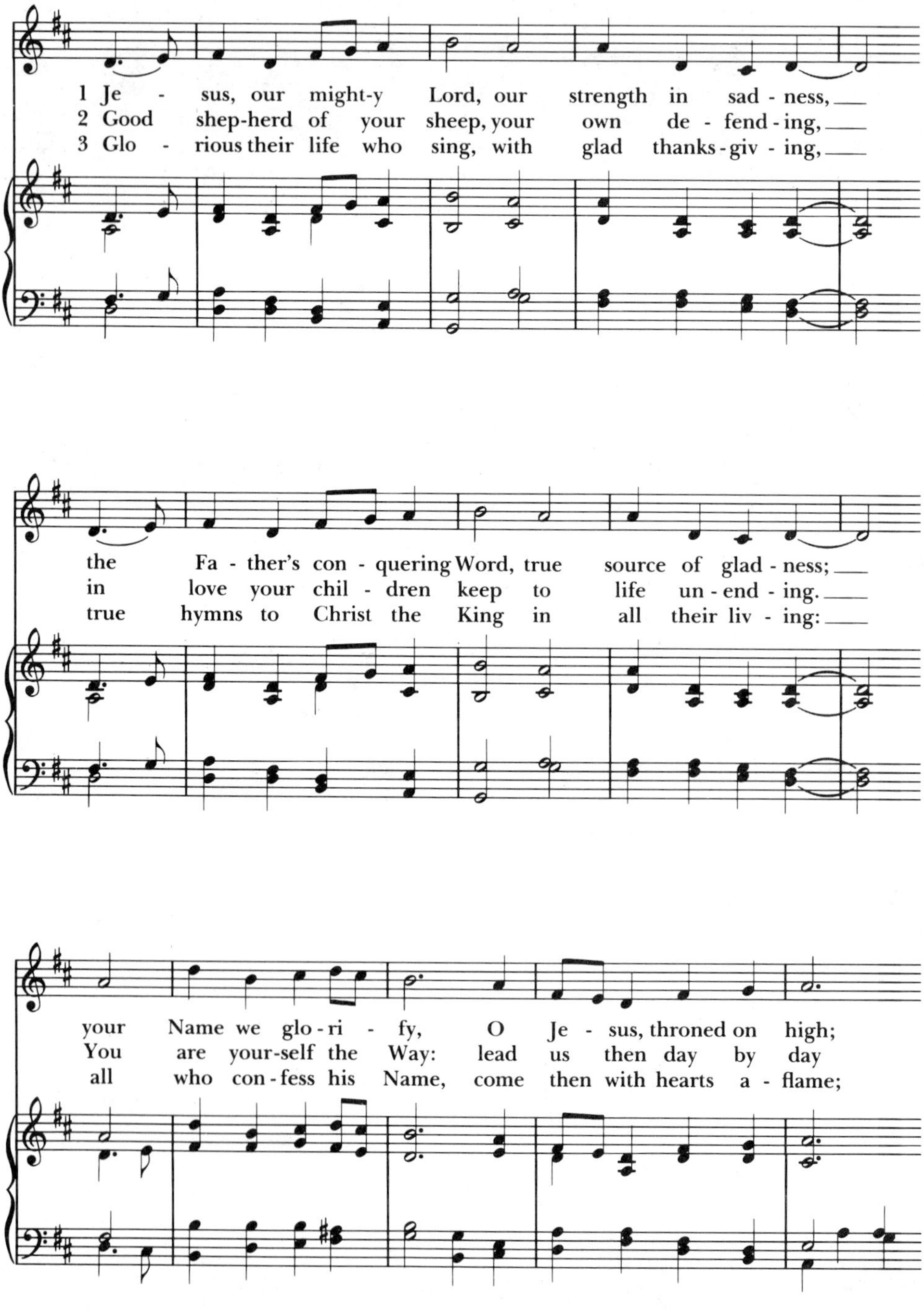
1 Je - sus, our might-y Lord, our strength in sad - ness,
2 Good shep-herd of your sheep, your own de - fend - ing,
3 Glo - rious their life who sing, with glad thanks-giv - ing,
the Fa - ther's con - quering Word, true source of glad - ness;
in love your chil - dren keep to life un - end - ing.
true hymns to Christ the King in all their liv - ing:
your Name we glo - ri - fy, O Je - sus, throned on high;
You are your-self the Way: lead us then day by day
all who con - fess his Name, come then with hearts a - flame;

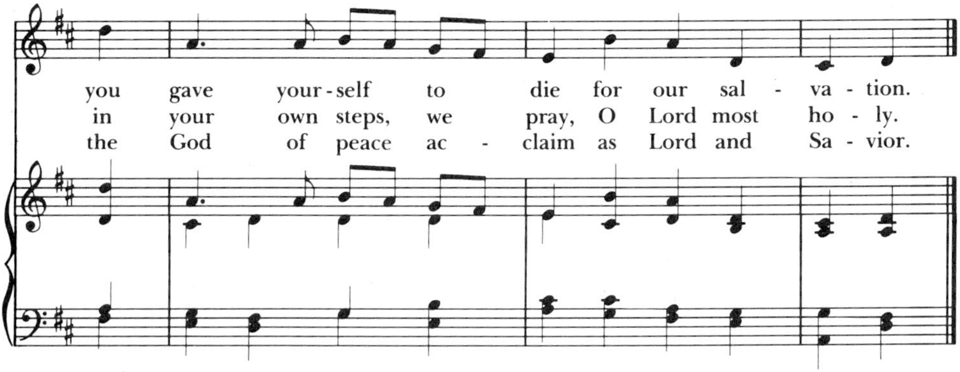
you gave your-self to die for our sal - va - tion.
in your own steps, we pray, O Lord most ho - ly.
the God of peace ac - claim as Lord and Sa - vior.

Alternative tune: *St. Dunstan's*, 564.

Words: Clement of Alexandria (170?-220?); para. F. Bland Tucker (1895-1984), rev.
Music: *Monk's Gate*, Sussex folk melody; adapt. and harm. Ralph Vaughan Williams (1872-1958)

𝅗𝅥=66
11 11. 12 11

Jesus Christ our Lord

479

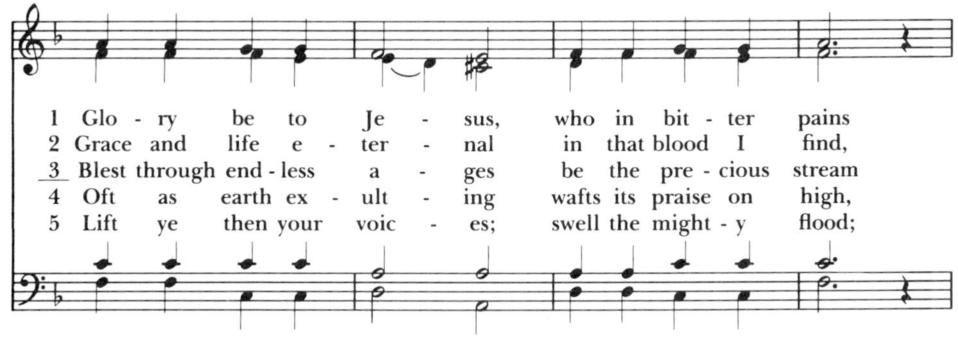
1 Glo - ry be to Je - sus, who in bit - ter pains
2 Grace and life e - ter - nal in that blood I find,
3 Blest through end - less a - ges be the pre - cious stream
4 Oft as earth ex - ult - ing wafts its praise on high,
5 Lift ye then your voic - es; swell the might - y flood;

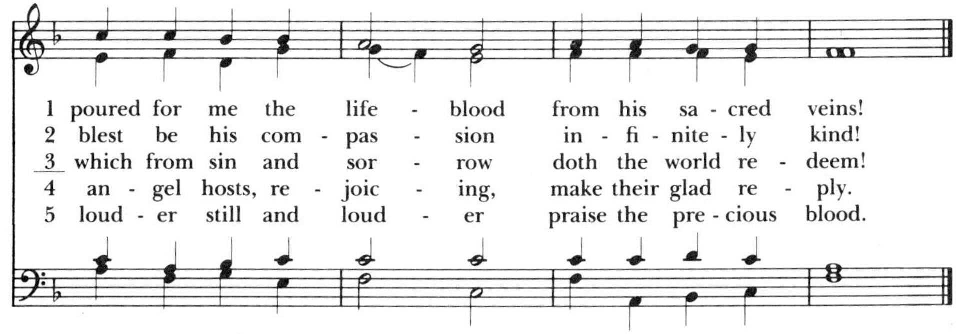
1 poured for me the life - blood from his sa - cred veins!
2 blest be his com - pas - sion in - fi - nite - ly kind!
3 which from sin and sor - row doth the world re - deem!
4 an - gel hosts, re - joic - ing, make their glad re - ply.
5 loud - er still and loud - er praise the pre - cious blood.

Words: Italian, 18th cent.; tr. Edward Caswall (1814-1878), alt.
Music: *Wem in Leidenstagen*, Friedrich Filitz (1804-1860)

𝅗𝅥=56
65. 65

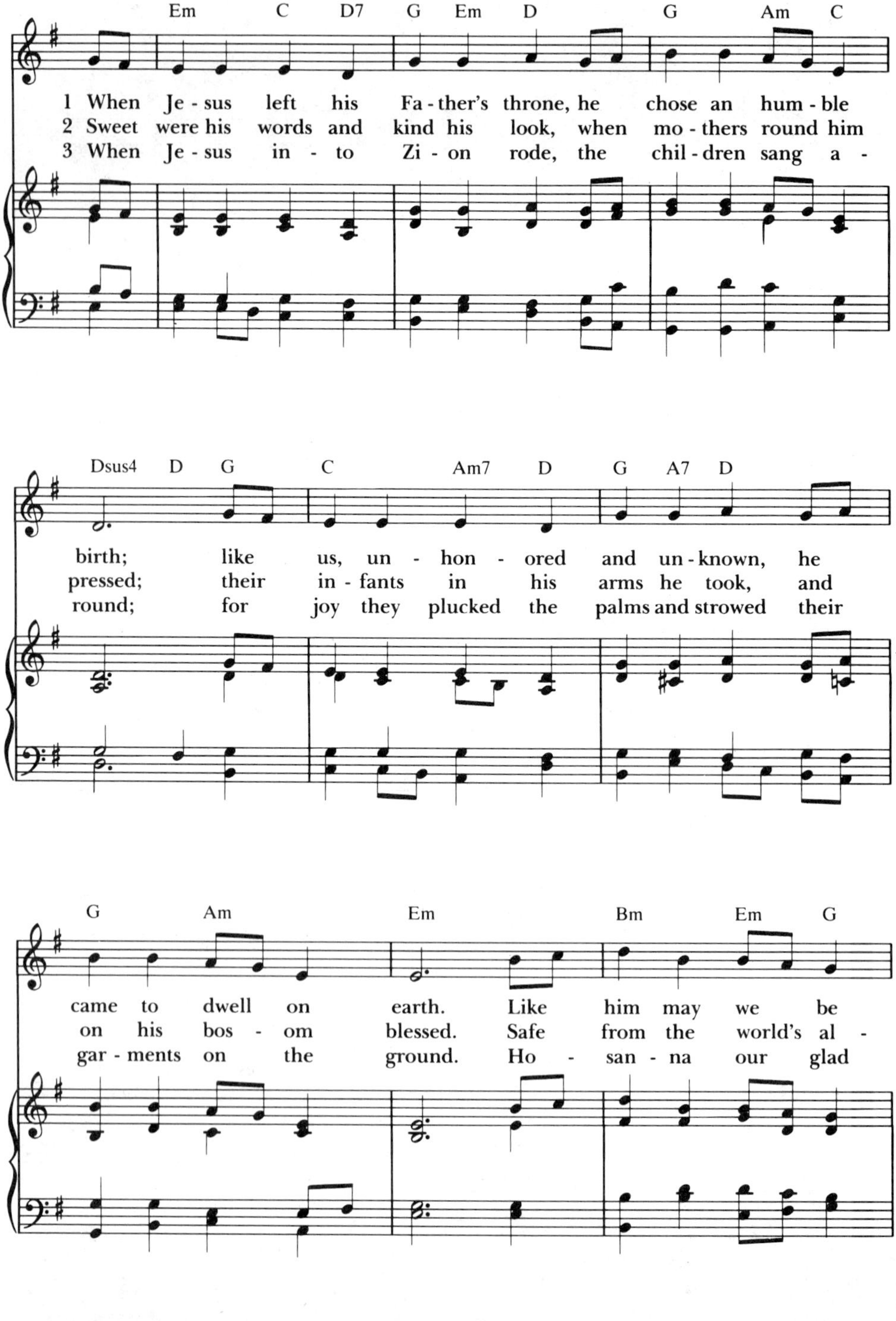
Em C D7 G Em D G Am C
1 When Je - sus left his Fa - ther's throne, he chose an hum - ble
2 Sweet were his words and kind his look, when mo - thers round him
3 When Je - sus in - to Zi - on rode, the chil - dren sang a -
Dsus4 D G C Am7 D G A7 D
birth; like us, un - hon - ored and un - known, he
pressed; their in - fants in his arms he took, and
round; for joy they plucked the palms and strowed their
G Am Em Bm Em G
came to dwell on earth. Like him may we be
on his bos - om blessed. Safe from the world's al -
gar - ments on the ground. Ho - san - na our glad

Am D G C Dsus4 D G
found be - low, in wis - dom's path of peace; like
lur - ing harms, be - neath his watch - ful eye, thus
voic - es raise, ho - san - na to our King! Should

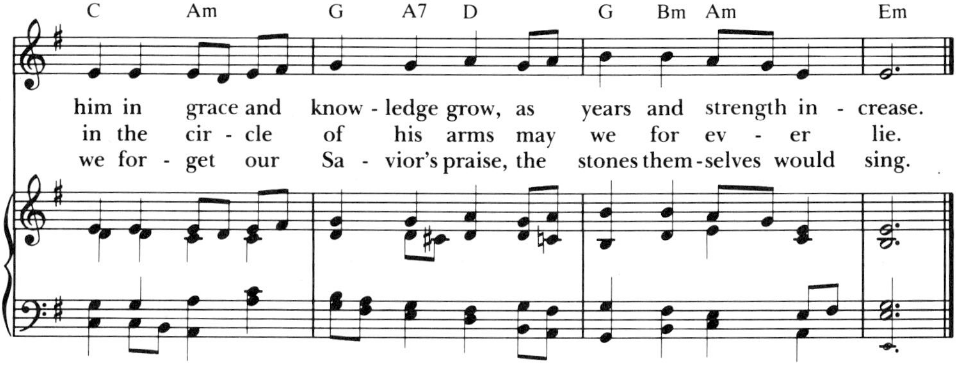
C Am G A7 D G Bm Am Em
him in grace and know - ledge grow, as years and strength in - crease.
in the cir - cle of his arms may we for ev - er lie.
we for - get our Sa - vior's praise, the stones them - selves would sing.

Words: James Montgomery (1771-1854)
Music: *Kingsfold*, English folk melody; adapt. and harm. Ralph Vaughan Williams (1872-1958)

𝅗𝅥 = 50
CMD

1 Re - joice, the Lord is King! Your Lord and King a - dore! Mor - tals, give thanks and sing, and tri - umph ev - er - more.
2 The Lord the Sa - vior reigns, the God of truth and love: when he had purged our stains, he took his seat a - bove.
3 His king-dom can - not fail; he rules o'er earth and heaven; the keys of death and hell to Christ the Lord are given.
4 Re - joice in glo - rious hope! Our Lord the Judge shall come, and take his ser - vants up to their e - ter - nal home.
Refrain
1-3
Lift up your heart! lift

up your voice! Re-joice! a-gain I say, re-joice!
Final Ending
up your heart! lift up your voice! Re-joice! a-
gain I say, re-joice!
poco rit.
a tempo

Words: Charles Wesley (1707-1788), alt.
Music: *Gopsal*, George Frideric Handel (1685-1759); arr. John Wilson (b. 1905)

𝅗𝅥=56
66. 66 with Refrain

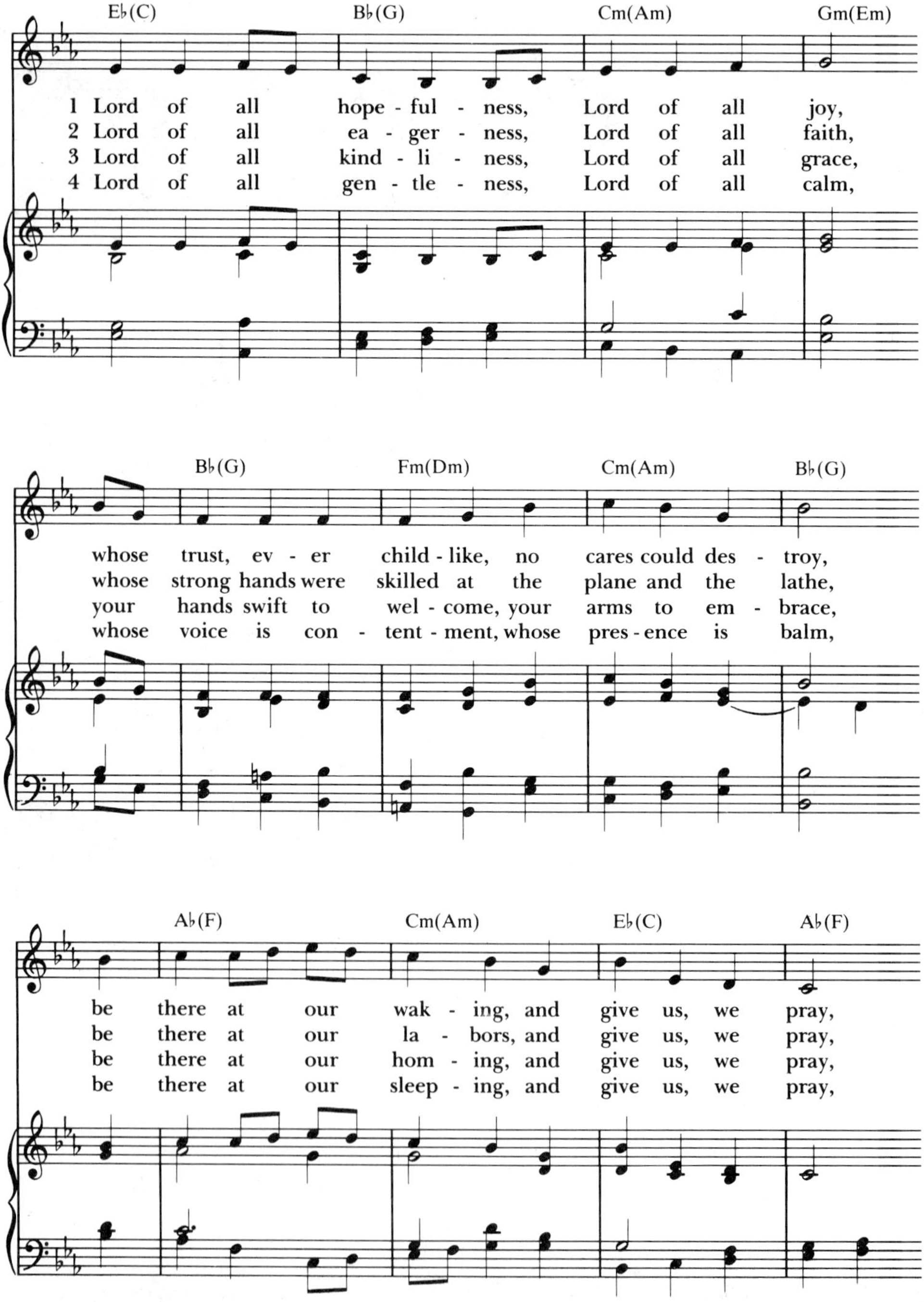
E♭(C) B♭(G) Cm(Am) Gm(Em)
1 Lord of all hope - ful - ness, Lord of all joy,
2 Lord of all ea - ger - ness, Lord of all faith,
3 Lord of all kind - li - ness, Lord of all grace,
4 Lord of all gen - tle - ness, Lord of all calm,
B♭(G) Fm(Dm) Cm(Am) B♭(G)
whose trust, ev - er child - like, no cares could des - troy,
whose strong hands were skilled at the plane and the lathe,
your hands swift to wel - come, your arms to em - brace,
whose voice is con - tent - ment, whose pres - ence is balm,
A♭(F) Cm(Am) E♭(C) A♭(F)
be there at our wak - ing, and give us, we pray,
be there at our la - bors, and give us, we pray,
be there at our hom - ing, and give us, we pray,
be there at our sleep - ing, and give us, we pray,

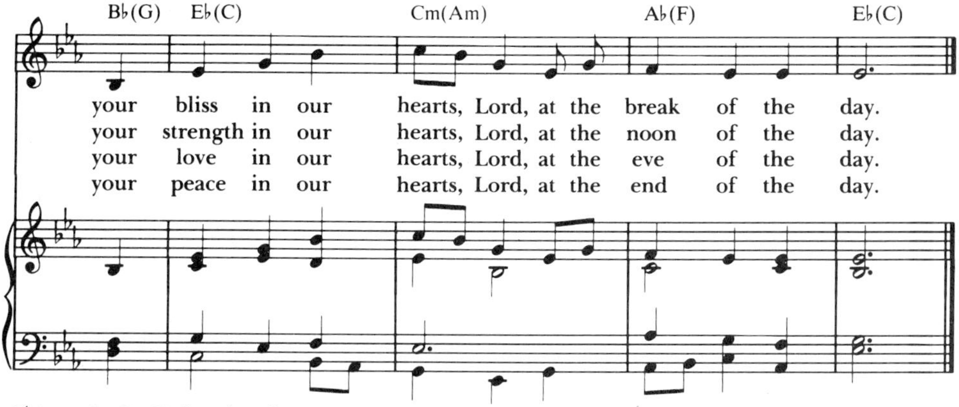
B♭(G) E♭(C) Cm(Am) A♭(F) E♭(C)
your bliss in our hearts, Lord, at the break of the day.
your strength in our hearts, Lord, at the noon of the day.
your love in our hearts, Lord, at the eve of the day.
your peace in our hearts, Lord, at the end of the day.

E♭(capo 3, C). Keyboard and guitar should not sound together. Another harmonization, 488.

Words: Jan Struther (1901-1953)
Music: *Slane,* Irish ballad melody; adapt. *The Church Hymnary,* 1927; harm. *Hymnal 1982*

♩=76
10 11. 11 12

Jesus Christ our Lord

483

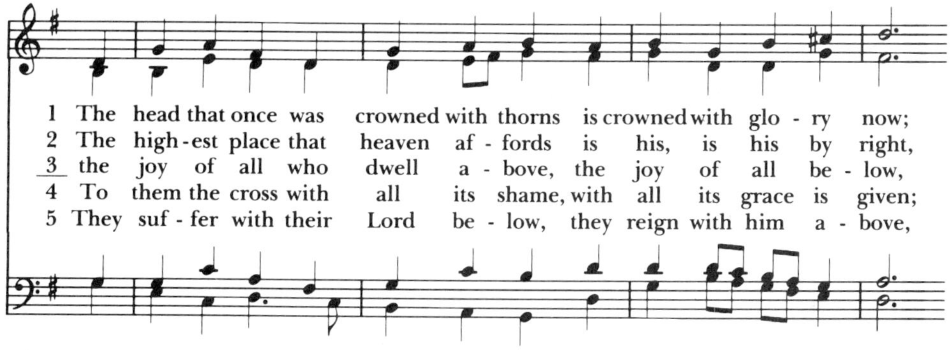
1 The head that once was crowned with thorns is crowned with glo - ry now;
2 The high - est place that heaven af - fords is his, is his by right,
3 the joy of all who dwell a - bove, the joy of all be - low,
4 To them the cross with all its shame, with all its grace is given;
5 They suf - fer with their Lord be - low, they reign with him a - bove,

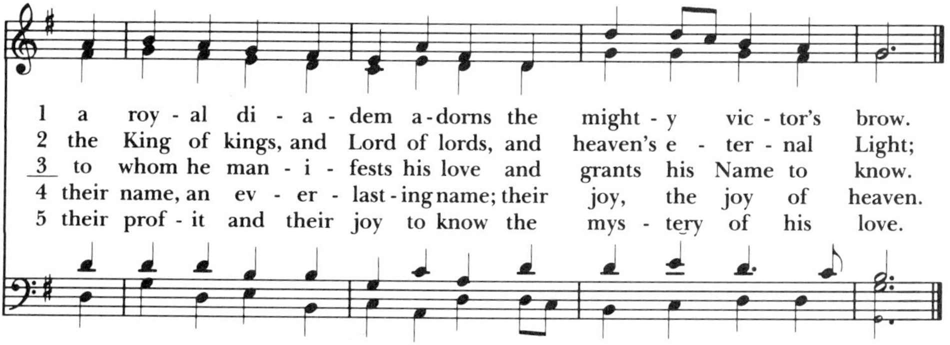
1 a roy - al di - a - dem a - dorns the might - y vic - tor's brow.
2 the King of kings, and Lord of lords, and heaven's e - ter - nal Light;
3 to whom he man - i - fests his love and grants his Name to know.
4 their name, an ev - er - last - ing name; their joy, the joy of heaven.
5 their prof - it and their joy to know the mys - tery of his love.

6 The cross he bore is life and health,
though shame and death to him:
his people's hope, his people's wealth,
their everlasting theme.

This music in F, 447.

Words: Thomas Kelly (1769-1855)
Music: *St. Magnus,* melody from *Divine Companion,* 1707; harm. William Henry Monk (1823-1889), after John Pyke Hullah (19th cent.)

♩=84
CM

1 Praise the Lord through ev - ery na - tion; his ho - ly
2 Je - sus, Lord, our Cap - tain glo - rious, o'er sin, and
arm hath wrought sal - va - tion; ex - alt him on his
death, and hell vic - to - rious, wis - dom and might to
Fa - ther's throne. Praise your King, ye Chris - tian le -
thee be - long: we con - fess, pro - claim, a - dore
gions, who now pre - pares in heaven - ly re -
thee; we bow the knee, we fall be - fore

gions un - fail - ing man - sions for his own: with
thee; thy love hence - forth shall be our song. The
voice and min - strel - sy ex - tol his ma - jes -
cross mean-while we bear, the crown ere-long to
ty: Al - le - lu - ia! His praise shall sound all
wear: Al - le - lu - ia! Thy reign ex - tend world
na - ture round, and hymns on ev - ery tongue a - bound.
with - out end; let praise from all to thee a - scend.

Alternative tune: *Wachet auf* (rhythmic), 485.

Words: Rhijnvis Feith (1753-1824); para. James Montgomery (1771-1854), alt.
Music: *Wachet auf,* melody Hans Sachs (1494-1576); adapt. Philipp Nicolai (1556-1608); arr. and harm. Johann Sebastian Bach (1685-1750)

♩=69
Irr.

1 Praise the Lord through ev - ery na - tion;
2 Je - sus, Lord, our Cap - tain glo - rious,
his ho - ly arm hath wrought sal - va - tion;
o'er sin, and death, and hell vic - to - rious,
ex - alt him
wis - dom and
on his Fa - ther's throne.
might to thee be - long:
Praise your King, ye Chris - tian
we con - fess, pro - claim, a -
le - gions,
dore thee;
who now pre - pares in heaven - ly re - gions
we bow the knee, we fall be - fore thee;

un - fail - ing man - sions for his own:
thy love hence - forth shall be our song.
with voice and min - strel - sy ex - tol his ma - jes - ty:
The cross mean-while we bear, the crown ere - long to wear:
Al - le - lu - ia! His praise shall sound all na - ture round,
Al - le - lu - ia! Thy reign ex - tend world with - out end;
and hymns on ev - ery tongue a - bound.
let praise from all to thee a - scend.

Alternative tune: *Wachet auf* (isometric), 484.

Words: Rhijnvis Feith (1753-1824); para. James Montgomery (1771-1854), alt.
Music: *Wachet auf,* melody Hans Sachs (1494-1576); adapt. Philipp Nicolai (1556-1608); harm. Jakob Praetorius (1586-1651)

𝅗𝅥=69
Irr.

1 Ho - san - na to the liv - ing Lord! Ho - san - na to the in - car - nate Word! To Christ, Cre - a - tor Sa - vior, King, let earth, let heaven, ho - san - na sing!
2 Ho - san - na Lord! thine an - gels cry; Ho - san - na Lord! thy saints re - ply; a - bove, be - neath us, and a - round, both dead and liv - ing swell the sound:
3 O Sa - vior, with pro - tect - ing care a - bide in this thy house of prayer, where we as - sem - bled in thy Name, in faith, thy part - ing prom - ise claim.
4 But, chief - est, in our cleans - ed breast, E - ter - nal! bid thy Spi - rit rest; and make our se - cret soul to be a tem - ple pure and wor - thy thee.
5 So in the last and dread - ful day, when earth and heaven shall melt a - way, thy flock, re - deemed from sin - ful stain, shall swell the sound of praise a - gain.
Refrain
Ho - san - na Lord! Ho - san - na in the high - est!

Words: Reginald Heber (1783-1826), alt.
Music: *Hosanna*, John Bacchus Dykes (1823-1876)

𝅗𝅥 = 52
LM with Refrain

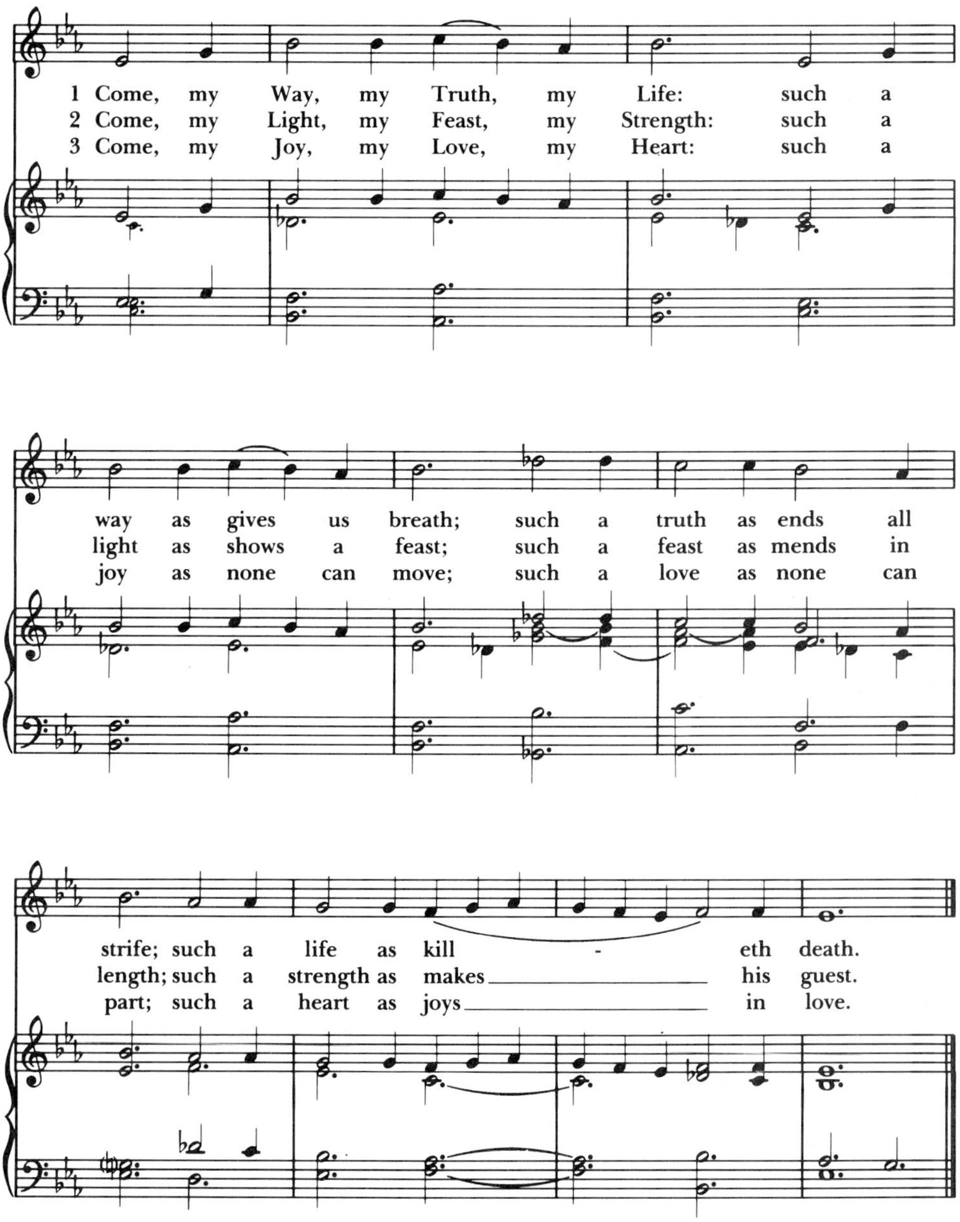
1 Come, my Way, my Truth, my Life: such a way as gives us breath; such a truth as ends all strife; such a life as kill - eth death.
2 Come, my Light, my Feast, my Strength: such a light as shows a feast; such a feast as mends in length; such a strength as makes his guest.
3 Come, my Joy, my Love, my Heart: such a joy as none can move; such a love as none can part; such a heart as joys in love.

Either version of the first measure may be used.

Words: George Herbert (1593-1633)
Music: *The Call,* Ralph Vaughan Williams (1872-1958)

𝅗𝅥. = 54
77. 77

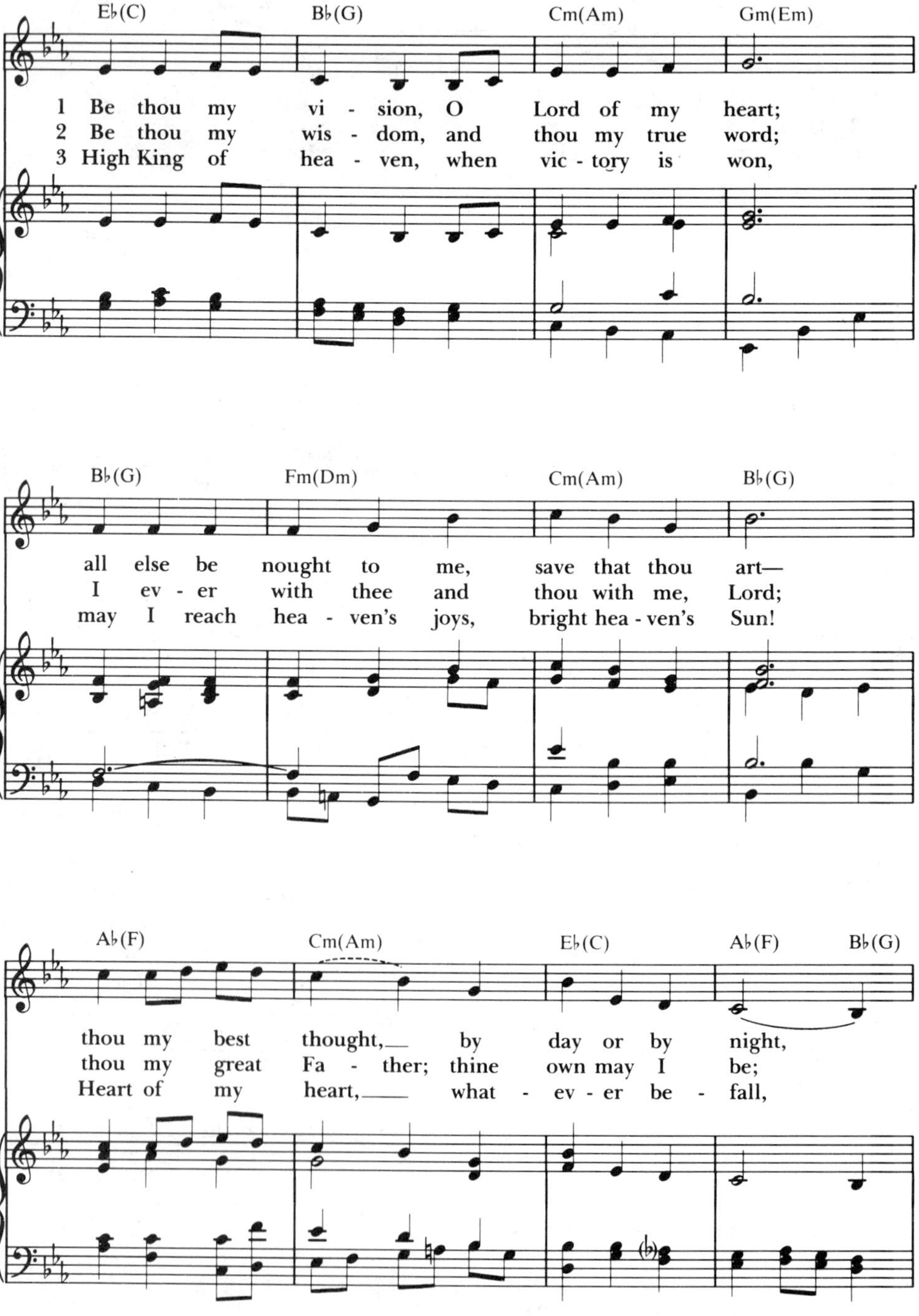
E♭(C) B♭(G) Cm(Am) Gm(Em)
1 Be thou my vi - sion, O Lord of my heart;
2 Be thou my wis - dom, and thou my true word;
3 High King of hea - ven, when vic - tory is won,
B♭(G) Fm(Dm) Cm(Am) B♭(G)
all else be nought to me, save that thou art—
I ev - er with thee and thou with me, Lord;
may I reach hea - ven's joys, bright hea - ven's Sun!
A♭(F) Cm(Am) E♭(C) A♭(F) B♭(G)
thou my best thought, by day or by night,
thou my great Fa - ther; thine own may I be;
Heart of my heart, what - ev - er be - fall,

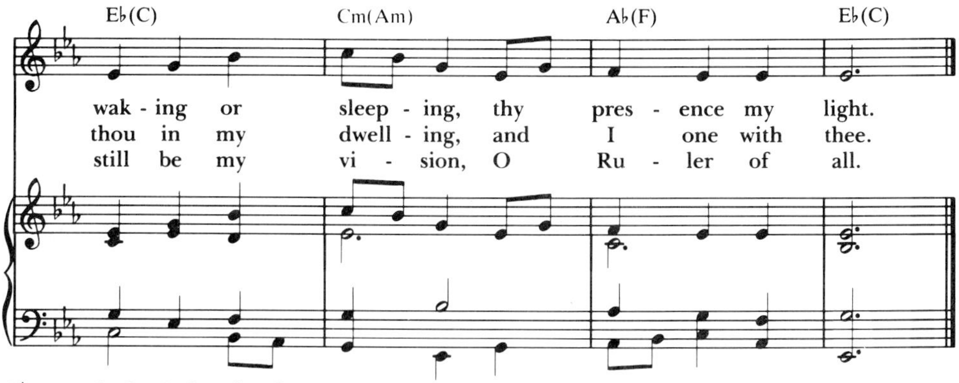
Eb(C) Cm(Am) Ab(F) Eb(C)
wak - ing or sleep - ing, thy pres - ence my light.
thou in my dwell - ing, and I one with thee.
still be my vi - sion, O Ru - ler of all.

Eb (capo 3, C). Keyboard and guitar should not sound together.
Another harmonization, 482.

Words: Irish, ca. 700; versified Mary Elizabeth Byrne (1880-1931); tr. Eleanor H. Hull (1860-1935), alt.
Music: *Slane,* Irish ballad melody; adapt. *The Church Hymnary,* 1927; harm. David Evans (1874-1948)

♩= 76
10 10. 9 10

Jesus Christ our Lord 489

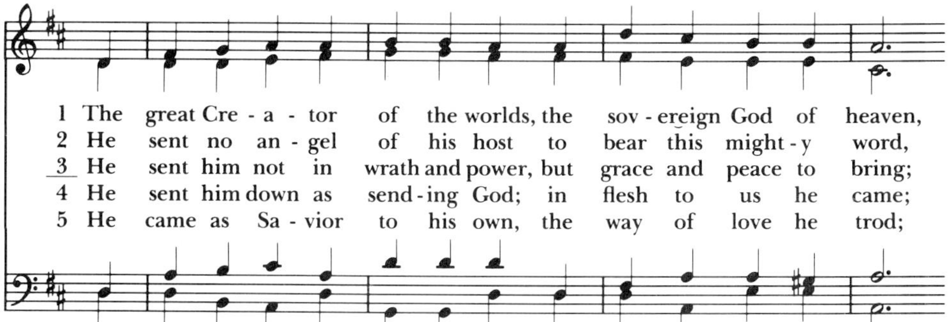
1 The great Cre - a - tor of the worlds, the sov - ereign God of heaven,
2 He sent no an - gel of his host to bear this might - y word,
3 He sent him not in wrath and power, but grace and peace to bring;
4 He sent him down as send - ing God; in flesh to us he came;
5 He came as Sa - vior to his own, the way of love he trod;

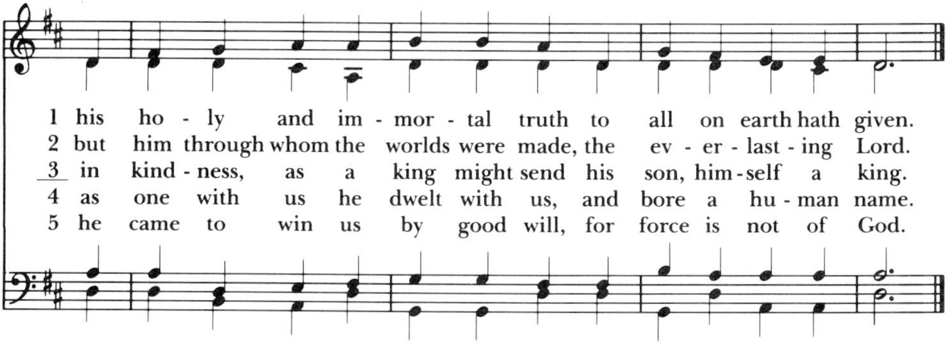
1 his ho - ly and im - mor - tal truth to all on earth hath given.
2 but him through whom the worlds were made, the ev - er - last - ing Lord.
3 in kind - ness, as a king might send his son, him - self a king.
4 as one with us he dwelt with us, and bore a hu - man name.
5 he came to win us by good will, for force is not of God.

6 Not to oppress, but summon all
their truest life to find,
in love God sent his Son to save,
not to condemn mankind.

Words: *Epistle to Diognetus,* ca. 150; tr. F. Bland Tucker (1895-1984), rev.
Music: *Tallis' Ordinal,* Thomas Tallis (1505?-1585)

♩= 80
CM

Jesus Christ our Lord

D♭(C) A♭(G) G♭(F) A♭(G)
1 I want to walk as a child of the light.
2 I want to see ___ the bright-ness of God.
3 I'm look - ing for ___ the com - ing of Christ.
B♭m(Am) Fm(Em) A♭(G) B♭m(Am)
I want to fol - low Je - sus.
I want to look at Je - sus.
I want to be with Je - sus.
D♭(C) Fm(Em) G♭(F) A♭(G)
God set the stars to give light to the world. The
Clear sun of right - eous - ness, shine on my path, and
When we have run ___ with pa - tience the race, we
D♭(C) A♭(G) E♭(D) A♭(G)
star of my life ___ is Je - sus.
show me the way to the Fa - ther.
shall know the joy ___ of Je - sus.

Refrain
D♭(C) G♭(F) D♭(C) Fm(Em)
In him there is no dark - ness at all. The
B♭m(Am) D♭(C)sus4 D♭(C) B♭(Am) A♭(G)
night and the day are both a - like. The
E♭m(Dm) D♭(C) G♭(F) A♭(G)
rit.
Lamb is the light of the ci - ty of God.
a tempo
D♭(C) A♭(G) G♭(F) A♭(G) D♭(C)
Shine in my heart, Lord Je - sus.

D♭ (capo 1, C). Keyboard and guitar should not sound together.

Words: Kathleen Thomerson (b. 1934)
Music: *Houston,* Kathleen Thomerson (b. 1934)

♩=96
Irr. with Refrain

1 Where is this stu - pen-dous stran - ger? Pro - phets, shep - herds, kings, ad - vise. Lead me to my Mas-ter's man - ger, show me where my Sa - vior lies.
2 O Most Might - y! O Most Ho - ly! Far be - yond the ser - aph's thought: art thou then so weak and low - ly as un - heed - ed pro - phets taught?
3 O the mag - ni - tude of meek - ness! Worth from worth im - mor - tal sprung; O the strength of in - fant weak - ness, if e - ter - nal is so young!
4 God all - boun - teous, all - cre - a - tive, whom no ills from good dis - suade, is in - car - nate, and a na - tive of the ve - ry world he made.

The fermata should be reserved for the final stanza.

Words: Christopher Smart (1722-1771), alt.
Music: *Kit Smart,* Alec Wyton (b. 1921)

♩=72
87. 87

Alternative accompaniment

The fermata should be reserved for the final stanza.

Music: *Kit Smart,* Alec Wyton (b. 1921) ♩= 72

1 Sing, ye faith - ful, sing with glad - ness, wake your no - blest,
2 Sing how he came forth from hea - ven, bowed him-self to
3 So, he tast - ed death for mor - tals, he, of hu - man -
4 Now on high, yet ev - er with us, from his Fa - ther's
sweet - est strain, with the prais - es of your Sa - vior
Beth - lehem's cave, stooped to wear the ser - vant's ves - ture,
kind the head, sin - less one, a - mong the sin - ful,
throne the Son rules and guides the world he ran - somed,
let his house re - sound a - gain; him let all your
bore the pain, the cross, the grave, passed with - in the
Prince of life, a - mong the dead; thus he wrought the
till the ap-point - ed work be done, till he see, re -

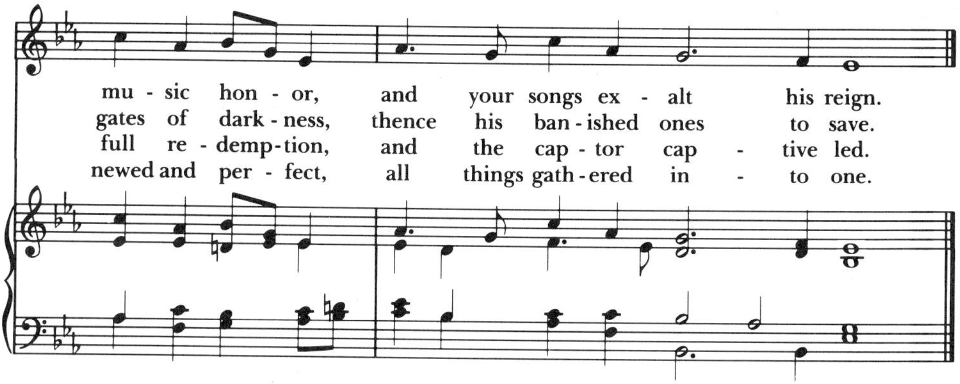
mu - sic hon - or, and your songs ex - alt his reign.
gates of dark - ness, thence his ban - ished ones to save.
full re - demp - tion, and the cap - tor cap - tive led.
newed and per - fect, all things gath - ered in - to one.

Words: John Ellerton (1826-1893), alt.
Music: *Finnian,* Christopher Dearnley (b. 1930)

𝅗𝅥=50
87. 87. 87

Jesus Christ our Lord

493

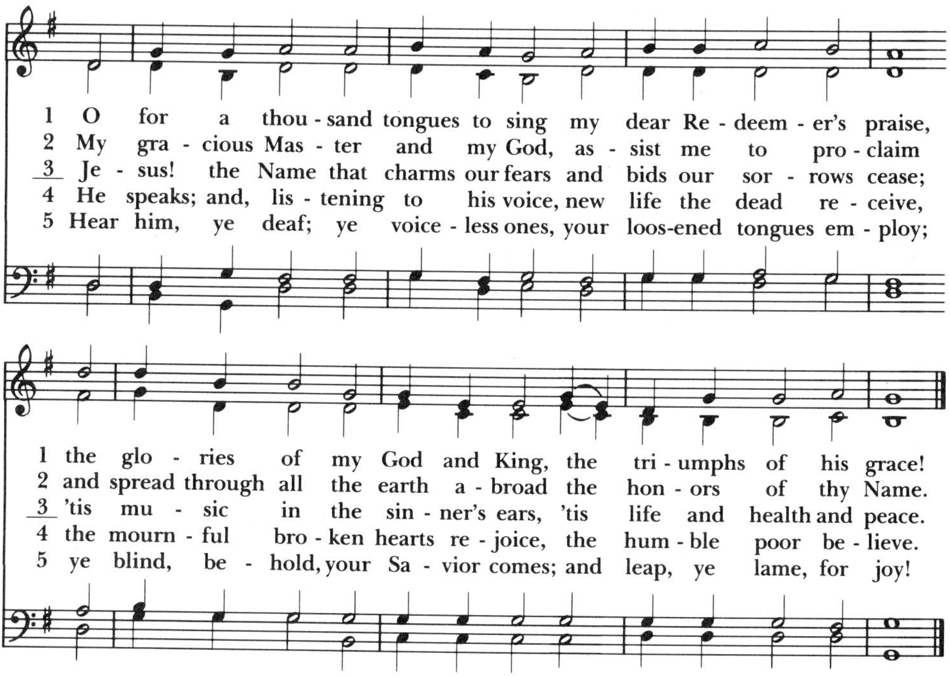
1 O for a thou - sand tongues to sing my dear Re - deem - er's praise,
2 My gra - cious Mas - ter and my God, as - sist me to pro - claim
3 Je - sus! the Name that charms our fears and bids our sor - rows cease;
4 He speaks; and, lis - tening to his voice, new life the dead re - ceive,
5 Hear him, ye deaf; ye voice - less ones, your loos-ened tongues em - ploy;
1 the glo - ries of my God and King, the tri - umphs of his grace!
2 and spread through all the earth a - broad the hon - ors of thy Name.
3 'tis mu - sic in the sin - ner's ears, 'tis life and health and peace.
4 the mourn - ful bro - ken hearts re - joice, the hum - ble poor be - lieve.
5 ye blind, be - hold, your Sa - vior comes; and leap, ye lame, for joy!

6 Glory to God and praise and love
be now and ever given
by saints below and saints above,
the Church in earth and heaven.

Words: Charles Wesley (1707-1788), alt.
Music: *Azmon,* Carl Gotthilf Gläser (1784-1829); adapt. and arr. Lowell Mason (1792-1872)

𝅗𝅥=84
CM

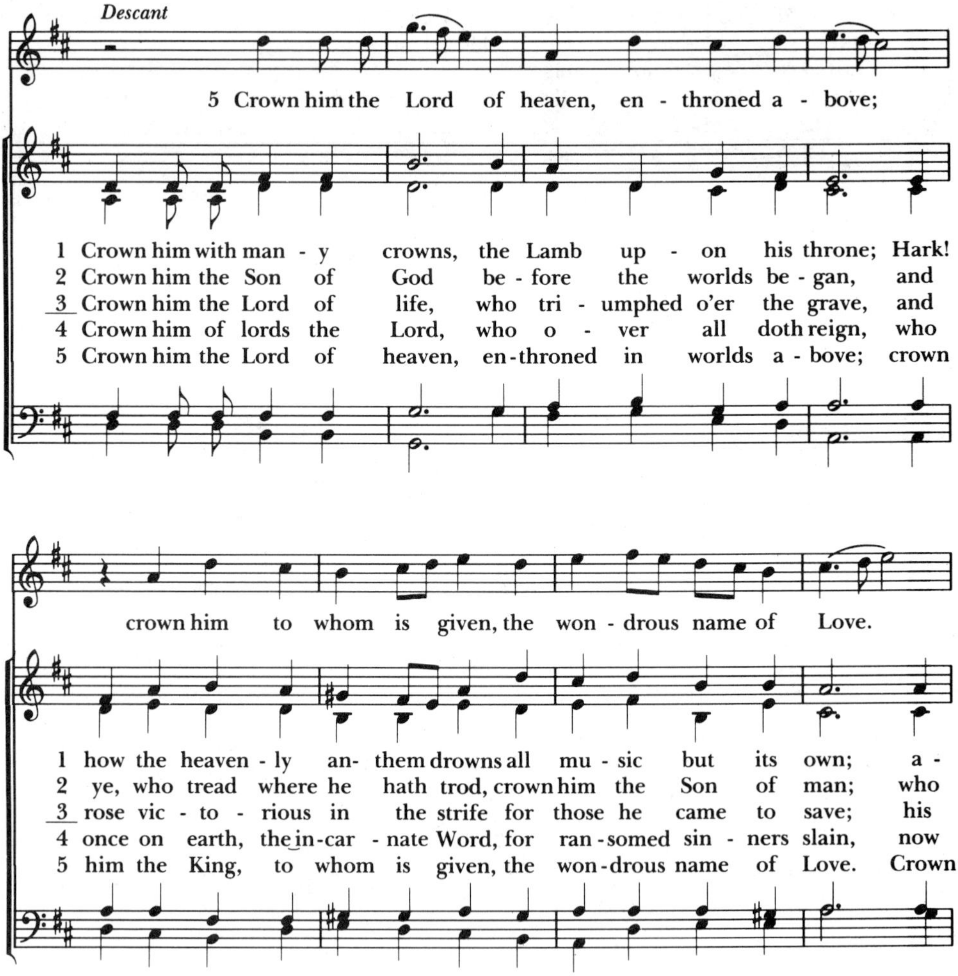
Descant
5 Crown him the Lord of heaven, en - throned a - bove;
1 Crown him with man - y crowns, the Lamb up - on his throne; Hark!
2 Crown him the Son of God be - fore the worlds be - gan, and
3 Crown him the Lord of life, who tri - umphed o'er the grave, and
4 Crown him of lords the Lord, who o - ver all doth reign, who
5 Crown him the Lord of heaven, en-throned in worlds a - bove; crown
crown him to whom is given, the won - drous name of Love.
1 how the heaven - ly an- them drowns all mu - sic but its own; a -
2 ye, who tread where he hath trod, crown him the Son of man; who
3 rose vic - to - rious in the strife for those he came to save; his
4 once on earth, the in-car - nate Word, for ran-somed sin - ners slain, now
5 him the King, to whom is given, the won-drous name of Love. Crown

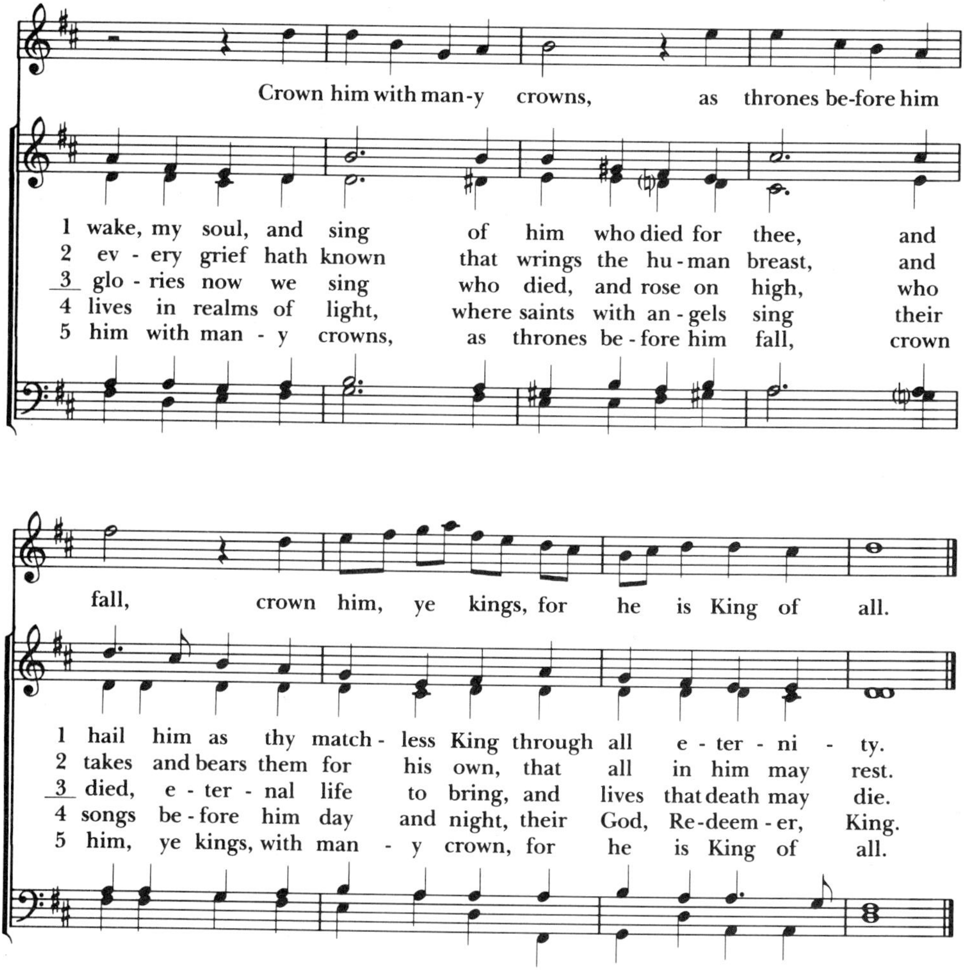
Crown him with man-y crowns, as thrones be-fore him
1 wake, my soul, and sing of him who died for thee, and
2 ev - ery grief hath known that wrings the hu - man breast, and
3 glo - ries now we sing who died, and rose on high, who
4 lives in realms of light, where saints with an - gels sing their
5 him with man - y crowns, as thrones be - fore him fall, crown
fall, crown him, ye kings, for he is King of all.
1 hail him as thy match - less King through all e - ter - ni - ty.
2 takes and bears them for his own, that all in him may rest.
3 died, e - ter - nal life to bring, and lives that death may die.
4 songs be - fore him day and night, their God, Re - deem - er, King.
5 him, ye kings, with man - y crown, for he is King of all.

Words: Matthew Bridges (1800-1894)
Music: *Diademata,* George Job Elvey (1816-1893); desc. Richard Proulx (b. 1937)

𝅗𝅥 = 56
SMD

Jesus Christ our Lord

1 Hail, thou once de - spis - ed Je - sus! Hail, thou Gal - i -
2 Pas - chal Lamb, by God ap - point - ed, all our sins on
3 Je - sus, hail! en - throned in glo - ry, there for ev - er
*4 Wor - ship, hon - or, power, and bless - ing thou art wor - thy

le - an King! Thou didst suf - fer to re - lease us;
thee were laid: by al - might - y love a - noint - ed,
to a - bide; all the heaven - ly hosts a - dore thee,
to re - ceive; high - est prais - es, with - out ceas - ing,

thou didst free sal - va - tion bring. Hail, thou u - ni - ver - sal
thou hast full a - tone - ment made. All thy peo - ple are for -
seat - ed at thy Fa - ther's side. There for sin - ners thou art
right it is for us to give. Help, ye bright an - gel - ic

Sa - vior, bear - er of our sin and shame! By thy mer - it
giv - en through the vir - tue of thy blood: o - pened is the
plead - ing: there thou dost our place pre - pare; ev - er for us
spi - rits, all your no - blest an - thems raise; help to sing our
we find fa - vor: life is giv - en through thy Name.
gate of hea - ven, re - con - ciled are we with God.
in - ter - ced - ing, till in glo - ry we ap - pear.
Sa - vior's mer - its, help to chant Em - man - uel's praise!

Another harmonization, 215.

Words: John Bakewell (1721-1819) and Martin Madan (1726-1790), alt.
Music: *In Babilone*, melody from *Oude en Nieuwe Hollantse Boerenlities en Contradanseu*, 1710; harm. Roy F. Kehl (b. 1935)

♩= 84
87. 87. D

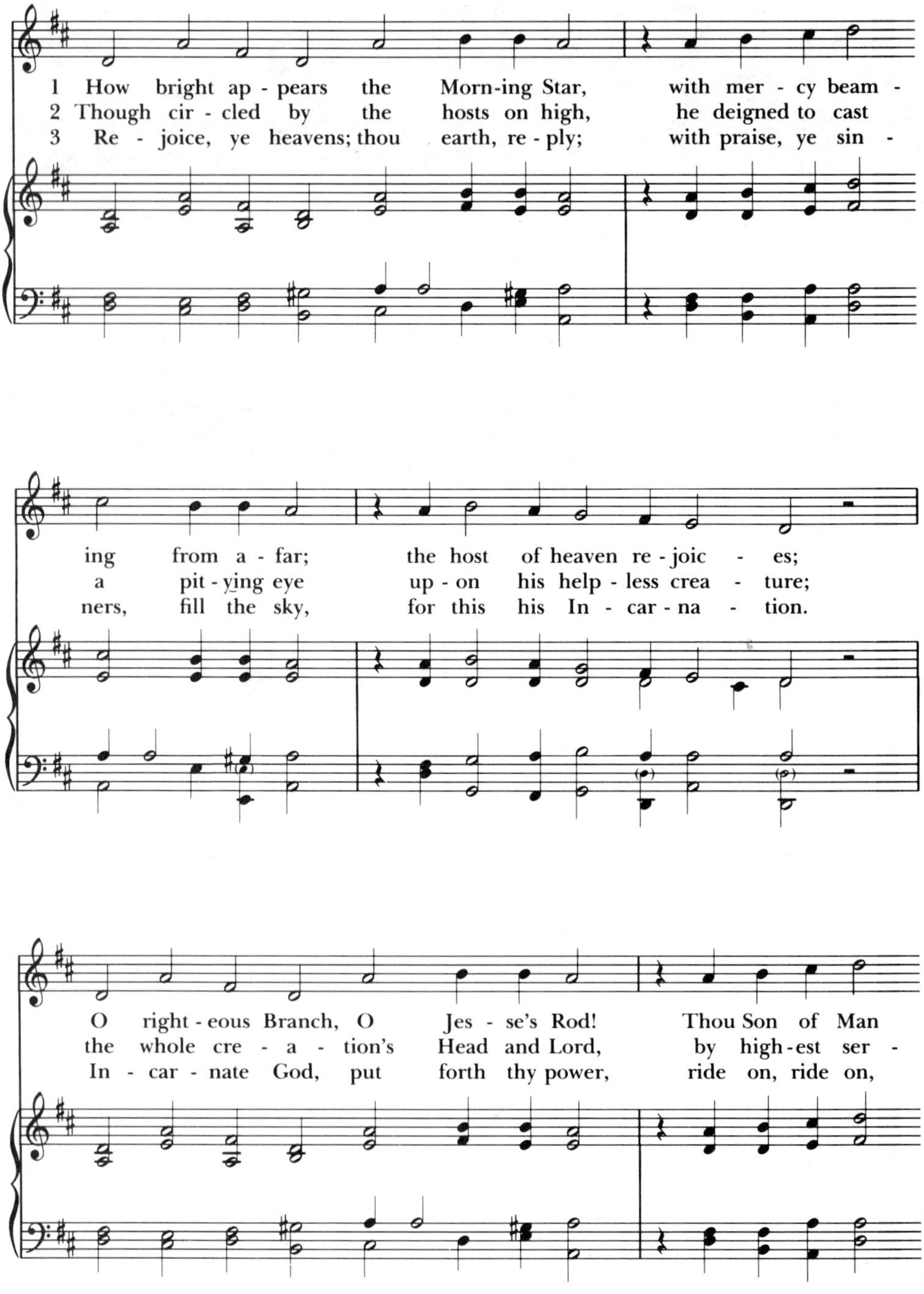
1 How bright ap - pears the Morn-ing Star, with mer - cy beam -
2 Though cir - cled by the hosts on high, he deigned to cast
3 Re - joice, ye heavens; thou earth, re - ply; with praise, ye sin -
ing from a - far; the host of heaven re - joic - es;
a pit - ying eye up - on his help - less crea - ture;
ners, fill the sky, for this his In - car - na - tion.
O right - eous Branch, O Jes - se's Rod! Thou Son of Man
the whole cre - a - tion's Head and Lord, by high - est ser -
In - car - nate God, put forth thy power, ride on, ride on,

and Son of God! We, too, will lift our voic - es:
a - phim a - dored, as - sumed our ve - ry na - ture;
great Con - quer - or, till all know thy sal - va - tion.
Je - sus, Je - sus! Ho - ly, ho - ly, yet most low - ly,
Je - sus, grant us, through thy mer - it, to in - her - it
A - men, a - men! Al - le - lu - ia, al - le - lu - ia!
draw thou near us; great Em - man - uel, come and hear us.
thy sal - va - tion; hear, O hear our sup - pli - ca - tion.
Praise be giv - en ev - er - more, by earth and hea - ven.

Alternative tune: *Wie schön leuchtet* (isometric), 497.

Words: William Mercer (1811-1873), after Philipp Nicolai (1556-1608)
Music: *Wie schön leuchtet,* melody att. Philipp Nicolai (1556-1608); harm. Johann Herman Schein (1586-1630)

𝅗𝅥 = 72
Irr.

1 How bright ap - pears the Morn-ing Star, with mer - cy beam - ing
2 Though cir - cled by the hosts on high, he deigned to cast a
3 Re - joice, ye heavens; thou earth, re - ply; with praise, ye sin - ners,
from a - far; the host of heaven re - joic - es;
pit - ying eye up - on his help - less crea - ture;
fill the sky, for this his In - car - na - tion.
O right-eous Branch, O Jes - se's Rod! Thou Son of Man and
the whole cre - a - tion's Head and Lord, by high-est ser - a -
In - car - nate God, put forth thy power, ride on, ride on, great
Son of God! We, too, will lift our voic - es:
phim a - dored, as - sumed our ve - ry na - ture;
Con - quer - or, till all know thy sal - va - tion.

Je - sus, Je - sus! Ho - ly ho - ly, yet most low - ly,
Je - sus, grant us, through thy mer - it, to in - her - it
A - men, a - men! Al - le - lu - ia, al - le - lu - ia!

draw thou near us; great Em - man - uel, come and hear us.
thy sal - va - tion; hear, O hear our sup - pli - ca - tion.
Praise be giv - en ev - er - more, by earth and hea - ven.

Alternative tune: *Wie schön leuchtet* (rhythmic), 496.

Words: William Mercer (1811-1873), after Philipp Nicolai (1556-1608)
Music: *Wie schön leuchtet*, melody att. Philipp Nicolai, (1556-1608); arr. and harm. Johann Sebastian Bach (1685-1750)

𝅗𝅥 = 72
Irr.

1 Be - neath the cross of Je - sus I fain would take my stand,
2 Up - on the cross of Je - sus mine eyes at times can see
3 I take, O cross, thy sha - dow for my a - bid - ing place;
the sha - dow of a might - y rock with - in a wea - ry land,
the ve - ry dy - ing form of one who suf - fered there for me;
I ask no o - ther sun - shine than the sun - shine of his face;
a home with - in the wil - der - ness, a rest up - on the way,
and from my smit - ten heart with tears two won - ders I con - fess:
con - tent to let my pride go by, to know no gain nor loss,
from the burn - ing of the noon - tide heat, and the bur - den of the day.
the ___ won - ders of re - deem - ing love, and ___ my un - wor - thi - ness.
my ___ sin - ful self my on - ly shame, my ___ glo - ry all the cross.

Words: Elizabeth Cecilia Clephane (1830-1869), alt.
Music: *St. Christopher*, Frederick Charles Maker (1844-1927)

𝅗𝅥 = 50
76. 86. 86. 86

Unison or harmony
Lord God, you now have set your ser - vant free to go in
peace as prom-ised in your word; my eyes have seen the
Sa - vior, Christ the Lord, pre-pared by you for all the
world to see, to shine on na-tions trapped in dark - est night,
the glo - ry of your peo - ple, and their light.

Words: Rae E. Whitney (b. 1927); para. of *The Song of Simeon*
Music: *Song 1*, melody and bass Orlando Gibbons (1583-1625); harm. Ralph Vaughan Williams (1872-1958)

♩= 90
10 10. 10 10. 10 10

1 Cre - a - tor Spi - rit, by whose aid the world's foun -
2 O Source of un - cre - at - ed light, the Fa - ther's
3 Plen - teous of grace, come from on high, rich in thy
da - tions first were laid, come, vis - it ev - ery hum - ble
prom - ised Par - a - clete, thrice ho - ly Fount, thrice ho - ly
seven - fold en - er - gy; make us e - ter - nal truth re -
mind; come, pour thy joys on hu - man - kind; from sin and
Fire, our hearts with heaven - ly love in - spire; come, and thy
ceive, and prac - tice all that we be - lieve; give us thy -
sor - row set us free, and make thy tem - ples wor - thy thee.
sa - cred unc - tion bring to sanc - ti - fy us while we sing.
self, that we may see the Fa - ther and the Son by thee.

Words: John Dryden (1631-1700); tr. of *Veni Creator Spiritus*
Music: *Surrey*, melody Henry Carey (1690?-1743)

𝅗𝅥=40
88. 88. 88

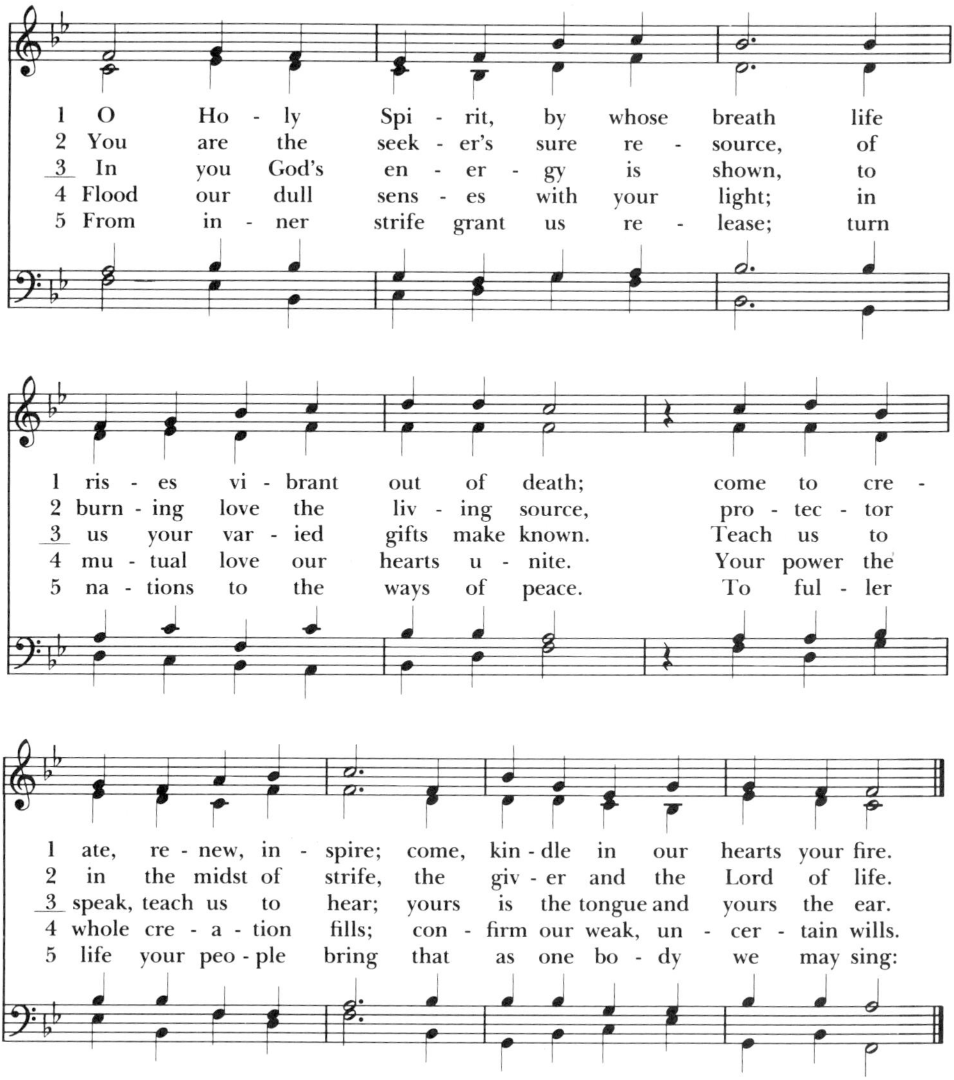
1 O Ho - ly Spi - rit, by whose breath life
2 You are the seek - er's sure re - source, of
3 In you God's en - er - gy is shown, to
4 Flood our dull sens - es with your light; in
5 From in - ner strife grant us re - lease; turn
1 ris - es vi - brant out of death; come to cre -
2 burn - ing love the liv - ing source, pro - tec - tor
3 us your var - ied gifts make known. Teach us to
4 mu - tual love our hearts u - nite. Your power the
5 na - tions to the ways of peace. To ful - ler
1 ate, re - new, in - spire; come, kin - dle in our hearts your fire.
2 in the midst of strife, the giv - er and the Lord of life.
3 speak, teach us to hear; yours is the tongue and yours the ear.
4 whole cre - a - tion fills; con - firm our weak, un - cer - tain wills.
5 life your peo - ple bring that as one bo - dy we may sing:

6 Praise to the Father, Christ, his Word,
and to the Spirit: God the Lord,
to whom all honor, glory be
both now and for eternity.

Alternative tune: *Veni Creator Spiritus*, 502 and 504.

Words: Att. Rabanus Maurus (776-856); tr. John Webster Grant (b. 1919), alt.; para. of *Veni Creator Spiritus* 𝅗𝅥=50
Music: *Komm, Gott Schöpfer*, melody from *Eyn Enchiridion*, 1524; harm. *The Lutheran Hymnal*, 1941 LM

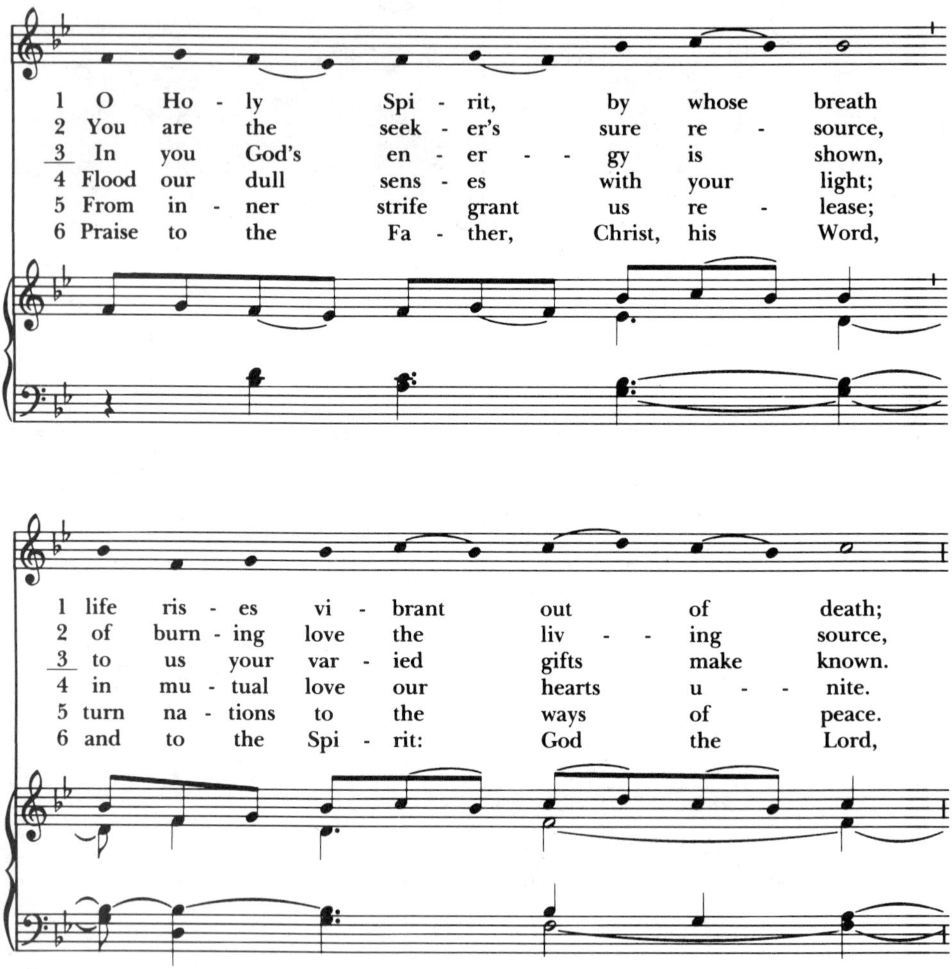
1 O Ho - ly Spi - rit, by whose breath
2 You are the seek - er's sure re - source,
3 In you God's en - er - - gy is shown,
4 Flood our dull sens - es with your light;
5 From in - ner strife grant us re - lease;
6 Praise to the Fa - ther, Christ, his Word,
1 life ris - es vi - brant out of death;
2 of burn - ing love the liv - - ing source,
3 to us your var - ied gifts make known.
4 in mu - tual love our hearts u - - nite.
5 turn na - tions to the ways of peace.
6 and to the Spi - rit: God the Lord,

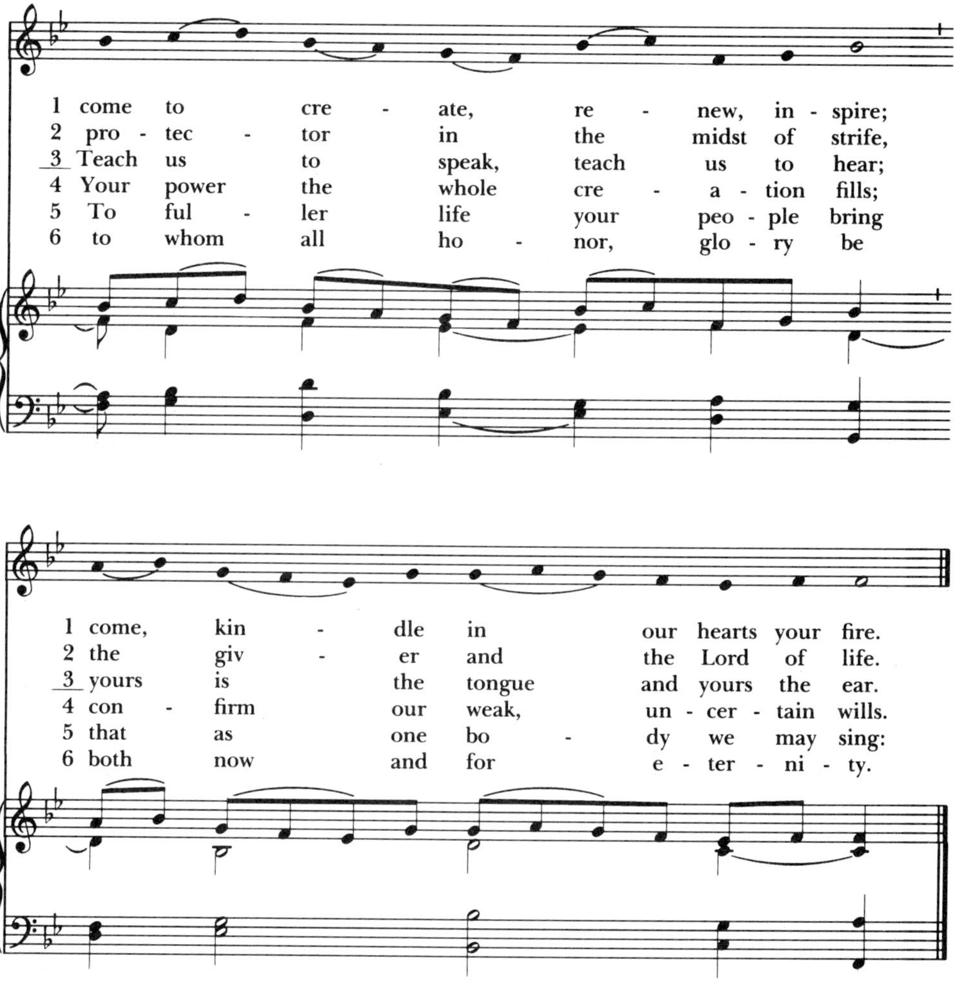
1 come to cre - ate, re - new, in - spire;
2 pro - tec - tor in the midst of strife,
3 Teach us to speak, teach us to hear;
4 Your power the whole cre - a - tion fills;
5 To ful - ler life your peo - ple bring
6 to whom all ho - nor, glo - ry be
1 come, kin - dle in our hearts your fire.
2 the giv - er and the Lord of life.
3 yours is the tongue and yours the ear.
4 con - firm our weak, un - cer - tain wills.
5 that as one bo - dy we may sing:
6 both now and for e - ter - ni - ty.

Another accompaniment, 504. Alternative tune: *Komm, Gott Schöpfer,* 501.

Words: Att. Rabanus Maurus (776-856); tr. John Webster Grant (b. 1919), alt.; para. of *Veni Creator Spiritus*
Music: *Veni Creator Spiritus,* plainsong, Mode 8; acc. Richard Proulx (b. 1937) LM

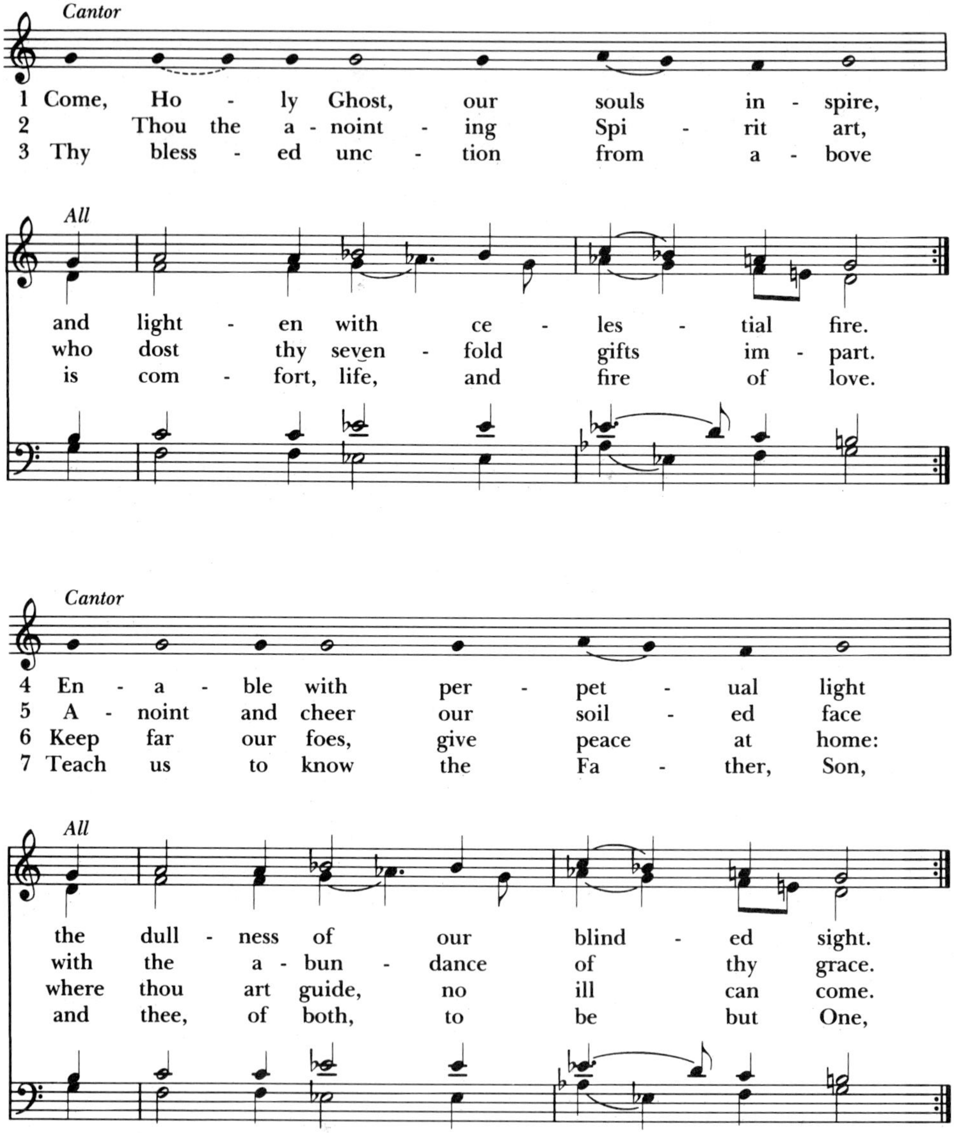
Cantor
1 Come, Ho - ly Ghost, our souls in - spire,
2 Thou the a - noint - ing Spi - rit art,
3 Thy bless - ed unc - tion from a - bove
All
and light - en with ce - les - tial fire.
who dost thy seven - fold gifts im - part.
is com - fort, life, and fire of love.
Cantor
4 En - a - ble with per - pet - ual light
5 A - noint and cheer our soil - ed face
6 Keep far our foes, give peace at home:
7 Teach us to know the Fa - ther, Son,
All
the dull - ness of our blind - ed sight.
with the a - bun - dance of thy grace.
where thou art guide, no ill can come.
and thee, of both, to be but One,

Cantor
8 that through the a - ges all a - long,
All
this may be our end - less song:
Cantor
9 praise to thy e - ter - nal mer - it,
All
Fa - ther, Son, and Ho - ly Spi - rit.

Alternative tune: *Veni Creator Spiritus,* 502 and 504.

Words: Latin, 9th cent.; tr. John Cosin (1594-1672); para. of *Veni Creator Spiritus.* ♩= 132
Music: *Come Holy Ghost,* John Henry Hopkins Jr. (1820-1891); adapt. and harm. David Hurd (b. 1950) 88

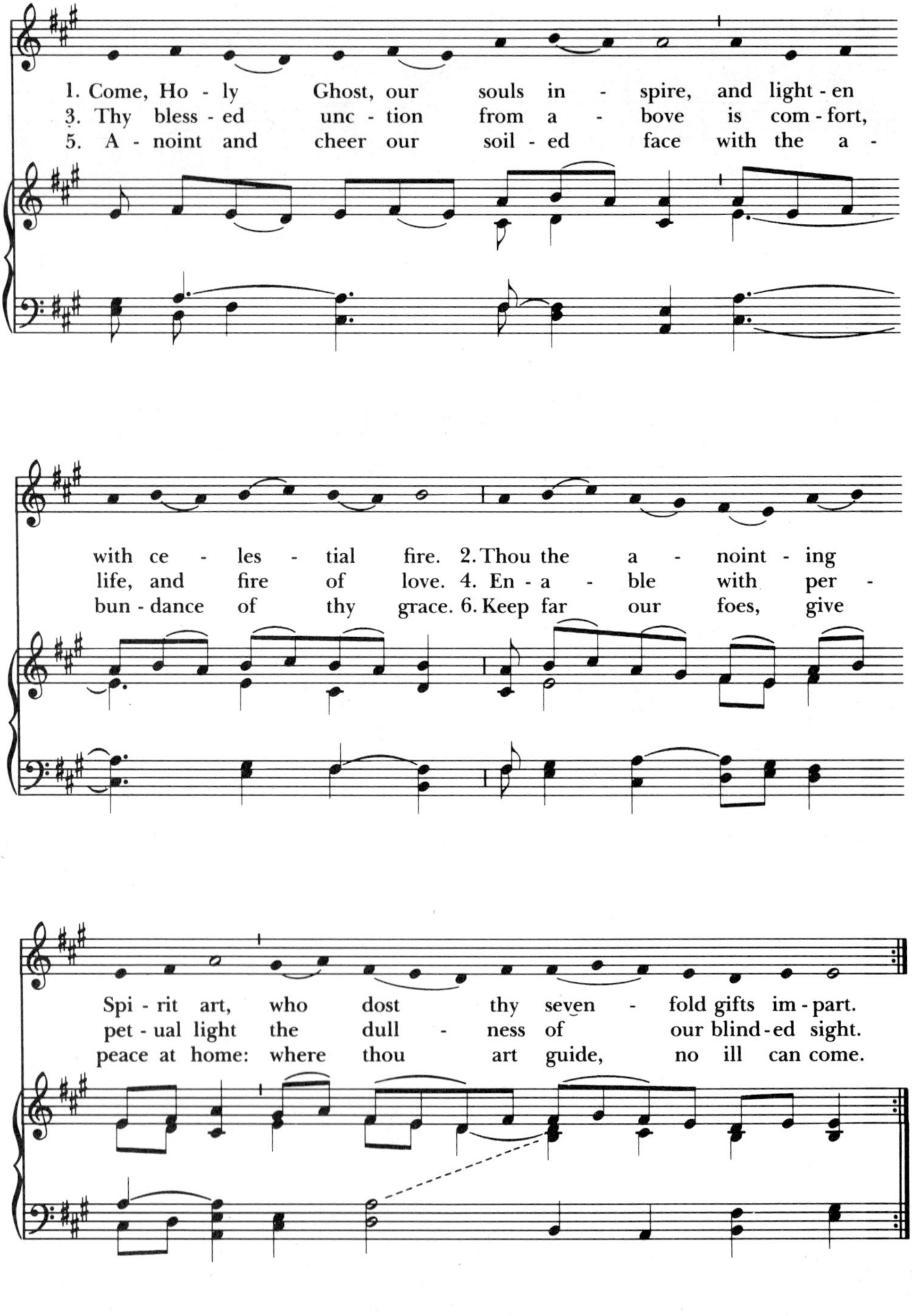
1. Come, Ho - ly Ghost, our souls in - spire, and light - en
3. Thy bless - ed unc - tion from a - bove is com - fort,
5. A - noint and cheer our soil - ed face with the a -
with ce - les - tial fire. 2. Thou the a - noint - ing
life, and fire of love. 4. En - a - ble with per -
bun - dance of thy grace. 6. Keep far our foes, give
Spi - rit art, who dost thy seven - fold gifts im - part.
pet - ual light the dull - ness of our blind - ed sight.
peace at home: where thou art guide, no ill can come.

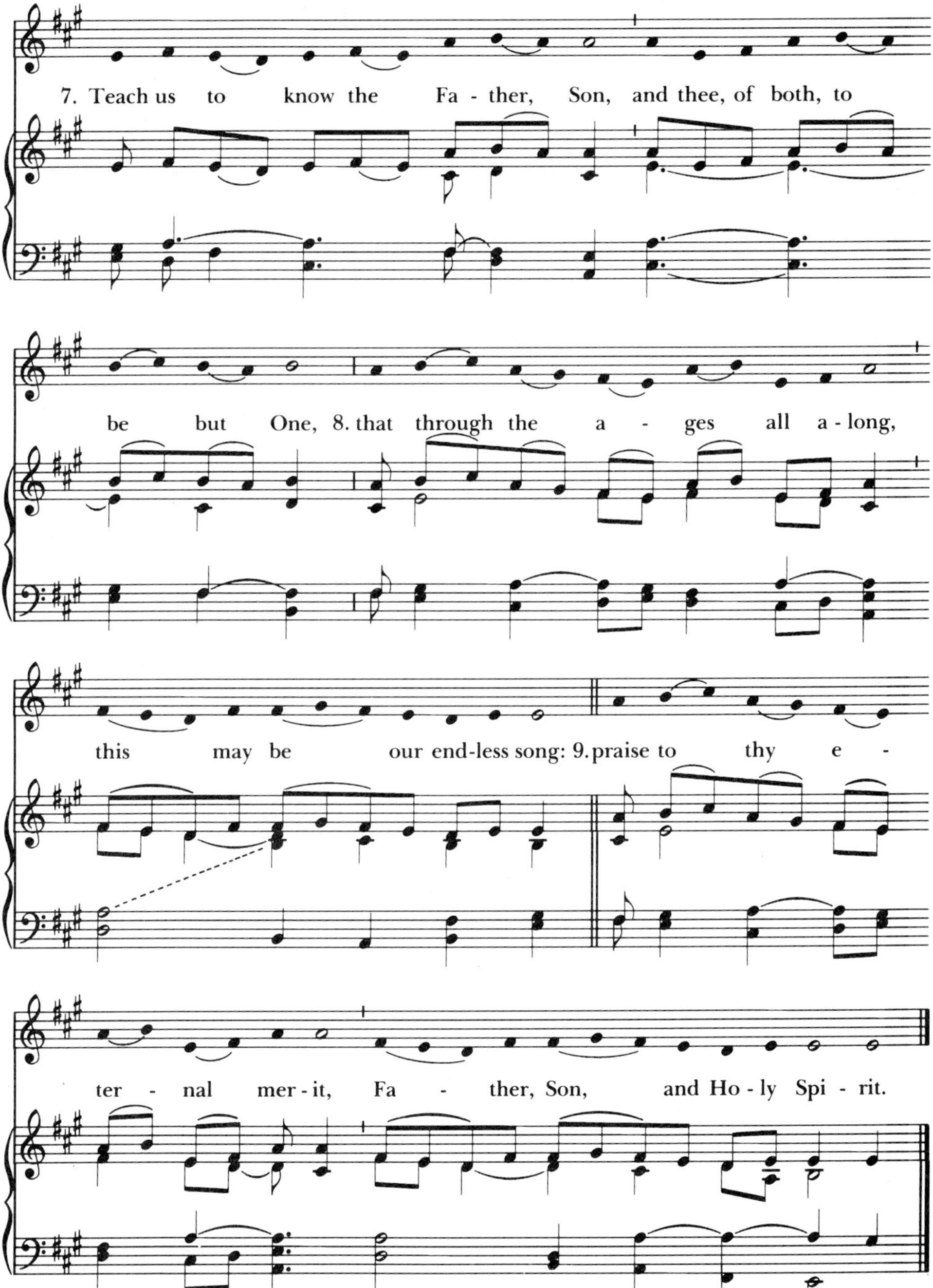
7. Teach us to know the Fa - ther, Son, and thee, of both, to
be but One, 8. that through the a - ges all a - long,
this may be our end-less song: 9. praise to thy e -
ter - nal mer - it, Fa - ther, Son, and Ho - ly Spi - rit.

Another accompaniment, 502. Alternative tune: *Come Holy Ghost,* 503.

Words: Latin, 9th cent.; tr. John Cosin (1594-1672); para. of *Veni Creator Spiritus*
Music: *Veni Creator Spiritus,* plainsong, Mode 8; acc. Charles Winfred Douglas (1867-1944)

LM

1 O Spi - rit of Life, O Spi - rit of God, in
2 O Spi - rit of Life, O Spi - rit of God, in -
3 O Spi - rit of Life, O Spi - rit of God, make
4 O Spi - rit of Life, O Spi - rit of God, en -
ev - ery need thou bring - est aid; thou com - est
crease our faith in our dear Lord; un - less thy
us to love thy sa - cred word; the ho - ly
light - en us by that same word; teach us to
forth from God's great throne, from God, the Fa - ther and the
grace the power should give, none can be - lieve in Christ and
flame of love im - part, that char - i - ty may warm each
know the Fa - ther's love, and his dear Son, who reigns a -

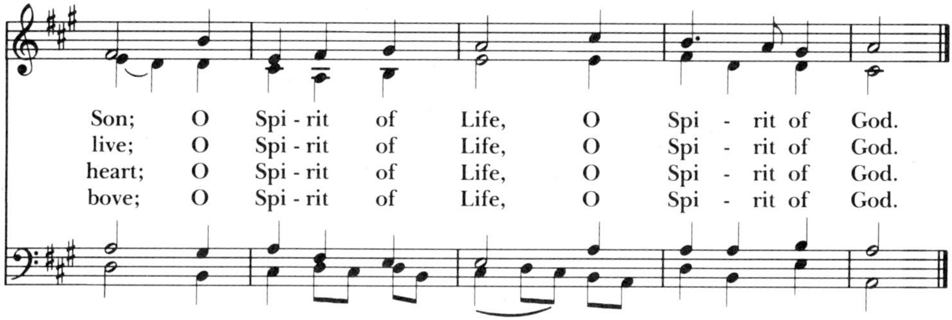
Son; O Spi - rit of Life, O Spi - rit of God.
live; O Spi - rit of Life, O Spi - rit of God.
heart; O Spi - rit of Life, O Spi - rit of God.
bove; O Spi - rit of Life, O Spi - rit of God.

Words: Johann Niedling (1602-1668); tr. John Caspar Mattes (1876-1948), alt.
Music: *O heiliger Geist*, melody from *Geistliche Kirchengesang*, 1623; harm. Johann Sebastian Bach (1685-1750); arr. Alastair Cassels-Brown (b. 1927)

♩= 88
10 8. 88. 10

1 Praise the Spi - rit in cre - a - tion, breath of God, life's
2 Praise the Spi - rit, close com - pan - ion of our in - most
3 Praise the Spi - rit, who en - light - ened priests and pro - phets
4 Tell of how the a - scend - ed Je - sus armed a peo - ple
5 Pray we then, O Lord the Spi - rit, on our lives de -
6 Praise, O praise the Ho - ly Spi - rit, praise the Fa - ther,
1 or - i - gin: Spi - rit, mov - ing on the wat - ers,
2 thoughts and ways; who, in show - ing us God's won - ders,
3 with the word; his the truth be - hind the wis - doms
4 for his own; how a hun - dred men and wo - men
5 scend in might; let your flame break out with - in us,
6 praise the Word, Source, and Truth, and In - spi - ra - tion,

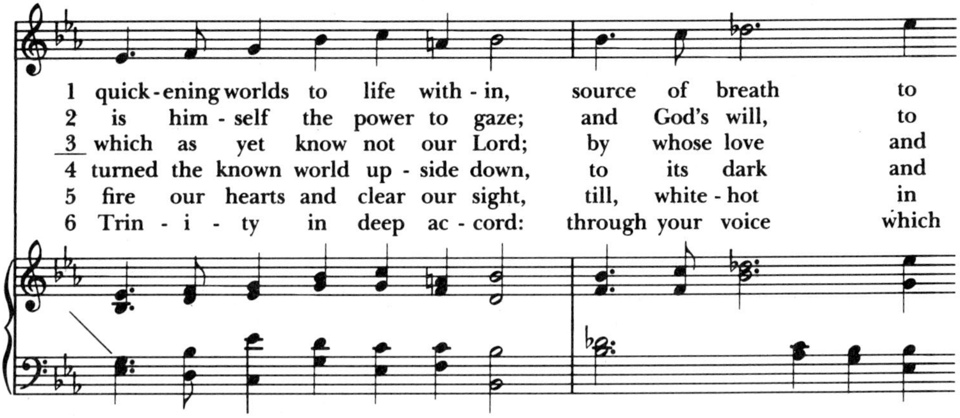
1 quick-ening worlds to life with-in, source of breath to
2 is him-self the power to gaze; and God's will, to
3 which as yet know not our Lord; by whose love and
4 turned the known world up-side down, to its dark and
5 fire our hearts and clear our sight, till, white-hot in
6 Trin-i-ty in deep ac-cord: through your voice which

1 all things breath-ing, life in whom all lives be-gin.
2 those who lis-ten, by a still small voice con-veys.
3 power, in Je-sus God him-self was seen and heard.
4 fur-thest cor-ners by the wind of hea-ven blown.
5 your pos-ses-sion, we, too, set the world a-light.
6 speaks with-in us we, your crea-tures, call you Lord.

Alternative tune: *Julion,* 507.

Words: Michael Hewlett (b. 1916), alt.
Music: *Finnian,* Christopher Dearnley (b. 1930)

𝅗𝅥=50
87. 87. 87

Introduction
1 Praise the Spi - rit in cre - a - tion, breath of
2 Praise the Spi - rit, close com - pan - ion of our
3 Praise the Spi - rit, who en - light - ened priests and
4 Tell of how the a - scend - ed Je - sus armed a
5 Pray we then, O Lord the Spi - rit, on our
6 Praise, O praise the Ho - ly Spi - rit, praise the
1 God, life's or - i - gin: Spi - rit, mov - ing on the
2 in - most thoughts and ways; who, in show - ing us God's
3 pro - phets with the word; his the truth be - hind the
4 peo - ple for his own; how a hun - dred men and
5 lives de - scend in might; let your flame break out with -
6 Fa - ther, praise the Word, Source, and Truth, and In - spi -

1 wat - ers, quick-ening worlds to life with - in, source of
2 won - ders, is him - self the power to gaze; and God's
3 wis - doms which as yet know not our Lord; by whose
4 wo - men turned the known world up - side down, to its
5 in us, fire our hearts and clear our sight, till, white -
6 ra - tion, Trin - i - ty in deep ac - cord: through your
1 breath to all things breath-ing, life in whom all lives be - gin.
2 will, to those who lis - ten, by a still small voice con - veys.
3 love and power, in Je - sus God him - self was seen and heard.
4 dark and fur - thest cor - ners by the wind of hea - ven blown.
5 hot in your pos - ses - sion, we, too, set the world a - light.
6 voice which speaks with - in us we, your crea - tures, call you Lord.
Interlude/Conclusion

The descant at 268 may be played on a solo instrument here. Alternative tune: *Finnian,* 506.

Words: Michael Hewlett (b. 1916), alt.
Music: *Julion,* David Hurd (b. 1950)

♩=72
87. 87. 87

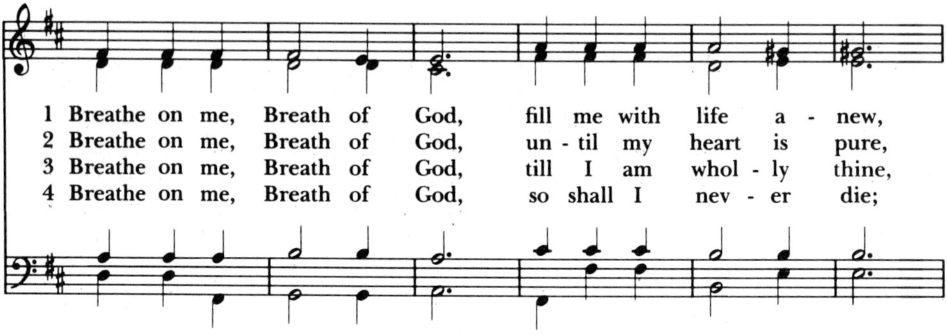
1 Breathe on me, Breath of God, fill me with life a - new,
2 Breathe on me, Breath of God, un - til my heart is pure,
3 Breathe on me, Breath of God, till I am whol - ly thine,
4 Breathe on me, Breath of God, so shall I nev - er die;

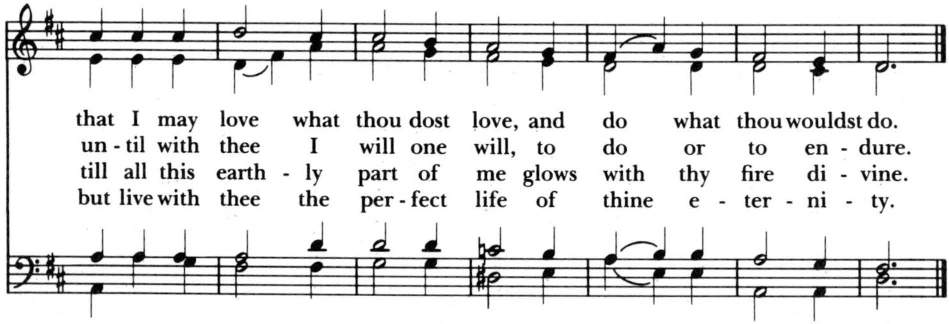
that I may love what thou dost love, and do what thou wouldst do.
un - til with thee I will one will, to do or to en - dure.
till all this earth - ly part of me glows with thy fire di - vine.
but live with thee the per - fect life of thine e - ter - ni - ty.

Words: Edwin Hatch (1835-1889), alt.
Music: *Nova Vita,* Lister R. Peace (1885-1969)

♩.=108
SM

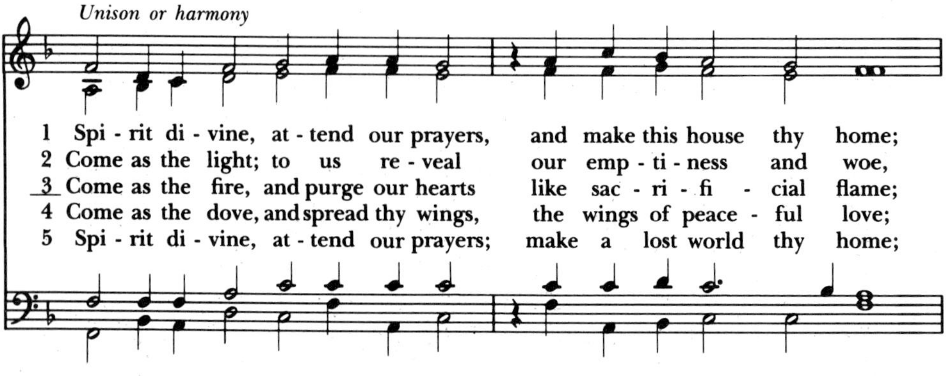
Unison or harmony
1 Spi - rit di - vine, at - tend our prayers, and make this house thy home;
2 Come as the light; to us re - veal our emp - ti - ness and woe,
3 Come as the fire, and purge our hearts like sac - ri - fi - cial flame;
4 Come as the dove, and spread thy wings, the wings of peace - ful love;
5 Spi - rit di - vine, at - tend our prayers; make a lost world thy home;

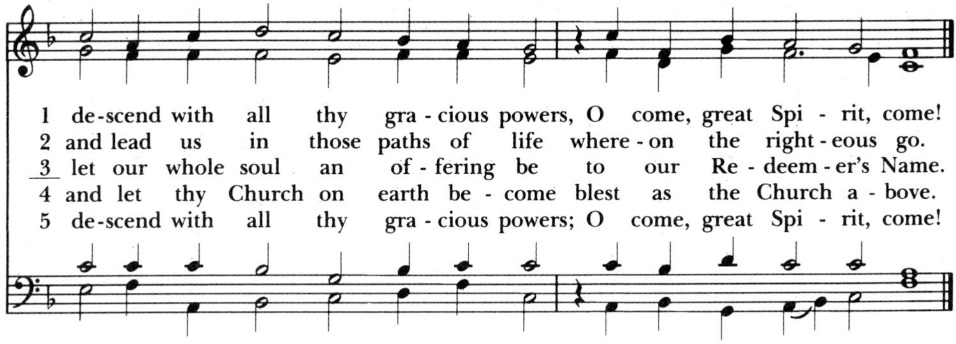
1 de-scend with all thy gra - cious powers, O come, great Spi - rit, come!
2 and lead us in those paths of life where - on the right - eous go.
3 let our whole soul an of - fering be to our Re - deem - er's Name.
4 and let thy Church on earth be - come blest as the Church a - bove.
5 de-scend with all thy gra - cious powers; O come, great Spi - rit, come!

Another harmonization, 374.

Words: Andrew Reed (1787-1862)
Music: *Nun danket all und bringet Ehr,* melody att. Johann Cruger (1598-1662)

𝅗𝅥=58
CM

The Holy Spirit 510

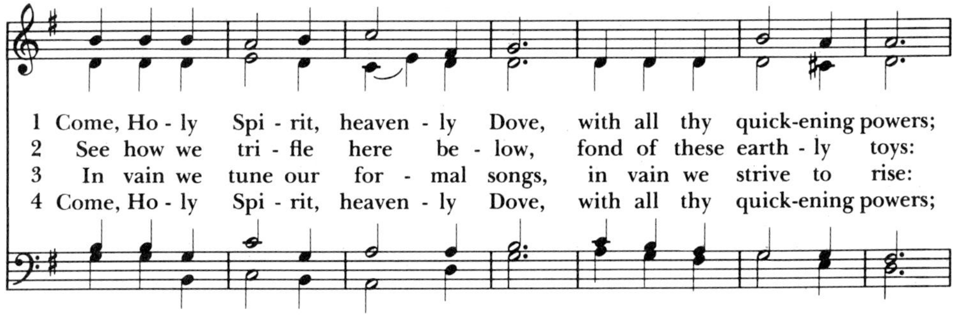
1 Come, Ho - ly Spi - rit, heaven - ly Dove, with all thy quick-ening powers;
2 See how we tri - fle here be - low, fond of these earth - ly toys:
3 In vain we tune our for - mal songs, in vain we strive to rise:
4 Come, Ho - ly Spi - rit, heaven - ly Dove, with all thy quick-ening powers;

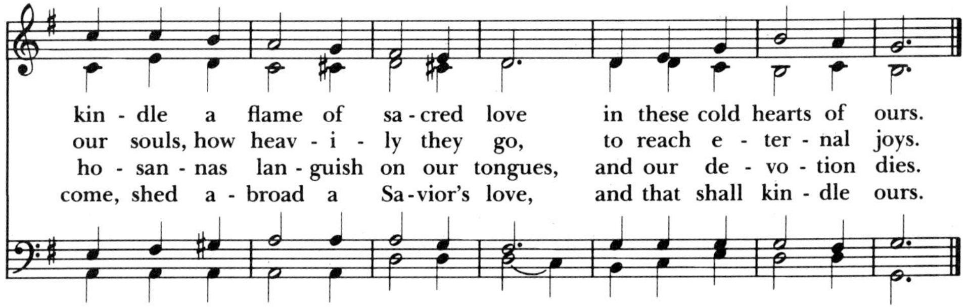
kin - dle a flame of sa - cred love in these cold hearts of ours.
our souls, how heav - i - ly they go, to reach e - ter - nal joys.
ho - san - nas lan - guish on our tongues, and our de - vo - tion dies.
come, shed a - broad a Sa - vior's love, and that shall kin - dle ours.

Another harmonization, 343.

Words: Isaac Watts (1674-1748), alt.
Music: *Saint Agnes,* John Bacchus Dykes (1823-1876)

♩=108
CM

1 Ho - ly Spi - rit, ev - er liv - ing as the Church's very life; Holy Spirit, ev - er striv-ing
2 Ho - ly Spi - rit, ev - er work-ing through the Church's min - is - try; quick-ening, strength-ening and ab - solv-ing,
through her in a cease - less strife; Ho - ly Spi - rit, ev - er
set - ting cap - tive sin - ners free; Ho - ly Spi - rit, ev - er
form-ing in the Church the mind of Christ; thee we praise with
bind-ing age to age, and soul to soul, in a fel - low -

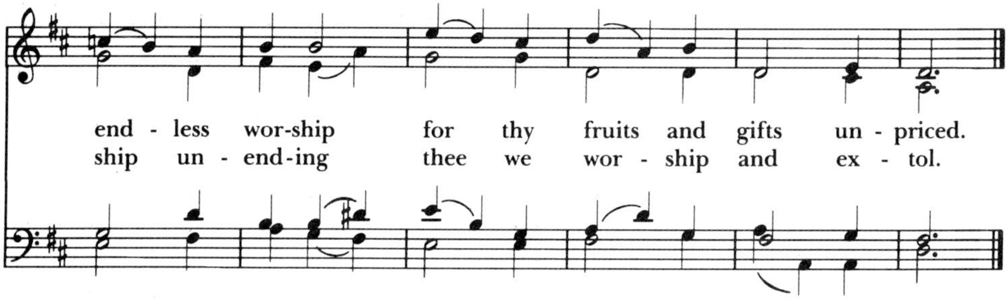
end - less wor-ship for thy fruits and gifts un - priced.
ship un - end-ing thee we wor - ship and ex - tol.

This music in C, 523.

Words: Timothy Rees (1874-1939), alt.
Music: *Abbot's Leigh,* Cyril Vincent Taylor (b. 1907)

♩= 92
87. 87. D

The Holy Spirit 512

1 Come, Gra - cious Spi - rit, heaven - ly Dove, with light and
2 The light of truth to us dis - play, and make us
3 Lead us to Christ, the liv - ing way, nor let us
4 Lead us to heaven, that we may share full - ness of
com - fort from a - bove; be thou our guard - ian,
know and choose thy way; plant ho - ly fear in
from his pre - cepts stray; lead us to ho - li -
joy for ev - er there; lead us to God, our
thou our guide o'er ev - ery thought and step pre - side.
ev - ery heart, that we from thee may ne'er de - part.
ness, the road that we must take to dwell with God.
fin - al rest, to be with him for ev - er blest.

Words: Simon Browne (1680-1732), alt.
Music: *Mendon,* melody from *Methodist Harmonist,* 1821; adapt. and harm. Lowell Mason (1792-1872)

♩= 96
LM

1 Like the mur-mur of the dove's song, like the chal - lenge of her flight, like the vig - or of the wind's rush, like the new flame's ea - ger might: come, Ho - ly Spi - rit, come.
2 To the mem-bers of Christ's Bo - dy, to the branch - es of the Vine, to the Church in faith as - sem - bled, to her midst as gift and sign: come, Ho - ly Spi - rit, come.
3 With the heal - ing of di - vi - sion, with the cease - less voice of prayer, with the power to love and wit - ness, with the peace be - yond com - pare: come, Ho - ly Spi - rit, come.

Phrase 1 of each stanza may be sung by one group, with a contrasted group singing phrase 2, and all joining for the final phrase.

Words: Carl P. Daw, Jr. (b. 1944)
Music: *Bridegroom,* Peter Cutts (b. 1937)

♩=90
87. 87. 6

1 To thee, O Com-fort-er di-vine, for all thy grace and power be-nign, sing we al-le-lu-ia! al-le-lu-ia!
2 To thee, whose faith-ful love had place in God's great cov-e-nant of grace, sing we al-le-lu-ia! al-le-lu-ia!
3 To thee, whose faith-ful power doth heal, en-light-en, sanc-ti-fy, and seal, sing we al-le-lu-ia! al-le-lu-ia!
4 To thee, by Je-sus Christ sent down, of all his gifts the sum and crown, sing we al-le-lu-ia! al-le-lu-ia!

Words: Frances Ridley Havergal (1836-1879)
Music: *St. Bartholomew's,* David McKinley Williams (1887-1978)

𝅗𝅥=60
88. 10

515

1 Ho - ly Ghost, dis - pel our sad - ness;
2 Au - thor of the new cre - a - tion,
pierce the clouds of na - ture's night;
come with unc - tion and with power.
come, thou source of joy and glad - ness,
Make our hearts thy ha - bi - ta - tion;
breathe thy life, and spread thy light.
with thy grace our spi - rits shower.

From the height which knows no mea - sure,
Hear, oh, hear our sup - pli - ca - tion,
as a gra - cious shower de - scend,
bless - ed Spi - rit, God of peace!
bring - ing down the rich - est trea - sure
Rest up - on this con - gre - ga - tion,
we can wish, or God can send.
with the full - ness of thy grace.

Words Paul Gerhardt (1607-1676); tr. John Christian Jacobi (1670-1750), alt.
Music: *Geneva*, George Henry Day (1883-1966)

𝅗𝅥=48
87. 87. D

1 Come down, O Love di - vine, seek thou this soul of mine,
2 O let it free - ly burn, till earth - ly pas - sions turn
3 And so the yearn - ing strong, with which the soul will long,
and vis - it it with thine own ar - dor glow - ing;
to dust and ash - es in its heat con - sum - ing;
shall far out - pass the power of hu - man tell - ing;
O Com-fort - er, draw near, with - in my heart ap - pear,
and let thy glo - rious light shine ev - er on my sight,
for none can guess its grace, till Love cre - ate a place
and kin - dle it, thy ho - ly flame be - stow - ing.
and clothe me round, the while my path il - lum - ing.
where - in the Ho - ly Spi - rit makes a dwell - ing.

Words: Bianco da Siena (d. 1434?); tr. Richard Frederick Littledale (1833-1890), alt.
Music: *Down Ampney,* Ralph Vaughan Williams (1872-1958)

𝅗𝅥=54
66. 11. D

1 How love - ly is thy dwell - ing - place, O Lord of hosts, to
2 Be - side thine al - tars, gra - cious Lord, the swal - lows find a
3 They who go through the des - ert vale will find it filled with
4 One day with - in thy courts ex - cels a thou-sand spent a -
me! My thirst - y soul de - sires and longs with -
nest; how hap - py they who dwell with thee and
springs, and they shall climb from height to height till
way; how hap - py they who keep thy laws nor
in thy courts to be; my ve - ry heart and
praise thee with - out rest, and hap - py they whose
Zi - on's tem - ple rings with praise to thee, in
from thy pre - cepts stray, for thou shalt sure - ly
flesh cry out, O liv - ing God, for thee.
hearts are set up - on the pil - grim's quest.
glo - ry throned, Lord God, great King of kings.
bless all those who live the words they pray.

Words: Para. of Psalm 84; sts. 1-2, *The Psalms of David in Meeter,* 1650; sts. 3-4, Carl P. Daw, Jr. (b. 1944)
Music: *Brother James' Air,* J. L. Macbeth Bain (1840?-1925)

♩=66
86. 86. 86

Descant
4 Here vouch-safe to all thy serv - ants what they ask of
1 Christ is made the sure foun - da - tion, Christ the head and
2 All that ded - i - cat - ed ci - ty, dear - ly loved of
3 To this tem - ple, where we call thee, come, O Lord of
4 Here vouch-safe to all thy serv-ants what they ask of
thee to gain; what they gain from thee, for ev - er
cor - ner - stone, cho - sen of the Lord, and pre - cious,
God on high, in ex - ult - ant ju - bi - la - tion
Hosts, to - day; with thy wont - ed lov - ing - kind - ness
thee to gain; what they gain from thee, for ev - er

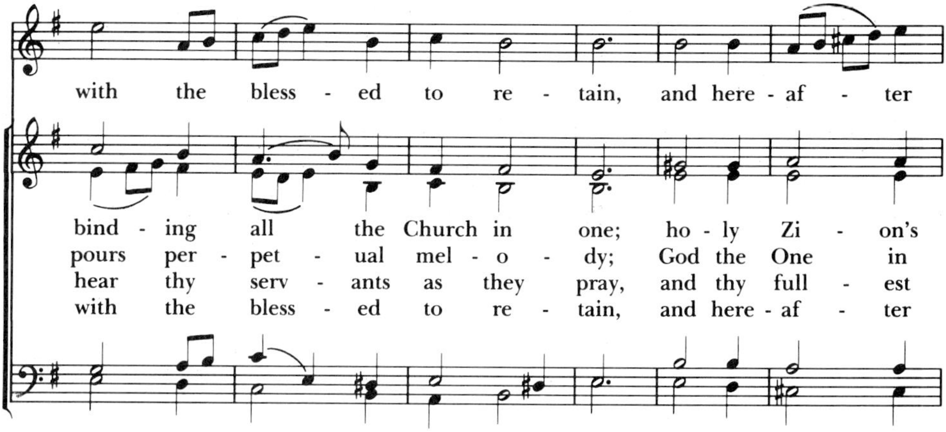
with the bless - ed to re - tain, and here - af - ter
bind - ing all the Church in one; ho - ly Zi - on's
pours per - pet - ual mel - o - dy; God the One in
hear thy serv - ants as they pray, and thy full - est
with the bless - ed to re - tain, and here - af - ter

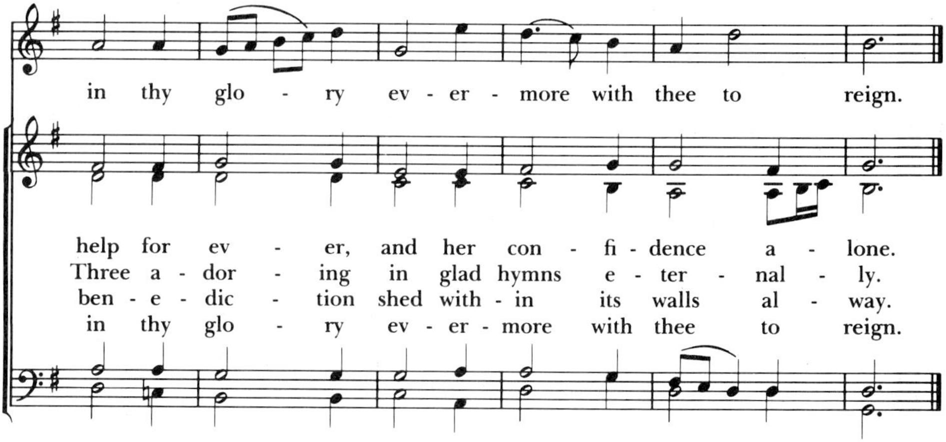
in thy glo - ry ev - er - more with thee to reign.
help for ev - er, and her con - fi - dence a - lone.
Three a - dor - ing in glad hymns e - ter - nal - ly.
ben - e - dic - tion shed with - in its walls al - way.
in thy glo - ry ev - er - more with thee to reign.

Alternative tunes: *Regent Square,* 368; *Urbs beata Jerusalem* (equalist), 519.

Words: Latin, ca. 7th cent.; tr. *Hymns Ancient and Modern,* 1861, after John Mason Neale (1818-1866), alt.

Music: *Westminster Abbey,* Henry Purcell (1659-1695), adapt.; desc. James Gillespie (b. 1929)

𝅗𝅥. = 44

87. 87. 87

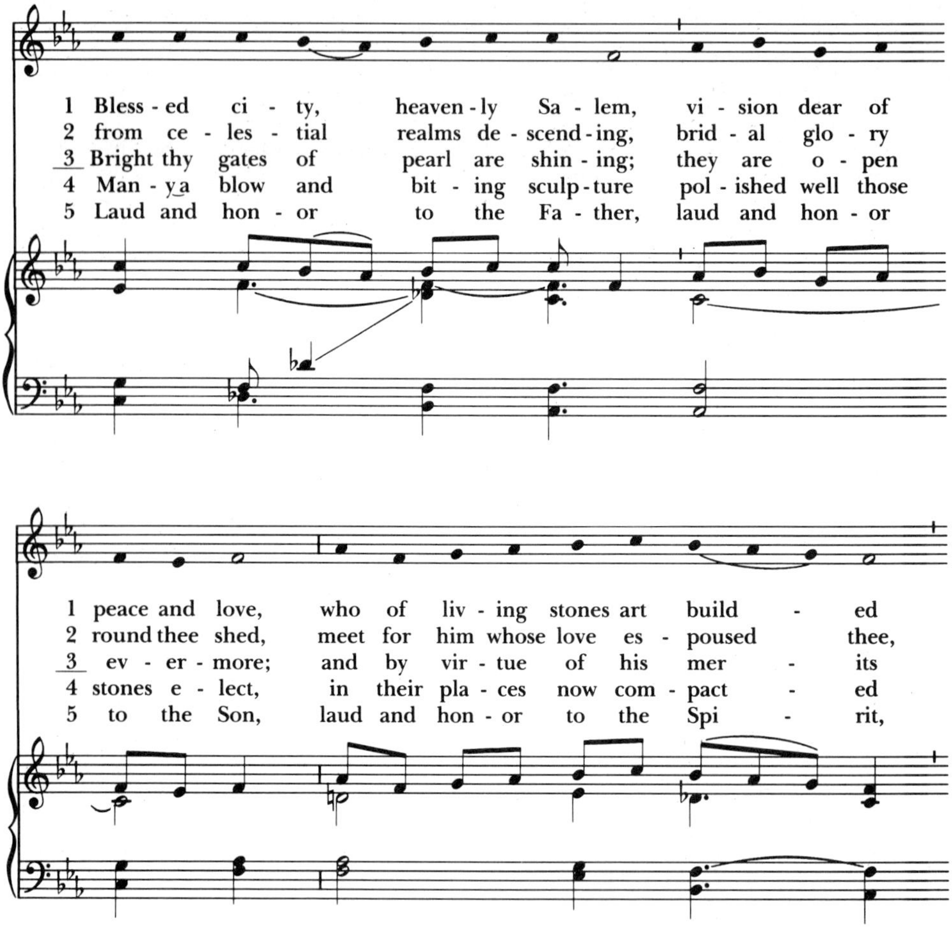
1 Bless - ed ci - ty, heaven - ly Sa - lem, vi - sion dear of
2 from ce - les - tial realms de - scend - ing, brid - al glo - ry
3 Bright thy gates of pearl are shin - ing; they are o - pen
4 Man - y a blow and bit - ing sculp - ture pol - ished well those
5 Laud and hon - or to the Fa - ther, laud and hon - or
1 peace and love, who of liv - ing stones art build - ed
2 round thee shed, meet for him whose love es - poused thee,
3 ev - er - more; and by vir - tue of his mer - its
4 stones e - lect, in their pla - ces now com - pact - ed
5 to the Son, laud and hon - or to the Spi - rit,

1 in the height of heaven a - bove, and, with an - gel
2 to thy Lord shalt thou be led; all thy streets and
3 thith - er faith - ful souls do soar, who, for Christ's dear
4 by the heaven - ly Ar - chi - tect, who there - with hath
5 ev - er Three, and ev - er One, con - sub - stan - tial,

1 hosts en - cir - cled, as a bride dost earth - ward move;
2 all thy bul-warks of pure gold are fa - shion - ed.
3 Name, in this world pain and tri - bu - la - tion bore.
4 willed for ev - er that his pal - ace should be decked.
5 co - e - ter - nal, while un - end - ing a - ges run.

Alternative accompaniment, 122. Alternative tunes: *Oriel,* 520; *Westminster Abbey,* 518; *Urbs beata Jerusalem* (proportional rhythm), 622.

Words: Latin, ca. 7th cent.; tr. *Hymns Ancient and Modern,* 1861, after John Mason Neale (1818-1866), alt.
Music: *Urbs beata Jerusalem,* plainsong, Mode 2; Nevers MS., 13th cent.; acc. Charles Winfred Douglas (1867-1944)

87. 87. 87

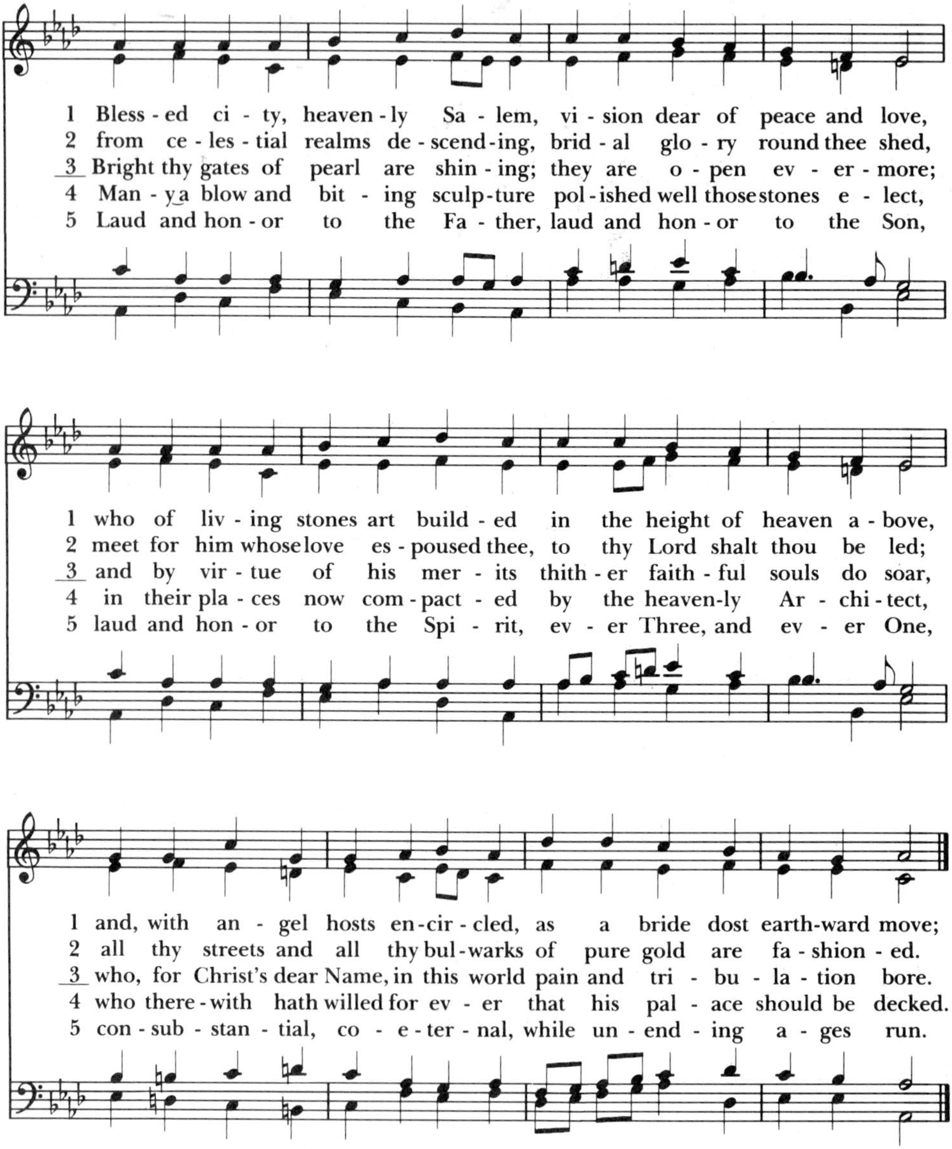
1 Bless - ed ci - ty, heaven - ly Sa - lem, vi - sion dear of peace and love,
2 from ce - les - tial realms de - scend - ing, brid - al glo - ry round thee shed,
3 Bright thy gates of pearl are shin - ing; they are o - pen ev - er - more;
4 Man - y a blow and bit - ing sculp - ture pol - ished well those stones e - lect,
5 Laud and hon - or to the Fa - ther, laud and hon - or to the Son,
1 who of liv - ing stones art build - ed in the height of heaven a - bove,
2 meet for him whose love es - poused thee, to thy Lord shalt thou be led;
3 and by vir - tue of his mer - its thith - er faith - ful souls do soar,
4 in their pla - ces now com - pact - ed by the heaven-ly Ar - chi - tect,
5 laud and hon - or to the Spi - rit, ev - er Three, and ev - er One,
1 and, with an - gel hosts en - cir - cled, as a bride dost earth-ward move;
2 all thy streets and all thy bul - warks of pure gold are fa - shion - ed.
3 who, for Christ's dear Name, in this world pain and tri - bu - la - tion bore.
4 who there - with hath willed for ev - er that his pal - ace should be decked.
5 con - sub - stan - tial, co - e - ter - nal, while un - end - ing a - ges run.

Alternative tunes: *Urbs beata Jerusalem* (equalist), 519; *Westminster Abbey,* 518.

Words: Latin, ca. 7th cent.; tr. *Hymns Ancient and Modern,* 1861, after John Mason Neale (1818-1866), alt. 𝅗𝅥=46

Music: *Oriel,* Caspar Ett (1788-1847) 87. 87. 87

Descant
4 O Judge di - vine of hu - man strife! O
1 Put forth, O God, thy Spi - rit's might and
2 Let works of dark - ness dis - ap - pear be -
3 Let what a - pos - tles learned of thee be
4 O Judge di - vine of hu - man strife! O
Van - quish - er of pain! To know thee is e -
bid thy Church in - crease, in breadth and length, in
fore thy con - quering light; let ha - tred and tor -
ours from age to age; their stead - fast faith our
Van - quish - er of pain! To know thee is e -
ter - nal life, to serve thee, to reign.
depth and height, her u - ni - ty and peace.
ment - ing fear pass with the pass - ing night.
u - ni - ty, their peace our her - it - age.
ter - nal life, to serve thee is to reign.

Words: Howard Chandler Robbins (1876-1952)
Music: *Chelsea Square*, Howard Chandler Robbins (1876-1952);
harm. Ray Francis Brown (1897-1964); desc. Lois Fyfe (b. 1927)

𝅗𝅥 = 46
CM

Descant
4 Blest in - hab - it - ants of Zi - on, washed in the Re - deem - er's blood! Whom their souls re - ly on, makes them kings and priests to God.
1 Glo - rious things of thee are spo - ken, Zi - on, ci - ty of our God; he whose word can - not be bro - ken formed thee for his own a - bode;
2 See! the streams of liv - ing wa - ters, spring - ing from e - ter - nal love, well sup - ply thy sons and daugh - ters and all fear of want re - move.
3 Round each ha - bi - ta - tion hov - ering, see the cloud and fire ap - pear for a glo - ry and a cov - ering, show - ing that the Lord is near.
4 Blest in - hab - it - ants of Zi - on, washed in the Re - deem - er's blood! Je - sus, whom their souls re - ly on, makes them kings and priests to God.

'Tis his love his peo - ple raise o - ver
on the Rock of A - ges found - ed, what can shake thy
Who can faint, when such a riv - er ev - er will their
Thus de - riv - ing from their ban - ner, light by night, and
'Tis his love his peo - ple rais - es o - ver self to
self to reign: and as priests, his
sure re - pose? With sal - va - tion's walls sur -
thirst as - suage? Grace which, like the Lord, the
shade by day, safe they feed up - on the
reign as kings: and as priests, his sol - emn
sol - emn prais - es each an of - fering brings.
round - ed, thou may'st smile at all thy foes.
giv - er, nev - er fails from age to age.
man - na which he gives them when they pray.
prais - es each for a thank - of - fering brings.

Alternative tune: *Abbot's Leigh,* 523.

Words: John Newton (1725-1807), alt.
Music: *Austria,* Franz Joseph Haydn (1732-1809); desc. Michael E. Young (b. 1939)

𝅗𝅥=46
87. 87. D

1 Glo - rious things of thee are spo - ken, Zi - on, ci - ty
2 See! the streams of liv - ing wa - ters, spring - ing from e -
3 Round each ha - bi - ta - tion hov-ering, see the cloud and
4 Blest in - hab - it - ants of Zi - on, washed in the Re -
of our God; he whose word can - not be bro - ken
ter - nal love, well sup - ply thy sons and daugh - ters
fire ap - pear for a glo - ry and a cov - ering,
deem - er's blood! Je - sus, whom their souls re - ly on,
formed thee for his own a - bode; on the Rock of A - ges
and all fear of want re - move. Who can faint, when such a
show - ing that the Lord is near. Thus de - riv - ing from their
makes them kings and priests to God. 'Tis his love his peo - ple
found - ed, what can shake thy sure re - pose? With sal -
riv - er ev - er will their thirst as - suage? Grace which,
ban - ner, light by night, and shade by day, safe they
rais - es o - ver self to reign as kings: and as

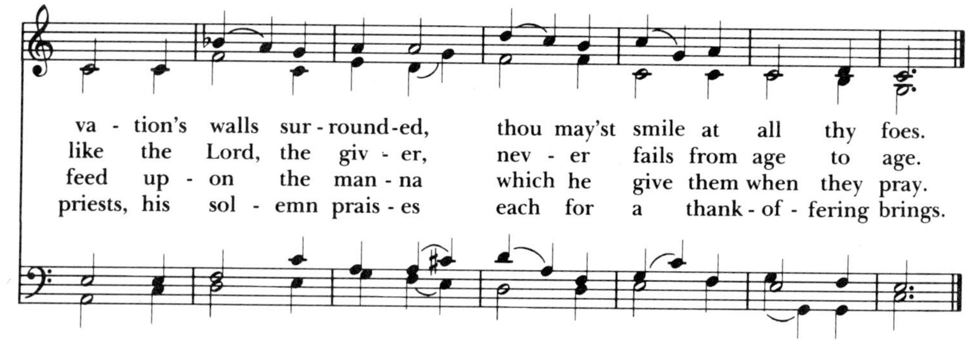
va - tion's walls sur - round-ed, thou may'st smile at all thy foes.
like the Lord, the giv - er, nev - er fails from age to age.
feed up - on the man - na which he give them when they pray.
priests, his sol - emn prais - es each for a thank - of - fering brings.

This music in D, 511. Alternative tune: *Austria*, 522.

Words: John Newton (1725-1807), alt.
Music: *Abbot's Leigh*, Cyril Vincent Taylor (b. 1907)

♩= 92
87. 87. D

The Church 524

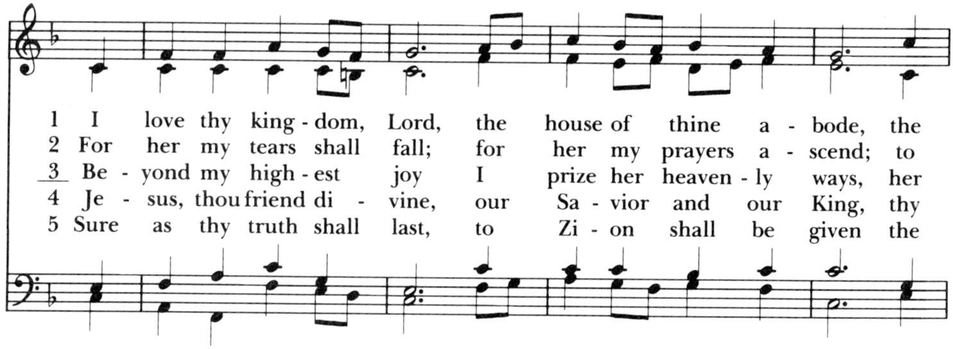
1 I love thy king - dom, Lord, the house of thine a - bode, the
2 For her my tears shall fall; for her my prayers a - scend; to
3 Be - yond my high - est joy I prize her heaven - ly ways, her
4 Je - sus, thou friend di - vine, our Sa - vior and our King, thy
5 Sure as thy truth shall last, to Zi - on shall be given the

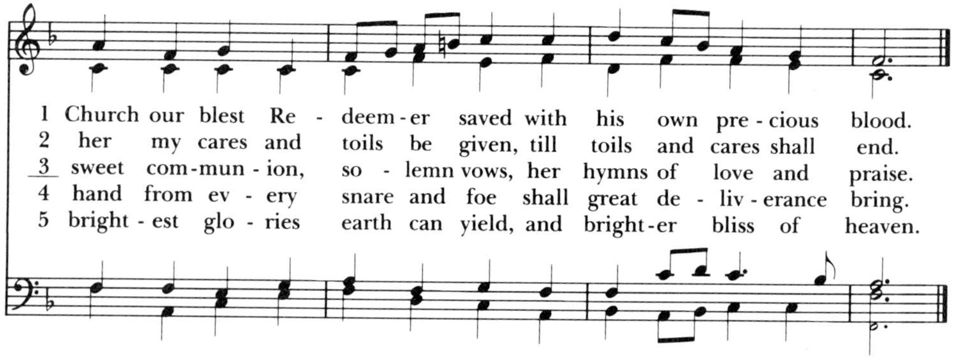
1 Church our blest Re - deem - er saved with his own pre - cious blood.
2 her my cares and toils be given, till toils and cares shall end.
3 sweet com - mun - ion, so - lemn vows, her hymns of love and praise.
4 hand from ev - ery snare and foe shall great de - liv - erance bring.
5 bright - est glo - ries earth can yield, and bright - er bliss of heaven.

This music in G, 411.

Words: Timothy Dwight (1725-1817)
Music: *St. Thomas (Williams)*, melody Aaron Williams (1731-1776); harm. Lowell Mason (1792-1872)

♩= 84
SM

1 The Church's one foun - da - tion is Je - sus Christ her Lord;
2 E - lect from ev - ery na - tion, yet one o'er all the earth,
3 Though with a scorn - ful won - der men see her sore op - pressed,
4 Mid toil and tri - bu - la - tion, and tu - mult of her war
5 Yet she on earth hath un - ion with God, the Three in One,
1 she is his new cre - a - tion by wa - ter and the word:
2 her char - ter of sal - va - tion, one Lord, one faith, one birth;
3 by schi - sms rent a - sun - der, by her - e - sies dis - tressed;
4 she waits the con - sum - ma - tion of peace for ev - er - more;
5 and mys - tic sweet com - mun - ion with those whose rest is won.
1 from heaven he came and sought her to be his ho - ly bride;
2 one ho - ly Name she bless - es, par - takes one ho - ly food,
3 yet saints their watch are keep - ing, their cry goes up, "How long?"
4 till with the vi - sion glo - rious her long - ing eyes are blessed,
5 O hap - py ones and ho - ly! Lord, give us grace that we

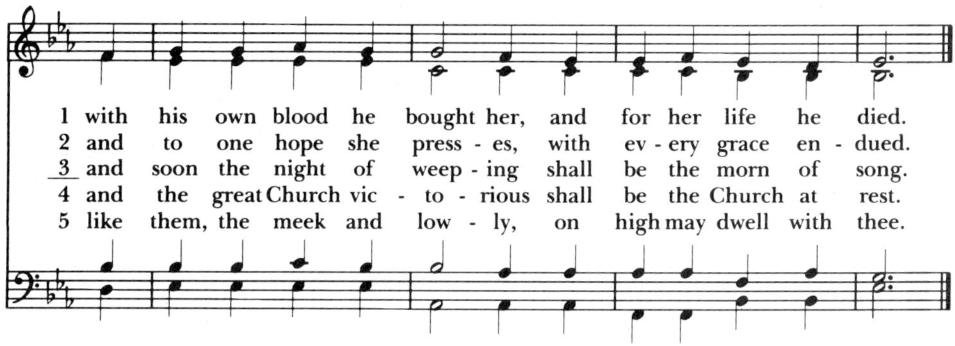
1 with his own blood he bought her, and for her life he died.
2 and to one hope she press - es, with ev - ery grace en - dued.
3 and soon the night of weep - ing shall be the morn of song.
4 and the great Church vic - to - rious shall be the Church at rest.
5 like them, the meek and low - ly, on high may dwell with thee.

Words: Samuel John Stone (1839-1900) — 𝅗𝅥=50
Music: *Aurelia,* Samuel Sebastian Wesley (1810-1876) — 76. 76. D

The Church

526

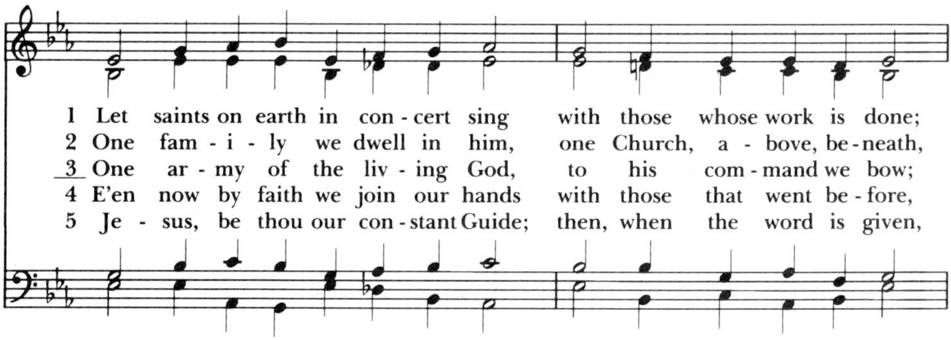
1 Let saints on earth in con - cert sing with those whose work is done;
2 One fam - i - ly we dwell in him, one Church, a - bove, be - neath,
3 One ar - my of the liv - ing God, to his com - mand we bow;
4 E'en now by faith we join our hands with those that went be - fore,
5 Je - sus, be thou our con - stant Guide; then, when the word is given,

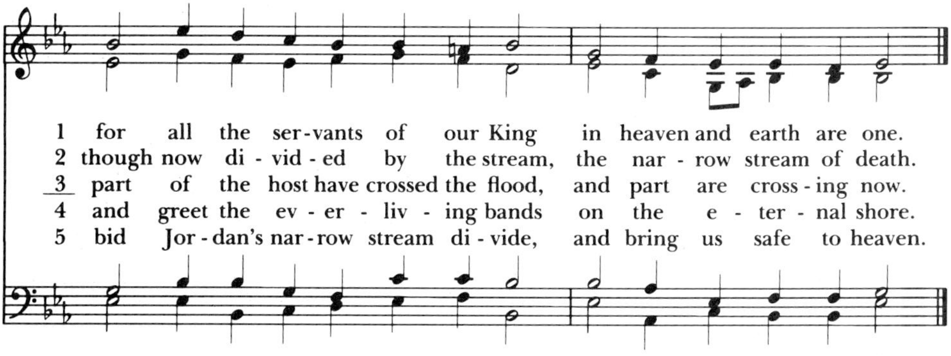
1 for all the ser - vants of our King in heaven and earth are one.
2 though now di - vid - ed by the stream, the nar - row stream of death.
3 part of the host have crossed the flood, and part are cross - ing now.
4 and greet the ev - er - liv - ing bands on the e - ter - nal shore.
5 bid Jor - dan's nar - row stream di - vide, and bring us safe to heaven.

A fauxbourdon setting, 709.

Words: Charles Wesley (1707-1788), alt. — 𝅘𝅥=88
Music: *Dundee,* melody from *The CL Psalmes of David,* 1615; harm. Thomas Ravenscroft (1592?-1635?), alt. — CM

1 Sing - ing songs of ex - pec - ta - tion, on - ward
2 One the light of God's own pres - ence, o'er his
3 One the strain the lips of thou - sands lift as
goes the pil - grim band, through the night of
ran - somed peo - ple shed, chas - ing far the
from the heart of one; one the con - flict,
doubt and sor - row, march - ing to the prom - ised land.
gloom and ter - ror, bright - ening all the path we tread:
one the per - il, one the march in God be - gun:
3

Clear be - fore us through the dark - ness gleams and
one the ob - ject of our jour - ney, one the
one the glad - ness of re - joic - ing on the
burns the guid - ing light: trust - ing God we
faith which nev - er tires, one the ear - nest
far e - ter - nal shore, where the one al -
march to - geth - er step - ping fear - less through the night.
look - ing for - ward, one the hope our God in - spires.
might - y Fa - ther reigns in love for ev - er - more.
3

Words: Bernard Severin Ingemann (1789-1862); tr. Sabine Baring-Gould (1834-1924), alt.
Music: *Ton-y-Botel*, Thomas John Williams (1869-1944)

𝅗𝅥 = 92
87. 87. D

1 Lord, you give the great com - mis - sion: "Heal the sick and
2 Lord, you call us to your serv - ice: "In my name bap -
3 Lord, you make the com - mon ho - ly: "This my bo - dy,
4 Lord, you show us love's true mea - sure: "Fa - ther, what they
5 Lord, you bless with words as - sur - ing: "I am with you
1 preach the word." Lest the Church ne - glect its mis - sion
2 tize and teach." That the world may trust your prom - ise,
3 this my blood." Let your priests, for earth's true glo - ry,
4 do, for - give." Yet we hoard as pri - vate trea - sure
5 to the end." Faith and hope and love re - stor - ing,
1 and the Gos - pel go un - heard, help us wit - ness to your
2 life a - bun - dant meant for each, give us all new fer - vor,
3 dai - ly lift life hea - ven - ward, ask - ing that the world a -
4 all that you so free - ly give. May your care and mer - cy
5 may we serve as you in - tend, and, a - mid the cares that

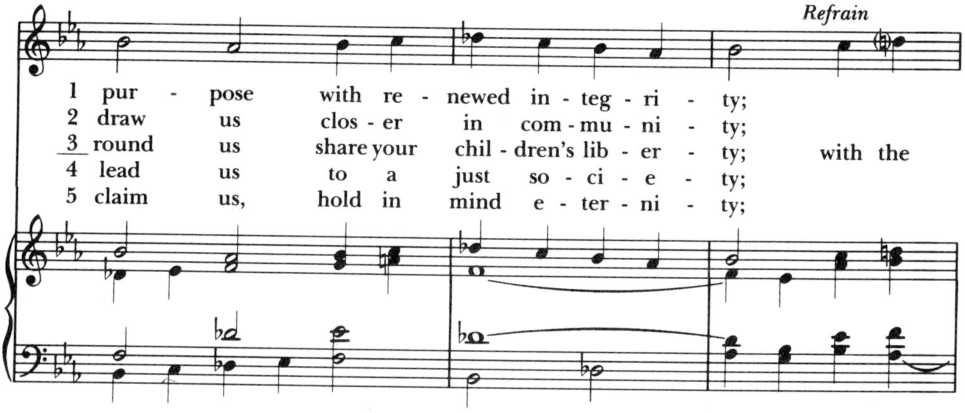
Refrain
1 pur - pose with re - newed in - teg - ri - ty;
2 draw us clos - er in com - mu - ni - ty;
3 round us share your chil - dren's lib - er - ty; with the
4 lead us to a just so - ci - e - ty;
5 claim us, hold in mind e - ter - ni - ty;

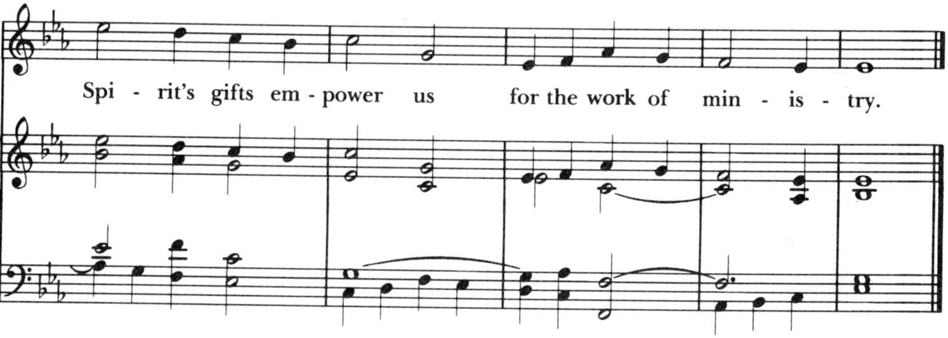
Spi - rit's gifts em - power us for the work of min - is - try.

Alternative tunes: *Hyfrydol,* 460; *Abbot's Leigh,* 523.

Words: Jeffery Rowthorn (b. 1934)
Music: *Rowthorn,* Alec Wyton (b. 1921)

♩= 108
87. 87. 87 with Refrain

529 The Church's Mission

Unison or harmony
C Bb F
1 In Christ there is no East or West, in
2 Join hands, dis - ci - ples of the faith, what -
3 In Christ now meet both East and West, in
Dm7 G7 C F C G C Am
him no South or North, but one great fel - low -
e'er your race may be! Who serves my Fa - ther
him meet South and North, all Christ - ly souls are
G7 C C G C
ship of love through - out the whole wide earth.
as his child is sure - ly kin to me.
one in him, through - out the whole wide earth.

Keyboard and guitar should not sound together.

Words: John Oxenham (1852-1941), alt.
Music: *McKee*, Afro-American spiritual; adapt. and harm. Harry T. Burleigh (1866-1949)

𝅗𝅥 = 48
CM

530 The Church's Mission

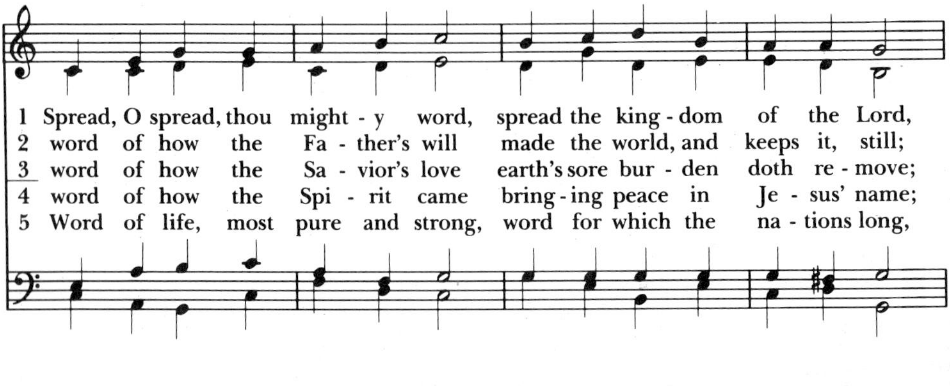
1 Spread, O spread, thou might - y word, spread the king - dom of the Lord,
2 word of how the Fa - ther's will made the world, and keeps it, still;
3 word of how the Sa - vior's love earth's sore bur - den doth re - move;
4 word of how the Spi - rit came bring - ing peace in Je - sus' name;
5 Word of life, most pure and strong, word for which the na - tions long,

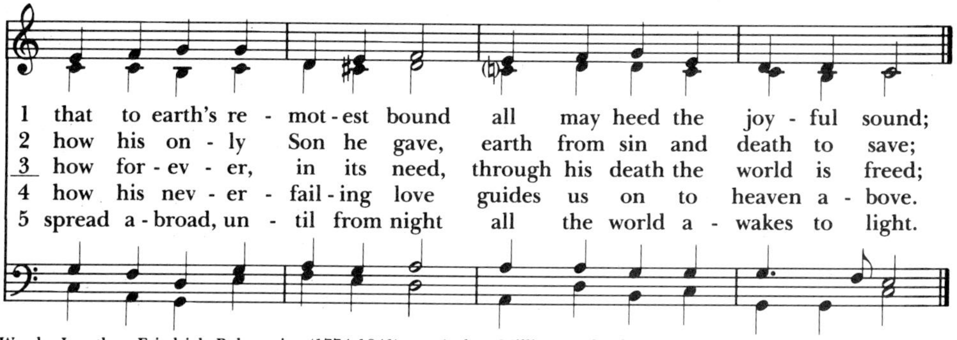
1 that to earth's re - mot - est bound all may heed the joy - ful sound;
2 how his on - ly Son he gave, earth from sin and death to save;
3 how for - ev - er, in its need, through his death the world is freed;
4 how his nev - er - fail - ing love guides us on to heaven a - bove.
5 spread a - broad, un - til from night all the world a - wakes to light.

Words: Jonathan Friedrich Bahnmaier (1774-1841); tr. Arthur William Farlander (1898-1952) and Charles Winfred Douglas (1867-1944), alt. St. 4, F. Bland Tucker (1895-1984)
Music: *Gott sei Dank,* melody from *Geistreiches Gesangbuch,* 1704; adapt. and harm. William Henry Havergal (1793-1870)

𝅗𝅥=52
77. 77

The Church's Mission

1 O Spi - rit of the liv - ing God, in all thy plen - i - tude of grace, wher - e'er the foot of man hath trod, de - scend on our a - pos - tate race.
2 Give tongues of fire and hearts of love, to preach the rec - on - cil - ing word; give power and unc - tion from a - bove, when - e'er the joy - ful sound is heard.
3 Be dark - ness, at thy com - ing, light; con - fu - sion, or - der in thy path; souls with - out strength in - spire with might, bid mer - cy tri - umph o - ver wrath.
4 Con - vert the na - tions! far and nigh the tri - umphs of the cross re - cord; the Name of Je - sus glo - ri - fy, till ev - ery peo - ple call him Lord.

Words: James Montgomery (1771-1854), alt.
Music: *Melcombe,* Samuel Webbe (1740-1816)

♩=96
LM

1 How won - drous and great thy works, God of praise!
2 To na - tions of earth thy light shall be shown;
How just, King of saints, and true are thy ways!
their wor - ship and vows shall come to thy throne:
O who shall not fear thee, and hon - or thy Name?
thy truth and thy judg - ments shall spread all a - broad,
Thou on - ly art ho - ly, thou on - ly su - preme.
till earth's ev - ery peo - ple con - fess thee their God.

Alternative tune: *Lyons,* 533.

Words: Henry Ustick Onderdonk (1759-1858), alt.; para. *The Song of the Redeemed*
Music: *Old 104th,* melody from *The Whole Booke of Psalmes,* 1621; harm. *Hymnal 1982*

𝅗𝅥. = 42
10 10. 11 11

1 How won - drous and great thy works, God of praise!
2 To na - tions of earth thy light shall be shown;
How just, King of saints, and true are thy ways!
their wor - ship and vows shall come to thy throne:
O who shall not fear thee, and hon - or thy Name?
thy truth and thy judg - ments shall spread all a - broad,
Thou on - ly, art ho - ly, thou on - ly, su - preme.
till earth's ev - ery peo - ple con - fess thee their God.

Alternative tune: *Old 104th,* 532.

Words: Henry Ustick Onderdonk (1759-1858), alt.; para. *The Song of the Redeemed*
Music: *Lyons,* att. Johann Michael Haydn (1737-1806)

𝅗𝅥. = 44
10 10. 11 11

1 God is work - ing his pur - pose out as
2 From ut - most east to ut - most west, wher -
3 March we forth in the strength of God, with the
4 All we can do is noth - ing worth un -
May be sung in canon
1 God is work - ing his
2 From ut - most east to
3 March we forth in the
4 All we can do is
year suc - ceeds to year: God is work-ing his
ev - er foot hath trod, by the mouth of man - y
ban - ner of Christ un - furled, that the light of the glo-rious
less God bless - es the deed; vain - ly we hope for the
pur - pose out as year suc-ceeds to year;
ut - most west, wher - ev - er foot hath trod, by the
strength of God, with the ban - ner of Christ un - furled, that the
noth - ing worth un - less God bless-es the deed;

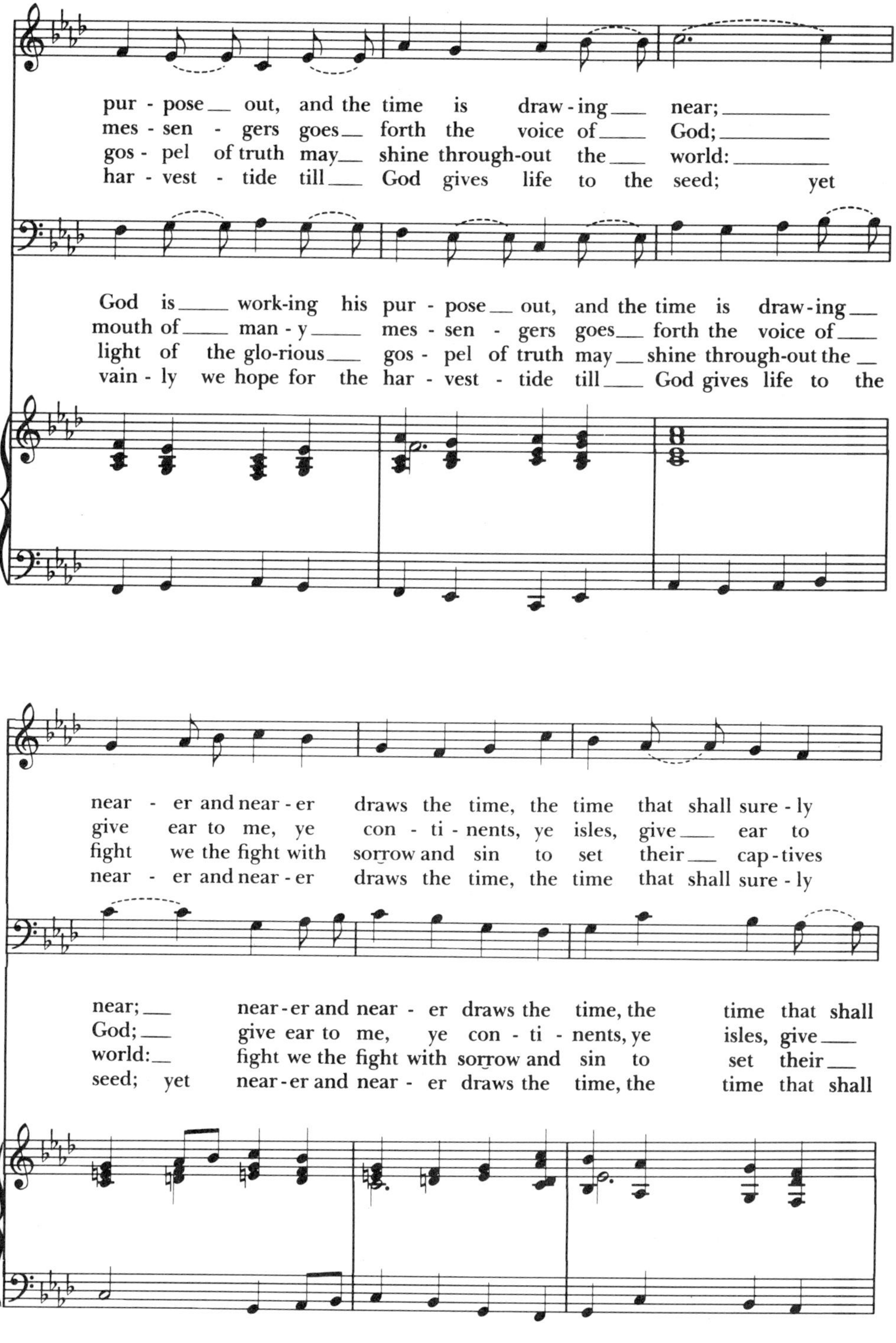
pur - pose out, and the time is draw - ing near;
mes - sen - gers goes forth the voice of God;
gos - pel of truth may shine through-out the world:
har - vest - tide till God gives life to the seed; yet
God is work-ing his pur - pose out, and the time is draw-ing
mouth of man - y mes - sen - gers goes forth the voice of
light of the glo-rious gos - pel of truth may shine through-out the
vain - ly we hope for the har - vest - tide till God gives life to the
near - er and near - er draws the time, the time that shall sure - ly
give ear to me, ye con - ti - nents, ye isles, give ear to
fight we the fight with sorrow and sin to set their cap - tives
near - er and near - er draws the time, the time that shall sure - ly
near; near - er and near - er draws the time, the time that shall
God; give ear to me, ye con - ti - nents, ye isles, give
world: fight we the fight with sorrow and sin to set their
seed; yet near - er and near - er draws the time, the time that shall

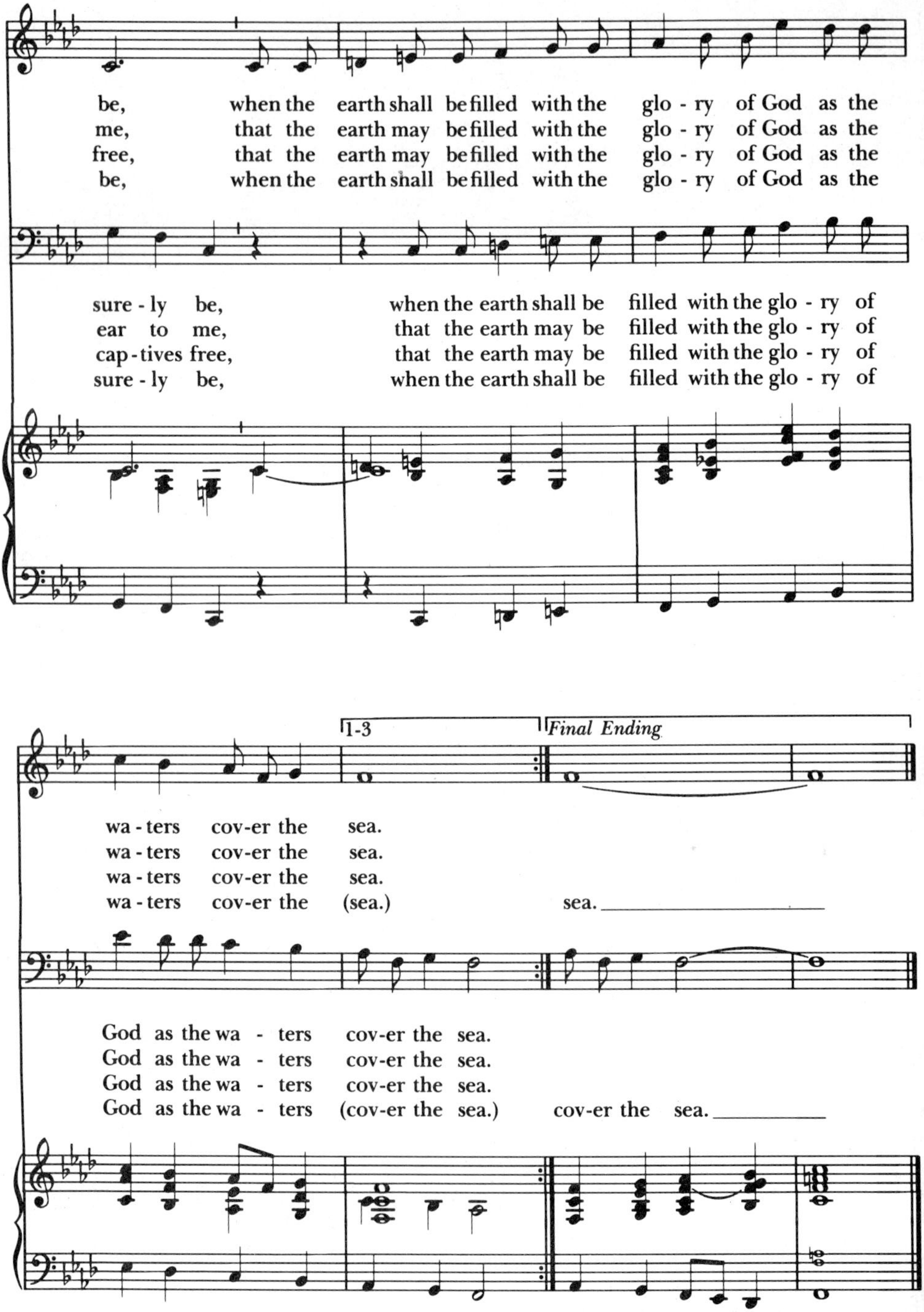

Words: Arthur Campbell Ainger (1841-1919), alt.
Music: *Purpose,* Martin Fallas Shaw (1875-1958)

𝅗𝅥=60
Irr.

1 Ye ser - vants of God, your Mas - ter pro - claim,
2 God rul - eth on high, al - might - y to save;
3 Sal - va - tion to God who sits on the throne!
4 Then let us a - dore, and give him his right:
and pub - lish a - broad his won - der - ful Name;
and still he is nigh: his pres - ence we have.
Let all cry a - loud, and hon - or the Son.
All glo - ry and power, all wis - dom and might,
the Name all - vic - to - rious of Je - sus ex - tol:
The great con - gre - ga - tion his tri - umph shall sing,
The prais - es of Je - sus the an - gels pro - claim,
and hon - or and bless - ing, with an - gels a - bove,
his king - dom is glo - rious; he rules o - ver all.
as - crib - ing sal - va - tion to Je - sus our King.
fall down on their fa - ces, and wor - ship the Lamb.
and thanks nev - er - ceas - ing and in - fi - nite love.

Words: Charles Wesley (1707-1788), alt.
Music: *Paderborn*, melody from *Catolisch-Paderbornisches Gesang-buch*, 1765; harm. Sydney Hugo Nicholson (1875-1947)

𝅗𝅥 = 100
10 10. 11 11

1 O - pen your ears, O faith-ful peo-ple, o - pen your ears and
2 They who have ears to hear the mes-sage, they who have ears, then
3 Is - ra - el comes to greet the Sa - vior, Ju - dah is glad to
4 O - pen your ears, O faith-ful peo-ple, o - pen your ears and
hear God's word. O - pen your hearts, O roy - al priest-hood,
let them hear. They who would learn the way of wis - dom,
see his day. From east and west the peo - ples trav - el,
hear God's word. O - pen your hearts, O roy - al priest-hood,
1-3
Final Ending
God has come to you.
let them hear God's word.
he will show the way.
God has come to (you.) you.
God has spo - ken to his peo - ple, Hal - le - lu -

jah! And his words are words of wis - dom,
Hal - le - lu - jah! Hal - le - lu - jah!
God has spo - ken
To - rah o - ra,
to his peo - ple,
To - rah o - ra,
Hal - le - lu - jah!
And his words are words of wis - dom, Hal - le - lu - jah!
To - rah o - ra, To - rah o - ra, Hal - le - lu - jah!
Da Capo
3

"Torah ora" is Hebrew for "The Law is our Light."

Words: Willard F. Jabusch (b. 1930), alt.
Music: *Torah song [Yisrael V'oraita]*, Hasidic melody; arr. Richard Proulx (b. 1937)

𝅗𝅥=63
98. 95 with Refrain

1 Christ for the world we sing! The world to
2 Christ for the world we sing! The world to
3 Christ for the world we sing! The world to
4 Christ for the world we sing! The world to
Christ we bring with lov - ing zeal; the poor, and
Christ we bring with fer - vent prayer; the way - ward
Christ we bring with one ac - cord; with us the
Christ we bring with joy - ful song; the new - born
them that mourn, the faint and o - ver - borne,
and the lost, by rest - less pas - sions tossed,
work to share, with us re - proach to dare,
souls, whose days, re - claimed from er - ror's ways,
sin - sick and sor - row-worn, whom Christ doth heal.
re - deemed at count - less cost from dark de - spair.
with us the cross to bear, for Christ our Lord.
in - spired with hope and praise, to Christ be - long.

This music in F, 365.

Words: Samuel Wolcott (1813-1886)
Music: *Moscow,* melody Felice de Giardini (1716-1796); harm. *The New Hymnal,* 1916 based on *Hymns Ancient and Modern,* 1875, and Lowell Mason (1792-1872)

𝅗𝅥. = 40
664. 6664

1 God of mer - cy, God of grace, show the bright - ness of thy
2 Let thy peo - ple praise thee, Lord; be by all that live a -
face. Shine up - on us, Sa - vior, shine, fill thy
dored. Let the na - tions shout and sing glo - ry
Church with light di - vine, and thy sav - ing health ex -
to their Sa - vior King; let all be, be - low, a -
tend un - to earth's re - mot - est end.
bove, one in joy, and light, and love.

This music in G, 416. Alternative tune: *Ratisbon,* 7.

Words: Henry Francis Lyte (1793-1847), alt.
Music: *Lucerna Laudoniae,* David Evans (1874-1948)

𝅗𝅥=84
77. 77. 77

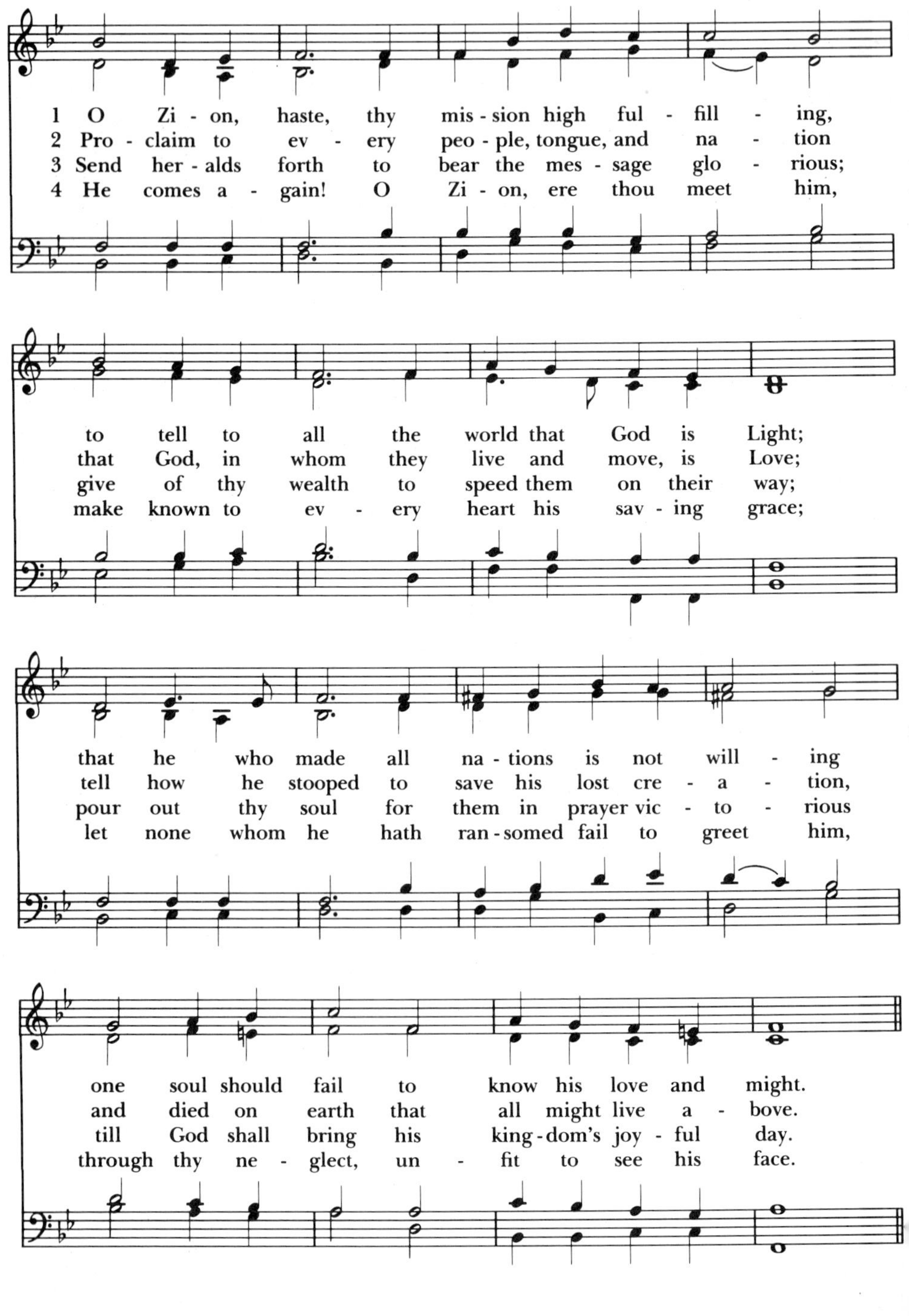
1 O Zi - on, haste, thy mis - sion high ful - fill - ing,
2 Pro - claim to ev - ery peo - ple, tongue, and na - tion
3 Send her - alds forth to bear the mes - sage glo - rious;
4 He comes a - gain! O Zi - on, ere thou meet him,
to tell to all the world that God is Light;
that God, in whom they live and move, is Love;
give of thy wealth to speed them on their way;
make known to ev - ery heart his sav - ing grace;
that he who made all na - tions is not will - ing
tell how he stooped to save his lost cre - a - tion,
pour out thy soul for them in prayer vic - to - rious
let none whom he hath ran - somed fail to greet him,
one soul should fail to know his love and might.
and died on earth that all might live a - bove.
till God shall bring his king - dom's joy - ful day.
through thy ne - glect, un - fit to see his face.

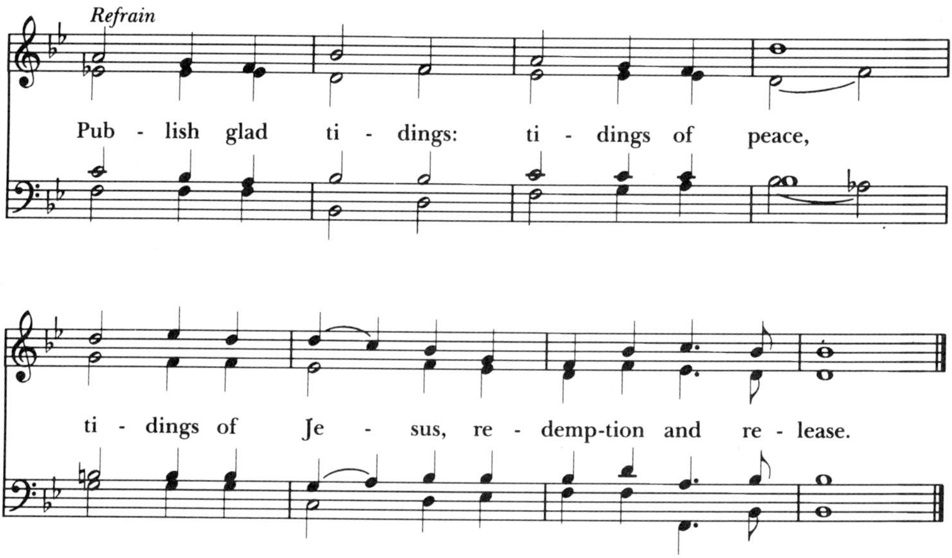
Refrain
Pub - lish glad ti - dings: ti - dings of peace,
ti - dings of Je - sus, re - demp-tion and re - lease.

Words: Mary Ann Thomson (1834-1923), alt.
Music: *Tidings,* James Walch (1837-1901)

𝅗𝅥=60
11 10. 11 10 with Refrain

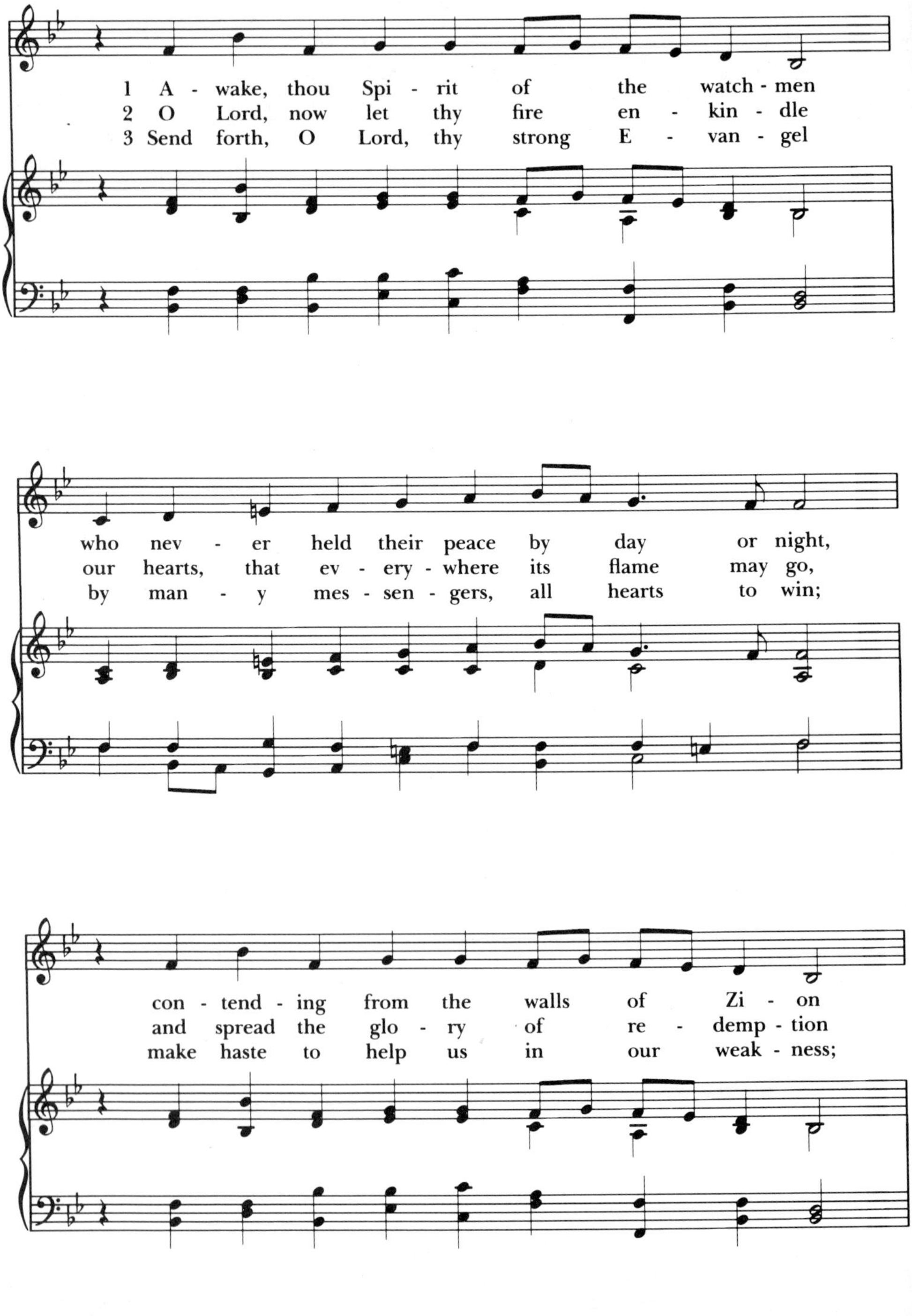
1 A - wake, thou Spi - rit of the watch - men
2 O Lord, now let thy fire en - kin - dle
3 Send forth, O Lord, thy strong E - van - gel
who nev - er held their peace by day or night,
our hearts, that ev - ery - where its flame may go,
by man - y mes - sen - gers, all hearts to win;
con - tend - ing from the walls of Zi - on
and spread the glo - ry of re - demp - tion
make haste to help us in our weak - ness;

a - gainst the foe, con - fid - ing in thy might.
till all the world thy sav - ing grace shall know.
break down the realm of Sa - tan, death, and sin:
Through - out the world their cry is ring - ing still,
O har - vest Lord, look down on us and view
the cir - cle of the earth shall then pro-claim
and bring - ing peo - ples to thy ho - ly will.
how white the fields; the la - bor - ers, how few!
thy king - dom, and the glo - ry of thy Name.

Words: Karl Heinrich von Bogatzky (1690-1774); tr. Arthur William Farlander (1898-1952) and Charles Winfred Douglas (1867-1944)

Music: *Dir, dir, Jehovah,* melody from *Hamburger Musikalisches handbuch,* 1690

𝅗𝅥 = 52

9 10. 9 10. 10 10

1 Come, la - bor on. Who dares stand i - dle
2 Come, la - bor on. The en - e - my is
3 Come, la - bor on. A - way with gloom - y
4 Come, la - bor on. Claim the high call - ing
5 Come, la - bor on. No time for rest, till
1 on the har - vest plain, while all a - round us
2 watch - ing night and day, to sow the tares, to
3 doubts and faith - less fear! No arm so weak but
4 an - gels can - not share— to young and old the
5 glows the west - ern sky, till the long sha - dows
1 waves the gold - en grain? And to each ser - vant
2 snatch the seed a - way; while we in sleep our
3 may do ser - vice here: by feeb - lest a - gents
4 Gos - pel glad - ness bear: re - deem the time; its
5 o'er our path - way lie, and a glad sound comes

1 does the Mas - ter say, "Go work to - day."
2 du - ty have for - got, he slum - bered not.
3 may our God ful - fill his right - eous will.
4 hours too swift - ly fly. The night draws nigh.
5 with the set - ting sun, "Ser - vants, well done."

Words: Jane Laurie Borthwick (1813-1897), alt.
Music: *Ora Labora*, Thomas Tertius Noble (1867-1953)

𝅗𝅥 = 60
4. 10 10. 10 4

1 Christ is the world's true Light, its Cap-tain of sal - va - tion,
2 In Christ all rac - es meet, their an - cient feuds for - get - ting,
3 One Lord, in one great Name u - nite us all who own thee;
the Day - star clear and bright of ev - ery race and na - - tion;
the whole round world com - plete, from sun-rise to its set - ting:
cast out our pride and shame that hin-der to en - throne thee;
new life, new hope a - wakes, for all who own his sway:
when Christ is throned as Lord all shall for - sake their fear,
the world has wait - ed long, has tra - vailed long in pain;
free - dom her bond - age breaks, and night is turned to day.
to plough-share beat the sword, to prun - ing - hook the spear.
to heal its an - cient wrong, come, Prince of Peace, and reign.

Words: George Wallace Briggs (1875-1959), alt.
Music: *St. Joan,* Percy E. B. Coller (b. 1895)

𝅗𝅥. = 42
67. 67. 66. 66

1 O Zi - on, tune thy voice, and raise thy hands on
2 He gilds thy morn - ing face with beams that can - not
3 In hon - or to his Name re - flect that sa - cred
4 There on his ho - ly hill a bright - er sun shall
high; tell all the earth thy joys, and boast sal -
fade; his all - re - splen - dent grace he pours a -
light; and loud that grace pro - claim, which makes thy
rise, and with his ra - diance fill those fair - er
va - tion nigh. Cheer - ful in God, a -
round thy head; the na - tions round thy
dark - ness bright; pur - sue his praise, till
pur - er skies; while round his throne ten
rise and shine, while rays di - vine stream all a - broad.
form shall view, with lus - ter new di - vine - ly crowned.
sov - ereign love in worlds a - bove the glo - ry raise.
thou - sand stars in no - bler spheres his in - fluence own.

Alternative tune: *Darwell's 148th*, 625.

Words: Philip Doddridge (1702-1751); based on *The Third Song of Isaiah*

Music: *Eastview*, J. V. Lee (1892-1959)

𝅗𝅥 = 58

66. 66 88

1 Je - sus shall reign wher - e'er the sun doth his suc -
2 To him shall end - less prayer be made, and prais - es
3 Peo - ple and realms of ev - ery tongue dwell on his
4 Bless - ings a - bound where - e'er he reigns: the pris - oners
5 Let ev - ery crea - ture rise and bring pe - cu - liar
1 ces - sive jour - neys run; his king - dom stretch from
2 throng to crown his head; his Name like sweet per -
3 love with sweet - est song; and in - fant voic - es
4 leap to lose their chains, the wea - ry find e -
5 hon - ors to our King; an - gels de - scend with
1 shore to shore, till moons shall wax and wane no more.
2 fume shall rise with ev - ery morn - ing sac - ri - fice.
3 shall pro - claim their ear - ly bless - ings on his Name.
4 ter - nal rest, and all who suf - fer want are blest.
5 songs a - gain, and earth re - peat the loud a - men.

Words: Isaac Watts (1674-1748), alt.
Music: *Duke Street,* John Hatton (d. 1793)

𝅗𝅥 = 72
LM

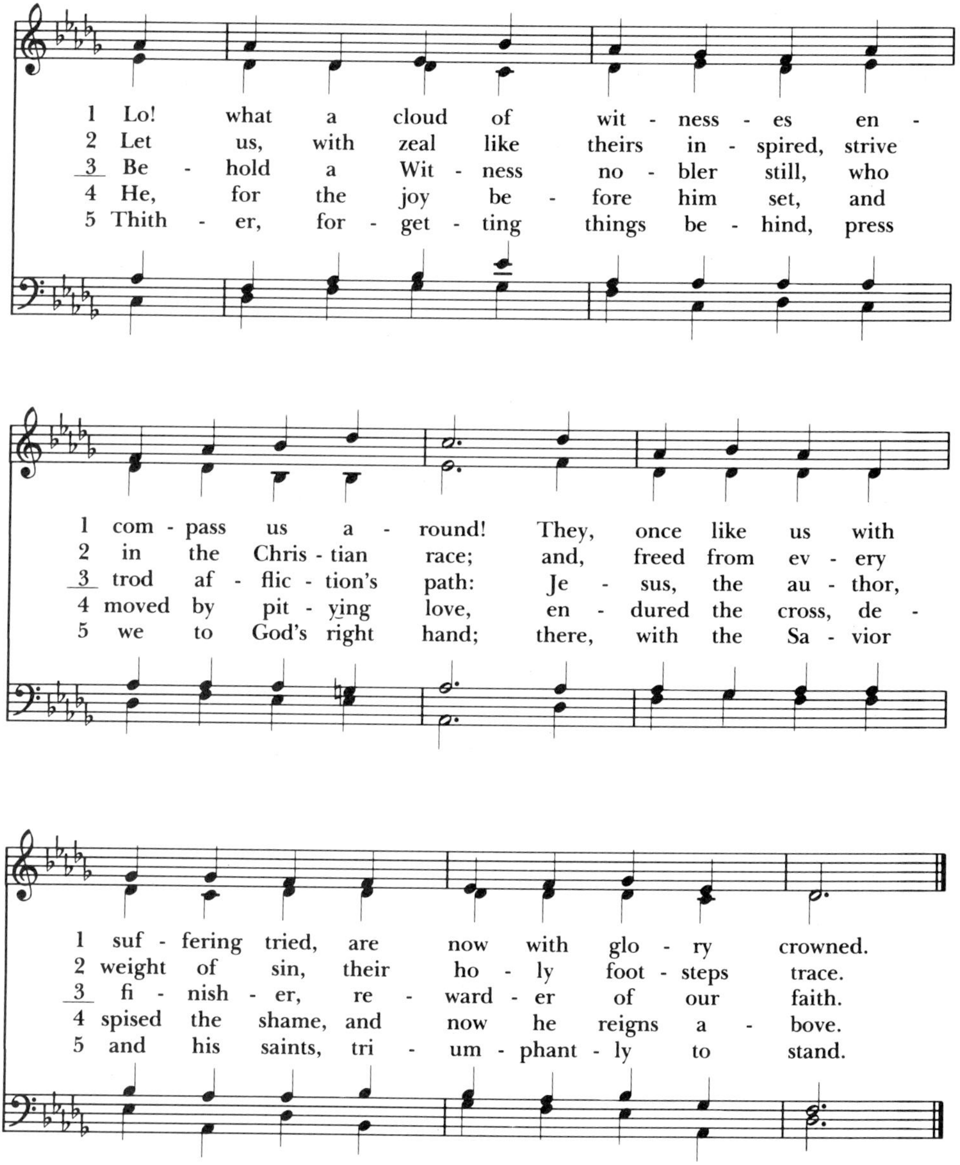
1 Lo! what a cloud of wit - ness - es en -
2 Let us, with zeal like theirs in - spired, strive
3 Be - hold a Wit - ness no - bler still, who
4 He, for the joy be - fore him set, and
5 Thith - er, for - get - ting things be - hind, press
1 com - pass us a - round! They, once like us with
2 in the Chris - tian race; and, freed from ev - ery
3 trod af - flic - tion's path: Je - sus, the au - thor,
4 moved by pit - ying love, en - dured the cross, de -
5 we to God's right hand; there, with the Sa - vior
1 suf - fering tried, are now with glo - ry crowned.
2 weight of sin, their ho - ly foot - steps trace.
3 fi - nish - er, re - ward - er of our faith.
4 spised the shame, and now he reigns a - bove.
5 and his saints, tri - um - phant - ly to stand.

Words: *Translations and Paraphrases,* 1745, alt.; para. of Hebrews 12:1-3
Music: *St. Fulbert,* Henry John Gauntlett (1805-1876)

𝅗𝅥=50
CM

1 A - wake, my soul, stretch ev - ery nerve, and press with
2 A cloud of wit - ness - es a - round hold thee in
3 'Tis God's all - an - i - mat - ing voice that calls thee
4 Then wake, my soul, stretch ev - ery nerve, and press with
vi - gor on; a heaven-ly race de - mands thy zeal, and
full sur - vey; for - get the steps al - read - y trod, and
from on high; 'tis his own hand pre - sents the prize to
vi - gor on; a heaven-ly race de - mands thy zeal, and
an im - mor - tal crown. and an im - mor - tal crown.
on - ward urge thy way. and on - ward urge thy way.
thine as - pir - ing eye. to thine as - pir - ing eye.
an im - mor - tal crown. and an im - mor - tal crown.

Words: Philip Doddridge (1702-1751)
Music: *Siroë,* George Frideric Handel (1685-1759); adapt. *Melodia Sacra,* 1815

♩=84
86. 866

1 A - wake, O sleep - er, rise from death, and Christ shall
2 To us on earth he came to bring from sin and
3 There is one Bo - dy and one hope, one Spi - rit
4 Then walk in love as Christ has loved, who died that
5 For us Christ lived, for us he died and con - quered
1 give you light, so learn his love— its length and
2 fear re - lease, to give the Spi - rit's u - ni -
3 and one call, one Lord, one Faith, and one Bap -
4 he might save; with kind and gen - tle hearts for -
5 in the strife. A - wake, a - rise, go forth in
1 breadth, its full - ness, depth, and height.
2 ty, the ve - ry bond of peace.
3 tism, one Fa - ther of us all.
4 give as God in Christ for - gave.
5 faith, and Christ shall give you life.

Words: F. Bland Tucker (1895-1984)
Music: *Marsh Chapel,* Max Miller (b. 1927)

♩=63
CM

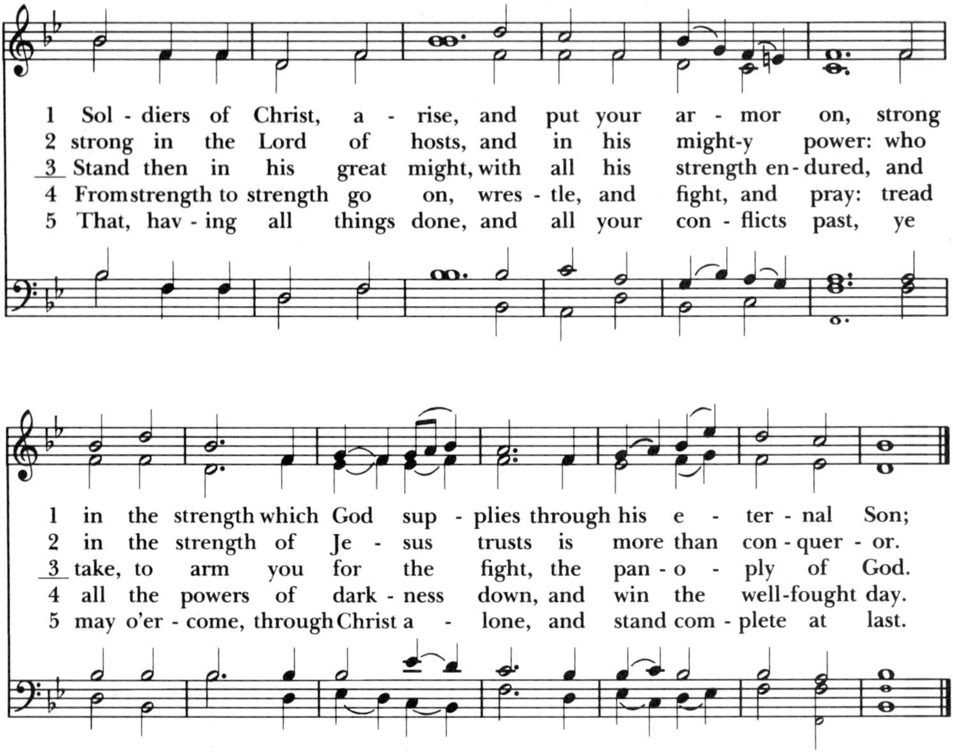
1 Sol - diers of Christ, a - rise, and put your ar - mor on, strong
2 strong in the Lord of hosts, and in his might-y power: who
3 Stand then in his great might, with all his strength en - dured, and
4 From strength to strength go on, wres - tle, and fight, and pray: tread
5 That, hav - ing all things done, and all your con - flicts past, ye
1 in the strength which God sup - plies through his e - ter - nal Son;
2 in the strength of Je - sus trusts is more than con - quer - or.
3 take, to arm you for the fight, the pan - o - ply of God.
4 all the powers of dark - ness down, and win the well-fought day.
5 may o'er - come, through Christ a - lone, and stand com - plete at last.

Words: Charles Wesley (1707-1788)
Music: *Silver Street,* Isaac Smith (1734?-1805)

𝅗=52
SM

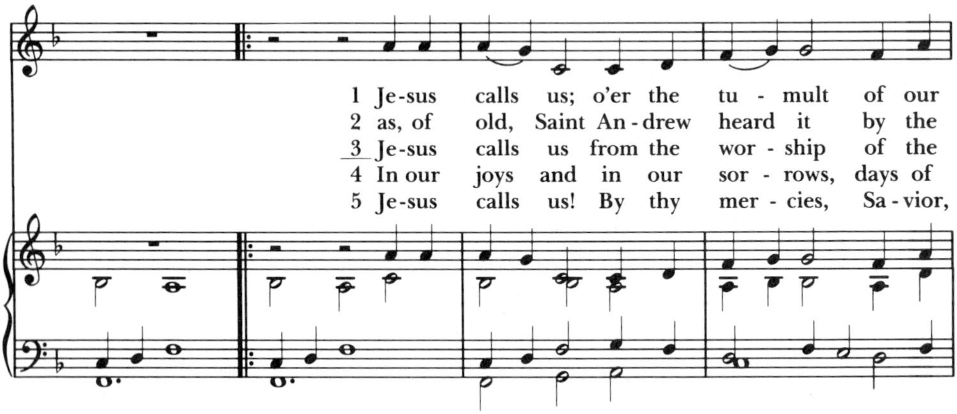
1 Je-sus calls us; o'er the tu - mult of our
2 as, of old, Saint An - drew heard it by the
3 Je-sus calls us from the wor - ship of the
4 In our joys and in our sor - rows, days of
5 Je-sus calls us! By thy mer - cies, Sa - vior,

1 life's wild, rest-less sea, day by day his clear voice
2 Gal - i - le - an lake, turned from home and toil and
3 vain world's gold-en store; from each i - dol that would
4 toil and hours of ease, still he calls, in cares and
5 may we hear thy call, give our hearts to thine o -
1 sound - eth, say - ing, "Chris - tian, fol - low me;" say - ing,
2 kin - dred, leav - ing all for his dear sake. leav - ing
3 keep us, say - ing, "Chris - tian, love me more." say - ing,
4 plea - sures, "Chris-tian, love me more than these." "Chris-tian,
5 be - dience, serve and love thee best of all. serve and
1-4
Final Ending
1 "Chris - tian, fol - low me;"
2 all for his dear sake.
3 "Chris - tian, love me more."
4 love me more than these."
5 love thee best of (all.) all.

Alternative tune: *Restoration,* 550.

Words: Cecil Frances Alexander (1818-1895), alt.
Music: *St. Andrew,* David Hurd (b. 1950)

𝅗𝅥=76
87. 877

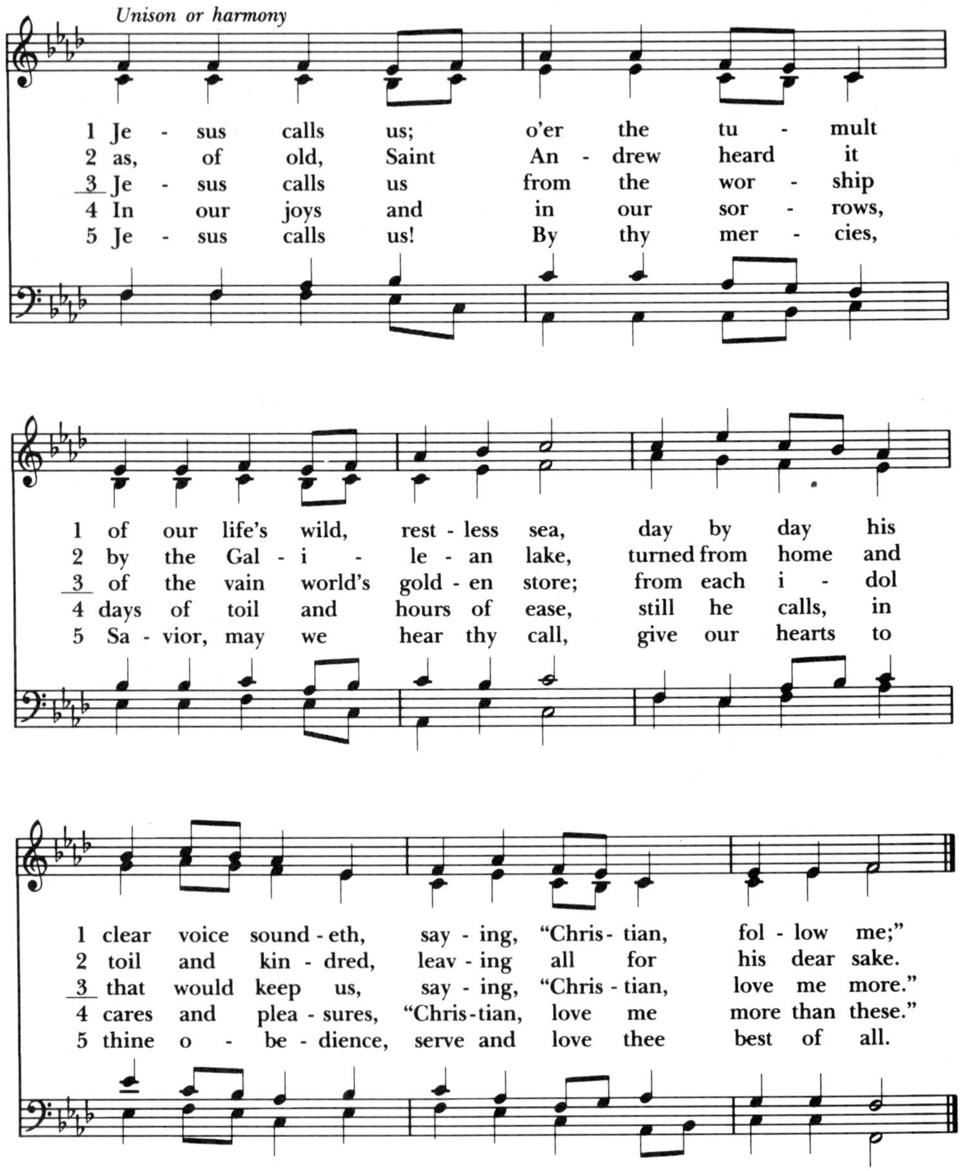
Unison or harmony
1 Je - sus calls us; o'er the tu - mult
2 as, of old, Saint An - drew heard it
3 Je - sus calls us from the wor - ship
4 In our joys and in our sor - rows,
5 Je - sus calls us! By thy mer - cies,
1 of our life's wild, rest - less sea, day by day his
2 by the Gal - i - le - an lake, turned from home and
3 of the vain world's gold - en store; from each i - dol
4 days of toil and hours of ease, still he calls, in
5 Sa - vior, may we hear thy call, give our hearts to
1 clear voice sound - eth, say - ing, "Chris - tian, fol - low me;"
2 toil and kin - dred, leav - ing all for his dear sake.
3 that would keep us, say - ing, "Chris - tian, love me more."
4 cares and plea - sures, "Chris - tian, love me more than these."
5 thine o - be - dience, serve and love thee best of all.

Alternative tune: *St. Andrew,* 549.

Words: Cecil Frances Alexander (1818-1895), alt.
Music: *Restoration,* melody from *The Southern Harmony,* 1835; harm. *Hymnal 1982,* after *The Southern Harmony,* 1835

𝅗𝅥=56
87. 87

Alternative accompaniment for unison singing

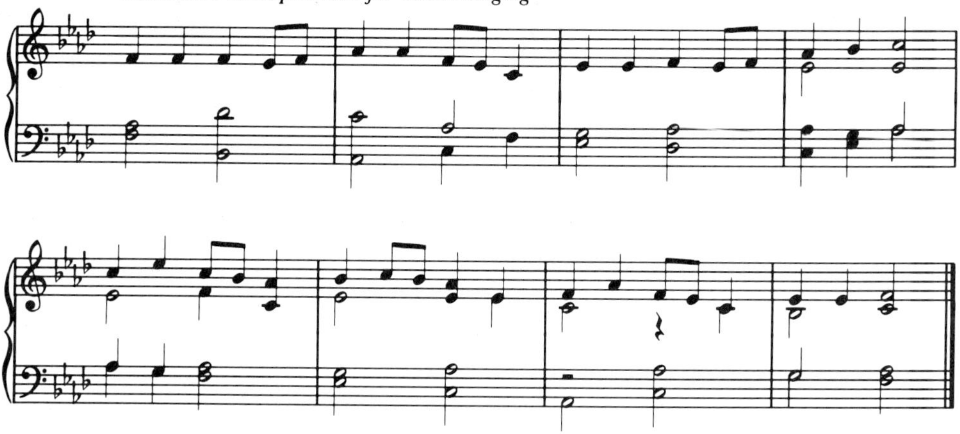

Music: *Restoration,* melody from *The Southern Harmony,* 1835; harm. Margaret W. Mealy (b. 1922) 𝅗𝅥=56

Christian Vocation and Pilgrimage 551

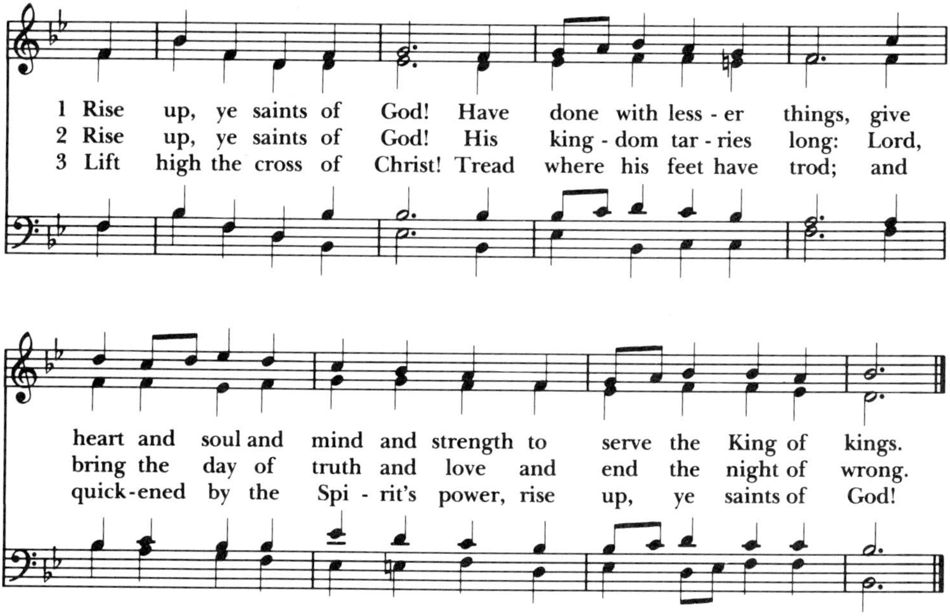
1 Rise up, ye saints of God! Have done with less - er things, give heart and soul and mind and strength to serve the King of kings.
2 Rise up, ye saints of God! His king - dom tar - ries long: Lord, bring the day of truth and love and end the night of wrong.
3 Lift high the cross of Christ! Tread where his feet have trod; and quick-ened by the Spi - rit's power, rise up, ye saints of God!

Words: William Pierson Merrill (1867-1954), alt.
Music: *Festal Song,* William H. Walter (1825-1893)

𝅗𝅥=52
SM

1 Fight the good fight with all thy might, Christ is thy
2 Run the straight race through God's good grace, lift up thine
*3 Cast care a - side, lean on thy Guide; his bound - less
*4 Faint not nor fear, his arms are near; he chan - geth

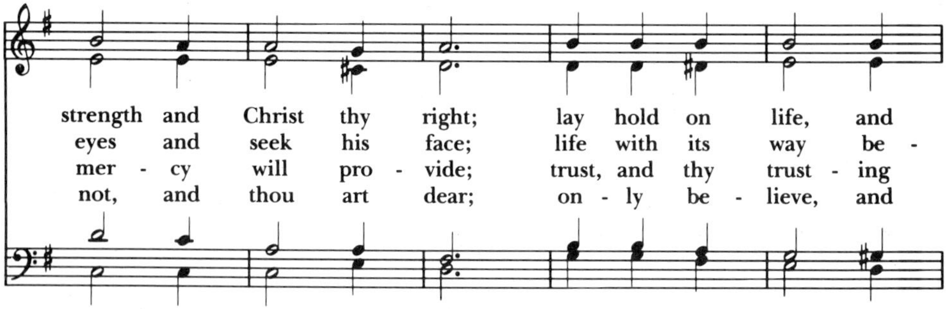
strength and Christ thy right; lay hold on life, and
eyes and seek his face; life with its way be -
mer - cy will pro - vide; trust, and thy trust - ing
not, and thou art dear; on - ly be - lieve, and

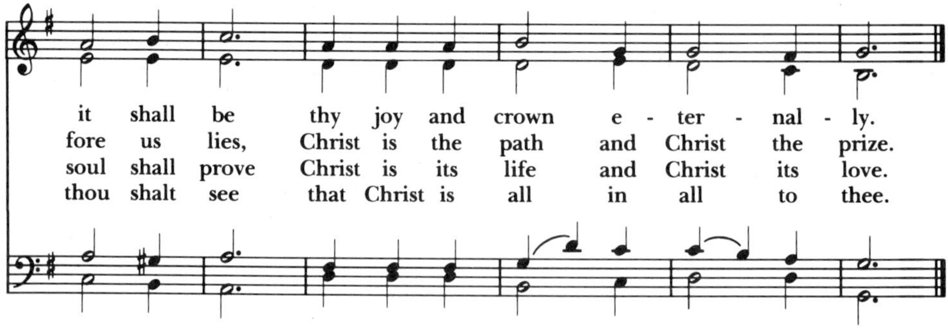
it shall be thy joy and crown e - ter - nal - ly.
fore us lies, Christ is the path and Christ the prize.
soul shall prove Christ is its life and Christ its love.
thou shalt see that Christ is all in all to thee.

Alternative tune: *Rushford,* 553.

Words: John Samuel Bewley Monsell (1811-1875), alt.
Music: *Pentecost,* William Boyd (1847-1928)

𝅗𝅥=46
LM

1 Fight the good fight with all thy might, Christ is thy strength and Christ thy right; lay hold on life, and it shall be thy joy and crown e - ter - nal - ly.
2 Run the straight race through God's good grace, lift up thine eyes and seek his face; life with its way be - fore us lies, Christ is the path and Christ the prize.
*3 Cast care a - side, lean on thy Guide; his bound - less mer - cy will pro-vide; trust, and thy trust - ing soul shall prove Christ is its life and Christ its love.
*4 Faint not nor fear, his arms are near; he chan - geth not, and thou art dear; on - ly be - lieve, and thou shalt see that Christ is all in all to thee.

Alternative tune: *Pentecost,* 552.

Words: John Samuel Bewley Monsell (1811-1875), alt.
Music: *Rushford,* Henry G. Ley (1887-1962)

𝅗𝅥 = 54
LM

G Em Bm* Em
'Tis the gift to be sim - ple, 'tis the gift to be free, 'tis the
Am A D
gift to come down where we ought to be, and
G Em Bm*
when we find our - selves in the place just right, 'twill
Am D G
be in the val - ley of love and de - light.

Bm* Em Bm* C
When true sim - plic - i - ty is gained to
G D G C
bow and to bend we shan't be a-shamed, to turn, turn, will
G Am D G C G
be our de-light till by turn - ing, turn - ing we come round right.

**Optional chord D. The following rhythm pattern for clapping or percussion instrument may be used for the Refrain:* 

Words: Shaker song, 18th cent.
Music: *Simple Gifts,* Shaker melody; acc. Margaret W. Mealy (b. 1922)

♩= 60
Irr. with Refrain

1 Lead on, O King e - ter - nal, the day of march has come;
2 Lead on, O King e - ter - nal, till sin's fierce war shall cease,
3 Lead on, O King e - ter - nal: we fol - low, not with fears;
hence - forth in fields of con - quest thy tents shall be our home:
and ho - li - ness shall whis - per the sweet a - men of peace;
for glad - ness breaks like morn - ing wher - e'er thy face ap - pears.
through days of prep - a - ra - tion thy grace has made us strong,
for not with swords loud clash - ing, nor roll of stir - ring drums,
Thy cross is lift - ed o'er us; we jour - ney in its light:
and now, O King e - ter - nal, we lift our bat - tle song.
but deeds of love and mer - cy, the heaven - ly king - dom comes.
the crown a - waits the con - quest; lead on, O God of might!

This music in D♭, 563.

Words: Ernest Warburton Shurtleff (1862-1917)
Music: *Lancashire,* Henry Thomas Smart (1813-1879)

𝅗𝅥=58
76. 76 D

1 Re - joice, ye pure in heart! Re - joice, give thanks, and sing! Your
2 With all the an - gel choirs, with all the saints of earth, pour
3 Your clear ho - san - nas raise, and al - le - lu - ias loud; while
4 Yes, on through life's long path, still chant - ing as ye go, from
5 Still lift your stand - ard high, still march in firm ar - ray, as
1 glo - rious ban - ner wave on high, the cross of Christ your King.
2 out the strains of joy and bliss, true rap - ture, no - blest mirth.
3 an - swering ech - oes up - ward float, like wreaths of in - cense cloud.
4 youth to age, by night and day, in glad - ness and in woe.
5 war - riors through the dark - ness toil, till dawns the gold - en day.
Refrain
Re - joice, re - joice, re - joice, give thanks, and sing.
re - joice, re - joice,

*6 At last the march shall end;
the wearied ones shall rest;
the pilgrims find their Father's house,
Jerusalem the blest.
Refrain

*7 Then on, ye pure in heart!
Rejoice, give thanks, and sing!
Your glorious banner wave on high
the cross of Christ your King.
Refrain

Alternative tune: *Vineyard Haven,* 557.

Words: Edward Hayes Plumptre (1821-1891)
Music: *Marion,* Arthur Henry Messiter (1834-1916)

𝅗𝅥=66
SM with Refrain

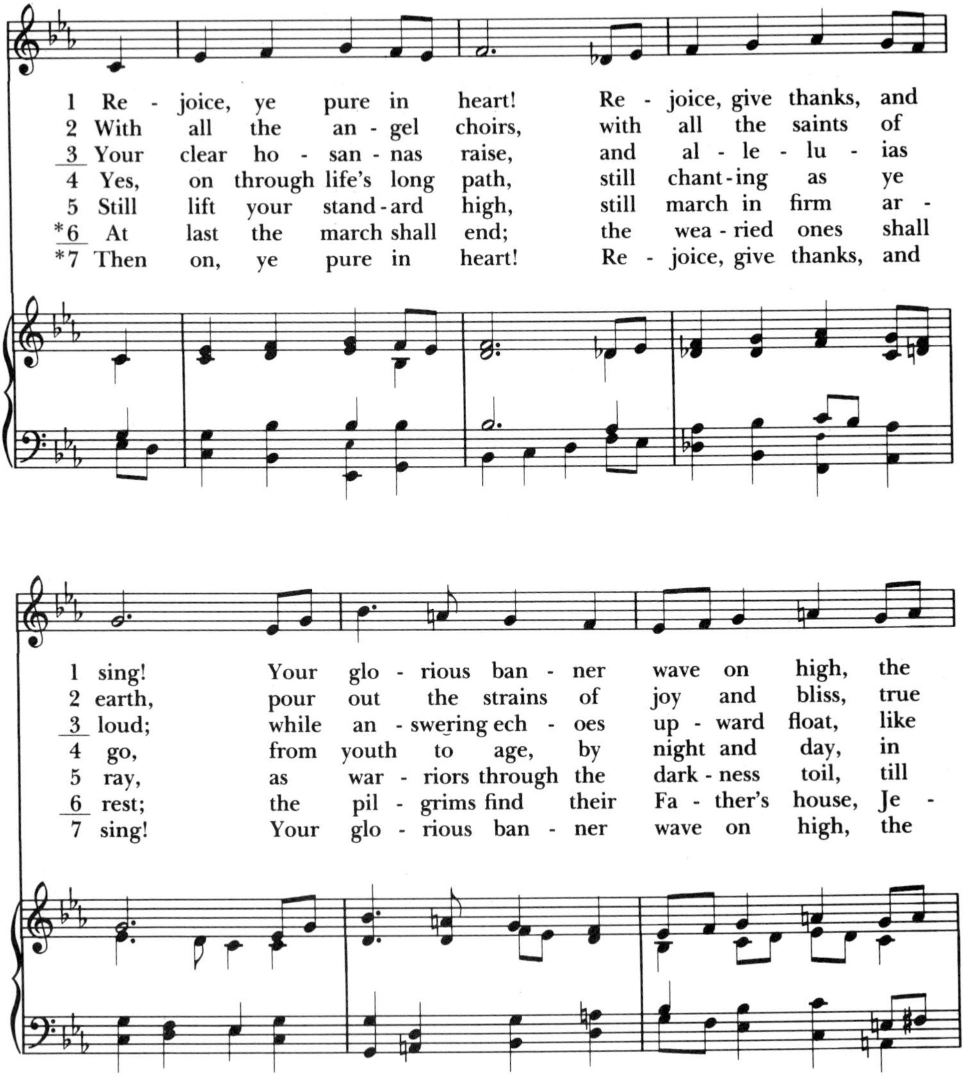
1 Re - joice, ye pure in heart! Re - joice, give thanks, and
2 With all the an - gel choirs, with all the saints of
3 Your clear ho - san - nas raise, and al - le - lu - ias
4 Yes, on through life's long path, still chant - ing as ye
5 Still lift your stand - ard high, still march in firm ar -
*6 At last the march shall end; the wea - ried ones shall
*7 Then on, ye pure in heart! Re - joice, give thanks, and
1 sing! Your glo - rious ban - ner wave on high, the
2 earth, pour out the strains of joy and bliss, true
3 loud; while an - swering ech - oes up - ward float, like
4 go, from youth to age, by night and day, in
5 ray, as war - riors through the dark - ness toil, till
6 rest; the pil - grims find their Fa - ther's house, Je -
7 sing! Your glo - rious ban - ner wave on high, the

Refrain
1 cross of Christ your King.
2 rap - ture, no - blest mirth.
3 wreaths of in - cense cloud.
4 glad - ness and in woe.
5 dawns the gold - en day.
6 ru - sa - lem the blest.
7 cross of Christ your King.
Ho - san - na, ho -
san - na! Re - joice, give thanks, and sing.

Alternative tune: *Marion,* 556.

Words: Edward Hayes Plumptre (1821-1891)
Music: *Vineyard Haven,* Richard Wayne Dirksen (b. 1921)

𝅗𝅥 = 54
SM with Refrain

1 Faith of our fa - thers! liv - ing still in spite of dun - geon,
2 Faith of our fa - thers! faith and prayer shall win all na - tions
3 Faith of our fa - thers! we will love both friend and foe in
fire, and sword: O how our hearts beat high with joy,
un - to thee; and through the truth that comes from God,
all our strife: and preach thee, too, as love knows how,
Refrain
when-e'er we hear that glo - rious word:
man - kind shall then in - deed be free.
by kind - ly deeds and vir - tuous life.
Faith of our fa - thers,
ho - ly faith! We will be true to thee till death.

Words: Frederick William Faber (1814-1863), alt.
Music: *St. Catherine*, Henri Frédéric Hemy (1818-1888); adapt. and arr. James G. Walton (1821-1905)

𝅗𝅥. = 44
88. 88. 88

1 Lead us, heaven - ly Fa - ther, lead us o'er the world's tem -
2 Sa - vior, breathe for - give - ness o'er us; all our weak - ness
3 Spi - rit of our God, de - scend - ing, fill our hearts with
pes - tuous sea; guard us, guide us, keep us, feed us,
thou dost know; thou didst tread this earth be - fore us;
heaven-ly joy; love with ev - ery pas - sion blend-ing
for we have no help but thee, yet pos - ses - sing
thou didst feel its keen - est woe; yet un - fear - ing,
plea - sure that can nev - er cloy; thus pro - vid - ed,
ev - ery bless - ing, if our God our Fa - ther be.
per - se - ver - ing, to thy pas - sion thou didst go.
par - doned, guid - ed, noth - ing can our peace des - troy.

Words: James Edmeston (1791-1867), alt.
Music: *Dulce carmen,* melody from *An Essay on the Church Plain Chant,* 1782; adapt. *Collection of Motetts or Antiphons,* ca. 1840; harm. William Henry Monk (1823-1889)

𝅗𝅥 = 52
87. 87. 87

Antiphon
Re-mem-ber your ser-vants, Lord, when you come in your kingly pow - er.
1. Bless-ed are the poor in spi - rit; for theirs is the kingdom of hea - ven.
2. Bless - ed are those who mourn; for they shall be com - fort - ed.
3. Bless - ed are the meek; for they shall in - her - it the earth.
4. Bless - ed are those who hunger and thirst af - ter right - eous-ness;

SATB
for they shall be sat - is - fied.
5. Bless - ed are the mer - ci - ful;
SATB
for they shall ob - tain mer - cy.
6. Bless - ed are the pure in heart;
Men U
for they shall see God.
7. Bless - ed are the peace - ma - kers;
for they shall be called the chil - dren of God.
Women U
8. Bless - ed are those who are perse - cut - ed for right - eous - ness' sake;

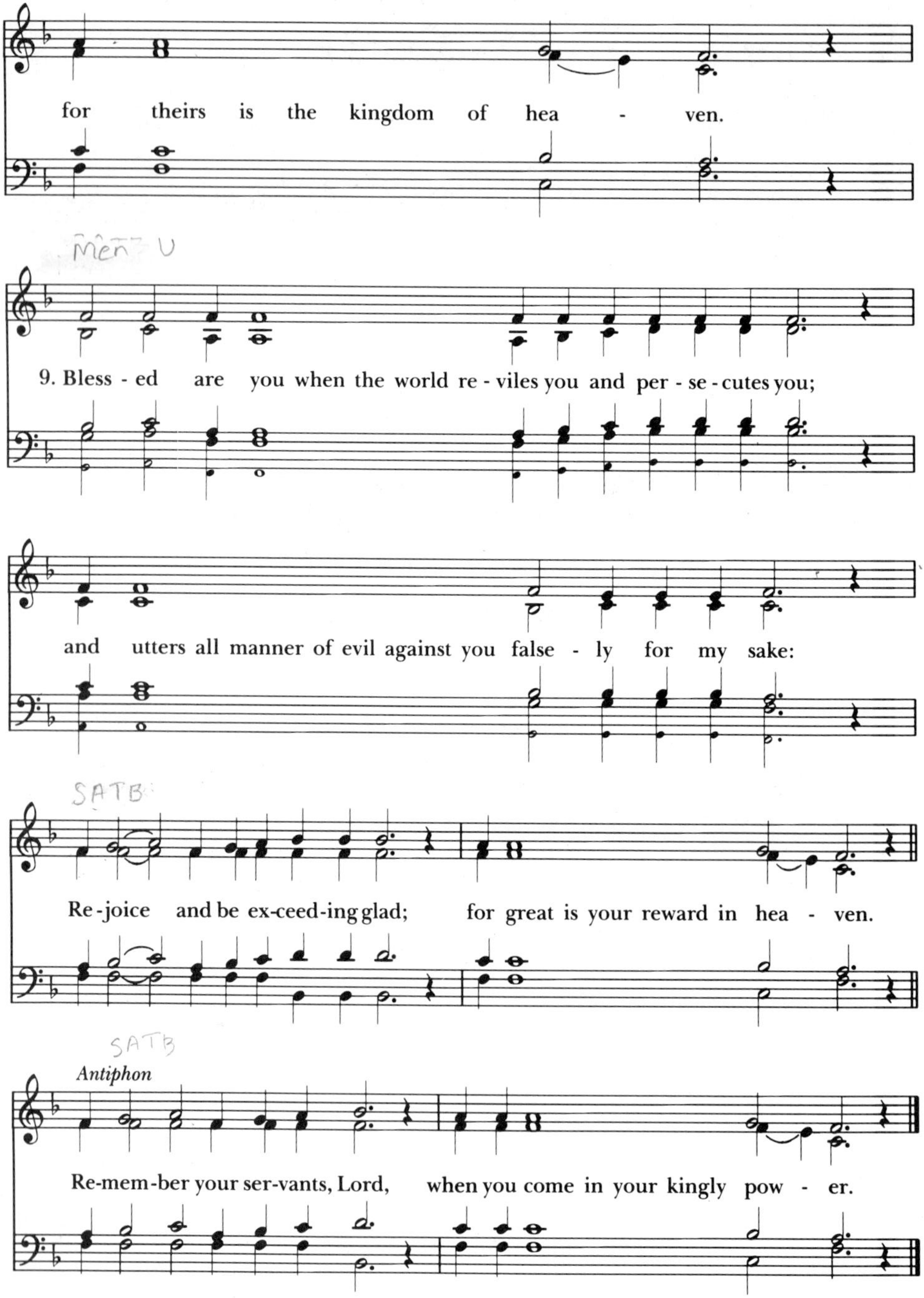
for theirs is the kingdom of hea - ven.
9. Bless - ed are you when the world re - viles you and per - se - cutes you;
and utters all manner of evil against you false - ly for my sake:
Re - joice and be ex-ceed-ing glad; for great is your reward in hea - ven.
Antiphon
Re-mem-ber your ser-vants, Lord, when you come in your kingly pow - er.

The second bass part is optional.

Words: Russian Orthodox liturgy; Matthew 5:3-12
Music: *Beatitudes,* Russian Orthodox hymn; arr. Richard Proulx (b. 1937)

𝅗𝅥 = 69
Irr. with Refrain

1 Stand up, stand up, for Je - sus, ye sold - iers of the cross;
2 Stand up, stand up, for Je - sus; the trum - pet call o - bey;
3 Stand up, stand up, for Je - sus; stand in his strength a - lone;
4 Stand up, stand up, for Je - sus: the strife will not be long:
lift high his roy - al ban - ner, it must not suf - fer loss:
forth to the might - y con - flict in this his glo - rious day:
the arm of flesh will fail you, ye dare not trust your own:
this day, the noise of bat - tle; the next, the vic - tor's song.
from vic - tory un - to vic - tory his ar - my shall he lead,
ye that are his now serve him a - gainst un - num - bered foes;
put on the Gos - pel ar - mor, and watch - ing un - to prayer,
To val - iant hearts tri - um - phant, a crown of life shall be;
till ev - ery foe is van - quished and Christ is Lord in - deed.
let cour - age rise with dan - ger, and strength to strength op - pose.
when du - ty calls, or dan - ger, be nev - er want - ing there.
they with the King of glo - ry shall reign e - ter - nal - ly.

Words: George Duffield, Jr. (1818-1888), alt.
Music: *Morning Light*, George James Webb (1803-1887)

𝅗𝅥 = 56
76. 76. D

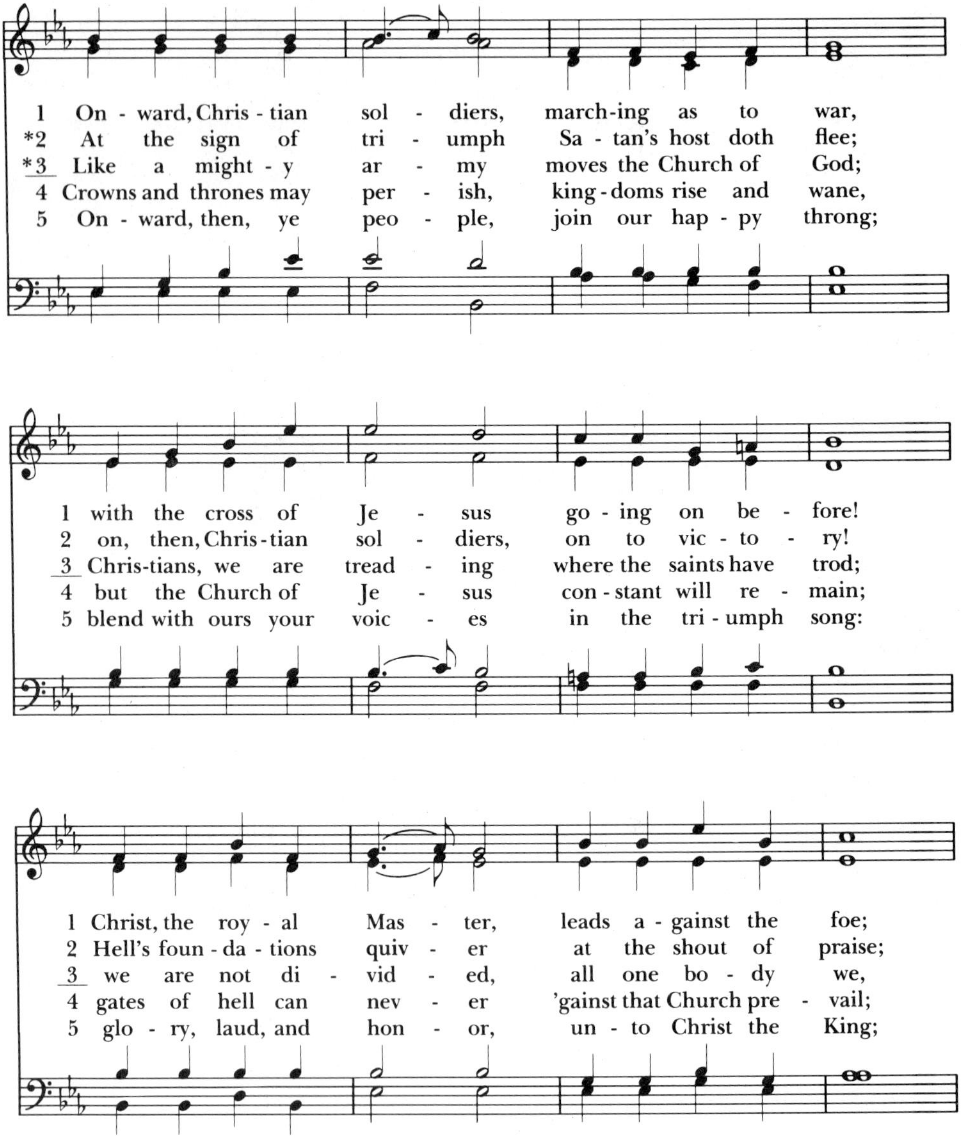
1 On - ward, Chris - tian sol - diers, march-ing as to war,
*2 At the sign of tri - umph Sa - tan's host doth flee;
*3 Like a might - y ar - my moves the Church of God;
4 Crowns and thrones may per - ish, king - doms rise and wane,
5 On - ward, then, ye peo - ple, join our hap - py throng;
1 with the cross of Je - sus go - ing on be - fore!
2 on, then, Chris - tian sol - diers, on to vic - to - ry!
3 Chris-tians, we are tread - ing where the saints have trod;
4 but the Church of Je - sus con - stant will re - main;
5 blend with ours your voic - es in the tri - umph song:
1 Christ, the roy - al Mas - ter, leads a - gainst the foe;
2 Hell's foun - da - tions quiv - er at the shout of praise;
3 we are not di - vid - ed, all one bo - dy we,
4 gates of hell can nev - er 'gainst that Church pre - vail;
5 glo - ry, laud, and hon - or, un - to Christ the King;

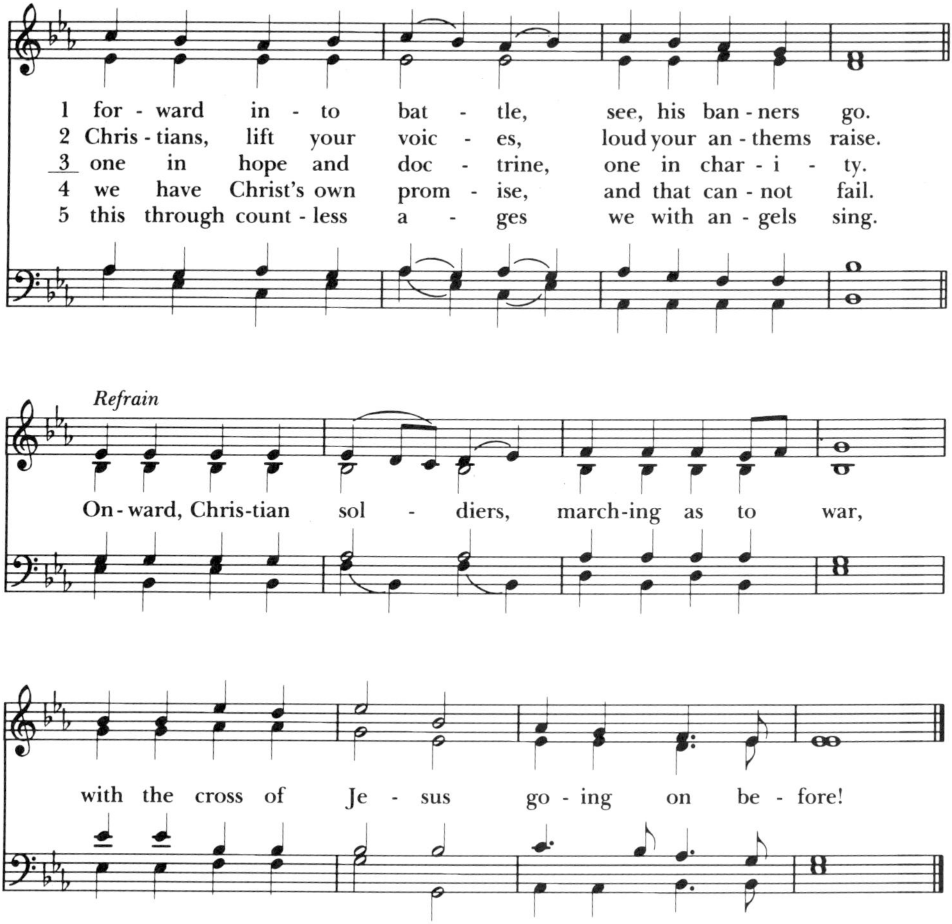
1 for - ward in - to bat - tle, see, his ban - ners go.
2 Chris - tians, lift your voic - es, loud your an - thems raise.
3 one in hope and doc - trine, one in char - i - ty.
4 we have Christ's own prom - ise, and that can - not fail.
5 this through count - less a - ges we with an - gels sing.
Refrain
On - ward, Chris - tian sol - diers, march - ing as to war,
with the cross of Je - sus go - ing on be - fore!

Words: Sabine Baring-Gould (1834-1924), alt.
Music: *St. Gertrude,* Arthur Seymour Sullivan (1842-1900)

𝅗𝅥 = 54
65. 65. D with Refrain

1 Go for-ward, Chris-tian sol - dier, be - neath his ban - ner true:
2 Go for-ward, Chris-tian sol - dier, fear not the se - cret foe;
3 Go for-ward, Chris-tian sol - dier, nor dream of peace-ful rest,
4 Go for-ward, Chris-tian sol - dier, fear not the gath-ering night:
the Lord him-self, thy Lead - er, shall all thy foes sub - due.
far more o'er thee are watch - ing than hu - man eyes can know:
till Sa - tan's host is van - quished and heaven is all pos - sessed;
the Lord has been thy shel - ter; the Lord will be thy light.
His love for-tells thy tri - als; he knows thine hour - ly need;
trust on - ly Christ, thy Cap - tain; cease not to watch and pray;
till Christ him-self shall call thee to lay thine ar - mor by,
When morn his face re - veal - eth thy dan - gers all are past:
he can with bread of hea - ven thy faint-ing spi - rit feed.
heed not the treach-erous voic - es that lure thy soul a - stray.
and wear in end - less glo - ry the crown of vic - to - ry.
O pray that faith and vir - tue may keep thee to the last!

This music in C, 555.

Words: Laurence Tuttiett (1825-1895)
Music: *Lancashire,* Henry Thomas Smart (1813-1879)

𝅗𝅥=58
76. 76. D

1 He who would val - iant be 'gainst all dis - as - ter,
2 Who so be - set him round with dis - mal sto - ries,
3 Since, Lord, thou dost de - fend us with thy Spi - rit,
let him in con - stan - cy fol - low the Mas - ter.
do but them - selves con-found, his strength the more is.
we know we at the end shall life in - her - it.
There's no dis - cour - age-ment shall make him once re - lent
No foes shall stay his might, though he with gi - ants fight;
Then fan - cies flee a - way; I'll fear not what men say,
his first a - vowed in - tent to be a pil - grim.
he will make good his right to be a pil - grim.
I'll la - bor night and day to be a pil - grim.

Alternative tune: *Monk's Gate,* 565.

Words: Percy Dearmer (1867-1936), after John Bunyan (1628-1688)
Music: *St. Dunstan's,* Charles Winfred Douglas (1867-1944)

♩= 120
65. 65. 6665

1 He who would val - iant be 'gainst all dis - as - ter,
2 Who so be - set him round with dis - mal sto - ries,
3 Since, Lord, thou dost de - fend us with thy Spi - rit,
let him in con - stan - cy fol - low the Mas - ter.
do but them-selves con - found, his strength the more is.
we know we at the end shall life in - her - it.
There's no dis-cour-age - ment shall make him once re - lent
No foes shall stay his might, though he with gi - ants fight;
Then fan-cies flee a - way; I'll fear not what men say,

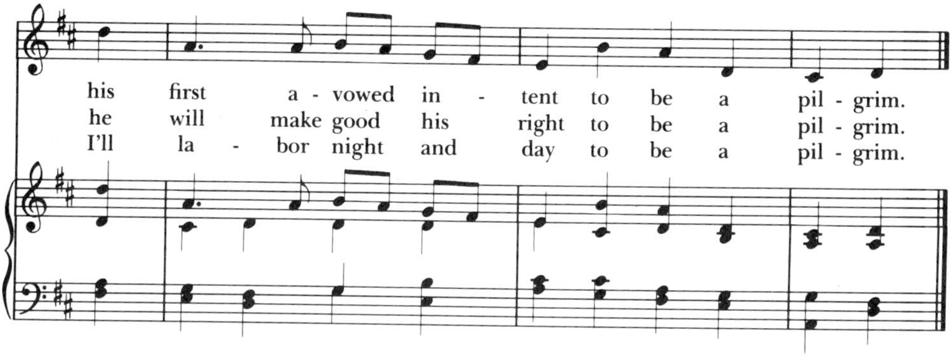
his first a - vowed in - tent to be a pil - grim.
he will make good his right to be a pil - grim.
I'll la - bor night and day to be a pil - grim.

Alternative tune: *St. Dunstan's* 564.

Words: Percy Dearmer (1868-1936), after John Bunyan (1628-1688)
Music: *Monk's Gate,* Sussex folk melody; adapt. and arr. Ralph Vaughan Williams (1872-1958)

𝅗𝅥 = 66
11 11. 12 11

1 From thee all skill and sci-ence flow, all pi - ty, care, and love,
2 And has-ten, Lord, that per-fect day when pain and death shall cease,
all calm and cour - age, faith and hope: O pour them from a - bove!
and thy just rule shall fill the earth with health and light and peace;
Im - part them, Lord, to each and all, as each and all shall need,
when ev - er - blue the sky shall gleam, and ev - er-green the sod,
to rise, like in - cense, each to thee, in no - ble thought and deed.
and our rude work de - face no more the hand - i - work of God.

Words: Charles Kingsley (1819-1875), alt.
Music: *The Church's Desolation,* traditional melody; harm. J. T. White (19th cent.); adapt. C. H. Cayce (19th-20th cent.)

𝅗𝅥 = 84
CMD

1 Thine arm, O Lord, in days of old was strong to heal and save;
2 And lo! thy touch brought life and health, gave hear - ing, strength, and sight;
3 Be thou our great de - liv - erer still, thou Lord of life and death;
it tri - umphed o'er dis - ease and death o'er dark-ness and the grave.
and youth re - newed and fren - zy calmed owned thee, the Lord of light:
re - store and quick - en, soothe and bless, with thine al - might - y breath:
To thee they went, the blind, the deaf, the pal - sied, and the lame,
and now, O Lord, be near to bless, al - might - y as of yore,
to hands that work and eyes that see, give wis - dom's heaven-ly lore,
the lep - er set a - part and shunned the sick with fe - vered frame.
in crowd - ed street, by rest - less couch, as by Gen - nes - aret's shore.
that whole and sick, and weak and strong, may praise thee ev - er - more.

Words: Edward Hayes Plumptre (1821-1891), alt.
Music: *St. Matthew,* from *Supplement to the New Version of Psalms by Dr. Brady and Mr. Tate,* 1708

♩=96
CMD

1 Fa - ther all lov - ing, who rul - est in ma - jes - ty,
2 Bless - ed Lord Je - sus, who cam - est in pov - er - ty,
3 Come, Ho - ly Spi - rit, cre - ate in us ho - li - ness,
4 Ho - li - est Trin - i - ty, per - fect in u - ni - ty,
judg - ment is thine, and con - demn - eth our pride;
shar - ing a sta - ble with beasts at thy birth,
lift up our lives to thy stand - ard of right;
bind in thy love ev - ery na - tion and race;
stir up our lead - ers and peo - ples to pen - i - tence,
stir us to work for thy jus - tice and char - i - ty,
stir ev - ery will to new ven - tures of faith - ful - ness,
may we a - dore thee for time and e - ter - ni - ty,
sor - row for sins that for ven - geance have cried.
tru - ly to care for the poor of the earth.
flood the whole Church with thy glo - ri - ous light.
Fa - ther, Re - deem - er, and Spi - rit of grace.

Words: Patrick Robert Norman Appleford (b. 1925), alt.
Music: *Was lebet,* melody from *Choral-Buch vor Johann Heinrich Reinhardt,* 1754; harm. Ralph Vaughan Williams (1872-1958)

♩= 104
12 10. 12 10

1 God the Om - ni - po - tent! King, who or - dain - est
2 God the All - mer - ci - ful! earth hath for - sak - en
3 God, the All - right - eous One! earth hath de - fied thee;
4 God the All - prov - i - dent! earth by thy chas - tening
thun - der thy clar - ion, the light - ning thy sword;
thy ways all ho - ly, and slight - ed thy word;
yet to e - ter - ni - ty stand - eth thy word,
yet shall to free - dom and truth be re - stored;
show forth thy pi - ty on high where thou reign - est:
bid not thy wrath in its ter - rors a - wak - en:
false - hood and wrong shall not tar - ry be - side thee:
through the thick dark - ness thy king - dom is haste - ning:
give to us peace in our time, O Lord.
give to us peace in our time, O Lord.
give to us peace in our time, O Lord.
thou wilt give peace in thy time, O Lord.

This music in C, 358.

Words: Sts. 1-2, Henry Fothergill Chorley (1808-1872), alt.; sts. 3-4, John Ellerton (1826-1893), alt.
Music: *Russia,* Alexis Lvov (1799-1870)

𝅗𝅥=58
11 10. 11 9

1 All who love and serve your ci - ty, all who
2 in your day of loss and sor - row, in your
3 In your day of wealth and plen - ty, wast - ed
4 For all days are days of judg - ment, and the
5 Ris - en Lord! shall yet the ci - ty be the
1 bear its dai - ly stress, all who cry for peace and
2 day of help-less strife, hon - or, peace, and love re -
3 work and wast - ed play, call to mind the word of
4 Lord is wait-ing still, draw - ing near a world that
5 ci - ty of de - spair? Come to - day, our Judge, our
1 jus - tice, all who curse and all who bless,
2 treat - ing, seek the Lord, who is your life.
3 Je - sus, "I must work while it is day."
4 spurns him, of - fering peace from Cal - vary's hill.
5 Glo - ry; be its name, "The Lord is there!"

Alternative tune: *Charlestown,* 571.

Words: Erik Routley (1917-1982), rev.
Music: *Birabus,* Peter Cutts (b. 1937)

𝅗𝅥 = 60
87. 87

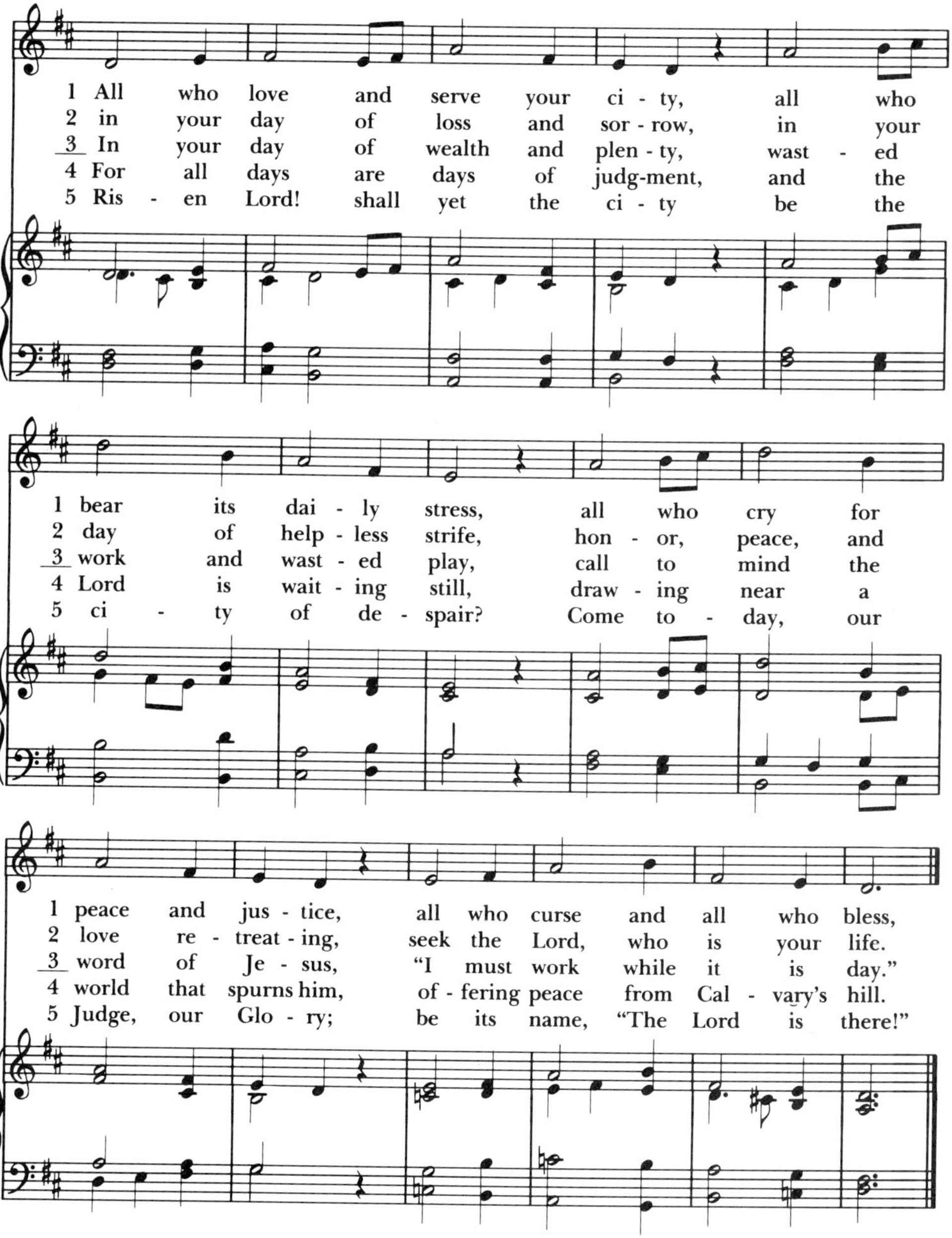
1 All who love and serve your ci - ty, all who
2 in your day of loss and sor - row, in your
3 In your day of wealth and plen - ty, wast - ed
4 For all days are days of judg-ment, and the
5 Ris - en Lord! shall yet the ci - ty be the
1 bear its dai - ly stress, all who cry for
2 day of help - less strife, hon - or, peace, and
3 work and wast - ed play, call to mind the
4 Lord is wait - ing still, draw - ing near a
5 ci - ty of de - spair? Come to - day, our
1 peace and jus - tice, all who curse and all who bless,
2 love re - treat - ing, seek the Lord, who is your life.
3 word of Je - sus, "I must work while it is day."
4 world that spurns him, of - fering peace from Cal - vary's hill.
5 Judge, our Glo - ry; be its name, "The Lord is there!"

Alternative tune: *Birabus*, 570.

Words: Erik Routley (1917-1982), rev.
Music: *Charlestown*, melody from *The Southern Harmony*, 1835; harm. Alastair Cassels-Brown (b. 1927)

𝅗𝅥=42
87. 87

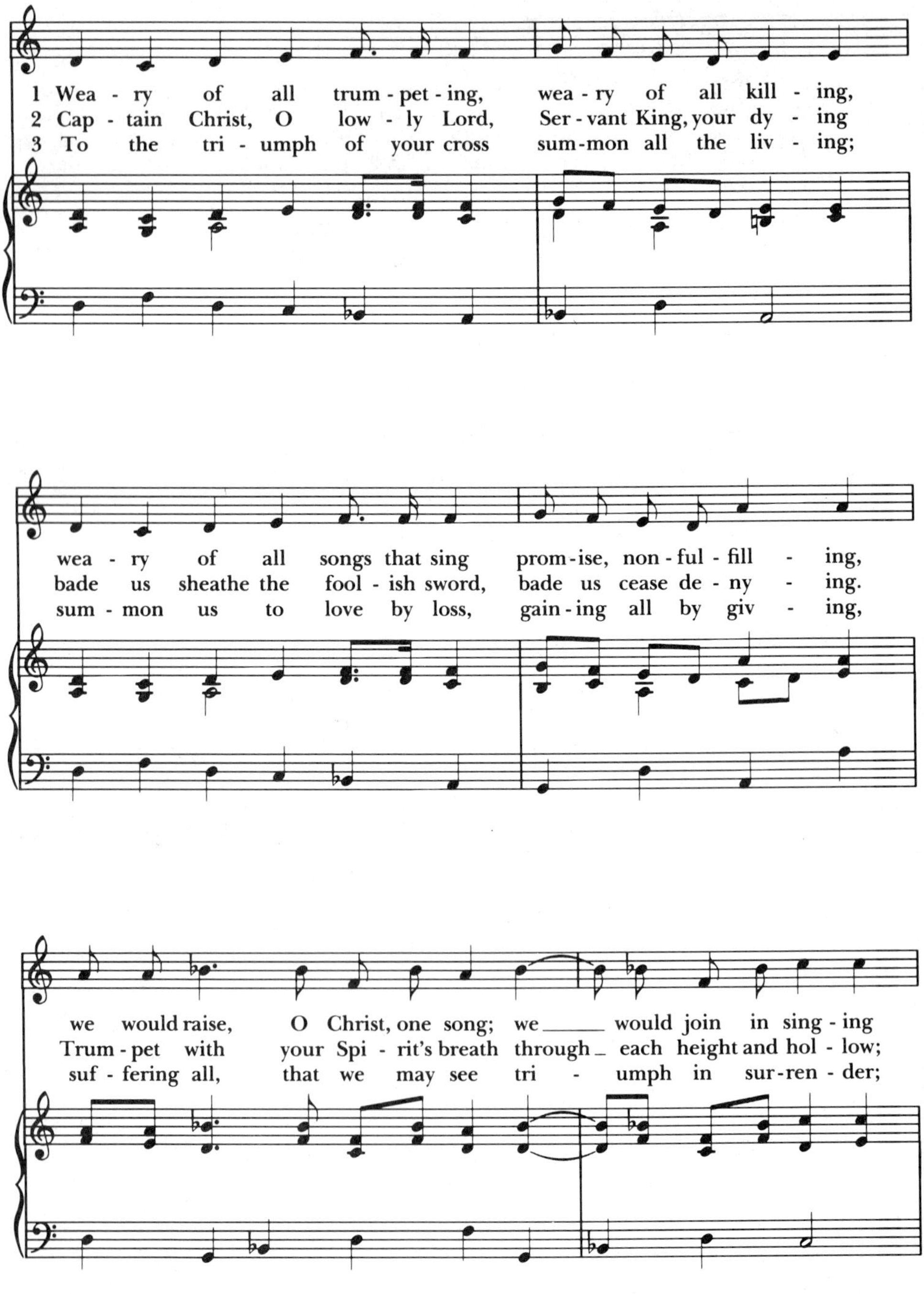
1 Wea - ry of all trum - pet - ing, wea - ry of all kill - ing,
2 Cap - tain Christ, O low - ly Lord, Ser - vant King, your dy - ing
3 To the tri - umph of your cross sum - mon all the liv - ing;
wea - ry of all songs that sing prom - ise, non - ful - fill - ing,
bade us sheathe the fool - ish sword, bade us cease de - ny - ing.
sum - mon us to love by loss, gain - ing all by giv - ing,
we would raise, O Christ, one song; we would join in sing - ing
Trum - pet with your Spi - rit's breath through each height and hol - low;
suf - fering all, that we may see tri - umph in sur - ren - der;

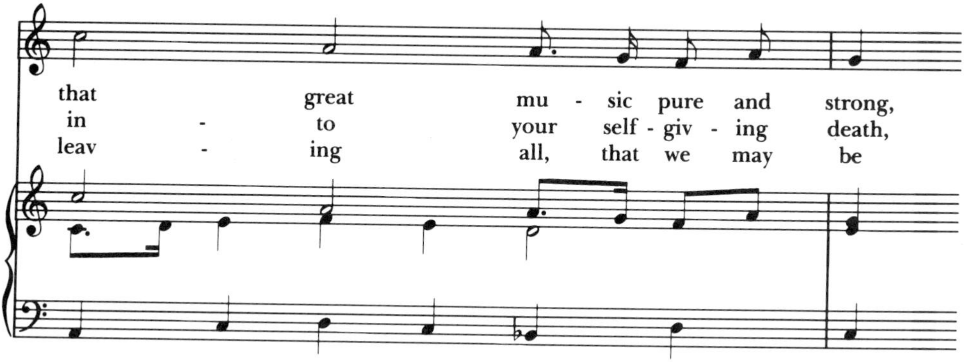
that great mu - sic pure and strong,
in - to your self - giv - ing death,
leav - ing all, that we may be

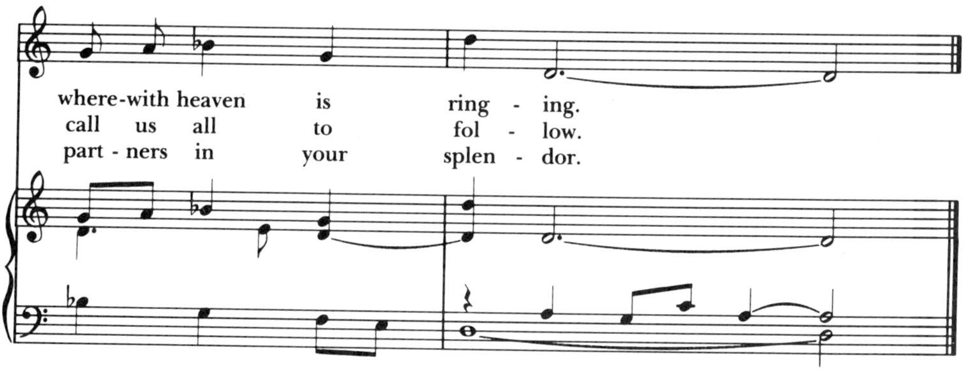
where-with heaven is ring - ing.
call us all to fol - low.
part - ners in your splen - dor.

Words: Martin H. Franzmann (1907-1976), alt.
Music: *Distler,* melody Hugo Distler (1908-1942); harm. Richard Proulx (b. 1937)

♩=72-84
76. 76. D

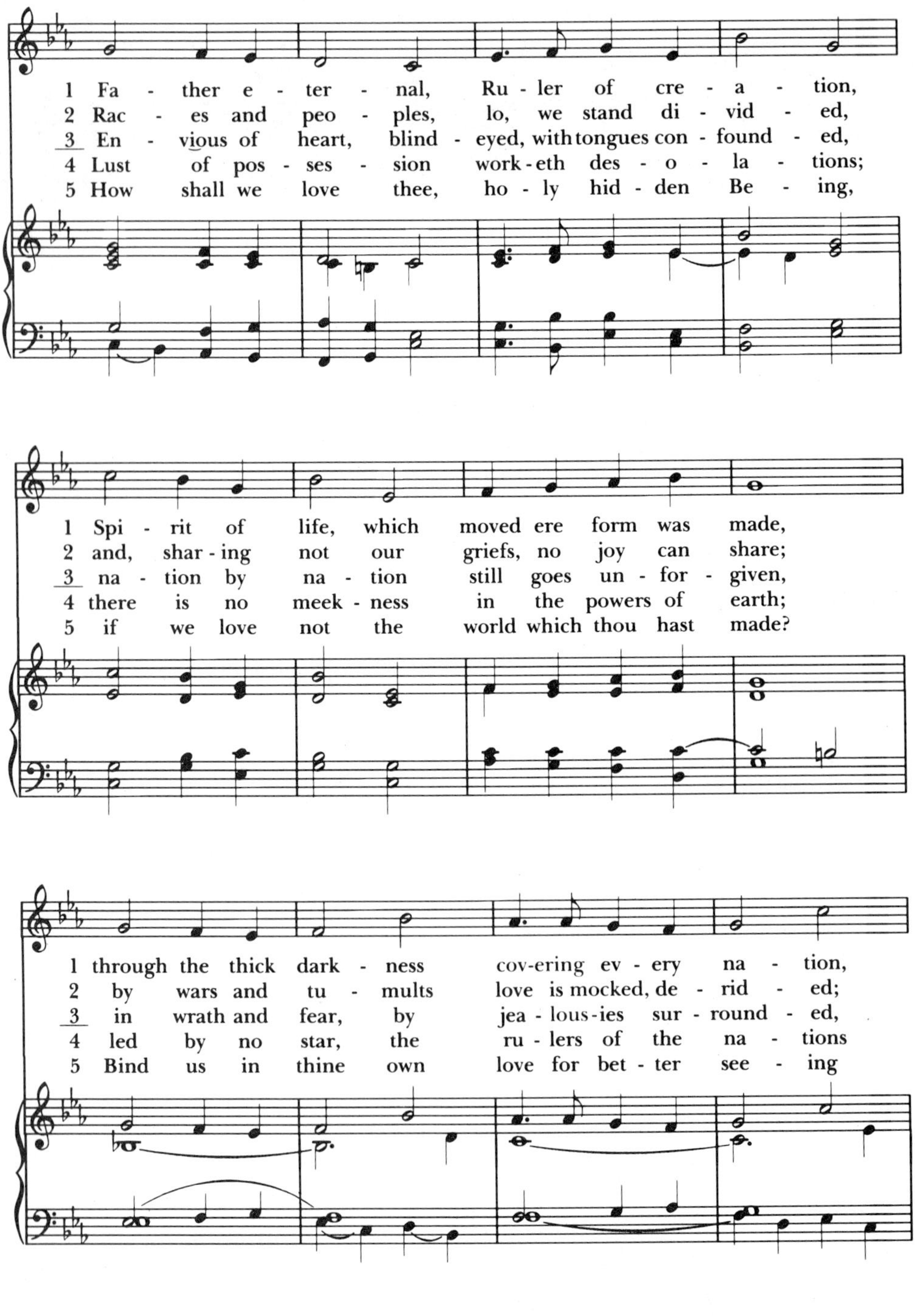
1 Fa - ther e - ter - nal, Ru - ler of cre - a - tion,
2 Rac - es and peo - ples, lo, we stand di - vid - ed,
3 En - vious of heart, blind - eyed, with tongues con - found - ed,
4 Lust of pos - ses - sion work - eth des - o - la - tions;
5 How shall we love thee, ho - ly hid - den Be - ing,
1 Spi - rit of life, which moved ere form was made,
2 and, shar - ing not our griefs, no joy can share;
3 na - tion by na - tion still goes un - for - given,
4 there is no meek - ness in the powers of earth;
5 if we love not the world which thou hast made?
1 through the thick dark - ness cov-ering ev - ery na - tion,
2 by wars and tu - mults love is mocked, de - rid - ed;
3 in wrath and fear, by jea - lous-ies sur - round - ed,
4 led by no star, the ru - lers of the na - tions
5 Bind us in thine own love for bet - ter see - ing

1 light to our blind - ness, O be thou our aid:
2 his sav - ing cross no na - tion yet will bear:
3 build - ing proud towers which shall not reach to heaven:
4 still fail to bring us to the bliss - ful birth:
5 thy Word made flesh, and in a man - ger laid:
Refrain
thy king - dom come, O Lord, thy will be done.

Words: Laurence Housman (1865-1959), alt.
Music: *Langham,* Geoffrey Turton Shaw (1879-1943)

𝅗𝅥 = 54
11 10. 11 10. 10

1 Be - fore thy throne, O God, we kneel: give us a con - science
2 Search out our hearts and make us true; help us to give to
3 For sins of heed - less word and deed, for pride am - bi - tious
4 Let the fierce fires which burn and try, our in - most spi - rits
quick to feel, a rea - dy mind to un - der - stand the
all their due. From love of plea - sure, lust of gold, from
to suc - ceed, for craft - y trade and sub - tle snare to
pu - ri - fy: con - sume the ill; purge out the shame; O
mean - ing of thy chas - tening hand; what - e'er the pain and
sins which make the heart grow cold, wean us and train us
catch the sim - ple un - a - ware, for lives be - reft of
God, be with us in the flame; a new - born peo - ple
shame may be, bring us, O Fa - ther, near - er thee.
with thy rod; teach us to know our faults, O God.
pur - pose high, for - give, for - give, O Lord, we cry.
may we rise, more pure, more true, more no - bly wise.

Alternative tune: *Vater unser im Himmelreich*, 575.

Words: William Boyd Carpenter (1841-1918), alt.
Music: *St. Petersburg*, Dimitri S. Bortniansky (1751-1825)

𝅗𝅥. = 40
88. 88. 88

1 Be - fore thy throne, O God, we kneel: give us a con-science
2 Search out our hearts and make us true; help us to give to
3 For sins of heed - less word and deed, for pride am - bi - tious
4 Let the fierce fires which burn and try, our in - most spi - rits
quick to feel, a rea - dy mind to un - der - stand
all their due. From love of plea - sure, lust of gold,
to suc - ceed, for craft - y trade and sub - tle snare
pu - ri - fy: con - sume the ill; purge out the shame;
the mean - ing of thy chas-tening hand; what - e'er the pain and
from sins which make the heart grow cold, wean us and train us
to catch the sim - ple un - a - ware, for lives be - reft of
O God, be with us in the flame; a new - born peo - ple
shame may be, bring us, O Fa - ther, near - er thee.
with thy rod; teach us to know our faults, O God.
pur - pose high, for - give, for - give, O Lord, we cry.
may we rise, more pure, more true, more no - bly wise.

Alernative tune: *St. Petersburg,* 574.

Words: William Boyd Carpenter (1841-1918), alt.
Music: *Vater unser im Himmelreich,* melody from *Geistliche lieder auffs new gebessert und gemehrt,* 1539; adapt. Martin Luther (1483-1546); harm. Hans Leo Hassler (1564-1612)

𝅗𝅥=48
88. 88. 88

Descant (after stanzas 2 and 3)
God is love, God is love,
Refrain
God is love, and where true love is
1-3
Final Ending
God him - self is there. there.
God him - self is there. there.
1 Here in Christ we gath - er, love of Christ our call - ing.
2 When we Chris-tians gath - er, mem-bers of one Bo - dy,
3 Grant us love's ful - fill - ment, joy with all the bless - ed,

Christ, our love, is with us, glad-ness be his greet - ing.
let there be in us no dis-cord but one spi - rit.
when we see your face, O Sa-vior, in its glo - ry.
Let us fear and love him, ho-ly God e - ter - nal.
Ban-ished now be an - ger, strife and ev-ery quar - rel.
Shine on us, O pur - est Light of all cre - a - tion,
Repeat Refrain
Lov-ing him, let each love Christ in one an - oth - er.
Christ, our God, be al - ways pres-ent here a - mong us.
be our bliss while end-less a-ges sing your prais - es.

This hymn is especially suitable for Maundy Thursday. The stanzas may be sung by cantor or choir.
Alternative tune: *Ubi caritas (Murray)*, 577.

Words: Latin; tr. James Quinn (b. 1919), alt.
Music: *Mandatum,* Richard Proulx (b. 1937)

𝅗𝅥=56
12. 12. 12. 12 with Refrain

Refrain
God is love, and where true love is God him-self is there.
1 Here in Christ we gath - er, love of Christ our call - ing.
2 When we Chris-tians gath - er, mem-bers of one Bo - dy,
3 Grant us love's ful-fill - ment, joy with all the bless - ed,
Christ, our love, is with us, glad-ness be his greet - ing.
let there be in us no dis-cord but one spi - rit.
when we see your face, O Sa-vior, in its glo - ry.
Let us fear and love him, ho-ly God e-ter - nal.
Ban-ished now be an - ger, strife and ev-ery quar - rel.
Shine on us, O pur - est Light of all cre-a - tion,

Repeat Refrain
Lov - ing him, let each love Christ in one an - oth - er.
Christ, our God, be al - ways pres - ent here a - mong us.
be our bliss while end - less a - ges sing your prais - es.

This is especially suitable for Maundy Thursday. The stanzas may be sung by cantor or choir.
Alternative tune: *Mandatum.* 576.

Words: Latin; tr. James Quinn (b. 1919), alt.
Music: *Ubi caritas (Murray),* A. Gregory Murray (b. 1905)

𝅗𝅥=48
12. 12. 12. 12 with Refrain

Christian Responsibility 578

Unison or harmony

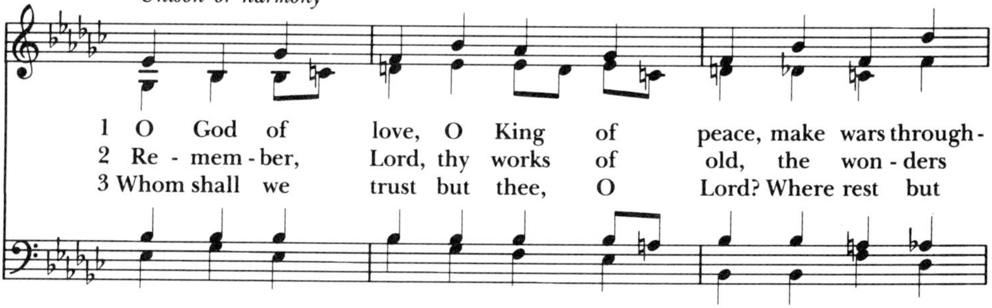
1 O God of love, O King of peace, make wars through -
2 Re - mem - ber, Lord, thy works of old, the won - ders
3 Whom shall we trust but thee, O Lord? Where rest but

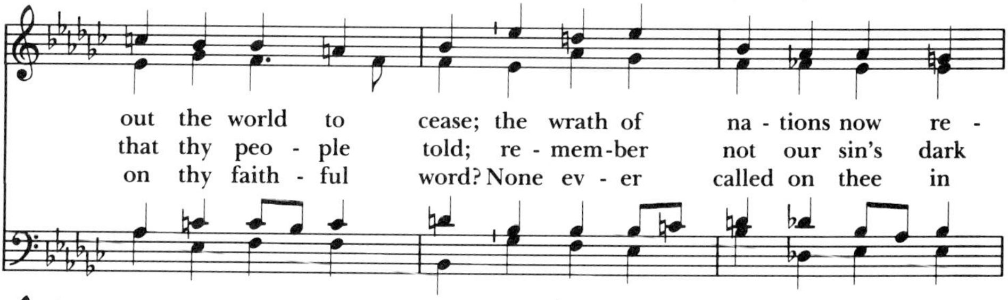
out the world to cease; the wrath of na - tions now re -
that thy peo - ple told; re - mem - ber not our sin's dark
on thy faith - ful word? None ev - er called on thee in

strain, give peace, O God, give peace a - gain!
stain, give peace, O God, give peace a - gain!
vain, give peace, O God, give peace a - gain!

The G♮ in the final chord should be reserved for stanza 3. This music in e, 434.

Words: Henry Williams Baker (1821-1877), alt.
Music: *Eltham,* melody Nathaiel Gawthorn (18th cent.); harm. Samuel Sebastian Wesley (1810-1876)

♩=88
LM

1 Al - might - y Fa - ther, strong to save, whose arm hath bound the
2 O Christ, the Lord of hill and plain o'er which our traf - fic
3 O Spi - rit, whom the Fa - ther sent to spread a - broad the
4 O Trin - i - ty of love and power, our peo - ple shield in
rest - less wave, who bidd'st the might - y o - cean deep its
runs a - main by moun - tain pass or val - ley low; wher -
firm - a - ment; O Wind of hea - ven, by thy might save
dan - ger's hour; from rock and tem - pest, fire and foe, pro -
own ap - point - ed li - mits keep: O hear us when we
ev - er, Lord, thy peo - ple go, pro - tect them by thy
all who dare the ea - gle's flight, and keep them by thy
tect them where - so - e'er they go; thus ev - er - more shall
cry to thee for those in per - il on the sea.
guard - ing hand from ev - ery per - il on the land.
watch - ful care from ev - ery per - il in the air.
rise to thee glad praise from space, air, land, and sea.

Words: Sts. 1 and 4, William Whiting (1825-1878), alt.; sts. 2-3, Robert Nelson Spencer (1877-1961), alt.
Music: *Melita*, John Bacchus Dykes (1823-1876)

𝅗𝅥=48
88. 88. 88

Unison

1 God, who stretched the span - gled hea - vens in - fi - nite in
*2 Proud-ly rise our mod - ern ci - ties, state - ly build-ings,
3 We have ven - tured worlds un - dreamed of since the child-hood
4 As each far ho - ri - zon beck - ons, may it chal - lenge

time and place, flung the suns in burn - ing ra - diance
row on row; yet their win - dows, blank, un - feel - ing,
of our race; known the ec - sta - sy of wing - ing
us a - new, chil - dren of cre - a - tive pur - pose,

through the si - lent fields of space: we, your chil - dren
stare on can - yoned streets be - low, where the lone - ly
through un - trav - eled realms of space; probed the se - crets
serv - ing o - thers, hon - oring you. May our dreams prove

in your like - ness, share in - ven - tive powers with you;
drift un - no - ticed in the ci - ty's ebb and flow,
of the at - om, yield - ing un - im - ag - ined power,
rich with prom - ise, each en - deav - or well be - gun:

Great Cre - a - tor, still cre - at - ing,
lost to pur - pose and to mean - ing,
fac - ing us with life's de - struc - tion
Great Cre - a - tor, give us guid - ance

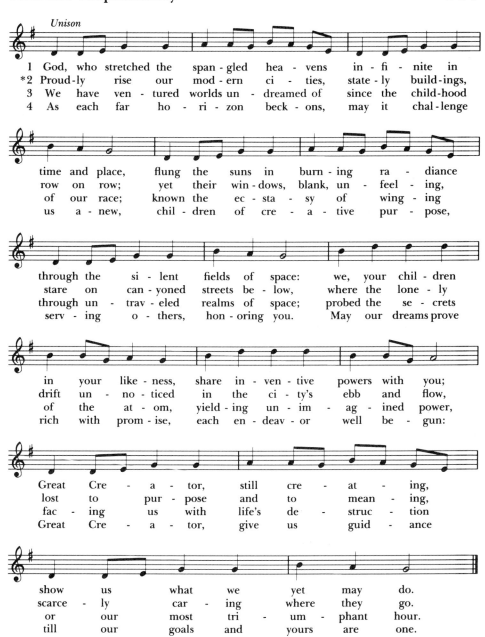

show us what we yet may do.
scarce - ly car - ing where they go.
or our most tri - um - phant hour.
till our goals and yours are one.

Words: Catherine Cameron (b. 1927), alt.
Music: *Holy Manna,* from *The Southern Harmony,* 1835

Harmony (the melody is in the tenor)

1 God, who stretched the span-gled hea-vens in-fi-nite in
*2 Proud-ly rise our mod-ern ci-ties, state-ly build-ings,
3 We have ven-tured worlds un-dreamed of since the child-hood
4 As each far ho-ri-zon beck-ons, may it chal-lenge
time and place, flung the suns in burn-ing ra-diance
row on row; yet their win-dows, blank, un-feel-ing,
of our race; known the ec-sta-sy of wing-ing
us a-new, chil-dren of cre-a-tive pur-pose,
through the si-lent fields of space: we, your chil-dren
stare on can-yoned streets be-low, where the lone-ly
through un-trav-eled realms of space; probed the se-crets
serv-ing o-thers, hon-oring you. May our dreams prove

in your like - ness, share in - ven - tive powers with you;
drift un - no - ticed in the ci - ty's ebb and flow,
of the at - om, yield - ing un - im - ag - ined power,
rich with prom - ise, each en - deav - or well be - gun:
Great Cre - a - tor, still cre - at - ing,
lost to pur - pose and to mean - ing,
fac - ing us with life's de - struc - tion
Great Cre - a - tor, give us guid - ance
show us what we yet may do.
scarce - ly car - ing where they go.
or our most tri - um - phant hour.
till our goals and yours are one.

Another accompaniment for unison singing, 238.

Words: Catherine Cameron (b. 1927), alt.
Music: *Holy Manna,* from *The Southern Harmony,* 1835

𝅗𝅥 = 52
87. 87. D

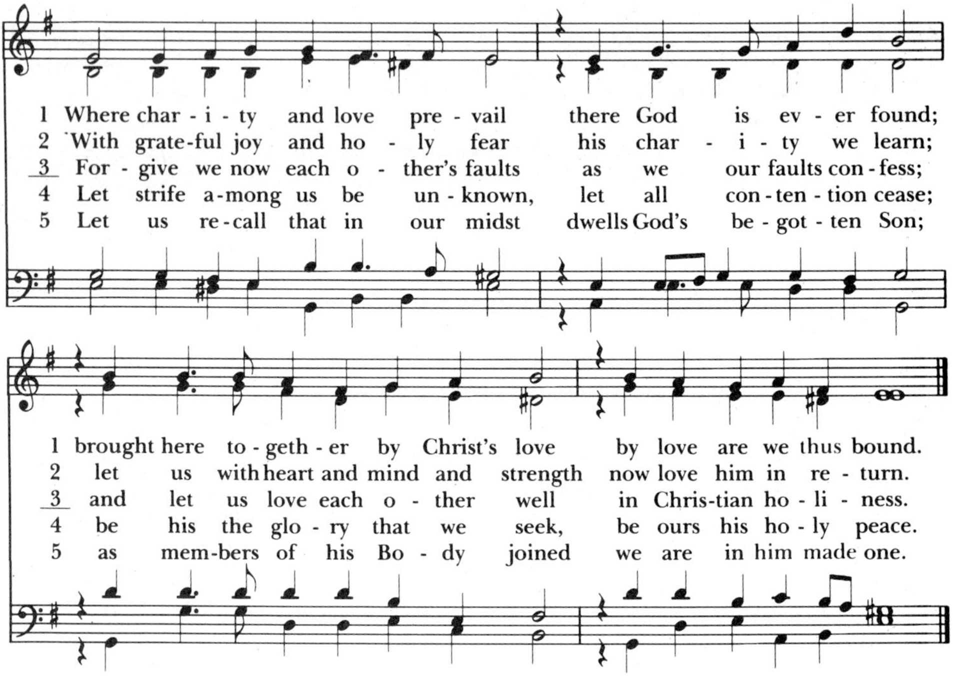
1 Where char - i - ty and love pre - vail there God is ev - er found;
2 With grate-ful joy and ho - ly fear his char - i - ty we learn;
3 For - give we now each o - ther's faults as we our faults con - fess;
4 Let strife a-mong us be un - known, let all con - ten - tion cease;
5 Let us re-call that in our midst dwells God's be - got - ten Son;
1 brought here to - geth - er by Christ's love by love are we thus bound.
2 let us with heart and mind and strength now love him in re - turn.
3 and let us love each o - ther well in Chris-tian ho - li - ness.
4 be his the glo - ry that we seek, be ours his ho - ly peace.
5 as mem-bers of his Bo - dy joined we are in him made one.

6 Love can exclude no race or creed
if honored be God's Name;
our common life embraces all
whose Father is the same.

This hymn is especially suitable for Maundy Thursday.

Words: Latin; tr. J. Clifford Evers (b. 1916)
Music: *Cheshire*, melody and bass from *The Whole Booke of Psalmes*, 1592, alt.; harm. *Hymns III*, 1979

♩=84
CM

582 Christian Responsibility

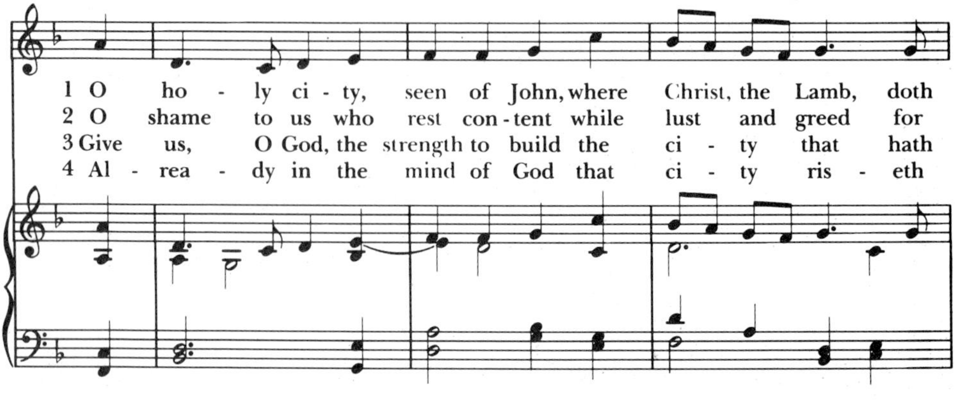
1 O ho - ly ci - ty, seen of John, where Christ, the Lamb, doth
2 O shame to us who rest con - tent while lust and greed for
3 Give us, O God, the strength to build the ci - ty that hath
4 Al - rea - dy in the mind of God that ci - ty ris - eth

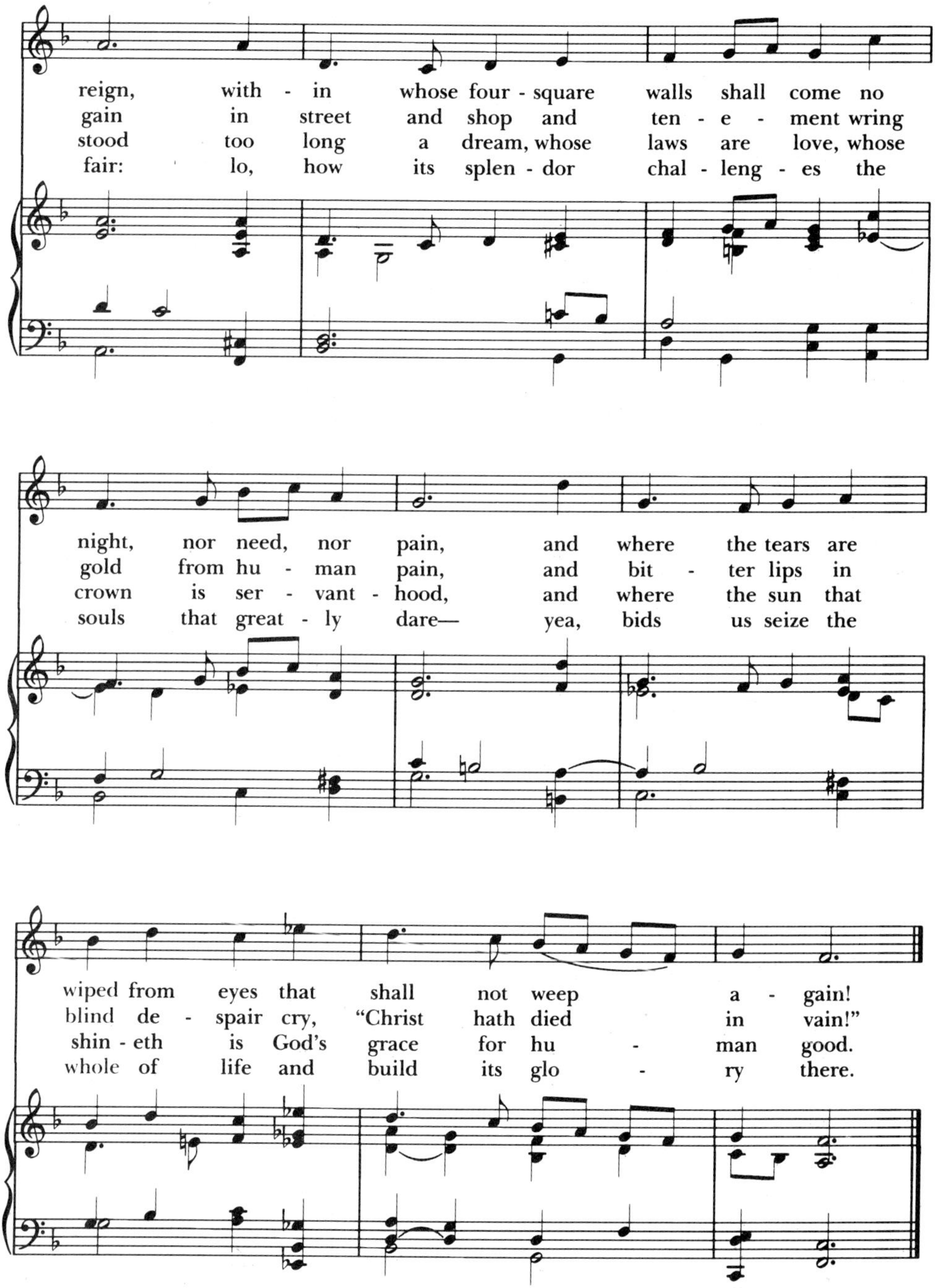
reign, with - in whose four - square walls shall come no
gain in street and shop and ten - e - ment wring
stood too long a dream, whose laws are love, whose
fair: lo, how its splen - dor chal - leng - es the
night, nor need, nor pain, and where the tears are
gold from hu - man pain, and bit - ter lips in
crown is ser - vant - hood, and where the sun that
souls that great - ly dare— yea, bids us seize the
wiped from eyes that shall not weep a - gain!
blind de - spair cry, "Christ hath died in vain!"
shin - eth is God's grace for hu - man good.
whole of life and build its glo - ry there.

Alternative tune: *Morning Song*, 583.

Words: Walter Russell Bowie (1882-1969), alt.
Music: *Sancta Civitas*, Herbert Howells (1892-1983)

♩=92
86. 86. 86

Fm(Em) D♭(C) E♭(D) A♭(G) Fm(Em) D♭(C)
1 O ho - ly ci - ty, seen of John, where Christ, the Lamb, doth
2 O shame to us who rest con - tent while lust and greed for
3 Give us, O God, the strength to build the ci - ty that hath
4 Al - rea - dy in the mind of God that ci - ty ris - eth
A♭(G) B♭m(Am) E♭(D) A♭(G)
reign, with - in whose four - square walls shall come no
gain in street and shop and ten - e - ment wring
stood too long a dream, whose laws are love, whose
fair: lo, how its splen - dor chal - leng - es the
Fm(Em) D♭(C) E♭(D) Fm(Em) A♭(G) B♭(Am)
night, nor need, nor pain, and where the tears are
gold from hu - man pain, and bit - ter lips in
crown is ser - vant - hood, and where the sun that
souls that great - ly dare— yea, bids us seize the

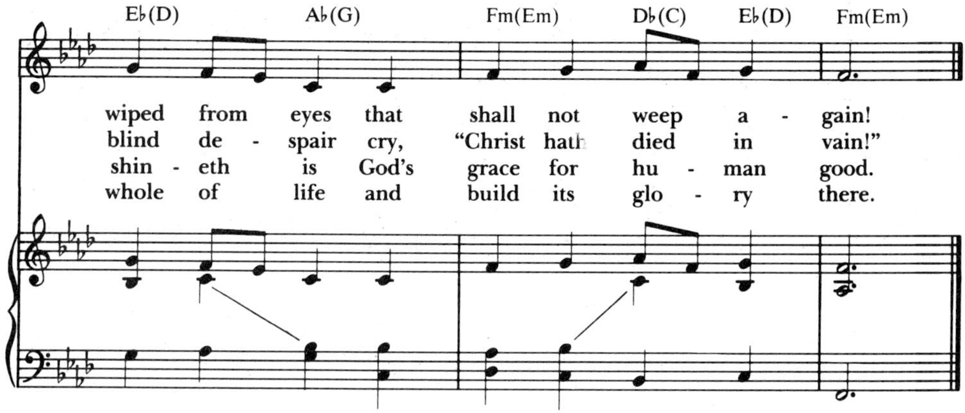
E♭(D) A♭(G) Fm(Em) D♭(C) E♭(D) Fm(Em)
wiped from eyes that shall not weep a - gain!
blind de - spair cry, "Christ hath died in vain!"
shin - eth is God's grace for hu - man good.
whole of life and build its glo - ry there.

Fm(capo 1, Em). Keyboard and guitar should not sound together. Another harmonization, 9.
Alternative tune: *Sancta Civitas,* 582.

Words: Walter Russell Bowie (1882-1969), alt.
Music: *Morning Song,* melody att. Elkanah Kelsay Dare (1782-1826); harm. Thomas Foster (b. 1938)

♩=92
86. 86. 86

Christian Responsibility 584

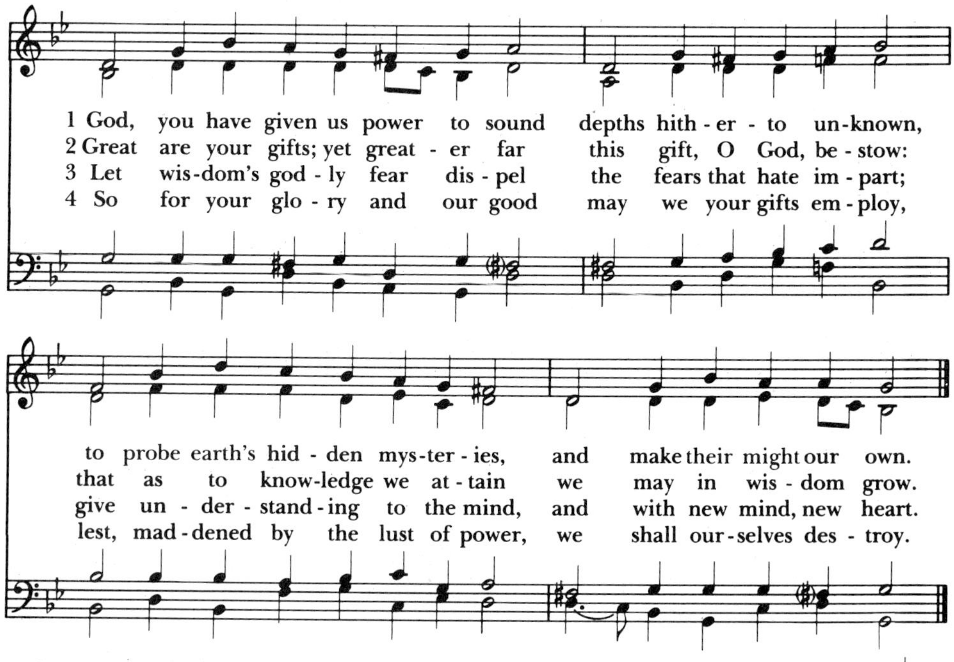
1 God, you have given us power to sound depths hith - er - to un - known,
2 Great are your gifts; yet great - er far this gift, O God, be - stow:
3 Let wis - dom's god - ly fear dis - pel the fears that hate im - part;
4 So for your glo - ry and our good may we your gifts em - ploy,
to probe earth's hid - den mys - ter - ies, and make their might our own.
that as to know - ledge we at - tain we may in wis - dom grow.
give un - der - stand - ing to the mind, and with new mind, new heart.
lest, mad - dened by the lust of power, we shall our - selves des - troy.

Words: George Wallace Briggs (1875-1959), alt.
Music: *Culross,* melody from *The Psalmes of David in Prose and Meeter,* 1635

♩=88
CM

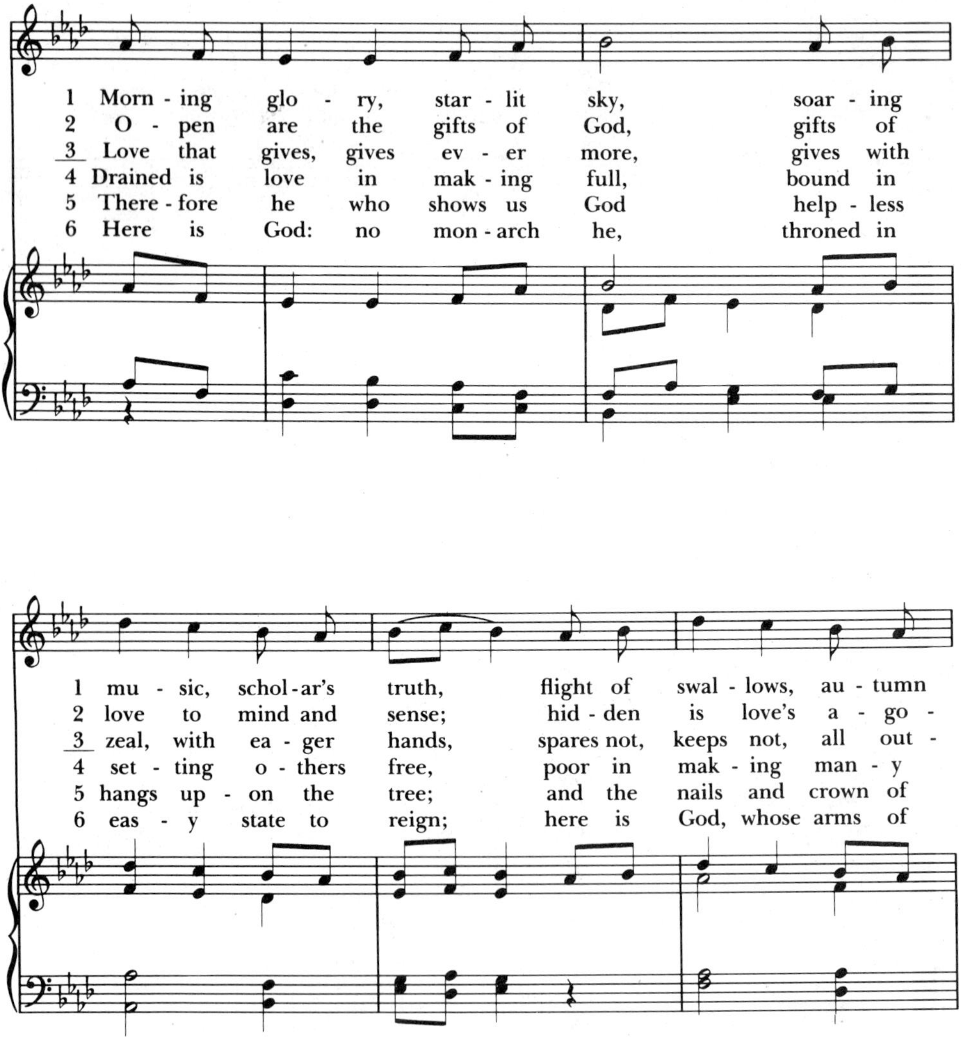
1 Morn - ing glo - ry, star - lit sky, soar - ing
2 O - pen are the gifts of God, gifts of
3 Love that gives, gives ev - er more, gives with
4 Drained is love in mak - ing full, bound in
5 There - fore he who shows us God help - less
6 Here is God: no mon - arch he, throned in
1 mu - sic, schol - ar's truth, flight of swal - lows, au - tumn
2 love to mind and sense; hid - den is love's a - go -
3 zeal, with ea - ger hands, spares not, keeps not, all out -
4 set - ting o - thers free, poor in mak - ing man - y
5 hangs up - on the tree; and the nails and crown of
6 eas - y state to reign; here is God, whose arms of

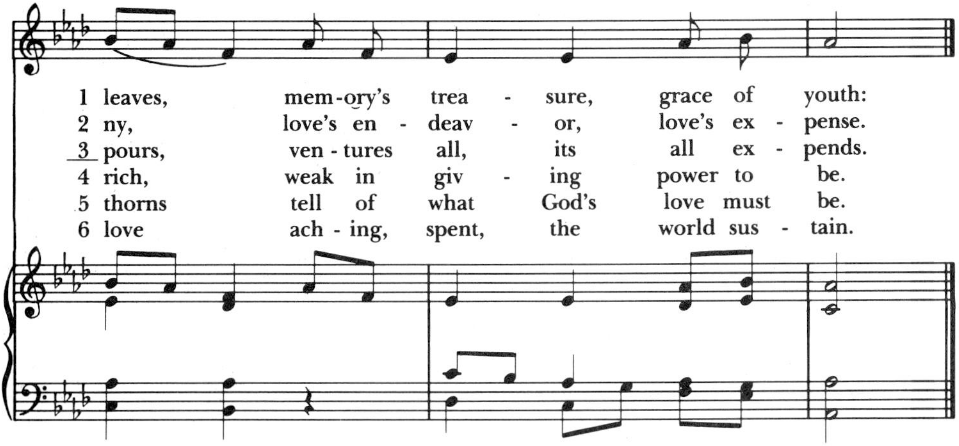
1 leaves, mem-ory's trea - sure, grace of youth:
2 ny, love's en - deav - or, love's ex - pense.
3 pours, ven-tures all, its all ex - pends.
4 rich, weak in giv - ing power to be.
5 thorns tell of what God's love must be.
6 love ach-ing, spent, the world sus - tain.

Words: W. H. Vanstone (b. 1923)
Music: *Bingham,* Dorothy Howell Sheets (b. 1915)

♩=84
77. 77

Alternative accompaniment

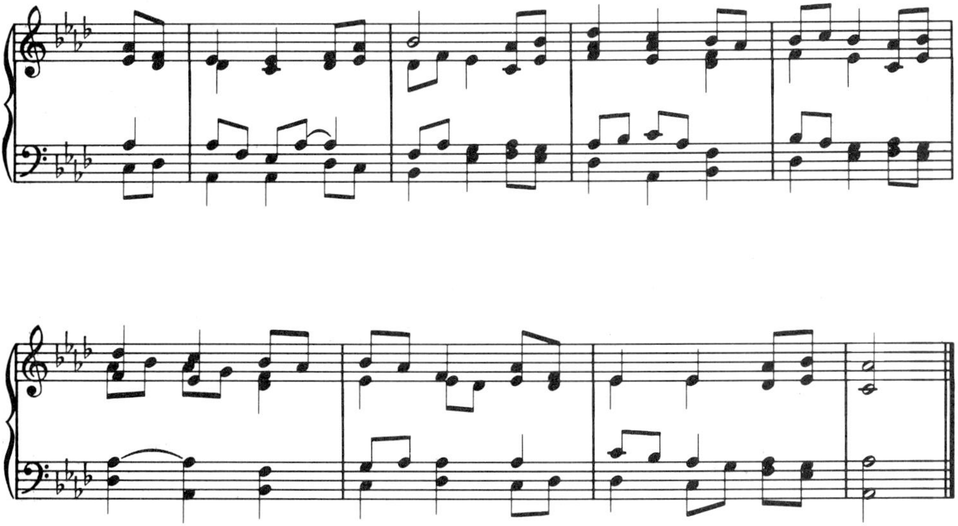

Music: *Bingham,* Dorothy Howell Sheets (b. 1915)

♩=84

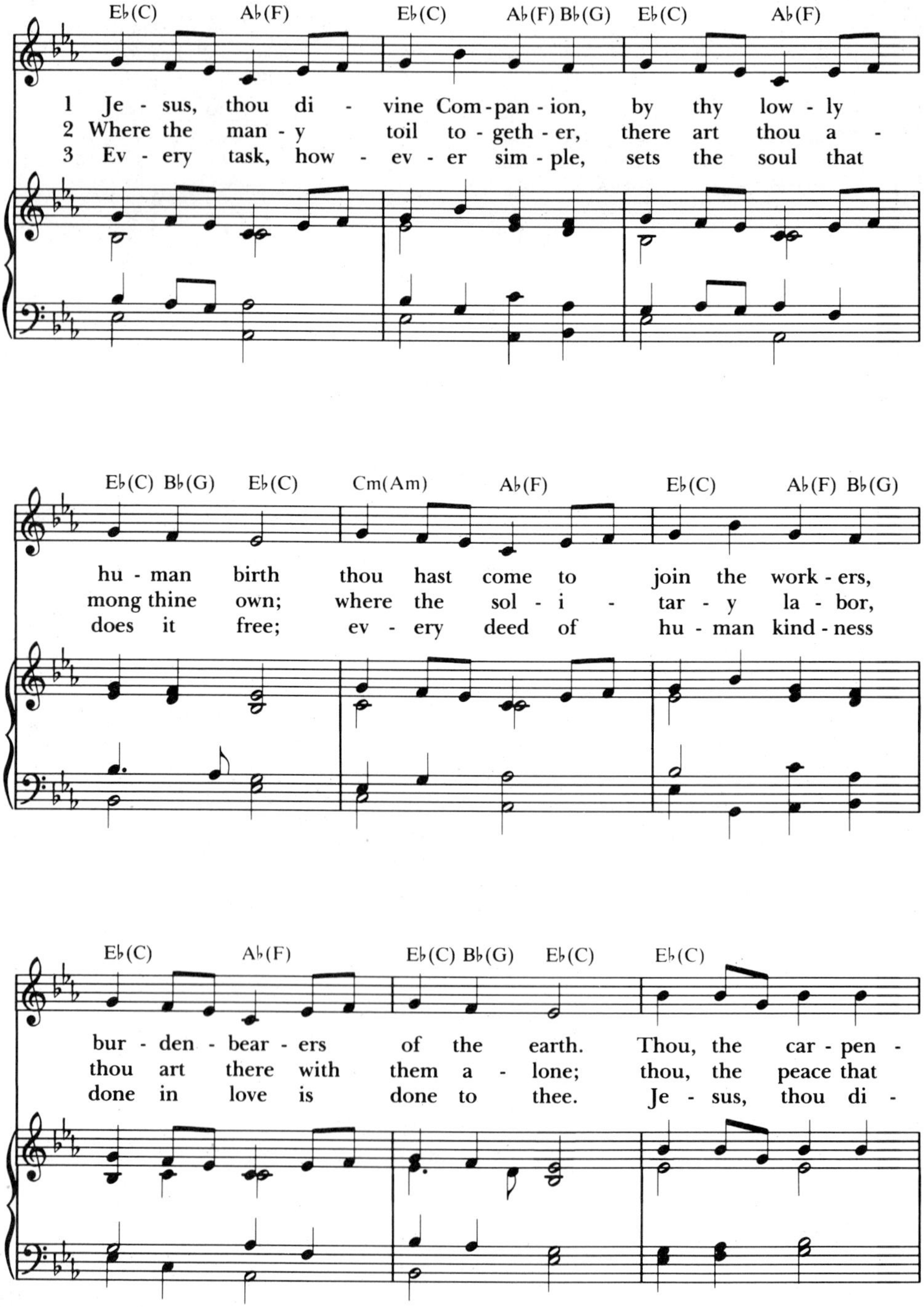
E♭(C) A♭(F) E♭(C) A♭(F) B♭(G) E♭(C) A♭(F)
1 Je - sus, thou di - vine Com - pan - ion, by thy low - ly
2 Where the man - y toil to - geth - er, there art thou a -
3 Ev - ery task, how - ev - er sim - ple, sets the soul that
E♭(C) B♭(G) E♭(C) Cm(Am) A♭(F) E♭(C) A♭(F) B♭(G)
hu - man birth thou hast come to join the work - ers,
mong thine own; where the sol - i - tar - y la - bor,
does it free; ev - ery deed of hu - man kind - ness
E♭(C) A♭(F) E♭(C) B♭(G) E♭(C) E♭(C)
bur - den - bear - ers of the earth. Thou, the car - pen -
thou art there with them a - lone; thou, the peace that
done in love is done to thee. Je - sus, thou di -

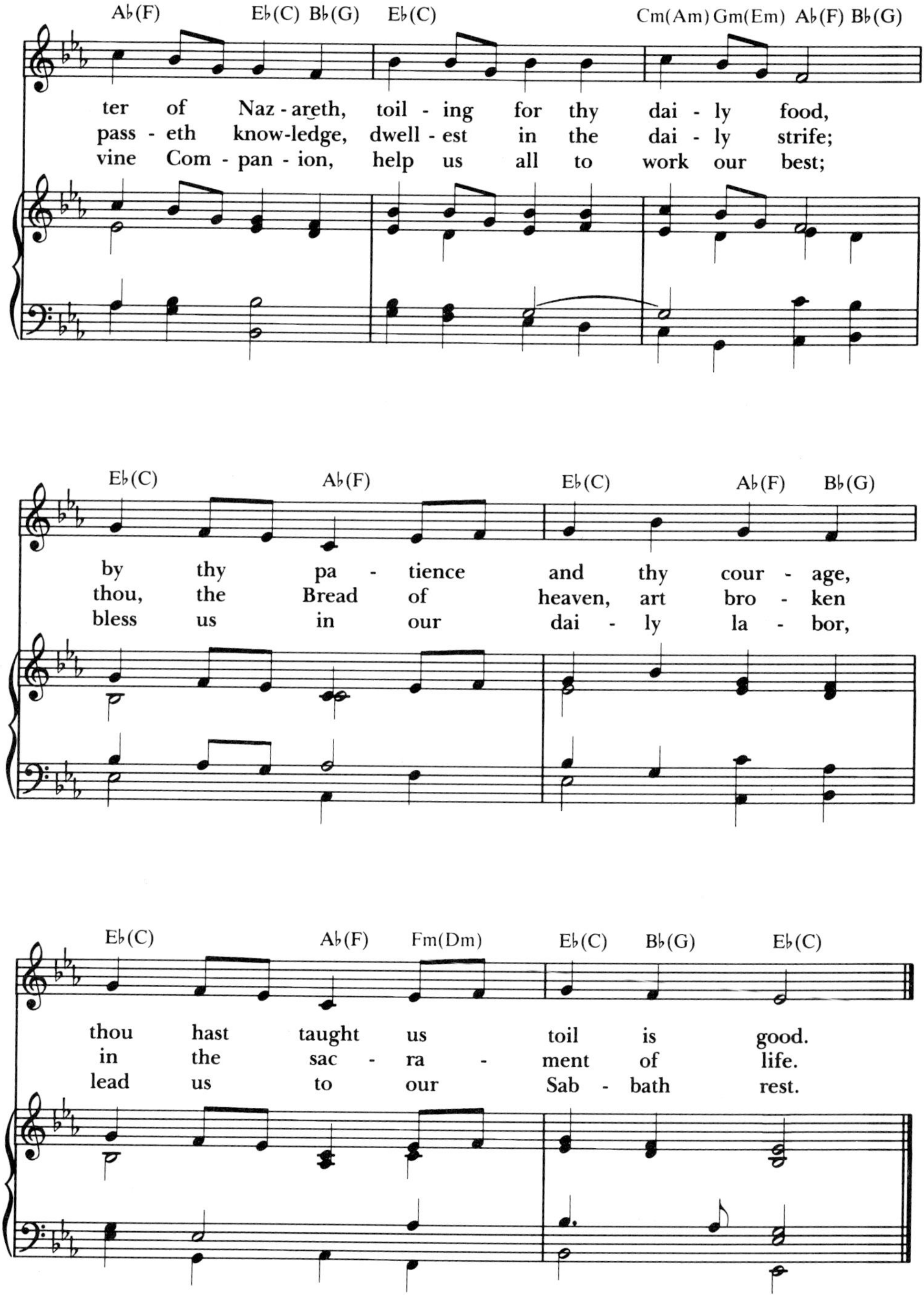
A♭(F) E♭(C) B♭(G) E♭(C) Cm(Am) Gm(Em) A♭(F) B♭(G)
ter of Naz-areth, toil-ing for thy dai-ly food,
pass-eth know-ledge, dwell-est in the dai-ly strife;
vine Com-pan-ion, help us all to work our best;
E♭(C) A♭(F) E♭(C) A♭(F) B♭(G)
by thy pa-tience and thy cour-age,
thou, the Bread of heaven, art bro-ken
bless us in our dai-ly la-bor,
E♭(C) A♭(F) Fm(Dm) E♭(C) B♭(G) E♭(C)
thou hast taught us toil is good.
in the sac-ra-ment of life.
lead us to our Sab-bath rest.

E♭ (capo 3, C).

Words: Henry Van Dyke (1852-1933), alt.
Music: *Pleading Savior*, melody from *The Christian Lyre*, 1830; harm. Richard Proulx (b. 1937)

𝅗𝅥 = 50
87. 87 D

1 Our Fa - ther, by whose Name all fa - ther-hood is known,
2 O Christ, thy - self a child with - in an earth - ly home,
3 O Spi - rit, who dost bind our hearts in u - ni - ty,
who dost in love pro - claim each fam - i - ly thine own,
with heart still un - de - filed, thou didst to man-hood come;
who teach-est us to find the love from self set free,
bless thou all par - ents, guard - ing well, with con-stant love as
our chil-dren bless, in ev - ery place, that they may all be -
in all our hearts such love in - crease, that ev - ery home, by
sen - ti - nel, the homes in which thy peo - ple dwell.
hold thy face, and know-ing thee may grow in grace.
this re - lease, may be the dwell-ing place of peace.

Words: F. Bland Tucker (1895-1984)
Music: *Rhosymedre,* John Edwards (1806-1885)

𝅗𝅥=50
66. 66. 888

1 Al-might-y God, your word is
2 Let not our self - ish - ness and
3 Let not the world's de - ceit - ful
cast like seed up - on the ground, now let the dew of heaven de -
hate this ho - ly seed re - move, but give it root in ev - ery
cares the ris - ing plant des - troy, but let it yield a hun-dred -
scend and right-eous fruits a - bound.
heart to bring forth fruits of love.
fold the fruits of peace and (joy.) joy.
1-2
Final Ending

Alternative tune: *Walden,* 589.

Words: John Cawood (1775-1852), alt.
Music: *Call Street,* Roy Henry Johnson (b. 1933)

♩=60-72
CM

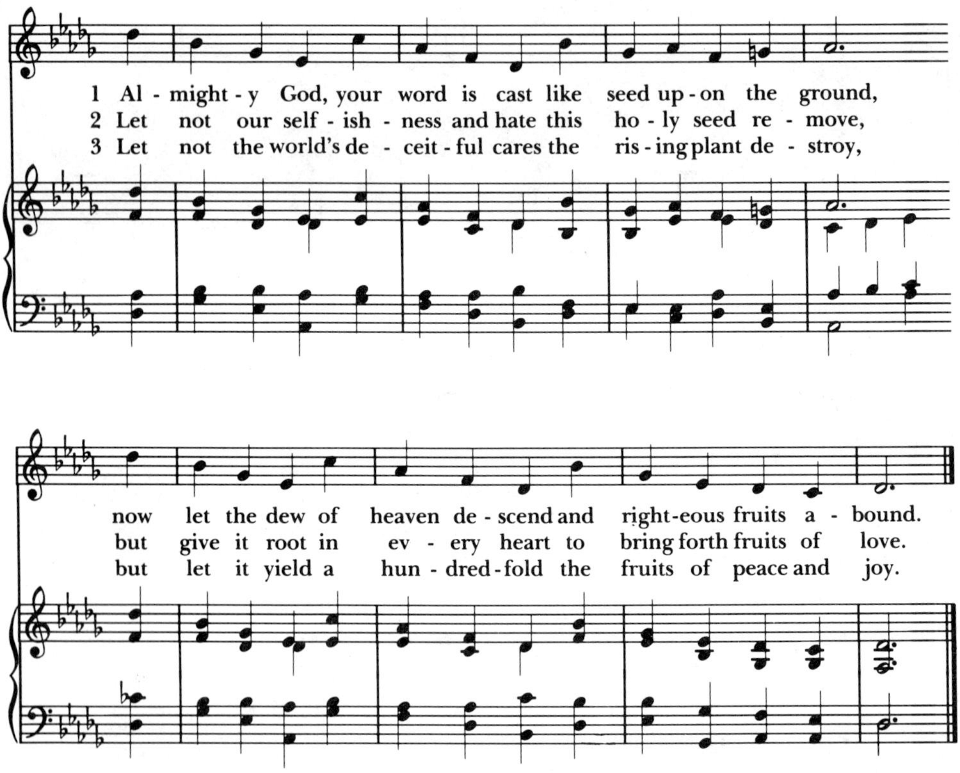
1 Al - might - y God, your word is cast like seed up - on the ground,
2 Let not our self - ish - ness and hate this ho - ly seed re - move,
3 Let not the world's de - ceit - ful cares the ris - ing plant de - stroy,
now let the dew of heaven de - scend and right - eous fruits a - bound.
but give it root in ev - ery heart to bring forth fruits of love.
but let it yield a hun - dred - fold the fruits of peace and joy.

Alternative tune: *Call Street,* 588.

Words: John Cawood (1775-1852), alt.
Music: *Walden,* Jane Manton Marshall (b. 1924)

♩=80
CM

590

Christian Responsibility

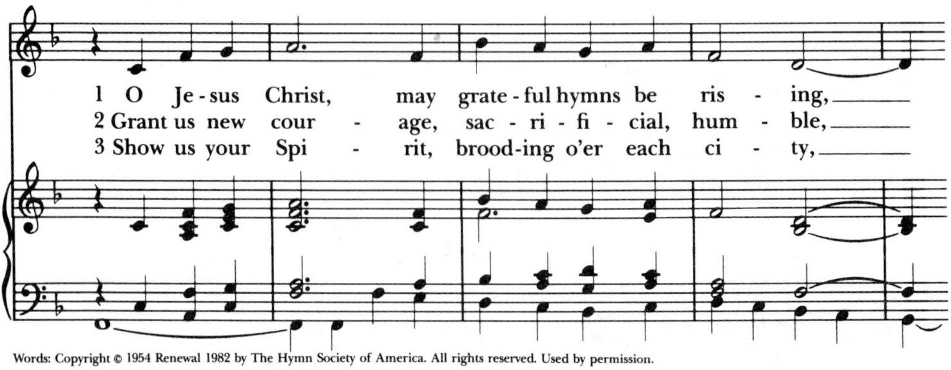
1 O Je - sus Christ, may grate - ful hymns be ris - ing,
2 Grant us new cour - age, sac - ri - fi - cial, hum - ble,
3 Show us your Spi - rit, brood - ing o'er each ci - ty,

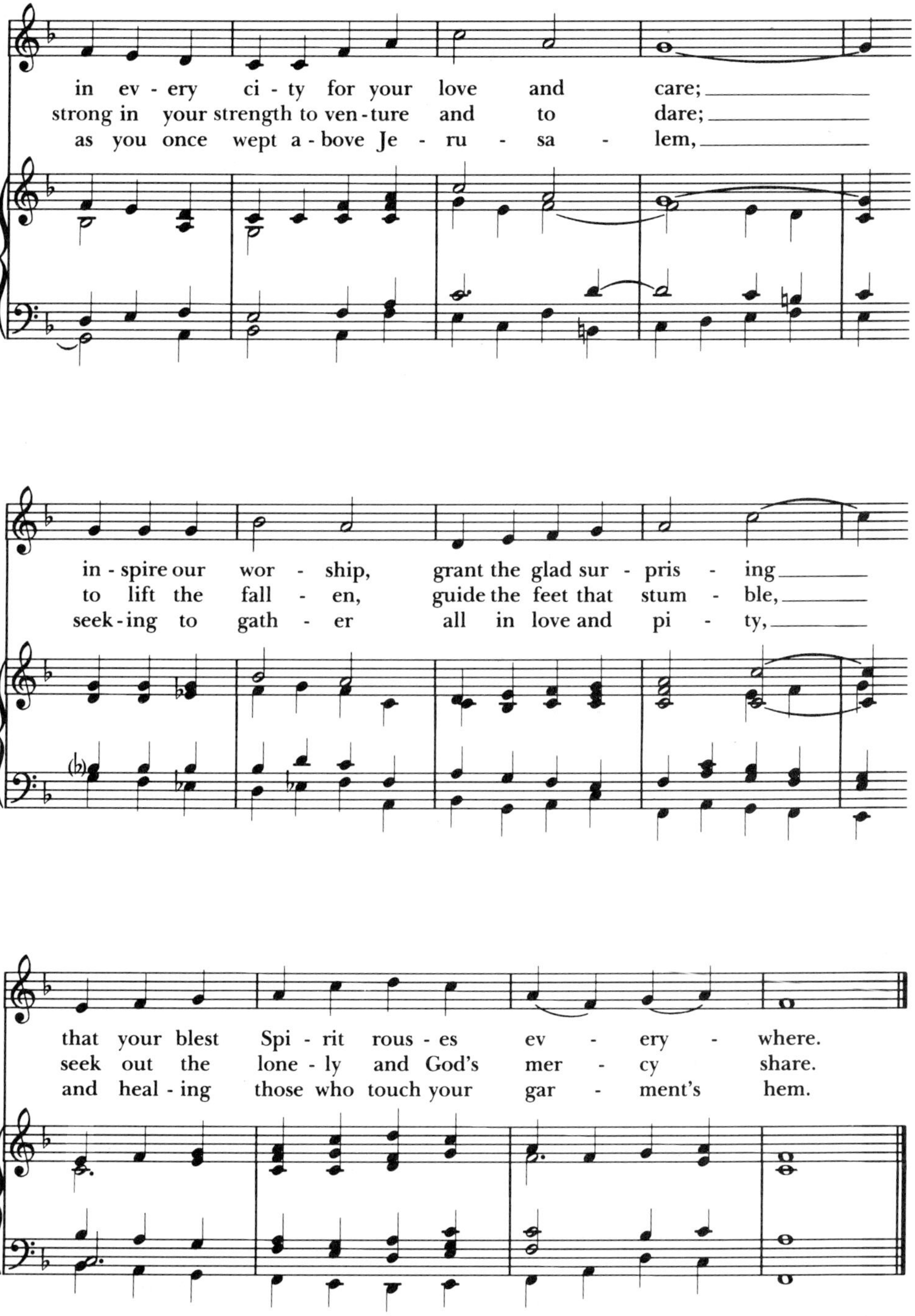
in ev - ery ci - ty for your love and care;
strong in your strength to ven - ture and to dare;
as you once wept a - bove Je - ru - sa - lem,
in - spire our wor - ship, grant the glad sur - pris - ing
to lift the fall - en, guide the feet that stum - ble,
seek - ing to gath - er all in love and pi - ty,
that your blest Spi - rit rous - es ev - ery - where.
seek out the lone - ly and God's mer - cy share.
and heal - ing those who touch your gar - ment's hem.

Words: Bradford Gray Webster (b. 1898), alt.
Music: *Charterhouse,* David Evans (1874-1948)

𝅗𝅥 = 50
11 10. 11 10

1 O God of earth and al - tar, bow down and hear our cry,
2 From all that ter - ror teach - es, from lies of tongue and pen,
3 Tie in a liv - ing teth - er the prince and priest and thrall,
our earth - ly ru - lers fal - ter, our peo - ple drift and die;
from all the eas - y speech - es that com-fort cru - el men,
bind all our lives to - geth - er, smite us and save us all;
the walls of gold en - tomb us, the swords of scorn di - vide,
from sale and prof - a - na - tion of hon - or, and the sword,
in ire and ex - ul - ta - tion a - flame with faith, and free,

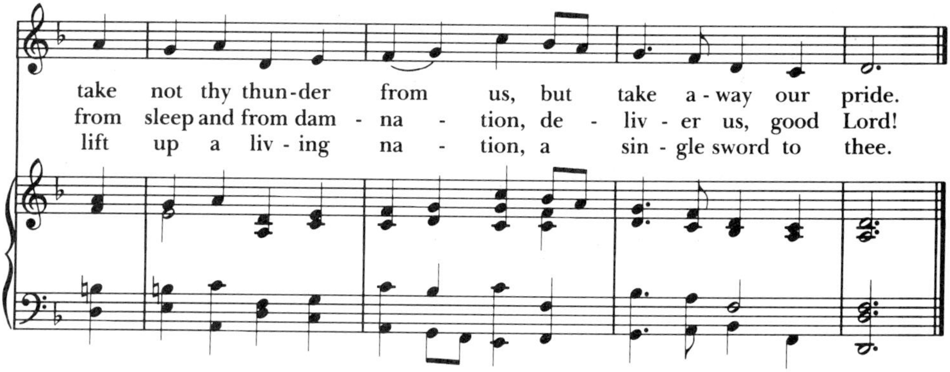
take not thy thun-der from us, but take a-way our pride.
from sleep and from dam - na - tion, de - liv - er us, good Lord!
lift up a liv-ing na - tion, a sin-gle sword to thee.

Alternative tune: *Llangloffan,* 607.

Words: Gilbert Keith Chesterton (1874-1936)
Music: *King's Lynn,* English melody; adapt. and harm. Ralph Vaughan Williams (1872-1958)

𝅗𝅥=60
76. 76. D

Christian Responsibility 592

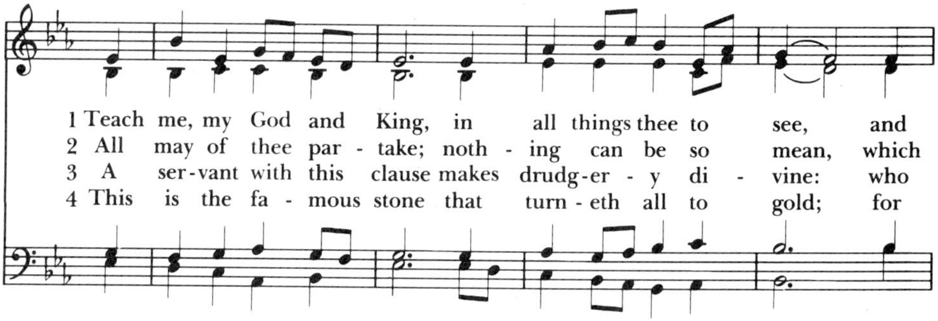
1 Teach me, my God and King, in all things thee to see, and
2 All may of thee par - take; noth - ing can be so mean, which
3 A ser-vant with this clause makes drudg-er - y di - vine: who
4 This is the fa - mous stone that turn-eth all to gold; for

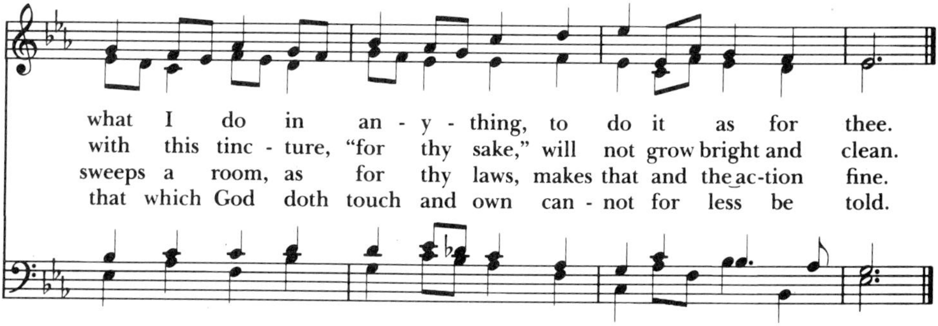
what I do in an - y - thing, to do it as for thee.
with this tinc - ture, "for thy sake," will not grow bright and clean.
sweeps a room, as for thy laws, makes that and the ac-tion fine.
that which God doth touch and own can - not for less be told.

Words: George Herbert (1593-1633)
Music: *Carlisle,* Charles Lockhart (1745-1815)

𝅗𝅥=88
SM

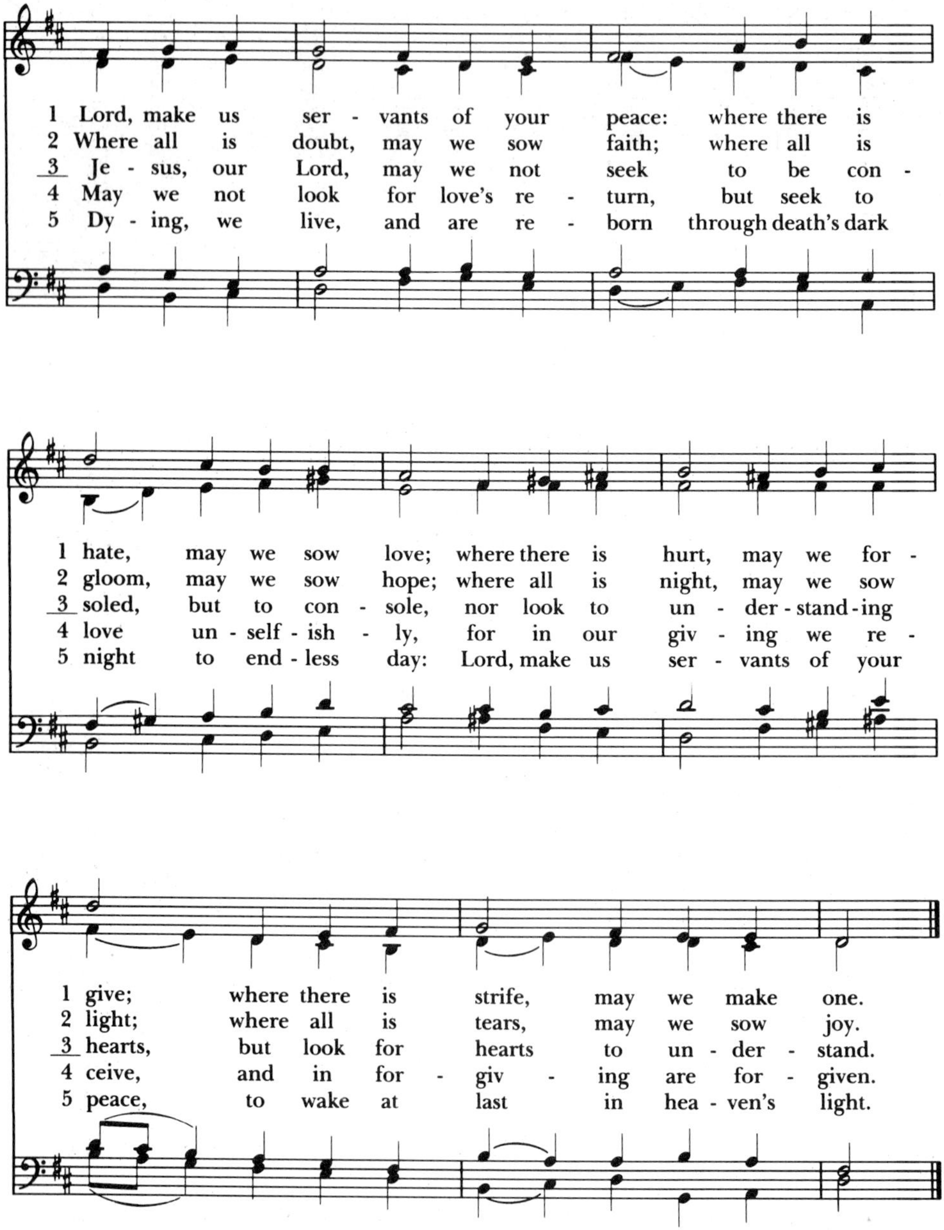
1 Lord, make us ser - vants of your peace: where there is
2 Where all is doubt, may we sow faith; where all is
3 Je - sus, our Lord, may we not seek to be con -
4 May we not look for love's re - turn, but seek to
5 Dy - ing, we live, and are re - born through death's dark
1 hate, may we sow love; where there is hurt, may we for -
2 gloom, may we sow hope; where all is night, may we sow
3 soled, but to con - sole, nor look to un - der - stand - ing
4 love un - self - ish - ly, for in our giv - ing we re -
5 night to end - less day: Lord, make us ser - vants of your
1 give; where there is strife, may we make one.
2 light; where all is tears, may we sow joy.
3 hearts, but look for hearts to un - der - stand.
4 ceive, and in for - giv - ing are for - given.
5 peace, to wake at last in hea - ven's light.

This music in D♭, 649.

Words: James Quinn (b. 1919), based on prayer att. Francis of Assisi (1182-1226)
Music: *Dickinson College*, Lee Hastings Bristol, Jr. (1923-1979)

♩= 108
LM

1 God of grace and God of glo - ry, on thy peo - ple pour thy power;
2 Lo! the hosts of e - vil round us scorn thy Christ, as - sail his ways!
3 Cure thy chil - dren's war - ring mad - ness, bend our pride to thy con - trol;
4 Save us from weak res - ig - na - tion to the e - vils we de - plore;
crown thine an - cient Church's sto - ry; bring her bud to glo - rious flower.
From the fears that long have bound us free our hearts to faith and praise:
shame our wan - ton, self - ish glad - ness, rich in things and poor in soul.
let the gift of thy sal - va - tion be our glo - ry ev - er - more.
Grant us wis - dom, grant us cour - age, for the fac - ing of this
grant us wis - dom, grant us cour - age for the liv - ing of these
Grant us wis - dom, grant us cour - age, lest we miss thy king-dom's
Grant us wis - dom, grant us cour - age, serv - ing thee whom we a -
hour, for the fac - ing of this hour.
days, for the liv - ing of these days.
goal, lest we miss thy king - dom's goal.
dore, serv - ing thee whom we a - dore.

Alternative tune: *Mannheim,* 595.

Words: Harry Emerson Fosdick (1878-1969), alt.
Music: *Cwm Rhondda,* John Hughes (1873-1932)

♩=96
87. 87. 877

1 God of grace and God of glo - ry, on thy peo - ple
2 Lo! the hosts of e - vil round us scorn thy Christ, as -
3 Cure thy chil - dren's war - ring mad - ness, bend our pride to
4 Save us from weak res - ig - na - tion to the e - vils
pour thy power; crown thine an - cient Church's sto - ry;
sail his ways! From the fears that long have bound us
thy con - trol; shame our wan - ton, self - ish glad - ness,
we de - plore; let the gift of thy sal - va - tion
bring her bud to glo - rious flower. Grant us wis - dom,
free our hearts to faith and praise: grant us wis - dom,
rich in things and poor in soul. Grant us wis - dom,
be our glo - ry ev - er - more. Grant us wis - dom,
grant us cour - age, for the fac - ing of this hour.
grant us cour - age for the liv - ing of these days.
grant us cour - age, lest we miss thy king - dom's goal.
grant us cour - age, serv - ing thee whom we a - dore.

Alternative tune: *Cwm Rhondda,* 594.

Words: Harry Emerson Fosdick (1878-1969), alt.
Music: *Mannheim,* melody from *Vierstimmiges Choralbuch,* 1847; harm. Lowell Mason (1792-1872)

𝅗𝅥=52
87. 87. 87

1 Judge e - ter - nal, throned in splen - dor, Lord of lords and
2 Still the wea - ry folk are pin - ing for the hour that
3 Crown, O God, thine own en - deav - or; cleave our dark - ness
King of kings, with thy liv - ing fire of judg - ment
brings re - lease, and the ci - ty's crowd - ed clang - or
with thy sword; feed all those who do not know thee
purge this land of bit - ter things; sol - ace all its
cries a - loud for sin to cease; and the home - steads
with the rich - ness of thy word; cleanse the bo - dy
wide do - min - ion with the heal - ing of thy wings.
and the wood-lands plead in si - lence for their peace.
of this na - tion through the glo - ry of the Lord.

Words: Henry Scott Holland (1847-1918), alt.
Music: *Komm, o komm, du Geist des Lebens,* melody from *Neu-vermehrtes und zu Ubung Christl. Gottseligkeit eingerichtetes Meiningisches Gesangbuch,* 1693

𝅗𝅥 = 50
87. 87. 87

Introduction
1 O day of peace that dim-ly shines through all our
2 Then shall the wolf dwell with the lamb, nor shall the
hopes and prayers and dreams, guide us to jus - tice, truth, and
fierce de - vour the small; as beasts and cat - tle calm - ly
love, de - liv - ered from our self - ish schemes. May swords of
graze, a lit - tle child shall lead them all. Then en - e -

hate fall from our hands, our hearts from en - - vy find re -
mies shall learn to love, all crea - tures find their true ac -
lease, till by God's grace our war - ring world shall see Christ's
cord; the hope of peace shall be ful - filled, for all the
1
prom-ised reign of peace.
earth shall know the (Lord.)
Interlude
Final Ending
Lord.

Words: Carl P. Daw, Jr. (b. 1944)
Music: *Jerusalem,* Charles Hubert Hastings Parry (1848-1918); arr. Janet Wyatt (b. 1934)

♩=48
LMD

1 Lord Christ, when first thou cam'st to earth, up - on a cross they
2 O awe - ful Love, which found no room in life where sin de -
3 New ad - vent of the love of Christ, shall we a - gain re -
4 O wound-ed hands of Je - sus, build in us thy new cre -
bound thee, and mocked thy sav - ing king-ship then
nied thee, and, doomed to death, must bring to doom
fuse thee, till in the night of hate and war
a - tion; our pride is dust, our vaunt is stilled,
by thorns with which they crowned thee: and still our wrongs
the powers which cru - ci - fied thee, till not a stone
we per - ish as we lose thee? From old un - faith
we wait thy rev - e - la - tion: O love that tri -

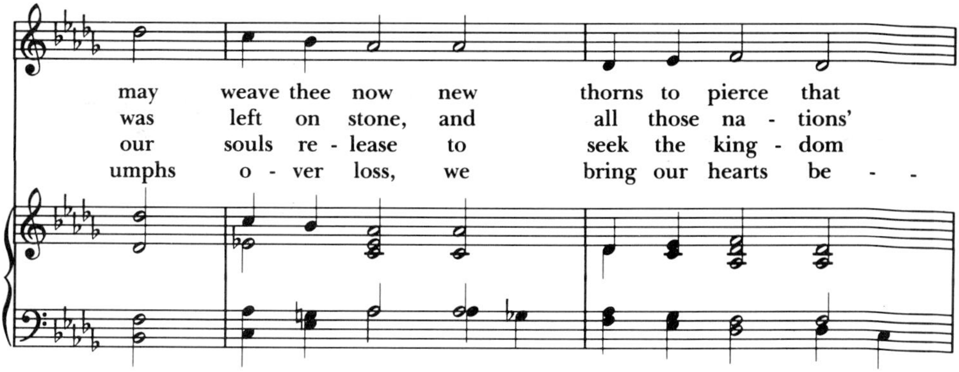
may weave thee now new thorns to pierce that
was left on stone, and all those na - tions'
our souls re - lease to seek the king - dom
umphs o - ver loss, we bring our hearts be - -

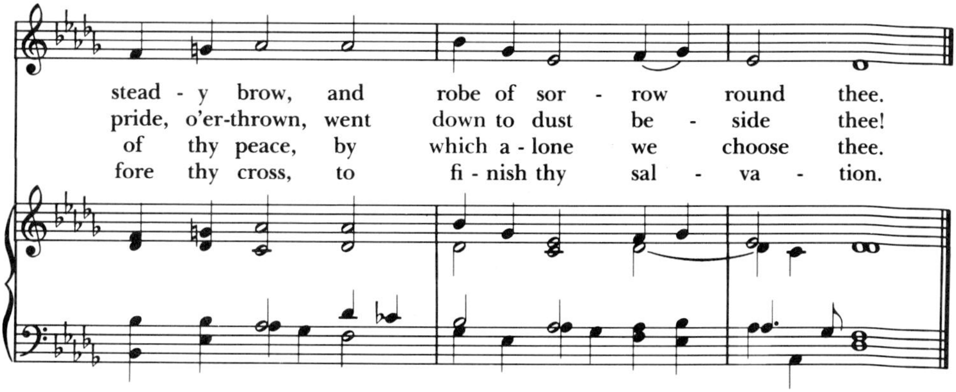
stead - y brow, and robe of sor - row round thee.
pride, o'er-thrown, went down to dust be - side thee!
of thy peace, by which a - lone we choose thee.
fore thy cross, to fi - nish thy sal - va - tion.

This music in D, 408.

Words: Walter Russell Bowie (1882-1969), alt.
Music: *Mit Freuden zart,* melody from "Une pastourelle gentille," 1529; adapt. *Pseaumes cinquante de David,* 1547, and *Kirchengeseng darinnen die Heubtartickel des Christlichen Glaubens gefasset,* 1566; harm. Ralph Vaughan Williams (1872-1958), after Heinrich Reimann (19th cent.)

𝅗𝅥 = 62
87. 87. 887

Introduction
1 Lift ev-ery voice and sing till earth and hea - ven ring, ring with the
2 Ston - y the road we trod, bit - ter the chas-tening rod, felt in the
3 God of our wea - ry years, God of our si - lent tears, thou who hast

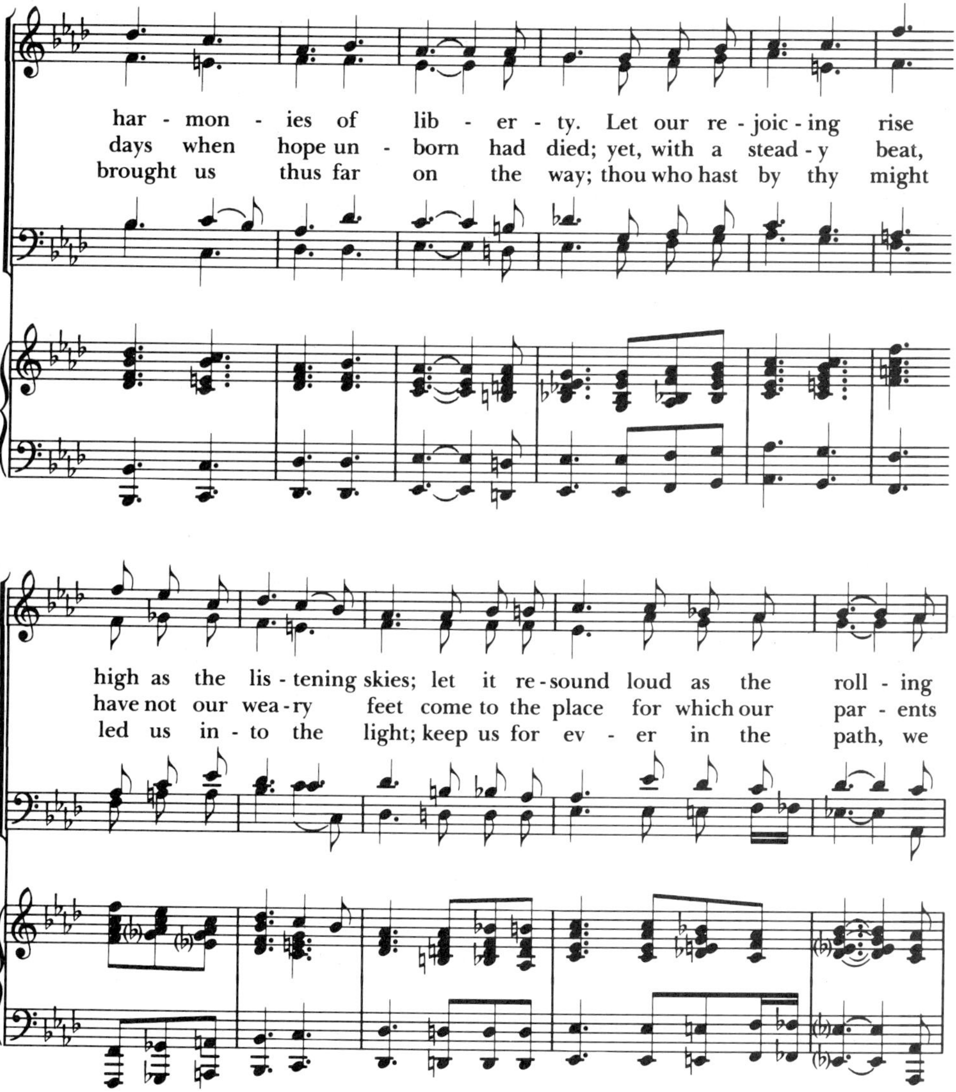
har - mon - ies of lib - er - ty. Let our re - joic - ing rise
days when hope un - born had died; yet, with a stead - y beat,
brought us thus far on the way; thou who hast by thy might
high as the lis - tening skies; let it re - sound loud as the roll - ing
have not our wea - ry feet come to the place for which our par - ents
led us in - to the light; keep us for ev - er in the path, we

sea. Sing a song full of the faith that the dark past has
sighed? We have come o - ver a way that with tears has been
pray. Lest our feet stray from the pla - ces, our God, where we
taught us; sing a song full of the hope that the pres-ent has
wa - tered; we have come, tread-ing our path through the blood of the
met thee; lest, our hearts drunk with the wine of the world we for -

brought us; fac-ing the ris - ing sun of our new
slaugh - tered, out from the gloom - y past, till now we
get thee; sha-dowed be - neath thy hand may we for
day be - gun, let us march on, till vic - to - ry is won.
stand at last where the white gleam of our bright star is cast.
ev - er stand, true to our God, true to our na - tive land.

Words: James Weldon Johnson (1871-1938)
Music: *Lift Every Voice,* J. Rosamond Johnson (1873-1954)

♩. = 80
Irr.

600

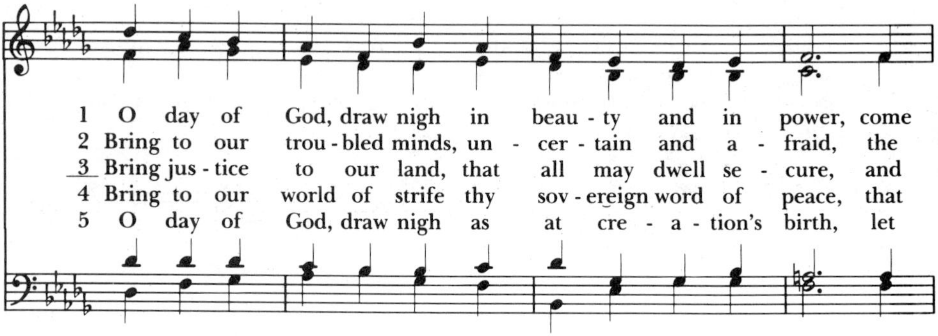
1 O day of God, draw nigh in beau - ty and in power, come
2 Bring to our trou - bled minds, un - cer - tain and a - fraid, the
3 Bring jus - tice to our land, that all may dwell se - cure, and
4 Bring to our world of strife thy sov - ereign word of peace, that
5 O day of God, draw nigh as at cre - a - tion's birth, let

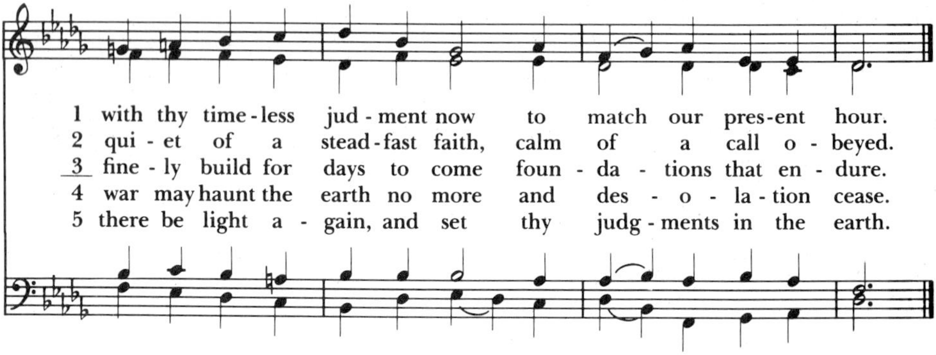
1 with thy time - less jud - ment now to match our pres - ent hour.
2 qui - et of a stead - fast faith, calm of a call o - beyed.
3 fine - ly build for days to come foun - da - tions that en - dure.
4 war may haunt the earth no more and des - o - la - tion cease.
5 there be light a - gain, and set thy judg - ments in the earth.

Alternative tune: *St. Michael,* 601.

Words: Robert Balgarnie Young Scott (b. 1899)
Music: *Bellwoods,* James Hopkirk (1908-1972)

𝅗𝅥=58
SM

601

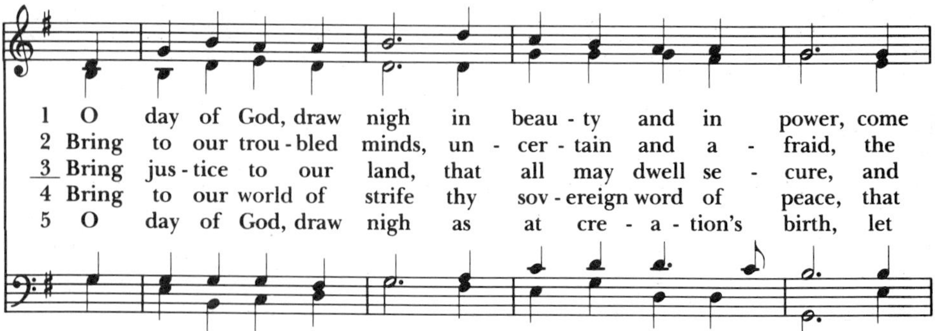
1 O day of God, draw nigh in beau - ty and in power, come
2 Bring to our trou - bled minds, un - cer - tain and a - fraid, the
3 Bring jus - tice to our land, that all may dwell se - cure, and
4 Bring to our world of strife thy sov - ereign word of peace, that
5 O day of God, draw nigh as at cre - a - tion's birth, let

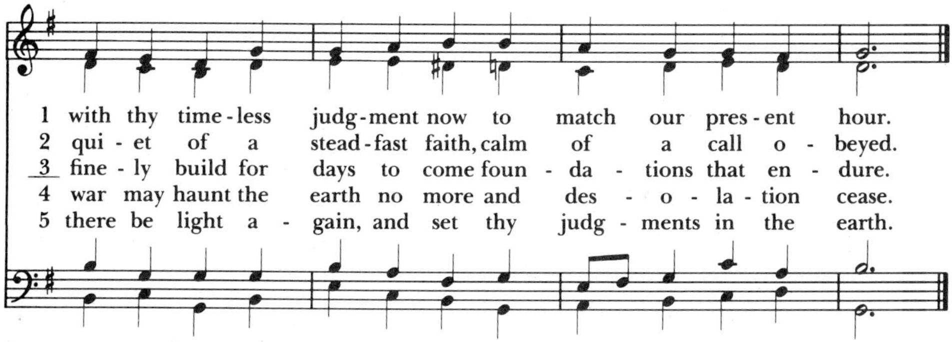
1 with thy time-less judg-ment now to match our pres-ent hour.
2 qui-et of a stead-fast faith, calm of a call o-beyed.
3 fine-ly build for days to come foun-da-tions that en-dure.
4 war may haunt the earth no more and des-o-la-tion cease.
5 there be light a-gain, and set thy judg-ments in the earth.

Alternative tune: *Bellwoods,* 600.

Words: Robert Balgarnie Young Scott (b. 1899) 𝅗𝅥=54
Music: *St. Michael,* Louis Bourgeois (1510?-1561?); harm. William Henry Monk (1823-1889) SM

Christian Responsibility 602

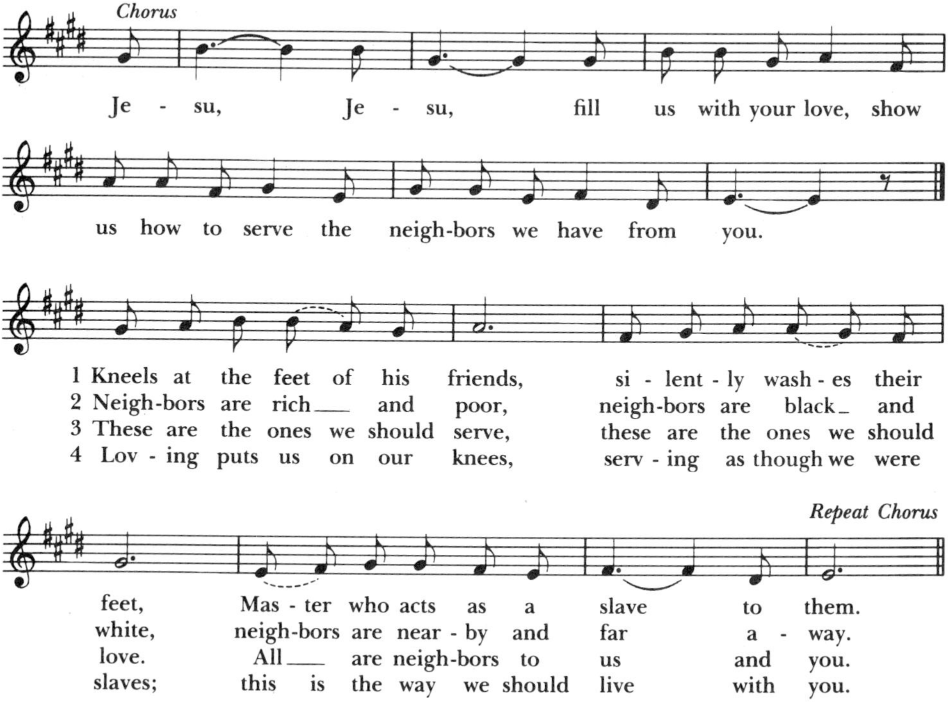
Chorus
Je-su, Je-su, fill us with your love, show us how to serve the neigh-bors we have from you.
1 Kneels at the feet of his friends, si-lent-ly wash-es their feet, Mas-ter who acts as a slave to them.
2 Neigh-bors are rich ___ and poor, neigh-bors are black _ and white, neigh-bors are near-by and far a-way.
3 These are the ones we should serve, these are the ones we should love. All ___ are neigh-bors to us and you.
4 Lov-ing puts us on our knees, serv-ing as though we were slaves; this is the way we should live with you.
Repeat Chorus

Words: Ghanaian; tr. Thomas Stevenson Colvin (b. 1925), alt. 𝅗𝅥.=72
Music: *Chereponi [Jesu, Jesu],* Ghanaian folk song; adapt. Thomas Stevenson Colvin (b. 1925) Irr.

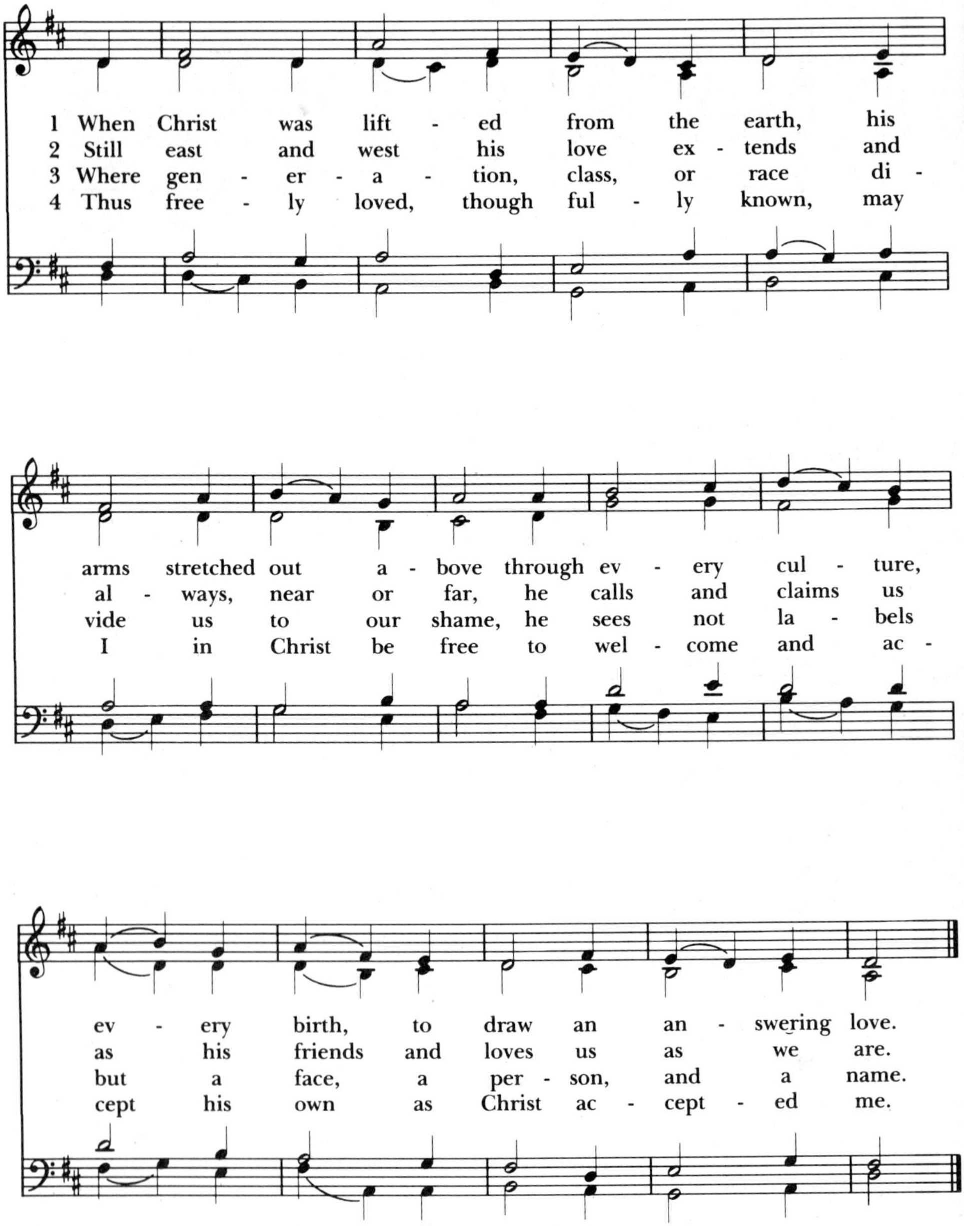
1 When Christ was lift - ed from the earth, his
2 Still east and west his love ex - tends and
3 Where gen - er - a - tion, class, or race di -
4 Thus free - ly loved, though ful - ly known, may
arms stretched out a - bove through ev - ery cul - ture,
al - ways, near or far, he calls and claims us
vide us to our shame, he sees not la - bels
I in Christ be free to wel - come and ac -
ev - ery birth, to draw an an - swering love.
as his friends and loves us as we are.
but a face, a per - son, and a name.
cept his own as Christ ac - cept - ed me.

Alternative tune: *San Rocco,* 604.

Words: Brian A. Wren (b. 1936)
Music: *St. Botolph,* Gordon Slater (1896-1979)

𝅗𝅥. = 40
CM

1 When Christ was lift - ed from the earth, his arms stretched out a - bove through ev - ery cul - ture, ev - ery birth, to draw an an - swering love. (love.)
2 Still east and west his love ex - tends and al - ways, near or far, he calls and claims us as his friends and loves us as we are. (are.)
3 Where gen - er - a - tion, class, or race di - vide us to our shame, he sees not la - bels but a face, a per - son, and a name. (name.)
4 Thus free - ly loved, though ful - ly known, may I in Christ be free to wel - come and ac - cept his own as Christ ac - cept - ed (me.) me.
Optional interlude between stanzas
Ending

This music in D♭, 253. Alternative tune: *St. Botolph,* 603.

Words: Brian A. Wren (b. 1936)
Music: *San Rocco,* Derek Williams (b. 1945)

𝅗𝅥 = 48
CM

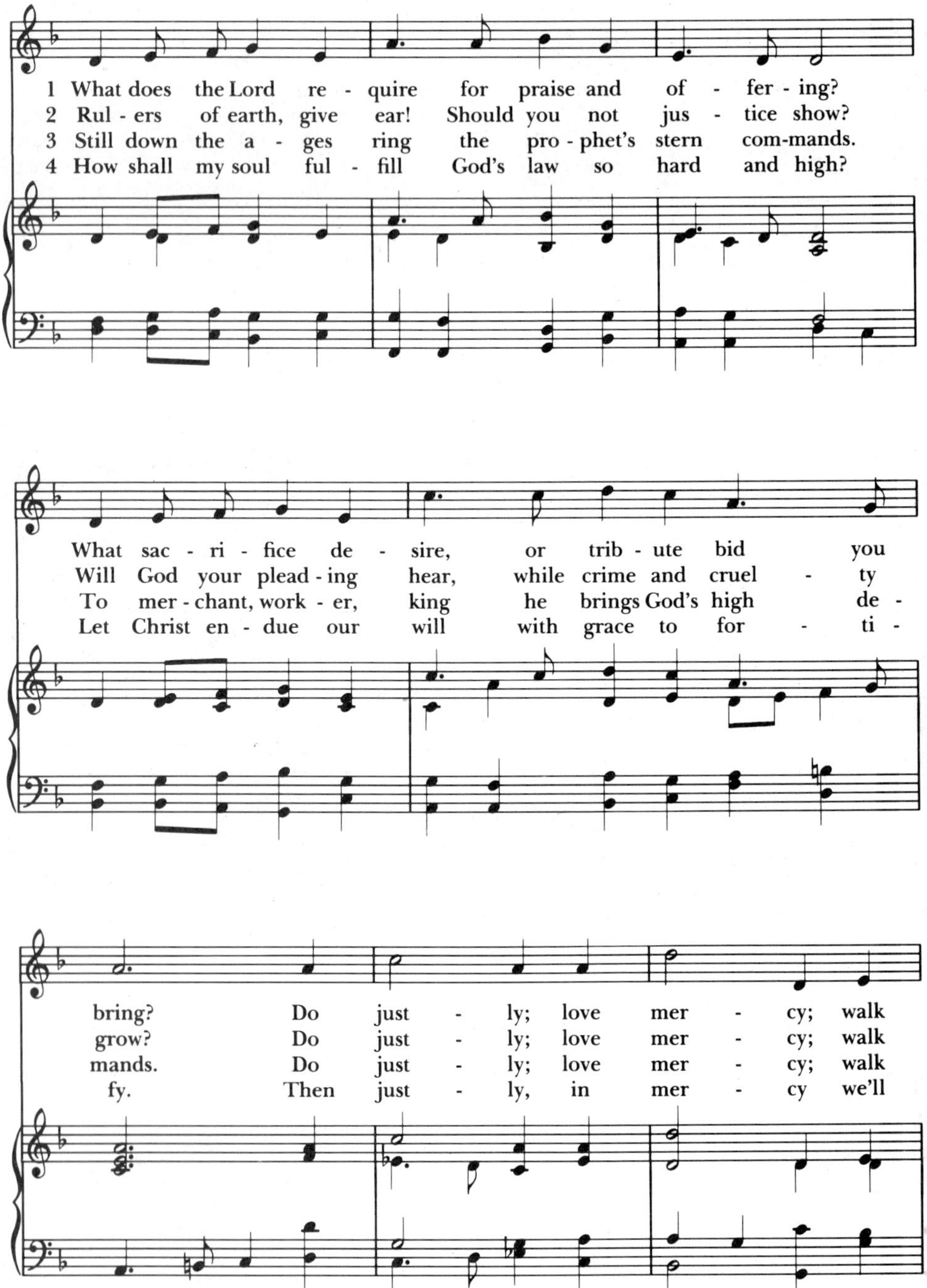
1 What does the Lord re - quire for praise and of - fer - ing?
2 Rul - ers of earth, give ear! Should you not jus - tice show?
3 Still down the a - ges ring the pro - phet's stern com-mands.
4 How shall my soul ful - fill God's law so hard and high?
What sac - ri - fice de - sire, or trib - ute bid you
Will God your plead - ing hear, while crime and cruel - ty
To mer - chant, work - er, king he brings God's high de -
Let Christ en - due our will with grace to for - ti -
bring? Do just - ly; love mer - cy; walk
grow? Do just - ly; love mer - cy; walk
mands. Do just - ly; love mer - cy; walk
fy. Then just - ly, in mer - cy we'll

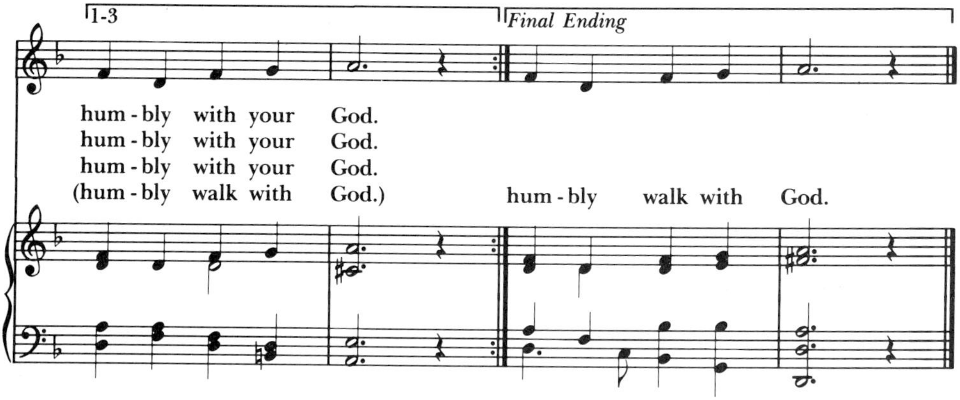
1-3
Final Ending
hum - bly with your God.
hum - bly with your God.
hum - bly with your God.
(hum - bly walk with God.)
hum - bly walk with God.

Words: Albert F. Bayly (b. 1901), alt.
Music: *Sharpthorne,* Erik Routley (1917-1982)

𝅗𝅥=50
66. 66. 33. 6

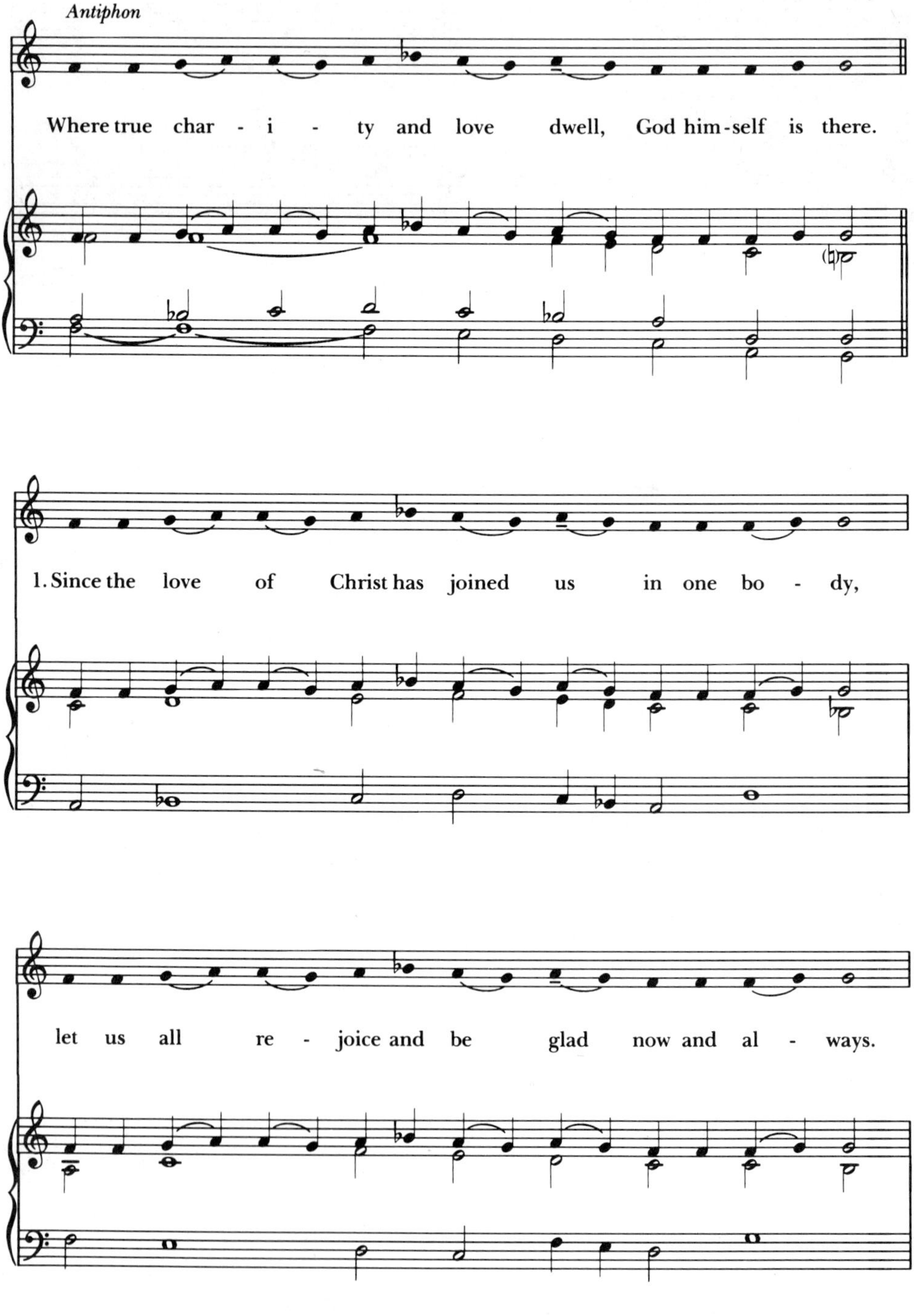
Antiphon
Where true char - i - ty and love dwell, God him-self is there.
1. Since the love of Christ has joined us in one bo - dy,
let us all re - joice and be glad now and al - ways.

And as we hear and love our Lord, the liv - ing God,
so let us in sin - cer - i - ty love all peo - ple.
Antiphon
Where true char - i - ty and love dwell, God him - self is there.

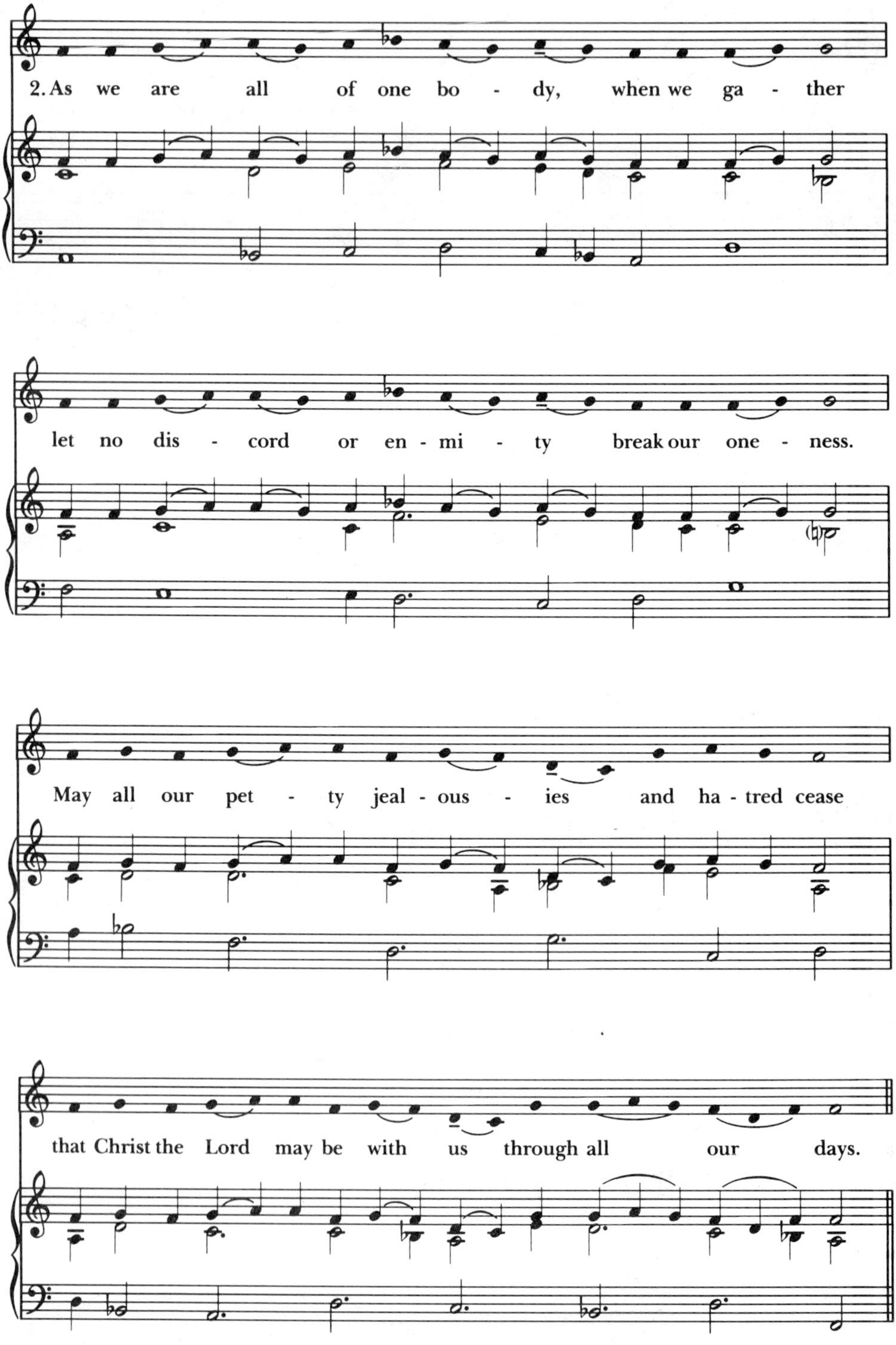
2. As we are all of one bo - dy, when we ga - ther
let no dis - cord or en - mi - ty break our one - ness.
May all our pet - ty jeal - ous - ies and ha - tred cease
that Christ the Lord may be with us through all our days.

Antiphon
Where true char - i - ty and love dwell, God him-self is there.
3. Now we pray that with the bless - ed you grant us grace
to see your ex - alt - ed glo - ry, O Christ our God,

our bound-less source of joy and truth, of peace and love,

for ev - er and for ev - er - more, world with - out end.

Antiphon

Where true char - i - ty and love dwell, God him-self is there.

This hymn is especially suitable for Maundy Thursday.

Words: Latin; tr. Joyce MacDonald Glover (b. 1923)
Music: *Ubi caritas*, plainsong, Mode 6; acc. David Hurd (b. 1950)

12. 12. 12. 12 with Refrain

607

1 O God of ev - ery na - tion, of ev - ery race and land,
2 From search for wealth and pow - er and scorn of truth and right,
3 Lord, strength-en all who la - bor that we may find re - lease
4 Keep bright in us the vi - sion of days when war shall cease,
re - deem the whole cre - a - tion with your al - might - y hand;
from trust in bombs that show - er de - struc-tion through the night,
from fear of rat - tling sa - ber, from dread of war's in - crease;
when ha - tred and di - vi - sion give way to love and peace,
where hate and fear di - vide us and bit - ter threats are hurled,
from pride of race and na - tion and blind - ness to your way,
when hope and cour - age fal - ter, your still small voice be heard;
till dawns the morn - ing glo - rious when truth and jus - tice reign
in love and mer - cy guide us and heal our strife - torn world.
de - liv - er ev - ery na - tion, e - ter - nal God, we pray!
with faith that none can al - ter, your ser - vants un - der - gird.
and Christ shall rule vic - to - rious o'er all the world's do - main.

Another harmonization, 68.

Words: William Watkins Reid, Jr. (b. 1923), alt.
Music: *Llangloffan*, melody from *Hymnau a Thonau er Gwasanaeth yr Eglwys yng Nghymru*, 1865; harm. *The English Hymnal*, 1906

𝅗𝅥=60
76. 76. D

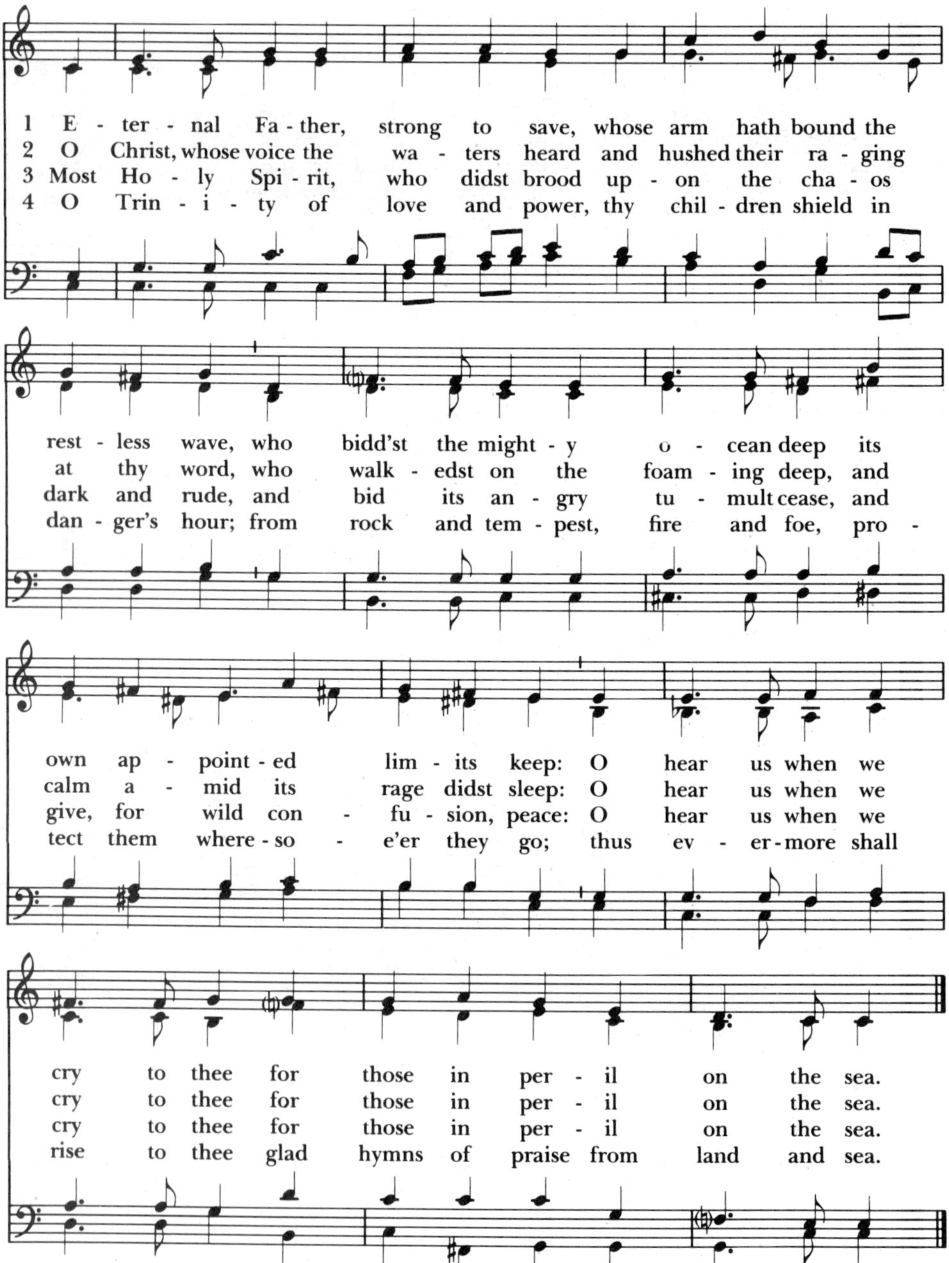
1 E - ter - nal Fa - ther, strong to save, whose arm hath bound the
2 O Christ, whose voice the wa - ters heard and hushed their ra - ging
3 Most Ho - ly Spi - rit, who didst brood up - on the cha - os
4 O Trin - i - ty of love and power, thy chil - dren shield in
rest - less wave, who bidd'st the might - y o - cean deep its
at thy word, who walk - edst on the foam - ing deep, and
dark and rude, and bid its an - gry tu - mult cease, and
dan - ger's hour; from rock and tem - pest, fire and foe, pro -
own ap - point - ed lim - its keep: O hear us when we
calm a - mid its rage didst sleep: O hear us when we
give, for wild con - fu - sion, peace: O hear us when we
tect them where - so - e'er they go; thus ev - er-more shall
cry to thee for those in per - il on the sea.
cry to thee for those in per - il on the sea.
cry to thee for those in per - il on the sea.
rise to thee glad hymns of praise from land and sea.

Words: William Whiting (1825-1878), alt.
Music: *Melita,* John Bacchus Dykes (1823-1876)

𝅗𝅥 = 48
88. 88. 88

1 Where cross the crowd - ed ways of life, where sound the
2 In haunts of wretch - ed - ness and need, on sha - dowed
3 The cup of wa - ter given for thee still holds the
4 O Mas - ter, from the moun - tain side, make haste to
5 till all the world shall learn thy love, and fol - low
1 cries of race and clan, a - bove the noise of
2 thresh - olds dark with fears, from paths where hide the
3 fresh - ness of thy grace; yet long these mul - ti -
4 heal these hearts of pain; a - mong these rest - less
5 where thy feet have trod; till glo - rious from thy
1 self - ish strife, we hear thy voice, O Son of Man.
2 lures of greed, we catch the vi - sion of thy tears.
3 tudes to see the true com - pas - sion of thy face.
4 throngs a - bide, O tread the ci - ty's streets a - gain;
5 heaven a - bove, shall come the ci - ty of our God.

Words: Frank Mason North (1850-1935), alt.
Music: *Gardiner*, from *Sacred Melodies*, 1815; arr. William Gardiner (1770-1853)

♩=96
LM

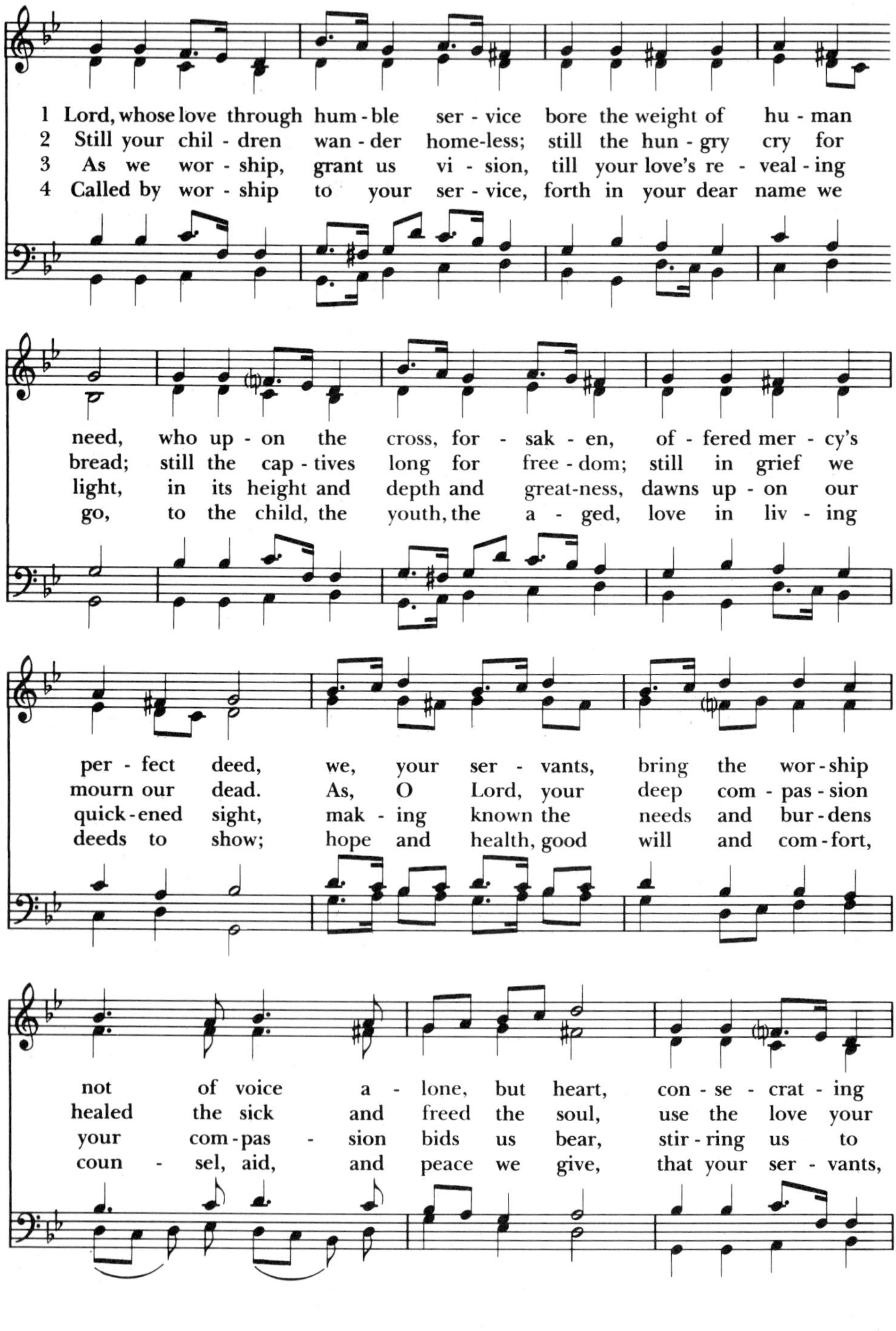
1 Lord, whose love through humble service bore the weight of human
2 Still your children wander homeless; still the hungry cry for
3 As we worship, grant us vision, till your love's revealing
4 Called by worship to your service, forth in your dear name we
need, who upon the cross, forsaken, offered mercy's
bread; still the captives long for freedom; still in grief we
light, in its height and depth and greatness, dawns upon our
go, to the child, the youth, the aged, love in living
perfect deed, we, your servants, bring the worship
mourn our dead. As, O Lord, your deep compassion
quickened sight, making known the needs and burdens
deeds to show; hope and health, good will and comfort,
not of voice alone, but heart, consecrating
healed the sick and freed the soul, use the love your
your compassion bids us bear, stirring us to
counsel, aid, and peace we give, that your servants,

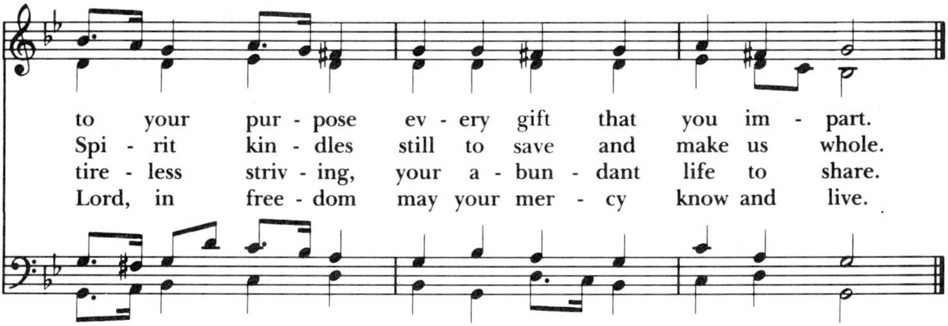
to your pur - pose ev - ery gift that you im - part.
Spi - rit kin - dles still to save and make us whole.
tire - less striv - ing, your a - bun - dant life to share.
Lord, in free - dom may your mer - cy know and live.

Words: Albert F. Bayly (b. 1901), alt.
Music: *Blaenhafren,* Welsh melody

𝅗𝅥=46
87. 87. D

Christian Responsibility

611

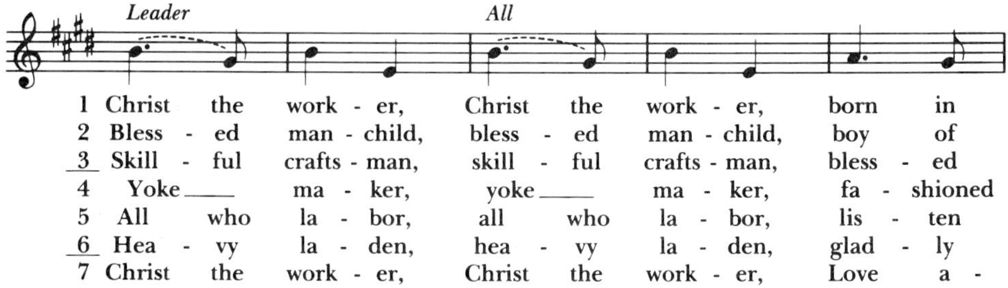
Leader
All
1 Christ the work - er, Christ the work - er, born in
2 Bless - ed man - child, bless - ed man - child, boy of
3 Skill - ful crafts - man, skill - ful crafts - man, bless - ed
4 Yoke ma - ker, yoke ma - ker, fa - shioned
5 All who la - bor, all who la - bor, lis - ten
6 Hea - vy la - den, hea - vy la - den, glad - ly
7 Christ the work - er, Christ the work - er, Love a -

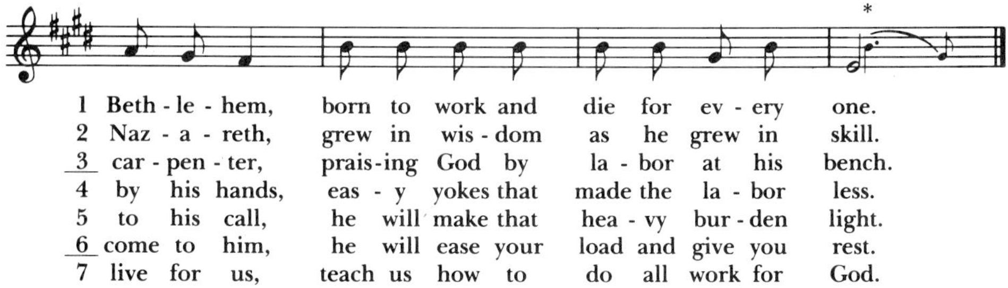
*
1 Beth - le - hem, born to work and die for ev - ery one.
2 Naz - a - reth, grew in wis - dom as he grew in skill.
3 car - pen - ter, prais - ing God by la - bor at his bench.
4 by his hands, eas - y yokes that made the la - bor less.
5 to his call, he will make that hea - vy bur - den light.
6 come to him, he will ease your load and give you rest.
7 live for us, teach us how to do all work for God.

**The leader may begin successive stanzas here.*

Words: Ghanaian work song; tr. Thomas Stevenson Colvin (b. 1925), alt.
Music: *African Work Song,* African work song; adapt. Thomas Stevenson Colvin (b. 1925)

♩=92
444. 9

1 Gra - cious Spi - rit, Ho - ly Ghost,
2 Love is kind, and suf - fers long,
3 Pro - phe - cy will fade a - way,
4 Faith and hope and love we see,
taught by thee we cov - et most, of thy gifts at
love is meek, and thinks no wrong, love than death it -
melt - ing in the light of day; love will ev - er
join - ing hand in hand, a - gree, but the great - est
Pen - te - cost, ho - ly, heaven - ly love.
self more strong; there - fore, give us love.
with us stay; there - fore, give us love.
of the three, and the best, is love.

Words: Christopher Wordsworth (1807-1885)
Music: *Troen,* Daniel Moe (b. 1926)

♩=c. 92
777. 5

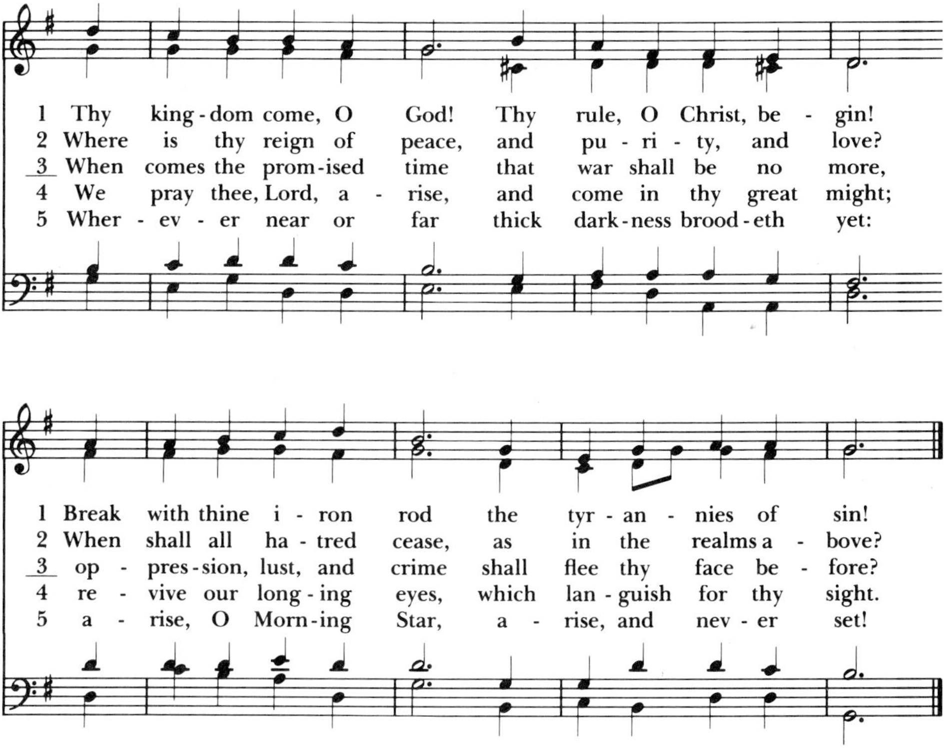
1 Thy king-dom come, O God! Thy rule, O Christ, be - gin!
2 Where is thy reign of peace, and pu - ri - ty, and love?
3 When comes the prom-ised time that war shall be no more,
4 We pray thee, Lord, a - rise, and come in thy great might;
5 Wher - ev - er near or far thick dark-ness brood-eth yet:
1 Break with thine i - ron rod the tyr - an - nies of sin!
2 When shall all ha - tred cease, as in the realms a - bove?
3 op - pres-sion, lust, and crime shall flee thy face be - fore?
4 re - vive our long-ing eyes, which lan-guish for thy sight.
5 a - rise, O Morn-ing Star, a - rise, and nev - er set!

Words: Lewis Hensley (1824-1905), alt.
Music: *St. Cecilia,* Leighton George Hayne (1836-1883)

𝅗𝅥=54
66. 66

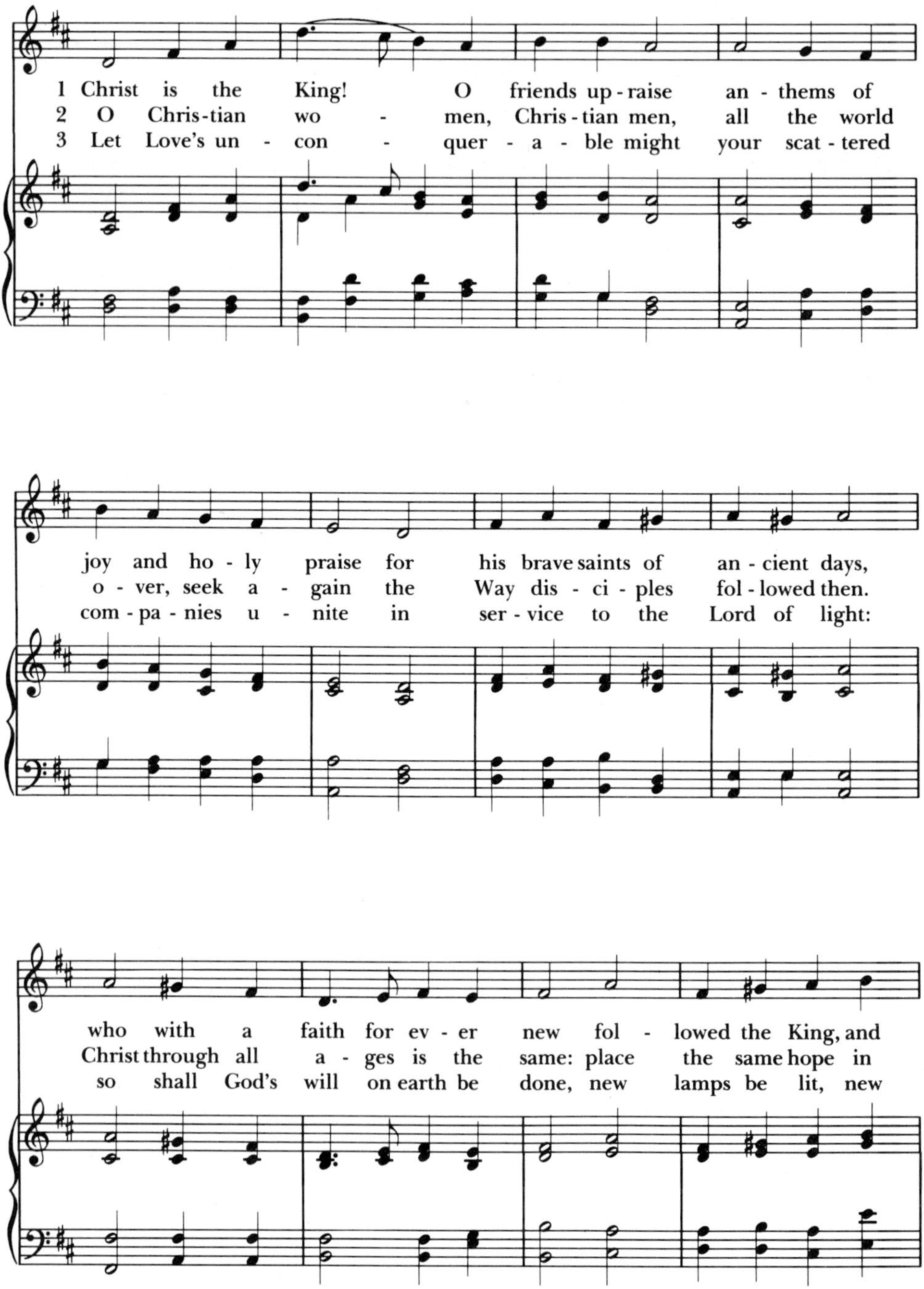
1 Christ is the King! O friends up - raise an - thems of
2 O Chris - tian wo - men, Chris - tian men, all the world
3 Let Love's un - con - quer - a - ble might your scat - tered
joy and ho - ly praise for his brave saints of an - cient days,
o - ver, seek a - gain the Way dis - ci - ples fol - lowed then.
com - pa - nies u - nite in ser - vice to the Lord of light:
who with a faith for ev - er new fol - lowed the King, and
Christ through all a - ges is the same: place the same hope in
so shall God's will on earth be done, new lamps be lit, new

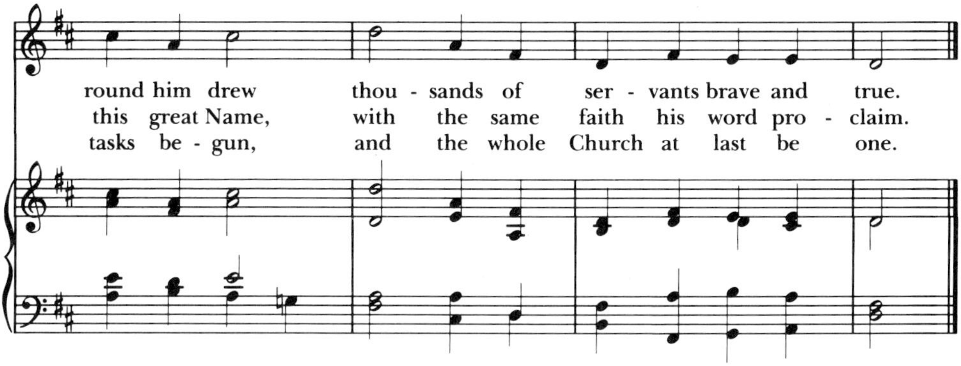
round him drew thou - sands of ser - vants brave and true.
this great Name, with the same faith his word pro - claim.
tasks be - gun, and the whole Church at last be one.

Words: George Kennedy Allen Bell (1883-1958) 𝅗𝅥 = 66
Music: *Christus Rex,* David McKinley Williams (1887-1978) 888. 888

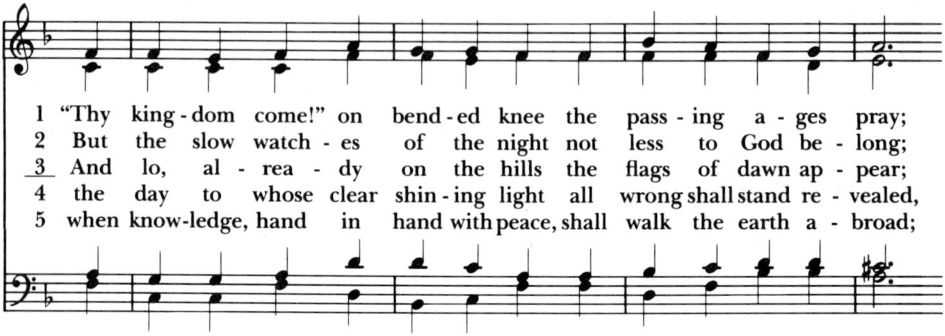
1 "Thy king-dom come!" on bend-ed knee the pass-ing a-ges pray;
2 But the slow watch-es of the night not less to God be-long;
3 And lo, al-rea-dy on the hills the flags of dawn ap-pear;
4 the day to whose clear shin-ing light all wrong shall stand re-vealed,
5 when know-ledge, hand in hand with peace, shall walk the earth a-broad;

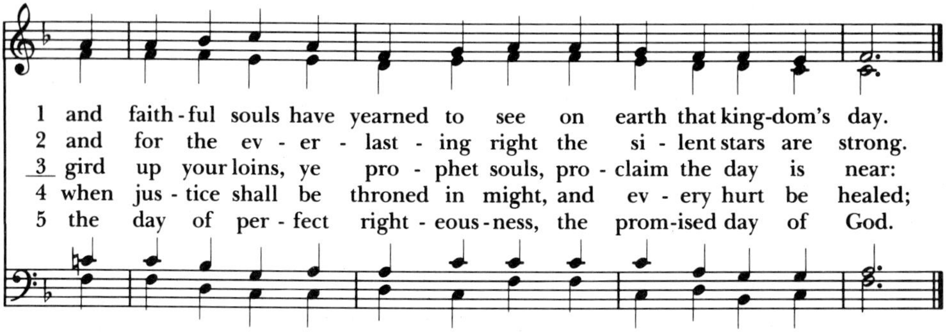
1 and faith-ful souls have yearned to see on earth that king-dom's day.
2 and for the ev-er-last-ing right the si-lent stars are strong.
3 gird up your loins, ye pro-phet souls, pro-claim the day is near:
4 when jus-tice shall be throned in might, and ev-ery hurt be healed;
5 the day of per-fect right-eous-ness, the prom-ised day of God.

Alternative tune: *St. Flavian* (original rhythm), 332.

Words: Frederick Lucian Hosmer (1840-1929) ♩=80

Music: *St. Flavian,* melody from *Day's Psalter,* 1562; adapt. and harm. Richard Redhead (1820-1901) CM

616 The Kingdom of God

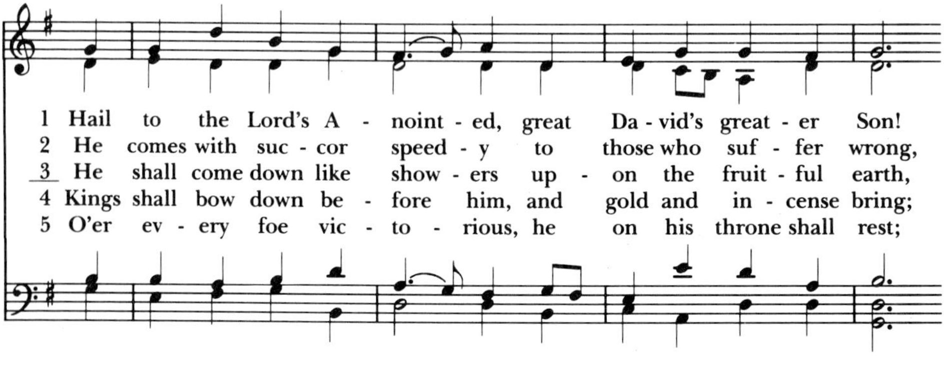
1 Hail to the Lord's A-noint-ed, great Da-vid's great-er Son!
2 He comes with suc-cor speed-y to those who suf-fer wrong,
3 He shall come down like show-ers up-on the fruit-ful earth,
4 Kings shall bow down be-fore him, and gold and in-cense bring;
5 O'er ev-ery foe vic-to-rious, he on his throne shall rest;

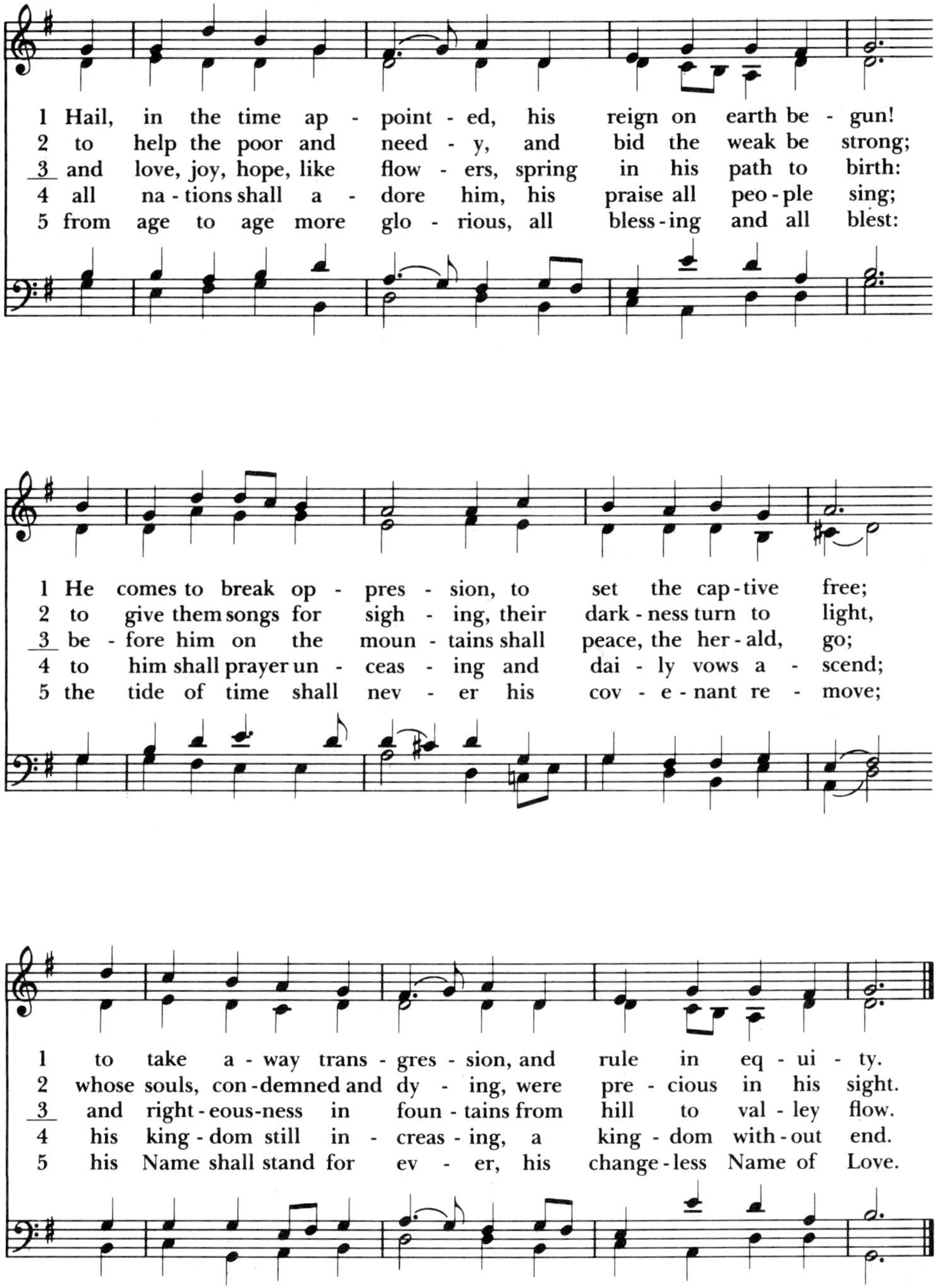
1 Hail, in the time ap - point - ed, his reign on earth be - gun!
2 to help the poor and need - y, and bid the weak be strong;
3 and love, joy, hope, like flow - ers, spring in his path to birth:
4 all na - tions shall a - dore him, his praise all peo - ple sing;
5 from age to age more glo - rious, all bless - ing and all blest:
1 He comes to break op - pres - sion, to set the cap - tive free;
2 to give them songs for sigh - ing, their dark - ness turn to light,
3 be - fore him on the moun - tains shall peace, the her - ald, go;
4 to him shall prayer un - ceas - ing and dai - ly vows a - scend;
5 the tide of time shall nev - er his cov - e - nant re - move;
1 to take a - way trans - gres - sion, and rule in eq - ui - ty.
2 whose souls, con - demned and dy - ing, were pre - cious in his sight.
3 and right - eous - ness in foun - tains from hill to val - ley flow.
4 his king - dom still in - creas - ing, a king - dom with - out end.
5 his Name shall stand for ev - er, his change - less Name of Love.

Another harmonization, 48.

Words: James Montgomery (1771-1854); para. of Psalm 72
Music: *Es flog ein kleins Waldvögelein,* German folk song; adapt. and harm. *A Student's Hymnal,* 1923, after Henry Walford Davies (1869-1941)

𝅗𝅥=54
76. 76. D

Unison or harmony
1 E - ter - nal Ru - ler of the cease - less round
2 We would be one in ha - tred of all wrong,
3 Oh, clothe us with thy heaven - ly ar - mor, Lord,
of cir - cling plan - ets sing - ing on their way,
one in the love of all things sweet and fair,
thy trust - y shield, thy sword of love di - vine;
guide of the na - - tions from the night pro - found
one with the joy that break - eth in - to song,
our in - spi - ra - - tion be thy con - stant word,
in - to the glo - ry of the per - fect day;
one with the grief that trem - bleth in - to prayer;
we ask no vic - to - ries that are not thine;

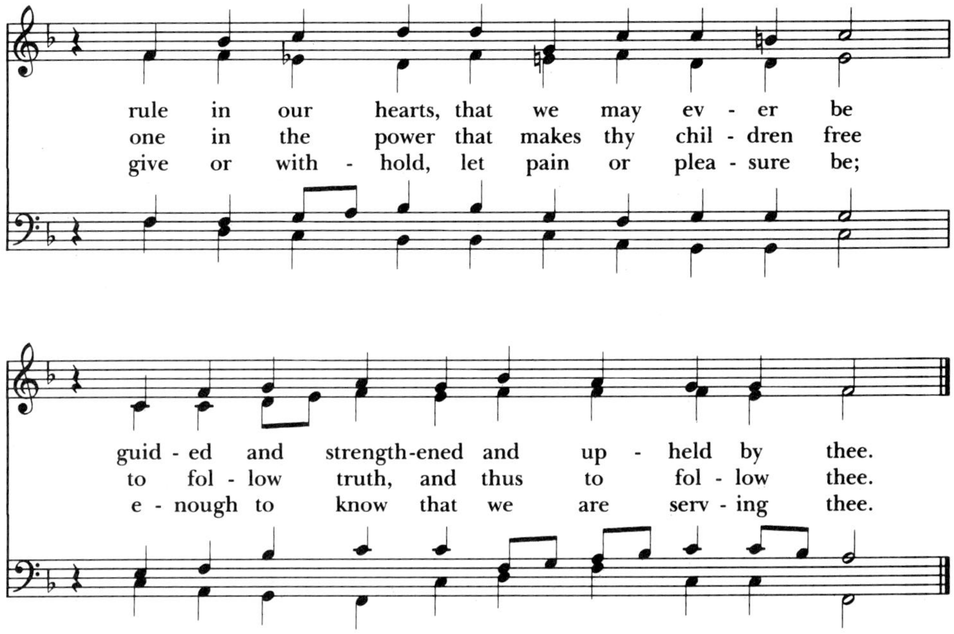
rule in our hearts, that we may ev - er be
one in the power that makes thy chil - dren free
give or with - hold, let pain or plea - sure be;
guid - ed and strength-ened and up - held by thee.
to fol - low truth, and thus to fol - low thee.
e - nough to know that we are serv - ing thee.

Words: John White Chadwick (1840-1904), alt.
Music: *Song 1*, melody and bass Orlando Gibbons (1583-1625);
harm. Ralph Vaughan Williams (1872-1958), rev.

♩=90
10 10. 10 10. 10 10

Unison
1 Ye watch - ers and ye ho - ly ones, bright
2 O high - er than the cher - u - bim, more
3 Re - spond, ye souls in end - less rest, ye
4 O friends, in glad - ness let us sing, su -
Harmony
ser - aphs, cher - u - bim, and thrones, raise the
glo - rious than the ser - a - phim, lead their
pa - tri - archs and pro - phets blest, Al - le -
per - nal an - thems ech - o - ing, Al - le -
Unison
glad strain, Al - le - lu - - ia! Cry
prais - es, Al - le - lu - - ia! Thou
lu - - ia, al - le - lu - - ia! Ye
lu - - ia, al - le - lu - - ia! To
out, do - min - ions, prince-doms, powers, vir - -
bear - er of the e - ter - nal Word, most
ho - ly twelve, ye mar - tyrs strong, all
God the Fa - ther, God the Son, and

Harmony
tues, arch - an - gels, an - gels' choirs, Al - le -
gra - cious, mag - ni - fy the Lord, Al - le -
saints tri - um - phant, raise the song, Al - le -
God the Spi - rit, Three in One, Al - le -
lu - ia, al - le - lu - ia, al - le - lu - ia,
lu - ia, al - le - lu - ia, al - le - lu - ia,
lu - ia, al - le - lu - ia, al - le - lu - ia,
lu - ia, al - le - lu - ia, al - le - lu - ia,
Unison
al - le - lu - ia, al - le - lu - - ia!
al - le - lu - ia, al - le - lu - - ia!
al - le - lu - ia, al - le - lu - - ia!
al - le - lu - ia, al - le - lu - - ia!

This music in D, 400.

Words: John Athelstan Laurie Riley (1858-1945)
Music: *Lasst uns erfreuen*, melody from *Auserlesene Catholische Geistliche Kirchengeseng*, 1623; adapt. and harm. Ralph Vaughan Williams (1872-1958)

𝅗𝅥=72
88. 44. 88 with Refrain

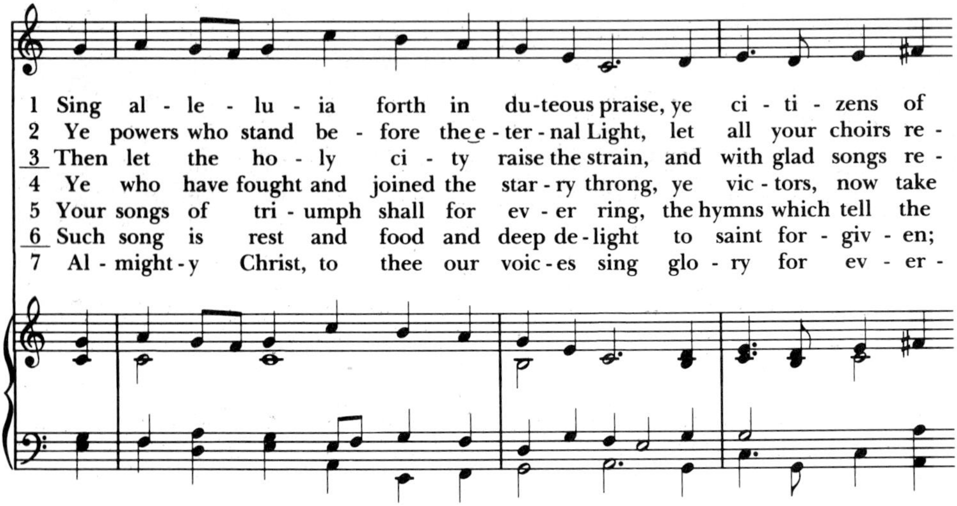
1 Sing al - le - lu - ia forth in du-teous praise, ye ci - ti - zens of
2 Ye powers who stand be - fore the e - ter - nal Light, let all your choirs re -
3 Then let the ho - ly ci - ty raise the strain, and with glad songs re -
4 Ye who have fought and joined the star - ry throng, ye vic - tors, now take
5 Your songs of tri - umph shall for ev - er ring, the hymns which tell the
6 Such song is rest and food and deep de - light to saint for - giv - en;
7 Al - might - y Christ, to thee our voic - es sing glo - ry for ev - er -

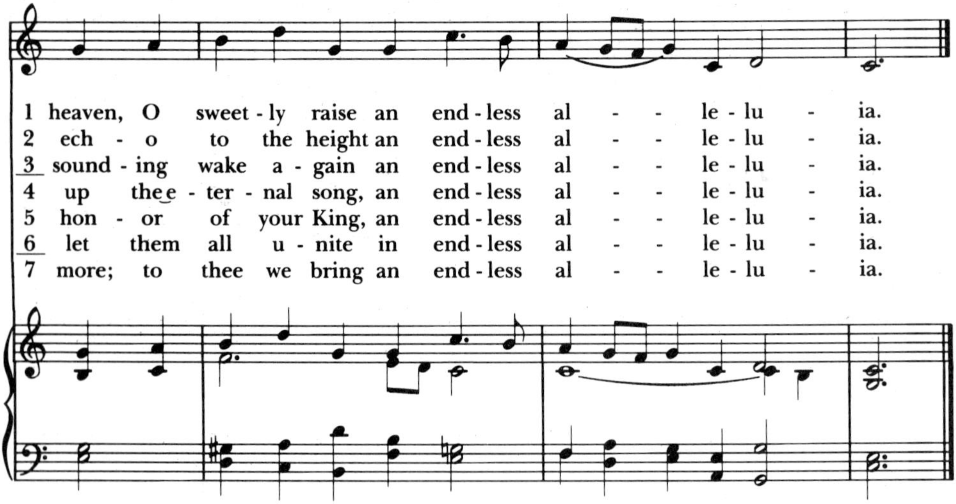
1 heaven, O sweet - ly raise an end - less al - - le - lu - ia.
2 ech - o to the height an end - less al - - le - lu - ia.
3 sound - ing wake a - gain an end - less al - - le - lu - ia.
4 up the e - ter - nal song, an end - less al - - le - lu - ia.
5 hon - or of your King, an end - less al - - le - lu - ia.
6 let them all u - nite in end - less al - - le - lu - ia.
7 more; to thee we bring an end - less al - - le - lu - ia.

Words: Latin, 5th-8th cent.; ver. *Hymnal 1940*
Music: *Martins*, Percy Carter Buck (1871-1947)

𝅗𝅥=60
10 10. 7

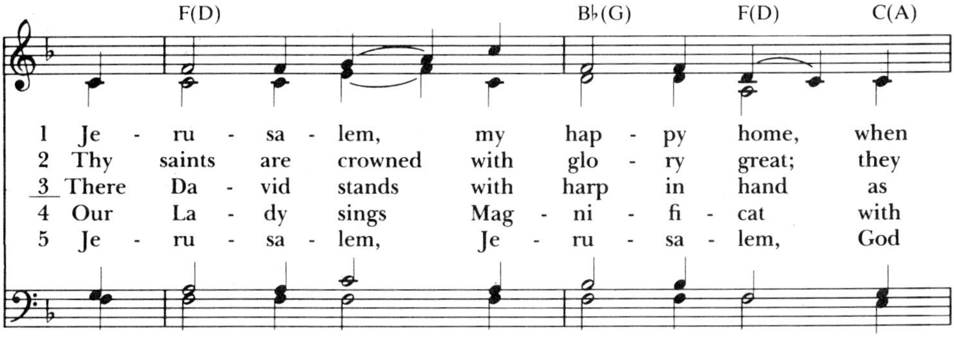
F(D) B♭(G) F(D) C(A)
1 Je - ru - sa - lem, my hap - py home, when
2 Thy saints are crowned with glo - ry great; they
3 There Da - vid stands with harp in hand as
4 Our La - dy sings Mag - ni - fi - cat with
5 Je - ru - sa - lem, Je - ru - sa - lem, God

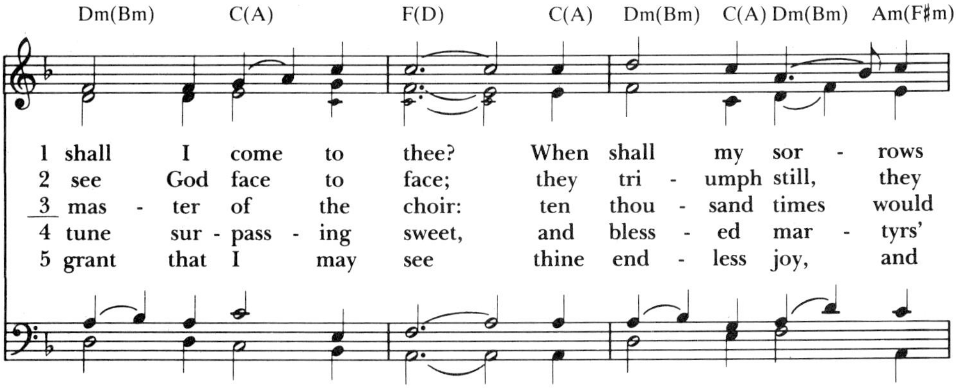
Dm(Bm) C(A) F(D) C(A) Dm(Bm) C(A) Dm(Bm) Am(F♯m)
1 shall I come to thee? When shall my sor - rows
2 see God face to face; they tri - umph still, they
3 mas - ter of the choir: ten thou - sand times would
4 tune sur - pass - ing sweet, and bless - ed mar - tyrs'
5 grant that I may see thine end - less joy, and

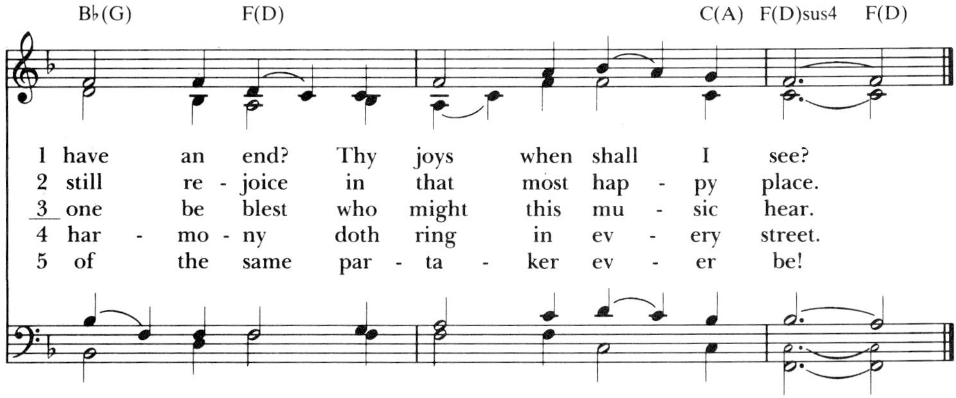
B♭(G) F(D) C(A) F(D)sus4 F(D)
1 have an end? Thy joys when shall I see?
2 still re - joice in that most hap - py place.
3 one be blest who might this mu - sic hear.
4 har - mo - ny doth ring in ev - ery street.
5 of the same par - ta - ker ev - er be!

F(capo 3, D).

Words: F. B. P. (ca. 16th cent.), alt.
Music: *Land of Rest,* American folk hymn; adapt. and harm. Annabel Morris Buchanan (1889-1983)

𝅗𝅥. = 50
CM

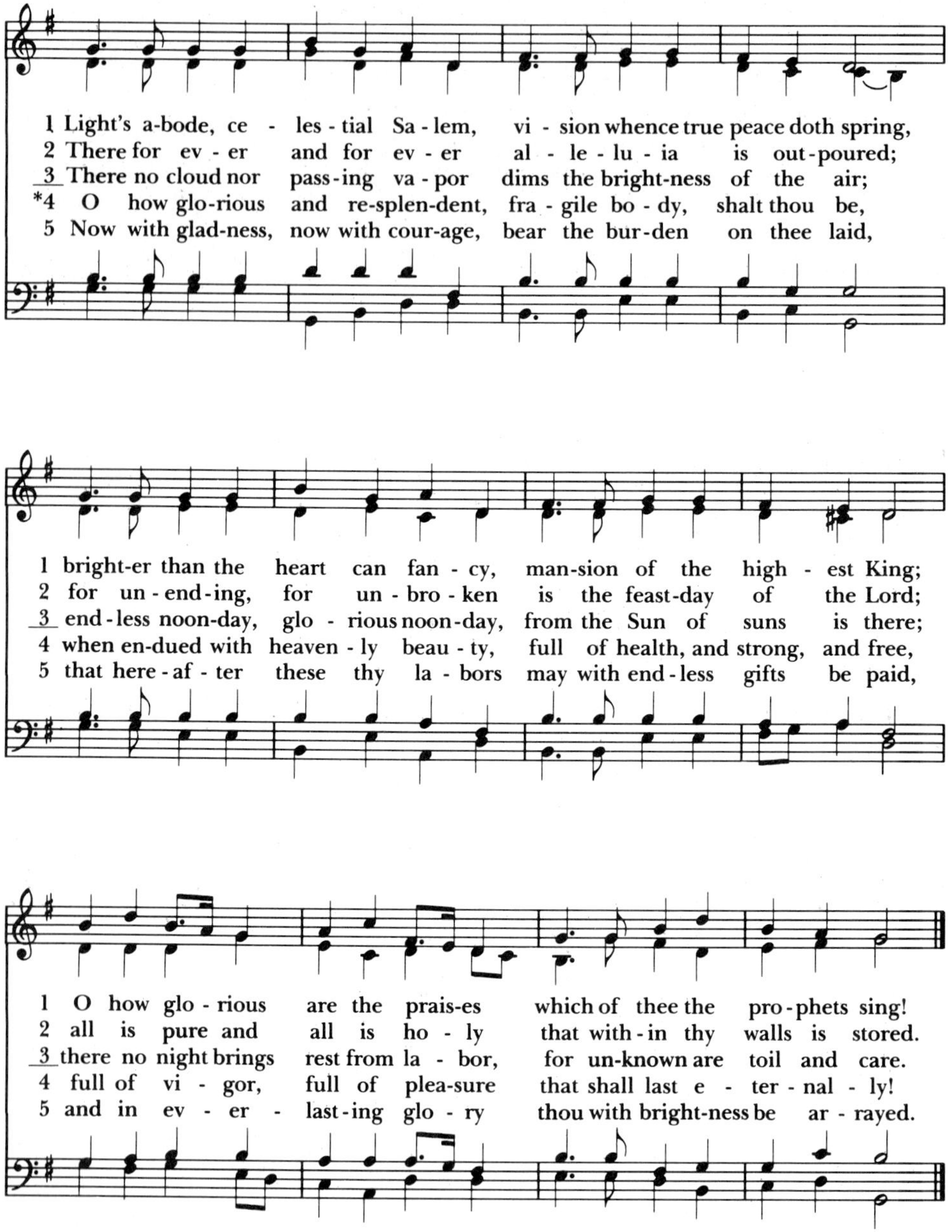
1 Light's a-bode, ce - les - tial Sa - lem, vi - sion whence true peace doth spring,
2 There for ev - er and for ev - er al - le - lu - ia is out-poured;
3 There no cloud nor pass-ing va - por dims the bright-ness of the air;
*4 O how glo-rious and re-splen-dent, fra - gile bo - dy, shalt thou be,
5 Now with glad-ness, now with cour-age, bear the bur-den on thee laid,
1 bright-er than the heart can fan - cy, man-sion of the high - est King;
2 for un - end-ing, for un - bro - ken is the feast-day of the Lord;
3 end-less noon-day, glo - rious noon-day, from the Sun of suns is there;
4 when en-dued with heaven - ly beau - ty, full of health, and strong, and free,
5 that here - af - ter these thy la - bors may with end - less gifts be paid,
1 O how glo - rious are the prais-es which of thee the pro-phets sing!
2 all is pure and all is ho - ly that with-in thy walls is stored.
3 there no night brings rest from la - bor, for un-known are toil and care.
4 full of vi - gor, full of plea-sure that shall last e - ter - nal - ly!
5 and in ev - er - last-ing glo - ry thou with bright-ness be ar - rayed.

Alternative tune: *Urbs beata Jerusalem* (proportional rhythm), 622.

Words: Latin, 15th cent.; tr. John Mason Neale (1818-1866), alt.
Music: *Rhuddlan*, Welsh melody

𝅗𝅥=52
87. 87. 87

1 Light's a - bode, ce - les - tial Sa - lem, vi - sion whence true peace doth spring,
2 There for ev - er and for ev - er al - le - lu - ia is out - poured;
3 There no cloud nor pass - ing va - por dims the bright - ness of the air;
*4 O how glo - rious and re - splen - dent, frag - ile bo - dy, shalt thou be,
5 Now with glad - ness, now with cour - age, bear the bur - den on thee laid,
(Accompaniment optional)
1 bright - er than the heart can fan - cy, man - sion of the high - est King;
2 for un - end - ing, for un - bro - ken is the feast - day of the Lord;
3 end - less noon - day, glo - rious noon - day, from the Sun of suns is there;
4 when en - dued with heaven - ly, beau - ty, full of health, and strong, and free,
5 that here - af - ter these thy la - bors may with end - less gifts be paid,
1 O how glo - rious are the prais - es which of thee the pro - phets sing!
2 all is pure and all is ho - ly that with - in thy walls is stored.
3 there no night brings rest from la - bor, for un - known are toil and care.
4 full of vi - gor, full of plea - sure that shall last e - ter - nal - ly!
5 and in ev - er - last - ing glo - ry thou with bright - ness be ar - rayed.

Alternative tunes: *Urbs beata Jerusalem* (equalist rhythm), 519; *Rhuddlan,* 621.

Words: Latin, 15th cent.; tr. John Mason Neale (1818-1866), alt.
Music: *Urbs beata Jerusalem,* plainsong, Mode 2, Nevers MS., 13th cent; ver. Schola Antiqua, 1983; acc. Alec Wyton (b. 1921)

𝅗𝅥=60
87. 87. 87

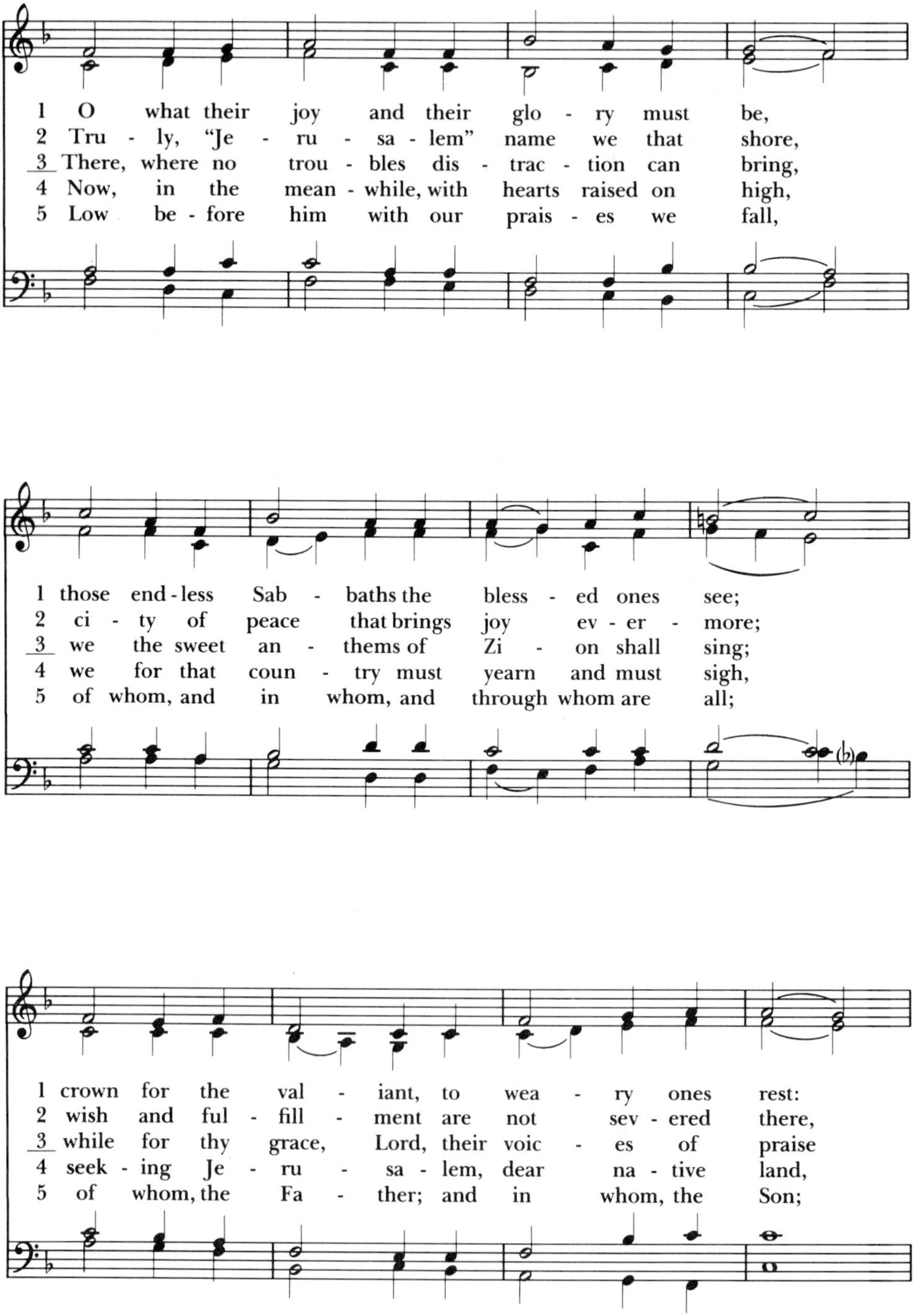
1 O what their joy and their glo - ry must be,
2 Tru - ly, "Je - ru - sa - lem" name we that shore,
3 There, where no trou - bles dis - trac - tion can bring,
4 Now, in the mean - while, with hearts raised on high,
5 Low be - fore him with our prais - es we fall,
1 those end - less Sab - baths the bless - ed ones see;
2 ci - ty of peace that brings joy ev - er - more;
3 we the sweet an - thems of Zi - on shall sing;
4 we for that coun - try must yearn and must sigh,
5 of whom, and in whom, and through whom are all;
1 crown for the val - iant, to wea - ry ones rest:
2 wish and ful - fill - ment are not sev - ered there,
3 while for thy grace, Lord, their voic - es of praise
4 seek - ing Je - ru - sa - lem, dear na - tive land,
5 of whom, the Fa - ther; and in whom, the Son;

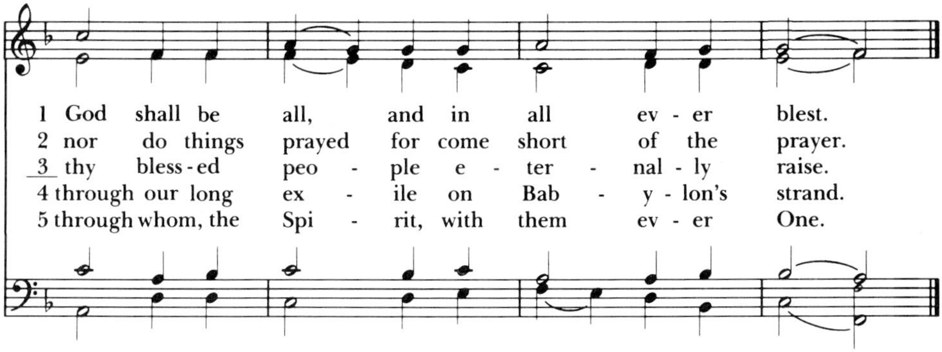
1 God shall be all, and in all ev - er blest.
2 nor do things prayed for come short of the prayer.
3 thy bless - ed peo - ple e - ter - nal - ly raise.
4 through our long ex - ile on Bab - y - lon's strand.
5 through whom, the Spi - rit, with them ev - er One.

Another harmonization, 348.

Words: Peter Abelard (1079-1142); tr. John Mason Neale (1818-1866), alt.
Music: *O quanta qualia,* melody from *Antiphoner,* 1681; harm. John Bacchus Dykes (1823-1876)

𝅗𝅥 = 54
10 10. 10 10

624

1 Je - ru - sa - lem the gold - en, with milk and hon - ey blest,
2 They stand, those halls of Zi - on, all ju - bi - lant with song,
3 There is the throne of Da - vid; and there, from care re - leased,
4 Oh, sweet and bless - ed coun - try, the home of God's e - lect!
be - neath thy con - tem - pla - tion sink heart and voice op - pressed:
and bright with man - y an an - gel, and all the mar - tyr throng:
the shout of them that tri - umph, the song of them that feast;
Oh, sweet and bless - ed coun - try that ea - ger hearts ex - pect!
I know not, oh, I know not, what joys a - wait us there;
the Prince is ev - er in them, the day - light is se - rene;
and they who with their Lead - er have con - quered in the fight,
Je - sus, in mer - cy bring us to that dear land of rest,
what ra - dian - cy of glo - ry, what bliss be - yond com - pare!
the pas - tures of the bless - ed are decked in glo - rious sheen.
for ev - er and for ev - er are clad in robes of white.
who art, with God the Fa - ther, and Spi - rit, ev - er blest.

Words: Bernard of Cluny (12th cent.); tr. John Mason Neale (1818-1866), alt.
St. 4, *Hymns Ancient and Modern,* 1861
Music: *Ewing,* Alexander Ewing (1830-1895)

𝅗𝅥=52
76. 76. D

Descant
4 My soul, bear thou thy part, tri - umph in God a - bove: and
with a well - tuned heart sing thou the songs of love! Let all thy
days till life shall end, what - e'er he send, be filled with praise.
1 Ye ho - ly an - gels bright, who wait at God's right hand, or
2 Ye bless - ed souls at rest, who ran this earth-ly race and
3 Ye saints, who toil be - low, a - dore your heaven-ly King, and
4 My soul, bear thou thy part, tri - umph in God a - bove: and
through the realms of light fly at your Lord's com - mand, as - sist our
now, from sin re - leased, be - hold the Sa - vior's face, God's prais - es
on - ward as ye go some joy - ful an - them sing; take what he
with a well-tuned heart sing thou the songs of love! Let all thy
song, for else the theme too high doth seem for mor - tal tongue.
sound, as in his sight with sweet de - light ye do a - bound.
gives and praise him still, through good or ill, who ev - er lives!
days till life shall end, what - e'er he send, be filled with praise.

Words: Richard Baxter (1615-1691); rev. John Hampden Gurney (1802-1862)
Music: *Darwall's 148th,* melody and bass John Darwall (1731-1789); harm. William Henry Monk (1823-1889), alt.; desc. Sydney Hugo Nicholson (1875-1947)

𝅗𝅥=52
66. 66. 44. 44

626 Holy Scripture

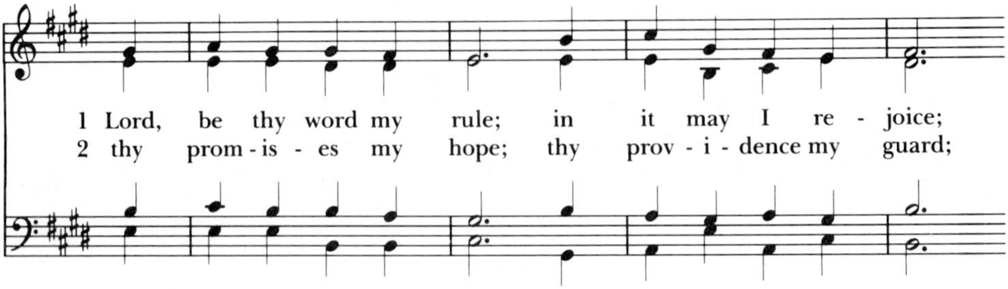
1 Lord, be thy word my rule; in it may I re - joice;
2 thy prom - is - es my hope; thy prov - i - dence my guard;

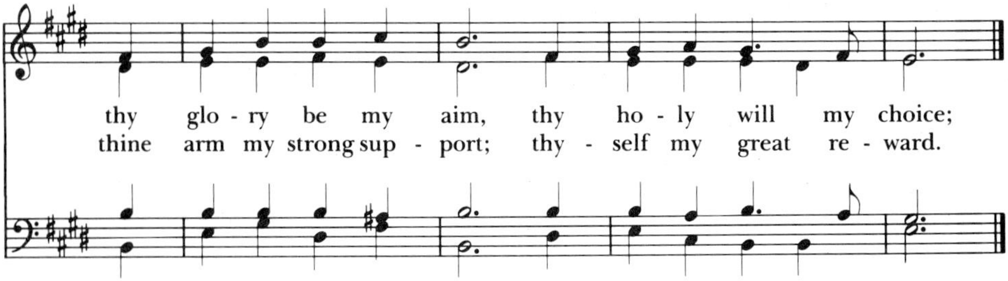
thy glo - ry be my aim, thy ho - ly will my choice;
thine arm my strong sup - port; thy - self my great re - ward.

Words: Christopher Wordsworth (1807-1885)
Music: *Quam dilecta,* Henry Lascelles Jenner (1820-1898)

𝅗𝅥=52
66. 66

627 Holy Scripture

Unison or harmony

1 Lamp of our feet, where - by we trace our path when wont to stray;
2 bread of our souls, where - on we feed, true man - na from on high;
3 pil - lar of fire, through watch - es dark, and ra - diant cloud by day;
4 word of the ev - er - liv - ing God, will of his glo - rious Son;
5 Lord, grant us all a - right to learn the wis - dom it im - parts;

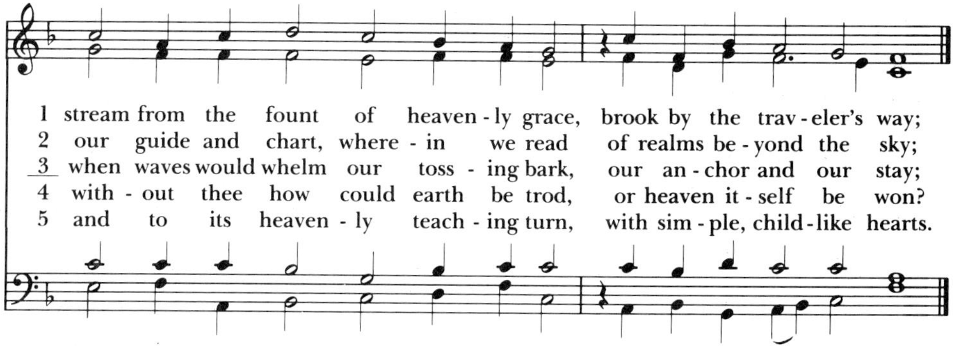
1 stream from the fount of heaven - ly grace, brook by the trav - eler's way;
2 our guide and chart, where - in we read of realms be - yond the sky;
3 when waves would whelm our toss - ing bark, our an - chor and our stay;
4 with - out thee how could earth be trod, or heaven it - self be won?
5 and to its heaven - ly teach - ing turn, with sim - ple, child - like hearts.

Another harmonization, 374.

Words: Bernard Barton (1784-1849)
Music: *Nun danket all und bringet Ehr,* melody att. Johann Cruger (1598-1662), alt.

𝅗𝅥=58
CM

Holy Scripture 628

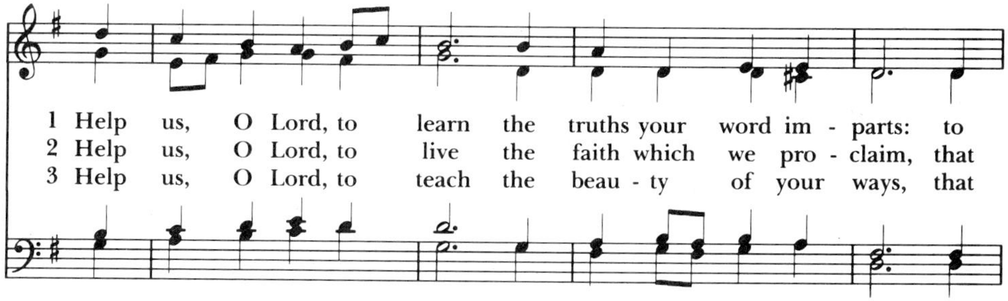
1 Help us, O Lord, to learn the truths your word im - parts: to
2 Help us, O Lord, to live the faith which we pro - claim, that
3 Help us, O Lord, to teach the beau - ty of your ways, that

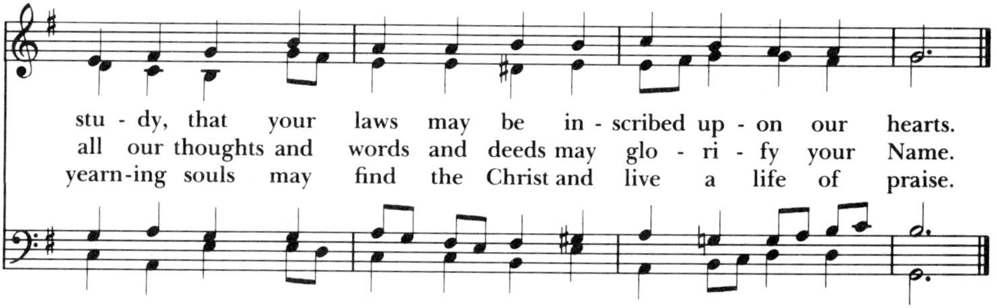
stu - dy, that your laws may be in - scribed up - on our hearts.
all our thoughts and words and deeds may glo - ri - fy your Name.
yearn-ing souls may find the Christ and live a life of praise.

Words: William Watkins Reid, Jr. (b. 1923), alt.
Music: *St. Ethelwald,* William Henry Monk (1823-1889)

𝅗𝅥=56
SM

Introduction
1 We lim - it not the
2 Who dares to bind to
3 O Fa - ther, Son, and
truth of God to our poor reach of mind, to
one's own sense the or - a - cles of heaven, for
Spi - rit, send us in - crease from a - bove; en -
no - tions of our day and place, crude, par - tial, and con -
all the na - tions, tongues, and climes and all the a - ges
large, ex - pand all liv - ing souls to com - pre - hend your

fined; no, let a new and bet - ter hope with -
given? That u - ni - verse, how much un - known! The
love; and make us all go on to know with
in our hearts be stirred; the Lord has yet more
o - cean un - ex - plored! the Lord has yet more
no - bler powers con - ferred— the Lord has yet more
light and truth to break forth from his word.
light and truth to break forth from his word.
light and truth to break forth from his word.
Interlude/Conclusion

The introduction, interlude, and conclusion may be omitted.

Words: George Rawson (1807-1889), alt.
Music: *Halifax,* George Frideric Handel (1685-1759); adapt. and arr. David Hurd (b. 1950)

♩=138
CMD

1 Thanks to God whose Word was spo - ken in the deed that
2 Thanks to God whose Word In - car - nate heights and depths of
*3 Thanks to God whose word was writ - ten in the Bi - ble's
*4 Thanks to God whose word is pub - lished in the tongues of
5 Thanks to God whose Word is an - swered by the Spi - rit's
1 made the earth. His the voice that called a na - tion;
2 life did share. Deeds and words and death and ris - ing,
3 sa - cred page, rec - ord of the rev - e - la - tion
4 ev - ery race. See its glo - ry un - di - mi - nished
5 voice with - in. Here we drink of joy un - mea - sured,
1 his the fires that tried her worth. God has spo - ken:
2 grace in hu - man form de - clare. God has spo - ken:
3 show - ing God to ev - ery age. God has spo - ken:
4 by the change of time or place. God has spo - ken:
5 life re-deemed from death and sin. God is speak - ing:

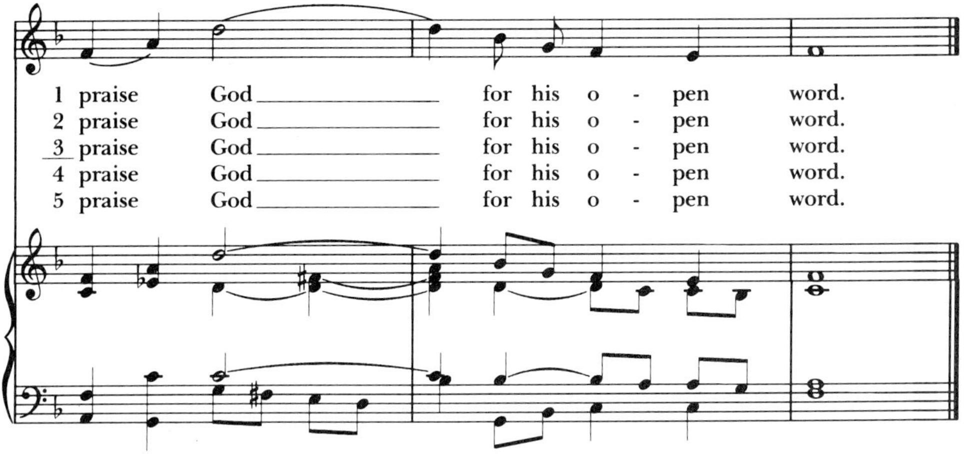
1 praise God for his o - pen word.
2 praise God for his o - pen word.
3 praise God for his o - pen word.
4 praise God for his o - pen word.
5 praise God for his o - pen word.

Words: R. T. Brooks (b. 1918), alt.
Music: *Wylde Green,* Peter Cutts (b. 1937)

♩= 90
87. 87 with Refrain

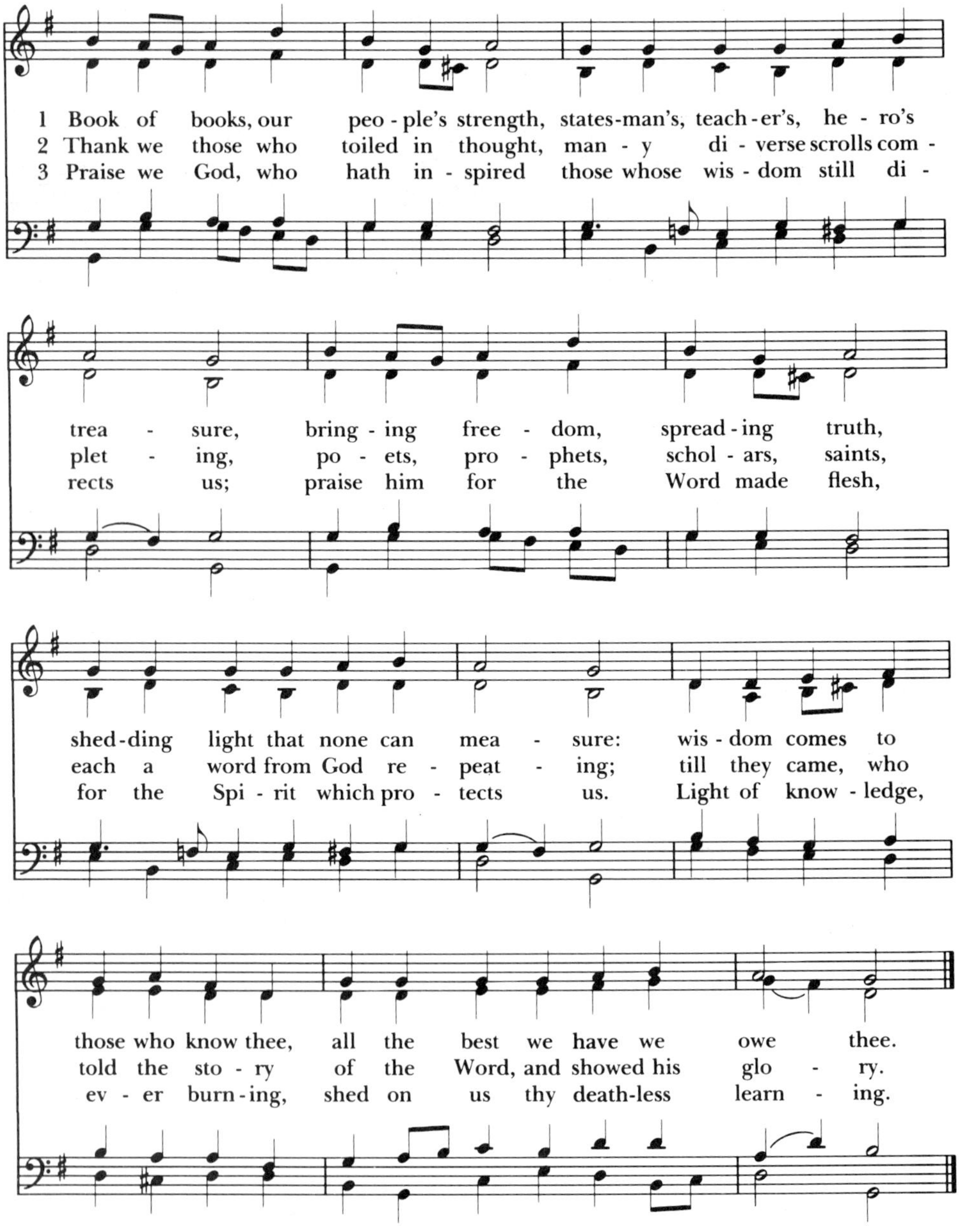
1 Book of books, our peo - ple's strength, states-man's, teach - er's, he - ro's
2 Thank we those who toiled in thought, man - y di - verse scrolls com -
3 Praise we God, who hath in - spired those whose wis - dom still di -
trea - sure, bring - ing free - dom, spread - ing truth,
plet - ing, po - ets, pro - phets, schol - ars, saints,
rects us; praise him for the Word made flesh,
shed - ding light that none can mea - sure: wis - dom comes to
each a word from God re - peat - ing; till they came, who
for the Spi - rit which pro - tects us. Light of know - ledge,
those who know thee, all the best we have we owe thee.
told the sto - ry of the Word, and showed his glo - ry.
ev - er burn - ing, shed on us thy death-less learn - ing.

Words: Percy Dearmer (1867-1936)
Music: *Liebster Jesu,* melody Johann Rudolph Ahle (1625-1673); alt. *Das grosse Cantional oder Kirchen-Gesangbuch,* 1687; harm. George Herbert Palmer (1846-1926)

𝅗𝅥 = 46
78. 78. 88

1 O Christ, the Word In - car - nate, O Wis - dom from on high,
2 The Church from our dear Mas - ter re - ceived the word di - vine,
3 O make thy Church, dear Sa - vior, a lamp of pur - est gold,
O Truth, un - changed, un - chang - ing, O Light of our dark sky;
and still that light is lift - ed o'er all the earth to shine.
to bear be - fore the na - tions thy true light as of old;
we praise thee for the ra - diance that from the scrip-ture's page,
It is the chart and com - pass that o'er life's surg - ing sea,
O teach thy wan-dering pil - grims by this their path to trace,
a lan - tern to our foot - steps, shines on from age to age.
mid mists and rocks and quick-sands, still guides, O Christ, to thee.
till, clouds and dark-ness end - ed, they see thee face to face.

This music in D, 255.

Words: William Walsham How (1823-1897), alt.
Music: *Munich,* melody from *Neu-vermehrtes und zu Übung Christl. Gottseligkeit eingerichtetes Meiningisches Gesangbuch,* 1693; adapt. and harm. Felix Mendelssohn (1809-1847)

𝅗𝅥 = 50
76. 76. D

1 Word of God, come down on earth,
2 Word e - ter - nal, throned on high,
3 Word that caused blind eyes to see,
4 Word that speaks your Fa - ther's love,
liv - ing rain from heaven de - scend - ing;
Word that brought to life cre - a - tion,
speak and heal our mor - tal blind - ness;
one with him be - yond all tell - ing,
touch our hearts and bring to birth
Word that came from heaven to die,
deaf we are: our heal - er be;
Word that sends us from a - bove

faith and hope and love un - end - ing.
cru - ci - fied for our sal - va - tion,
loose our tongues to tell your kind - ness.
God the Spi - rit, with us dwell - ing,
Word al - might - y, we re - vere you;
sav - ing Word, the world re - stor - ing,
Be our Word in pi - ty spo - ken;
Word of truth, to all truth lead us,
Word made flesh, we long to hear you.
speak to us, your love out - pour - ing.
heal the world, by our sin brok - en.
Word of life, with one Bread feed us.

A single stanza may be used as a sequence hymn. Alternative tune: *Liebster Jesu,* 631.

Words: James Quinn (b. 1919)
Music: *Mt. St. Alban NCA,* Richard Wayne Dirksen (b. 1921)

♩= 96
78. 78. 88

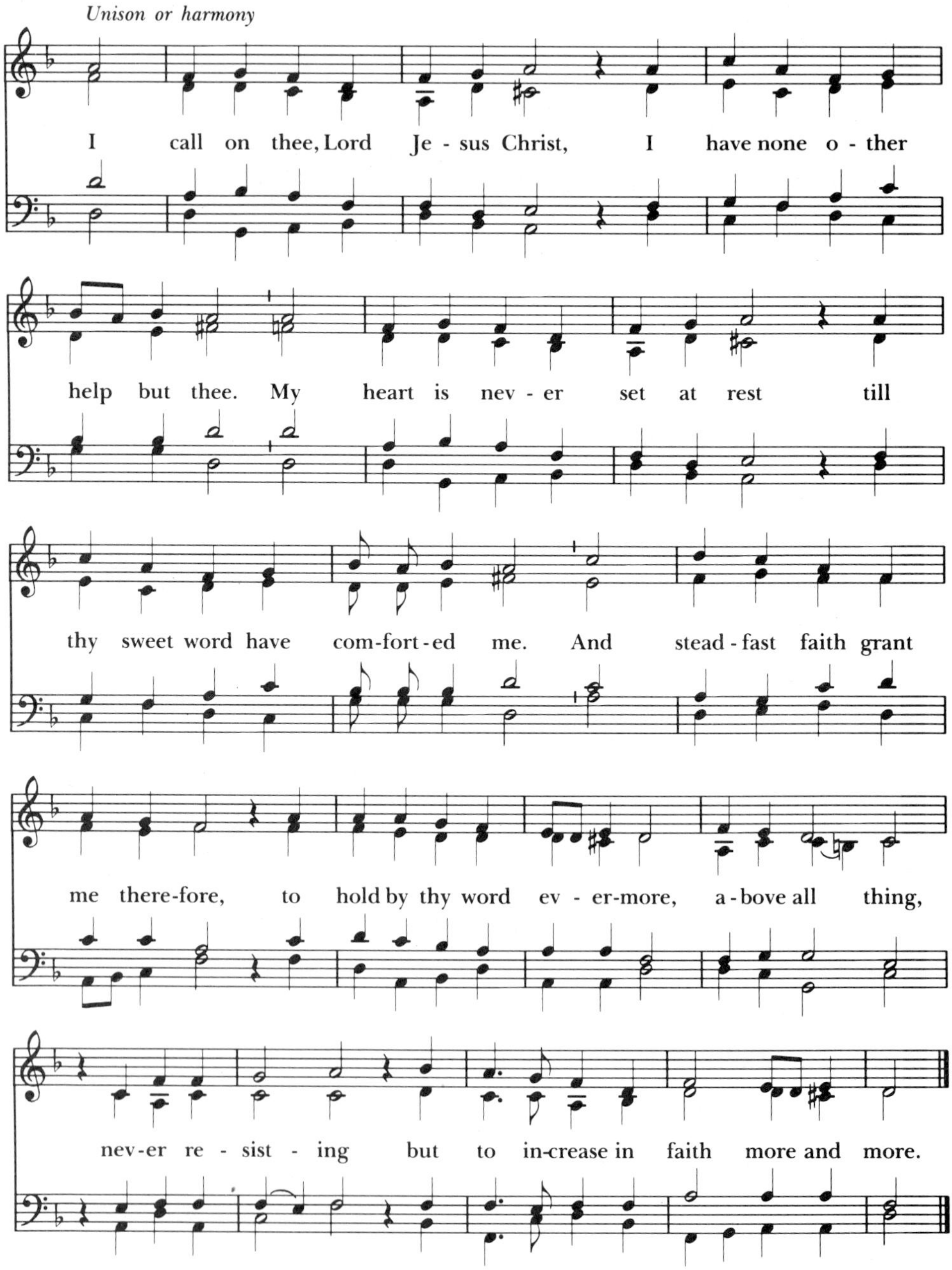
Unison or harmony
I call on thee, Lord Je - sus Christ, I have none o - ther
help but thee. My heart is nev - er set at rest till
thy sweet word have com-fort - ed me. And stead - fast faith grant
me there-fore, to hold by thy word ev - er-more, a - bove all thing,
nev-er re - sist - ing but to in-crease in faith more and more.

Words: Miles Coverdale (1487-1568)
Music: *Ich ruf zu dir*, melody from *Geistliche Lieder*, 1533;
harm. *Thuringer Evangelisches Gesangbuch*, 1928

𝅗𝅥 = 50
Irr.

Unison or harmony
1 If thou but trust in God to guide thee, and hope in him through
2 Sing, pray, and keep his ways un - swerv - ing; so do thine own part
all thy ways, he'll give thee strength what - e'er be - tide thee,
faith - ful - ly, and trust his word, though un - de - serv - ing;
and bear thee through the e - vil days. Who trusts in God's un -
thou yet shalt find it true for thee; God nev - er yet for -
chang - ing love builds on a rock that nought can move.
sook in need the soul that trust - ed him in - deed.

Words: Georg Neumark (1621-1681); tr. Catherine Winkworth (1827-1878), alt.
Music: *Wer nur den lieben Gott,* Georg Neumark (1621-1681)

♩= 108
98. 98. 88

D G C G Em G Am Bm
1 How firm a foun - da - tion, ye saints of the Lord,
2 "Fear not, I am with thee; O be not dis - mayed!
3 "When through the deep wa - ters I call thee to go,
4 "When through fier - - y tri - als thy path - way shall lie,
5 "The soul that to Je - sus hath fled for re - pose,
D7sus4 C G Em G D7 G
1 is laid for your faith in his ex - cel - lent word!
2 For I am thy God, and will still give thee aid;
3 the riv - ers of woe shall not thee o - ver - flow;
4 my grace, all suf - fi - cient, shall be thy sup - ply;
5 I will not, I will not de - sert to its foes;
Bm Em Bm Am Bm
1 What more can he say than to you he hath said,
2 I'll strength - en thee, help thee, and cause thee to stand,
3 for I will be with thee, thy trou - bles to bless,
4 the flame shall not hurt thee; I on - ly de - sign
5 that soul, though all hell shall en - deav - or to shake,

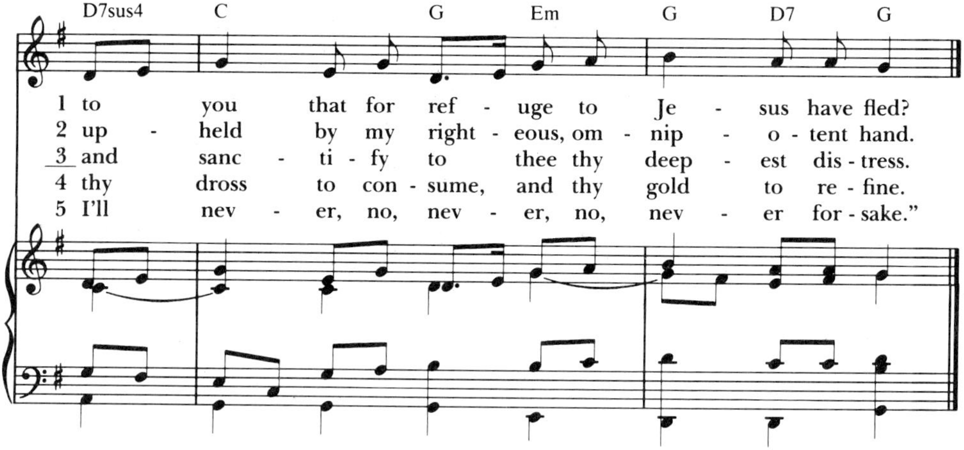
D7sus4 C G Em G D7 G
1 to you that for ref - uge to Je - sus have fled?
2 up - held by my right - eous, om - nip - o - tent hand.
3 and sanc - ti - fy to thee thy deep - est dis - tress.
4 thy dross to con - sume, and thy gold to re - fine.
5 I'll nev - er, no, nev - er, no, nev - er for - sake."

Optional Interlude

Alternative tune: *Lyons*, 637.

Words: K. in John Rippon's *Selection*, 1787, alt.
Music: *Foundation*, melody from *The Sacred Harp*, 1844; harm. Calvin Hampton (1938-1984)

♩= 88
11 11. 11 11

Alternative accompaniment

Music: *Foundation*, melody from *The Sacred Harp*, 1844; harm. Eugene W. Hancock (b. 1929)

♩= 88

Descant
5 "The soul that to Je - sus hath fled for re - pose,
1 How firm a foun - da - tion, ye saints of the Lord,
2 "Fear not, I am with thee; O be not dis - mayed!
3 "When through the deep wa - ters I call thee to go,
4 "When through fier - y tri - als thy path - way shall lie,
5 "The soul that to Je - sus hath fled for re - pose,
5 I will not, I will not de - sert to its foes;
1 is laid for your faith in his ex - cel - lent word!
2 For I am thy God, and will still give thee aid;
3 the riv - ers of woe shall not thee o - ver - flow;
4 my grace, all suf - fi - cient, shall be thy sup - ply;
5 I will not, I will not de - sert to its foes;

5 soul to shake, no,
1 What more can he say than to you he hath said,
2 I'll strength - en thee, help thee, and cause thee to stand,
3 for I will be with thee, thy trou - bles to bless,
4 the flame shall not hurt thee; I on - ly de - sign
5 that soul, though all hell shall en - deav - or to shake,
5 I'll nev - er, no, nev - er, no, nev - er for - sake."
1 to you that for ref - uge to Je - sus have fled?
2 up - held by my right - eous, om - nip - o - tent hand.
3 and sanc - ti - fy to thee thy deep - est dis - tress.
4 thy dross to con - sume, and thy gold to re - fine.
5 I'll nev - er, no, nev - er, no, ne - ver for - sake."

Alternative tune: *Foundation,* 636.

Words: K. in John Rippon's *Selection,* 1787, alt.
Music: *Lyons,* att. Johann Michael Haydn (1737-1806); desc. Lois Fyfe (b. 1927)

♩. = 44
11 11. 11 11

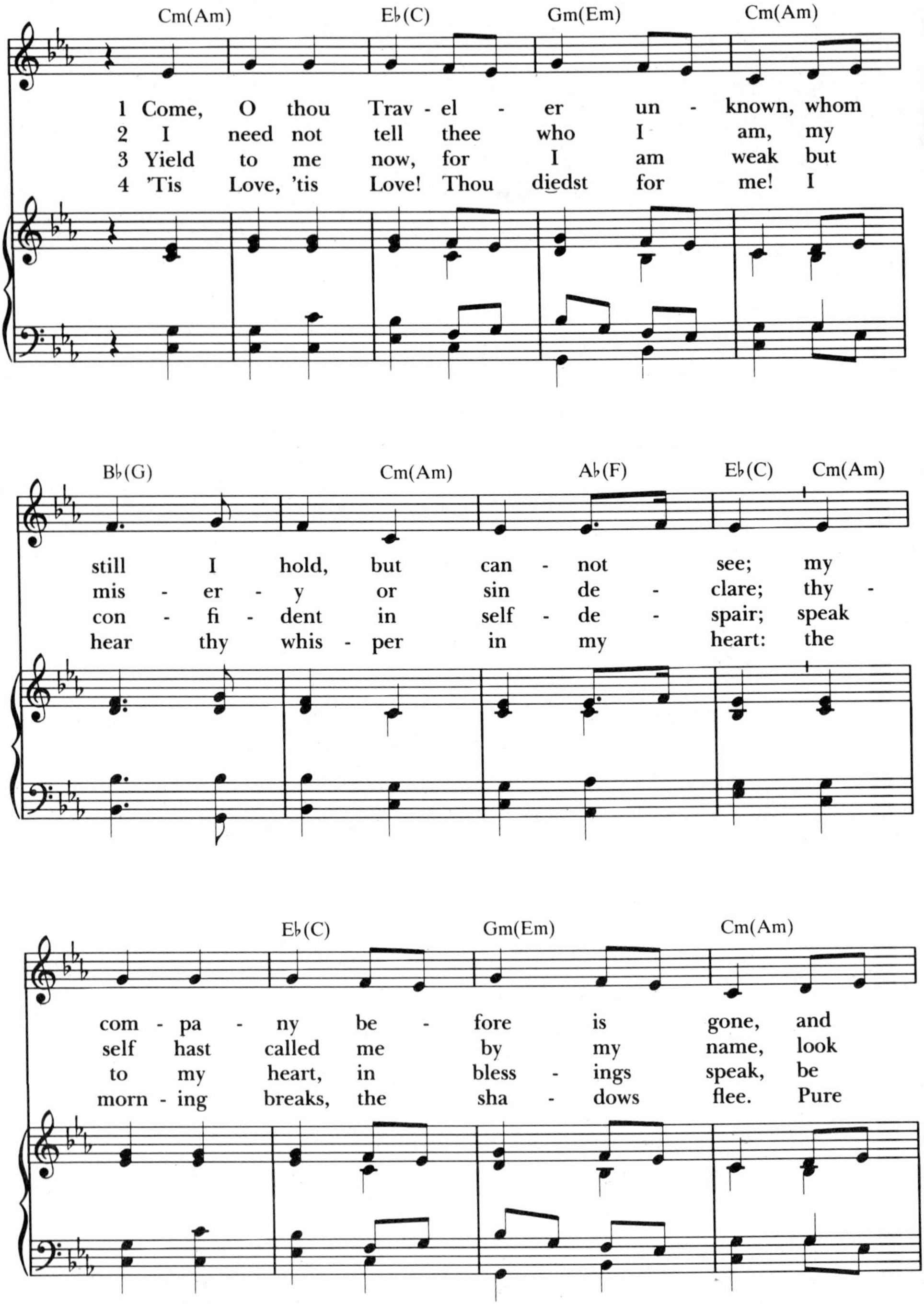
Cm(Am) E♭(C) Gm(Em) Cm(Am)
1 Come, O thou Trav - el - er un - known, whom
2 I need not tell thee who I am, my
3 Yield to me now, for I am weak but
4 'Tis Love, 'tis Love! Thou diedst for me! I
B♭(G) Cm(Am) A♭(F) E♭(C) Cm(Am)
still I hold, but can - not see; my
mis - er - y or sin de - clare; thy -
con - fi - dent in self - de - spair; speak
hear thy whis - per in my heart: the
E♭(C) Gm(Em) Cm(Am)
com - pa - ny be - fore is gone, and
self hast called me by my name, look
to my heart, in bless - ings speak, be
morn - ing breaks, the sha - dows flee. Pure

B♭(G) Cm(Am) A♭(F) E♭(C)
I am left a - lone with thee. With
on thy hands, and read it there. But
con - quered by my in - stant prayer. Speak,
U - ni - ver - sal Love thou art; thy
A♭(F) Gm(Em) Cm(Am)
thee all night I mean to stay, and
who, I ask thee, who art thou? Tell
or thou nev - er hence shalt move, and
mer - cies nev - er shall re - move, thy
E♭(C) Fm(Dm) Gm(Em) E♭(C) Cm(Am)
wres - tle till the break of day.
me thy name, and tell me now.
tell me, if thy name is Love.
na - ture and thy name is Love.

Cm (capo 3, Am). Alternative tune: *Woodbury*, 639.

Words: Charles Wesley (1707-1788), alt.
Music: *Vernon,* traditional melody; harm. att. Lucius Chapin (1760-1842); arr. *Hymnal 1982*

𝅗𝅥 = 52
88. 88. 88

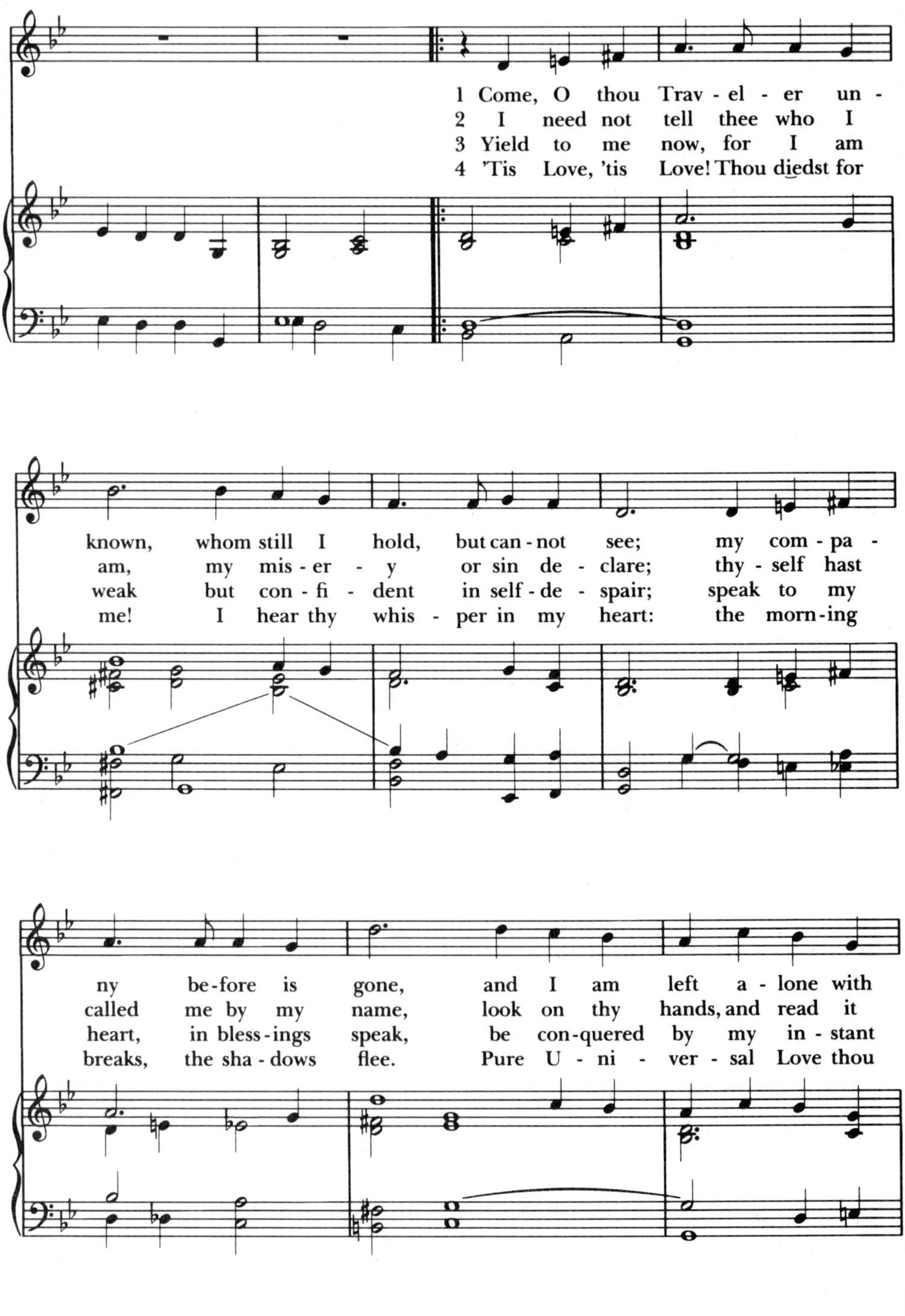
1 Come, O thou Trav - el - er un -
2 I need not tell thee who I
3 Yield to me now, for I am
4 'Tis Love, 'tis Love! Thou diedst for
known, whom still I hold, but can - not see; my com - pa -
am, my mis - er - y or sin de - clare; thy - self hast
weak but con - fi - dent in self - de - spair; speak to my
me! I hear thy whis - per in my heart: the morn - ing
ny be - fore is gone, and I am left a - lone with
called me by my name, look on thy hands, and read it
heart, in bless - ings speak, be con - quered by my in - stant
breaks, the sha - dows flee. Pure U - ni - ver - sal Love thou

thee. With thee all night I mean to stay, and wres - tle till the break of day.
there. But who, I ask thee, who are thou? Tell me thy name, and tell me now.
prayer. Speak, or thou nev - er hence shalt move, and tell me, if thy name is Love.
art; thy mer - cies nev - er shall re - move, thy na - ture and thy name is (Love.)
1-3
Final Ending
Love.

Alternative tune: *Vernon,* 638.

Words: Charles Wesley (1707-1788), alt.
Music: *Woodbury,* Eric Routley (1917-1982)

𝅗𝅥=60
88. 88. 88

1 Watch-man, tell us of the night, what its signs of prom-ise
2 Watch-man, tell us of the night; high-er yet that star a -
3 Watch-man, tell us of the night, for the morn-ing seems to
are. Trav - eler, o'er yon moun-tain's height, see that glo - ry -
scends. Trav - eler, bless - ed - ness and light, peace and truth its
dawn. Trav - eler, dark - ness takes its flight, doubt and ter - ror
beam - ing star. Watch-man, does its beau - teous ray
course por - tends. Watch-man, will its beams a - lone
are with - drawn. Watch-man, let thy wan - derings cease;
aught of joy or hope fore - tell? Trav - eler, yes; it
gild the spot that gave them birth? Trav - eler, a - ges
hie thee to thy qui - et home. Trav - eler, lo! the

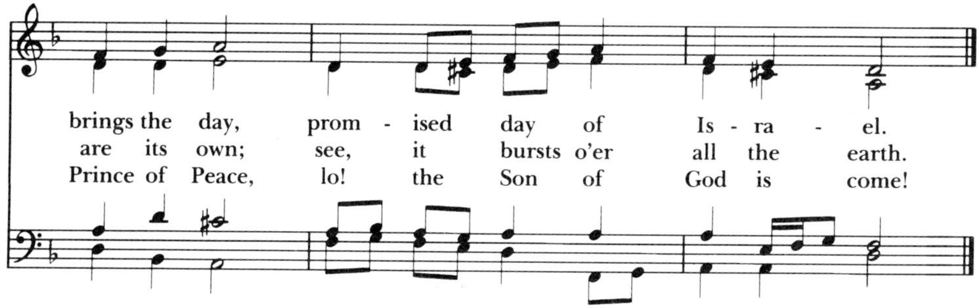
brings the day, prom - ised day of Is - ra - el.
are its own; see, it bursts o'er all the earth.
Prince of Peace, lo! the Son of God is come!

Two groups may sing antiphonally, alternating by sentences. This music in e, 699.

Words: John Bowring (1792-1872)
Music: *Aberystwyth,* Joseph Parry (1841-1903)

𝅗𝅥 = 44
77. 77. D

The Christian Life

641

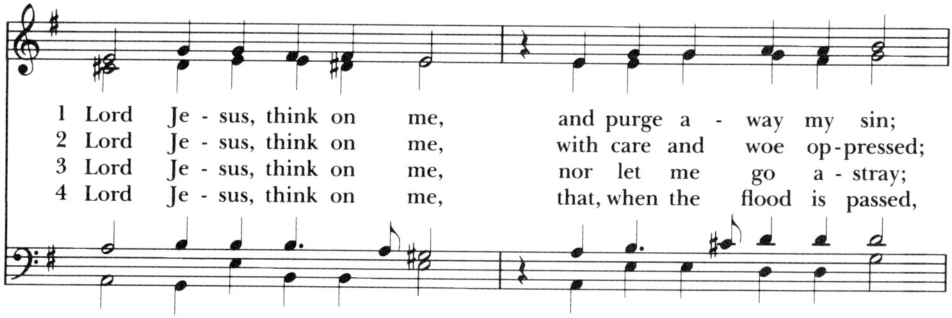
1 Lord Je - sus, think on me, and purge a - way my sin;
2 Lord Je - sus, think on me, with care and woe op - pressed;
3 Lord Je - sus, think on me, nor let me go a - stray;
4 Lord Je - sus, think on me, that, when the flood is passed,

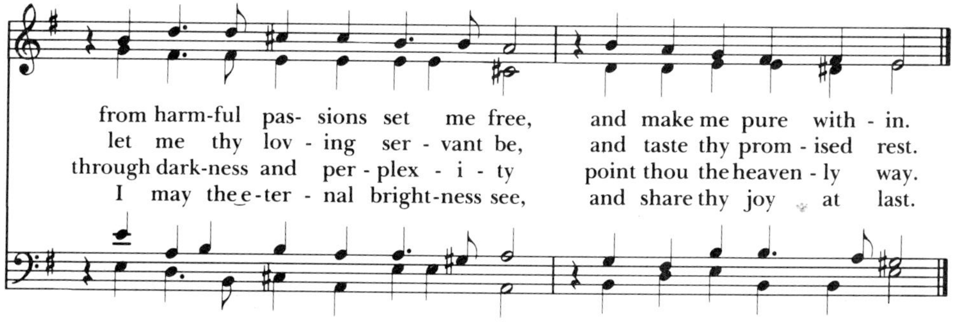
from harm-ful pas- sions set me free, and make me pure with - in.
let me thy lov - ing ser - vant be, and taste thy prom - ised rest.
through dark-ness and per - plex - i - ty point thou the heaven - ly way.
I may the e - ter - nal bright-ness see, and share thy joy at last.

Alternative tune: *St. Bride,* 666.

Words: Synesius of Cyrene (375?-414?); tr. Allen William Chatfield (1808-1896), alt.
Music: *Southwell,* from *Daman's Psalter,* 1579; adapt. *Hymnal 1982*

♩ = 80
SM

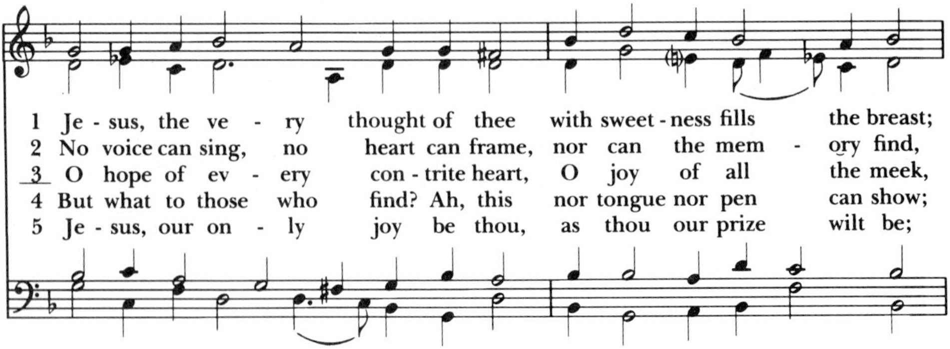
1 Je - sus, the ve - ry thought of thee with sweet - ness fills the breast;
2 No voice can sing, no heart can frame, nor can the mem - ory find,
3 O hope of ev - ery con - trite heart, O joy of all the meek,
4 But what to those who find? Ah, this nor tongue nor pen can show;
5 Je - sus, our on - ly joy be thou, as thou our prize wilt be;

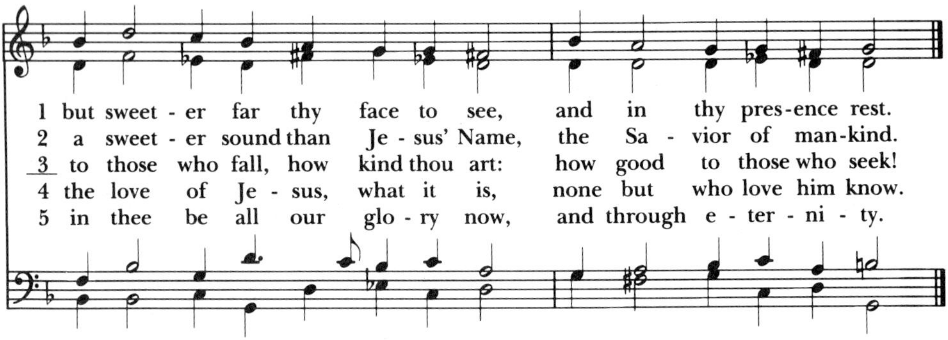
1 but sweet - er far thy face to see, and in thy pres-ence rest.
2 a sweet - er sound than Je - sus' Name, the Sa - vior of man-kind.
3 to those who fall, how kind thou art: how good to those who seek!
4 the love of Je - sus, what it is, none but who love him know.
5 in thee be all our glo - ry now, and through e - ter - ni - ty.

Alternative tune: *Windsor* (isometric), 643.

Words: Latin, 12th cent.; st. 5, Latin, 15th cent.; tr. Edward Caswall (1814-1878), alt.
Music: *Windsor*, melody William Damon (1540?-1591?); harm. Thomas Este (1540?-1608?)

♩=84
CM

Unison or harmony

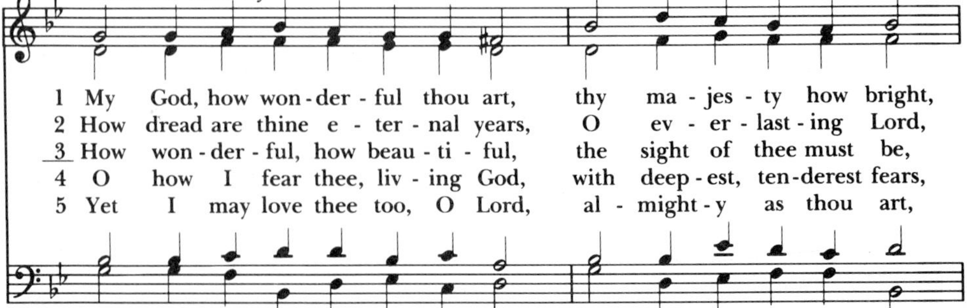
1 My God, how won - der - ful thou art, thy ma - jes - ty how bright,
2 How dread are thine e - ter - nal years, O ev - er - last - ing Lord,
3 How won - der - ful, how beau - ti - ful, the sight of thee must be,
4 O how I fear thee, liv - ing God, with deep - est, ten-derest fears,
5 Yet I may love thee too, O Lord, al - might - y as thou art,

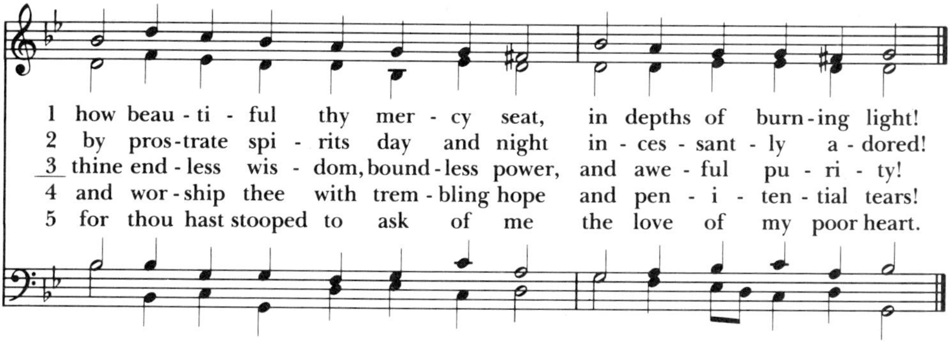
1 how beau - ti - ful thy mer - cy seat, in depths of burn - ing light!
2 by pros - trate spi - rits day and night in - ces - sant - ly a - dored!
3 thine end - less wis - dom, bound - less power, and awe - ful pu - ri - ty!
4 and wor - ship thee with trem - bling hope and pen - i - ten - tial tears!
5 for thou hast stooped to ask of me the love of my poor heart.

Alternative tune: *Windsor* (rhythmic), 642.

Words: Frederick William Faber (1814-1863)
Music: *Windsor,* melody William Damon (1540?-1591?), alt.; harm. *Booke of Musicke,* 1591

♩= 84
CM

The Christian Life

644

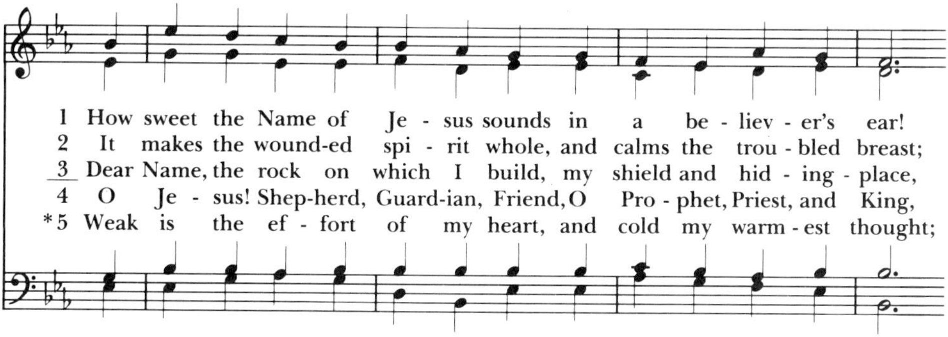
1 How sweet the Name of Je - sus sounds in a be - liev - er's ear!
2 It makes the wound-ed spi - rit whole, and calms the trou - bled breast;
3 Dear Name, the rock on which I build, my shield and hid - ing - place,
4 O Je - sus! Shep-herd, Guard-ian, Friend, O Pro - phet, Priest, and King,
*5 Weak is the ef - fort of my heart, and cold my warm - est thought;

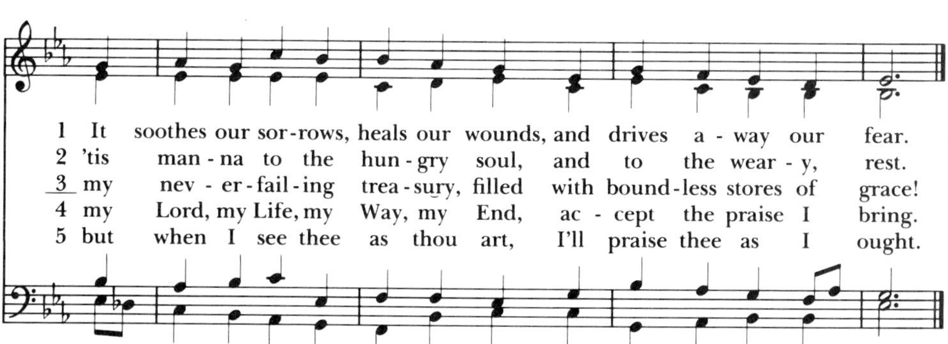
1 It soothes our sor - rows, heals our wounds, and drives a - way our fear.
2 'tis man - na to the hun - gry soul, and to the wear - y, rest.
3 my nev - er - fail - ing trea - sury, filled with bound - less stores of grace!
4 my Lord, my Life, my Way, my End, ac - cept the praise I bring.
5 but when I see thee as thou art, I'll praise thee as I ought.

Words: John Newton (1725-1807), alt.
Music: *St. Peter,* Alexander Robert Reinagle (1799-1877)

♩= 88
CM

1 The King of love my shep - herd is, whose good - ness
2 Where streams of liv - ing wa - ter flow, my ran - somed
*3 Per - verse and fool - ish oft I strayed, but yet in
*4 In death's dark vale I fear no ill with thee, dear
5 Thou spread'st a ta - ble in my sight; thy unc - tion
6 And so through all the length of days thy good - ness
1 fail - eth nev - er; I noth - ing lack if
2 soul he lead - eth, and where the ver - dant
3 love he sought me, and on his shoul - der
4 Lord, be - side me; thy rod and staff my
5 grace be - stow - eth; and oh, what trans - port
6 fail - eth nev - er: Good Shep - herd, may I

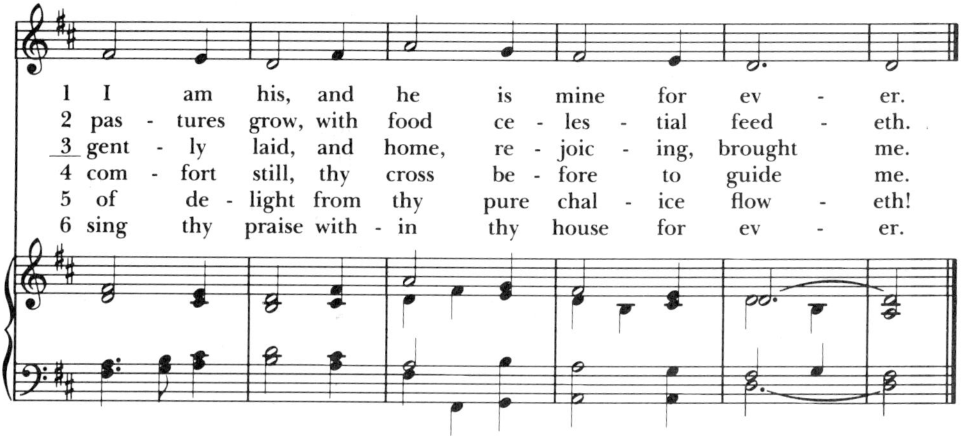
1 I am his, and he is mine for ev - er.
2 pas - tures grow, with food ce - les - tial feed - eth.
3 gent - ly laid, and home, re - joic - ing, brought me.
4 com - fort still, thy cross be - fore to guide me.
5 of de - light from thy pure chal - ice flow - eth!
6 sing thy praise with - in thy house for ev - er.

Alternative tune: *Dominus regit me,* 646.

Words: Henry Williams Baker (1821-1877); para. of Psalm 23
Music: *St. Columba,* Irish melody; harm. *Hymnal 1982*

♩= 100
87. 87

Descant
6 And so through all the length of days thy
1 The King of love my shep - herd is, whose
2 Where streams of liv - ing wa - ter flow, my
*3 Per - verse and fool - ish oft I strayed, but
*4 In death's dark vale I fear no ill with
5 Thou spread'st a ta - ble in my sight; thy
6 good - ness fail - eth nev - er: Good Shep-herd, may I
1 good - ness fail - eth nev - er; I noth - ing lack if
2 ran - somed soul he lead - eth, and where the ver - dant
3 yet in love he sought me, and on his shoul-der
4 thee, dear Lord, be - side me; thy rod and staff my
5 unc - tion grace be - stow - eth; and oh, what trans-port

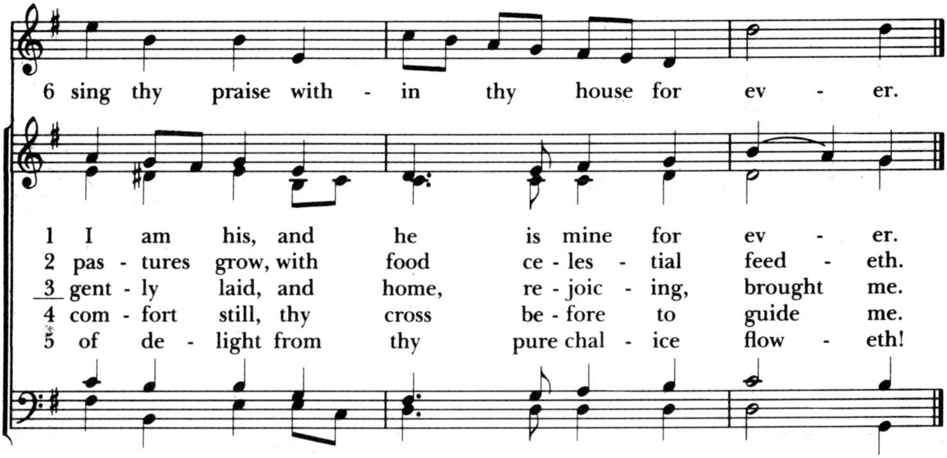
6 sing thy praise with - in thy house for ev - er.
1 I am his, and he is mine for ev - er.
2 pas - tures grow, with food ce - les - tial feed - eth.
3 gent - ly laid, and home, re - joic - ing, brought me.
4 com - fort still, thy cross be - fore to guide me.
5 of de - light from thy pure chal - ice flow - eth!

6 And so through all the length of days
thy goodness faileth never:
Good shepherd, may I sing thy praise
within thy house for ever.

Alternative tune: *St. Columba*, 645.

Words: Henry Williams Baker (1821-1877); para. of Psalm 23 — 𝅗𝅥=48
Music: *Dominus regit me*, John Bacchus Dykes (1823-1876); desc. David Willcocks (b. 1919) — 87. 87

1 I know not where the road will lead I follow day by day,
2 And some I love have reached the end, but some with me may stay,
3 The count-less hosts lead on be-fore, I must not fear nor stray;
or where it ends: I on-ly know I walk the King's high-way.
their faith and hope still guid-ing me: I walk the King's high-way.
with them, the pil-grims of the faith, I walk the King's high-way.
I know not if the way is long, and no one else can say;
The way is truth, the way is love, for light and strength I pray,
Through light and dark the road leads on till dawns the end-less day,
but rough or smooth, up hill or down, I walk the King's high-way.
and through the years of life, to God I walk the King's high-way.
when I shall know why in this life I walk the King's high-way.

Words: Evelyn Atwater Cummins (1891-1971)
Music: *Laramie,* Arnold George Henry Bode (1866-1952)

𝅗𝅥=60
CMD

Fm(Dm) Cm(Am) Fm(Dm) C(A) C7(A7) Fm(Dm)
1 When Is - rael was in E - gypt's land, let my peo-ple go;
2 The Lord told Mo - ses what to do, let my peo-ple go;
3 They jour-neyed on at his com - mand, let my peo-ple go;
4 Oh, let us all from bond - age flee, let my peo-ple go;
Fm(Dm) Cm(Am) Fm(Dm) C(A) C7(A7) Fm(Dm)
op-pressed so hard they could not stand, let my peo-ple go.
to lead the chil - dren of Is - rael through, let my peo-ple go.
and came at length to Ca - naan's land, let my peo-ple go.
and let us all in Christ be free, let my peo-ple go.
Refrain
Fm(Dm) B♭m(Gm) C(A) Fm(Dm)
Go down, Mo - ses, way down in E - gypt's land;
Fm7(Dm7) Ddim7(Bdim7) B♭m7 (Gm7) Fm(Dm) C7(A7) Fm(Dm)
tell old Pha - raoh to let my peo - ple go.

Fm (capo 3, Dm).

Words: Afro-American spiritual

Music: *Go Down, Moses,* Afro-American spiritual; arr. Horace Clarence Boyer (b. 1935)

𝅗𝅥 = 54

85. 85 with Refrain

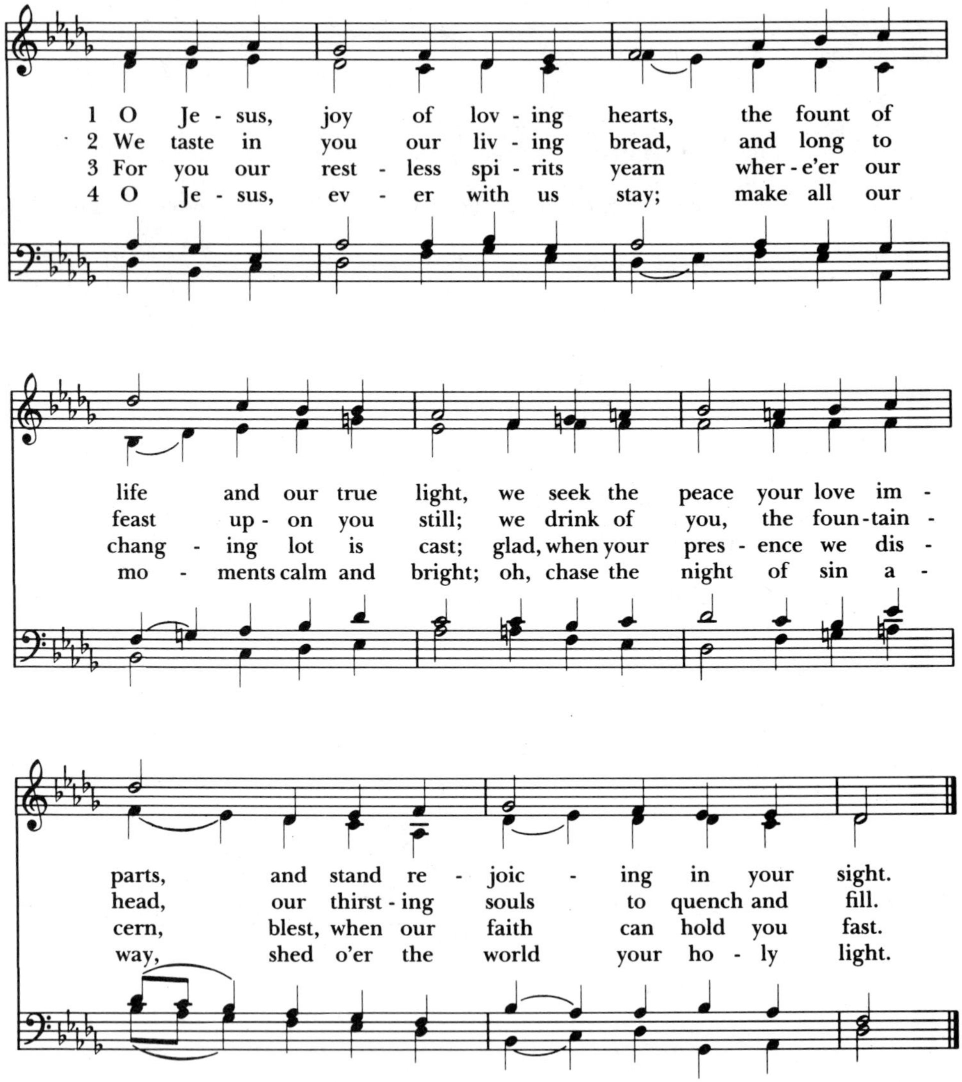
1 O Je - sus, joy of lov - ing hearts, the fount of
2 We taste in you our liv - ing bread, and long to
3 For you our rest - less spi - rits yearn wher - e'er our
4 O Je - sus, ev - er with us stay; make all our
life and our true light, we seek the peace your love im -
feast up - on you still; we drink of you, the foun - tain -
chang - ing lot is cast; glad, when your pres - ence we dis -
mo - ments calm and bright; oh, chase the night of sin a -
parts, and stand re - joic - ing in your sight.
head, our thirst - ing souls to quench and fill.
cern, blest, when our faith can hold you fast.
way, shed o'er the world your ho - ly light.

This music in D, 593. Alternative tune: *Jesu dulcis memoria,* 650.

Words: Att. Bernard of Clairvaux (1091-1153); tr. and para. Ray Palmer (1808-1887), alt.
Music: *Dickinson College,* Lee Hastings Bristol, Jr. (1923-1979)

♩= 108
LM

1 O Je - sus, joy of lov - ing hearts, the fount of life and
2 We taste in you our liv - ing bread, and long to feast up -
3 For you our rest - less spi - rits yearn wher - e'er our chang - ing
4 O Je - sus, ev - er with us stay; make all our mo - ments
our true light, we seek the peace your love im -
on you still; we drink of you, the foun - tain -
lot is cast; glad, when your pres - ence we dis -
calm and bright; oh, chase the night of sin a -
parts, and stand re - joic - ing in your sight.
head, our thirst - ing souls to quench and fill.
cern, blest, when our faith can hold you fast.
way, shed o'er the world your ho - ly light.

Other accompaniments, 18 and 134. Alternative tune: *Dickinson College,* 649.

Words: Att. Bernard of Clairvaux (1091-1153); tr. and para. Ray Palmer (1808-1887), alt.
Music: *Jesu dulcis memoria,* plainsong, Mode 2; acc. Gerard Farrell (b. 1919) LM

1 This is my Fa - ther's world, and to my lis - tening ears
2 This is our Fa - ther's world, oh, let us not for - get
all na - ture sings and round me rings the mu - sic of the spheres.
that though the wrong is great and strong, God is our Fa - ther yet.
This is my Fa - ther's world: I rest me in the thought of
He trusts us with his world, to keep it clean and fair, all
rocks and trees, of skies and seas, his hand the won - ders wrought.
earth and trees, all skies and seas, all crea - tures ev - ery - where.

Words: St. 1, Maltbie D. Babcock (1858-1901); st. 2, Mary Babcock Crawford (b. 1909)
Music: *Mercer Street,* Malcolm Williamson (b. 1931)

♩=72
SMD

652

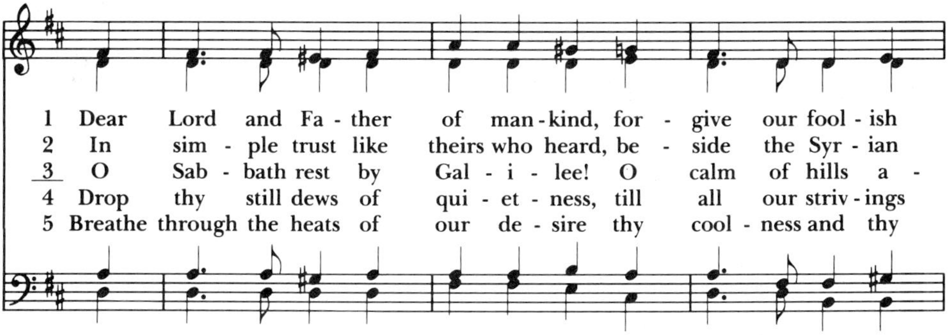
1 Dear Lord and Fa - ther of man - kind, for - give our fool - ish
2 In sim - ple trust like theirs who heard, be - side the Syr - ian
3 O Sab - bath rest by Gal - i - lee! O calm of hills a -
4 Drop thy still dews of qui - et - ness, till all our striv - ings
5 Breathe through the heats of our de - sire thy cool - ness and thy

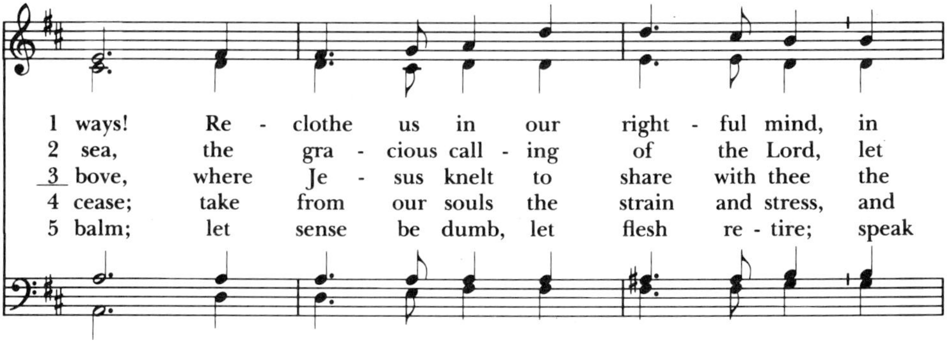
1 ways! Re - clothe us in our right - ful mind, in
2 sea, the gra - cious call - ing of the Lord, let
3 bove, where Je - sus knelt to share with thee the
4 cease; take from our souls the strain and stress, and
5 balm; let sense be dumb, let flesh re - tire; speak

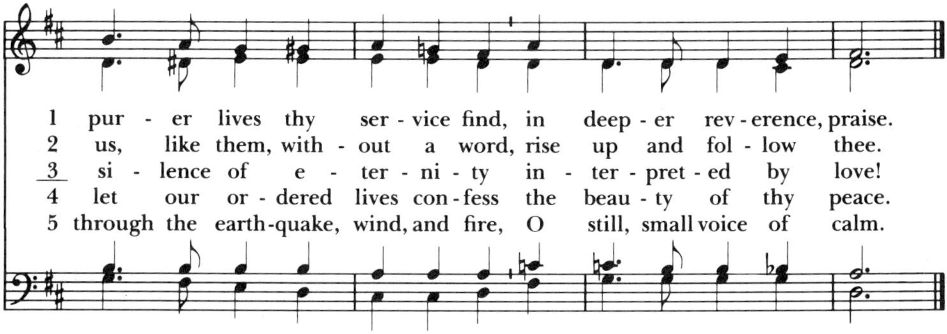
1 pur - er lives thy ser - vice find, in deep - er rev - erence, praise.
2 us, like them, with - out a word, rise up and fol - low thee.
3 si - lence of e - ter - ni - ty in - ter - pret - ed by love!
4 let our or - dered lives con - fess the beau - ty of thy peace.
5 through the earth - quake, wind, and fire, O still, small voice of calm.

Alternative tune: *Repton*, 653.

Words: John Greenleaf Whittier (1807-1892), alt.
Music: *Rest*, Frederick Charles Maker (1844-1927)

𝅗𝅥=50
86. 886

1 Dear Lord and Fa - ther of man-kind, for -
2 In sim - ple trust like theirs who heard, be -
3 O Sab - bath rest by Gal - i - lee! O
4 Drop thy still dews of qui - et - ness, till
5 Breathe through the heats of our de - sire thy
1 give our fool - ish ways! Re - clothe us in our
2 side the Syr - ian sea, the gra - cious call - ing
3 calm of hills a - bove, where Je - sus knelt to
4 all our striv - ings cease; take from our souls the
5 cool - ness and thy balm; let sense be dumb, let
1 right - ful mind, in pur - er lives thy ser - vice find, in
2 of the Lord, let us, like them, with - out a word, rise
3 share with thee the si - lence of e - ter - ni - ty in -
4 strain and stress, and let our or - dered lives con - fess the
5 flesh re - tire; speak through the earth-quake, wind, and fire, O

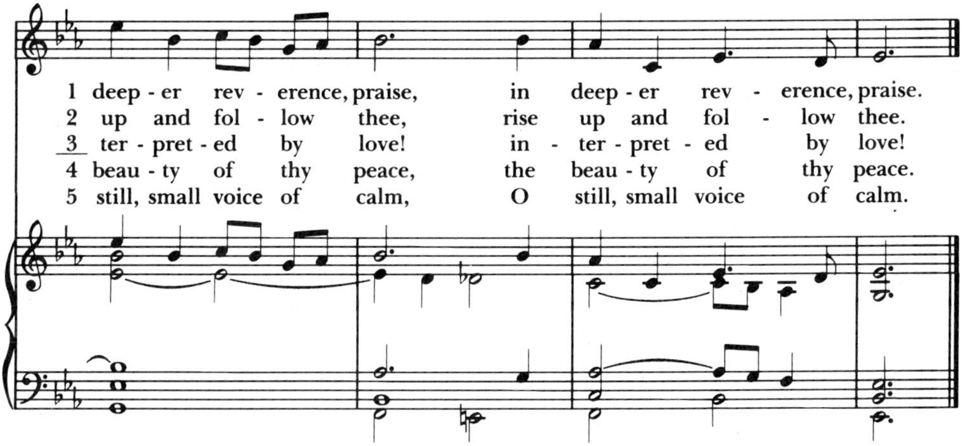
1 deep - er rev - erence, praise, in deep - er rev - erence, praise.
2 up and fol - low thee, rise up and fol - low thee.
3 ter - pret - ed by love! in - ter - pret - ed by love!
4 beau - ty of thy peace, the beau - ty of thy peace.
5 still, small voice of calm, O still, small voice of calm.

Alternative tune: *Rest,* 652.

Words: John Greenleaf Whittier (1807-1892), alt.
Music: *Repton,* Charles Hubert Hastings Parry (1848-1918), alt.

𝅗𝅥=48
86. 886

The Christian Life 654

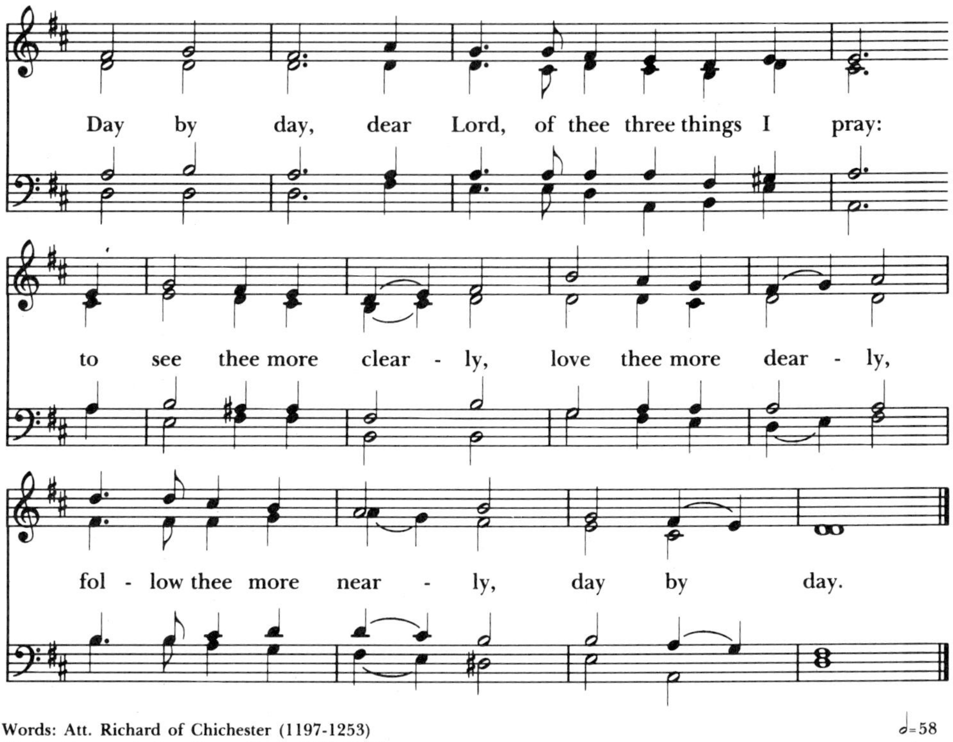
Day by day, dear Lord, of thee three things I pray:
to see thee more clear - ly, love thee more dear - ly,
fol - low thee more near - ly, day by day.

Words: Att. Richard of Chichester (1197-1253)
Music: *Sumner,* Arthur Henry Biggs (1906-1954)

𝅗𝅥=58
Irr.

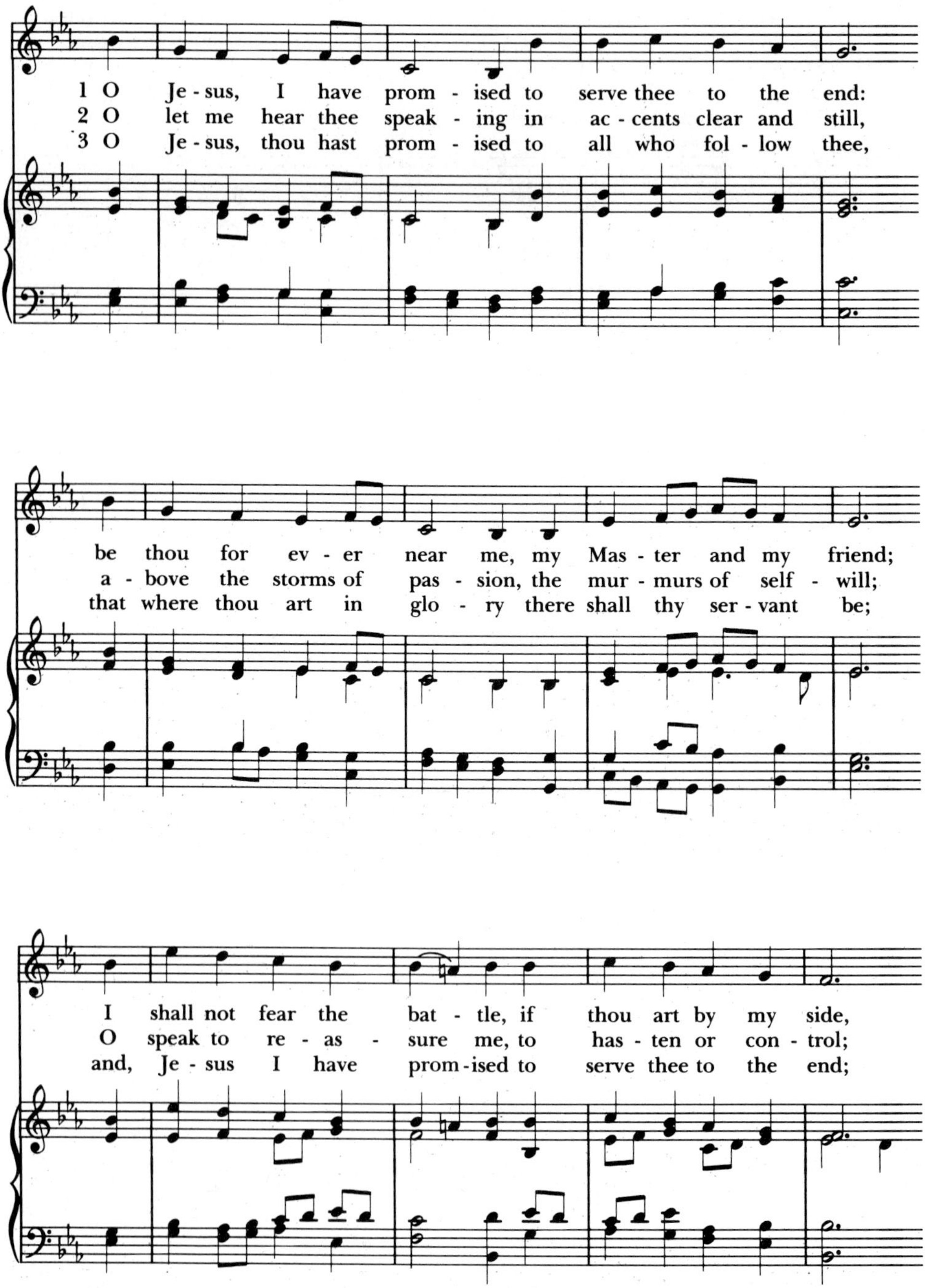
1 O Je - sus, I have prom - ised to serve thee to the end:
2 O let me hear thee speak - ing in ac - cents clear and still,
3 O Je - sus, thou hast prom - ised to all who fol - low thee,
be thou for ev - er near me, my Mas - ter and my friend;
a - bove the storms of pas - sion, the mur - murs of self - will;
that where thou art in glo - ry there shall thy ser - vant be;
I shall not fear the bat - tle, if thou art by my side,
O speak to re - as - sure me, to has - ten or con - trol;
and, Je - sus I have prom - ised to serve thee to the end;

nor wan - der from the path - way, if thou wilt be my guide.
O speak, and make me lis - ten, thou guard - ian of my soul.
O give me grace to fol - low, my Mas - ter and my friend.

Words: John Ernest Bode (1816-1874), alt.
Music: *Nyland,* Finnish folk melody; adapt. and harm. David Evans (1874-1948)

𝅗𝅥=48
76. 76. D

The Christian Life

656

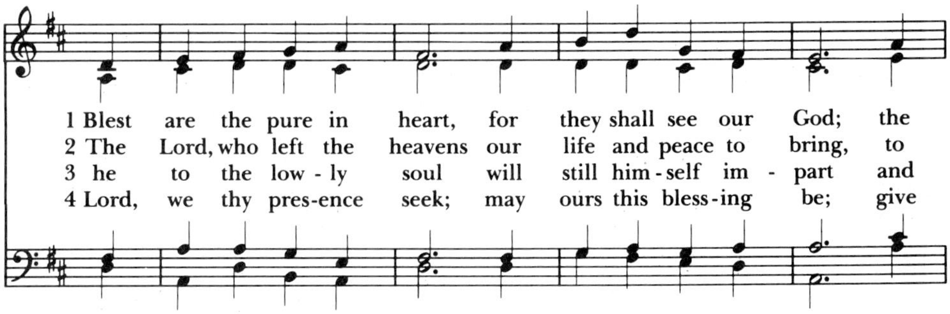
1 Blest are the pure in heart, for they shall see our God; the
2 The Lord, who left the heavens our life and peace to bring, to
3 he to the low - ly soul will still him - self im - part and
4 Lord, we thy pres-ence seek; may ours this bless-ing be; give

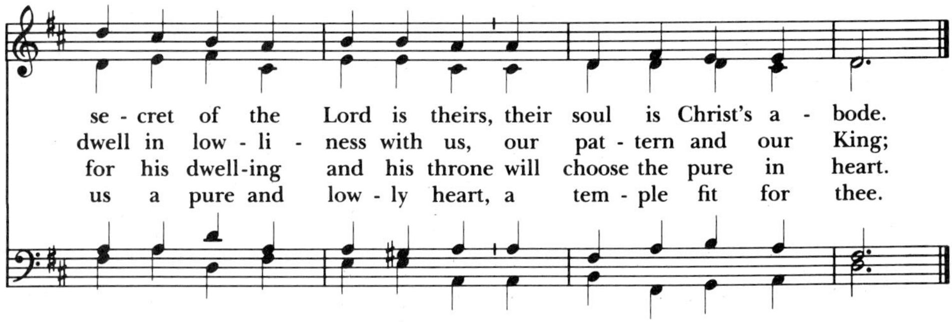
se - cret of the Lord is theirs, their soul is Christ's a - bode.
dwell in low - li - ness with us, our pat - tern and our King;
for his dwell-ing and his throne will choose the pure in heart.
us a pure and low - ly heart, a tem - ple fit for thee.

Words: Sts. 1 and 3, John Keble (1792-1866), alt.; st. 2 and 4, William John Hall (1793-1861), alt.
Music: *Franconia,* melody Johann Balthasar König (1691-1758);
adapt. and harm. William Henry Havergal (1793-1870)

𝅗𝅥=56
SM

1 Love di - vine, all loves ex - cell - ing, joy of heaven, to
2 Come, al - might - y to de - liv - er, let us all thy
3 Fi - nish then thy new cre - a - tion; pure and spot - less
earth come down, fix in us thy hum - ble dwell - ing, all thy
life re - ceive; sud - den - ly re - turn, and nev - er, nev - er -
let us be; let us see thy great sal - va - tion per - fect -
faith - ful mer - cies crown. Je - sus, thou art all com - pas - sion,
more thy tem - ples leave. Thee we would be al - way bless - ing,
ly re - stored in thee: changed from glo - ry in - to glo - ry,
pure, un - bound - ed love thou art;
serve thee as thy hosts a - bove,
till in heaven we take our place,
vis - it us with
pray, and praise thee
till we cast our

thy sal - va - tion, en - ter ev - ery trem-bling heart.
with - out ceas - ing, glo - ry in thy per - fect love.
crowns be - fore thee, lost in won - der, love, and praise.

Words: Charles Wesley (1707-1788)
Music: *Hyfrydol*, Rowland Hugh Prichard (1811-1887)

♩=112
87. 87. D

The Christian Life 658

1 As longs the deer for cool - ing streams in
2 For thee, my God, the liv - ing God, my
3 Why rest - less, why cast down, my soul? Hope
4 To Fa - ther, Son, and Ho - ly Ghost, the

parched and bar - ren ways, so longs my soul, O
thirst - y soul doth pine: O when shall I be -
still, and thou shalt sing the praise of him who
God whom we a - dore, be glo - ry, as it

God, for thee and thy re - fresh - ing grace.
hold thy face, thou Ma - jes - ty di - vine?
is thy God, thy health's e - ter - nal spring.
was, is now, and shall be ev - er - more.

Words: *New Version of the Psalms of David*, 1696, alt.; para. of Psalm 42:1-7
Music: *Martyrdom*, melody and bass Hugh Wilson (1764-1824); adapt. and harm. Robert Smith (1780-1829)

♩.=44
CM

1 O Mas - ter, let me walk with thee
2 (Help me the slow of heart to) move
3 (Teach me thy pa - tience; still with) thee
4 (in hope that sends a shin - ing) ray
in low - ly paths of ser - vice free;
by some clear, win - ning word of love;
in clos - er, dear - er com - pa - ny,
far down the fu - ture's broad - ening way,
tell me thy se - cret; help me bear
teach me the way - ward feet to stay,
in work that keeps faith sweet and strong,
in peace that on - ly thou canst give,

the strain of toil, the fret of care.
and guide them in the home - ward way.
in trust that tri - umphs o - ver wrong,
with thee, O Mas - ter, let me live.

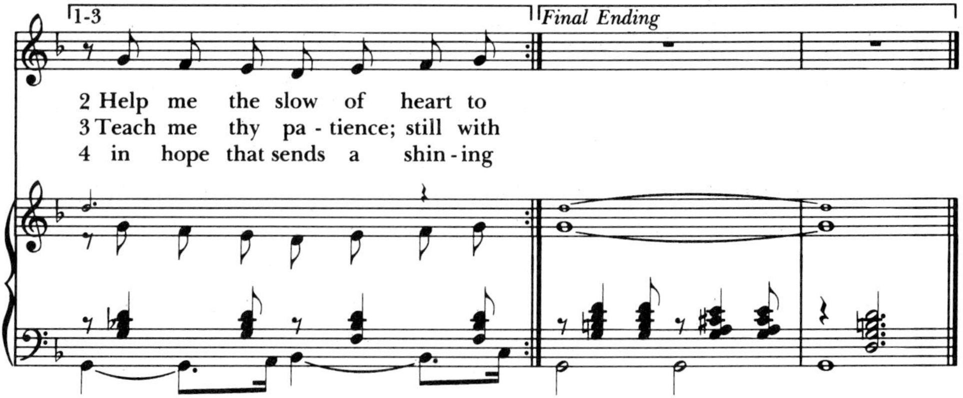
1-3
Final Ending
2 Help me the slow of heart to
3 Teach me thy pa - tience; still with
4 in hope that sends a shin - ing

The obbligato in the right hand of the accompaniment may be played by an assistant, sung by sopranos, or played on a solo instrument. Alternative tune: *Maryton,* 660.

Words: Washington Gladden (1836-1918)
Music: *de Tar,* Calvin Hampton (1938-1984)

♩= 72
LM

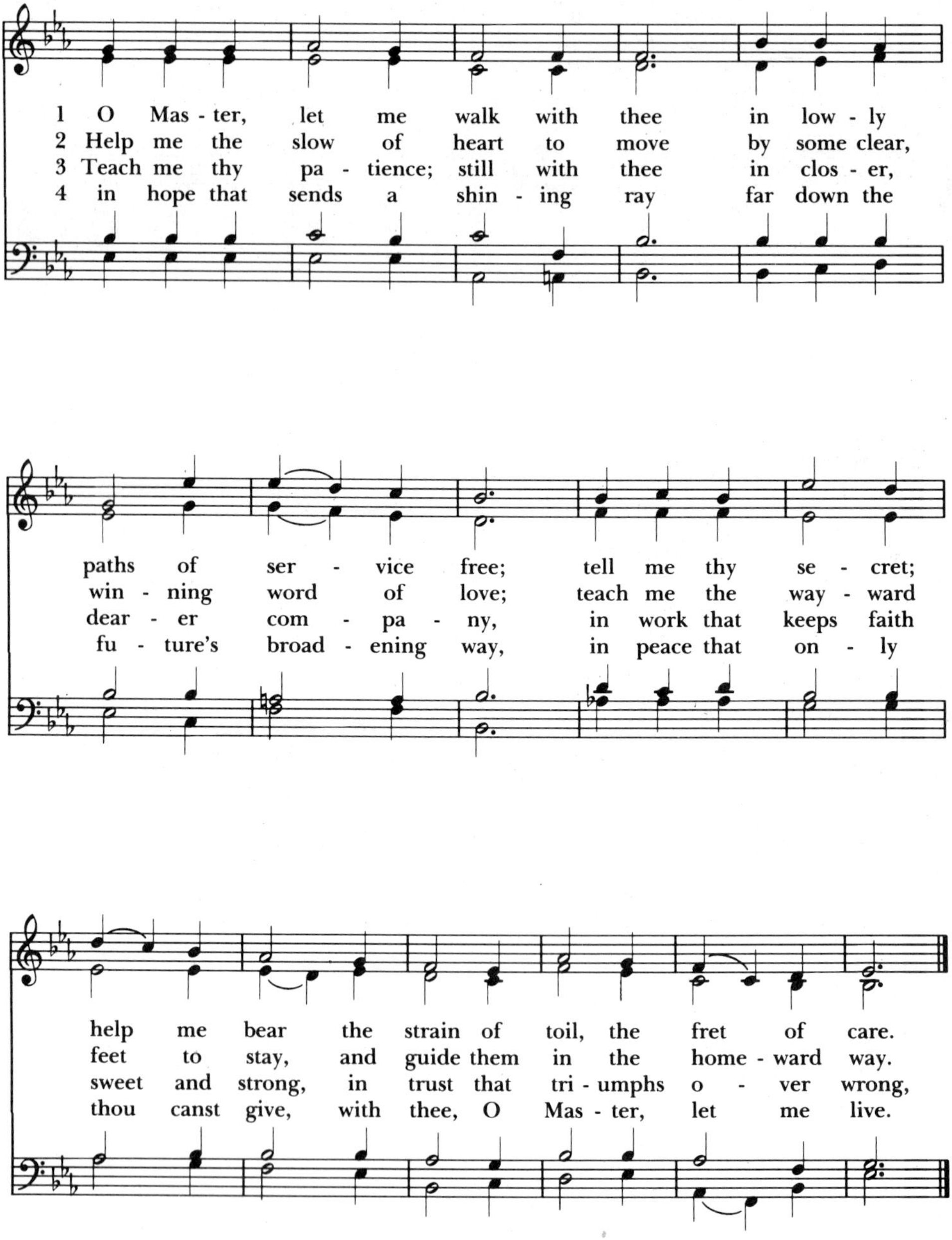
1 O Mas - ter, let me walk with thee in low - ly
2 Help me the slow of heart to move by some clear,
3 Teach me thy pa - tience; still with thee in clos - er,
4 in hope that sends a shin - ing ray far down the
paths of ser - vice free; tell me thy se - cret;
win - ning word of love; teach me the way - ward
dear - er com - pa - ny, in work that keeps faith
fu - ture's broad - ening way, in peace that on - ly
help me bear the strain of toil, the fret of care.
feet to stay, and guide them in the home - ward way.
sweet and strong, in trust that tri - umphs o - ver wrong,
thou canst give, with thee, O Mas - ter, let me live.

Alternative tune: *de Tar,* 659.

Words: Washington Gladden (1836-1918)
Music: *Maryton,* Henry Percy Smith (1825-1898)

♩= 100
LM

1 They cast their nets in Gal - i - lee just
2 Con - tent - ed, peace - ful fish - er - men, be -
3 Young John who trimmed the flap - ping sail, home -
4 The peace of God, it is no peace, but
off the hills of brown; such hap - py,
fore they ev - er knew the peace of
less, in Pat - mos died. Pe - ter, who
strife closed in the sod. Yet let us
sim - ple fish - er - folk, be - fore the Lord came down.
God that filled their hearts brim - ful, and broke them too.
hauled the teem - ing net, head - down was cru - ci - fied.
pray for but one thing— the mar - vel-ous peace of God.

Words: William Alexander Percy (1885-1942), alt.
Music: *Georgetown*, David McKinley Williams (1887-1978)

𝅗𝅥=56
CM

1 A - bide with me: fast falls the e - ven - tide;
2 I need thy pres - ence ev - ery pass - ing hour;
3 I fear no foe, with thee at hand to bless;
4 Hold thou thy cross be - fore my clos - ing eyes;
the dark - ness deep - ens; Lord, with me a - bide:
what but thy grace can foil the tempt-er's power?
ills have no weight, and tears no bit - ter - ness.
shine through the gloom, and point me to the skies;
when o - ther help - ers fail and com-forts flee,
Who, like thy - self, my guide and stay can be?
Where is death's sting? where, grave, thy vic - to - ry?
heaven's morn - ing breaks, and earth's vain sha - dows flee;
help of the help - less, O a - bide with me.
Through cloud and sun - shine, Lord, a - bide with me.
I tri - umph still, if thou a - bide with me.
in life, in death, O Lord, a - bide with me.

Words: Henry Francis Lyte (1793-1847)
Music: *Eventide,* William Henry Monk (1823-1889)

𝅗𝅥 = 54
10 10. 10 10

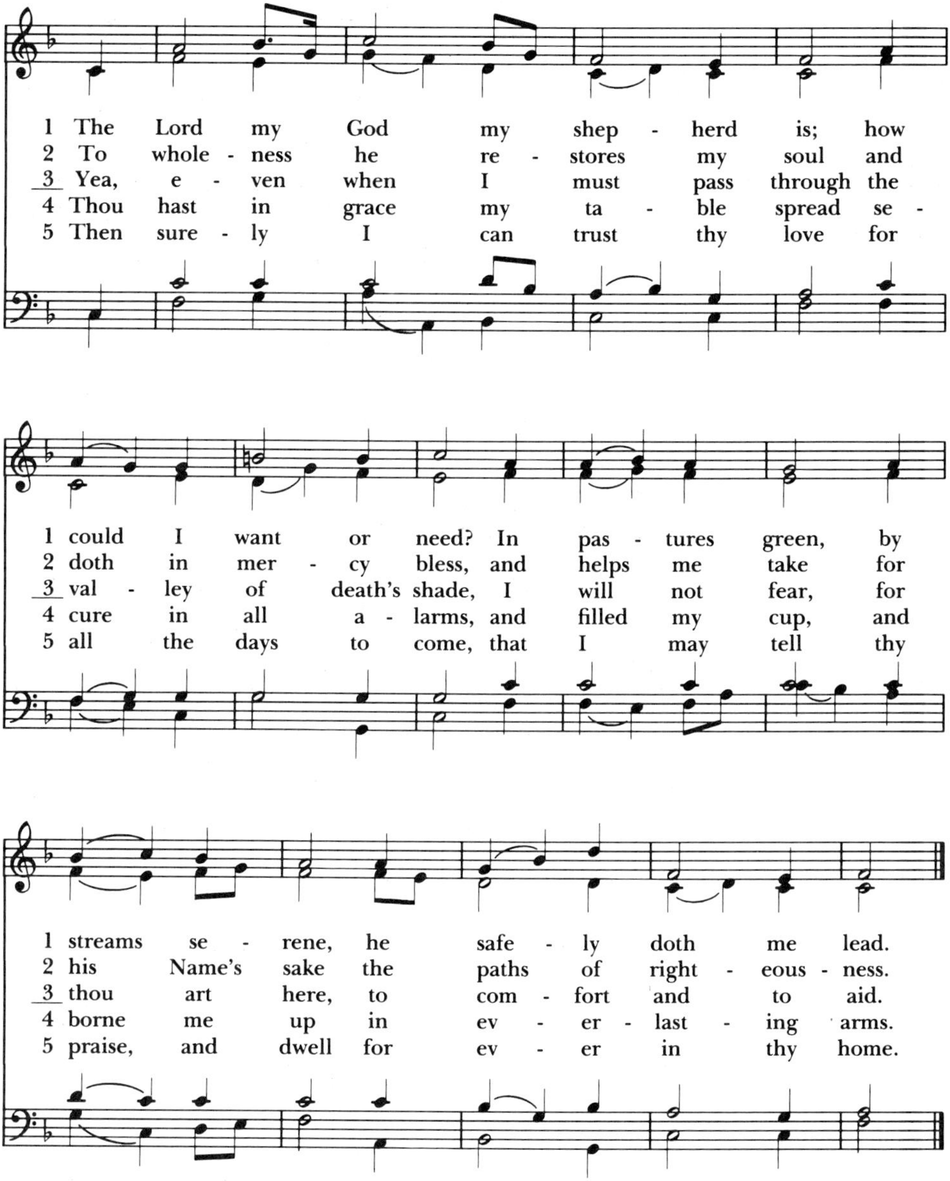
1 The Lord my God my shep - herd is; how
2 To whole - ness he re - stores my soul and
3 Yea, e - ven when I must pass through the
4 Thou hast in grace my ta - ble spread se -
5 Then sure - ly I can trust thy love for
1 could I want or need? In pas - tures green, by
2 doth in mer - cy bless, and helps me take for
3 val - ley of death's shade, I will not fear, for
4 cure in all a - larms, and filled my cup, and
5 all the days to come, that I may tell thy
1 streams se - rene, he safe - ly doth me lead.
2 his Name's sake the paths of right - eous - ness.
3 thou art here, to com - fort and to aid.
4 borne me up in ev - er - last - ing arms.
5 praise, and dwell for ev - er in thy home.

Words: F. Bland Tucker (1895-1984); para. of Psalm 23
Music: *Crimond,* melody Jesse Seymour Irvine (1836-1887); harm. *Hymnal 1982*

♩=84
CM

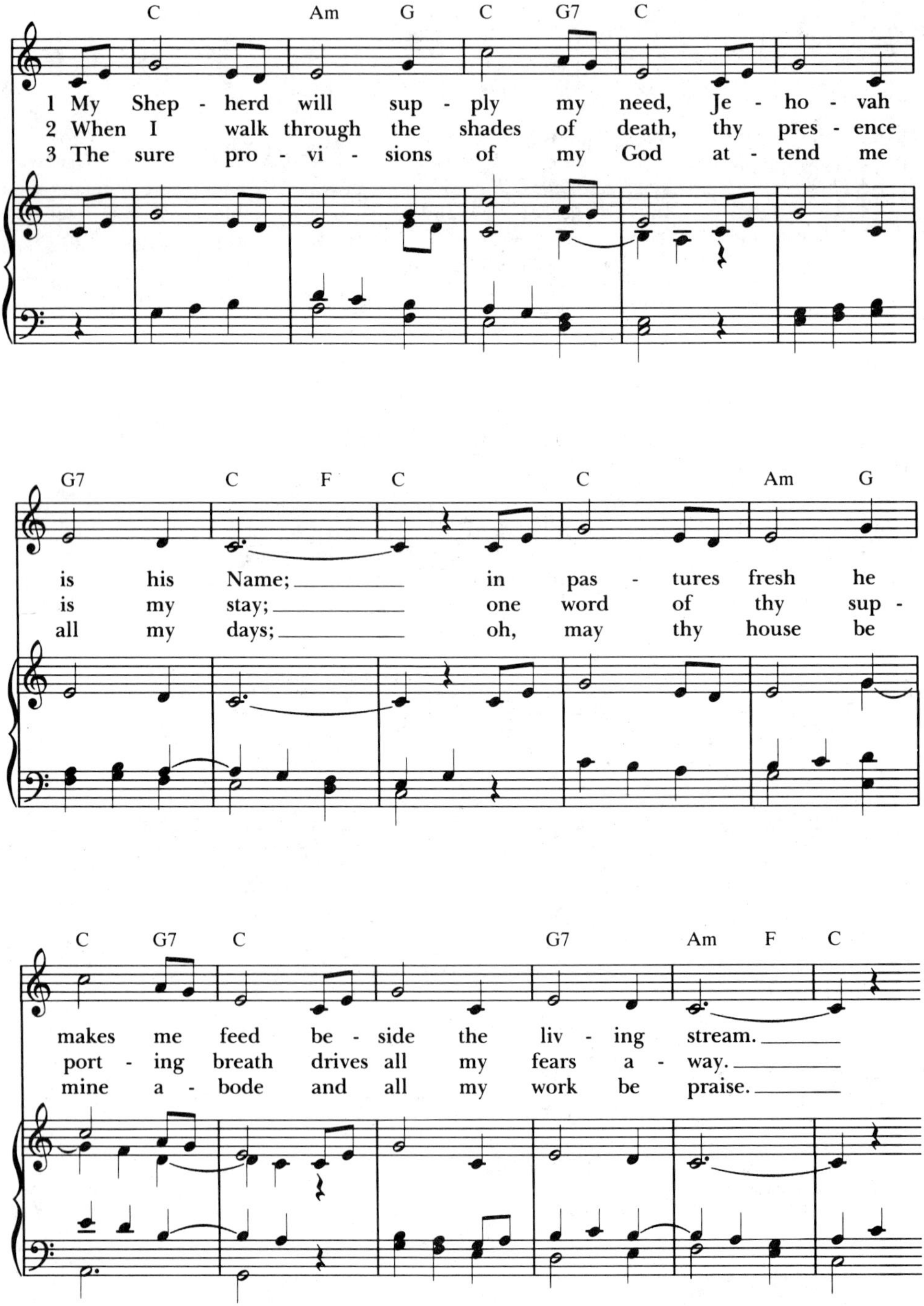
C Am G C G7 C
1 My Shep - herd will sup - ply my need, Je - ho - vah
2 When I walk through the shades of death, thy pres - ence
3 The sure pro - vi - sions of my God at - tend me
G7 C F C C Am G
is his Name; in pas - tures fresh he
is my stay; one word of thy sup -
all my days; oh, may thy house be
C G7 C G7 Am F C
makes me feed be - side the liv - ing stream.
port - ing breath drives all my fears a - way.
mine a - bode and all my work be praise.

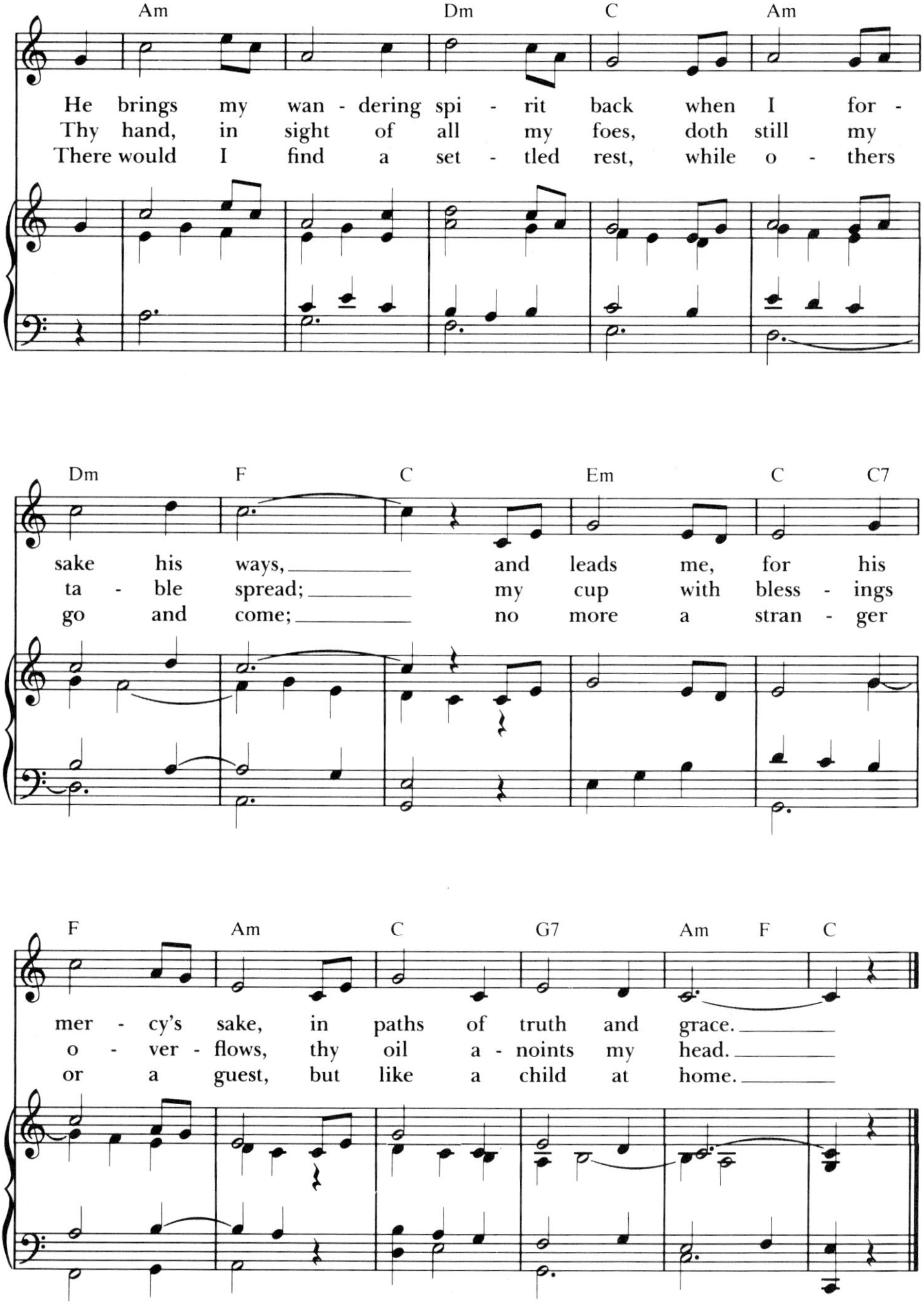
Am Dm C Am
He brings my wan - dering spi - rit back when I for -
Thy hand, in sight of all my foes, doth still my
There would I find a set - tled rest, while o - thers
Dm F C Em C C7
sake his ways, and leads me, for his
ta - ble spread; my cup with bless - ings
go and come; no more a stran - ger
F Am C G7 Am F C
mer - cy's sake, in paths of truth and grace.
o - ver - flows, thy oil a - noints my head.
or a guest, but like a child at home.

Keyboard and guitar should not sound together.

Words: Isaac Watts (1674-1748); para. of Psalm 23
Music: *Resignation*, American folk melody, acc. David Hurd (b. 1950)

♩= 120
CMD

1 All my hope on God is found - ed; he doth still my
2 Mor - tal pride and earth - ly glo - ry, sword and crown be -
3 God's great good - ness e'er en - dur - eth, deep his wis - dom
4 Dai - ly doth the al - might - y Giv - er boun - teous gifts on
5 Still from earth to God e - ter - nal sac - ri - fice of
1 trust re - new, me through change and chance he
2 tray our trust; though with care and toil we
3 pass - ing thought: splen - dor, light, and life at -
4 us be - stow; his de - sire our soul de -
5 praise be done, high a - bove all prais - es
1 guid - eth, on - ly good and on - ly true. God un -
2 build them, tower and tem - ple fall to dust. But God's
3 tend him, beau - ty spring - eth out of nought. Ev - er -
4 light - eth, plea - sure leads us where we go. Love doth
5 prais - ing for the gift of Christ, his son. Christ doth

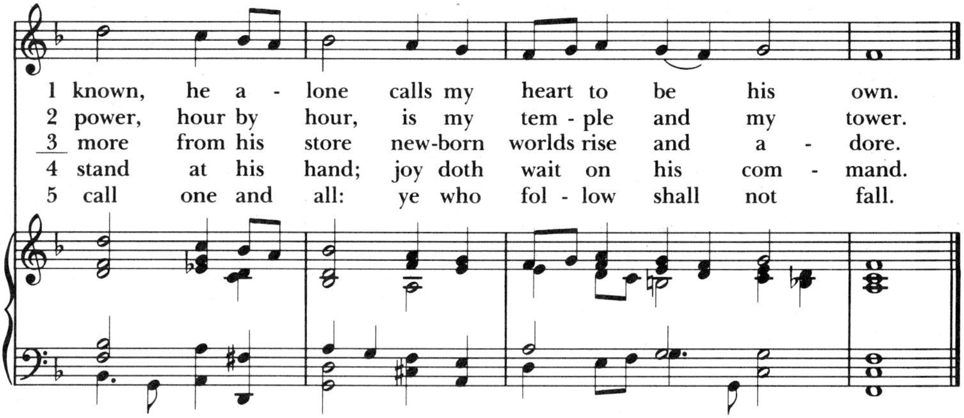
1 known, he a - lone calls my heart to be his own.
2 power, hour by hour, is my tem - ple and my tower.
3 more from his store new-born worlds rise and a - dore.
4 stand at his hand; joy doth wait on his com - mand.
5 call one and all: ye who fol - low shall not fall.

Words: Robert Seymour Bridges (1844-1930), alt., after Joachim Neander (1650-1680) ♩= 120
Music: *Michael,* Herbert Howells (1892-1983) 87. 87. 337

The Christian Life 666

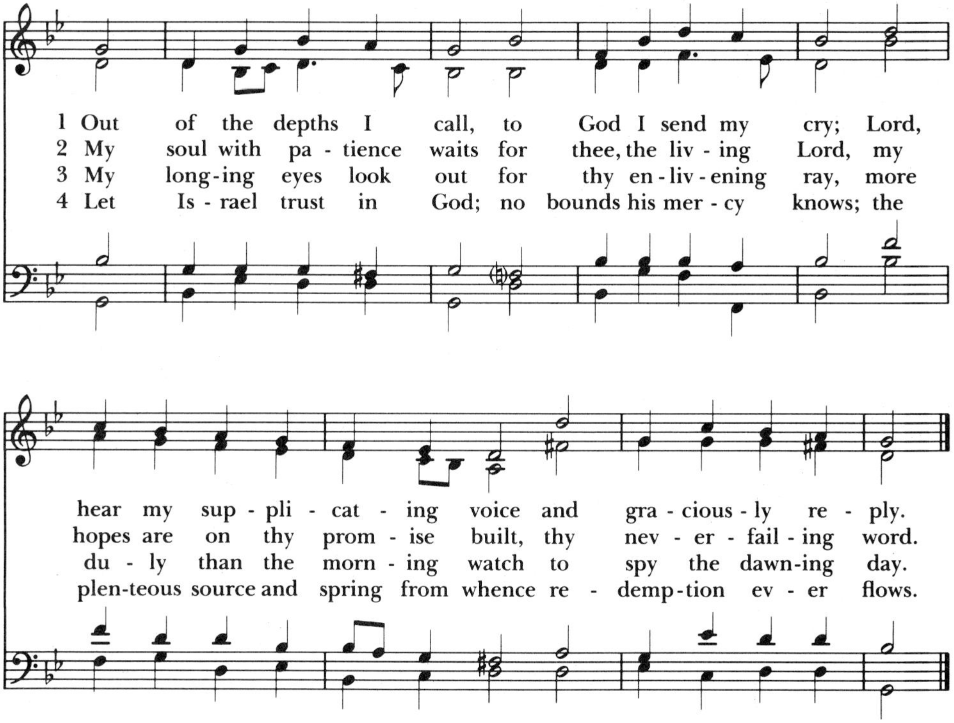
1 Out of the depths I call, to God I send my cry; Lord, hear my sup - pli - cat - ing voice and gra - cious - ly re - ply.
2 My soul with pa - tience waits for thee, the liv - ing Lord, my hopes are on thy prom - ise built, thy nev - er - fail - ing word.
3 My long-ing eyes look out for thy en - liv - ening ray, more du - ly than the morn - ing watch to spy the dawn-ing day.
4 Let Is - rael trust in God; no bounds his mer - cy knows; the plen-teous source and spring from whence re - demp-tion ev - er flows.

Alternative tunes: *Franconia,* 656; *Southwell,* 641.

Words: *A Supplement to the New Version of the Psalms,* 1698, alt.; para. of Psalm 130 𝅗𝅥= 46
Music: *St. Bride,* Samuel Howard (1710-1782) SM

1 Some - times a light sur - pris - es the Chris - tian while he sings;
2 In ho - ly con - tem - pla - tion we sweet - ly then pur - sue
3 It can bring with it noth - ing but he will bear us through:
4 Though vine nor fig tree nei - ther their wont - ed fruit should bear,
it is the Lord who ris - es with heal - ing in his wings:
the theme of God's sal - va - tion, and find it ev - er new;
who gives the lil - ies cloth - ing will clothe his peo - ple, too:
though all the fields should with - er, nor flocks nor herds be there;
when com - forts are de - clin - ing, he grants the soul a - gain
set free from pres - ent sor - row, we cheer - ful - ly can say,
be - neath the spread - ing hea - vens no crea - ture but is fed;
yet, God the same a - bid - ing, his praise shall tune my voice;

a sea - son of clear shin - ing, to cheer it af - ter rain.
let the un - known to - mor - row bring with it what it may.
and he who feeds the rav - ens will give his chil - dren bread.
for, while in him con - fid - ing, I can - not but re - joice.

Words: William Cowper (1731-1800)
Music: *Light,* melody from *The Christian Lyre,* 1830; harm. Charles Winfred Douglas (1867-1944)

𝅗𝅥=56
76. 76. D

The Christian Life 668

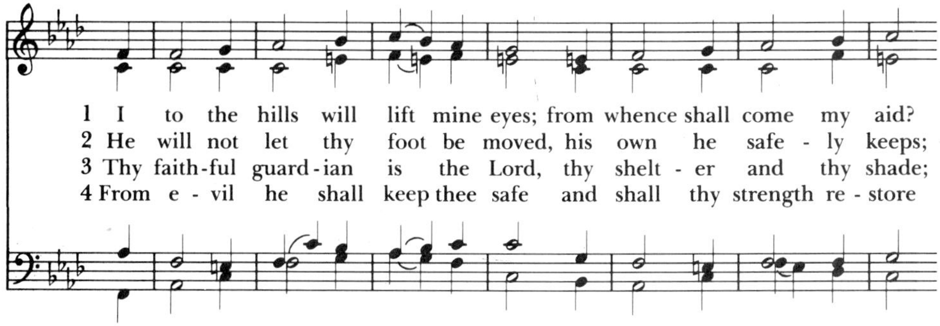
1 I to the hills will lift mine eyes; from whence shall come my aid?
2 He will not let thy foot be moved, his own he safe - ly keeps;
3 Thy faith - ful guard - ian is the Lord, thy shelt - er and thy shade;
4 From e - vil he shall keep thee safe and shall thy strength re - store

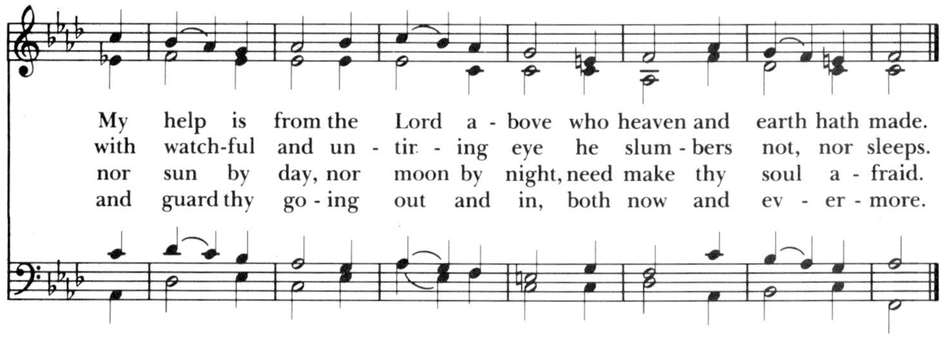
My help is from the Lord a - bove who heaven and earth hath made.
with watch - ful and un - tir - ing eye he slum - bers not, nor sleeps.
nor sun by day, nor moon by night, need make thy soul a - fraid.
and guard thy go - ing out and in, both now and ev - er - more.

Alternative tune: *Dundee,* 709.

Words: *The Psalms of David in Meeter,* 1650, alt.; st. 4, F. Bland Tucker (1895-1984); para. of Psalm 121
Music: *Burford,* from *A Book of Psalmody,* 1718

♩=88
CM

1 Com - mit thou all that grieves thee and fills thy heart with
2 O trust the Lord then whol - ly, if thou wouldst be se -
3 Thy last - ing truth and mer - cy, O Fa - ther, see a -
4 Hope on, then, bro - ken spi - rit; hope on, be not a -
care to him whose faith - ful mer - cy the
cure; his work must thou con - sid - er for
right the needs of all thy chil - dren, their
fraid: fear not the griefs that plague thee and
skies a - bove de - clare, who gives the winds their
thy work to en - dure. What prof - it doth it
an - guish or de - light: what lov - ing wis - dom
keep thy heart dis - mayed: thy God, in his great
cours - es, who points the clouds their way; 'tis
bring thee to pine in grief and care? God
choos - eth, re - deem - ing might will do, and
mer - - cy, will save thee, hold thee fast, and

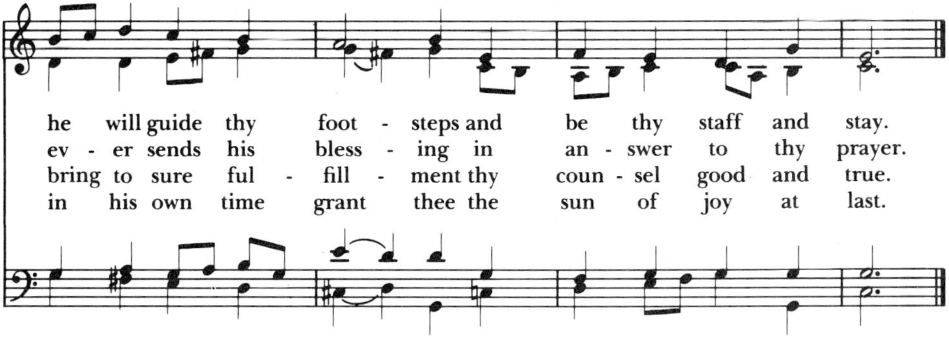
he will guide thy foot - steps and be thy staff and stay.
ev - er sends his bless - ing in an - swer to thy prayer.
bring to sure ful - fill - ment thy coun - sel good and true.
in his own time grant thee the sun of joy at last.

Alternative tune, *Herzlich tut mich verlangen* (rhythmic), 169.

Words: Paul Gerhardt (1607-1676); tr. Arthur William Farlander (1898-1952) and Charles Winfred Douglas (1867-1944), alt.
Music: *Herzlich tut mich verlangen [Passion Chorale]*, Hans Leo Hassler (1564-1612); adapt. and harm. Johann Sebastian Bach (1685-1750)

♩=72
76. 76. D

The Christian Life 670

Unison or harmony

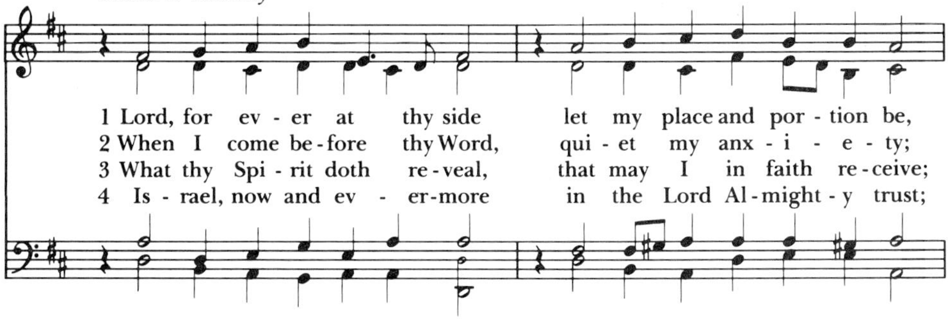
1 Lord, for ev - er at thy side let my place and por - tion be,
2 When I come be - fore thy Word, qui - et my anx - i - e - ty;
3 What thy Spi - rit doth re - veal, that may I in faith re - ceive;
4 Is - rael, now and ev - er-more in the Lord Al - might - y trust;

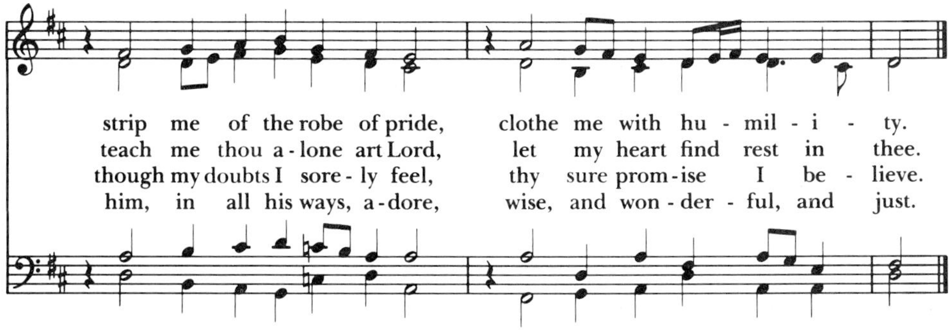
strip me of the robe of pride, clothe me with hu - mil - i - ty.
teach me thou a - lone art Lord, let my heart find rest in thee.
though my doubts I sore - ly feel, thy sure prom - ise I be - lieve.
him, in all his ways, a - dore, wise, and won - der - ful, and just.

Words: Sts. 1 and 4, James Montgomery (1771-1854), alt.; sts. 2-3, Charles P. Price (b. 1920)
Music: *Song 13*, melody and bass Orlando Gibbons (1583-1625); harm. *Songs of Praise*, 1931, alt.

♩=88
77. 77

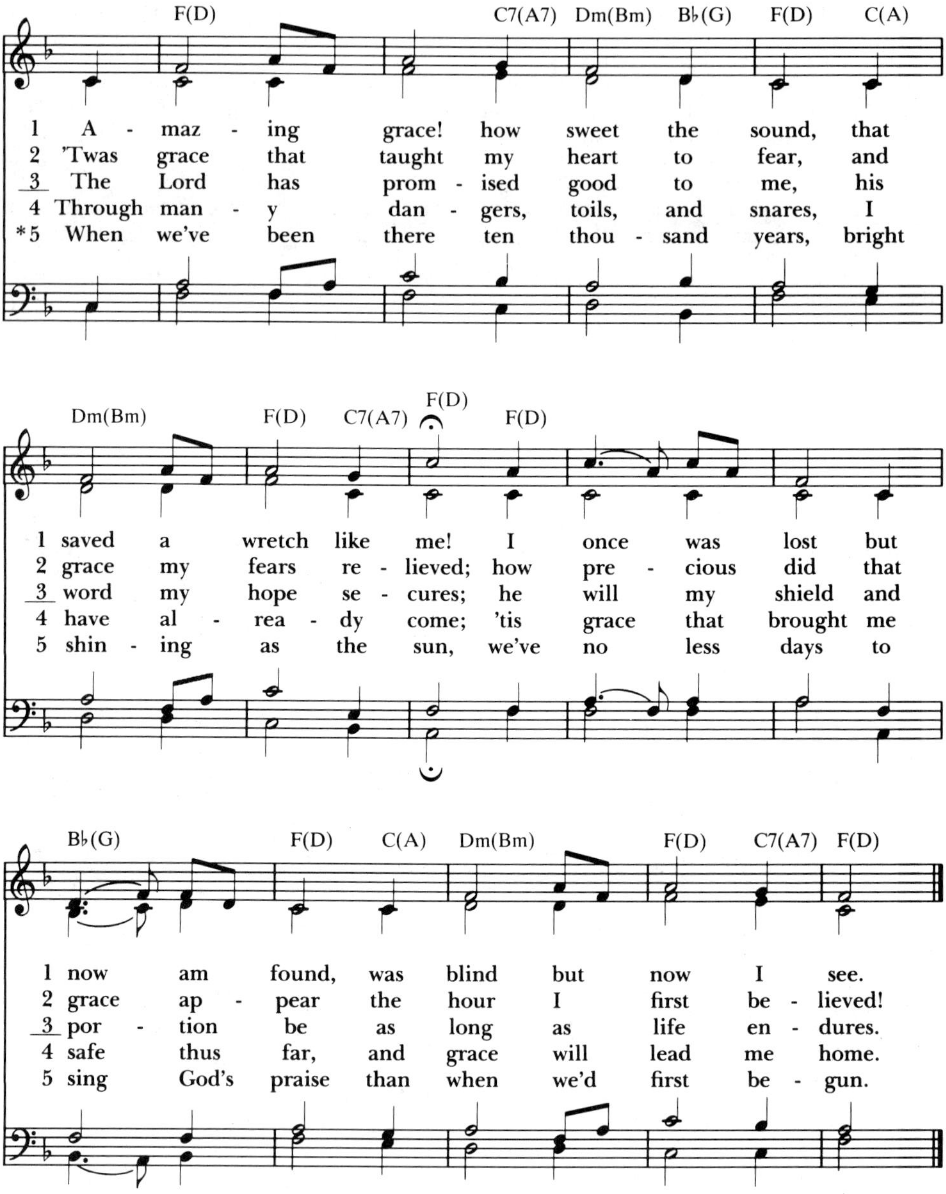
F(D) C7(A7) Dm(Bm) B♭(G) F(D) C(A)
1 A - maz - ing grace! how sweet the sound, that
2 'Twas grace that taught my heart to fear, and
3 The Lord has prom - ised good to me, his
4 Through man - y dan - gers, toils, and snares, I
*5 When we've been there ten thou - sand years, bright
Dm(Bm) F(D) C7(A7) F(D) F(D)
1 saved a wretch like me! I once was lost but
2 grace my fears re - lieved; how pre - cious did that
3 word my hope se - cures; he will my shield and
4 have al - rea - dy come; 'tis grace that brought me
5 shin - ing as the sun, we've no less days to
B♭(G) F(D) C(A) Dm(Bm) F(D) C7(A7) F(D)
1 now am found, was blind but now I see.
2 grace ap - pear the hour I first be - lieved!
3 por - tion be as long as life en - dures.
4 safe thus far, and grace will lead me home.
5 sing God's praise than when we'd first be - gun.

F (capo 3, D). The melody may be sung in canon at distances of either two or three beats.

Words: John Newton (1725-1807), alt.; st. 5, John Rees (19th cent.)
Music: *New Britain,* from *Virginia Harmony,* 1831; adapt. att. Edwin Othello Excell (1851-1921); harm. Austin Cole Lovelace (b. 1919)

♩= 108
CM

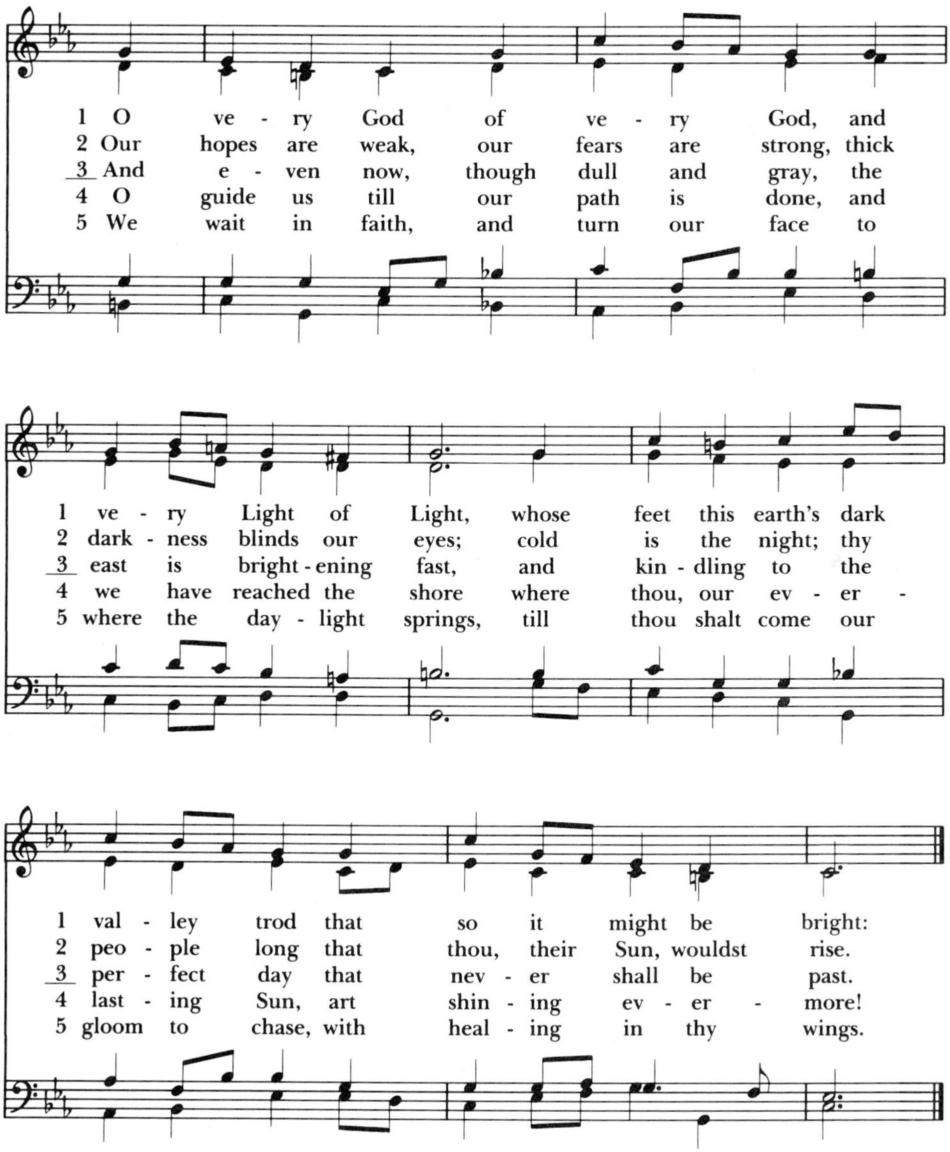
1 O ve - ry God of ve - ry God, and
2 Our hopes are weak, our fears are strong, thick
3 And e - ven now, though dull and gray, the
4 O guide us till our path is done, and
5 We wait in faith, and turn our face to
1 ve - ry Light of Light, whose feet this earth's dark
2 dark - ness blinds our eyes; cold is the night; thy
3 east is bright - ening fast, and kin - dling to the
4 we have reached the shore where thou, our ev - er -
5 where the day - light springs, till thou shalt come our
1 val - ley trod that so it might be bright:
2 peo - ple long that thou, their Sun, wouldst rise.
3 per - fect day that nev - er shall be past.
4 last - ing Sun, art shin - ing ev - er - more!
5 gloom to chase, with heal - ing in thy wings.

Words: John Mason Neale (1818-1866)
Music: *Bangor,* from *A Compleat Melody or Harmony of Zion,* 1734

♩= 72
CM

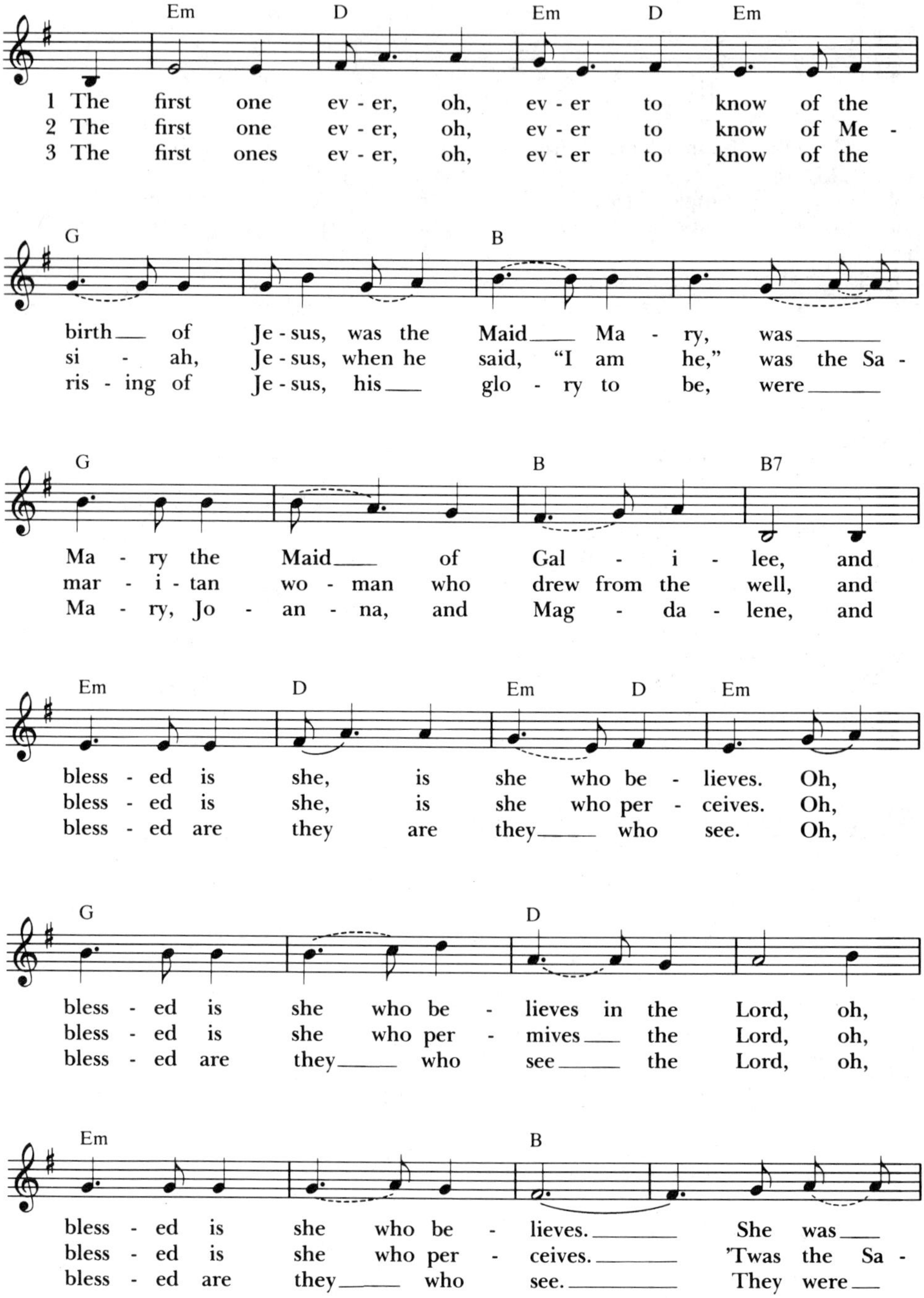
Em D Em D Em
1 The first one ev - er, oh, ev - er to know of the
2 The first one ev - er, oh, ev - er to know of Me -
3 The first ones ev - er, oh, ev - er to know of the
G B
birth of Je - sus, was the Maid Ma - ry, was
si - ah, Je - sus, when he said, "I am he," was the Sa -
ris - ing of Je - sus, his glo - ry to be, were
G B B7
Ma - ry the Maid of Gal - i - lee, and
mar - i - tan wo - man who drew from the well, and
Ma - ry, Jo - an - na, and Mag - da - lene, and
Em D Em D Em
bless - ed is she, is she who be - lieves. Oh,
bless - ed is she, is she who per - ceives. Oh,
bless - ed are they are they who see. Oh,
G D
bless - ed is she who be - lieves in the Lord, oh,
bless - ed is she who per - mives the Lord, oh,
bless - ed are they who see the Lord, oh,
Em B
bless - ed is she who be - lieves. She was
bless - ed is she who per - ceives. 'Twas the Sa -
bless - ed are they who see. They were

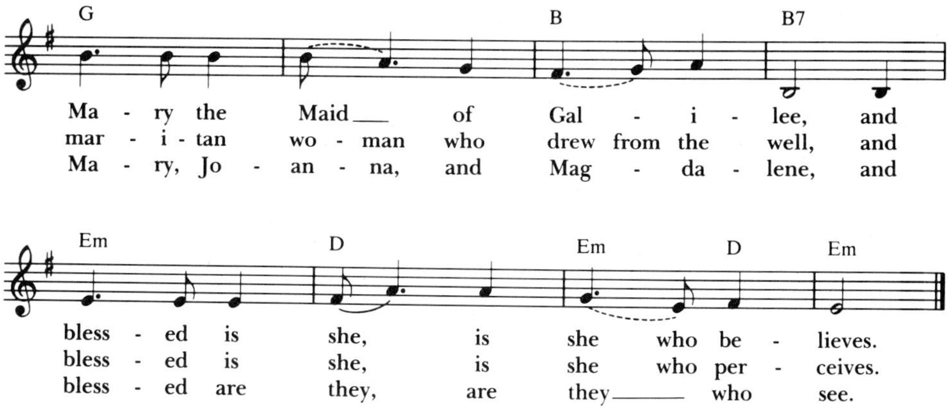
G
B
B7
Ma - ry the Maid___ of Gal - i - lee, and
mar - i - tan wo - man who drew from the well, and
Ma - ry, Jo - an - na, and Mag - da - lene, and
Em
D
Em
D
Em
bless - ed is she, is she who be - lieves.
bless - ed is she, is she who per - ceives.
bless - ed are they, are they___ who see.

Words: Linda Wilberger Egan (b. 1946), alt.
Music: *Ballad,* Linda Wilberger Egan (b. 1946)

𝅗𝅥. = 46
Irr.

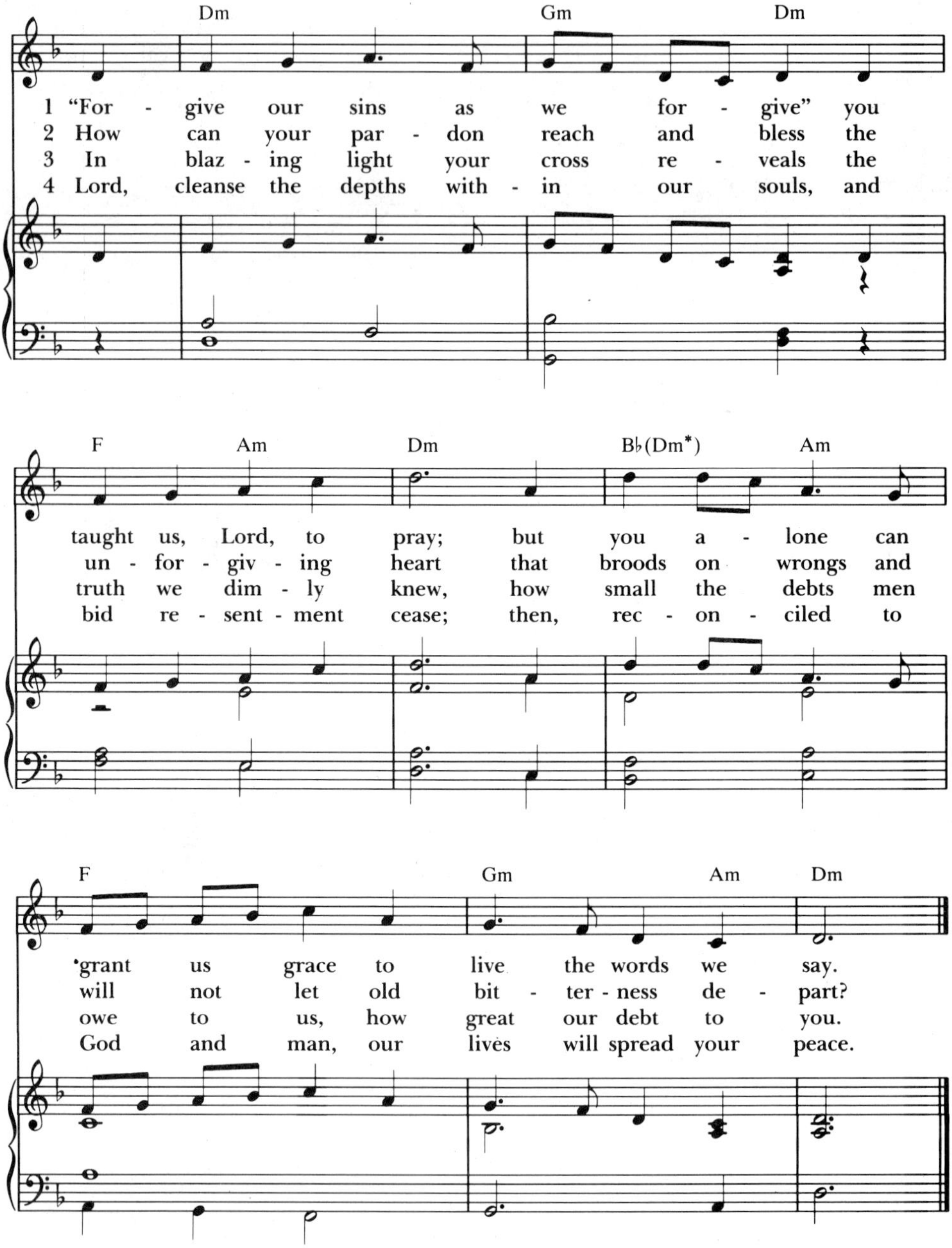
Dm Gm Dm
1 "For - give our sins as we for - give" you
2 How can your par - don reach and bless the
3 In blaz - ing light your cross re - veals the
4 Lord, cleanse the depths with - in our souls, and
F Am Dm B♭(Dm*) Am
taught us, Lord, to pray; but you a - lone can
un - for - giv - ing heart that broods on wrongs and
truth we dim - ly knew, how small the debts men
bid re - sent - ment cease; then, rec - on - ciled to
F Gm Am Dm
grant us grace to live the words we say.
will not let old bit - ter - ness de - part?
owe to us, how great our debt to you.
God and man, our lives will spread your peace.

Denotes optional chord

Words: Rosamond E. Herklots (b. 1905)
Music *Detroit,* from *Supplement to Kentucky Harmony,* 1820; harm. Margaret W. Mealy (b. 1922)

𝅗𝅥=50
CM

Fm(Dm) Bb m(Gm) Cm(Am) Fm(Dm)
1 Take up your cross, the Sa - vior said, if
2 Take up your cross, let not its weight fill
3 Take up your cross, heed not the shame, and
4 Take up your cross, then, in his strength, and
5 Take up your cross, and fol - low Christ, nor
Db(Bb) Ab(F) Db(Bb) Fm(Dm) Ab(F) Fm7(Dm7) Cm(Am) Db(Bb) Cm(Am)
1 you would my dis - ci - ple be; take up your cross with
2 your weak spi - rit with a - larm; his strength shall bear your
3 let your fool - ish heart be still; the Lord for you ac -
4 calm - ly ev - ery dan - ger brave: it guides you to a -
5 think till death to lay it down; for on - ly those who
Db(Bb) Ab(F) Fm(Dm) Db(Bb) Bb m(Gm) Fm(Dm) Cm(Am) Fm(Dm)
1 will - ing heart, and hum - bly fol - low af - ter me.
2 spi - rit up, and brace your heart, and nerve your arm.
3 cept - ed death up - on a cross, on Cal - vary's hill.
4 bun - dant life and leads to vic - tory o'er the grave.
5 bear the cross may hope to wear the glo - rious crown.

Fm (capo 3, Dm). Another harmonization, 147.

Words: Charles William Everest (1814-1877), alt.
Music: *Bourbon*, melody att. Freeman Lewis (1780-1859); harm. John Leon Hooker (b. 1944)

♩= 69
LM

Refrain
There is a balm in Gil - e - ad, to
make the wound - ed whole, there is a
balm in Gil - e - ad, to
1
heal the sin - sick
soul. There is a
2
heal the sin - sick soul.

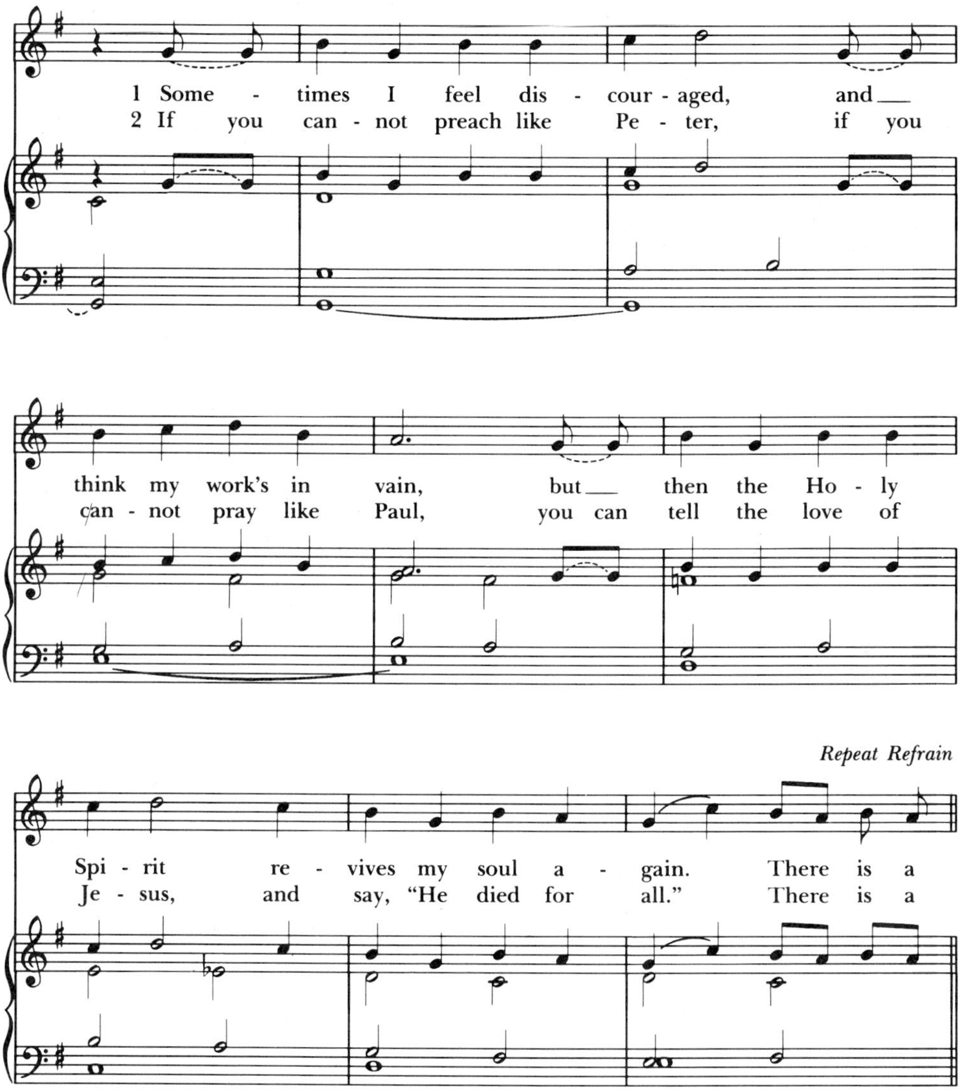
1 Some - times I feel dis - cour - aged, and___
2 If you can - not preach like Pe - ter, if you
think my work's in vain, but___ then the Ho - ly
can - not pray like Paul, you can tell the love of
Repeat Refrain
Spi - rit re - vives my soul a - gain. There is a
Je - sus, and say, "He died for all." There is a

Words: Afro-American spiritual
Music: *Balm in Gilead*, Afro-American spiritual; acc. David Hurd (b. 1950)

𝅗𝅥 = 50
Irr. with Refrain

Unison or harmony

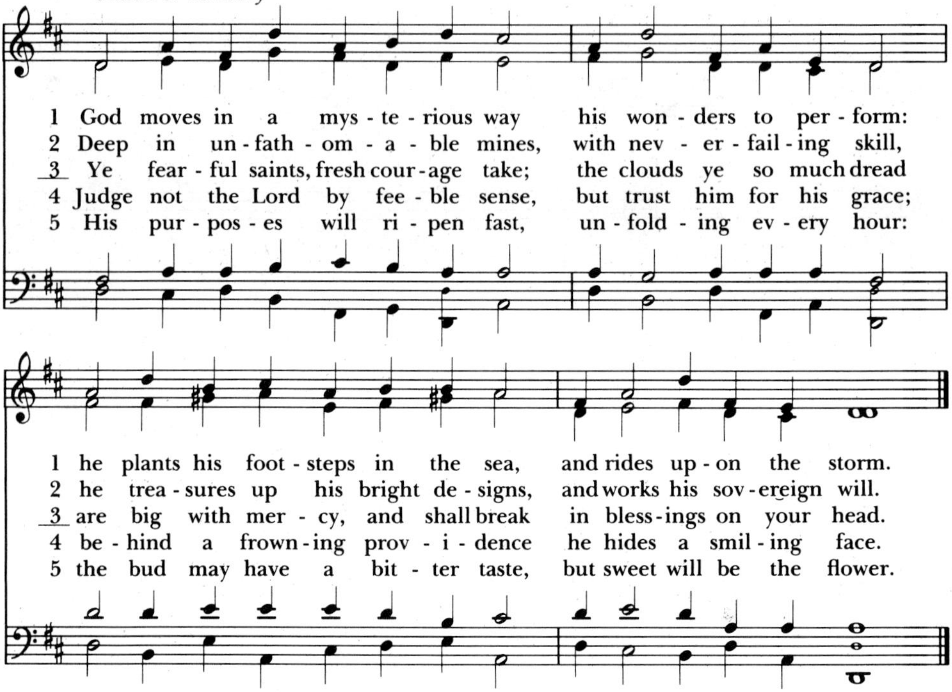
1 God moves in a mys - te - rious way his won - ders to per - form:
2 Deep in un - fath - om - a - ble mines, with nev - er - fail - ing skill,
3 Ye fear - ful saints, fresh cour - age take; the clouds ye so much dread
4 Judge not the Lord by fee - ble sense, but trust him for his grace;
5 His pur - pos - es will ri - pen fast, un - fold - ing ev - ery hour:
1 he plants his foot - steps in the sea, and rides up - on the storm.
2 he trea - sures up his bright de - signs, and works his sov - ereign will.
3 are big with mer - cy, and shall break in bless - ings on your head.
4 be - hind a frown - ing prov - i - dence he hides a smil - ing face.
5 the bud may have a bit - ter taste, but sweet will be the flower.

6 Blind unbelief is sure to err,
and scan his work in vain;
God is his own interpreter,
and he will make it plain.

This music in C, 50.

Words: William Cowper (1731-1800)
Music: *London New,* melody from *The Psalmes of David in Prose and Meeter,* 1635; harm. John Playford (1623-1686)

♩=88
CM

1 Sure - ly it is God who saves me;
2 Make his deeds known to the peo - ples;

trust-ing him, I shall not fear. For the Lord de-fends and
tell out his ex-alt-ed Name. Praise the Lord, who has done
shields me and his sav-ing help is near. So re-
great things; all his works his might pro-claim. Zi-on,
joice as you draw wa-ter from sal-va-tion's liv-ing spring; in the
lift your voice in sing-ing; for with you has come to dwell, in your
day of your de-liv-erance thank the Lord, his mer-cies sing.
ve-ry midst, the great and Ho-ly One of Is-ra-el.

Alternative tune: *Thomas Merton*, 679.

Words: Carl P. Daw, Jr. (b. 1944); para. of *The First Song of Isaiah*
Music: *College of Preachers,* Arthur Rhea (b. 1919)

♩=c. 54
87. 87. D

E B C♯m E F♯m A B
1 Sure - ly it is God ___ who saves me; trust-ing him, I shall not
2 Make his deeds _ known to the peo - ples; tell out his ex - alt - ed
E B7 E B C♯m E F♯m
fear. For the Lord de - fends and shields me and his sav - ing
Name. Praise the Lord, who has done great things; all his works his
A B E B7sus4 E F♯m E C♯m
help is near. So re - joice as you draw wa - ter from sal -
might pro - claim. Zi - on, lift your voice in sing - ing; for with
A E A B E C♯m
va - tion's liv - ing spring; in the day of your de -
you has come to dwell, in your ve - ry midst, the

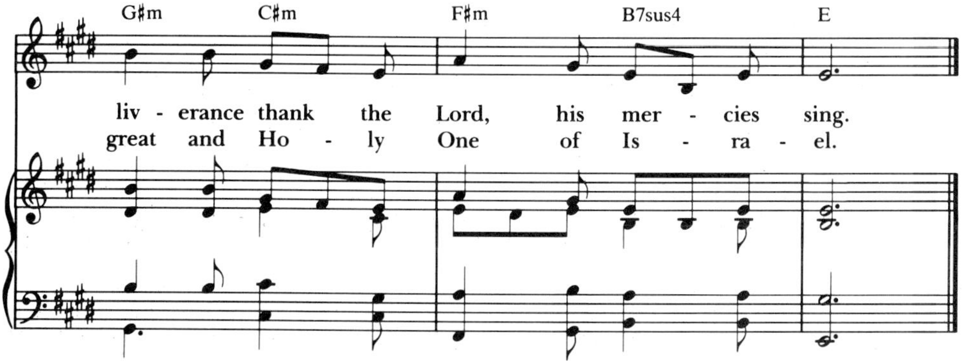

G♯m C♯m F♯m B7sus4 E
liv - erance thank the Lord, his mer - cies sing.
great and Ho - ly One of Is - ra - el.

If keyboard and guitar do not sound together, then: C♯m *may be played* E; F♯m *played* A; *and* G♯m *played* B. Alternative tune: *College of Preachers,* 678.

Words: Carl P. Daw, Jr. (b. 1944); para. of *The First Song of Isaiah* ♩. = 48-52
Music: *Thomas Merton,* Ray W. Urwin (b. 1950) 87. 87. D

The Christian Life 680

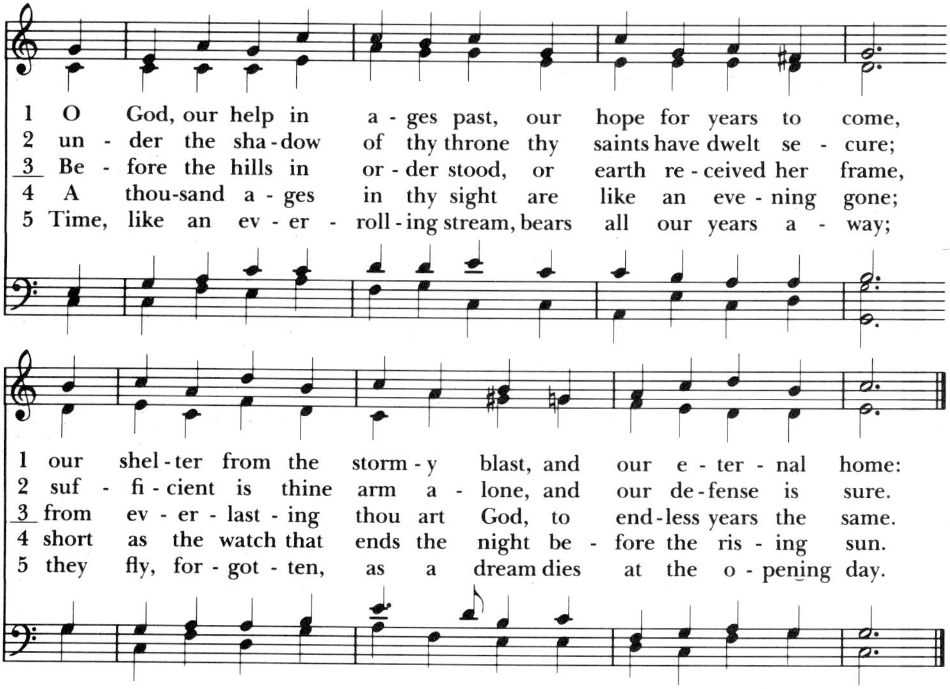

1 O God, our help in a - ges past, our hope for years to come,
2 un - der the sha - dow of thy throne thy saints have dwelt se - cure;
3 Be - fore the hills in or - der stood, or earth re - ceived her frame,
4 A thou-sand a - ges in thy sight are like an eve - ning gone;
5 Time, like an ev - er - roll - ing stream, bears all our years a - way;
1 our shel - ter from the storm - y blast, and our e - ter - nal home:
2 suf - fi - cient is thine arm a - lone, and our de - fense is sure.
3 from ev - er - last - ing thou art God, to end - less years the same.
4 short as the watch that ends the night be - fore the ris - ing sun.
5 they fly, for - got - ten, as a dream dies at the o - pening day.

6 O God, our help in ages past,
our hope for years to come,
be thou our guide while life shall last,
and our eternal home.

Words: Isaac Watts (1674-1748), alt.; para. of Psalm 90:1-5 ♩ = 72
Music: *St. Anne,* melody att. William Croft (1678-1727), alt.; harm. William Henry Monk (1823-1889) CM

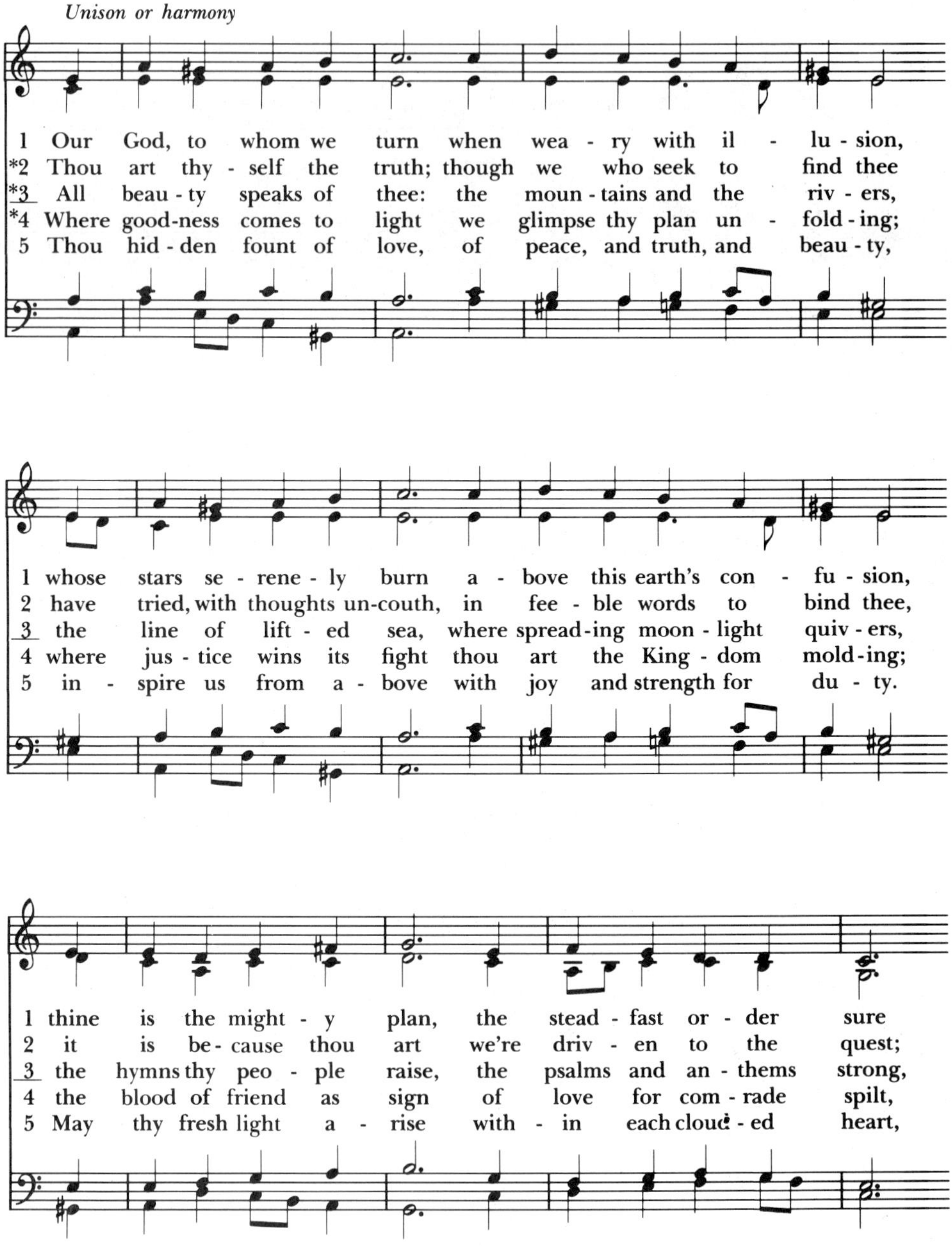
Unison or harmony
1 Our God, to whom we turn when wea - ry with il - lu - sion,
*2 Thou art thy - self the truth; though we who seek to find thee
*3 All beau - ty speaks of thee: the moun - tains and the riv - ers,
*4 Where good-ness comes to light we glimpse thy plan un - fold - ing;
5 Thou hid - den fount of love, of peace, and truth, and beau - ty,
1 whose stars se - rene - ly burn a - bove this earth's con - fu - sion,
2 have tried, with thoughts un-couth, in fee - ble words to bind thee,
3 the line of lift - ed sea, where spread-ing moon - light quiv - ers,
4 where jus - tice wins its fight thou art the King - dom mold-ing;
5 in - spire us from a - bove with joy and strength for du - ty.
1 thine is the might - y plan, the stead - fast or - der sure
2 it is be- cause thou art we're driv - en to the quest;
3 the hymns thy peo - ple raise, the psalms and an - thems strong,
4 the blood of friend as sign of love for com - rade spilt,
5 May thy fresh light a - rise with - in each cloud - ed heart,

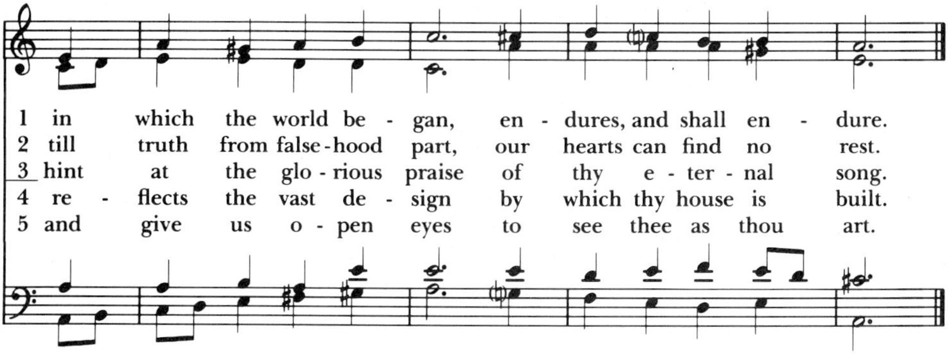
1 in which the world be - gan, en - dures, and shall en - dure.
2 till truth from false-hood part, our hearts can find no rest.
3 hint at the glo - rious praise of thy e - ter - nal song.
4 re - flects the vast de - sign by which thy house is built.
5 and give us o - pen eyes to see thee as thou art.

Words: Edward Grubb (1854-1939), alt.
Music: *O Gott, du frommer Gott,* melody from *Neu ordentlich Gesangbuch,* 1646; harm. Johann Sebastian Bach (1685-1750), alt.

♩=92
67. 67. 66. 66

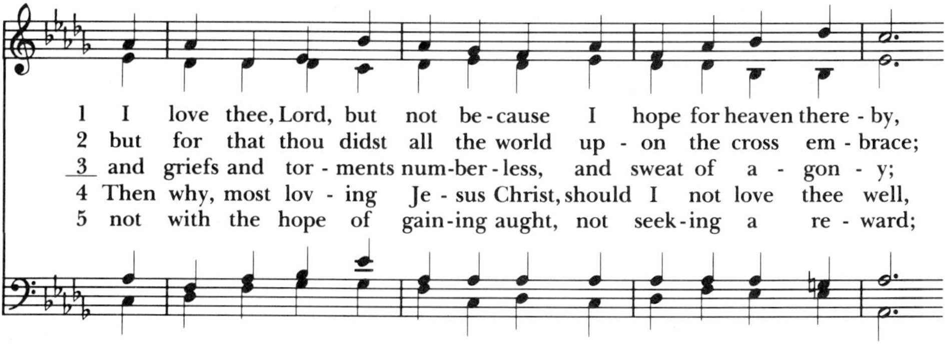
1 I love thee, Lord, but not be-cause I hope for heaven there - by,
2 but for that thou didst all the world up - on the cross em - brace;
3 and griefs and tor - ments num-ber-less, and sweat of a - gon - y;
4 Then why, most lov - ing Je - sus Christ, should I not love thee well,
5 not with the hope of gain-ing aught, not seek-ing a re - ward;

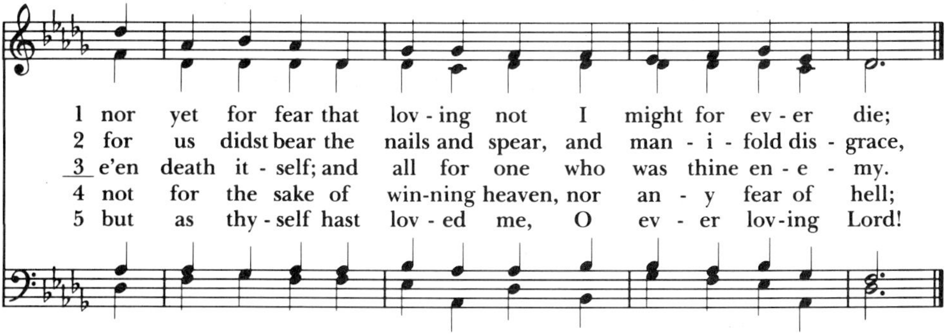
1 nor yet for fear that lov - ing not I might for ev - er die;
2 for us didst bear the nails and spear, and man - i - fold dis - grace,
3 e'en death it - self; and all for one who was thine en - e - my.
4 not for the sake of win-ning heaven, nor an - y fear of hell;
5 but as thy - self hast lov - ed me, O ev - er lov-ing Lord!

6 E'en so I love thee, and will love,
and in thy praise will sing,
solely because thou art my God
and my eternal King.

Music: Spanish, 17th cent.; tr. Edward Caswall (1814-1878); adapt. Percy Dearmer (1867-1936), alt.
Music: *St. Fulbert,* Henry John Gauntlett (1805-1876)

𝅗𝅥=50
CM

683 The Christian Life

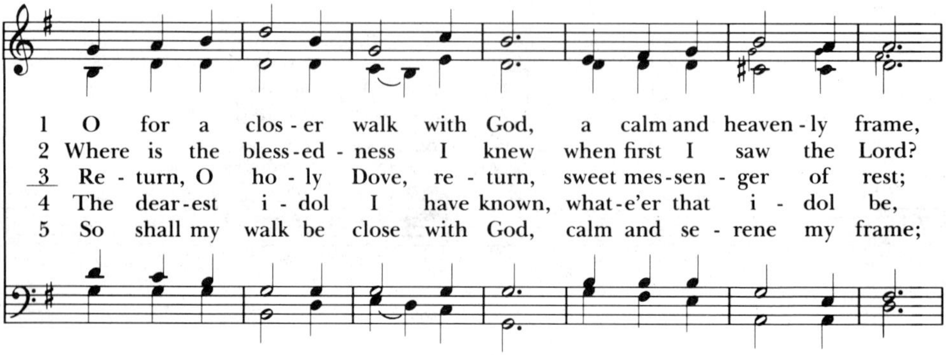
1 O for a clos - er walk with God, a calm and heaven - ly frame,
2 Where is the bless-ed - ness I knew when first I saw the Lord?
3 Re - turn, O ho - ly Dove, re - turn, sweet mes-sen - ger of rest;
4 The dear-est i - dol I have known, what-e'er that i - dol be,
5 So shall my walk be close with God, calm and se - rene my frame;

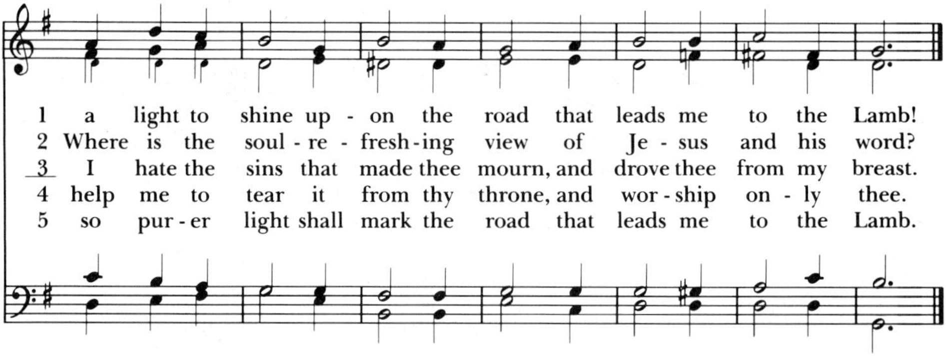
1 a light to shine up - on the road that leads me to the Lamb!
2 Where is the soul - re - fresh-ing view of Je - sus and his word?
3 I hate the sins that made thee mourn, and drove thee from my breast.
4 help me to tear it from thy throne, and wor-ship on - ly thee.
5 so pur - er light shall mark the road that leads me to the Lamb.

Words: William Cowper (1731-1800), alt.
Music: *Beatitudo,* John Bacchus Dykes (1823-1876)

𝅗𝅥. = 40
CM

684 The Christian Life

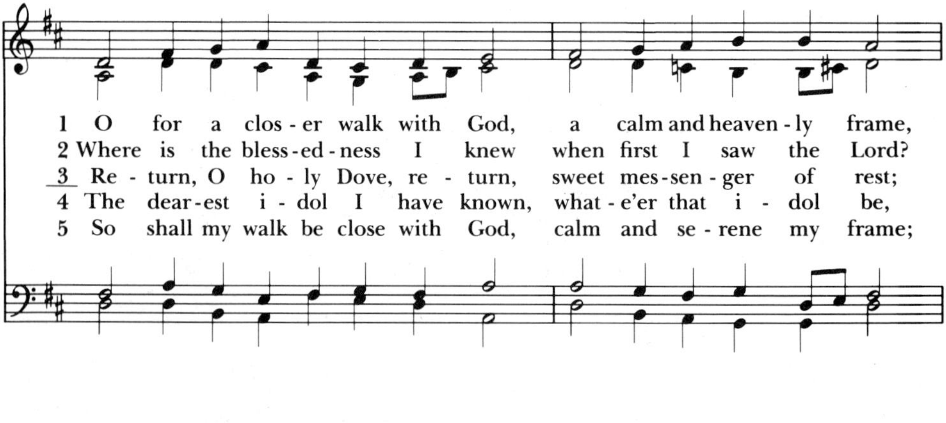
1 O for a clos - er walk with God, a calm and heaven - ly frame,
2 Where is the bless-ed-ness I knew when first I saw the Lord?
3 Re - turn, O ho - ly Dove, re - turn, sweet mes-sen - ger of rest;
4 The dear-est i - dol I have known, what - e'er that i - dol be,
5 So shall my walk be close with God, calm and se - rene my frame;

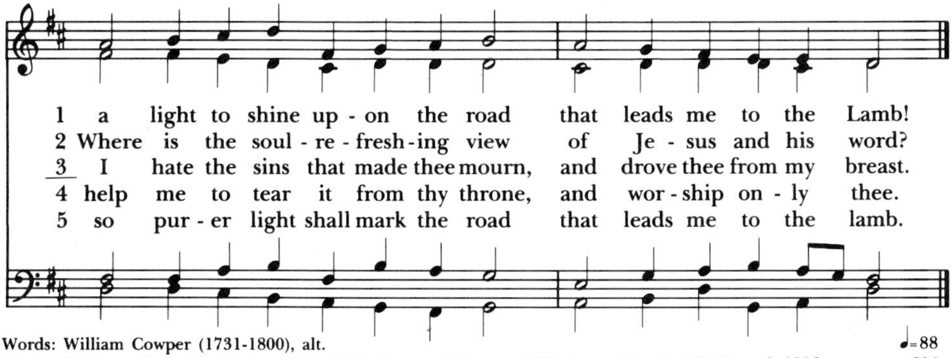
1 a light to shine up-on the road that leads me to the Lamb!
2 Where is the soul-re-fresh-ing view of Je-sus and his word?
3 I hate the sins that made thee mourn, and drove thee from my breast.
4 help me to tear it from thy throne, and wor-ship on-ly thee.
5 so pur-er light shall mark the road that leads me to the lamb.

Words: William Cowper (1731-1800), alt.
Music: *Caithness,* from *The Psalmes of David in Prose and Meeter,* 1635; harm. *The English Hymnal,* 1906

♩=88
CM

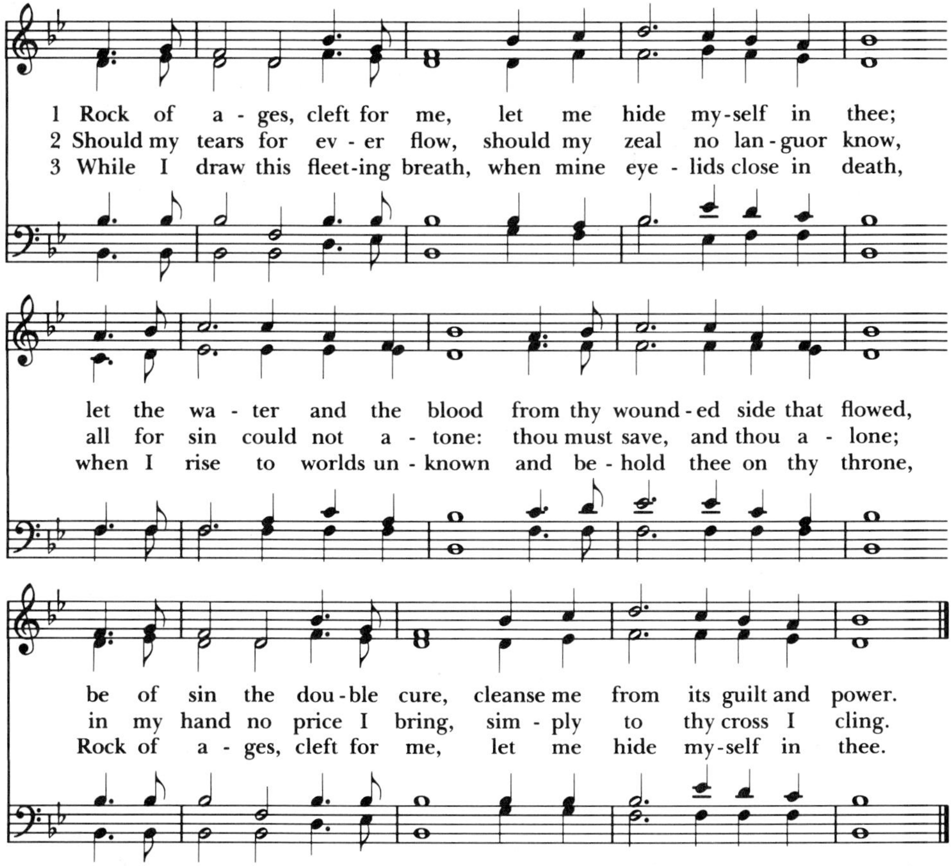
1 Rock of a-ges, cleft for me, let me hide my-self in thee;
2 Should my tears for ev-er flow, should my zeal no lan-guor know,
3 While I draw this fleet-ing breath, when mine eye-lids close in death,
let the wa-ter and the blood from thy wound-ed side that flowed,
all for sin could not a-tone: thou must save, and thou a-lone;
when I rise to worlds un-known and be-hold thee on thy throne,
be of sin the dou-ble cure, cleanse me from its guilt and power.
in my hand no price I bring, sim-ply to thy cross I cling.
Rock of a-ges, cleft for me, let me hide my-self in thee.

Words: Augustus Montague Toplady (1740-1778), alt.
Music: *Toplady,* Thomas Hastings (1784-1872)

𝅗𝅥=69
77. 77. 77

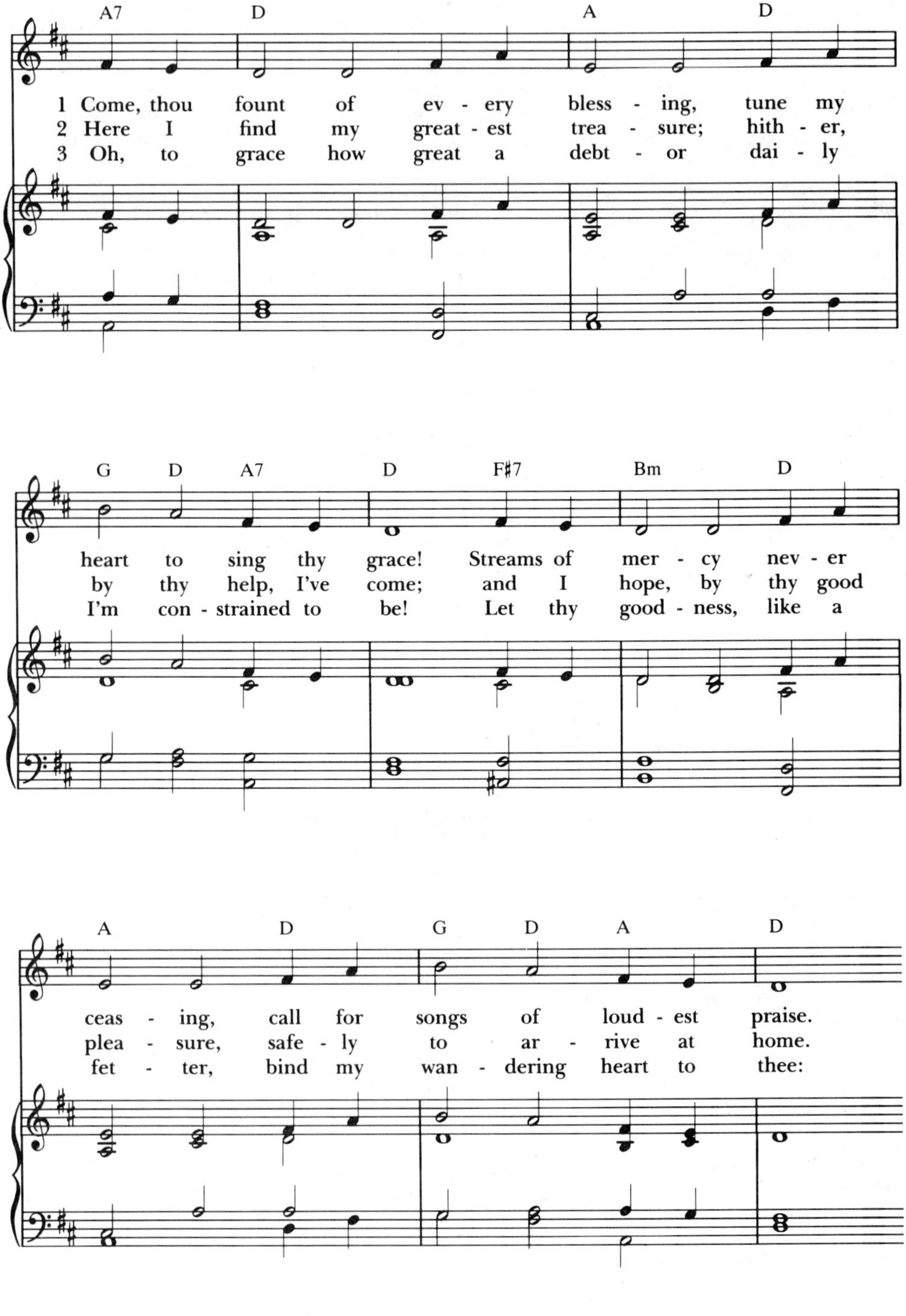
A7 D A D
1 Come, thou fount of ev - ery bless - ing, tune my
2 Here I find my great - est trea - sure; hith - er,
3 Oh, to grace how great a debt - or dai - ly
G D A7 D F♯7 Bm D
heart to sing thy grace! Streams of mer - cy nev - er
by thy help, I've come; and I hope, by thy good
I'm con - strained to be! Let thy good - ness, like a
A D G D A D
ceas - ing, call for songs of loud - est praise.
plea - sure, safe - ly to ar - rive at home.
fet - ter, bind my wan - dering heart to thee:

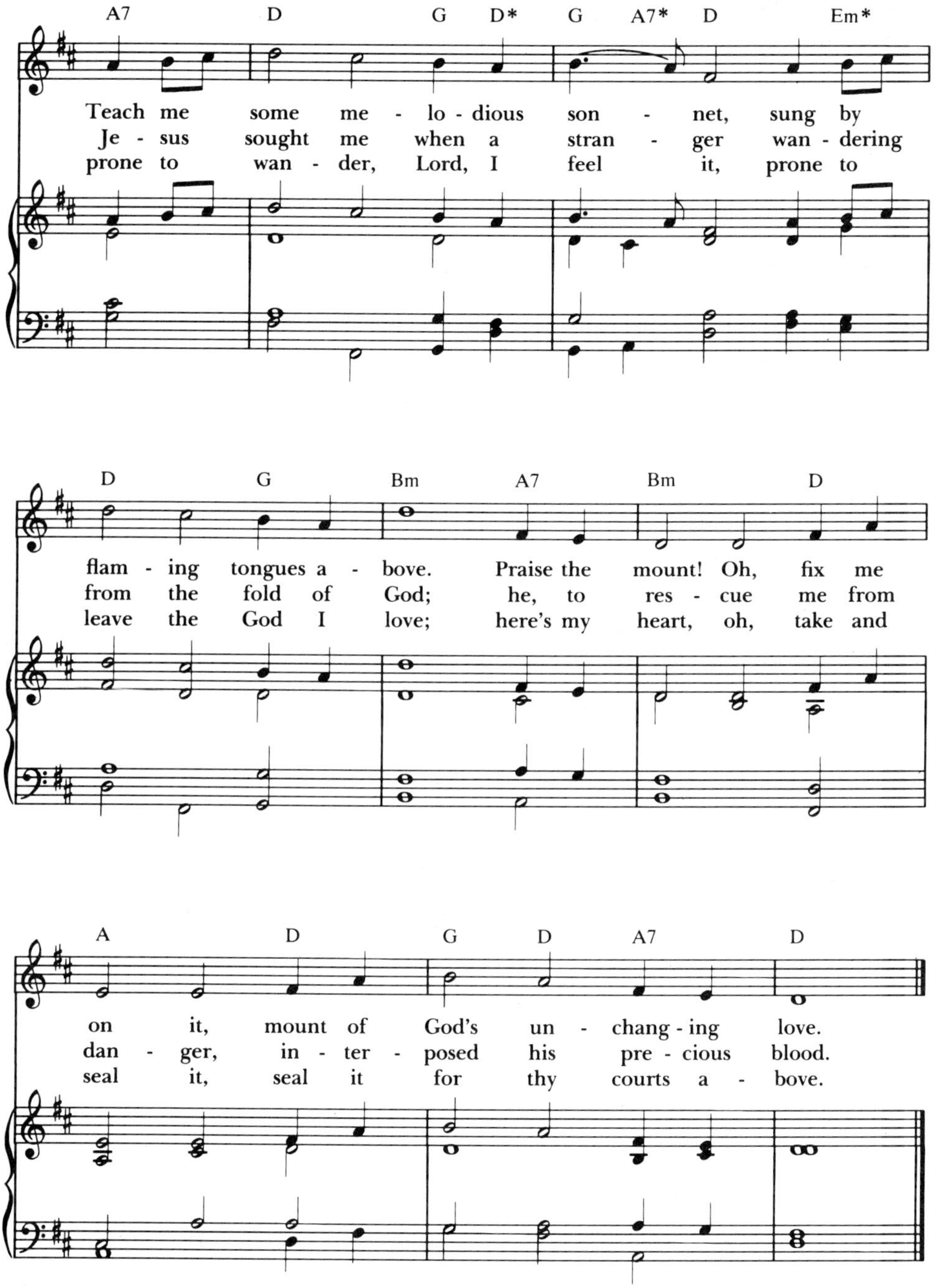
A7 D G D* G A7* D Em*
Teach me some me - lo - dious son - net, sung by
Je - sus sought me when a stran - ger wan - dering
prone to wan - der, Lord, I feel it, prone to
D G Bm A7 Bm D
flam - ing tongues a - bove. Praise the mount! Oh, fix me
from the fold of God; he, to res - cue me from
leave the God I love; here's my heart, oh, take and
A D G D A7 D
on it, mount of God's un - chang - ing love.
dan - ger, in - ter - posed his pre - cious blood.
seal it, seal it for thy courts a - bove.

**Denotes optional chords.*

Words: Robert Robinson (1735-1790), alt.
Music: *Nettleton,* melody from *A Repository of Sacred Music, Part II,* 1813; harm. Gerre Hancock (b. 1934)

♩= 100
87. 87. D

1 A might - y for - tress is our God, a bul - wark
2 Did we in our own strength con - fide, our striv - ing
3 And though this world, with dev - ils filled, should threat - en
4 That word a - bove all earth - ly powers, no thanks to
nev - er fail - ing; our help - er he a - mid the flood
would be los - ing; were not the right man on our side,
to un - do us; we will not fear, for God hath willed
them, a - bid - eth; the Spi - rit and the gifts are ours
of mor - tal ills pre - vail - ing: for still our an - cient foe
the man of God's own choos - ing: dost ask who that may be?
his truth to tri - umph through us; the prince of dark - ness grim,
through him who with us sid - eth: let goods and kin - dred go,

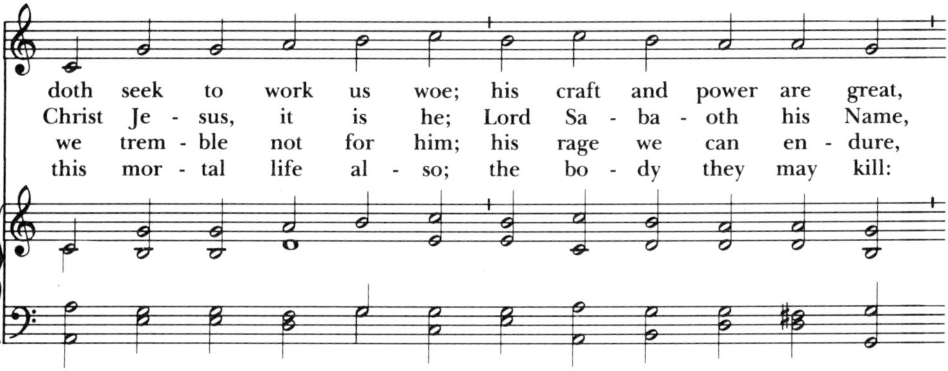
doth seek to work us woe; his craft and power are great,
Christ Je - sus, it is he; Lord Sa - ba - oth his Name,
we trem - ble not for him; his rage we can en - dure,
this mor - tal life al - so; the bo - dy they may kill:

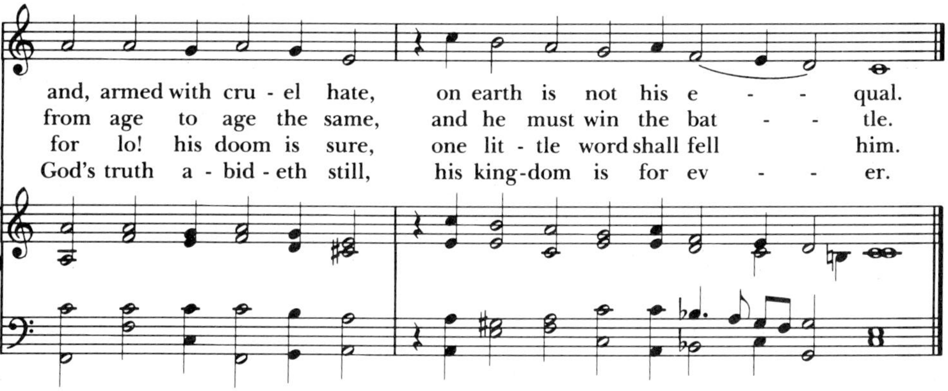
and, armed with cru - el hate, on earth is not his e - - qual.
from age to age the same, and he must win the bat - - tle.
for lo! his doom is sure, one lit - tle word shall fell him.
God's truth a - bid - eth still, his king-dom is for ev - - er.

Alternative tune: *Ein feste Burg* (isometric), 688.

Words: Martin Luther (1483-1546); tr. Frederic Henry Hedge (1805-1890); based on Psalm 46
Music: *Ein feste Burg*, melody Martin Luther (1483-1546); 𝅗𝅥=100
harm. Hans Leo Hassler (1564-1612), alt. 87. 87. 66. 66. 7

1 A might - y for - tress is our God, a bul - wark nev - er
2 Did we in our own strength con - fide, our striv - ing would be
3 And though this world, with dev - ils filled, should threat - en to un -
4 That word a - bove all earth - ly powers, no thanks to them, a -
fail - ing; our help - er he a - mid the flood
los - - ing; were not the right man on our side,
do us; we will not fear, for God hath willed
bid - eth; the Spi - rit and the gifts are ours
of mor - tal ills pre - vail - ing: for still our an - cient foe
the man of God's own choos - ing: dost ask who that may be?
his truth to tri - umph through us; the prince of dark - ness grim,
through him who with us sid - eth: let goods and kin - dred go,
doth seek to work us woe; his craft and power are great,
Christ Je - sus, it is he; Lord Sa - ba - oth his Name,
we trem - ble not for him; his rage we can en - dure,
this mor - tal life al - so; the bo - dy they may kill:

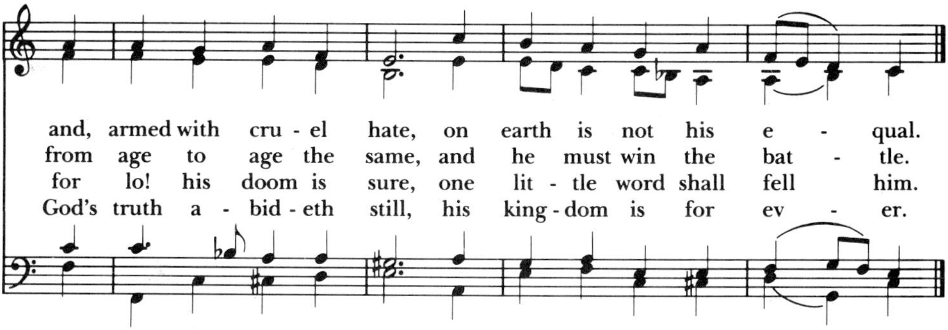
and, armed with cru - el hate, on earth is not his e - qual.
from age to age the same, and he must win the bat - tle.
for lo! his doom is sure, one lit - tle word shall fell him.
God's truth a - bid - eth still, his king - dom is for ev - er.

Alternative tune: *Ein feste Burg* (rhythmic), 687.

Words: Martin Luther (1483-1546); tr. Frederick Henry Hedge (1805-1890); based on Psalm 46
Music: *Ein feste Burg,* melody Martin Luther (1483-1546); harm. Johann Sebastian Bach (1685-1750)

♩=88
87. 87. 66. 66. 7

The Christian Life 689

1 I sought the Lord, and af - ter - ward I knew he moved my soul to seek him, seek - ing me; it was not I that found, O Sa - vior true; no, I was found of thee.
2 Thou didst reach forth thy hand and mine en - fold; I walked and sank not on the storm-vexed sea; 'twas not so much that I on thee took hold, as thou, dear Lord, on me.
3 I find, I walk, I love, but oh, the whole of love is but my an - swer, Lord, to thee; for thou wert long be - fore - hand with my soul, al - ways thou lov - edst me.

Words: Anon., *Pilgrim Hymnal,* 1904
Music: *Faith,* J. Harold Moyer (b. 1927)

𝅗𝅥=66
10. 10. 10. 6

1 Guide me, O thou great Je - ho - vah, pil - grim through this
2 O - pen now the crys - tal foun - tain, whence the heal - ing
3 When I tread the verge of Jor - dan, bid my anx - ious
bar - ren land; I am weak, but thou art might - y;
stream doth flow; let the fire and cloud - y pil - lar
fears sub - side; death of death, and hell's de - struc - tion,
hold me with thy power - ful hand; bread of hea - ven,
lead me all my jour - ney through; strong de - liv - erer,
land me safe on Ca - naan's side; songs of prais - es,
bread of hea - ven, feed me now and ev - er -
strong de - liv - erer, be thou still my strength and
songs of prais - es, I will ev - er give to

more, feed me now and ev - er - more.
shield, be thou still my strength and shield.
thee, I will ev - er give to thee.

Words: William Williams (1717-1791); tr. Peter Williams (1722-1796), alt.
Music: *Cwm Rhondda,* John Hughes (1873-1932)

♩=96
87. 87. 877

691

1 My faith looks up to thee, thou Lamb of Cal - va - ry,
2 May thy rich grace im-part strength to my faint - ing heart,
3 While life's dark maze I tread, and griefs a - round me spread,
Sa - vior di - vine! Now hear me while I pray, take all my
my zeal in - spire; as thou hast died for me, O may my
be thou my guide; bid dark-ness turn to day; wipe sor-row's
guilt a - way; O let me from this day be whol - ly thine.
love to thee pure, warm, and change-less be, a liv - ing fire.
tears a - way, nor let me ev - er stray from thee a - side.

Words: Ray Palmer (1808-1887)
Music: *Olivet,* Lowell Mason (1792-1872)

𝅗𝅥=56
664. 6664

1 I heard the voice of Je - sus say, "Come un - to me and rest;
2 I heard the voice of Je - sus say, "Be - hold, I free - ly give
3 I heard the voice of Je - sus say, "I am this dark world's light;
and in your wea - ri - ness lay down your head up - on my breast."
the liv - ing wa - ter; thirst - y one, stoop down and drink, and live."
look un - to me, your morn shall rise, and all your day be bright."
*
I came to Je - sus as I was, so wea - ry, worn, and sad;
I came to Je - sus, and I drank of that life - giv - ing stream;
I looked to Je - sus, and I found in him my Star, my Sun;
I found in him a rest - ing place, and he has made me glad.
my thirst was quenched, my soul re - vived, and now I live in him.
and in that light of life I'll walk till pil - grim days are done.

The bracketed notes are to be treated as triplet groups. This music in d, 170.
Alternative tune: *Kingsfold,* 480.

Words: Horatius Bonar (1808-1889), alt.
Music: *The Third Tune,* Thomas Tallis (1505?-1585); ed. John Wilson (b. 1905)

♩=82
CMD

D A D A
1 Just as I am, with - out one plea, but that thy
2 Just as I am, though tossed a - bout with man - y a
*3 Just as I am, poor, wretch - ed, blind; sight, rich - es,
4 Just as I am: thou wilt re - ceive; wilt wel - come,
5 Just as I am, thy love un - known has bro - ken
A7 G D D
1 blood was shed for me, and that thou bidd'st me
2 con - flict, man - y a doubt; fight - ings and fears with -
3 heal - ing of the mind, yea, all I need, in
4 par - don, cleanse, re - lieve, be - cause thy prom - ise
5 ev - ery bar - rier down; now to be thine, yea,
G D A D
1 come to thee, O Lamb of God, I come, I come.
2 in, with - out, O Lamb of God, I come, I come.
3 thee to find, O Lamb of God, I come, I come.
4 I be - lieve, O Lamb of God, I come, I come.
5 thine a - lone, O Lamb of God, I come, I come.

6 Just as I am, of thy great love
the breadth, length, depth, and height to prove,
here for a season, then above:
O Lamb of God, I come, I come.

Words: Charlotte Elliott (1789-1871)
Music: *Woodworth*, William Batchelder Bradbury (1816-1868)

𝅗𝅥. = 46
LM

God be in my head, and in my un - der - stand - ing;
God be in mine eyes, and in my look - ing;
God be in my mouth, and in my speak - ing;
God be in my heart, and in my think - ing;
God be at mine end, and at my de - part - ing.

Words: *Sarum Primer,* 1514
Music: *Lytlington,* Sydney Hugo Nicholson (1875-1947)

𝅗𝅥=60
Irr.

1 By gra - cious powers so won - der - ful - ly shel - tered,
2 Yet is this heart by its old foe tor - ment - ed,
3 And when this cup you give is filled to brim - ming
4 Yet when a - gain in this same world you give us
and con - fi - dent - ly wait - ing come what may,
still e - vil days bring bur - dens hard to bear;
with bit - ter suf - fering, hard to un - der - stand,
the joy we had, the bright - ness of your Sun,
we know that God is with us night and morn - ing,
O give our fright - ened souls the sure sal - va - tion,
we take it thank - ful - ly and with - out trem - bling,
we shall re - mem - ber all the days we lived through,
and nev - er fails to greet us each new day.
for which, O Lord, you taught us to pre - pare.
out of so good and so be - loved a hand.
and our whole life shall then be yours a - lone.

Alternative tune: *Le Cénacle*, 696.

Words: F. Pratt Green (b. 1903), after Dietrich Bonhoeffer (1906-1945)
Music: *Intercessor*, Charles Hubert Hastings Parry (1848-1918)

♩= 100
11 10. 11 10

1 By gra - cious powers so won - der - ful - ly
2 Yet is this heart by its old foe tor -
3 And when this cup you give is filled to
4 Yet when a - gain in this same world you
shel - tered, and con - - - fi - dent - ly wait - ing come what
ment - ed, still e - - - vil days bring bur - dens hard to
brim - ming with bit - - - ter suf - fering, hard to un - der -
give us the joy we had, the bright-ness of your
simile
may, we know that God is with us night and
bear; O give our fright - ened souls the sure sal -
stand, we take it thank - ful - ly and with-out
Sun, we shall re - mem - ber all the days we

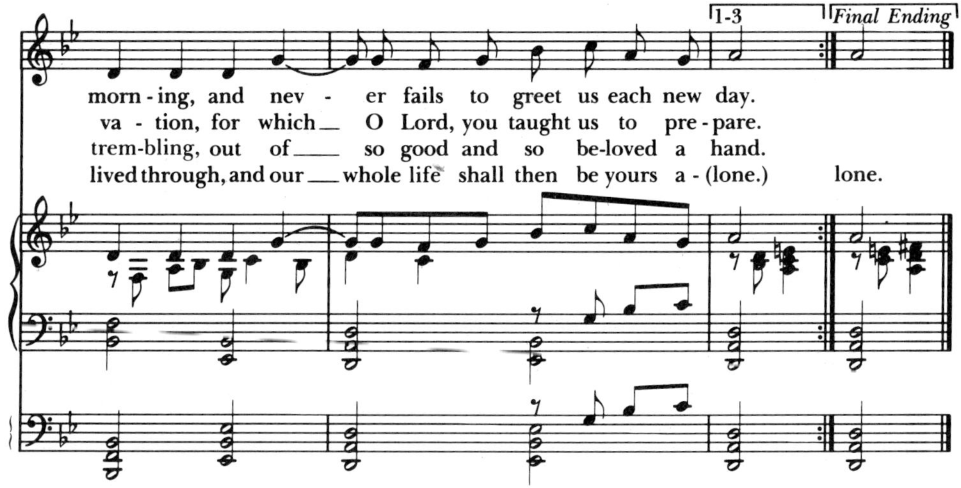
1-3
Final Ending
morn - ing, and nev - er fails to greet us each new day.
va - tion, for which O Lord, you taught us to pre - pare.
trem-bling, out of so good and so be-loved a hand.
lived through, and our whole life shall then be yours a - (lone.) lone.

When piano is used, left hand plays the bottom staff. Alternative tune: *Intercessor,* 695.

Words: F. Pratt Green (b. 1903), after Dietrich Bonhoeffer (1906-1945)
Music: *Le Cénacle,* Joseph Gelineau (b. 1920)

♩=72
11 10. 11 10

The Christian Life

697

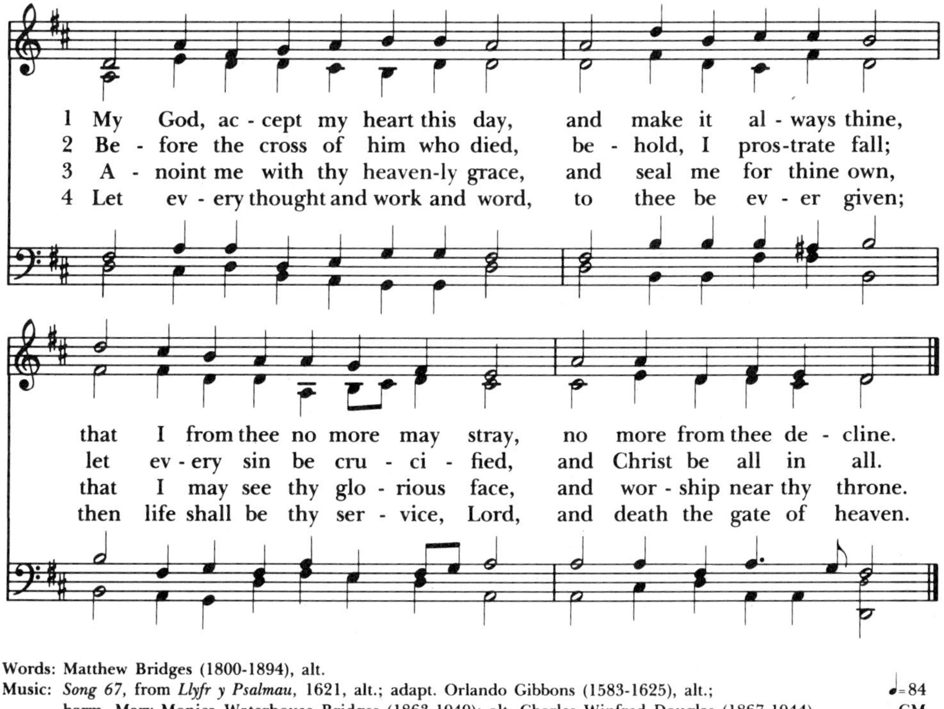
1 My God, ac - cept my heart this day, and make it al - ways thine,
2 Be - fore the cross of him who died, be - hold, I pros-trate fall;
3 A - noint me with thy heaven-ly grace, and seal me for thine own,
4 Let ev - ery thought and work and word, to thee be ev - er given;
that I from thee no more may stray, no more from thee de - cline.
let ev - ery sin be cru - ci - fied, and Christ be all in all.
that I may see thy glo - rious face, and wor - ship near thy throne.
then life shall be thy ser - vice, Lord, and death the gate of heaven.

Words: Matthew Bridges (1800-1894), alt.
Music: *Song 67,* from *Llyfr y Psalmau,* 1621, alt.; adapt. Orlando Gibbons (1583-1625), alt.; harm. Mary Monica Waterhouse Bridges (1863-1949); alt. Charles Winfred Douglas (1867-1944)

♩=84
CM

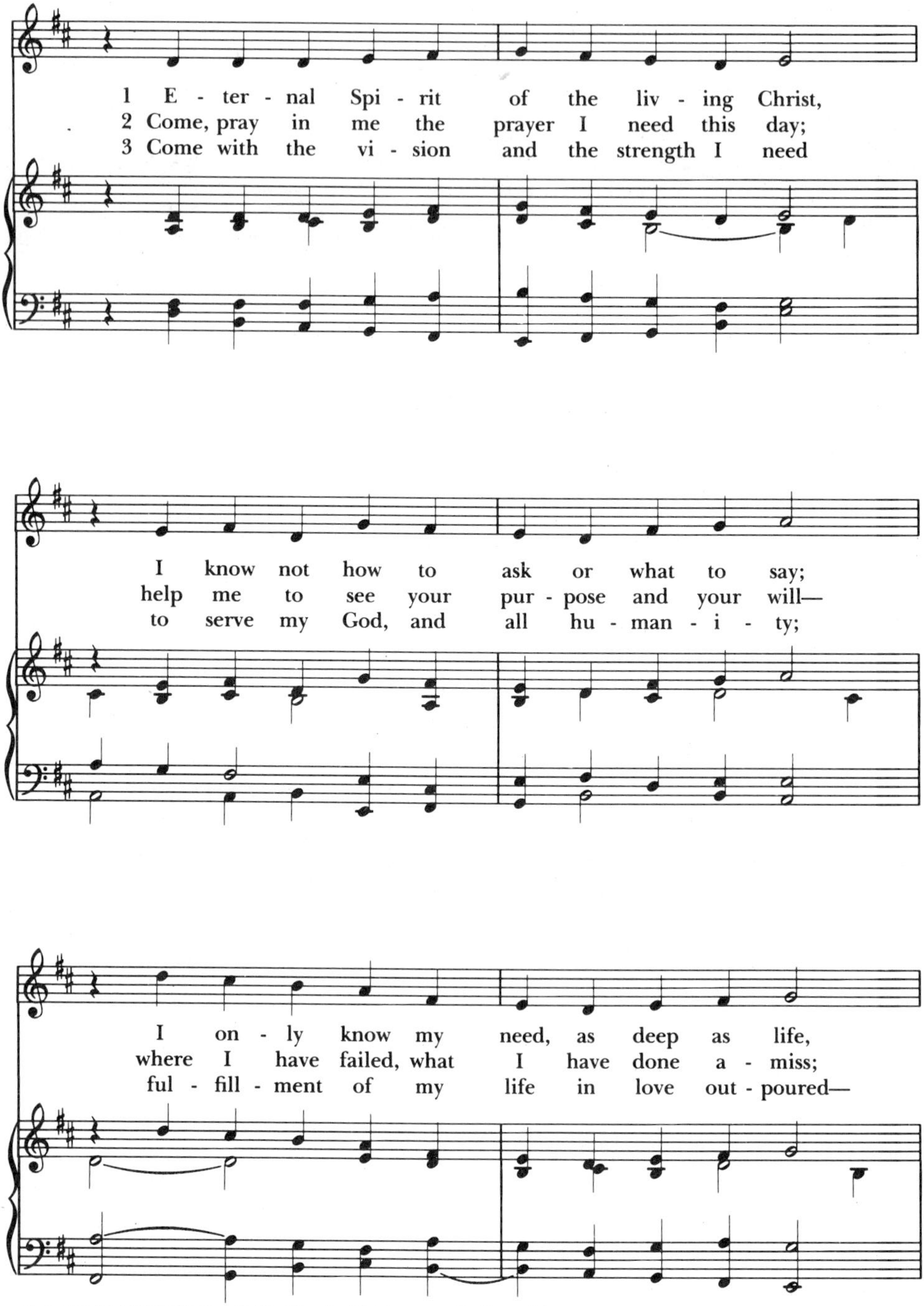
1 E - ter - nal Spi - rit of the liv - ing Christ,
2 Come, pray in me the prayer I need this day;
3 Come with the vi - sion and the strength I need
I know not how to ask or what to say;
help me to see your pur - pose and your will—
to serve my God, and all hu - man - i - ty;
I on - ly know my need, as deep as life,
where I have failed, what I have done a - miss;
ful - fill - ment of my life in love out - poured—

and on - ly you can teach me how to pray.
held in for - giv - ing love, let me be still.
my life in you, O Christ, your love in me.

Words: Frank von Christierson (b. 1900), rev.
Music: *Flentge,* Carl Flentge Schalk (b. 1929)

𝅗𝅥=c. 48
10 10. 10 10

1 Je - sus, Lov - er of my soul, let me to thy bos - om
2 O - ther ref - uge have I none, hangs my help - less soul on
3 Plen - teous grace with thee is found, grace to cleanse from ev - ery
fly, while the near - er wa - ters roll, while the tem - pest
thee; leave, ah! leave me not a - lone, still sup - port and
sin; let the heal - ing streams a - bound, make and keep me
still is high: hide me, O my Sa - vior, hide,
com - fort me! All my trust on thee is stayed;
pure with - in. Thou of life the foun - tain art,
till the storm of life be past; safe in - to the
all my help from thee I bring; cov - er my de -
free - ly let me take of thee: spring thou up with -

ha - ven guide, O re - ceive my soul at last.
fense - less head with the sha - dow of thy wing.
in my heart, rise to all e - ter - ni - ty.

This music in d, 640.

Words: Charles Wesley (1707-1788), alt.
Music: *Aberystwyth,* Joseph Parry (1841-1903)

𝅗𝅥=44
77. 77. D

The Christian Life

700

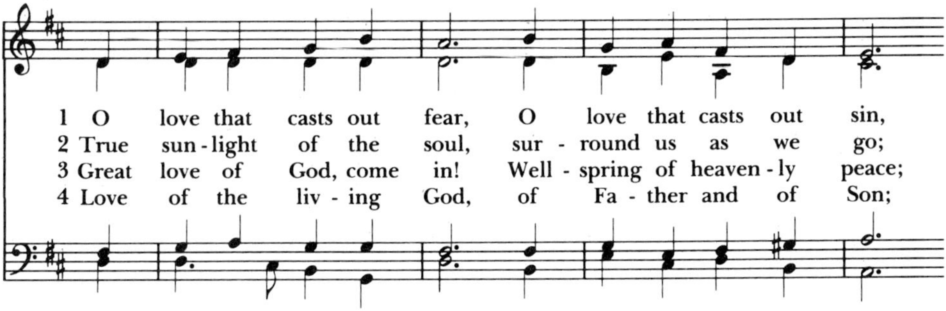
1 O love that casts out fear, O love that casts out sin,
2 True sun - light of the soul, sur - round us as we go;
3 Great love of God, come in! Well - spring of heaven - ly peace;
4 Love of the liv - ing God, of Fa - ther and of Son;

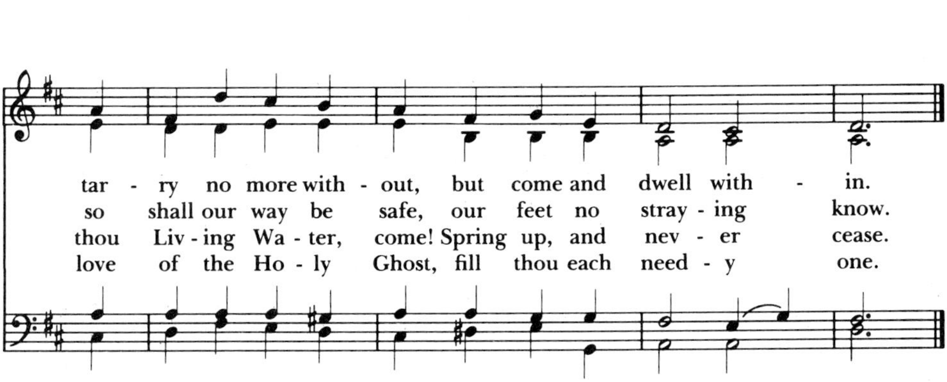
tar - ry no more with - out, but come and dwell with - in.
so shall our way be safe, our feet no stray - ing know.
thou Liv - ing Wa - ter, come! Spring up, and nev - er cease.
love of the Ho - ly Ghost, fill thou each need - y one.

Words: Horatius Bonar (1808-1889)
Music: *Moseley,* Henry Thomas Smart (1813-1879)

𝅗𝅥=54
66. 66

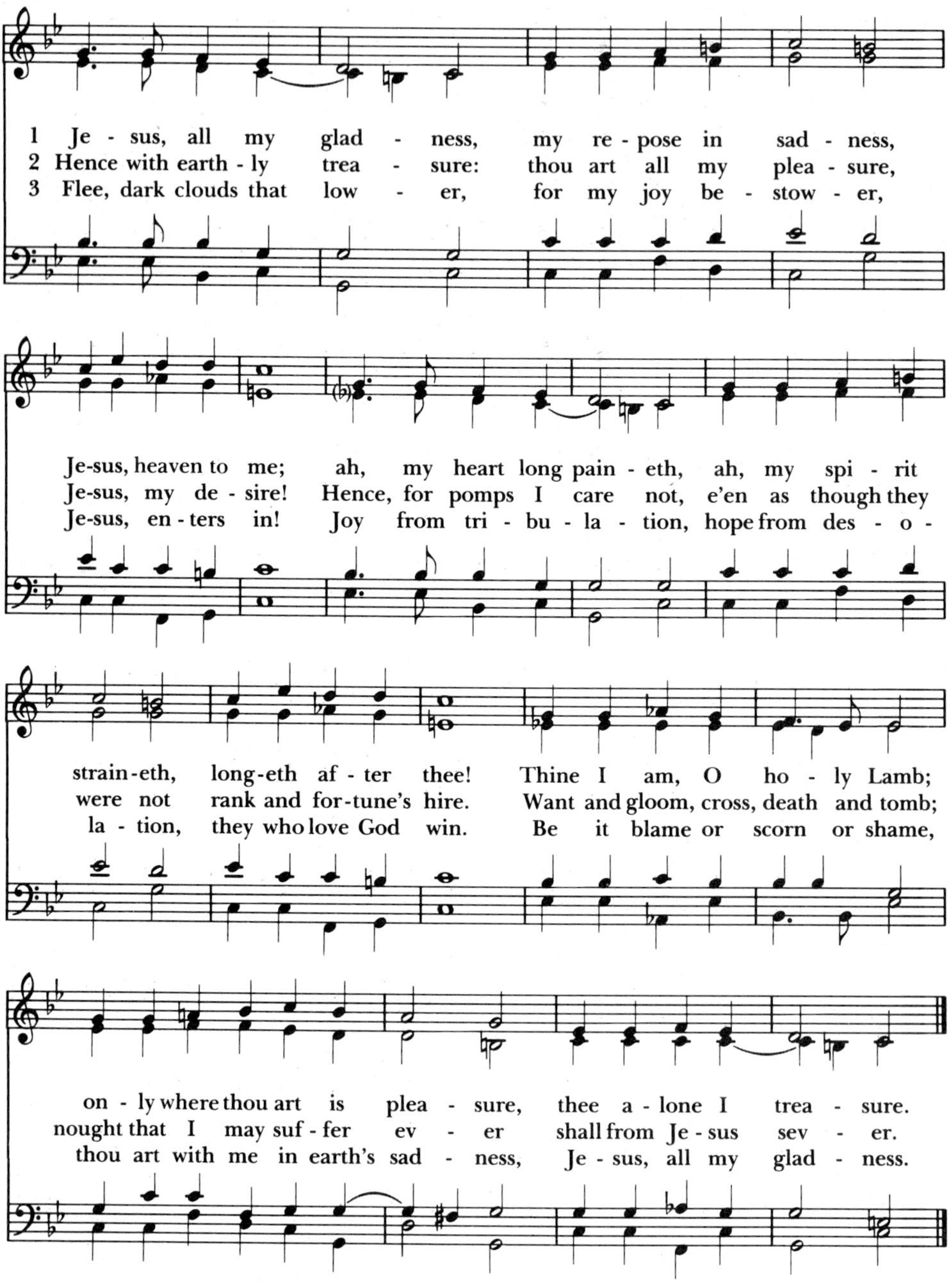
1 Je - sus, all my glad - ness, my re - pose in sad - ness,
2 Hence with earth - ly trea - sure: thou art all my plea - sure,
3 Flee, dark clouds that low - er, for my joy be - stow - er,
Je-sus, heaven to me; ah, my heart long pain - eth, ah, my spi - rit
Je-sus, my de - sire! Hence, for pomps I care not, e'en as though they
Je-sus, en - ters in! Joy from tri - bu - la - tion, hope from des - o -
strain-eth, long-eth af - ter thee! Thine I am, O ho - ly Lamb;
were not rank and for-tune's hire. Want and gloom, cross, death and tomb;
la - tion, they who love God win. Be it blame or scorn or shame,
on - ly where thou art is plea - sure, thee a - lone I trea - sure.
nought that I may suf - fer ev - er shall from Je - sus sev - er.
thou art with me in earth's sad - ness, Je - sus, all my glad - ness.

Words: Johann Franck (1618-1677); tr. Arthur Wellesley Wotherspoon (1853-1936), alt.
Music: *Jesu, meine Freude,* Johann Cruger (1598-1662), alt.

𝅗𝅥=46
665. 665. 786

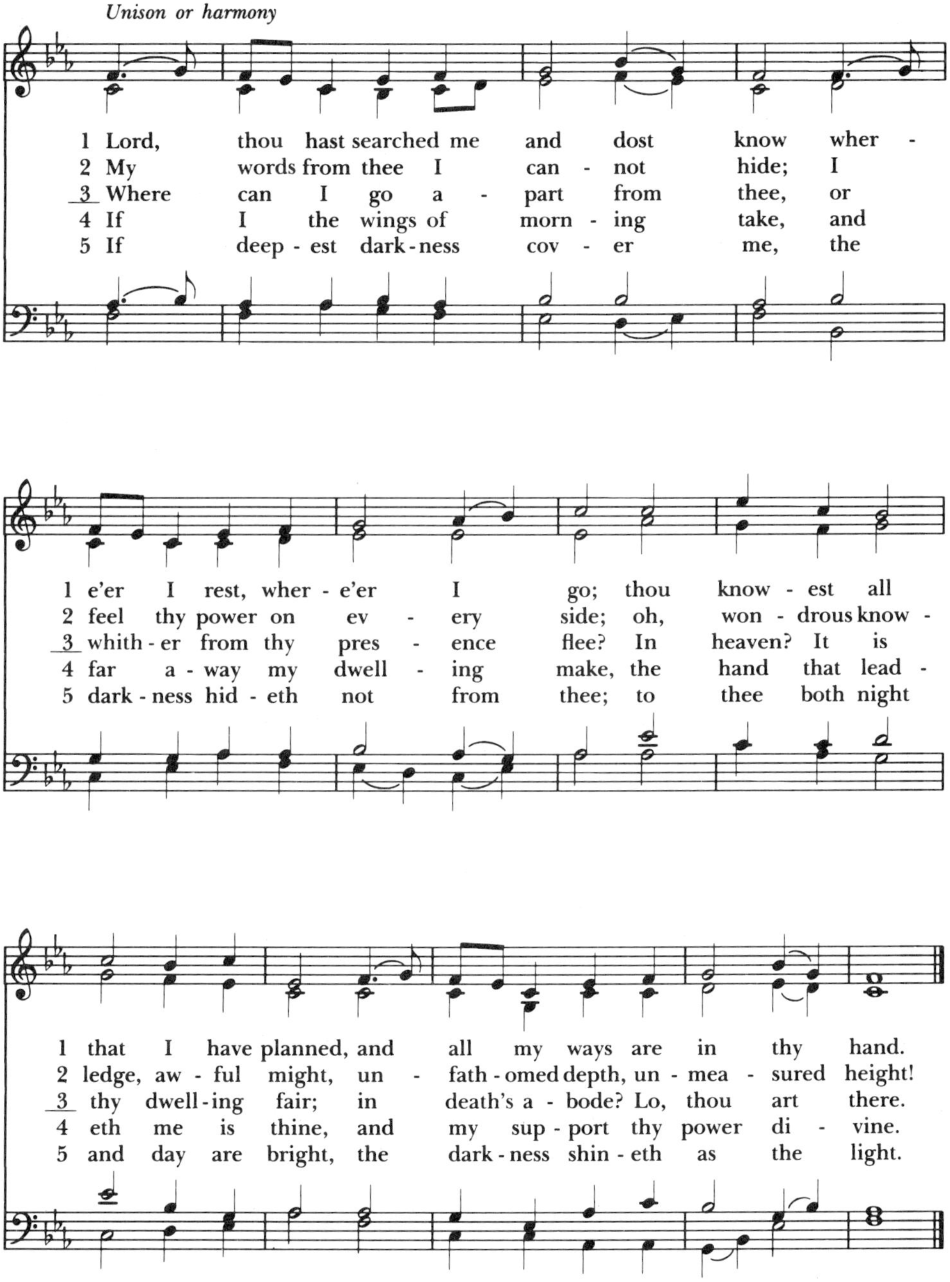
Unison or harmony
1 Lord, thou hast searched me and dost know wher -
2 My words from thee I can - not hide; I
3 Where can I go a - part from thee, or
4 If I the wings of morn - ing take, and
5 If deep - est dark - ness cov - er me, the
1 e'er I rest, wher - e'er I go; thou know - est all
2 feel thy power on ev - ery side; oh, won - drous know -
3 whith - er from thy pres - ence flee? In heaven? It is
4 far a - way my dwell - ing make, the hand that lead -
5 dark - ness hid - eth not from thee; to thee both night
1 that I have planned, and all my ways are in thy hand.
2 ledge, aw - ful might, un - fath - omed depth, un - mea - sured height!
3 thy dwell - ing fair; in death's a - bode? Lo, thou art there.
4 eth me is thine, and my sup - port thy power di - vine.
5 and day are bright, the dark - ness shin - eth as the light.

Words: *The Psalter Hymnal*, 1927; para. of Psalm 139:1-11
Music: *Tender Thought*, from *Kentucky Harmony*, 1816

𝅗𝅥=56
LM

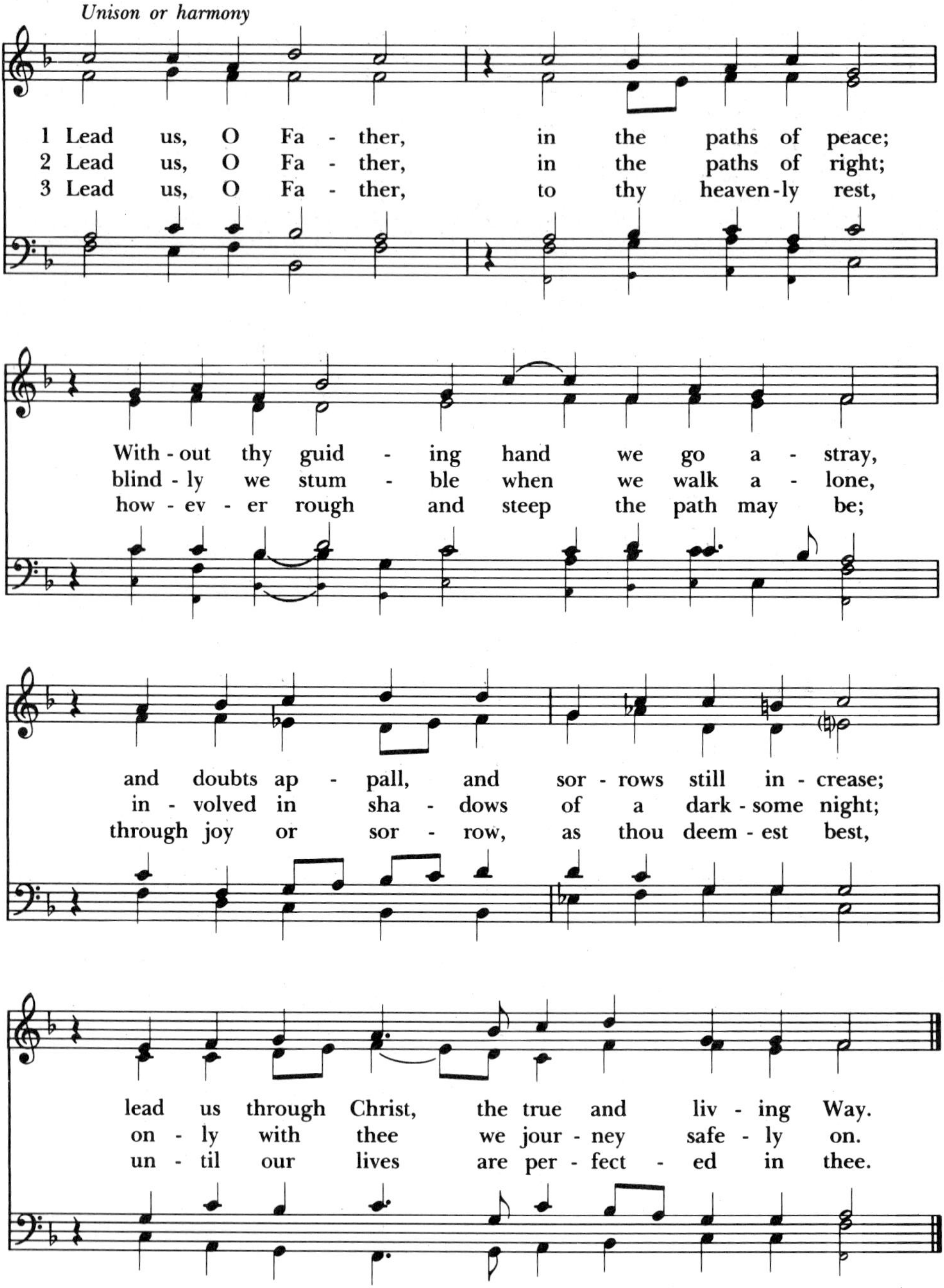
Unison or harmony
1 Lead us, O Fa - ther, in the paths of peace;
2 Lead us, O Fa - ther, in the paths of right;
3 Lead us, O Fa - ther, to thy heaven-ly rest,
With-out thy guid - ing hand we go a - stray,
blind - ly we stum - ble when we walk a - lone,
how - ev - er rough and steep the path may be;
and doubts ap - pall, and sor - rows still in - crease;
in - volved in sha - dows of a dark - some night;
through joy or sor - row, as thou deem - est best,
lead us through Christ, the true and liv - ing Way.
on - ly with thee we jour - ney safe - ly on.
un - til our lives are per - fect - ed in thee.

Words: William Henry Burleigh (1812-1871), alt.
Music: *Song 22,* melody and bass Orlando Gibbons (1583-1625)

♩=88
10 10. 10 10

1 O thou who cam - est from a - bove the fire ce -
2 There let it for thy glo - ry burn with ev - er
3 Je - sus, con - firm my heart's de - sire to work, and
*4 Still let me prove thy per - fect will, my acts of
les - tial to im - part, kin - dle a flame of
bright, un - dy - ing blaze, and trem - bling to its
speak, and think for thee; still let me guard the
faith and love re - peat, till death thy end - less
sa - cred love up - on the al - tar of my heart.
source re - turn in hum - ble prayer and fer - vent praise.
ho - ly fire and still stir up the gift in me.
mer - cies seal, and make the sac - ri - fice com - plete.

Words: Charles Wesley (1707-1788), alt.
Music: *Hereford,* Samuel Sebastian Wesley (1810-1876)

♩=92
LM

Unison or harmony
1 As those of old their first fruits brought of vine-yard, flock, and
*2 A world in need now sum-mons us to la-bor, love, and
3 With grat-i-tude and hum-ble trust we bring our best to
field to God, the giv-er of all good, the
give; to make our life an of-fer-ing to
thee to serve thy cause and share thy love with
source of boun-teous yield; so we to-day our
God that all may live; the Church of Christ is
all hu-man-i-ty. O thou who gav-est
first fruits bring, the wealth of this good land, of
call-ing us to make the dream come true: a
us thy-self in Je-sus Christ thy Son, help

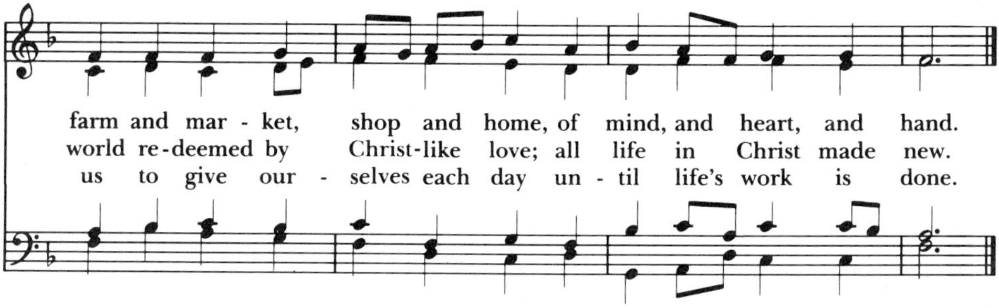
farm and mar - ket, shop and home, of mind, and heart, and hand.
world re-deemed by Christ-like love; all life in Christ made new.
us to give our - selves each day un - til life's work is done.

Words: Frank von Christierson (b. 1900), alt. 𝅗𝅥=48
Music: *Forest Green,* English melody; adapt. and harm. Ralph Vaughan Williams (1872-1958) CMD

The Christian Life 706

1 In your mer - cy, Lord, you called me, taught my
2 Lord, I did not free - ly choose you till by
3 Now my heart sets none a - bove you, for your
sin - filled heart and mind, else this world had
grace you set me free; for my heart would
grace a - lone I thirst, know - ing well, that
still en-thralled me, and to glo - ry kept me blind.
still re - fuse you had your love not cho - sen me.
if I love you, you, O Lord, have loved me first.

Words: Josiah Conder (1789-1855); alt. Charles P. Price (b. 1920) 𝅗𝅥=50
Music: *Halton Holgate,* William Boyce (1711-1779) 87. 87

1 Take my life, and let it be con - se - crat - ed, Lord, to thee;
2 Take my voice, and let me sing al - ways, on - ly, for my King;
take my mo - ments and my days, let them flow in cease - less praise.
take my in - tel - lect, and use ev - ery power as thou shalt choose.
Take my hands, and let them move at the im - pulse of thy love;
Take my will, and make it thine; it shall be no long - er mine.
take my heart, it is thine own; it shall be thy roy - al throne.
Take my - self, and I will be ev - er, on - ly, all for thee.

Alternative tune: *Aberystwyth,* 699.

Words: Frances Ridley Havergal (1836-1879), alt.
Music: *Hollingside,* John Bacchus Dykes (1823-1876)

𝅗𝅥 = 46
77. 77. D

1 Sa - vior, like a shep-herd lead us; much we need thy
2 Ear - ly let us seek thy fa - vor, ear - ly let us
ten - der care; in thy plea - sant pas - tures feed us;
learn thy will; do thou, Lord, our on - ly Sa - vior,
for our use thy folds pre - pare. Bless - ed Je - sus!
with thy love our bos - oms fill. Bless - ed Je - sus!
Bless - ed Je - sus! Thou hast bought us, thine we are.
Bless - ed Je - sus! Thou hast loved us: love us still.

Words: *Hymns for the Young,* ca. 1830, alt.
Music: *Sicilian Mariners,* Sicilian melody, from *The European Magazine and London Review,* 1792

♩=69
87. 87. 87

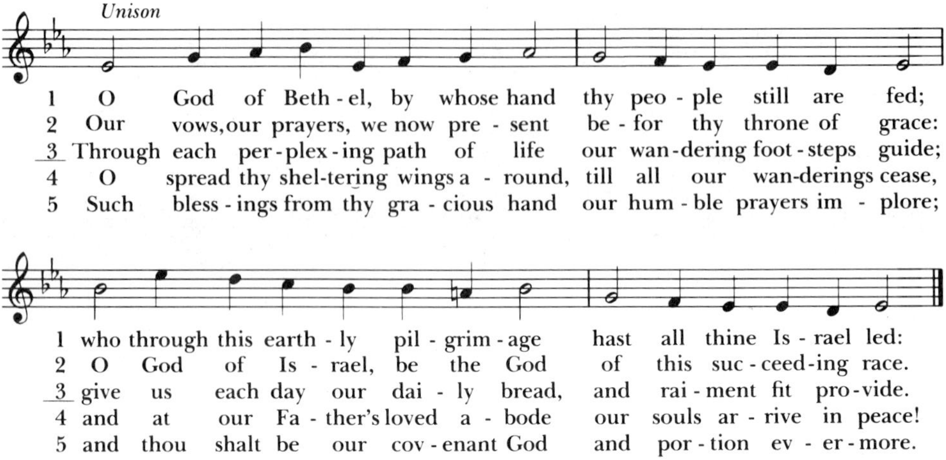
Unison
1 O God of Beth-el, by whose hand thy peo-ple still are fed;
2 Our vows, our prayers, we now pre-sent be-for thy throne of grace:
3 Through each per-plex-ing path of life our wan-dering foot-steps guide;
4 O spread thy shel-tering wings a-round, till all our wan-derings cease,
5 Such bless-ings from thy gra-cious hand our hum-ble prayers im-plore;
1 who through this earth-ly pil-grim-age hast all thine Is-rael led:
2 O God of Is-rael, be the God of this suc-ceed-ing race.
3 give us each day our dai-ly bread, and rai-ment fit pro-vide.
4 and at our Fa-ther's loved a-bode our souls ar-rive in peace!
5 and thou shalt be our cov-enant God and por-tion ev-er-more.

Words: Philip Doddridge (1702-1751), alt.
Music: *Dundee*, melody from *The CL Psalmes of David*, 1615;
fauxbourdon *The Psalmes of David in Prose and Meeter*, 1635

♩=88
CM

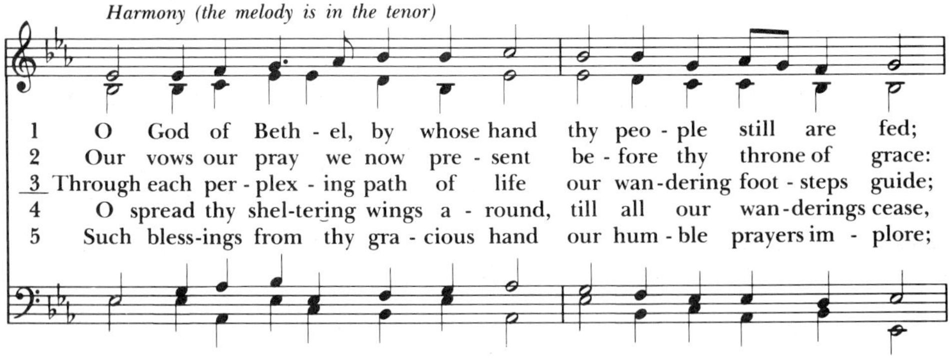
Harmony (the melody is in the tenor)
1 O God of Beth-el, by whose hand thy peo-ple still are fed;
2 Our vows our pray we now pre-sent be-fore thy throne of grace:
3 Through each per-plex-ing path of life our wan-dering foot-steps guide;
4 O spread thy shel-tering wings a-round, till all our wan-derings cease,
5 Such bless-ings from thy gra-cious hand our hum-ble prayers im-plore;

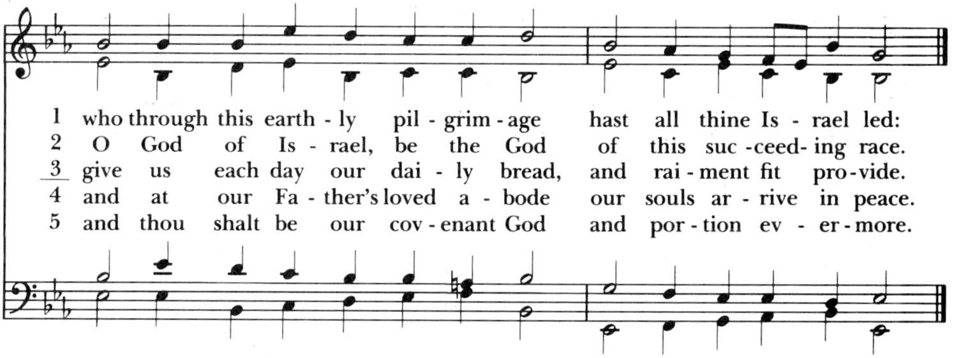
1 who through this earth - ly pil - grim - age hast all thine Is - rael led:
2 O God of Is - rael, be the God of this suc - ceed - ing race.
3 give us each day our dai - ly bread, and rai - ment fit pro - vide.
4 and at our Fa - ther's loved a - bode our souls ar - rive in peace.
5 and thou shalt be our cov - enant God and por - tion ev - er - more.

Another harmonization, 526.

Words: Philip Doddridge (1702-1751), alt.
Music: *Dundee,* melody from *The CL Psalmes of David,* 1615; fauxbourdon *The Psalmes of David in Prose and Meeter,* 1635

♩.= 88
CM

Rounds and Canons

710

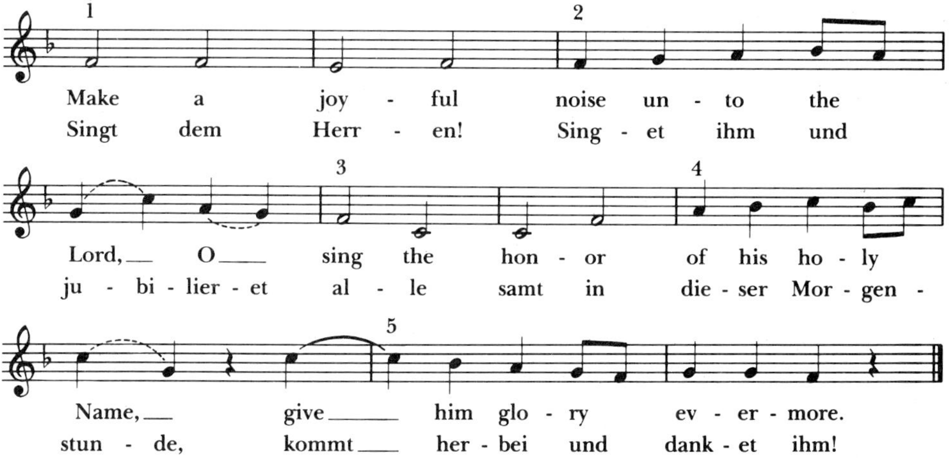
1
2
Make a joy - ful noise un - to the
Singt dem Herr - en! Sing - et ihm und
3
4
Lord, O sing the hon - or of his ho - ly
ju - bi - lier - et al - le samt in die - ser Mor - gen -
5
Name, give him glo - ry ev - er - more.
stun - de, kommt her - bei und dank - et ihm!

Words: German; adapt. Ann M. Gilman (b. 1932) and Lawrence Gilman (b. 1930)
Music: *Singt dem Herren,* Michael Praetorius (1571-1621)

𝅗𝅥= 100
Irr.

1
D F♯m G D
1 Seek ye first the king - dom of God
2 Ask, and it shall be giv - en un - to you,
G D Asus4 A D F♯m
and its right - eous - ness, and all these things shall be
seek, and ye shall find, knock, and the door shall be
G D G D Asus4 A7 D
add - ed un - to you; Al - le - lu, al - le - lu - ia!
o - pened un - to you; Al - le - lu, al - le - lu - ia!

Refrain
2
D F♯m G D
Al - le - lu - ia,
G D Asus4 A D F♯m
al - le - lu - ia, al - le -
G D G D Asus4 A7 D
lu - ia! Al - le - lu, al - le - lu - ia!

This may be sung in two part canon at the distance of eight measures.

Words: St. 1, Matthew 6:33; adapt. Karen Lafferty (20th cent.). St. 2, Matthew 7:7.
Stanza 2 is not part of the hymn as originally written.
Music: *Seek Ye First,* Karen Lafferty (20th cent.)

♩=66
13. 11. 7 with Alleluias

712

Rounds and Canons

1
Do - na no - bis pa - cem, pa-cem. Do - na no - bis
pa - cem. 2 Do - na no - bis pa - cem.
Do - na no - bis pa - cem. 3 Do - na
no - bis pa - cem. Do - na no - bis pa - cem.

Words: Traditional Latin
Music: *Dona nobis pacem,* traditional canon

♩= 84
Irr.

713

Rounds and Canons

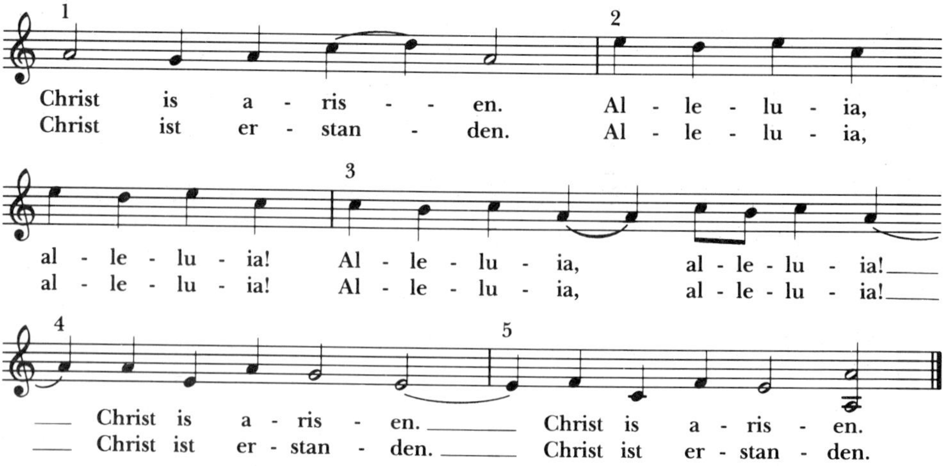
1 2 3 4 5
Christ is a - ris - - en. Al - le - lu - ia,
Christ ist er - stan - den. Al - le - lu - ia,
al - le - lu - ia! Al - le - lu - ia, al - le - lu - ia!
al - le - lu - ia! Al - le - lu - ia, al - le - lu - ia!
Christ is a - ris - en. Christ is a - ris - en.
Christ ist er - stan - den. Christ ist er - stan - den.

Words: German, ca. 1529, adapt.
Music: *Christ is arisen,* Richard Rudolf Klein (b. 1921); based on the chorale *Christ ist erstanden*

𝅗𝅥= 66
Irr.

Rounds and Canons 714

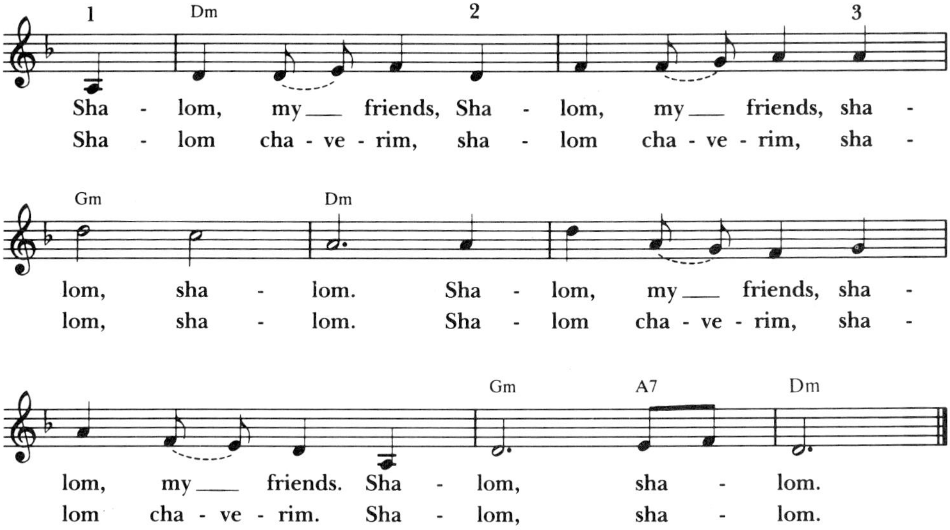
1 Dm 2 3
Sha - lom, my ___ friends, Sha - lom, my ___ friends, sha -
Sha - lom cha - ve - rim, sha - lom cha - ve - rim, sha -
Gm Dm
lom, sha - lom. Sha - lom, my ___ friends, sha -
lom, sha - lom. Sha - lom cha - ve - rim, sha -
Gm A7 Dm
lom, my ___ friends. Sha - lom, sha - lom.
lom cha - ve - rim. Sha - lom, sha - lom.

Words: Israeli round
Music: *Shalom chaverim,* Hebrew melody

𝅗𝅥=42
Irr.

Rounds and Canons 715

1 2
When Je - sus wept, the fall - ing tear in
3
mer - cy flowed be - yond all bound; when Je - sus groaned, a
4
trem-bling fear seized all the guilt - y world a - round.

Words: *The New England Psalm Singer,* 1770
Music: *When Jesus Wept,* William Billings (1746-1800)

𝅗𝅥=100
LM

1 God bless our na - tive land; firm may she ev - er stand
2 For her our prayers shall rise to God, a - bove the skies;
Trumpets
through storm and night: when the wild
on him we wait; thou who art
tem - pests rave, ru - ler of wind and wave,
ev - er nigh, guard - ing with watch - ful eye,
do thou our coun - try save by thy great might.
to thee a - loud we cry, God save the state!

Another harmonization, 717.

Words: Siegfried August Mahlmann (1771-1826); tr. Charles Timothy Brooks (1813-1883) and John Sullivan Dwight (1812-1893), alt.
Music: *America*, from *Thesaurus Musicus*, 1745

♩=96
664. 6664

717

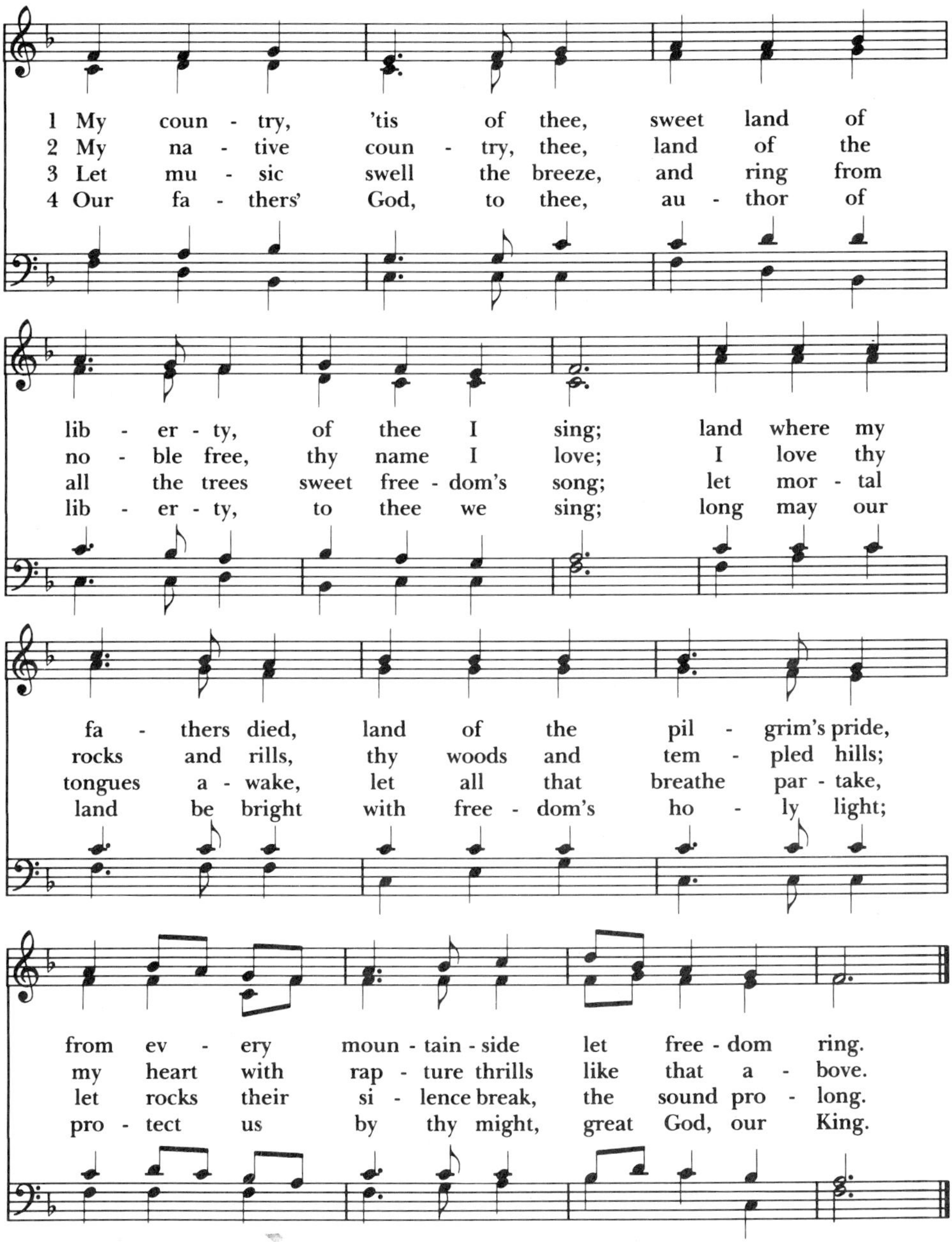
1 My coun - try, 'tis of thee, sweet land of lib - er - ty, of thee I sing; land where my fa - thers died, land of the pil - grim's pride, from ev - ery moun - tain - side let free - dom ring.
2 My na - tive coun - try, thee, land of the no - ble free, thy name I love; I love thy rocks and rills, thy woods and tem - pled hills; my heart with rap - ture thrills like that a - bove.
3 Let mu - sic swell the breeze, and ring from all the trees sweet free - dom's song; let mor - tal tongues a - wake, let all that breathe par - take, let rocks their si - lence break, the sound pro - long.
4 Our fa - thers' God, to thee, au - thor of lib - er - ty, to thee we sing; long may our land be bright with free - dom's ho - ly light; pro - tect us by thy might, great God, our King.

Another harmonization, 716.

Words: Samuel Francis Smith (1808-1895)
Music: *America*, from *Thesaurus Musicus*, 1745

♩=96
664. 6664

Trumpets
1 God of our fa - thers, whose al - might - y
2 Thy love di - vine hath led us in the
3 From war's a - larms, from dead - ly pes - ti -
4 Re - fresh thy peo - ple on their toil - some
hand leads forth in beau - ty all the star - ry band
past, in this free land by thee our lot is cast;
lence, be thy strong arm our ev - er sure de - fense;
way, lead us from night to nev - er - end - ing day;
of shin - ing worlds in splen - dor through the skies,
be thou our ru - ler, guard - ian, guide, and stay,
thy true re - li - gion in our hearts in - crease,
fill all our lives with love and grace di - vine,
our grate - ful songs be - fore thy throne a - rise.
thy word our law, thy paths our cho - sen way.
thy boun - teous good - ness nour - ish us in peace.
and glo - ry, laud, and praise be ev - er thine.

Words: Daniel Crane Roberts (1841-1907)
Music: *National Hymn*, George William Warren (1828-1902)

𝅗𝅥=66
10 10. 10 10

1 O beau - ti - ful for spa - cious skies, for am - ber waves of grain,
2 O beau - ti - ful for he - roes proved in lib - er - at - ing strife,
3 O beau - ti - ful for pa - triot dream that sees be - yond the years
for pur - ple moun - tain ma - jes - ties a - bove the fruit - ed plain!
who more than self their coun - try loved, and mer - cy more than life!
thine al - a - bas - ter ci - ties gleam, un - dimmed by hu - man tears!
A - mer - i - ca! A - mer - i - ca! God shed his grace on thee,
A - mer - i - ca! A - mer - i - ca! God mend thine ev - ery flaw,
A - mer - i - ca! A - mer - i - ca! God shed his grace on thee,
and crown thy good with bro - ther-hood from sea to shin - ing sea.
con - firm thy soul in self - con - trol, thy lib - er - ty in law.
and crown thy good with bro - ther-hood from sea to shin - ing sea.

Words: Katherine Lee Bates (1859-1929), alt.
Music: *Materna*, Samuel Augustus Ward (1848-1903)

𝅗𝅥=60
CMD

1 O say can you see, by the dawn's ear - ly light,
2 O thus be it ev - er, when free - men shall stand
what so proud - ly we hailed at the twi - light's last gleam - ing,
be - tween their loved homes and the war's des - o - lat - tion!
whose broad stripes and bright stars, through the per - il - lous fight,
Blest with vic - tory and peace, may the heaven - re - scued land
o'er the ram - parts we watched, were so gal - lant - ly stream - ing?
praise the Power that hath made and pre - served us a na - tion!

And the rock - ets' red glare, the bombs burst - ing in air,
Then — con - quer we must, when our cause it is just,
gave proof through the night that our flag was still there.
and this be our mot - to, "In God is our trust."
O — say does that star - span - gled ban - ner yet wave
And the star - span - gled ban - ner in tri - umph shall wave
o'er the land of the free and the home of the brave?
o'er the land of the free and the home of the brave!

Words: Francis Scott Key (1779-1843)
Music: *National Anthem*, source unknown, ca. 18th cent.

♩= 92
Irr.

Indexes

Copyright Acknowledgments

The following texts are copyrighted by The Church Pension Fund:
16(Sts.1-3), 17(1-3), 18, 19(1-2), 20(1-2), 25, 26, 38(1-4), 39(1-4), 40(1-4), 41(1-4), 44(1-3), 45(1-3), 48(4), 56, 60, 63, 64, 81(3), 91, 121, 139, 152, 153, 159, 162, 164, 165, 166, 173(1,4), 176(3), 177(3), 193, 220, 221, 231, 232, 233, 234, 261, 262, 282, 283, 302, 303, 314(1-3), 319, 320, 329, 330, 331, 353, 356, 364(6-8), 366, 375, 390, 421, 428, 443, 475(1,2,4), 478, 489, 499, 530, 540, 579(2,3), 619, 647, 663, 668(4), 669.

The following musical settings are copyrighted by The Church Pension Fund:
9, 37, 107, 153, 157, 163, 185, 187, 312, 316, 403, 454, 514, 515, 532, 542, 564, 614, 647, 654, 661.

The following harmonizations and accompaniments are copyrighted by The Church Pension Fund:
8, 25, 27, 43, 105, 149, 159, 166 (alternative accompaniment), 172, 184, 201, 203, 215, 257 (alternative harmonization), 314, 319, 330, 359, 364, 366, 404, 439, 504, 505, 519, 571, 622, 667, 697.

Individual copyright acknowledgments are as follows:

1 Words: By permission of Oxford University Press. Music: Harmonization by permission of Oxford University Press.
2 Words: By permission of Oxford University Press. Music: Melody rhythmic version © 1984, Schola Antiqua Inc. Used by permission. Accompaniment © 1984, Roy F. Kehl.
3 Words: Sts.2-4 Copyright © 1972, Peter J. Scagnelli. From *Catholic Liturgy Book*. Used by permission.
4 Words: Sts.2-4 Copyright © 1972, Peter J. Scagnelli. From *Catholic Liturgy Book*. Used by permission. Music: Accompaniment © 1984, Howard Don Small.
5 Music: Accompaniment copyright © 1985, G.I.A. Publications, Inc.
6 Music: Copyright by Edward B. Marks Music Company, New York, NY. International Copyright Secured. ALL RIGHTS RESERVED. Used by permission.
8 Words: By permission of David Higham Associates Limited, London.
9 Words: By permission of Hodder and Stoughton Limited.
12 Words: © 1982, Charles P. Price. Music: Harmonization by permission of Oxford University Press.
13 Words: © 1982, Charles P. Price. Music: Accompaniment © 1984, Richard Solly.
14 Words: St.3 © 1982, Charles P. Price.
15 Words: St.3 © 1982, James Waring McCrady. Music: Accompaniment © 1984, Gerard Farrell.
16 Words: St.4 © 1982, Anne LeCroy. Music: Accompaniment © 1984, David Hurd.
17 Words: St.4 © 1982, Anne LeCroy. Music: By permission of Oxford University Press.
18 Music: Accompaniment © 1984, McNeil Robinson II.
19 Words: St.3 © 1982, James Waring McCrady. Music: Accompaniment © 1984, Gerard Farrell.
20 Words: St.3 © 1982, James Waring McCrady.
21 Words: St.3 © 1982, James Waring McCrady.
22 Words: St.3 © 1982, James Waring McCrady. Music: Accompaniment © 1984, Roy F. Kehl. Alternative accompaniment © 1984, David Shuler.
23 Words: © 1982, Charles P. Price.
26 Music: Accompaniment © Bruce Neswick.
27 Words: © 1982, Anne LeCroy.
28 Words: © 1982, Anne LeCroy.
30 Music: Accompaniment copyright © 1970 by H. W. Gray, a division of Belwin-Mills Publishing Corp. Used with permission. All rights reserved.
31 Words: © 1982, Anne LeCroy. Music: Reprinted from the *New Catholic Hymnal* by permission of the publishers, Faber Music Ltd., London.
32 Words: © 1982, Anne LeCroy. Music: Melody rhythmic version © 1984, Schola Antiqua Inc. Used by permission. Accompaniment © 1984, Roy F. Kehl.
33 Words: © 1982, Anne LeCroy. Music: Accompaniment copyright © 1985, G.I.A. Publications, Inc.
34 Words: © 1982, Anne LeCroy. Music: © 1984, Richard W. Dirksen.
35 Words: © 1982, Anne LeCroy. Music: Copyright © 1985, G.I.A. Publications, Inc.
38 Words: St.5 © 1982, Anne LeCroy. Music: Accompaniment © 1984, Richard Solly.
39 Words: St.5 © 1982, Anne LeCroy. Music: By permission of Oxford University Press.
40 Words: St.5 © 1982, Charles P. Price. Music: Accompaniment © 1984, James McGregor.
41 Words: St.5 © 1982, Charles P. Price. Music: Copyright © 1985, G.I.A. Publications, Inc.
44 Words: St.4 © 1982, James Waring McCrady. Music: Accompaniment © 1984, James McGregor.
45 Words: St.4 © 1972, James Waring McCrady. Music: Accompaniment © 1984, James McGregor.
48 Words: St.3 © 1982, Charles P. Price.
49 Music: Copyright © 1977 by Hinshaw Music, Inc. Used by permission.
51 Words: By permission of John E. Bowers. Music: © 1984, Richard W. Dirksen.
52 Music: Copyright © 1936 Ascherberg, Hopwood and Crew Limited, Chappell Music Limited London. Reproduced by permission.
53 Music: Harmonization © 1984, Jack W. Burnam.
54 Words: Sts.3-4 © 1982, James Waring McCrady.
55 Words: © 1982, Charles P. Price. Music: Accompaniment © 1984, David Hurd.
56 Music: Both accompaniments copyright © 1975, G.I.A. Publications, Inc.
59 Music: Descant used by permission of Cambridge University Press.
60 Music: Accompaniment © 1984, Bruce Neswick.
61 Words: © 1982, Carl P. Daw, Jr.
62 Words: © 1982, Carl P. Daw, Jr.
63 Music: Accompaniment © 1984, Howard Don Small.
65 Words: © 1982, Charles P. Price. Music: Arrangement reprinted from AMERICAN LUTHERAN HYMNAL, Copyright © 1930. by permission of Augsburg Publishing House.
69 Words: © 1971, Carol C. Stone. Music: Harmonization © 1971, Norman Mealy.
70 Words: By permission of Margaret Waters. Music: © 1983, Robert J. Powell.
74 Words: Copyright © 1974 by Hope Publishing Company, Carol Stream, IL 60188. All Rights Reserved. Used by Permission. Music: Harmonization © 1984, Ronald Arnatt.
75 Music: © 1938, H. Hugh Bancroft.
77 Music: Accompaniment © 1984, Carol Doran.
78 Music: By permission of Oxford University Press.
80 Words: Translation copyright © 1978, LUTHERAN BOOK OF WORSHIP. Used by permission of Augsburg Publishing House.
82 Music: Harmonization © 1984, Bruce Neswick.
84 Music: By permission of Oxford University Press.
85 Words: Copyright © 1978, Lutheran Book of Worship. Used by permission. Music: Accompaniment © 1984, Bruce Neswick.
86 Words: Copyright © 1978, Lutheran Book of Worship. Used by permission. Music: By permission of Oxford University Press.
88 Music: By permission of Oxford University Press.
92 Words: Copyright by G. Schirmer, Inc. Reprinted by permission. Music: Used by arrangement with G. Schirmer, Inc.
94 Music: Descant by permission of Novello and Company Limited.
95 Music: Copyright © 1985, Theodore Presser Co. Used by permission of the publisher.
96 Words: By permission of Fleming H. Revell Company.
97 Music: Harmonization © 1984, Jack H. Burnam.
98 Words: From The Oxford Book of Carols © 1964, Oxford University Press. Music: By permission of Oxford University Press.
99 Music: Arrangement © 1984, Horace Clarence Boyer.
101 Music: Harmonization by permission of Oxford University Press.
102 Words: St.3 © 1982, James Waring McCrady. Music: Copyright © 1957, Novello and Company Limited. Used by permission.
103 Words: Copyright © 1964, G.I.A. Publications, Inc. Music: Accompaniment © 1984, David Hurd.
104 Words: Copyright © 1961 by Richard Wilbur. Reprinted from his volume, *Advice to a Prophet and other Poems* by permission of Harcourt Brace Jovanovich, Inc. Music: Copyright © 1984, G.I.A. Publications, Inc.
105 Words: By permission of Fleming H. Revell Company.

109 Music: Alternative setting with descant by permission of Oxford University Press.
110 Music: Harmonization © 1941, Leo Sowerby.
113 Words, Music: Copyright © 1954, University of New Mexico Press. Used by permission.
114 Words: English text by J. E. Middleton. Used by permission of The Frederick Harris Music Co., Limited. Music: Setting Copyright © 1978, LUTHERAN BOOK OF WORSHIP. Used by permission of Augsburg Publishing House. Alternative setting based on an arrangement by Healy Willan. Copyright © 1954 by The Frederick Harris Music Co., Limited. Used by permission.
116 Music: By permission of Oxford University Press.
118 Music: Alternative harmonization © 1984, Thomas Foster.
120 Words: From *English Praise*. By permission of Oxford University Press. Music: By permission of Oxford University Press.
122 Music: Accompaniment © 1984, Jackson Hill.
123 Music: Melody rhythmic version © 1984, Schola Antiqua Inc. Used by permission. Accompaniment copyright © 1985, G.I.A. Publicaitons, Inc. Alternative accompaniment © 1984, Jackson Hill.
125 Music: Music Copyright © 1964 by Abingdon Press. Used by permission.
127 Music: Harmonization by permission of K. D. Smith.
129 Words: Copyright © 1977 by Hope Publishing Company, Carol Stream, IL 60188. All Rights Reserved. Used by Permission. Music: Copyright © 1985 by Hope Publishing Company, Carol Stream, IL 60188. All Rights Reserved. Used by Permission.
130 Words, Music: Copyright © 1977 by Hope Publishing Company, Carol Stream, IL 60188. All Rights Reserved. Used by Permission.
131 Words: Reprinted from *The Hymn Book of the Anglican Church of Canada and the United Church of Canada*. Used by permission. Music: Accompaniment © 1984, Carol Doran.
132 Words: Reprinted from *The Hymn Book of the Anglican Church of Canada and the United Church of Canada*. Used by permission.
133 Music: © 1982, Cary Ratcliff.
134 Music: Accompaniment © 1984, James McGregor.
136 Music: Accompaniment © 1984, Roy F. Kehl. Alternative accompaniment © 1984, Thomas Foster.
137 Music: Descant by permission of Royal School of Church Music.
140 Music: Harmonization © 1984, Roy F. Kehl.
143 Words: By permission of Oxford University Press.
144 Words: © 1982, Anne LeCroy. Music: By permission of Oxford University Press.
145 Words: From *The Oxford Book of Carols* © 1964, Oxford University Press. Music: By permission of Oxford University Press.
146 Words: Copyright © by James Quinn, SJ. Printed by permission of Geoffrey Chapman, a division of Cassell Ltd. Music: Accompaniment © 1984, Roy F. Kehl. Alternative accompaniment © 1984, Morgan Simmons.
147 Words: Copyright © by James Quinn, SJ. Printed by permission of Geoffrey Chapman, a division of Cassell Ltd. Music: harmonization © 1984, Thomas Foster.
148 Words: By permission of J. Donald P. Hughes.
149 Words: © 1982, Thomas H. Cain.
155 Music: Melody rhythmic version © 1984, Schola Antiqua Inc. Used by permission. Accompaniment copyright © 1985, G.I.A. Publications, Inc.
156 Music: Copyright © 1941 by H. W. Gray, a division of Belwin-Mills Publishing Corp. Copyright renewed. Used with permission. All rights reserved.
161 Words: © 1971, John Webster Grant. Music: Melody rhythmic version © 1984, Schola Antiqua Inc. Used by permission. Accompaniment © 1983, David Hurd.
162 Music: Accompaniment © 1983, David Hurd. Alternative accompaniment copyright © 1985, G.I.A. Publications, Inc.
165 Music: Melody rhythmic transcription © 1984, Schola Antiqua Inc. Used by permission. Accompaniment © 1984, David Hurd.
166 Music: Accompaniment © 1984, David Hurd.
170 Words: Copyright © 1973 by Hope Publishing Company, Carol Stream, IL 60188. All Rights Reserved. Used by Permission. Music: By permission of Oxford University Press.
173 Words: Sts.2–3 © 1982, James Waring McCrady.
175 Words, Music: By permission of Oxford University Press.
176 Words: Sts.1–2 from *A Monastic Breviary*, copyright © 1976 by Holy Cross Publications. All rights reserved. Music: © 1984, Robert N. Roth.
177 Words: Sts. 1-2 from *A Monastic Breviary*, copyright © 1976 by Holy Cross Publications. All rights reserved. Music: Copyright © 1983 by Hank Beebe. All Rights Reserved. Used by Permission.
178 Words: Copyright © 1973, The Word of God. All Rights Reserved. P.O.Box 8617, Ann Arbor, MI 48107, U.S.A. Music: Melody copyright © 1973, The Word of God. All Rights Reserved. P.O.Box 8617, Ann Arbor, MI 48107, U.S.A. Arrangement copyright © 1979, Celebration. P.O. Box 309 Aliquippa, PA 15001, USA. All rights reserved. Used by permission.
182 Words: Copyright © 1975 by Hope Publishing Company, Carol Stream, IL 60188. All Rights Reserved. Used by Permission.
183 Music: Accompaniment copyright © 1985, G.I.A. Publications, Inc.
187 Words: By permission of Burns & Oates.
189 Music: Copyright © 1970, Robert Sherlaw Johnson. All Rights Reserved. Used by permission.
190 Music: © 1984, Thomas Foster.
192 Words: By permission of A. R. Mowbray & Co. Ltd. From *The Cowley Carol Book* by G. R. Woodward and C. Wood.
193 Music: Alternative accompaniment © 1982 by John Erickson.
195 Music: Copyright © 1985 by Hope Publishing Company, Carol Stream, IL 60188. All Rights Reserved. Used by Permission.
196 Words: Copyright © 1980 by John Bennett. Music: Copyright © 1983 by Henmar Press Inc. Used by permission of C. F. Peters Corporation.
197 Words: Copyright © 1980 by John Bennett. Music: Copyright © 1984 by Hope Publishing Company, Carol Stream, IL 60188. All Rights Reserved. Used by Permission.
201 Words: By permission of Oxford University Press.
202 Music: Melody rhythmic reconstruction © 1960. A. Gregory Murray. Used by permission. Accompaniment © 1984, Roy F. Kehl.
204 Words: From *The Oxford Book of Carols* © 1964, Oxford University Press. Music: Harmonization based on "Variation sur un Noël" for organ by Marcel Dupré, copyright © Alphonse Leduc, Paris. Used by permission. Adaptation © 1983, Roy F. Kehl. Used by permission. Alternative harmonization © 1984, George Mims.
205 Words: By permission of Hymns Ancient & Modern Limited. St.5, Copyright © 1971 by Walton Music Corporation. Used by permission.
206 Music: Both accompaniments copyright © 1975, G.I.A. Publications, Inc.
207 Music: Descant by permission of Hymns Ancient & Modern Limited.
209 Music: By permission of Oxford University Press.
210 Music: Descant by permission of Oxford University Press.
211 Words: From *The Oxford Book of Carols* © 1964, Oxford University Press. Music: Copyright © 1960 by H. W. Gray, a division of Belwin-Mills Publishing Corp. All rights reserved. Used by permission.
213 Music: Harmonization © 1984, Jack W. Burnam.
216 Words, Music: By permission of Oxford University Press.
217 Music: Accompaniment © 1984, Bruce Neswick.
218 Music: Copyright © 1947, Mercury Music Corporation. Used by permission. A subsidiary of Theodore Presser Company.
220 Music: Accompaniment © 1984, Richard Solly.
221 Music: By permission of Oxford University Press.
222 Words: © 1979, Albert F. Bayly. Used by permission of Oxford University Press.
223 Words: By permission of Burns & Oates. Music: Accompaniment © 1984, Gerard Farrell.
224 Words: By permission of Burns & Oates. Music: Setting from: Worship Supplement © 1969, Concordia Publishing House. Used by permission.
225 Words, Music: By permission of Oxford University Press.
226 Words: © 1982, Charles P. Price. Music: From *Liedboek Voor De Kerken* © 1973, Interkerkelijke Stichting voor het Kerkelied.
227 Words: © 1982, Charles P. Price. Music: Copyright © 1983 by Henmar Press Inc. Used by permission of C.F. Peters Corporation.
228 Words: © 1971, John Webster Grant.
229 Music: © 1984, M. Lee Suitor.
230 Words: By permission of Oxford University Press. Music: Copyright © 1983 by H. W. Gray, a division of Belwin-Mills Publishing Corp. All rights reserved. Used with permission.
231 Music: By permission of Oxford University Press.
232 Music: Harmonization by permission of Oxford University Press.
233 Music: Melody rhythmic reconstruction © 1960, A. Gregory Murray. Used by permission. Accompaniment © 1984, David Hurd.
234 Music: By permission of Oxford University Press.
236 Words: © 1971, John Webster Grant. Music: Accompaniment © 1984, Howard Don Small. Alternative accompaniment © 1984, Morgan F. Simmons.
238 Music: Accompaniment © 1984, Margaret W. Mealy.
240 Music: © 1983, David Childs.
241 Music: Descant by permission of Oxford University Press.

242 Music: Copyright © 1984, G.I.A. Publications, Inc.
243 Words: By permission of Oxford University Press. Music: Alternative harmonization © 1984, Eugene W. Hancock.
245 Words: From *Sing Glorias for All His Saints.* Copyright 1983, F. Samuel Janzow. Used by permission.
246 Words: By permission of Oxford University Press. Music: © 1983, Wilbur Held.
247 Music: Harmonization by permission of Oxford University Press.
250 Words: © 1969, Concordia Publishing House. Used by permission. Music: © 1984, Alfred V. Fedak.
253 Music: © 1968, Derek Williams.
254 Music: © 1984, Richard W. Dirksen.
256 Words: © 1980, Gracia Grindal. Music: © 1984, M. Lee Suitor.
260 Words: Copyright © 1979 by Hymn Society of America, Texas Christian University, Fort Worth, TX 76129. All rights reserved. Used by permission.
261 Music: Melody rhythmic version © 1984, Schola Antiqua Inc. Used by permission. Accompaniment © 1984, Thomas Foster.
262 Music: Copyright © 1983 by Hank Beebe. All Rights Reserved. Used by Permission.
263 Words: Sts.1,3,4 By permission of Hymns Ancient & Modern Limited. St.2 © 1982, Anne LeCroy. Music: Accompaniment © 1984, Bruce Neswick.
264 Words: Sts.1,3,4 By permission of Hymns Ancient & Modern Limited. St.2 © 1982, Anne LeCroy.
265 Music: Copyright © 1961, B. Feldman & Co. Ltd., trading as H. Freeman & Co. Reproduced by permission of EMI Music Publishing Ltd.,138–140 Charing Cross Road, London WC2H OLD, England.
266 Words: © 1982, Carl P. Daw, Jr. Music: Harmonization © 1984, Jack W. Burnam.
268 Music: Copyright © 1983, G.I.A. Publications, Inc.
270 Music: Copyright © 1961, B. Feldman & Co. Ltd., trading as H. Freeman & Co. Reproduced by permission of EMI Music Publishing Ltd.,138–140 Charing Cross Road, London WC2H OLD, England.
271 Music: Accompaniment copyright © 1985, G.I.A. Publications, Inc.
272 Music: Harmonization by permission of Oxford University Press.
273 Words: © 1982, Anne LeCroy. Accompaniment © 1984, David Hurd.
274 Words: © 1982, Anne LeCroy. Music: From *Liedboek Voor De Kerken* © 1973, Interkerkelijke Stichting voor het Kerkelied.
276 Music: Harmonization © 1984, Margaret W. Mealy.
277 Words: Used by permission of the Reverend Roland F. Palmer. Music: © 1985, Skinner Chavez-Mélo.
278 Words: By permission of Oxford University Press.
282 Music: By permission of Oxford University Press.
283 Music: Melody rhythmic version © 1984, Schola Antiqua Inc. Used by permission. Accompaniment © 1984, David Hurd.
284 Words: St.4 © 1982, Charles P. Price.
287 Music: By permission of Oxford University Press.
289 Music: By permission of Oxford University Press.
290 Music: Descant copyright © 1953, Novello & Company Limited. Used by permission.
293 Music: By permission of Oxford University Press.
294 Words: © 1982, Michael Saward. Music: © 1983, David Charles Walker.
295 Words: Copyright © 1962, World Library Publications, 3815 N. Willow Rd. Schiller Park, IL 60176. ALL RIGHTS RESERVED. USED WITH PERMISSION.
296 Words: Used by permission of the author.
297 Words: Reprinted and used from THE WORSHIPBOOK – SERVICES AND HYMNS, © 1972, The Westminster Press.
299 Words: By permission of Mary Arthur.
300 Music: By permission of Oxford University Press.
303 Music: Copyright © 1973, Elkan-Vogel Company. Used by permission of the publisher.
304 Words: Copyright © 1971 by Hope Publishing Company, Carol Stream, IL 60188. All Rights Reserved. Used by Permission. Music: Copyright © 1938 by J. Fischer & Bro., a division of Belwin-Mills Publishing Corp. Copyright renewed. Used with permission. All rights reserved.
305 Words: By permission of Oxford University Press. Music: Copyright © 1969 by H. W. Gray, a division of Belwin-Mills Publishing Corp. All rights reserved. Used with permission.
306 Words: By permission of Oxford University Press. Music: © 1941, Mrs. Alfred M. Smith.
308 Words: By permission of Oxford University Press.
309 Words: By permission of Oxford University Press.
311 Music: Accompaniment © 1984, Roy F. Kehl.
312 Words: By permission of Oxford University Press.
315 Words: By permission of Hymns Ancient and Modern Limited. Music: From *Hymns for Church and School,* 1964.
317 Music: Copyright © Sydney Watson. Used by permission.
318 Music: © 1970, Warren Swenson.
319 Music: Percussion part copyright © 1984, David Hurd.
320 Music: Accompaniment © 1984, David Hurd.
322 Music: Copyright © 1985, G.I.A. Publications, Inc.
325 Music: Harmonization © 1985, David Hurd.
326 Music: Copyright © 1957, Novello & Company Limited. Used by permission.
327 Music: © 1981, David Ashley White.
329 Music: Accompaniment © 1984, Jackson Hill.
333 Words, Music: Coyright © 1969 by Hope Publishing Company, Carol Stream, IL 60188. All Rights Reserved. Used by Permission.
334 Words: By permission of H. C. A. Gaunt.
335 Words: Copyright © 1971, G.I.A. Publications, Inc. Music: © 1970, 1975, Celebration. P.O. Box 309 Aliquippa, PA 15001, USA. All rights reserved. Used by permission.
336 Words: Sts.2–3 © 1982, Charles P. Price.
340 Words: By Louis F. Benson. Used by permission of Robert F. Jeffery. Music: © 1970, I-to Loh.
341 Words: Copyright © by Louis F. Benson. Used by permission of Robert F. Jeffery.
342 Words: By permission of the Estate of Frank W. Price. Music: Harmonization © 1984, I-to Loh.
343 Music: Copyright © 1985, G.I.A. Publications, Inc.
346 Words: By permission of the Executor of Mrs. V. M. Pocknee, deceased.
347 Words: By permission of Mildred E. Peacey. Music: Copyright © 1985 by Hope Publishing Company, Carol Stream, IL 60188. All Rights Reserved. Used by Permission.
348 Words: Copyright © 1979 by Hope Publishing Company, Carol Stream, IL 60188. All Rights Reserved. Used by Permission.
350 Music: © 1984, Gerre Hancock.
352 Words: Sts.1–3 © 1982, Charles P. Price.
354 Words: By permission of Theodore Marier. Music: Accompaniment © 1984, David Hurd. Alternative accompaniment copyright © 1985, G.I.A. Publications, Inc.
357 Music: Accompaniment copyright © 1985, G.I.A. Publications, Inc.
358 Words: © 1982, Carl P. Daw, Jr.
359 Words: St.3 © 1982, Carl P. Daw, Jr.
361 Music: Melody rhythmic version © 1984, Schola Antiqua Inc. Used by permission. Accompaniment © 1984. David Hurd. Alternative accompaniment © 1985, John Blackley.
363 Music: Copyright © 1984 by H. W. Gray Co., a division of Belwin-Mills Publishing Corp. Used with permission. All Rights Reserved.
368 Music: Descant © 1953, Novello & Company Limited. Used by permission.
369 Music: Both settings copyright © 1977 by Hope Publishing Company, Carol Stream, IL 60188. International Rights Secured. All Rights Reserved. Used by Permission.
373 Music: Used by permission of David N. Johnson.
376 Words: Reprinted with the permission of Charles Scribner's Sons.
379 Words: Copyright held by A. R. Mowbray & Co. Ltd. Music: Copyright © 1942 • Renewal 1970 by Hope Publishing Company, Carol Stream, IL 60188. All Rights Reserved. Used by Permission.
381 Words: From WORSHIP SUPPLEMENT. Copyright © 1969, Concordia Publishing House. Used by permission.
382 Music: © 1976, David Charles Walker.
390 Music: Descant copyright © 1953, Novello and Company Limited. Used by permission.
392 Music: Copyright © 1974, Harold Flammer, Inc., Delaware Water Gap, PA 18327. All Rights Reserved. Used with permission.
393 Music: From *Union Songster,* Copyright © 1960, Conference of American Rabbis. Used by permission.
394 Words: Copyright © 1979 by The Hymn Society of America, Texas Christian University, Fort Worth, TX 76129. All rights reserved. Used by permission. Music: By permission of Oxford University Press.
395 Words: Copyright © 1979 by The Hymn Society of America, Texas Christian University, Fort Worth, TX 76129. All rights reserved. Used by permission. Music: Copyright © 1983, G.I.A. Publications, Inc.
398 Music: By permission of Oxford University Press.
399 Words: © 1969, James Quinn, SJ, printed by permission of Geoffrey Chapman, a division of Cassell Ltd. Music: Copyright © 1980, G.I.A. Publications, Inc.
400 Words: Copyright © 1985 by G. Schirmer. Used by arrangement with G. Schirmer, Inc. Music: By permission of Oxford University Press.
402 Music: Copyright © 1976 by Hinshaw Music, Inc. Used by Permission.
404 Words: Reproduced with the kind permission of T & T Clark Limited, Edinburgh.
405 Music: Used by arrangement with G. Schirmer, Inc. Descant copyright © 1979, G.I.A. Publications, Inc.
406 Music: © 1940, Mrs. Alfred M. Smith.

407 Music: Copyright © 1975, 1980, G.I.A. Publications, Inc.
410 Music: Descant by permission of Novello and Company, Limited.
412 Words, Music: Copyright Augsburg Publishing House. Used by permission.
413 Words: Copyright © 1974 by Hope Publishing Company. Music: Copyright © 1977 by Hope Publishing Company, Carol Stream, IL 60188. International Copyright Secured. All Rights Reserved.
414 Used by Permission. Music: Descant by permission of Oxford University Press.
416 Music: By permission of Oxford University Press.
417 Words, Music: Reprinted from LUTHERAN BOOK OF WORSHIP, © 1978. By permission of Augsburg Publishing House on behalf of the publishers and copyright holders.
418 Words: Reprinted from LUTHERAN BOOK OF WORSHIP, © 1978. By permission of Augsburg Publishing House on behalf of the publishers and copyright holders. Music: © 1984, Peter R. Hallock.
420 Words: Copyright © 1972 by Hope Publishing Company, Carol Stream, IL 60188. All Rights Reserved. Used by Permission.
422 Words: © 1982, George B. Caird.
424 Words: Copyright © 1970 by Hope Publishing Company, Carol Stream, IL 60188. All Rights Reserved. Used by Permission. Music: © 1960, Francis Jackson.
426 Music: By permission of Hymns Ancient & Modern Limited.
429 Music: Harmony Copyright © 1964, Abingdon Press. Used by permission.
430 Music: Setting from: *Worship Supplement* © 1969, Concordia Publishing House. Used by permission.
431 Words: Copyright © 1981 by Hope Publishing Company, Carol Stream, IL 60188. All Rights Reserved. Used by Permission. Music: Copyright © 1985, G.I.A. Publications, Inc.
433 Words: Used by permission with G. Schirmer Inc.
435 Music: By permission of Oxford University Press.
437 Words: Copyright © 1962 by Hope Publishing Company, Carol Stream, IL 60188. All Rights Reserved. Used by Permission.
438 Words: Copyright © 1962 by Hope Publishing Company, Carol Stream, IL 60188. All Rights Reserved. Used by Permission. Music: Both settings by permission of Oxford University Press.
439 Music: Harmonization by Young, copyright © 1964 by Abingdon Press. Used by permission.
442 Music: © 1983, Bruce Neswick.
443 Music: © 1984, Ronald Arnatt.
444 Words: © 1973, Michael A. Perry. Music: Published by permission of the Executors of the late Dr. Basil Harwood. Originally composed for the hymn, "Thy hand, O God, has guided."
447 Words: Copyright © Australian Hymn Book Co. Used by Permission.
449 Music: By permission of Hymns Ancient & Modern Limited.
450 Music: Descant copyright © 1979, G.I.A. Publications, Inc.
452 Words: Copyright © 1969 by Hope Publishing Company, Carol Stream, IL 60188. All Rights Reserved. Used by Permission.
453 Music: Copyright © 1971 by Walton Music Corporation. International Copyright Secured. All Rights Reserved. Used by permission.
455 Music: Reprinted from the *New Catholic Hymnal* by permission of the publishers, Faber Music Ltd., London.
456 Music: Copyright © 1973, Concordia Publishing House. Used by permission.
458 Music: Copyright © 1924, John Ireland. By permission of executors of N. Kirby deceased.
459 Words: Reprinted by permission of Morehouse-Barlow Co., Inc. Music: Arrangement © 1985, David Hurd.
463 Words: Reprinted by permission of Faber and Faber Ltd. from COLLECTED POEMS by W. H. Auden. Music: Copyright © 1985, G.I.A. Publications, Inc.
464 Words: Reprinted by permission of Faber and Faber Ltd. from COLLECTED POEMS by W. H. Auden. Music: Copyright © 1972, The Westminster Press; from THE WORSHIP BOOK – SERVICES AND HYMNS. Used by permission.
465 Words: © 1982, Christopher Idle.
466 Words: © 1982, Christopher Idle. Music: Copyright © 1984, G.I.A. Publications, Inc.
468 Music: Accompaniment © 1984, Jack W. Burnam.
469 Music: Copyright © 1977, G.I.A. Publications.
472 Words: Copyright © 1954. Renewal 1982 by The Hymn Society of America, Texas Christian University, Fort Worth, TX 76129. All rights reserved. Used by permission.
473 Words, Music: By permission of Hymns Ancient & Modern Ltd. Descant copyright © 1985, G.I.A. Publications, Inc.
475 Words: St.3 By permission of David D. Coffin.
476 Words: © 1980, Elizabeth J. Cosnett. Music: By permission of Oxford University Press.
477 Music: Descant copyright © 1979, G.I.A. Publications, Inc.
478 Music: By permission of Oxford University Press.
480 Music: By permission of Oxford University Press.
481 Words: By permission of Oxford University Press. Music: Arrangement by permission of Oxford University Press.
482 Words: By permission of Oxford University Press.
487 Music: Copyright © 1911 by Stainer and Bell Ltd. All Rights Reserved. Used by permission.
488 Words: This hymn appears courtesy of the Estate of Eleanor Hull and Chatto & Windus Ltd. Music: By permission of Oxford University Press.
490 Words, Music: Copyright © 1970, 1975, Celebration. P.O. Box 309 Aliquippa, PA 15001, USA. All Rights Reserved. Used by permission.
491 Music: Copyright © 1969 by Hope Publishing Company, Carol Stream, IL 60188. International Copyright Secured. All Rights Reserved. Used by Permission.
492 Music: By permission of Oxford University Press.
494 Music: Descant copyright © 1970, Augsburg Publishing House. Used by permission.
495 Music: Harmonization © 1984, Roy F. Kehl.
499 Music: From *Hymns for Church and School*, 1964.
501 Words: © 1971, John Webster Grant.
502 Words: © 1971, John Webster Grant. Music: Accompaniment copyright © 1985, G.I.A. Publications, Inc.
503 Music: Harmonization © 1985, David Hurd.
505 Words: Reprinted by permission from *The Common Service Book of the Lutheran Church*, copyright 1917 and 1918 by The United Lutheran Church of America, a predecessor of the Lutheran Church in America.
506 Words, Music: By permission of Oxford University Press.
507 Words: By permission of Oxford University Press. Music: Copyright © 1983, G.I.A. Publications, Inc.
511 Words: Copyright held by A. R. Mowbray & Co. Ltd. Music: Copyright © 1942, Renewal 1970 by Hope Publishing Company, Carol Stream, IL 60188. All Rights Reserved. Used by Permission.
513 Words: © 1982, Carl P. Daw, Jr. Music: Copyright © 1969 by Hope Publishing Company, Carol Stream, IL 60188. All Rights Reserved. Used by Permission.
516 Music: By permission of Oxford University Press.
517 Words: Sts.3–4 © 1982, Carl P. Daw, Jr. Music: By permission of Oxford University Press.
518 Music: Descant by permission of Church Society, London.
521 Music: Melody by permission of the Estate of Howard C. Robbins. Harmonization copyright © 1940, Estate of Ray F. Brown. Used by permission. Descant © 1944, The Cumberland Press. All Rights Reserved. Used by Permission.
522 Music: Descant copyright © 1979, G.I.A. Publications, Inc.
523 Music: Copyright © 1942. Renewal 1970 by Hope Publishing Company, Carol Stream, IL 60188. All Rights Reserved. Used by Permission.
528 Words: © 1978, Jeffery W. Rowthorn. Music: Copyright © 1985 by Hope Publishing Company, Carol Stream, IL 60188. All Rights Reserved. Used by Permission.
529 Words: Reprinted by permission of The American Tract Society, Garland, Texas. Music: Copyright © 1940, Henry T. Burleigh. Used by permission of the Estate of Henry T. Burleigh.
534 Music: By permission of Oxford University Press.
536 Words: © 1966, 1984 by Willard F. Jabusch. Music: Arrangement copyright © 1985, G.I.A. Publications, Inc.
538 Music: By permission of Oxford University Press.
542 Words: By permission of Oxford University Press.
543 Music: By permission of the United Reformed Church in the United Kingdom.
547 Words: Copyright © 1980, Augsburg Publishing House. Used by permission. Music: © 1984, Max Miller.
549 Music: Copyright © 1983, G.I.A. Publications, Inc.
550 Music: Alternative harmonization © 1984, Margaret W. Mealy.
551 Words: Used by permission of The Presbyterian Outlook, Richmond, VA.
553 Music: Copyright © 1936 Ascherberg, Hopwood and Crew Limited, Chappell Music Limited London. Reproduced by Permission.
554 Music: Accompaniment © 1984, Margaret W. Mealy.
557 Music: Copyright © 1974, Harold Flammer, Inc., Delaware Water Gap, PA 18327. All Rights Reserved. Used with permission.
560 Music: Copyright © 1985, G.I.A. Publications, Inc.
564 Words: By permission of Oxford University Press.
565 Words, Music: By permission of Oxford University Press.
568 Words: By permission of The United Society for the Propagation of the Gospel.
570 Words: Copyright © 1969 by Galliard Ltd. All Rights Reserved. Used by permission. Music: Copyright © 1969 by Hope Publishing Company, Carol Stream, IL 60188. All Rights Reserved. Used by Permission.

571 Words: Copyright © 1969 by Galliard Ltd. All Rights Reserved. Used by permission.
572 Words: By permission of Inter-Lutheran Commission on Worship. Music: Melody copyright © 1972 by Chantry Music Press, Inc. Used by permission. Harmonization copyright © 1975, G.I.A. Publications, Inc.
573 Words: By permission of Oxford University Press. Music: Used by permission of the United Nations Association.
576 Words: © 1969, James Quinn, SJ, printed by permission of Geoffrey Chapman, a division of Cassell Ltd. Music: Copyright © 1985, G.I.A. Publications, Inc.
577 Words: © 1969, James Quinn, SJ, printed by permission of Geoffrey Chapman, a division of Cassell Ltd. Music: By permission of A. Gregory Murray.
580 Words: Copyright © 1967 Copyright by Hope Publishing Company, Carol Stream, IL 60188. All Rights Reserved. Used by Permission.
581 Words: Copyright © 1961–62, World Library Publications, 3815 N. Willow Rd. Schiller Park, IL 60176. ALL RIGHTS RESERVED. USED BY PERMISSION.
582 Words: From HYMNS OF THE CHRISTIAN LIFE, edited by Milton S. Littlefield. Copyright 1910 by Harper & Row, Publishers, Inc. Courtesy of the publishers. Music: Copyright © 1968, Novello & Company Limited. Used by permission.
583 Words: From HYMNS OF THE CHRISTIAN LIFE, edited by Milton S. Littlefield. Copyright 1910 by Harper & Row, Publishers, Inc. Courtesy of the publishers. Music: Harmonization © 1984, Thomas Foster.
584 Words: By permission of Oxford University Press.
585 Words: By permission of J. W. Shore. Music: © 1984, Dorothy Howell Sheets.
586 Words: Copyright © 1909, 1911 by Charles Scribner's Sons. © Renewed. Reprinted by permission of Charles Scribner's Sons. Music: Harmonization Copyright © 1985, G.I.A. Publications, Inc.
588 Music: © 1984, Roy Johnson.
589 Music: © 1983, Jane M. Marshall.
590 Words: Copyright © 1954. Renewal 1982 by The Hymn Society of America, Texas Christian University, Fort Worth, TX 76129. All rights reserved. Used by permission. Music: By permission of Oxford University Press.
591 Words, Music: By permission of Oxford University Press.
593 Words: Copyright ©, James Quinn, SJ, printed by permission of Geoffrey Chapman, a division of Cassell Ltd. Music: Copyright © 1962, Theodore Presser Co. Used by permission of the publisher.
594 Words: By permission of the author.
595 Words: By permission of the author.
597 Words: © 1982, Carl P. Daw, Jr. Music: Copyright © 1977, Roberton Publications. Used by permission of the publisher.
598 Words: By permission of the family of Walter Russell Bowie.
599 Words, Music: Copyright © 1921 by Edward B. Marks Music Company. Copyright Renewed. International Copyright Secured. ALL RIGHTS RESERVED. Used by permission.
600 Words: Copyright © Emmanuel College, Toronto. Used by permission. Music: Copyright © 1938, Estate of James Hopkirk.
601 Words: Copyright © Emmanuel College, Toronto. Used by permission.
602 Words, Music: Copyright © 1969 by Hope Publishing Company, Carol Stream, IL 60188. International Copyright Secured. All Rights Reserved. Used by permission.
603 Words: Copyright © 1980 by Hope Publishing Company, Carol Stream, IL 60188. All Rights Reserved. Used by Permission. Music: By permission of Oxford University Press.
604 Words: Copyright © 1980 by Hope Publishing Company, Carol Stream, IL 60188. All Rights Reserved. Used by Permission. Music: © 1968, Derek Williams.
605 Words: © 1949, Albert F. Bayly. Used by permission of Oxford University Press. Music: Copyright © 1969 by Hope Publishing Company, Carol Stream, IL 60188. All Rights Reserved. Used by Permission.
606 Words: © 1982, Joyce M. Glover. Music: Accompaniment © 1984, David Hurd.
607 Words: Copyright © 1958 by The Hymn Society of America, Texas Christian University, Fort Worth, TX 76129. All rights reserved. Used by permission.
610 Words: Copyright © 1961, Albert F. Bayly. Used by permission of Oxford University Press.
611 Words, Music: Copyright © 1969 by Hope Publishing Company, Carol Stream, IL 60188. International Copyright Secured. All Rights Reserved. Used by Permission.
612 Music: © 1984, Daniel Moe.
614 Words: By permission of Oxford University Press.
617 Music: From *Hymns for Church and School,* 1964.
618 Words, Music: By permission of Oxford University Press.
620 Music: Copyright © 1938 by J. Fischer & Bro., a division of Belwin-Mills Publishing Corp. Copyright renewed. Used with permission. All rights reserved.
622 Music: Melody rhythmic version © 1984, Schola Antiqua Inc. Used by permission.
625 Music: Descant by permission of Hymns Ancient & Modern Limited.
628 Words: Copyright © 1959 by The Hymn Society of America, Texas Christian University, Fort Worth, TX 76129. All rights reserved. Used by permission.
629 Music: Arrangement copyright © 1985, David Hurd.
630 Words: Copyright © 1954. Renewal 1982 by Hope Publishing Company. Music: Copyright © 1966 by Hope Publishing Company, Carol Stream, IL 60188. International Copyright Secured. Used by Permission.
631 Words: By permission of Oxford University Press.
633 Words: © 1969, James Quinn, SJ, printed by permission of Geoffrey Chapman, a division of Cassell Ltd. Music: © 1984, Richard W. Dirksen.
636 Music: Harmonization © 1984, Calvin Hampton. Alternative harmonization © 1984, Eugene W. Hancock.
637 Music: Descant copyright © 1974, The Cumberland Press. All Rights Reserved. Used by Permission.
639 Music: Copyright © 1971 by Carl Fischer, Inc., New York. All Rights Reserved. Used by Permission.
646 Music: Descant by permission of Oxford University Press.
648 Music: Arrangement © 1984, Horace Clarence Boyer.
649 Words: Adapted text from *ICEL Resource Collection of Hymns and Service Music for the Liturgy* © 1981, International Committee on English in the Liturgy, Inc. All rights reserved. Music: Copyright © 1962, Theodore Presser Co. Used by permission of the Publisher.
650 Words: Adapted text from *ICEL Resource Collection of Hymns and Service Music for the Liturgy* © 1981. International Committee on English in the Liturgy, Inc. All rights reserved. Music: Accompaniment © 1984, Gerard Farrell.
651 Words: St.2 Used by permission of Mary Babcock Crawford. Music: Copyright © 1975 by Hope Publishing Company, Carol Stream, IL 60188. International Copyright Secured. All Rights Reserved. Used by Permission.
655 Music: Harmonization by permission of Oxford University Press.
659 Music: Copyright © 1973. Concordia Publishing House. Used by permission.
661 Words: Copyright by Edward B. Marks Music Corporation. Used by permission.
664 Music: Accompaniment © 1985, David Hurd.
665 Music: Copyright © 1968, Novello & Company Limited. Used by permission.
670 Words: Sts.2–3 © 1982, Charles P. Price.
671 Music: Harmonization copyright © 1974 by Abingdon Press. Used by permission.
673 Words, Music: © 1983, Linda Wilberger Egan.
674 Words: By permission of Oxford University Press.
675 Music: Harmonization © 1984, John Hooker.
676 Music: Accompaniment © 1982, David Hurd.
678 Words: Copyright © 1982, Carl P. Daw, Jr. Music: Copyright © 1985, Arthur Rhea.
679 Words: © 1982, Carl P. Daw, Jr. Music: © 1984, Ray W. Urwin.
681 Words: By permission of Heckford, Norton & Co., Solicitors.
682 Words: By permission of Oxford University Press.
686 Music: Harmonization copyright © 1971 by Walton Music Corporation. International Copyright Secured. All Rights Reserved. Used by permission.
689 Music: Copyright © 1969 by Harold Press, Scottsdale, PA 15683.
692 Music: By permission of Oxford University Press.
694 Music: By permission of The Royal School of Church Music.
695 Words: Copyright © 1974 by Hope Publishing Company, Carol Stream, IL 60188. All Rights Reserved. Used by Permission.
696 Words: Copyright © 1974 by Hope Publishing Company, Carol Stream, IL 60188. All Rights Reserved. Used by Permission. Music: By permission of the Rev. Joseph Gelineau, Maret sur Loring, France.
698 Words: Copyright © 1976 by The Hymn Society of America, Texas Christian University, Fort Worth, TX 76129. All Rights Reserved. Used by permission. Music: © 1979, Carl Schalk.
702 Music: Arrangement as in *Hymnal for Colleges and Schools* (1956), edited by E. Harold Geer. Copyright © Yale University Press. Used by permission.
705 Words: Copyright © 1961 by The Hymn Society of America, Texas Christian University, Fort Worth, TX 76129. All rights reserved. Used by permission. Music: By permission of Oxford University Press.
706 Words: © 1982, Charles P. Price.
710 Words: Adaptation from *Song and Spirit,* copyright © 1976, The Council for Religion in Independent Schools.
711 Words: St.1 Copyright © 1972, Maranatha! Music. Music: Copyright © 1972, Maranatha! Music. All Rights Reserved. International Copyright Secured. Used by permission.
713 Music: By permission of Richard Rudolf Klein.

General Performance Notes

Hymn singing is not one kind of music making, but many kinds. One requirement of all hymns is that they can be performed by groups of people who do not have the benefit of regular rehearsal. Thus, memorability and simplicity are important to good hymn tunes. It is *purpose*, rather than musical style, which unites them into a genre. In fact, a wide variety of styles and methods should characterize hymnody.

Some hymns are dignified, some are dancelike; some delight us and set our toes tapping, some express our sorrow. Some hymns may include parts to be sung by a soloist or choir. Some may have specially composed introductions or interludes. Some may be sung in canon. Some are ancient, some contemporary. In hymn singing, voices may be divided by range or location. Contrast may be made between low and high voices, one side and the other, choir and congregation, or voices and instruments. Some hymns are unison song while others are works to be sung in harmony. Accompaniment may incorporate a variety of instruments and may utilize a variety of textures. If organ is used, it should be used imaginatively. Although keyboard accompaniments are provided for almost every hymn in this book, other instrumental parts are often included. These parts might serve as models for creating alternative accompaniments by local musicians using resources at hand. Some hymns might sound best with no accompaniment at all; in this instance, leadership should be provided by a cantor or song leader.

Where appropriate, *The Hymnal 1982* includes chord symbols for the guitar. On occasion the use of a capo is suggested, allowing the guitarist the convenience of playing the music in the most comfortable hand position. The printed key is always listed first; the key for use with the capo is indicated next in parentheses.

Wherever possible, the words of the hymns have been printed within the musical systems. For increased legibility, most music has been notated predominatly with black notes (quarters).

Every hymn has its basis in song and dance, in melodic and rhythmic pattern. Generally, singers should be encouraged to feel the rhythm of hymns in large units: one large pulse to a bar rather than three, or two pulses rather than four. A large pulse means that at any tempo every hymn will be sung with a sense of movement and vitality and thus with grace and vigor. This does not mean that every hymn will be fast, for hymn singing should encompass a wide variety of tempi. It is essential that singers and accompanists pay close attention to the words of a hymn so that the phrasing of the music reflects the phrasing of the text.

Metronome markings have been provided for most hymns. These suggest both a performance tempo and a good practice tempo for the accompanist. The size and resonance of the room, the number of singers, the accompanying instrument(s), the relative familiarity of the hymn, and the occasion may modify tempo in actual congregational performance.

Two historic families of hymns must receive special comment here because they have been the subjects of significant research since the publication of *The Hymnal 1940*. These are the chant hymns and the chorales. Both groups are large and varied.

The performance of equalist chant hymns remains basically the same as indicated in *The Hymnal 1940*. However, to indicate more clearly the flow of the musical line the notation has been simplified by using note heads without stems. The open note head indicates a duration double that of the black note head. An incise on the top line of the staff indicates a slight break in momentum. Vertical members within the staff indicate breathing places. In chant hymns of this type, flow and flexibility are preeminent qualities.

Although chant hymns in other than equalist realization rarely appear in contemporary hymnals, they are a major component of the repertoire. In the present hymnal there are also examples of chant hymns in syllabic (see 202) and proportional rhythms (see 165), and hymns in rhythmic modes (see 82). They are notated in the usual method to indicate duration, primarily with quarter and eighth notes. Incises are used as described above. Short strokes beneath notes in proportional hymns clarify the pulse (see 165). Full bar lines are used in hymns in rhythmic modes. The performance of most rhythmic chant hymns should be at once both spirited and graceful. Often light percussion accompaniment will help achieve this goal. Keyboard accompaniment is optional for all chant hymns. A few chant hymns notated in equalist manner may be performed in rhythmic fashion and vice versa. These are marked accordingly (see 26 and 82).

The chorales may be divided into two groups, usually called isometric (see 688) and rhythmic (see 687). The isometric chorales may be sung either in unison or in harmony and should move along with deliberation and momentum. Congregational singing of rhythmic chorales assumes unison singing with well-articulated rhythms and clear phrasing. To help in the performance of these chorales, bar lines have been placed at the ends of phrases. Occasionally, the congregation might sing one version in alternation with the choir singing the other.

Another application of alternative performance practice is possible with chant hymns and chorales derived from them: See 54, *Nun komm, der Heiden Heiland* and 55, *Veni Redemptor gentium*; 501, *Komm Gott Schöpfer* and 502, *Veni Creator Spiritus*; 183–186, *Victimae Paschali laudes, Christ ist erstanden*, and *Christ lag in Todesbanden*. This practice requires careful preparation.

Variety and flexibility have been important criteria in the selection of materials for this book. Every hymn is valuable, but this does not mean that every one will be useful everywhere. However, hymn singing in our churches will only attain its full potential and richness when the people of God are encouraged to feast on the larger banquet rather than limit themselves to the familiar fare.

Index of Hymns for use with Children

Hymnody is perhaps more important to very young Christians than it is to the mature members of the congregation. Hymns help to incorporate children into the worshiping community. By joining in the singing children can experience a fullness of participation difficult for them to feel in some other parts of the liturgy. Hymns tell the story of the faith, provide vehicles for the liberation of soul and spirit, and teach theology and church history. They can both educate and form young Christians.

This index is for use with children in kindergarten and lower primary grades. It is comprehensive, covering the entire liturgical range, so that children may be continuously included in the hymns of corporate worship. It is not meant to be exclusive; hymns which are particular favorites in a congregation may also be used.

Do not try to teach many hymns to younger children—that comes later when facility in reading develops—rather help them to know well a limited number. Similarly, do not try to use all stanzas since one stanza is often sufficient. Young children memorize readily and should be given the opportunity to learn a stanza of each hymn through its repeated use. Text and music together will penetrate to the heart and become part of the person. A number of hymns with refrains (designated by an asterisk) have been included. Refrains are quickly learned, enabling very young children to sing part of a complex hymn. Sometimes the word "Alleluia" or a repeated phrase such as "May Jesus Christ be praised" may be taught in refrain fashion.

The texts of the hymns in this index were chosen for their immediacy and for their ability to touch a child's life. Clarity of image, sustaining power, and honest sentiment were also sought. If the leader is comfortable with foreign languages, children will enjoy learning the rounds and canons in their original languages.

The hymn music was evaluated with consideration of the child's need for melodic strength and integrity (those qualities which make a tune singable), a range which is not extreme, and rhythmic clarity. These qualities are not necessarily the same as "simplicity"; young children are natural mimics, and can easily learn strong rhythms and melodies which are demonstrated for them. Christmas hymns have not been included in this index since virtually every Christmas hymn is a child's hymn, and the custom of the local community should guide those selections.

8 Morning has broken
35 Christ, mighty Savior, Light of all creation
43 All praise to thee, my God, this night
54 Savior of the nations, come!
56 O come, O come, Emmanuel*
60 Creator of the stars of night
66 Come, thou long-expected Jesus
69 What is the crying at Jordan?
70 Herald, sound the note of judgment*
124 What star is this, with beams so bright
150 Forty days and forty nights
155 All glory, laud, and honor*
172 Were you there when they crucified my Lord?
175 Hail thee, festival day! *Easter**
178 Alleluia, alleluia! Give thanks to the risen Lord*
187 Through the Red Sea brought at last, Alleluia!
(Alleluias taught as a refrain)
204 Now the green blade riseth from the buried grain
207 Jesus Christ is risen today, Alleluia!*
(Alleluias taught as a refrain)
213 Come away to the skies
214 Hail the day that sees him rise, Alleluia!*
(Alleluias taught as a refrain)
216 Hail thee, festival day! *Ascension**
225 Hail thee, festival day! *Pentecost**
226 Come, thou Holy Spirit bright
247 Lully, lullay, thou little tiny child*
266 Nova, nova*
277 Sing of Mary, pure and lowly
287 For all the saints, who from their labors rest
291 We plow the fields, and scatter*
294 Baptized in water
304 I come with joy to meet my Lord
322 When Jesus died to save us
324 Let all mortal flesh keep silence
325 Let us break bread together on our knees*
335 I am the bread of life*
341 For the bread which you have broken
362 Holy, holy holy! Lord God Almighty!
365 Come, thou almighty King
381 Thy strong word did cleave the darkness*
382 King of glory, King of peace
383 Fairest Lord Jesus
384 Fairest Lord Jesus
396 Now thank we all our God
397 Now thank we all our God
400 All creatures of our God and King*
(Alleluias taught as a refrain)
405 All things bright and beautiful*
416 For the beauty of the earth*
425 Sing now with joy unto the Lord
427 When morning gilds the skies*
("May Jesus Christ be praised!" taught as a refrain)
436 Lift up your heads, ye mighty gates
439 What wondrous love is this
453 As Jacob with travel was weary one day*
468 It was poor little Jesus*
473 Lift high the cross*
480 When Jesus left his Father's throne
487 Come, my Way, my Truth, my Life
488 Be thou my vision, O Lord of my heart
490 I want to walk as a child of the light*
493 O for a thousand tongues to sing
529 In Christ there is no East or West
536 God has spoken to his people*
537 Christ for the world we sing!
538 God of mercy, God of grace
554 'Tis the gift to be simple
556 Rejoice, ye pure in heart!*
557 Rejoice, ye pure in heart*
570 All who love and serve your city
571 All who love and serve your city
593 Lord, make us servants of your peace
602 Jesu, Jesu, fill us with your love*
611 Christ the worker
618 Ye watchers and ye holy ones*
(Alleluias taught as a refrain)
620 Jerusalem, my happy home
641 Lord Jesus, think on me
645 The King of love my shepherd is
646 The King of love my shepherd is
648 When Israel was in Egypt's land*
651 This is my Father's world
661 They cast their nets in Galilee
663 The Lord my God my shepherd is
664 My Shepherd will supply my need
671 Amazing grace! how sweet the sound
676 There is a balm in Gilead*
678 Surely it is God who saves me
679 Surely it is God who saves me
680 O God, our help in ages past
690 Guide me, O thou great Jehovah
708 Savior, like a shepherd lead us
710 Make a joyful noise unto the Lord
(Singt dem Herren!)
711 Seek ye first the kingdom of God*
712 Dona nobis pacem
713 Christ is arisen (Christ ist erstanden)
714 Shalom, my friends (Shalom chaverim)
715 When Jesus wept, the falling tear

Metrical Psalms and Hymns based on Psalms

Index of Scriptural References

Proverbs

Song of Solomon

Isaiah

Jeremiah

Lamentations

Ezekiel

Daniel

Mark

Luke

Acts

Romans

1 Corinthians

2 Corinthians

Galatians

Ephesians

Philippians

Index of Hymns on the Consultation on Ecumenical Hymnody List

Index of Authors, Translators, and Sources

Herbert, George (1593-1633) 382, 402, 403, 487, 592
Herklots, Rosamond E. (b. 1905) 246, 674
Herman, Nikolaus (1480?-1561) 201
Hernaman, Claudia Frances (1838-1898) 142
Hewlett, Michael (b. 1916) 506, 507
Hilary of Poitiers (4th cent.) 223, 224
Hispanic folk song 113
Holland, Henry Scott (1847-1918) 596
Holmes, Oliver Wendell (1809-1894) 419
Hopkins, John Henry, Jr. (1820-1891) 128, 336
Hosmer, Frederick Lucian (1840-1929) 615
Housman, Laurence (1865-1959) 133, 134, 573
How, William Walsham (1823-1897) 52, 254, 287, 632
Hughes, David W. (1911-1967) 148
Hull, Eleanor H. (1860-1935) 488
Hume, Ruth Fox (1922-1980) 103
Humphreys, Charles William (1840-1921) 312, 326
Hunterian MS. 83, 15th cent. 266
Hymnal 1940 56, 60, 81, 152, 193, 233, 234, 282, 283, 314, 320, 329, 330, 331, 390, 475, 619
Hymnal 1982 16, 17, 19, 20, 38, 39, 40, 41, 44, 45, 48, 63, 64, 91, 159, 162, 165, 166, 176, 177, 231, 232, 261, 262, 314, 320, 364
Hymn Book of the Anglican Church of Canada and the United church of Canada, The, 1971 131, 132
Hymns Ancient and Modern, 1861 59, 124, 127, 136, 137, 244, 248, 249, 263, 264, 518, 519, 520, 624
Hymns for the Festivals and Saints' Days of the Church of England, 1846 267
Hymns for the Young, ca. 1830 708

Idle, Christopher (b. 1938) 465, 466
Ingemann, Bernard Severin (1789-1862) 527
Irish, ca. 700 488
Isaiah 9:2-7 125, 126
Israeli round 714
Italian, 18th cent. 479

Jabusch, Willard F. (b. 1930) 536
Jacobi, Jon Christian (1670-1750) 515
Janzow, F. Samuel (b. 1913) 245
Jenkins, William Vaughan (1868-1920) 350
Jervois, William Henry Hammond (1852-1905) 338
Jewish liturgy, Medieval 372
John of Damascus (8th cent.) 198, 199, 200, 210
John 6 335
Johnson, James Weldon (1871-1938) 599
Joseph, Jane M. (1894-1929) 92
Joseph the Hymnographer (9th cent.) 237

K. 636, 637
Keble, John (1792-1866) 10, 656
Kelly, Thomas (1769-1855) 471, 483
Ken, Thomas (1637-1711) 11, 43, 380
Kethe, William (d. 1608?) 377, 378
Key, Francis Scott (1779-1843) 720
Kingo, Thomas Hansen (1634-1703) 298
Kingsley, Charles (1819-1875) 566
Kitchin, George William (1827-1912) 473
Knox, Ronald A. (1888-1957) 187

Lafferty, Karen (20th cent.) 711
Landsberg, Max (1845-1928) 372
Latin 16, 17, 31, 32, 47, 144, 190, 236, 273, 274, 354, 356, 576, 577, 581, 606
Latin, 5th cent. 193
Latin, 5th-8th cent. 619
Latin, 6th cent. 3, 4, 27, 28, 29, 30, 40, 41, 44, 45, 143
Latin, ca. 6th cent. 59, 85, 86
Latin, ca. 7th cent. 63, 64, 518, 519, 520
Latin, 7th-8th cent. 202, 263, 264
Latin, Medieval 220, 221
Latin, 9th cent. 60, 503, 504
Latin, ca. 9th cent. 56, 360, 361
Latin, 10th cent. 1, 2, 38, 39, 133, 134
Latin, 11th cent. 122, 123
Latin, 12th cent. 226, 227, 228, 235, 238, 239, 244, 642
Latin, 13th cent. 159
Latin, 14 cent. 103, 207
Latin, 15th cent. 98, 136, 137, 248, 249, 448, 449, 621, 622, 642
Latin, 1632 174
Latin, 1661 308, 309
Latin, 1695 208
Laurenti, Laurentius (1660-1772) 68
Layritz, Friedrich (1808-1859) 81
LeCroy, Anne K. (b. 1930) 16, 17, 27, 28, 31, 32, 33, 34, 35, 38, 39, 144, 263, 264, 273, 274
Lew, Timothy T'ing Fang (1892-1947) 342
Littledale, Richard Frederick (1833-1890) 516
Liturgy of St. Basil 346
Liturgy of St. James 324, 326
London carol, 18th cent. 105
Luther, Martin (1483-1546) 54. 80, 139, 151, 185, 186, 319, 687, 688
Lutheran Book of Worship, 1978 80
Lyra Davidica, 1708 207
Lyte, Henry Francis (1793-1847) 410, 538, 662

Maclagan, William Dalrymple (1826-1910) 285, 349
Madan, Martin (1726-1790) 495
Mahlmann, Siegfried August (1771-1826) 716
Mann, Newton M. (1836-1926) 372
Mant, Richard (1776-1848) 279, 367, 414
Marier, Theodore (b. 1912) 354
Marriott, John (1780-1825) 371
Mason, Jackson (1833-1889) 235
Massie, Richard (1800-1887) 185, 186
Mattes, John Caspar (1876-1948) 505
Matthew 5:3-12 560
Matthew 6:33 711
Matthew 7:7 711
Mauburn, Jean (1460-1503) 97
Maurus, Rabanus (776-856) 282, 283, 501, 502

McCrady, James Waring (b. 1938) 14, 15, 19, 20, 21, 22, 44, 45, 54, 102, 173
McDougall, Alan G. (1875-1964) 33, 34, 35
Mealy, Norman (b. 1923) 205
Mercer, William (1811-1873) 496, 497
Merrill, William Pierson (1867-1954) 551
Micklem, Caryl (b. 1925) 369
Middleton, Jesse Edgar (1872-1960) 114
Milligan, James Lewis (1876-1961) 75
Milman, Henry Hart (1791-1868) 156
Milton, John (1608-1674) 389, 462
Mohr, Joseph (1792-1848) 111
Monastic Breviary, A, 1976 176, 177
Monsell, John Samuel Bewley (1811-1875) 552, 553
Montgomery, James (1771-1854) 93, 171, 343, 411, 426, 480, 484, 485, 616, 670
Morison, John (1749-1798) 125, 126
Moultrie, Gerard (1829-1885) 324
Mozarabic, 10th cent. 33, 34, 35

Neale, John Mason (1818-1866) 3, 4, 14, 15, 21, 22, 29, 30, 82, 107, 122, 123, 131, 132, 136, 137, 154, 155, 165, 166, 198, 199, 200, 202, 203, 206, 210, 237, 238, 239, 263, 264, 270, 271, 272, 327, 328, 518, 519, 520, 621, 622, 623, 624, 672
Neander, Joachim (1650-1680) 390, 665
Nelson, Horatio Bolton (1823-1913) 231, 232
Neumark, Georg (1621-1681) 635
New England Psalm Singer, The, 1770 715
New Version of the Psalms of David, 1696 658
Newbolt, Michael Robert (1874-1956) 473
Newman, John Henry (1801-1890) 445, 446
Newton, John (1725-1807) 351, 522, 523, 644, 671
New York, 1850 383, 384
Nicolai, Philipp (1556-1608) 61, 62, 496, 497
Niedling, Johann (1602-1668) 505
Noel, Caroline Maria (1817-1877) 435
North, Frank Mason (1850-1935) 609

O Gracious Light 25, 26, 36, 37
Oakeley, Frederick (1802-1880) 83
Olearius, Johann G. (1611-1684) 67
Olivers, Thomas (1725-1799) 401
Onderdonk, Henry Ustick (1759-1858) 532, 533
Osler, Edward (1798-1863) 332
Oxenham, John (1852-1941) 529

Pagura, Frederico J. (b. 1923) 74
Palmer, Edmund Stuart (1856-1931) 357
Palmer, Ray (1808-1887) 649, 650, 691
Palmer, Roland Ford (b. 1891) 277
Paraphrases, 1781 447
Patrick (372-466) 370
Peacey, John Raphael (1896-1971) 347
Percy, William Alexander (1885-1942) 661
Perronet, Edward (1726-1792) 450, 451
Perry, Michael A. (b. 1942) 444
Phos hilaron 25, 26, 36, 37
Piae Cantiones, 1582 92, 270
Pierpoint, Folliot Sandford (1835-1917) 416
Pilgrim Hymnal, 1904 689
Plumptre, Edward Hayes (1821-1891) 556, 557, 567
Pocknee, Cyril E. (1906-1980) 346
Pott, Francis (1832-1909) 208
Praise the Lord, 1972 146, 147
Price, Charles P. (b. 1920) 12, 13, 18, 23, 40, 41, 48, 55, 65, 226, 227, 284, 336, 352, 670, 706
Price, Frank (1895-1974) 342
Prudentius, Marcus Aurelius Clemens (348-410?) 82, 127
Psalm 19 431
Psalm 19:1-6 409
Psalm 23 645, 646, 663, 664
Psalm 42:1-7 658
Psalm 46 687, 688
Psalm 72 616
Psalm 84 517
Psalm 90:1-5 680
Psalm 95 (Venite) 399
Psalm 98 413
Psalm 100 377, 378, 391
Psalm 103:1-5 411
Psalm 117 380
Psalm 118:19-29 157
Psalm 121 668
Psalm 130 151, 666
Psalm 136 389
Psalm 139:1-11 702
Psalm 145 404
Psalm 145:1-12 414
Psalm 146 429
Psalm 148 373, 432
Psalm 150 432
Psalms, Hymns and Anthems, 1774 229
Psalms of David in Meeter, The, 1650 517, 668
Psalter Hymnal, The, 1927 702

Quinn, James (b. 1919) 399, 576, 577, 593, 633

Rawson, George (1807-1889) 629
Reed, Andrew (1787-1862) 509
Rees, John (19th cent.) 671
Rees, Timothy (1874-1939) 379, 511
Reid, William Watkins, Jr. (b. 1923) 607, 628
Revelation 5:12-13 417, 418
Reynolds, William M. (1812-1876) 54
Rhys, John Howard (b. 1917) 443
Richard of Chichester (1197-1253) 654
Riley, John Athelstan Laurie (1858-1945) 308, 309, 618
Rinckart, Martin (1586-1649) 396, 397
Rist, Johann (1607-1667) 91, 173
Robb, John Donald (b. 1892) 113
Robbins, Howard Chandler (1876-1952) 108, 163, 406, 407, 459, 521
Roberts, Daniel Crane (1841-1907) 718
Robinson, Robert (1735-1790) 686
Roh, Jan (1485?-1547) 53

Romans 8:34-39 447
Rossetti, Christina (1830-1894) 84, 112
Routley, Erik (1830-1894) 413, 570, 571
Rowthorn, Jeffery (b. 1934) 394, 395, 528
Russell, Arthur T. (1806-1874) 219
Russian Orthodox liturgy 560
Rygh, George Alfred Taylor (1860-1942) 298

Sarum Primer, 1514 694
Saward, Michael (b. 1932) 294
Scagnelli, Peter (b. 1949) 3, 4
Schenck, Theobald Heinrich (1656-1727) 286
Schulz-Widmar, Russell (b. 1944) 319, 353
Schütz, Johann Jacob (1640-1690) 375, 408
Scott, Lesbia (b. 1898) 293
Scott, Robert Balgarnie Young (b. 1899) 600, 601
Sears, Edmund H. (1810-1876) 89, 90
Sedulius, Caelius (5th cent.) 77, 131, 132
Selection, 1787 636, 637
Shaker song, 18th cent. 554
Shurtleff, Ernest Warburton (1862-1917) 555
Slovak, 17th cent. 250
Smart, Christopher (1722-1771) 212, 240, 241, 386, 387, 491
Smith, Horace (1836-1922) 251
Smith, Samuel Francis (1808-1895) 717
Smith, Walter Chalmers (1824-1908) 423
Smyttan, George Hunt (1822-1870) 150
Song of Creation, A 428
Song of Mary, The 437, 438
Song of Simeon, The 499
Song of the Redeemed, The 532, 533
Song of Zechariah, The 444
Song to the Lamb, A 374
Source unknown, 19th cent. 110
Southern Harmony, 1835 213
Spaeth, Harriet Reynolds Krauth (1845-1925) 81
Spanish, 17th cent. 682
Sparrow-Simpson, William J. (1860-1952) 160
Spencer, Robert Nelson (1877-1961) 579
Stone, Samuel John (1839-1900) 525
Struther, Jan (1901-1953) 243, 482
Studdert-Kennedy, Geoffrey Anketel (1883-1929) 9
Supplement to the New Version of the Psalms of David, A, 1698 364, 666
Synesius of Cyrene (375?-414?) 641
Syriac Liturgy of Malabar 312

Tate, Nahum (1625-1715) 94, 95
Te Deum 364, 366
Terry, Charles Sanford (1864-1936) 201
Tersteegen, Gerhardt (1697-1769) 475
Theodulph of Orleans (d. 821) 154, 155
Third Song of Isaiah, The 543
Thomas Aquinas (1225?-1274) 310, 311, 314, 320, 329, 330, 331
Thomerson, Kathleen (b. 1934) 490
Thomson, Mary Ann (1834-1923) 539
Thring, Godfrey (1823-1903) 454
Timms, George B. (b. 1910) 120, 230, 278
Tisserand, Jean (15th cent.) 203, 206
Toolan, Suzanne (b. 1927) 335
Toplady, Augustus Montague (1740-1778) 685
Traditional carol 101
Translations and Paraphrases, 1745 545
Tucker, F. Bland (1895-1984) 25, 26, 121, 135, 139, 164, 220, 221, 268, 269, 302, 303, 322, 356, 366, 421, 428, 443, 477, 478, 489, 530, 547, 587, 663, 668
Turton, William Harry (1856-1938) 315
Tuttiett, Laurence (1825-1895) 563

Vajda, Jaroslav J. (b. 1919) 250, 333
Van Dyke, Henry (1852-1933) 376, 586
Vanstone, W. H. (b. 1923) 585
Veni Creator Spiritus 500, 501, 502, 503, 504
Veni Sancte Spiritus 226, 227
von Bogatzky, Karl Heinrich (1690-1774) 540
von Christierson, Frank (b. 1900) 698, 705
von Spee, Friedrich (1591-1635) 173, 211

Wade, John Francis (1711-1786) 83
Walworth, Clarence Augustus (1820-1900) 366
Waters, Moir A. J. (1906-1980) 70
Watts, Isaac (1674-1748) 50, 100, 253, 321, 369, 374, 380, 391, 392, 398, 429, 434, 474, 510, 544, 664, 680
Webb, Benjamin (1819-1885) 217, 218, 220, 221, 448, 449
Webster, Bradford Gray (b. 1898) 590
Weisse, Michael (1480-1534) 184
Weissel, Georg (1590-1635) 436
Wesley, Charles (1707-1788) 6, 7, 49, 57, 58, 66, 87, 188, 189, 207, 214, 300, 352, 481, 493, 526, 535, 548, 638, 639, 657, 699, 704
Wesley, John (1703-1791) 429
Whiting, William (1825-1878) 579, 608
Whitney, Rae E. (b. 1927) 499
Whittier, John Greenleaf (1807-1892) 652, 653
Wigbert [Wipo of Burgundy] (d. 1050?) 183
Wilbur, Richard (b. 1921) 104
Williams, George W. (b. 1922) 260
Williams, Peter (1722-1796) 690
Williams, William (1717-1791) 690
Winkworth, Catherine (1827-1878) 53, 67, 151, 184, 339, 396, 397, 436, 440, 635
Wither, George (1588-1667) 430
Wolcott, Samuel (1813-1886) 537
Woodward, George R (1848-1934) 192
Wordsworth, Christopher (1807-1885) 48, 88, 135, 191, 215, 275, 612, 626
Work, John W. (b. 1901) 99
Wortman, Denis (1835-1922) 359
Wotherspoon, Arthur Wellesley (1835-1936) 701
Wren, Brian A. (b. 1936) 129, 130, 182, 304, 603, 604

Young, John Freeman (1820-1885) 111

Index of Composers, Arrangers, and Sources

Hallock, Peter R. (b. 1923) 418
Hamburger Musikalsiches handbuch, 1690 540
Hampton, Calvin (1938-1984) 403, 407, 456, 469, 636, 659
Hancock, Eugene W. (b. 1929) 243, 636
Hancock, Gerre (b. 1934) 350, 686
Handel, George Frideric (1685-1759) 100, 459, 481, 546, 629
Harding, James Proctor (1850-1911) 117
Harmonia Sacra, ca. 1760 188, 257
Harwood, Basil (1859-1949) 285, 444, 448
Hasidic melody 536
Hassler, Hans Leo (1564-1612) 80, 132, 168, 169, 184, 185, 298, 319, 575, 669, 687
Hastings, Thomas (1784-1872) 685
Hatton, John (d. 1793) 544
Havergal, William Henry (1793-1870) 7, 47, 66, 127, 414, 530, 656
Haweis, Thomas (1734-1820) 72, 212
Haydn, Franz Joseph (1732-1809) 28, 29, 409, 522
Haydn, Johann Michael (1737-1806) 533, 637
Hayes, William (1706-1777) 387
Hayne, Leighton George (1836-1883) 613
Hebrew melody 372, 393, 401, 714
Heinlein, Paul (1626-1686) 323
Held, Wilbur (b. 1914) 246
Helmore, Thomas (1811-1890) 56
Hemy, Henri Frédéric (1818-1888) 558
Herbst, Martin (1654-1681) 150
Hermann, Nikolaus (1480?-1561) 201
Hill, Jackson (b. 1941) 122, 123, 329
Hillert, Richard (b. 1923) 417
Hilton, John (1599-1657) 140
Himlischer Lieder, 1641 173
Hintze, Jakob (1622-1702) 135, 174
Hispanic folk melody 113
Hodges, Edward (1796-1867) 376
Holden, Oliver (1765-1844) 450
Holst, Gustav Theodore (1874-1934) 92, 112
Hooker, John Leon (b. 1944) 675
Hopkins, Edward John (1818-1901) 345
Hopkins, John Henry (1861-1945) 293
Hopkins, John Henry, Jr. (1820-1891) 128, 503
Hopkirk, James (1908-1972) 600
Horsley, William (1774-1858) 167
Howard, Samuel (1710-1782) 666
Howells, Herbert (1892-1983) 582, 665
Hughes, John (1873-1932) 594, 690
Hullah, John Pyke (19th cent.) 447, 483
Hundert Arien, 1694 187, 269
Hunterian MS., 15th cent. 266
Hurd, David (b. 1950) 16, 35, 41, 55, 103, 104, 161, 162, 166, 233, 268, 273, 283, 319, 320, 322, 325, 354, 361, 395, 459, 463, 503, 507, 549, 606, 629, 664, 676
Hutchings, Arthur (b. 1906) 17, 120
Hymnal 1940 166, 299, 330
Hymnal 1982 10, 25, 43, 67, 173, 185, 201, 203, 235, 257, 319, 364, 415, 482, 532, 550, 638, 641, 645, 663
Hymnau a Thonau er Gwasanaeth yr Eglwys yng Nghymru, 1865 68, 607
Hymns Ancient and Modern, 1875 20, 137, 353, 365, 371, 372, 401, 537
Hymns Ancient and Modern, 1916 228
Hymns Ancient and Modern, 1922 94
Hymns Ancient and Modern, Historical Edition, 1909 348
Hymns Ancient and Modern, Revised, 1950 72, 193, 207, 284, 449
Hymns and Sacred Poems, 1749 428
Hymns III, 1979 581

Ireland, John (1879-1962) 458
Irish ballad melody 482, 488
Irish melody 69, 370, 645
Irvine, Jesse Seymour (1836-1887) 663
Isaac, Heinrich (1450?-1517) 46, 309

Jackisch, Frederick (b. 1922) 114
Jackson, Francis (b. 1917) 424
Jacob, Gordon (b. 1895) 517
Jenner, Henry Lascelles (1820-1898) 626
Johnson, David N. (b. 1922) 373, 412
Johnson, J. Rosamond (1873-1954) 599
Johnson, Robert Sherlaw (b. 1932) 189
Johnson, Roy Henry (b. 1933) 588
Jones, W. Thomas (b. 1956) 49
Jones, William (1726-1800) 73

Katholisches Gesangbuch, 1686 366
Katholisches Gesangbuch, 1863 210
Kehl, Roy F. (b. 1935) 2, 22, 32, 136, 140, 146, 202, 204, 311, 495
Keiser, Marilyn J. (b. 1941) 213
Kentucky Harmony, 1816 243, 702
Kievan chant 355
King, Charles John (1859-1934) 426
Kirchengeseng darinnen die Heubtartickel des Christlichen Glaubens gefasset, 1566 408, 598
Kirkpatrick, William James (1838-1921) 101
Klein, Richard Rudolf (b. 1921) 713
Klosterneuburger Hymnar, 1336 22
Knapp, William (1698-1768) 20, 137, 353
Kocher, Conrad (1786-1872) 119, 269, 288, 366
König, Johann Balthasar (1691-1758) 244, 334, 656
Koralbok for Svenska Kyrkan, 1939 65
Kremser, Eduard (1838-1914) 433

Lafferty, Karen (20th cent.) 711
Lang, Craig Sellar (1891-1971) 72, 94, 290, 326, 368, 390, 410
Laudi Spirituali, 14th cent. 239
Layriz, Friedrich (1808-1859) 338
Lee, J. V. (1892-1959) 543

Metrical Index of Tunes

Index of Tune Names

Index of First Lines